Dragonball

STORY AND ART BY

AKIRA TORIYAMA

DRAGON BALL 3-IN-1 EDITION 2

SHONEN JUMP Manga Omnibus Edition
A compilation of the graphic novel volumes 4–6

STORY AND ART **AKIRA TORIYAMA**

TRANSLATION **Mari Morimoto**
ENGLISH ADAPTATION **Gerard Jones**
TOUCH-UP ART & LETTERING **Wayne Truman**
DESIGN **Sean Lee** (Manga Edition)
Shawn Carrico (Omnibus Edition)
EDITOR **Jason Thompson** (Manga Edition)
Mike Montesa (Omnibus Edition)

Printed in Canada

Published by VIZ Media, LLC
P.O. Box 77010
San Francisco, CA 94107

10 9 8
Omnibus edition first printing, September 2013
Eighth printing, March 2022

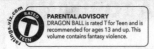

PARENTAL ADVISORY
DRAGON BALL is rated T for Teen and is
recommended for ages 13 and up. This
volume contains fantasy violence.

Dragonball

VOLUME 4
STRONGEST UNDER THE HEAVENS

VOLUME 5
THE RED RIBBON ARMY

VOLUME 6
BULMA RETURNS

STORY AND ART BY

AKIRA TORIYAMA

SHONEN JUMP Manga Omnibus Edition

CONTENTS

VOLUME 5
THE RED RIBBON ARMY

VOLUME 6
BULMA RETURNS

CAST OF CHARACTERS

Bulma
A genius inventor, Bulma met Goku on her quest for the seven magical Dragon Balls.

Pu'ar
Yamcha's shapeshifting friend.

Yamcha
Yamcha used to be a desert bandit, but he went to the city to be Bulma's boyfriend. He uses "Fist of the Wolf Fang" kung-fu.

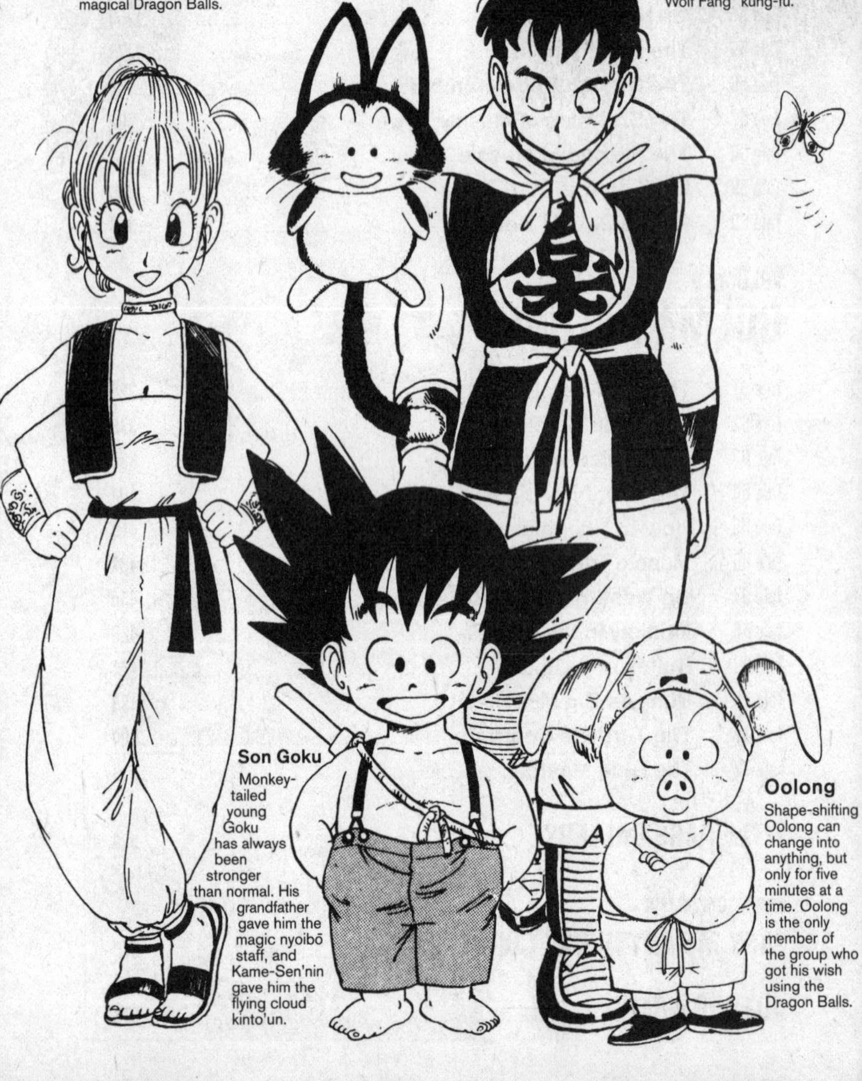

Son Goku
Monkey-tailed young Goku has always been stronger than normal. His grandfather gave him the magic nyoibō staff, and Kame-Sen'nin gave him the flying cloud kinto'un.

Oolong
Shape-shifting Oolong can change into anything, but only for five minutes at a time. Oolong is the only member of the group who got his wish using the Dragon Balls.

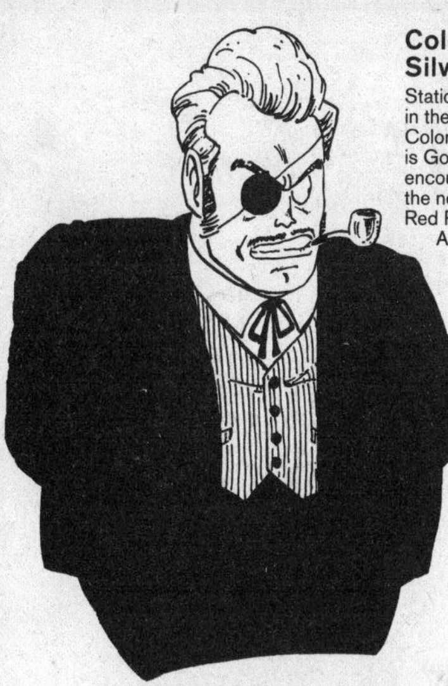

Commander Red

The ultimate authority of the Red Ribbon Army, he wants to gather all seven Dragon Balls so that his wish can be granted.

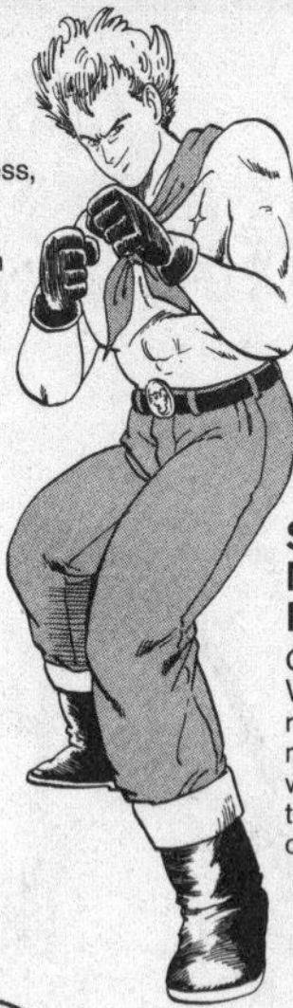

Colonel Silver

Stationed out in the wilderness, Colonel Silver is Goku's first encounter with the nefarious Red Ribbon Army.

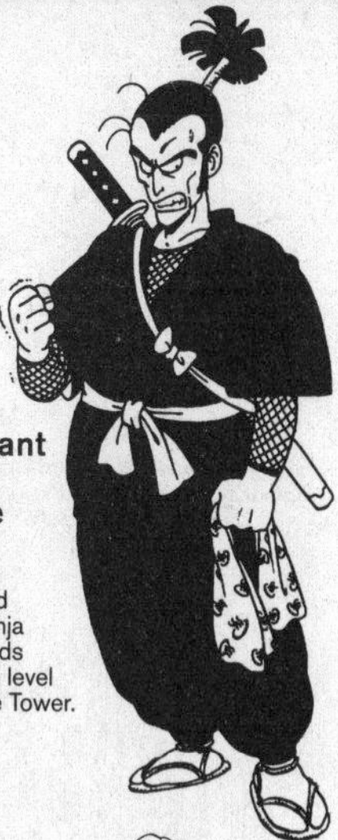

Sergeant Major Purple

General White's right-hand man, a ninja who guards the fourth level of Muscle Tower.

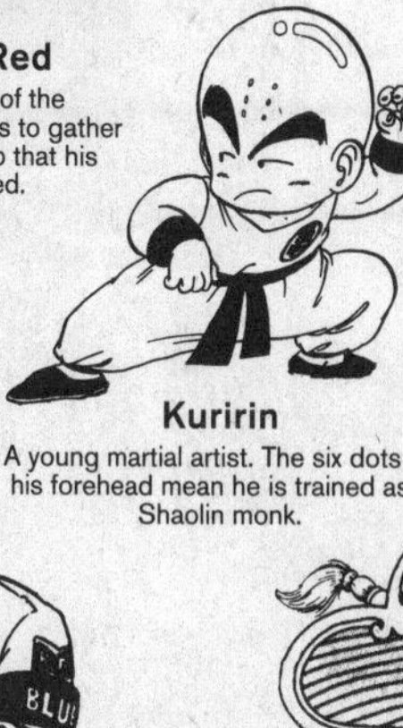

Kuririn

A young martial artist. The six dots on his forehead mean he is trained as a Shaolin monk.

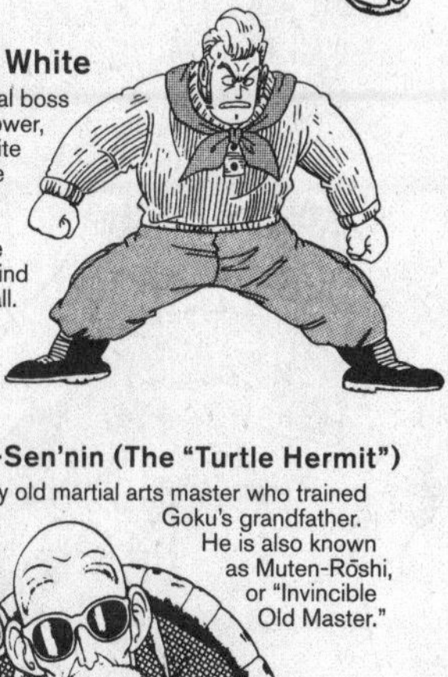

General White

The diabolical boss of Muscle Tower, General White is forcing the peaceful residents of Jingle Village to help him find a Dragon Ball.

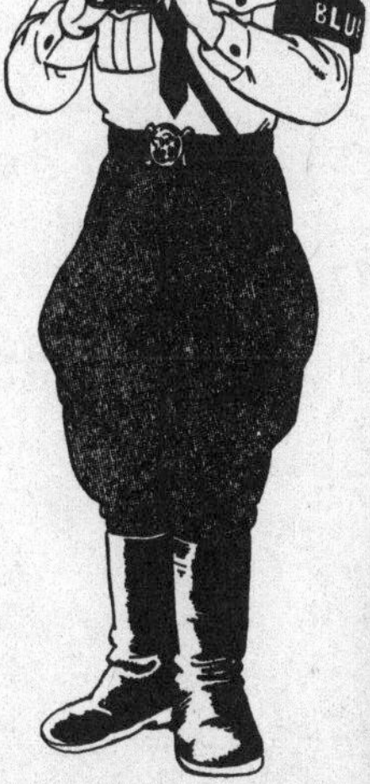

General Blue

One of the leaders of the Red Ribbon Army, cruel General Blue likes things neat and tidy.

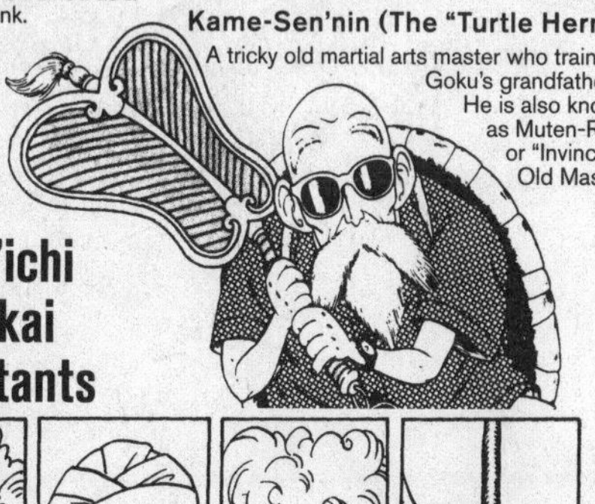

Kame-Sen'nin (The "Turtle Hermit")

A tricky old martial arts master who trained Goku's grandfather. He is also known as Muten-Rōshi, or "Invincible Old Master."

Tenka'ichi Budōkai Contestants

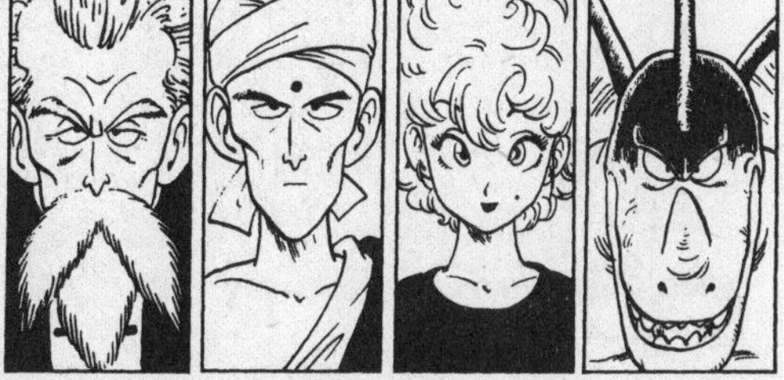

Jackie Chun   Namu   Ran Fuan   Giran

Dragonball

VOLUME 4

STRONGEST UNDER
THE HEAVENS

Tale 37
Match No. 2

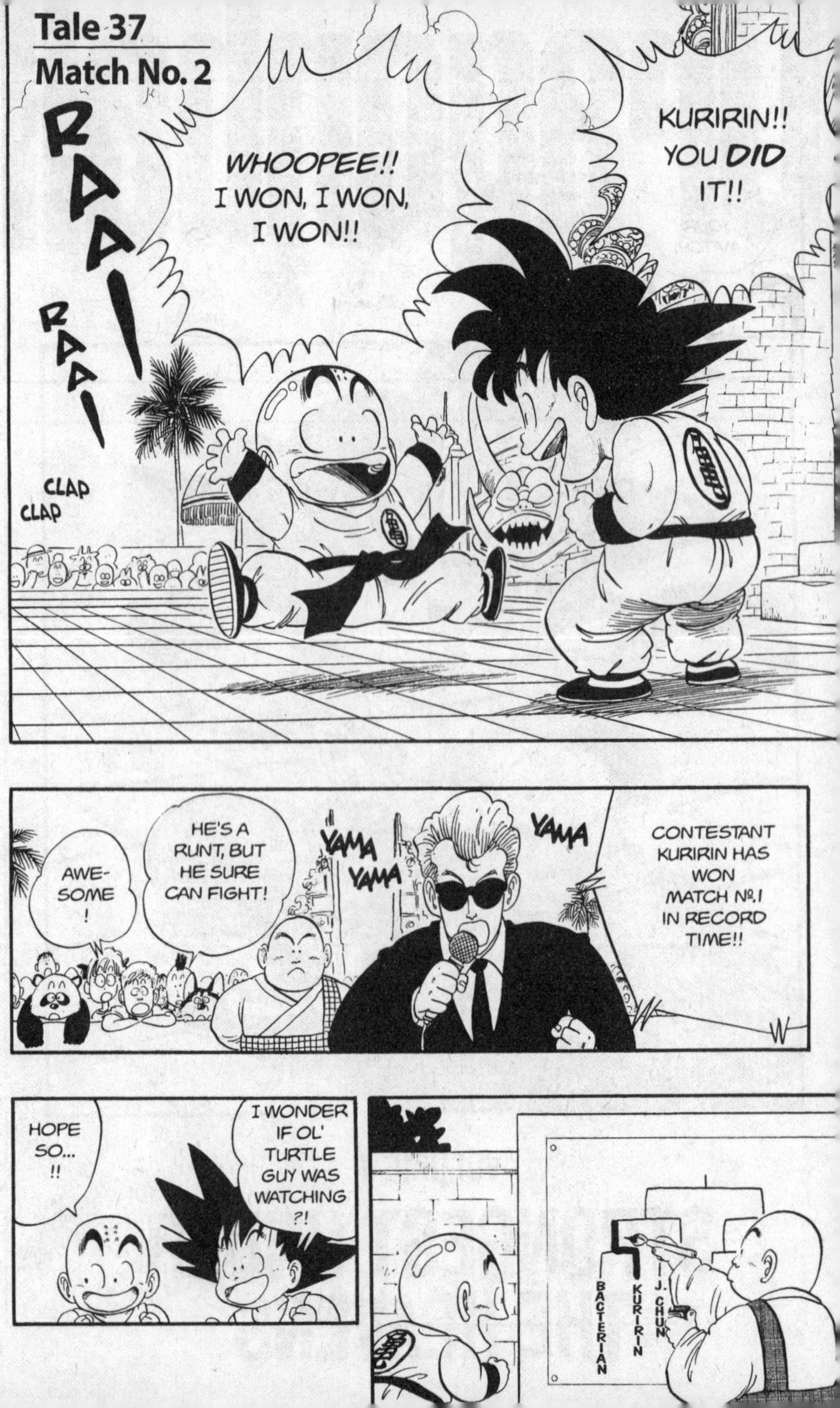
KURIRIN!! YOU DID IT!!
WHOOPEE!! I WON, I WON, I WON!!
RAAAI
RAAAI
CLAP CLAP
CONTESTANT KURIRIN HAS WON MATCH No.1 IN RECORD TIME!!
YAMA
YAMA YAMA
HE'S A RUNT, BUT HE SURE CAN FIGHT!
AWE-SOME!
J. CHUN
KURIRIN
BACTERIAN
I WONDER IF OL' TURTLE GUY WAS WATCHING?!
HOPE SO...!!

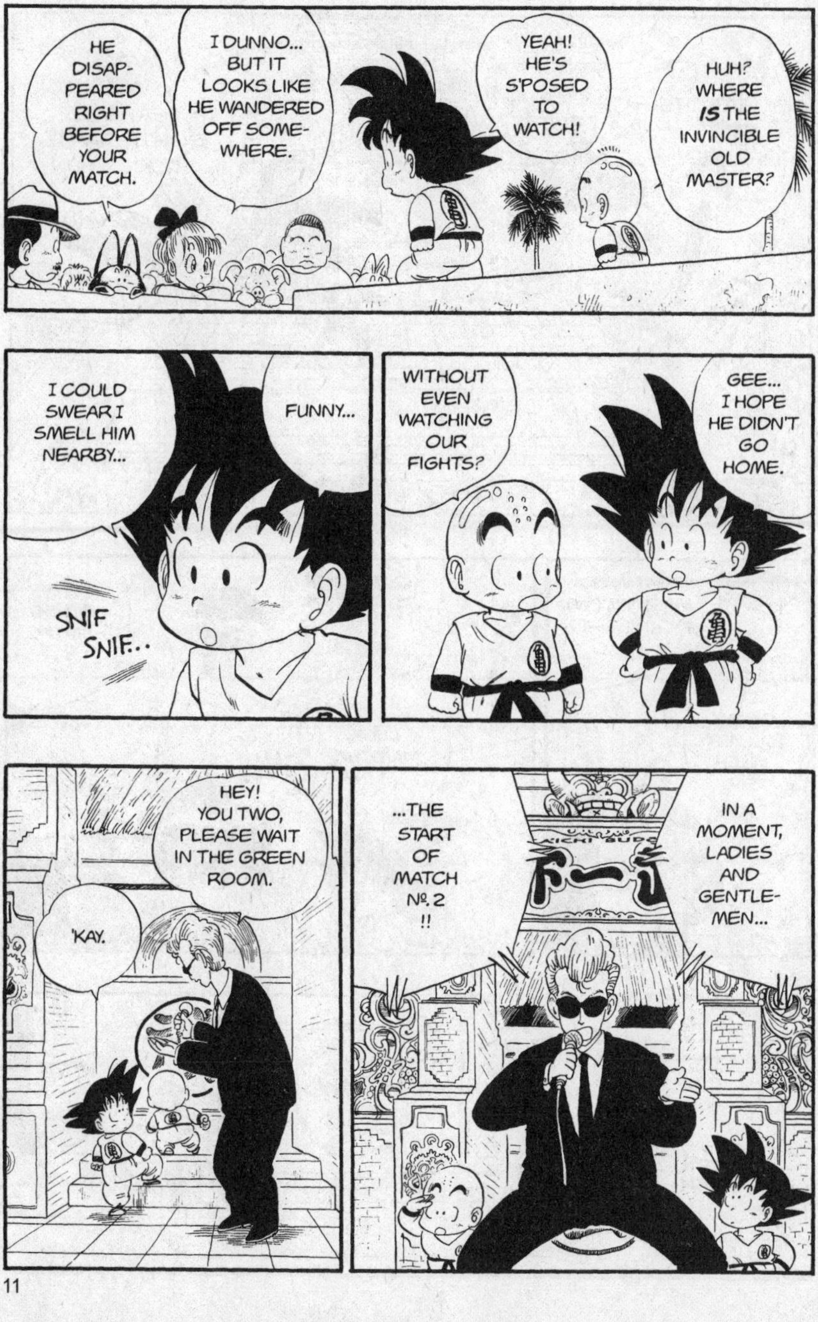
HUH? WHERE *IS* THE INVINCIBLE OLD MASTER?
YEAH! HE'S S'POSED TO WATCH!
I DUNNO... BUT IT LOOKS LIKE HE WANDERED OFF SOME-WHERE.
HE DISAP-PEARED RIGHT BEFORE YOUR MATCH.
GEE... I HOPE HE DIDN'T GO HOME.
WITHOUT EVEN WATCHING OUR FIGHTS?
FUNNY...
I COULD SWEAR I SMELL HIM NEARBY...
SNIF SNIF...
IN A MOMENT, LADIES AND GENTLE-MEN...
...THE START OF MATCH №. 2 !!
HEY! YOU TWO, PLEASE WAIT IN THE GREEN ROOM.
'KAY.

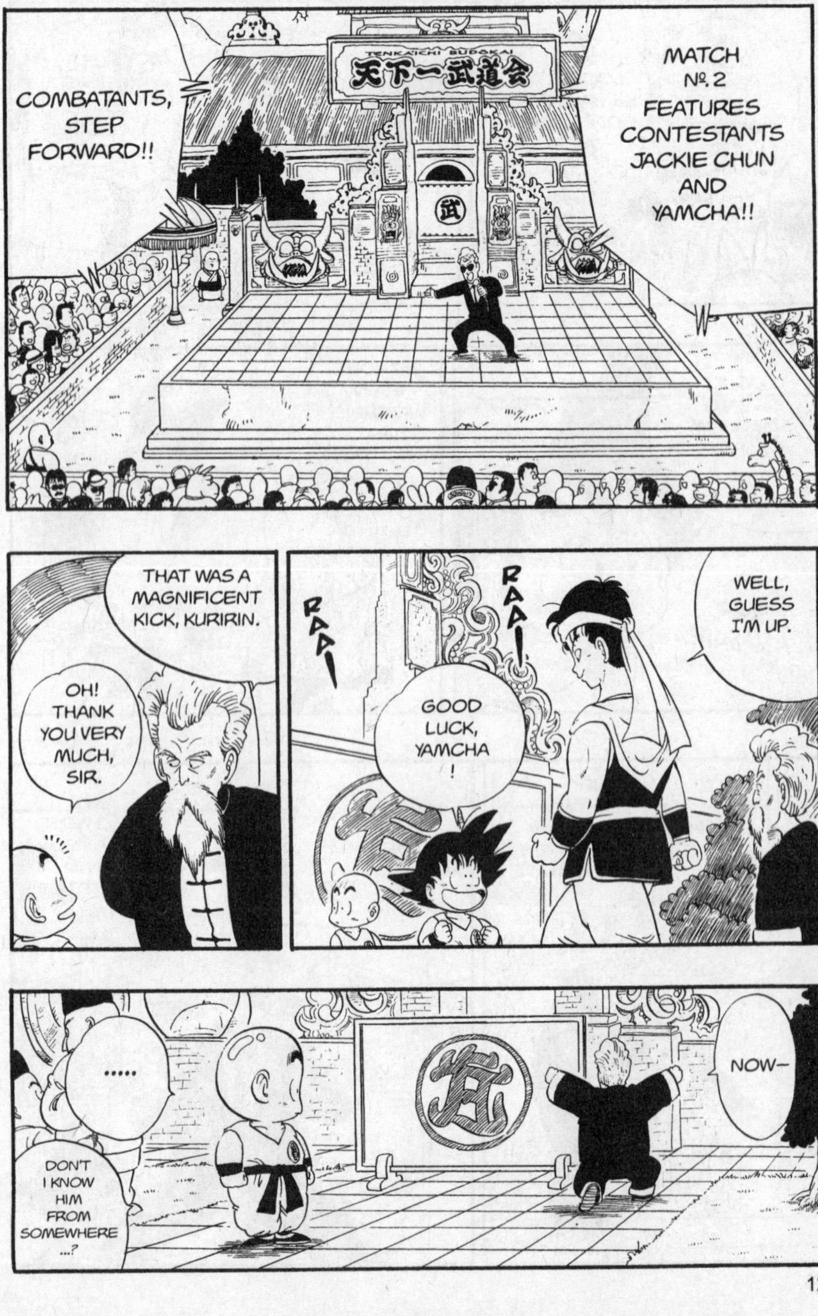

TENKAICHI BUDOKAI
天下一武道会
MATCH №.2 FEATURES CONTESTANTS JACKIE CHUN AND YAMCHA!!
COMBATANTS, STEP FORWARD!!
武
WELL, GUESS I'M UP.
RAA!
RAA!
GOOD LUCK, YAMCHA!
THAT WAS A MAGNIFICENT KICK, KURIRIN.
OH! THANK YOU VERY MUCH, SIR.
NOW—
.....
DON'T I KNOW HIM FROM SOMEWHERE...?

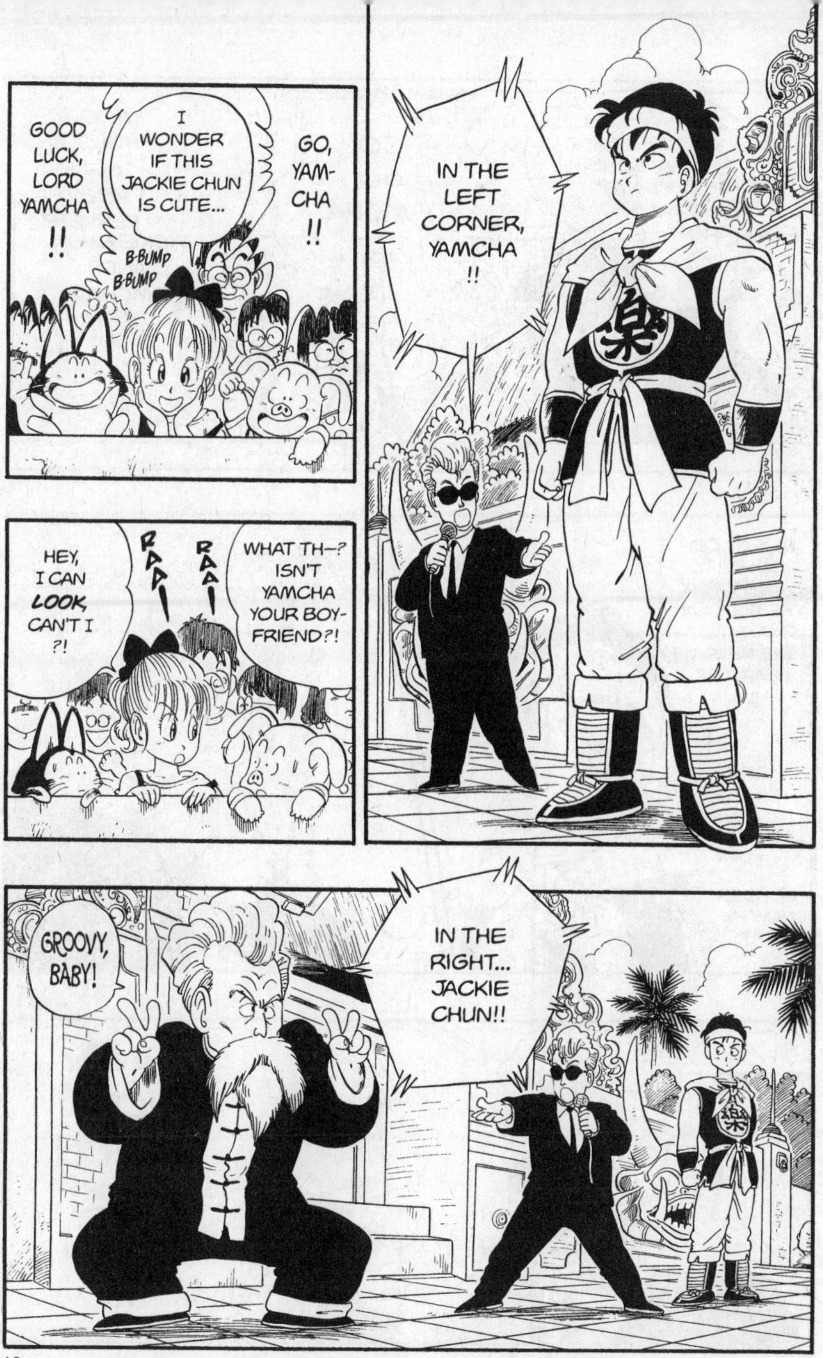
IN THE LEFT CORNER, YAMCHA!!
GO, YAM-CHA!!
I WONDER IF THIS JACKIE CHUN IS CUTE...
B-BUMP B-BUMP
GOOD LUCK, LORD YAMCHA!!
WHAT TH—? ISN'T YAMCHA YOUR BOY-FRIEND?!
RAA!
RAA!
HEY, I CAN LOOK, CAN'T I?!
IN THE RIGHT... JACKIE CHUN!!
GROOVY, BABY!

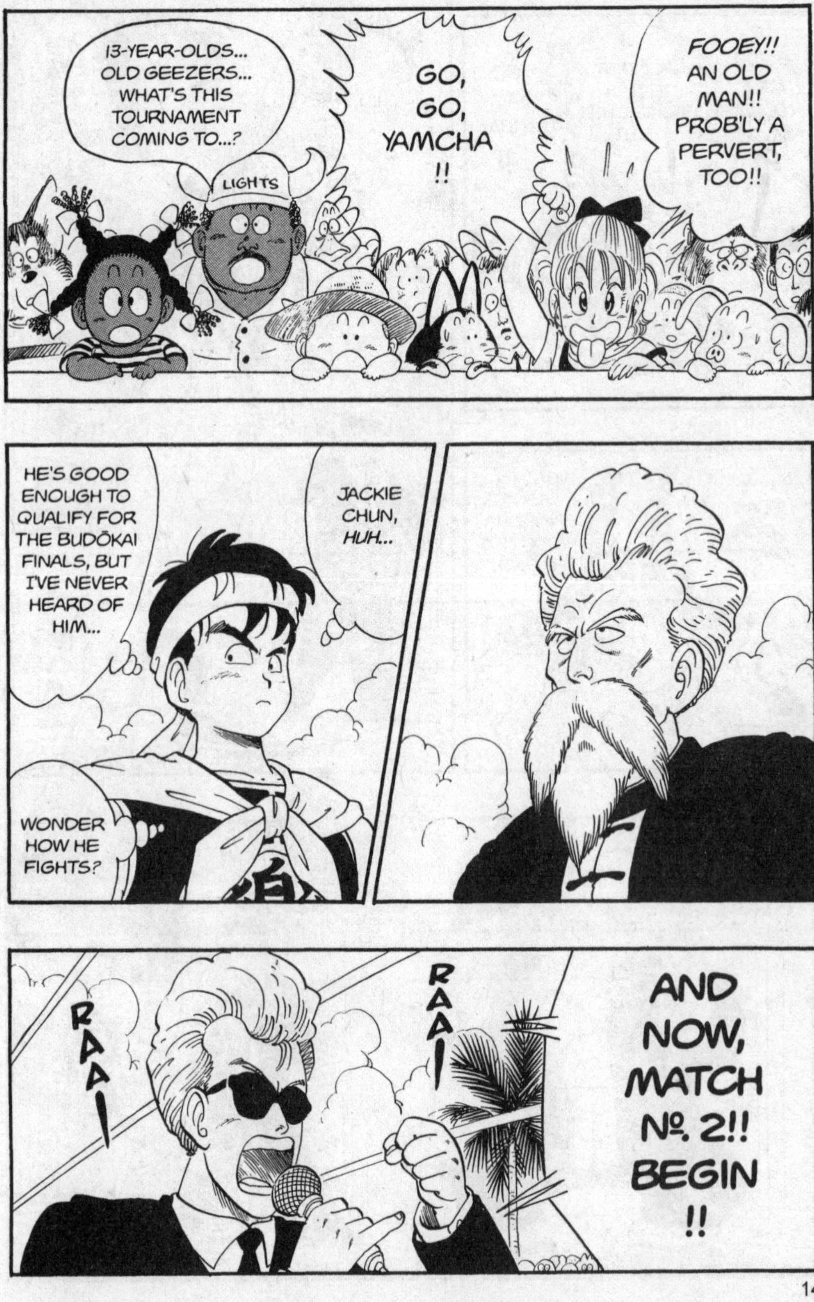
FOOEY!! AN OLD MAN!! PROB'LY A PERVERT, TOO!!
GO, GO, YAMCHA!!
LIGHTS
13-YEAR-OLDS... OLD GEEZERS... WHAT'S THIS TOURNAMENT COMING TO...?
JACKIE CHUN, HUH...
HE'S GOOD ENOUGH TO QUALIFY FOR THE BUDŌKAI FINALS, BUT I'VE NEVER HEARD OF HIM...
WONDER HOW HE FIGHTS?
AND NOW, MATCH №. 2!! BEGIN!!
RAA!
RAA!

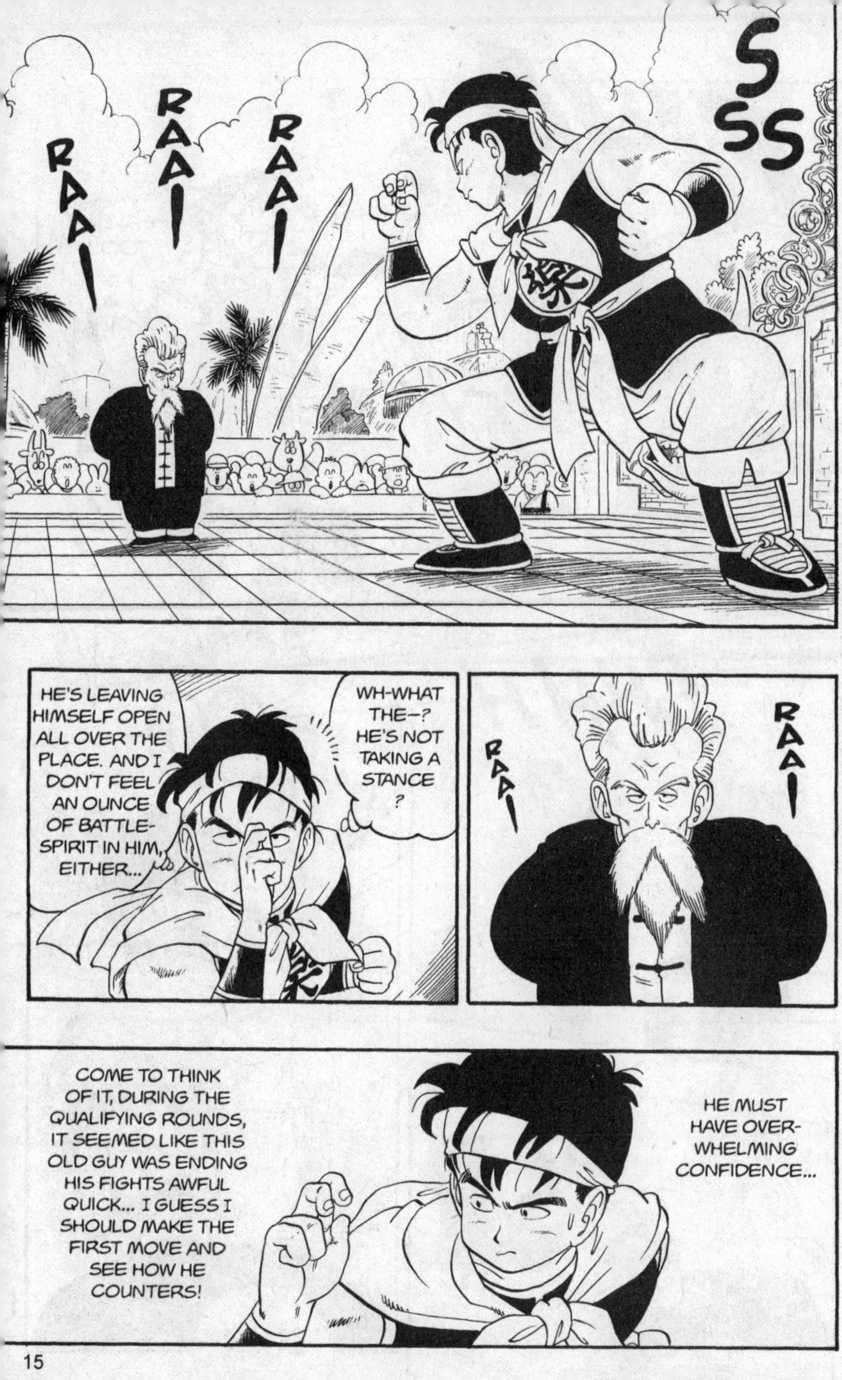
S SS
RAAI
RAAI
RAAI
RAAI
RAAI
WH-WHAT THE--? HE'S NOT TAKING A STANCE?
HE'S LEAVING HIMSELF OPEN ALL OVER THE PLACE. AND I DON'T FEEL AN OUNCE OF BATTLE-SPIRIT IN HIM, EITHER...
HE MUST HAVE OVER-WHELMING CONFIDENCE...
COME TO THINK OF IT, DURING THE QUALIFYING ROUNDS, IT SEEMED LIKE THIS OLD GUY WAS ENDING HIS FIGHTS AWFUL QUICK... I GUESS I SHOULD MAKE THE FIRST MOVE AND SEE HOW HE COUNTERS!

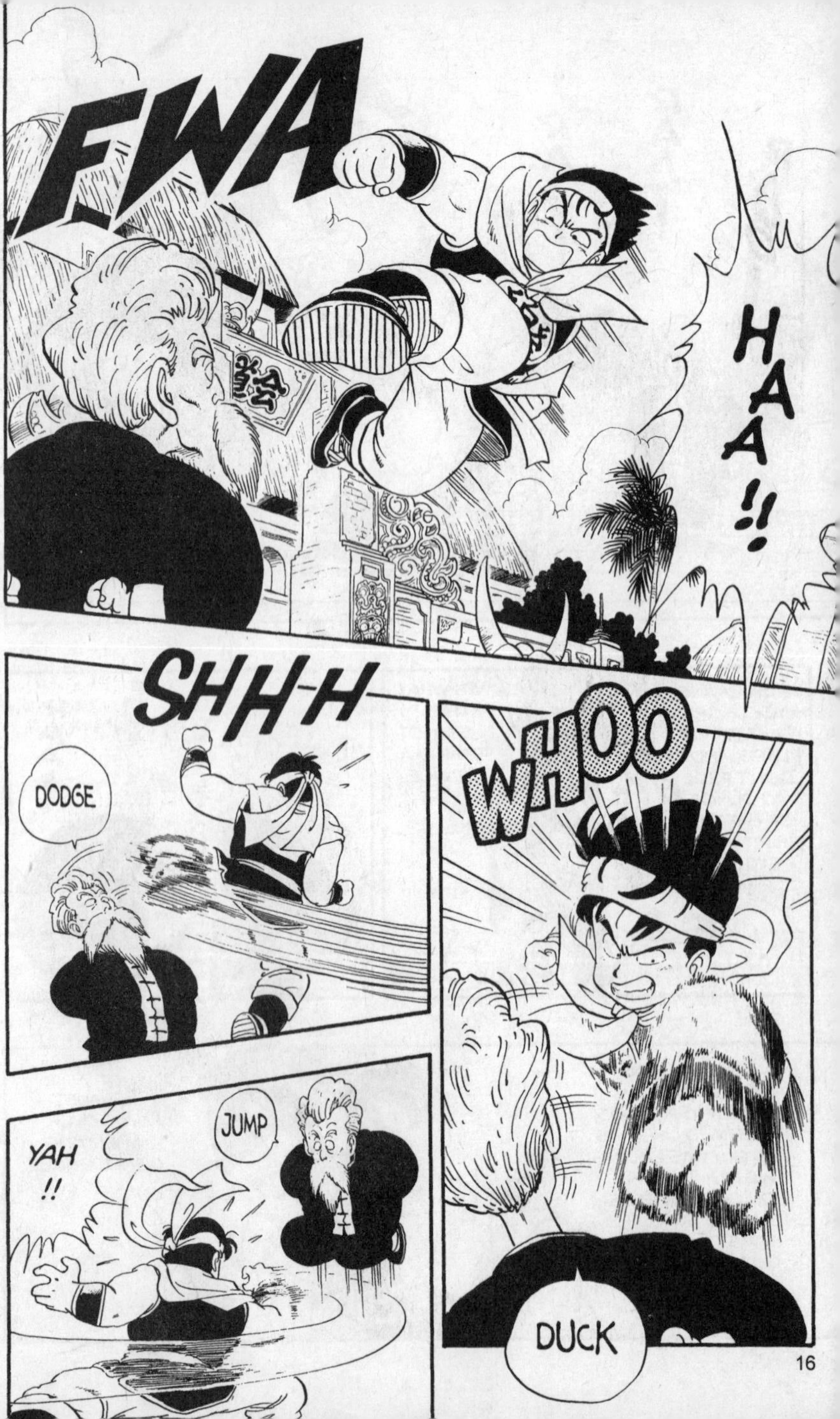
FWA
HAA!!
WHOO
DUCK
SHH-H
DODGE
JUMP
YAH!!

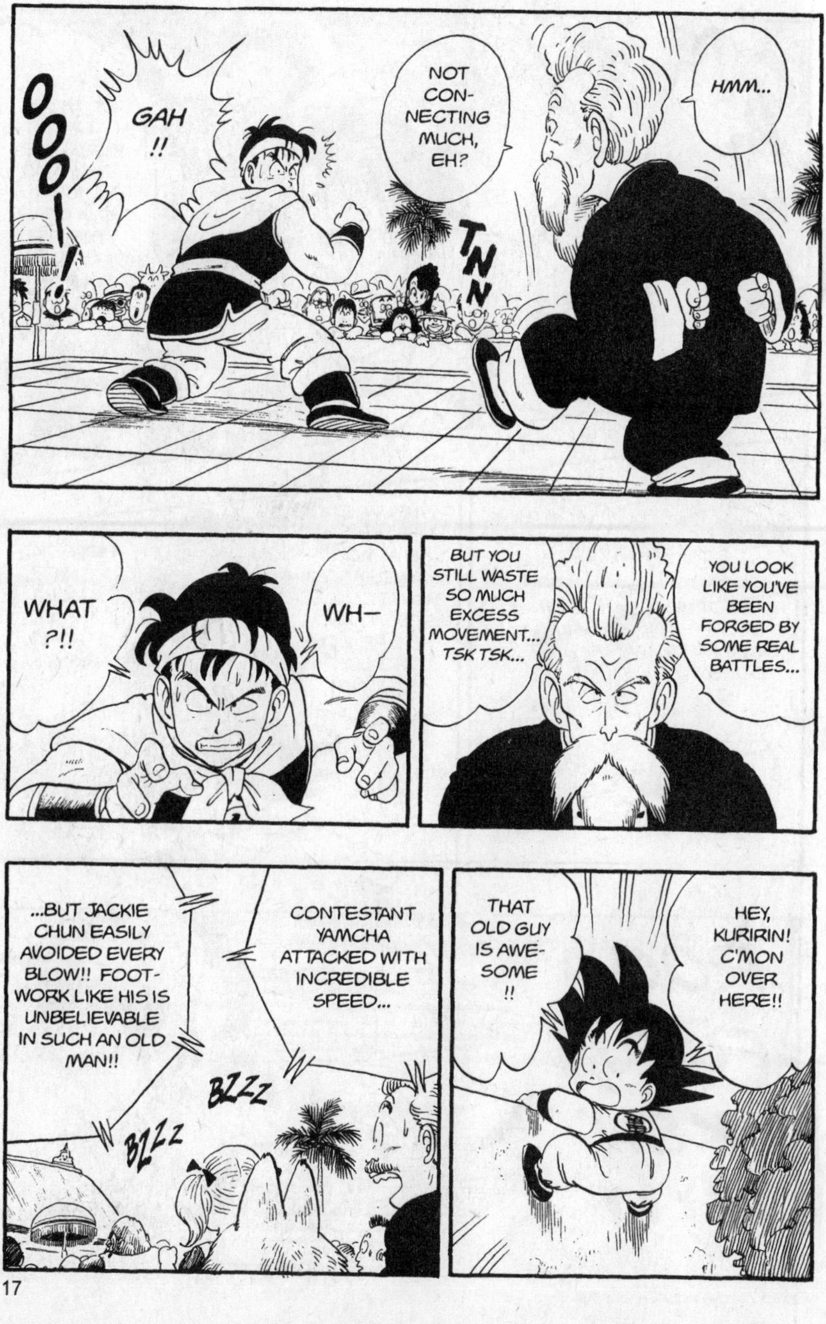
HMM...
NOT CON-NECTING MUCH, EH?
TNN
GAH!!
OOOI!
YOU LOOK LIKE YOU'VE BEEN FORGED BY SOME REAL BATTLES...
BUT YOU STILL WASTE SO MUCH EXCESS MOVEMENT... TSK TSK...
WH—
WHAT?!!
HEY, KURIRIN! C'MON OVER HERE!!
THAT OLD GUY IS AWE-SOME!!
CONTESTANT YAMCHA ATTACKED WITH INCREDIBLE SPEED...
...BUT JACKIE CHUN EASILY AVOIDED EVERY BLOW!! FOOT-WORK LIKE HIS IS UNBELIEVABLE IN SUCH AN OLD MAN!!
BZZZ
BZZZ

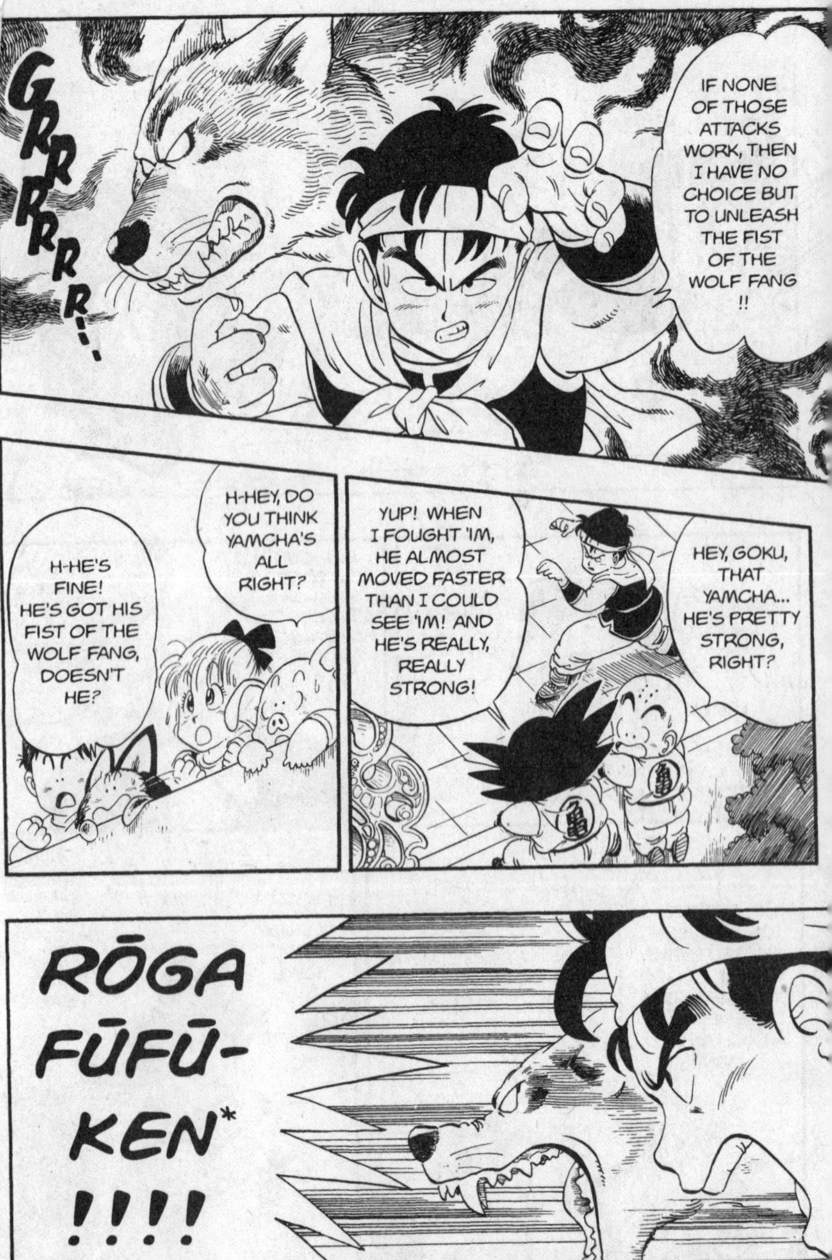
IF NONE OF THOSE ATTACKS WORK, THEN I HAVE NO CHOICE BUT TO UNLEASH THE FIST OF THE WOLF FANG !!
GRRRRRR...
HEY, GOKU, THAT YAMCHA... HE'S PRETTY STRONG, RIGHT?
YUP! WHEN I FOUGHT 'IM, HE ALMOST MOVED FASTER THAN I COULD SEE 'IM! AND HE'S REALLY, REALLY STRONG!
H-HEY, DO YOU THINK YAMCHA'S ALL RIGHT?
H-HE'S FINE! HE'S GOT HIS FIST OF THE WOLF FANG, DOESN'T HE?
RŌGA FŪFŪ-KEN* !!!!

*FIST OF THE WOLF FANG GALE

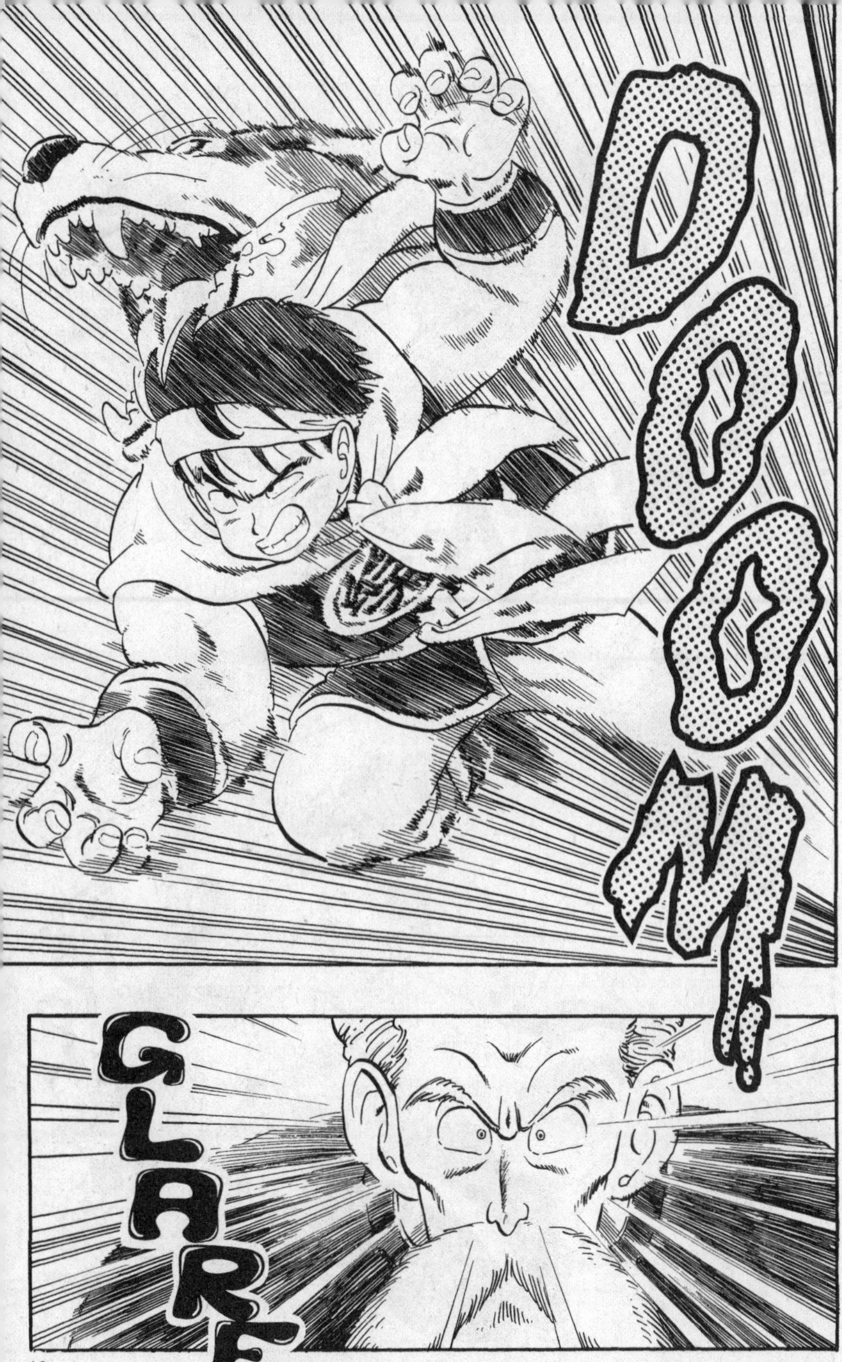
DOOOM!
GLARE

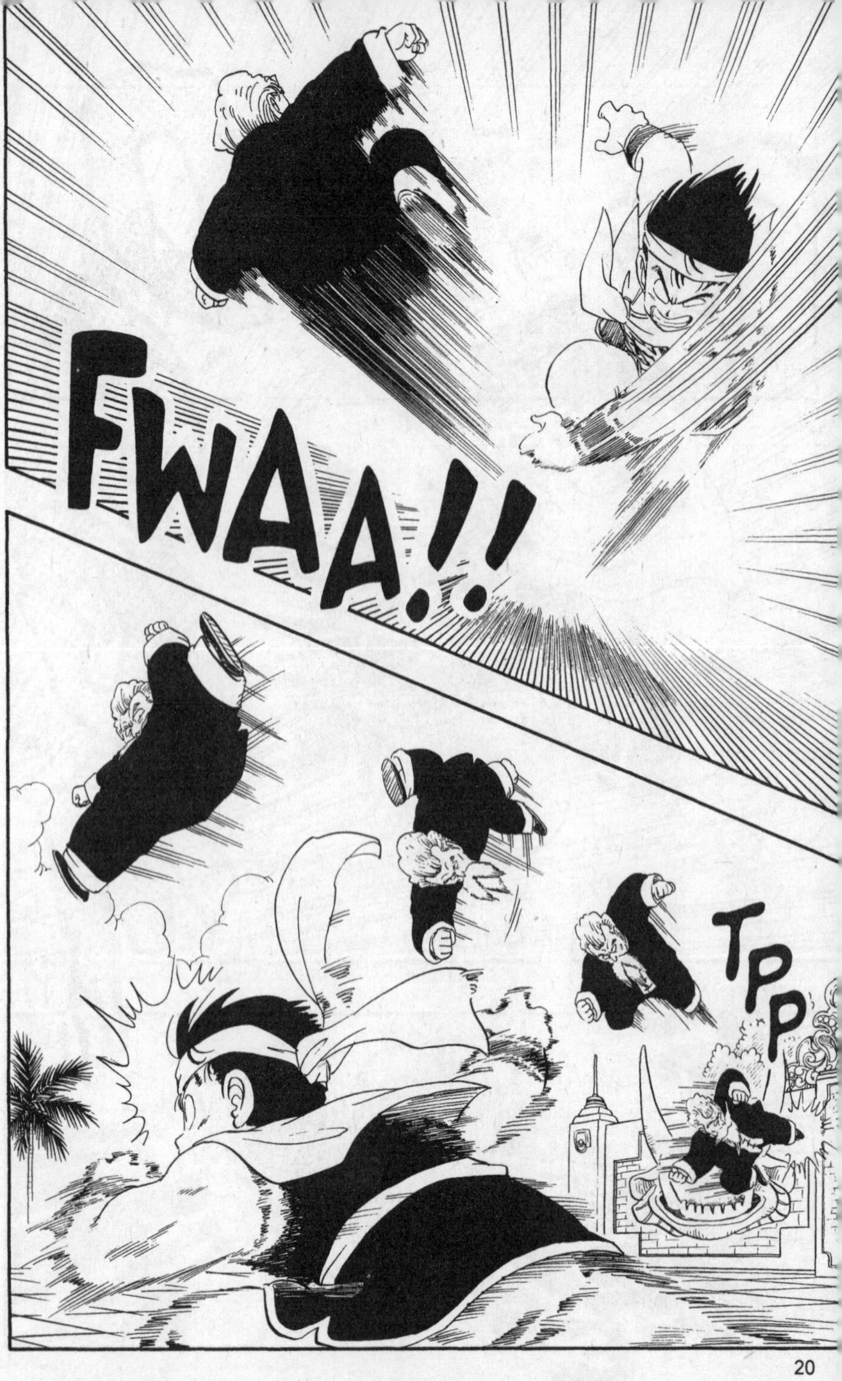
FWAA!!
TPP

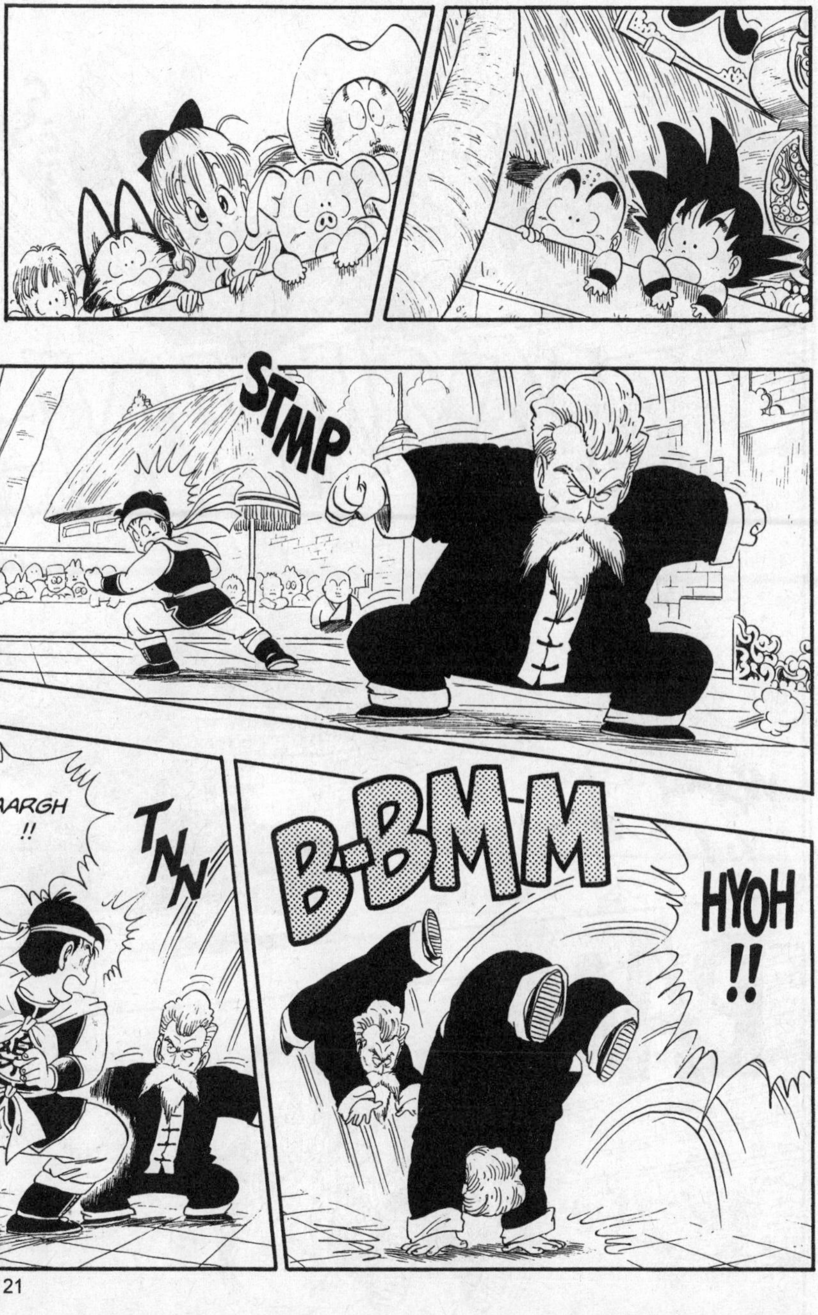
STMP
HYOH!!
B-BMM
TNN
AARGH!!

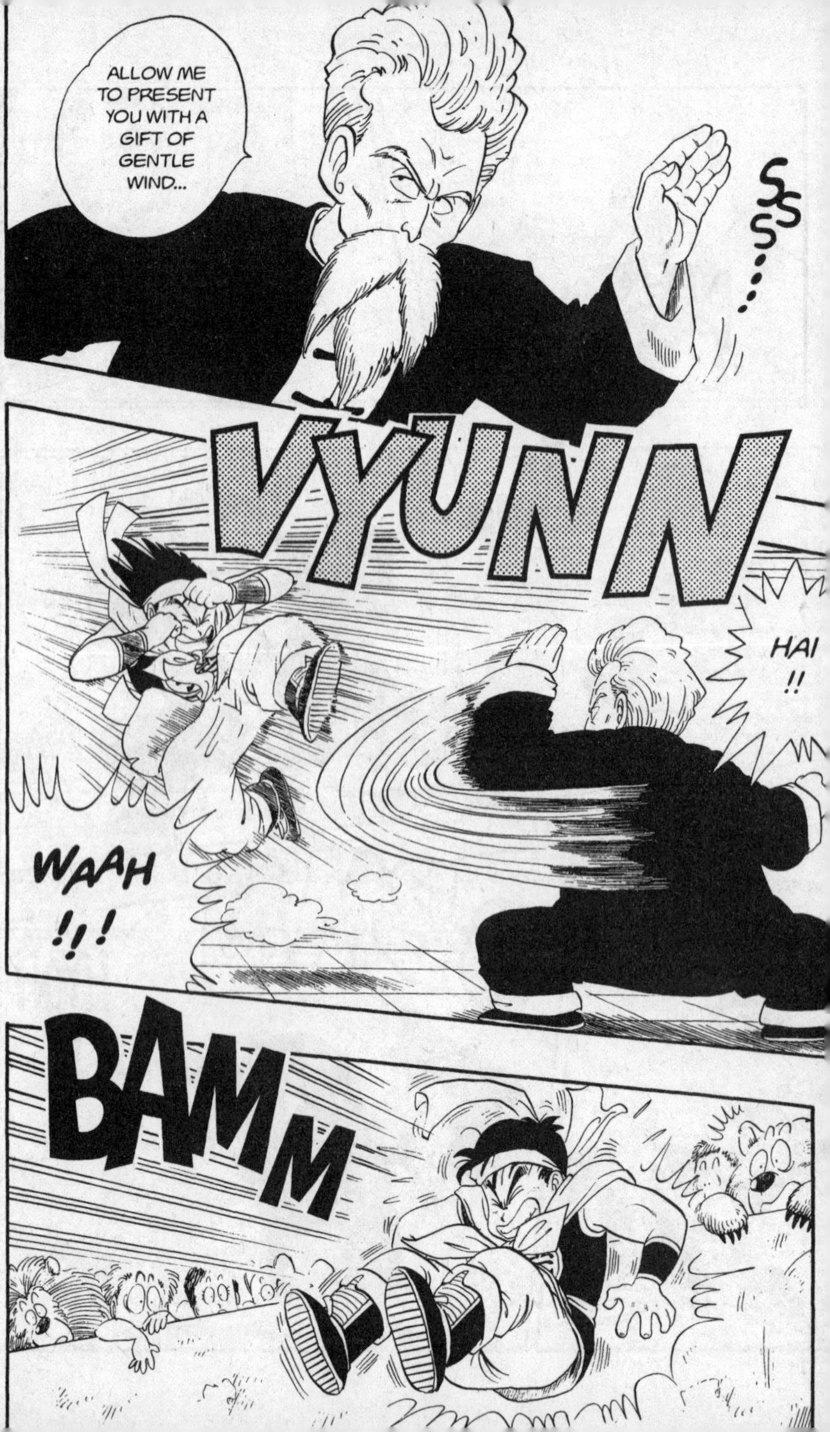

ALLOW ME TO PRESENT YOU WITH A GIFT OF GENTLE WIND...
SSS...
VYUNN
HAI !!
WAAH !!!
BAMM

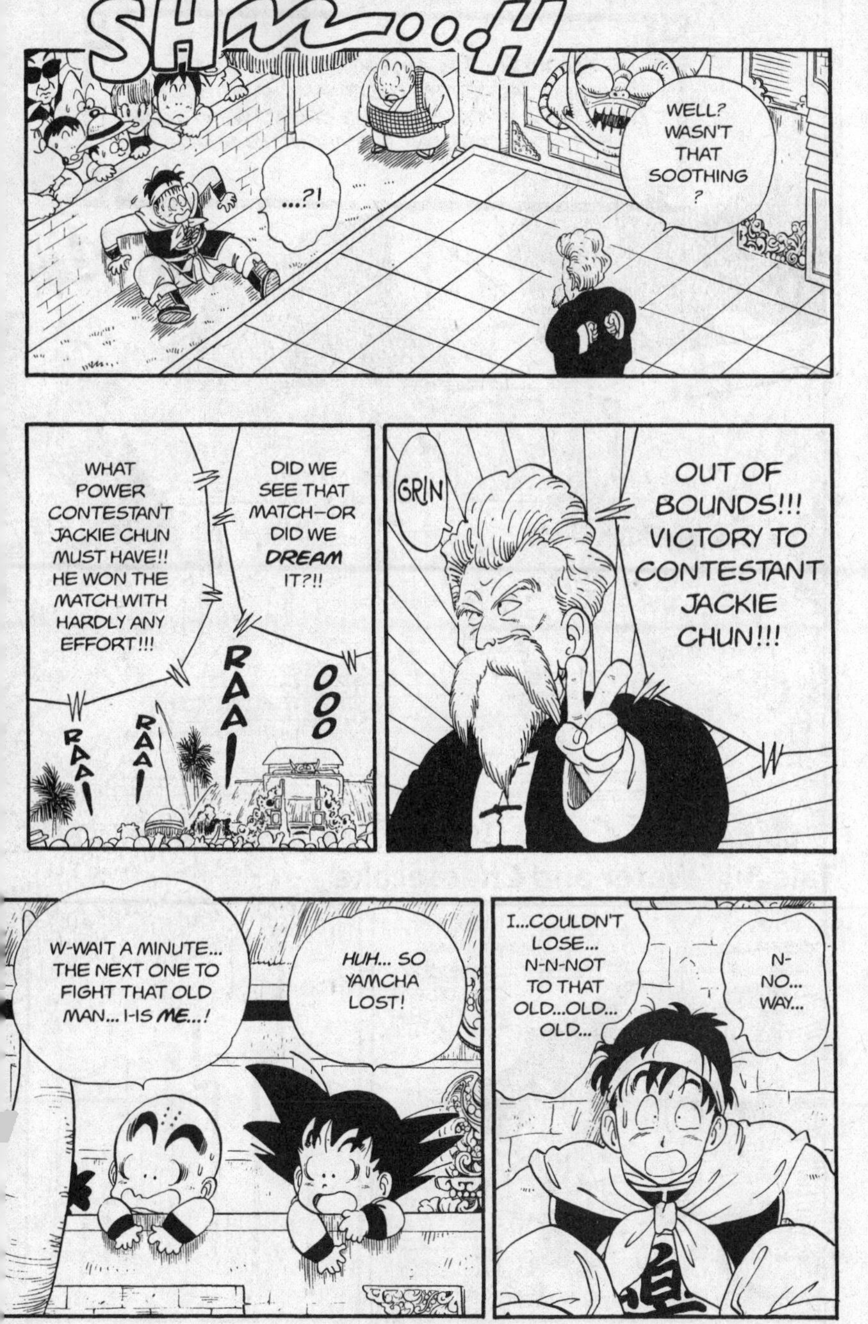
SHOO..H
WELL? WASN'T THAT SOOTHING ?
...?!
GRIN
OUT OF BOUNDS!!! VICTORY TO CONTESTANT JACKIE CHUN!!!
DID WE SEE THAT MATCH—OR DID WE *DREAM* IT?!!
WHAT POWER CONTESTANT JACKIE CHUN MUST HAVE!! HE WON THE MATCH WITH HARDLY ANY EFFORT!!!
RAA!
RAA!
RAA!
OOO
N-NO... WAY...
I...COULDN'T LOSE... N-N-NOT TO THAT OLD...OLD... OLD...
HUH... SO YAMCHA LOST!
W-WAIT A MINUTE... THE NEXT ONE TO FIGHT THAT OLD MAN... I-IS *ME*...!

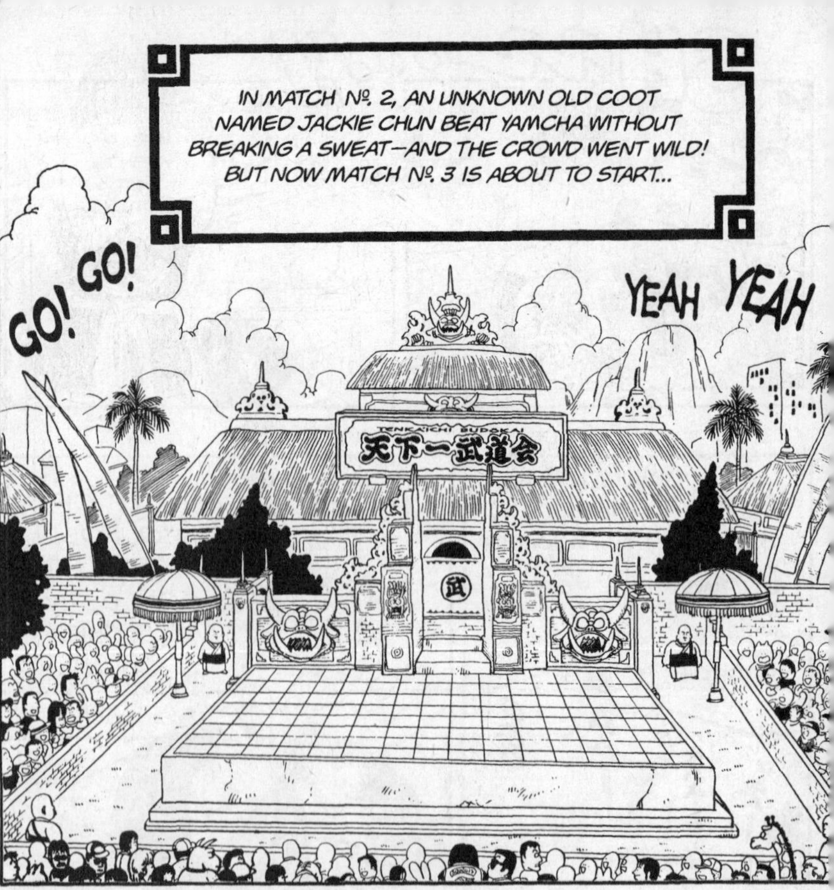
IN MATCH №. 2, AN UNKNOWN OLD COOT NAMED JACKIE CHUN BEAT YAMCHA WITHOUT BREAKING A SWEAT—AND THE CROWD WENT WILD! BUT NOW MATCH №. 3 IS ABOUT TO START...
YEAH YEAH
GO! GO!
TENKAICHI BUDOKAI
天下一武道会
武

Tale 38 • Water and Cheesecake

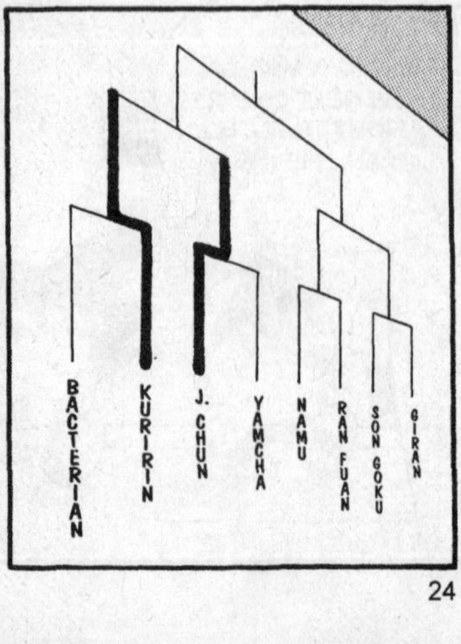
BACTERIAN
KURIRIN
J. CHUN
YAMCHA
NAMU
RAN FUAN
SON GOKU
GIRAN

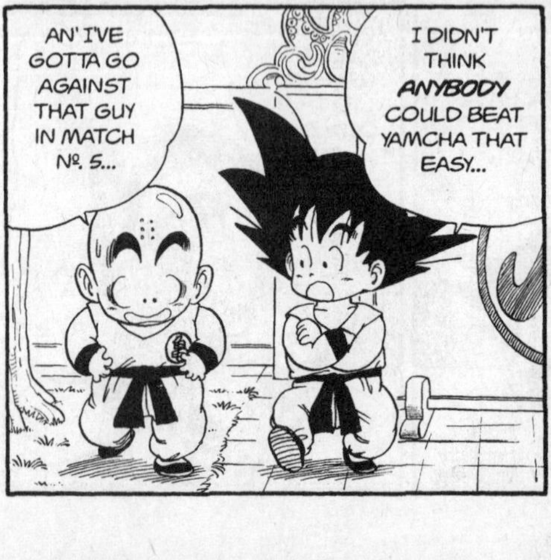
I DIDN'T THINK ANYBODY COULD BEAT YAMCHA THAT EASY...
AN' I'VE GOTTA GO AGAINST THAT GUY IN MATCH №. 5...

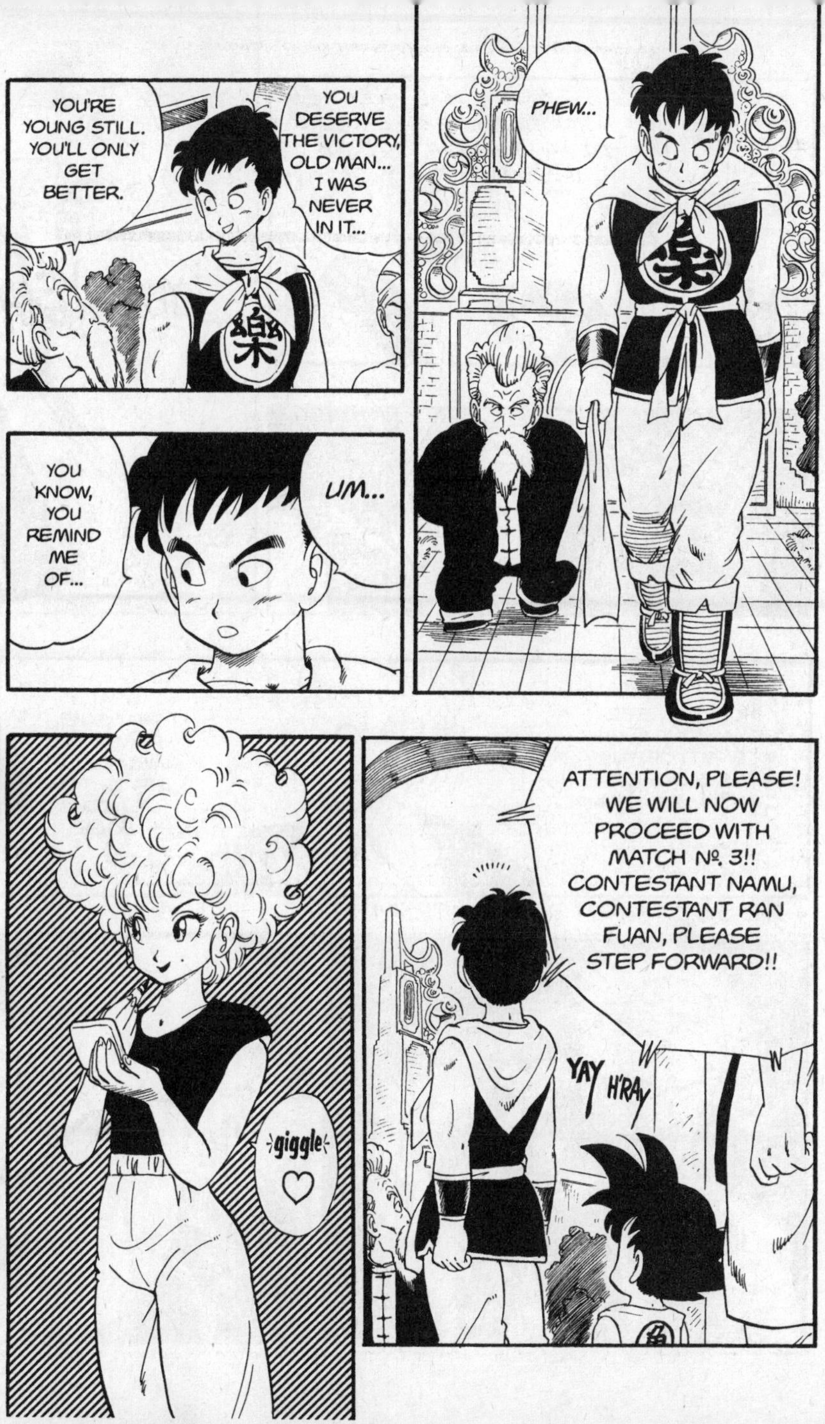
PHEW...
YOU DESERVE THE VICTORY, OLD MAN... I WAS NEVER IN IT...
YOU'RE YOUNG STILL. YOU'LL ONLY GET BETTER.
UM...
YOU KNOW, YOU REMIND ME OF...
ATTENTION, PLEASE! WE WILL NOW PROCEED WITH MATCH №. 3!! CONTESTANT NAMU, CONTESTANT RAN FUAN, PLEASE STEP FORWARD!!
YAY
H'RAY
giggle ♡

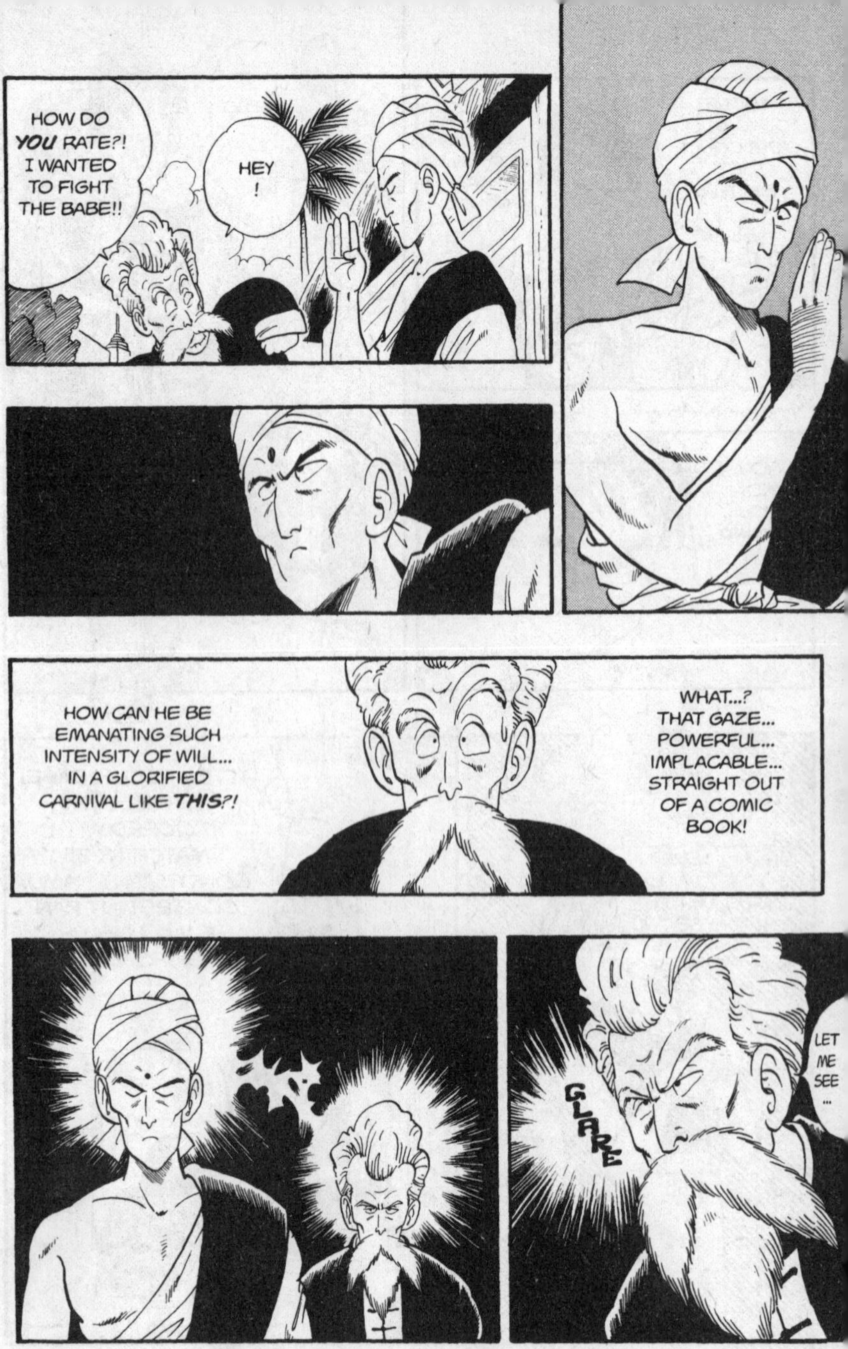
HEY !
HOW DO YOU RATE?! I WANTED TO FIGHT THE BABE!!
WHAT...? THAT GAZE... POWERFUL... IMPLACABLE... STRAIGHT OUT OF A COMIC BOOK!
HOW CAN HE BE EMANATING SUCH INTENSITY OF WILL... IN A GLORIFIED CARNIVAL LIKE THIS?!
LET ME SEE ...
GLARE

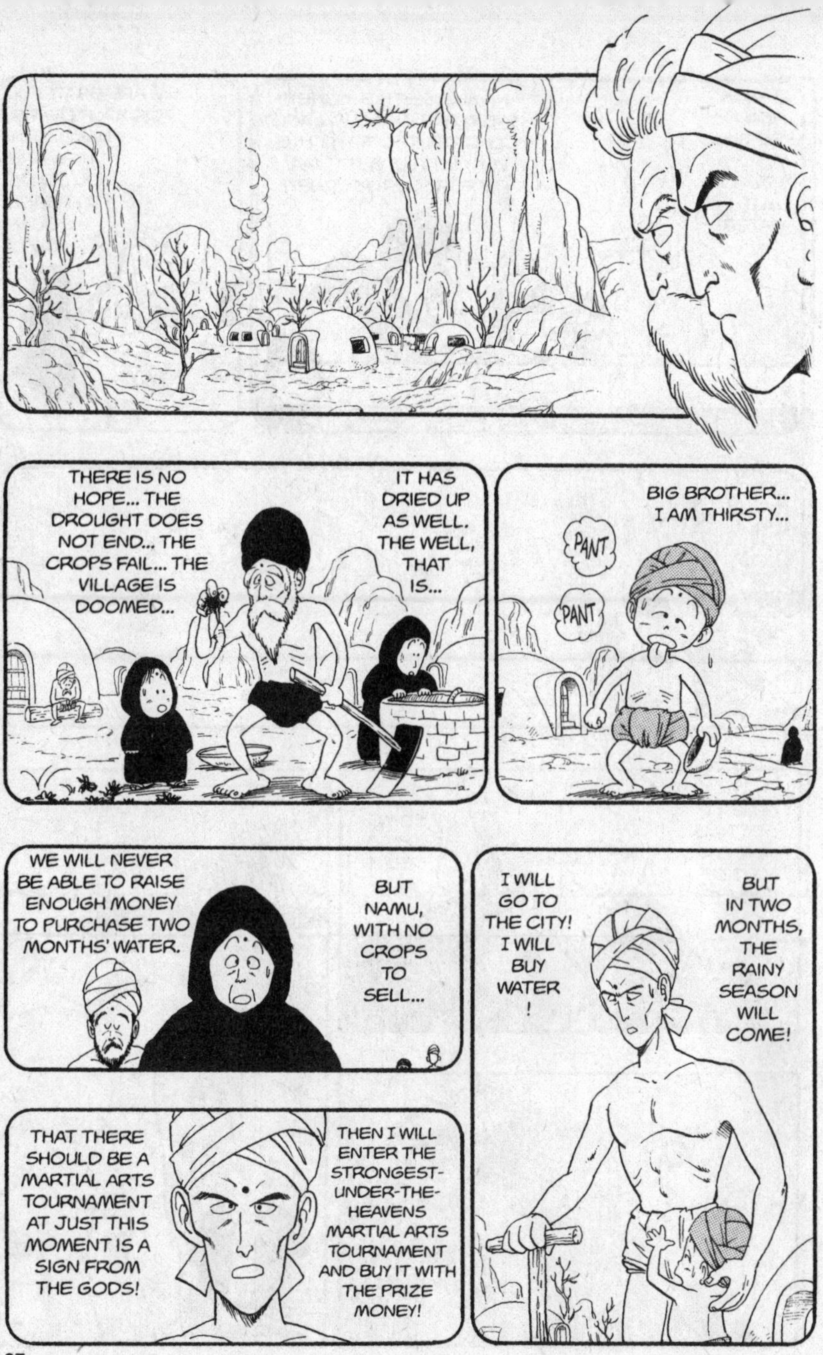
PANT
PANT
BIG BROTHER... I AM THIRSTY...
IT HAS DRIED UP AS WELL. THE WELL, THAT IS...
THERE IS NO HOPE... THE DROUGHT DOES NOT END... THE CROPS FAIL... THE VILLAGE IS DOOMED...
BUT IN TWO MONTHS, THE RAINY SEASON WILL COME!
I WILL GO TO THE CITY! I WILL BUY WATER!
BUT NAMU, WITH NO CROPS TO SELL...
WE WILL NEVER BE ABLE TO RAISE ENOUGH MONEY TO PURCHASE TWO MONTHS' WATER.
THEN I WILL ENTER THE STRONGEST-UNDER-THE-HEAVENS MARTIAL ARTS TOURNAMENT AND BUY IT WITH THE PRIZE MONEY!
THAT THERE SHOULD BE A MARTIAL ARTS TOURNAMENT AT JUST THIS MOMENT IS A SIGN FROM THE GODS!

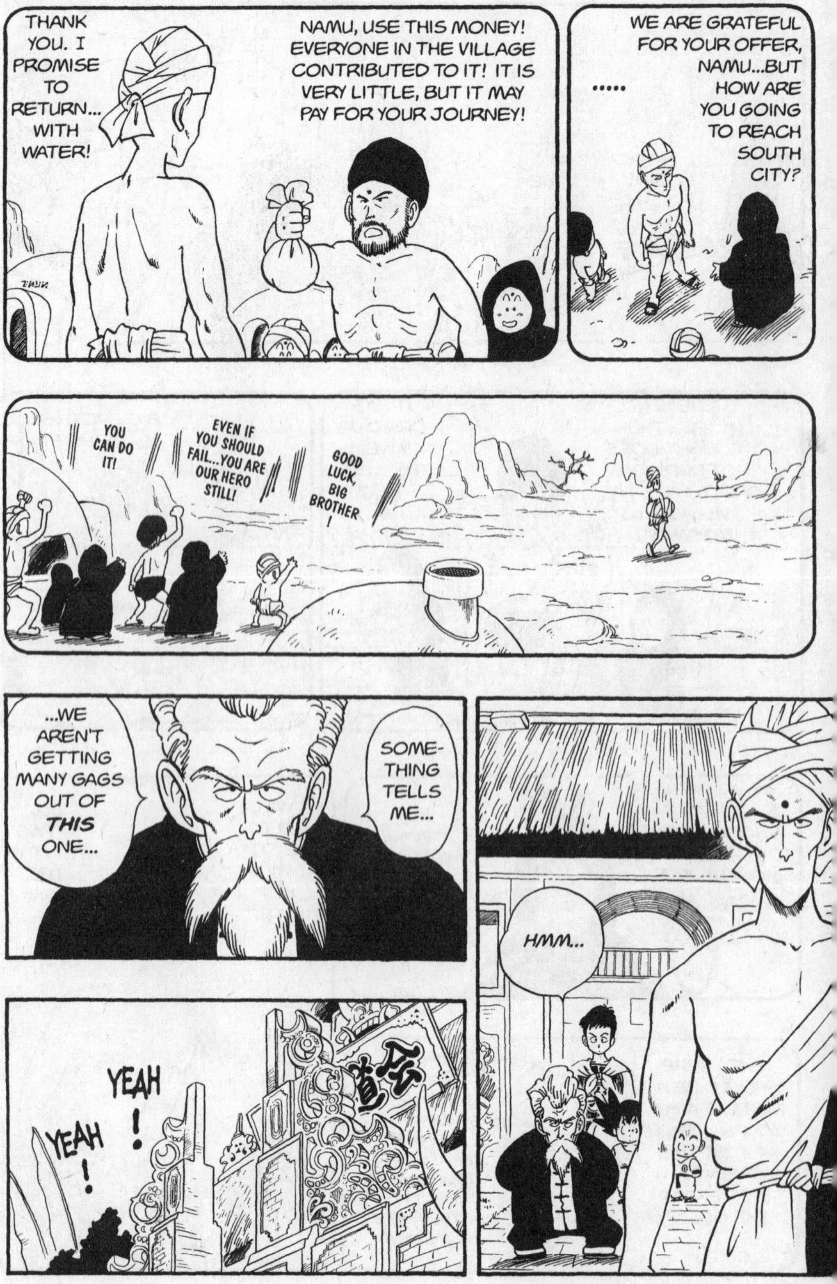
WE ARE GRATEFUL FOR YOUR OFFER, NAMU...BUT HOW ARE YOU GOING TO REACH SOUTH CITY?
.....
NAMU, USE THIS MONEY! EVERYONE IN THE VILLAGE CONTRIBUTED TO IT! IT IS VERY LITTLE, BUT IT MAY PAY FOR YOUR JOURNEY!
THANK YOU. I PROMISE TO RETURN... WITH WATER!
GOOD LUCK, BIG BROTHER!
EVEN IF YOU SHOULD FAIL...YOU ARE OUR HERO STILL!
YOU CAN DO IT!
HMM...
SOMETHING TELLS ME...
...WE AREN'T GETTING MANY GAGS OUT OF THIS ONE...
YEAH!
YEAH!

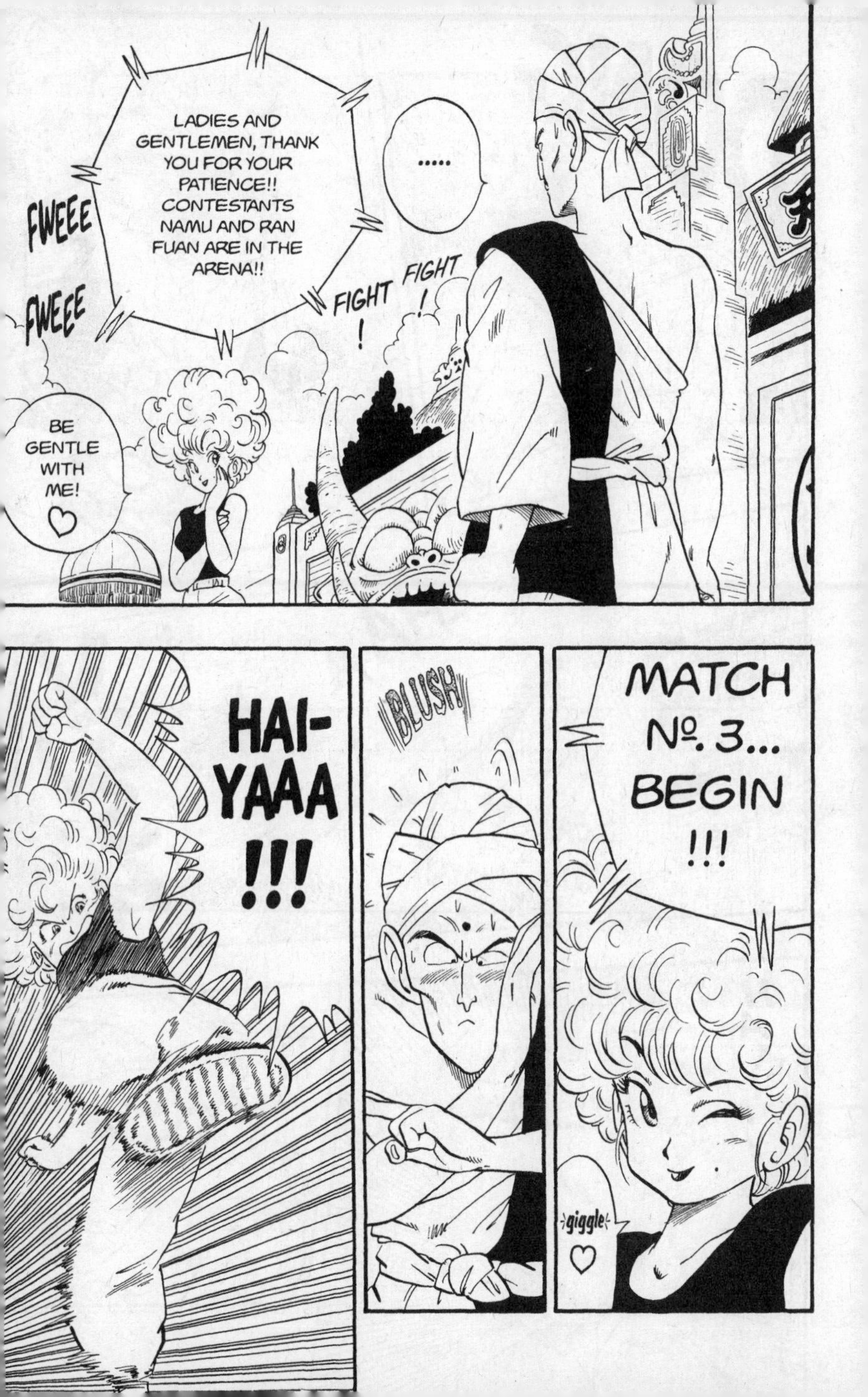
LADIES AND GENTLEMEN, THANK YOU FOR YOUR PATIENCE!! CONTESTANTS NAMU AND RAN FUAN ARE IN THE ARENA!!
.....
FIGHT! FIGHT!
FWEEE FWEEE
BE GENTLE WITH ME! ♡
MATCH №. 3... BEGIN!!!
giggle ♡
BLUSH
HAI-YAAA!!!

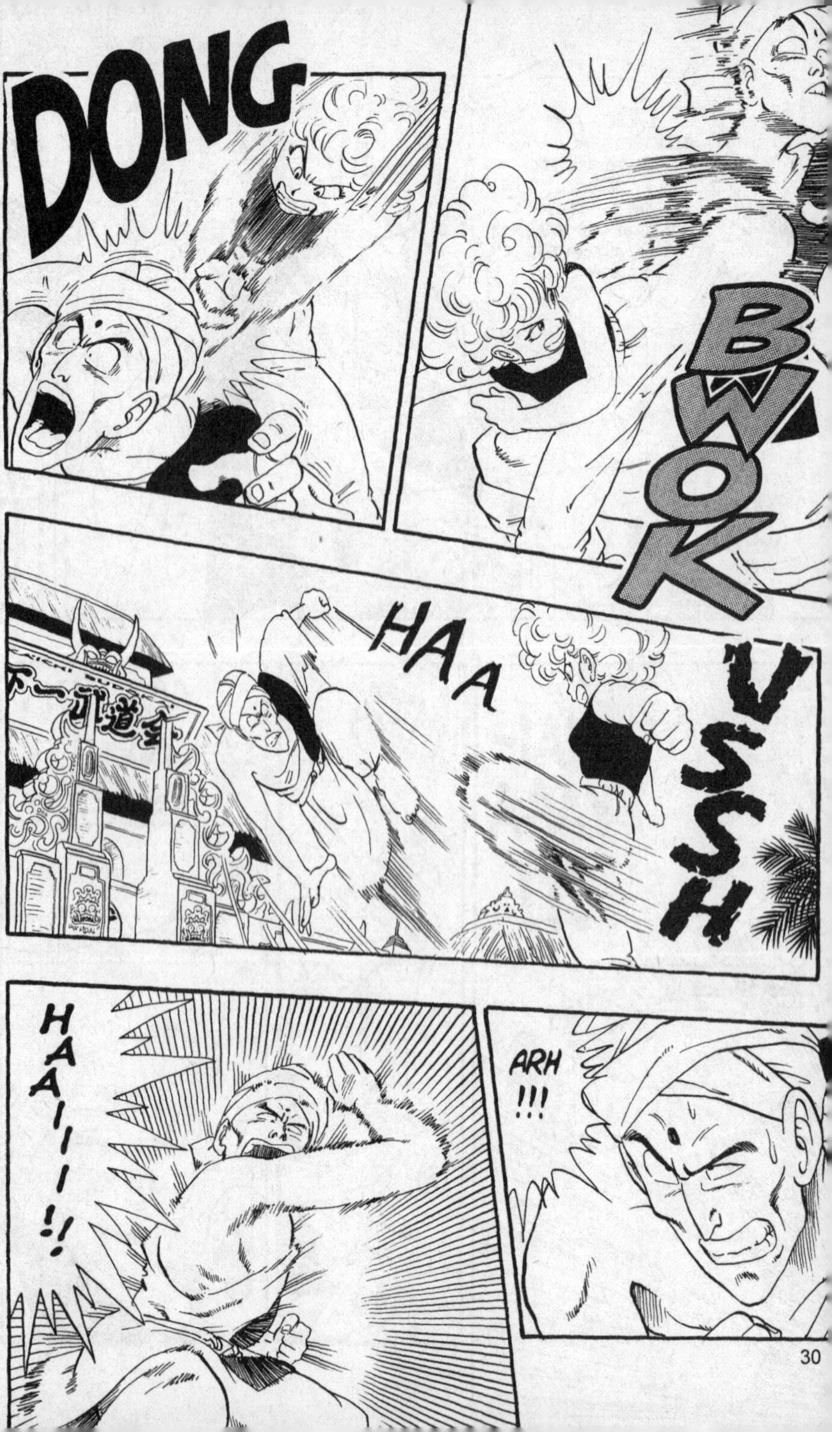
BWOK
DONG
VSSH
HAA
ARH !!!
HAAIII!!

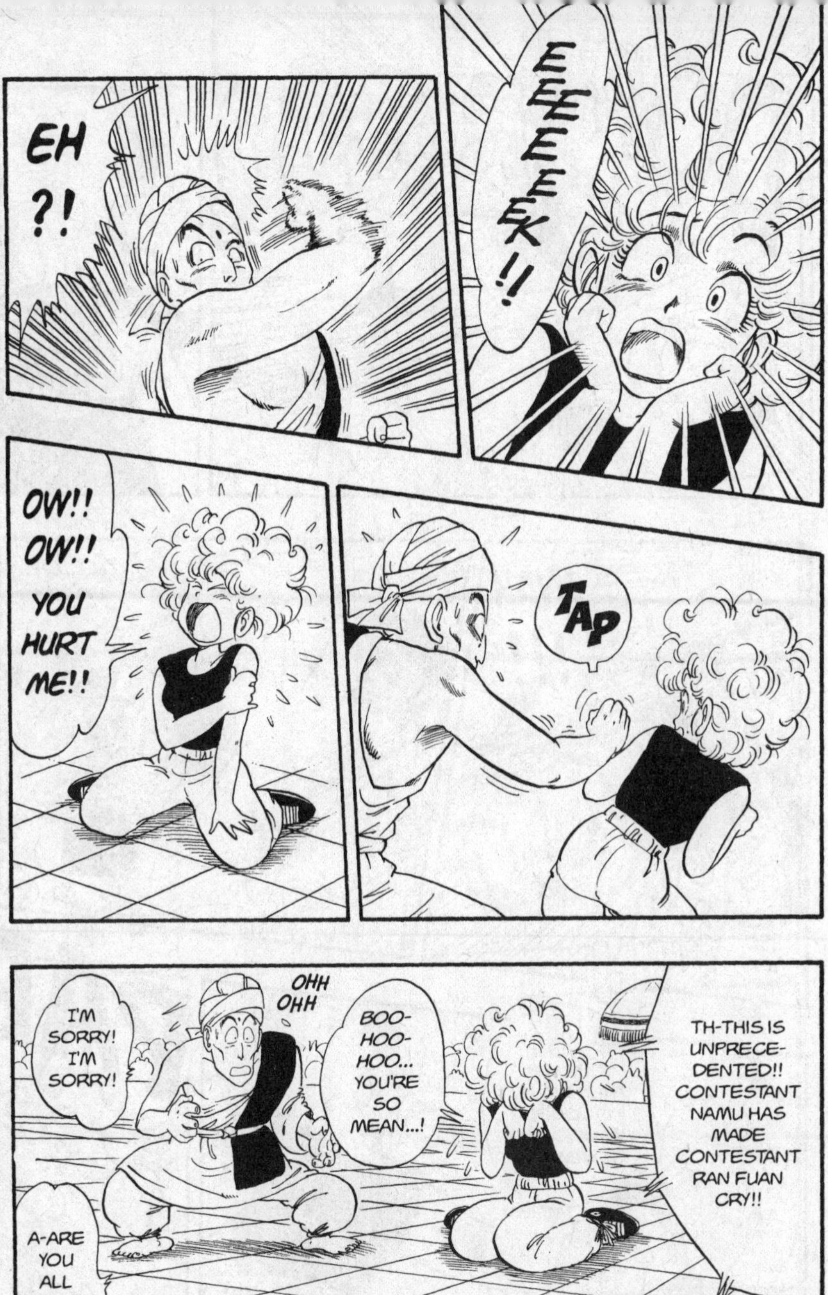
EEEEEEK!!
EH ?!
TAP
OW!! OW!! YOU HURT ME!!
TH-THIS IS UNPRECE-DENTED!! CONTESTANT NAMU HAS MADE CONTESTANT RAN FUAN CRY!!
BOO-HOO-HOO... YOU'RE SO MEAN...!
OHH OHH
I'M SORRY! I'M SORRY!
A-ARE YOU ALL RIGHT?

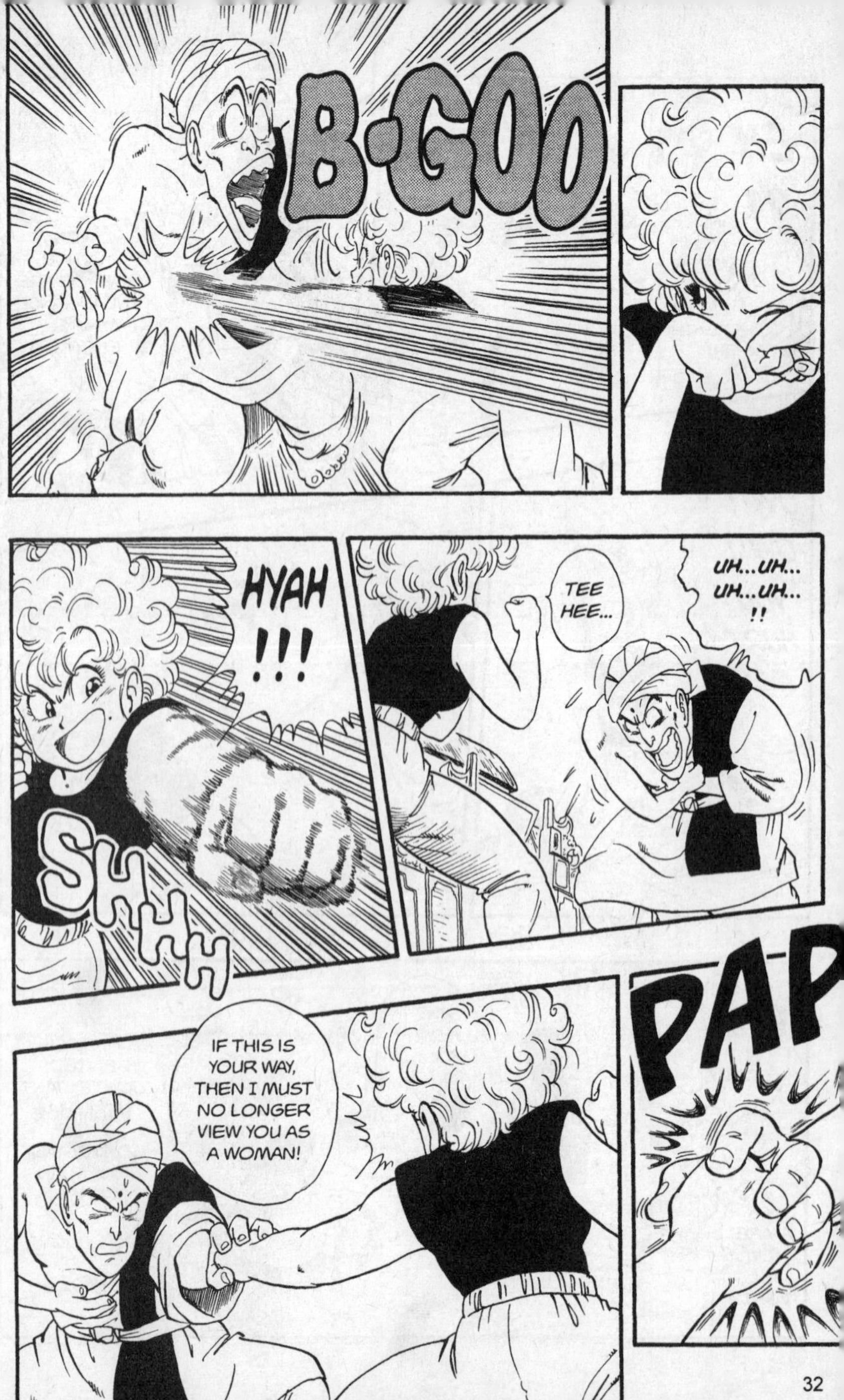
B-GOO
UH...UH... UH...UH... !!
TEE HEE...
HYAH !!!
SHHHH
PAP
IF THIS IS YOUR WAY, THEN I MUST NO LONGER VIEW YOU AS A WOMAN!

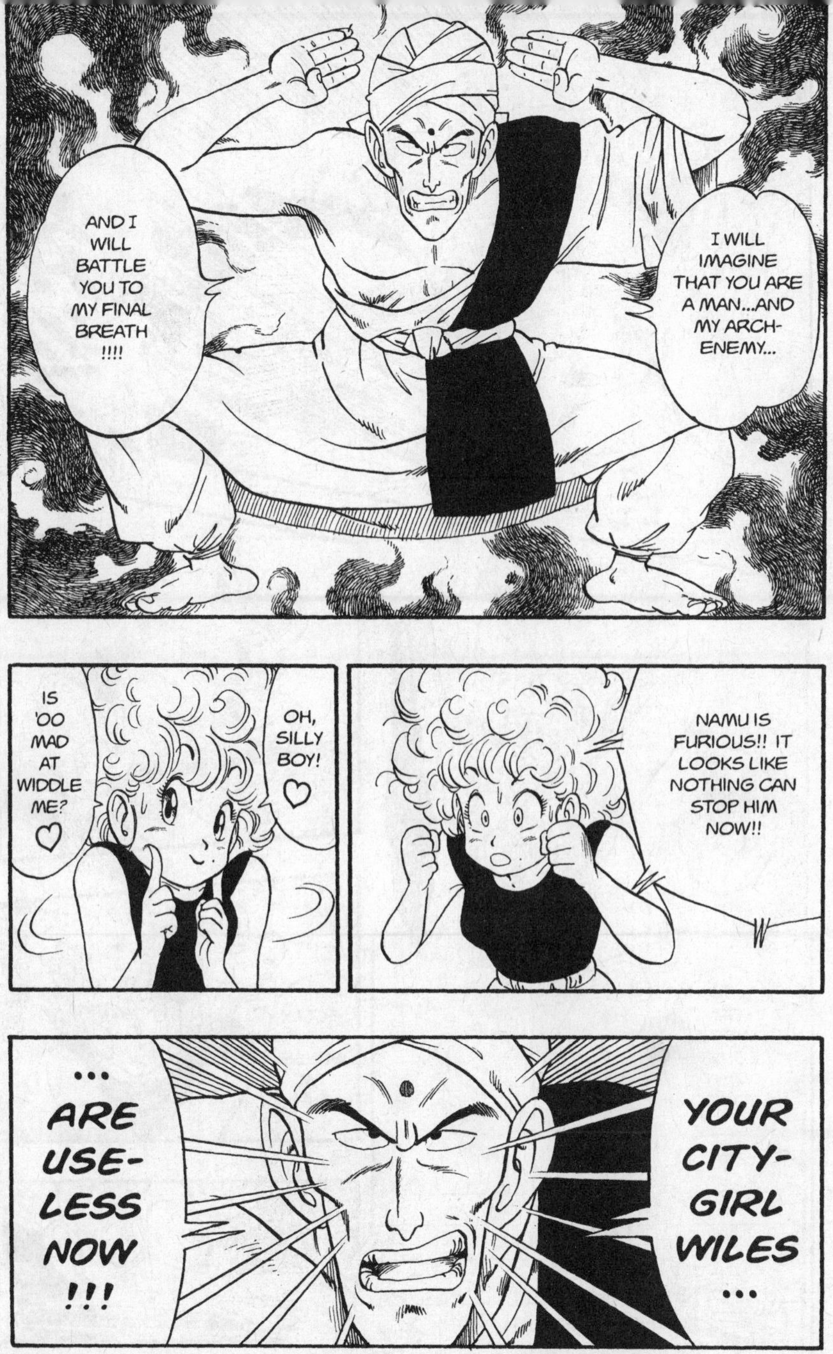
I WILL IMAGINE THAT YOU ARE A MAN...AND MY ARCH-ENEMY...
AND I WILL BATTLE YOU TO MY FINAL BREATH !!!!
NAMU IS FURIOUS!! IT LOOKS LIKE NOTHING CAN STOP HIM NOW!!
OH, SILLY BOY! ♡
IS 'OO MAD AT WIDDLE ME? ♡
YOUR CITY-GIRL WILES...
...ARE USE-LESS NOW!!!

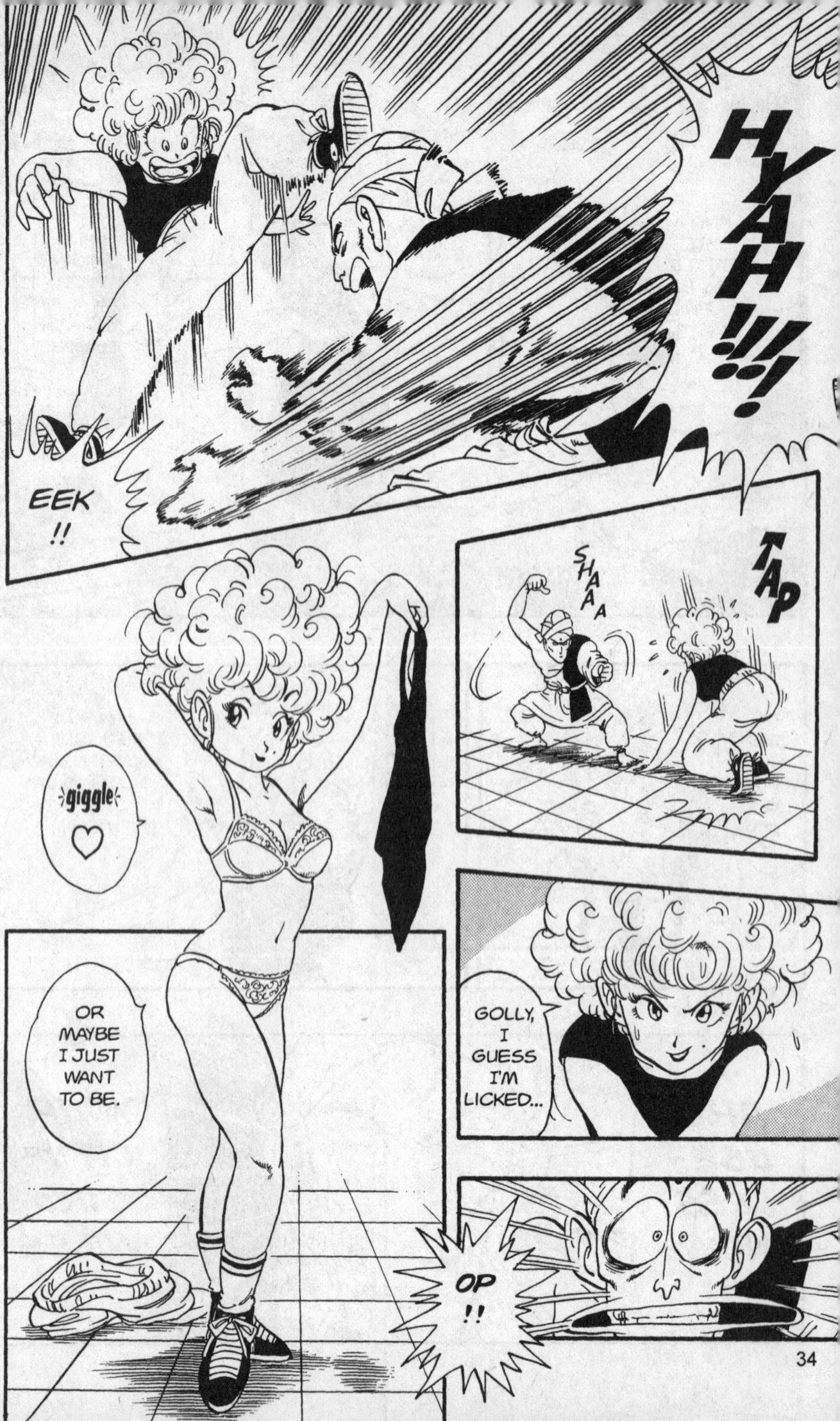
HYAH!!!!
EEK !!
TAP
SHAAA
GOLLY, I GUESS I'M LICKED...
giggle ♡
OR MAYBE I JUST WANT TO BE.
OP !!

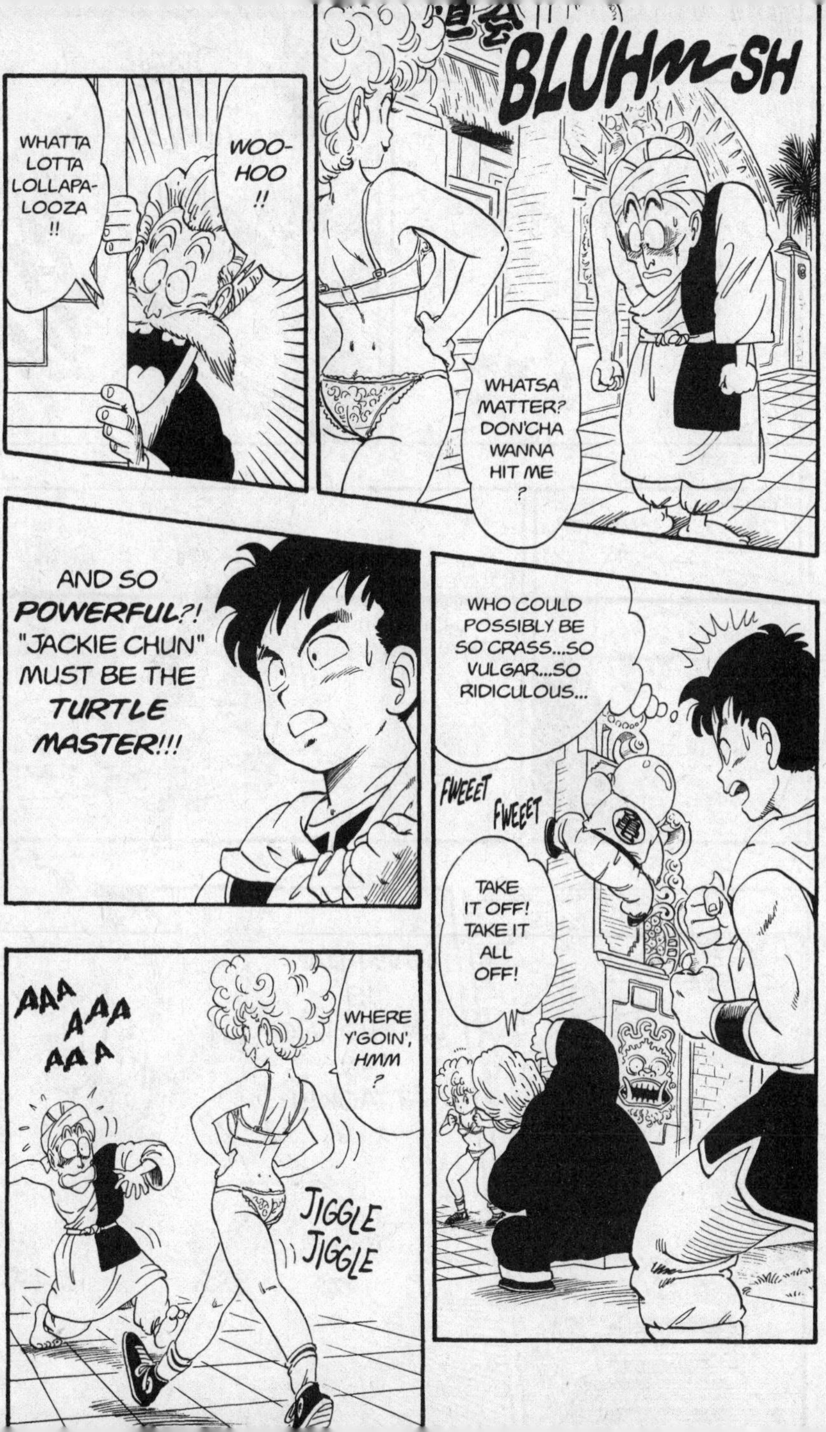
BLUHM-SH
WHATSA MATTER? DON'CHA WANNA HIT ME ?
WOO-HOO !!
WHATTA LOTTA LOLLAPA-LOOZA !!
WHO COULD POSSIBLY BE SO CRASS...SO VULGAR...SO RIDICULOUS...
FWEEET FWEEET
TAKE IT OFF! TAKE IT ALL OFF!
AND SO POWERFUL?! "JACKIE CHUN" MUST BE THE TURTLE MASTER!!!
WHERE Y'GOIN', HMM ?
AAA AAA AAA
JIGGLE JIGGLE

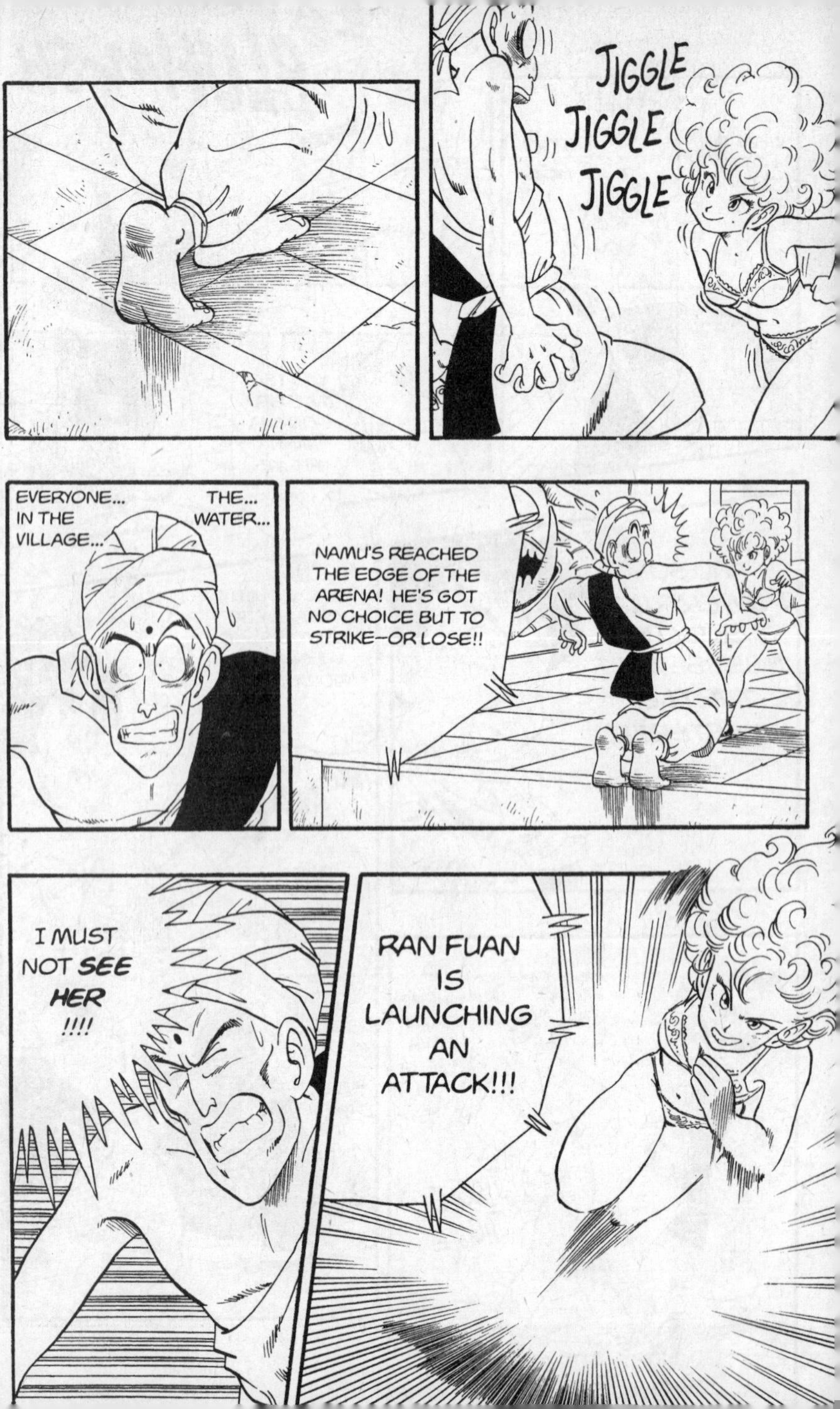
JIGGLE
JIGGLE
JIGGLE
NAMU'S REACHED THE EDGE OF THE ARENA! HE'S GOT NO CHOICE BUT TO STRIKE--OR LOSE!!
EVERYONE... IN THE VILLAGE...
THE... WATER...
RAN FUAN IS LAUNCHING AN ATTACK!!!
I MUST NOT SEE HER !!!!

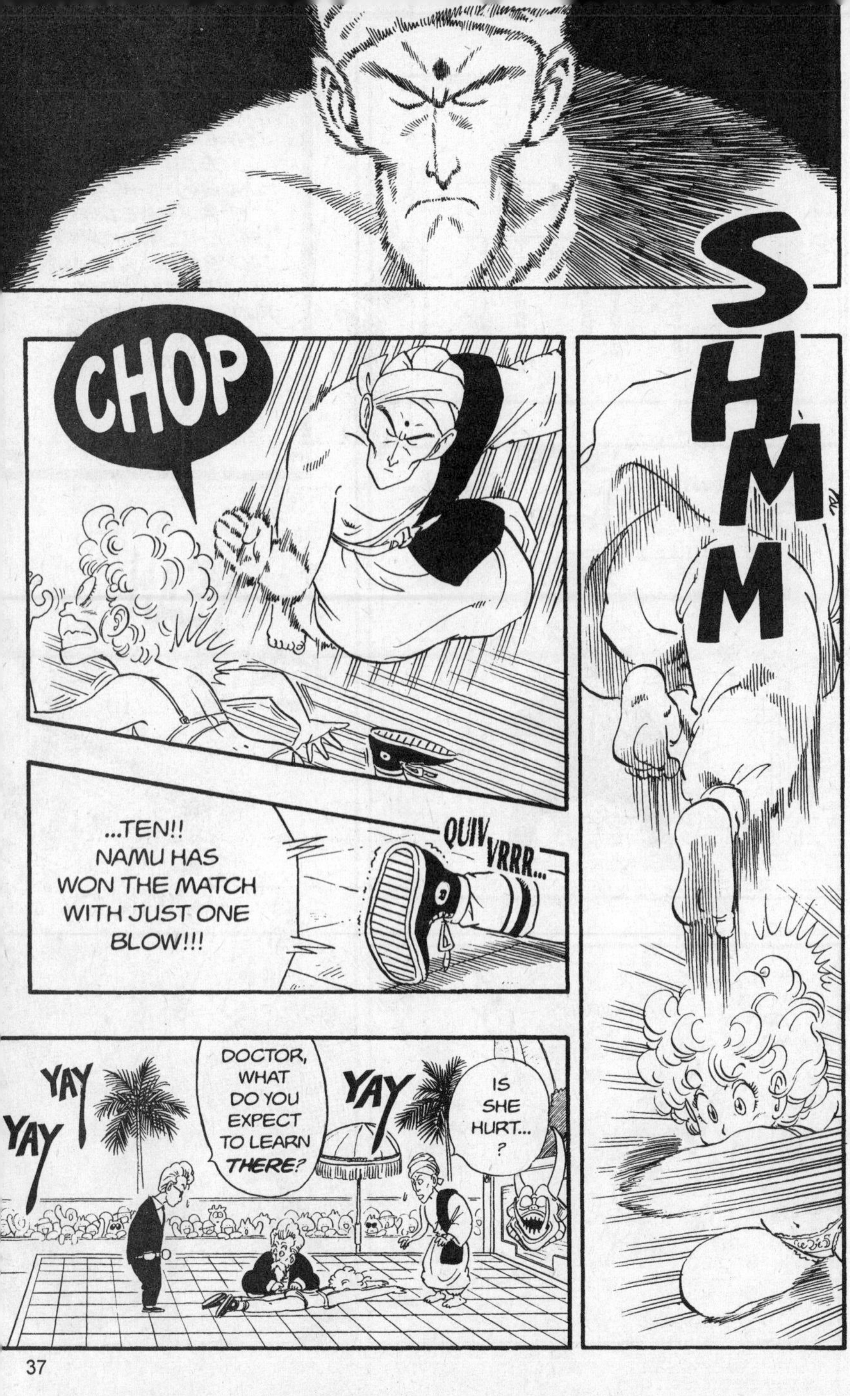
SHMM
CHOP
QUIVVRRR...
...TEN!! NAMU HAS WON THE MATCH WITH JUST ONE BLOW!!!
IS SHE HURT...?
YAY
DOCTOR, WHAT DO YOU EXPECT TO LEARN THERE?
YAY
YAY

Tale 39
Monster Smash!

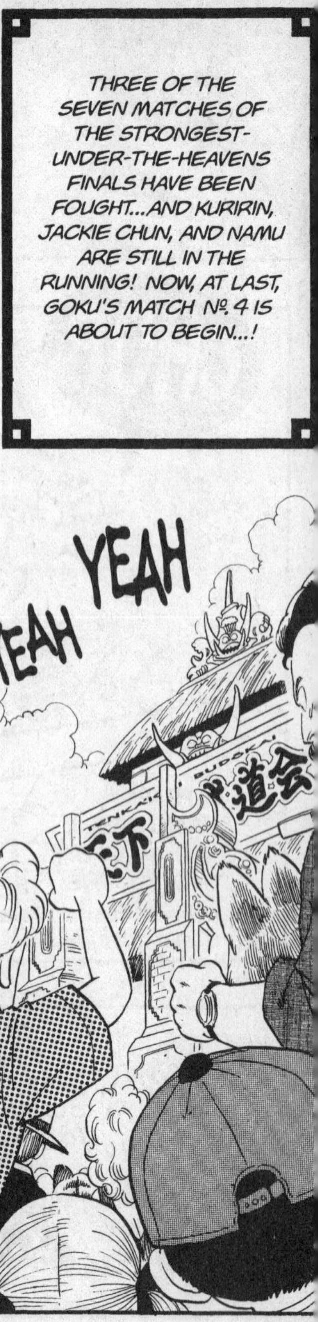
THREE OF THE SEVEN MATCHES OF THE STRONGEST-UNDER-THE-HEAVENS FINALS HAVE BEEN FOUGHT...AND KURIRIN, JACKIE CHUN, AND NAMU ARE STILL IN THE RUNNING! NOW, AT LAST, GOKU'S MATCH №. 4 IS ABOUT TO BEGIN...!
YEAH
YEAH

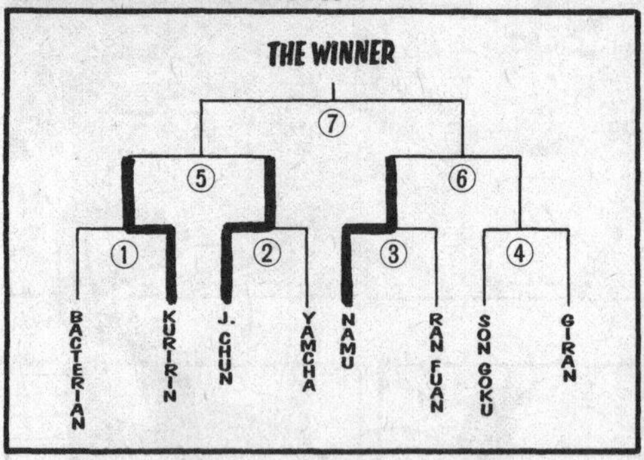
THE WINNER
⑦
⑤
⑥
①
②
③
④
BACTERIAN
KURIRIN
J. CHUN
YAMCHA
NAMU
RAN FUAN
SON GOKU
GIRAN

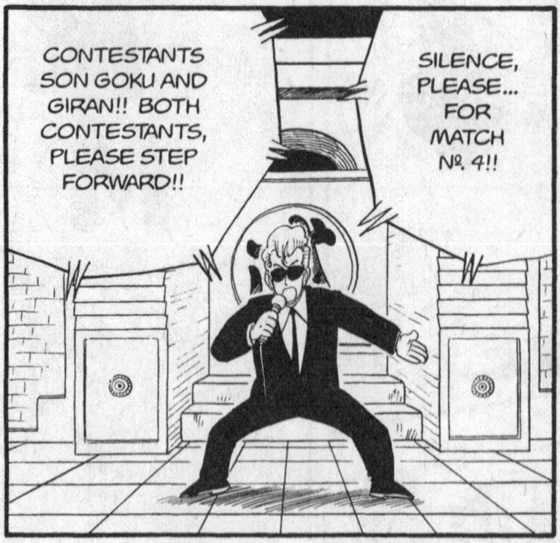
SILENCE, PLEASE... FOR MATCH №. 4!!
CONTESTANTS SON GOKU AND GIRAN!! BOTH CONTESTANTS, PLEASE STEP FORWARD!!

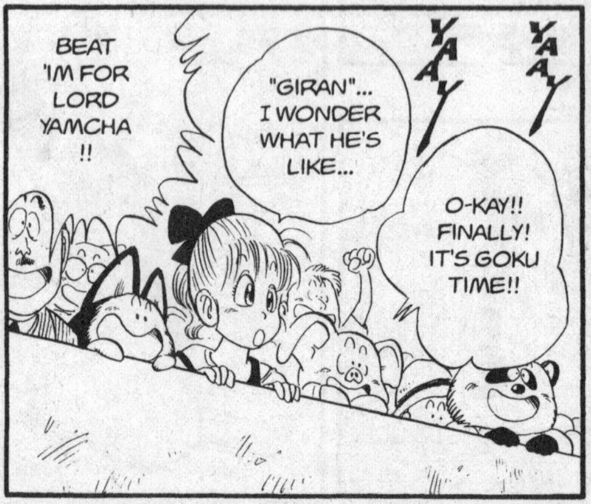
YAAAY
YAAAY
"GIRAN"... I WONDER WHAT HE'S LIKE...
BEAT 'IM FOR LORD YAMCHA !!
O-KAY!! FINALLY! IT'S GOKU TIME!!

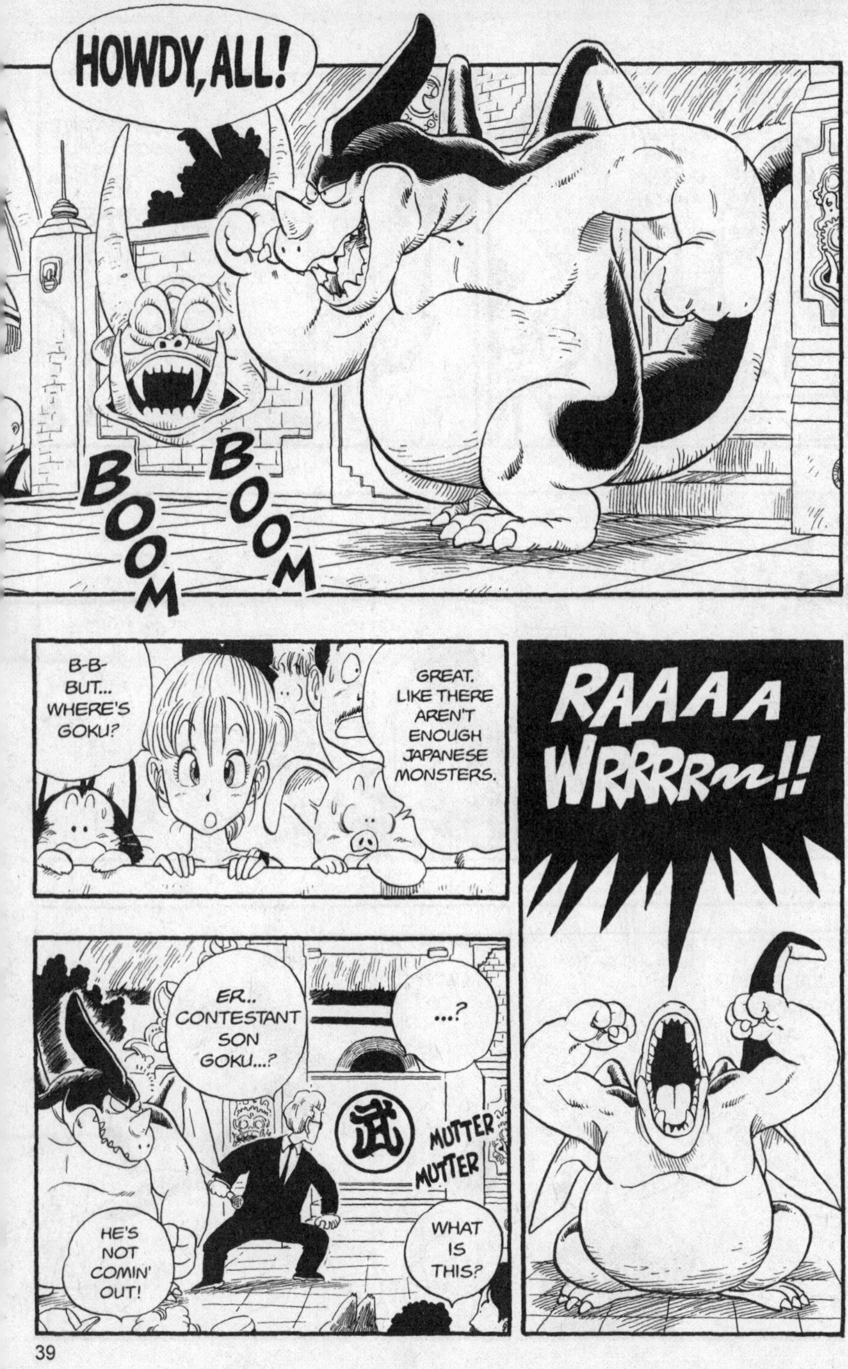
HOWDY, ALL!
BOOM
BOOM
RAAAA WRRRRn!!
GREAT. LIKE THERE AREN'T ENOUGH JAPANESE MONSTERS.
B-B-BUT... WHERE'S GOKU?
...?
ER.. CONTESTANT SON GOKU...?
MUTTER MUTTER
WHAT IS THIS?
HE'S NOT COMIN' OUT!

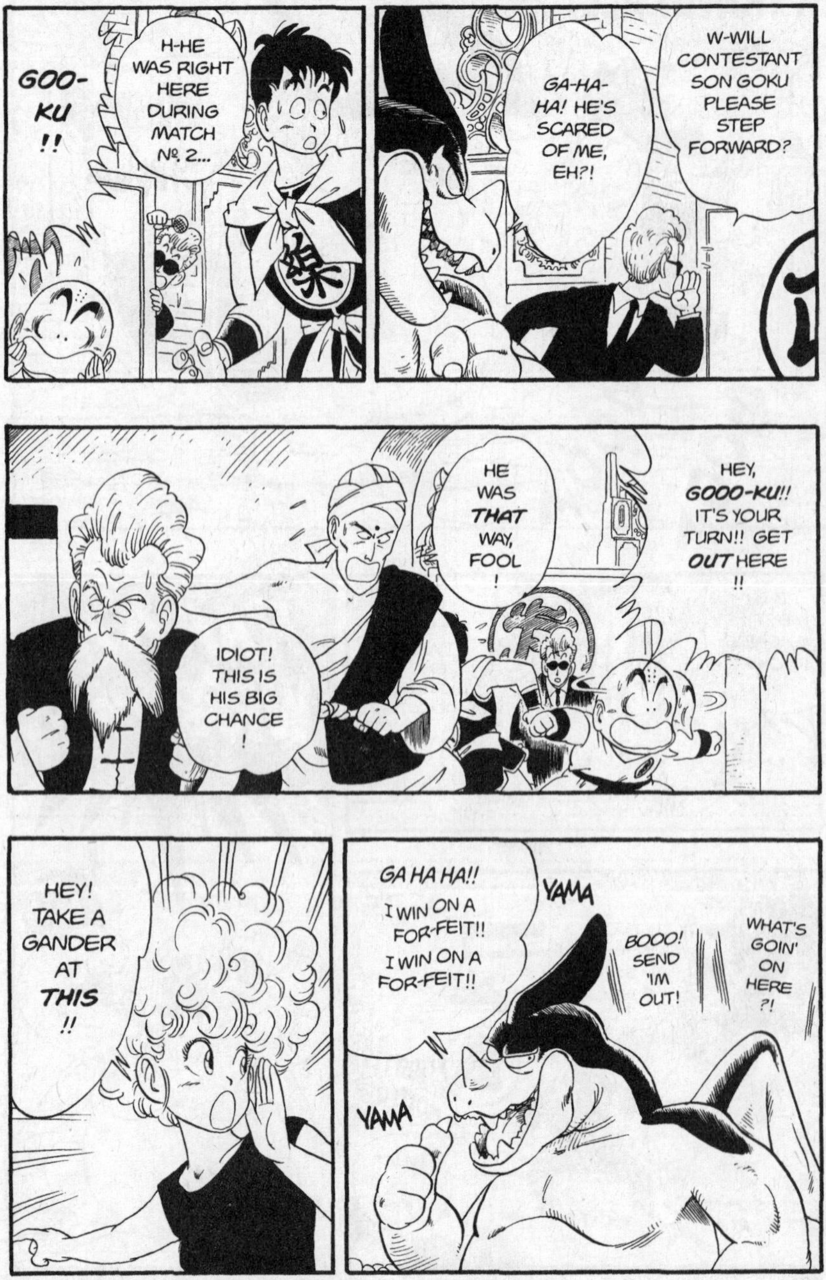
W-WILL CONTESTANT SON GOKU PLEASE STEP FORWARD?
GA-HA-HA! HE'S SCARED OF ME, EH?!
H-HE WAS RIGHT HERE DURING MATCH №. 2...
GOO-KU!!
HEY, GOOO-KU!! IT'S YOUR TURN!! GET OUT HERE!!
HE WAS THAT WAY, FOOL!
IDIOT! THIS IS HIS BIG CHANCE!
WHAT'S GOIN' ON HERE?!
BOOO! SEND 'IM OUT!
YAMA
GA HA HA!! I WIN ON A FOR-FEIT!! I WIN ON A FOR-FEIT!!
YAMA
HEY! TAKE A GANDER AT THIS!!

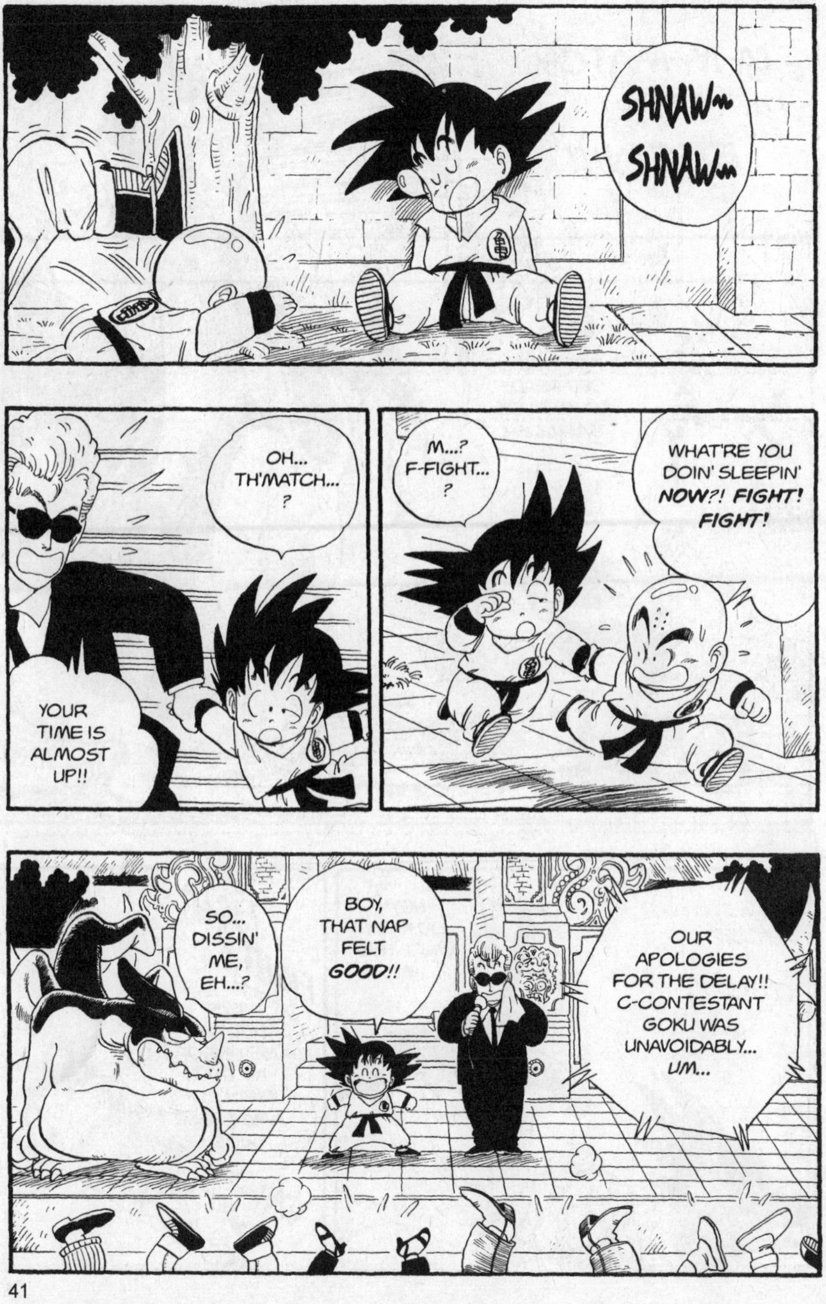
SHNAW... SHNAW...
WHAT'RE YOU DOIN' SLEEPIN' *NOW?! FIGHT! FIGHT!*
M...? F-FIGHT...?
OH... TH'MATCH...?
YOUR TIME IS ALMOST UP!!
OUR APOLOGIES FOR THE DELAY!! C-CONTESTANT GOKU WAS UNAVOIDABLY... *UM...*
BOY, THAT NAP FELT *GOOD!!*
SO... DISSIN' ME, EH...?

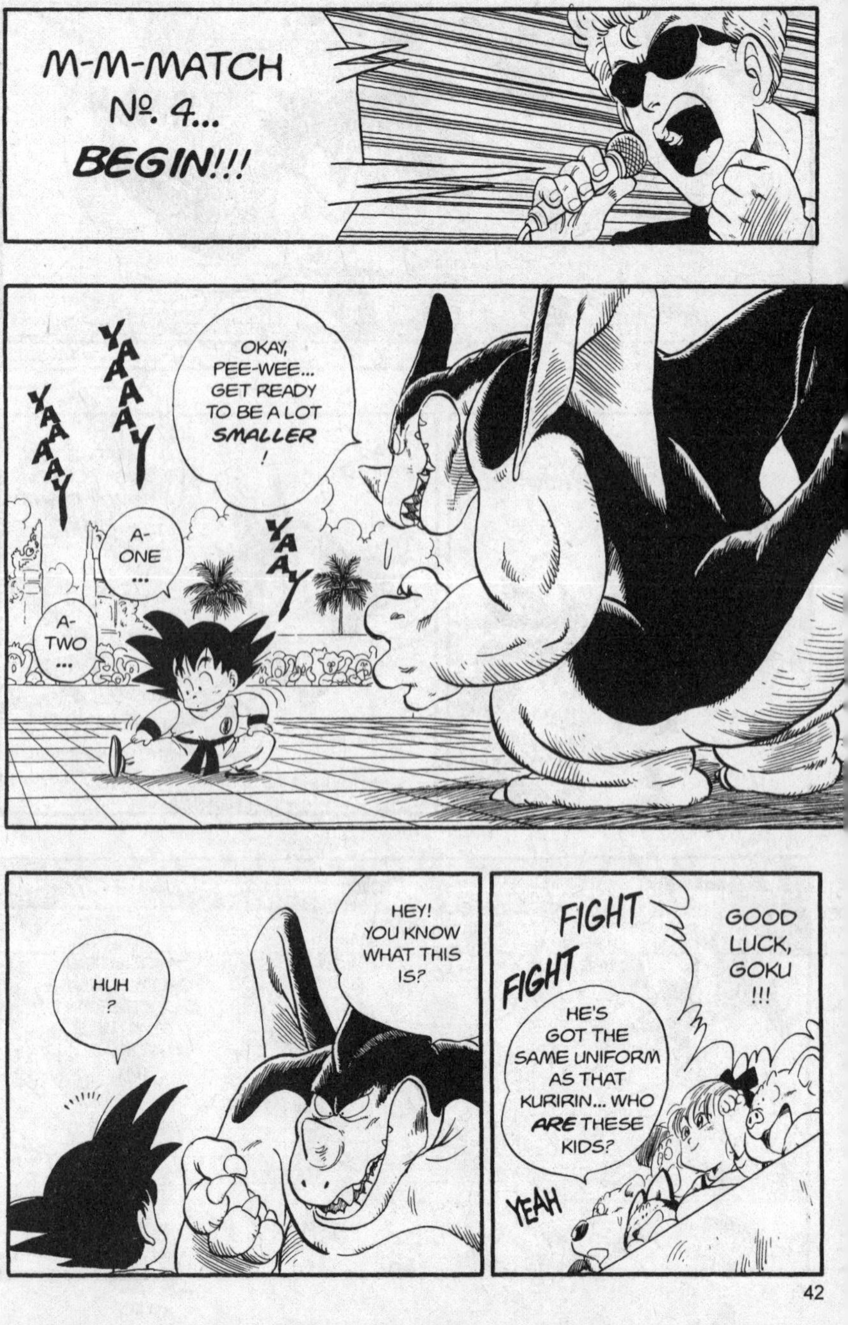
M-M-MATCH №. 4... BEGIN!!!
OKAY, PEE-WEE... GET READY TO BE A LOT SMALLER!
YAAAAY
YAAAAY
YAAAY
A-ONE...
A-TWO...
GOOD LUCK, GOKU!!!
FIGHT
FIGHT
HE'S GOT THE SAME UNIFORM AS THAT KURIRIN... WHO ARE THESE KIDS?
YEAH
HEY! YOU KNOW WHAT THIS IS?
HUH?

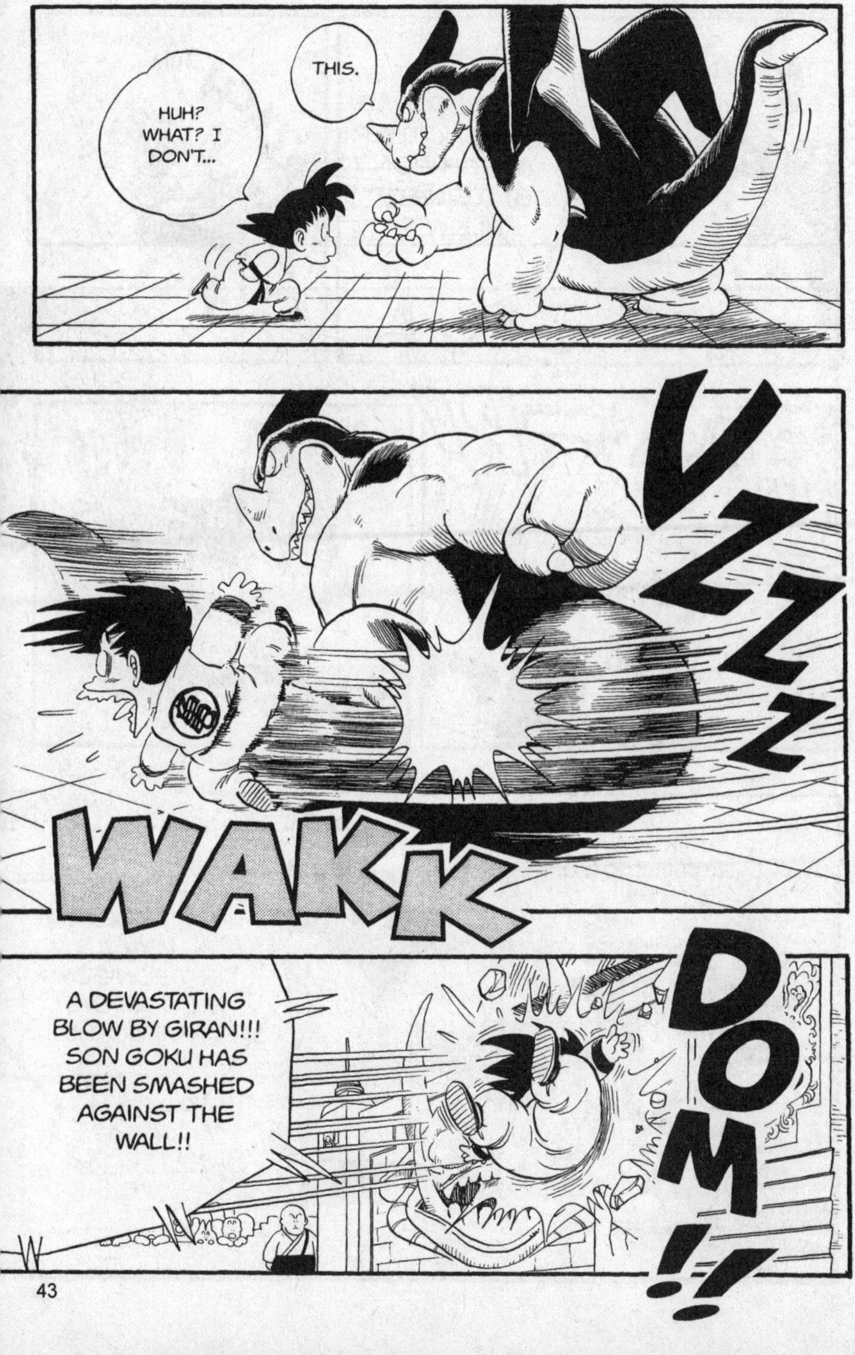
THIS.
HUH? WHAT? I DON'T...
VZZZZ
WAKK
DOM!!
A DEVASTATING BLOW BY GIRAN!!! SON GOKU HAS BEEN SMASHED AGAINST THE WALL!!

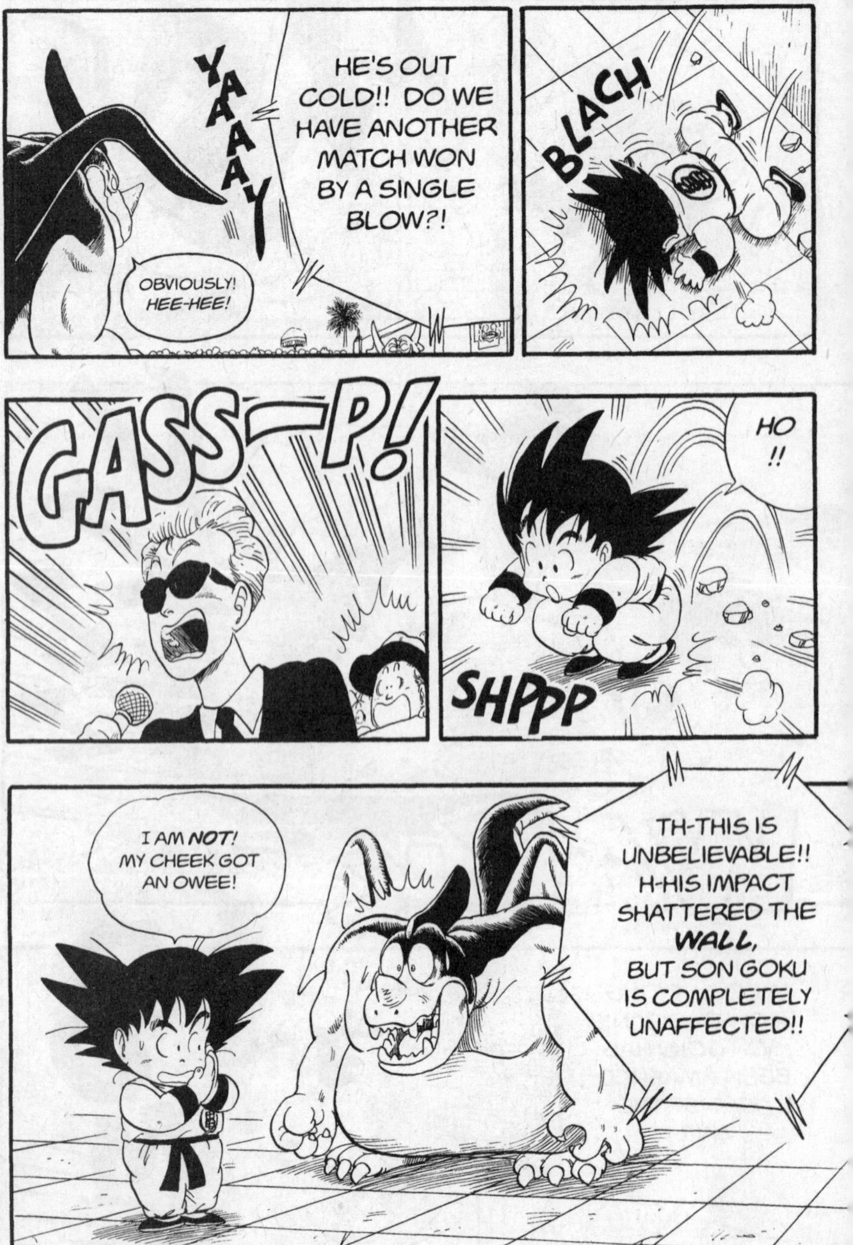
BLACH
HE'S OUT COLD!! DO WE HAVE ANOTHER MATCH WON BY A SINGLE BLOW?!
YAAAAY
OBVIOUSLY! HEE-HEE!
HO !!
SHPPP
GASS—P!
TH-THIS IS UNBELIEVABLE!! H-HIS IMPACT SHATTERED THE WALL, BUT SON GOKU IS COMPLETELY UNAFFECTED!!
I AM NOT! MY CHEEK GOT AN OWEE!

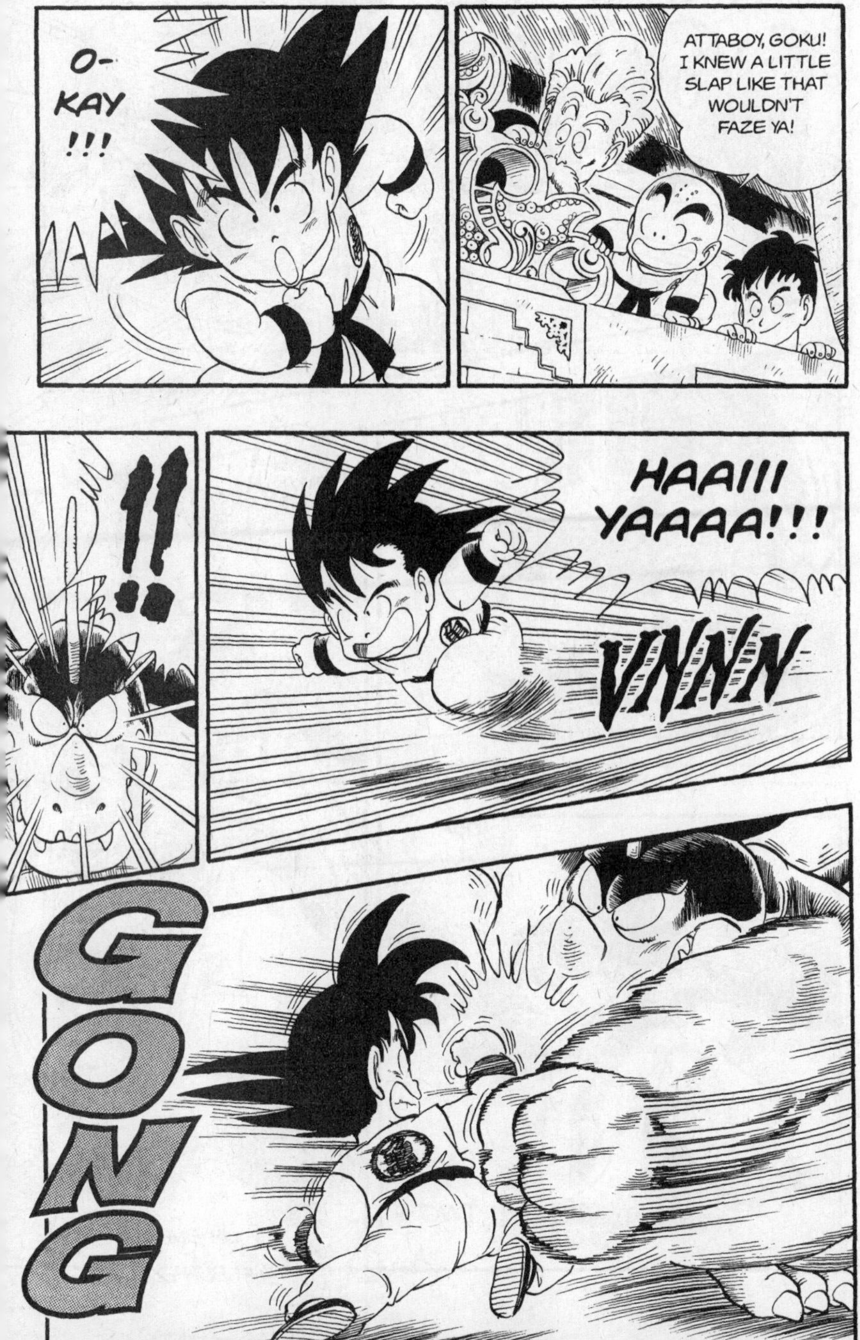
ATTABOY, GOKU! I KNEW A LITTLE SLAP LIKE THAT WOULDN'T FAZE YA!
O-KAY!!!
HAAIII YAAAA!!!
VNNN
!!
GONG

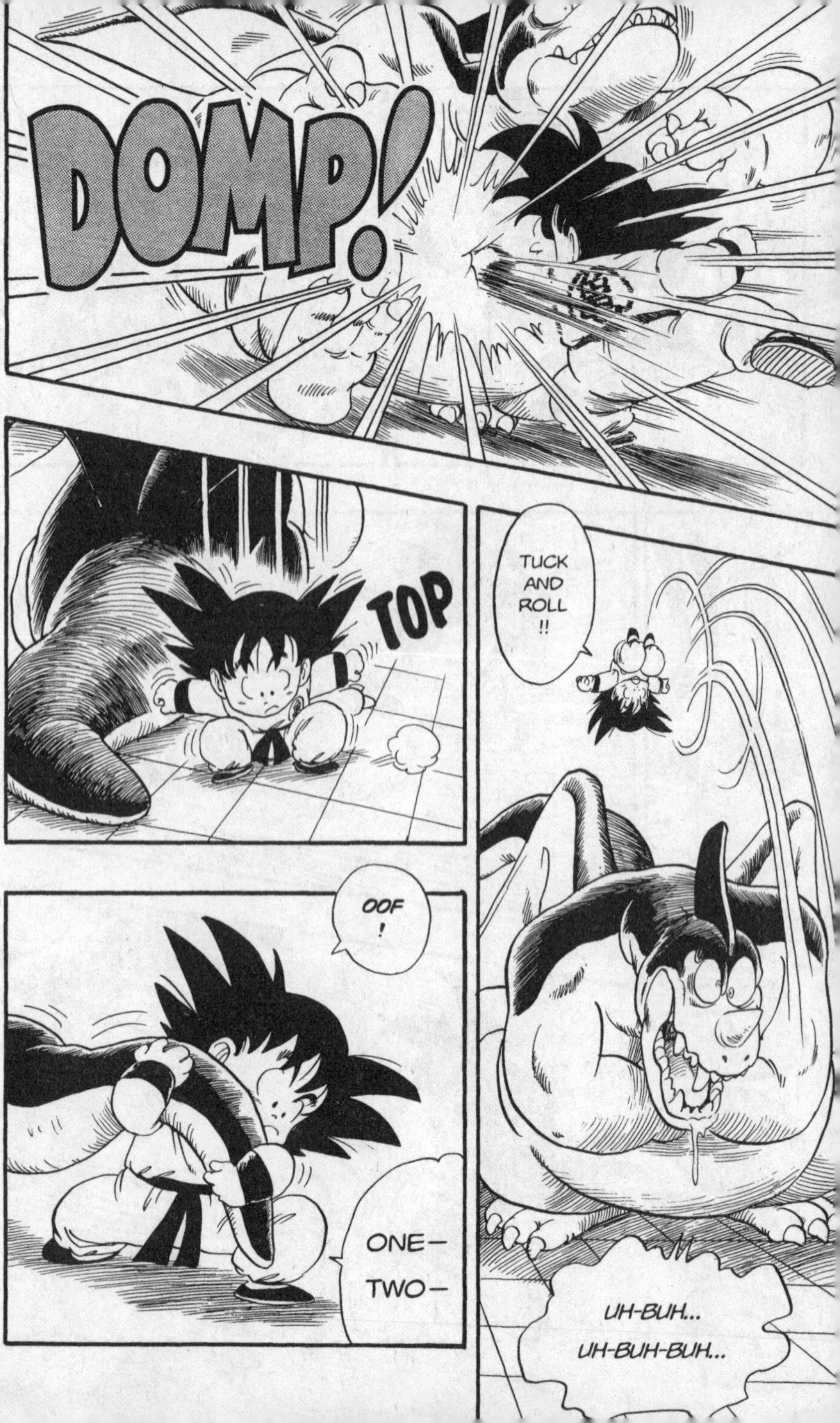
DOMP!
TUCK AND ROLL !!
UH-BUH...
UH-BUH-BUH...
TOP
OOF !
ONE—
TWO—

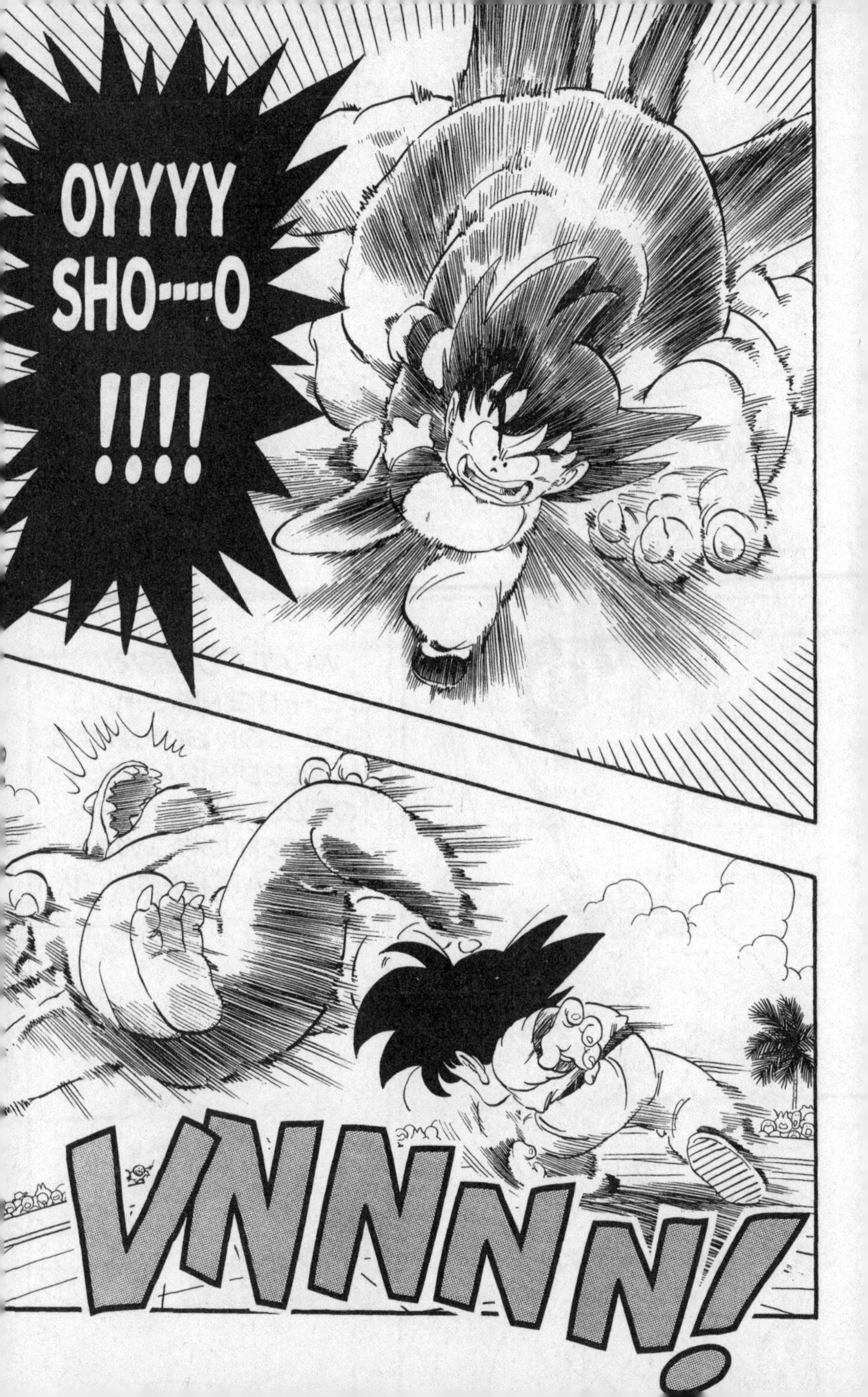
OYYYY SHO----O !!!!
VNNNN!

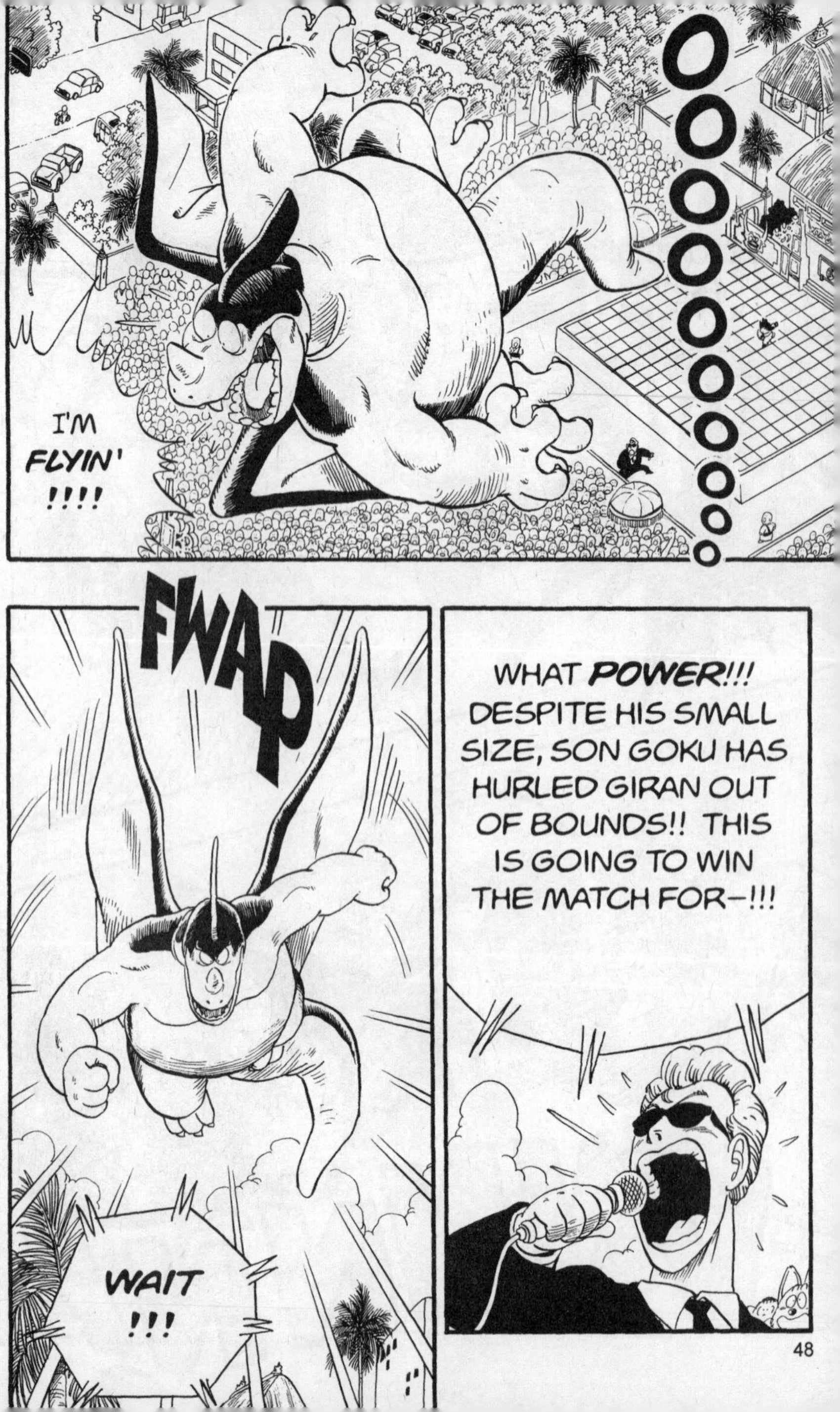
OOOOOOOOOOOO
I'M FLYIN' !!!!
WHAT POWER!!! DESPITE HIS SMALL SIZE, SON GOKU HAS HURLED GIRAN OUT OF BOUNDS!! THIS IS GOING TO WIN THE MATCH FOR-!!!
FWAP
WAIT !!!

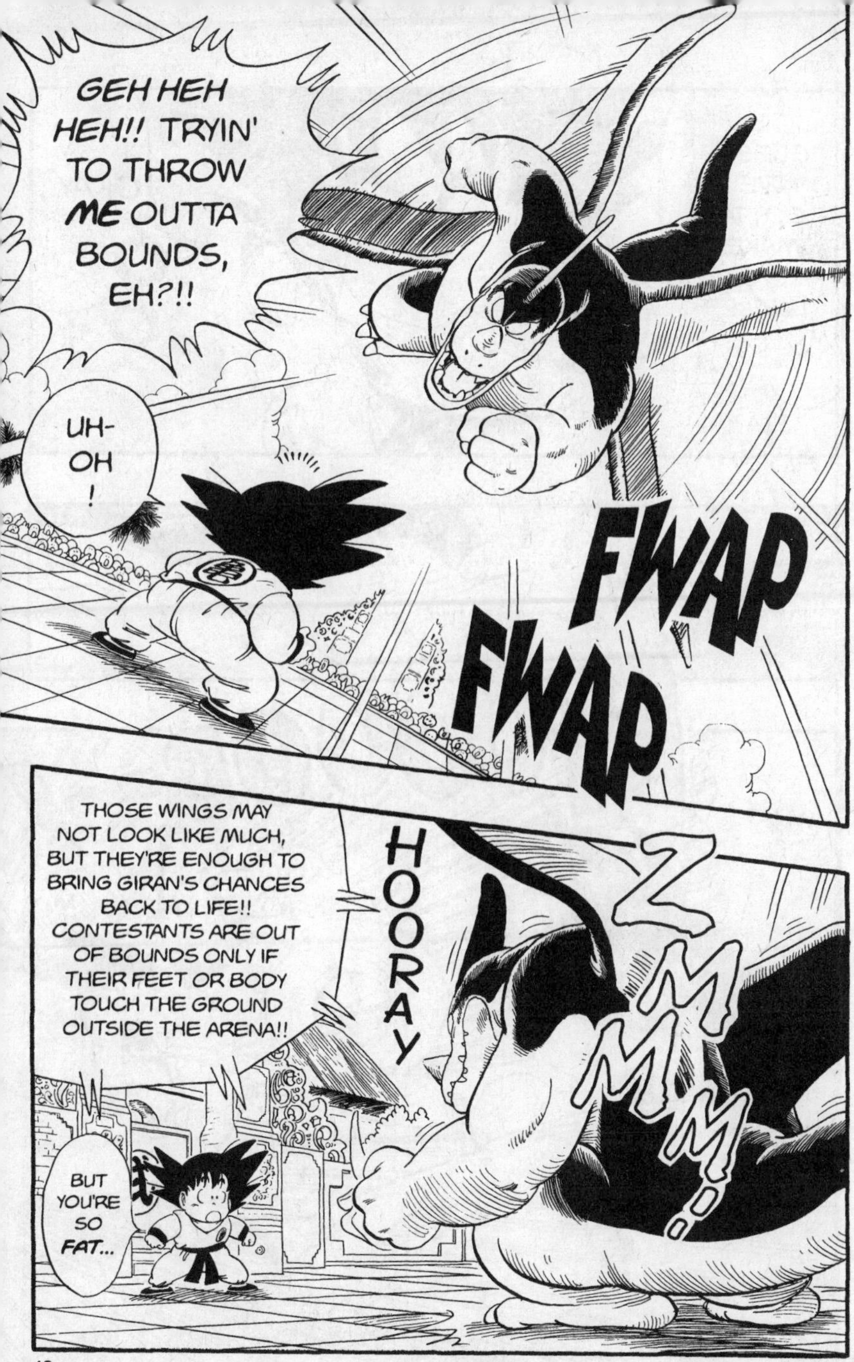
GEH HEH HEH!! TRYIN' TO THROW *ME* OUTTA BOUNDS, EH?!!
UH-OH !
FWAP
FWAP
HOORAY
ZMMMM...
THOSE WINGS MAY NOT LOOK LIKE MUCH, BUT THEY'RE ENOUGH TO BRING GIRAN'S CHANCES BACK TO LIFE!! CONTESTANTS ARE OUT OF BOUNDS ONLY IF THEIR FEET OR BODY TOUCH THE GROUND OUTSIDE THE ARENA!!
BUT YOU'RE SO *FAT*...

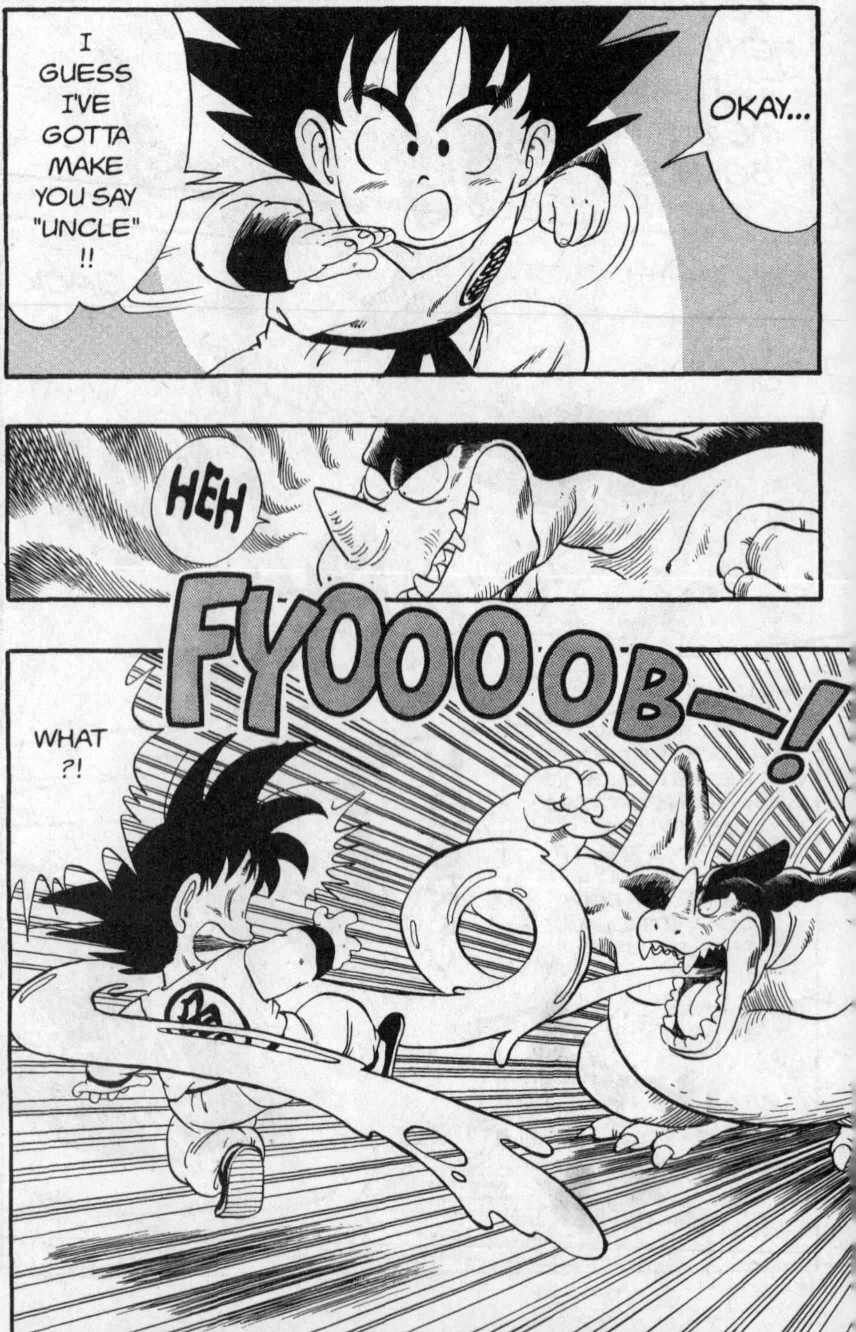

OKAY...
I GUESS I'VE GOTTA MAKE YOU SAY "UNCLE" !!
HEH
FYOOOOB—!
WHAT ?!

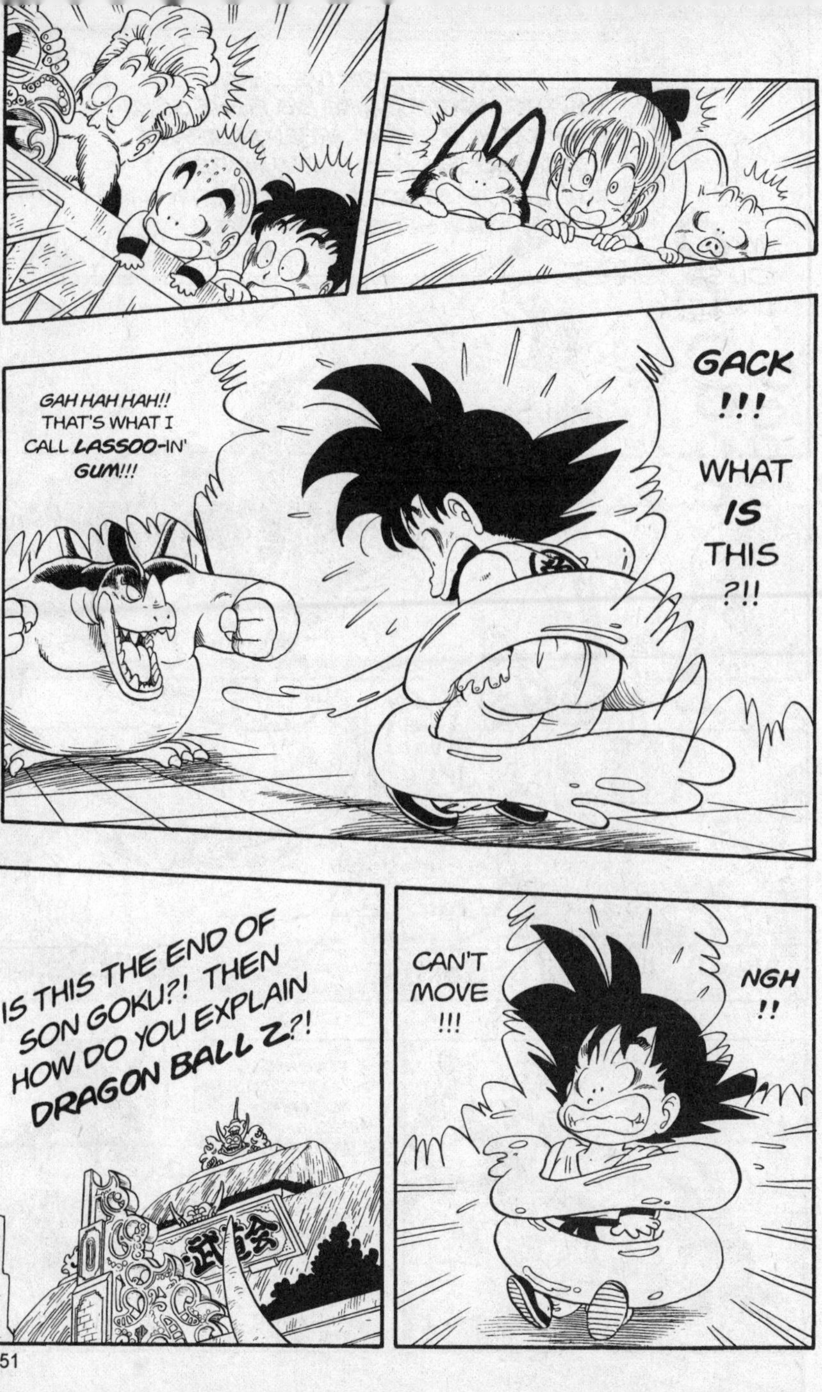
GACK !!!
WHAT IS THIS ?!!
GAH HAH HAH!! THAT'S WHAT I CALL LASSOO-IN' GUM!!!
NGH !!
CAN'T MOVE !!!
IS THIS THE END OF SON GOKU?! THEN HOW DO YOU EXPLAIN DRAGON BALL Z?!

Tale 40 • The Tail of Goku

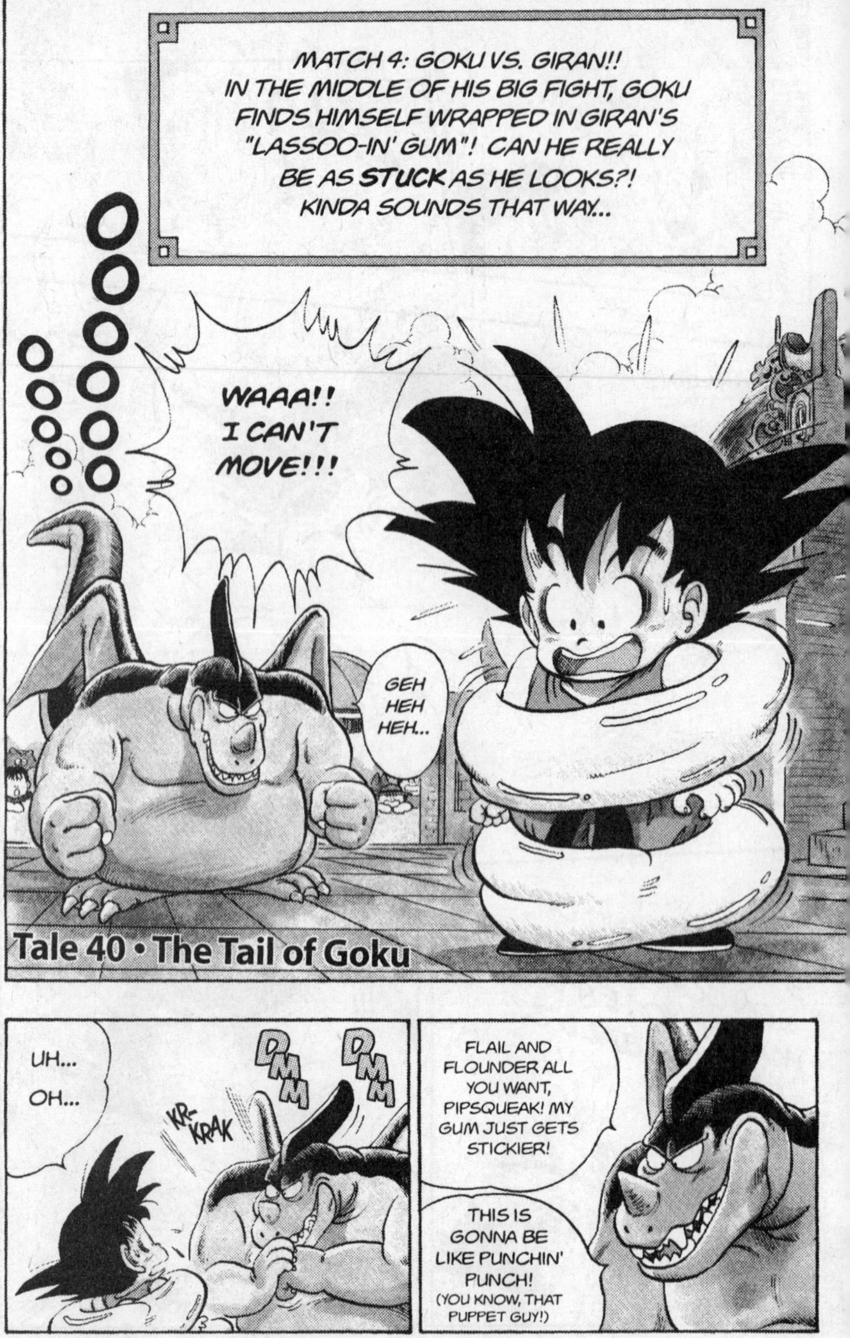
MATCH 4: GOKU VS. GIRAN!! IN THE MIDDLE OF HIS BIG FIGHT, GOKU FINDS HIMSELF WRAPPED IN GIRAN'S "LASSOO-IN' GUM"! CAN HE REALLY BE AS **STUCK** AS HE LOOKS?! KINDA SOUNDS THAT WAY...
WAAA!! I CAN'T MOVE!!!
OOOOOOOOOOOOOOOO
GEH HEH HEH...
Tale 40 • The Tail of Goku
FLAIL AND FLOUNDER ALL YOU WANT, PIPSQUEAK! MY GUM JUST GETS STICKIER!
THIS IS GONNA BE LIKE PUNCHIN' PUNCH! (YOU KNOW, THAT PUPPET GUY!)
DMM
DMM
KR-KRAK
UH... OH...

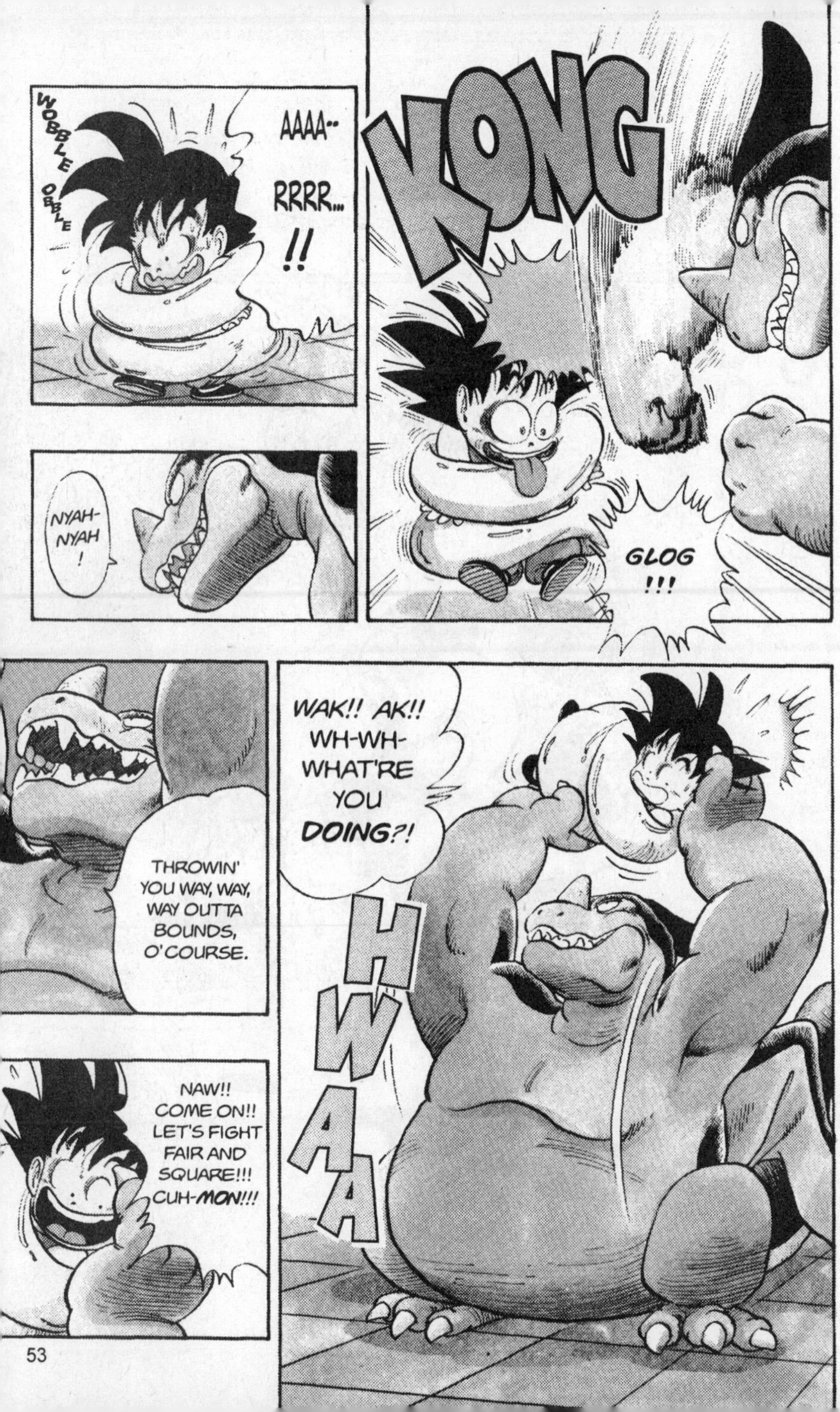
KONG
GLOG !!!
WOBBLE OBBLE
AAAA-- RRRR... !!
NYAH-NYAH!
WAK!! AK!! WH-WH-WHAT'RE YOU DOING?!
HWAAA
THROWIN' YOU WAY, WAY, WAY OUTTA BOUNDS, O'COURSE.
NAW!! COME ON!! LET'S FIGHT FAIR AND SQUARE!!! CUH-MON!!!

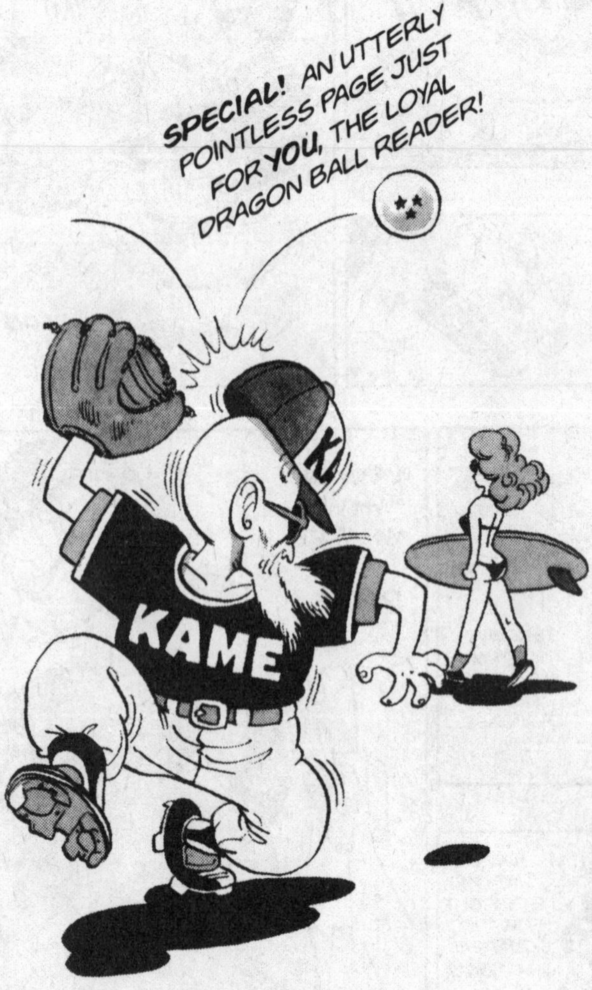
SPECIAL! AN UTTERLY POINTLESS PAGE JUST FOR YOU, THE LOYAL DRAGON BALL READER!
KAME
KA

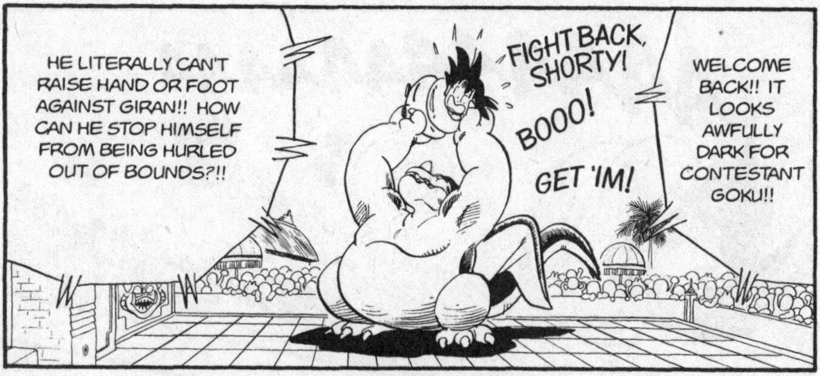
WELCOME BACK!! IT LOOKS AWFULLY DARK FOR CONTESTANT GOKU!!
FIGHT BACK, SHORTY!
BOOO!
GET 'IM!
HE LITERALLY CAN'T RAISE HAND OR FOOT AGAINST GIRAN!! HOW CAN HE STOP HIMSELF FROM BEING HURLED OUT OF BOUNDS?!!
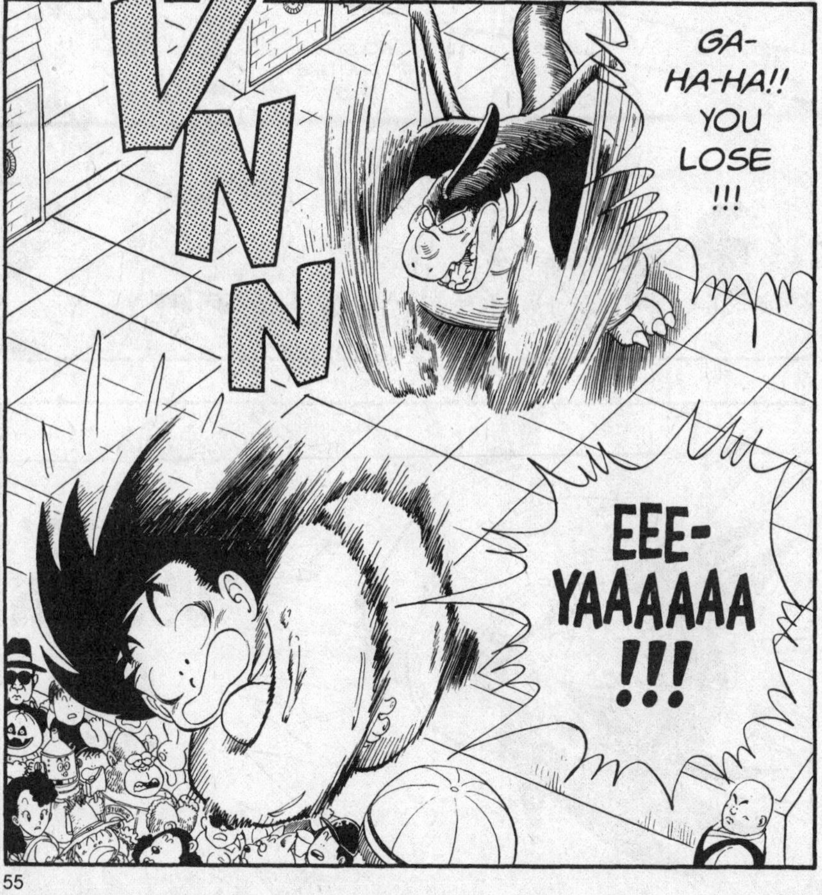
GA-HA-HA!! YOU LOSE !!!
VNNN
EEE-YAAAAAA !!!

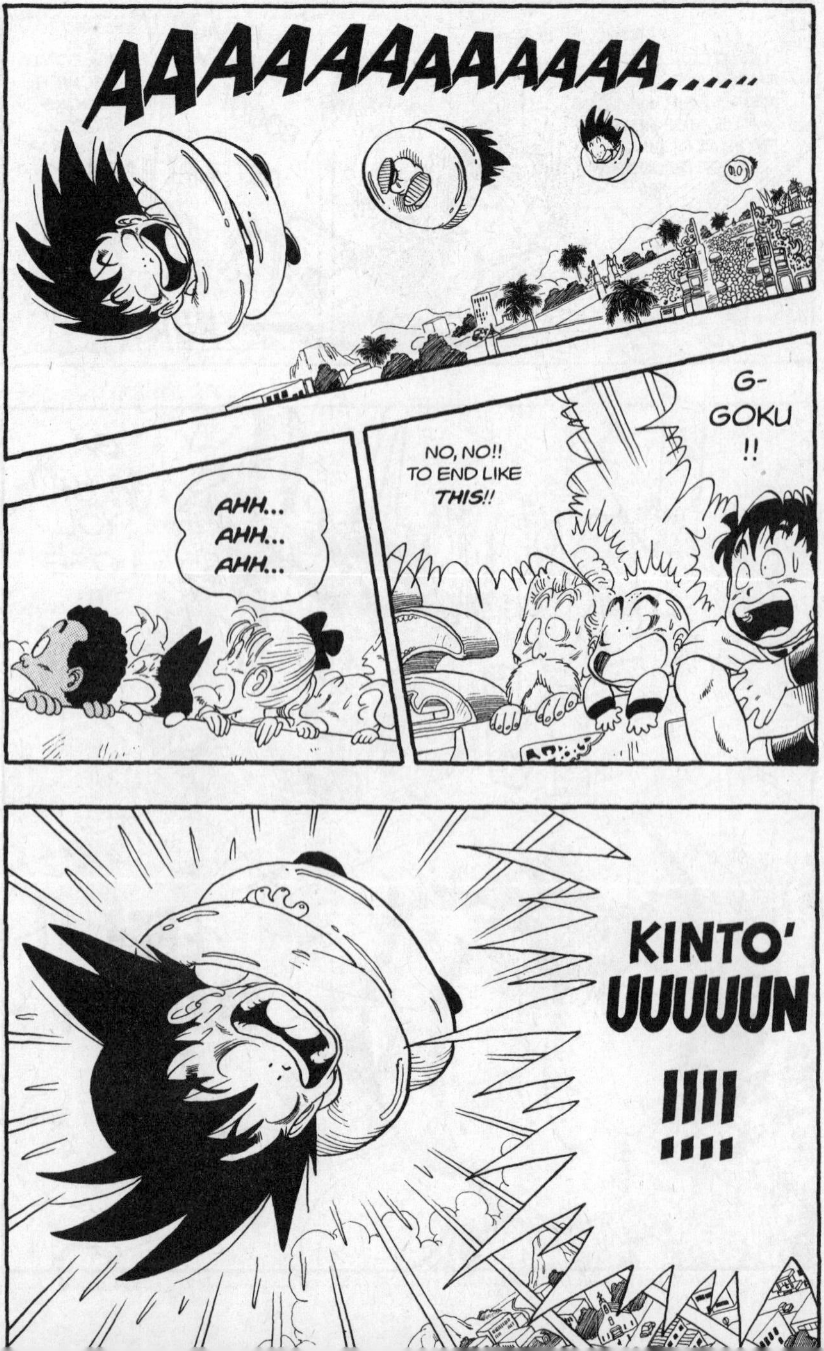
AAAAAAAAAAAA......
G-GOKU!!
NO, NO!! TO END LIKE THIS!!
AHH... AHH... AHH...
KINTO' UUUUUN!!!!!!!!

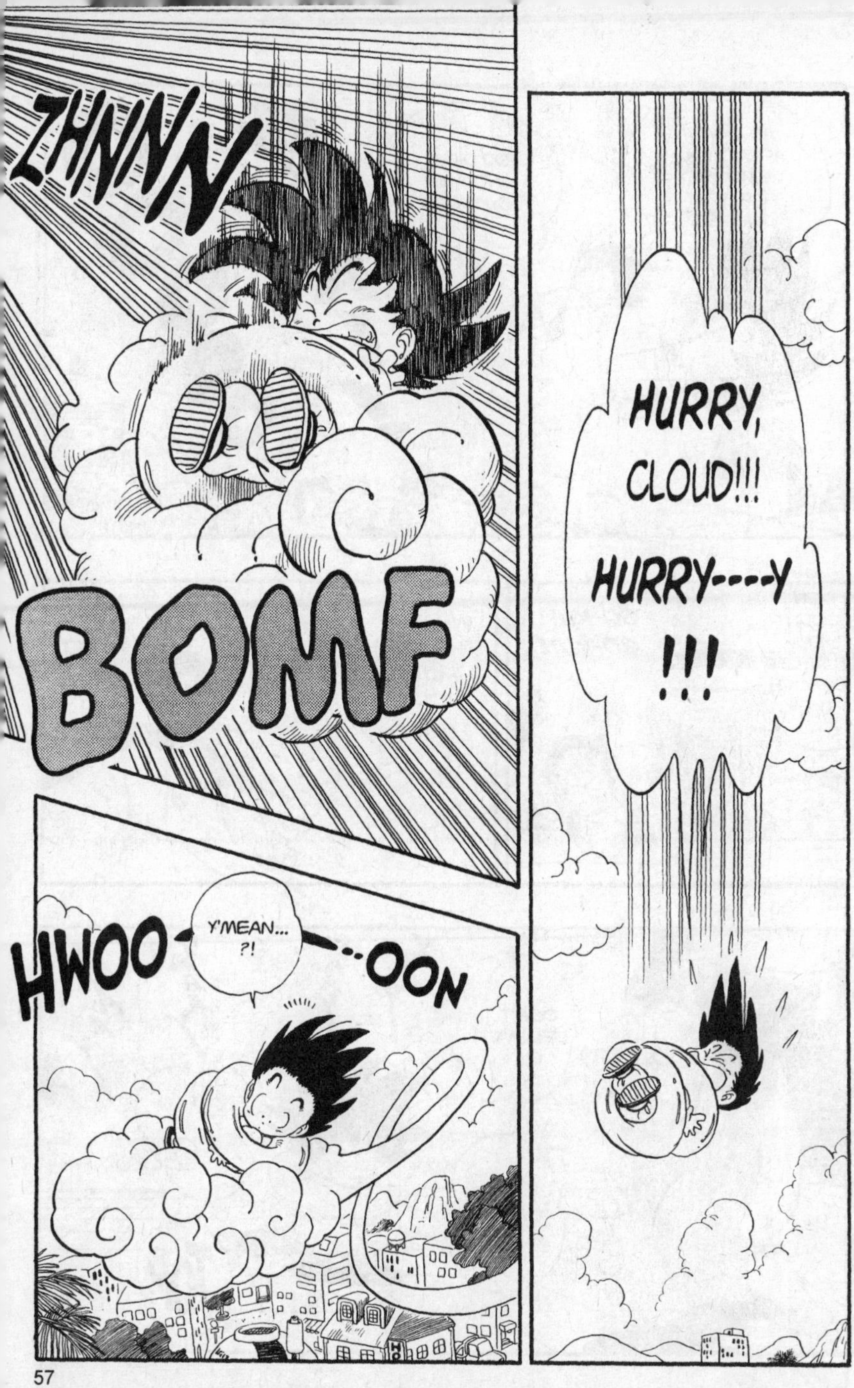
HURRY, CLOUD!!! HURRY----Y !!!
ZHNNN
BOMF
HWOO--OON
Y'MEAN... ?!

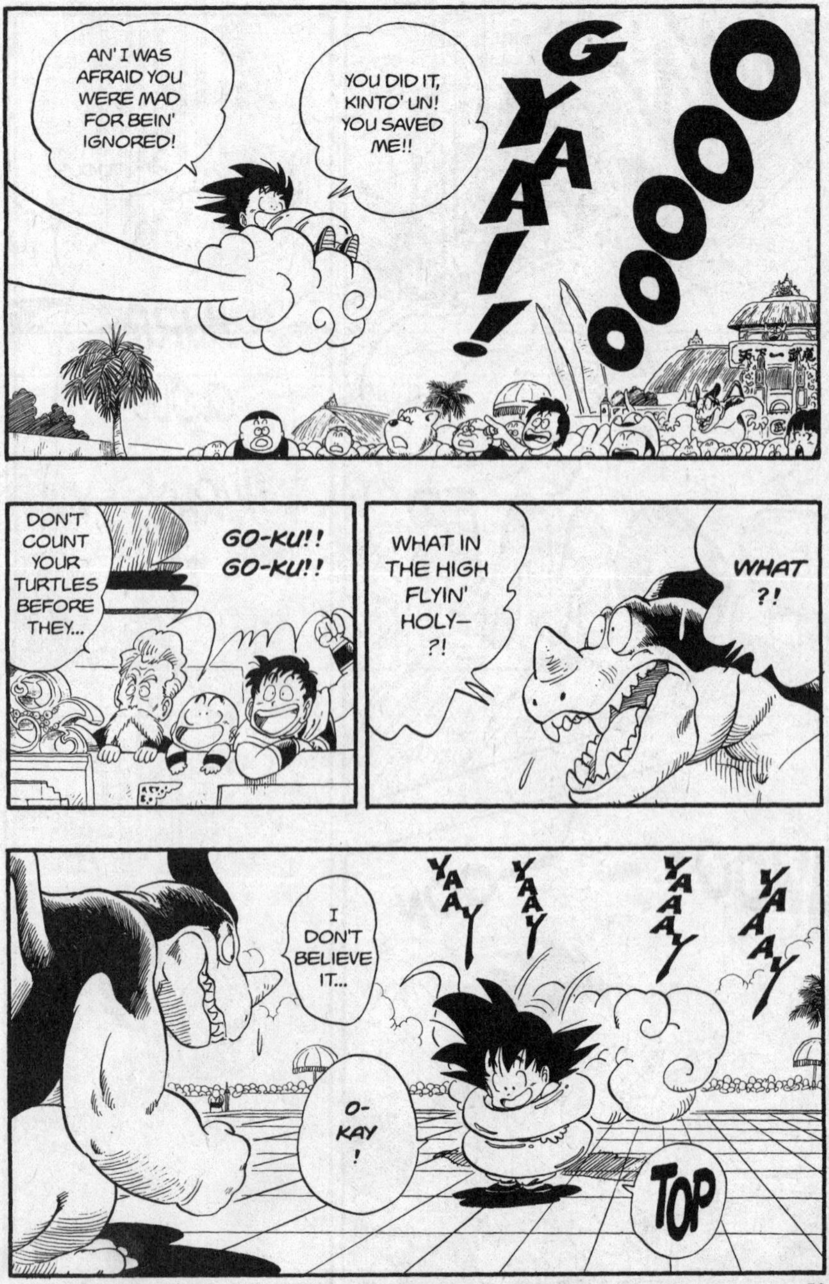
GYAA!!
OOOOOO
YOU DID IT, KINTO' UN! YOU SAVED ME!!
AN' I WAS AFRAID YOU WERE MAD FOR BEIN' IGNORED!
WHAT ?!
WHAT IN THE HIGH FLYIN' HOLY— ?!
GO-KU!! GO-KU!!
DON'T COUNT YOUR TURTLES BEFORE THEY...
YAAAY
YAAAY
YAAY
YAAY
TOP
O-KAY!
I DON'T BELIEVE IT...

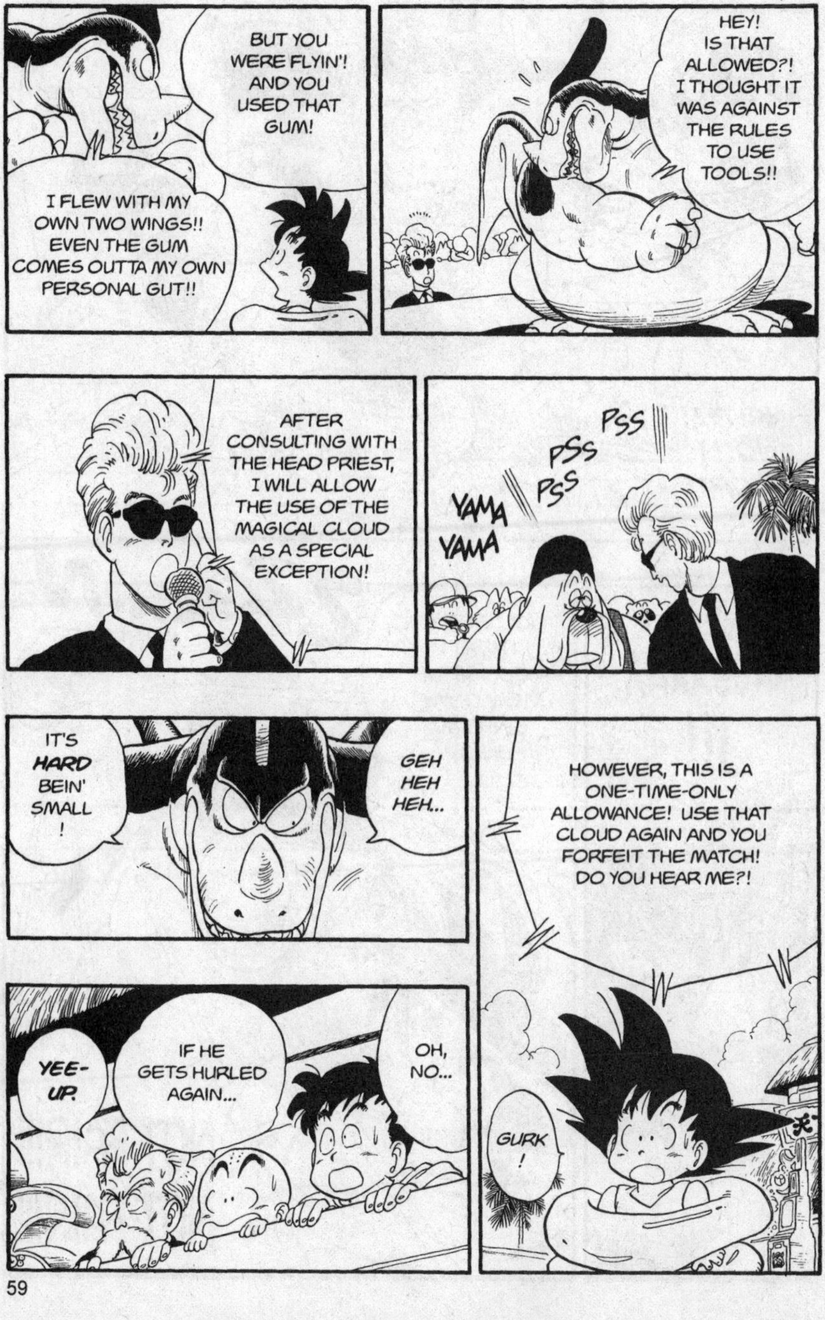
HEY! IS THAT ALLOWED?! I THOUGHT IT WAS AGAINST THE RULES TO USE TOOLS!!
BUT YOU WERE FLYIN'! AND YOU USED THAT GUM!
I FLEW WITH MY OWN TWO WINGS!! EVEN THE GUM COMES OUTTA MY OWN PERSONAL GUT!!
PSS
PSS
PSS
YAMA YAMA
AFTER CONSULTING WITH THE HEAD PRIEST, I WILL ALLOW THE USE OF THE MAGICAL CLOUD AS A SPECIAL EXCEPTION!
HOWEVER, THIS IS A ONE-TIME-ONLY ALLOWANCE! USE THAT CLOUD AGAIN AND YOU FORFEIT THE MATCH! DO YOU HEAR ME?!
GURK!
GEH HEH HEH...
IT'S HARD BEIN' SMALL!
OH, NO...
IF HE GETS HURLED AGAIN...
YEE-UP.

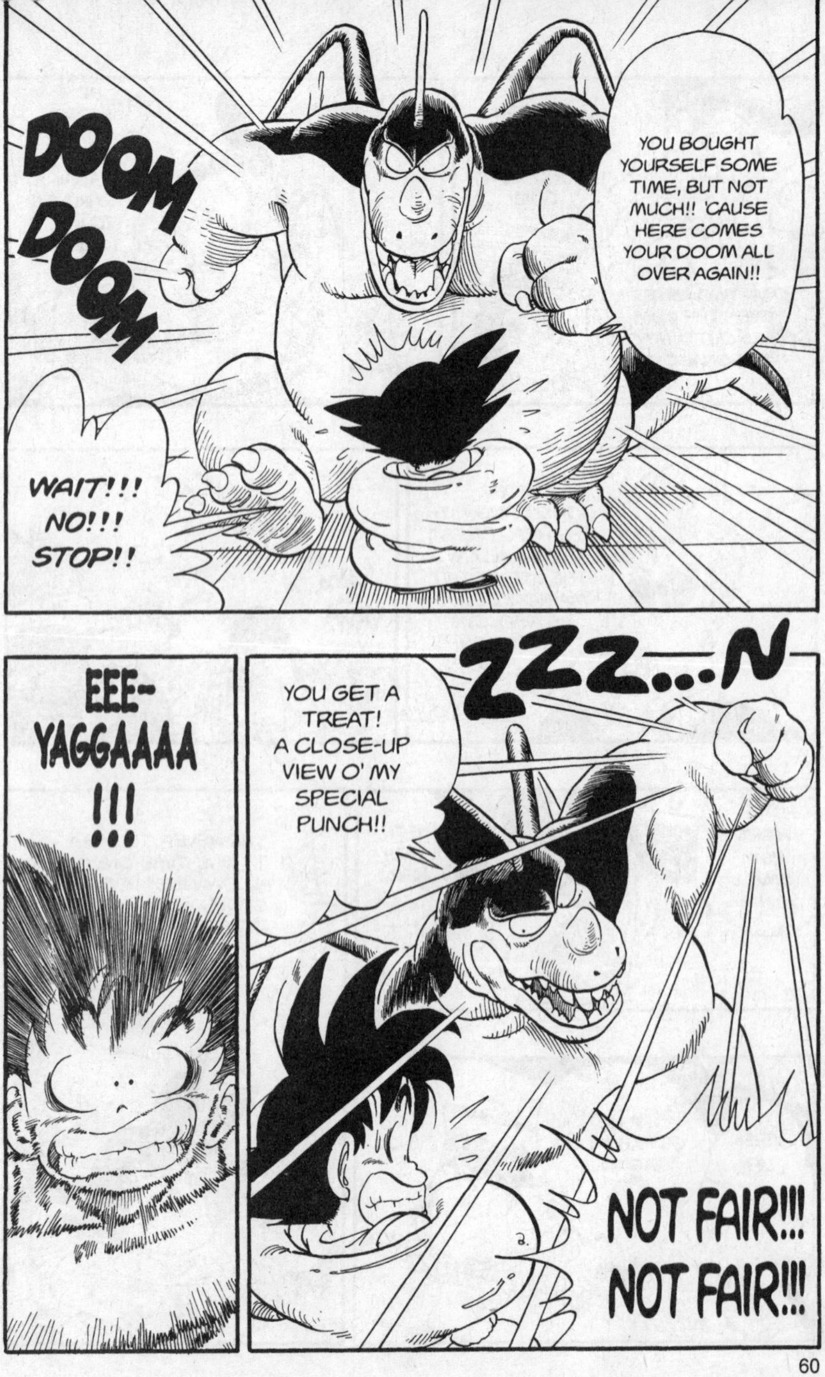
YOU BOUGHT YOURSELF SOME TIME, BUT NOT MUCH!! 'CAUSE HERE COMES YOUR DOOM ALL OVER AGAIN!!
DOOM DOOM DOOM
WAIT!!! NO!!! STOP!!
ZZZ...N
YOU GET A TREAT! A CLOSE-UP VIEW O' MY SPECIAL PUNCH!!
NOT FAIR!!! NOT FAIR!!!
EEE-YAGGAAAA!!!

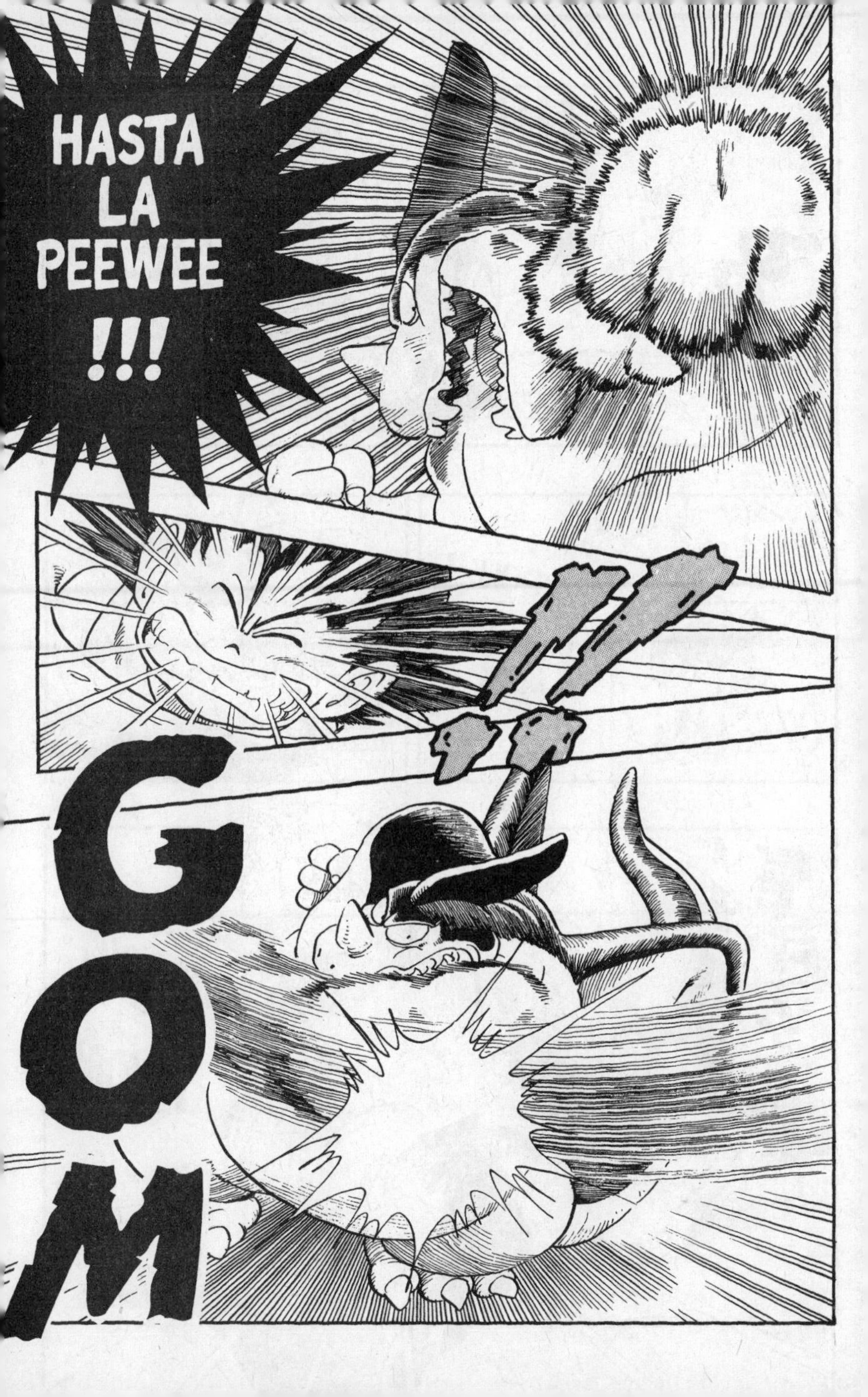
HASTA LA PEEWEE !!!
GOM

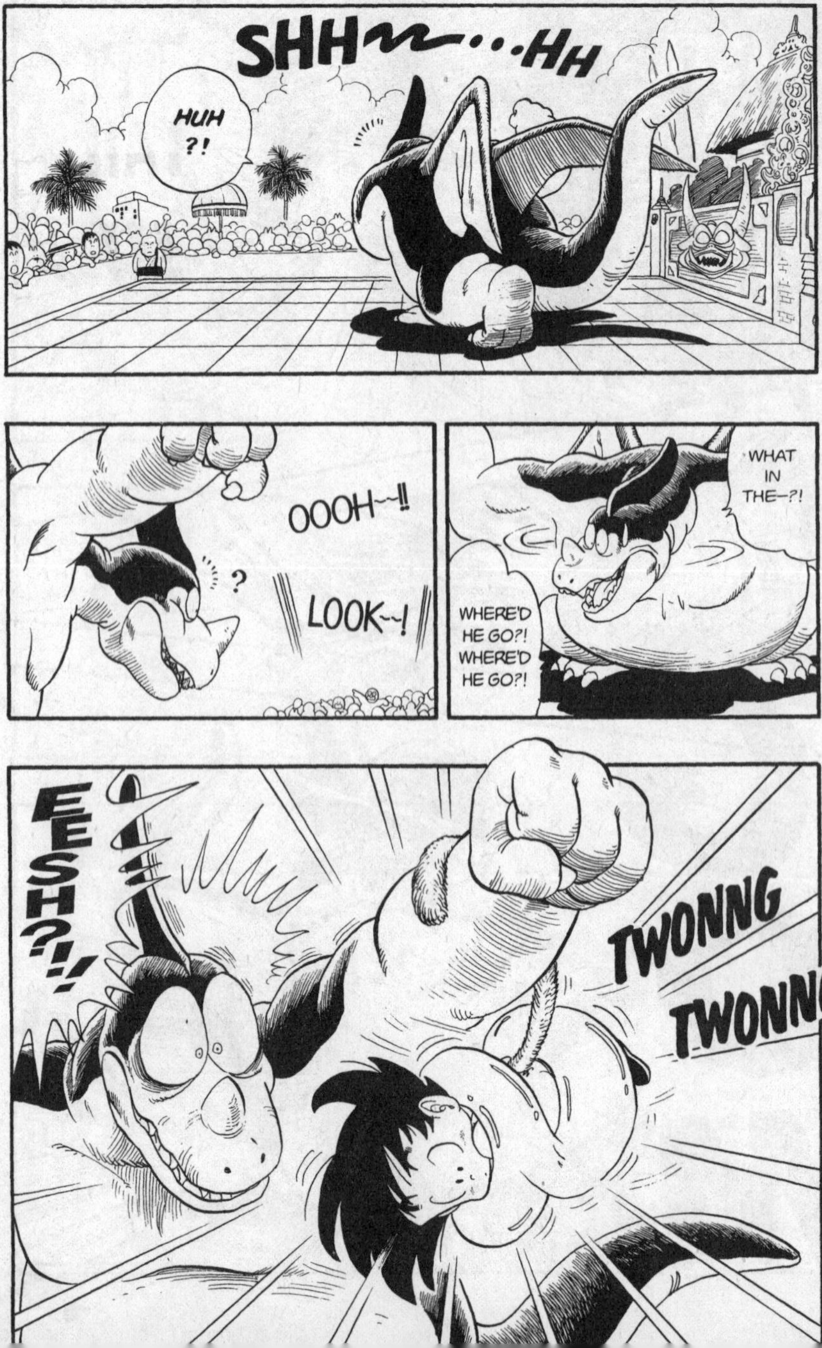
SHH~~...HH
HUH ?!
WHAT IN THE—?!
WHERE'D HE GO?! WHERE'D HE GO?!
OOOH~~!!
?
LOOK~~!
EESH?!!
TWONNG
TWONNG

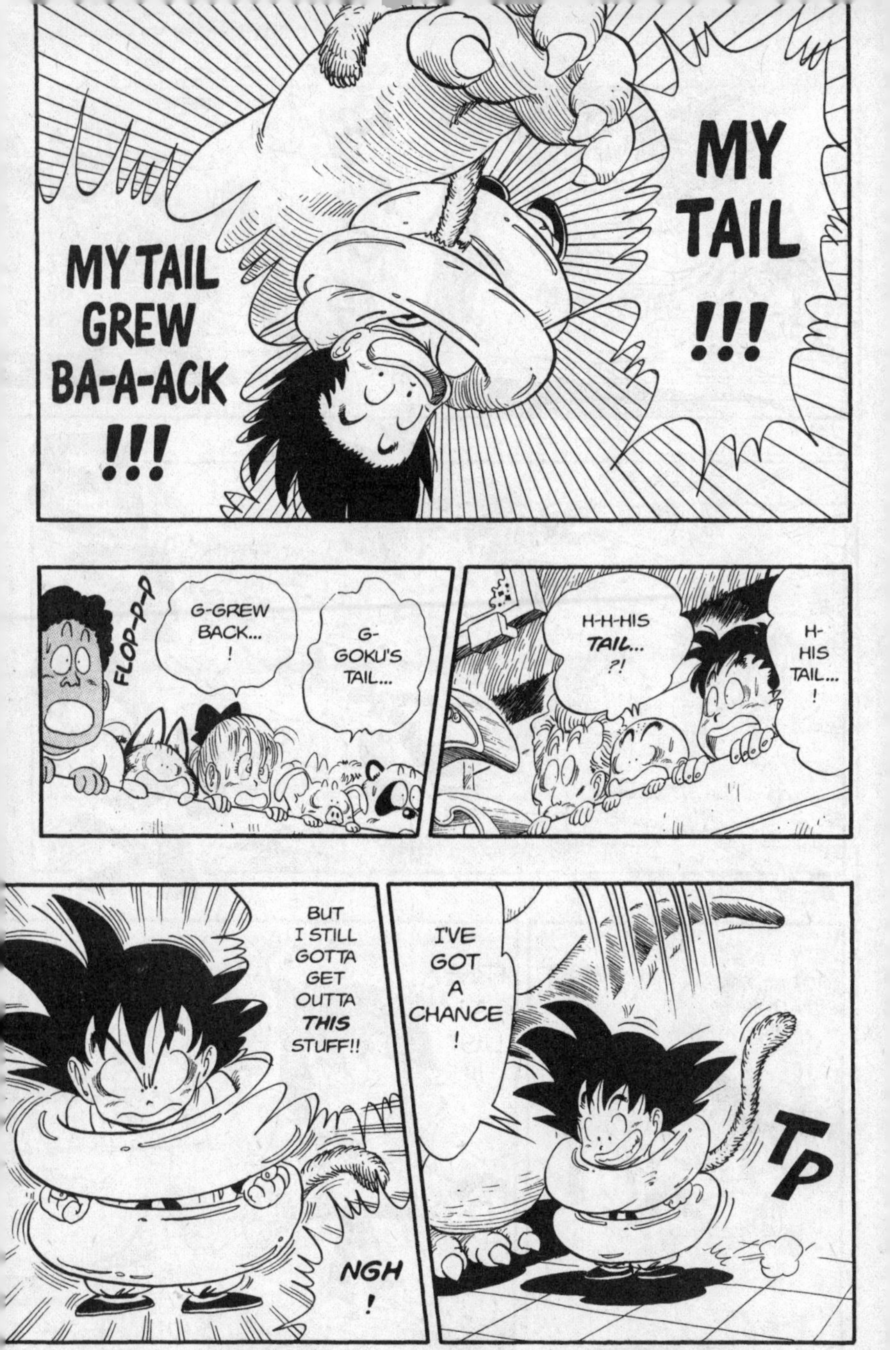
MY TAIL !!!
MY TAIL GREW BA-A-ACK !!!
H-HIS TAIL... !
H-H-HIS TAIL... ?!
G-GOKU'S TAIL...
G-GREW BACK... !
FLOP-P-P
TP
I'VE GOT A CHANCE !
BUT I STILL GOTTA GET OUTTA THIS STUFF!!
NGH !

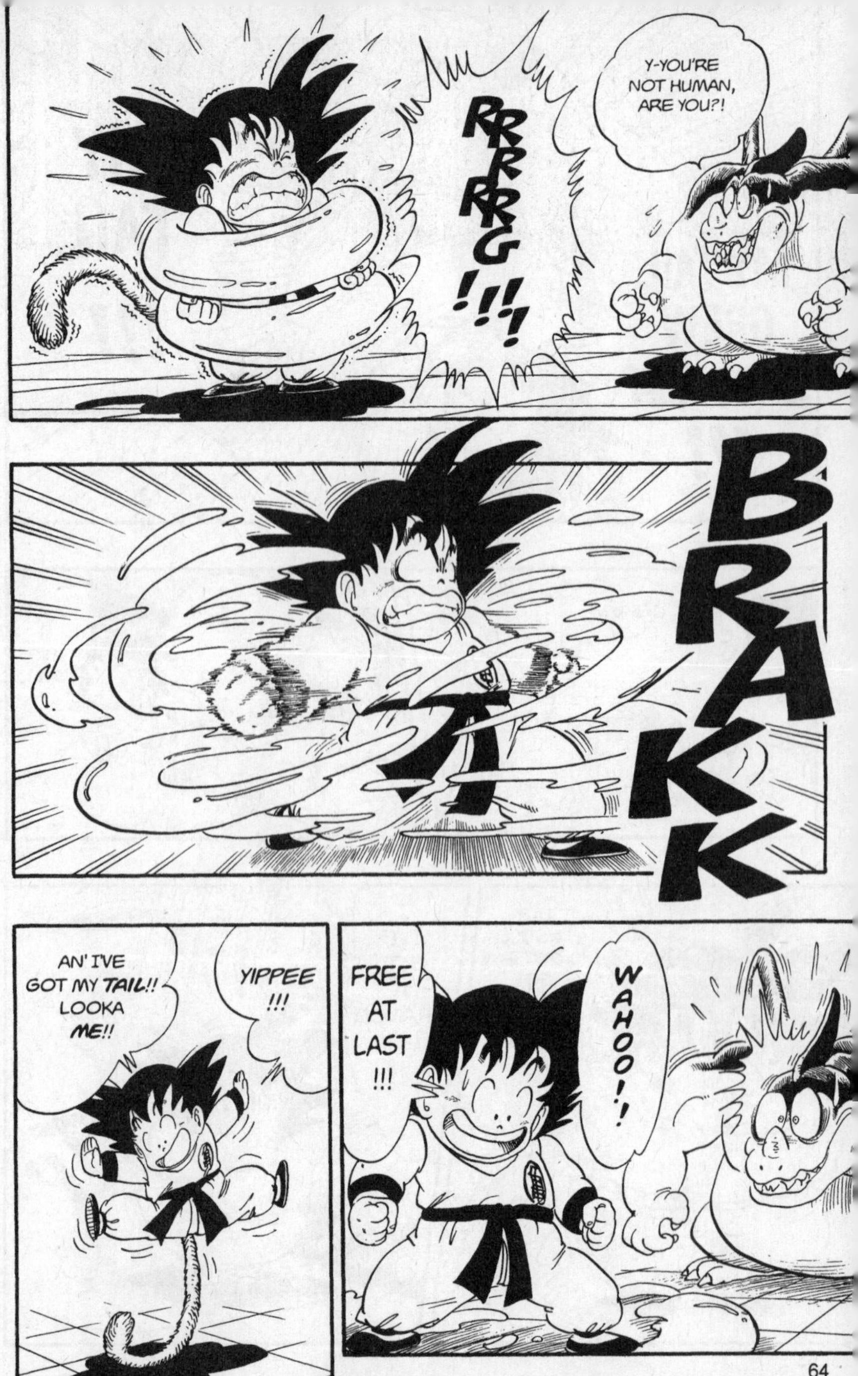

Y-YOU'RE NOT HUMAN, ARE YOU?!
RRRRRG!!!!
BRAKK
WAHOO!!
FREE AT LAST!!!
YIPPEE!!!
AN' I'VE GOT MY *TAIL*!! LOOKA *ME*!!

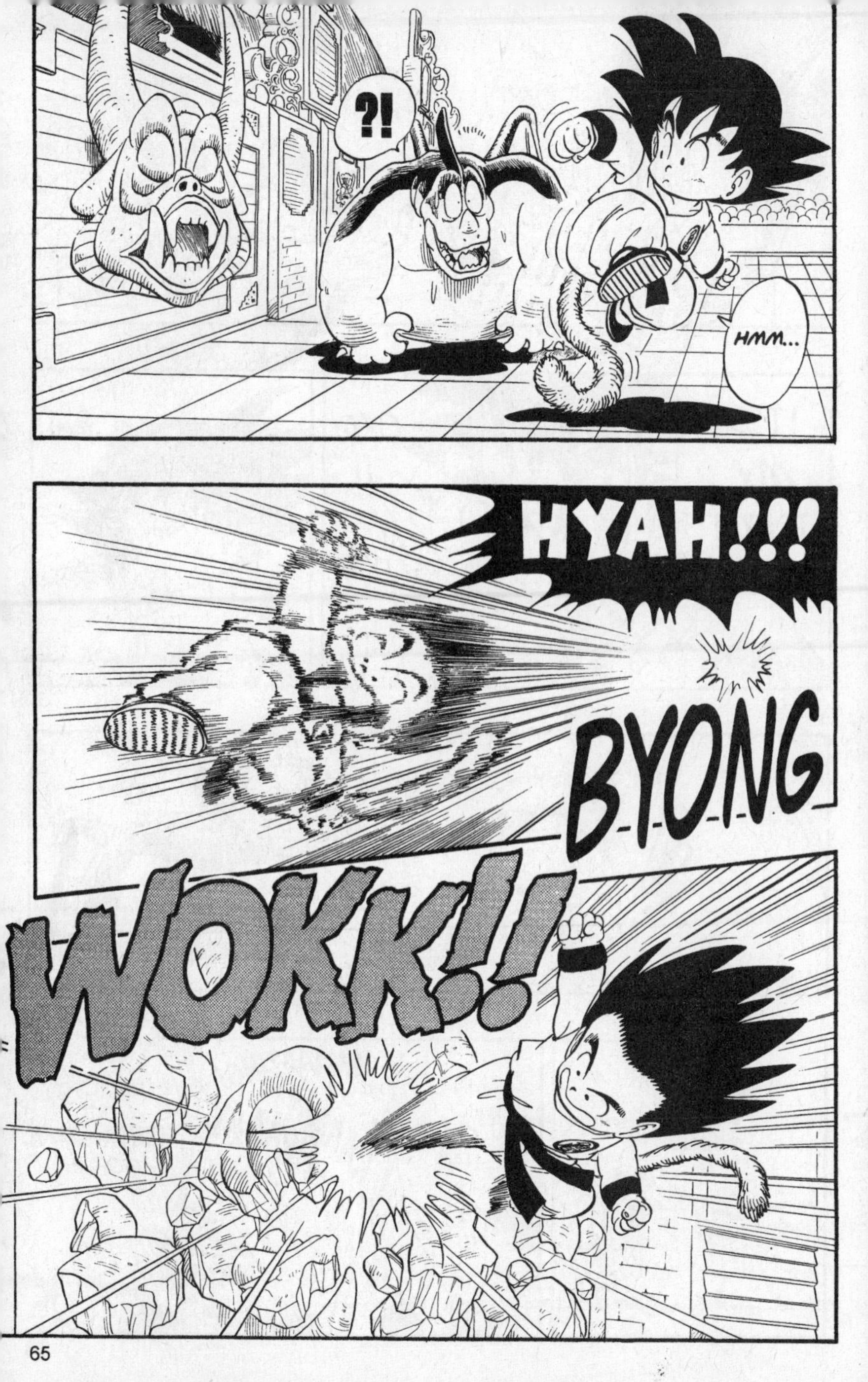
HMM...
?!
HYAH!!!
BYONG
WOKK!!

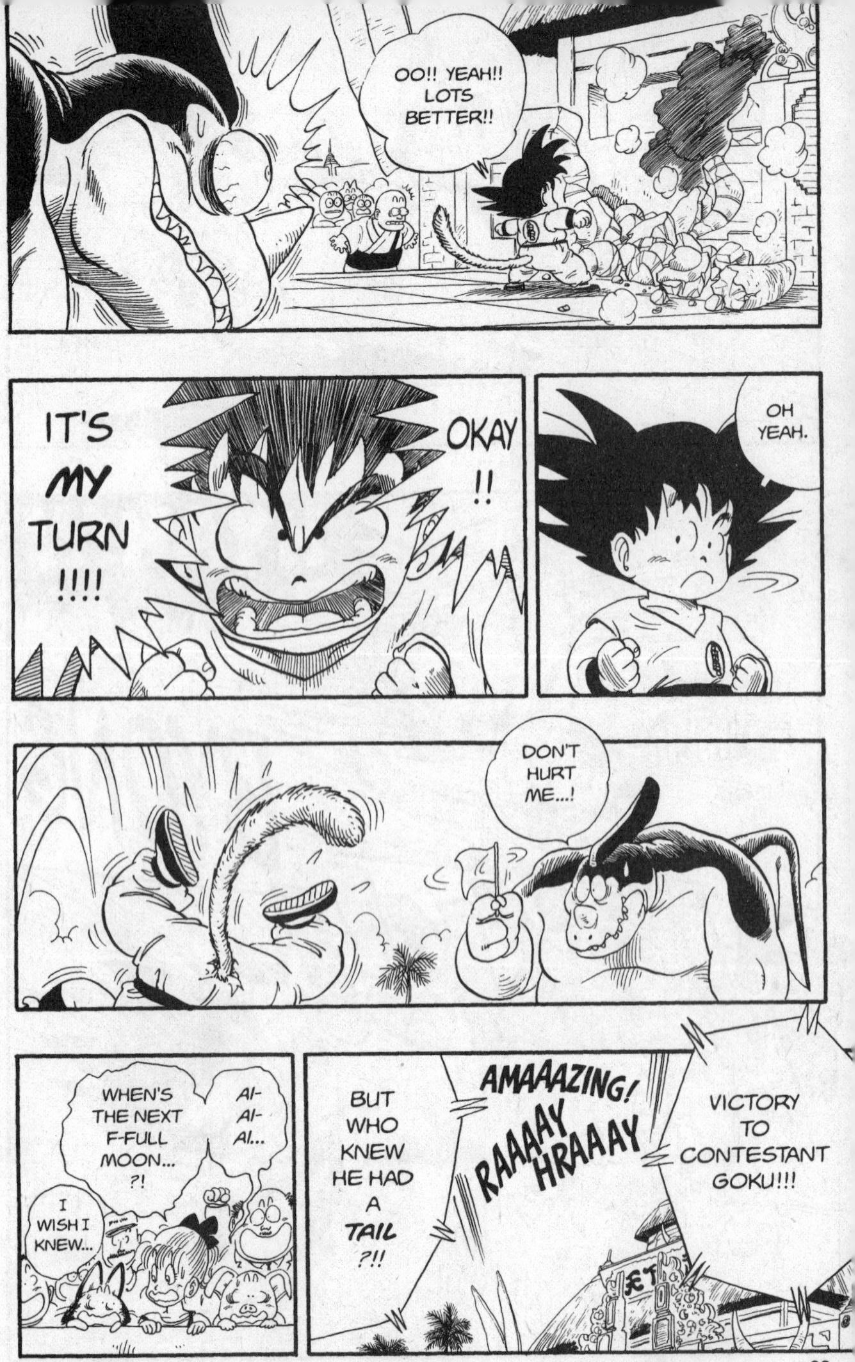
OO!! YEAH!! LOTS BETTER!!
OH YEAH.
OKAY!!
IT'S MY TURN!!!!
DON'T HURT ME...!
VICTORY TO CONTESTANT GOKU!!!
AMAAAZING!
RAAAAY HRAAAY
BUT WHO KNEW HE HAD A TAIL?!!
AI- AI- AI...
WHEN'S THE NEXT F-FULL MOON...?!
I WISH I KNEW...

Tale 41
Kuririn vs. Jackie Chun

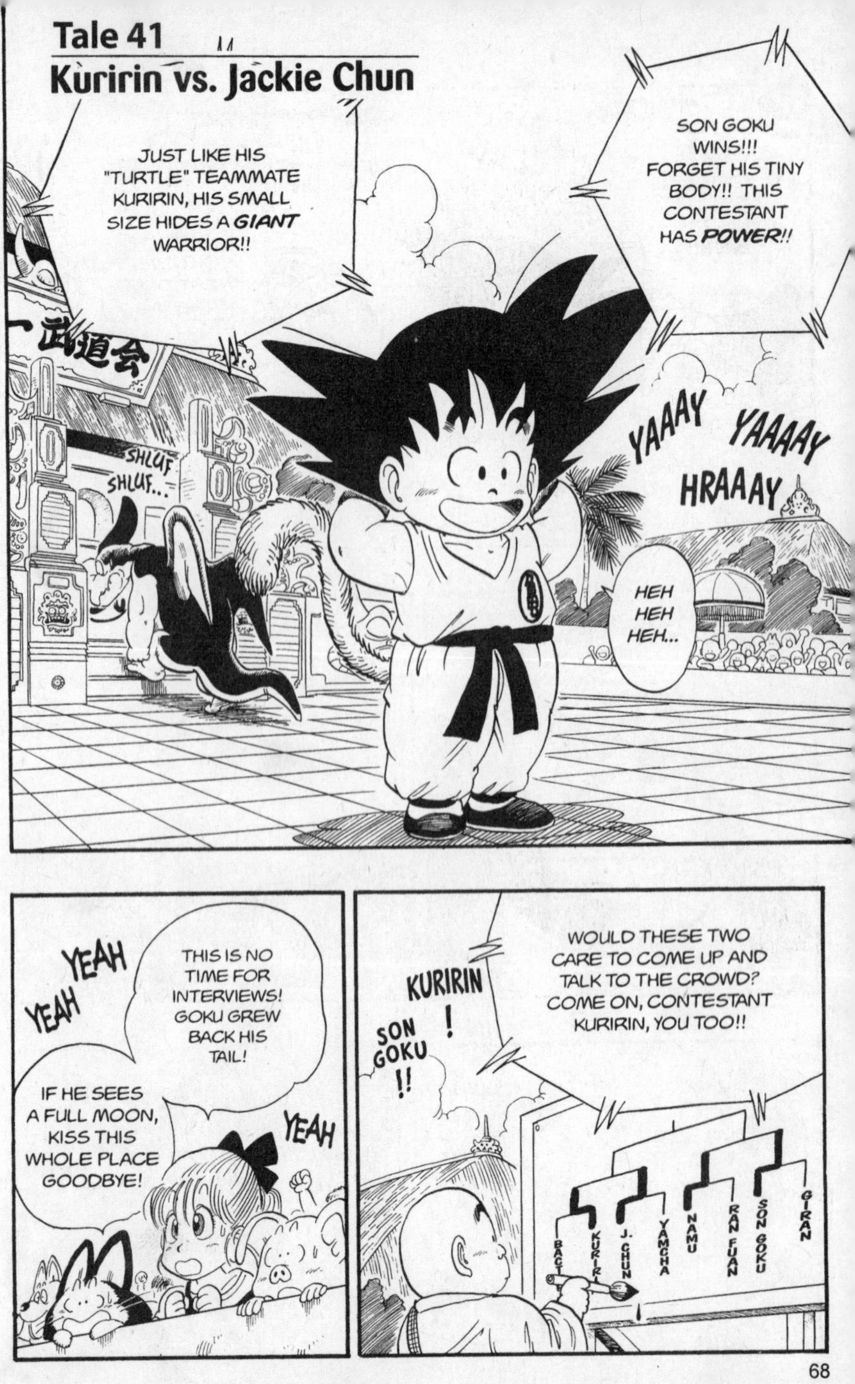

SON GOKU WINS!!! FORGET HIS TINY BODY!! THIS CONTESTANT HAS **POWER**!!
JUST LIKE HIS "TURTLE" TEAMMATE KURIRIN, HIS SMALL SIZE HIDES A ***GIANT*** WARRIOR!!
YAAAAY
YAAAY
HRAAAY
HEH HEH HEH...
SHLUF SHLUF...
WOULD THESE TWO CARE TO COME UP AND TALK TO THE CROWD? COME ON, CONTESTANT KURIRIN, YOU TOO!!
KURIRIN!
SON GOKU!!
GIRAN
SON GOKU
RAN FUAN
NAMU
YAMCHA
J. CHUN
KURIRI
BACT
THIS IS NO TIME FOR INTERVIEWS! GOKU GREW BACK HIS TAIL!
YEAH
YEAH
IF HE SEES A FULL MOON, KISS THIS WHOLE PLACE GOODBYE!
YEAH

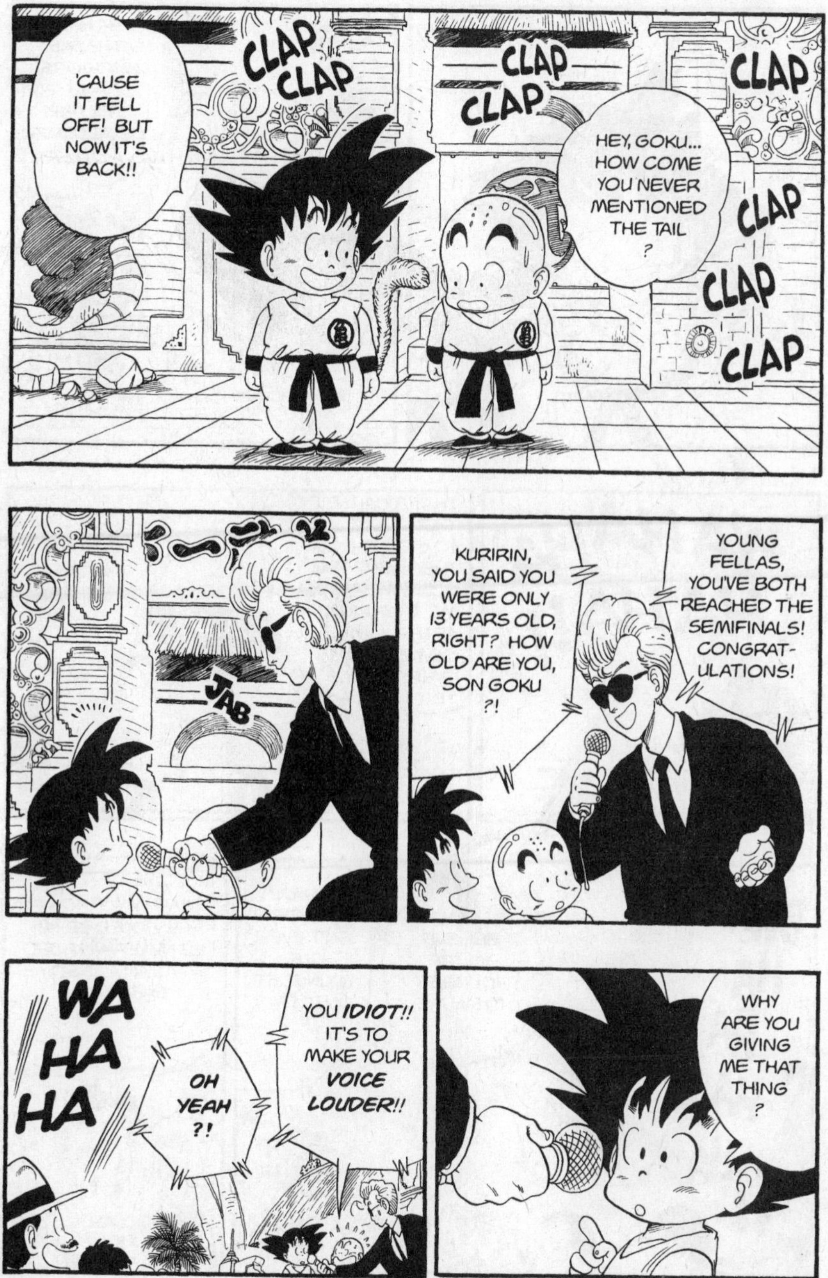
CLAP
CLAP CLAP
HEY, GOKU... HOW COME YOU NEVER MENTIONED THE TAIL?
CLAP CLAP
CLAP
CLAP CLAP
'CAUSE IT FELL OFF! BUT NOW IT'S BACK!!
YOUNG FELLAS, YOU'VE BOTH REACHED THE SEMIFINALS! CONGRATULATIONS!
KURIRIN, YOU SAID YOU WERE ONLY 13 YEARS OLD, RIGHT? HOW OLD ARE YOU, SON GOKU?!
JAB
WHY ARE YOU GIVING ME THAT THING?
YOU IDIOT!! IT'S TO MAKE YOUR VOICE LOUDER!!
OH YEAH?!
WA HA HA

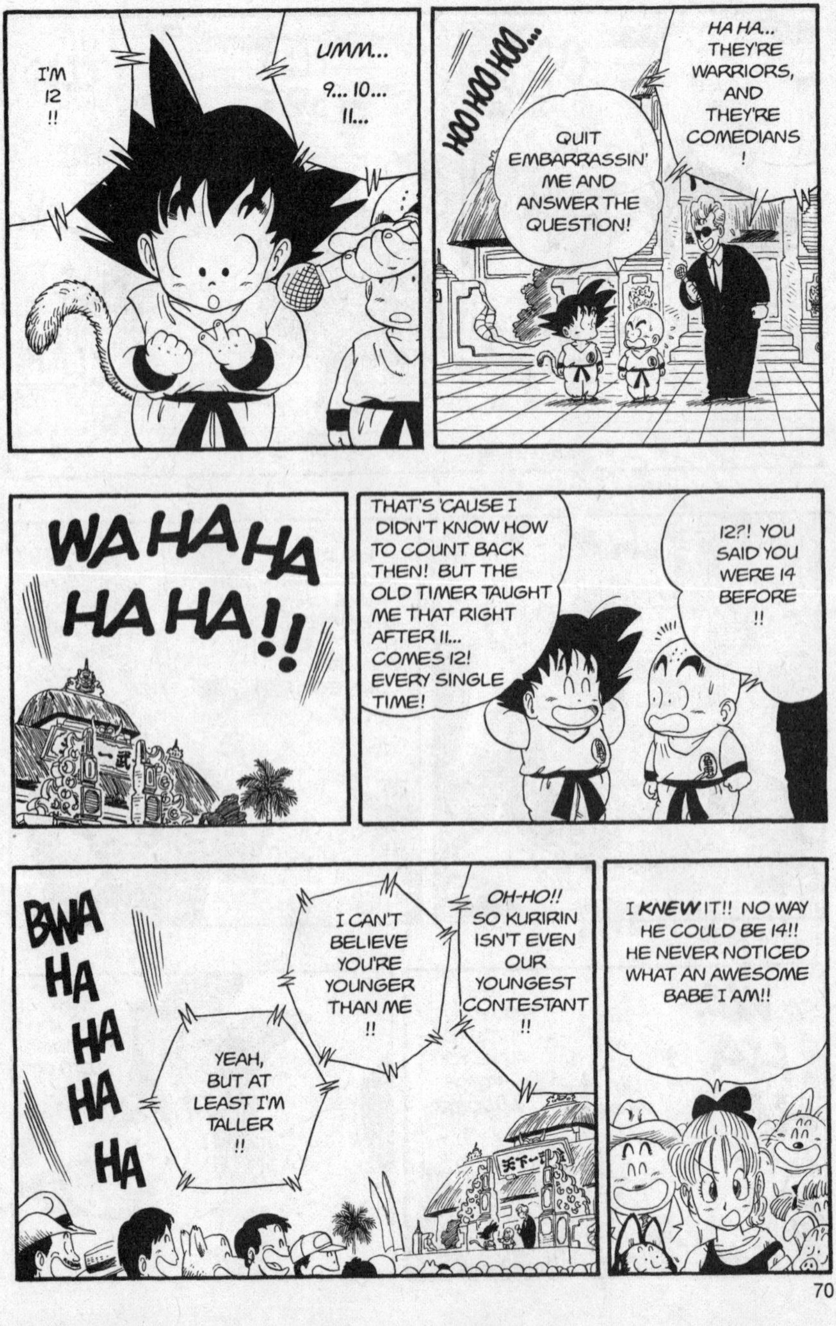
HA HA... THEY'RE WARRIORS, AND THEY'RE COMEDIANS!
QUIT EMBARRASSIN' ME AND ANSWER THE QUESTION!
HOO HOO HOO...
UMM... 9... 10... 11...
I'M 12!!
12?! YOU SAID YOU WERE 14 BEFORE!!
THAT'S 'CAUSE I DIDN'T KNOW HOW TO COUNT BACK THEN! BUT THE OLD TIMER TAUGHT ME THAT RIGHT AFTER 11... COMES 12! EVERY SINGLE TIME!
WAHAHA HAHA!!
I KNEW IT!! NO WAY HE COULD BE 14!! HE NEVER NOTICED WHAT AN AWESOME BABE I AM!!
OH-HO!! SO KURIRIN ISN'T EVEN OUR YOUNGEST CONTESTANT!!
I CAN'T BELIEVE YOU'RE YOUNGER THAN ME!!
YEAH, BUT AT LEAST I'M TALLER!!
BWA HA HA HA HA HA

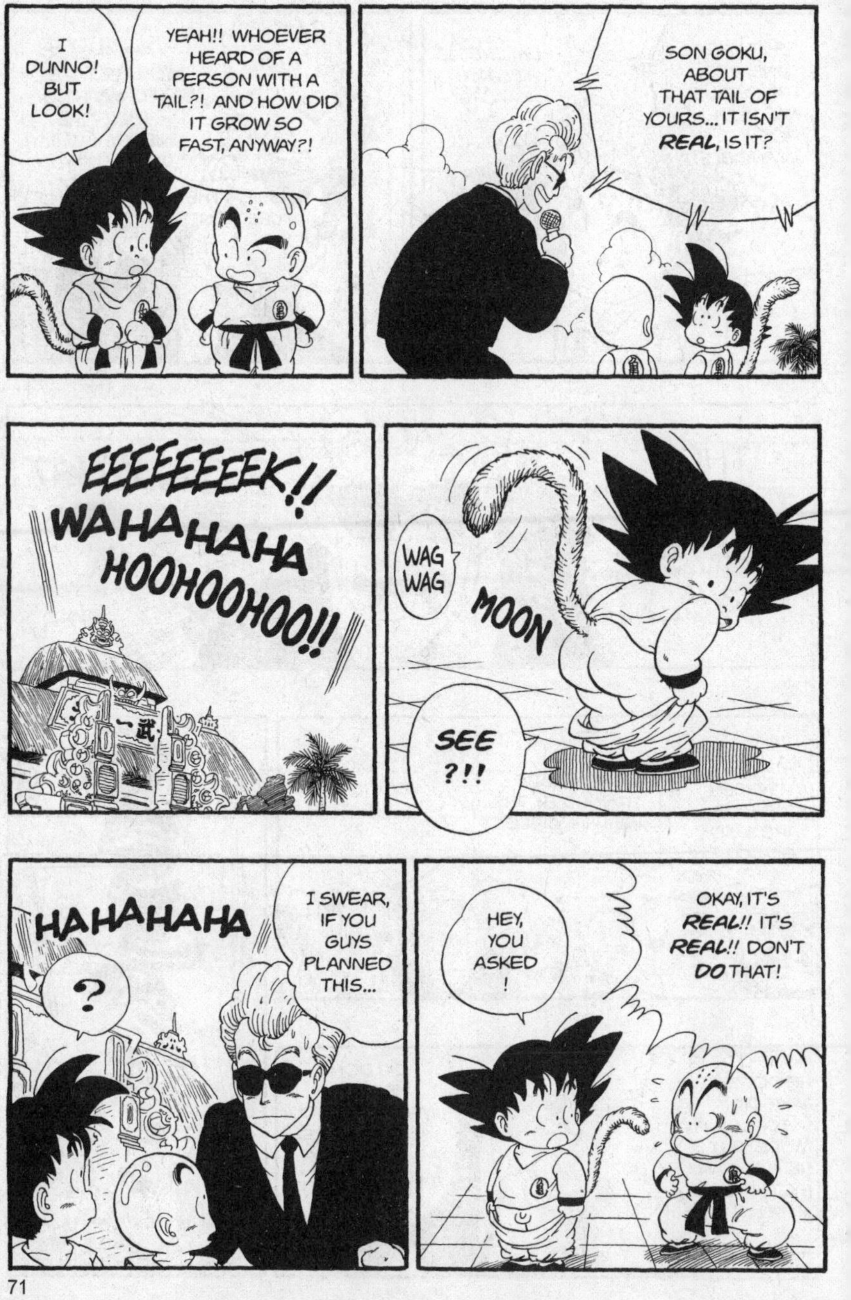
SON GOKU, ABOUT THAT TAIL OF YOURS... IT ISN'T REAL, IS IT?
YEAH!! WHOEVER HEARD OF A PERSON WITH A TAIL?! AND HOW DID IT GROW SO FAST, ANYWAY?!
I DUNNO! BUT LOOK!
WAG WAG
MOON
SEE ?!!
EEEEEEEEEK!!
WAHAHAHAHA
HOOHOOHOO!!
OKAY, IT'S REAL!! IT'S REAL!! DON'T DO THAT!
HEY, YOU ASKED!
I SWEAR, IF YOU GUYS PLANNED THIS...
HAHAHAHA
?

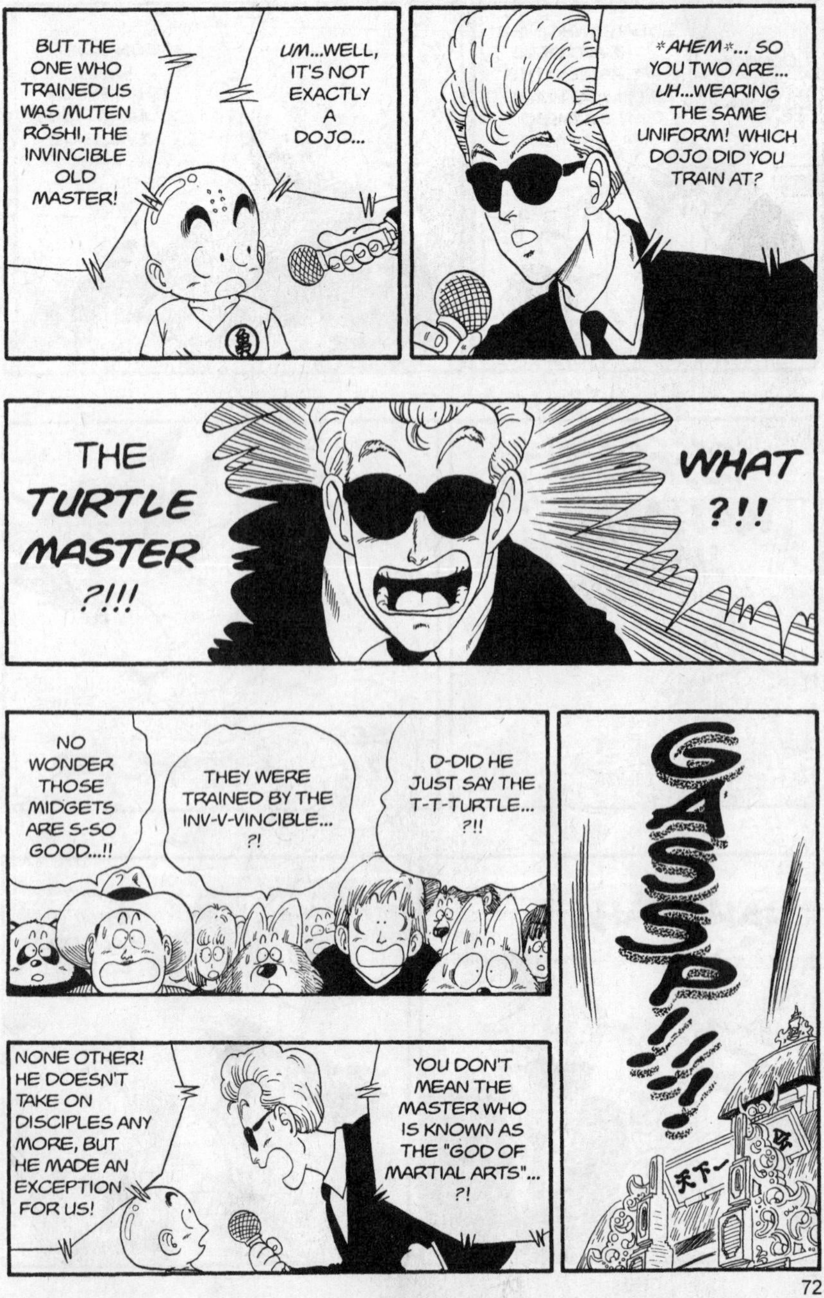
AHEM... SO YOU TWO ARE... UH...WEARING THE SAME UNIFORM! WHICH DOJO DID YOU TRAIN AT?
UM...WELL, IT'S NOT EXACTLY A DOJO...
BUT THE ONE WHO TRAINED US WAS MUTEN RŌSHI, THE INVINCIBLE OLD MASTER!
WHAT ?!!
THE TURTLE MASTER ?!!!
GASSP!!!!
天下一
D-DID HE JUST SAY THE T-T-TURTLE... ?!!
THEY WERE TRAINED BY THE INV-V-VINCIBLE... ?!
NO WONDER THOSE MIDGETS ARE S-SO GOOD...!!
YOU DON'T MEAN THE MASTER WHO IS KNOWN AS THE "GOD OF MARTIAL ARTS"... ?!
NONE OTHER! HE DOESN'T TAKE ON DISCIPLES ANY MORE, BUT HE MADE AN EXCEPTION FOR US!

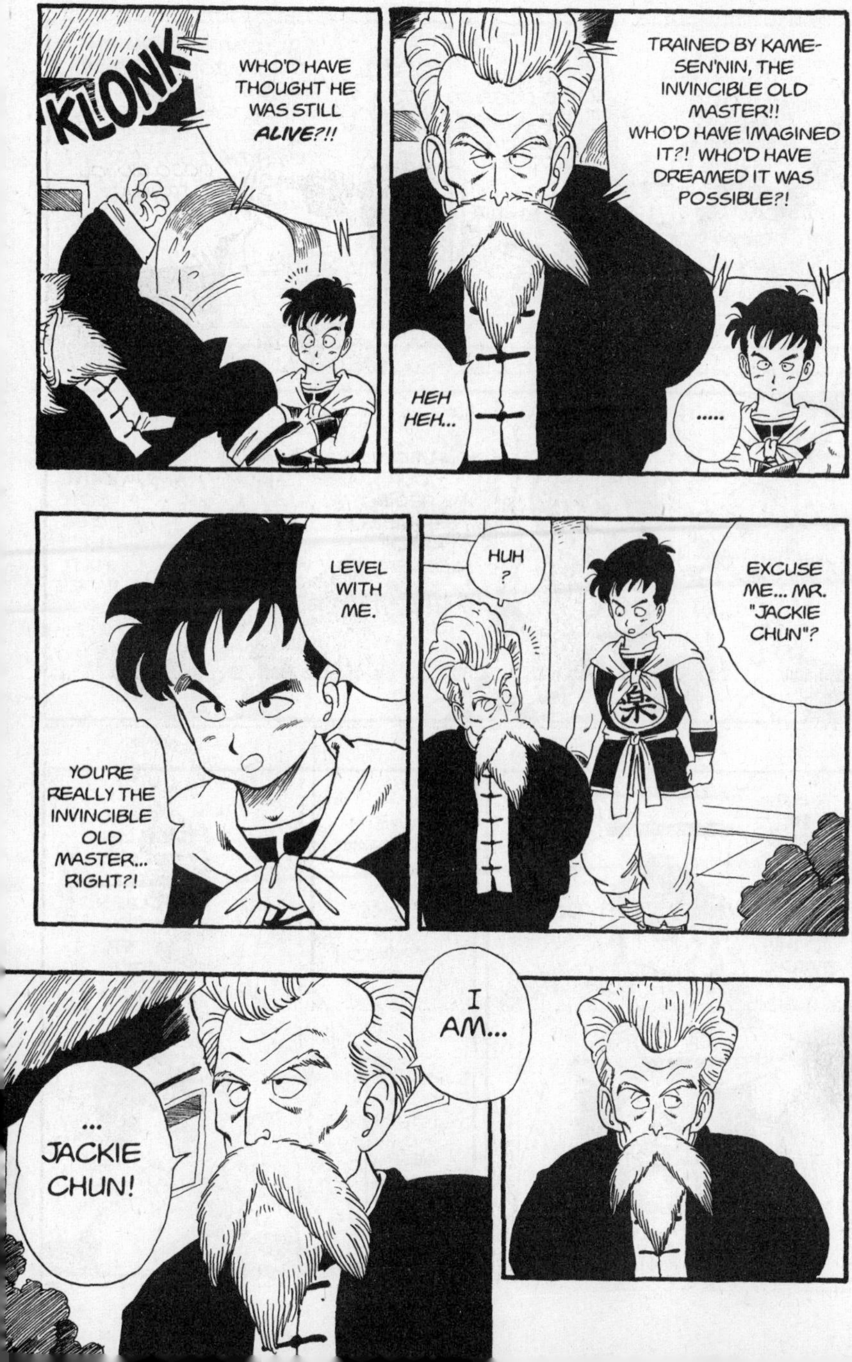
TRAINED BY KAME-SEN'NIN, THE INVINCIBLE OLD MASTER!! WHO'D HAVE IMAGINED IT?! WHO'D HAVE DREAMED IT WAS POSSIBLE?!
.....
HEH HEH...
WHO'D HAVE THOUGHT HE WAS STILL *ALIVE*?!!
KLONK
EXCUSE ME... MR. "JACKIE CHUN"?
HUH ?
LEVEL WITH ME.
YOU'RE REALLY THE INVINCIBLE OLD MASTER... RIGHT?!
I AM...
... JACKIE CHUN!

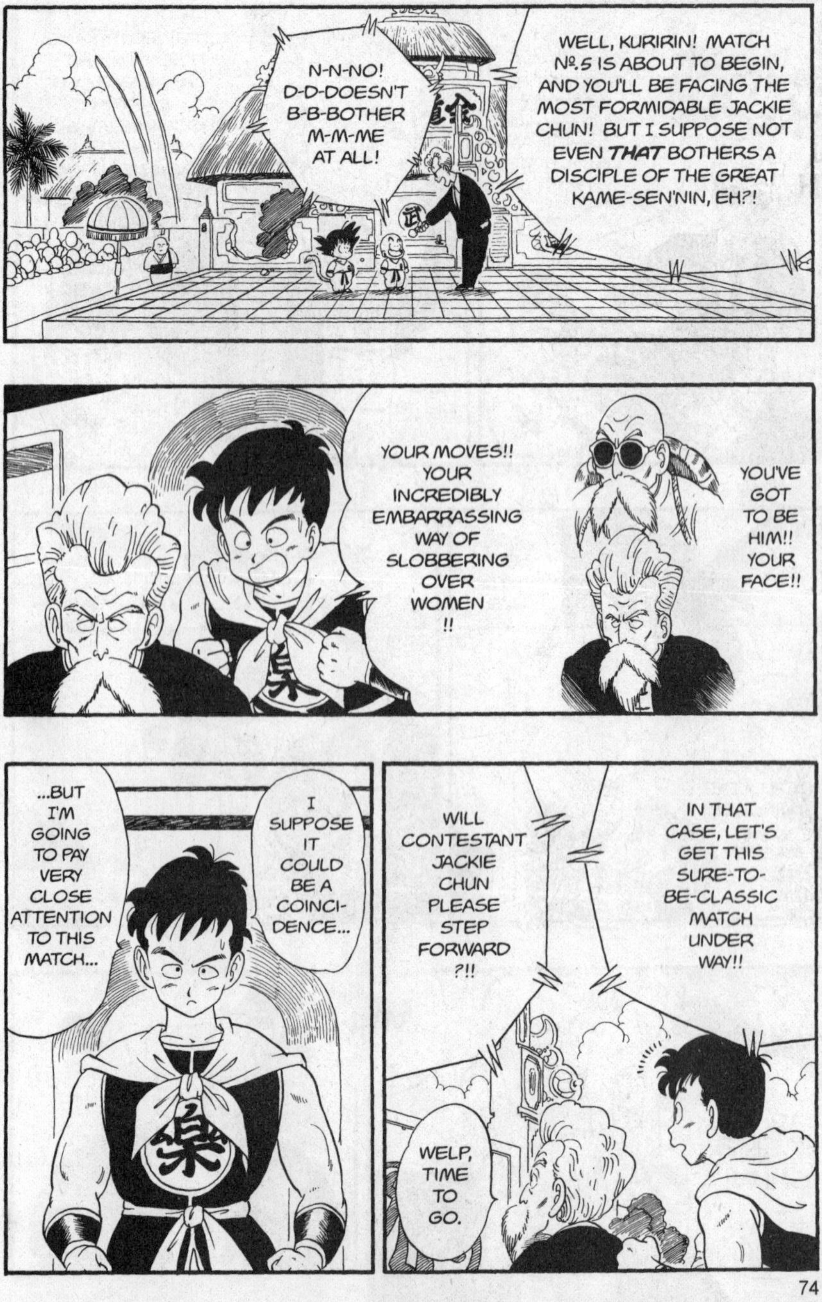
WELL, KURIRIN! MATCH №.5 IS ABOUT TO BEGIN, AND YOU'LL BE FACING THE MOST FORMIDABLE JACKIE CHUN! BUT I SUPPOSE NOT EVEN *THAT* BOTHERS A DISCIPLE OF THE GREAT KAME-SEN'NIN, EH?!
N-N-NO! D-D-DOESN'T B-B-BOTHER M-M-ME AT ALL!
YOU'VE GOT TO BE HIM!! YOUR FACE!!
YOUR MOVES!! YOUR INCREDIBLY EMBARRASSING WAY OF SLOBBERING OVER WOMEN !!
IN THAT CASE, LET'S GET THIS SURE-TO-BE-CLASSIC MATCH UNDER WAY!!
WILL CONTESTANT JACKIE CHUN PLEASE STEP FORWARD ?!!
WELP, TIME TO GO.
I SUPPOSE IT COULD BE A COINCIDENCE...
...BUT I'M GOING TO PAY VERY CLOSE ATTENTION TO THIS MATCH...

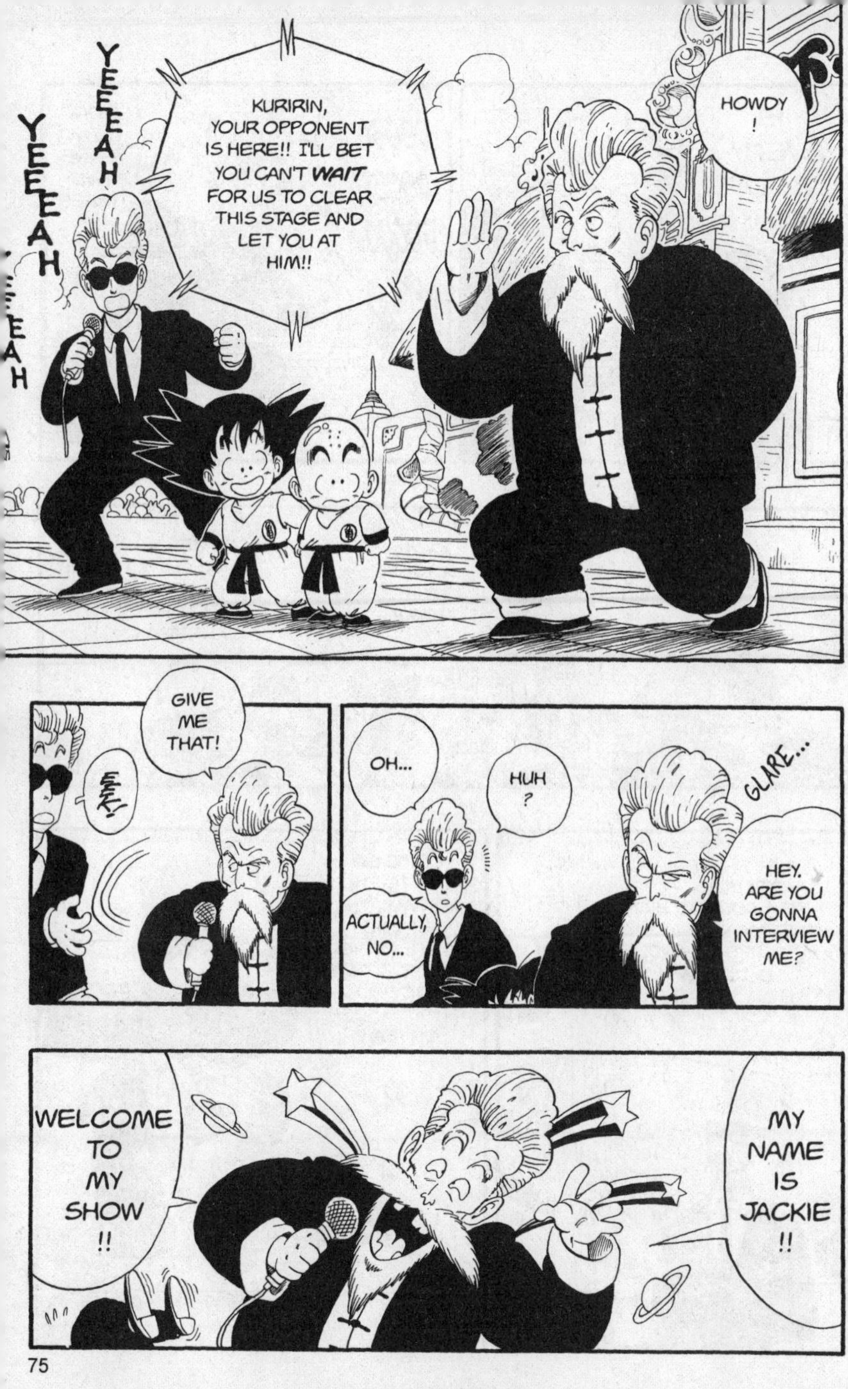
HOWDY!
KURIRIN, YOUR OPPONENT IS HERE!! I'LL BET YOU CAN'T **WAIT** FOR US TO CLEAR THIS STAGE AND LET YOU AT HIM!!
YEEEAH
YEEEEAH
GLARE...
HEY. ARE YOU GONNA INTERVIEW ME?
HUH?
OH...
ACTUALLY, NO...
GIVE ME THAT!
EEK!
MY NAME IS JACKIE!!
WELCOME TO MY SHOW!!

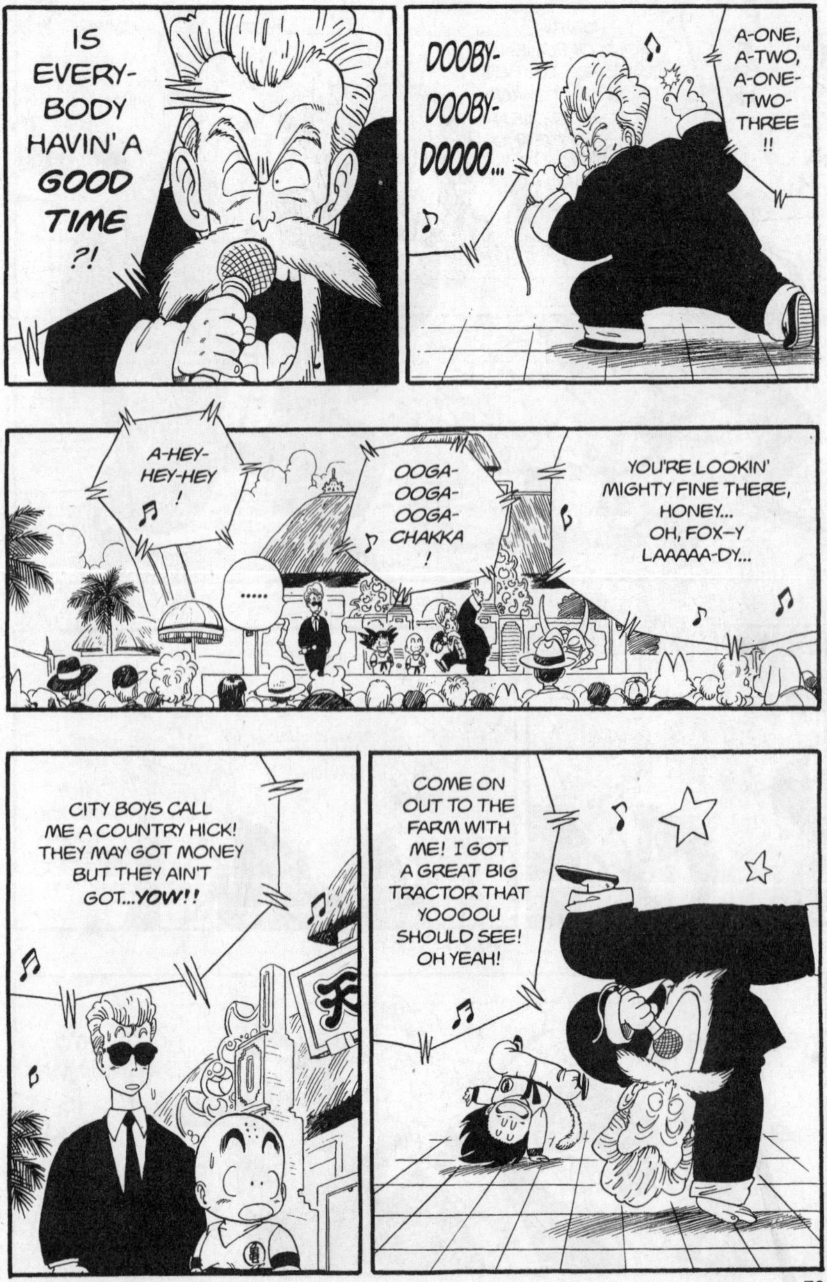
A-ONE, A-TWO, A-ONE-TWO-THREE!!
DOOBY-DOOBY-DOOOO...
IS EVERYBODY HAVIN' A GOOD TIME?!
YOU'RE LOOKIN' MIGHTY FINE THERE, HONEY... OH, FOX-Y LAAAAA-DY...
OOGA-OOGA-OOGA-CHAKKA!
A-HEY-HEY-HEY!
......
COME ON OUT TO THE FARM WITH ME! I GOT A GREAT BIG TRACTOR THAT YOOOOU SHOULD SEE! OH YEAH!
CITY BOYS CALL ME A COUNTRY HICK! THEY MAY GOT MONEY BUT THEY AIN'T GOT...YOW!!

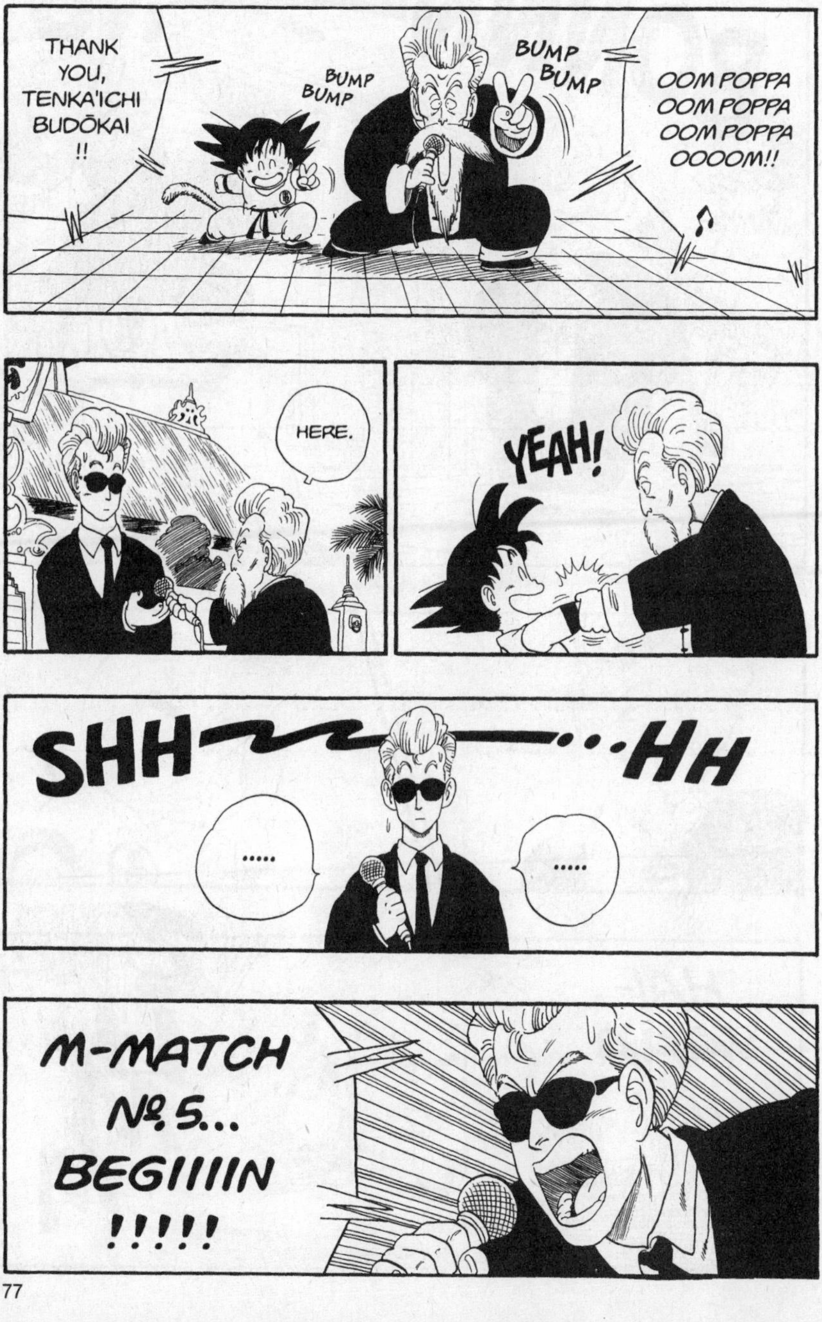
OOM POPPA OOM POPPA OOM POPPA OOOOM!!
BUMP BUMP
BUMP BUMP
THANK YOU, TENKA'ICHI BUDŌKAI !!
YEAH!
HERE.
SHH......HH
.....
.....
M-MATCH №. 5... BEGIIIIN !!!!!

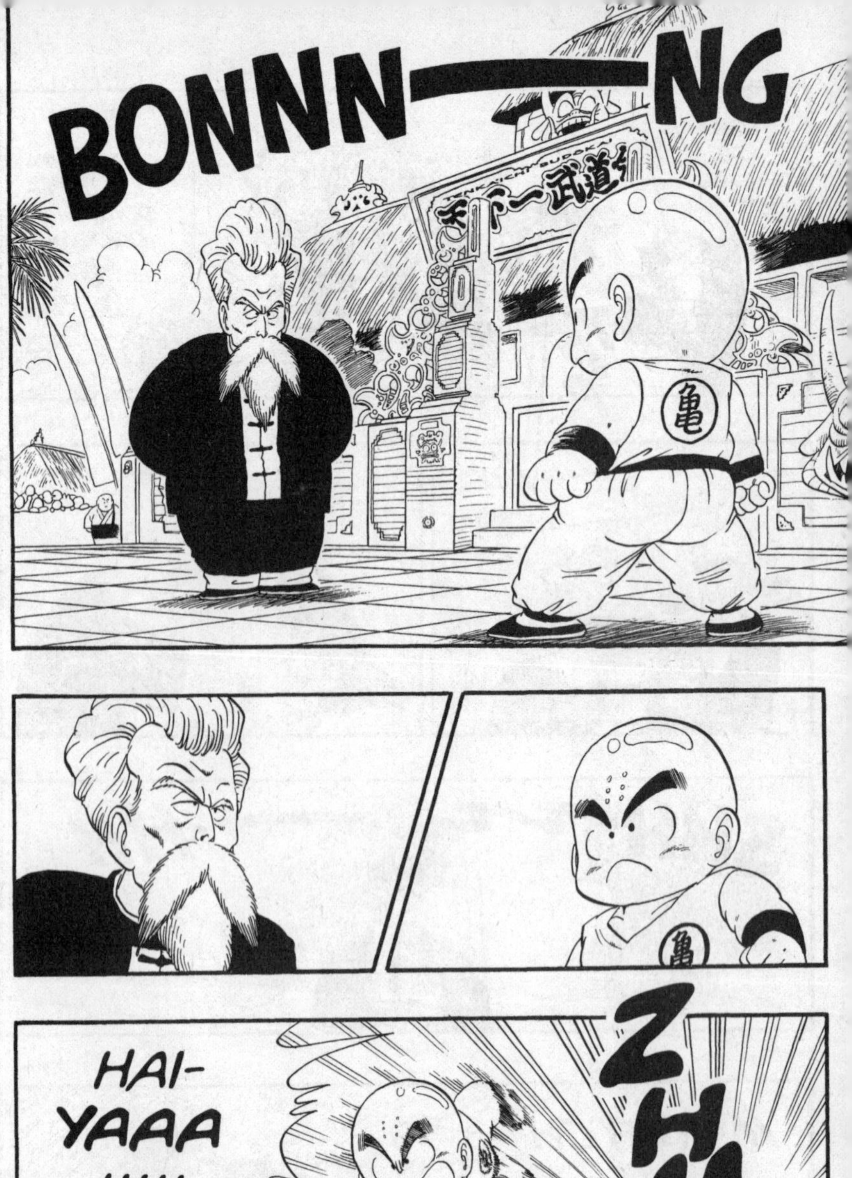
BONNN——NG
ZHMM
HAI-YAAA!!!!!

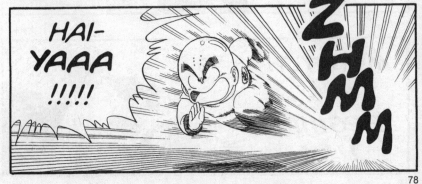

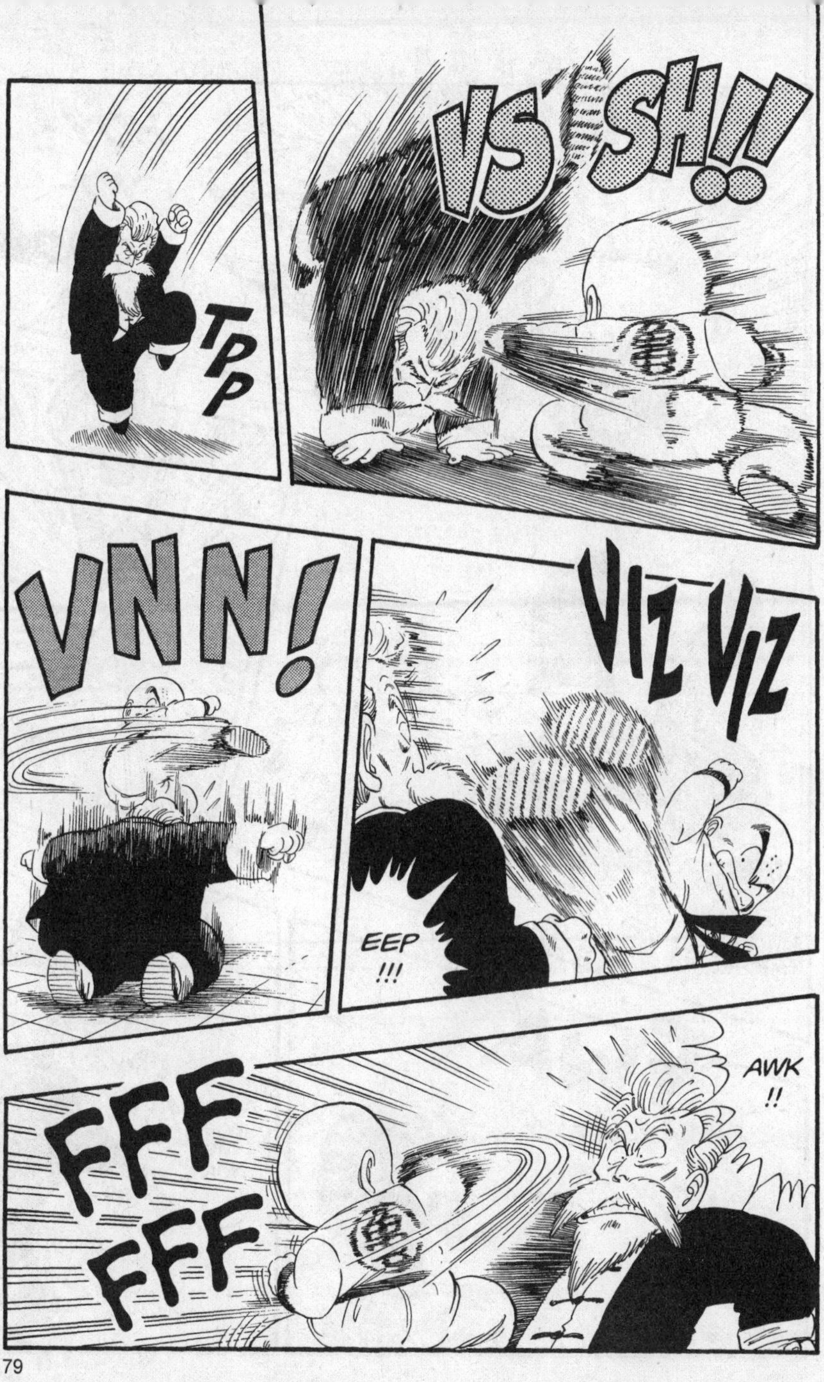
VSSH!!
TPP
VIZ VIZ
EEP!!!
VNN!
AWK!!
FFF FFF

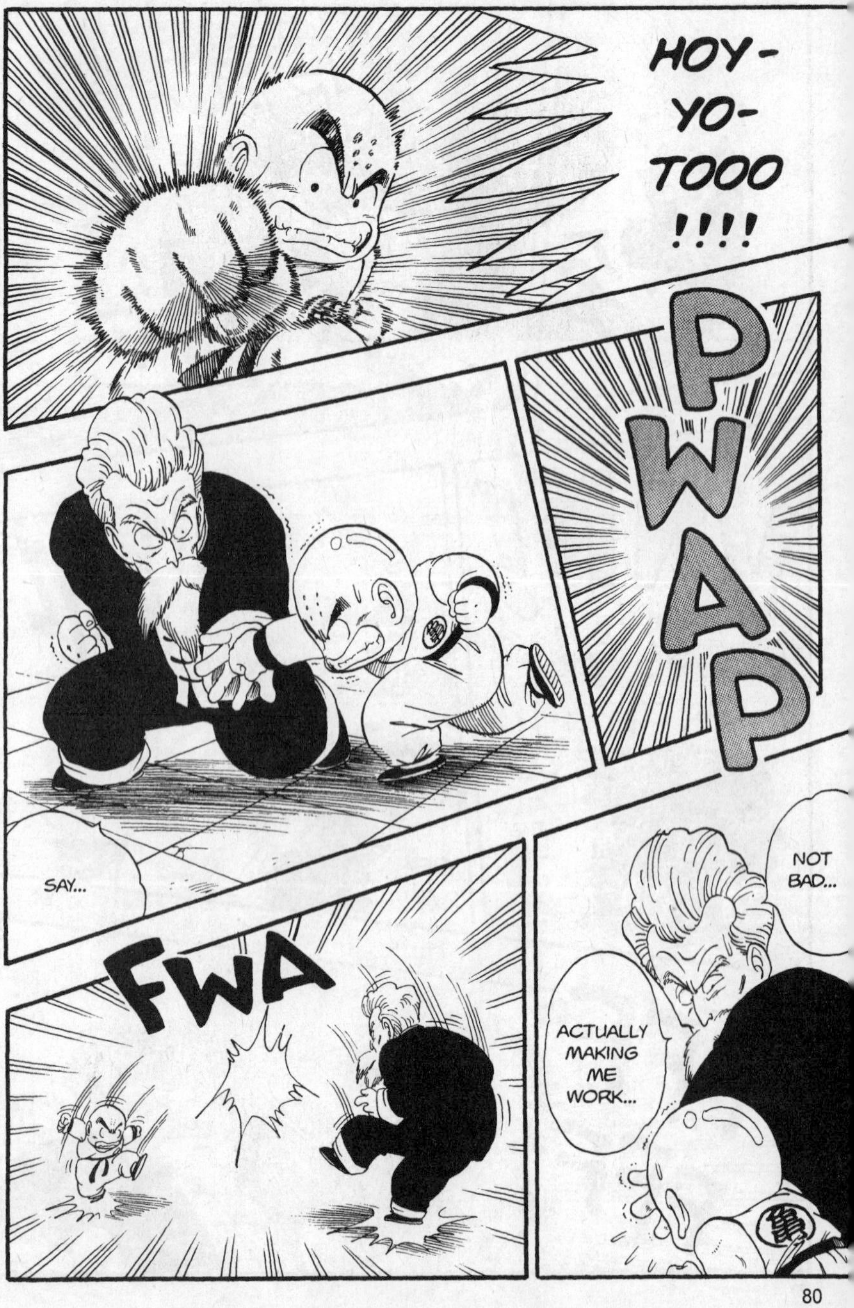
HOY-YO-TOOO!!!!
PWAP
NOT BAD...
ACTUALLY MAKING ME WORK...
SAY...
FWA

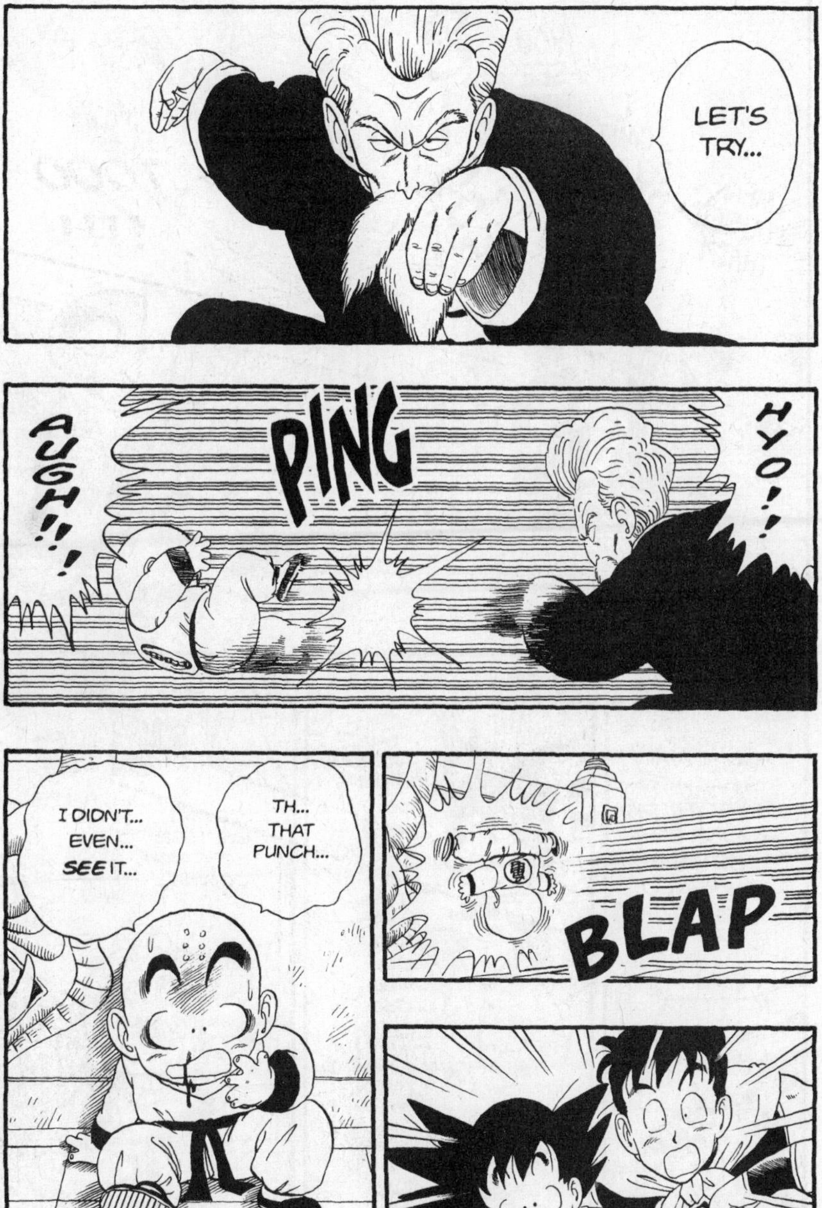
LET'S TRY...
HYO!!
PING
AUGH!!!
BLAP
TH... THAT PUNCH...
I DIDN'T... EVEN... SEE IT...

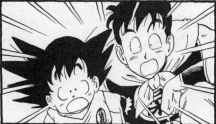

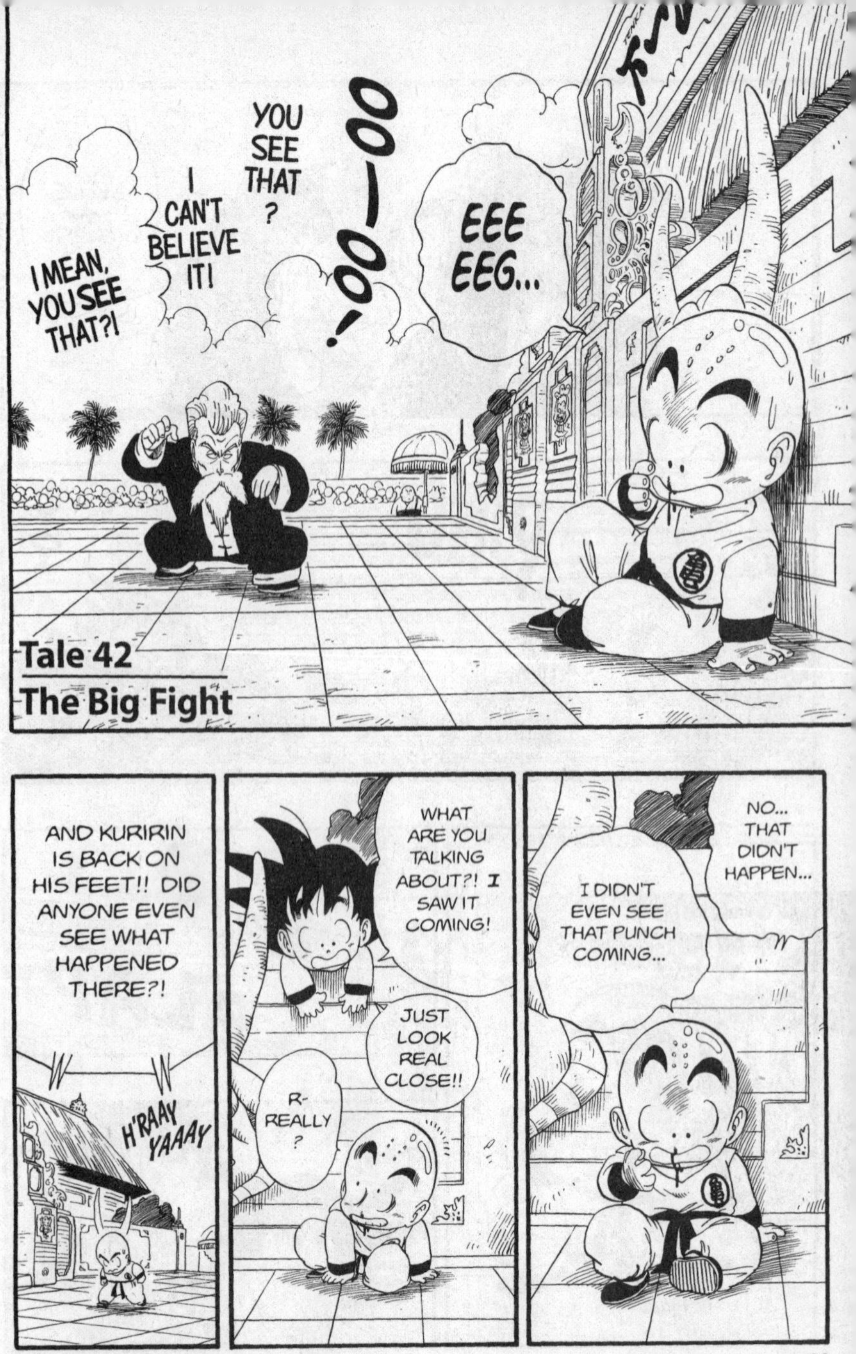
EEE EEG...
OOO-OOO!
YOU SEE THAT?
I CAN'T BELIEVE IT!
I MEAN, YOU SEE THAT?!
Tale 42
The Big Fight
NO... THAT DIDN'T HAPPEN...
I DIDN'T EVEN SEE THAT PUNCH COMING...
WHAT ARE YOU TALKING ABOUT?! I SAW IT COMING!
JUST LOOK REAL CLOSE!!
R-REALLY?
AND KURIRIN IS BACK ON HIS FEET!! DID ANYONE EVEN SEE WHAT HAPPENED THERE?!
H'RAAY YAAAY

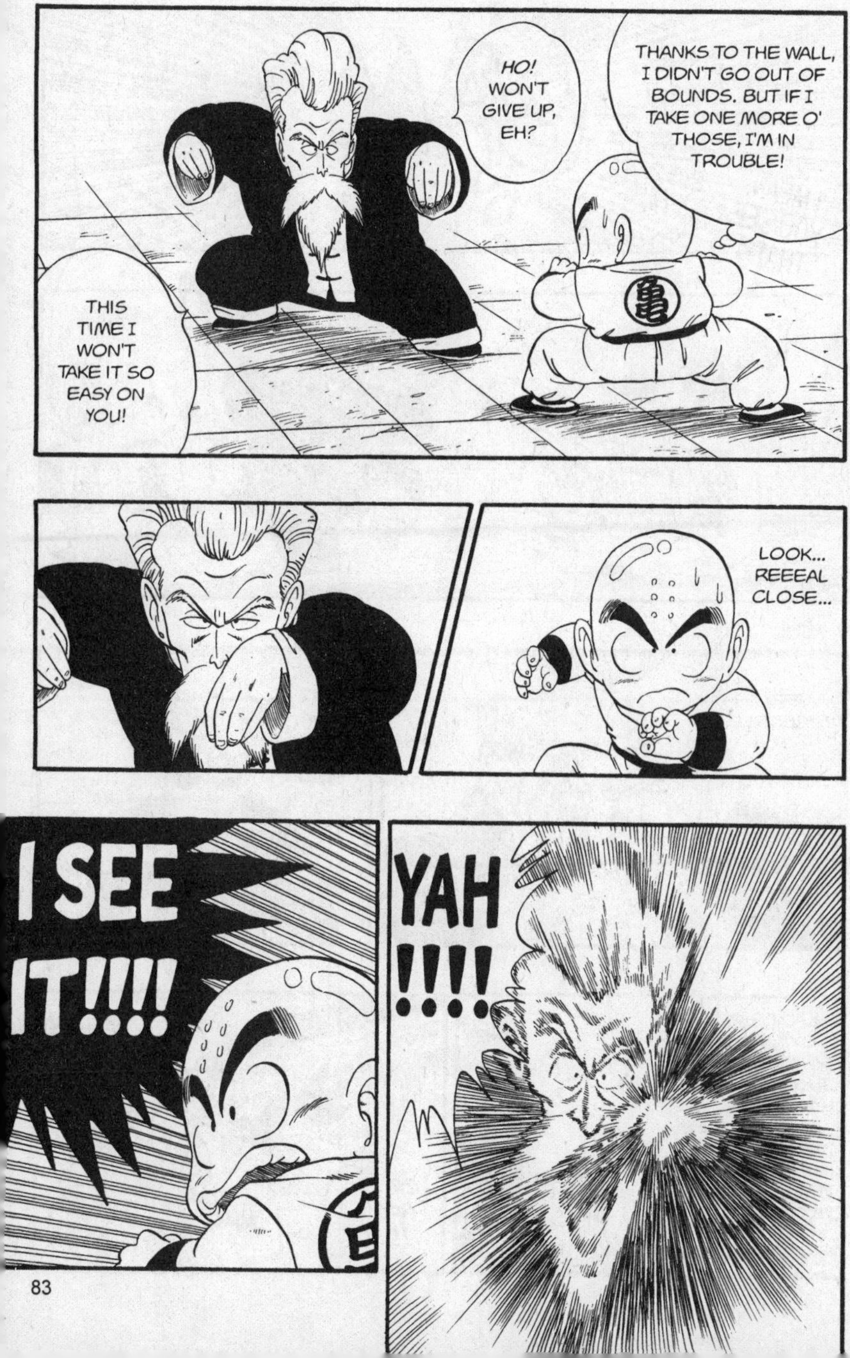
THANKS TO THE WALL, I DIDN'T GO OUT OF BOUNDS. BUT IF I TAKE ONE MORE O' THOSE, I'M IN TROUBLE!
HO! WON'T GIVE UP, EH?
THIS TIME I WON'T TAKE IT SO EASY ON YOU!
LOOK... REEEAL CLOSE...
YAH!!!!
I SEE IT!!!!

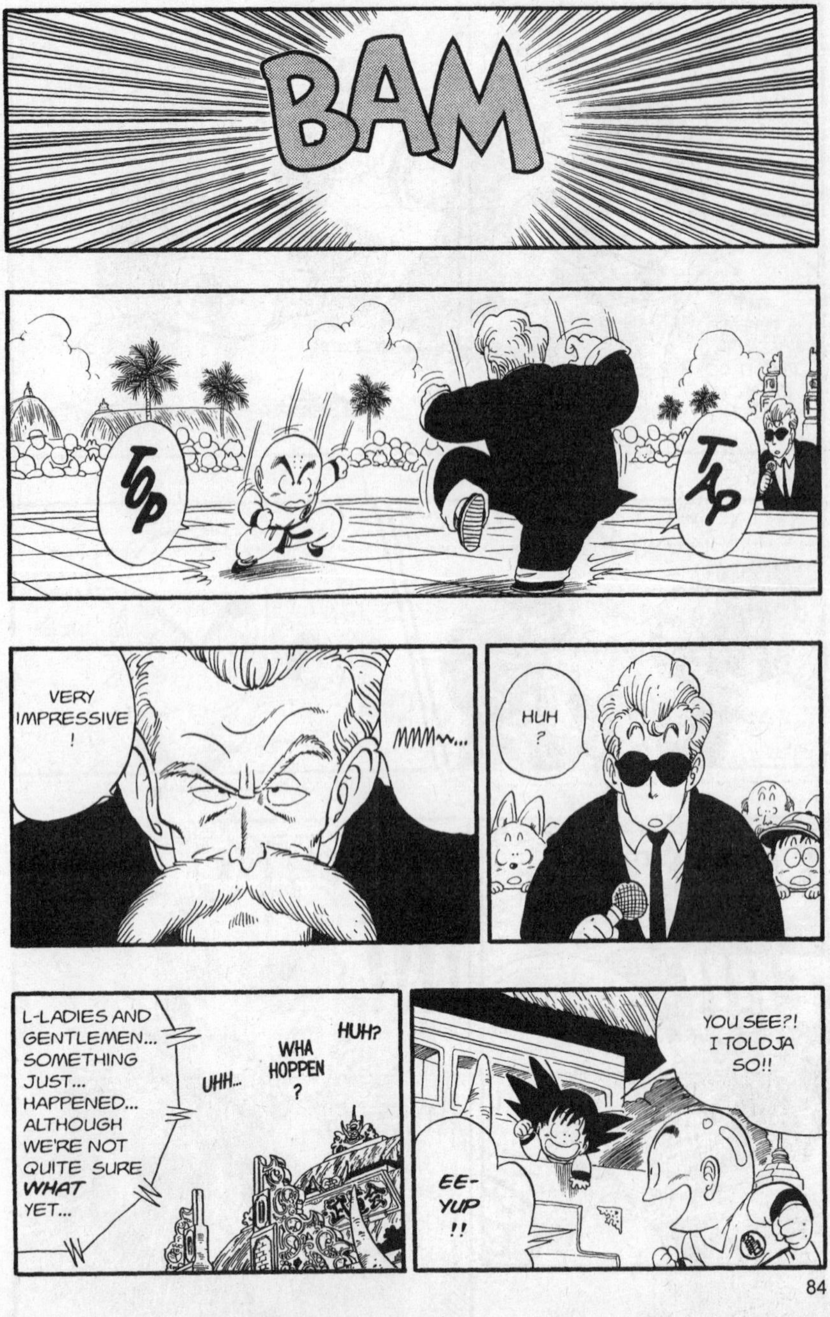
BAM
TAP
TOP
HUH ?
MMMM...
VERY IMPRESSIVE !
YOU SEE?! I TOLDJA SO!!
EE- YUP !!
HUH?
WHA HOPPEN ?
UHH...
L-LADIES AND GENTLEMEN... SOMETHING JUST... HAPPENED... ALTHOUGH WE'RE NOT QUITE SURE WHAT YET...

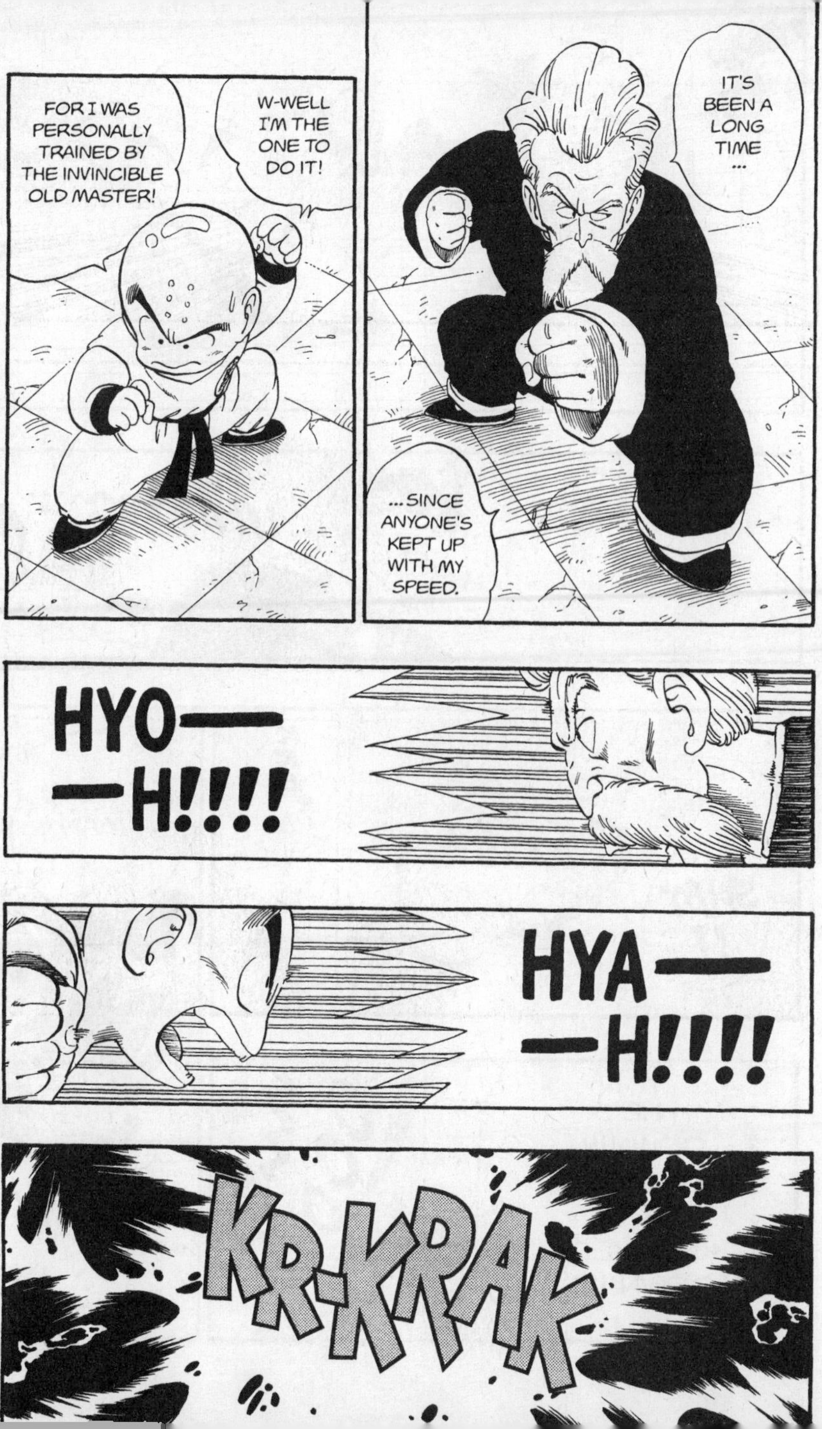
IT'S BEEN A LONG TIME ...
...SINCE ANYONE'S KEPT UP WITH MY SPEED.
W-WELL I'M THE ONE TO DO IT!
FOR I WAS PERSONALLY TRAINED BY THE INVINCIBLE OLD MASTER!
HYO——H!!!!
HYA——H!!!!
KR-KRAK

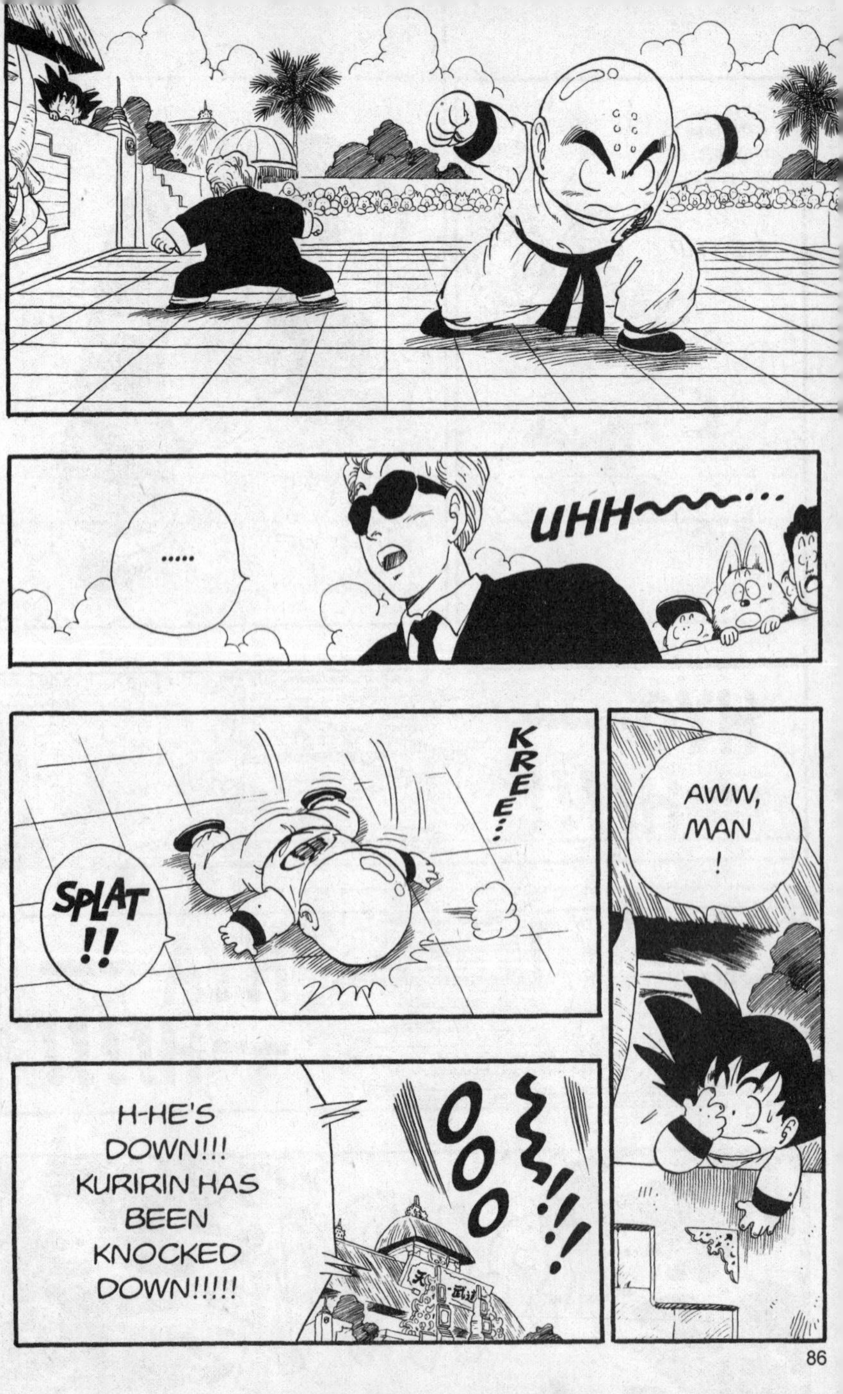
UHH~~~...
.....
AWW, MAN!
KREE...
SPLAT!!
OOO~!!!
H-HE'S DOWN!!! KURIRIN HAS BEEN KNOCKED DOWN!!!!!

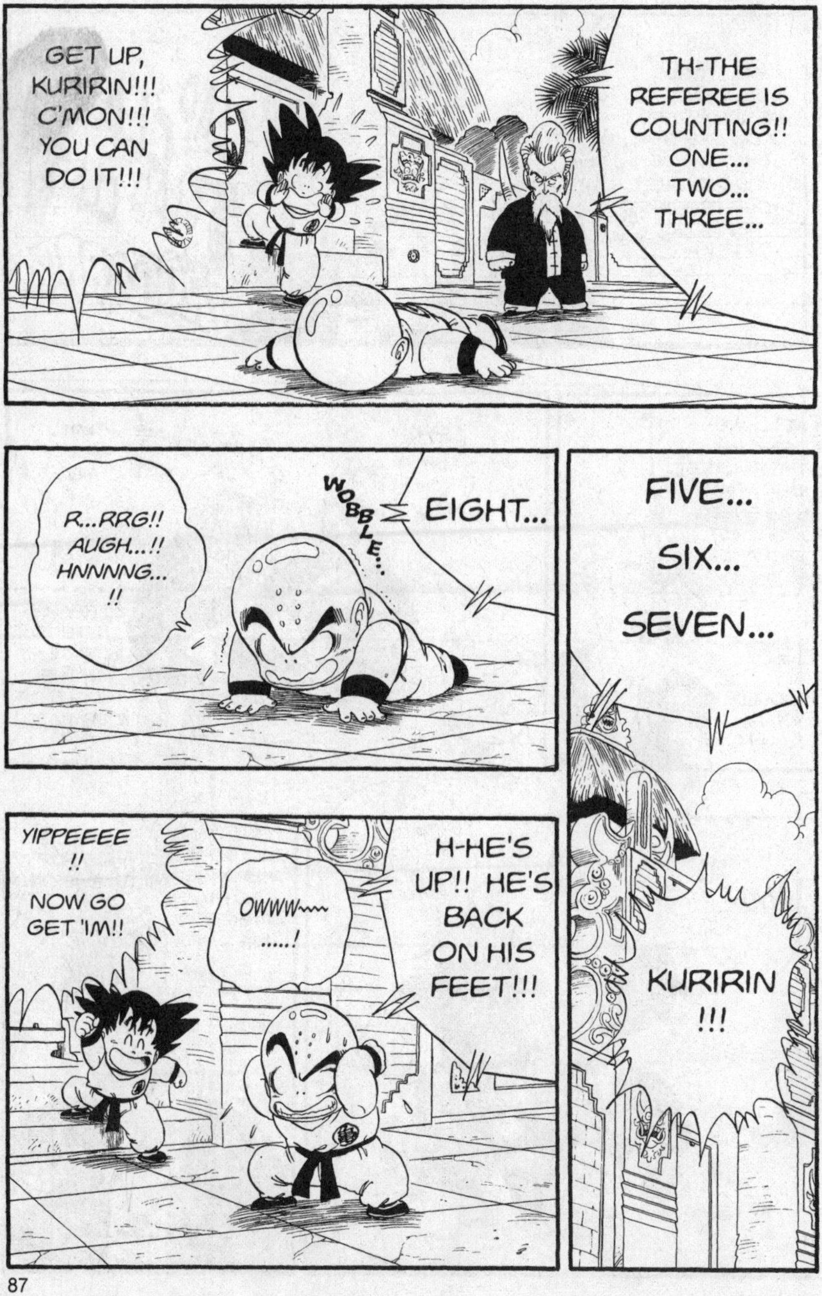
TH-THE REFEREE IS COUNTING!! ONE... TWO... THREE...
GET UP, KURIRIN!!! C'MON!!! YOU CAN DO IT!!!
FIVE... SIX... SEVEN...
KURIRIN !!!
EIGHT...
WOBBLE...
R...RRG!! AUGH...!! HNNNNG... !!
H-HE'S UP!! HE'S BACK ON HIS FEET!!!
OWWW~~ .....!
YIPPEEEE !!
NOW GO GET 'IM!!

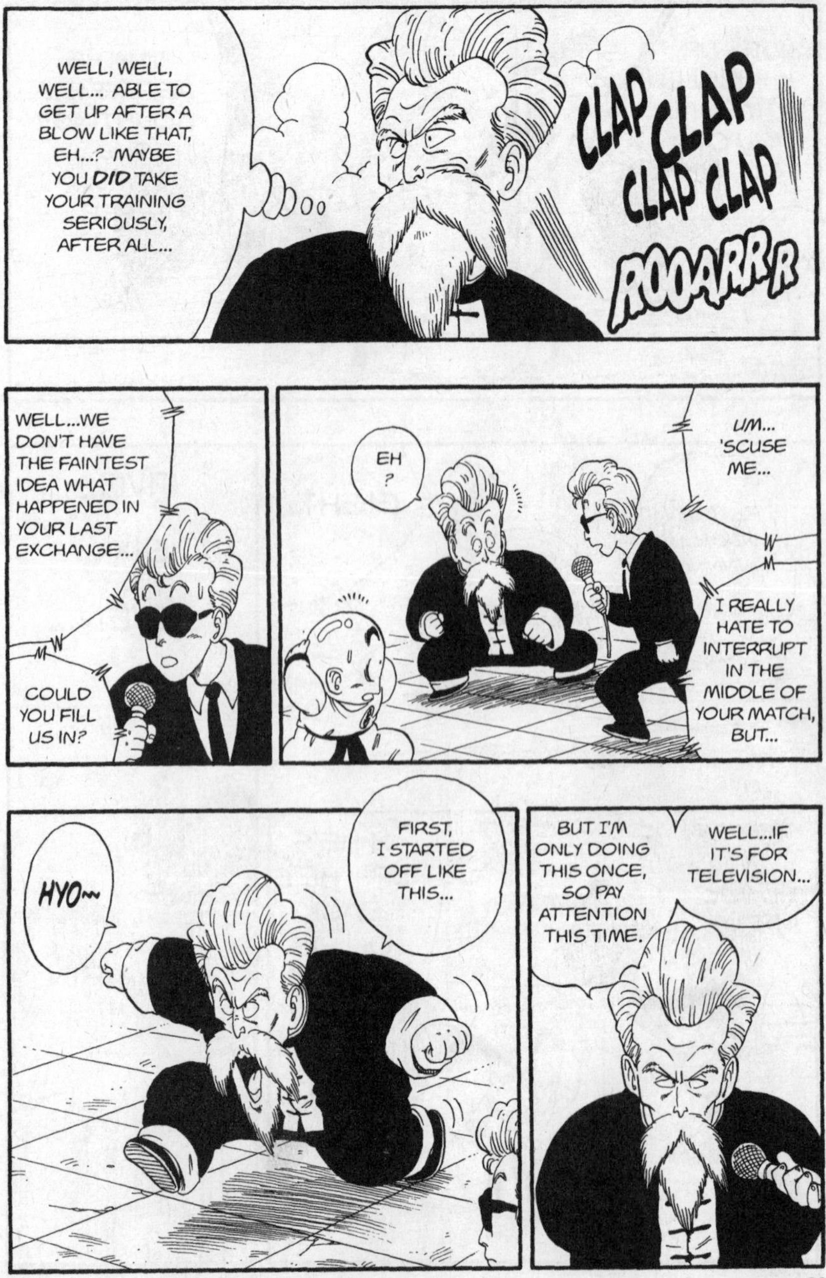
CLAP CLAP
CLAP CLAP
ROOARRR R
WELL, WELL, WELL... ABLE TO GET UP AFTER A BLOW LIKE THAT, EH...? MAYBE YOU ***DID*** TAKE YOUR TRAINING SERIOUSLY, AFTER ALL...
UM... 'SCUSE ME...
I REALLY HATE TO INTERRUPT IN THE MIDDLE OF YOUR MATCH, BUT...
EH ?
WELL...WE DON'T HAVE THE FAINTEST IDEA WHAT HAPPENED IN YOUR LAST EXCHANGE...
COULD YOU FILL US IN?
WELL...IF IT'S FOR TELEVISION...
BUT I'M ONLY DOING THIS ONCE, SO PAY ATTENTION THIS TIME.
FIRST, I STARTED OFF LIKE THIS...
HYO~~

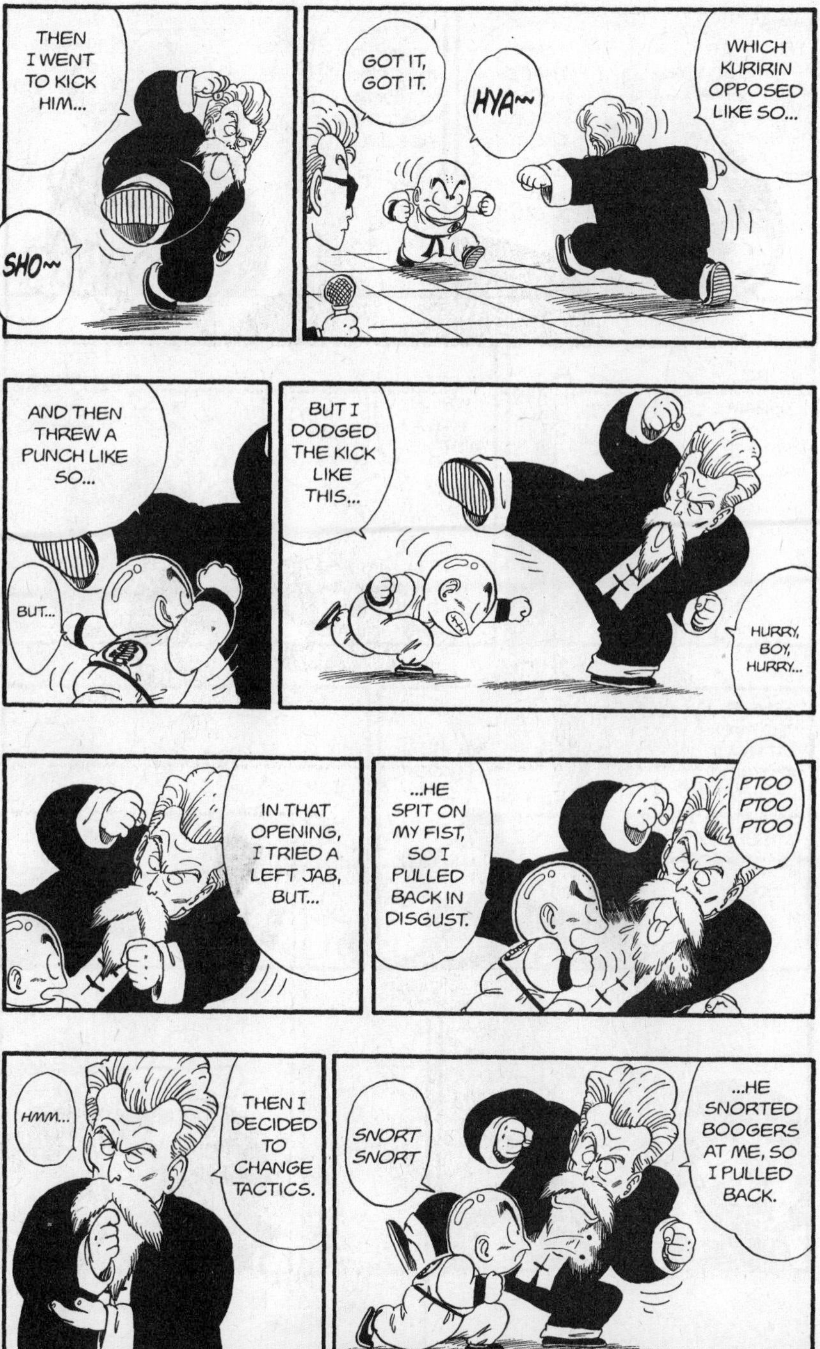
WHICH KURIRIN OPPOSED LIKE SO...
HYA~
GOT IT, GOT IT.
THEN I WENT TO KICK HIM...
SHO~
BUT I DODGED THE KICK LIKE THIS...
HURRY, BOY, HURRY...
AND THEN THREW A PUNCH LIKE SO...
BUT...
PTOO PTOO PTOO
...HE SPIT ON MY FIST, SO I PULLED BACK IN DISGUST.
IN THAT OPENING, I TRIED A LEFT JAB, BUT...
...HE SNORTED BOOGERS AT ME, SO I PULLED BACK.
SNORT SNORT
THEN I DECIDED TO CHANGE TACTICS.
HMM...

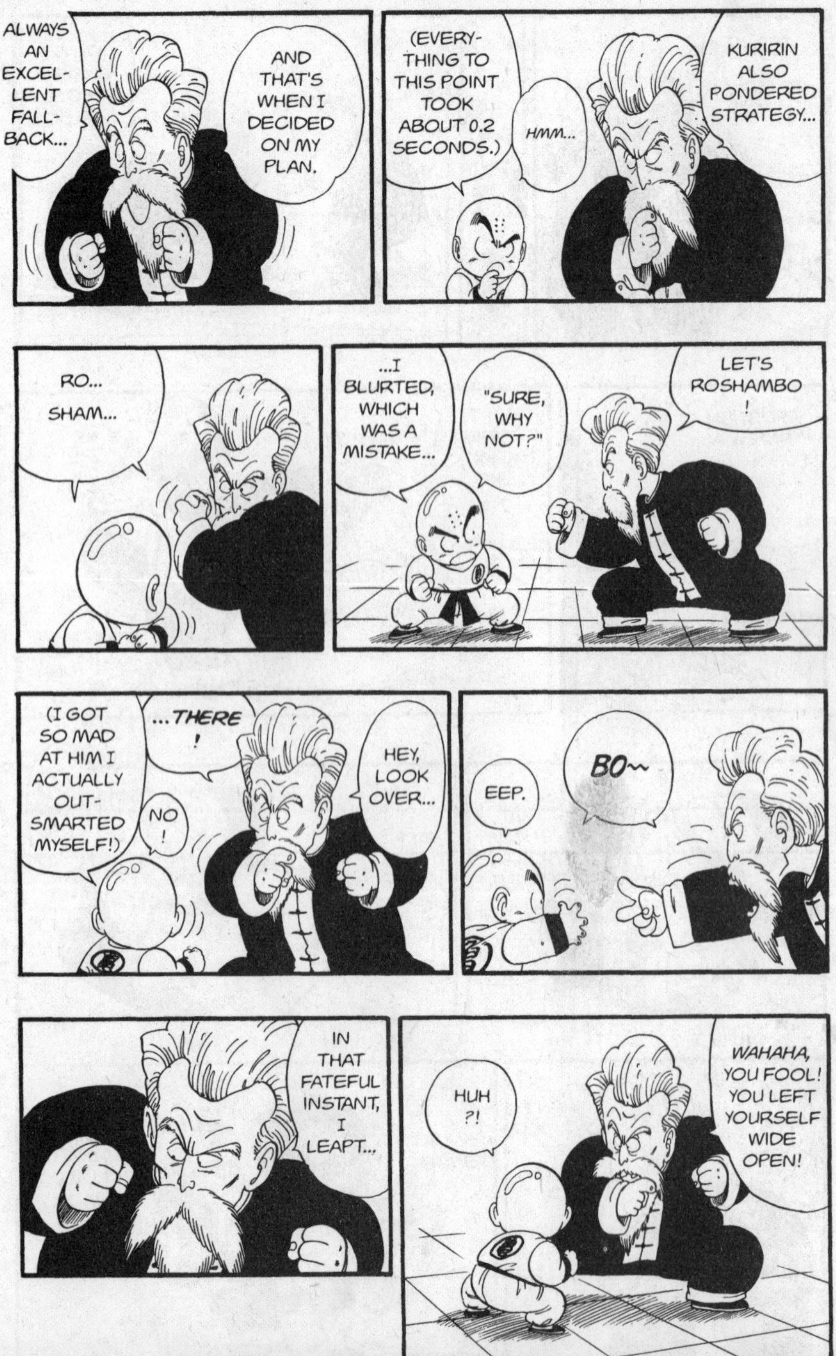

KURIRIN ALSO PONDERED STRATEGY...
HMM...
(EVERY-THING TO THIS POINT TOOK ABOUT 0.2 SECONDS.)
AND THAT'S WHEN I DECIDED ON MY PLAN.
ALWAYS AN EXCEL-LENT FALL-BACK...
LET'S ROSHAMBO!
"SURE, WHY NOT?"
...I BLURTED, WHICH WAS A MISTAKE...
RO... SHAM...
BO~
EEP.
HEY, LOOK OVER...
...THERE!
NO!
(I GOT SO MAD AT HIM I ACTUALLY OUT-SMARTED MYSELF!)
WAHAHA, YOU FOOL! YOU LEFT YOURSELF WIDE OPEN!
HUH?!
IN THAT FATEFUL INSTANT, I LEAPT...

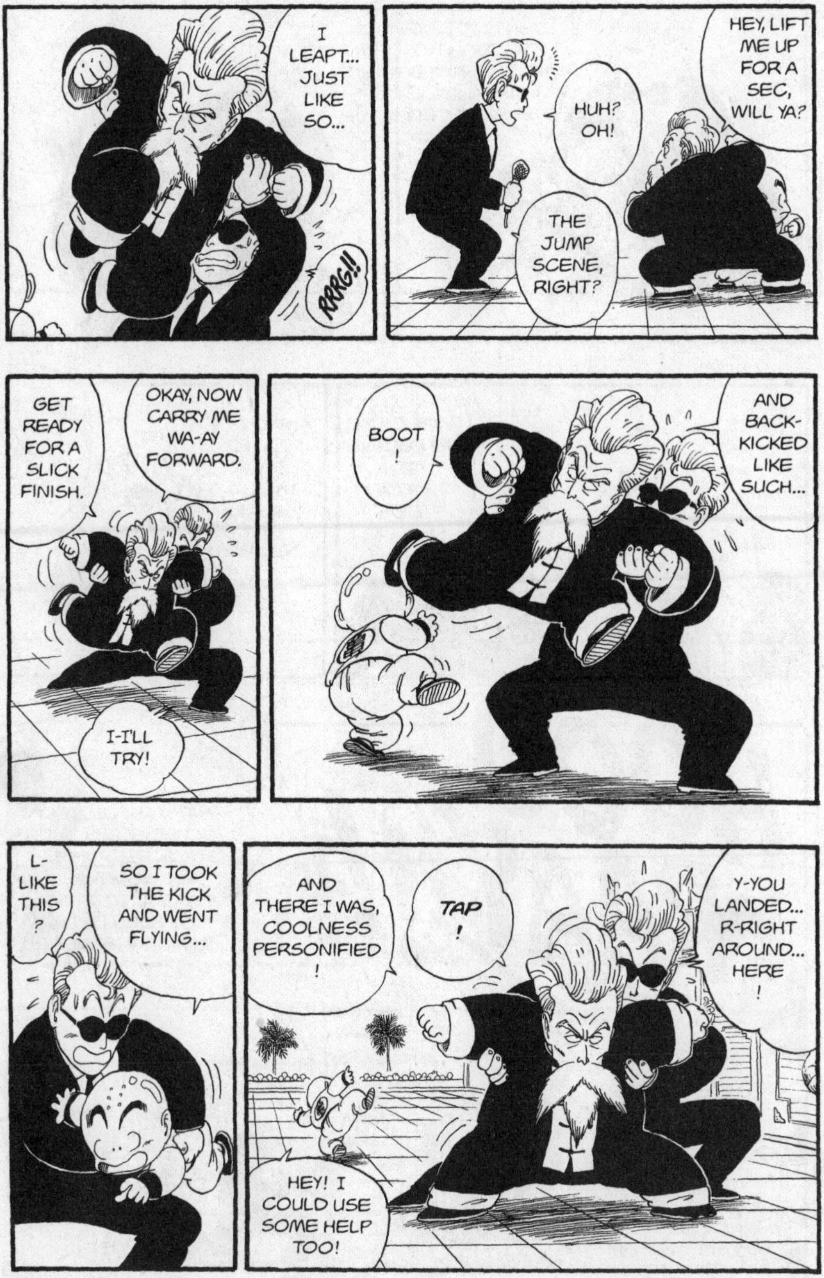
HEY, LIFT ME UP FOR A SEC, WILL YA?
HUH? OH!
THE JUMP SCENE, RIGHT?
I LEAPT... JUST LIKE SO...
RRRG!!
AND BACK-KICKED LIKE SUCH...
BOOT!
OKAY, NOW CARRY ME WA-AY FORWARD.
GET READY FOR A SLICK FINISH.
I-I'LL TRY!
Y-YOU LANDED... R-RIGHT AROUND... HERE!
TAP!
AND THERE I WAS, COOLNESS PERSONIFIED!
HEY! I COULD USE SOME HELP TOO!
SO I TOOK THE KICK AND WENT FLYING...
L-LIKE THIS?

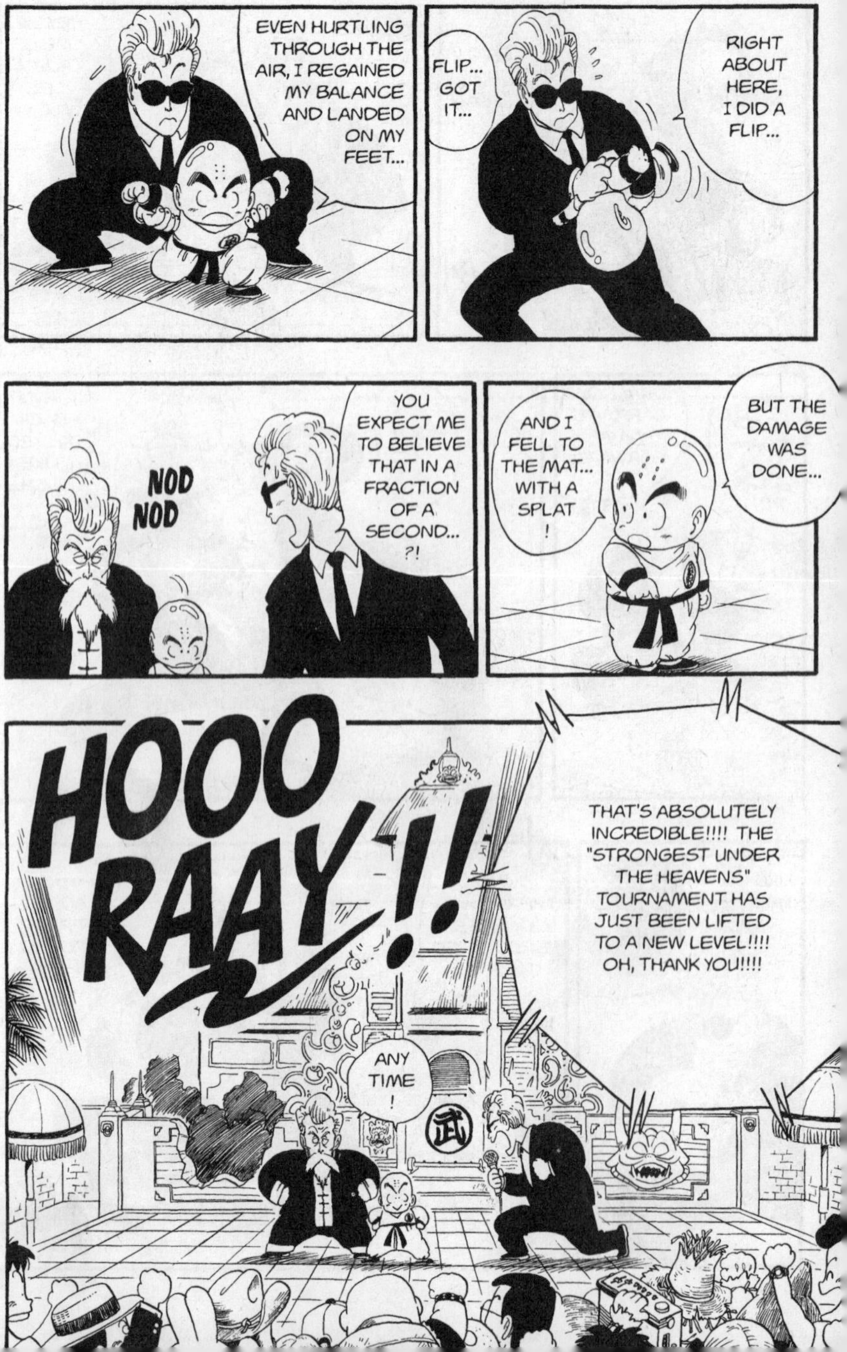
RIGHT ABOUT HERE, I DID A FLIP...
FLIP... GOT IT...
EVEN HURTLING THROUGH THE AIR, I REGAINED MY BALANCE AND LANDED ON MY FEET...
BUT THE DAMAGE WAS DONE...
AND I FELL TO THE MAT... WITH A SPLAT!
YOU EXPECT ME TO BELIEVE THAT IN A FRACTION OF A SECOND...?!
NOD NOD
THAT'S ABSOLUTELY INCREDIBLE!!!! THE "STRONGEST UNDER THE HEAVENS" TOURNAMENT HAS JUST BEEN LIFTED TO A NEW LEVEL!!!! OH, THANK YOU!!!!
HOOO RAAY!!
ANY TIME!

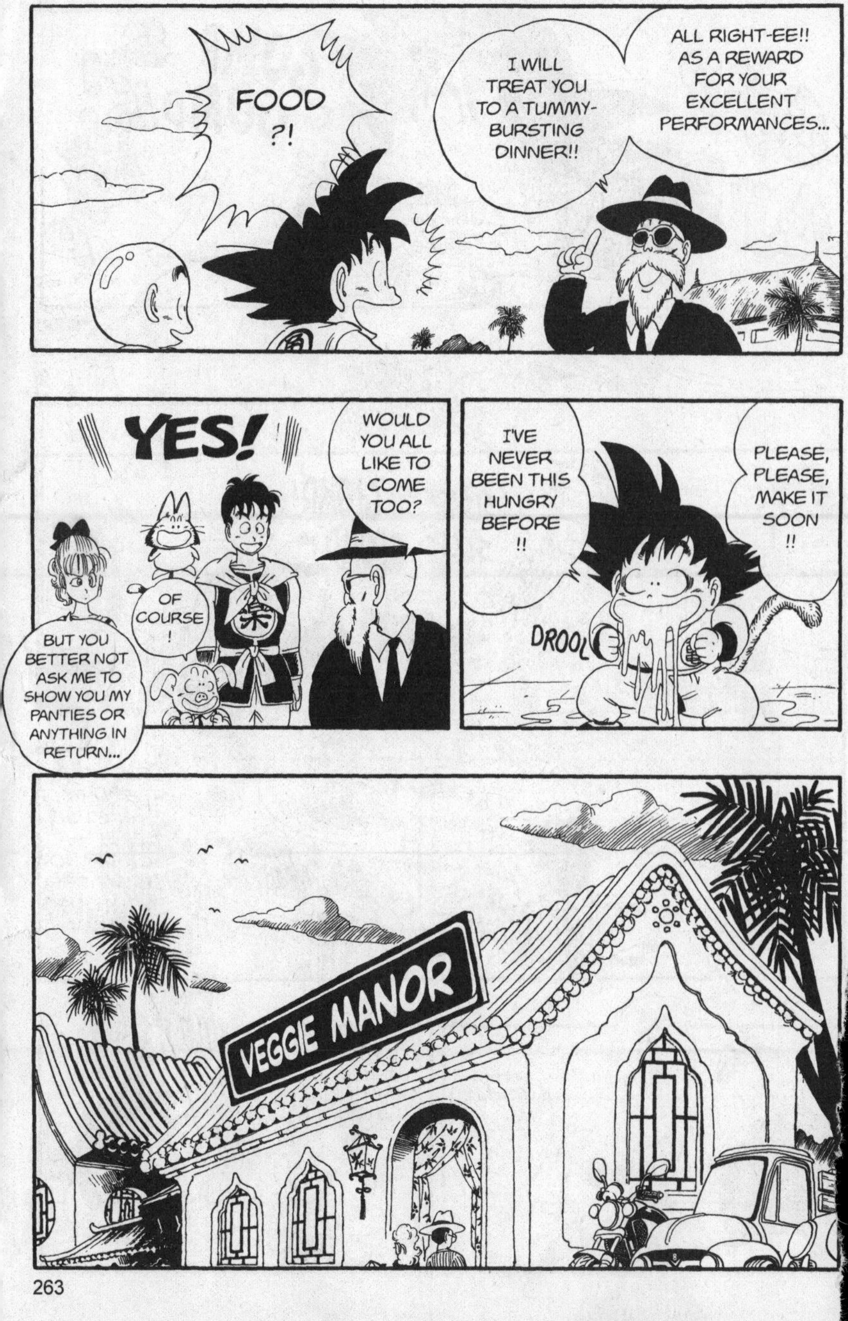
ALL RIGHT-EE!! AS A REWARD FOR YOUR EXCELLENT PERFORMANCES...
I WILL TREAT YOU TO A TUMMY-BURSTING DINNER!!
FOOD ?!
PLEASE, PLEASE, MAKE IT SOON !!
I'VE NEVER BEEN THIS HUNGRY BEFORE !!
DROOL
WOULD YOU ALL LIKE TO COME TOO?
YES!
OF COURSE !
BUT YOU BETTER NOT ASK ME TO SHOW YOU MY PANTIES OR ANYTHING IN RETURN...
VEGGIE MANOR

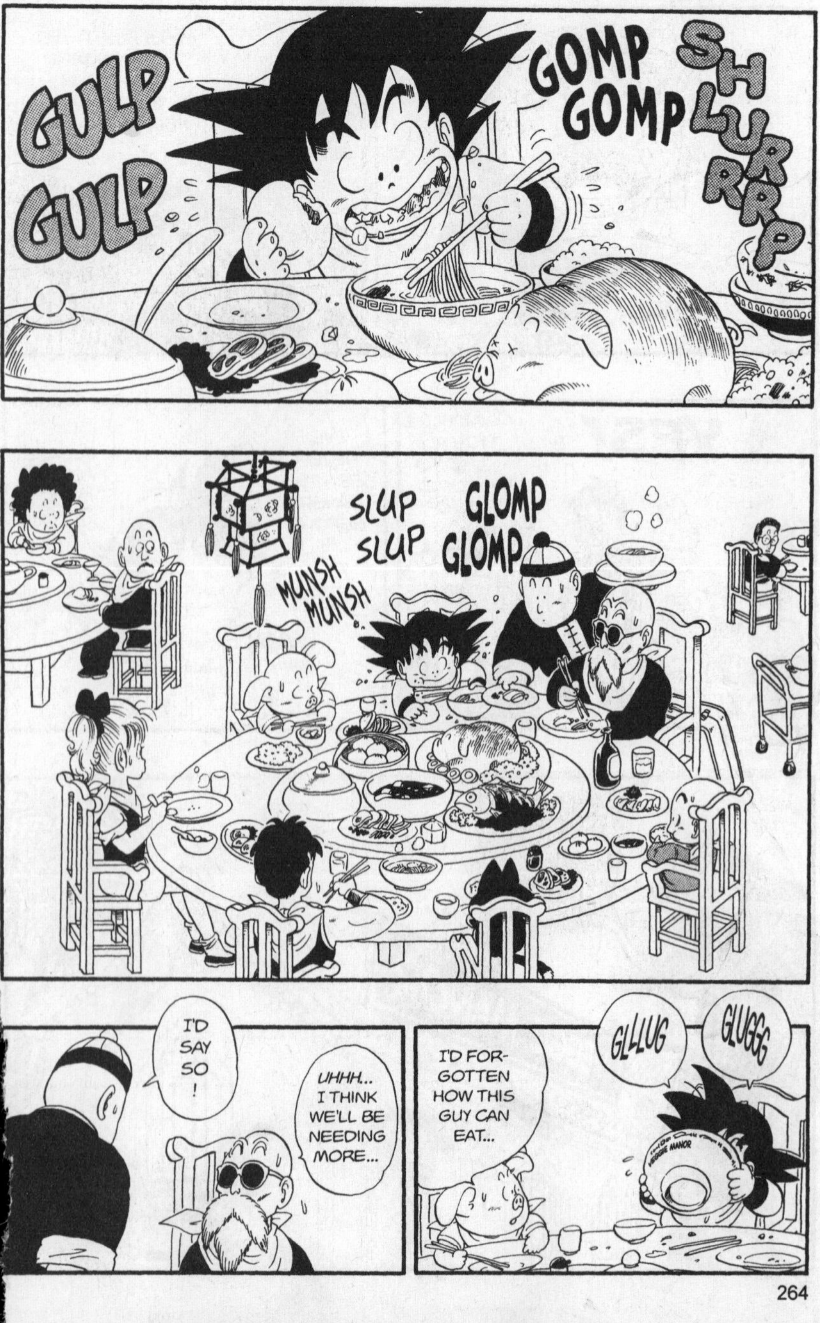
SHLURRRP
GOMP GOMP
GULP GULP
GLOMP GLOMP
SLUP SLUP
MUNSH MUNSH
GLUGGG
GLLLUG
I'D FOR-GOTTEN HOW THIS GUY CAN EAT...
VEGGIE MANOR
UHHH... I THINK WE'LL BE NEEDING MORE...
I'D SAY SO!

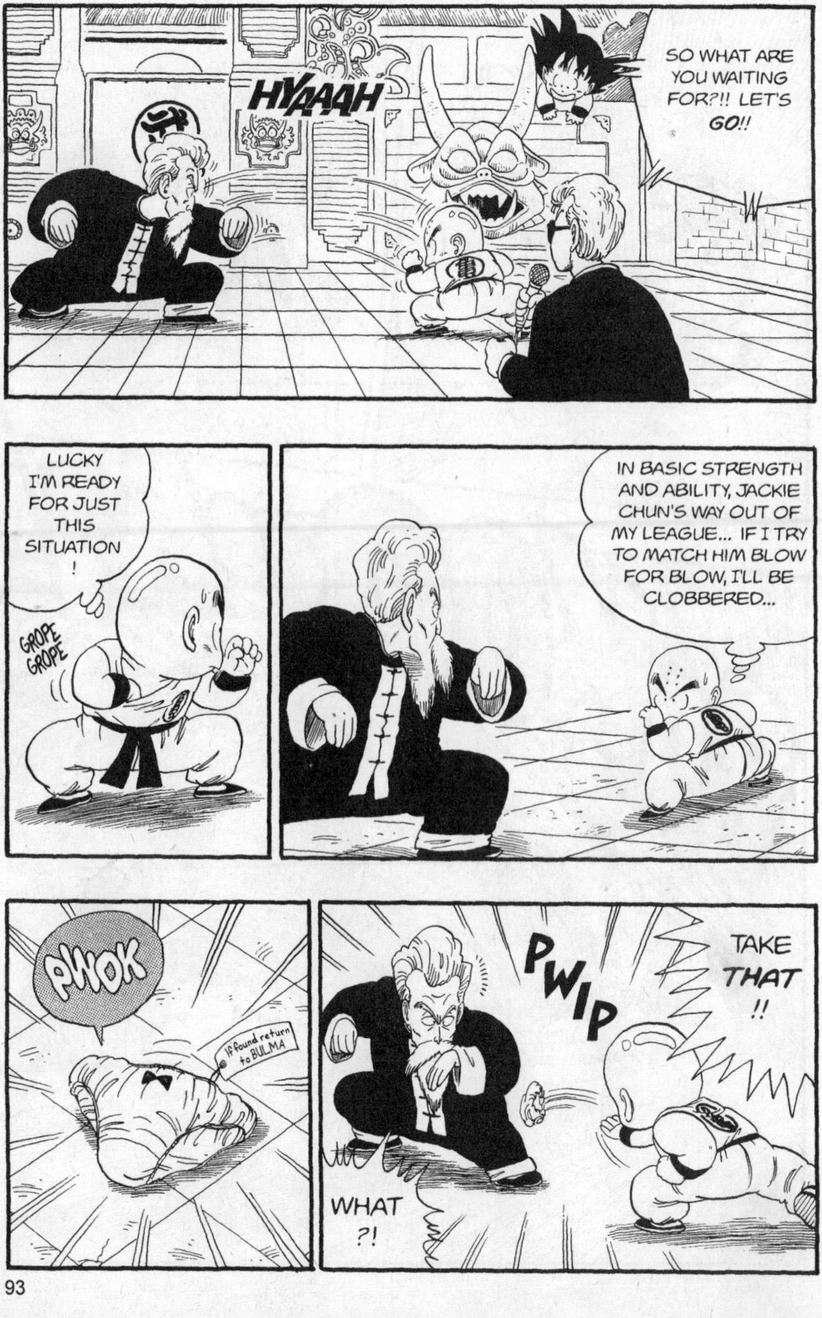
SO WHAT ARE YOU WAITING FOR?!! LET'S GO!!
HYAAAH
IN BASIC STRENGTH AND ABILITY, JACKIE CHUN'S WAY OUT OF MY LEAGUE... IF I TRY TO MATCH HIM BLOW FOR BLOW, I'LL BE CLOBBERED...
LUCKY I'M READY FOR JUST THIS SITUATION !
GROPE GROPE
TAKE THAT !!
PWIP
WHAT ?!
PWOK
If found return to BULMA

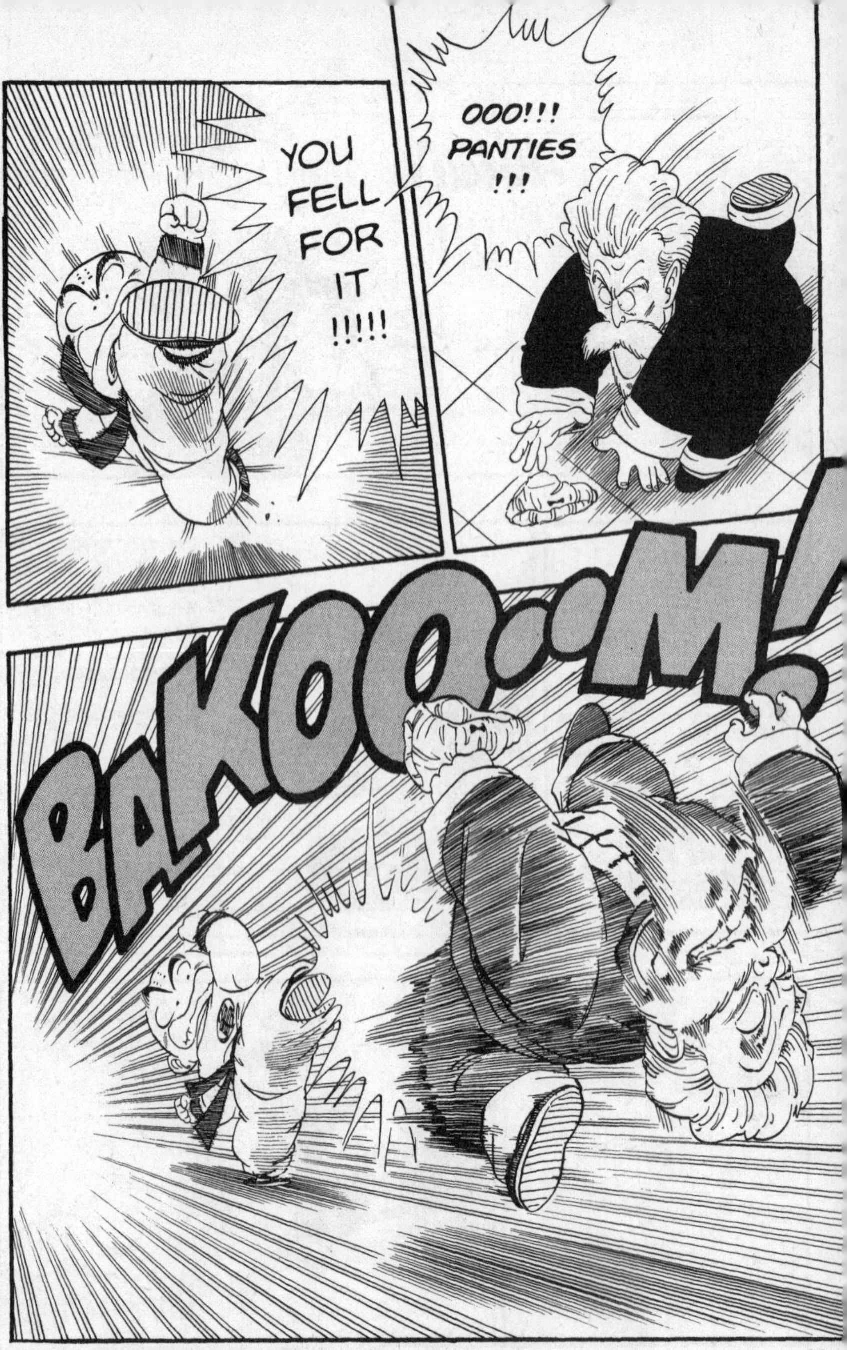
OOO!!! PANTIES !!!
YOU FELL FOR IT !!!!!
BAKOO..M!

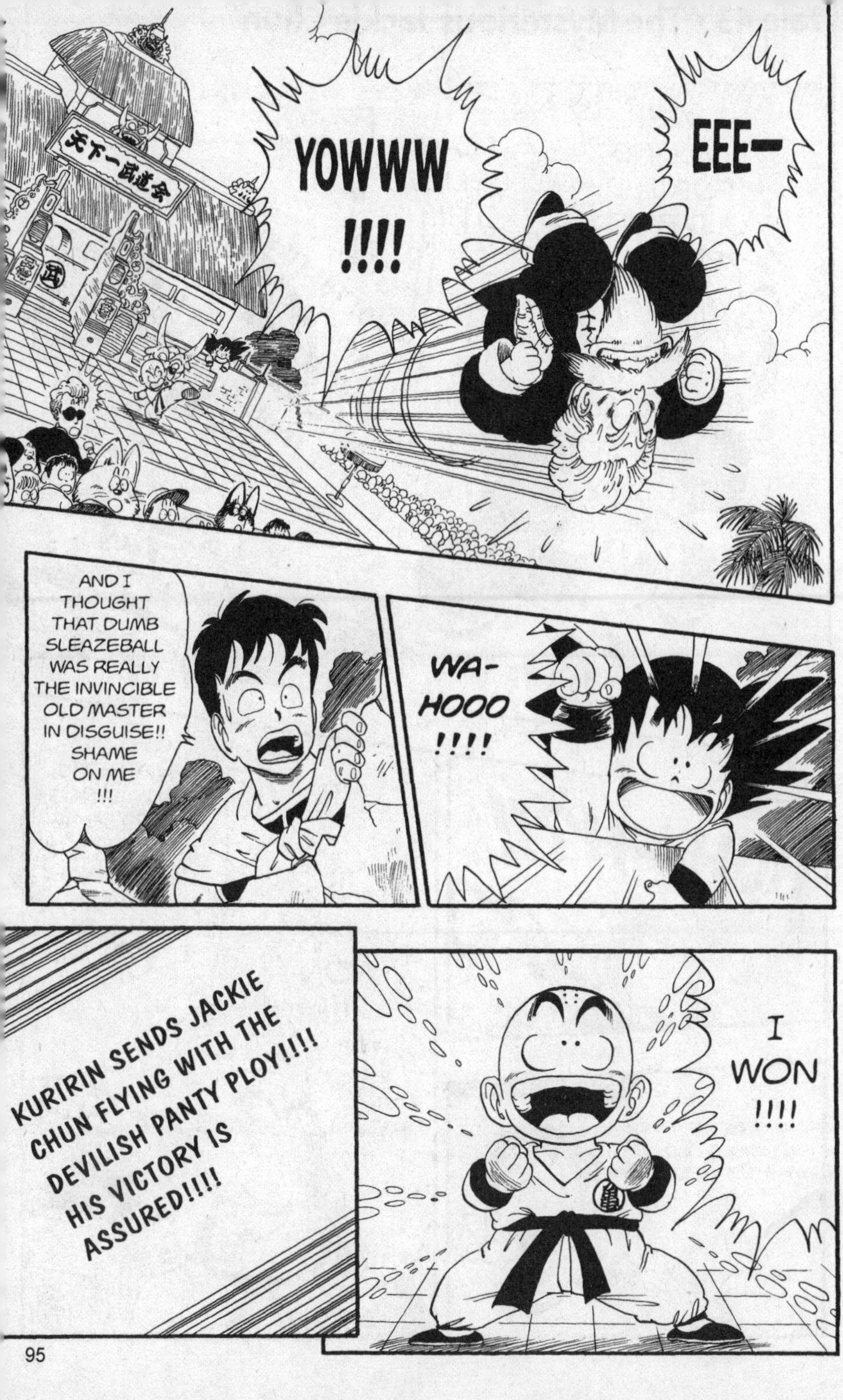
YOWWW !!!!
EEE—
天下一武道会
武
WA-HOOO !!!!
AND I THOUGHT THAT DUMB SLEAZEBALL WAS REALLY THE INVINCIBLE OLD MASTER IN DISGUISE!! SHAME ON ME !!!
I WON !!!!
KURIRIN SENDS JACKIE CHUN FLYING WITH THE DEVILISH PANTY PLOY!!!! HIS VICTORY IS ASSURED!!!!

Tale 43 • The Mysterious Jackie Chun

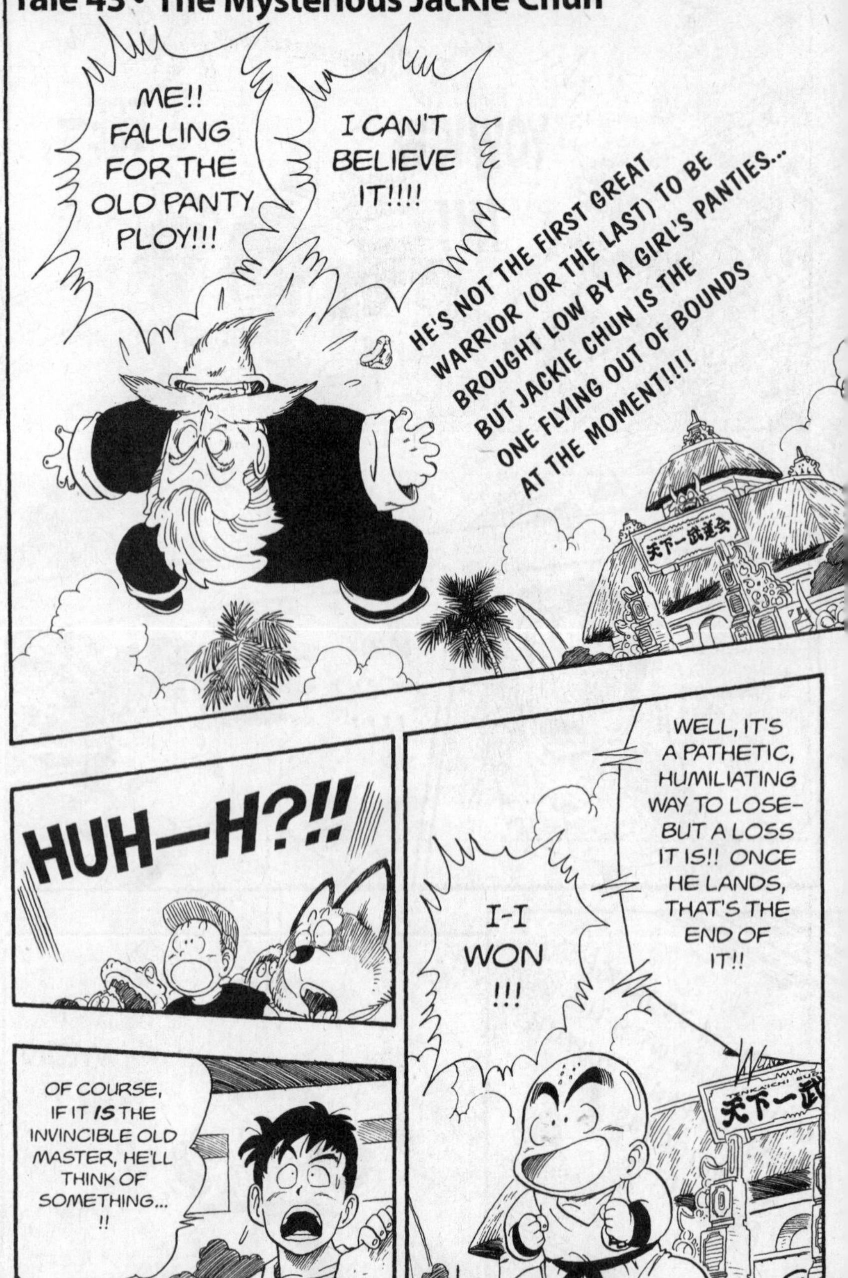
I CAN'T BELIEVE IT!!!!
ME!! FALLING FOR THE OLD PANTY PLOY!!!
HE'S NOT THE FIRST GREAT WARRIOR (OR THE LAST) TO BE BROUGHT LOW BY A GIRL'S PANTIES... BUT JACKIE CHUN IS THE ONE FLYING OUT OF BOUNDS AT THE MOMENT!!!!
天下一武道会
WELL, IT'S A PATHETIC, HUMILIATING WAY TO LOSE– BUT A LOSS IT IS!! ONCE HE LANDS, THAT'S THE END OF IT!!
I-I WON !!!
HUH–H?!!
OF COURSE, IF IT *IS* THE INVINCIBLE OLD MASTER, HE'LL THINK OF SOMETHING... !!

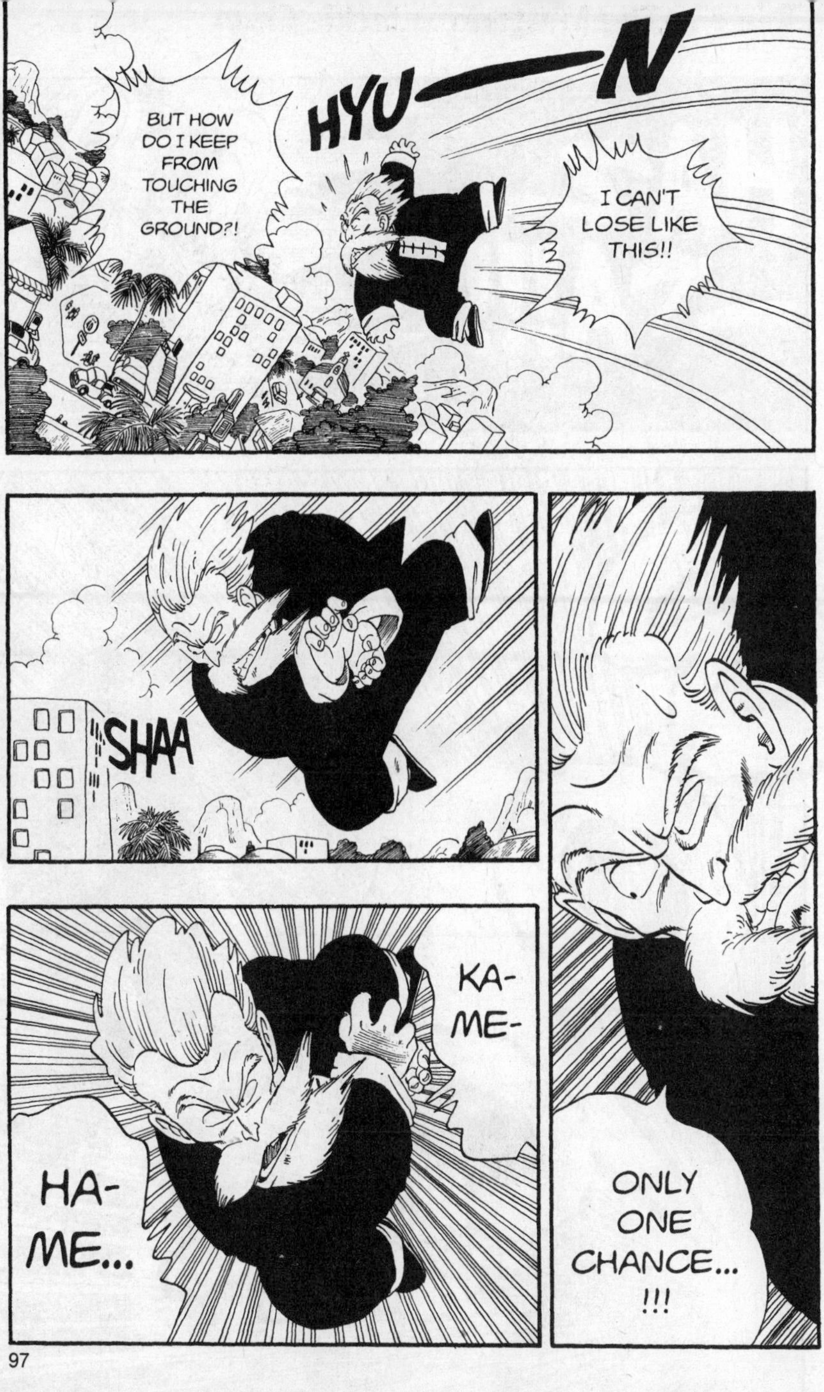
HYU—N
I CAN'T LOSE LIKE THIS!!
BUT HOW DO I KEEP FROM TOUCHING THE GROUND?!
ONLY ONE CHANCE... !!!
SHAA
KA- ME-
HA- ME...

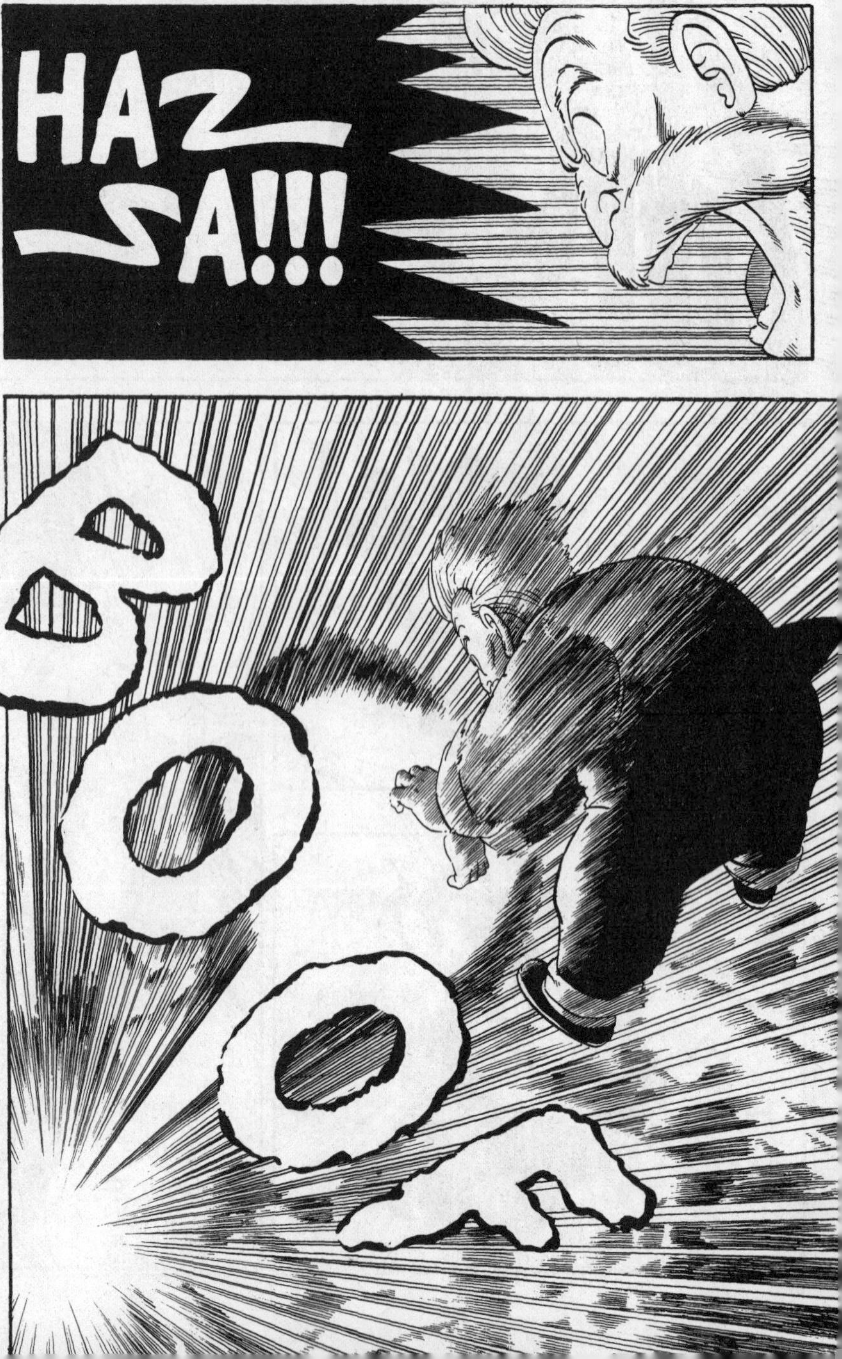
HAZ SA!!!
BOOM

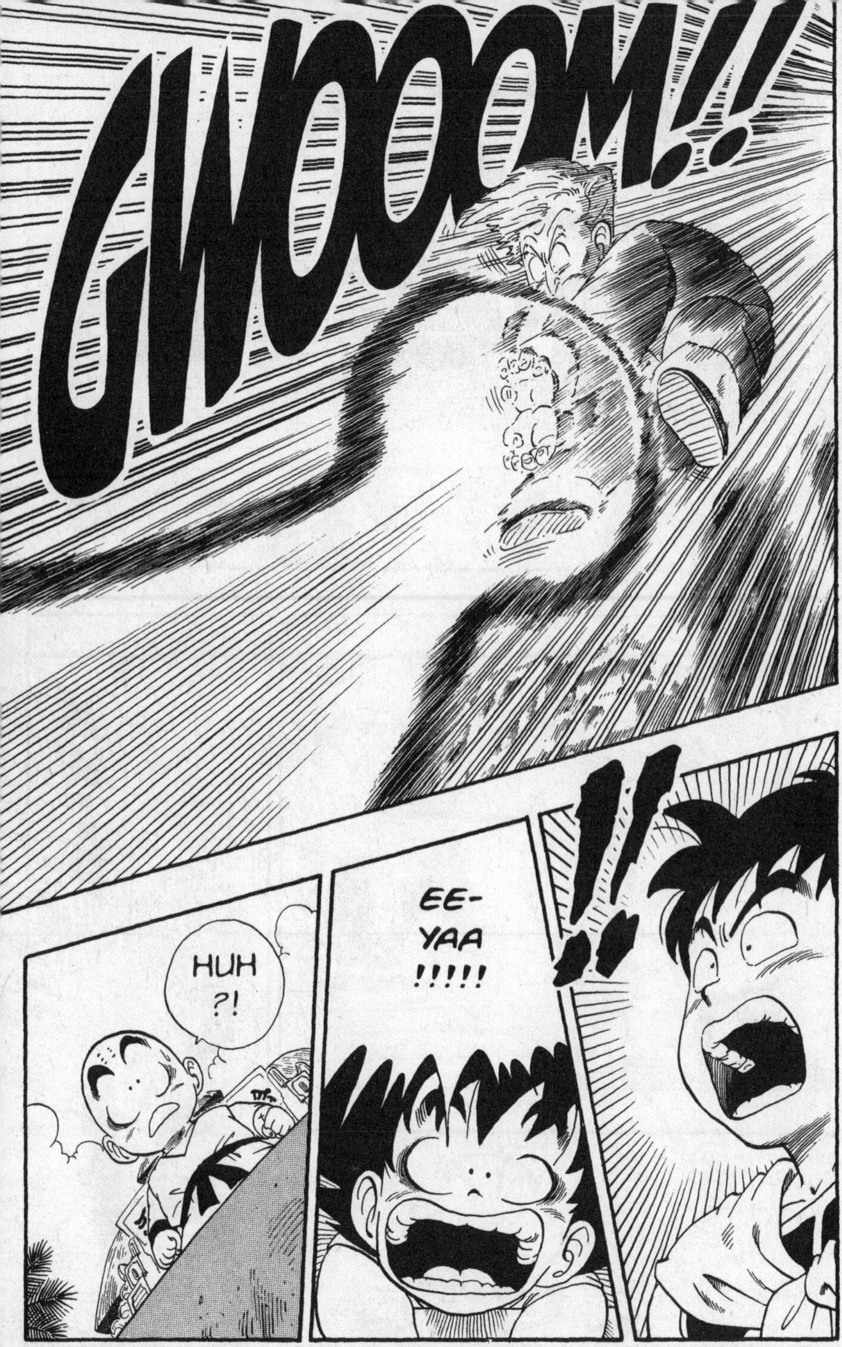
GWOOOM!!
!!
EE-
YAA
!!!!!
HUH
?!

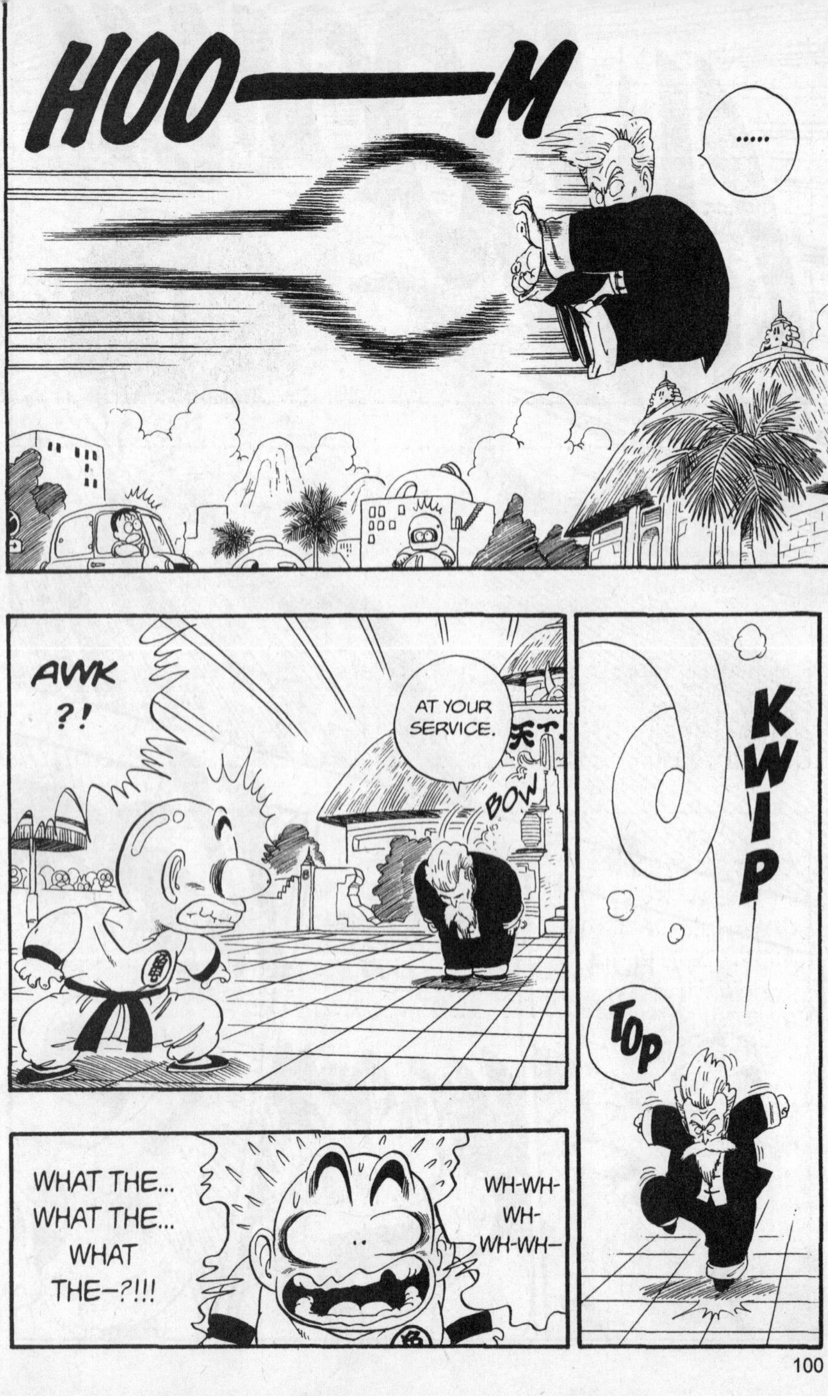
......
HOO—M
KWIP
TOP
AT YOUR SERVICE.
BOW
AWK ?!
WH-WH- WH- WH-WH-
WHAT THE... WHAT THE... WHAT THE-?!!!

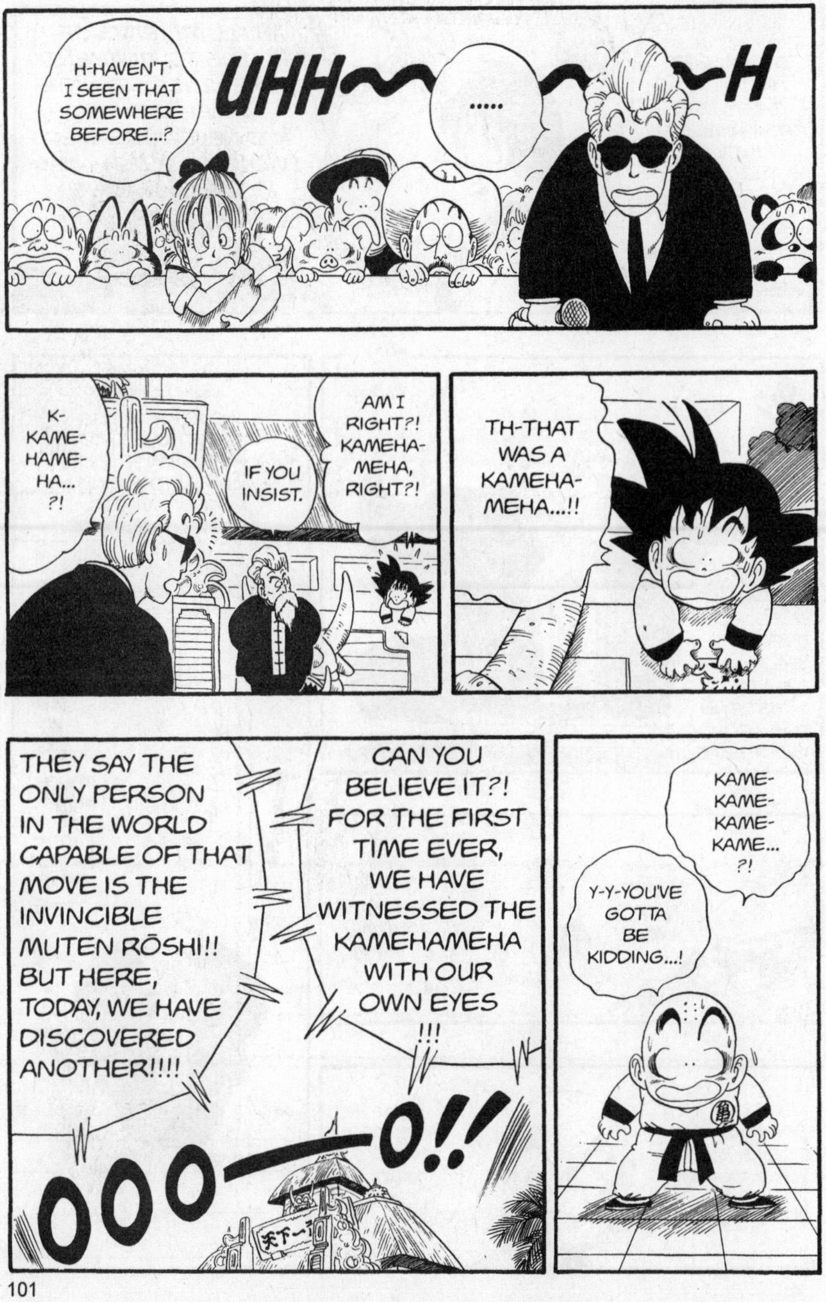
UHH~~~H
.....
H-HAVEN'T I SEEN THAT SOMEWHERE BEFORE...?
TH-THAT WAS A KAMEHA-MEHA...!!
AM I RIGHT?! KAMEHA-MEHA, RIGHT?!
IF YOU INSIST.
K-KAME-HAME-HA... ?!
KAME-KAME-KAME-KAME... ?!
Y-Y-YOU'VE GOTTA BE KIDDING...!
CAN YOU BELIEVE IT?! FOR THE FIRST TIME EVER, WE HAVE WITNESSED THE KAMEHAMEHA WITH OUR OWN EYES !!!
THEY SAY THE ONLY PERSON IN THE WORLD CAPABLE OF THAT MOVE IS THE INVINCIBLE MUTEN RŌSHI!! BUT HERE, TODAY, WE HAVE DISCOVERED ANOTHER!!!!
OOO—O!!

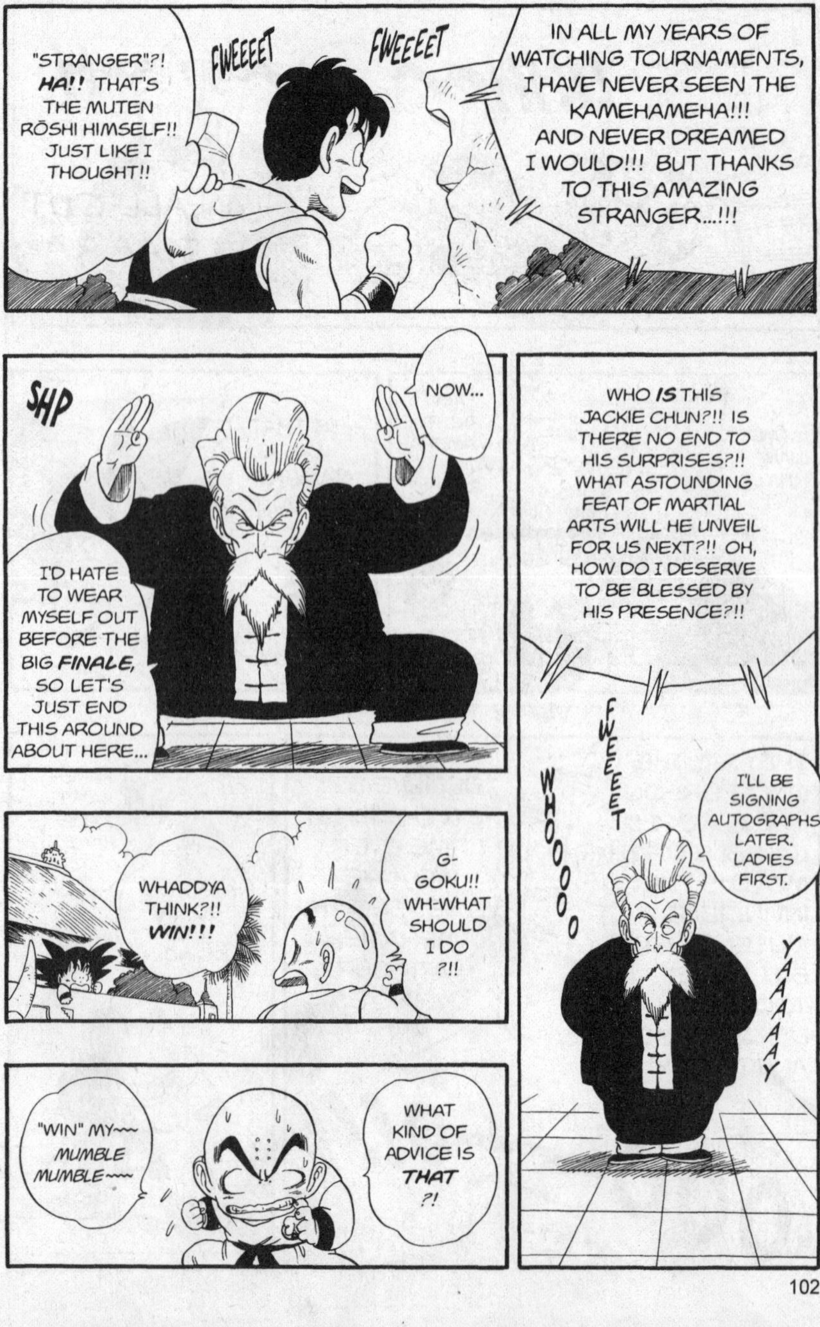

IN ALL MY YEARS OF WATCHING TOURNAMENTS, I HAVE NEVER SEEN THE KAMEHAMEHA!!! AND NEVER DREAMED I WOULD!!! BUT THANKS TO THIS AMAZING STRANGER...!!!
FWEEEET
FWEEEET
"STRANGER"?! **HA!!** THAT'S THE MUTEN RŌSHI HIMSELF!! JUST LIKE I THOUGHT!!
WHO **IS** THIS JACKIE CHUN?!! IS THERE NO END TO HIS SURPRISES?!! WHAT ASTOUNDING FEAT OF MARTIAL ARTS WILL HE UNVEIL FOR US NEXT?!! OH, HOW DO I DESERVE TO BE BLESSED BY HIS PRESENCE?!!
FWEEEET
WHOOOOOO
I'LL BE SIGNING AUTOGRAPHS LATER. LADIES FIRST.
YAAAAAY
NOW...
SHP
I'D HATE TO WEAR MYSELF OUT BEFORE THE BIG ***FINALE***, SO LET'S JUST END THIS AROUND ABOUT HERE...
G-GOKU!! WH-WHAT SHOULD I DO?!!
WHADDYA THINK?!! ***WIN!!!***
WHAT KIND OF ADVICE IS ***THAT***?!
"WIN" MY~~~ *MUMBLE MUMBLE*~~~

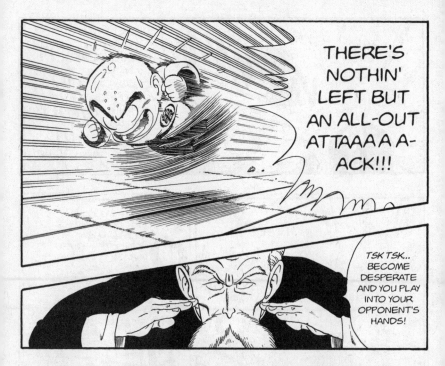

THERE'S NOTHIN' LEFT BUT AN ALL-OUT ATTAAAA A A-ACK!!!

TSK TSK... BECOME DESPERATE AND YOU PLAY INTO YOUR OPPONENT'S HANDS!

OWmmmW!!

EXCELLENT! TOO BAD YOUR OPPONENT ISN'T THE WALL! HO HO!

HO!

FWAK!

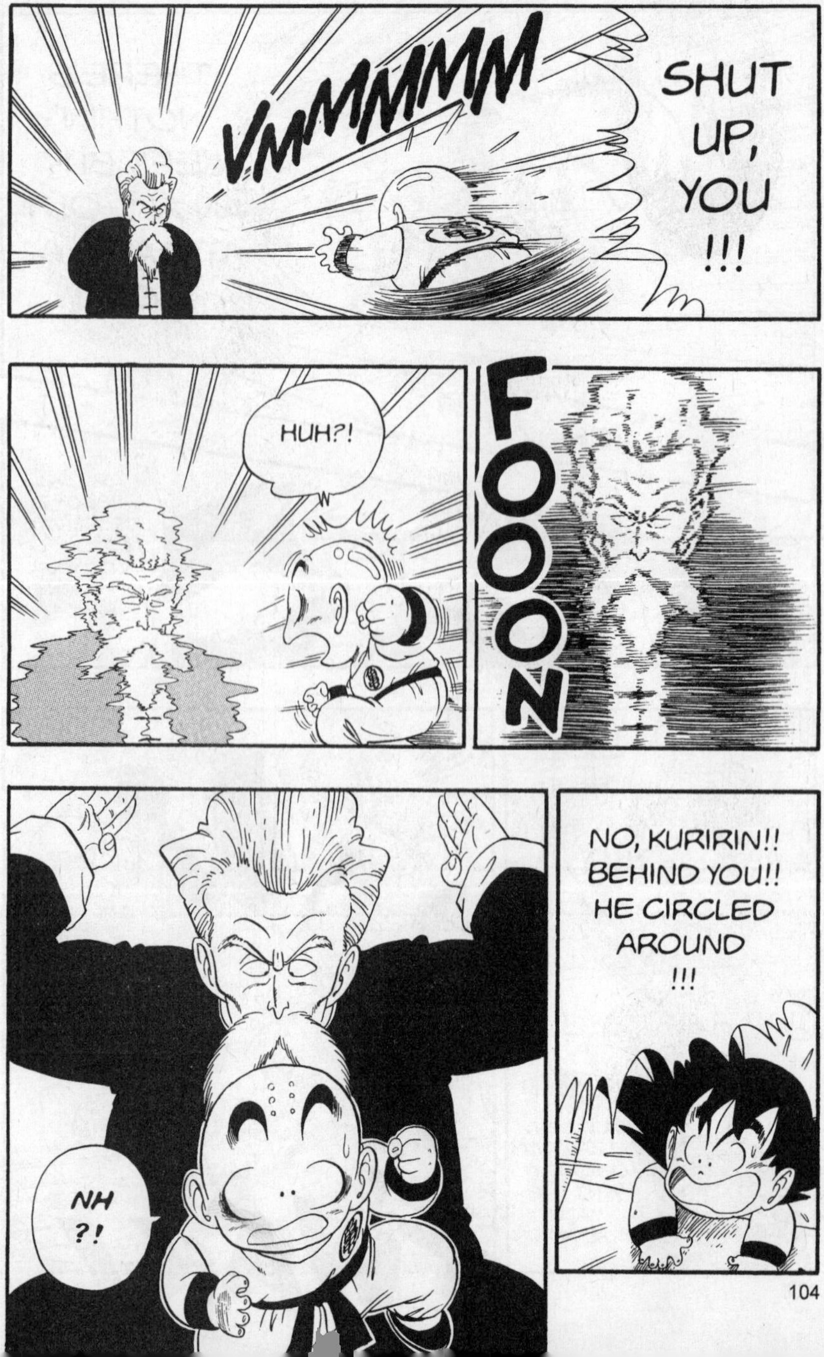
SHUT UP, YOU !!!
VMMMMM
FOOOON
HUH?!
NO, KURIRIN!! BEHIND YOU!! HE CIRCLED AROUND !!!
NH ?!

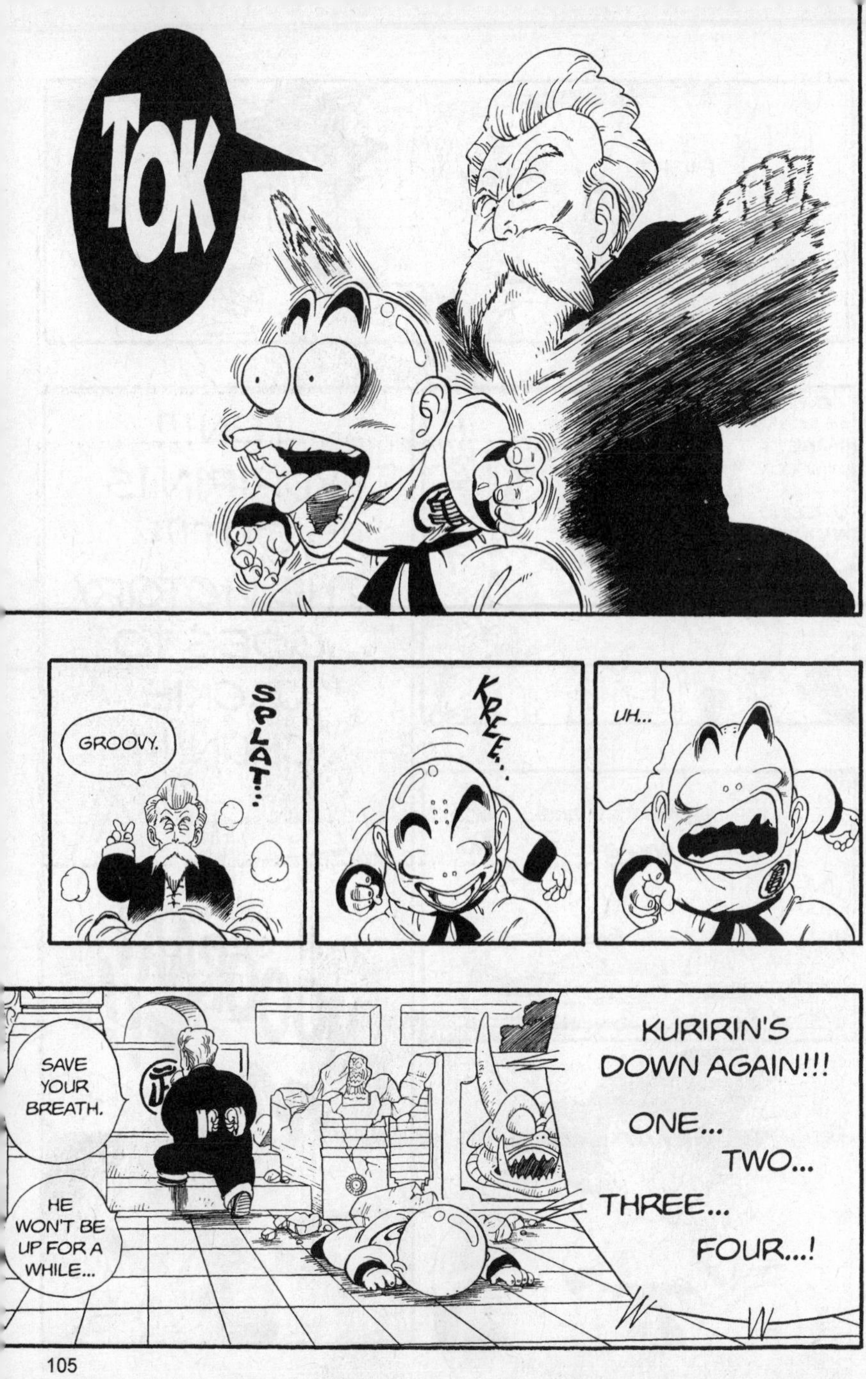
TOK
UH...
KREE...
SPLAT..
GROOVY.
KURIRIN'S DOWN AGAIN!!!
ONE...
TWO...
THREE...
FOUR...!
SAVE YOUR BREATH.
HE WON'T BE UP FOR A WHILE...

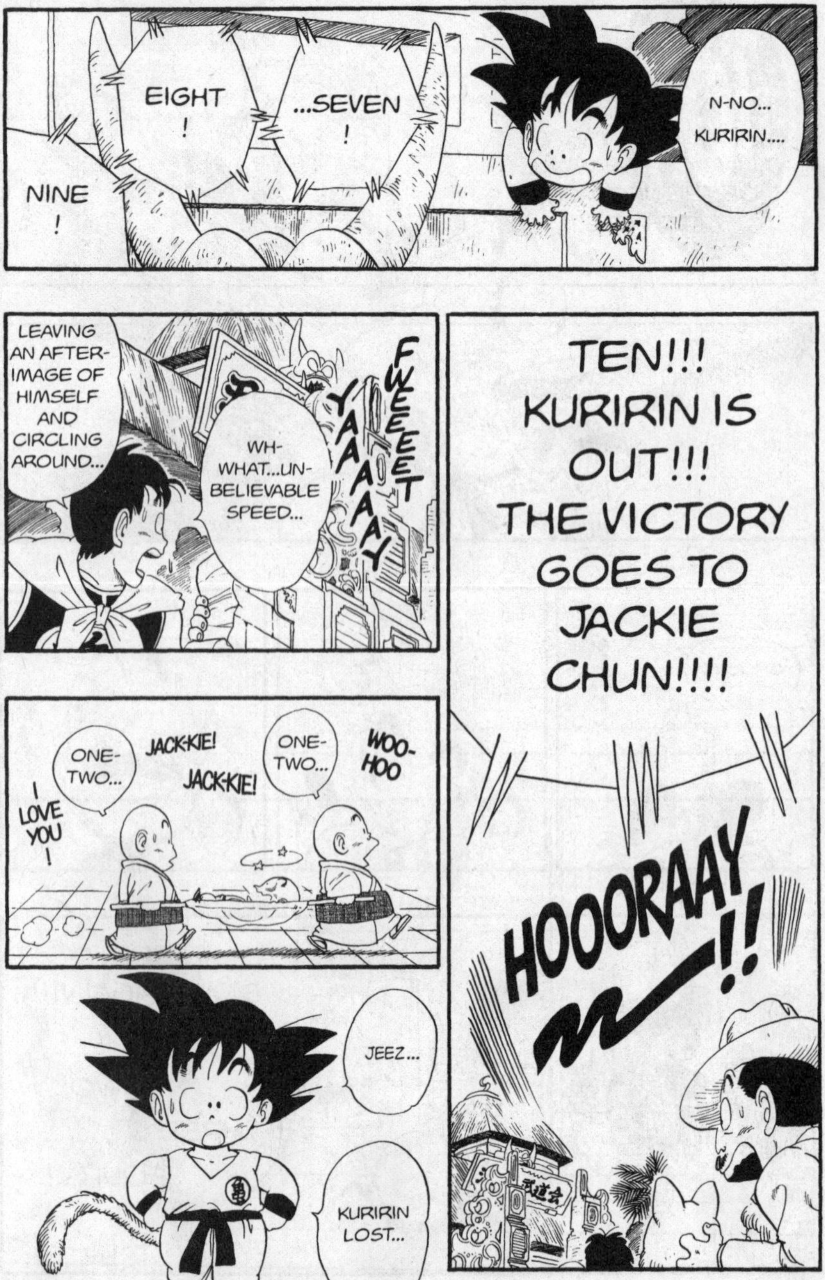
N-NO... KURIRIN....
...SEVEN !
EIGHT !
NINE !
TEN!!! KURIRIN IS OUT!!! THE VICTORY GOES TO JACKIE CHUN!!!!
HOOORAAY—!!
FWEEEET
YAAAAAAY
WH-WHAT...UN-BELIEVABLE SPEED...
LEAVING AN AFTER-IMAGE OF HIMSELF AND CIRCLING AROUND...
WOO-HOO
ONE-TWO...
JACK-KIE!
JACK-KIE!
ONE-TWO...
I LOVE YOU !
JEEZ...
KURIRIN LOST...

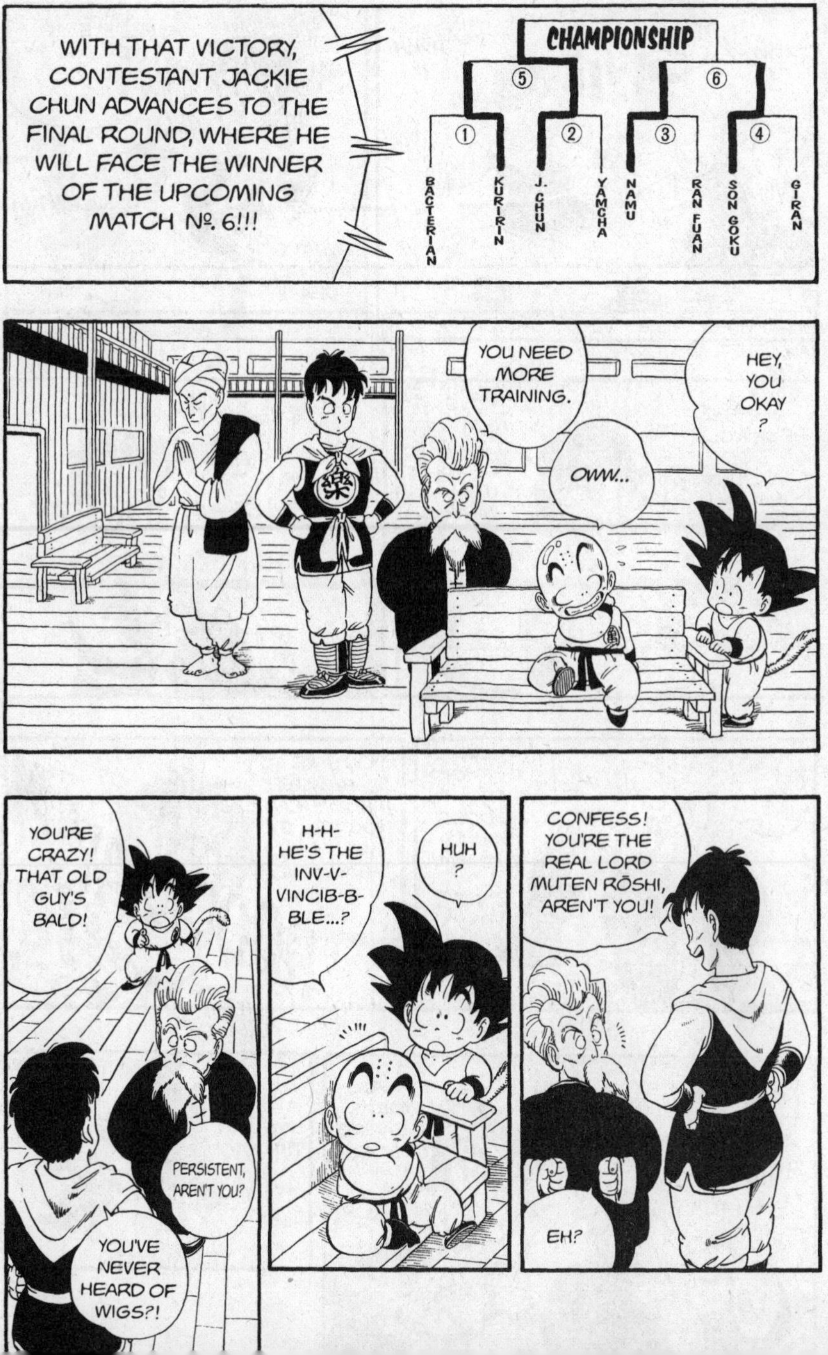
CHAMPIONSHIP
⑥
⑤
④
③
②
①
GIRAN
SON GOKU
RAN FUAN
NAMU
YAMCHA
J. CHUN
KURIRIN
BACTERIAN
WITH THAT VICTORY, CONTESTANT JACKIE CHUN ADVANCES TO THE FINAL ROUND, WHERE HE WILL FACE THE WINNER OF THE UPCOMING MATCH №. 6!!!
HEY, YOU OKAY?
OWW...
YOU NEED MORE TRAINING.
CONFESS! YOU'RE THE REAL LORD MUTEN RŌSHI, AREN'T YOU!
EH?
HUH?
H-H-HE'S THE INV-V-VINCIB-B-BLE...?
YOU'RE CRAZY! THAT OLD GUY'S BALD!
PERSISTENT, AREN'T YOU?
YOU'VE NEVER HEARD OF WIGS?!

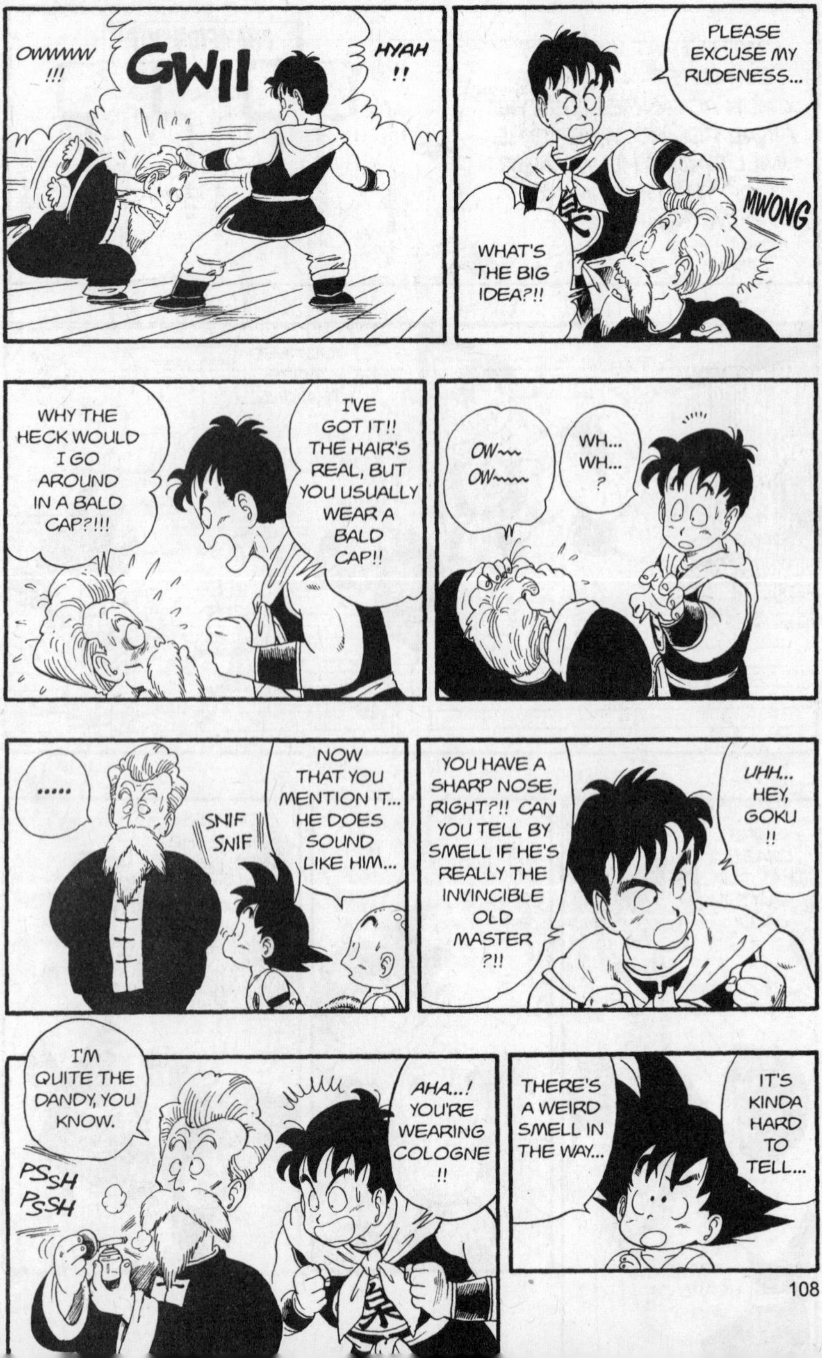
PLEASE EXCUSE MY RUDENESS...
MWONG
WHAT'S THE BIG IDEA?!!
HYAH !!
GWII
OWWWW !!!
WH... WH... ?
OW~~ OW~~
I'VE GOT IT!! THE HAIR'S REAL, BUT YOU USUALLY WEAR A BALD CAP!!
WHY THE HECK WOULD I GO AROUND IN A BALD CAP?!!!
UHH... HEY, GOKU !!
YOU HAVE A SHARP NOSE, RIGHT?!! CAN YOU TELL BY SMELL IF HE'S REALLY THE INVINCIBLE OLD MASTER ?!!
NOW THAT YOU MENTION IT... HE DOES SOUND LIKE HIM...
SNIF SNIF
......
IT'S KINDA HARD TO TELL...
THERE'S A WEIRD SMELL IN THE WAY...
AHA...! YOU'RE WEARING COLOGNE !!
I'M QUITE THE DANDY, YOU KNOW.
PSSH PSSH

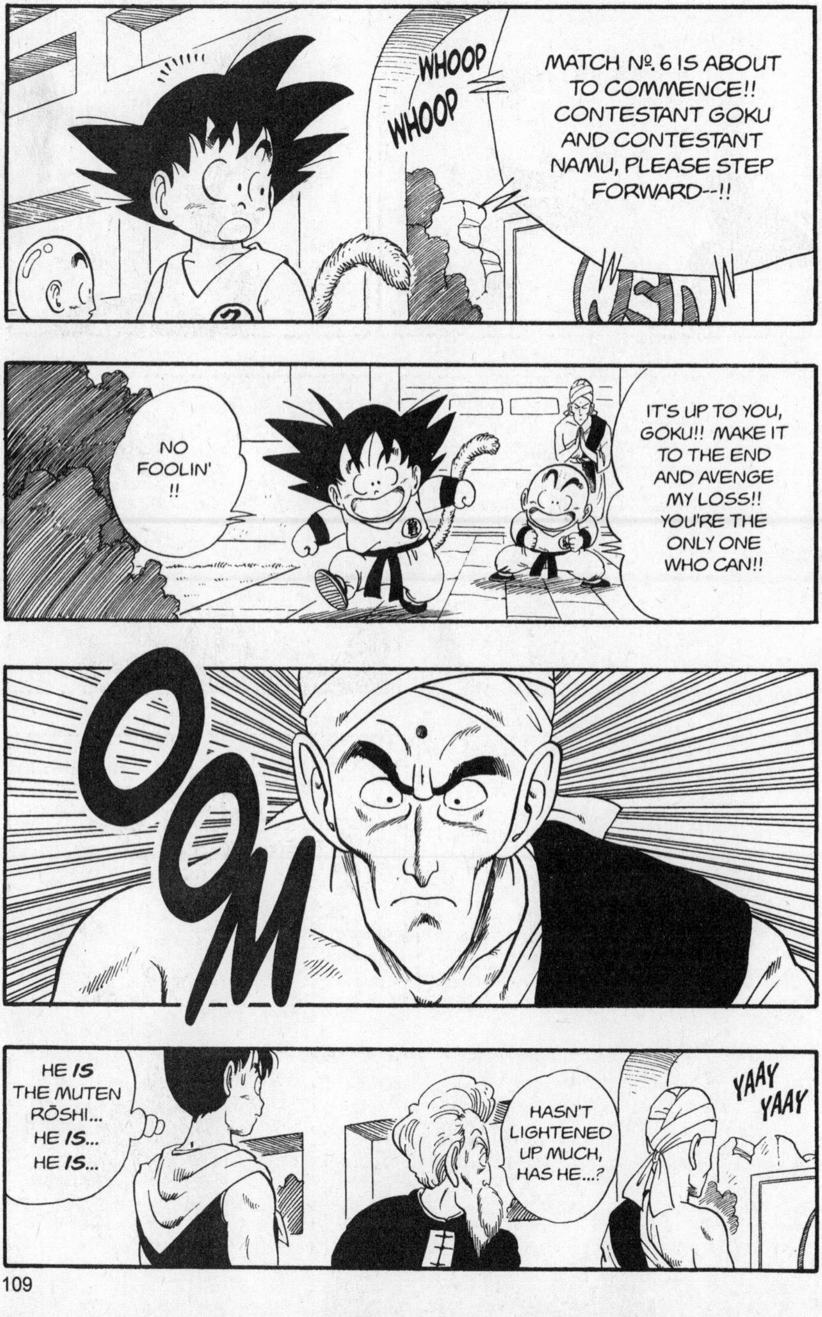
MATCH №. 6 IS ABOUT TO COMMENCE!! CONTESTANT GOKU AND CONTESTANT NAMU, PLEASE STEP FORWARD--!!
WHOOP WHOOP
IT'S UP TO YOU, GOKU!! MAKE IT TO THE END AND AVENGE MY LOSS!! YOU'RE THE ONLY ONE WHO CAN!!
NO FOOLIN' !!
OOM
YAAY YAAY
HASN'T LIGHTENED UP MUCH, HAS HE...?
HE *IS* THE MUTEN RŌSHI... HE *IS*... HE *IS*...

Tale 44
The Name of the Game Is Namu

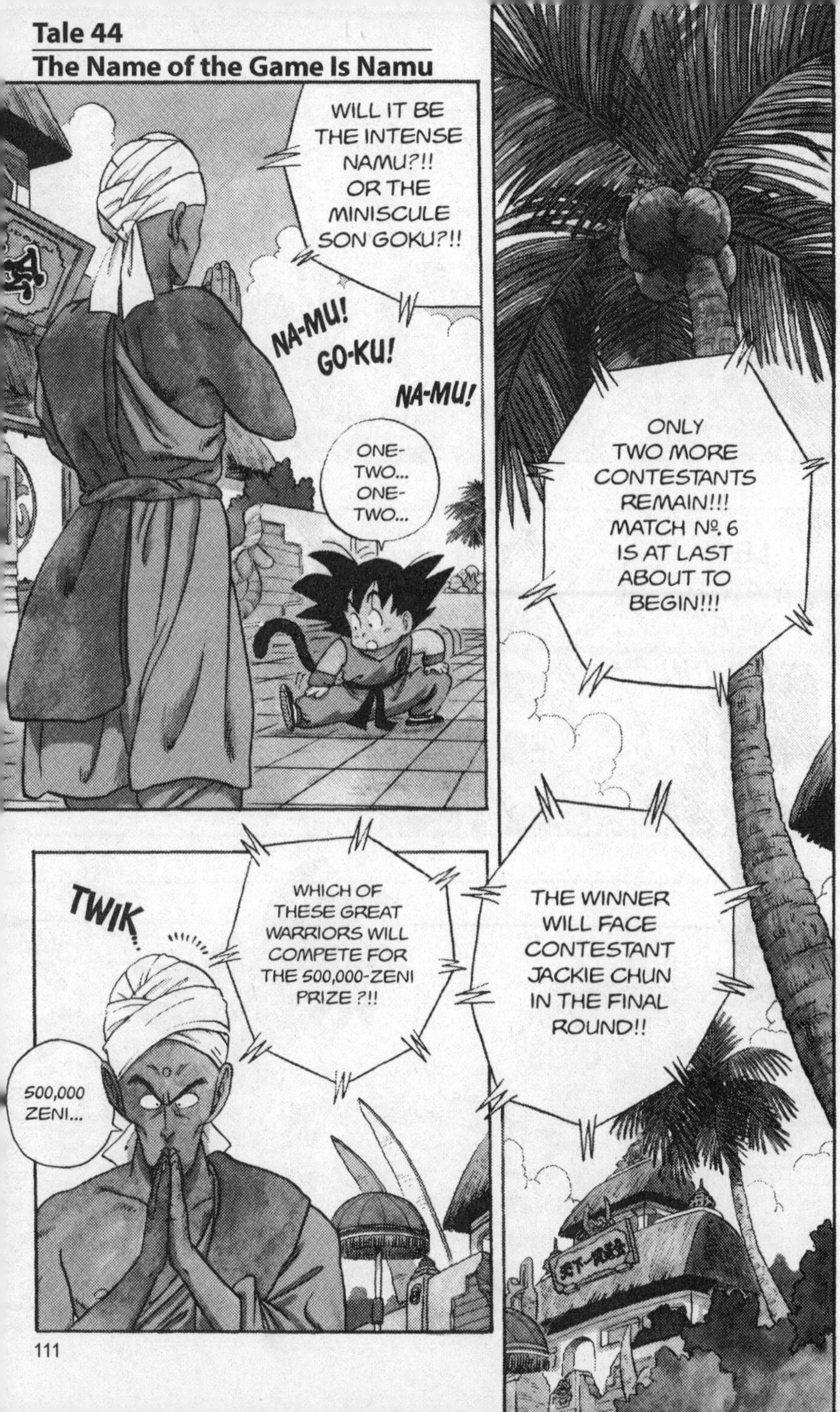
ONLY TWO MORE CONTESTANTS REMAIN!!! MATCH №. 6 IS AT LAST ABOUT TO BEGIN!!!
THE WINNER WILL FACE CONTESTANT JACKIE CHUN IN THE FINAL ROUND!!
WILL IT BE THE INTENSE NAMU?!! OR THE MINISCULE SON GOKU?!!
NA-MU!
GO-KU!
NA-MU!
ONE-TWO... ONE-TWO...
WHICH OF THESE GREAT WARRIORS WILL COMPETE FOR THE 500,000-ZENI PRIZE ?!!
TWIK
500,000 ZENI...

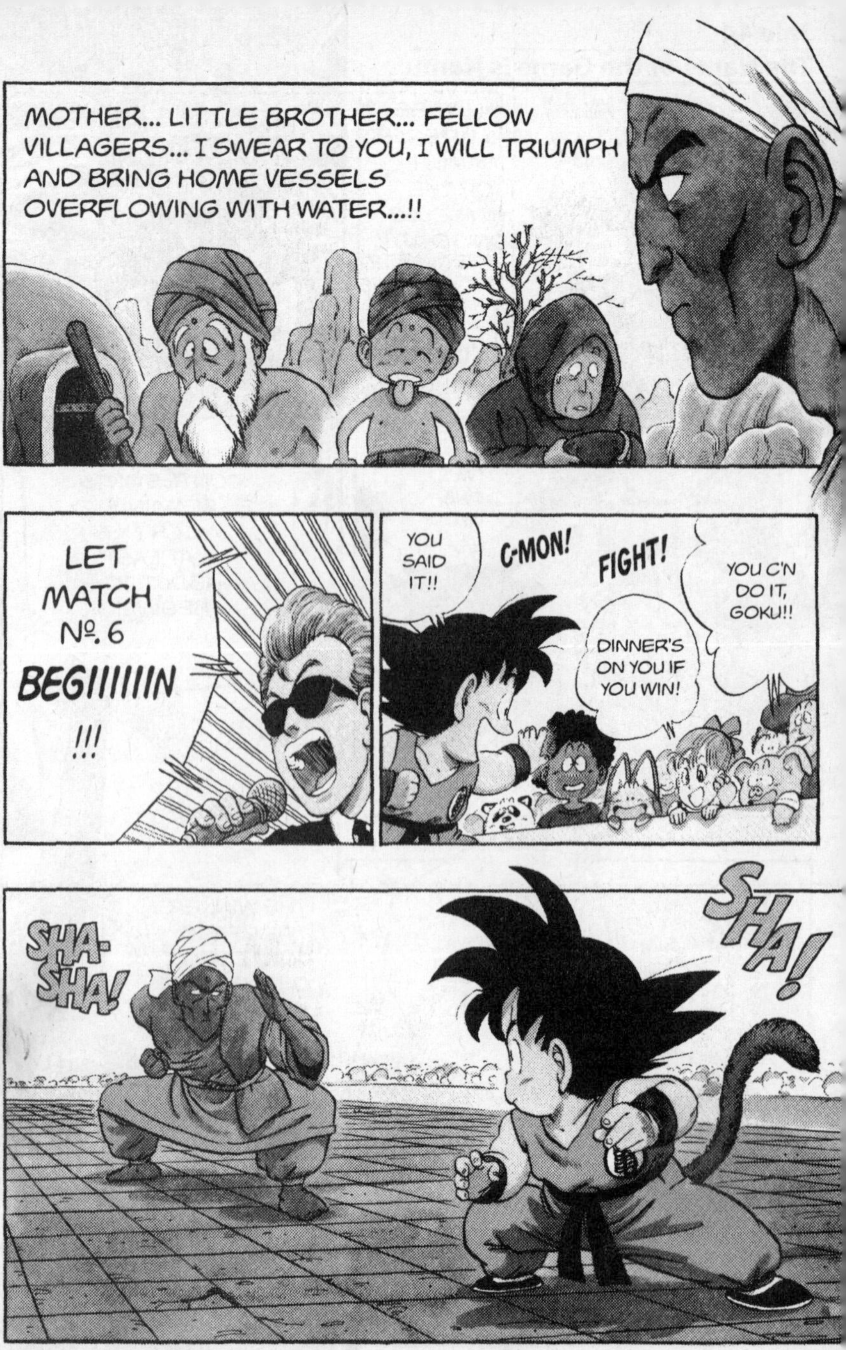

MOTHER... LITTLE BROTHER... FELLOW VILLAGERS... I SWEAR TO YOU, I WILL TRIUMPH AND BRING HOME VESSELS OVERFLOWING WITH WATER...!!
YOU C'N DO IT, GOKU!!
FIGHT!
C-MON!
YOU SAID IT!!
DINNER'S ON YOU IF YOU WIN!
LET MATCH №. 6 BEGIIIIIIN !!!
SHA!
SHA-SHA!

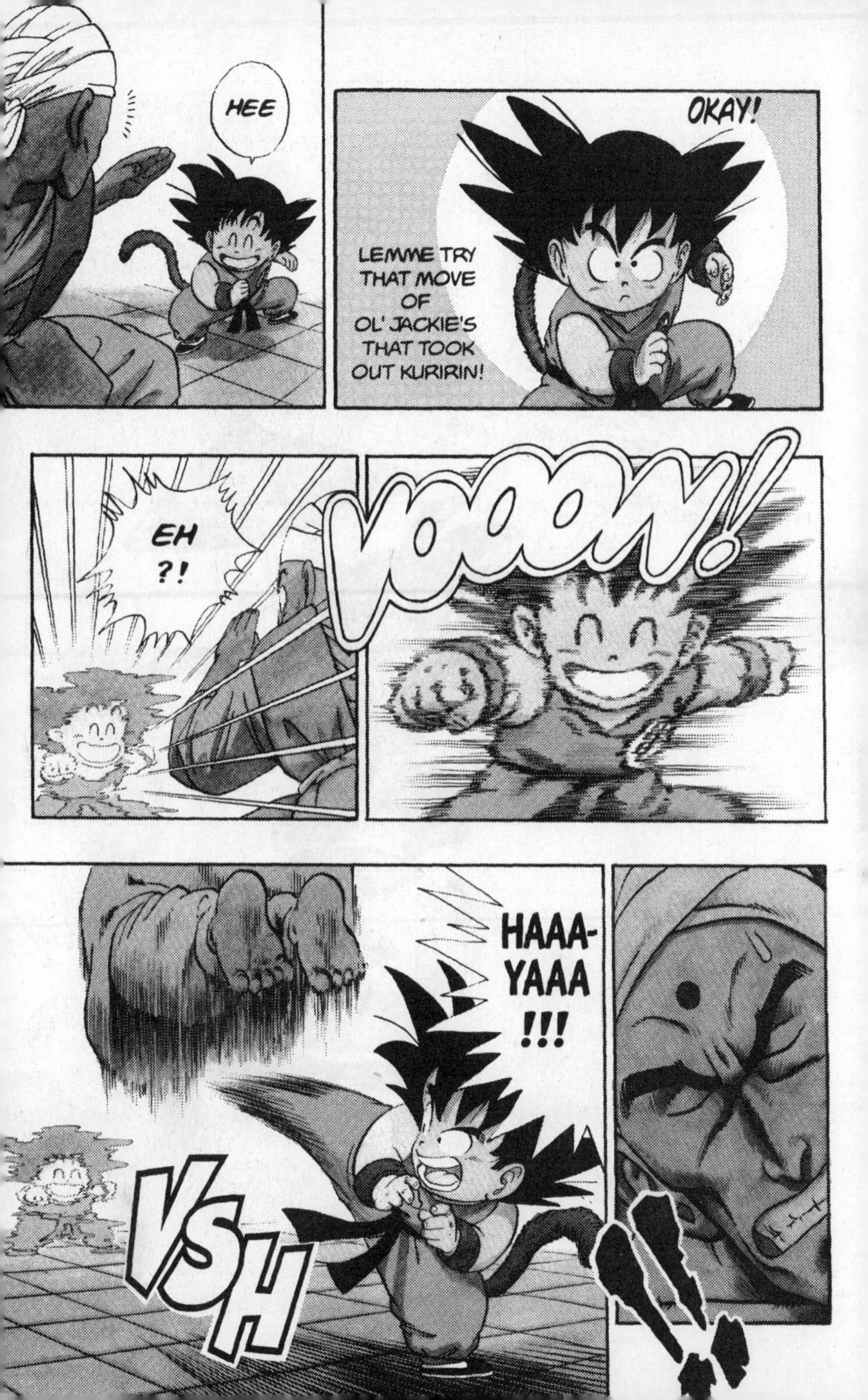

OKAY!
LEMME TRY THAT MOVE OF OL' JACKIE'S THAT TOOK OUT KURIRIN!
HEE
VOOOM!
EH?!
HAAA-YAAA!!!
VSH

BONUS!

WHEN THIS COMIC RAN IN SHONEN JUMP MAGAZINE, THERE WAS PROBABLY AN AD ON THIS PAGE!

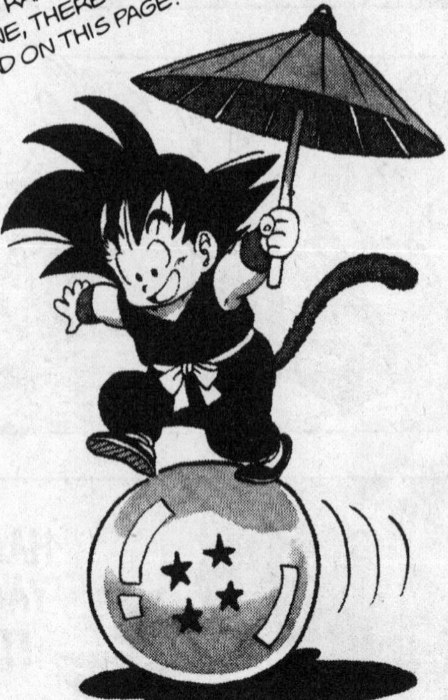

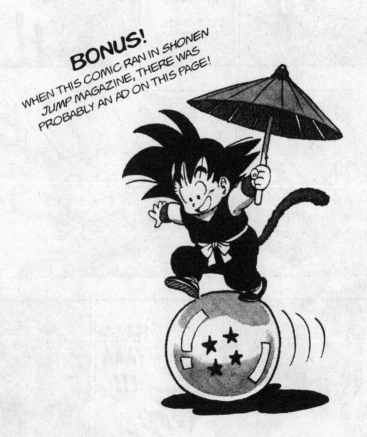

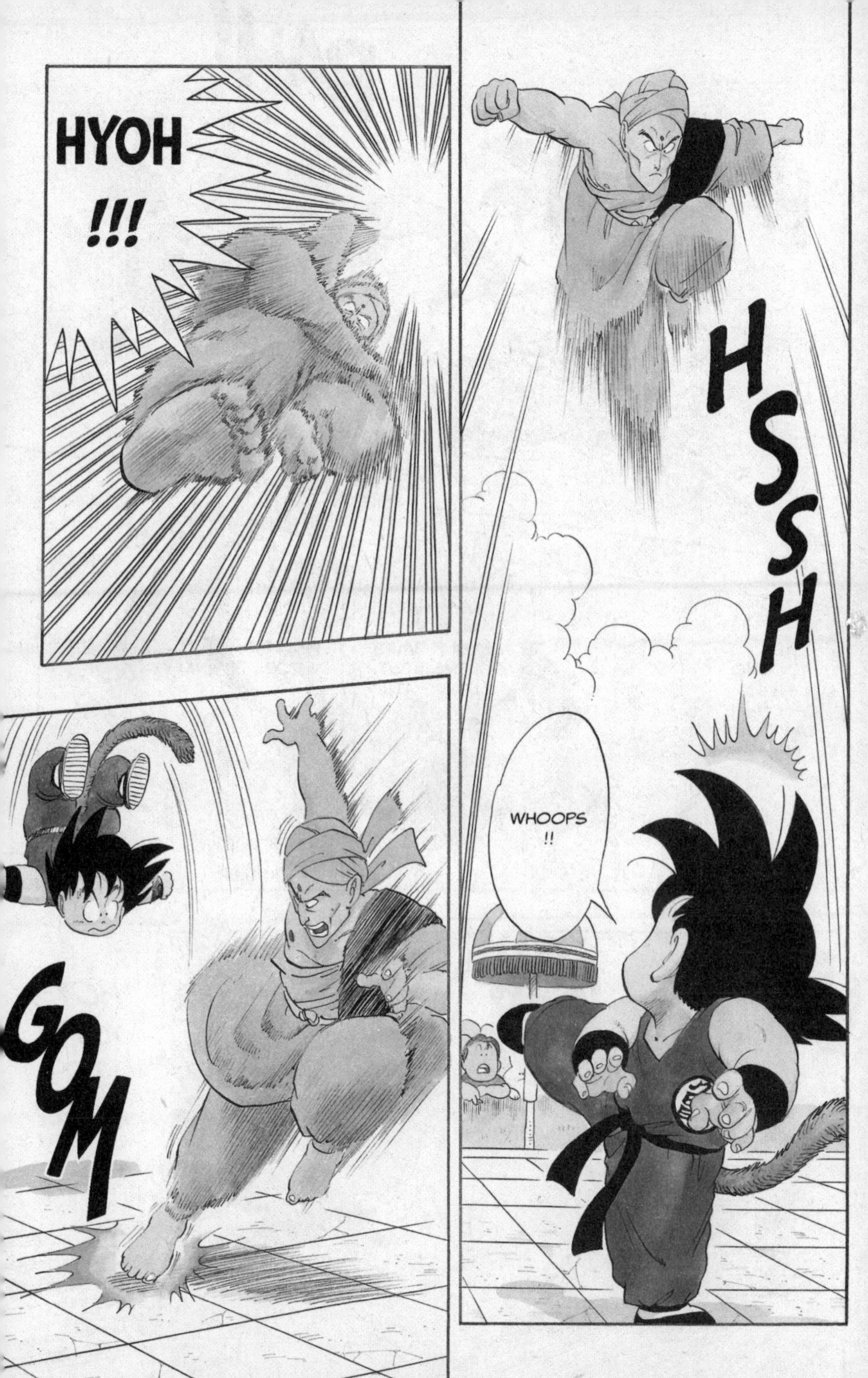
HSSH
WHOOPS !!
HYOH !!!
GOM

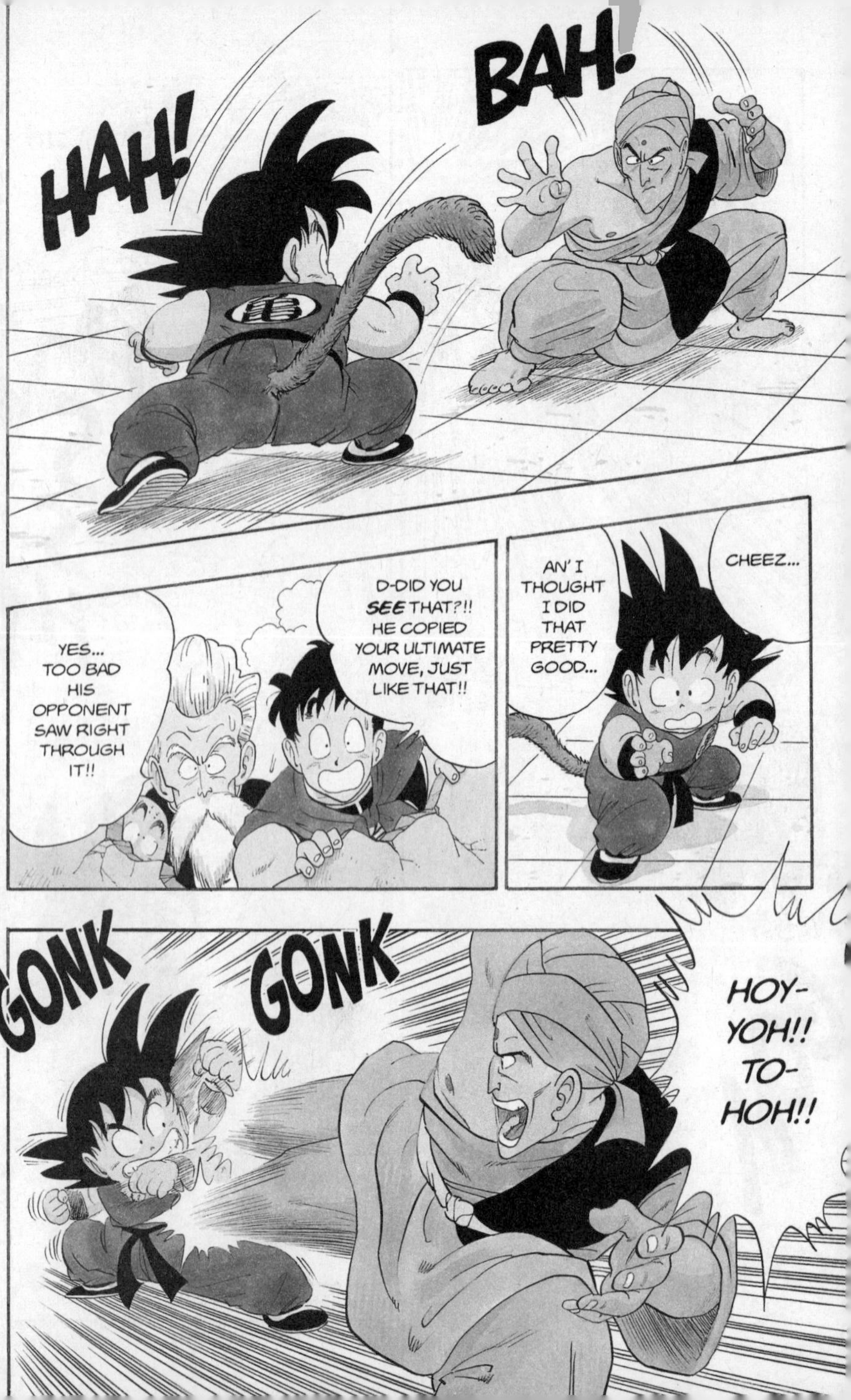
BAH!
HAH!
CHEEZ...
AN' I THOUGHT I DID THAT PRETTY GOOD...
D-DID YOU SEE THAT?!! HE COPIED YOUR ULTIMATE MOVE, JUST LIKE THAT!!
YES... TOO BAD HIS OPPONENT SAW RIGHT THROUGH IT!!
HOY-YOH!! TO-HOH!!
GONK
GONK

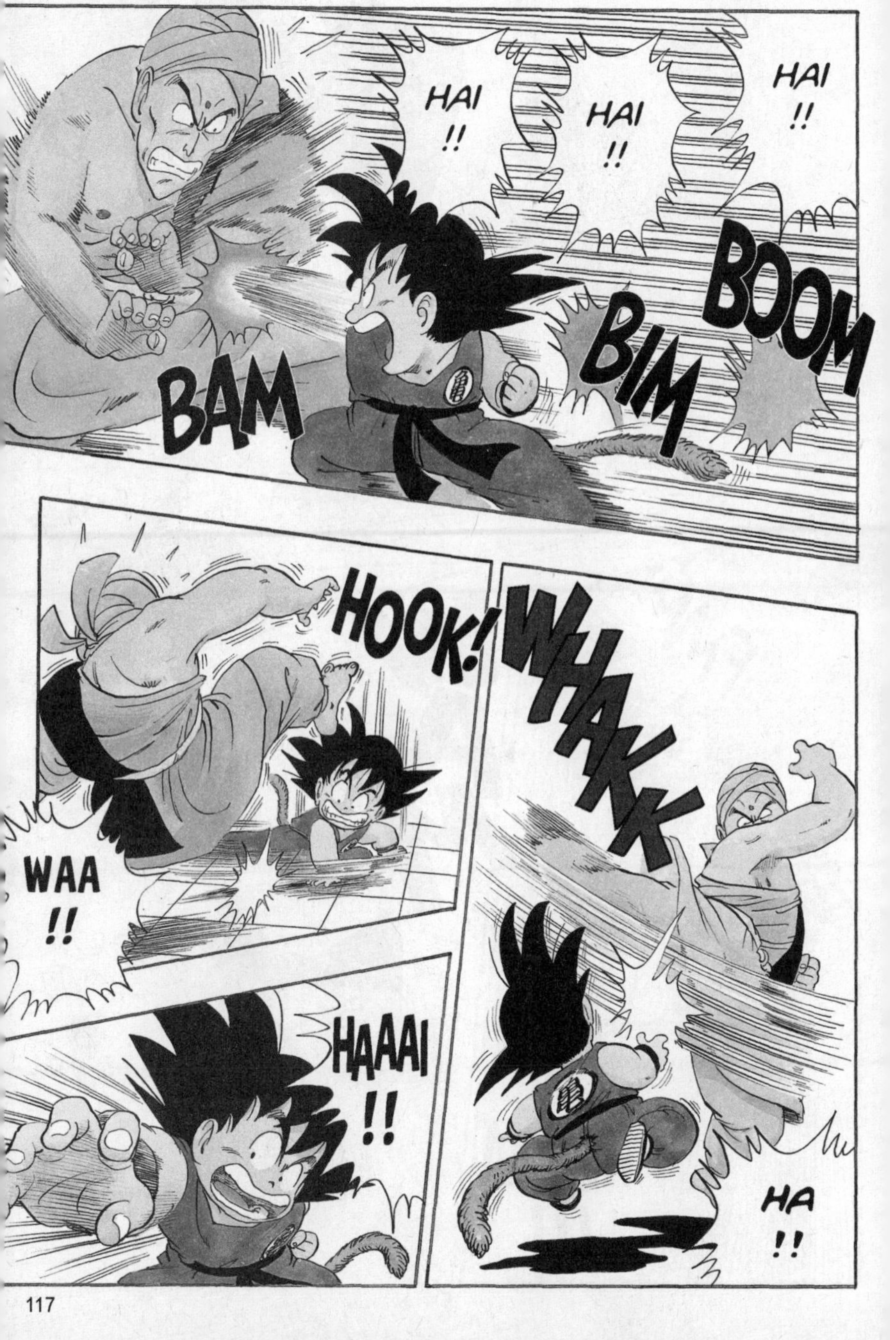
HAI !!
HAI !!
HAI !!
BOOM
BIM
BAM
WHAKK
HA !!
HOOK!
WAA !!
HAAAI !!

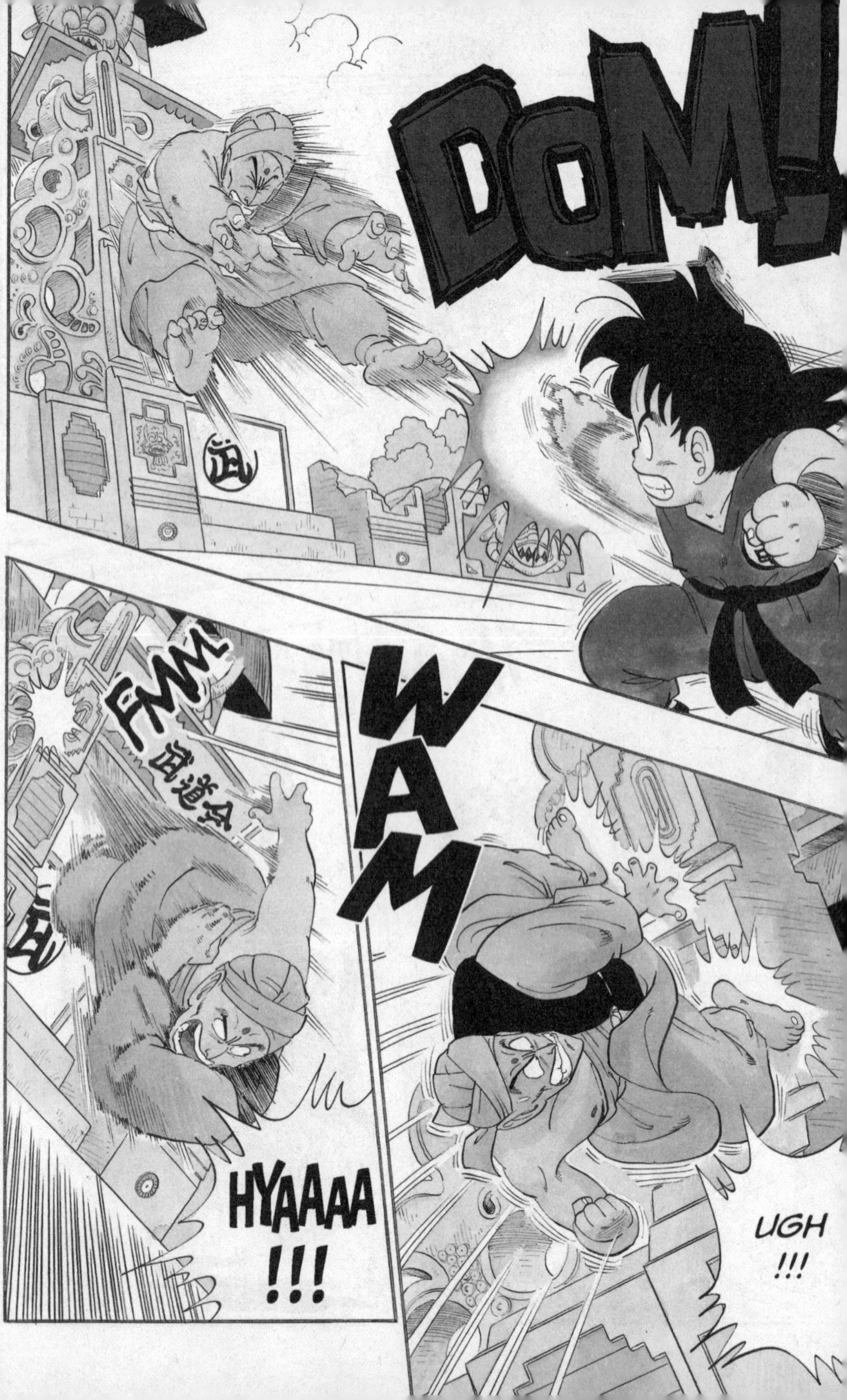
DOM!
WAM
UGH !!!
FWM
武道会
HYAAAA !!!

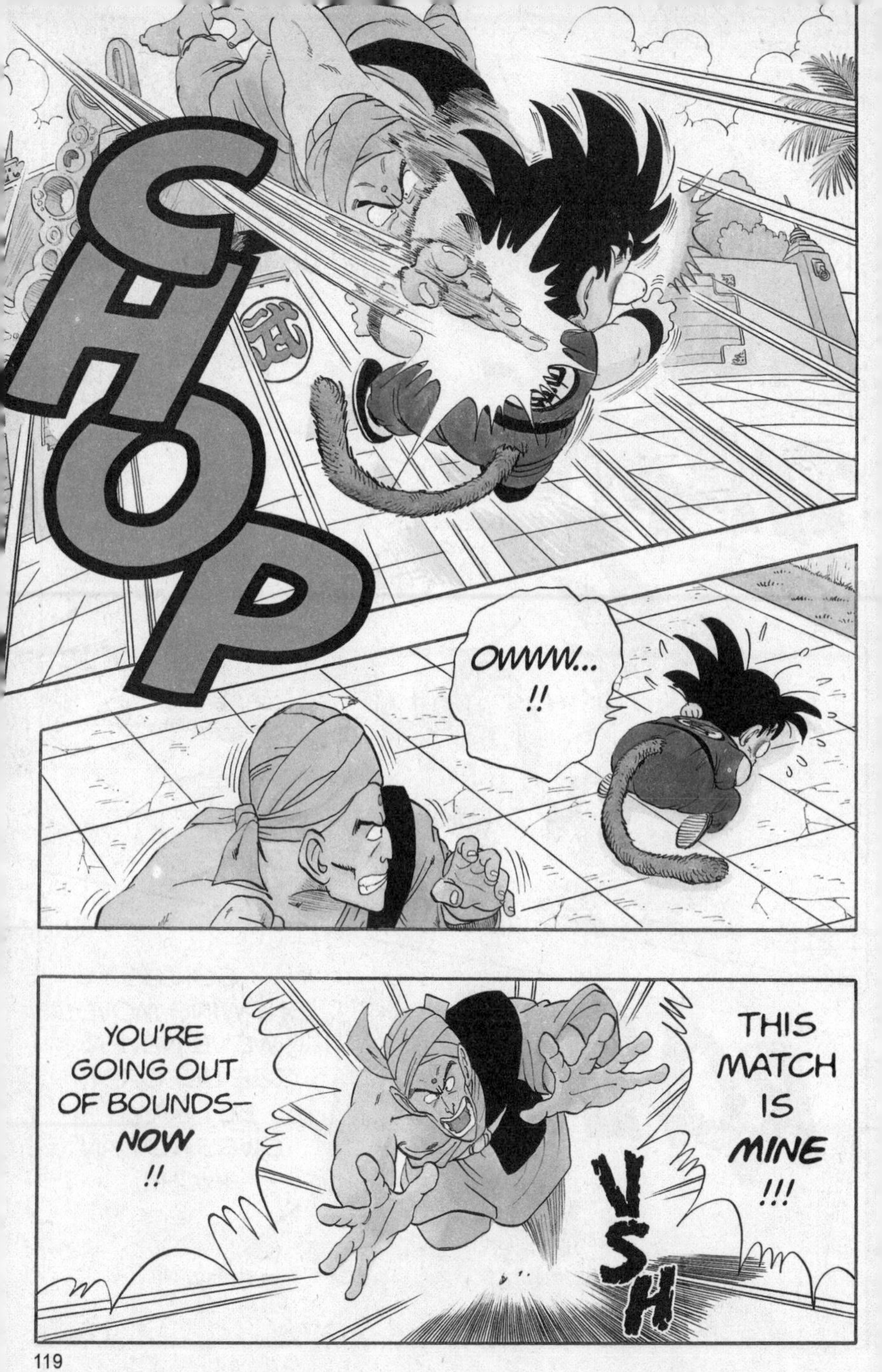
CHOP
OWWW... !!
THIS MATCH IS MINE !!!
VSH
YOU'RE GOING OUT OF BOUNDS— NOW !!

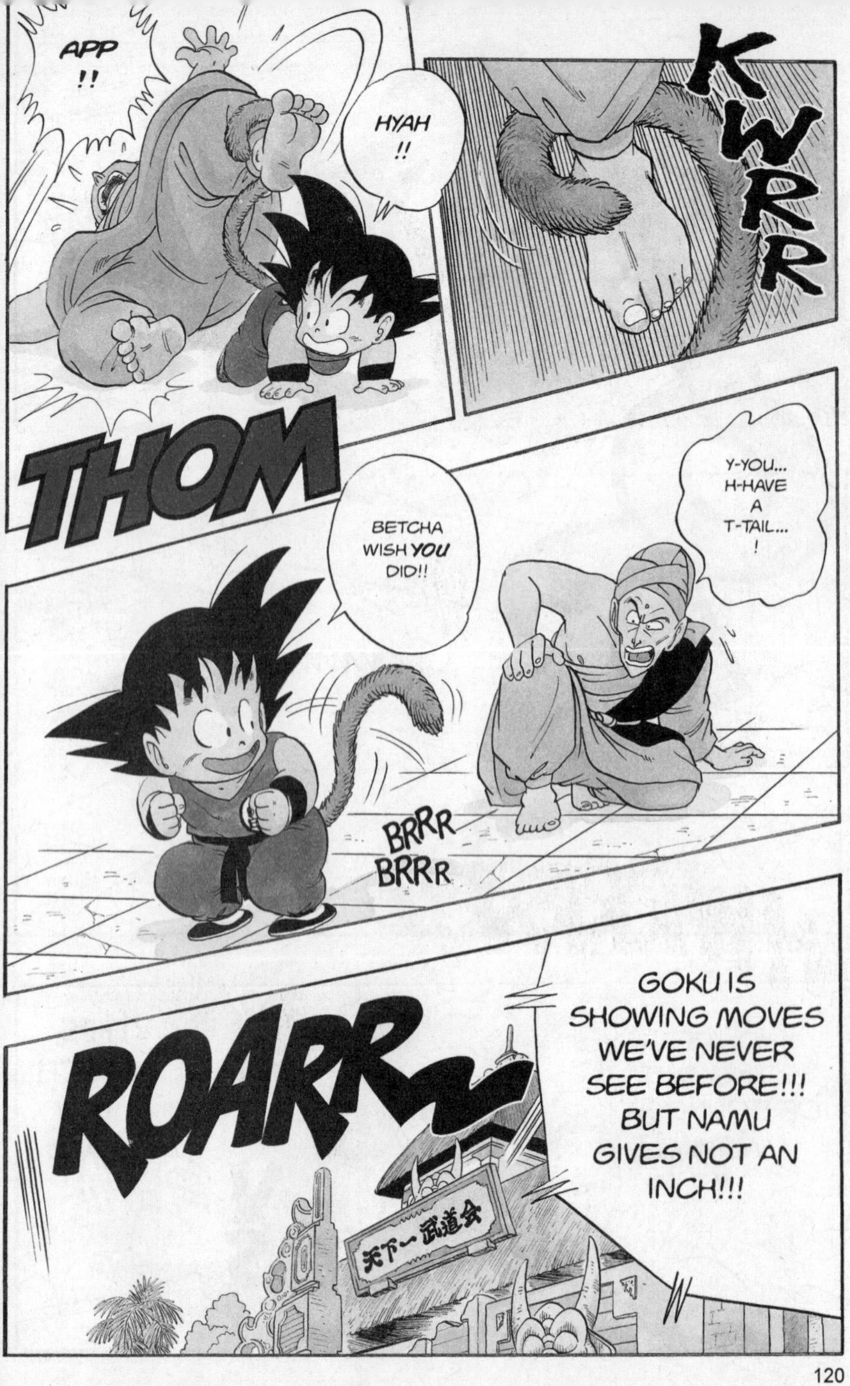
KWRR
HYAH !!
APP !!
THOM
Y-YOU... H-HAVE A T-TAIL... !
BETCHA WISH YOU DID!!
BRRR BRRR
GOKU IS SHOWING MOVES WE'VE NEVER SEE BEFORE!!! BUT NAMU GIVES NOT AN INCH!!!
ROARR
天下一武道会

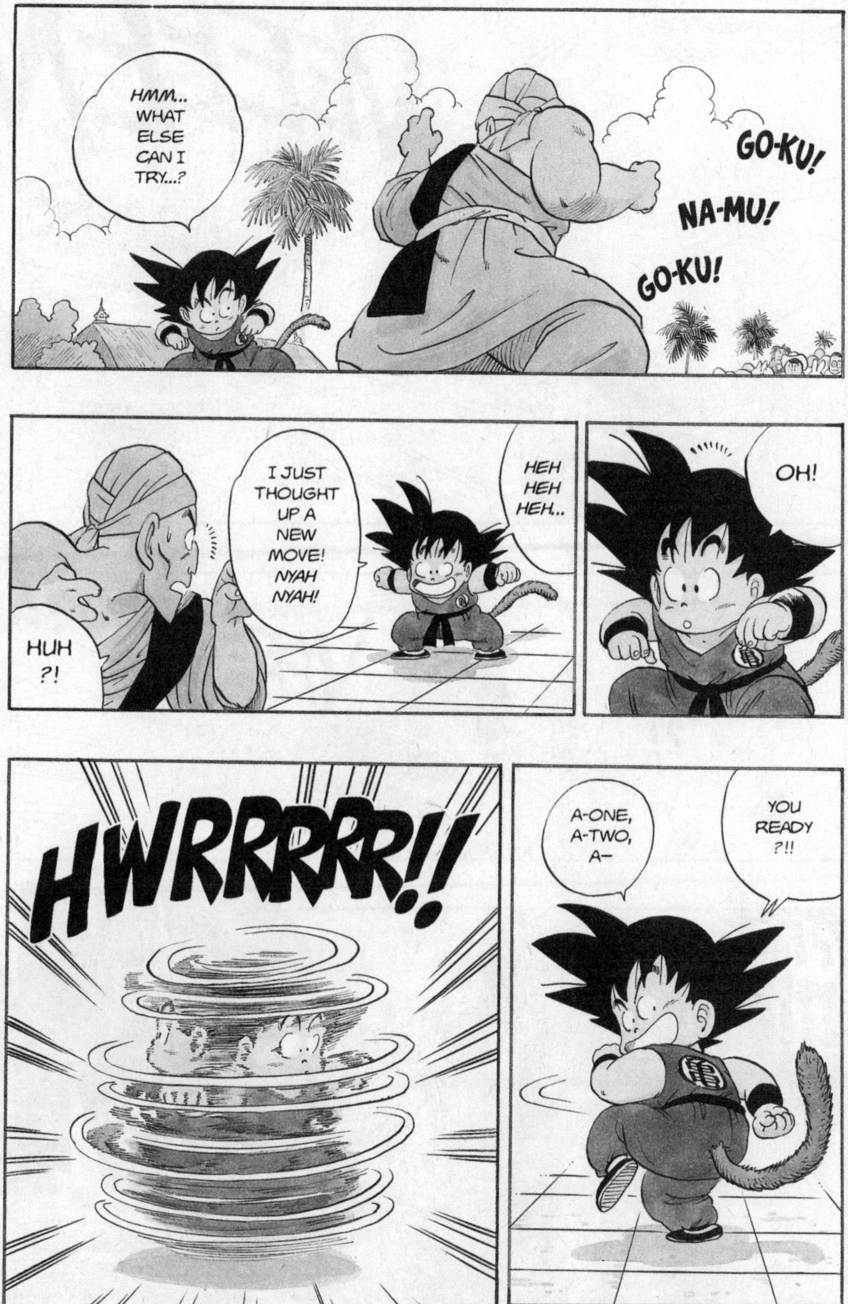
GO-KU!
NA-MU!
GO-KU!
HMM... WHAT ELSE CAN I TRY...?
OH!
HEH HEH HEH...
I JUST THOUGHT UP A NEW MOVE! NYAH NYAH!
HUH ?!
YOU READY ?!!
A-ONE, A-TWO, A—
HWRRRRR!!

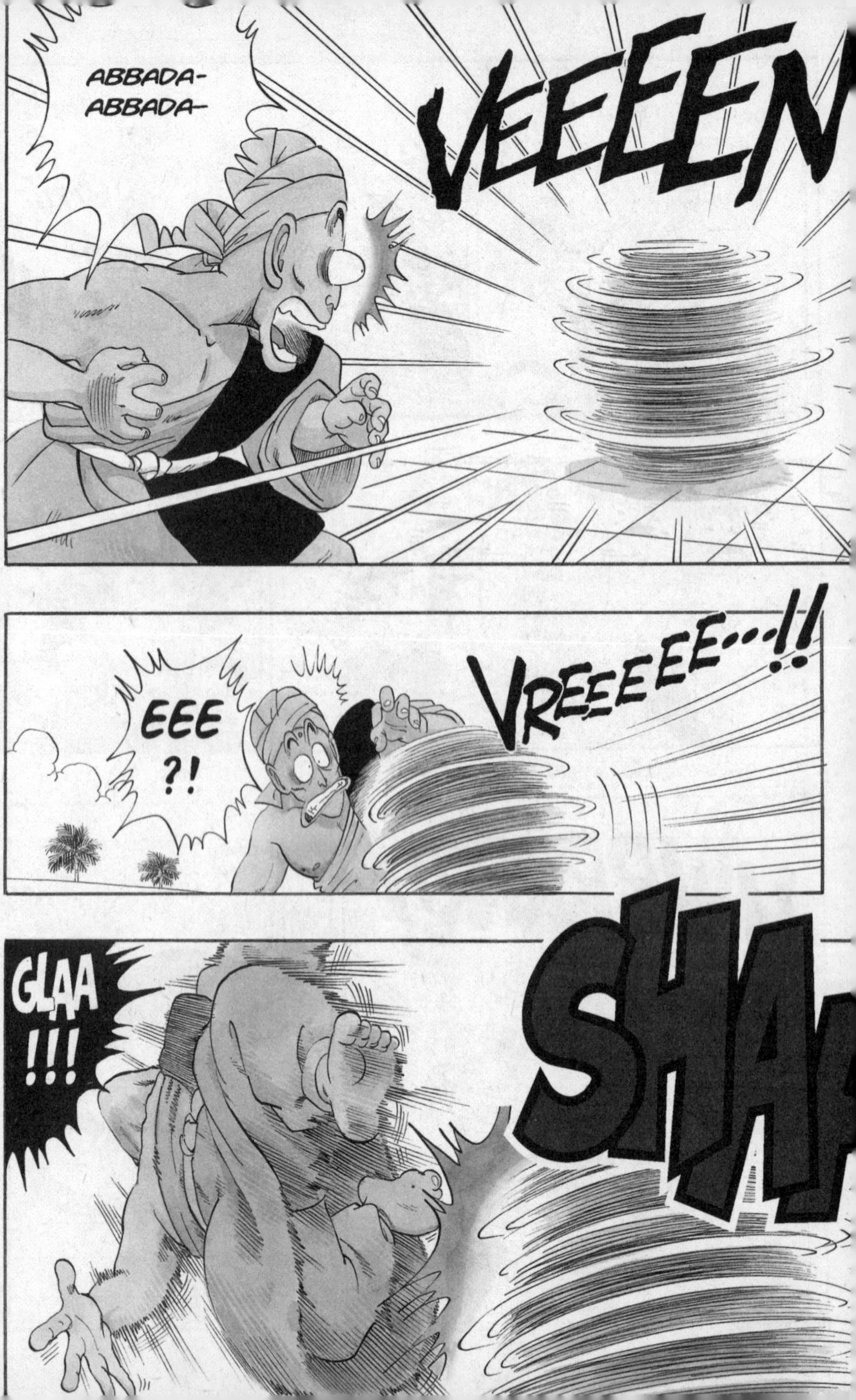
ABBADA-
ABBADA-
VEEEEN
VREEEEEE...!!
EEE ?!
SHA
GLAA !!!

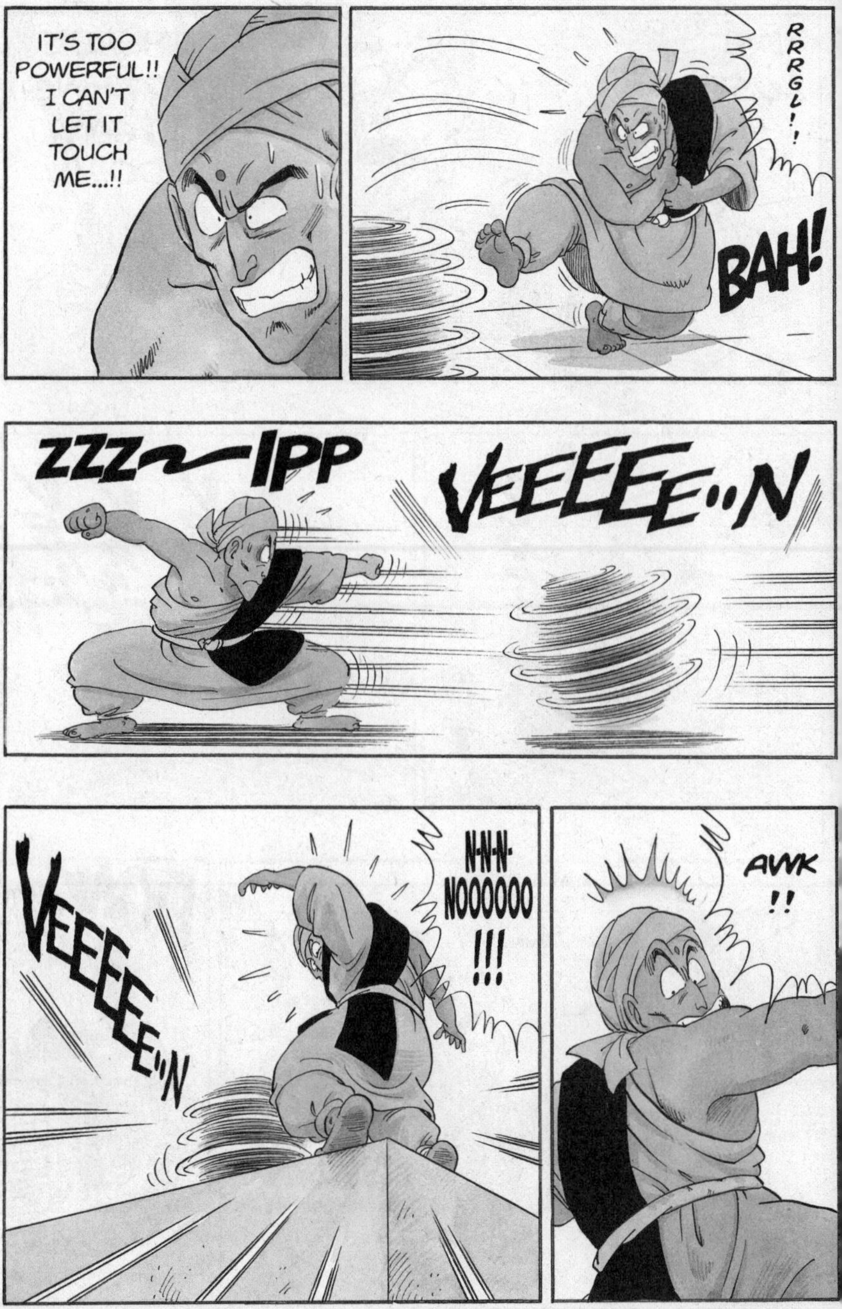
RRRGL!!
BAH!
IT'S TOO POWERFUL!! I CAN'T LET IT TOUCH ME...!!
VEEEEEE··N
ZZZ~IPP
AWK!!
N-N-N-NOOOOOO!!!
VEEEEEE··N

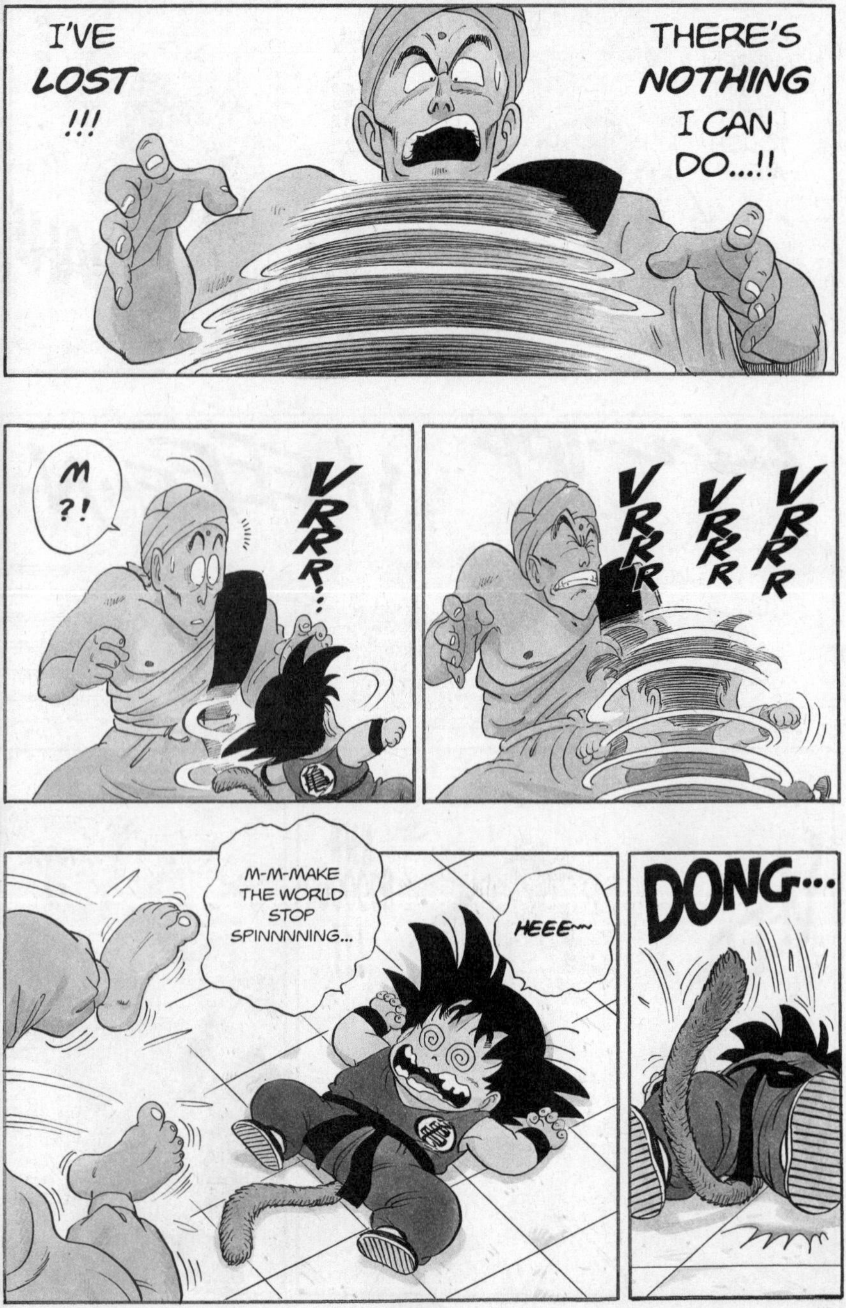
THERE'S NOTHING I CAN DO...!!
I'VE LOST !!!
VRRR
VRRR
VRRR
VRRR...
M ?!
DONG...
HEEE~~
M-M-MAKE THE WORLD STOP SPINNNNING...

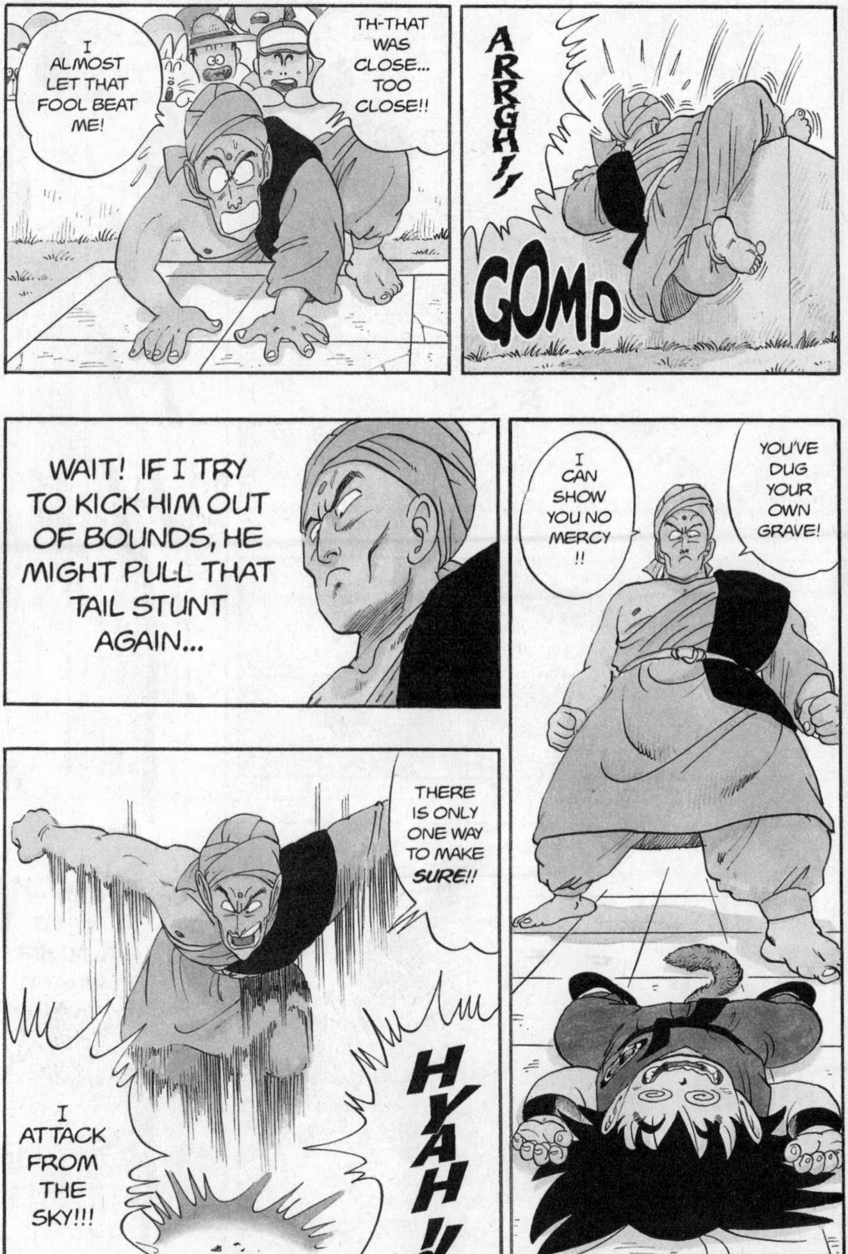
ARRGH!!
GOMP
TH-THAT WAS CLOSE... TOO CLOSE!!
I ALMOST LET THAT FOOL BEAT ME!
YOU'VE DUG YOUR OWN GRAVE!
I CAN SHOW YOU NO MERCY!!
WAIT! IF I TRY TO KICK HIM OUT OF BOUNDS, HE MIGHT PULL THAT TAIL STUNT AGAIN...
THERE IS ONLY ONE WAY TO MAKE SURE!!
HYAH!!
I ATTACK FROM THE SKY!!!

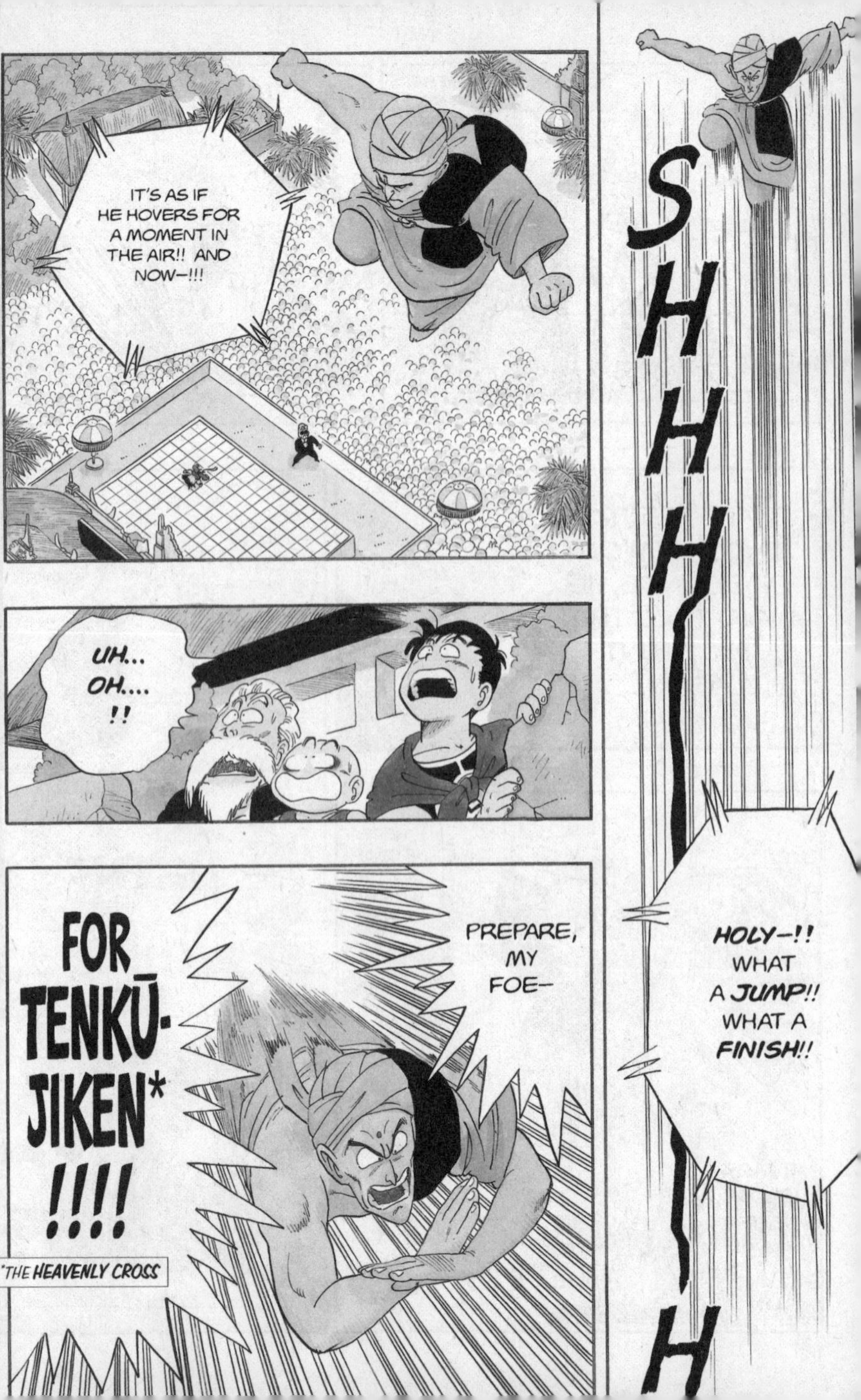
SHHH—H
HOLY—!! WHAT A JUMP!! WHAT A FINISH!!
IT'S AS IF HE HOVERS FOR A MOMENT IN THE AIR!! AND NOW—!!!
UH... OH.... !!
PREPARE, MY FOE—
FOR TENKŪ-JIKEN* !!!!
*THE HEAVENLY CROSS

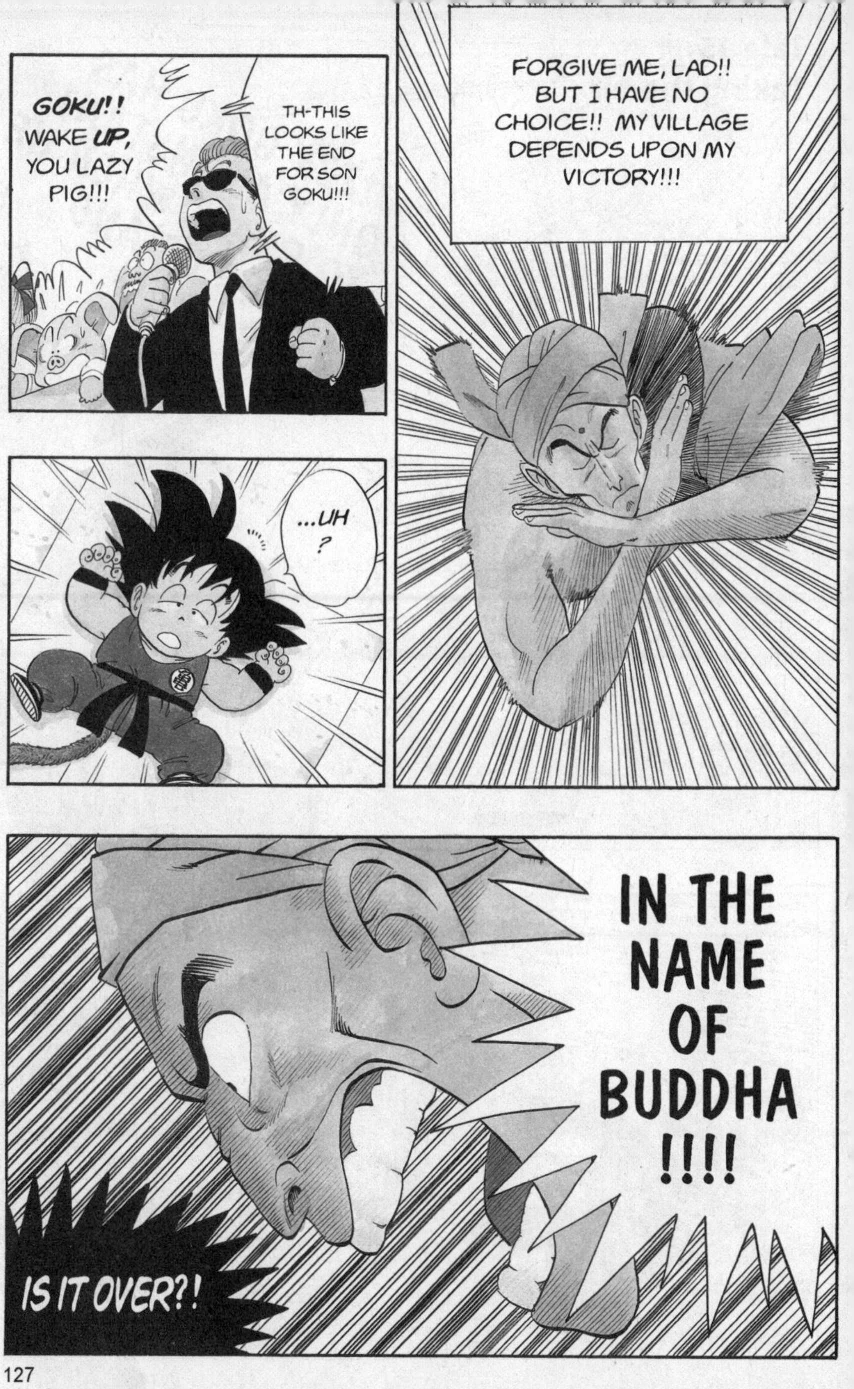
FORGIVE ME, LAD!! BUT I HAVE NO CHOICE!! MY VILLAGE DEPENDS UPON MY VICTORY!!!
TH-THIS LOOKS LIKE THE END FOR SON GOKU!!!
GOKU!! WAKE UP, YOU LAZY PIG!!!
...UH ?
IN THE NAME OF BUDDHA !!!!
IS IT OVER?!

Tale 45
Taking the Air

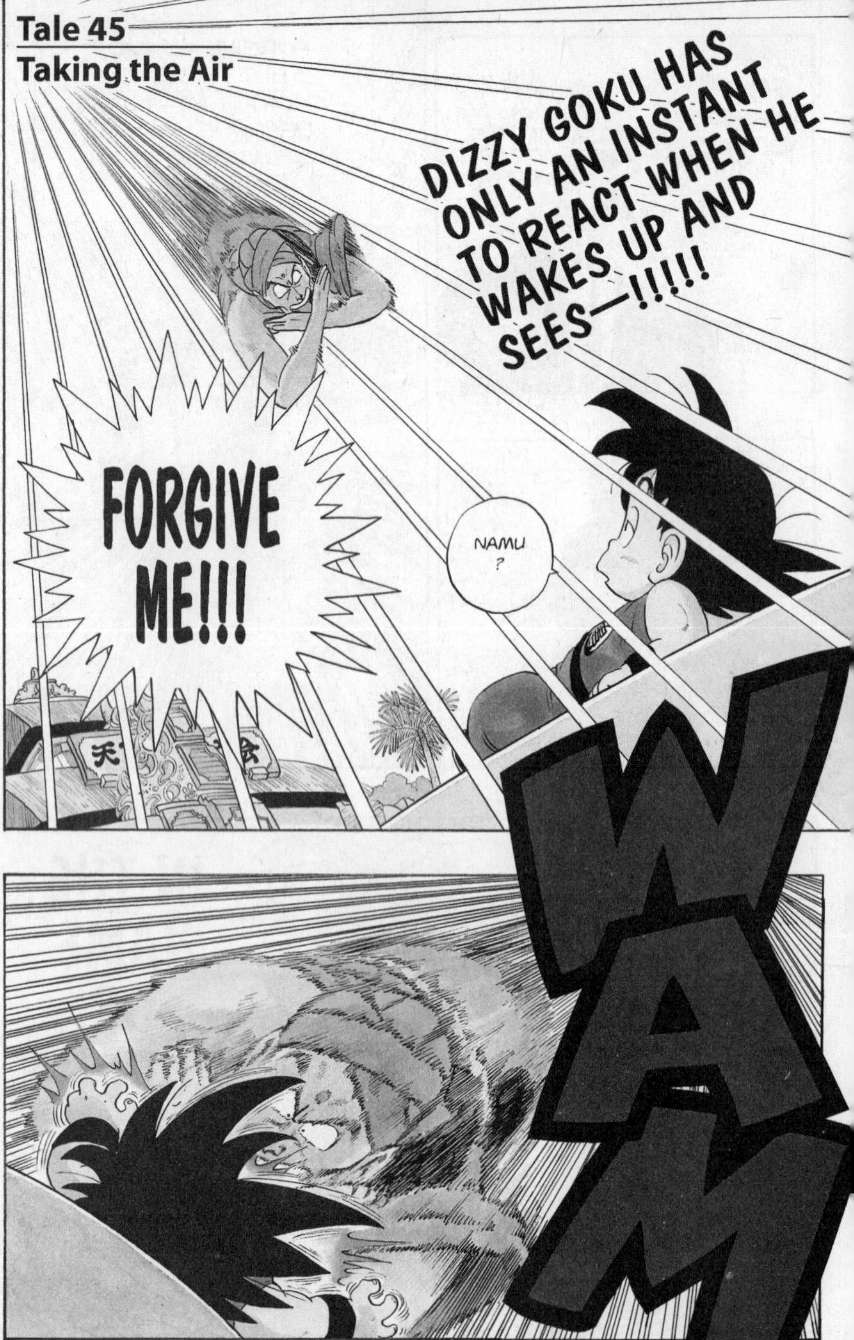
DIZZY GOKU HAS ONLY AN INSTANT TO REACT WHEN HE WAKES UP AND SEES—!!!!!
NAMU ?
FORGIVE ME!!!
WAM

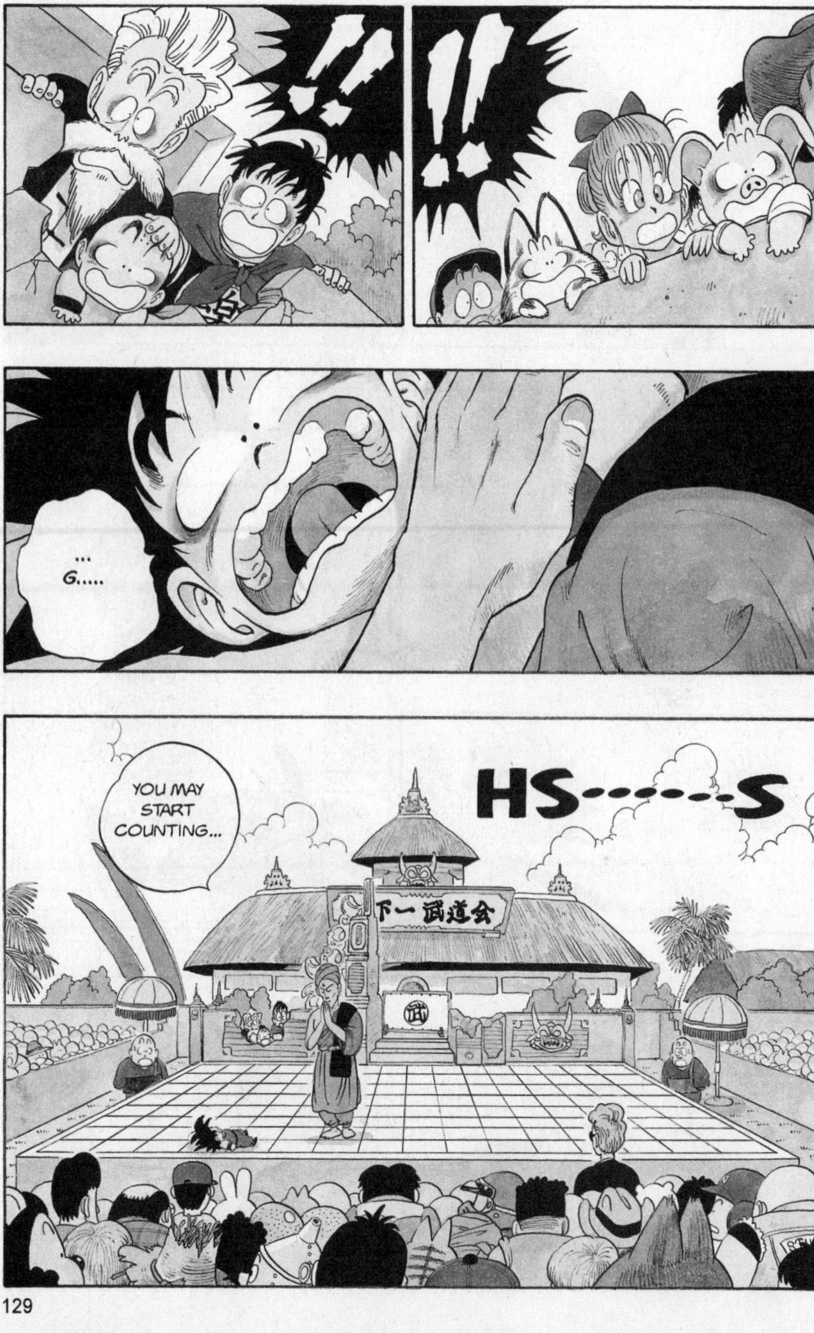
!!
!!
... G.....
HS------S
YOU MAY START COUNTING...

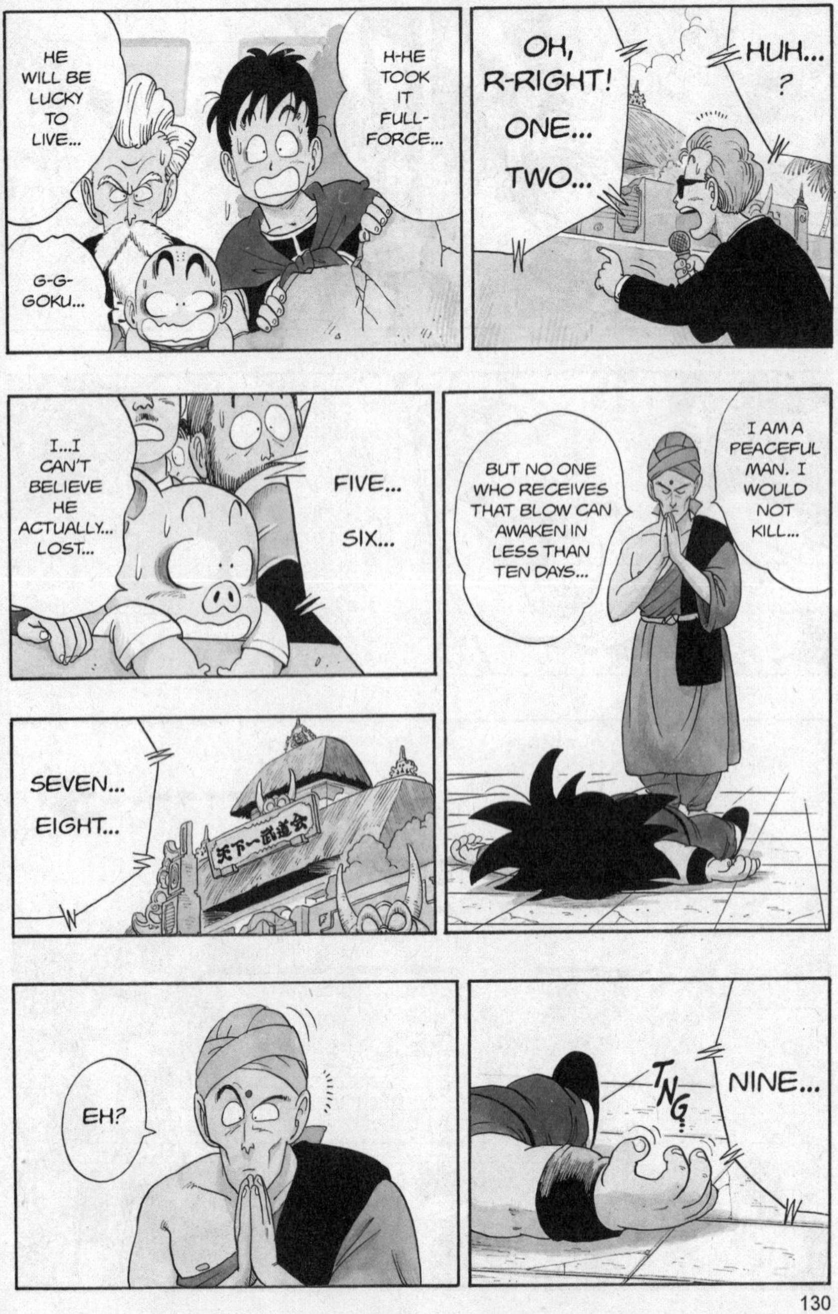
HUH...?
OH, R-RIGHT! ONE... TWO...
H-HE TOOK IT FULL-FORCE...
HE WILL BE LUCKY TO LIVE...
G-G-GOKU...
I AM A PEACEFUL MAN. I WOULD NOT KILL...
BUT NO ONE WHO RECEIVES THAT BLOW CAN AWAKEN IN LESS THAN TEN DAYS...
FIVE... SIX...
I...I CAN'T BELIEVE HE ACTUALLY... LOST...
SEVEN... EIGHT...
天下一武道会
NINE...
TNG...
EH?

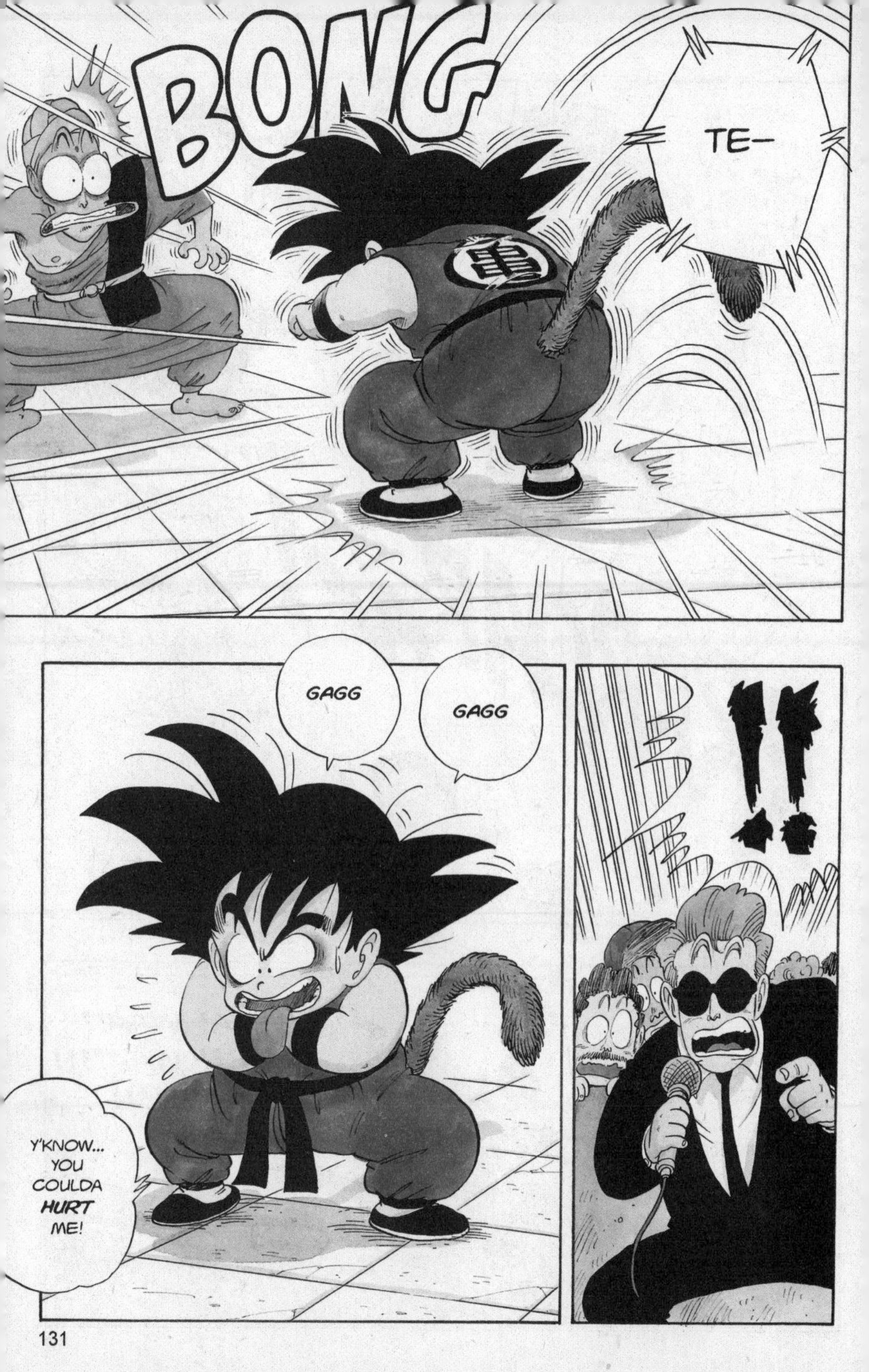
BONG
TE—
GAGG
GAGG
Y'KNOW... YOU COULDA HURT ME!
!!

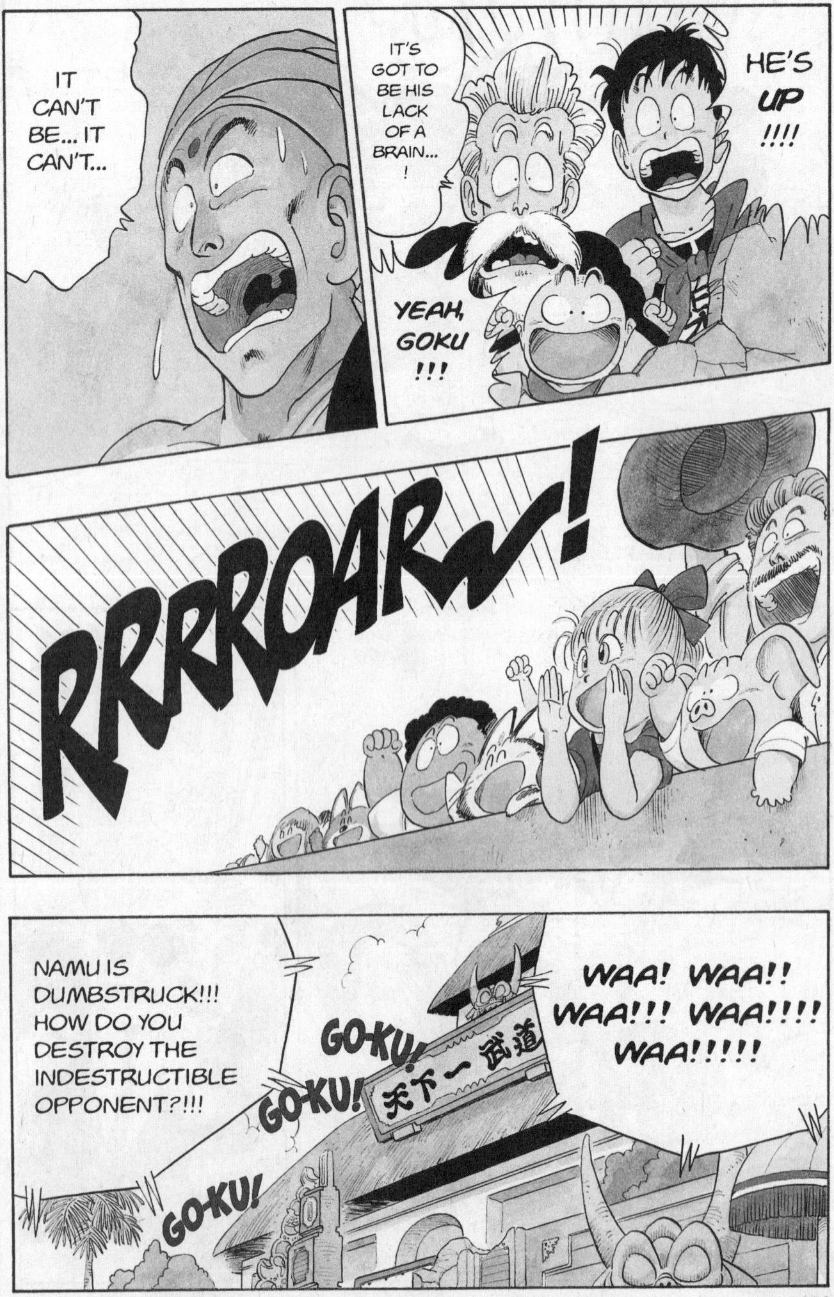
HE'S UP!!!!
IT'S GOT TO BE HIS LACK OF A BRAIN...!
YEAH, GOKU!!!
IT CAN'T BE... IT CAN'T...
RRRROARW!
WAA! WAA!! WAA!!! WAA!!!! WAA!!!!!
GO-KU!
GO-KU!
天下一武道
GO-KU!
NAMU IS DUMBSTRUCK!!! HOW DO YOU DESTROY THE INDESTRUCTIBLE OPPONENT?!!!

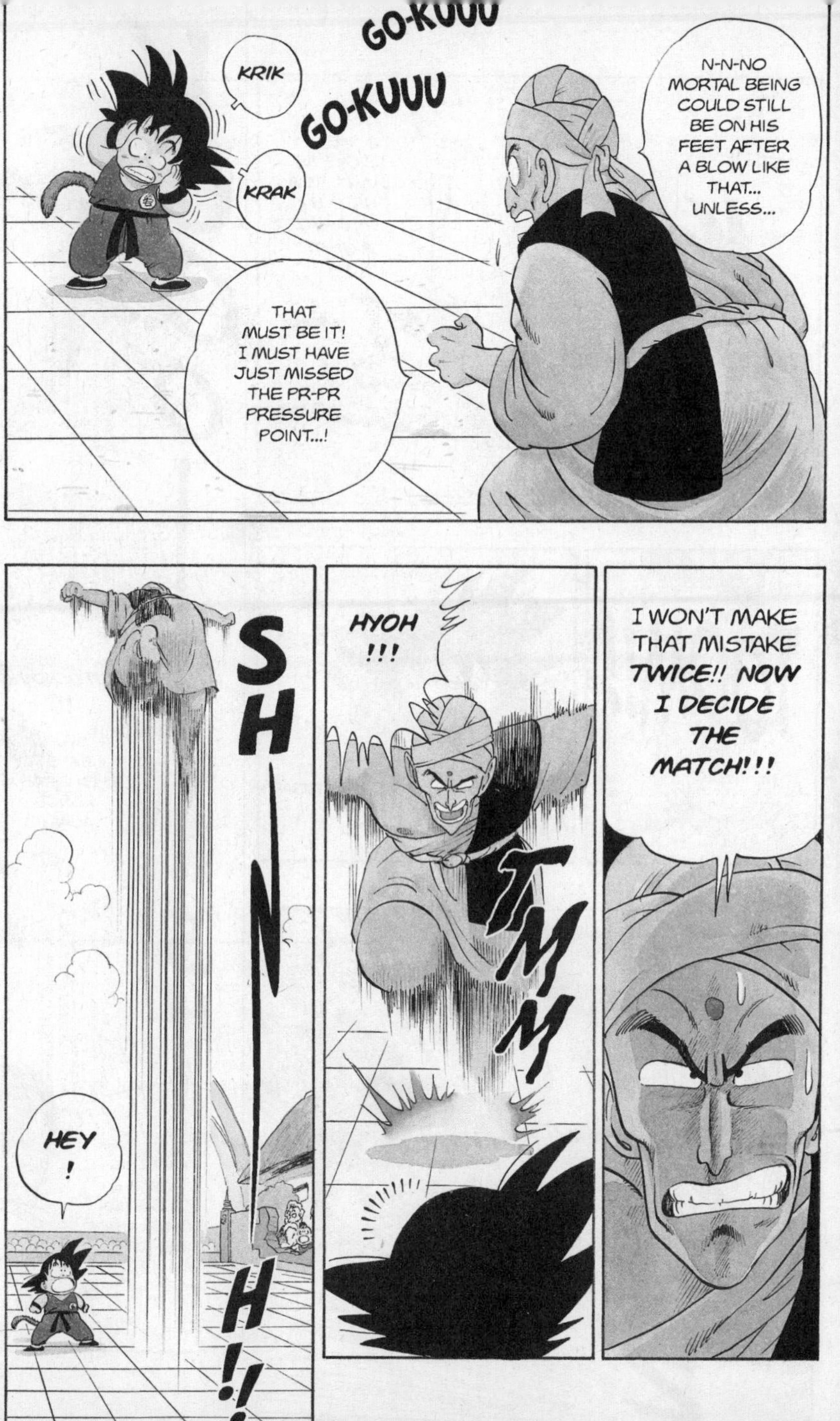
GO-KUUU
N-N-NO MORTAL BEING COULD STILL BE ON HIS FEET AFTER A BLOW LIKE THAT... UNLESS...
GO-KUUU
KRIK
KRAK
THAT MUST BE IT! I MUST HAVE JUST MISSED THE PR-PR PRESSURE POINT...!
I WON'T MAKE THAT MISTAKE TWICE!! NOW I DECIDE THE MATCH!!!
HYOH !!!
TMM
SHHH!!
HEY !

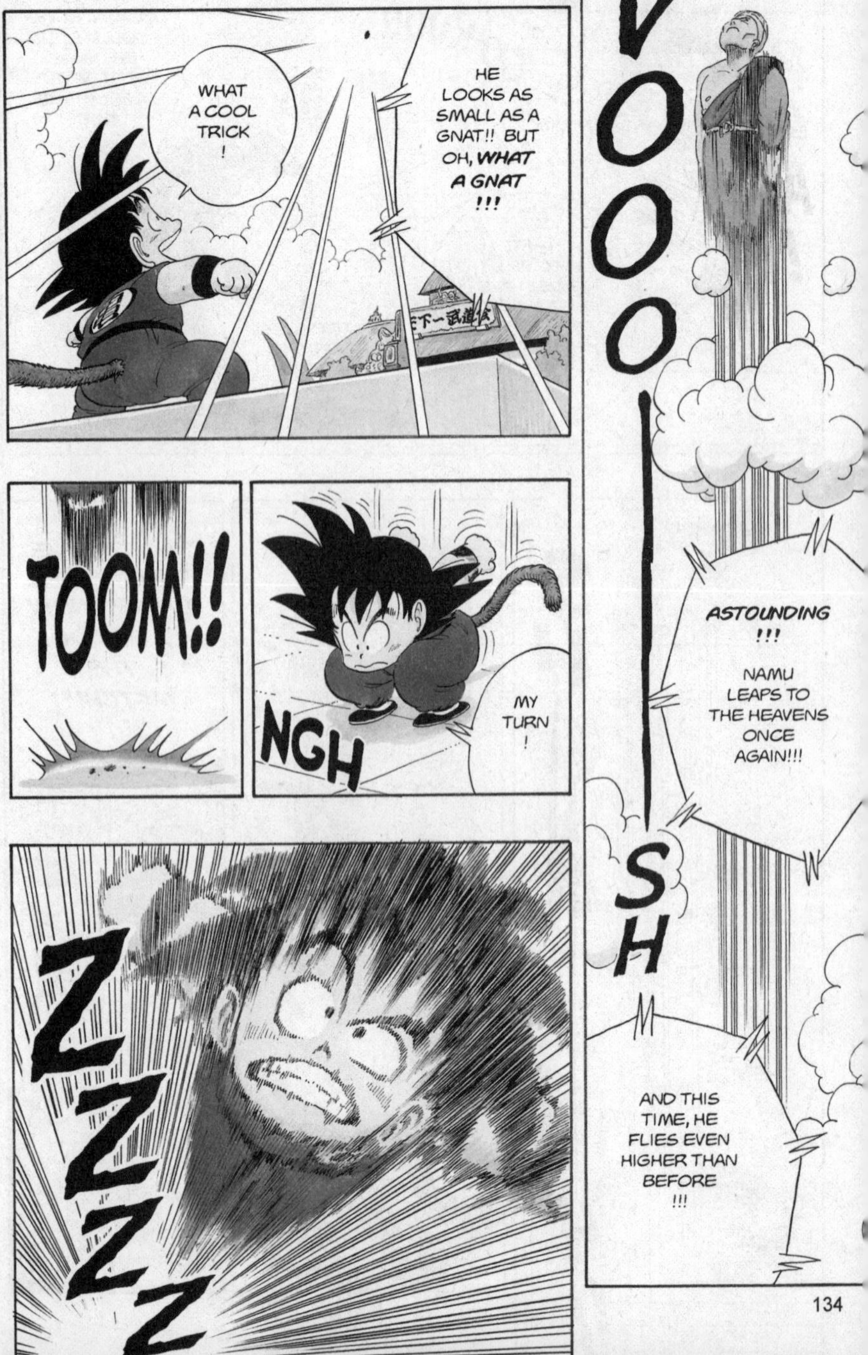
VOOOOSH
ASTOUNDING!!!
NAMU LEAPS TO THE HEAVENS ONCE AGAIN!!!
AND THIS TIME, HE FLIES EVEN HIGHER THAN BEFORE!!!
HE LOOKS AS SMALL AS A GNAT!! BUT OH, **WHAT A GNAT!!!**
WHAT A COOL TRICK!
NGH
MY TURN!
TOOM!!
ZZZZZ

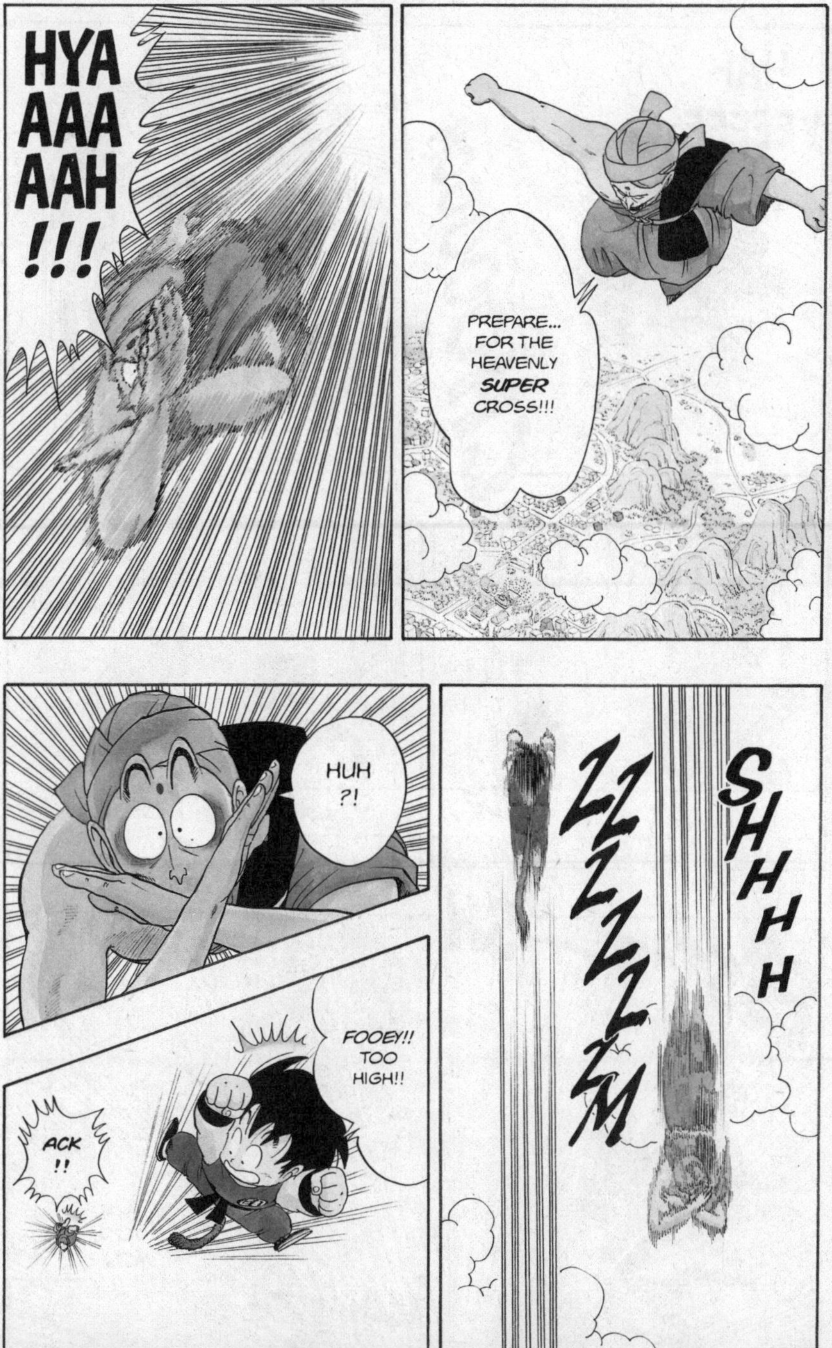
PREPARE... FOR THE HEAVENLY SUPER CROSS!!!
HYA AAA AAH !!!
SHHHH
ZZZZZM
HUH ?!
FOOEY!! TOO HIGH!!
ACK !!

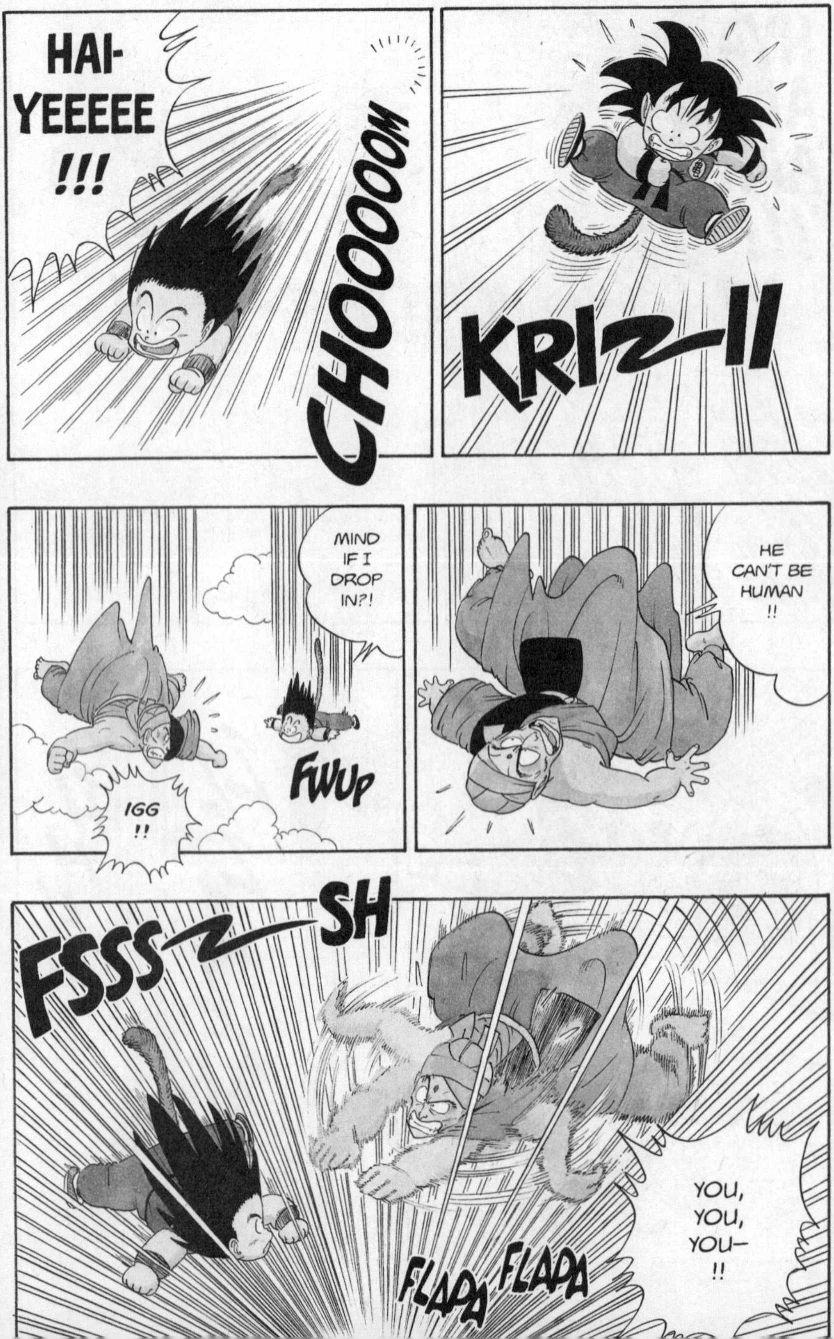
KRIZ-II
HAI-YEEEEE!!!
CHOOOOOM
HE CAN'T BE HUMAN!!
MIND IF I DROP IN?!
FWUP
IGG!!
FSSS-SH
YOU, YOU, YOU—!!
FLAPA FLAPA

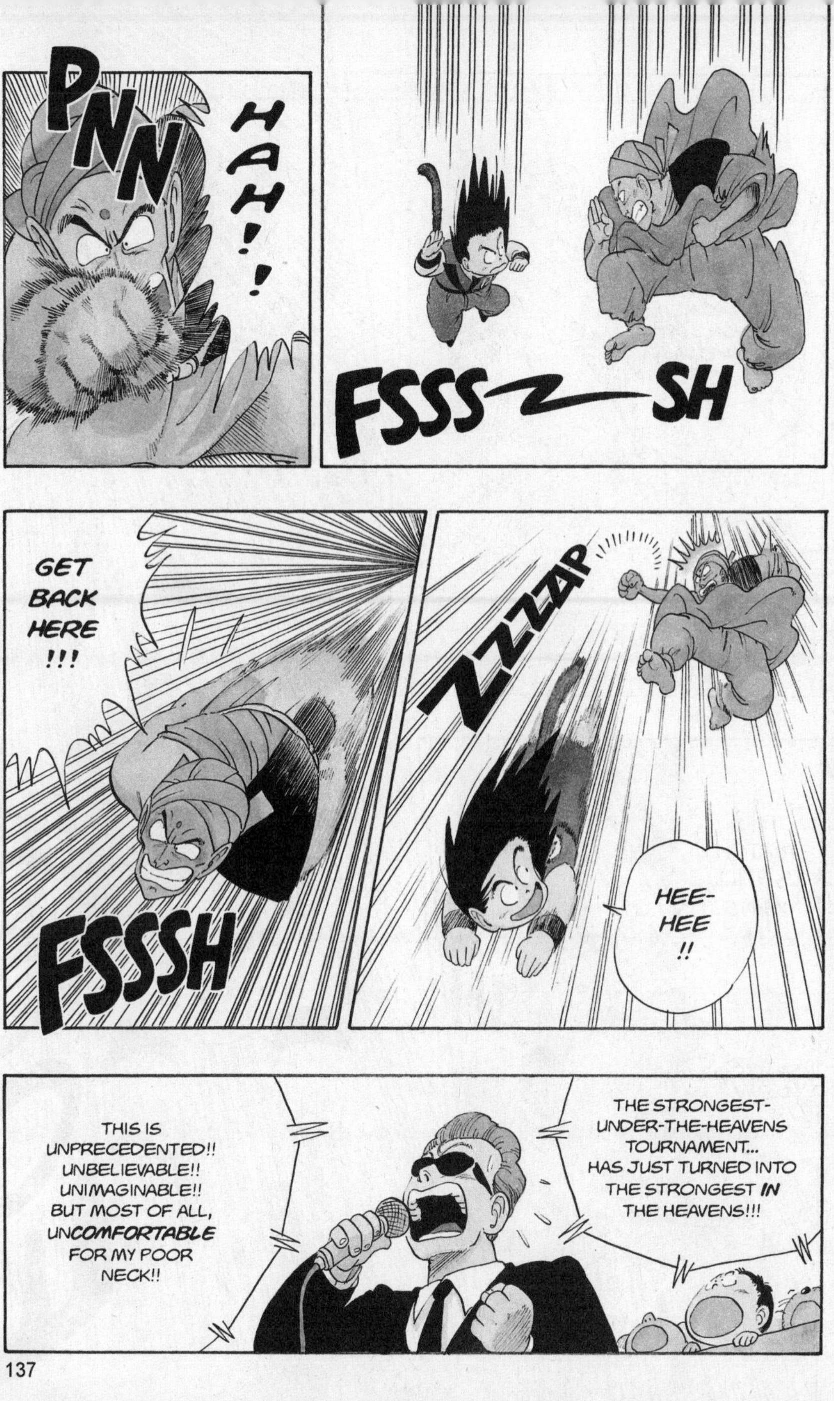
FSSS—SH
PNN
HAH!!
ZZZZAP
HEE-HEE!!
GET BACK HERE!!!
FSSSH
THE STRONGEST-UNDER-THE-HEAVENS TOURNAMENT... HAS JUST TURNED INTO THE STRONGEST *IN* THE HEAVENS!!!
THIS IS UNPRECEDENTED!! UNBELIEVABLE!! UNIMAGINABLE!! BUT MOST OF ALL, UN*COMFORTABLE* FOR MY POOR NECK!!

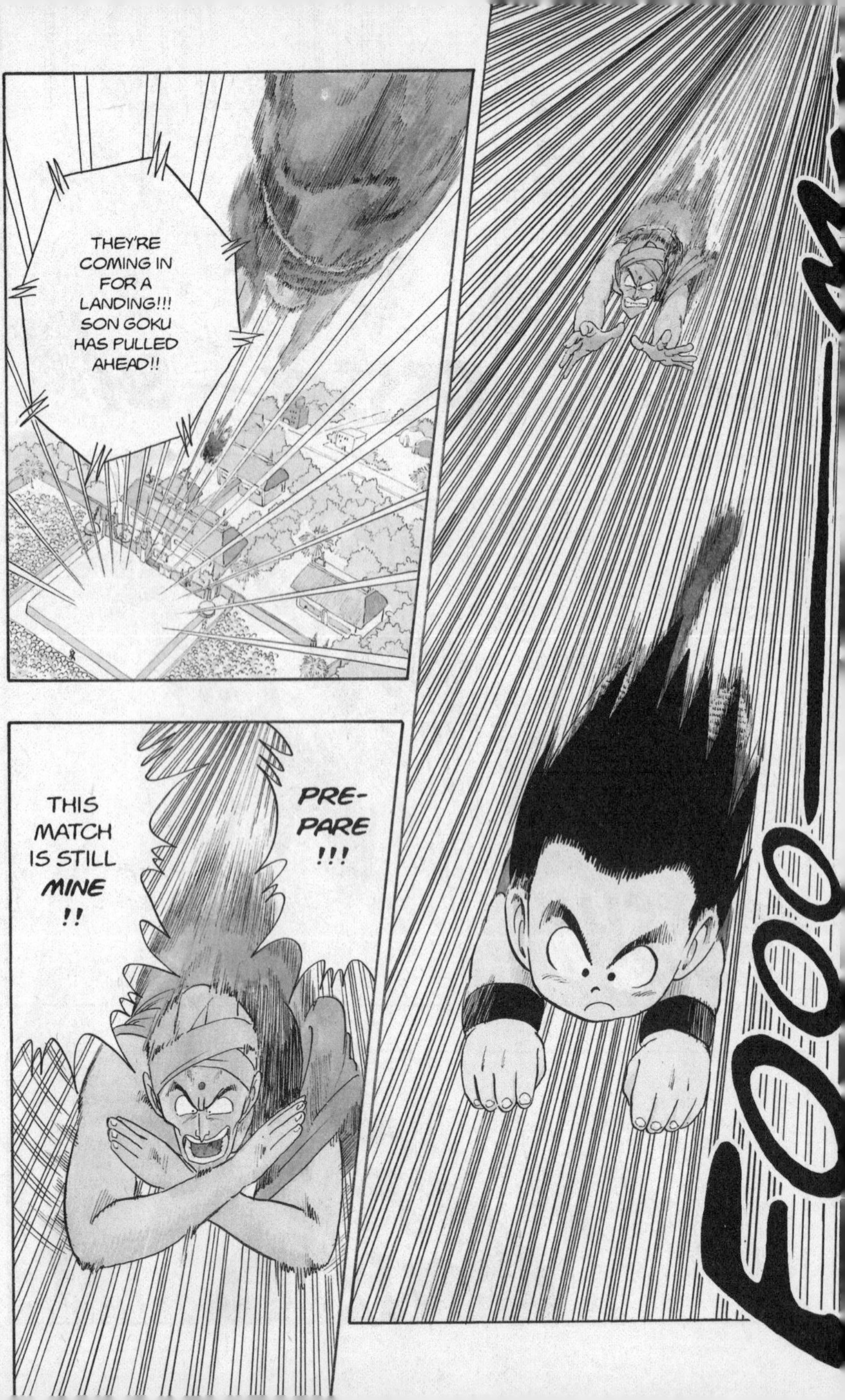
FOOO—
THEY'RE COMING IN FOR A LANDING!!! SON GOKU HAS PULLED AHEAD!!
PRE-PARE!!!
THIS MATCH IS STILL MINE!!

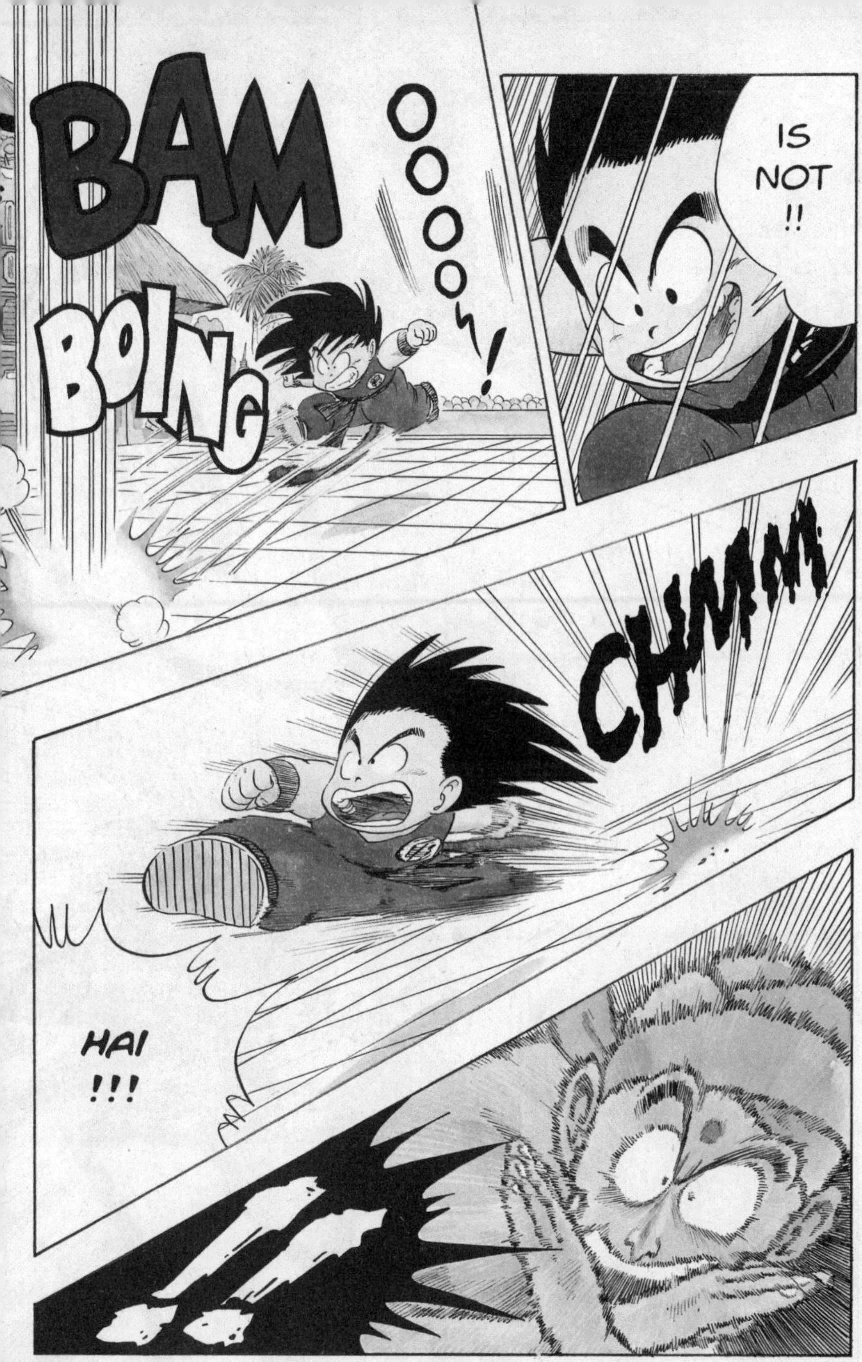
IS NOT !!
OOOOh!
BAM
BOING
CHMM
HAI !!!

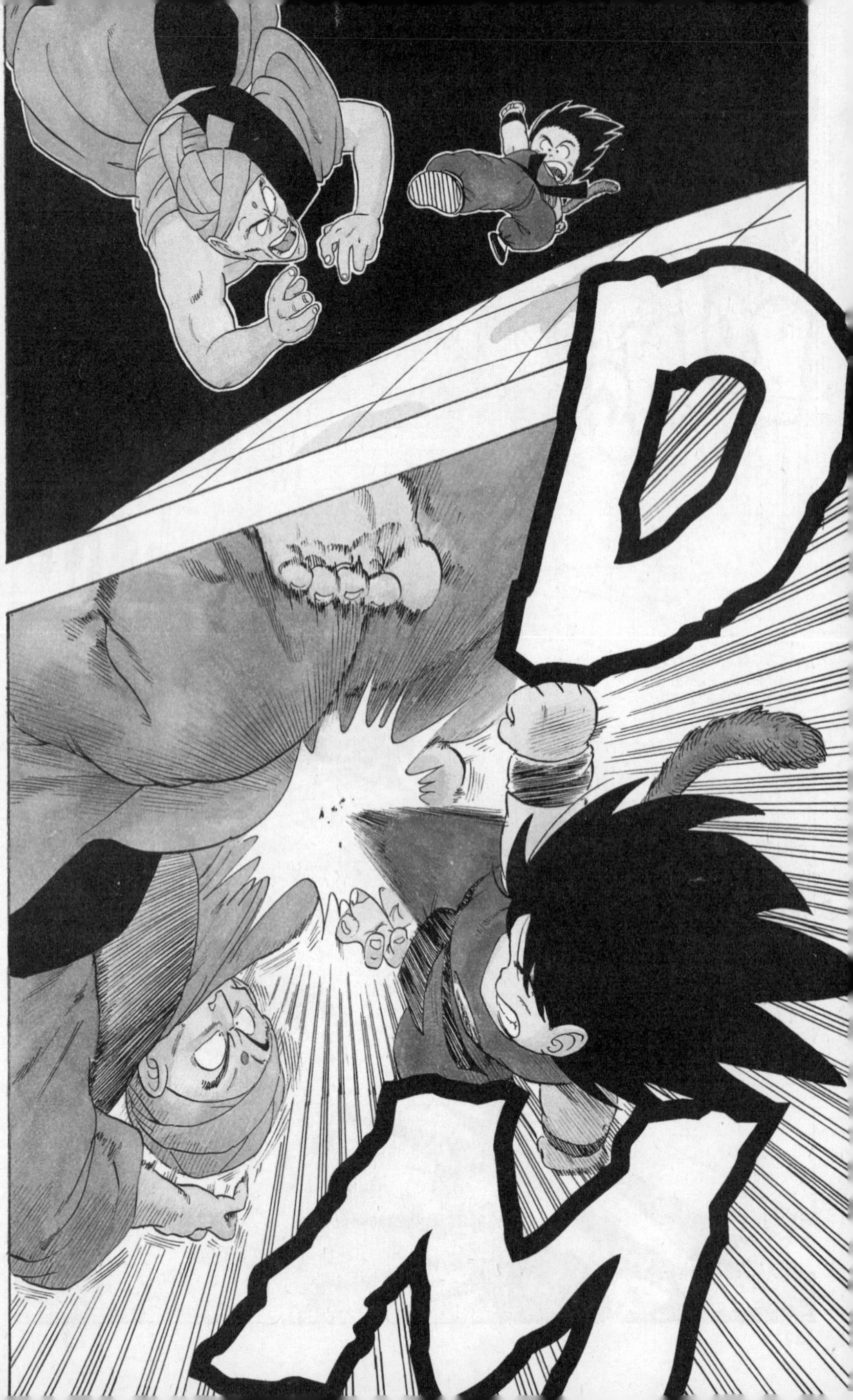
D

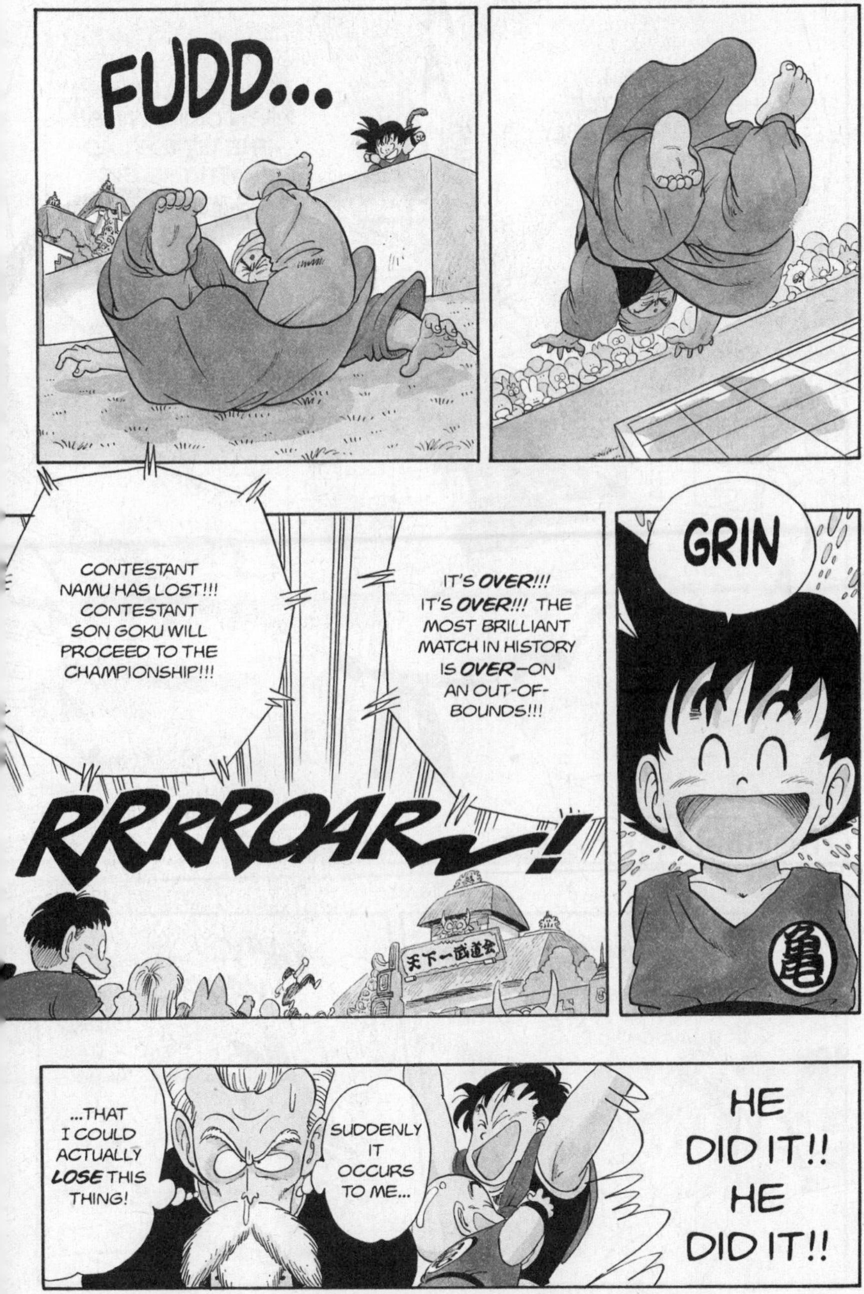
FUDD...
GRIN
IT'S OVER!!! IT'S OVER!!! THE MOST BRILLIANT MATCH IN HISTORY IS OVER—ON AN OUT-OF-BOUNDS!!!
CONTESTANT NAMU HAS LOST!!! CONTESTANT SON GOKU WILL PROCEED TO THE CHAMPIONSHIP!!!
RRRROAR!
天下一武道会
HE DID IT!! HE DID IT!!
SUDDENLY IT OCCURS TO ME...
...THAT I COULD ACTUALLY LOSE THIS THING!

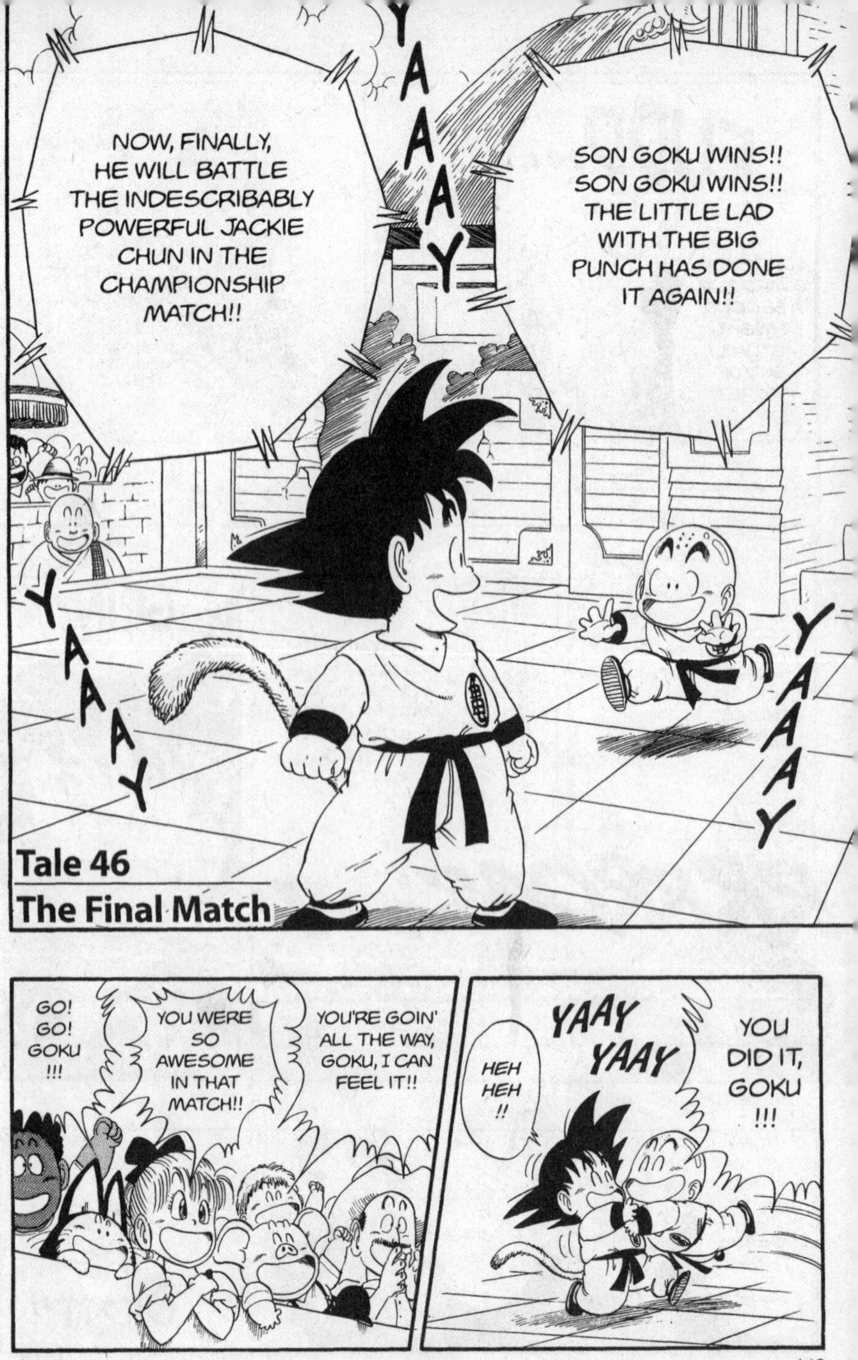

SON GOKU WINS!! SON GOKU WINS!! THE LITTLE LAD WITH THE BIG PUNCH HAS DONE IT AGAIN!!
YAAAY
NOW, FINALLY, HE WILL BATTLE THE INDESCRIBABLY POWERFUL JACKIE CHUN IN THE CHAMPIONSHIP MATCH!!
YAAAAY
YAAAAY
Tale 46
The Final Match
YAAY YAAY
YOU DID IT, GOKU !!!
HEH HEH !!
YOU'RE GOIN' ALL THE WAY, GOKU, I CAN FEEL IT!!
YOU WERE SO AWESOME IN THAT MATCH!!
GO! GO! GOKU !!!

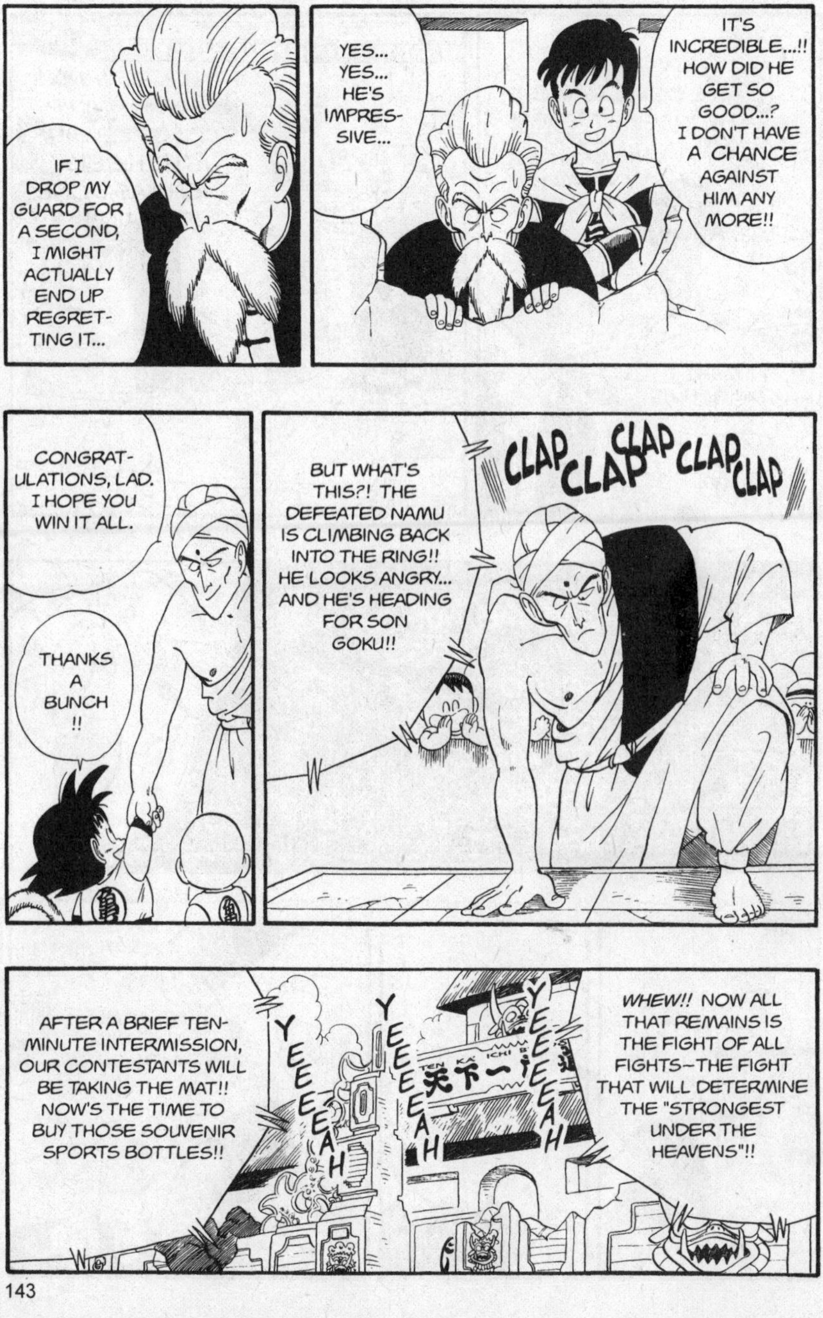
IT'S INCREDIBLE...!! HOW DID HE GET SO GOOD...? I DON'T HAVE A CHANCE AGAINST HIM ANY MORE!!
YES... YES... HE'S IMPRES-SIVE...
IF I DROP MY GUARD FOR A SECOND, I MIGHT ACTUALLY END UP REGRET-TING IT...
CLAP CLAP CLAP CLAP CLAP
BUT WHAT'S THIS?! THE DEFEATED NAMU IS CLIMBING BACK INTO THE RING!! HE LOOKS ANGRY... AND HE'S HEADING FOR SON GOKU!!
CONGRAT-ULATIONS, LAD. I HOPE YOU WIN IT ALL.
THANKS A BUNCH !!
WHEW!! NOW ALL THAT REMAINS IS THE FIGHT OF ALL FIGHTS—THE FIGHT THAT WILL DETERMINE THE "STRONGEST UNDER THE HEAVENS"!!
YEEEEAH
YEEEEAH
YEEEEAH
AFTER A BRIEF TEN-MINUTE INTERMISSION, OUR CONTESTANTS WILL BE TAKING THE MAT!! NOW'S THE TIME TO BUY THOSE SOUVENIR SPORTS BOTTLES!!

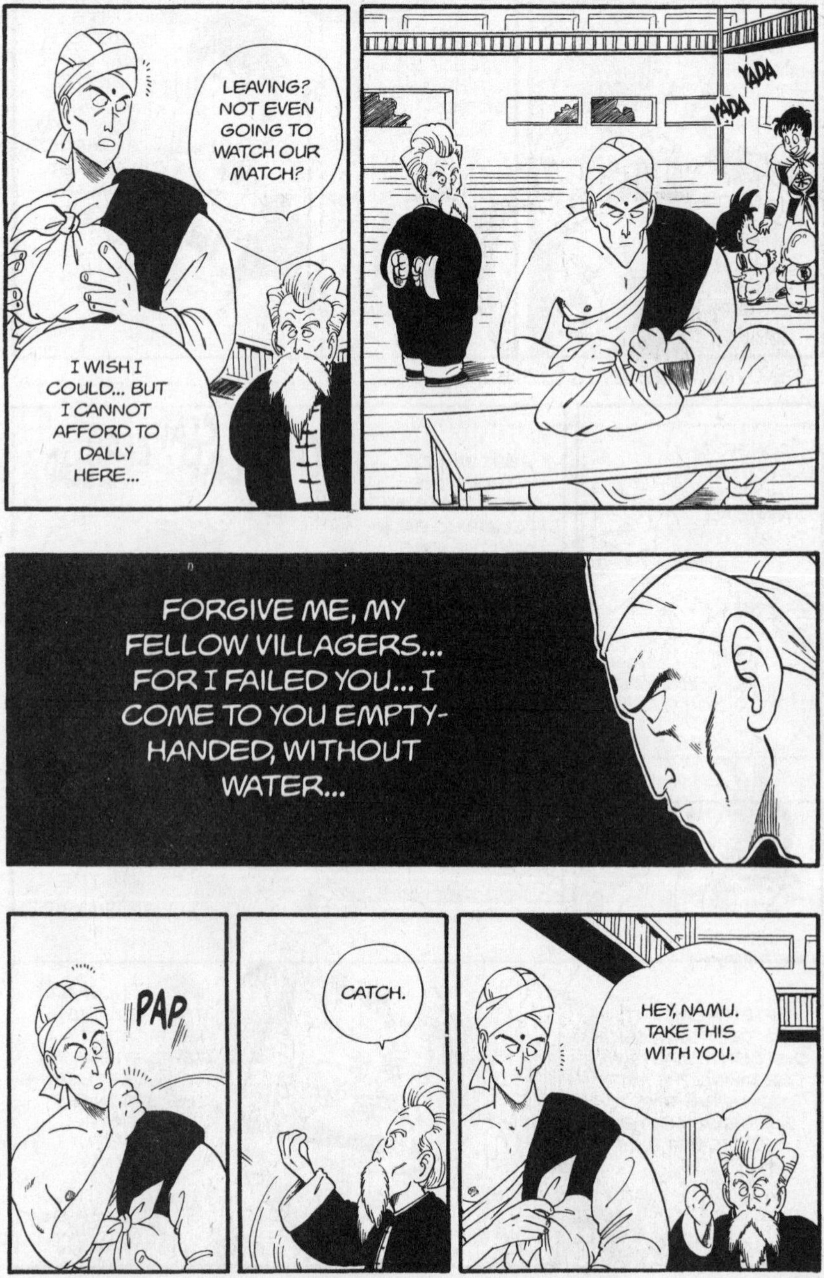
YADA
YADA
LEAVING? NOT EVEN GOING TO WATCH OUR MATCH?
I WISH I COULD... BUT I CANNOT AFFORD TO DALLY HERE...
FORGIVE ME, MY FELLOW VILLAGERS... FOR I FAILED YOU... I COME TO YOU EMPTY-HANDED, WITHOUT WATER...
HEY, NAMU. TAKE THIS WITH YOU.
CATCH.
PAP

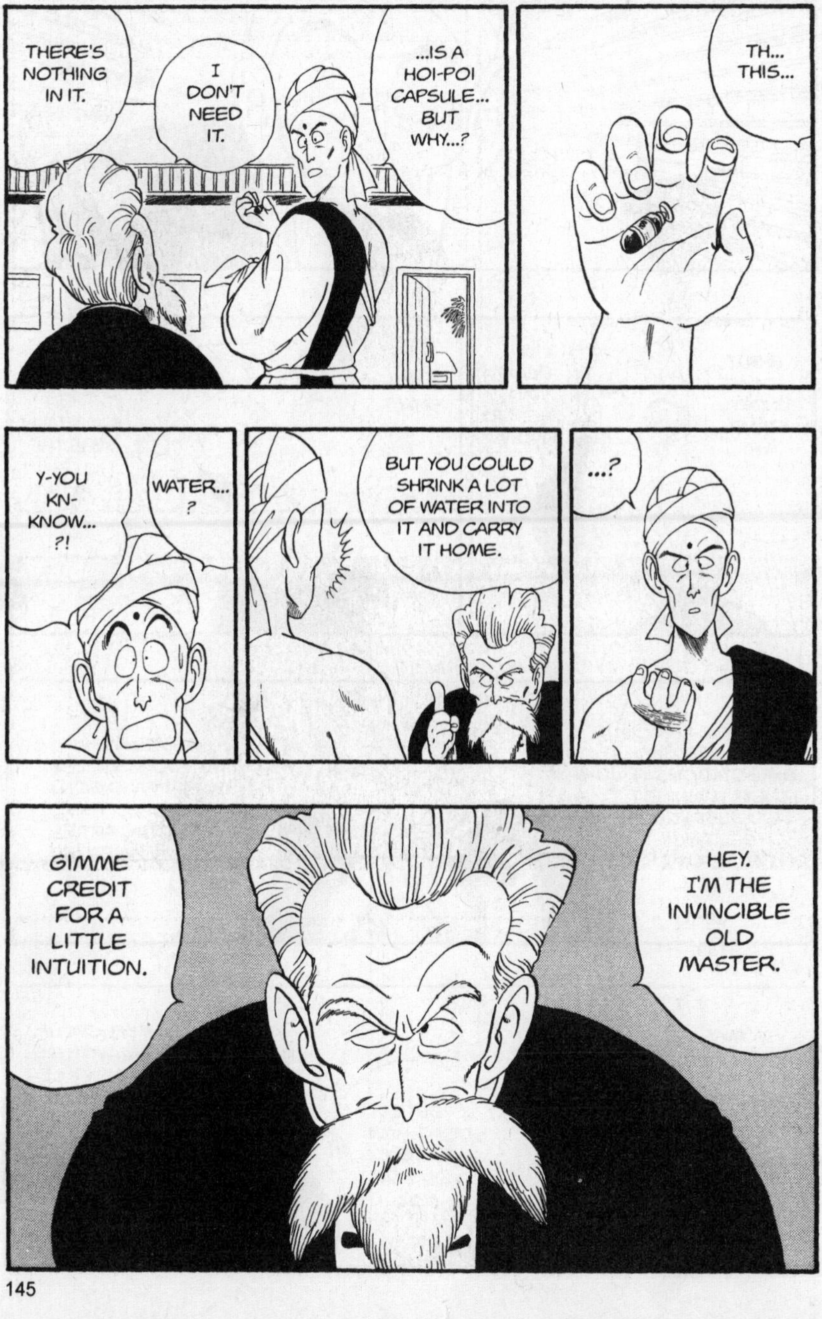
TH... THIS...
...IS A HOI-POI CAPSULE... BUT WHY...?
I DON'T NEED IT.
THERE'S NOTHING IN IT.
...?
BUT YOU COULD SHRINK A LOT OF WATER INTO IT AND CARRY IT HOME.
WATER...?
Y-YOU KN-KNOW...?!
HEY. I'M THE INVINCIBLE OLD MASTER.
GIMME CREDIT FOR A LITTLE INTUITION.

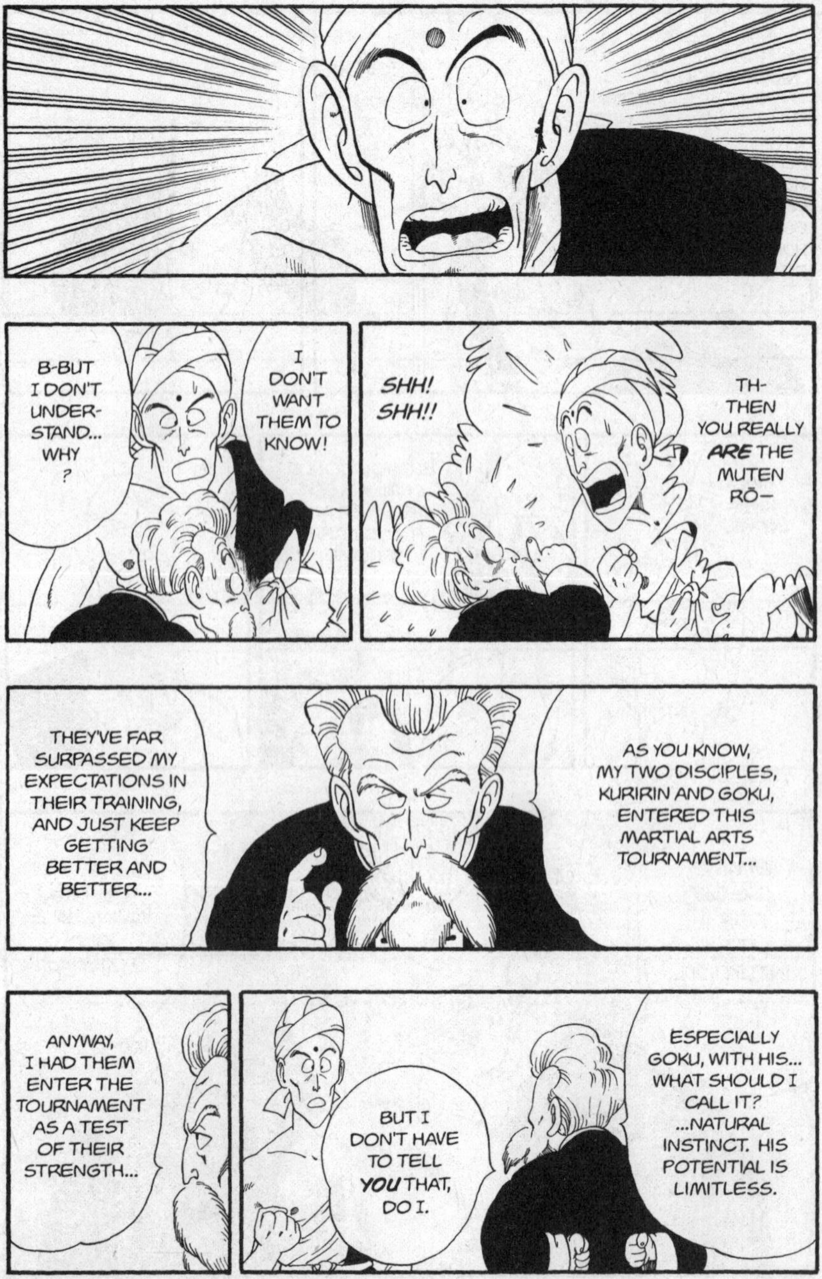
TH- THEN YOU REALLY ARE THE MUTEN RŌ-
SHH! SHH!!
I DON'T WANT THEM TO KNOW!
B-BUT I DON'T UNDER-STAND... WHY?
AS YOU KNOW, MY TWO DISCIPLES, KURIRIN AND GOKU, ENTERED THIS MARTIAL ARTS TOURNAMENT...
THEY'VE FAR SURPASSED MY EXPECTATIONS IN THEIR TRAINING, AND JUST KEEP GETTING BETTER AND BETTER...
ESPECIALLY GOKU, WITH HIS... WHAT SHOULD I CALL IT? ...NATURAL INSTINCT. HIS POTENTIAL IS LIMITLESS.
BUT I DON'T HAVE TO TELL YOU THAT, DO I.
ANYWAY, I HAD THEM ENTER THE TOURNAMENT AS A TEST OF THEIR STRENGTH...

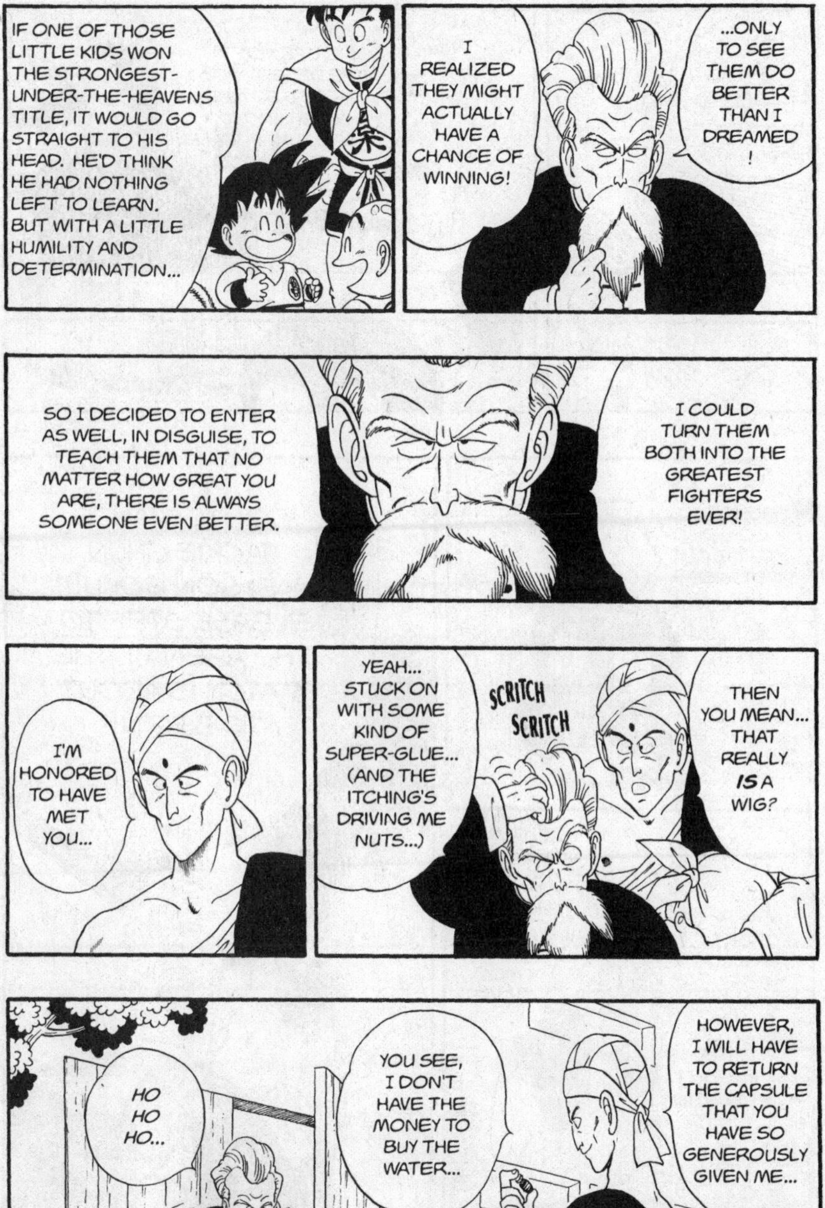
...ONLY TO SEE THEM DO BETTER THAN I DREAMED!
I REALIZED THEY MIGHT ACTUALLY HAVE A CHANCE OF WINNING!
IF ONE OF THOSE LITTLE KIDS WON THE STRONGEST-UNDER-THE-HEAVENS TITLE, IT WOULD GO STRAIGHT TO HIS HEAD. HE'D THINK HE HAD NOTHING LEFT TO LEARN. BUT WITH A LITTLE HUMILITY AND DETERMINATION...
I COULD TURN THEM BOTH INTO THE GREATEST FIGHTERS EVER!
SO I DECIDED TO ENTER AS WELL, IN DISGUISE, TO TEACH THEM THAT NO MATTER HOW GREAT YOU ARE, THERE IS ALWAYS SOMEONE EVEN BETTER.
THEN YOU MEAN... THAT REALLY *IS* A WIG?
SCRITCH
SCRITCH
YEAH... STUCK ON WITH SOME KIND OF SUPER-GLUE... (AND THE ITCHING'S DRIVING ME NUTS...)
I'M HONORED TO HAVE MET YOU...
HOWEVER, I WILL HAVE TO RETURN THE CAPSULE THAT YOU HAVE SO GENEROUSLY GIVEN ME...
YOU SEE, I DON'T HAVE THE MONEY TO BUY THE WATER...
HO HO HO...

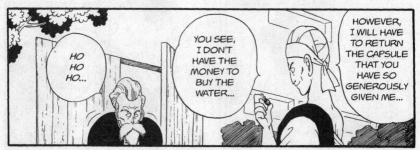

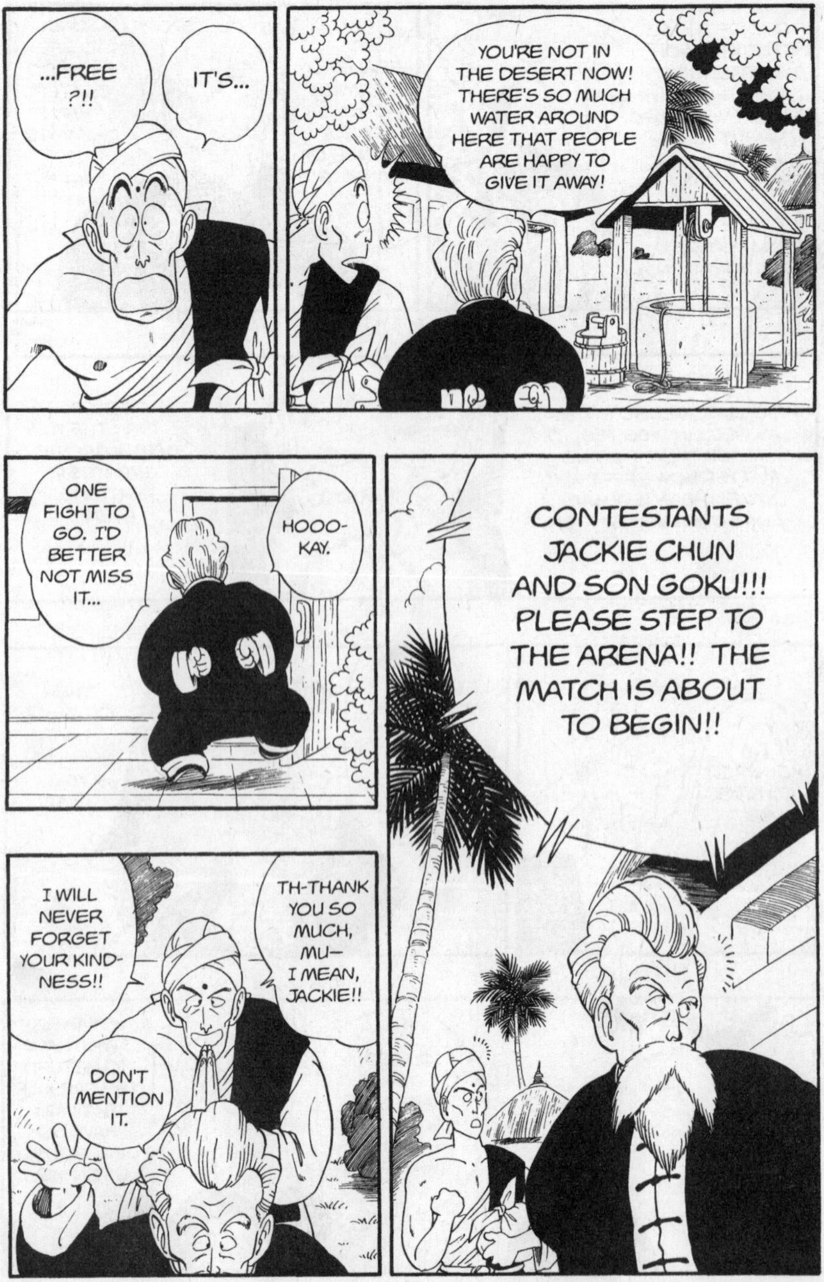
YOU'RE NOT IN THE DESERT NOW! THERE'S SO MUCH WATER AROUND HERE THAT PEOPLE ARE HAPPY TO GIVE IT AWAY!
IT'S...
...FREE ?!!
CONTESTANTS JACKIE CHUN AND SON GOKU!!! PLEASE STEP TO THE ARENA!! THE MATCH IS ABOUT TO BEGIN!!
HOOO-KAY.
ONE FIGHT TO GO. I'D BETTER NOT MISS IT...
TH-THANK YOU SO MUCH, MU— I MEAN, JACKIE!!
I WILL NEVER FORGET YOUR KIND-NESS!!
DON'T MENTION IT.

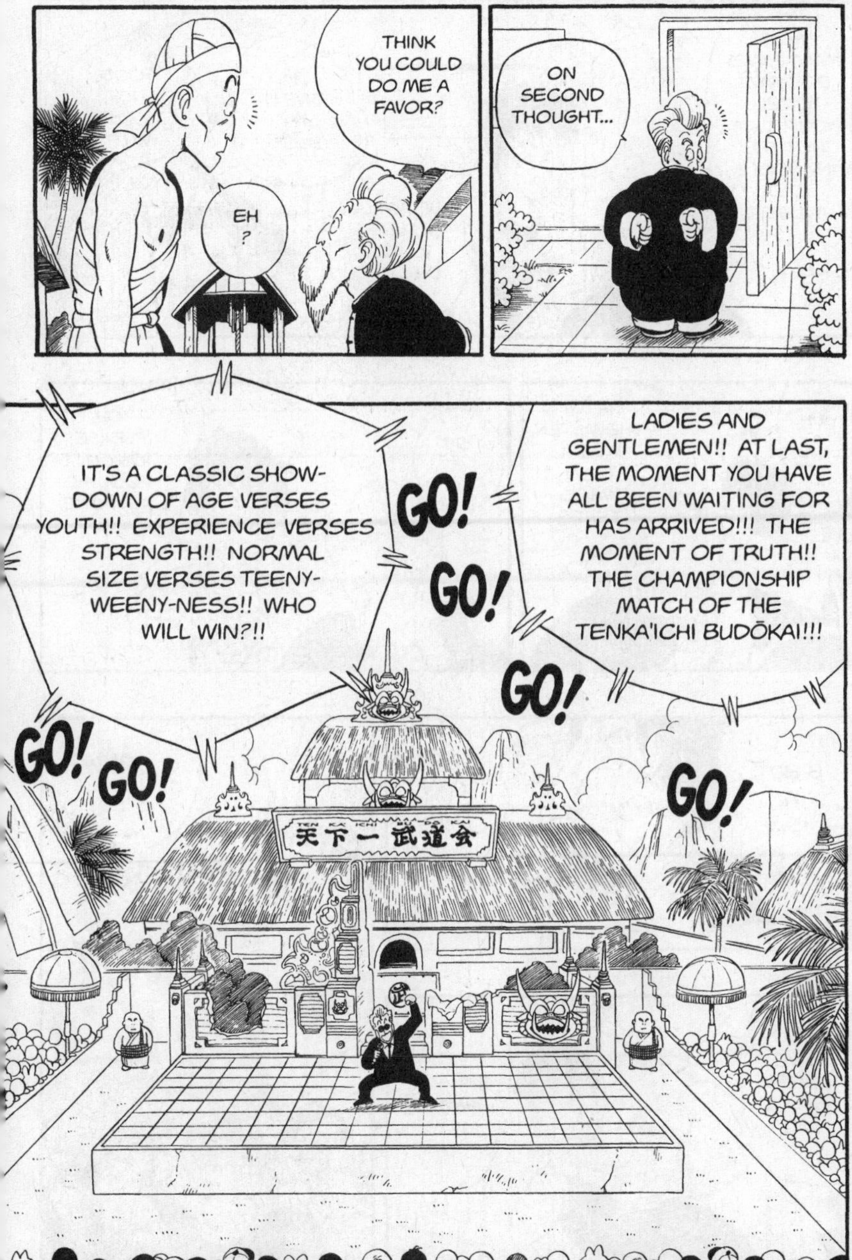
ON SECOND THOUGHT...
THINK YOU COULD DO ME A FAVOR?
EH ?
LADIES AND GENTLEMEN!! AT LAST, THE MOMENT YOU HAVE ALL BEEN WAITING FOR HAS ARRIVED!!! THE MOMENT OF TRUTH!! THE CHAMPIONSHIP MATCH OF THE TENKA'ICHI BUDŌKAI!!!
GO!
GO!
GO!
GO!
IT'S A CLASSIC SHOW-DOWN OF AGE VERSES YOUTH!! EXPERIENCE VERSES STRENGTH!! NORMAL SIZE VERSES TEENY-WEENY-NESS!! WHO WILL WIN?!!
GO!
GO!
天下一武道会

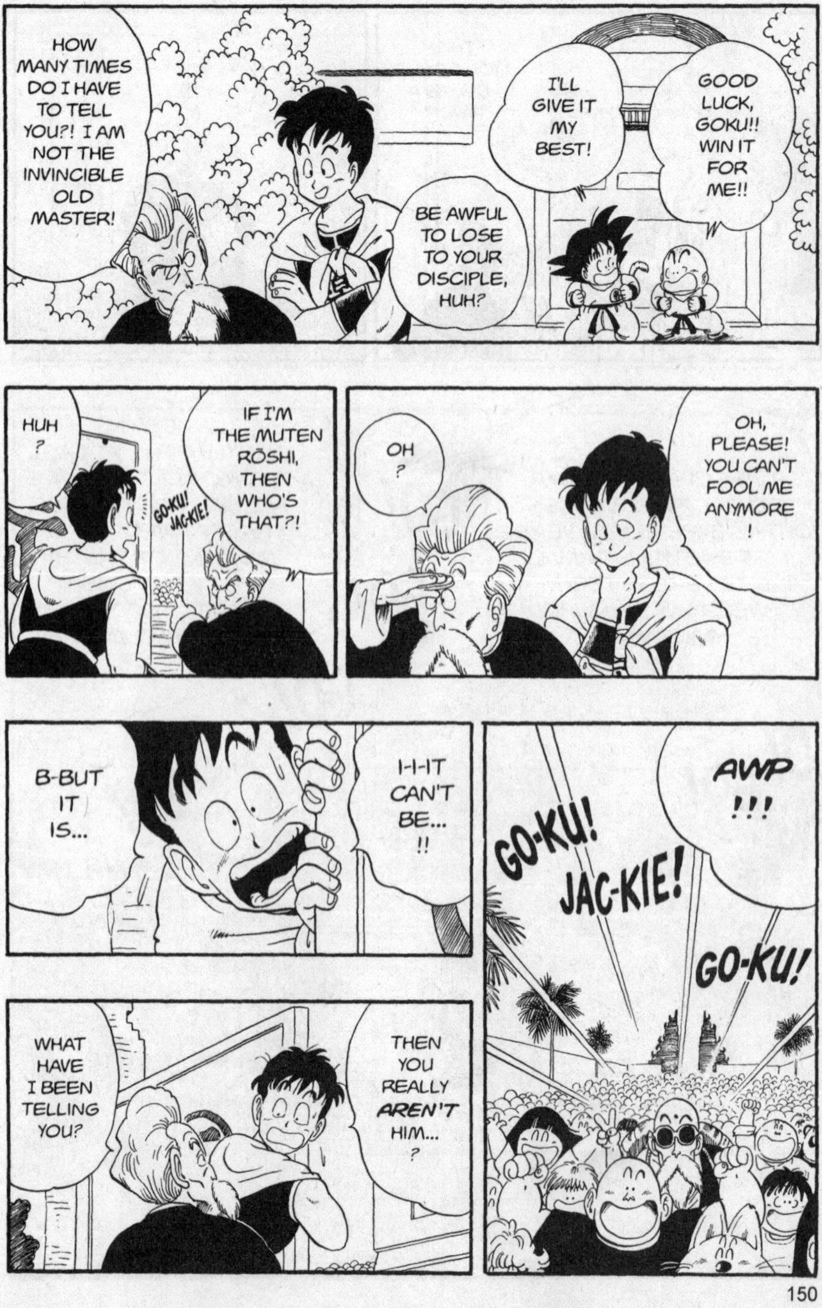
GOOD LUCK, GOKU!! WIN IT FOR ME!!
I'LL GIVE IT MY BEST!
BE AWFUL TO LOSE TO YOUR DISCIPLE, HUH?
HOW MANY TIMES DO I HAVE TO TELL YOU?! I AM NOT THE INVINCIBLE OLD MASTER!
OH, PLEASE! YOU CAN'T FOOL ME ANYMORE!
OH?
IF I'M THE MUTEN RŌSHI, THEN WHO'S THAT?!
GO-KU! JAC-KIE!
HUH?
AWP!!!
GO-KU!
JAC-KIE!
GO-KU!
I-I-IT CAN'T BE...!!
B-BUT IT IS...
THEN YOU REALLY *AREN'T* HIM...?
WHAT HAVE I BEEN TELLING YOU?

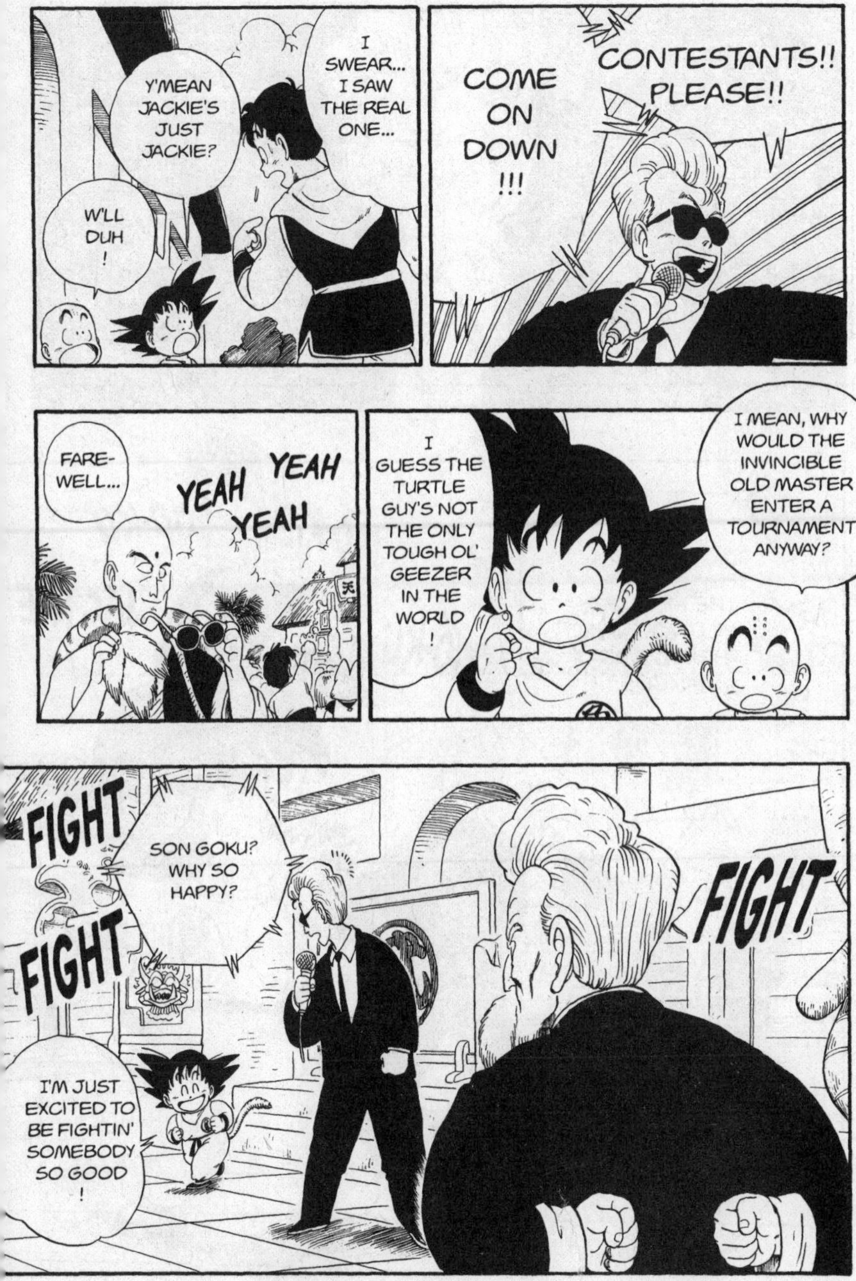
CONTESTANTS!! PLEASE!!
COME ON DOWN!!!
I SWEAR... I SAW THE REAL ONE...
Y'MEAN JACKIE'S JUST JACKIE?
W'LL DUH!
I MEAN, WHY WOULD THE INVINCIBLE OLD MASTER ENTER A TOURNAMENT ANYWAY?
I GUESS THE TURTLE GUY'S NOT THE ONLY TOUGH OL' GEEZER IN THE WORLD!
YEAH YEAH YEAH
FARE-WELL...
FIGHT
SON GOKU? WHY SO HAPPY?
FIGHT
FIGHT
I'M JUST EXCITED TO BE FIGHTIN' SOMEBODY SO GOOD!

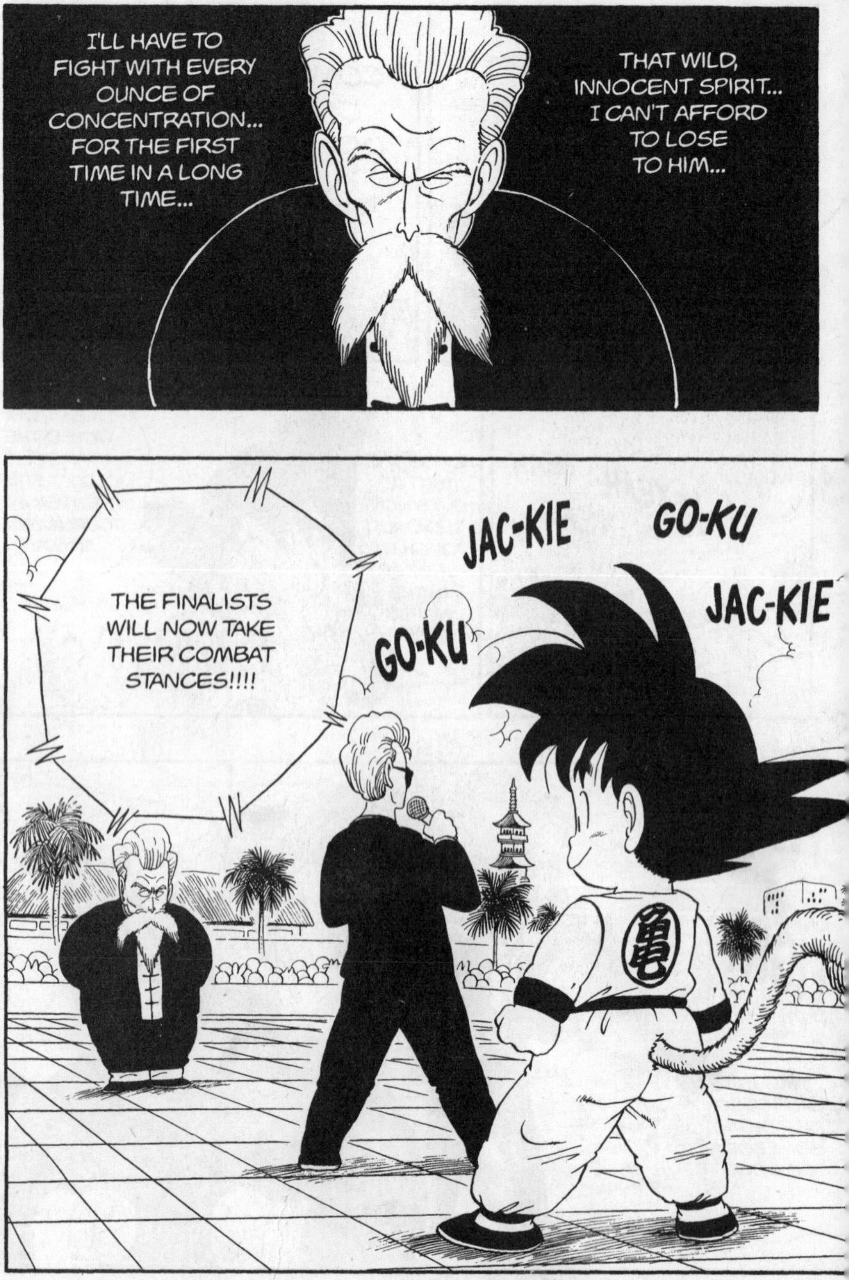
THAT WILD, INNOCENT SPIRIT... I CAN'T AFFORD TO LOSE TO HIM...
I'LL HAVE TO FIGHT WITH EVERY OUNCE OF CONCENTRATION... FOR THE FIRST TIME IN A LONG TIME...
GO-KU
JAC-KIE
JAC-KIE
GO-KU
THE FINALISTS WILL NOW TAKE THEIR COMBAT STANCES!!!!

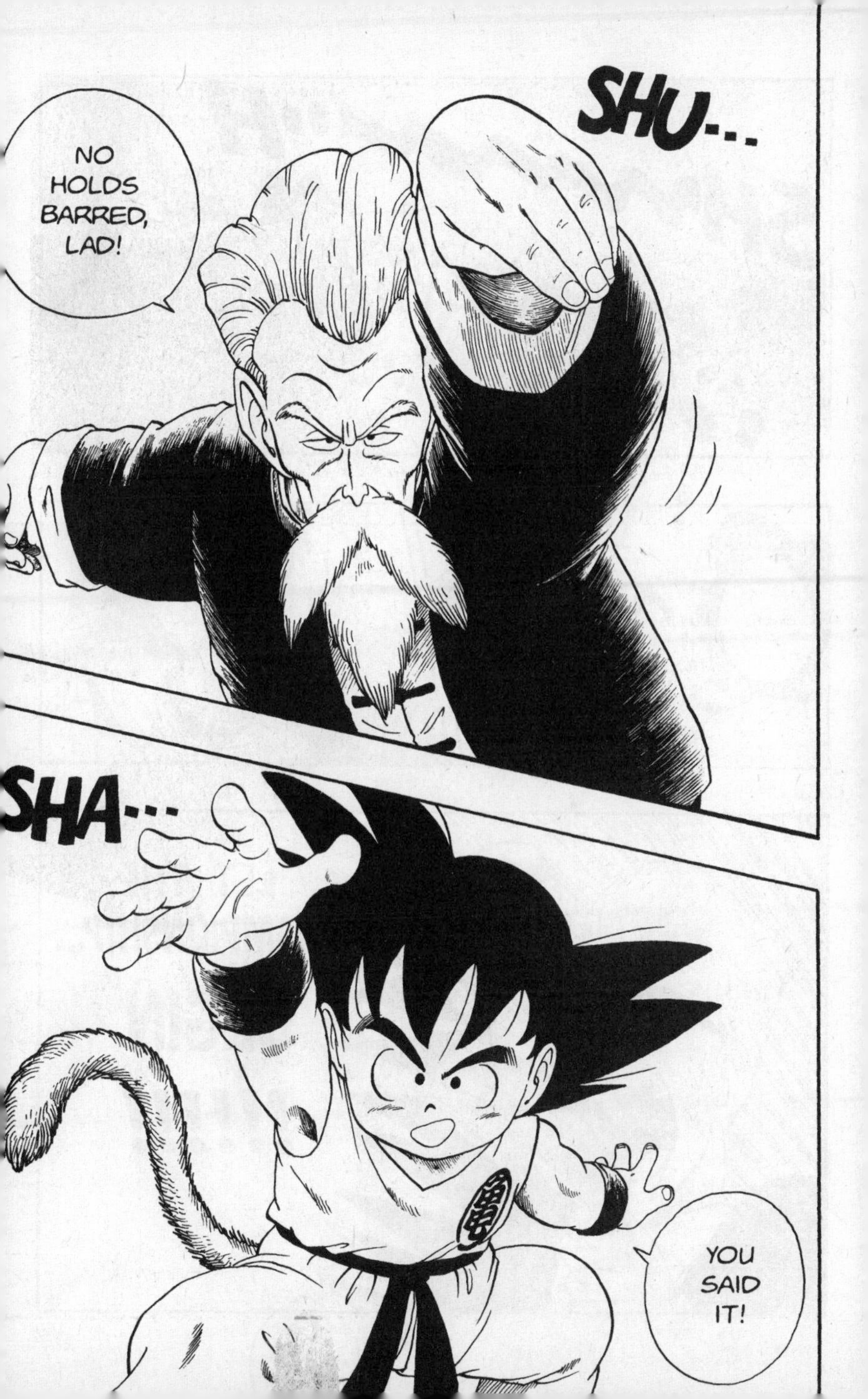
SHU...
NO HOLDS BARRED, LAD!
SHA...
YOU SAID IT!

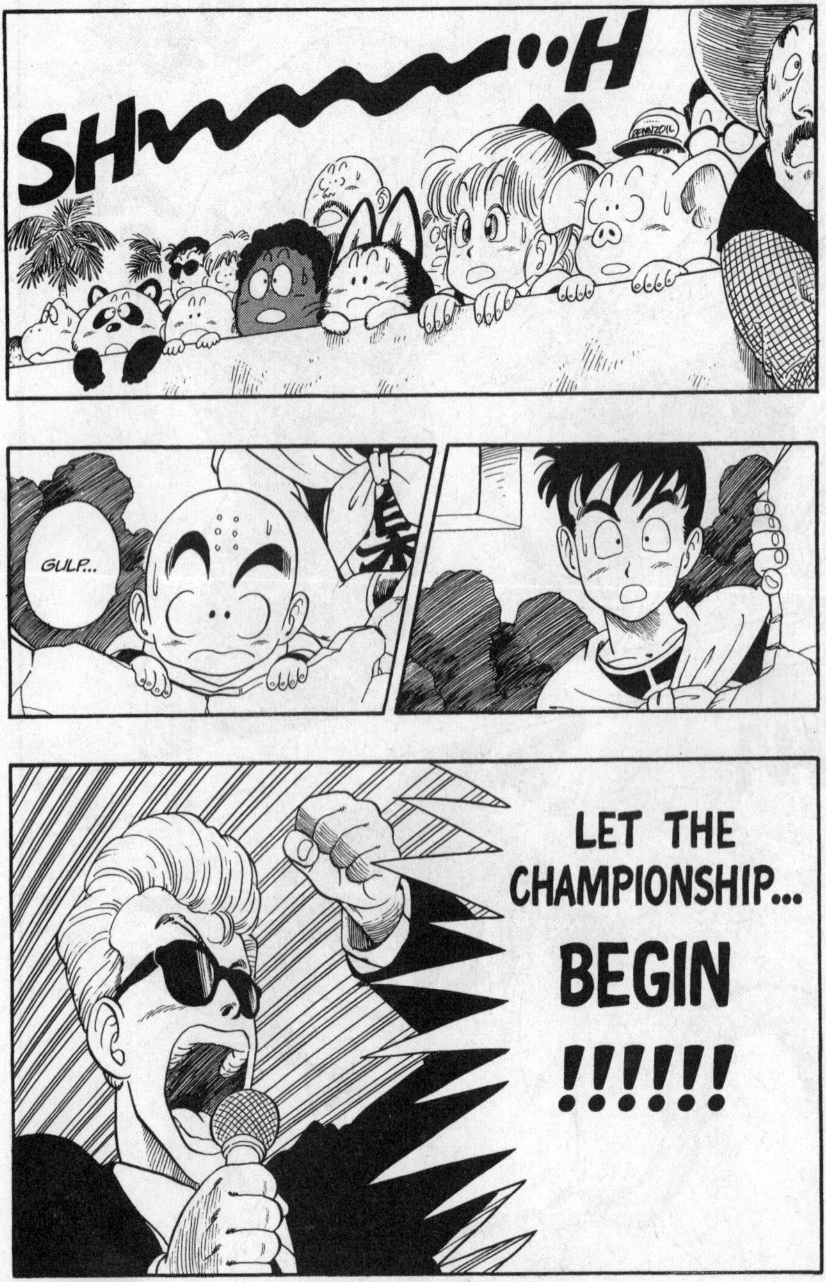
SHHHHHH••H
GULP...
LET THE CHAMPIONSHIP... BEGIN!!!!!!

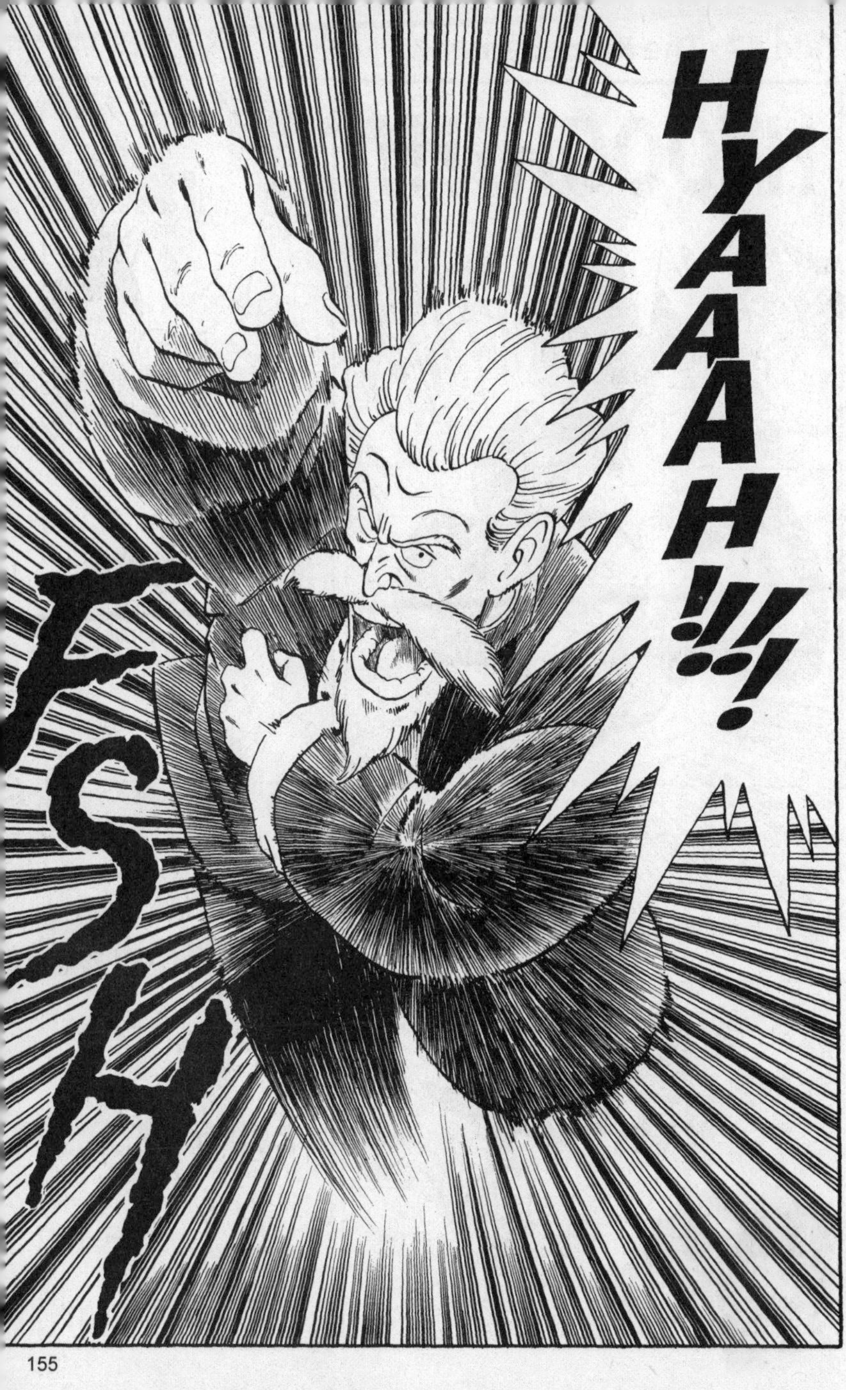
HYAAAH!!!!
FSH

Tale 47 • The Kamehameha

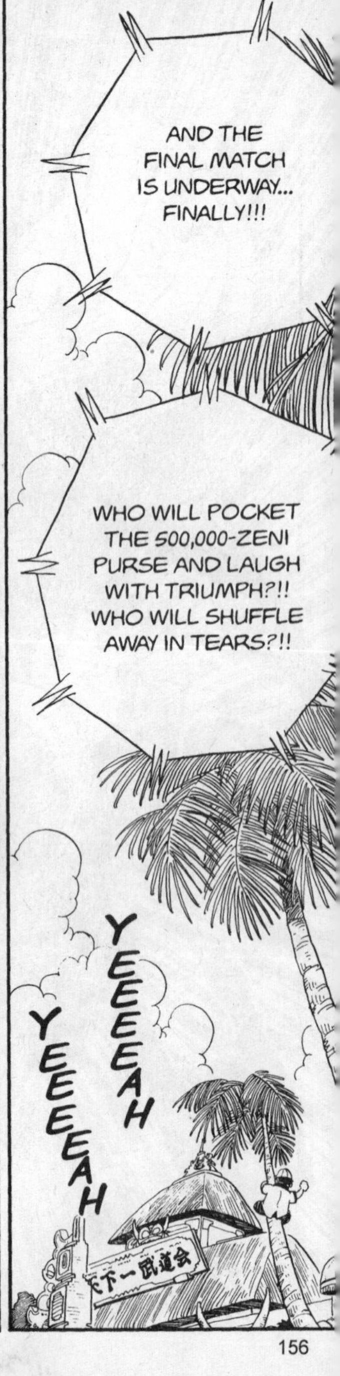
AND THE FINAL MATCH IS UNDERWAY... FINALLY!!!
WHO WILL POCKET THE 500,000-ZENI PURSE AND LAUGH WITH TRIUMPH?!! WHO WILL SHUFFLE AWAY IN TEARS?!!
YEEEEAH
YEEEEAH
天下一武道会

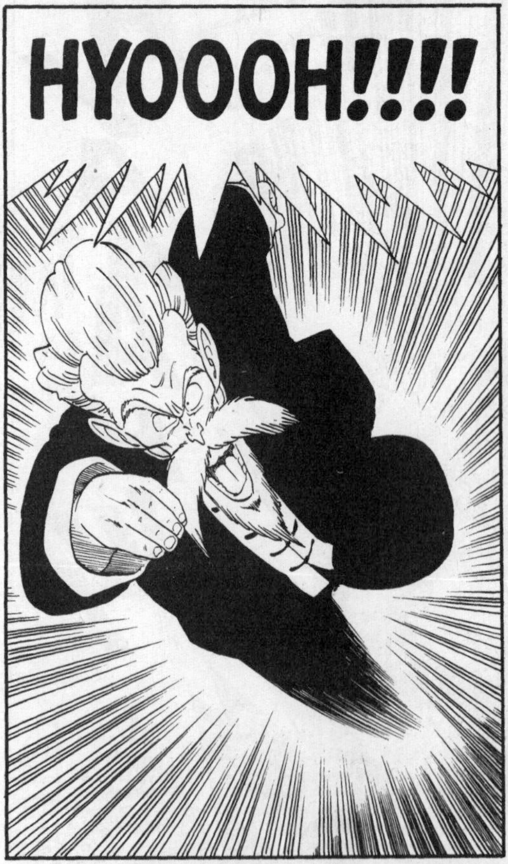
HYOOOH!!!!

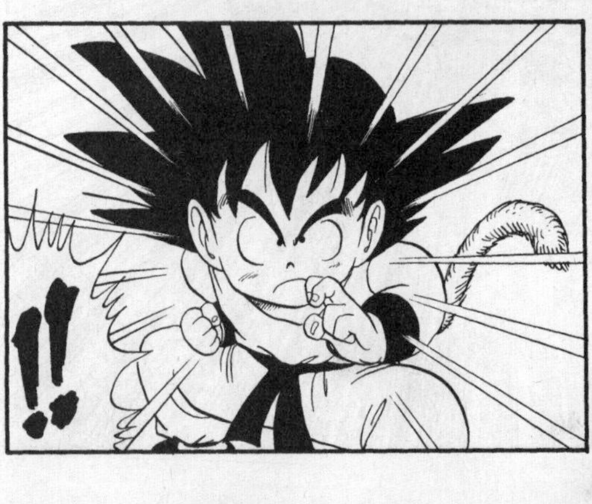
!!

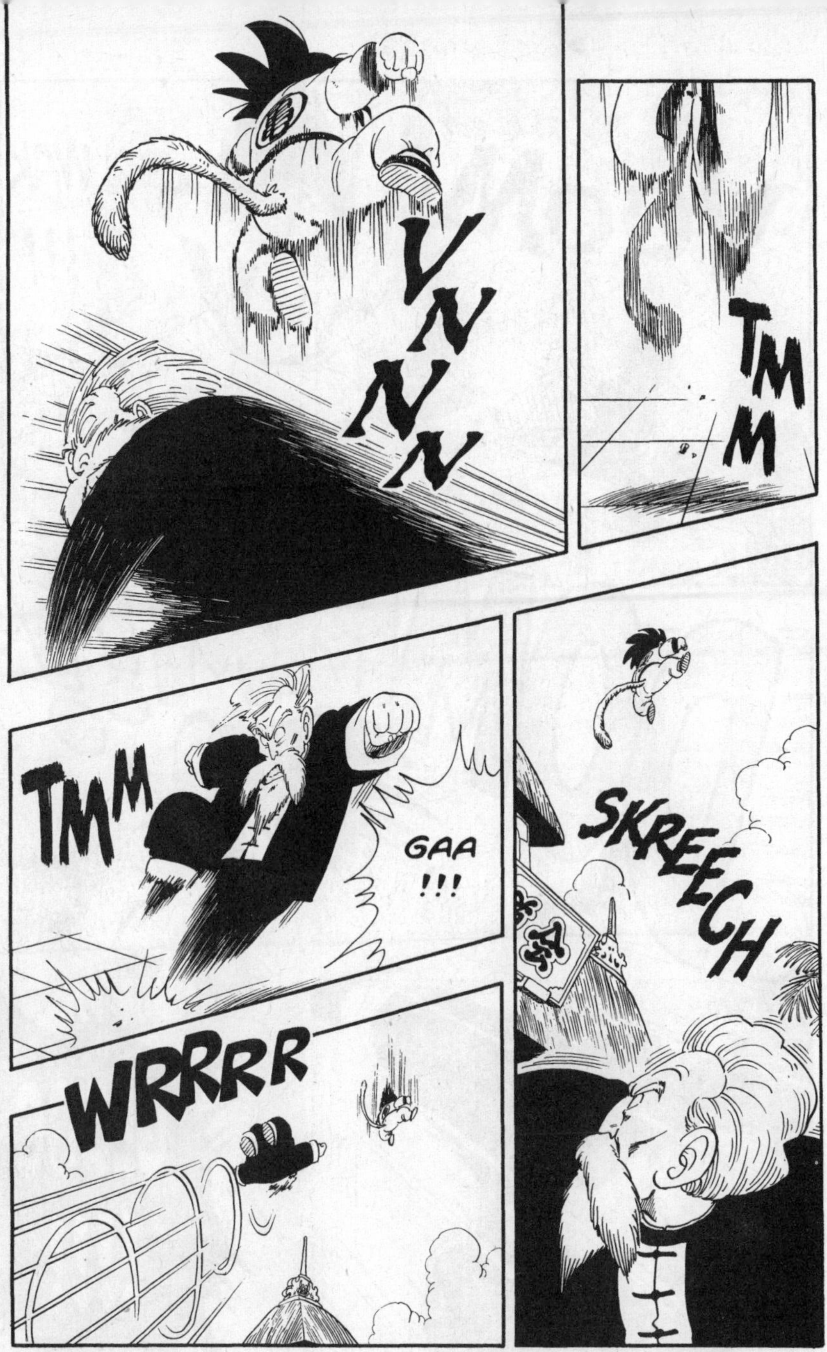
TMM M
VNNN
SKREECH
TMM
GAA !!!
WRRRR

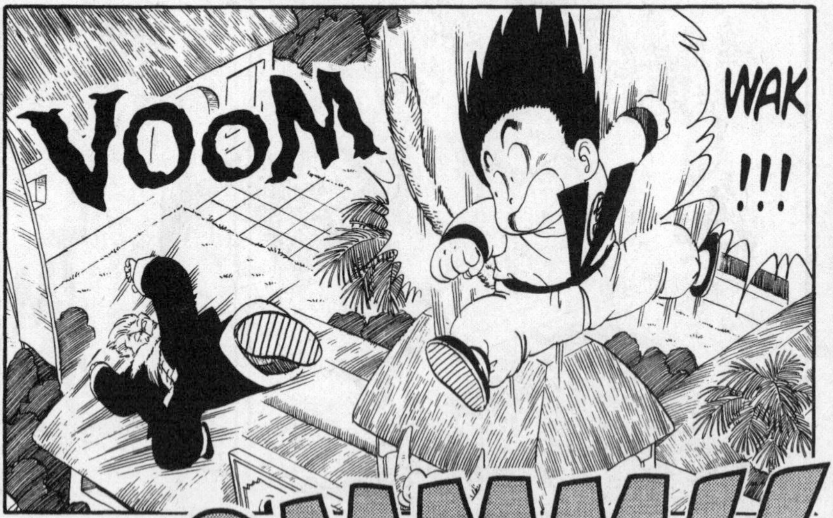
WAK
!!!
VOOM
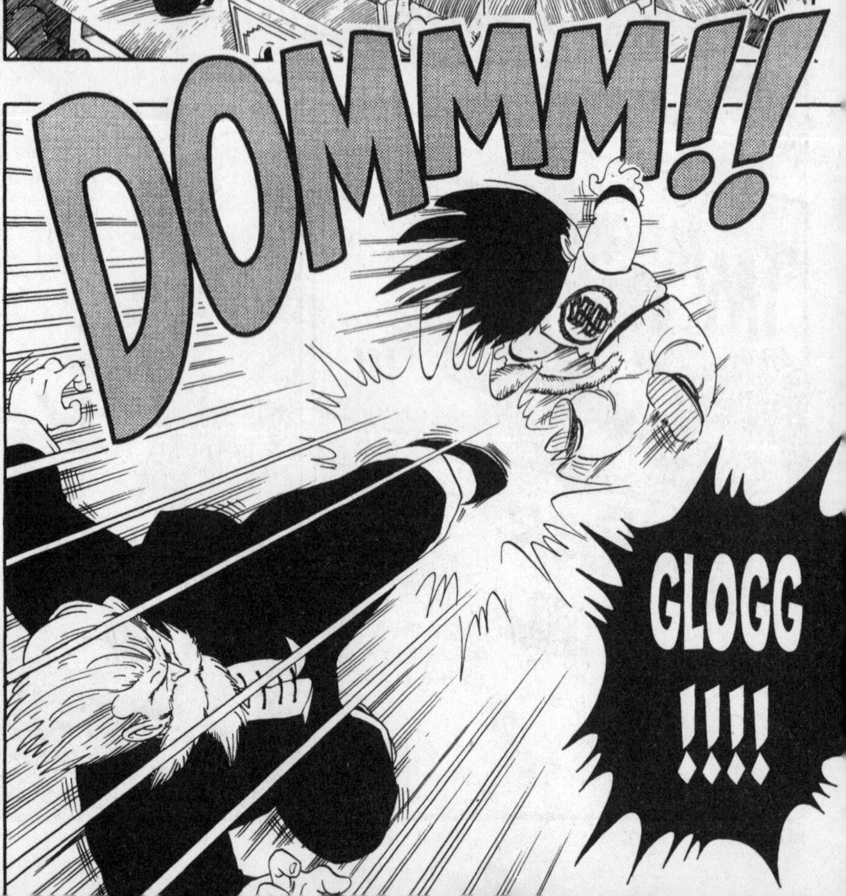
DOMMM!!
GLOGG
!!!!

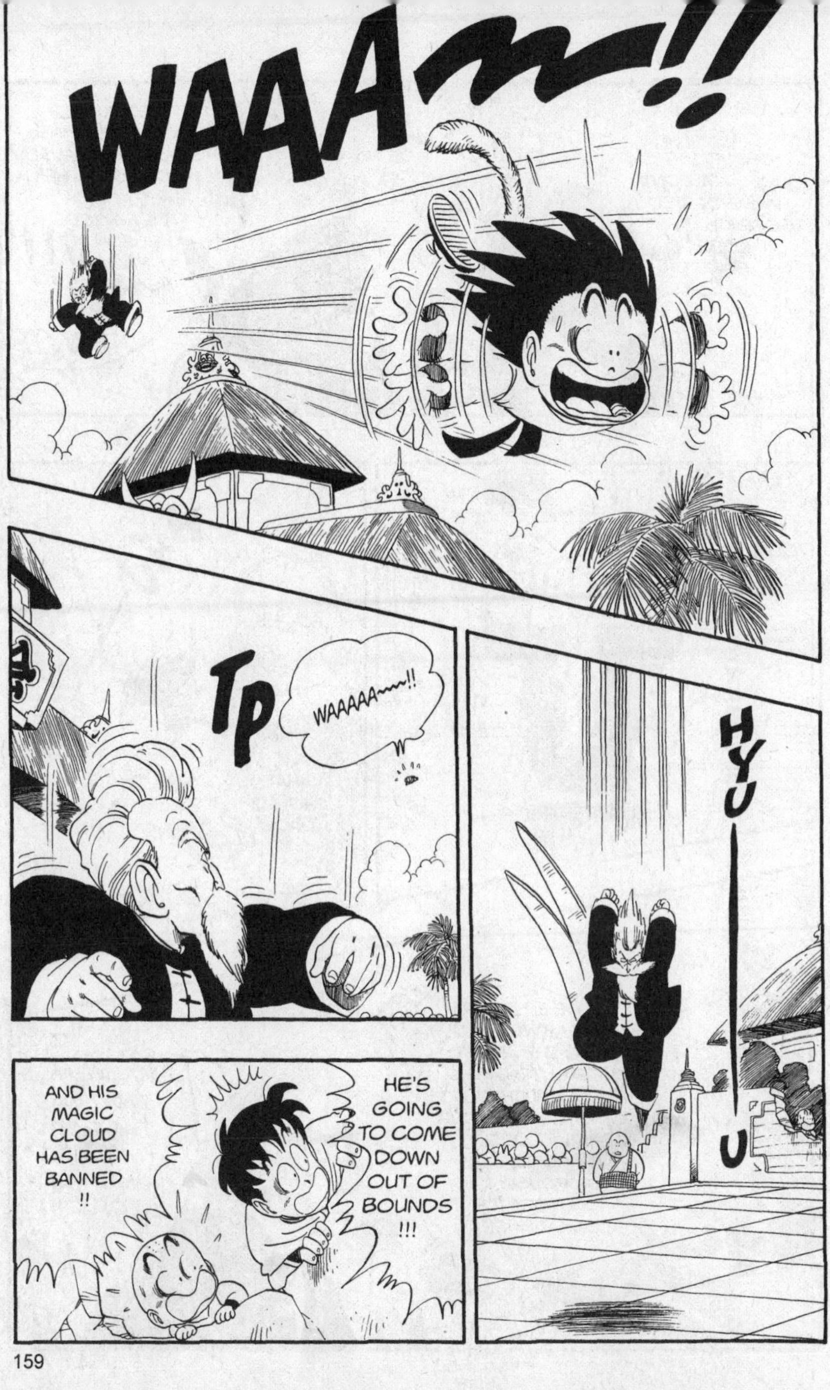
WAAAn~!!
HYU—U
Tp
WAAAAA~~!!
HE'S GOING TO COME DOWN OUT OF BOUNDS !!!
AND HIS MAGIC CLOUD HAS BEEN BANNED !!

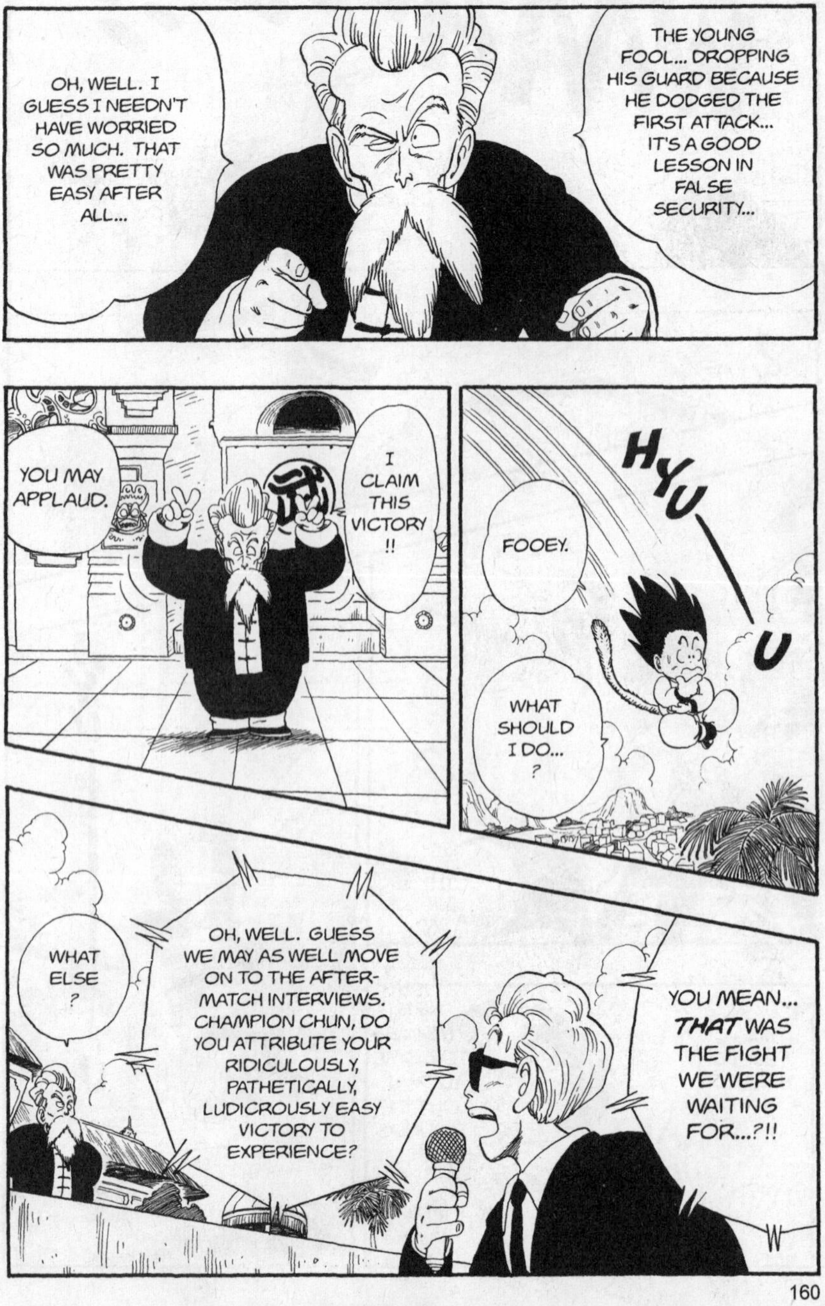
THE YOUNG FOOL... DROPPING HIS GUARD BECAUSE HE DODGED THE FIRST ATTACK... IT'S A GOOD LESSON IN FALSE SECURITY...
OH, WELL. I GUESS I NEEDN'T HAVE WORRIED SO MUCH. THAT WAS PRETTY EASY AFTER ALL...
HYU—U
FOOEY.
WHAT SHOULD I DO...?
I CLAIM THIS VICTORY!!
YOU MAY APPLAUD.
YOU MEAN... *THAT* WAS THE FIGHT WE WERE WAITING FOR...?!!
OH, WELL. GUESS WE MAY AS WELL MOVE ON TO THE AFTER-MATCH INTERVIEWS. CHAMPION CHUN, DO YOU ATTRIBUTE YOUR RIDICULOUSLY, PATHETICALLY, LUDICROUSLY EASY VICTORY TO EXPERIENCE?
WHAT ELSE?

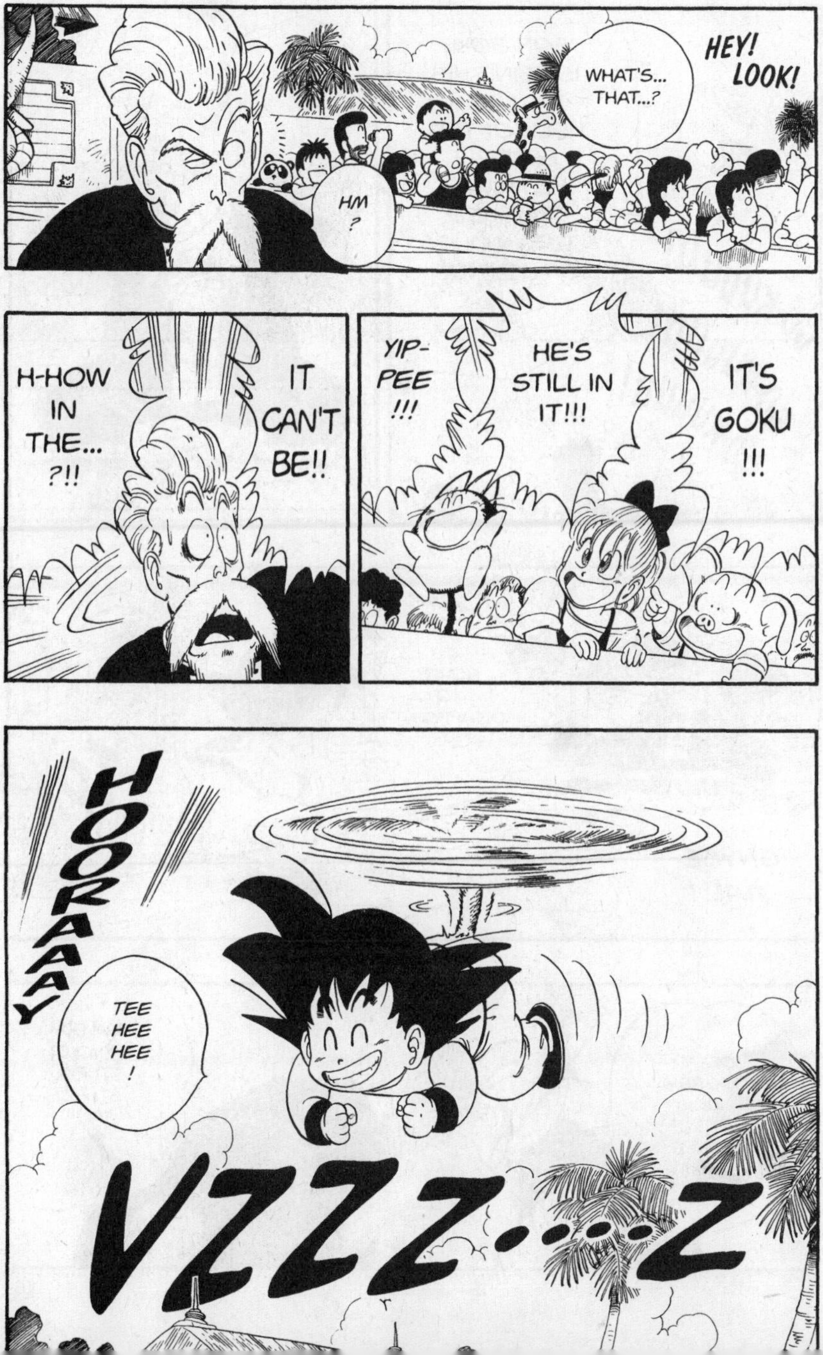
HEY! LOOK!
WHAT'S... THAT...?
HM?
IT'S GOKU!!!
HE'S STILL IN IT!!!
YIP-PEE!!!
IT CAN'T BE!!
H-HOW IN THE...?!!
HOORAAAY
TEE HEE HEE!
VZZZ...Z

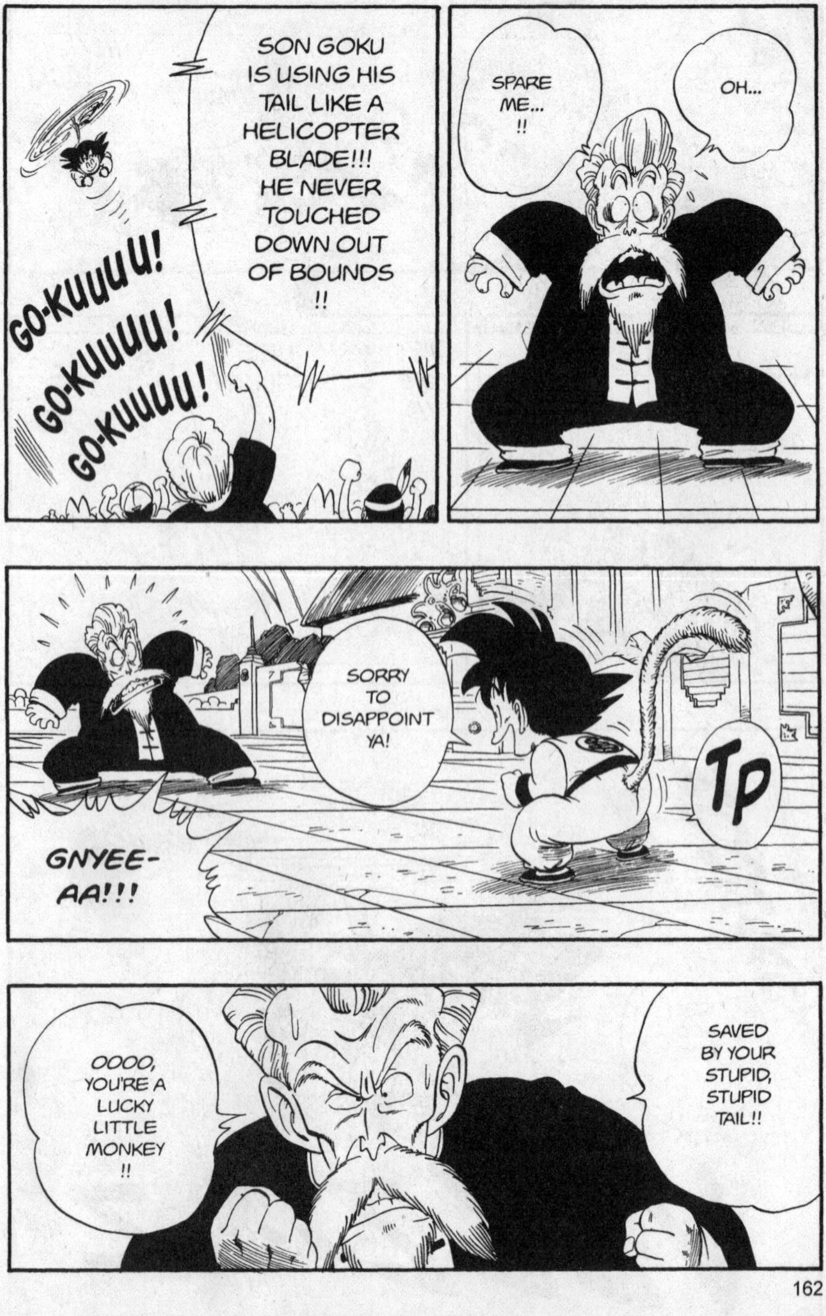
OH...
SPARE ME... !!
SON GOKU IS USING HIS TAIL LIKE A HELICOPTER BLADE!!! HE NEVER TOUCHED DOWN OUT OF BOUNDS !!
GO-KUUUU!
GO-KUUUU!
GO-KUUUU!
TP
SORRY TO DISAPPOINT YA!
GNYEE-AA!!!
SAVED BY YOUR STUPID, STUPID TAIL!!
OOOO, YOU'RE A LUCKY LITTLE MONKEY !!

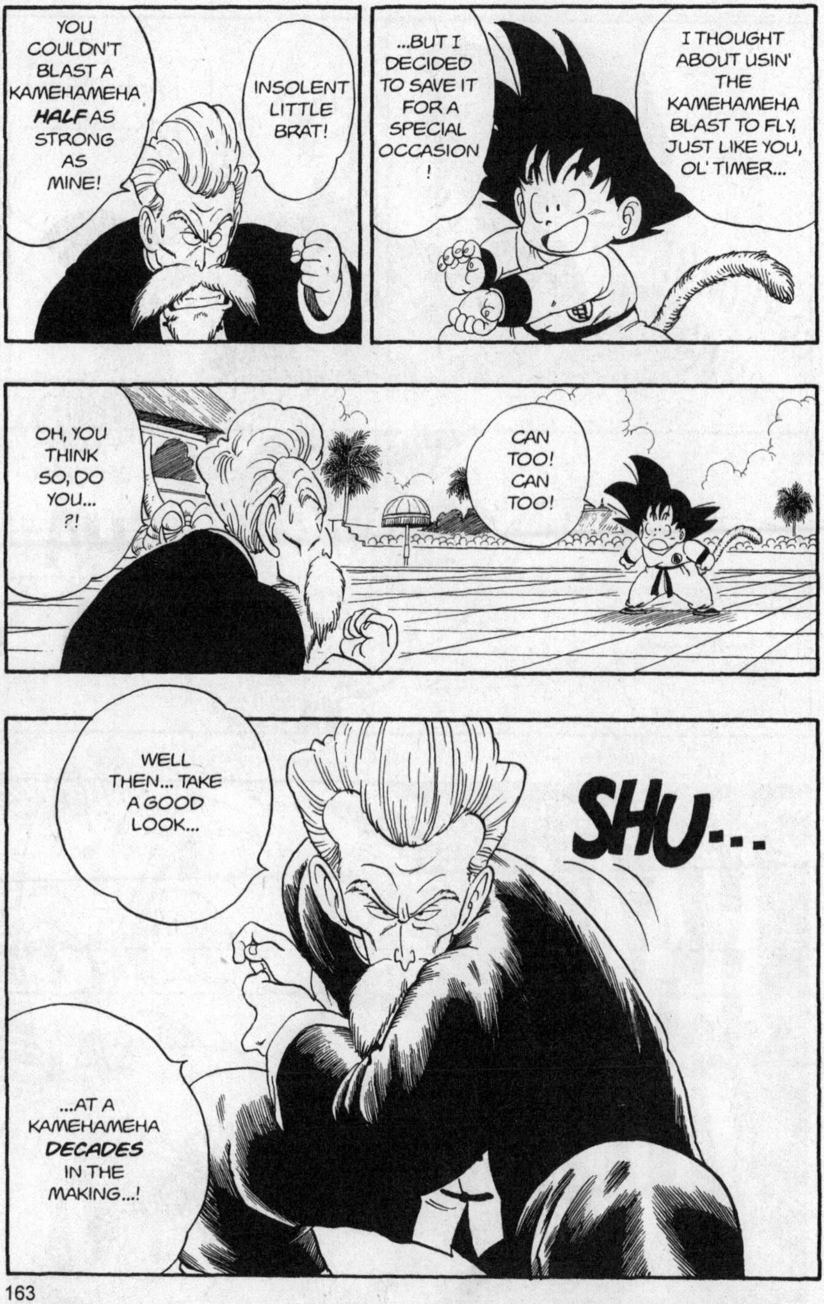
I THOUGHT ABOUT USIN' THE KAMEHAMEHA BLAST TO FLY, JUST LIKE YOU, OL' TIMER...
...BUT I DECIDED TO SAVE IT FOR A SPECIAL OCCASION!
INSOLENT LITTLE BRAT!
YOU COULDN'T BLAST A KAMEHAMEHA **HALF** AS STRONG AS MINE!
CAN TOO! CAN TOO!
OH, YOU THINK SO, DO YOU...?!
SHU...
WELL THEN... TAKE A GOOD LOOK...
...AT A KAMEHAMEHA **DECADES** IN THE MAKING...!

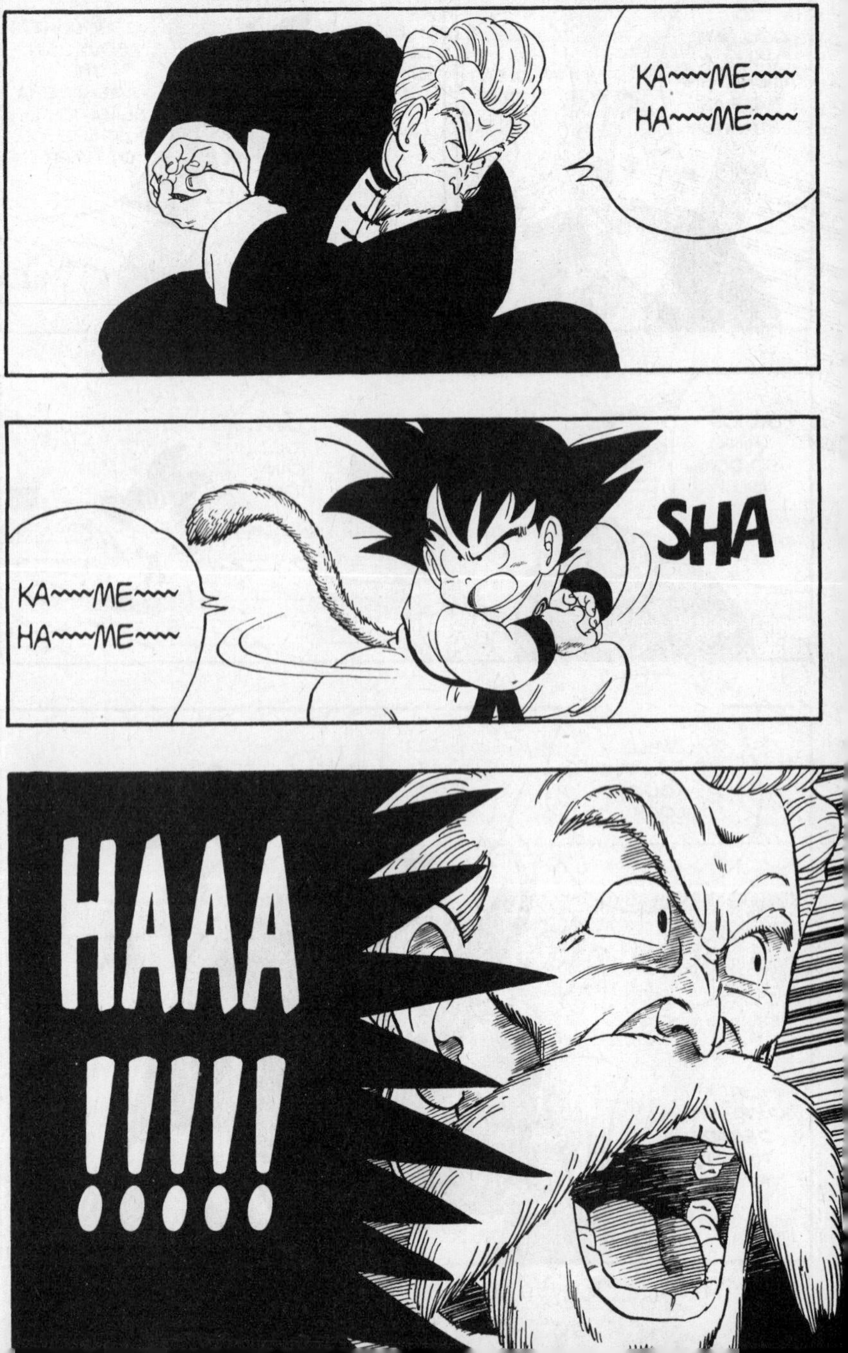
KA~~~ME~~~
HA~~~ME~~~
SHA
KA~~~ME~~~
HA~~~ME~~~
HAAA
!!!!!

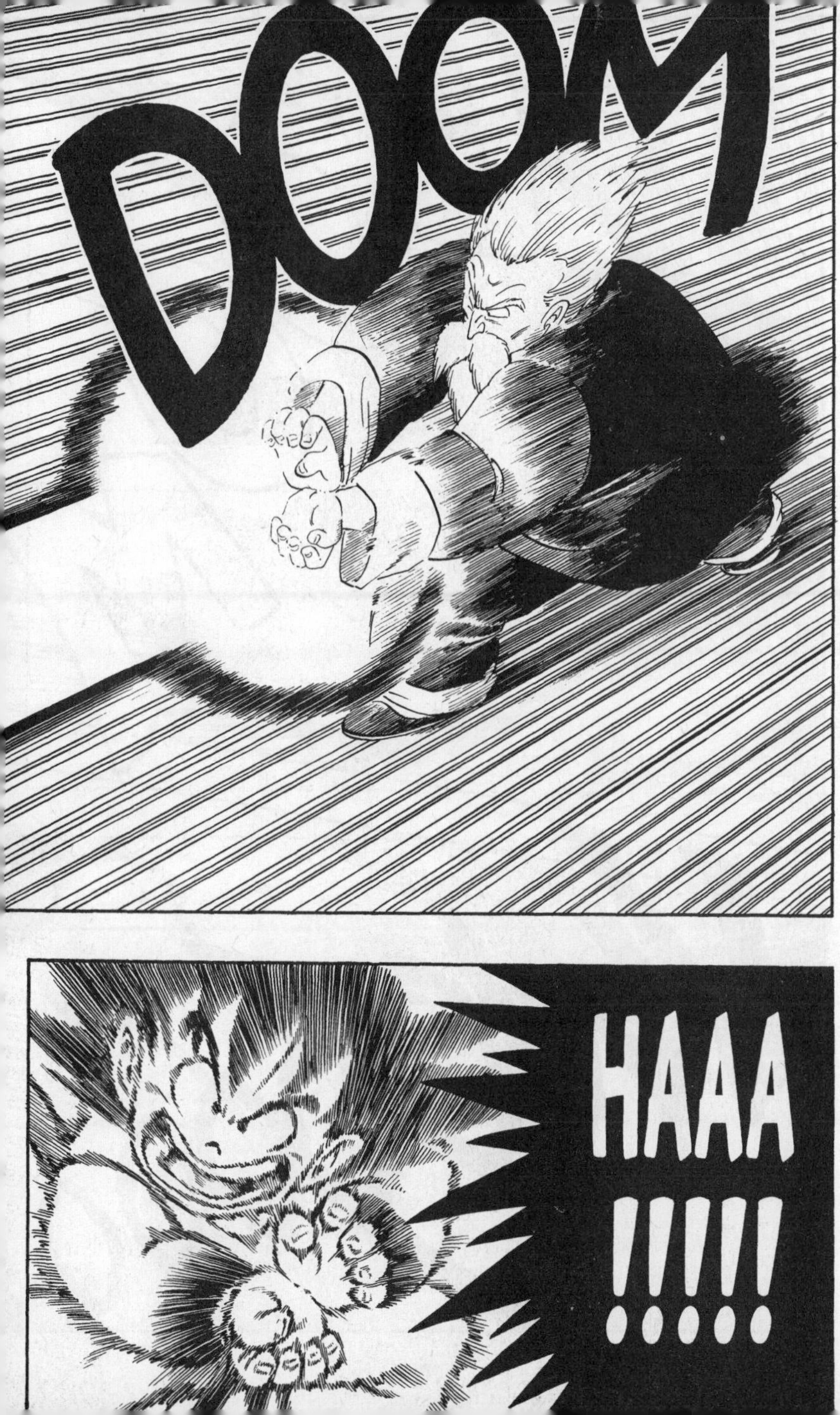
DOOM
HAAA!!!!!

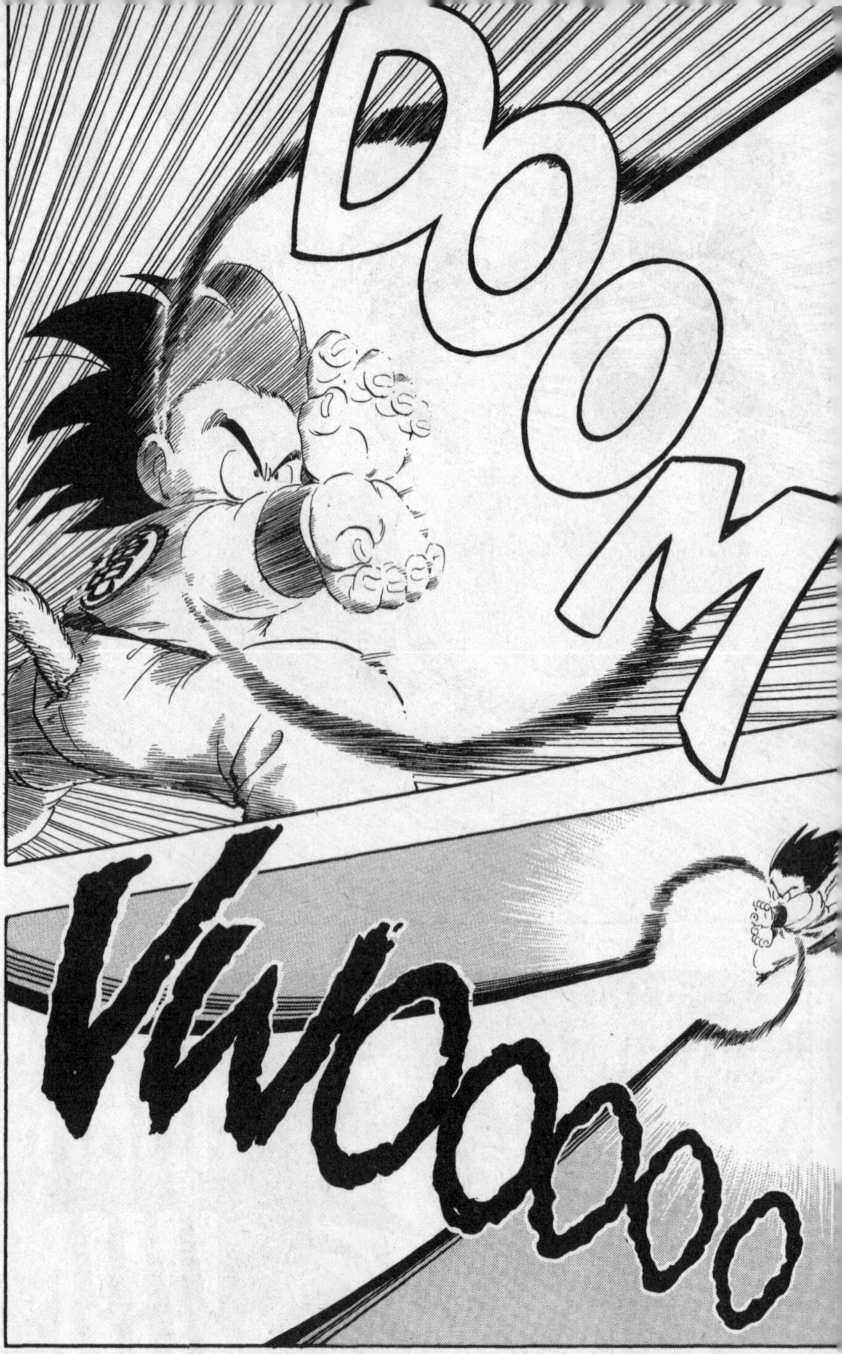
DOOOM
VWOOOOOO

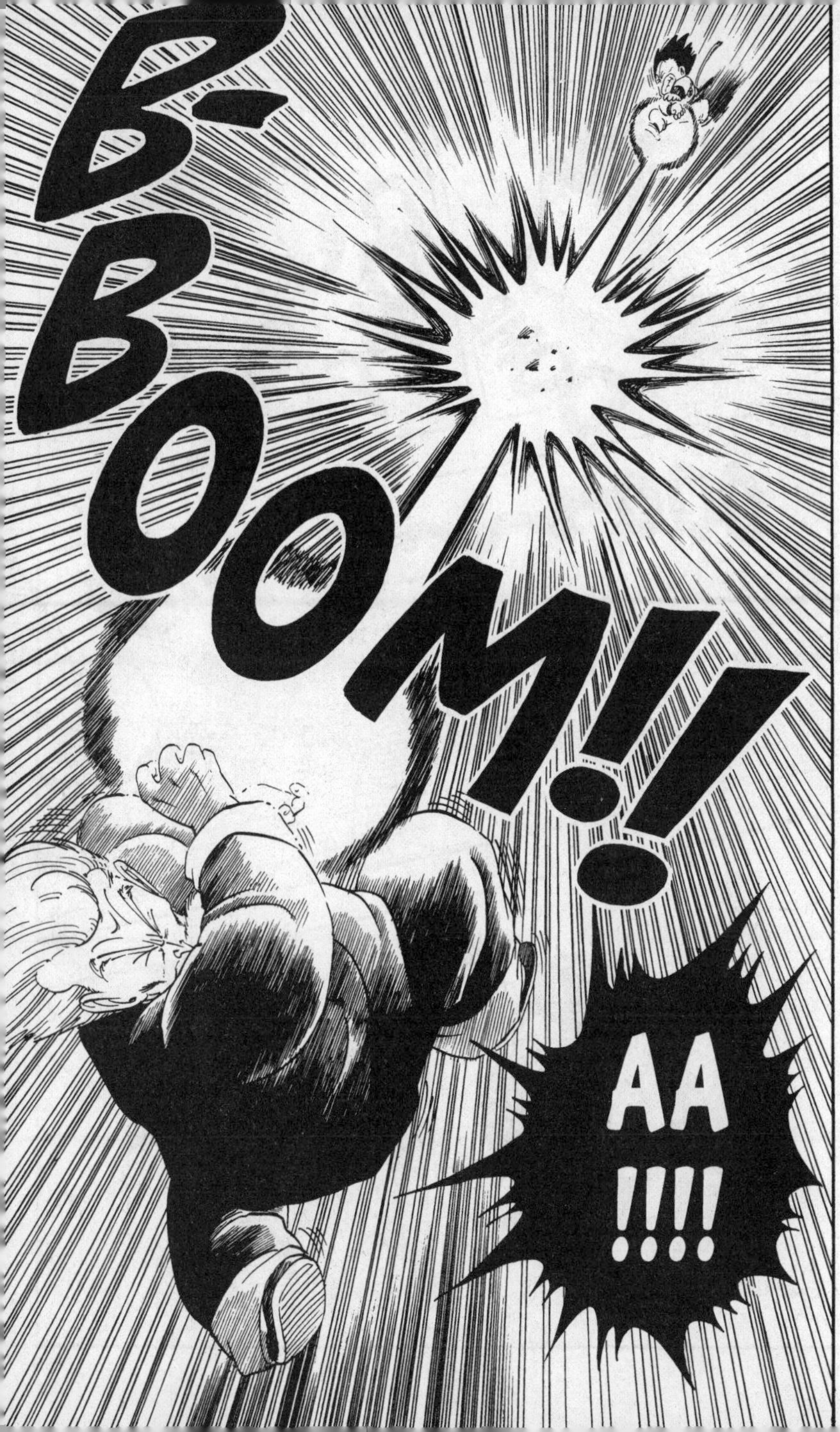
B-BOOM!!
AA
!!!!

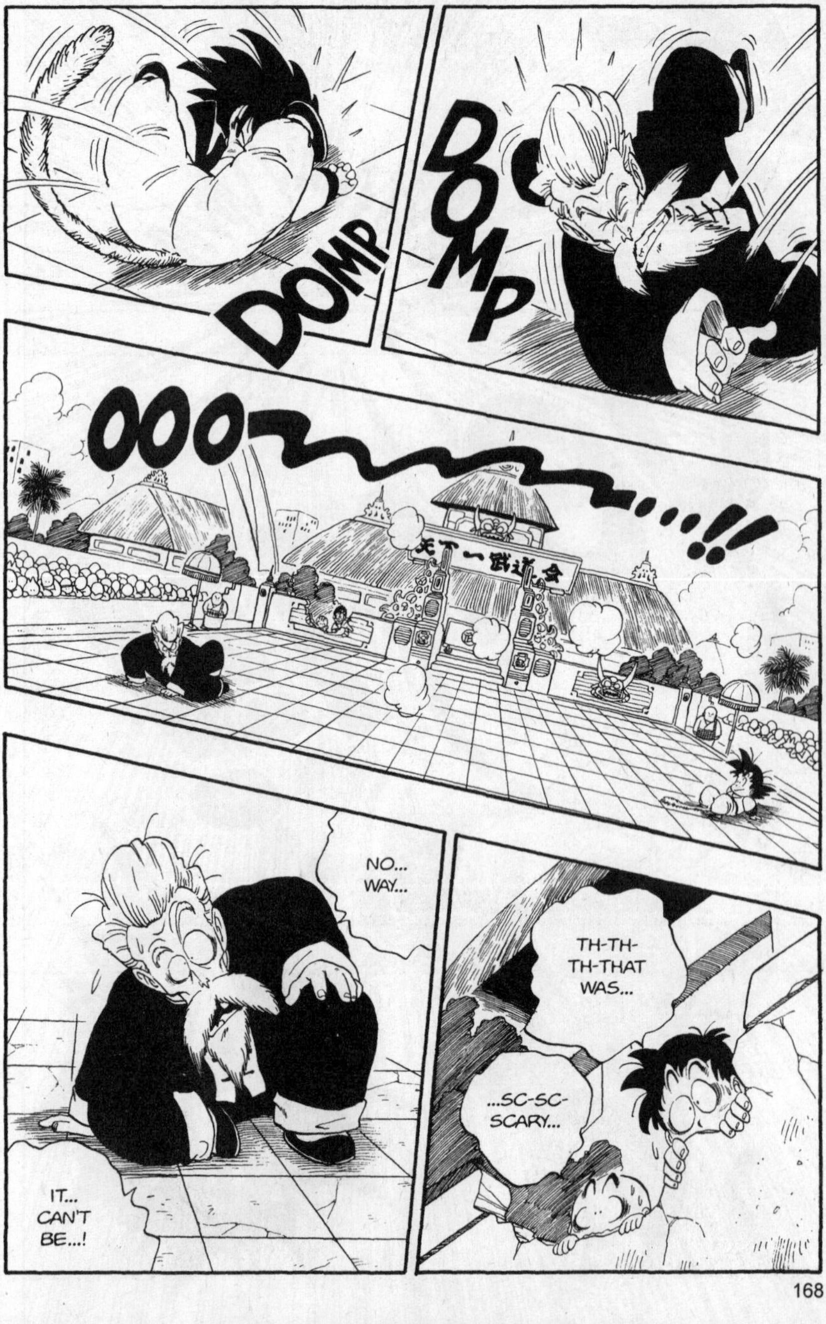
DOMP
DOMP
OOO~~~...!!!
天下一武道会
TH-TH-TH-THAT WAS...
...SC-SC-SCARY...
NO... WAY...
IT... CAN'T BE...!

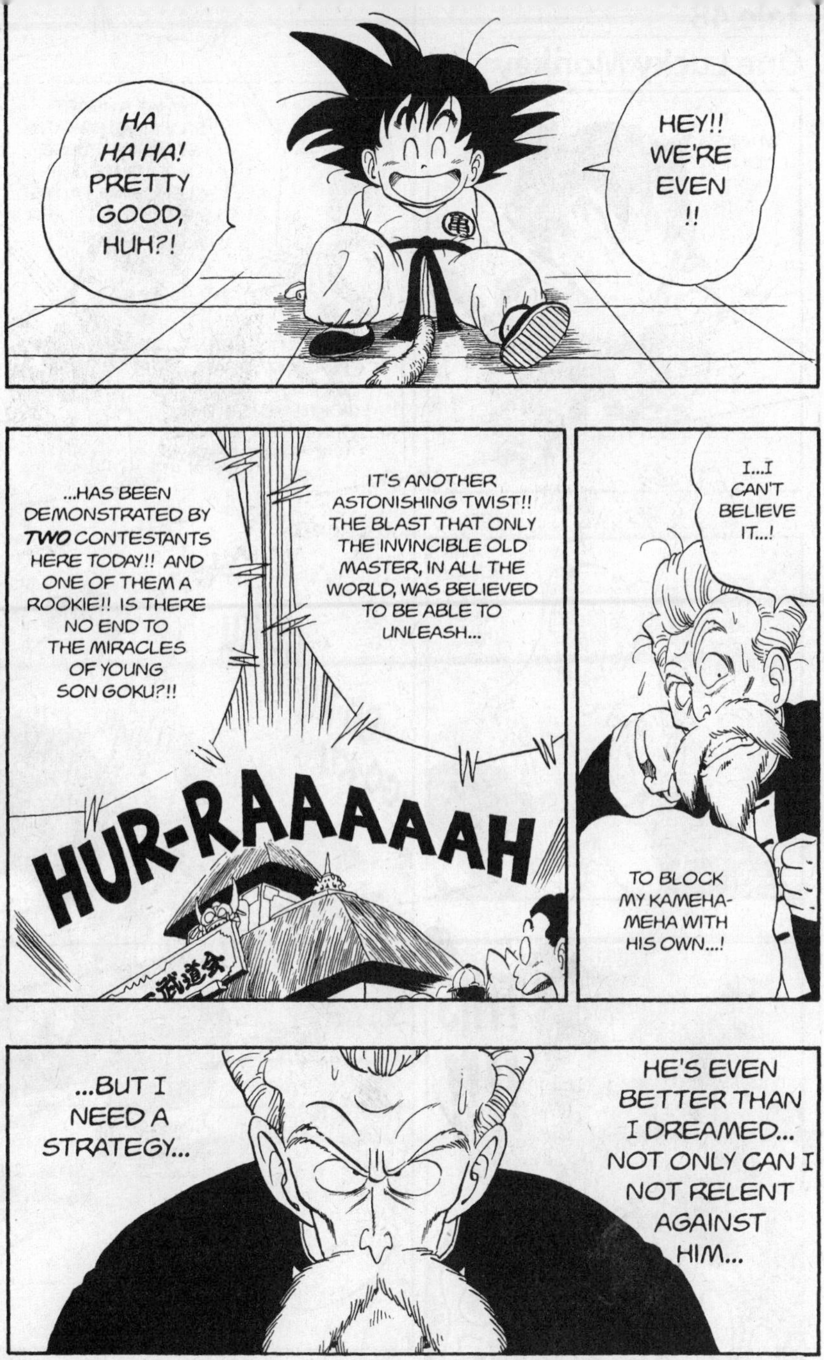

HEY!! WE'RE EVEN !!
HA HA HA! PRETTY GOOD, HUH?!
I...I CAN'T BELIEVE IT...!
TO BLOCK MY KAMEHA-MEHA WITH HIS OWN...!
IT'S ANOTHER ASTONISHING TWIST!! THE BLAST THAT ONLY THE INVINCIBLE OLD MASTER, IN ALL THE WORLD, WAS BELIEVED TO BE ABLE TO UNLEASH...
...HAS BEEN DEMONSTRATED BY **TWO** CONTESTANTS HERE TODAY!! AND ONE OF THEM A ROOKIE!! IS THERE NO END TO THE MIRACLES OF YOUNG SON GOKU?!!
HUR-RAAAAAH
武道会
HE'S EVEN BETTER THAN I DREAMED... NOT ONLY CAN I NOT RELENT AGAINST HIM...
...BUT I NEED A STRATEGY...

Tale 48
One Lucky Monkey

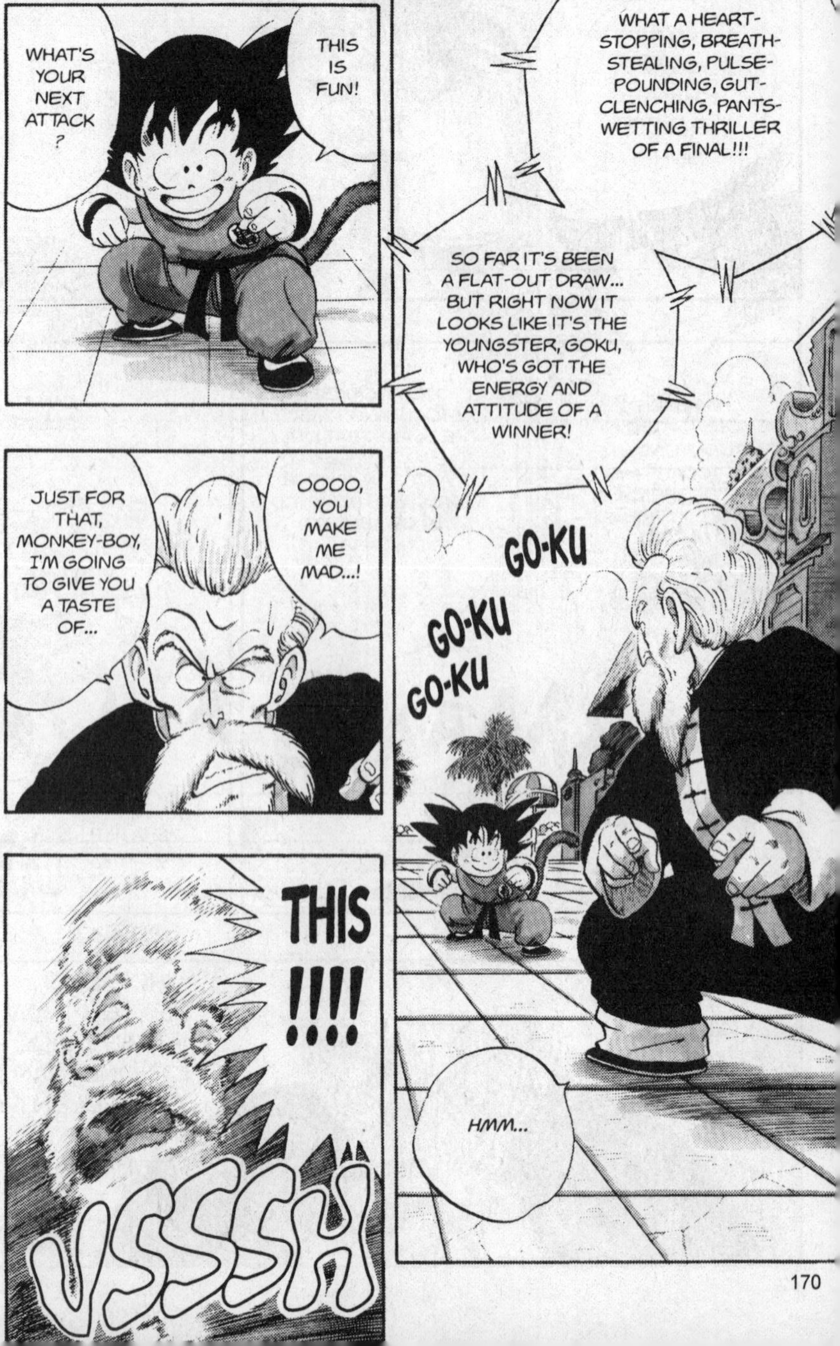
WHAT A HEART-STOPPING, BREATH-STEALING, PULSE-POUNDING, GUT-CLENCHING, PANTS-WETTING THRILLER OF A FINAL!!!
SO FAR IT'S BEEN A FLAT-OUT DRAW... BUT RIGHT NOW IT LOOKS LIKE IT'S THE YOUNGSTER, GOKU, WHO'S GOT THE ENERGY AND ATTITUDE OF A WINNER!
GO-KU
GO-KU
GO-KU
HMM...
THIS IS FUN!
WHAT'S YOUR NEXT ATTACK?
OOOO, YOU MAKE ME MAD...!
JUST FOR THAT, MONKEY-BOY, I'M GOING TO GIVE YOU A TASTE OF...
THIS!!!!
VSSSH

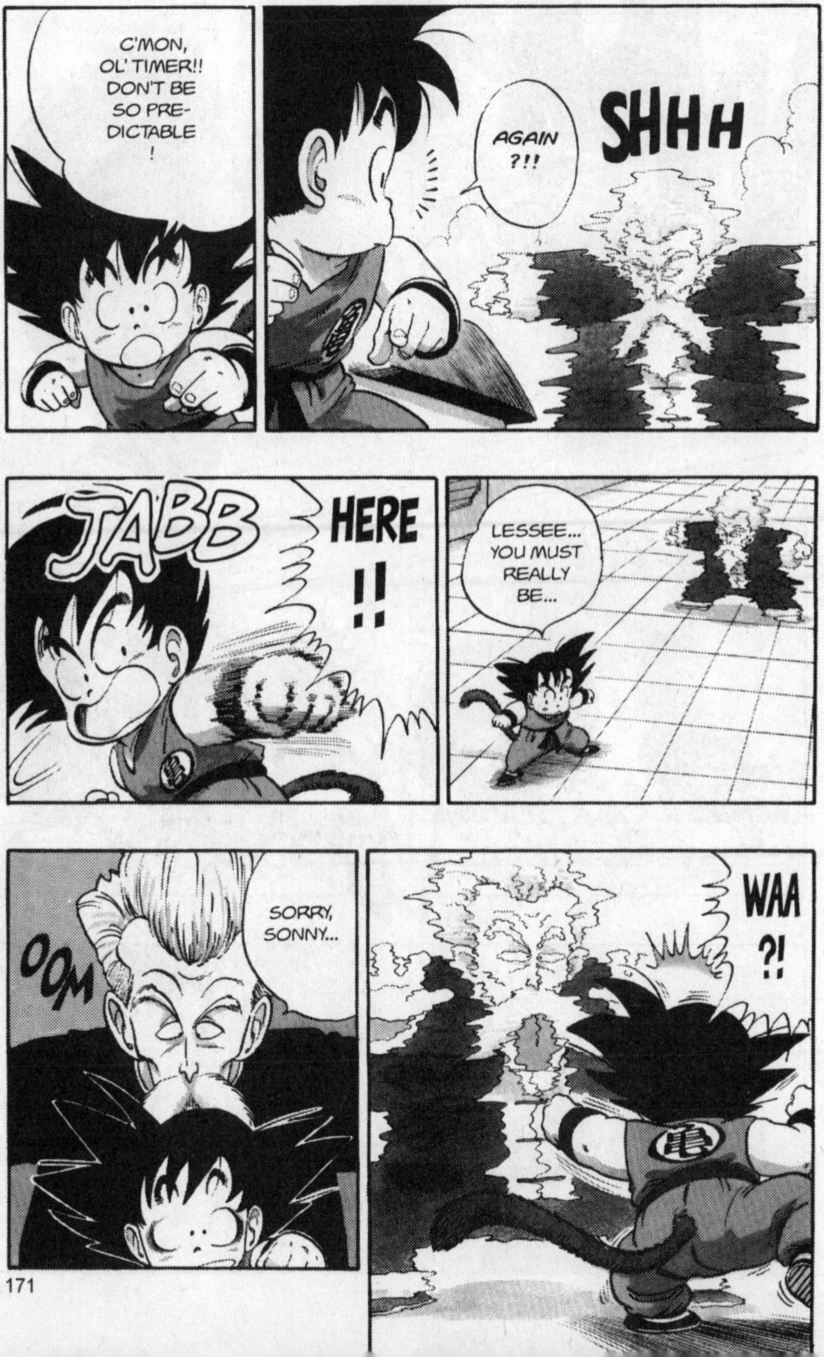
SHHH
AGAIN ?!!
C'MON, OL' TIMER!! DON'T BE SO PRE-DICTABLE !
LESSEE... YOU MUST REALLY BE...
HERE !!
JABB
WAA ?!
SORRY, SONNY...
OOM

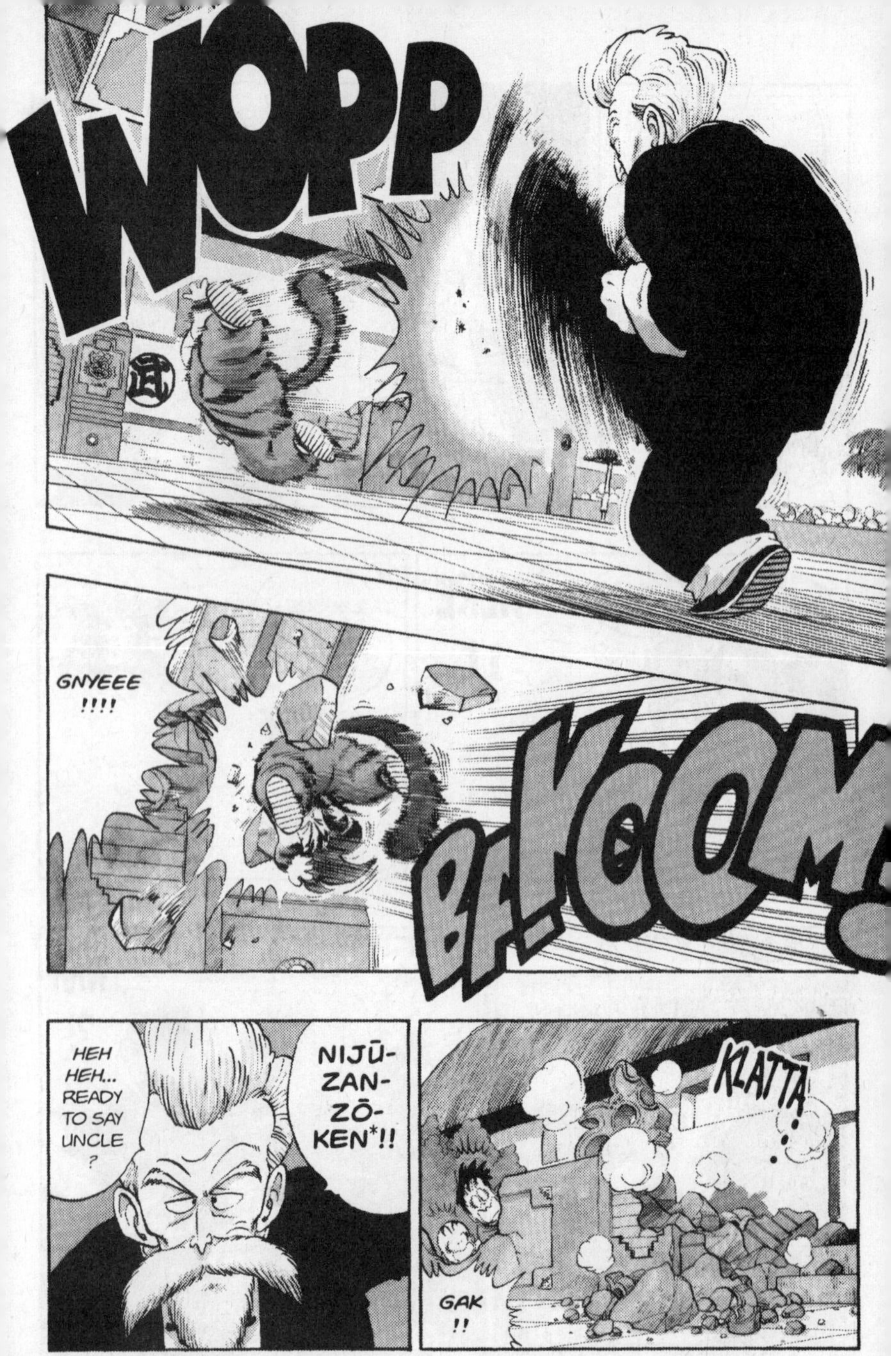
WOPP
GNYEEE !!!!
BA-VOOM
KLATTA
GAK !!
NIJŪ-ZAN-ZŌ-KEN*!!
HEH HEH... READY TO SAY UNCLE ?

* "DOUBLE-SHADOW ATTACK"

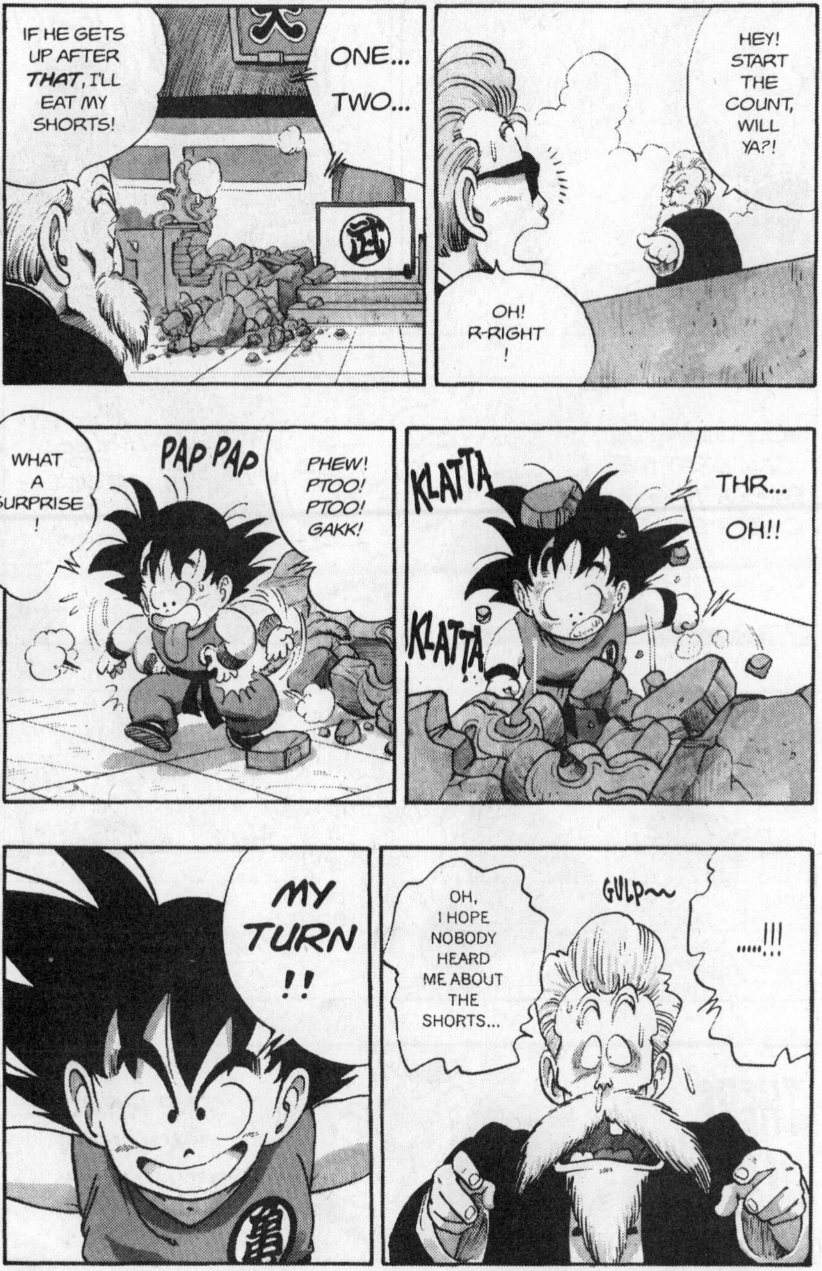
HEY! START THE COUNT, WILL YA?!
OH! R-RIGHT!
ONE... TWO...
IF HE GETS UP AFTER THAT, I'LL EAT MY SHORTS!
THR... OH!!
KLATTA
KLATTA
PHEW! PTOO! PTOO! GAKK!
PAP PAP
WHAT A SURPRISE!
.....!!!
GULP~~
OH, I HOPE NOBODY HEARD ME ABOUT THE SHORTS...
MY TURN!!

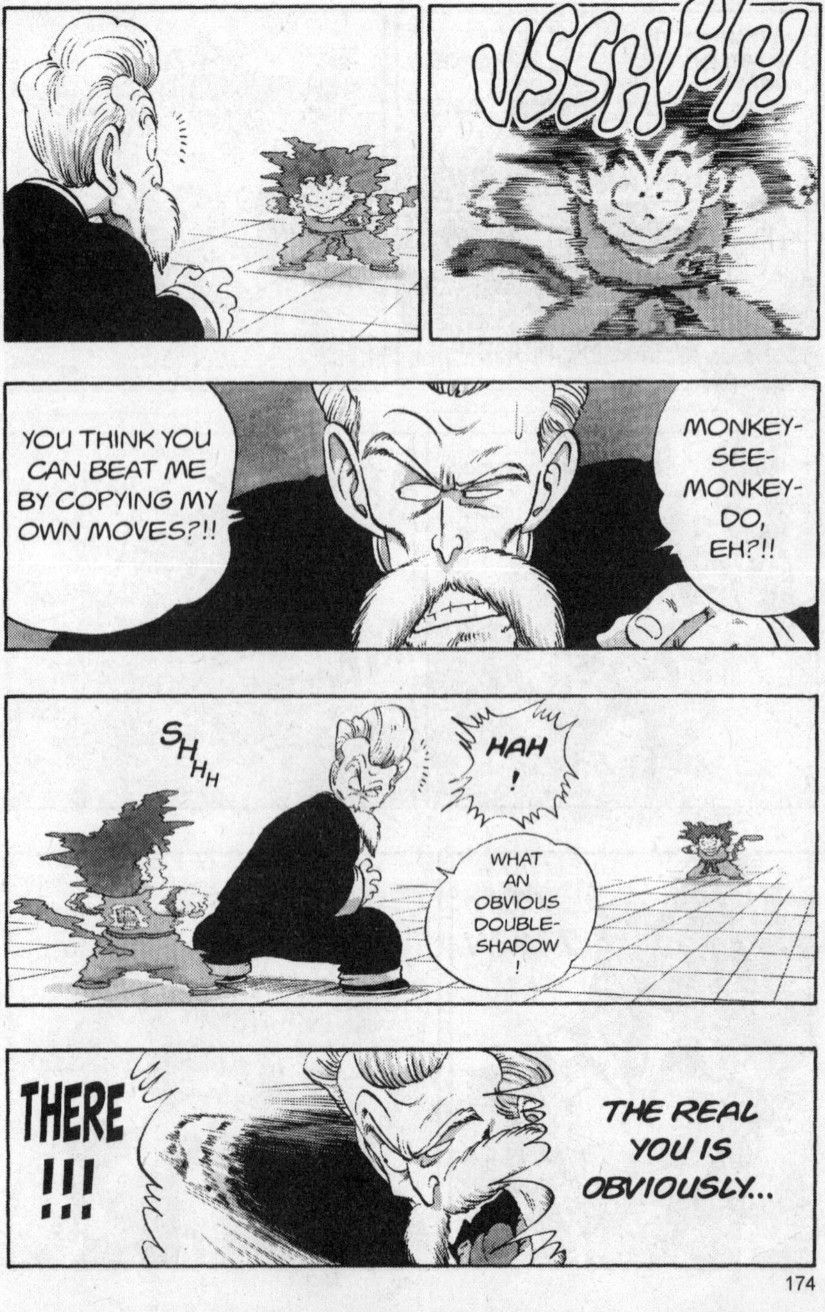

VSSHHHH
MONKEY-SEE-MONKEY-DO, EH?!!
YOU THINK YOU CAN BEAT ME BY COPYING MY OWN MOVES?!!
HAH!
SHHH
WHAT AN OBVIOUS DOUBLE-SHADOW!
THE REAL YOU IS OBVIOUSLY...
THERE!!!

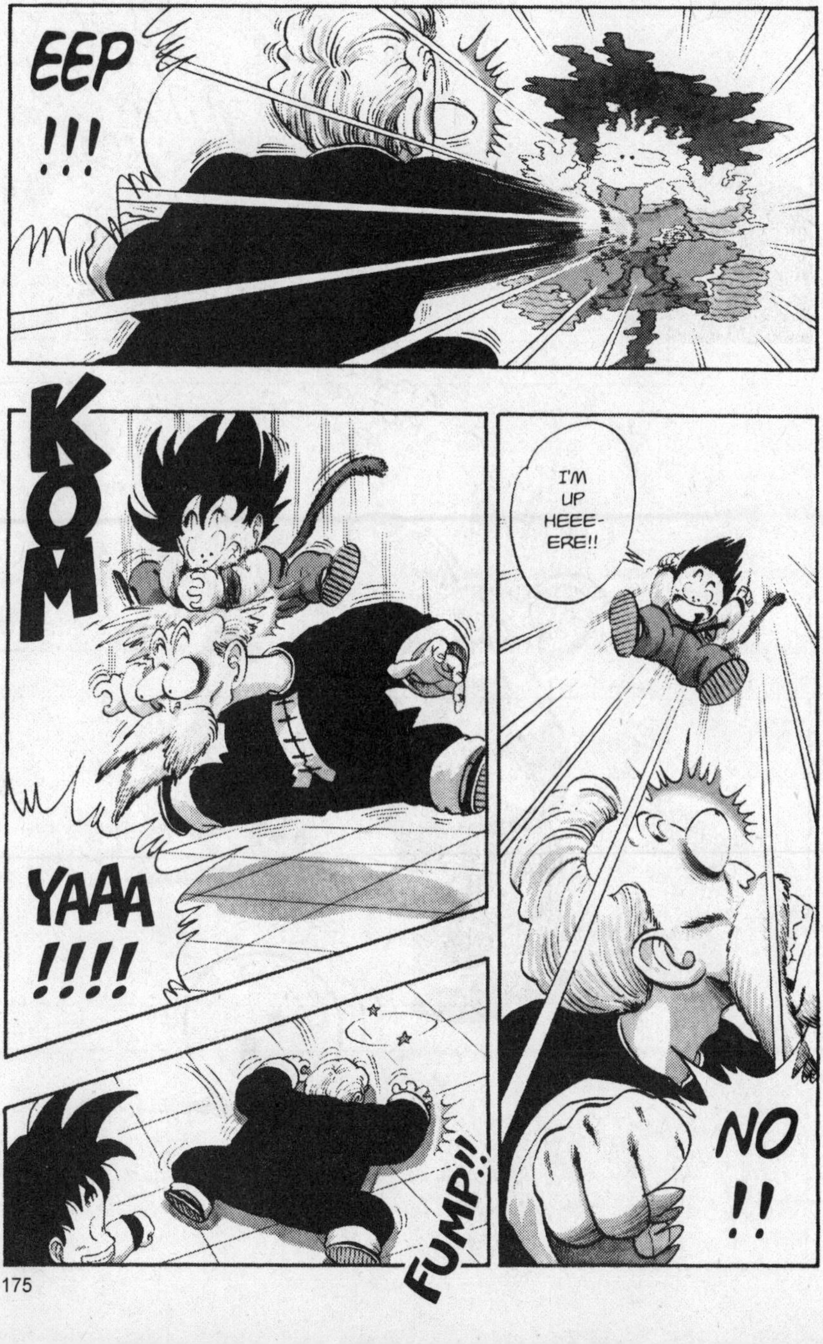
EEP!!!
I'M UP HEEEE-ERE!!
NO!!
KOM
YAAA!!!!
FUMP!!

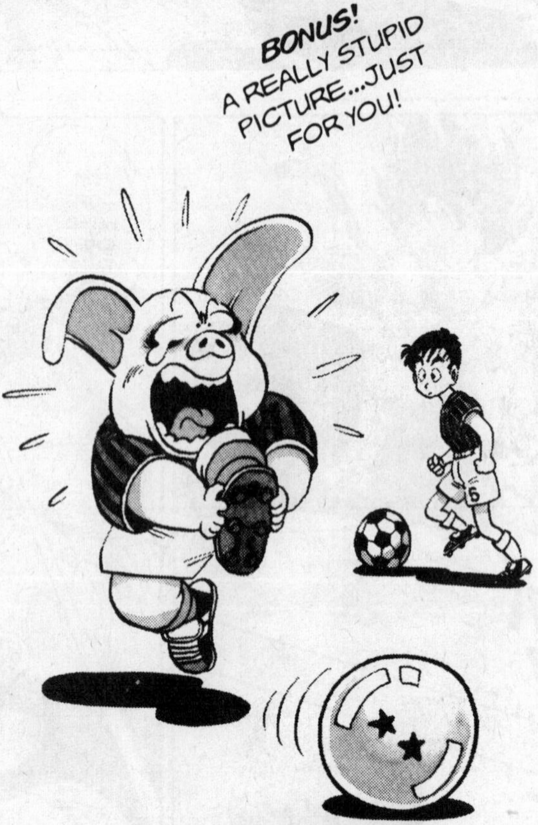
BONUS!
A REALLY STUPID PICTURE...JUST FOR YOU!
6

HOW'D YOU LIKE MY *TRIPLE SHADOW*?!!

CLOBBERIN' YOUR OWN MASTER'S HEAD...

LITTLE INGRATE...

WELL? HUH? DID YOU LIKE IT?

OWWWW!!

A-HA... A-HA-HAHA!

Y-YOU MUST'VE HIT ME HARDER'N I THOUGHT...

OOP!

GULP

MY MASTER'S THE TURTLE GUY!

HUH? HOW COME YOU'RE CALLIN' YOURSELF MY MASTER?

YOU'VE GOT A GREAT MASTER, BOY...

BUT ENOUGH WACKY MISUNDERSTANDINGS!!

177

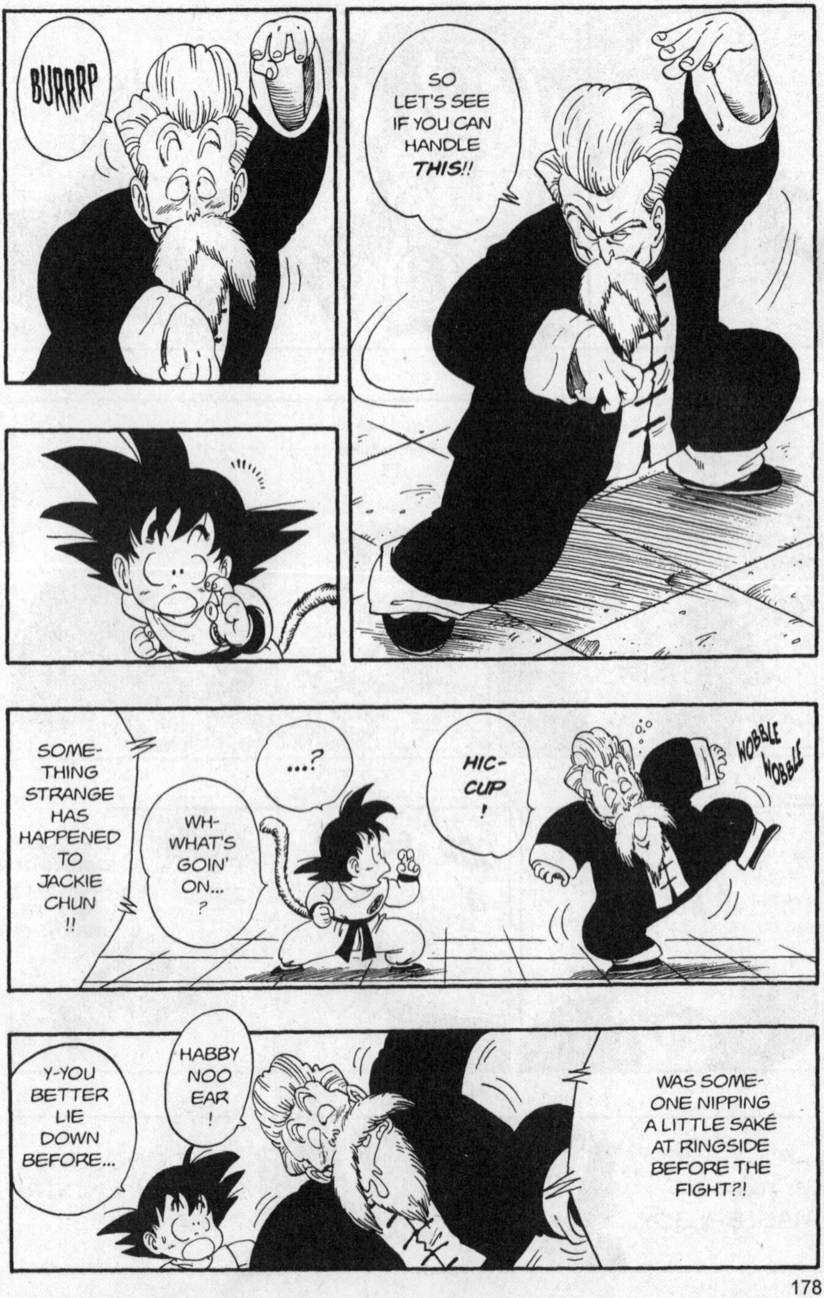
SO LET'S SEE IF YOU CAN HANDLE ***THIS!!***
BURRRP
WOBBLE WOBBLE
HIC-CUP!
...?
WH-WHAT'S GOIN' ON...?
SOME-THING STRANGE HAS HAPPENED TO JACKIE CHUN!!
WAS SOME-ONE NIPPING A LITTLE SAKÉ AT RINGSIDE BEFORE THE FIGHT?!
HABBY NOO EAR!
Y-YOU BETTER LIE DOWN BEFORE...

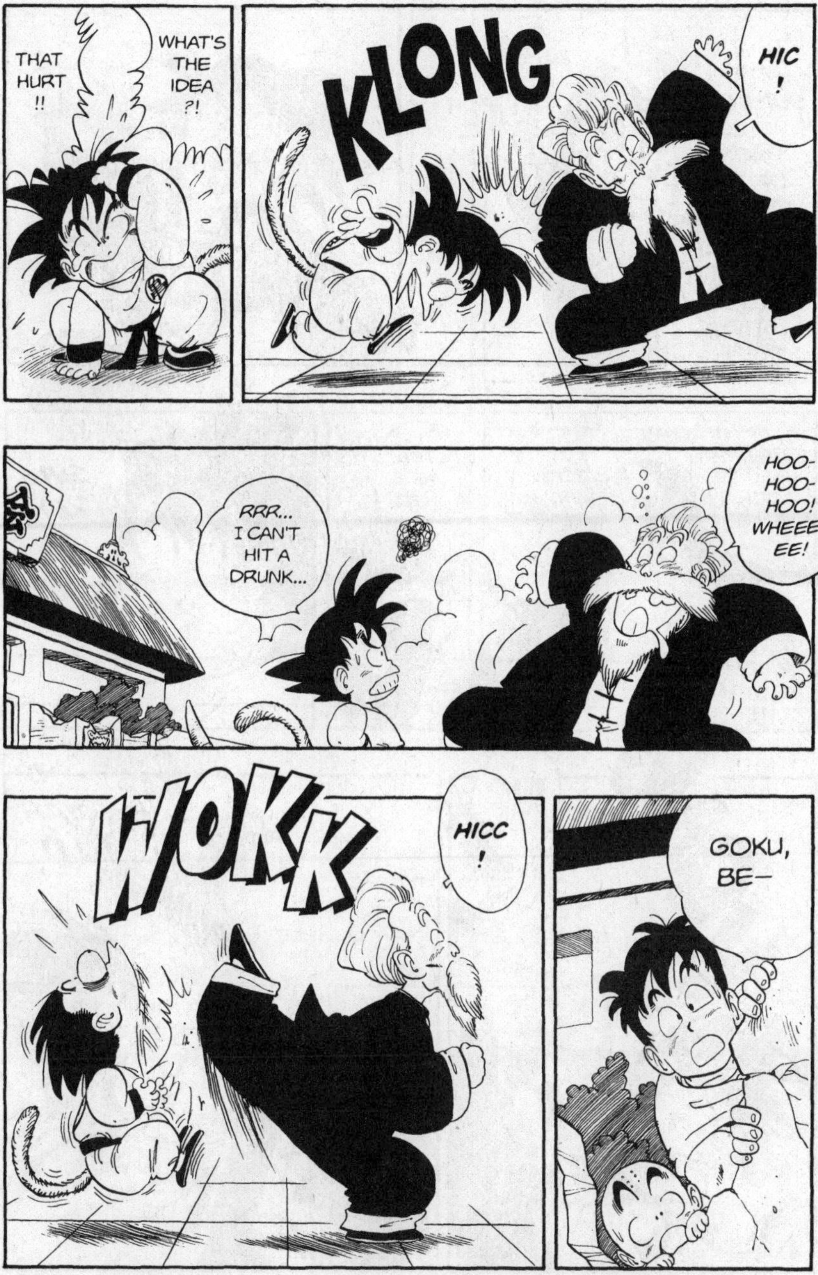
HIC!
KLONG
WHAT'S THE IDEA ?!
THAT HURT !!
HOO-HOO-HOO! WHEEEEE!
RRR... I CAN'T HIT A DRUNK...
GOKU, BE—
HICC!
WOKK

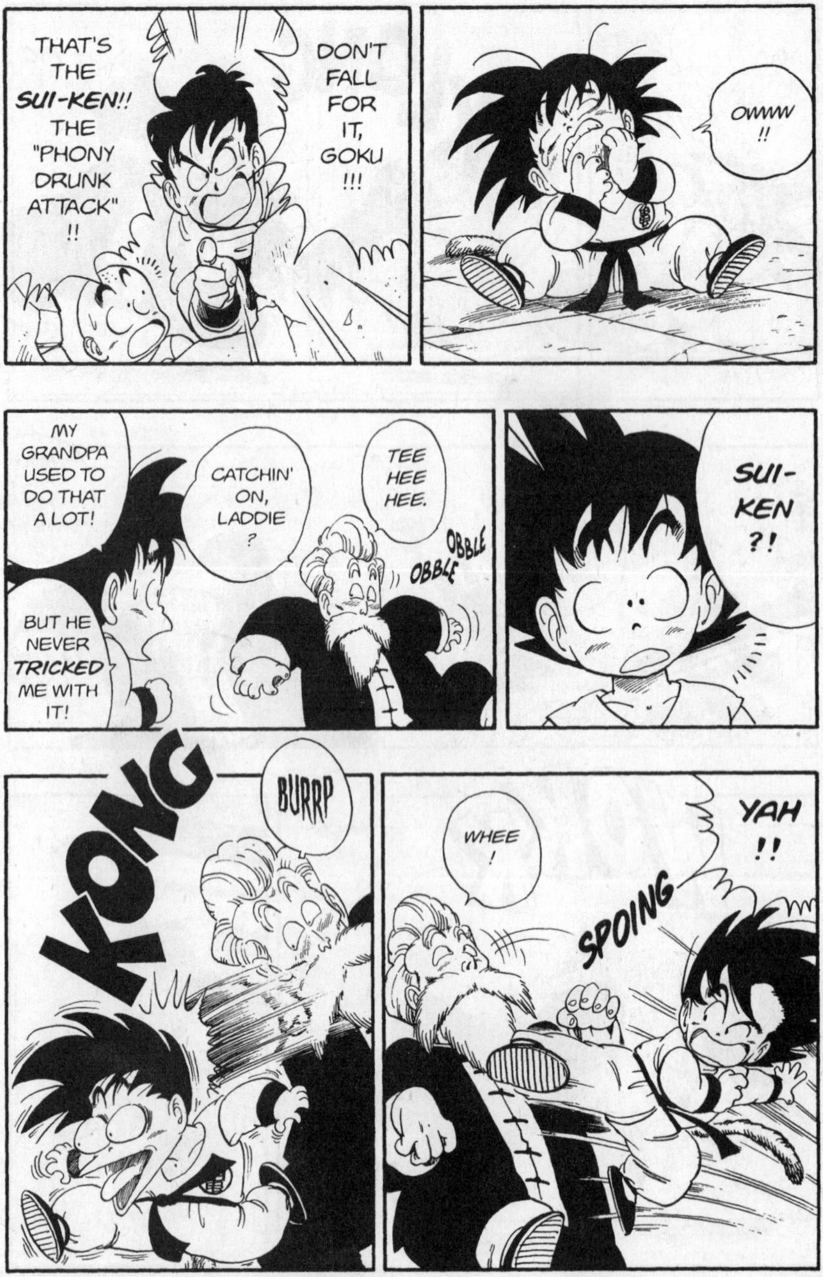
OWWW !!
DON'T FALL FOR IT, GOKU !!!
THAT'S THE SUI-KEN!! THE "PHONY DRUNK ATTACK" !!
SUI-KEN ?!
TEE HEE HEE.
OBBLE OBBLE
CATCHIN' ON, LADDIE ?
MY GRANDPA USED TO DO THAT A LOT!
BUT HE NEVER TRICKED ME WITH IT!
YAH !!
WHEE !
SPOING
BURRP
KONG

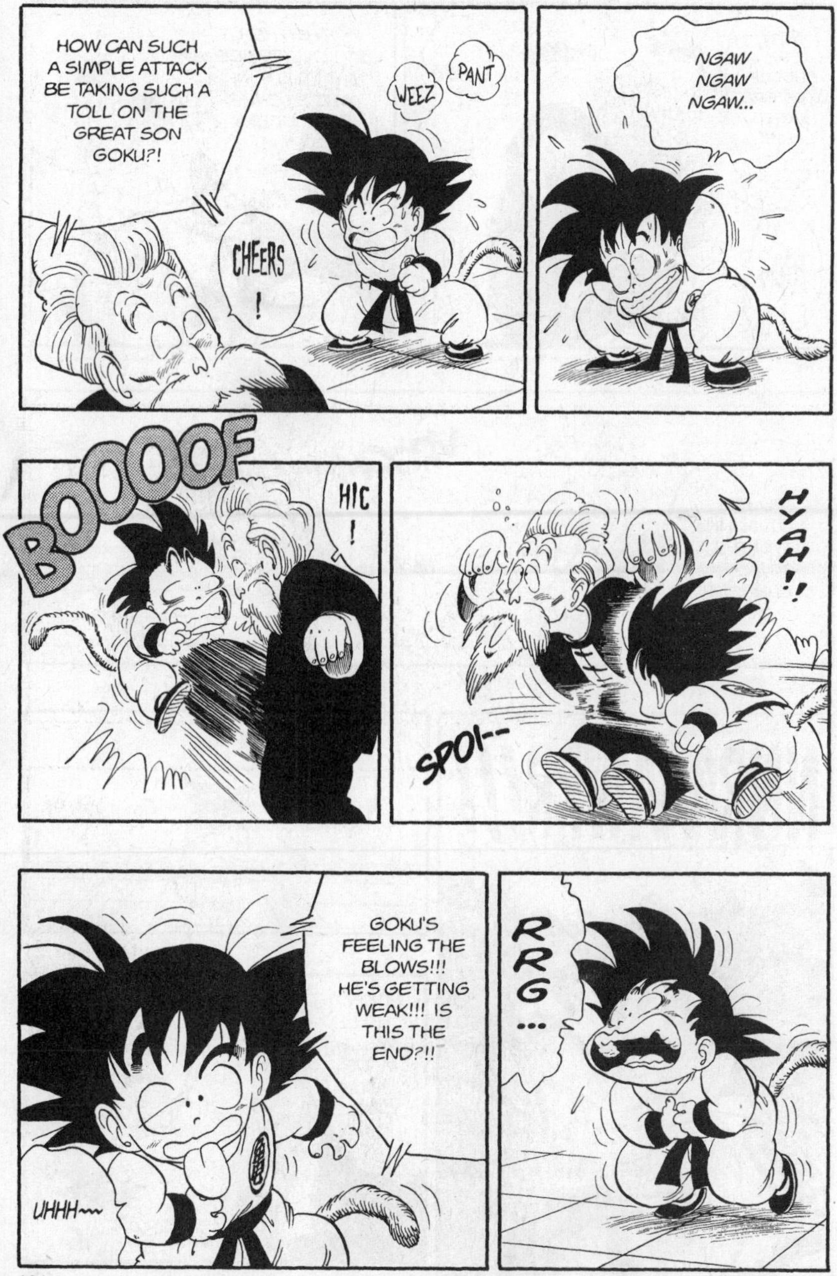
NGAW NGAW NGAW...
PANT
WEEZ
HOW CAN SUCH A SIMPLE ATTACK BE TAKING SUCH A TOLL ON THE GREAT SON GOKU?!
CHEERS!
HYAH!!
SPOI--
HIC!
BOOOOF
RRG...
GOKU'S FEELING THE BLOWS!!! HE'S GETTING WEAK!!! IS THIS THE END?!!
UHHH~~

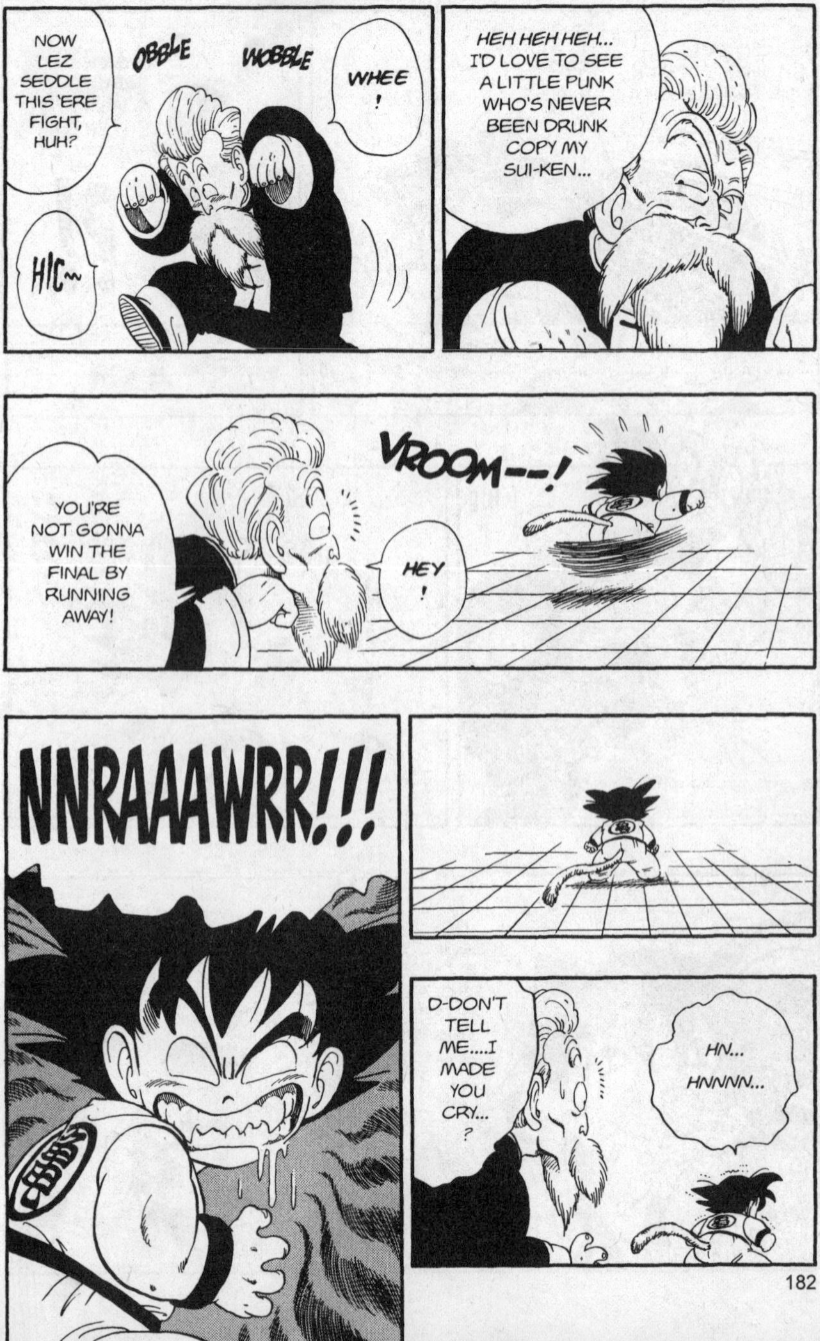
HEH HEH HEH... I'D LOVE TO SEE A LITTLE PUNK WHO'S NEVER BEEN DRUNK COPY MY SUI-KEN...
WHEE!
WOBBLE
OBBLE
NOW LEZ SEDDLE THIS 'ERE FIGHT, HUH?
HIC~
VROOM--!
HEY!
YOU'RE NOT GONNA WIN THE FINAL BY RUNNING AWAY!
HN... HNNNN...
D-DON'T TELL ME....I MADE YOU CRY...?
NNRAAAWRR!!!

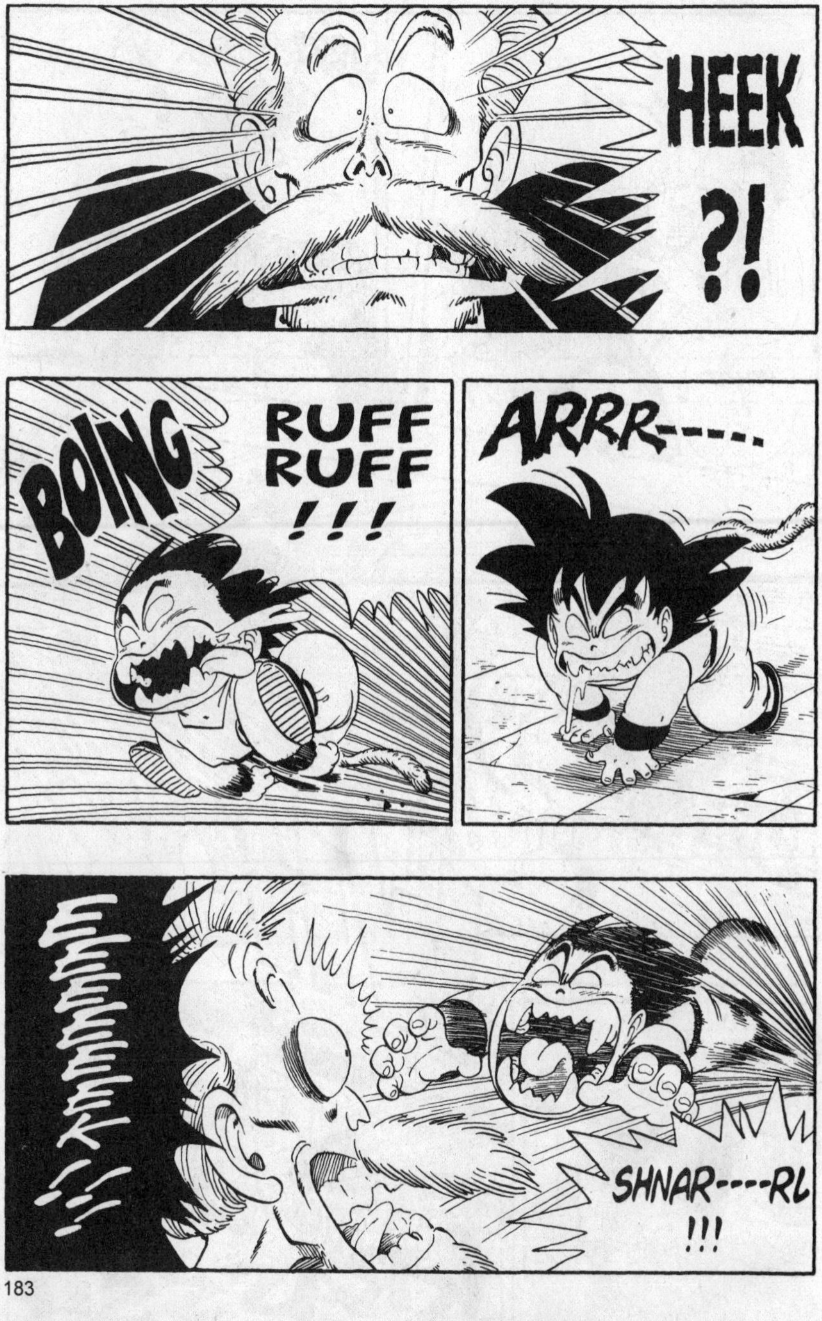
HEEK ?!
ARRR-----
RUFF RUFF !!!
BOING
SHNAR----RL !!!
EEEEEEK!!!

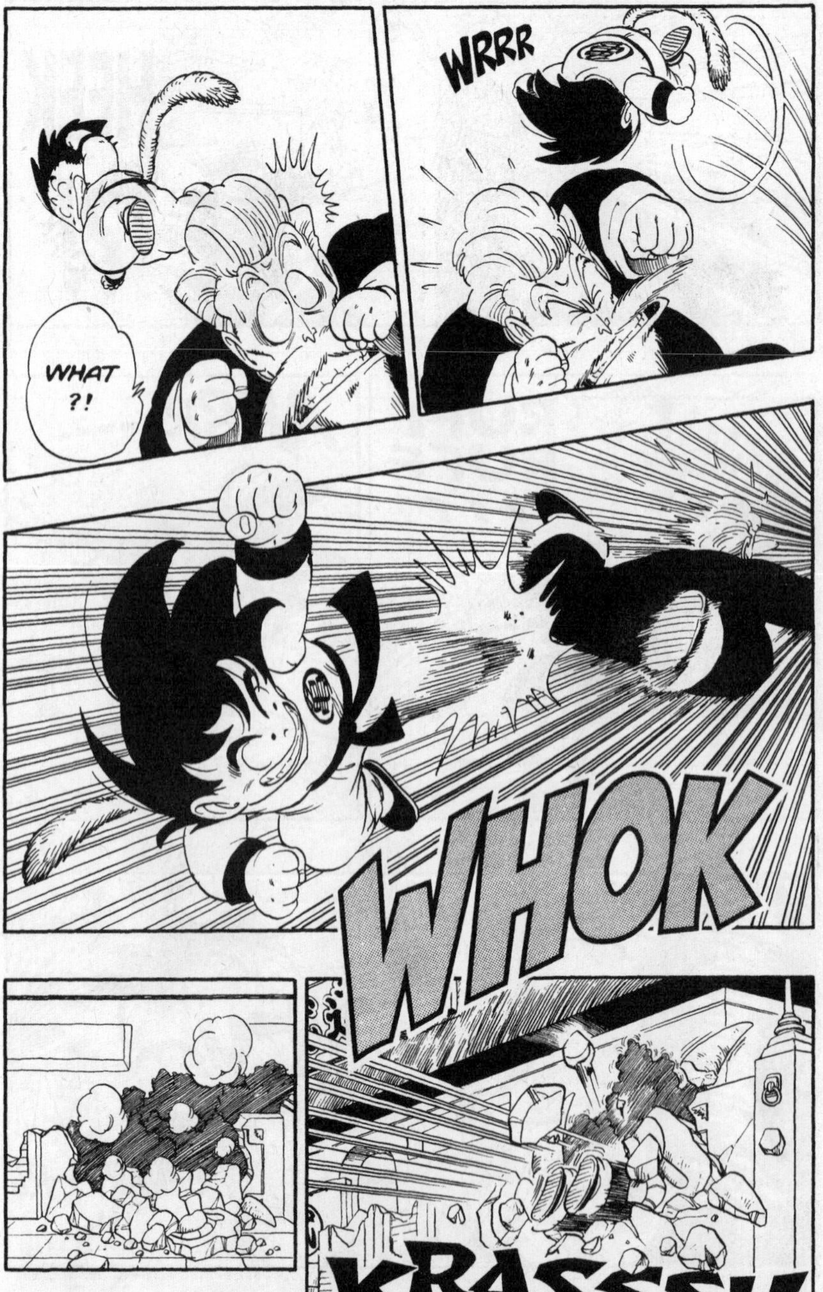
WRRR
WHAT ?!
WHOK
KRASSSH

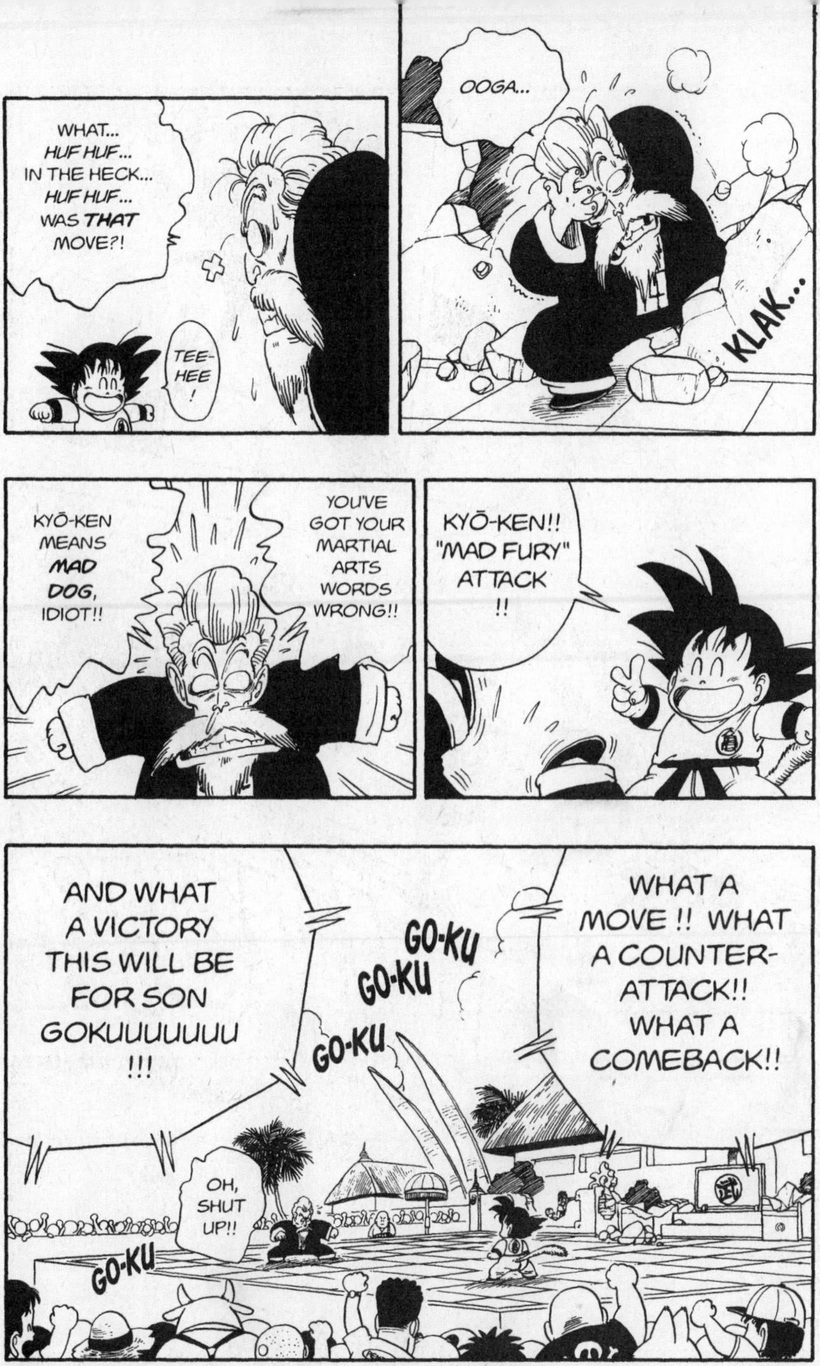
OOGA...
KLAK...
WHAT... HUF HUF... IN THE HECK... HUF HUF... WAS THAT MOVE?!
TEE-HEE!
KYŌ-KEN!! "MAD FURY" ATTACK!!
YOU'VE GOT YOUR MARTIAL ARTS WORDS WRONG!!
KYŌ-KEN MEANS MAD DOG, IDIOT!!
WHAT A MOVE!! WHAT A COUNTER-ATTACK!! WHAT A COMEBACK!!
GO-KU
GO-KU
GO-KU
AND WHAT A VICTORY THIS WILL BE FOR SON GOKUUUUUUU!!!
OH, SHUT UP!!
GO-KU

Dragonball

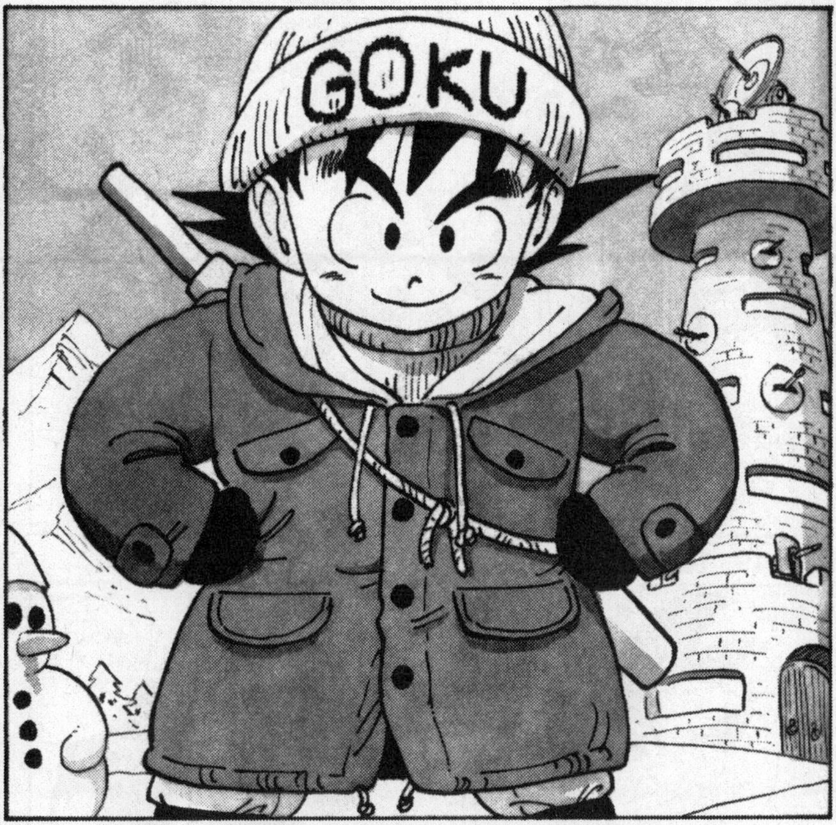
GOKU

VOLUME 5

THE RED RIBBON ARMY

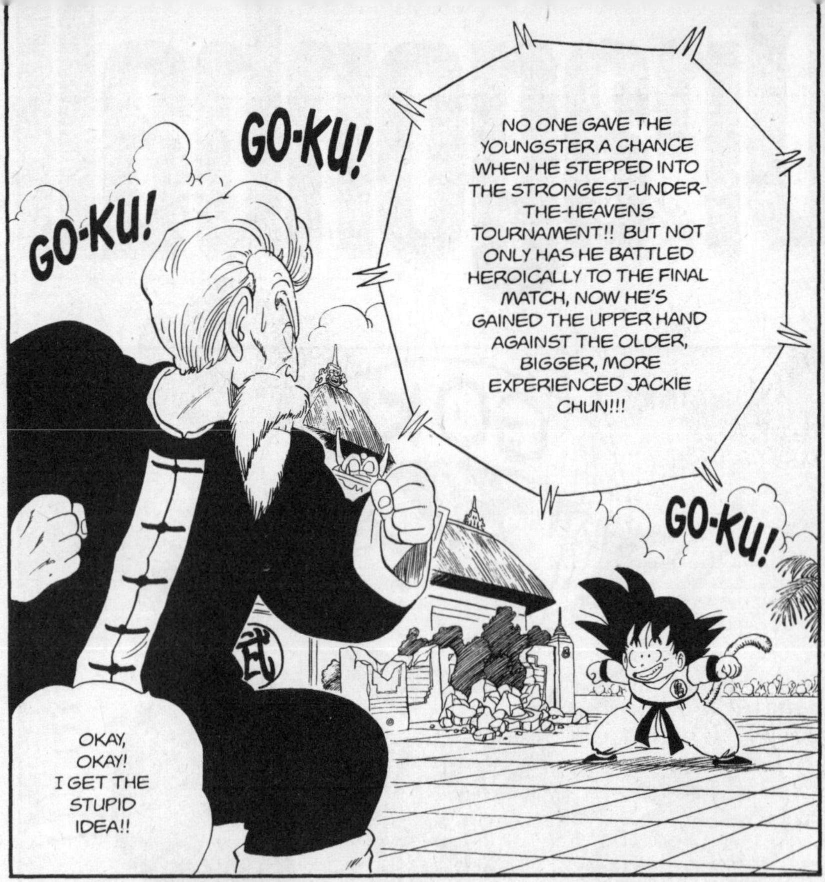
NO ONE GAVE THE YOUNGSTER A CHANCE WHEN HE STEPPED INTO THE STRONGEST-UNDER-THE-HEAVENS TOURNAMENT!! BUT NOT ONLY HAS HE BATTLED HEROICALLY TO THE FINAL MATCH, NOW HE'S GAINED THE UPPER HAND AGAINST THE OLDER, BIGGER, MORE EXPERIENCED JACKIE CHUN!!!
GO-KU!
GO-KU!
GO-KU!
OKAY, OKAY! I GET THE STUPID IDEA!!

Tale 49 · The Big Sleep

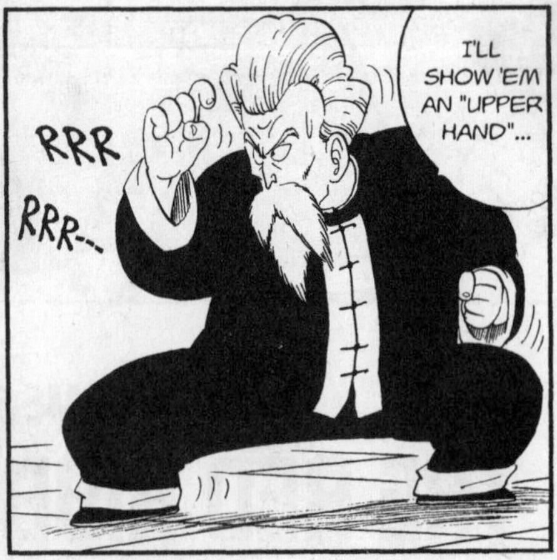
I'LL SHOW 'EM AN "UPPER HAND"...
RRR
RRR--.

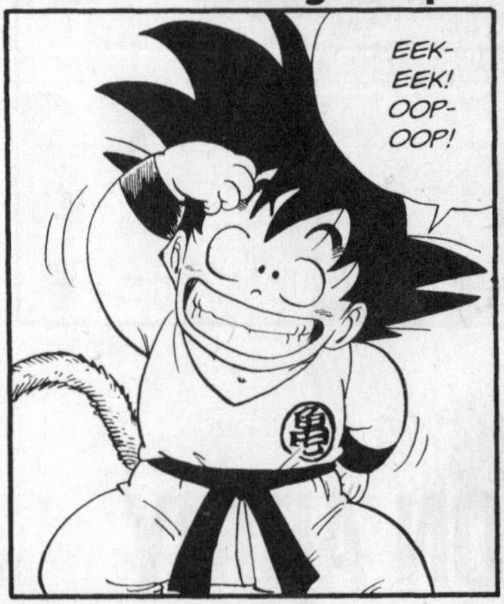
EEK-EEK! OOP-OOP!

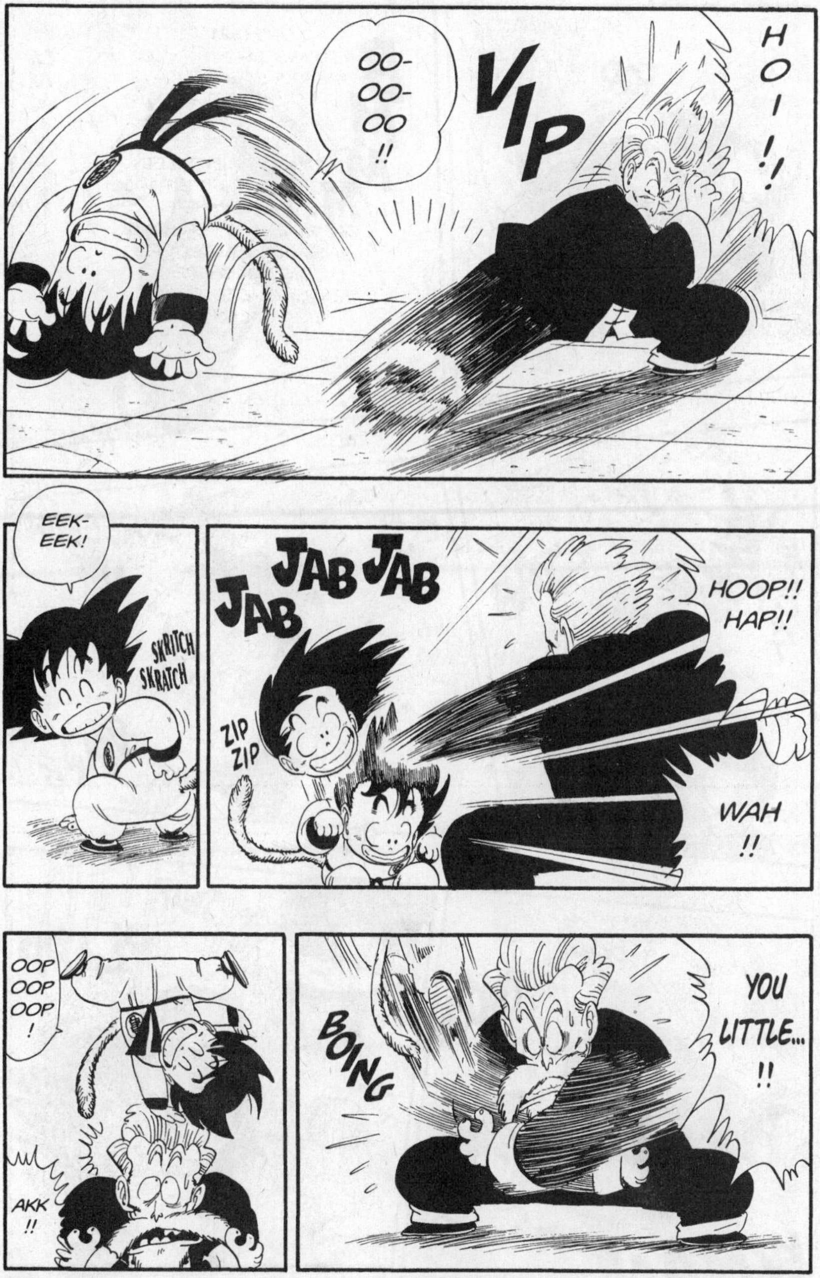
HO-I!!
VIP
OO-OO-OO!!
HOOP!! HAP!!
JAB JAB JAB
WAH!!
ZIP ZIP
EEK-EEK!
SKRITCH SKRATCH
YOU LITTLE...!!
BOING
OOP OOP OOP!
AKK!!

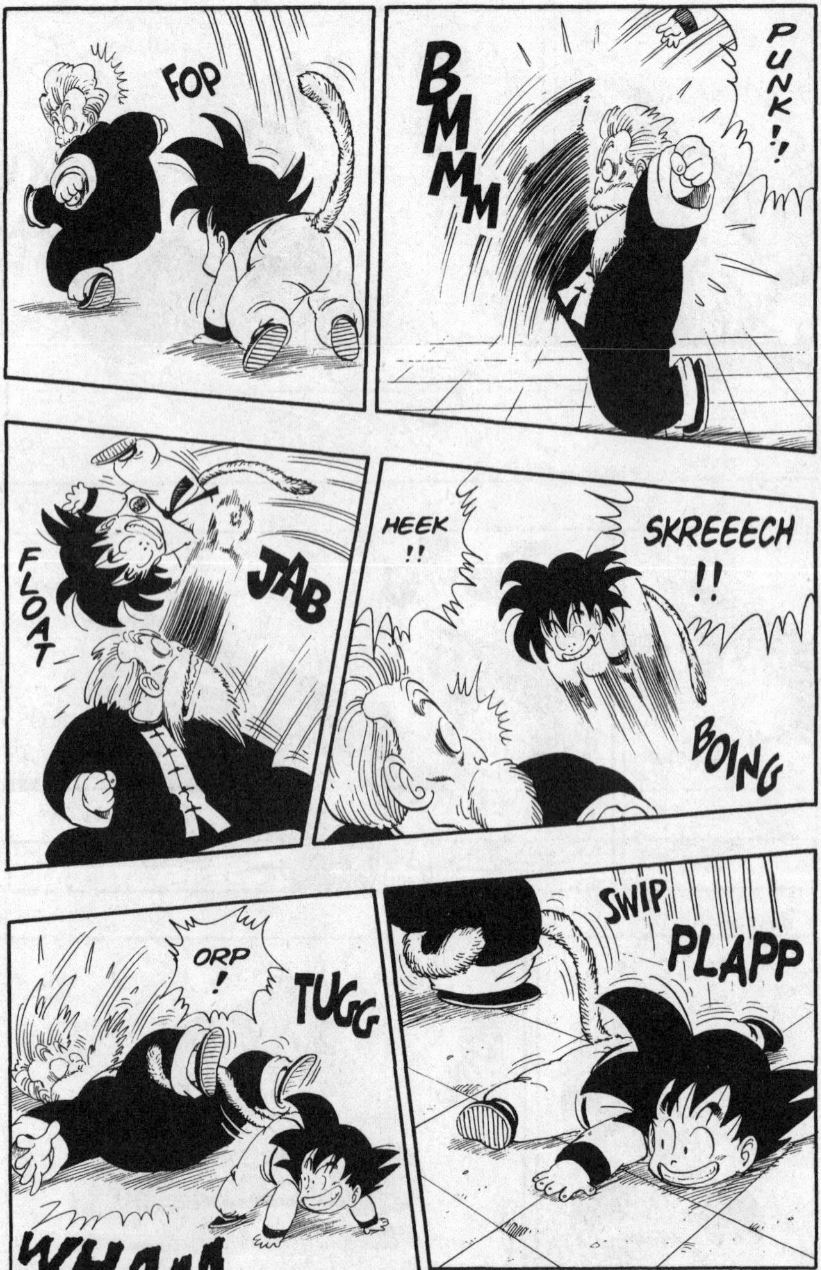
PUNK!!
BMMM
FOP
SKREEECH!!
HEEK!!
BOING
JAB
FLOAT
SWIP
PLAPP
ORP!
TUGG
WHAM

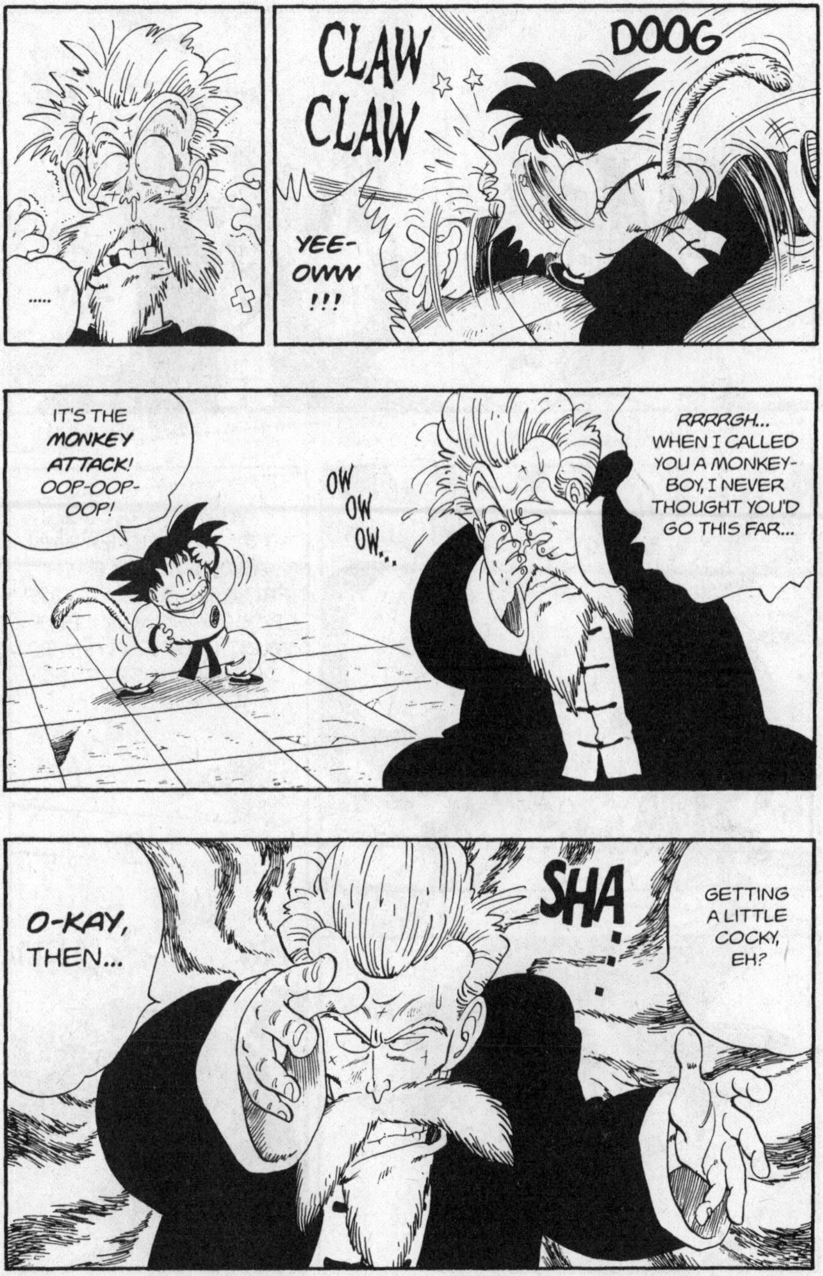
DOOG
CLAW CLAW
YEE-OWW !!!
.....
RRRRGH... WHEN I CALLED YOU A MONKEY-BOY, I NEVER THOUGHT YOU'D GO THIS FAR...
OW OW OW...
IT'S THE MONKEY ATTACK! OOP-OOP-OOP!
GETTING A LITTLE COCKY, EH?
SHA
O-KAY, THEN...

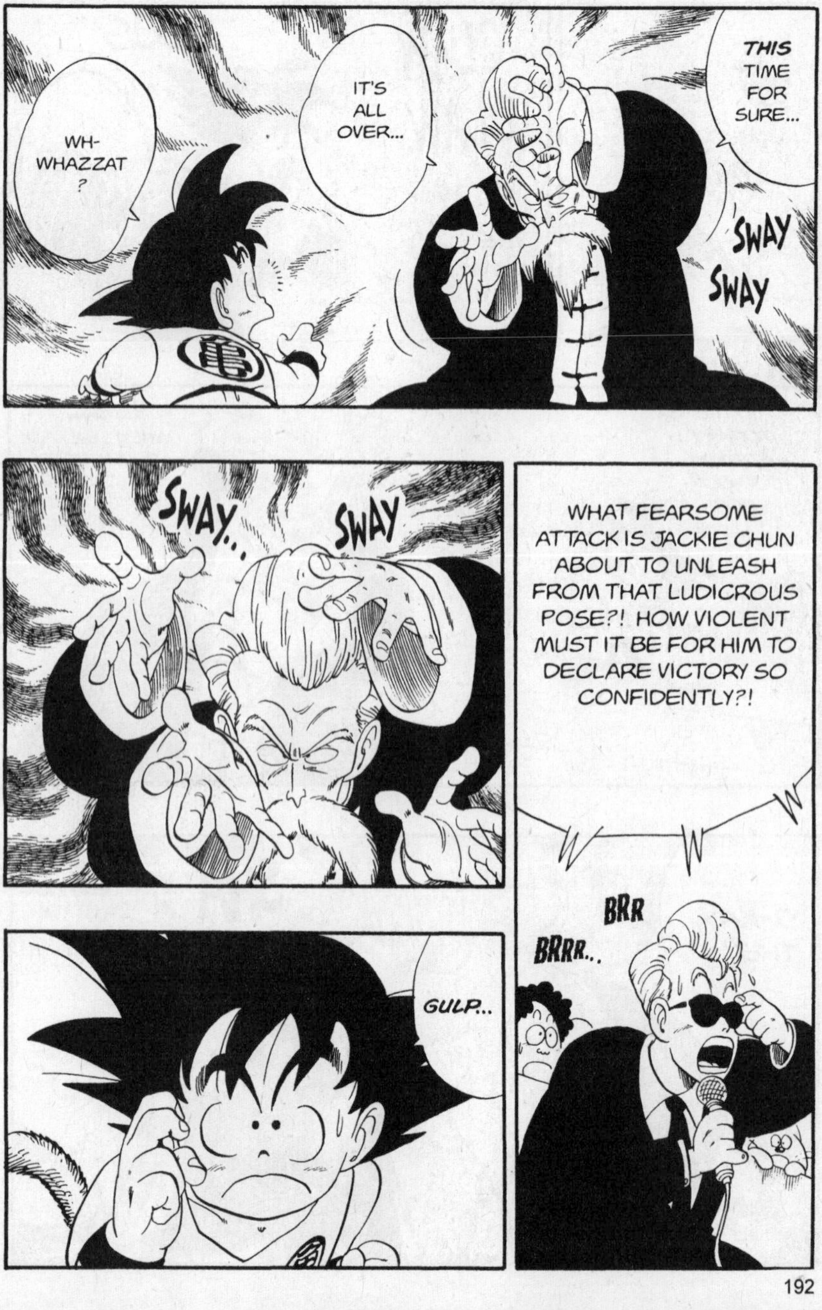
THIS TIME FOR SURE...
SWAY
SWAY
IT'S ALL OVER...
WH- WHAZZAT?
WHAT FEARSOME ATTACK IS JACKIE CHUN ABOUT TO UNLEASH FROM THAT LUDICROUS POSE?! HOW VIOLENT MUST IT BE FOR HIM TO DECLARE VICTORY SO CONFIDENTLY?!
BRR
BRRR...
SWAY
SWAY...
GULP...

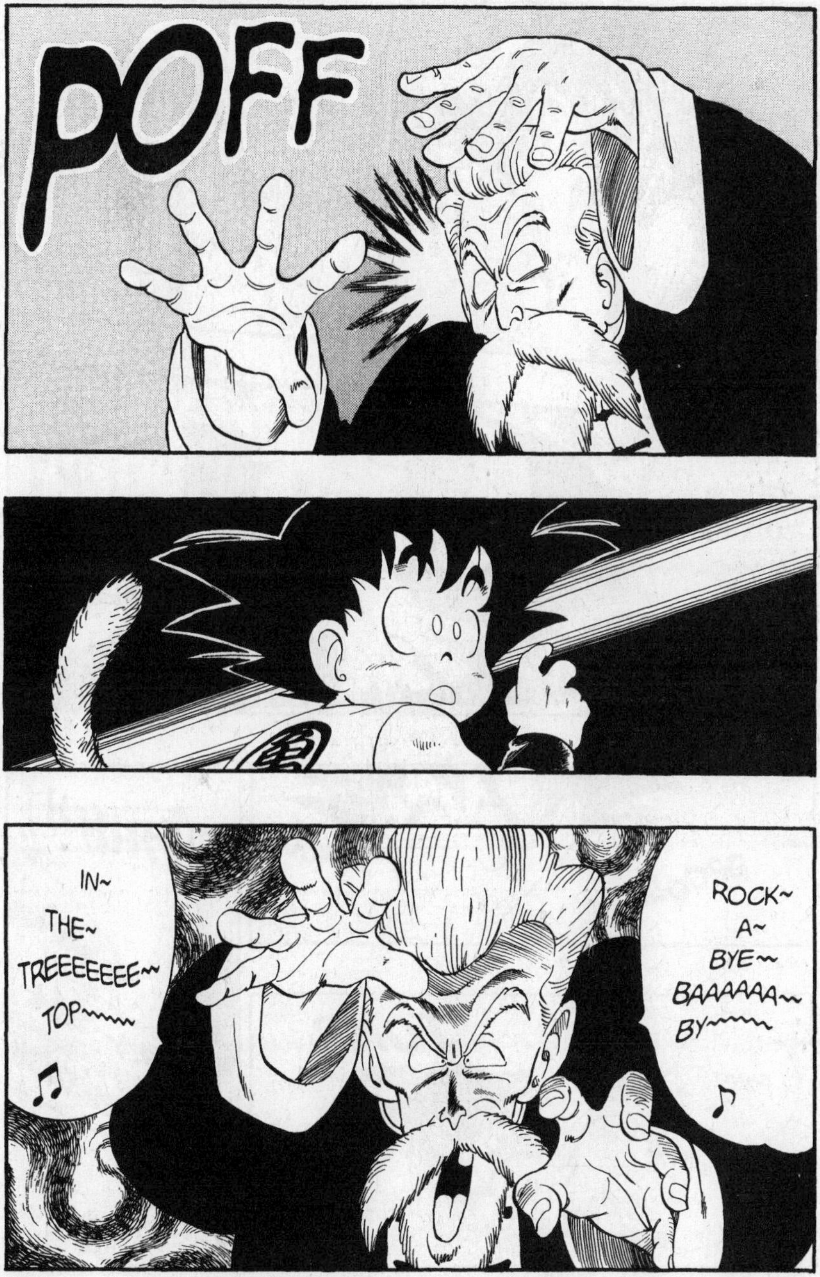
POFF
ROCK~
A~
BYE~
BAAAAAA~
BY~~~~
IN~
THE~
TREEEEEEE~
TOP~~~~~

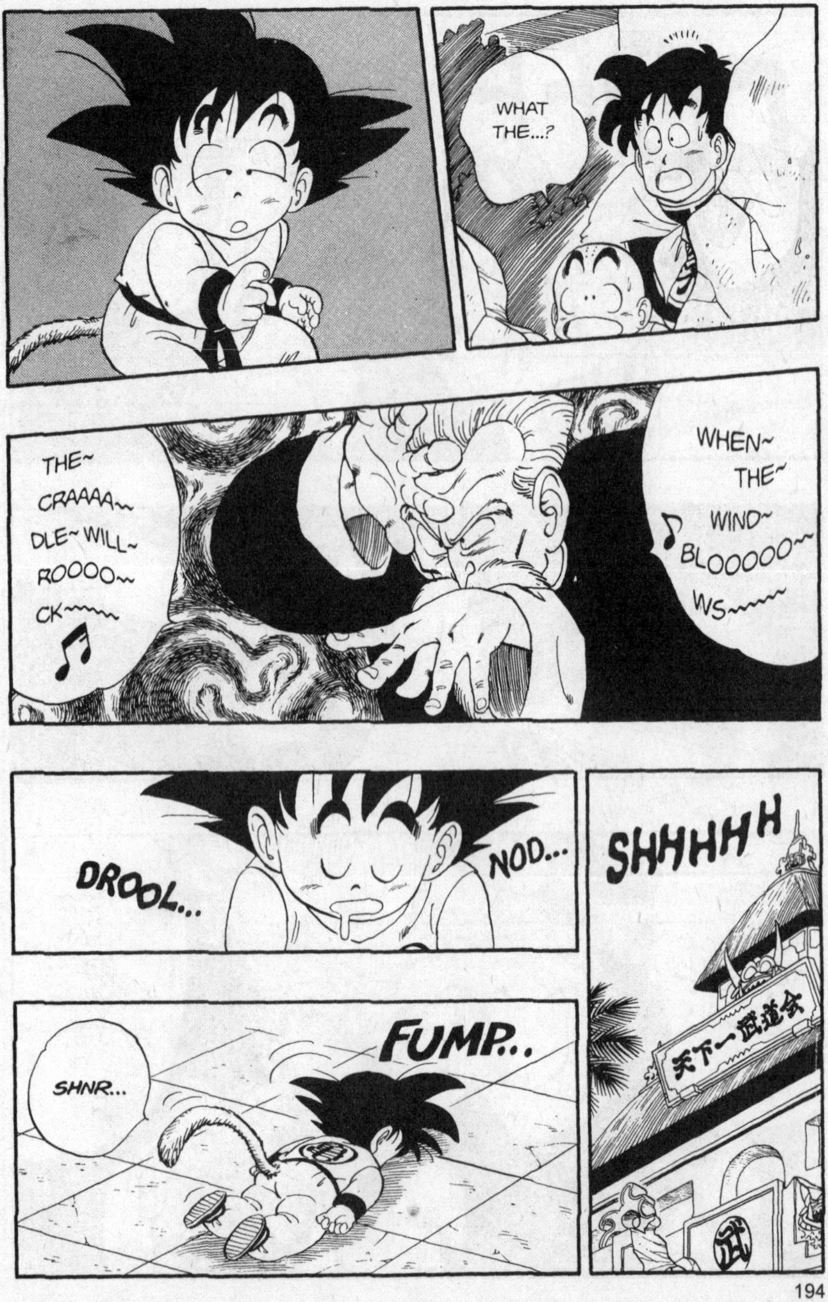
WHAT THE...?
WHEN~ THE~ WIND~ BLOOOOO~ WS~~~~
THE~ CRAAAA~ DLE~ WILL~ ROOOO~ CK~~~~
SHHHHH
天下一武道会
武
NOD...
DROOL...
FUMP...
SHNR...

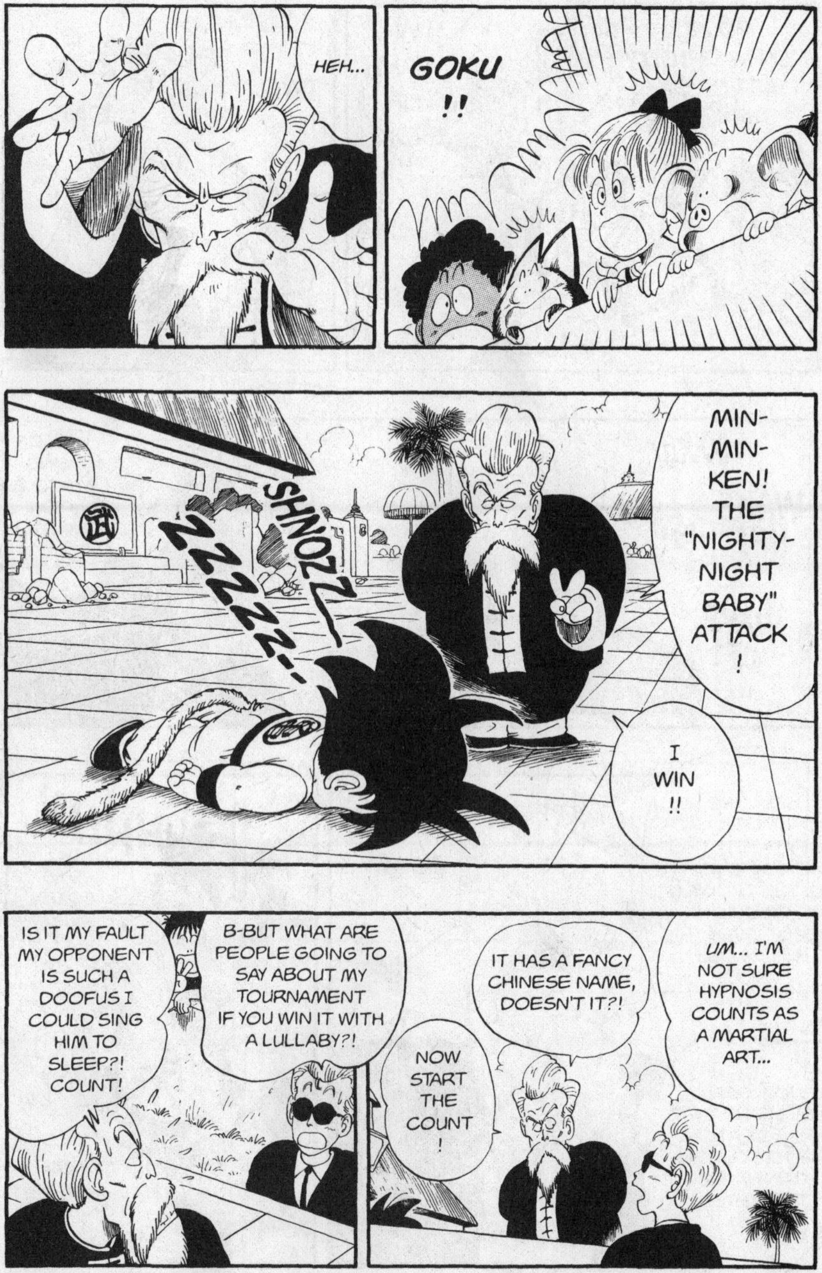
GOKU !!
HEH...
MIN-MIN-KEN! THE "NIGHTY-NIGHT BABY" ATTACK!
SHNOZZZ—ZZZZZ...
I WIN!!
UM... I'M NOT SURE HYPNOSIS COUNTS AS A MARTIAL ART...
IT HAS A FANCY CHINESE NAME, DOESN'T IT?!
NOW START THE COUNT!
B-BUT WHAT ARE PEOPLE GOING TO SAY ABOUT MY TOURNAMENT IF YOU WIN IT WITH A LULLABY?!
IS IT MY FAULT MY OPPONENT IS SUCH A DOOFUS I COULD SING HIM TO SLEEP?! COUNT!

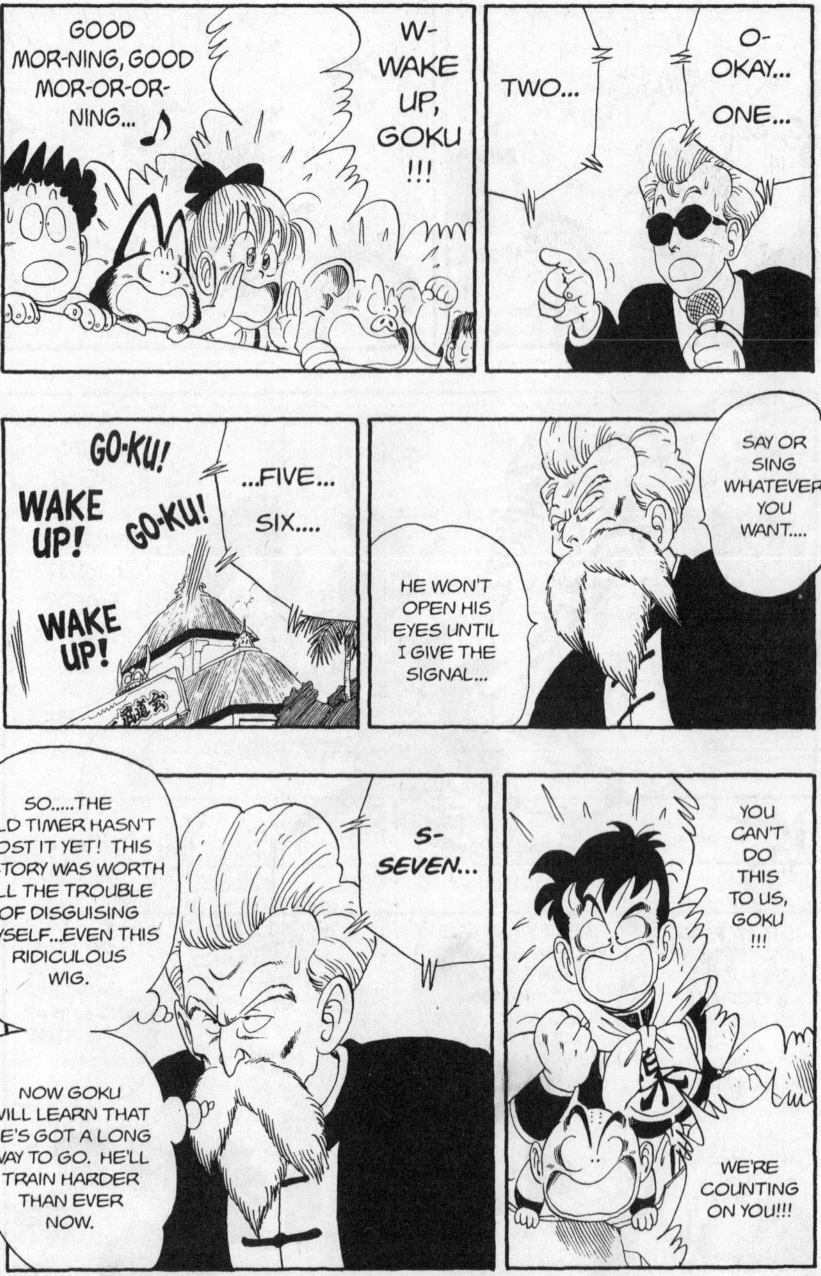
O- OKAY... ONE...
TWO...
W- WAKE UP, GOKU !!!
GOOD MOR-NING, GOOD MOR-OR-OR-NING... ♪
SAY OR SING WHATEVER YOU WANT....
HE WON'T OPEN HIS EYES UNTIL I GIVE THE SIGNAL...
...FIVE... SIX....
GO-KU!
WAKE UP!
GO-KU!
WAKE UP!
YOU CAN'T DO THIS TO US, GOKU !!!
WE'RE COUNTING ON YOU!!!
S- SEVEN...
SO.....THE OLD TIMER HASN'T LOST IT YET! THIS ICTORY WAS WORTH ALL THE TROUBLE OF DISGUISING MYSELF...EVEN THIS RIDICULOUS WIG.
NOW GOKU WILL LEARN THAT HE'S GOT A LONG WAY TO GO. HE'LL TRAIN HARDER THAN EVER NOW.

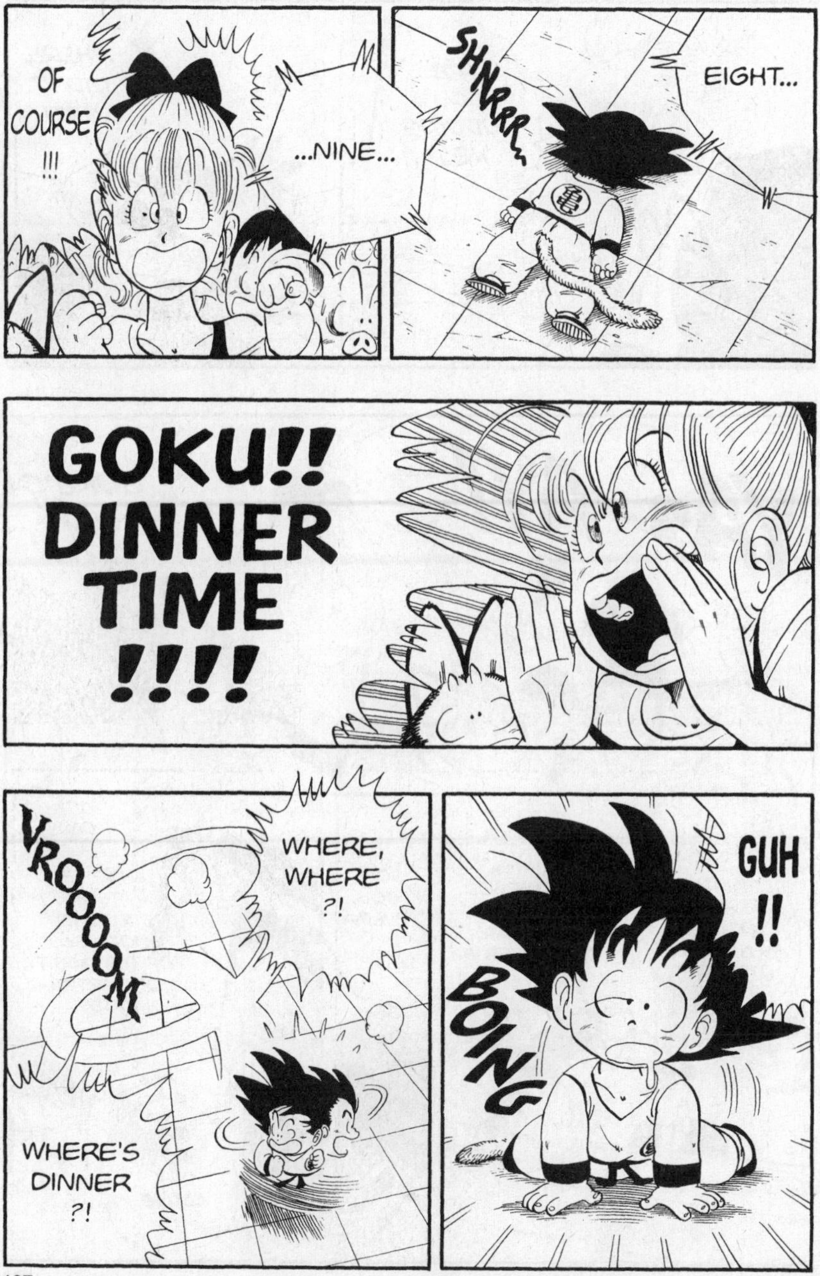
EIGHT...
SHNRRR
...NINE...
OF COURSE !!!
GOKU!! DINNER TIME !!!!
GUH !!
BOING
WHERE, WHERE ?!
VROOOOM
WHERE'S DINNER ?!

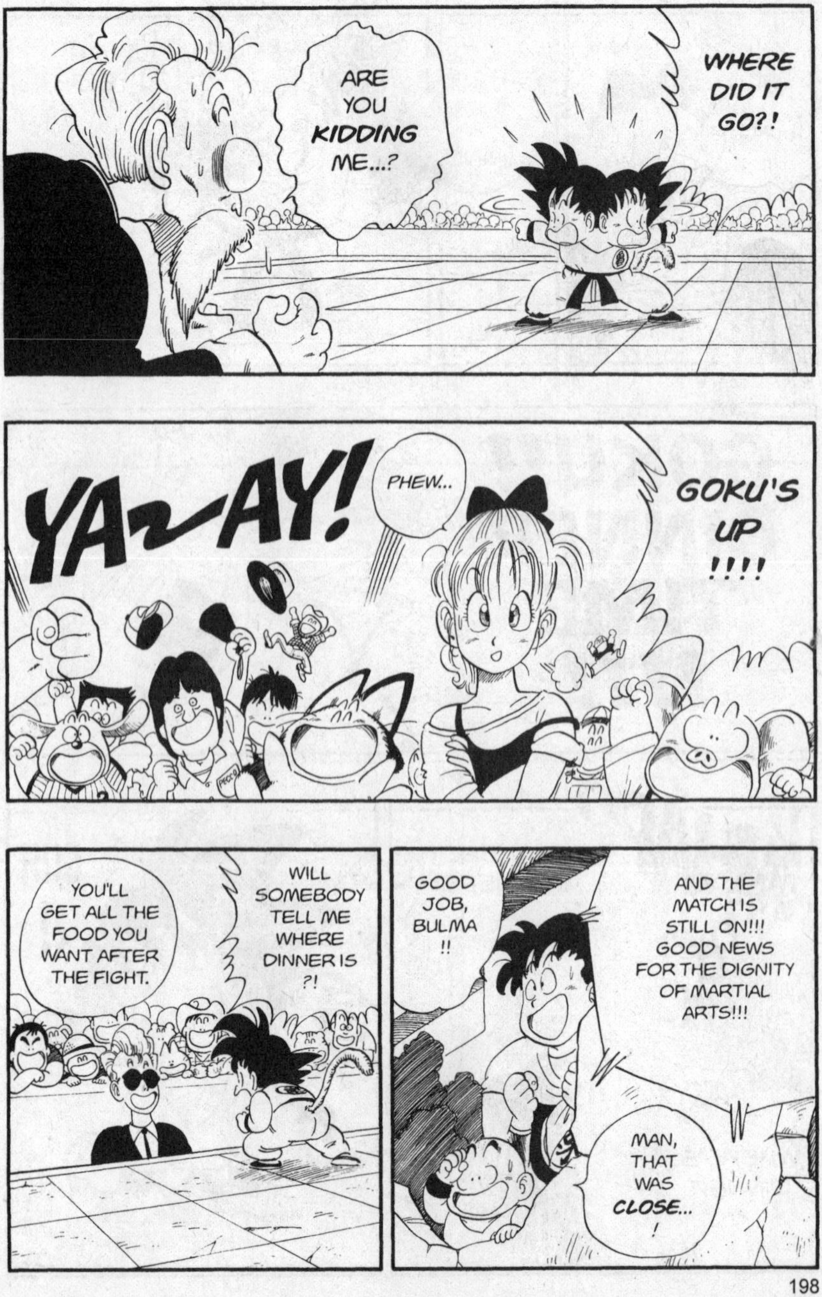
WHERE DID IT GO?!
ARE YOU KIDDING ME...?
GOKU'S UP !!!!
PHEW...
YA~AY!
AND THE MATCH IS STILL ON!!! GOOD NEWS FOR THE DIGNITY OF MARTIAL ARTS!!!
GOOD JOB, BULMA !!
MAN, THAT WAS CLOSE... !
WILL SOMEBODY TELL ME WHERE DINNER IS ?!
YOU'LL GET ALL THE FOOD YOU WANT AFTER THE FIGHT.

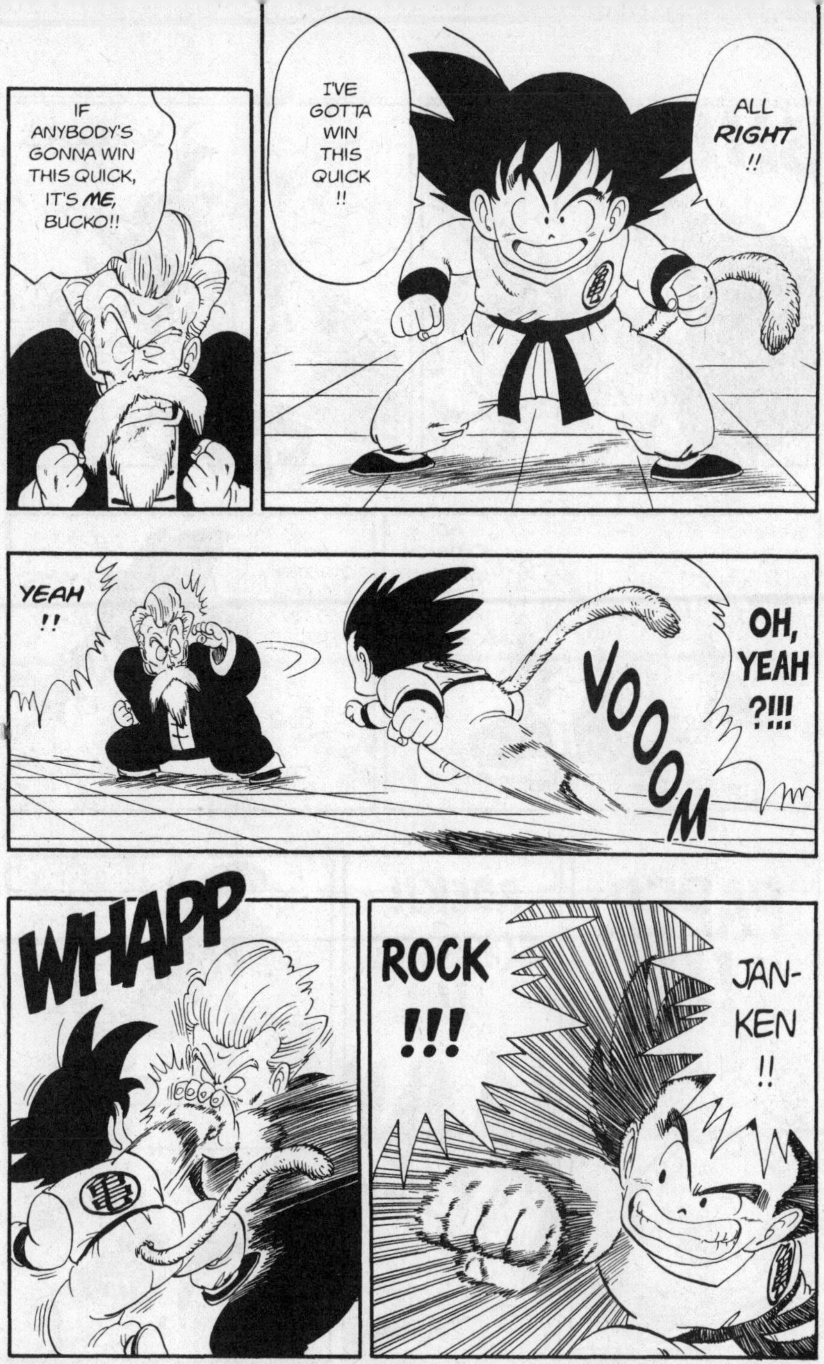
ALL RIGHT!!
I'VE GOTTA WIN THIS QUICK!!
IF ANYBODY'S GONNA WIN THIS QUICK, IT'S ME, BUCKO!!
OH, YEAH?!!!
VOOOM
YEAH!!
JAN-KEN!!
ROCK!!!
WHAPP

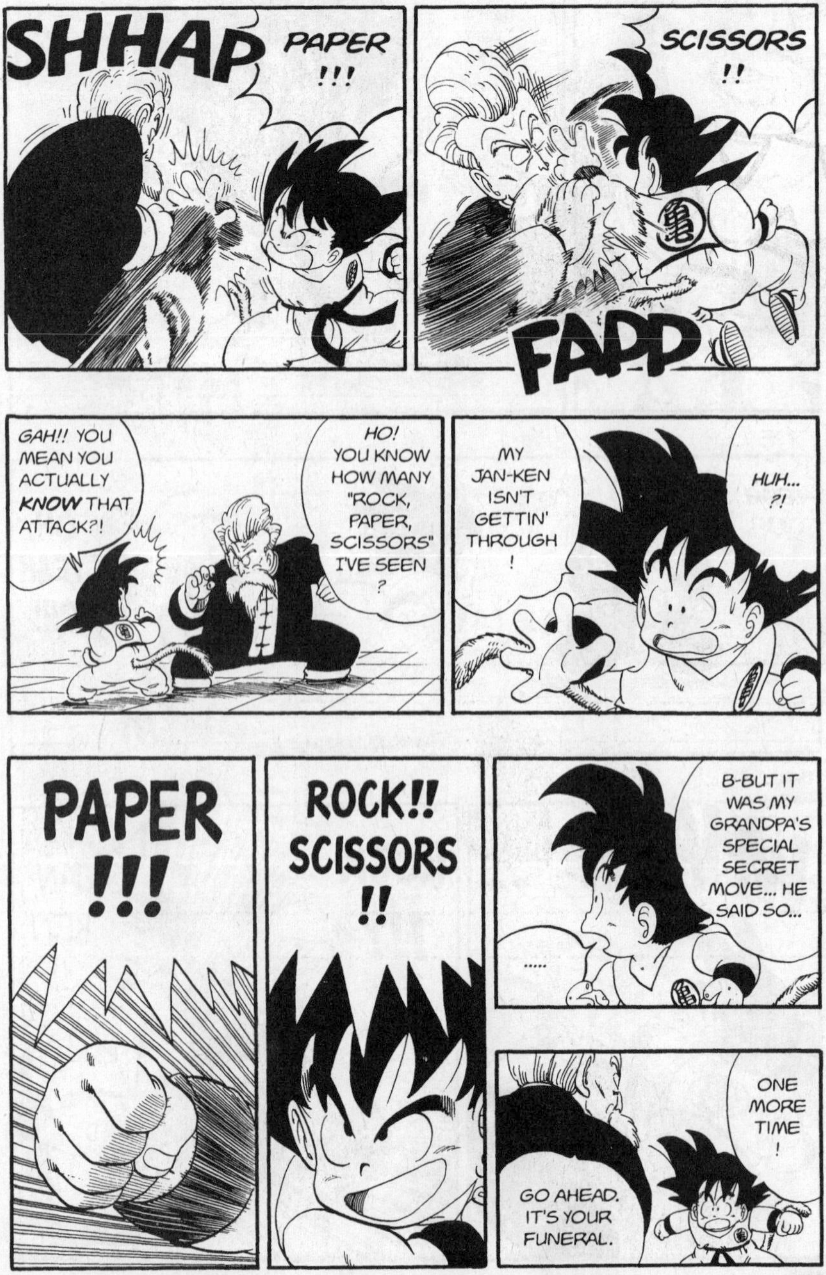
SCISSORS !!
FAPP
SHHAP
PAPER !!!
HUH... ?!
MY JAN-KEN ISN'T GETTIN' THROUGH !
HO! YOU KNOW HOW MANY "ROCK, PAPER, SCISSORS" I'VE SEEN ?
GAH!! YOU MEAN YOU ACTUALLY **KNOW** THAT ATTACK?!
B-BUT IT WAS MY GRANDPA'S SPECIAL SECRET MOVE... HE SAID SO...
.....
ONE MORE TIME !
GO AHEAD. IT'S YOUR FUNERAL.
ROCK!! SCISSORS !!
PAPER !!!

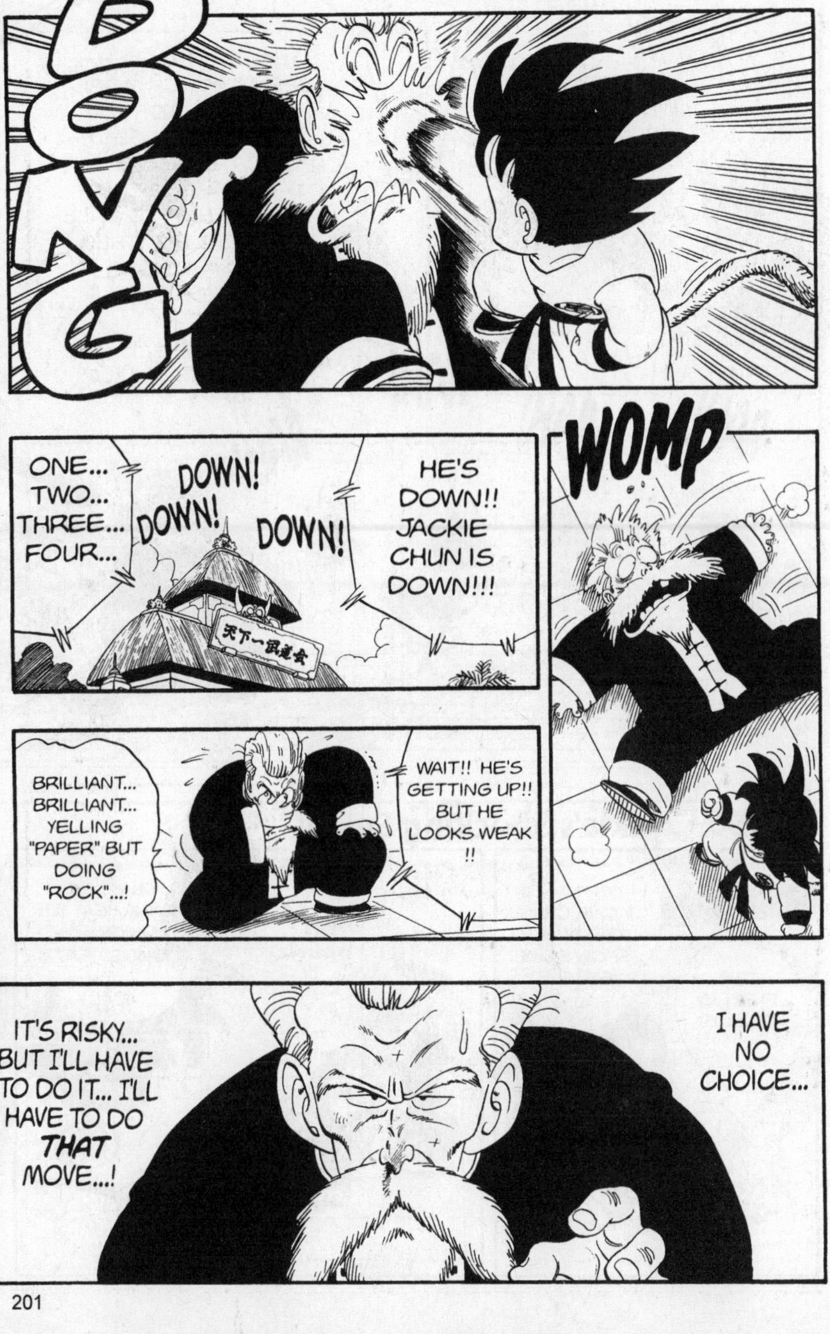
DOG
WOMP
HE'S DOWN!! JACKIE CHUN IS DOWN!!!
DOWN!
DOWN!
DOWN!
ONE... TWO... THREE... FOUR...
天下一武道会
WAIT!! HE'S GETTING UP!! BUT HE LOOKS WEAK!!
BRILLIANT... BRILLIANT... YELLING "PAPER" BUT DOING "ROCK"...!
I HAVE NO CHOICE...
IT'S RISKY... BUT I'LL HAVE TO DO IT... I'LL HAVE TO DO *THAT* MOVE...!

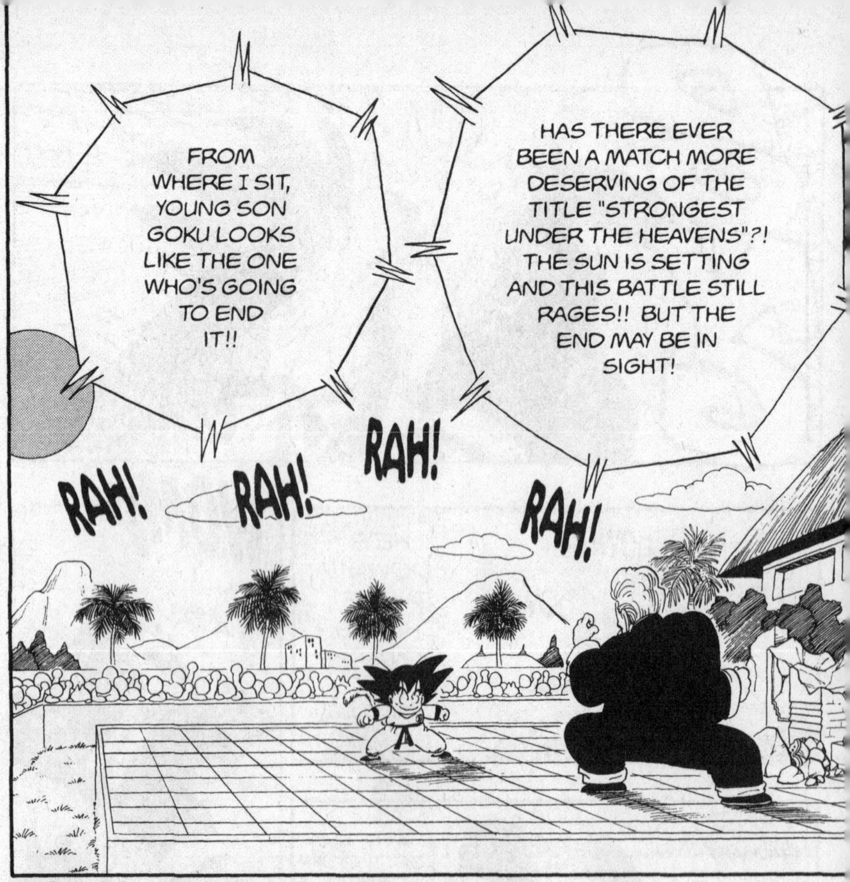
HAS THERE EVER BEEN A MATCH MORE DESERVING OF THE TITLE "STRONGEST UNDER THE HEAVENS"?! THE SUN IS SETTING AND THIS BATTLE STILL RAGES!! BUT THE END MAY BE IN SIGHT!
FROM WHERE I SIT, YOUNG SON GOKU LOOKS LIKE THE ONE WHO'S GOING TO END IT!!
RAH!
RAH!
RAH!
RAH!

Tale 50 • Jackie's Shocking Secret

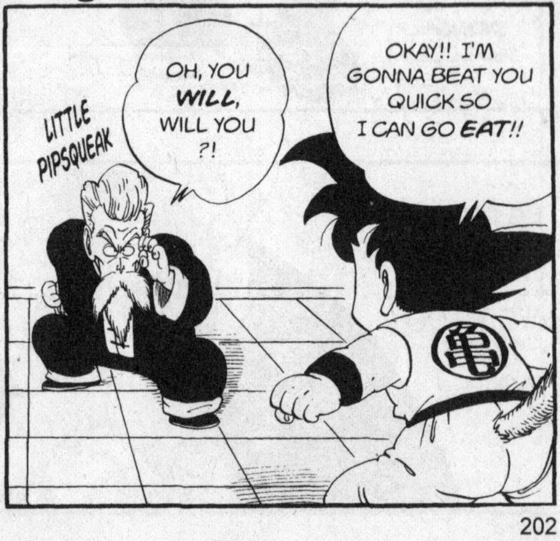
OKAY!! I'M GONNA BEAT YOU QUICK SO I CAN GO EAT!!
OH, YOU WILL, WILL YOU ?!
LITTLE PIPSQUEAK

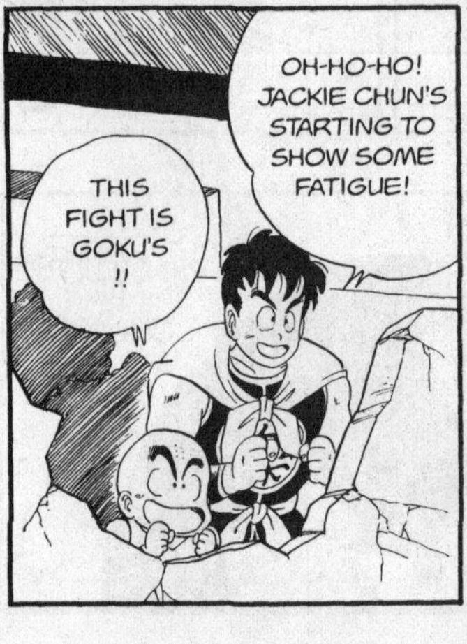
OH-HO-HO! JACKIE CHUN'S STARTING TO SHOW SOME FATIGUE!
THIS FIGHT IS GOKU'S !!

BUT GOKU'S YOUNG... HE'LL PROBABLY SURVIVE IT...

I HAVE NO CHOICE BUT TO RESORT TO *THAT* MOVE...

...BUT YOU'RE ABOUT TO LOSE.

I'M SORRY, SON...

HUH?

SNAP

BUT YOU ARE ONLY THE SECOND OPPONENT WHO HAS EVER FORCED ME TO USE THIS MOVE... AND THE FIRST ONE...

PERHAPS SO...

OOOO OOOO

THAT'S STUPID! I'M AHEAD! HE SAID SO!

LOSE?!

203

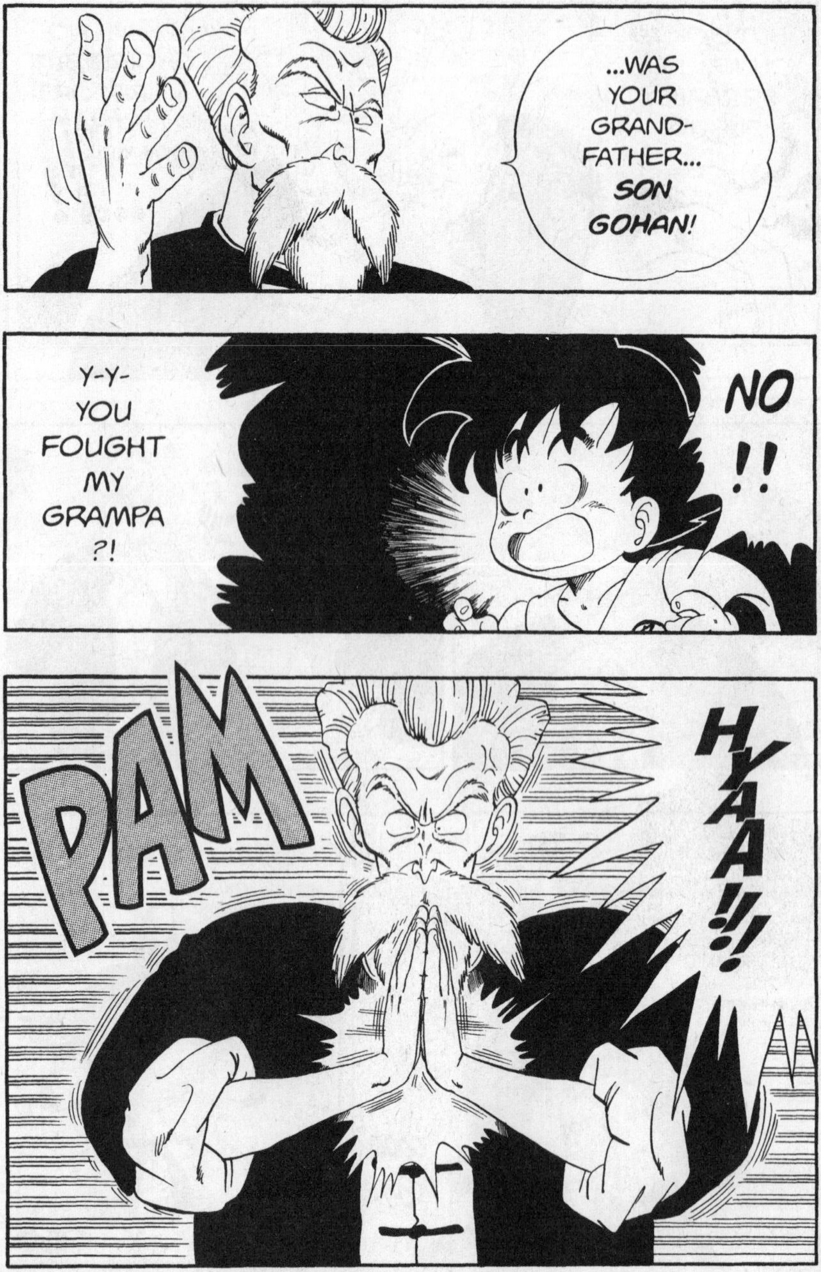
...WAS YOUR GRAND-FATHER... SON GOHAN!
NO !!
Y-Y-YOU FOUGHT MY GRAMPA ?!
HYAA!!!
PAM

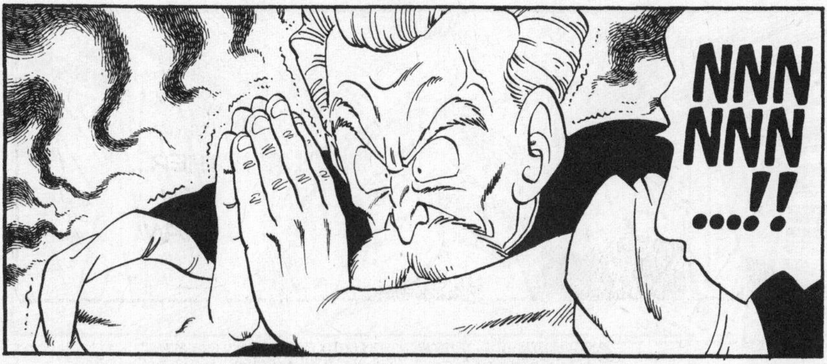
NNN
NNN
....!!

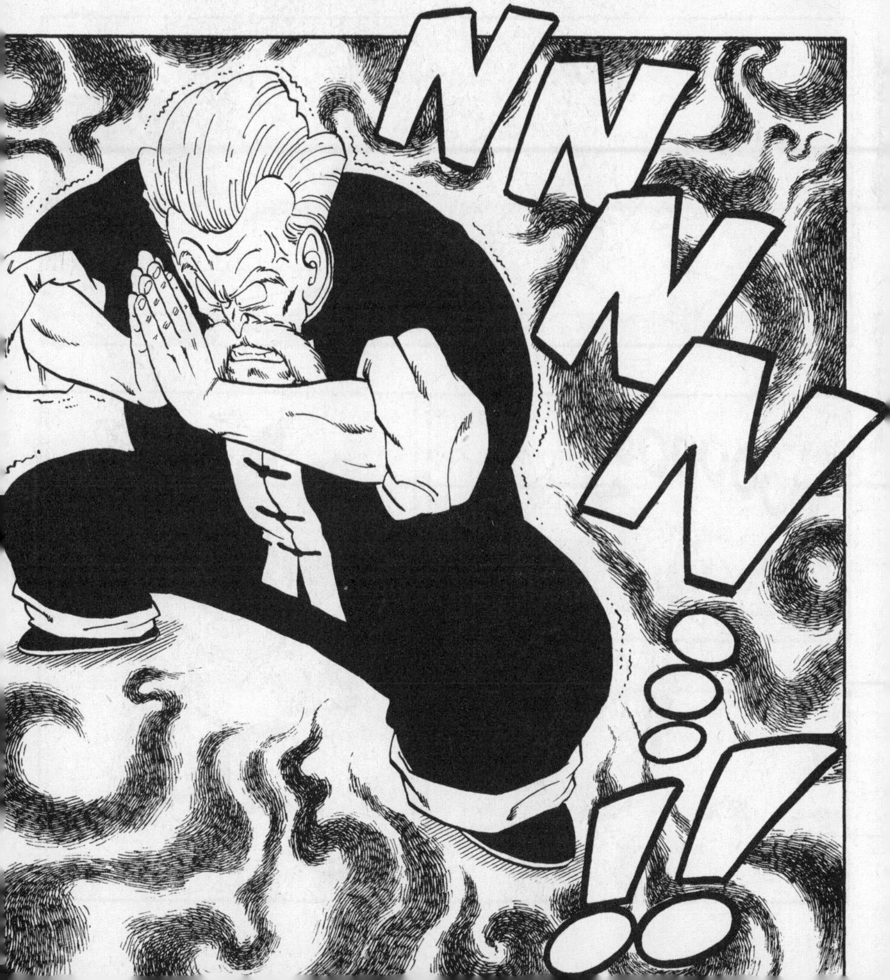
NNNNN...!!

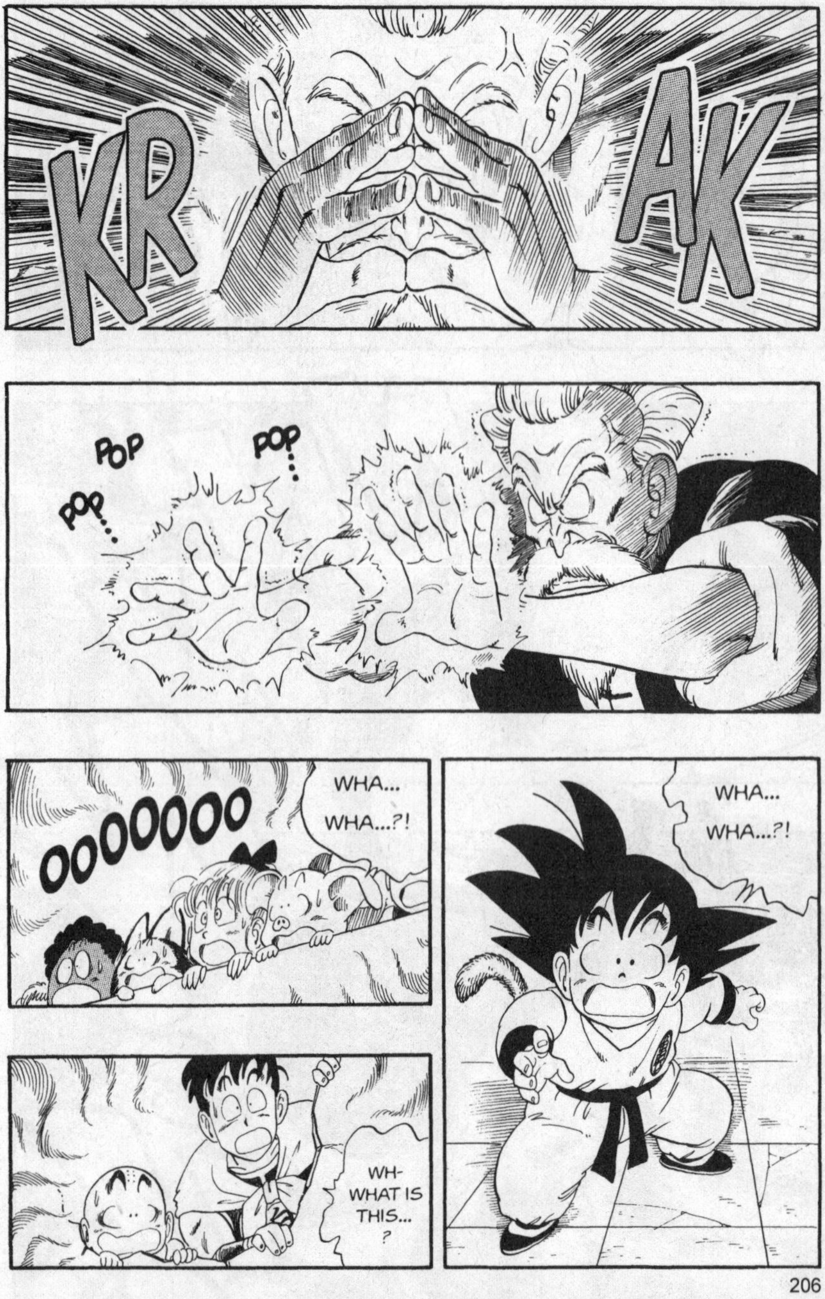
KR
AK
POP...
POP
POP...
WHA...
WHA...?!
WHA...
WHA...?!
OOOOOO
WH-
WHAT IS
THIS...
?

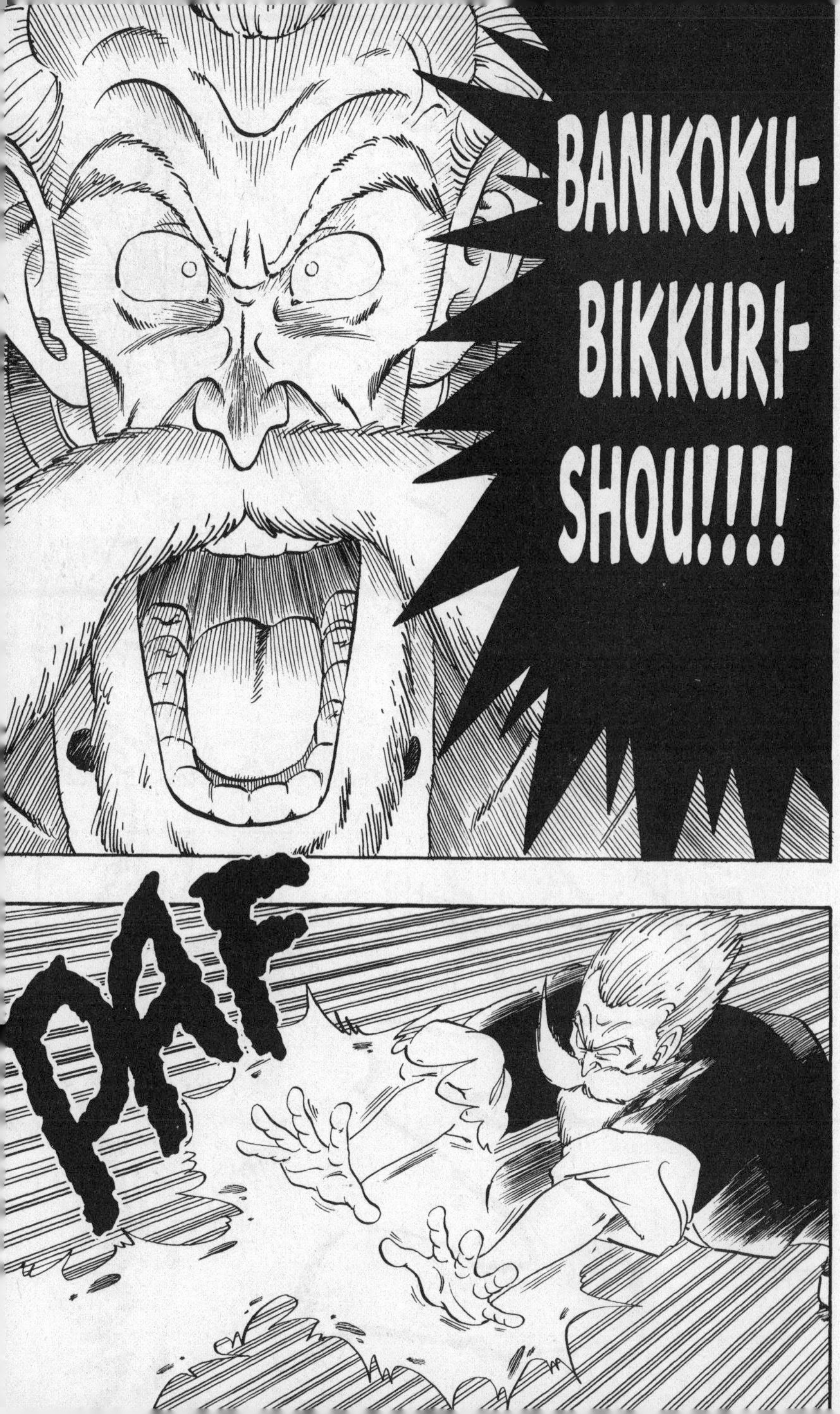
BANKOKU-
BIKKURI-
SHOU!!!!
PAF

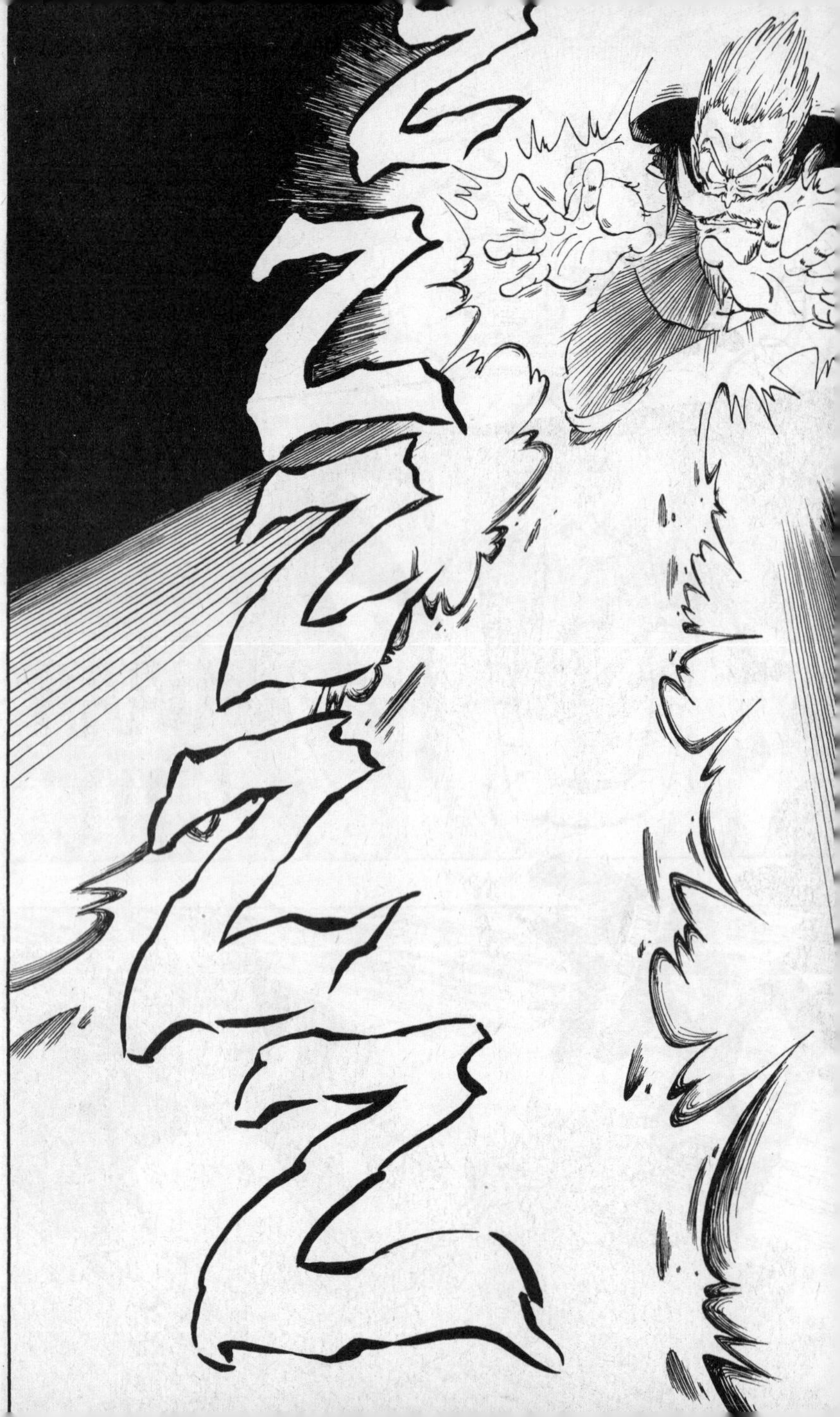

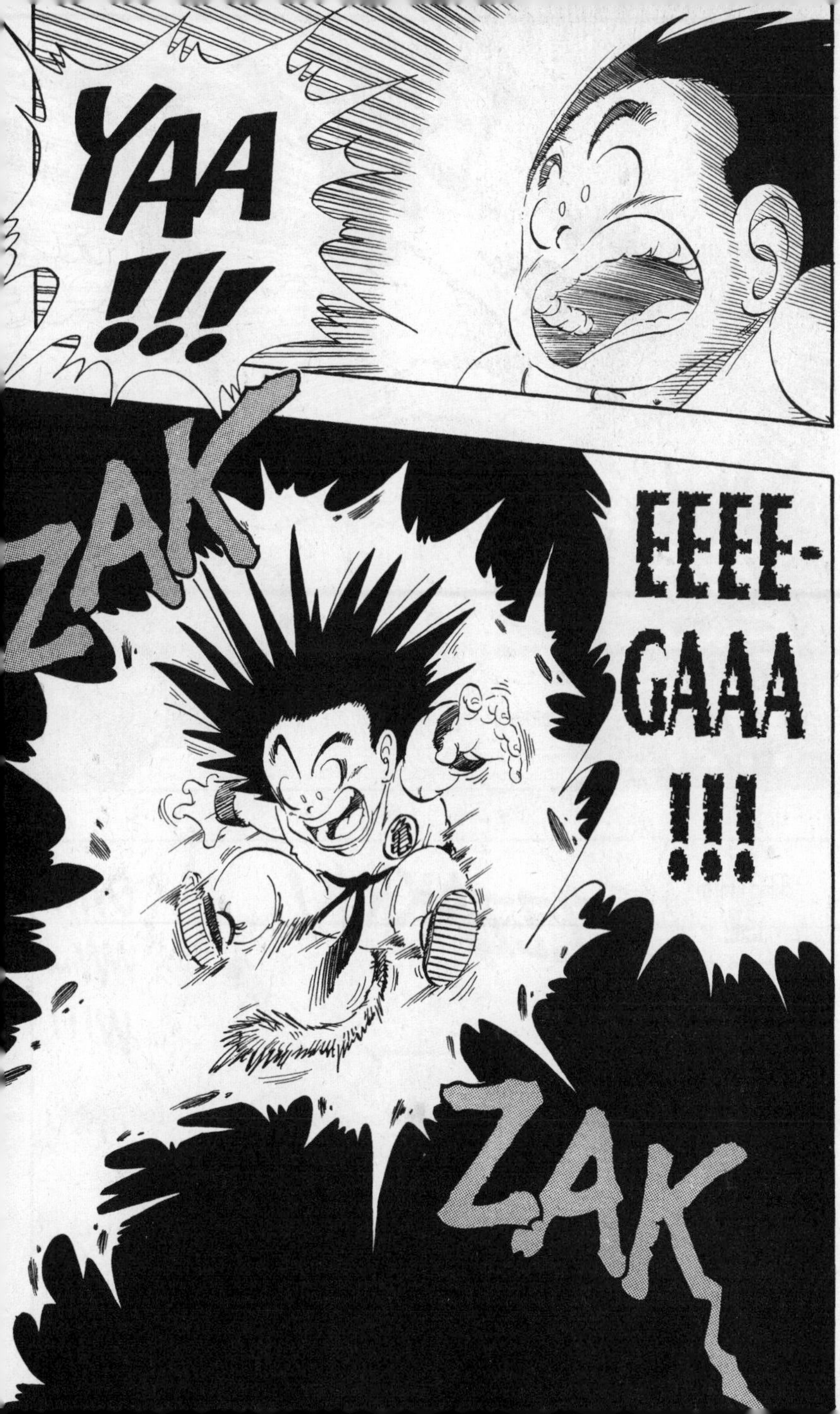
YAA!!!
ZAK
EEEE-GAAA!!!
ZAK

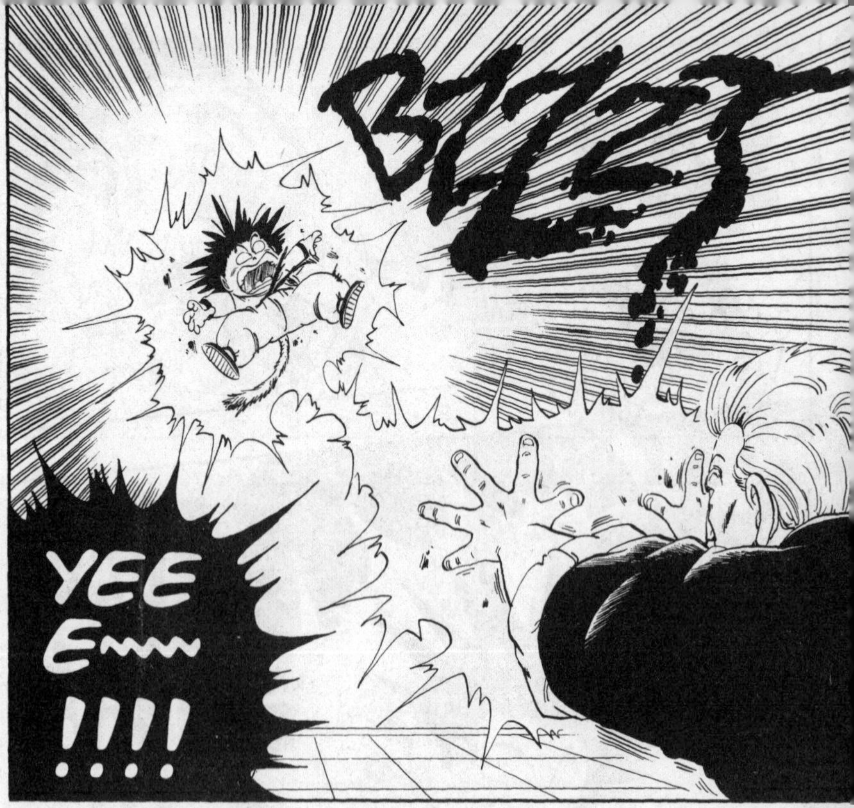
BZZT
YEEE~~~
!!!!

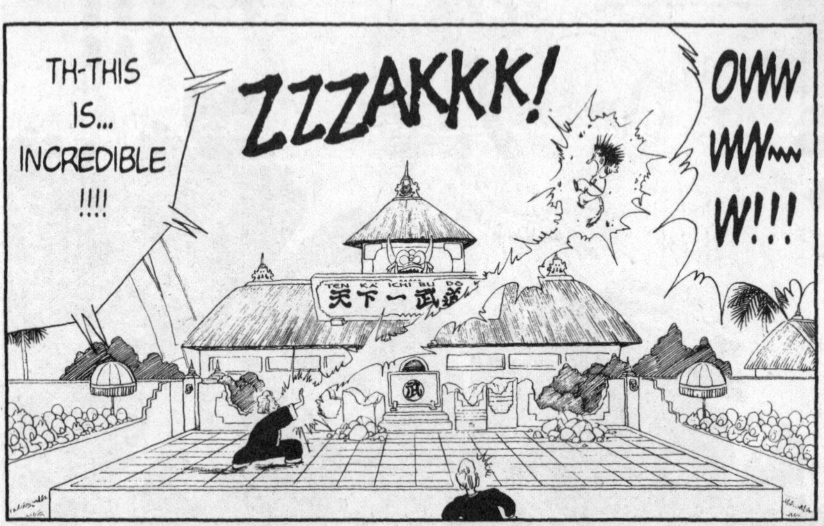
OWWWWW~~W!!!
ZZZAKKK!
TEN KA ICHI BU DO
天下一武道
TH-THIS IS... INCREDIBLE!!!!

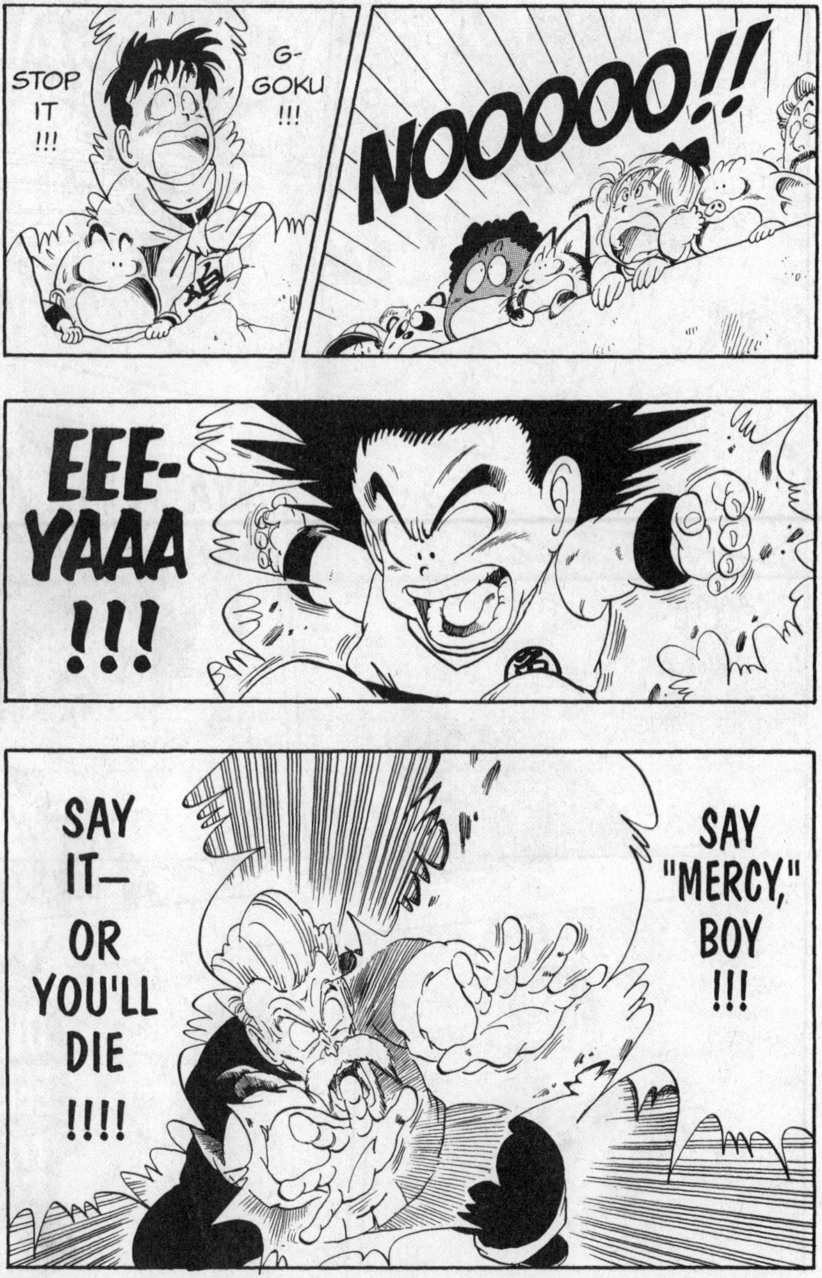
NOOOOO!!
G-GOKU!!!
STOP IT!!!
EEE-YAAA!!!
SAY "MERCY," BOY!!!
SAY IT—OR YOU'LL DIE!!!!

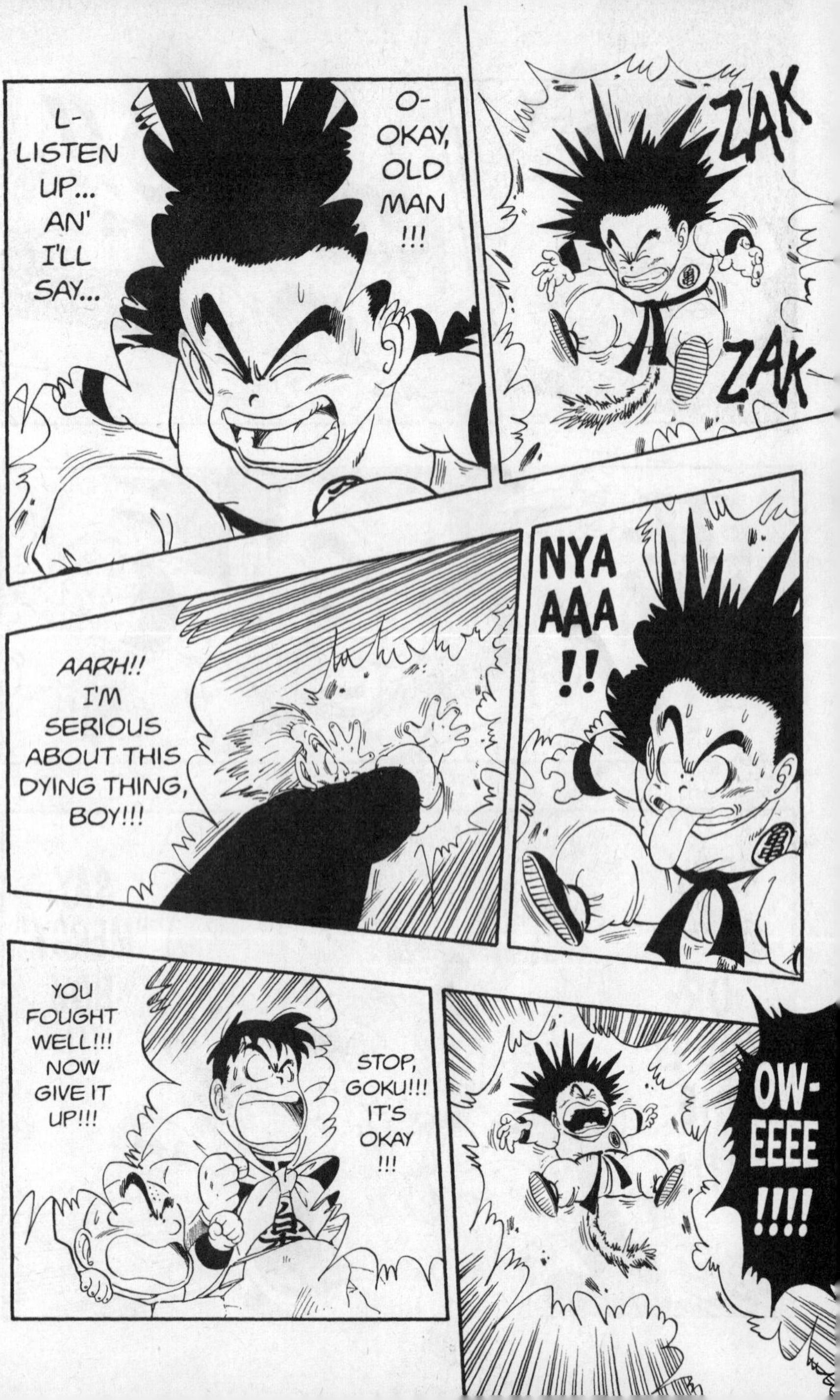
ZAK
ZAK
O- OKAY, OLD MAN!!!
L- LISTEN UP... AN' I'LL SAY...
NYA AAA!!
AARH!! I'M SERIOUS ABOUT THIS DYING THING, BOY!!!
OW-EEEE!!!!
STOP, GOKU!!! IT'S OKAY!!!
YOU FOUGHT WELL!!! NOW GIVE IT UP!!!

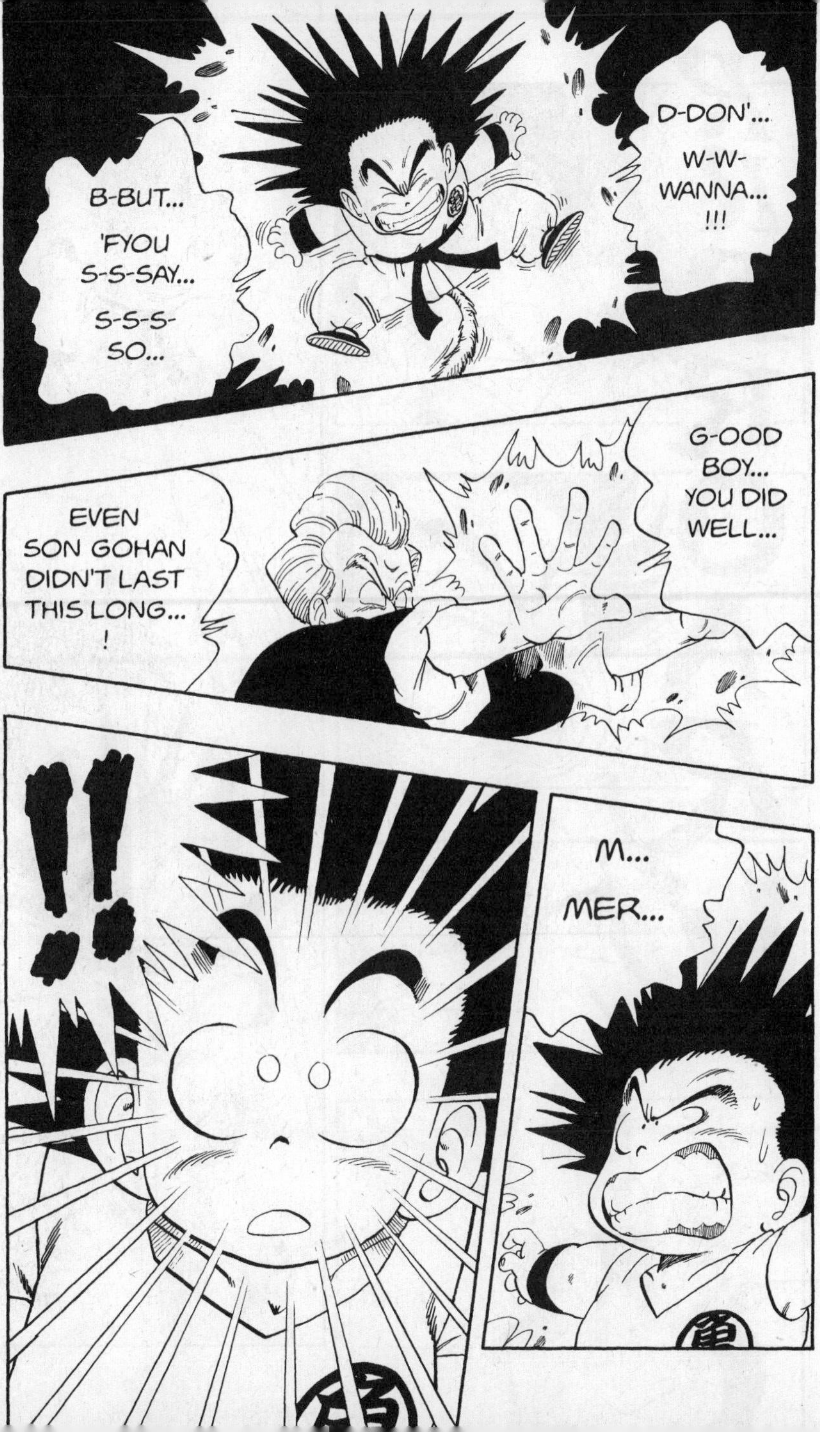
D-DON'... W-W-WANNA... !!!
B-BUT... 'FYOU S-S-SAY... S-S-S-SO...
G-OOD BOY... YOU DID WELL...
EVEN SON GOHAN DIDN'T LAST THIS LONG... !
M... MER...
!!

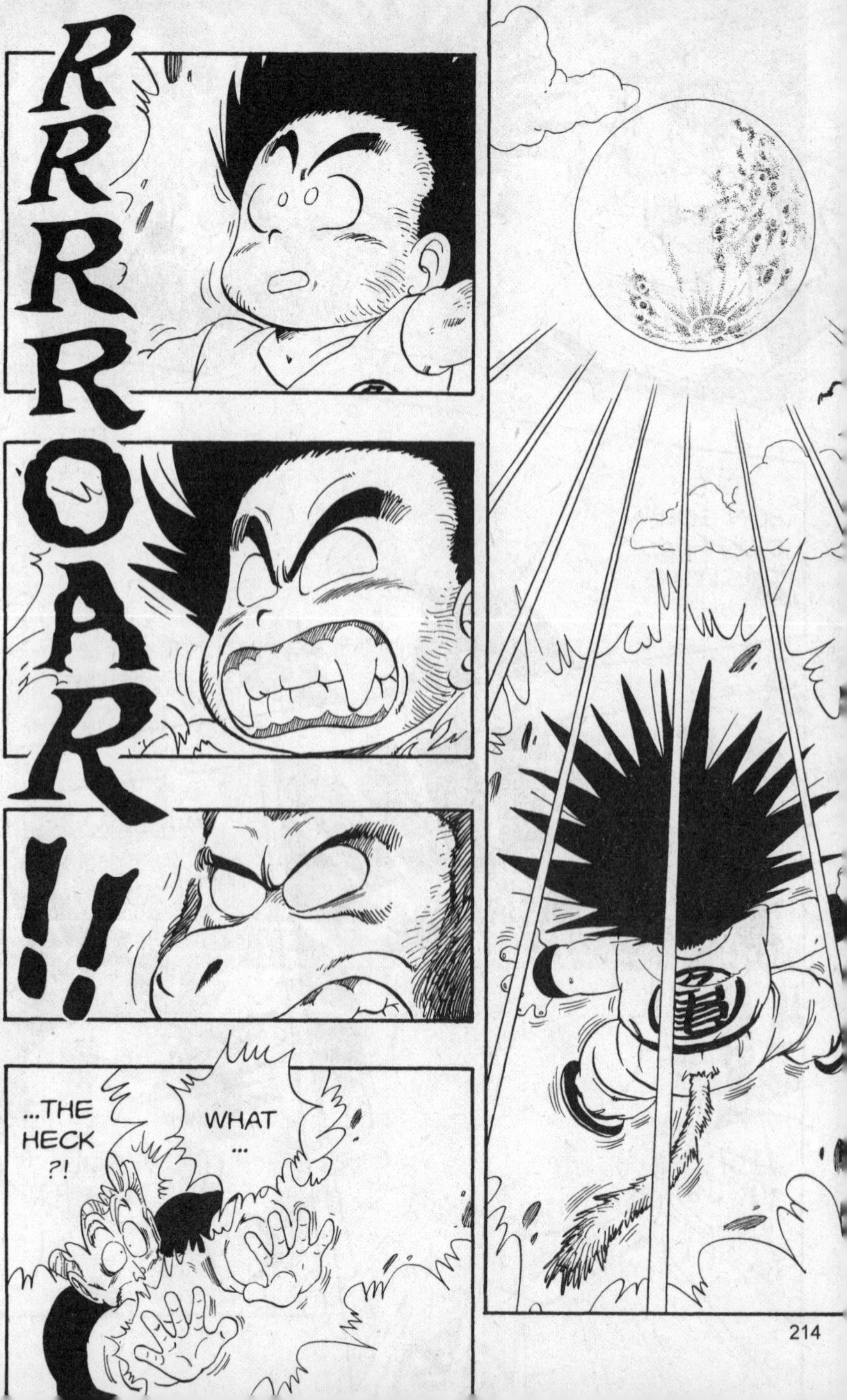
RRRROAR!!
WHAT ...
...THE HECK ?!

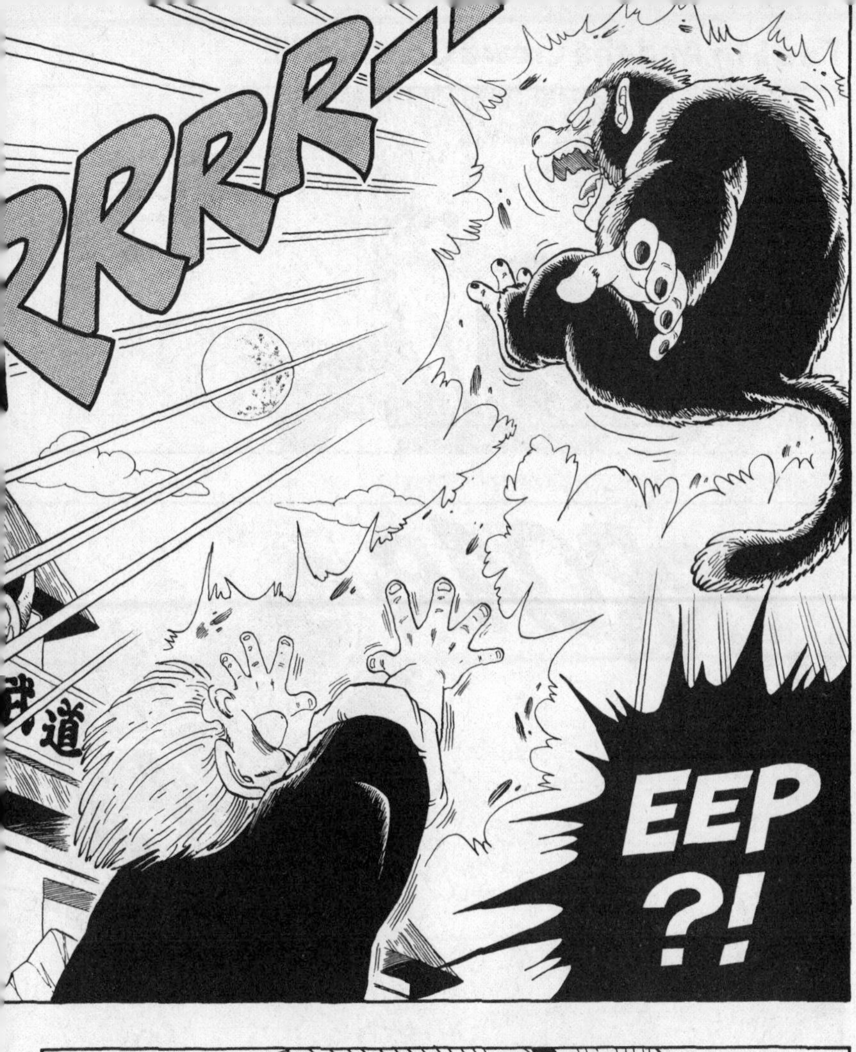
RRRR–
道
EEP ?!

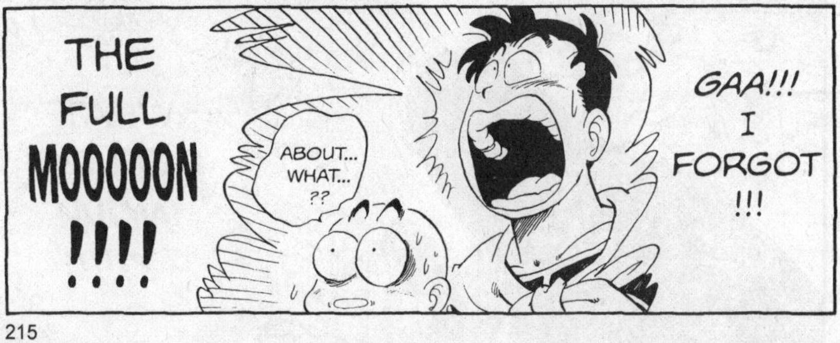
GAA!!! I FORGOT !!!
ABOUT... WHAT... ??
THE FULL MOOOOON !!!!

Tale 51 • And the Crowd Goes Wild!!!

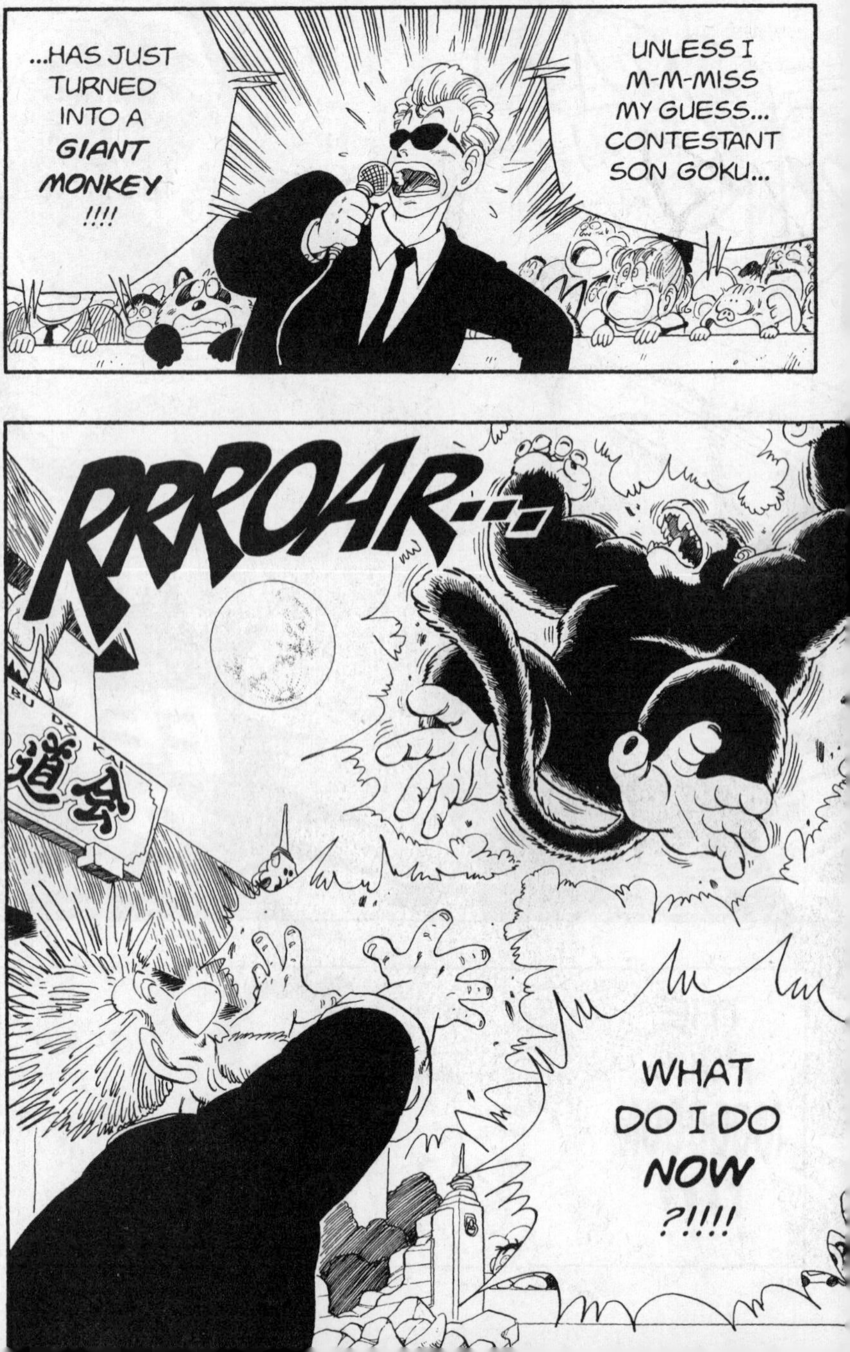
UNLESS I M-M-MISS MY GUESS... CONTESTANT SON GOKU...
...HAS JUST TURNED INTO A GIANT MONKEY !!!!
RRROAR...
BU DŌ KAI
WHAT DO I DO NOW ?!!!!

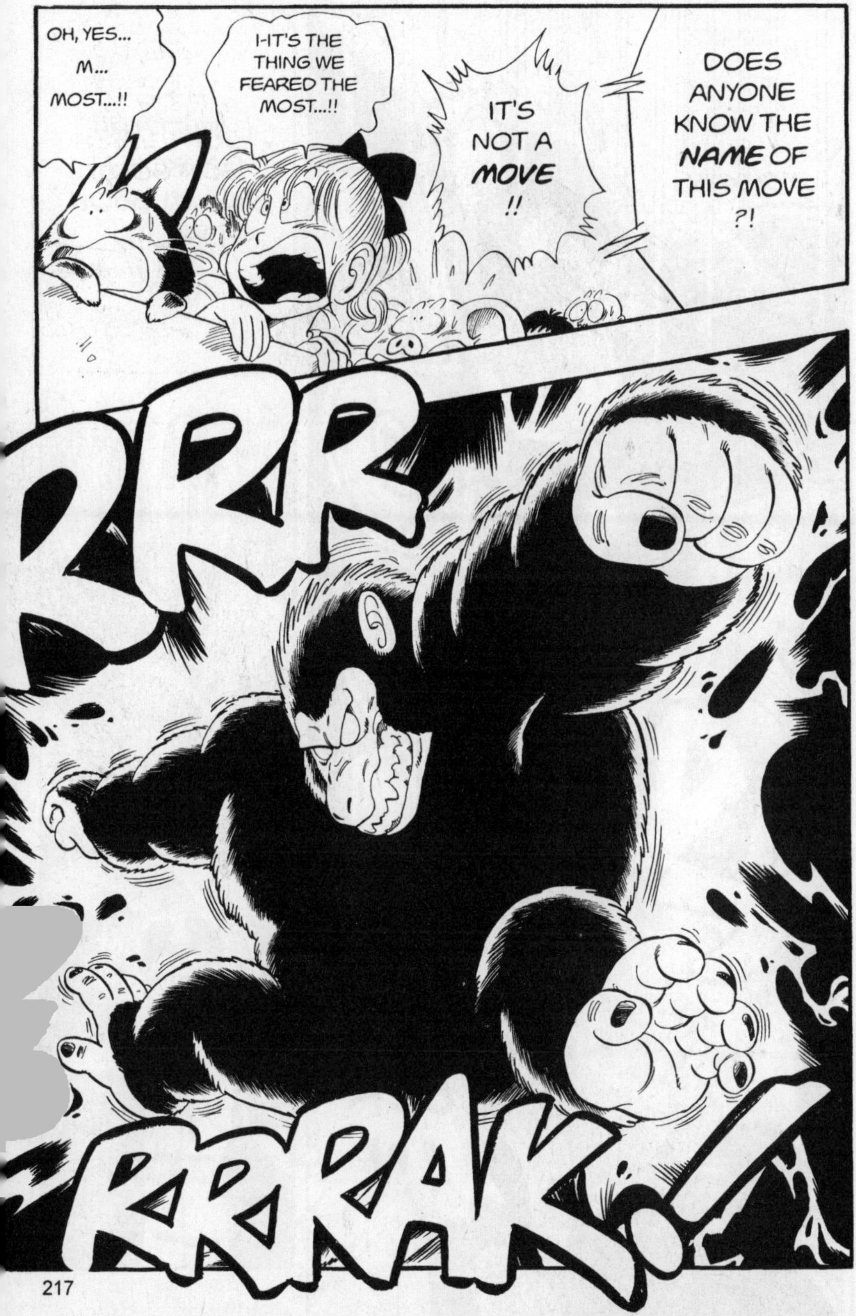
DOES ANYONE KNOW THE NAME OF THIS MOVE ?!
IT'S NOT A MOVE !!
I-IT'S THE THING WE FEARED THE MOST...!!
OH, YES... M... MOST...!!
RRR
RRRAK...!

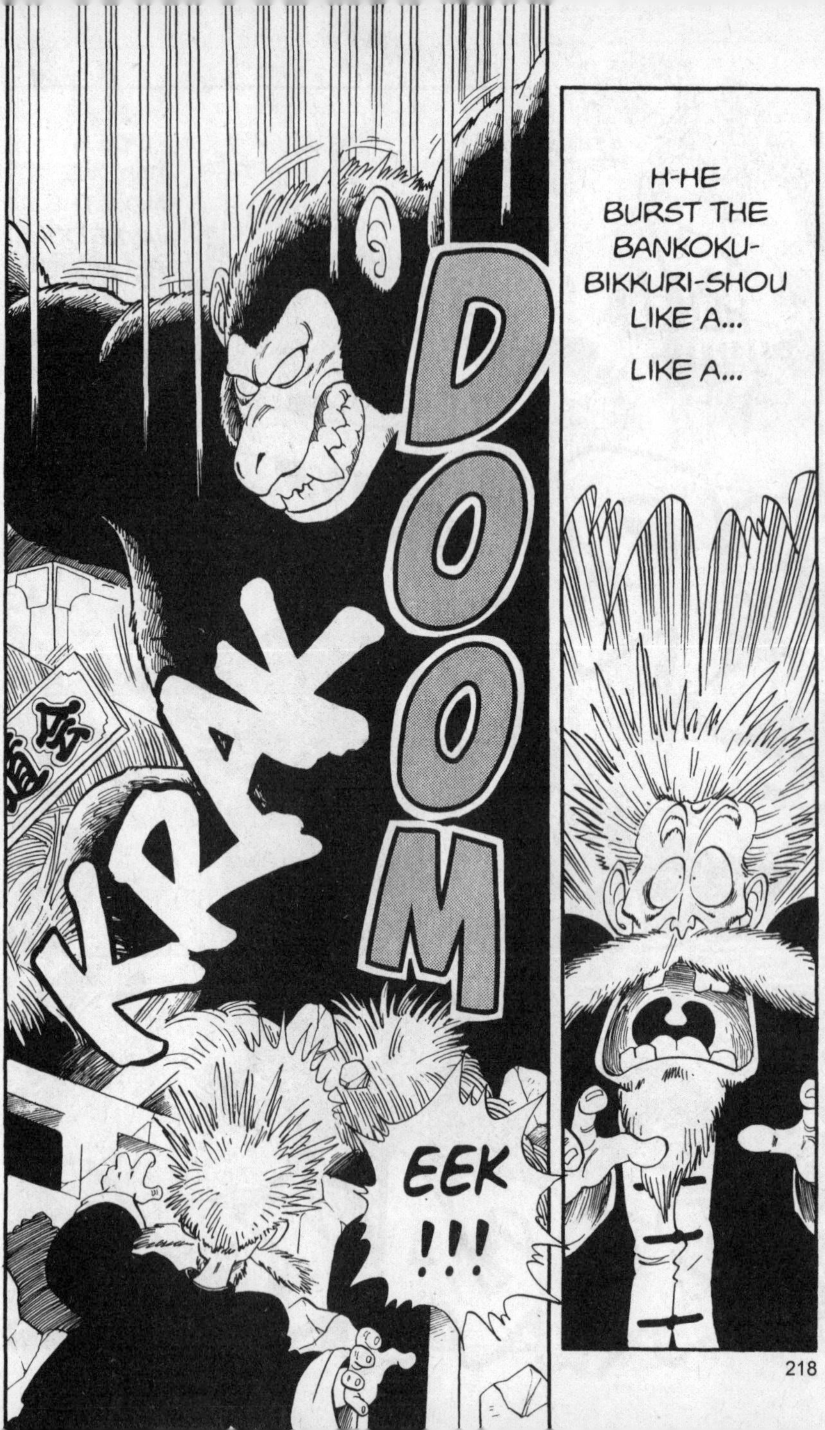
H-HE BURST THE BANKOKU-BIKKURI-SHOU LIKE A...
LIKE A...
DOOM
KRAK
EEK !!!

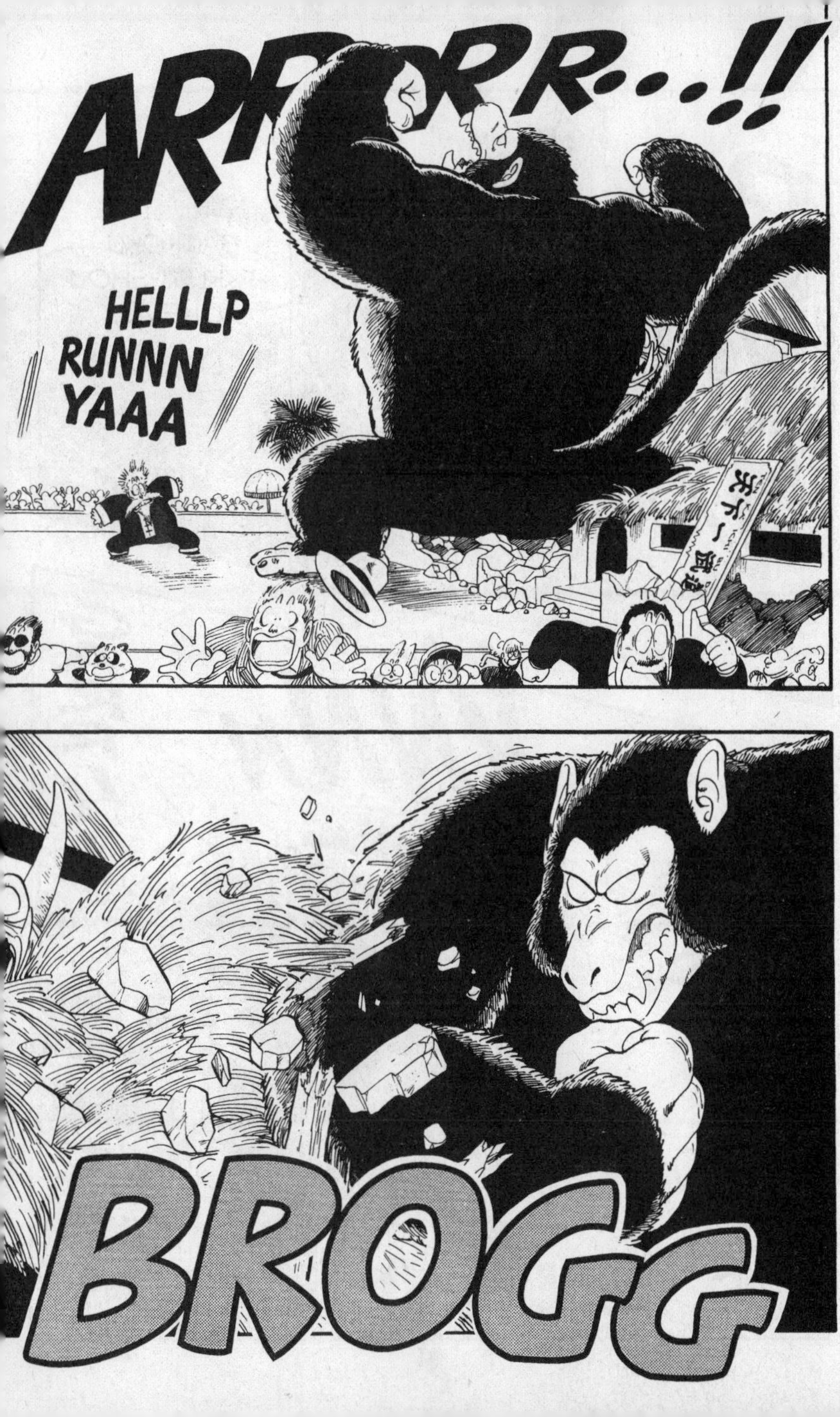
ARRRR..!!
HELLLP
RUNNN
YAAA
BROGG

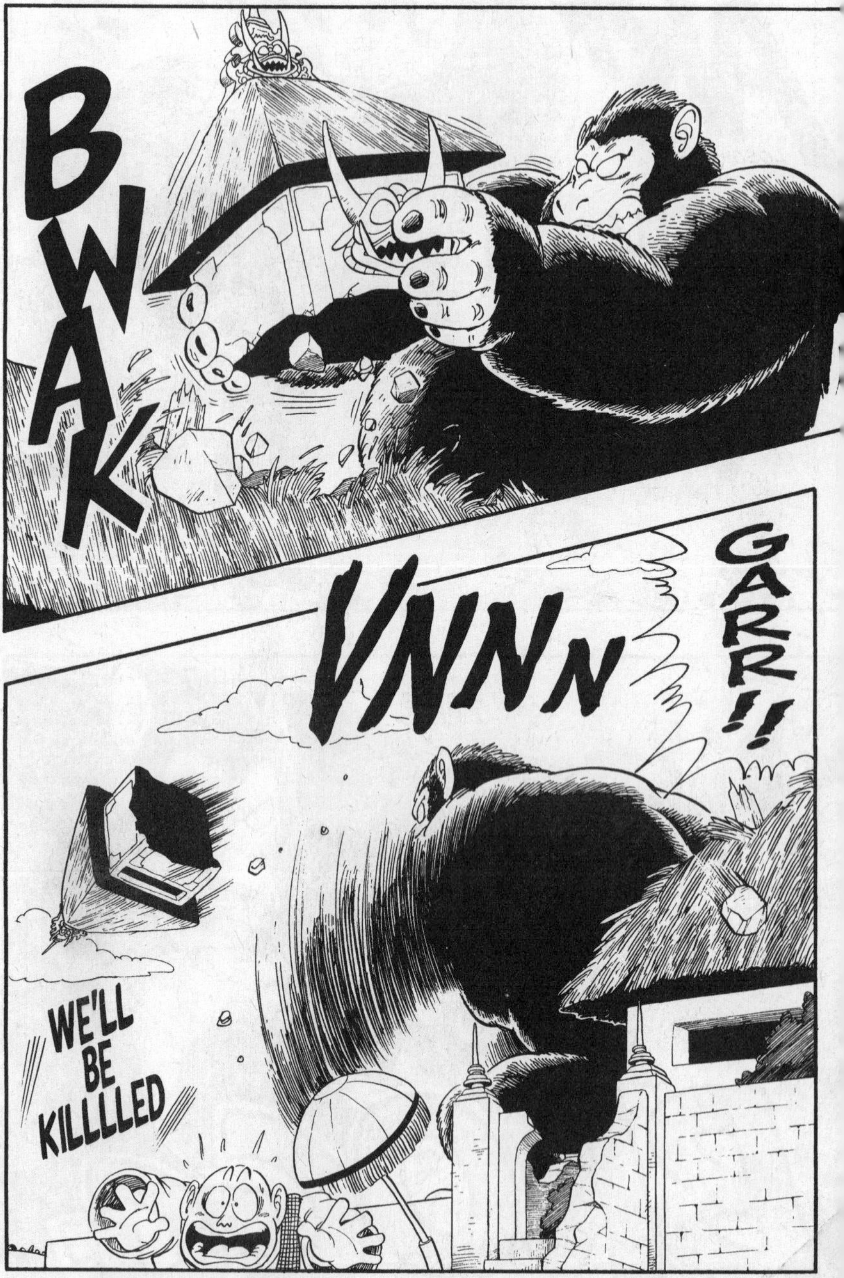
BWAK
GARR!!
VNNN
WE'LL BE KILLLLED

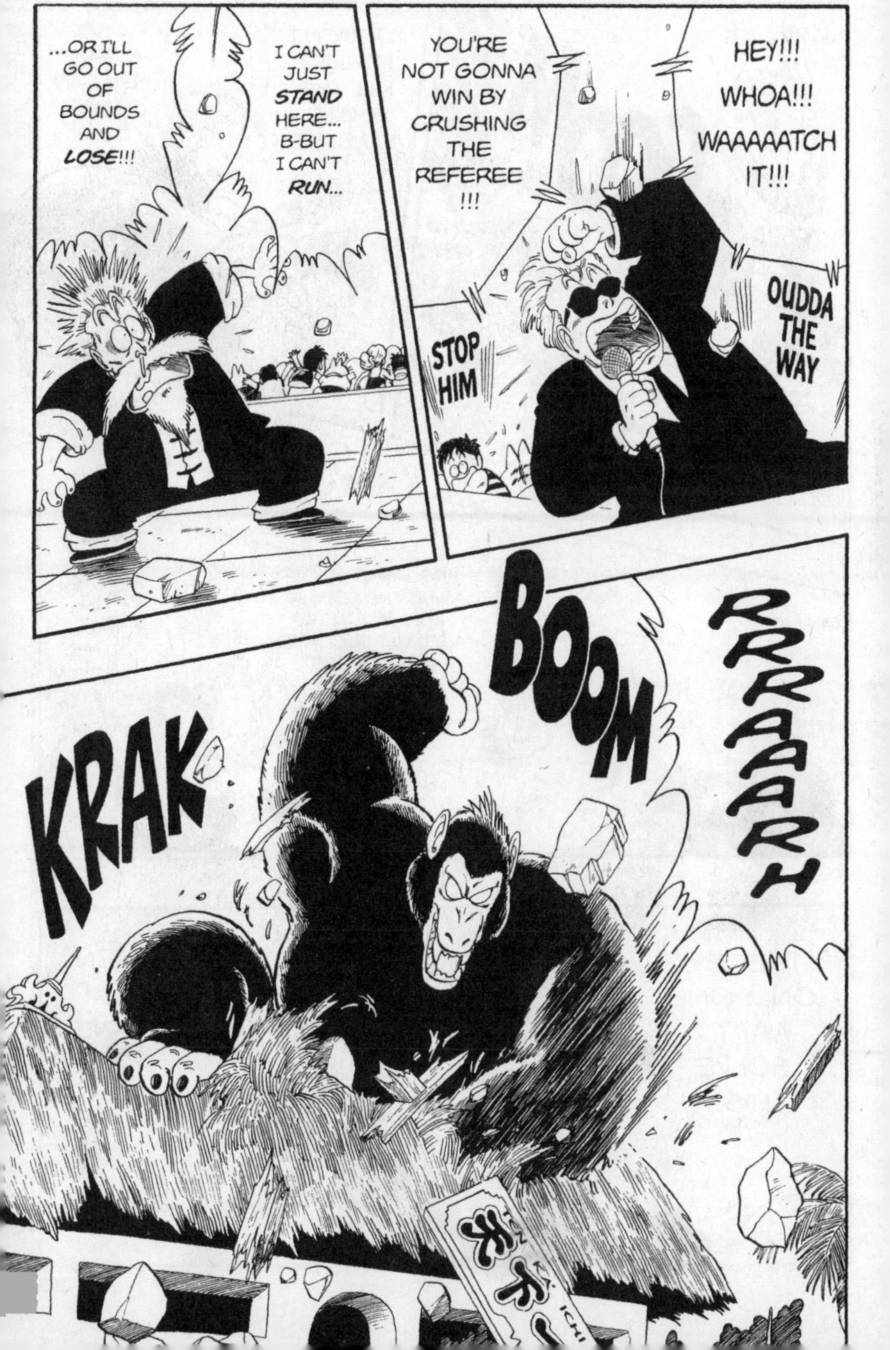
HEY!!! WHOA!!! WAAAAATCH IT!!!
YOU'RE NOT GONNA WIN BY CRUSHING THE REFEREE !!!
OUDDA THE WAY
STOP HIM
I CAN'T JUST STAND HERE... B-BUT I CAN'T RUN...
...OR I'LL GO OUT OF BOUNDS AND LOSE!!!
RRRAAARH
BOOM
KRAK

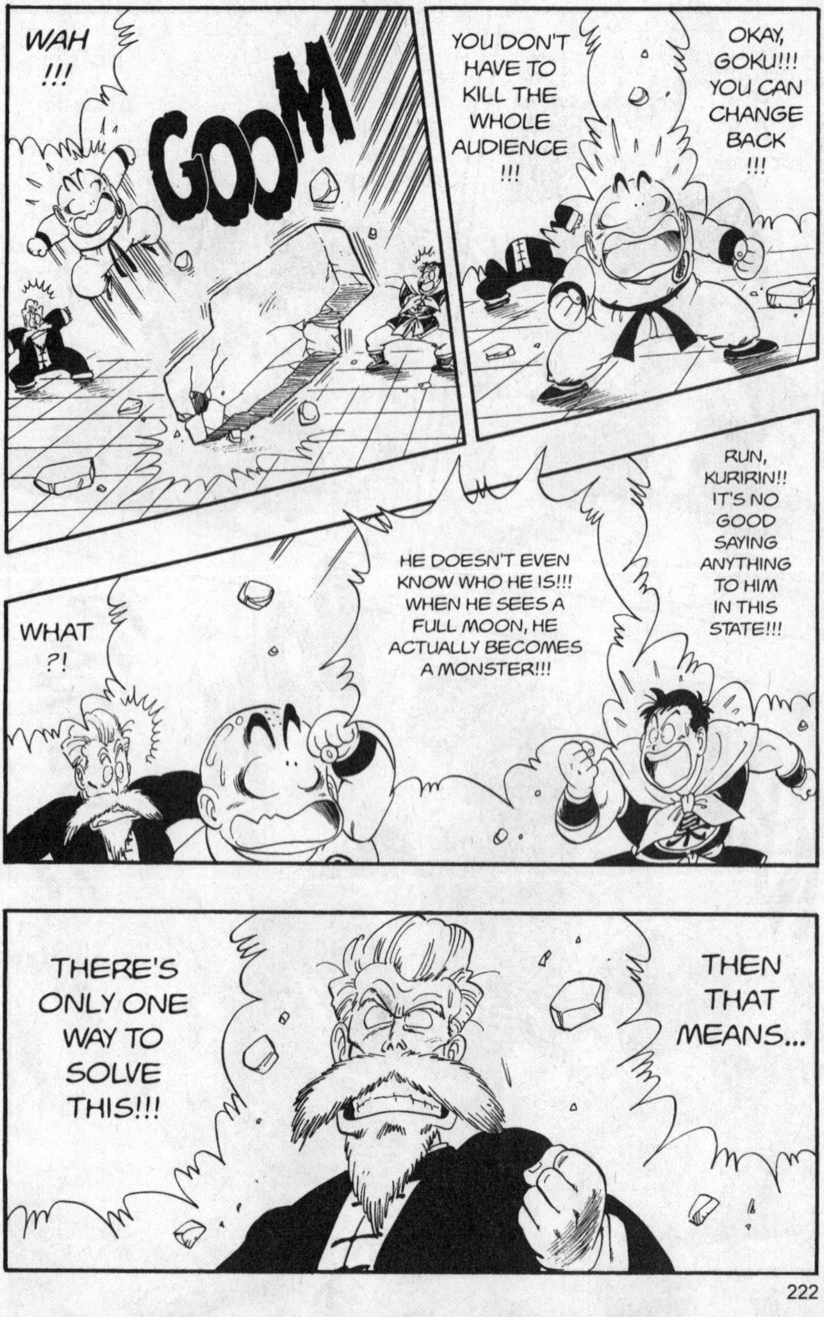
OKAY, GOKU!!! YOU CAN CHANGE BACK !!!
YOU DON'T HAVE TO KILL THE WHOLE AUDIENCE !!!
GOOM
WAH !!!
RUN, KURIRIN!! IT'S NO GOOD SAYING ANYTHING TO HIM IN THIS STATE!!!
HE DOESN'T EVEN KNOW WHO HE IS!!! WHEN HE SEES A FULL MOON, HE ACTUALLY BECOMES A MONSTER!!!
WHAT ?!
THEN THAT MEANS...
THERE'S ONLY ONE WAY TO SOLVE THIS!!!

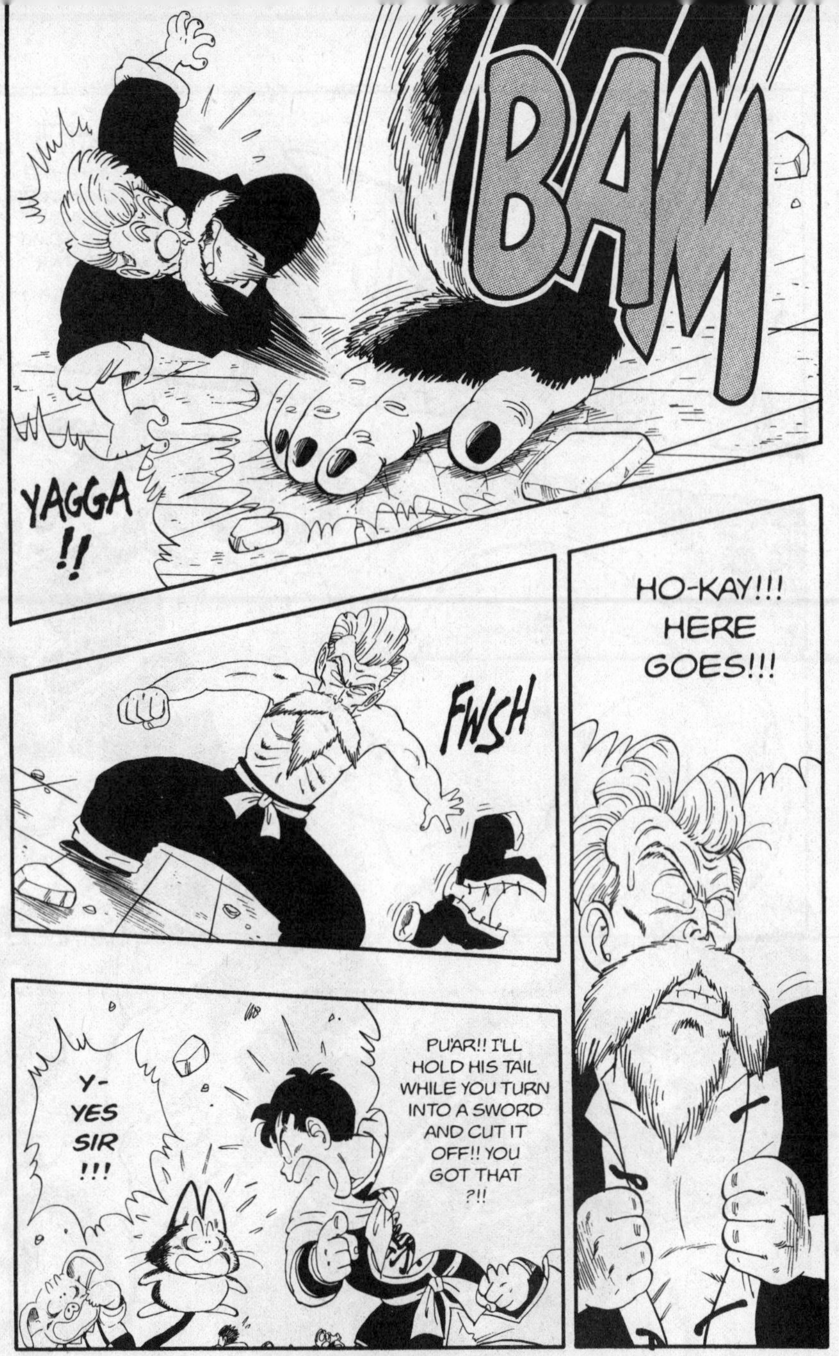
BAM
YAGGA !!
HO-KAY!!! HERE GOES!!!
FWSH
PU'AR!! I'LL HOLD HIS TAIL WHILE YOU TURN INTO A SWORD AND CUT IT OFF!! YOU GOT THAT ?!!
Y- YES SIR !!!

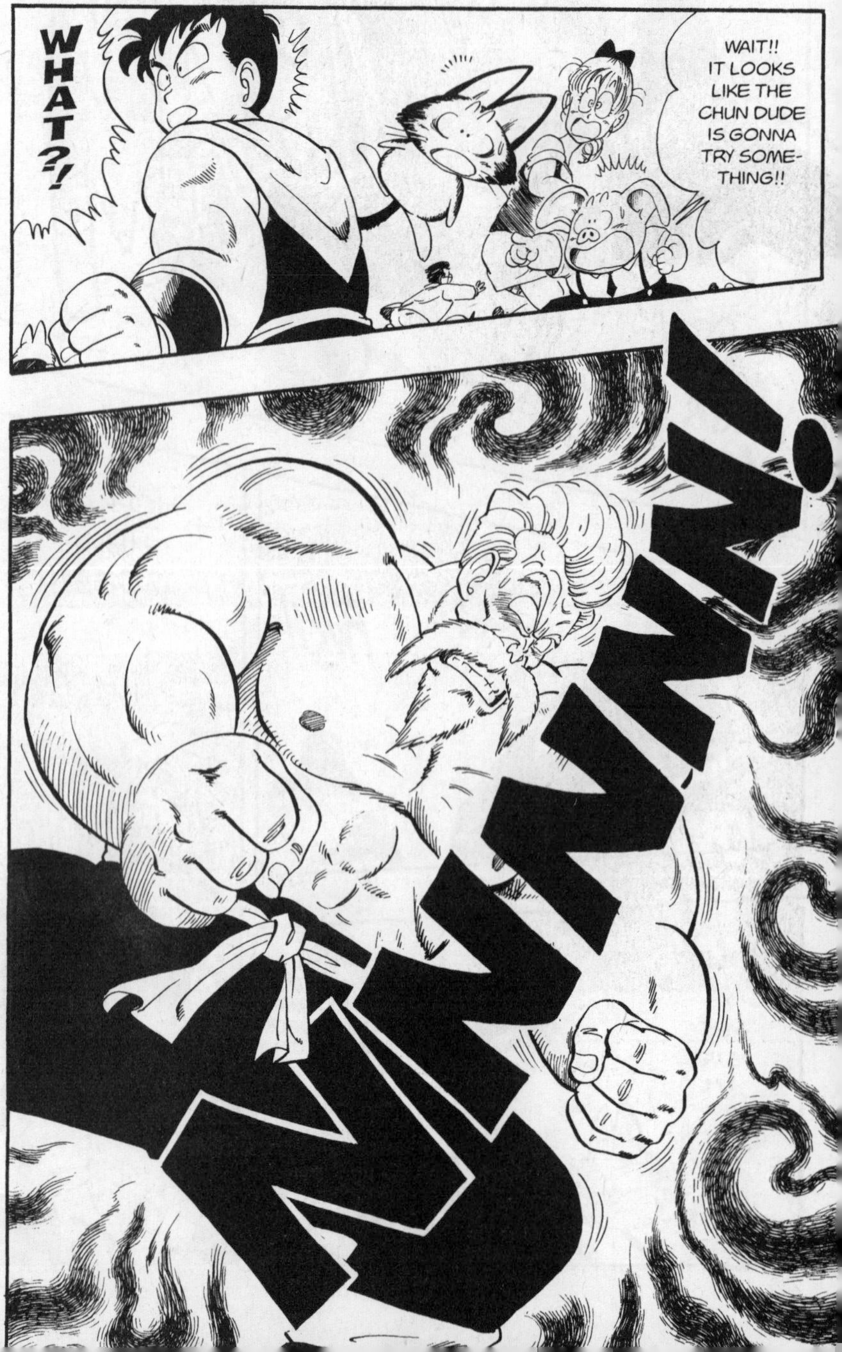
WAIT!! IT LOOKS LIKE THE CHUN DUDE IS GONNA TRY SOME-THING!!
WHAT?!

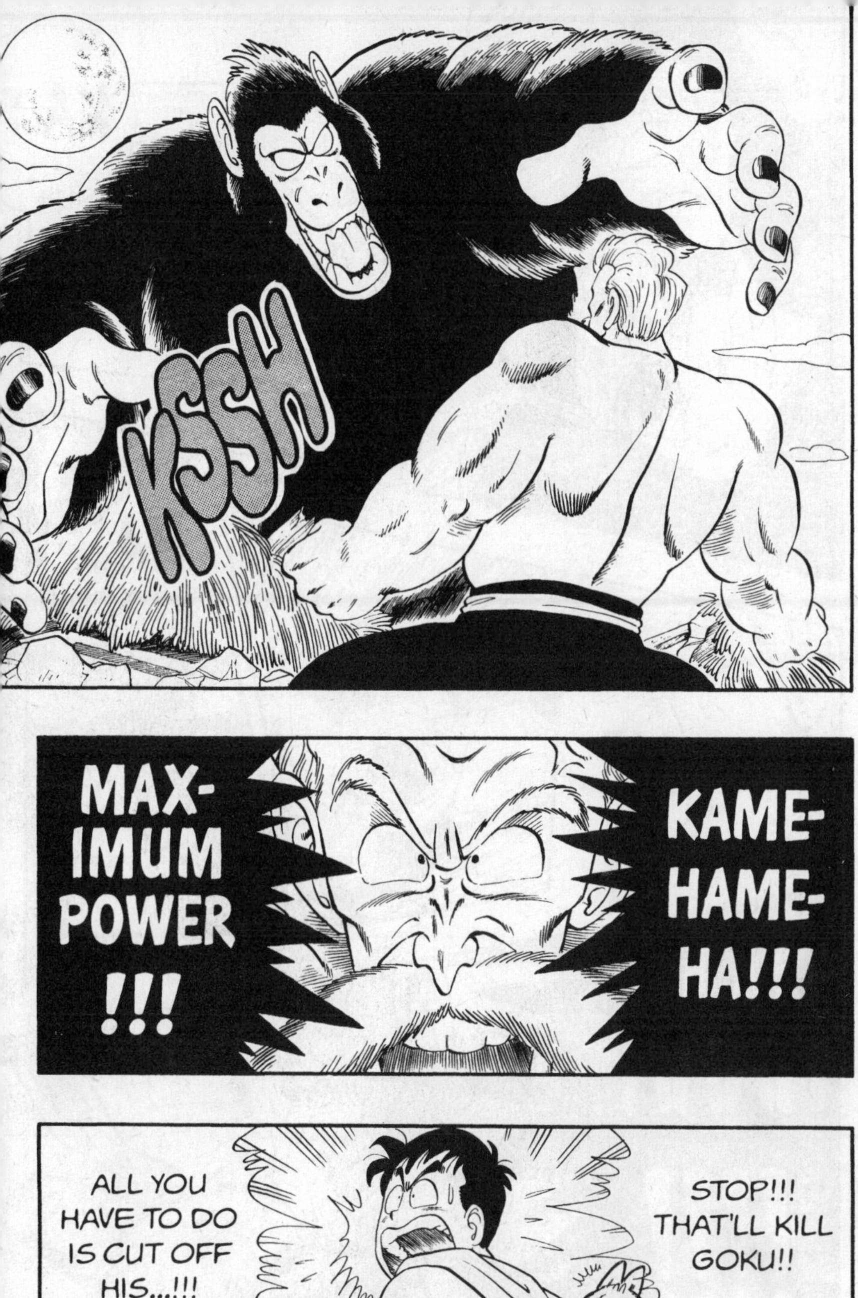
KSSH
KAME-HAME-HA!!!
MAX-IMUM POWER!!!
STOP!!! THAT'LL KILL GOKU!!
ALL YOU HAVE TO DO IS CUT OFF HIS...!!!

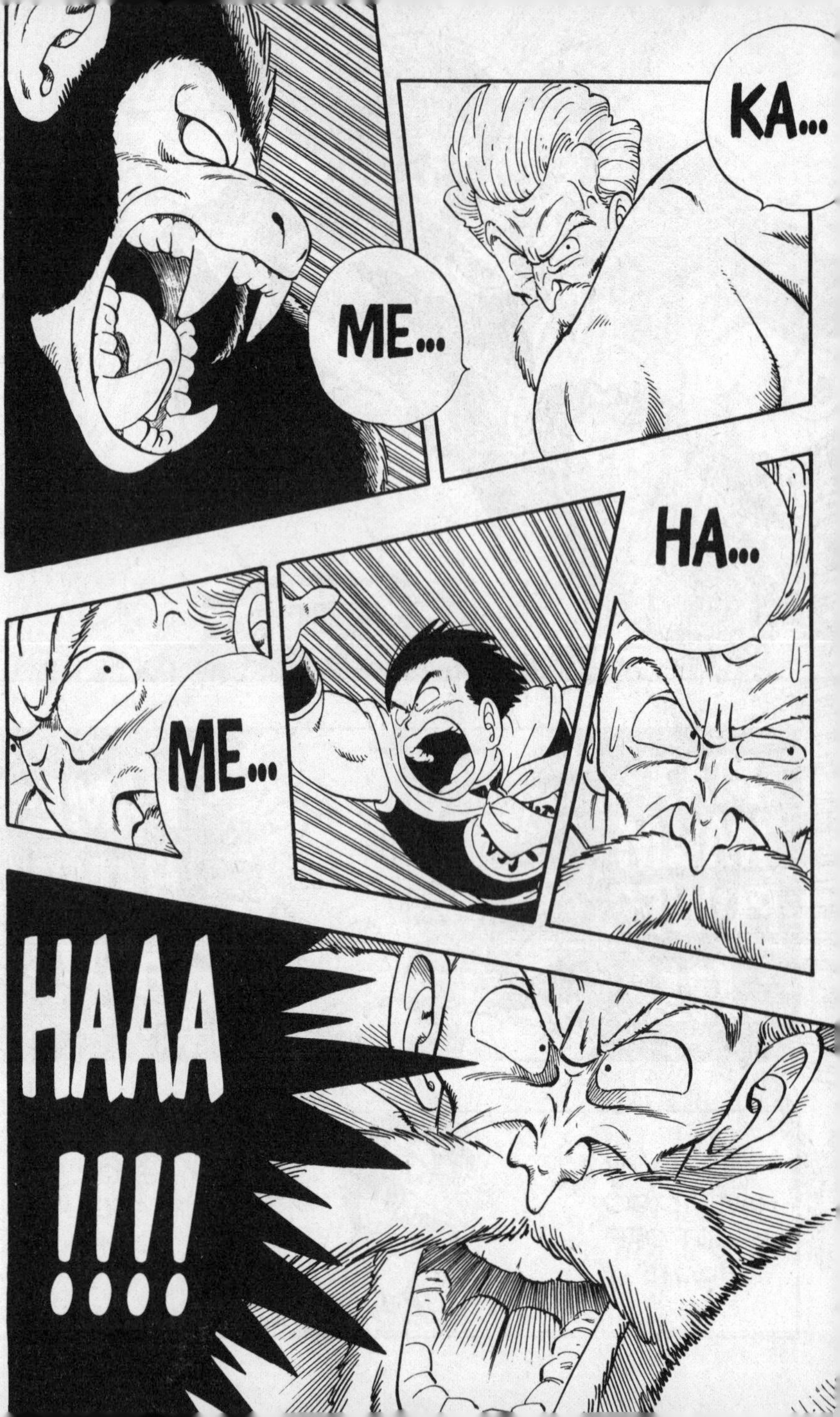
KA...
ME...
HA...
ME...
HAAA !!!!!

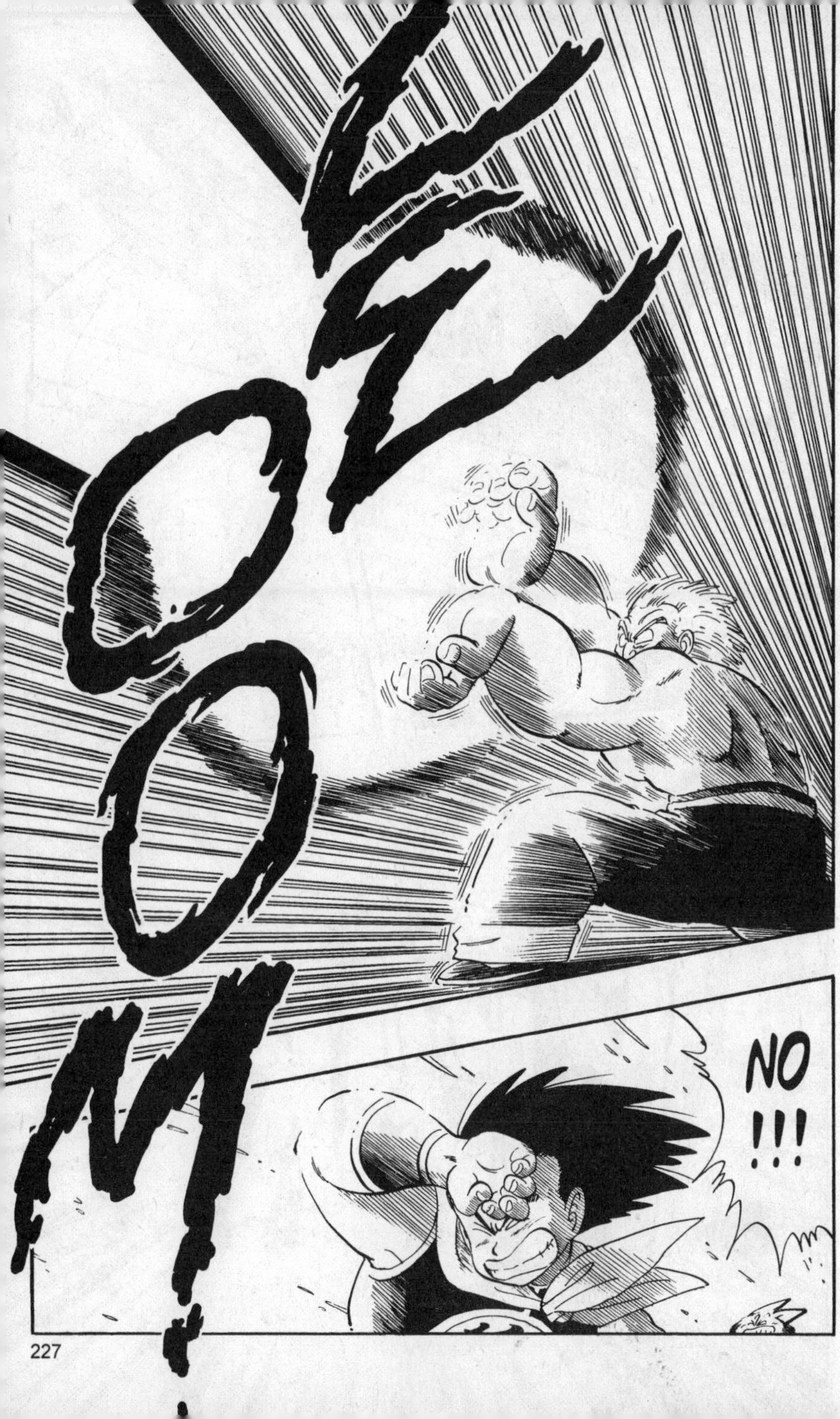
ZOOOM
NO !!!

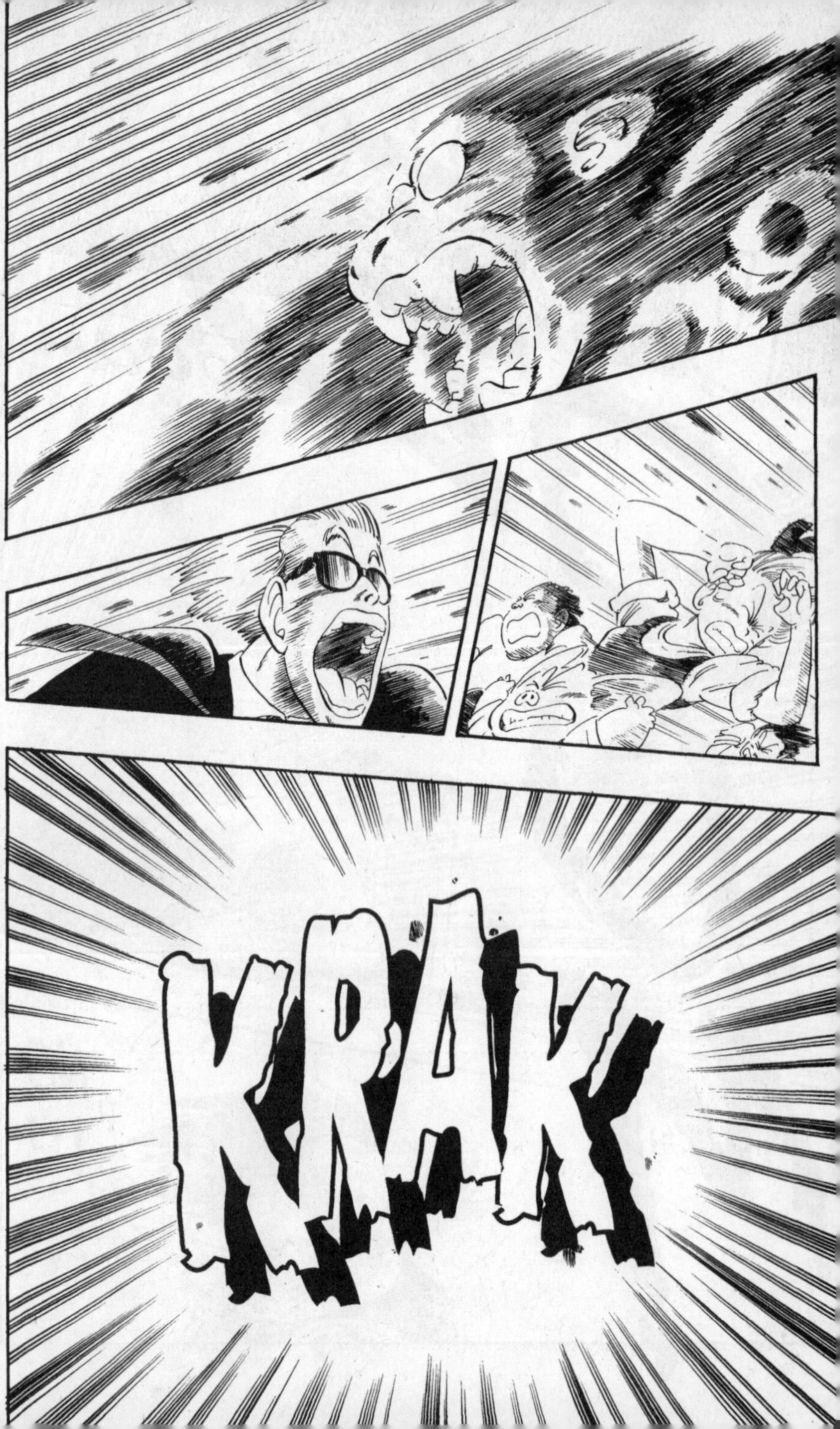
KRAK

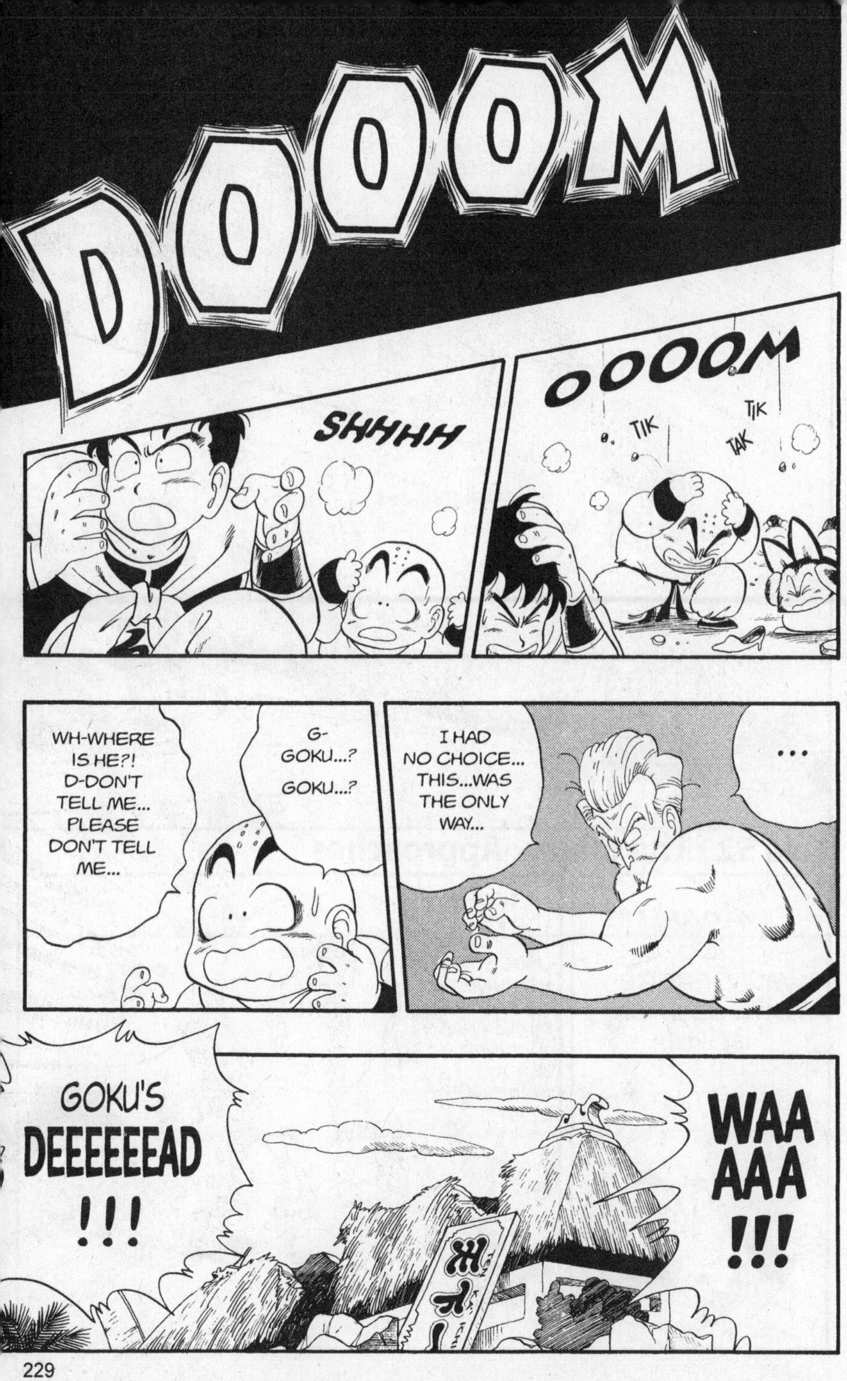
DOOOM
OOOOM
TIK
TAK
TIK
SHHHH
...
I HAD NO CHOICE... THIS...WAS THE ONLY WAY...
G- GOKU...? GOKU...?
WH-WHERE IS HE?! D-DON'T TELL ME... PLEASE DON'T TELL ME...
WAAAAA!!!
GOKU'S DEEEEEEAD!!!

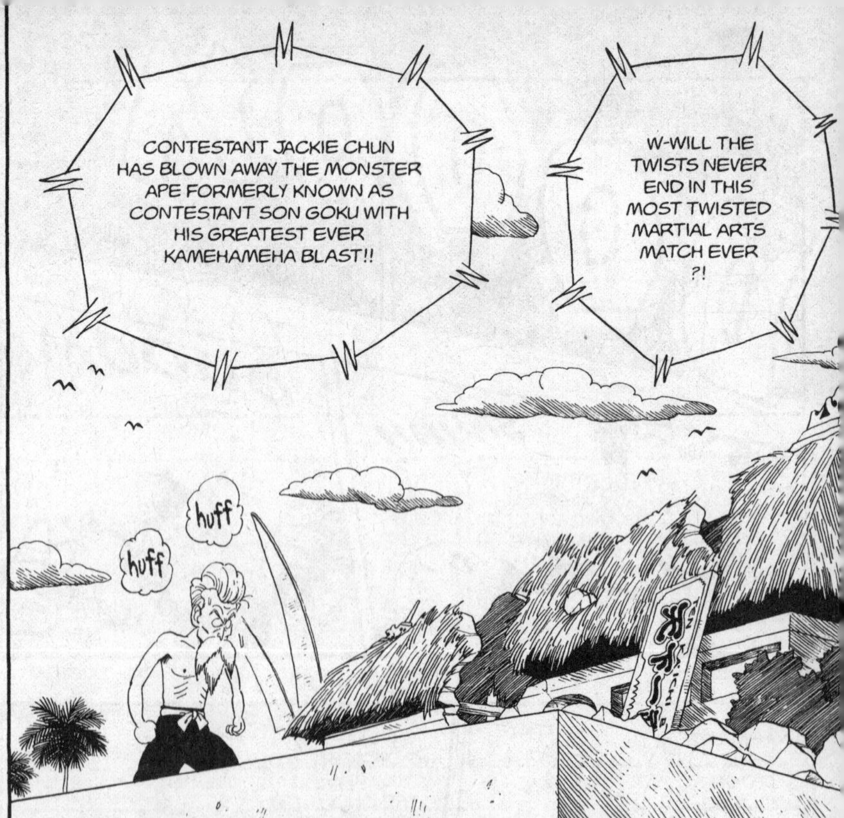
W-WILL THE TWISTS NEVER END IN THIS MOST TWISTED MARTIAL ARTS MATCH EVER ?!
CONTESTANT JACKIE CHUN HAS BLOWN AWAY THE MONSTER APE FORMERLY KNOWN AS CONTESTANT SON GOKU WITH HIS GREATEST EVER KAMEHAMEHA BLAST!!
huff
huff

Tale 52 • The Climax Approaches

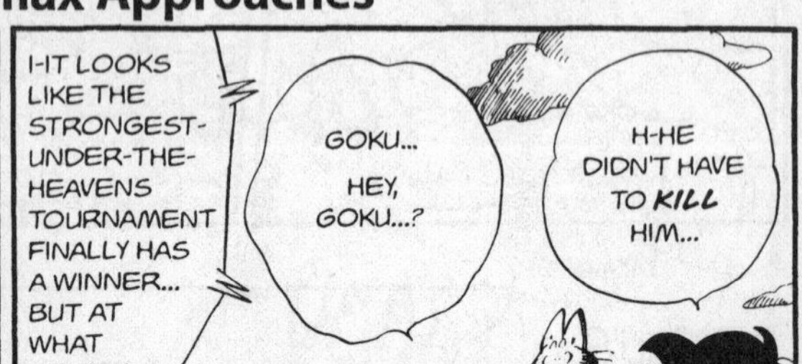
H-HE DIDN'T HAVE TO KILL HIM...
GOKU... HEY, GOKU...?
I-IT LOOKS LIKE THE STRONGEST-UNDER-THE-HEAVENS TOURNAMENT FINALLY HAS A WINNER... BUT AT WHAT COST?!
MURMUR
MURMUR

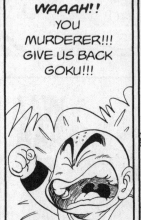

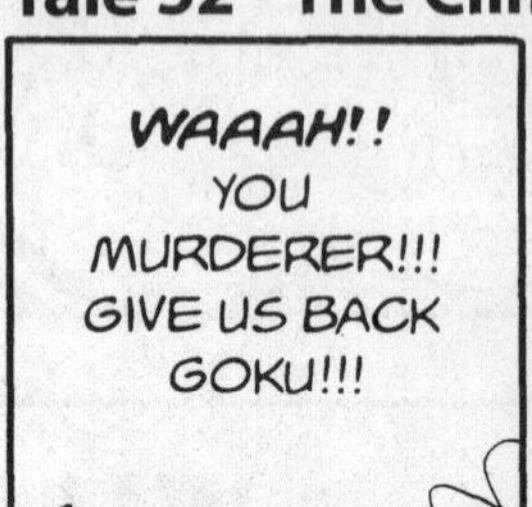
WAAAH!! YOU MURDERER!!! GIVE US BACK GOKU!!!

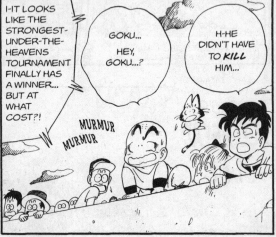

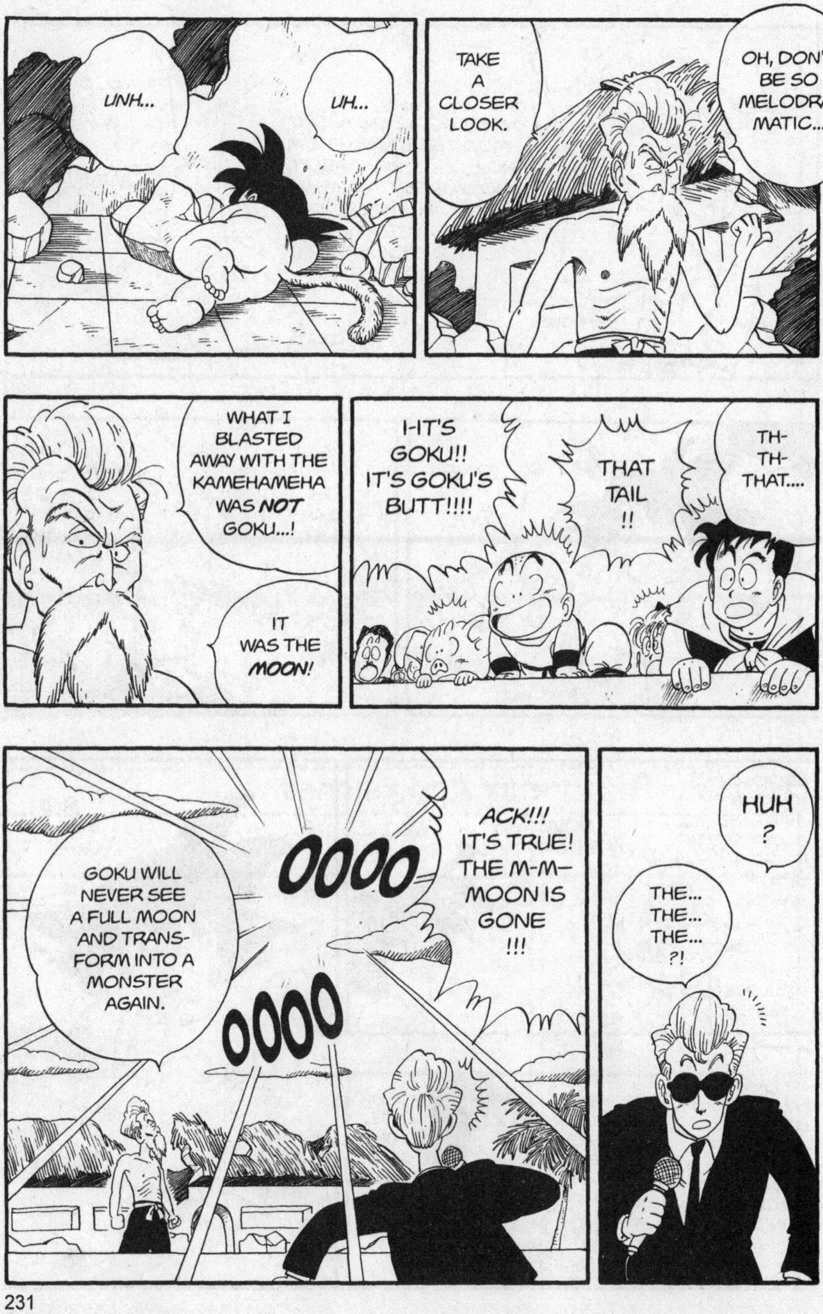
OH, DON'T BE SO MELODRAMATIC...
TAKE A CLOSER LOOK.
UH...
UNH...
TH-TH-THAT....
THAT TAIL!!
I-IT'S GOKU!! IT'S GOKU'S BUTT!!!!
WHAT I BLASTED AWAY WITH THE KAMEHAMEHA WAS *NOT* GOKU...!
IT WAS THE *MOON*!
HUH?
THE... THE... THE...?!
ACK!!! IT'S TRUE! THE M-M-MOON IS GONE!!!
OOOO
GOKU WILL NEVER SEE A FULL MOON AND TRANSFORM INTO A MONSTER AGAIN.
OOOO

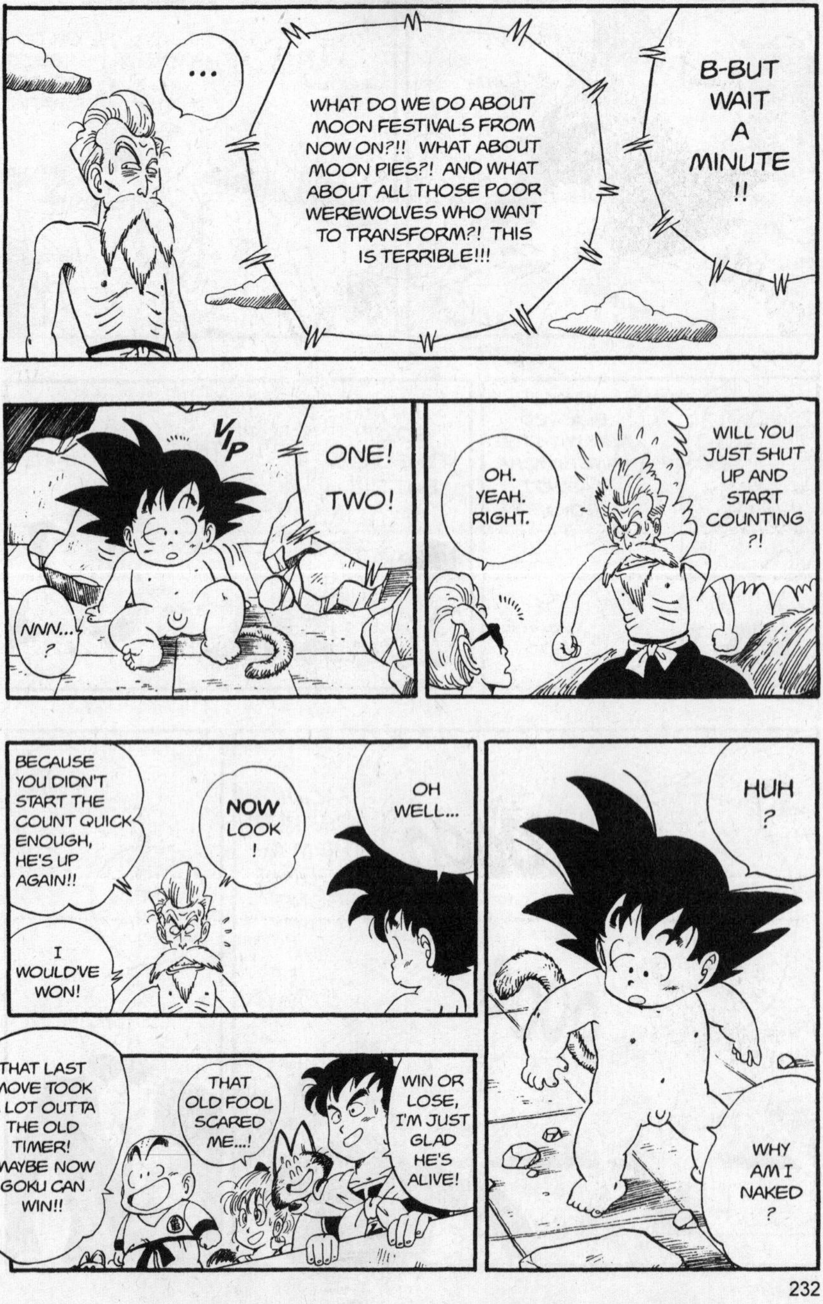

B-BUT WAIT A MINUTE !!
WHAT DO WE DO ABOUT MOON FESTIVALS FROM NOW ON?!! WHAT ABOUT MOON PIES?! AND WHAT ABOUT ALL THOSE POOR WEREWOLVES WHO WANT TO TRANSFORM?! THIS IS TERRIBLE!!!
...
WILL YOU JUST SHUT UP AND START COUNTING ?!
OH. YEAH. RIGHT.
ONE!
TWO!
VIP
NNN... ?
HUH ?
WHY AM I NAKED ?
OH WELL...
NOW LOOK !
BECAUSE YOU DIDN'T START THE COUNT QUICK ENOUGH, HE'S UP AGAIN!!
I WOULD'VE WON!
WIN OR LOSE, I'M JUST GLAD HE'S ALIVE!
THAT OLD FOOL SCARED ME...!
THAT LAST MOVE TOOK A LOT OUTTA THE OLD TIMER! MAYBE NOW GOKU CAN WIN!!

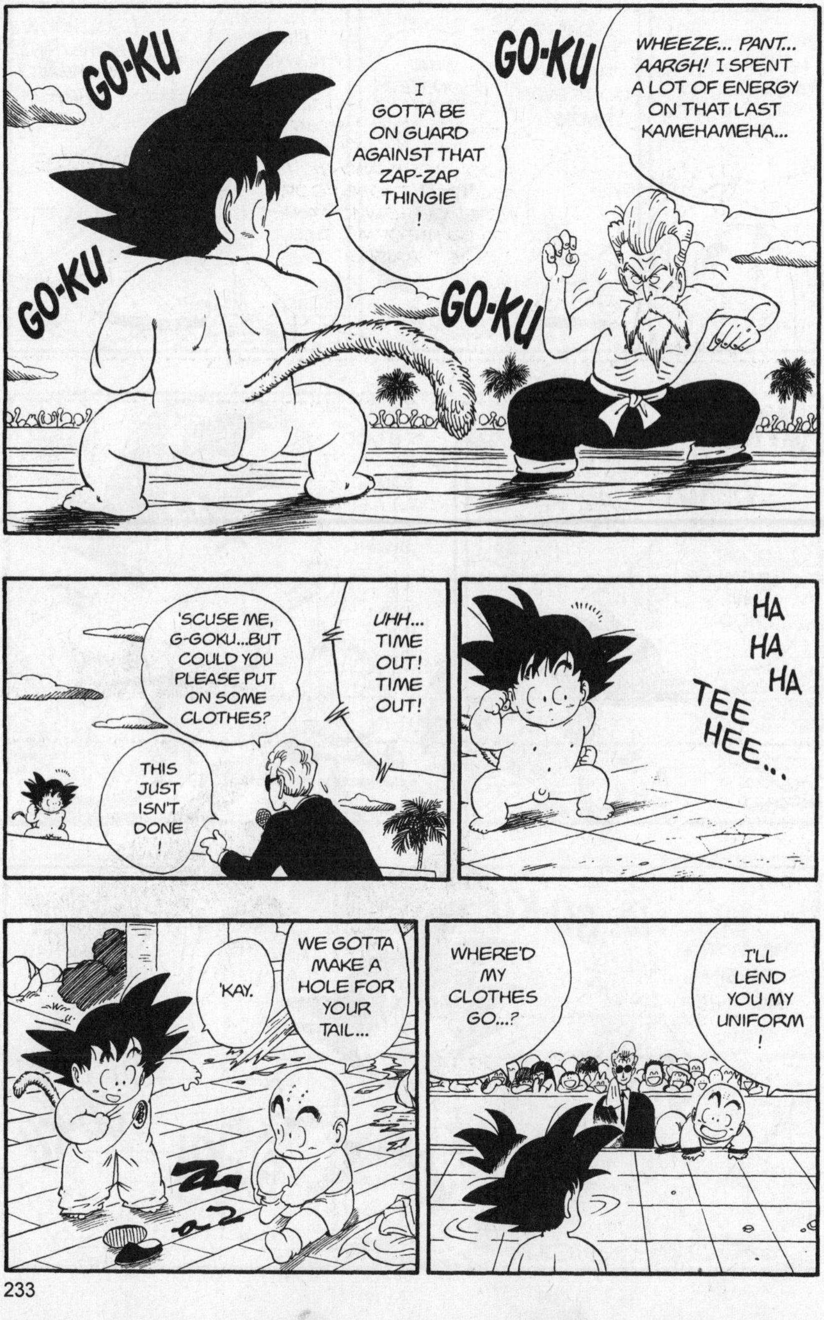
WHEEZE... PANT... AARGH! I SPENT A LOT OF ENERGY ON THAT LAST KAMEHAMEHA...
GO-KU
GO-KU
I GOTTA BE ON GUARD AGAINST THAT ZAP-ZAP THINGIE!
GO-KU
GO-KU
HA HA HA
TEE HEE...
UHH... TIME OUT! TIME OUT!
'SCUSE ME, G-GOKU...BUT COULD YOU PLEASE PUT ON SOME CLOTHES?
THIS JUST ISN'T DONE!
I'LL LEND YOU MY UNIFORM!
WHERE'D MY CLOTHES GO...?
WE GOTTA MAKE A HOLE FOR YOUR TAIL...
'KAY.

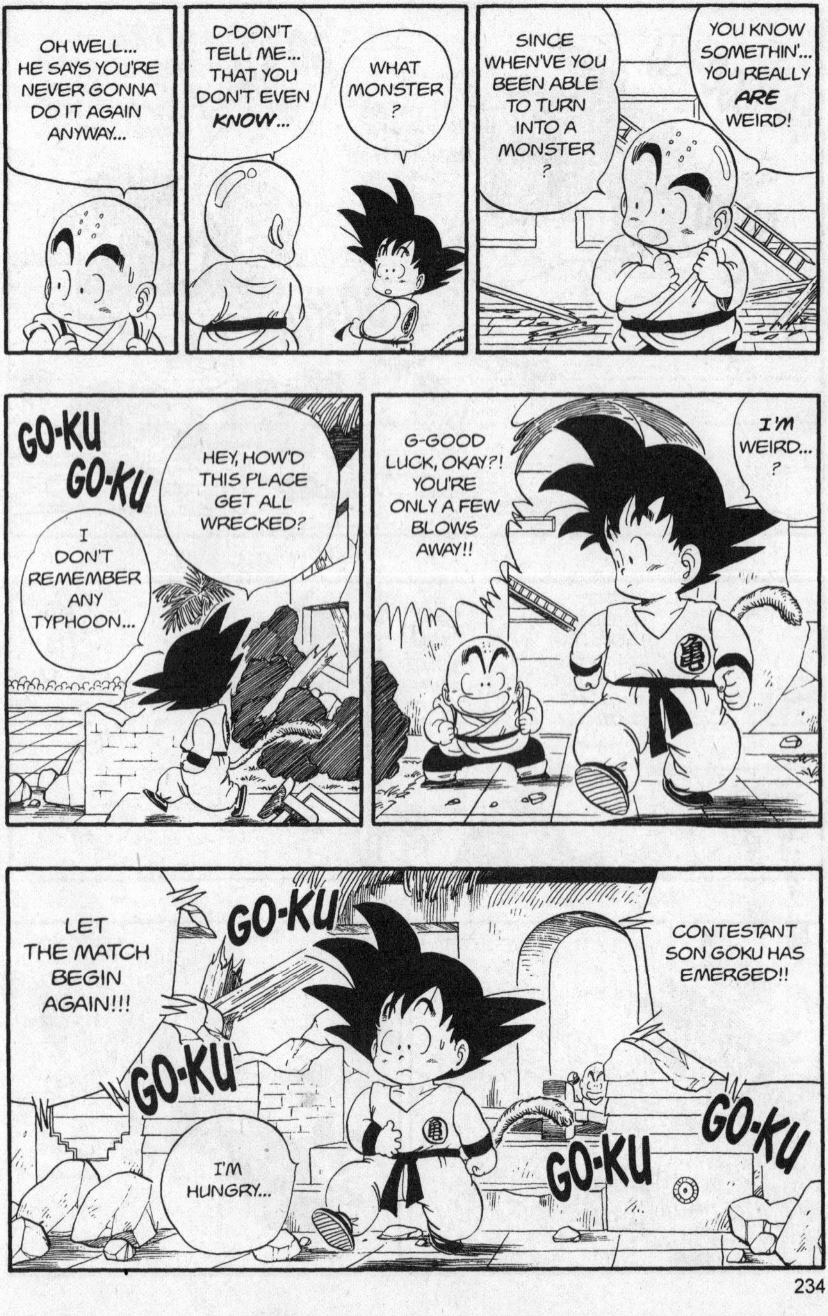
YOU KNOW SOMETHIN'... YOU REALLY ARE WEIRD!
SINCE WHEN'VE YOU BEEN ABLE TO TURN INTO A MONSTER?
WHAT MONSTER?
D-DON'T TELL ME... THAT YOU DON'T EVEN KNOW...
OH WELL... HE SAYS YOU'RE NEVER GONNA DO IT AGAIN ANYWAY...
I'M WEIRD...?
G-GOOD LUCK, OKAY?! YOU'RE ONLY A FEW BLOWS AWAY!!
HEY, HOW'D THIS PLACE GET ALL WRECKED?
GO-KU GO-KU
I DON'T REMEMBER ANY TYPHOON...
CONTESTANT SON GOKU HAS EMERGED!!
GO-KU
LET THE MATCH BEGIN AGAIN!!!
GO-KU
GO-KU
GO-KU
I'M HUNGRY...

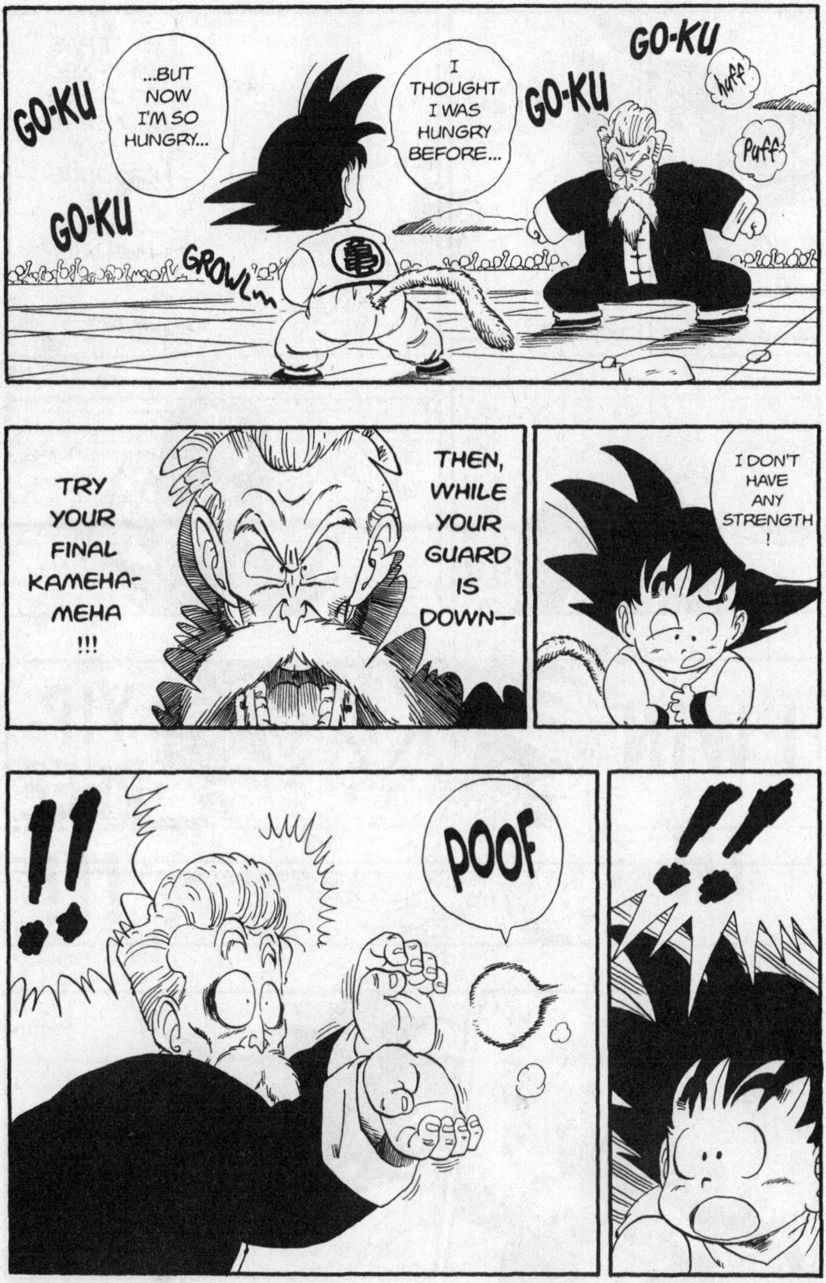
GO-KU
huff
puff
GO-KU
I THOUGHT I WAS HUNGRY BEFORE...
...BUT NOW I'M SO HUNGRY...
GO-KU
GO-KU
GROWL
I DON'T HAVE ANY STRENGTH!
THEN, WHILE YOUR GUARD IS DOWN—
TRY YOUR FINAL KAMEHA-MEHA!!!
!!
POOF
!!

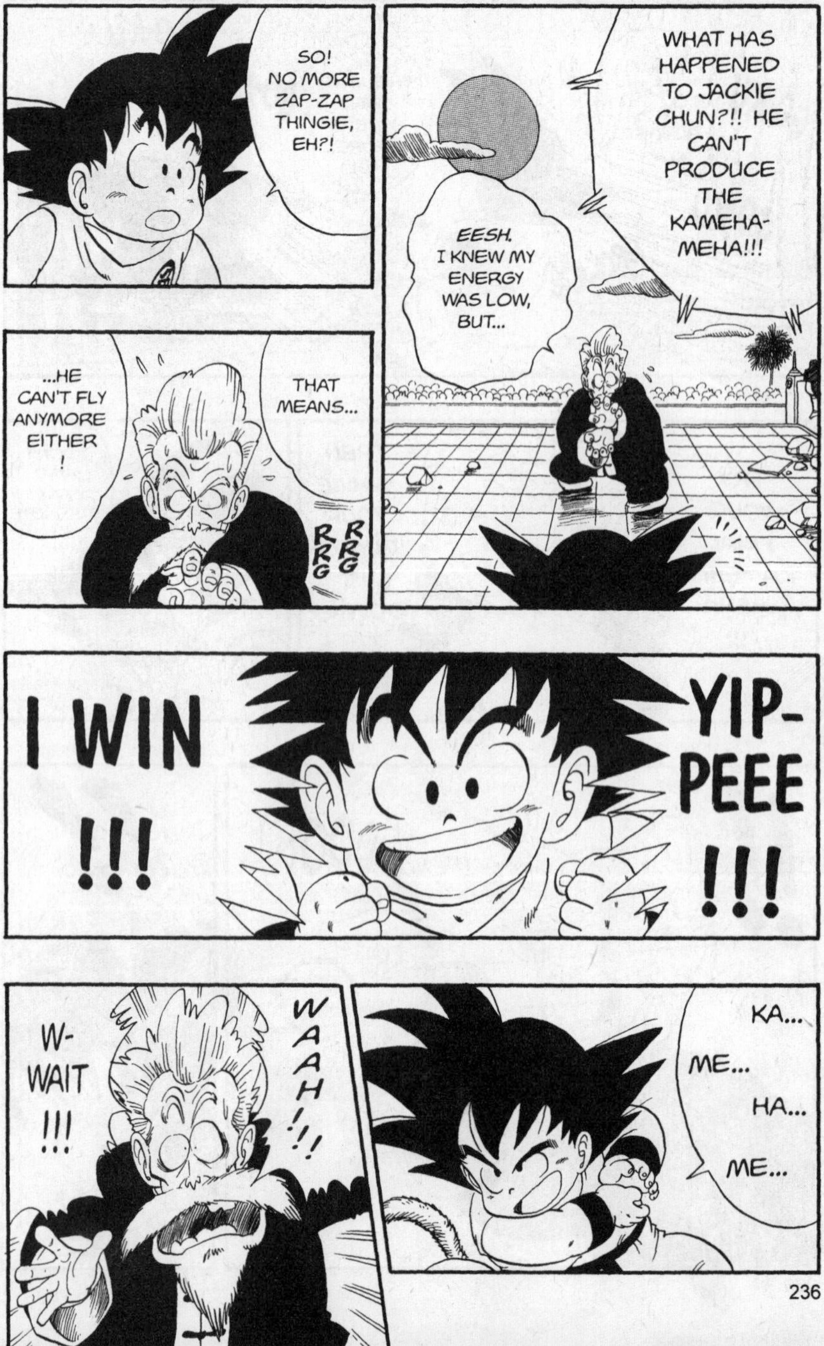
WHAT HAS HAPPENED TO JACKIE CHUN?!! HE CAN'T PRODUCE THE KAMEHA-MEHA!!!
EESH. I KNEW MY ENERGY WAS LOW, BUT...
SO! NO MORE ZAP-ZAP THINGIE, EH?!
THAT MEANS...
...HE CAN'T FLY ANYMORE EITHER!
RRG RRG
YIP-PEEE!!!
I WIN!!!
KA... ME... HA... ME...
WAAH!!!
W-WAIT!!!

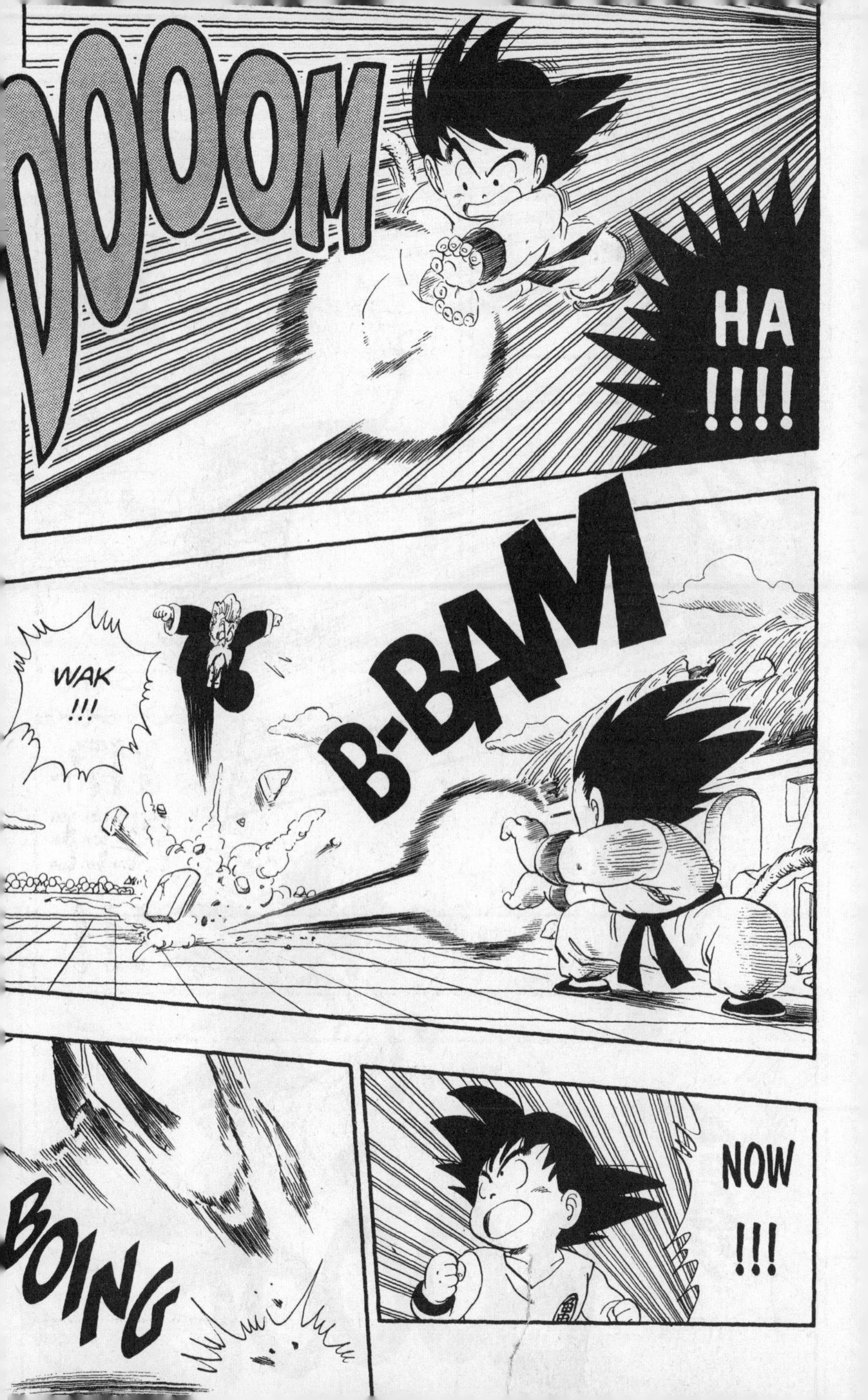
HA !!!!
DOOOM
B-BAM
WAK !!!
NOW !!!
BOING

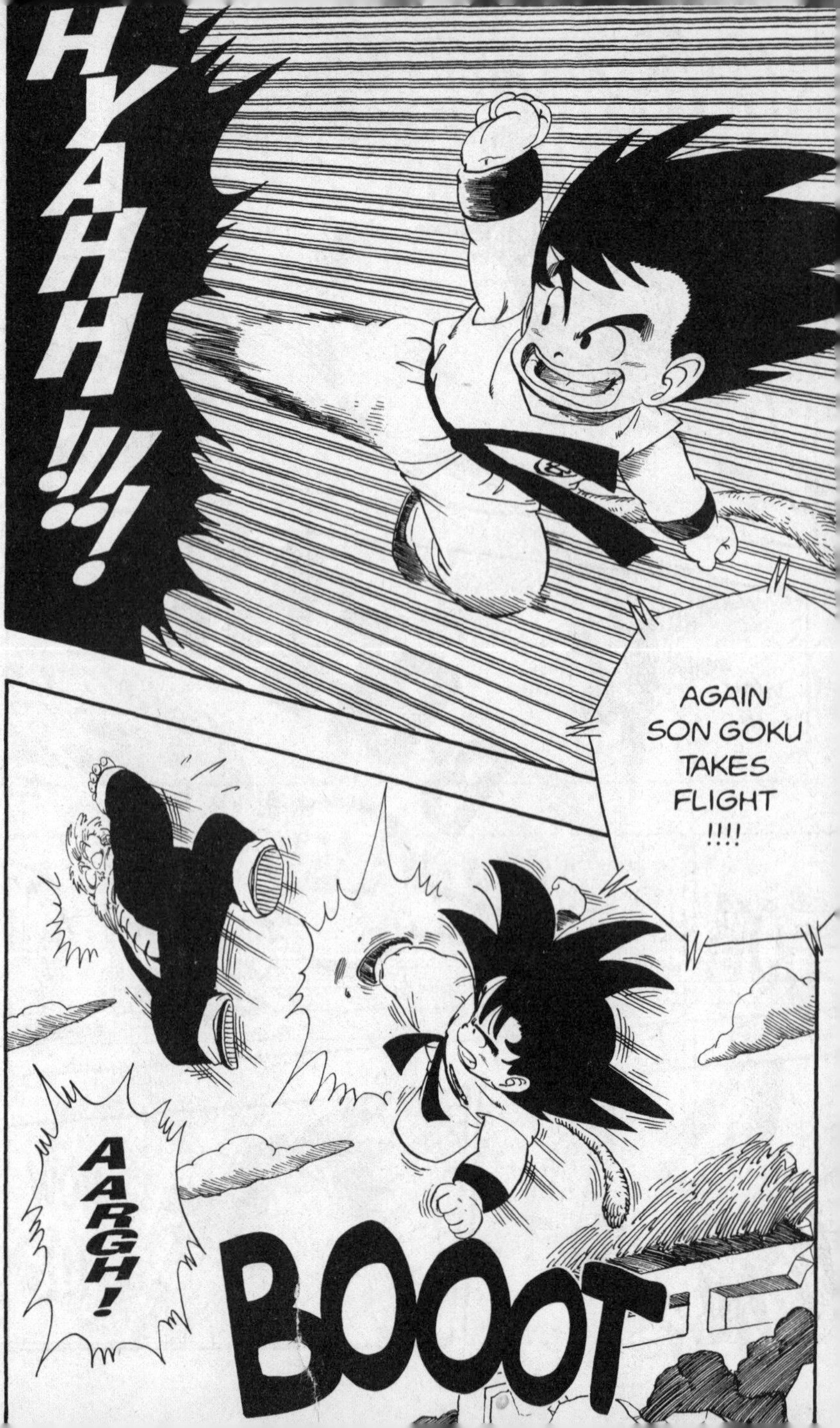
HYAHH!!!!
AGAIN SON GOKU TAKES FLIGHT !!!!
AARGH!
BOOOT

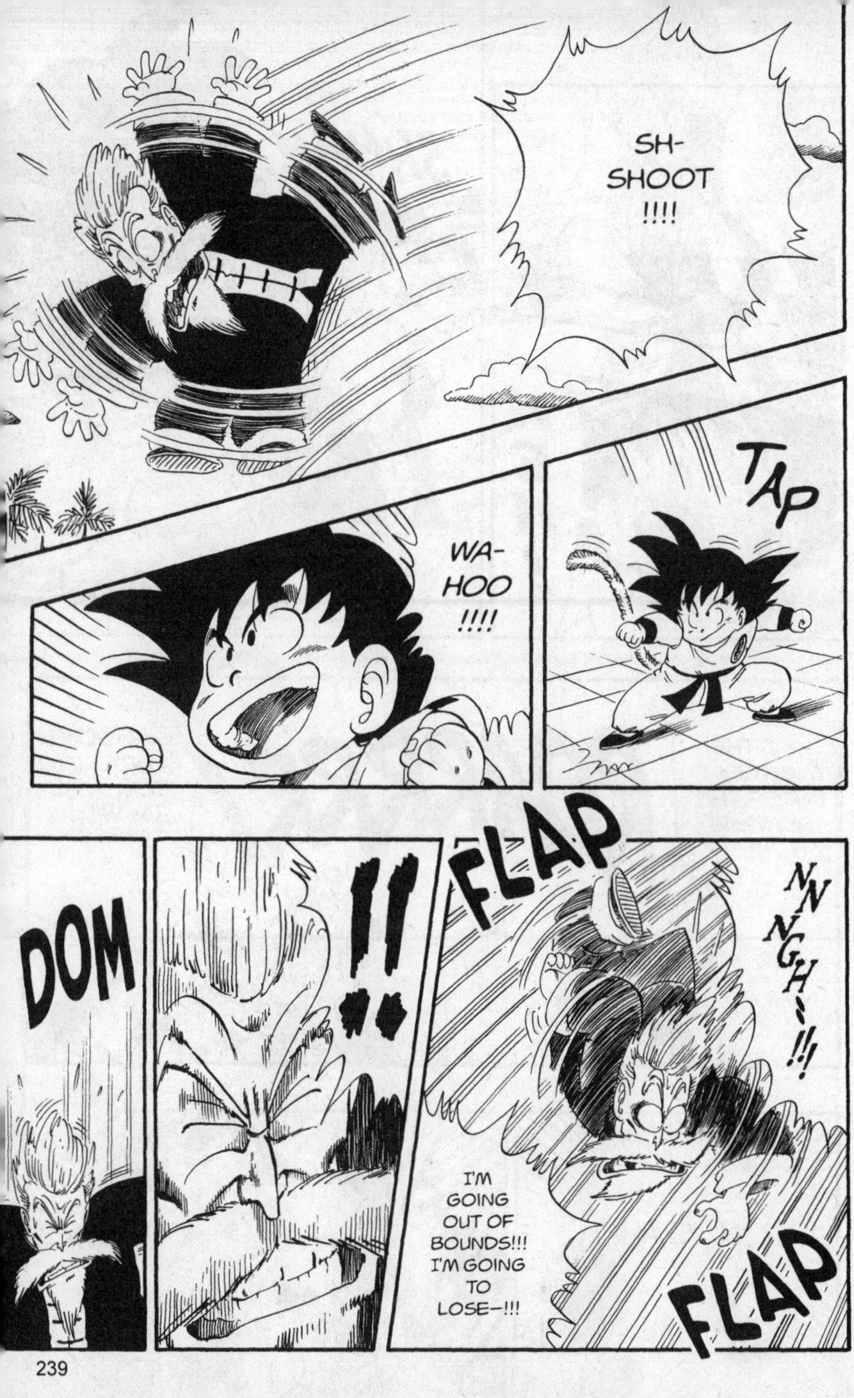
SH-SHOOT!!!!
TAP
WA-HOO!!!!
FLAP
NNNGH~!!!
I'M GOING OUT OF BOUNDS!!! I'M GOING TO LOSE-!!!
FLAP
!!!!
DOM

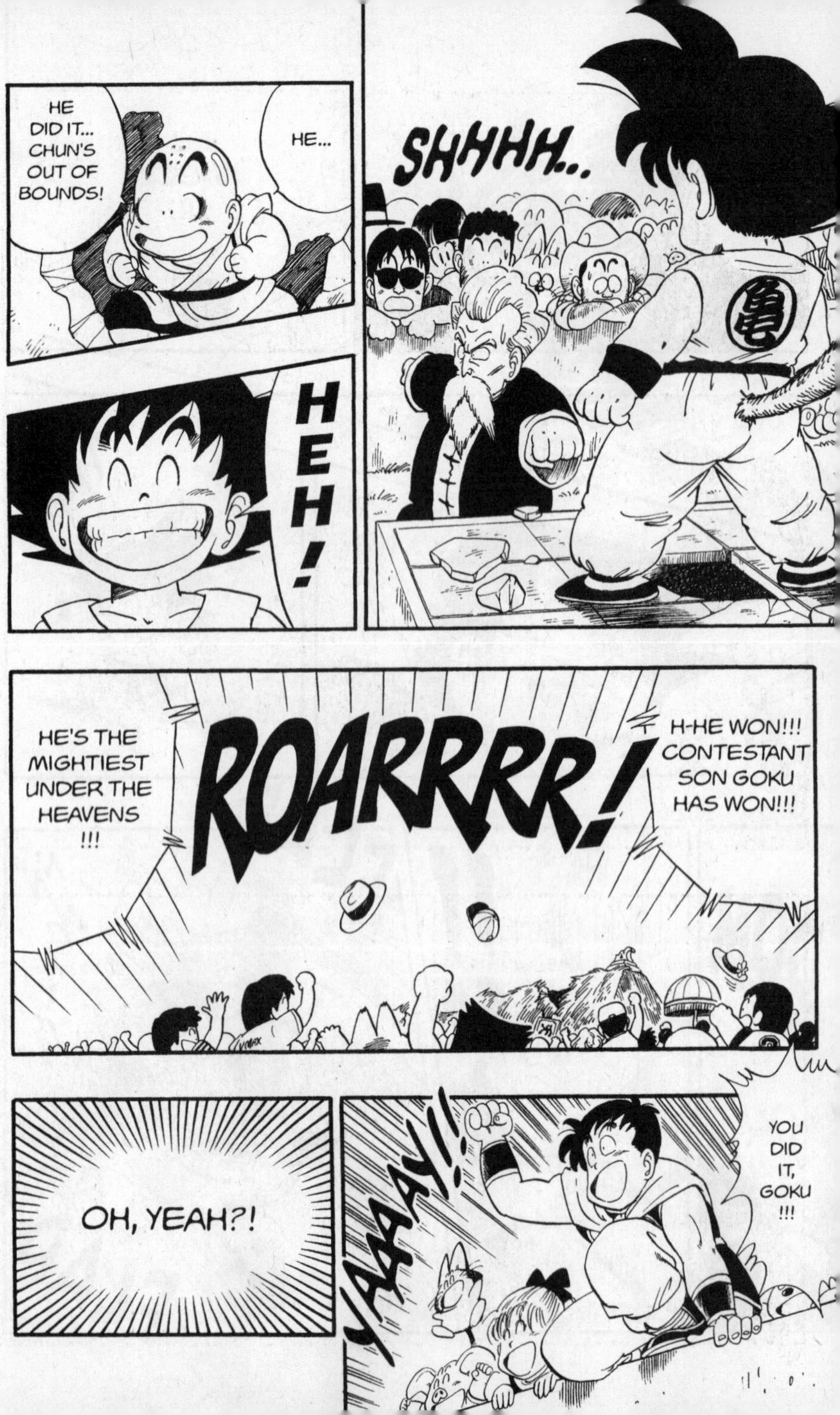
SHHHH...
HE...
HE DID IT... CHUN'S OUT OF BOUNDS!
HEH!
H-HE WON!!! CONTESTANT SON GOKU HAS WON!!!
ROARRRR!
HE'S THE MIGHTIEST UNDER THE HEAVENS !!!
YOU DID IT, GOKU !!!
YAAAAY!!
OH, YEAH?!

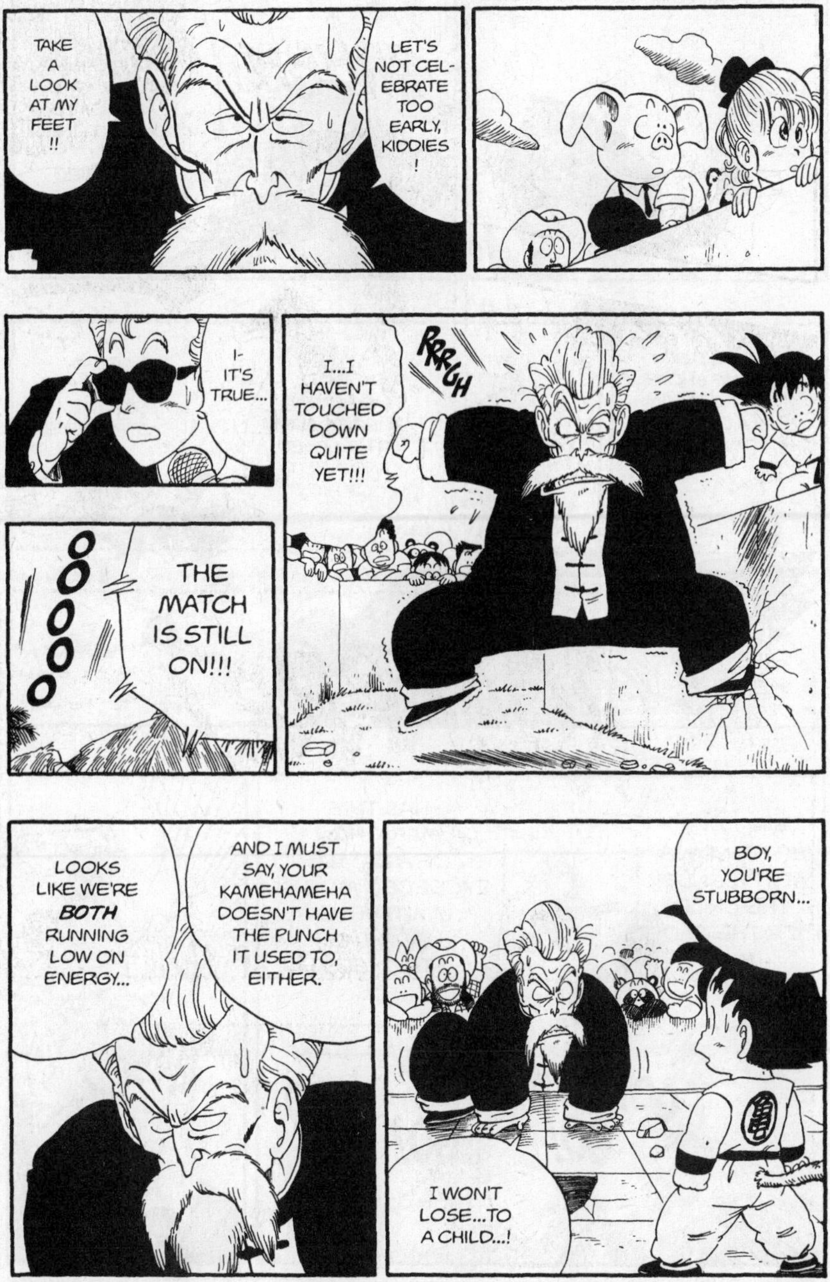
LET'S NOT CELEBRATE TOO EARLY, KIDDIES!
TAKE A LOOK AT MY FEET!!
RRRGH
I...I HAVEN'T TOUCHED DOWN QUITE YET!!!
I- IT'S TRUE...
THE MATCH IS STILL ON!!!
OOOOOO
BOY, YOU'RE STUBBORN...
I WON'T LOSE...TO A CHILD...!
AND I MUST SAY, YOUR KAMEHAMEHA DOESN'T HAVE THE PUNCH IT USED TO, EITHER.
LOOKS LIKE WE'RE BOTH RUNNING LOW ON ENERGY...

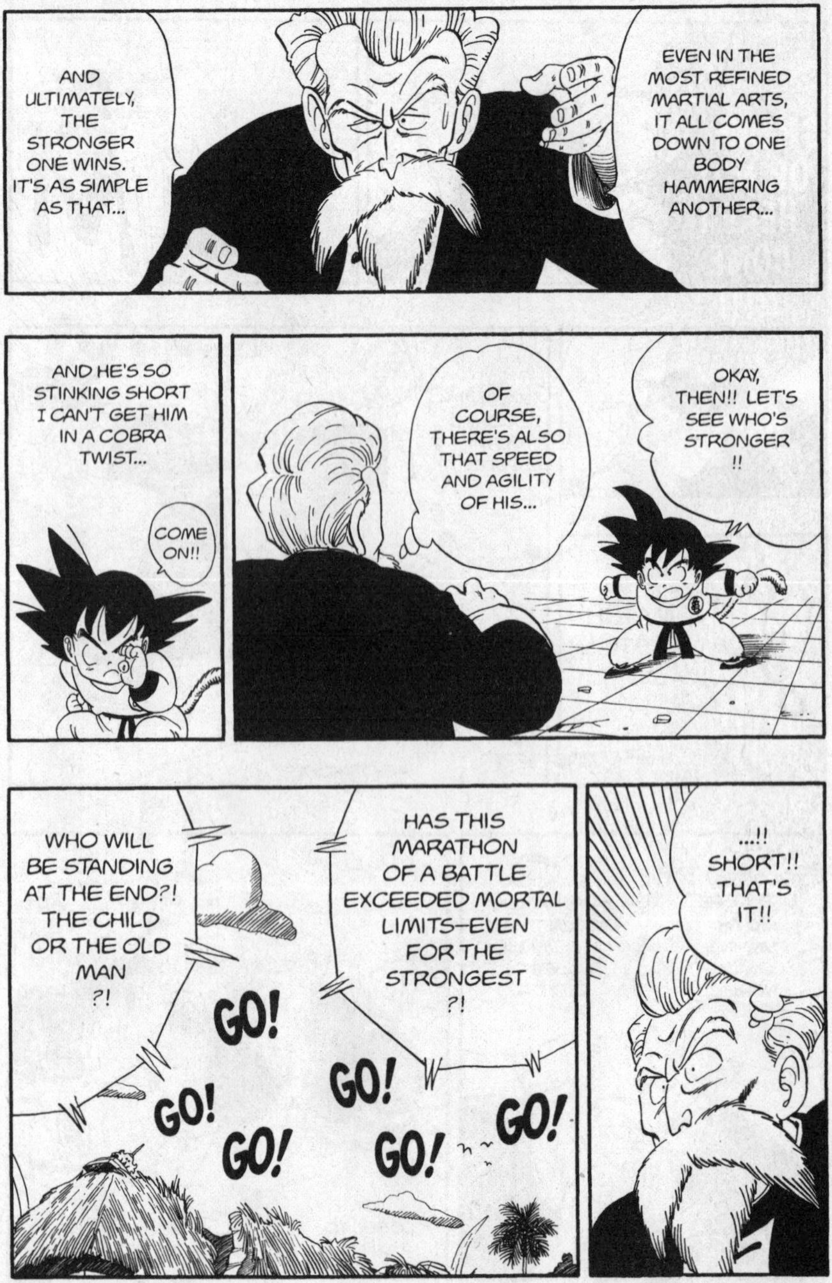
EVEN IN THE MOST REFINED MARTIAL ARTS, IT ALL COMES DOWN TO ONE BODY HAMMERING ANOTHER...
AND ULTIMATELY, THE STRONGER ONE WINS. IT'S AS SIMPLE AS THAT...
OKAY, THEN!! LET'S SEE WHO'S STRONGER !!
OF COURSE, THERE'S ALSO THAT SPEED AND AGILITY OF HIS...
AND HE'S SO STINKING SHORT I CAN'T GET HIM IN A COBRA TWIST...
COME ON!!
...!! SHORT!! THAT'S IT!!
HAS THIS MARATHON OF A BATTLE EXCEEDED MORTAL LIMITS—EVEN FOR THE STRONGEST ?!
WHO WILL BE STANDING AT THE END?! THE CHILD OR THE OLD MAN ?!
GO!
GO!
GO!
GO!
GO!
GO!

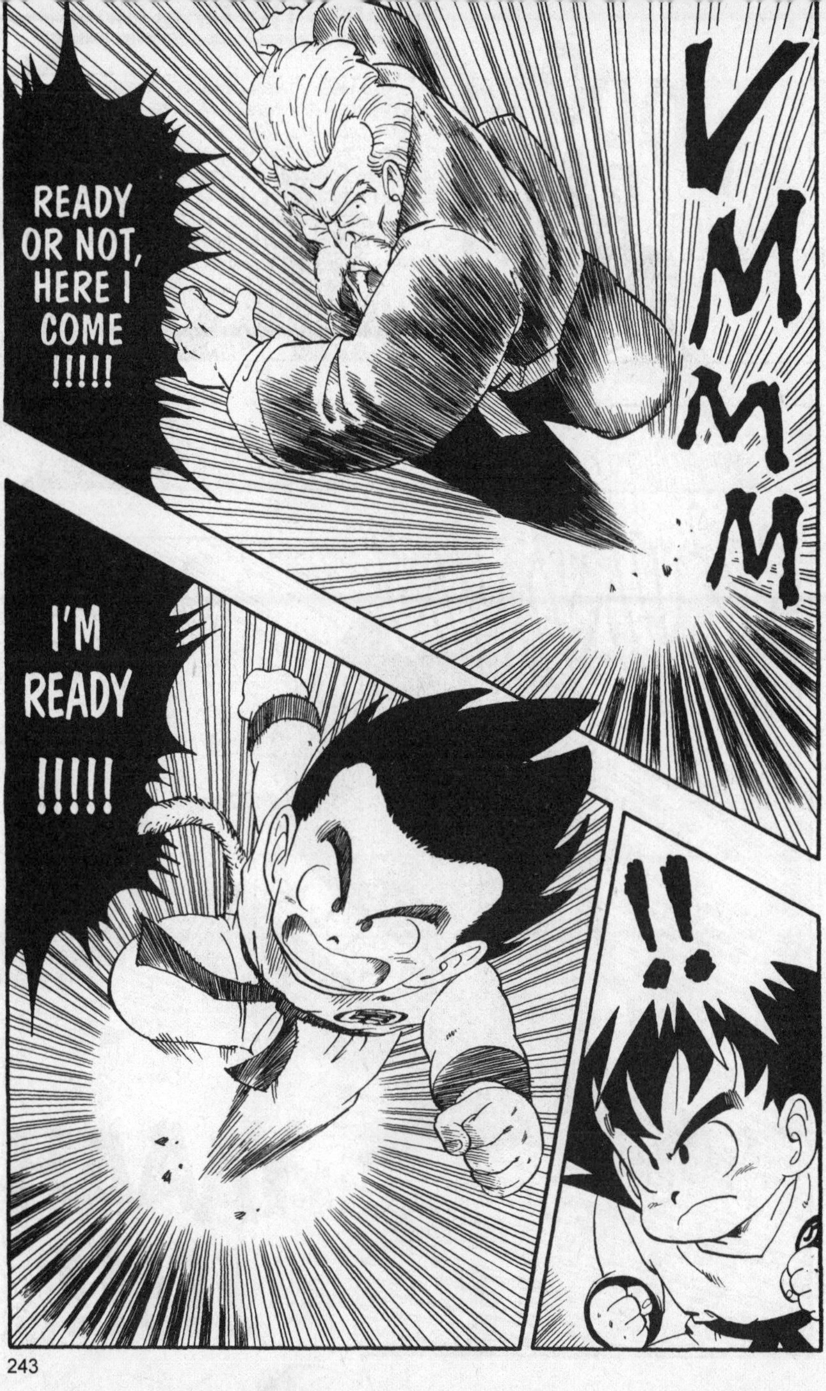
VMMM
READY OR NOT, HERE I COME!!!!!
!!
I'M READY!!!!!

Tale 53 • The Final Blow

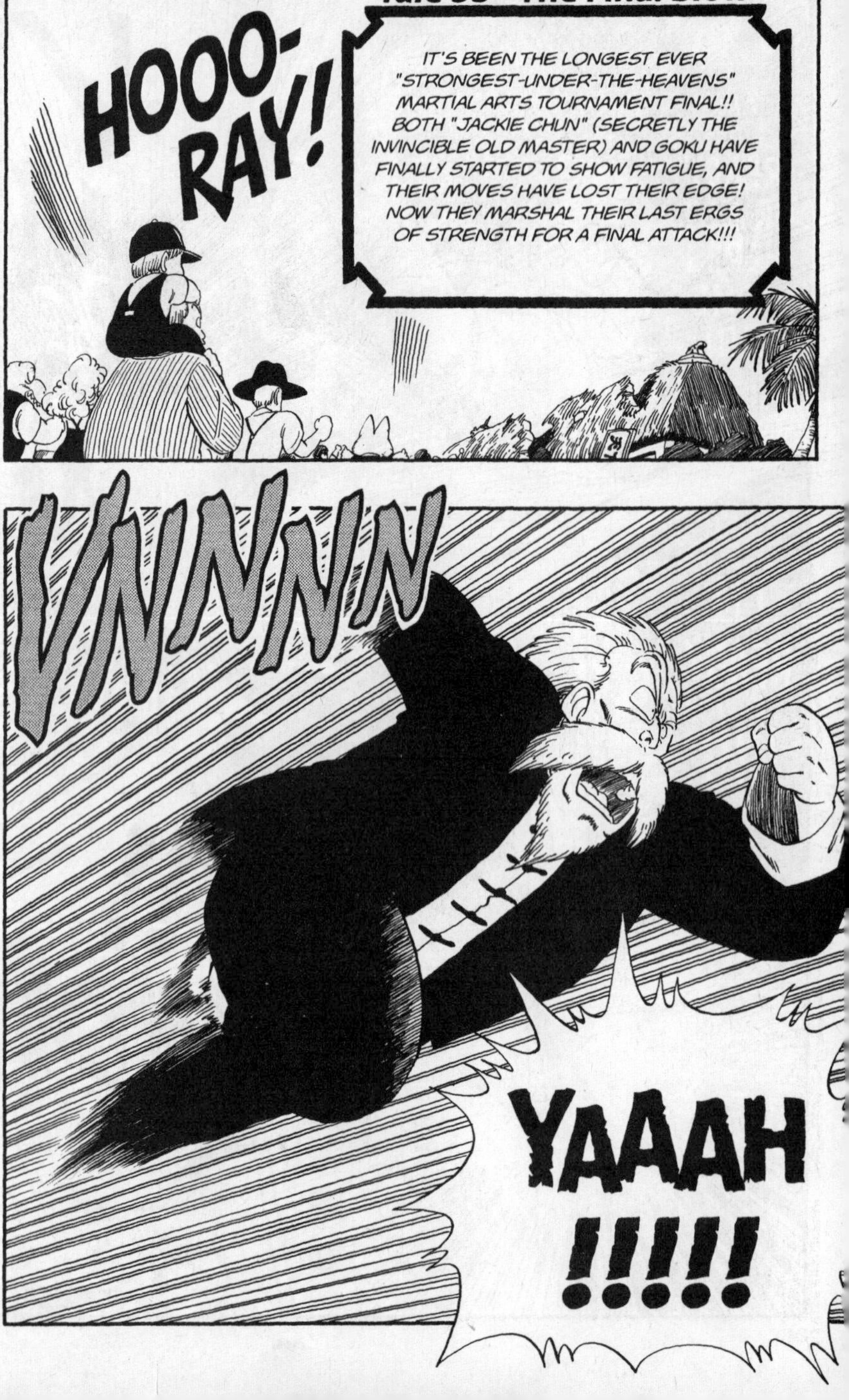
IT'S BEEN THE LONGEST EVER "STRONGEST-UNDER-THE-HEAVENS" MARTIAL ARTS TOURNAMENT FINAL!! BOTH "JACKIE CHUN" (SECRETLY THE INVINCIBLE OLD MASTER) AND GOKU HAVE FINALLY STARTED TO SHOW FATIGUE, AND THEIR MOVES HAVE LOST THEIR EDGE! NOW THEY MARSHAL THEIR LAST ERGS OF STRENGTH FOR A FINAL ATTACK!!!
HOOO-RAY!
VNNNN
YAAAH !!!!!

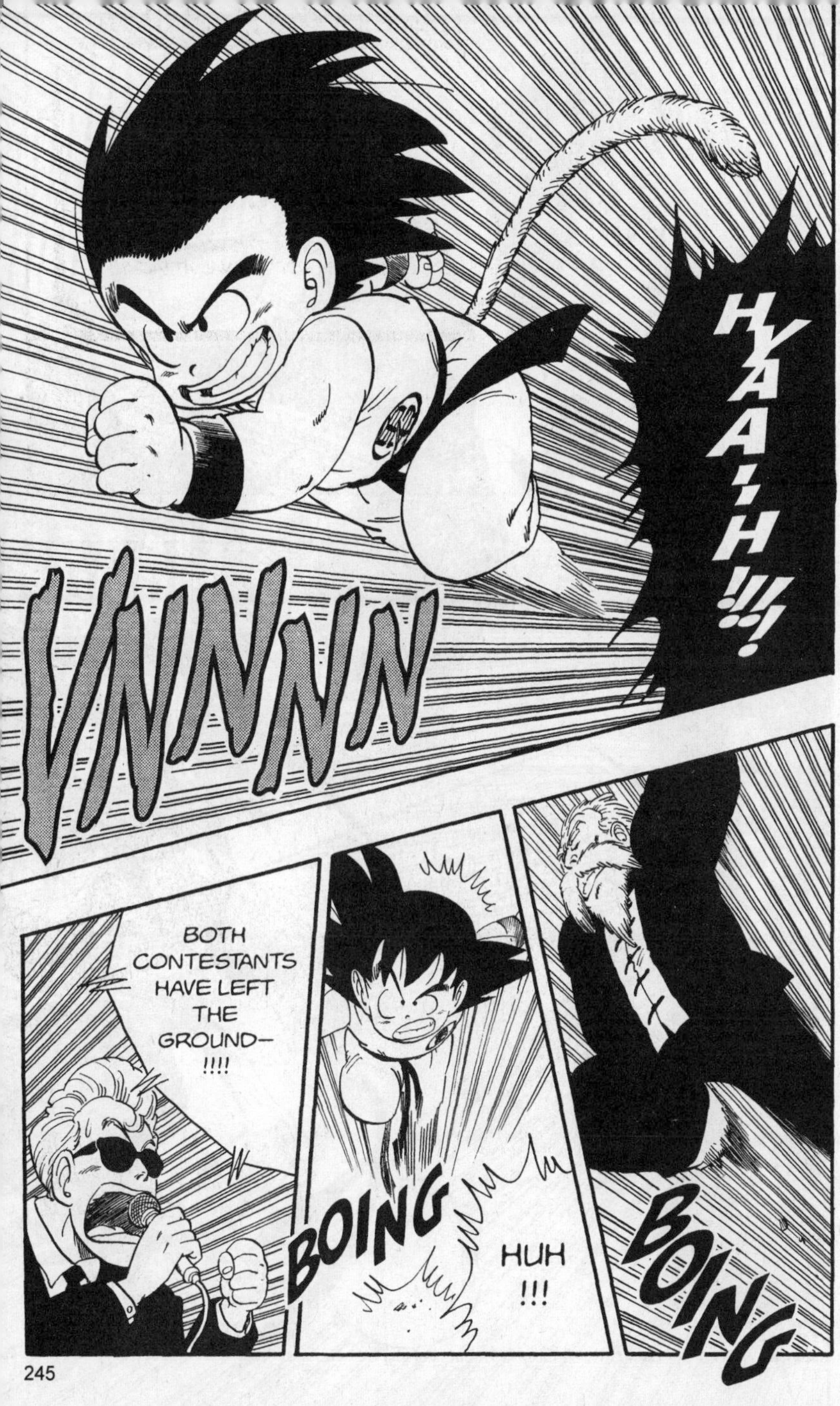
HYAAH!!!!
VNNNN
BOING
BOING
HUH !!!
BOTH CONTESTANTS HAVE LEFT THE GROUND—!!!!

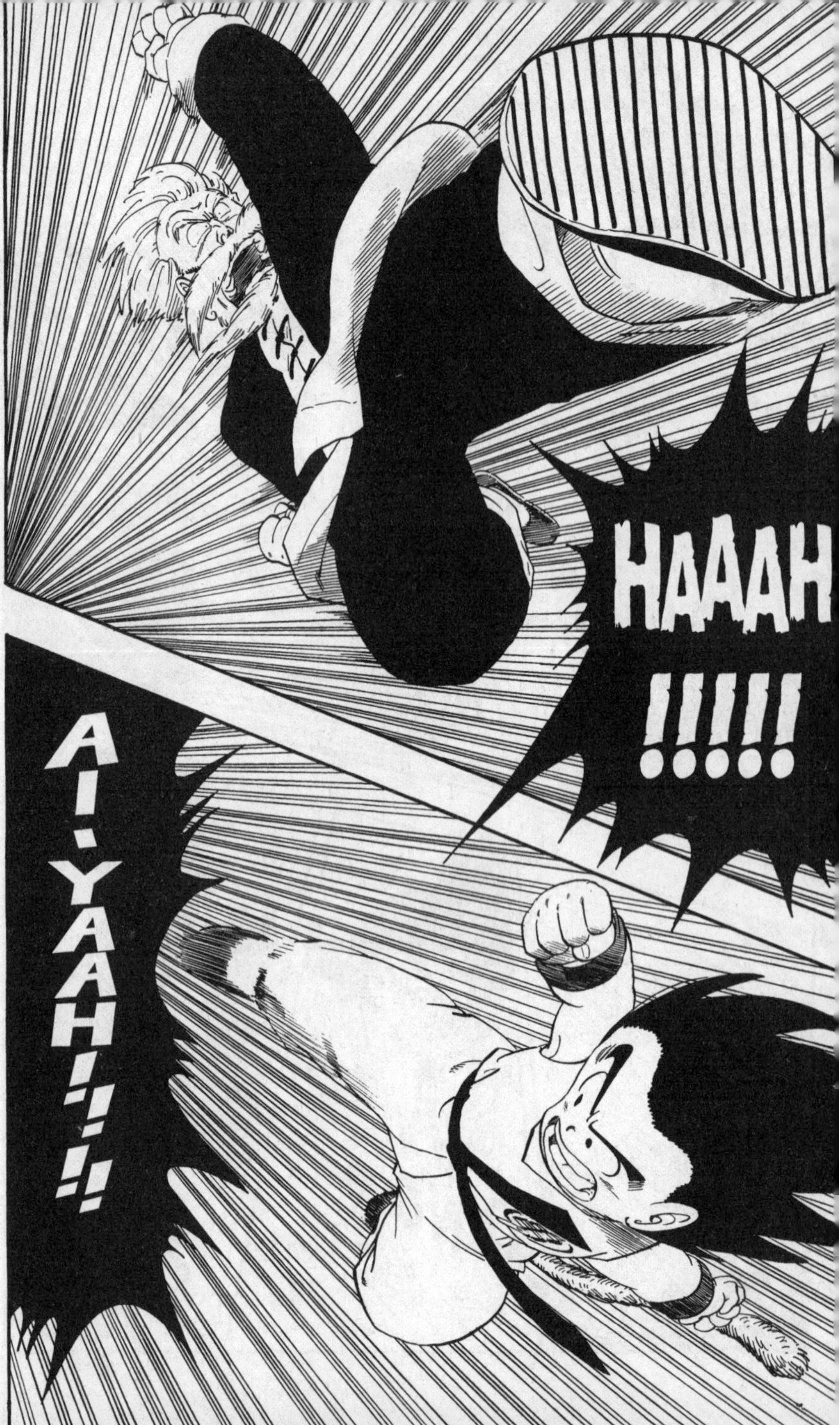
HAAAH!!!!!
AI-YAAH!!!!!

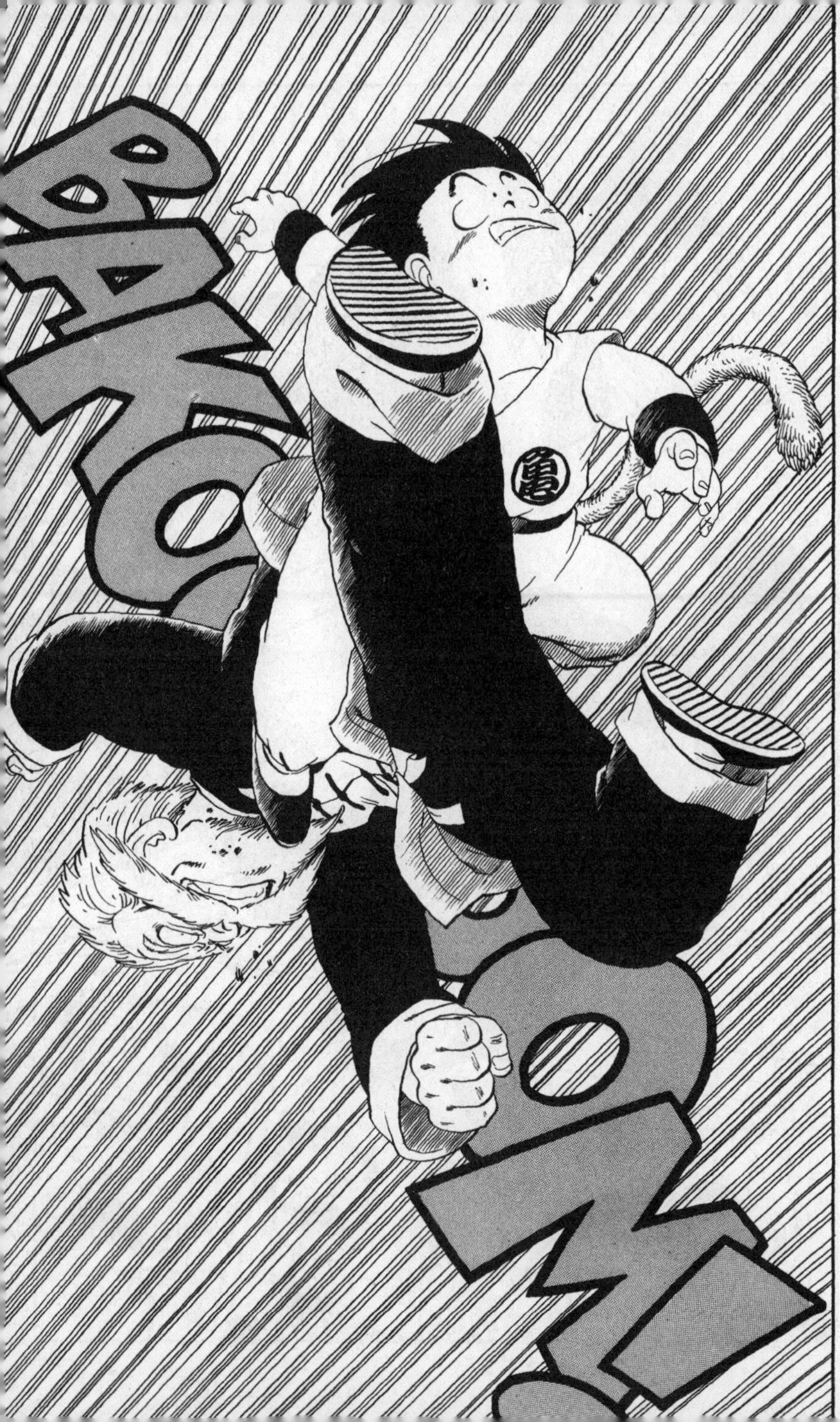
BAKOOM!

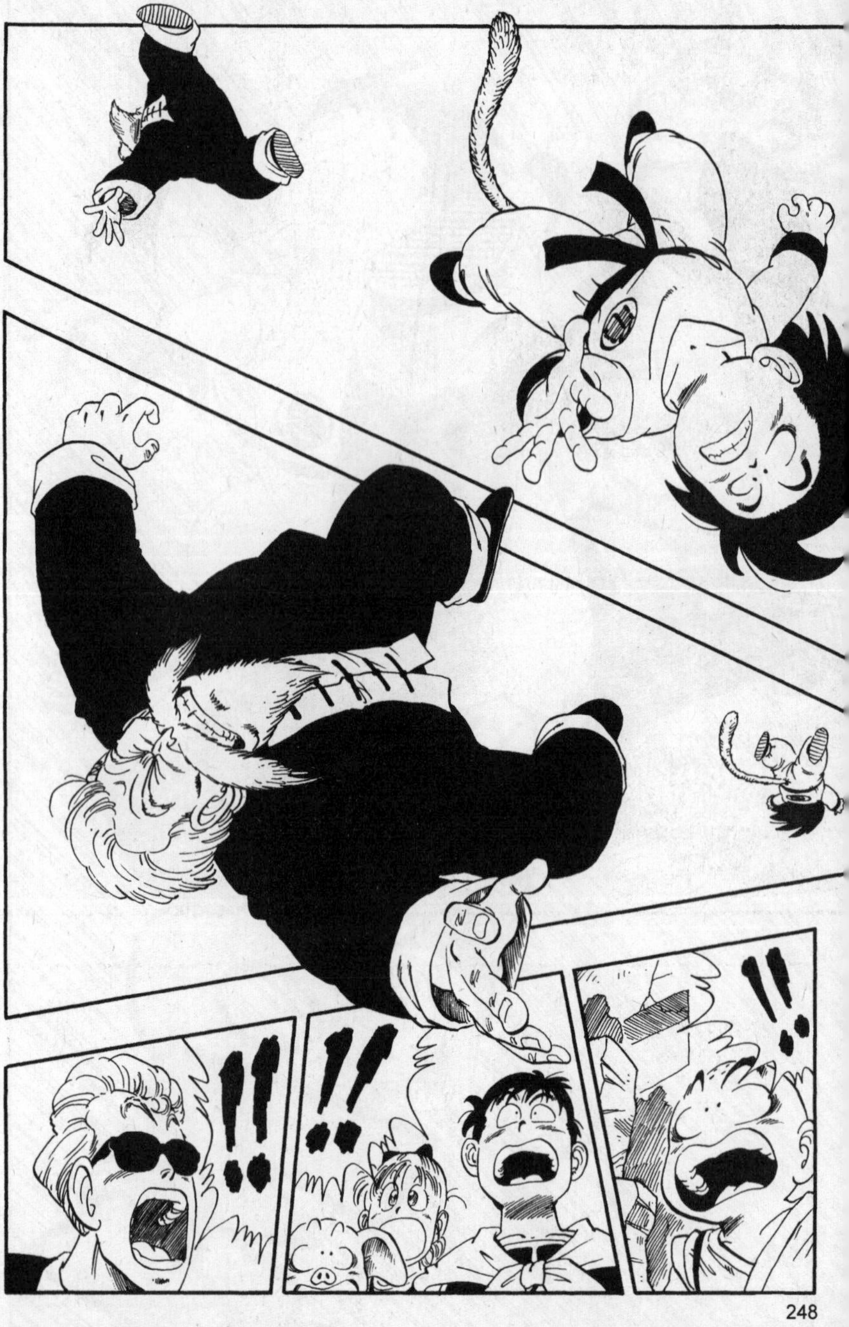
!!
!!
!!

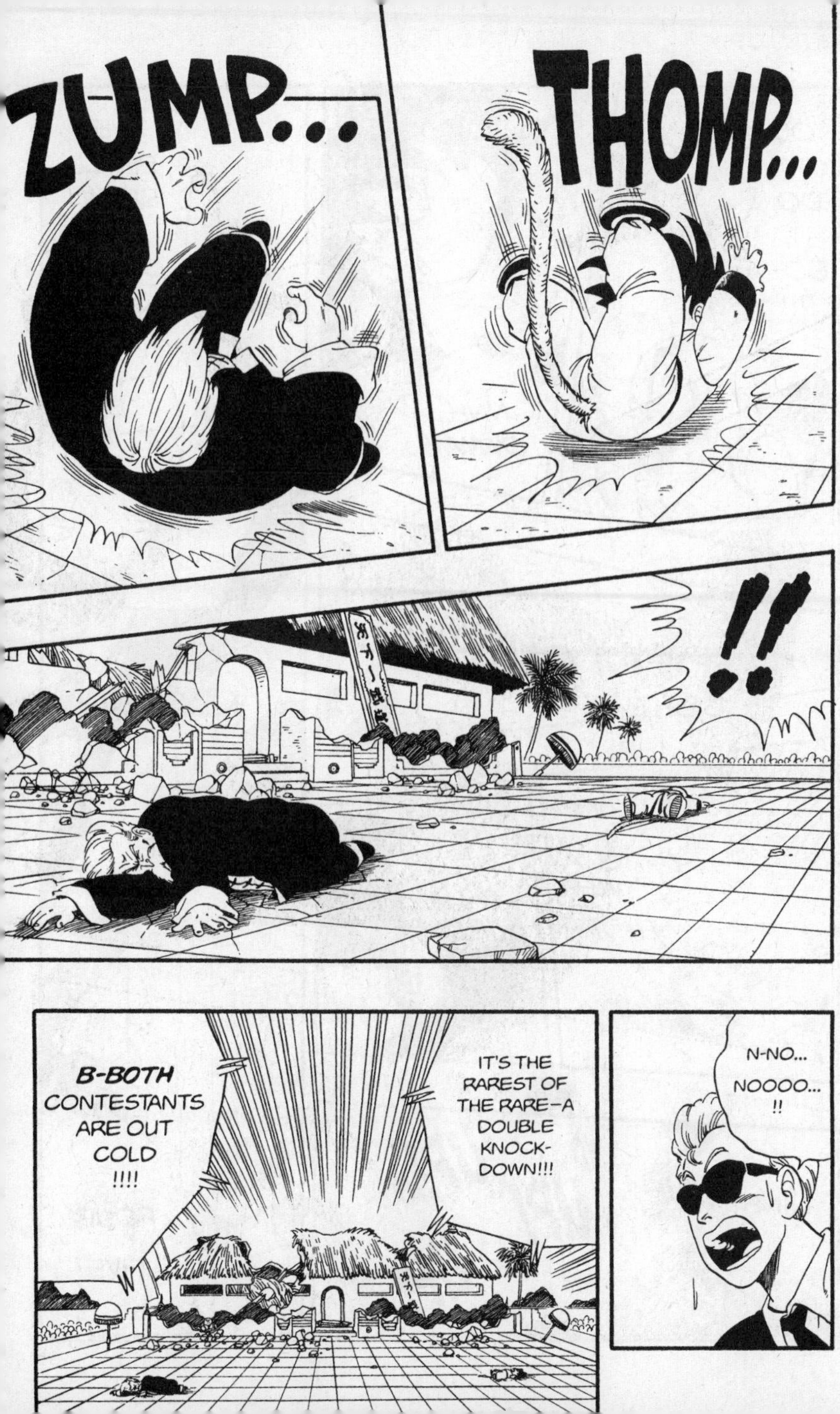
THOMP...
ZUMP...
!!
N-NO...
NOOOO... !!
IT'S THE RAREST OF THE RARE—A DOUBLE KNOCK-DOWN!!!
B-BOTH CONTESTANTS ARE OUT COLD !!!!

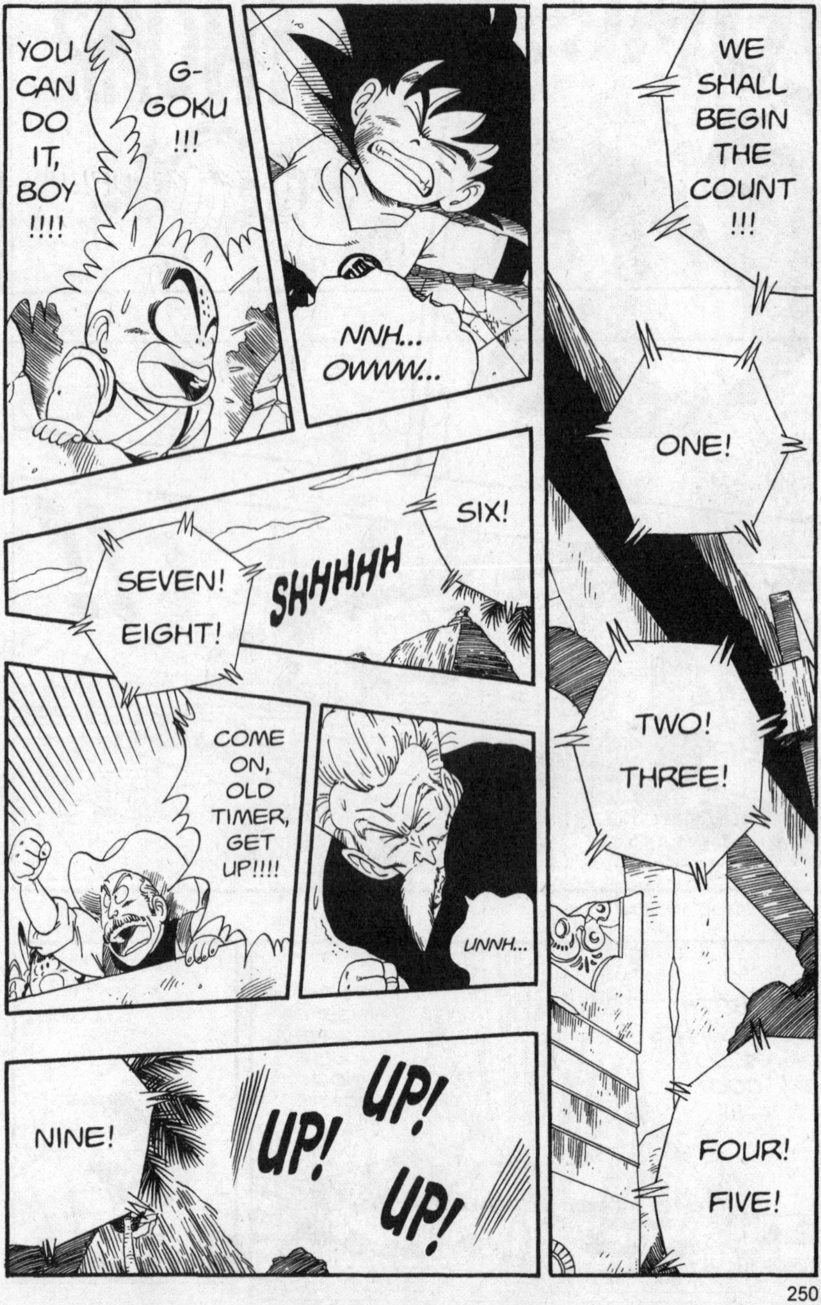
WE SHALL BEGIN THE COUNT !!!
ONE!
TWO! THREE!
FOUR! FIVE!
NNH... OWWW...
G-GOKU !!!
YOU CAN DO IT, BOY !!!!
SIX!
SHHHHH
SEVEN! EIGHT!
UNNH...
COME ON, OLD TIMER, GET UP!!!!
UP!
UP!
UP!
NINE!

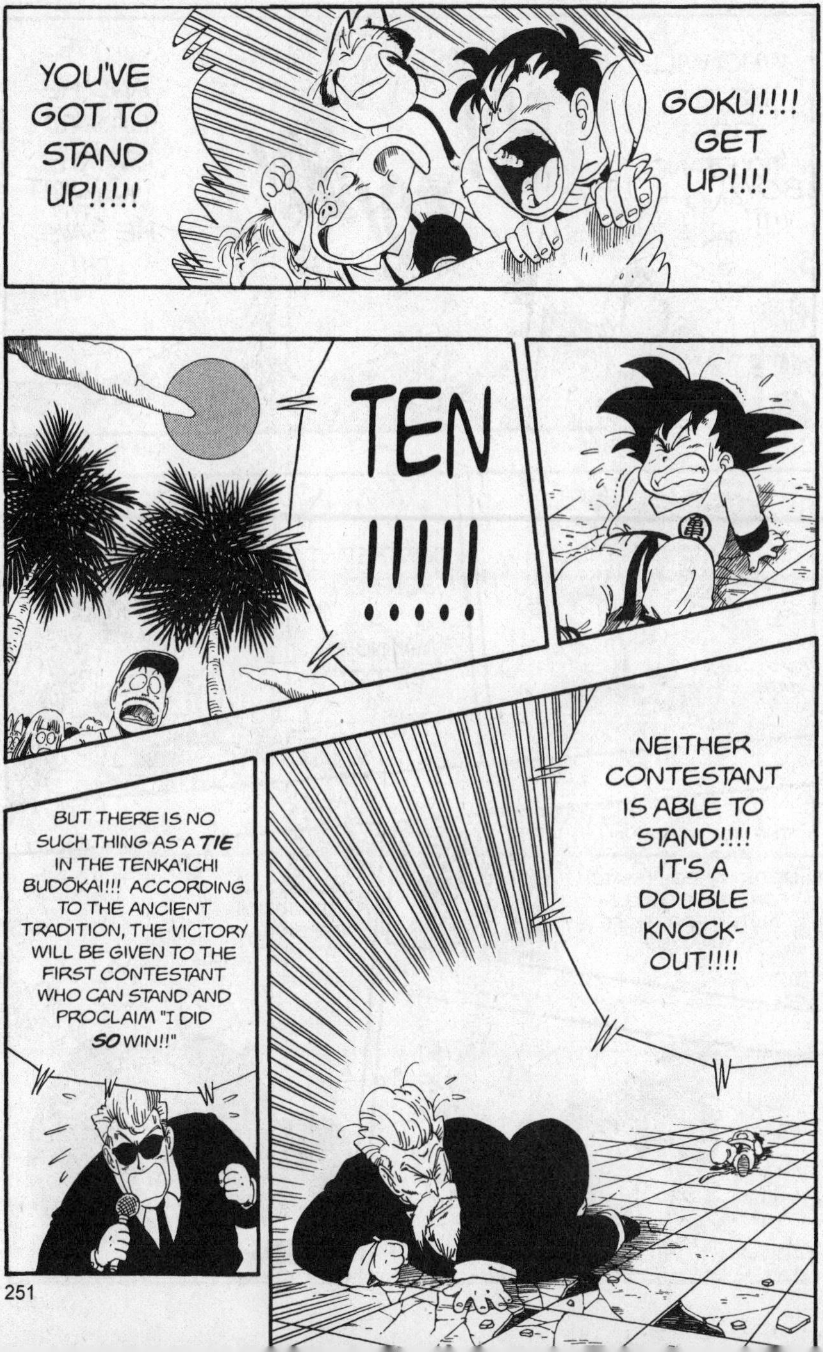
GOKU!!!! GET UP!!!!
YOU'VE GOT TO STAND UP!!!!!
TEN !!!!! .....
NEITHER CONTESTANT IS ABLE TO STAND!!!! IT'S A DOUBLE KNOCK-OUT!!!!
BUT THERE IS NO SUCH THING AS A *TIE* IN THE TENKA'ICHI BUDŌKAI!!!! ACCORDING TO THE ANCIENT TRADITION, THE VICTORY WILL BE GIVEN TO THE FIRST CONTESTANT WHO CAN STAND AND PROCLAIM "I DID *SO* WIN!!"

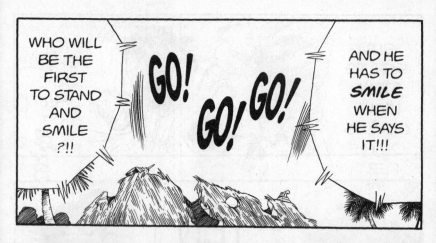

AND HE HAS TO SMILE WHEN HE SAYS IT!!!
GO! GO! GO!
WHO WILL BE THE FIRST TO STAND AND SMILE ?!!
CONTESTANT SON GOKU IS MAKING AN EFFORT !!!!
U- UGH... !!
JACKIE CHUN STRUGGLES DESPERATELY TO BEAT HIM!!!
ONE- TWO ONE- TWO
THE VICTOR IS FINALLY ABOUT TO BE DETERMINED!!!! WATCH FOR THOSE SMILES!!! LISTEN FOR THOSE WORDS!!!
JUST ONE MORE PUSH, GOKU !!!!
YOU CAN DO IT !!!!

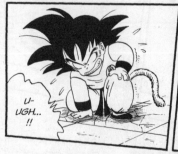

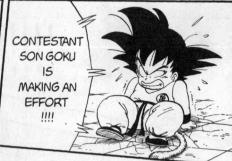

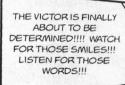

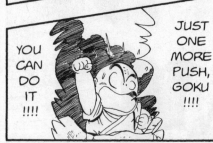

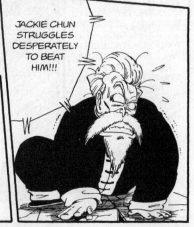

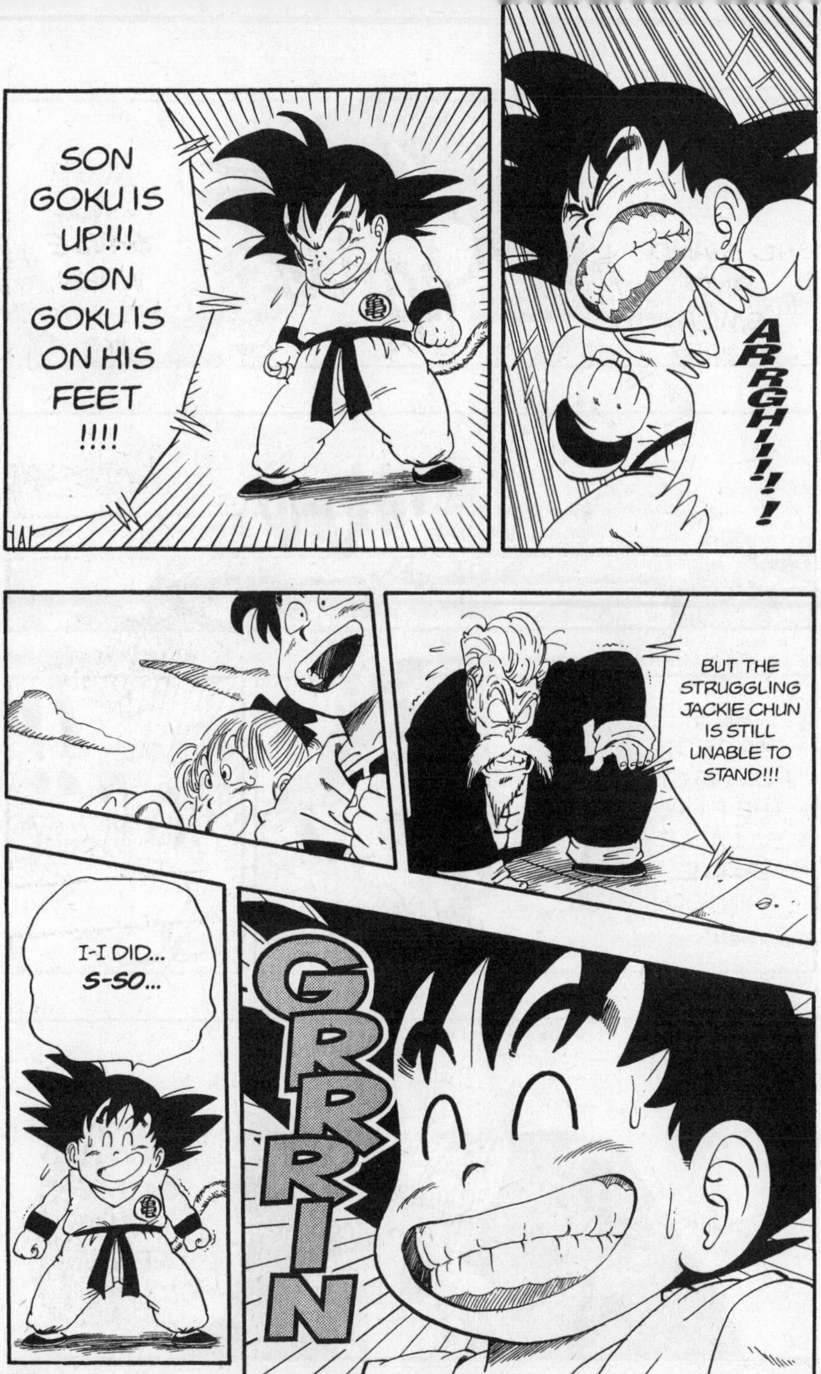
ARRGH!!!!
SON GOKU IS UP!!! SON GOKU IS ON HIS FEET !!!!
BUT THE STRUGGLING JACKIE CHUN IS STILL UNABLE TO STAND!!!
GRRRIN
I-I DID... S-SO...

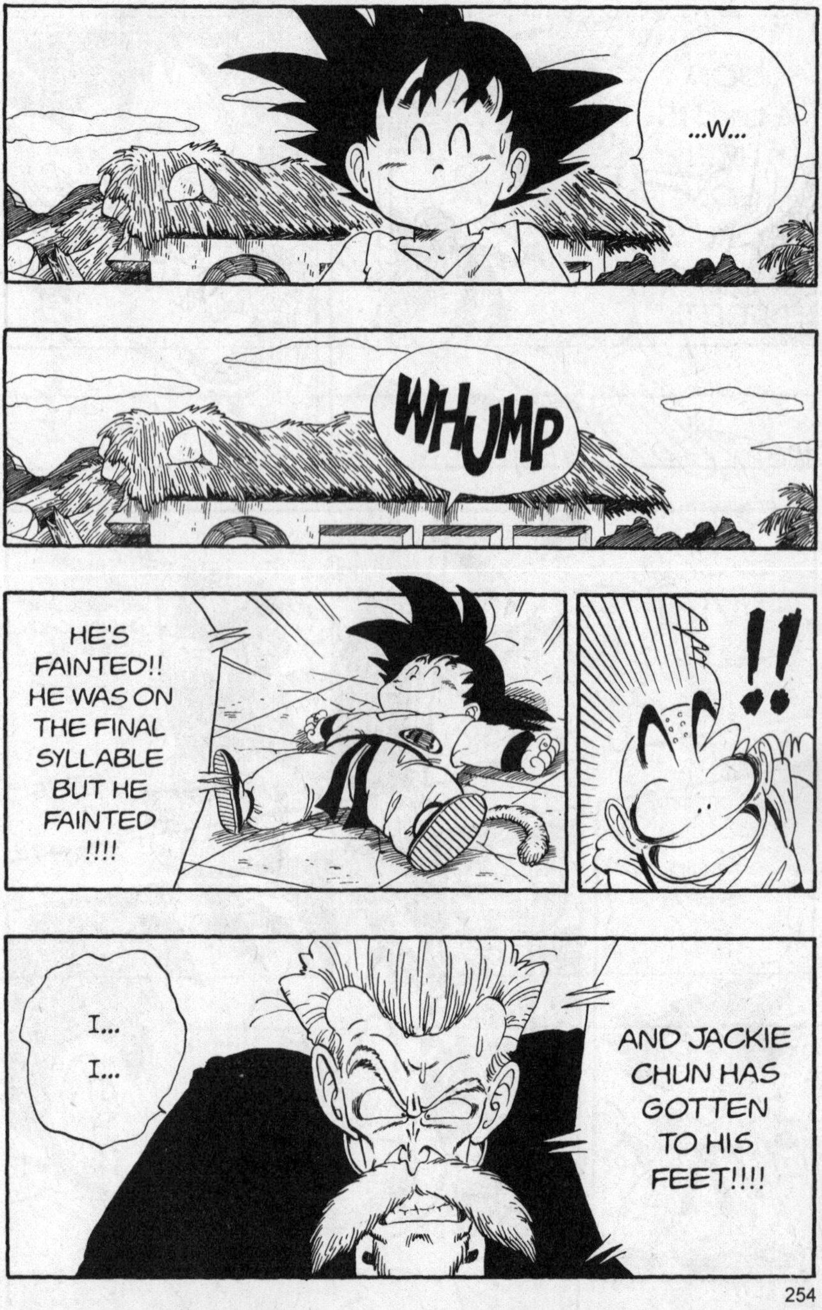
...W...
WHUMP
!!
HE'S FAINTED!! HE WAS ON THE FINAL SYLLABLE BUT HE FAINTED !!!!
AND JACKIE CHUN HAS GOTTEN TO HIS FEET!!!!
I... I...

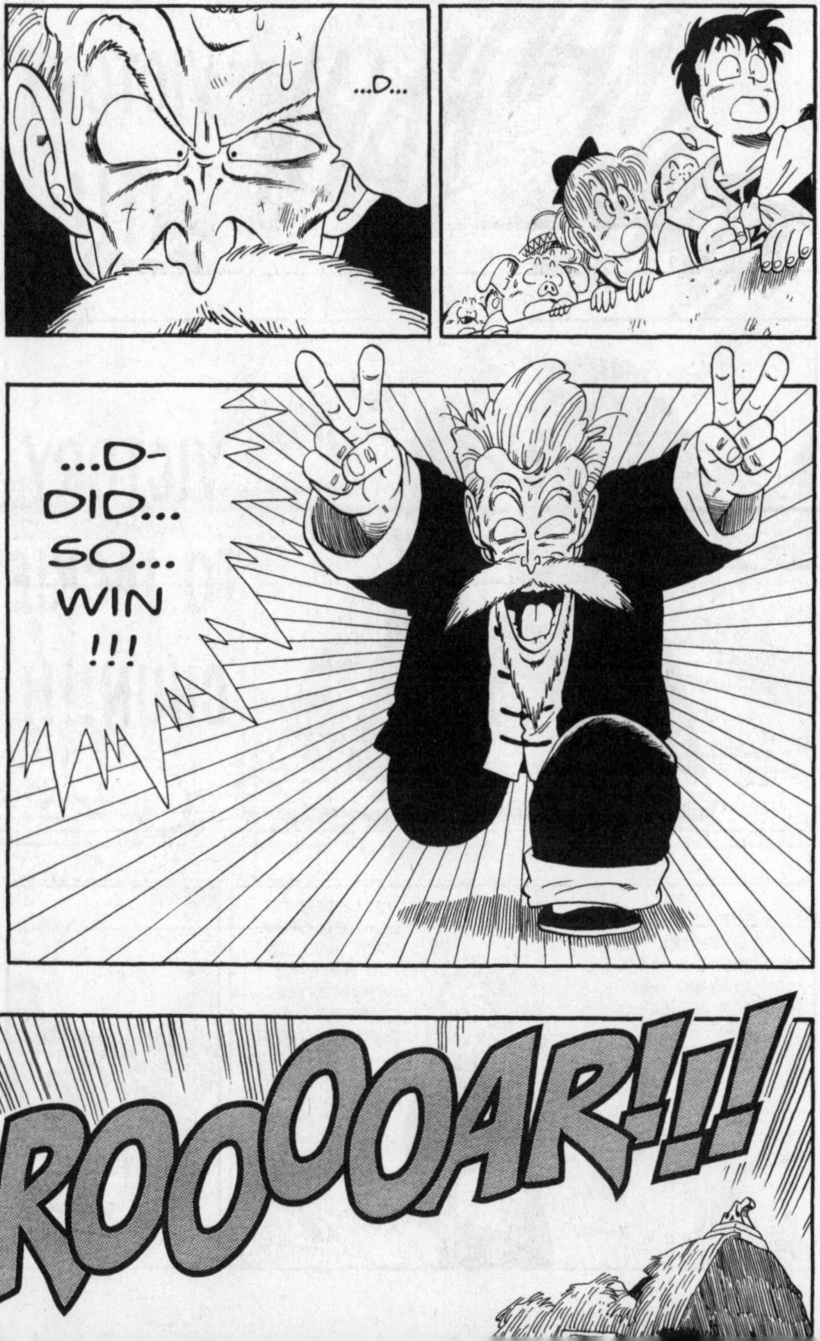
...D...
...D-DID... SO... WIN !!!
ROOOOAR!!!

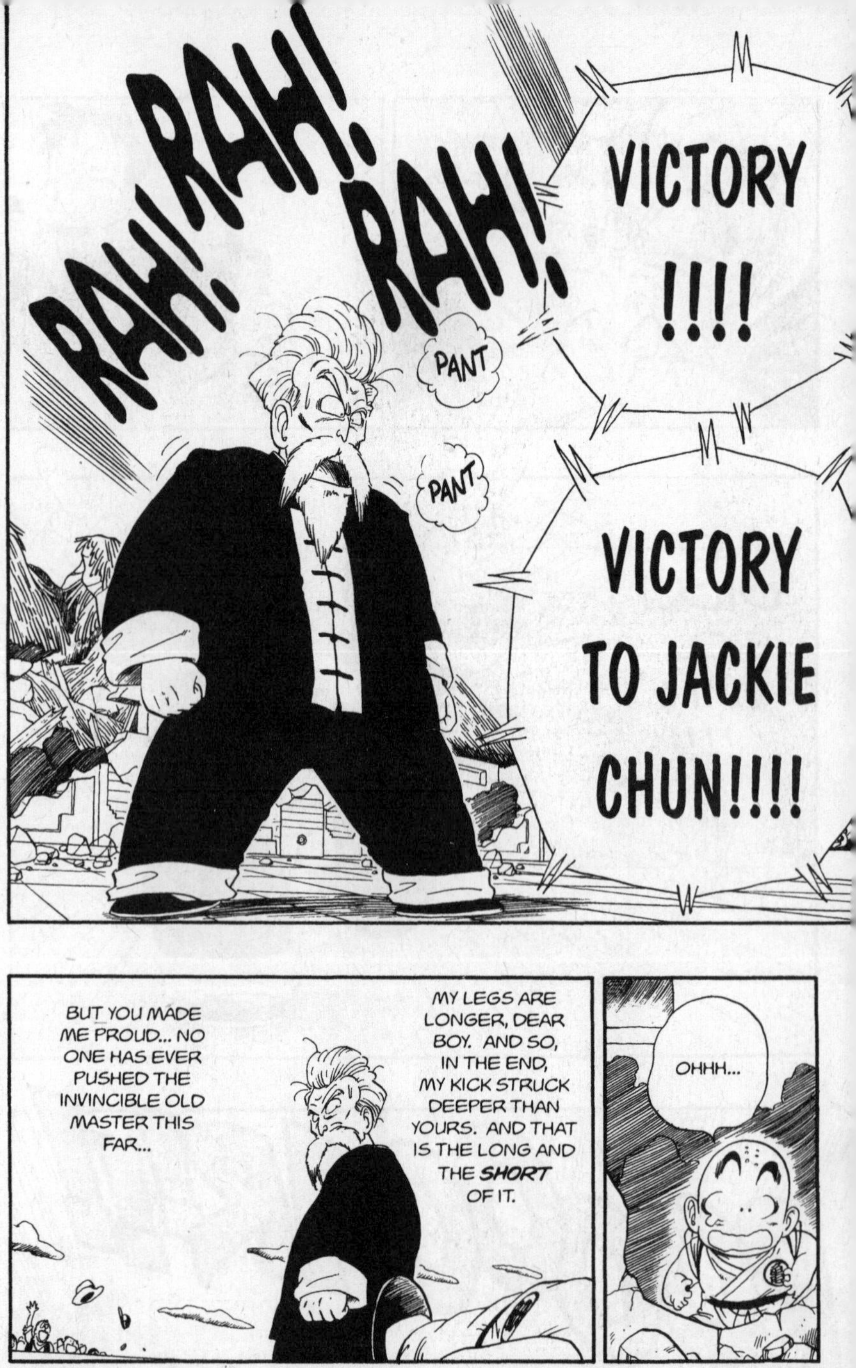
VICTORY !!!!
VICTORY TO JACKIE CHUN!!!!
RAH! RAH!
RAH! RAH!
PANT
PANT
OHHH...
MY LEGS ARE LONGER, DEAR BOY. AND SO, IN THE END, MY KICK STRUCK DEEPER THAN YOURS. AND THAT IS THE LONG AND THE *SHORT* OF IT.
BUT YOU MADE ME PROUD... NO ONE HAS EVER PUSHED THE INVINCIBLE OLD MASTER THIS FAR...

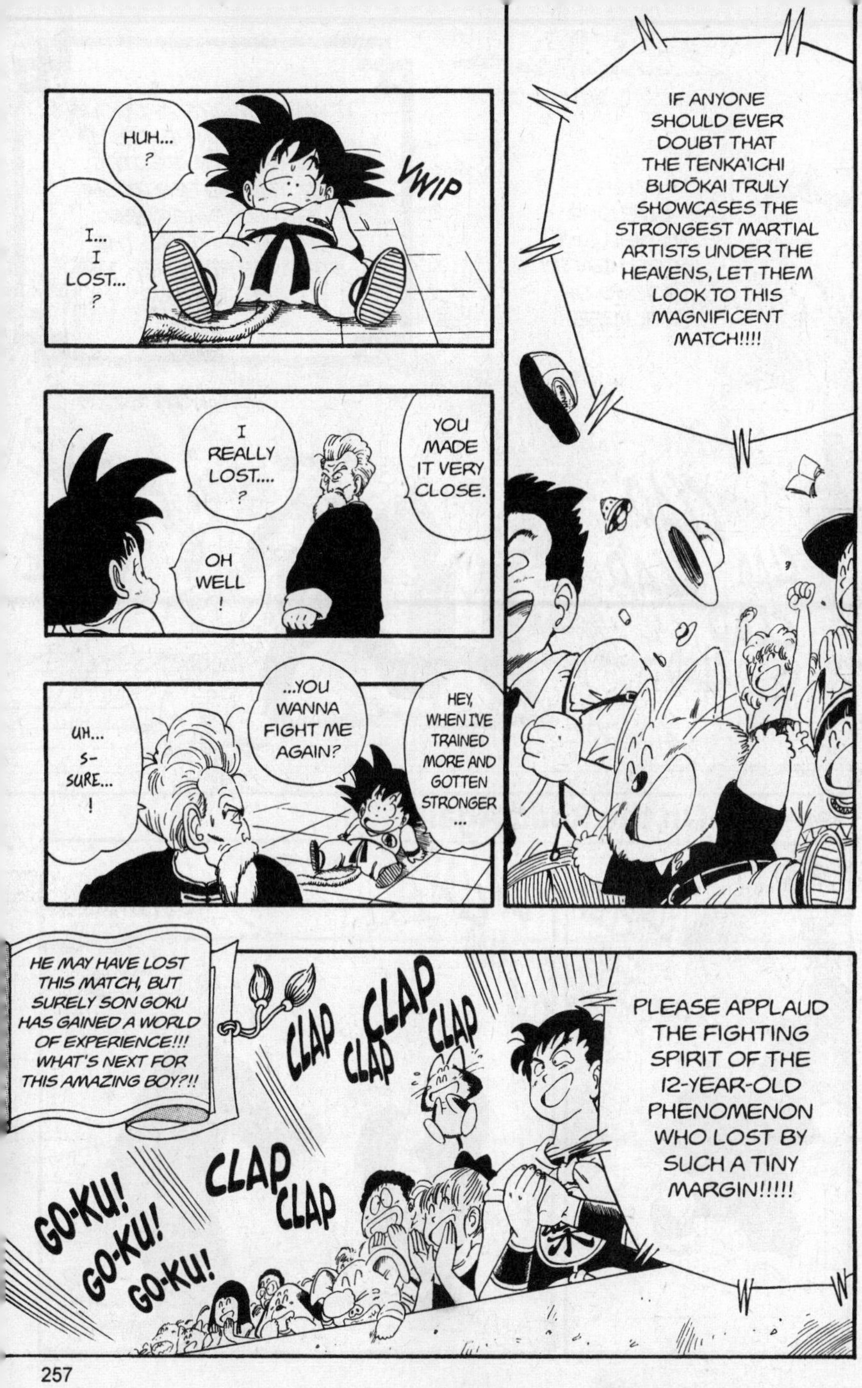
IF ANYONE SHOULD EVER DOUBT THAT THE TENKA'ICHI BUDŌKAI TRULY SHOWCASES THE STRONGEST MARTIAL ARTISTS UNDER THE HEAVENS, LET THEM LOOK TO THIS MAGNIFICENT MATCH!!!!
VWIP
HUH...?
I... I LOST...?
YOU MADE IT VERY CLOSE.
I REALLY LOST....?
OH WELL!
HEY, WHEN I'VE TRAINED MORE AND GOTTEN STRONGER...
...YOU WANNA FIGHT ME AGAIN?
UH... S-SURE...!
PLEASE APPLAUD THE FIGHTING SPIRIT OF THE 12-YEAR-OLD PHENOMENON WHO LOST BY SUCH A TINY MARGIN!!!!!
CLAP CLAP CLAP CLAP
HE MAY HAVE LOST THIS MATCH, BUT SURELY SON GOKU HAS GAINED A WORLD OF EXPERIENCE!!! WHAT'S NEXT FOR THIS AMAZING BOY?!!
CLAP CLAP
GO-KU! GO-KU! GO-KU!

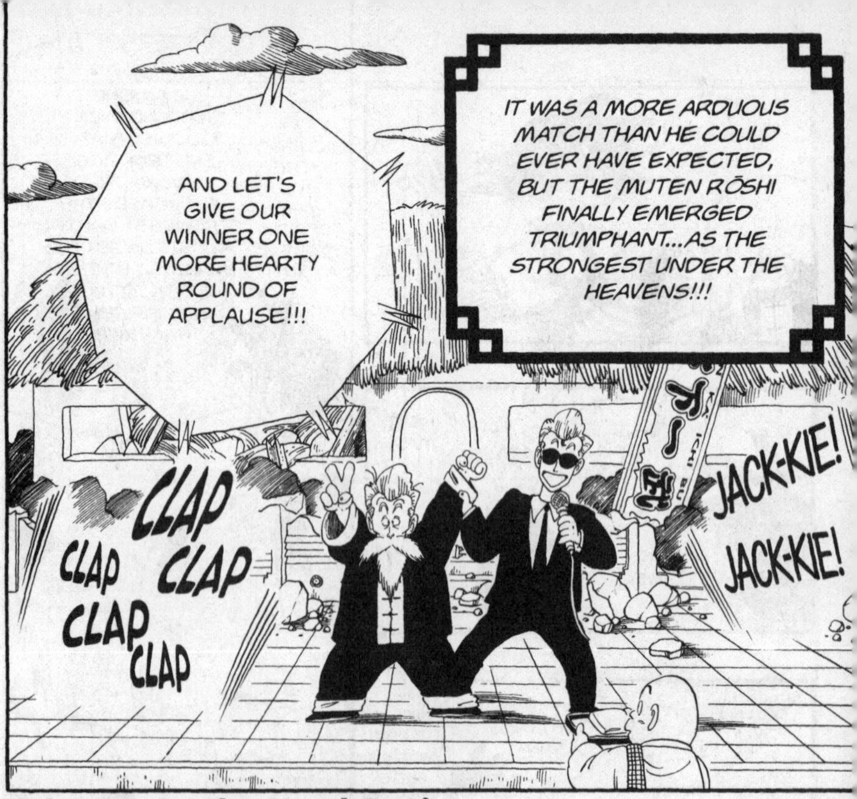
IT WAS A MORE ARDUOUS MATCH THAN HE COULD EVER HAVE EXPECTED, BUT THE MUTEN RŌSHI FINALLY EMERGED TRIUMPHANT...AS THE STRONGEST UNDER THE HEAVENS!!!
AND LET'S GIVE OUR WINNER ONE MORE HEARTY ROUND OF APPLAUSE!!!
JACK-KIE!
JACK-KIE!
CLAP
CLAP
CLAP
CLAP
CLAP

Tale 54 • On the Road Again

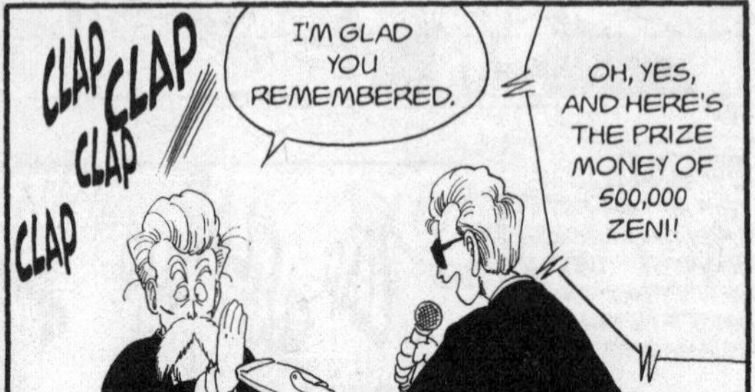
OH, YES, AND HERE'S THE PRIZE MONEY OF 500,000 ZENI!
I'M GLAD YOU REMEMBERED.
CLAP
CLAP
CLAP
CLAP

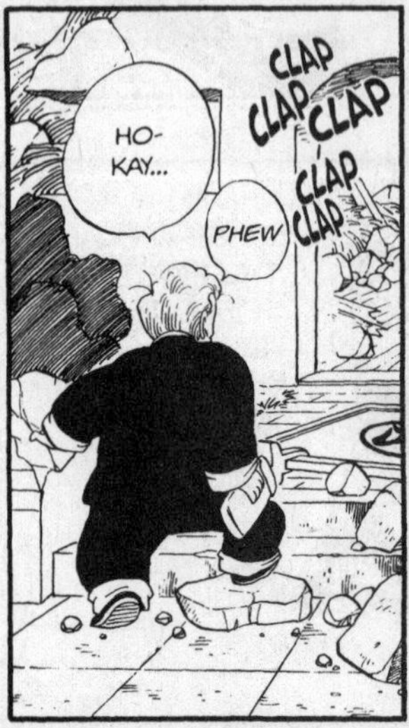
CLAP
CLAP
CLAP
CLAP
CLAP
PHEW
HO-KAY...

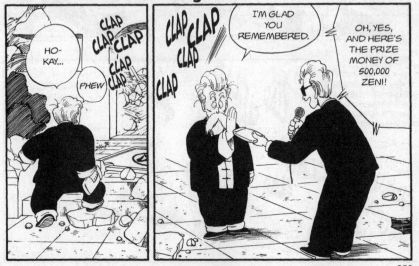

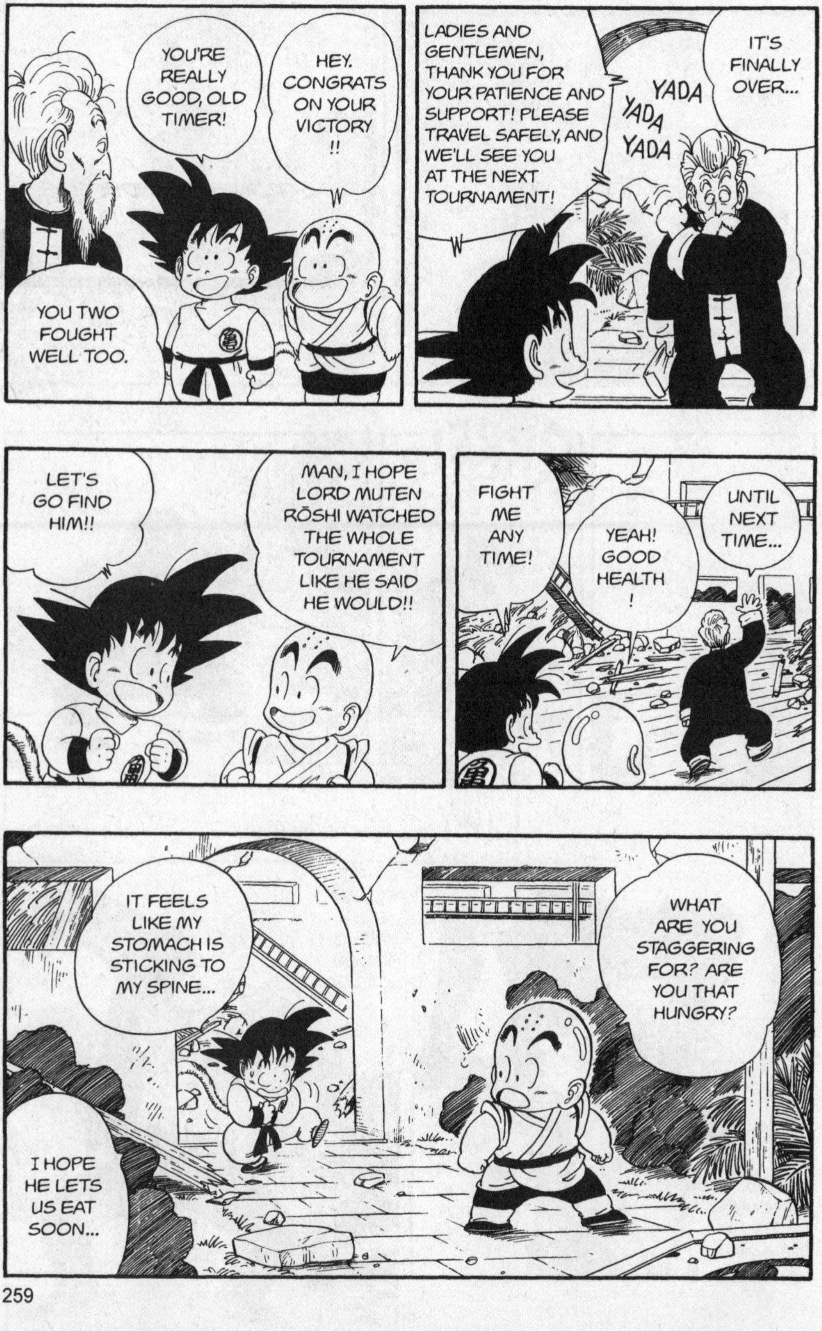
IT'S FINALLY OVER...
YADA YADA YADA
LADIES AND GENTLEMEN, THANK YOU FOR YOUR PATIENCE AND SUPPORT! PLEASE TRAVEL SAFELY, AND WE'LL SEE YOU AT THE NEXT TOURNAMENT!
HEY. CONGRATS ON YOUR VICTORY!!
YOU'RE REALLY GOOD, OLD TIMER!
YOU TWO FOUGHT WELL TOO.
UNTIL NEXT TIME...
YEAH! GOOD HEALTH!
FIGHT ME ANY TIME!
MAN, I HOPE LORD MUTEN RŌSHI WATCHED THE WHOLE TOURNAMENT LIKE HE SAID HE WOULD!!
LET'S GO FIND HIM!!
WHAT ARE YOU STAGGERING FOR? ARE YOU THAT HUNGRY?
IT FEELS LIKE MY STOMACH IS STICKING TO MY SPINE...
I HOPE HE LETS US EAT SOON...

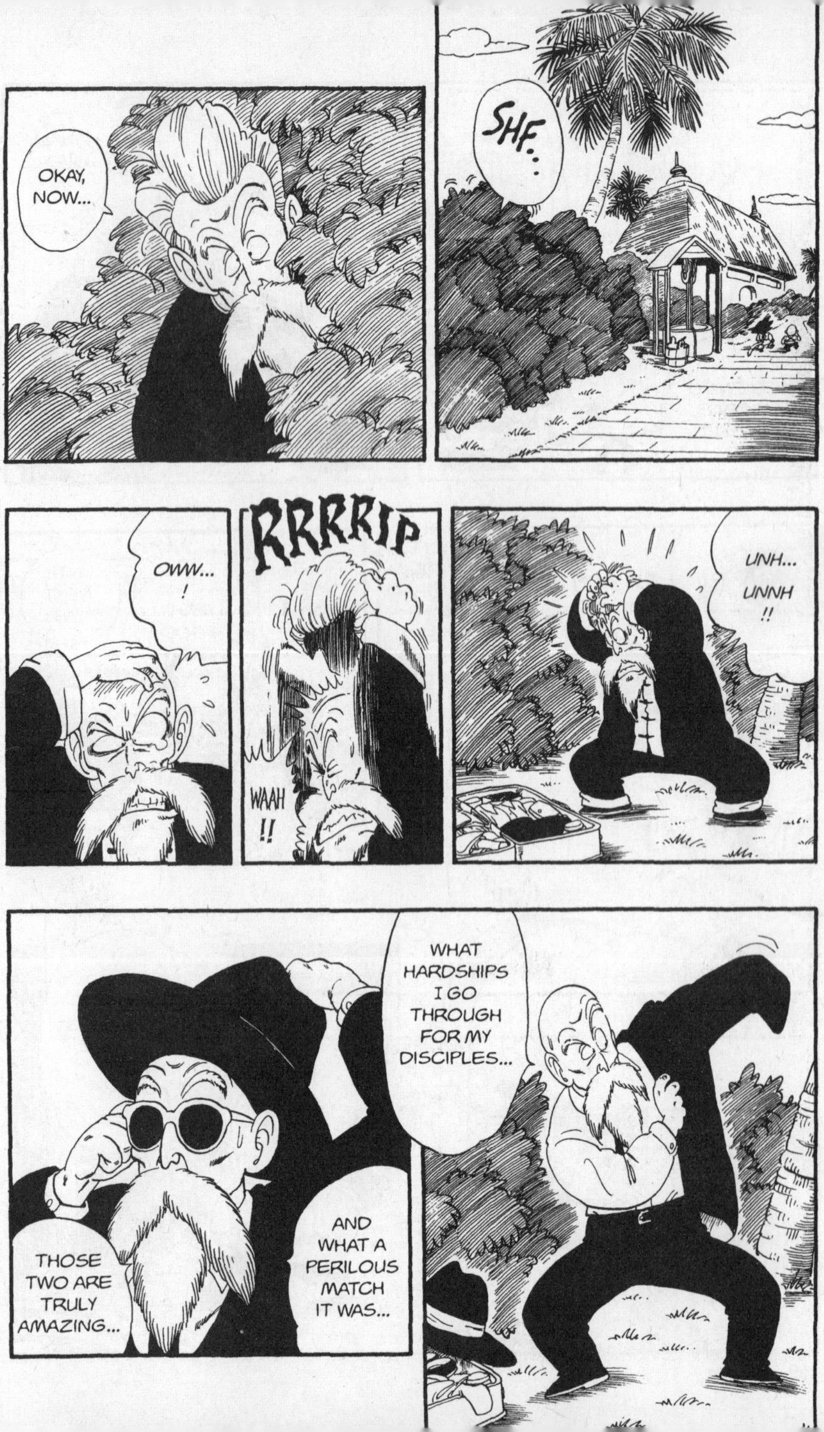
SHF...
OKAY, NOW...
UNH... UNNH !!
RRRRIP
WAAH !!
OWW... !
WHAT HARDSHIPS I GO THROUGH FOR MY DISCIPLES...
AND WHAT A PERILOUS MATCH IT WAS...
THOSE TWO ARE TRULY AMAZING...

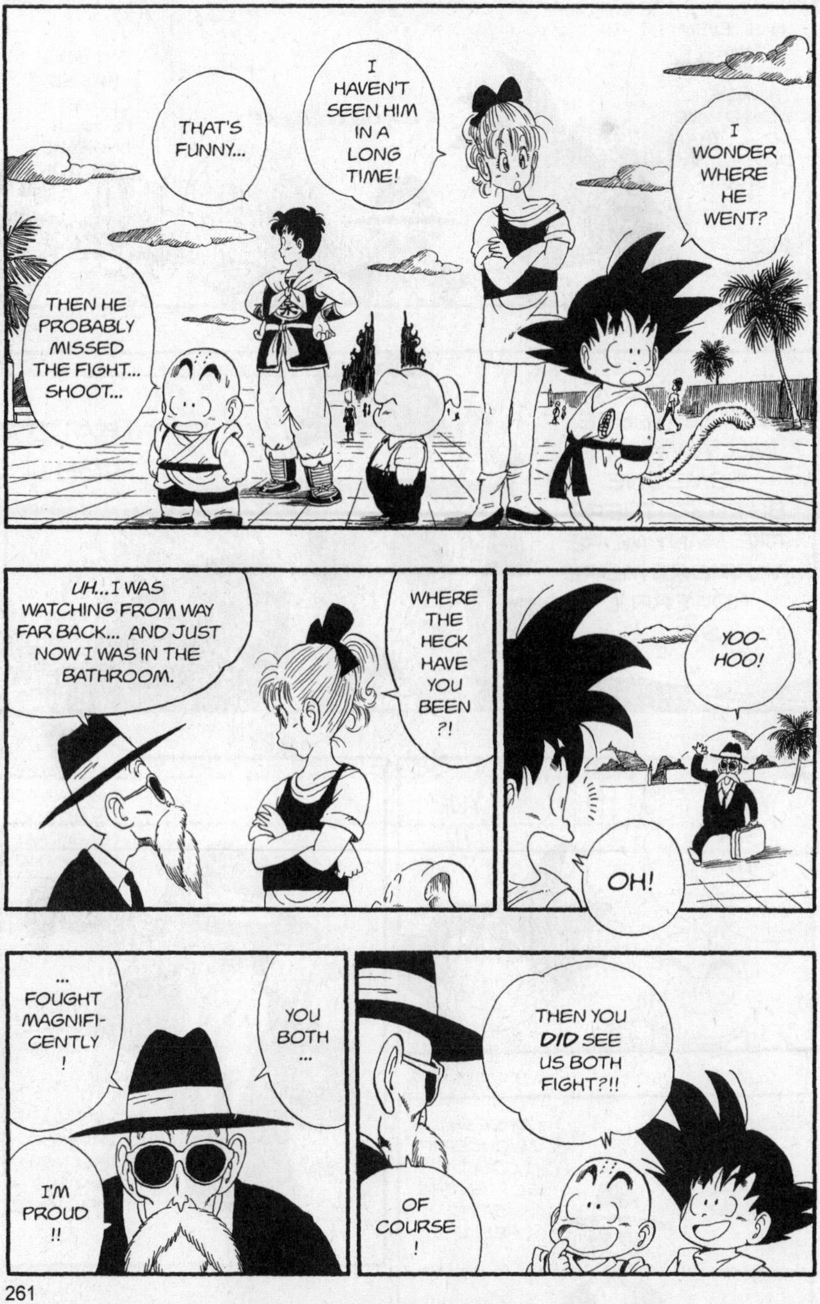
I WONDER WHERE HE WENT?
I HAVEN'T SEEN HIM IN A LONG TIME!
THAT'S FUNNY...
THEN HE PROBABLY MISSED THE FIGHT... SHOOT...
YOO-HOO!
OH!
WHERE THE HECK HAVE YOU BEEN?!
UH... I WAS WATCHING FROM WAY FAR BACK... AND JUST NOW I WAS IN THE BATHROOM.
THEN YOU ***DID*** SEE US BOTH FIGHT?!!
OF COURSE!
YOU BOTH...
...FOUGHT MAGNIFI-CENTLY!
I'M PROUD!!

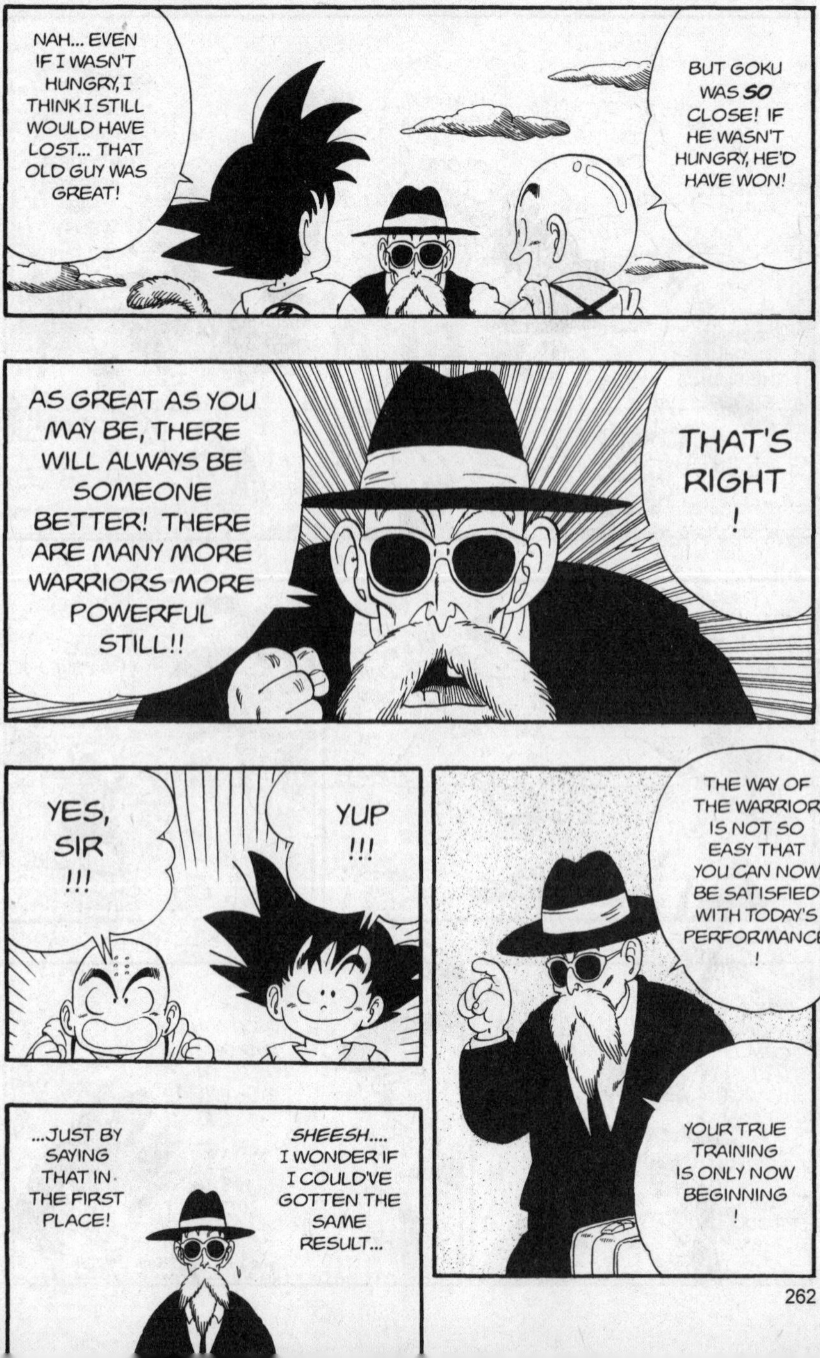
BUT GOKU WAS SO CLOSE! IF HE WASN'T HUNGRY, HE'D HAVE WON!
NAH... EVEN IF I WASN'T HUNGRY, I THINK I STILL WOULD HAVE LOST... THAT OLD GUY WAS GREAT!
THAT'S RIGHT!
AS GREAT AS YOU MAY BE, THERE WILL ALWAYS BE SOMEONE BETTER! THERE ARE MANY MORE WARRIORS MORE POWERFUL STILL!!
THE WAY OF THE WARRIOR IS NOT SO EASY THAT YOU CAN NOW BE SATISFIED WITH TODAY'S PERFORMANCE!
YOUR TRUE TRAINING IS ONLY NOW BEGINNING!
YUP!!!
YES, SIR!!!
SHEESH.... I WONDER IF I COULD'VE GOTTEN THE SAME RESULT...
...JUST BY SAYING THAT IN THE FIRST PLACE!

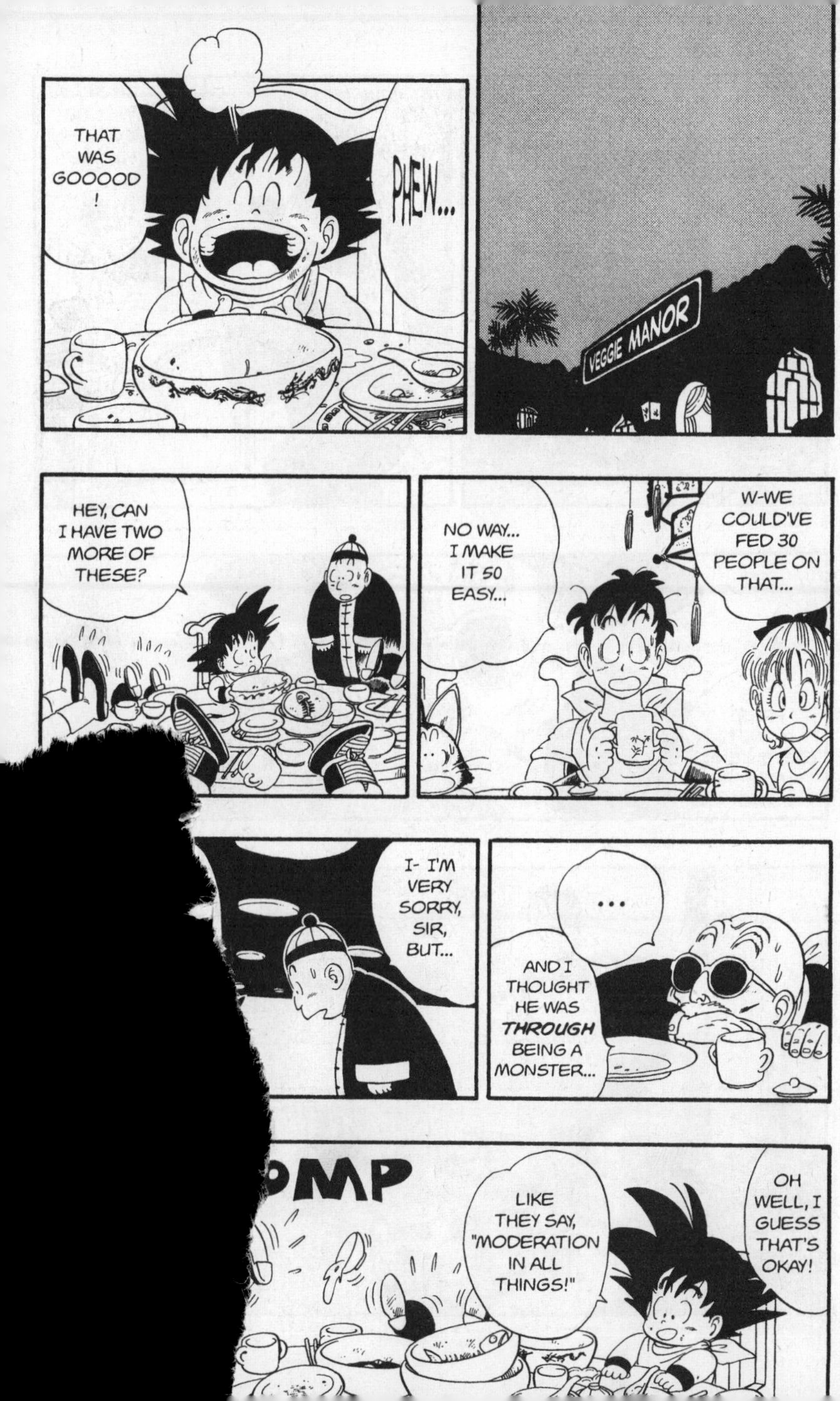
VEGGIE MANOR
PHEW...
THAT WAS GOOOOD!
W-WE COULD'VE FED 30 PEOPLE ON THAT...
NO WAY... I MAKE IT 50 EASY...
HEY, CAN I HAVE TWO MORE OF THESE?
...
AND I THOUGHT HE WAS **THROUGH** BEING A MONSTER...
I- I'M VERY SORRY, SIR, BUT...
OH WELL, I GUESS THAT'S OKAY!
LIKE THEY SAY, "MODERATION IN ALL THINGS!"
OMP

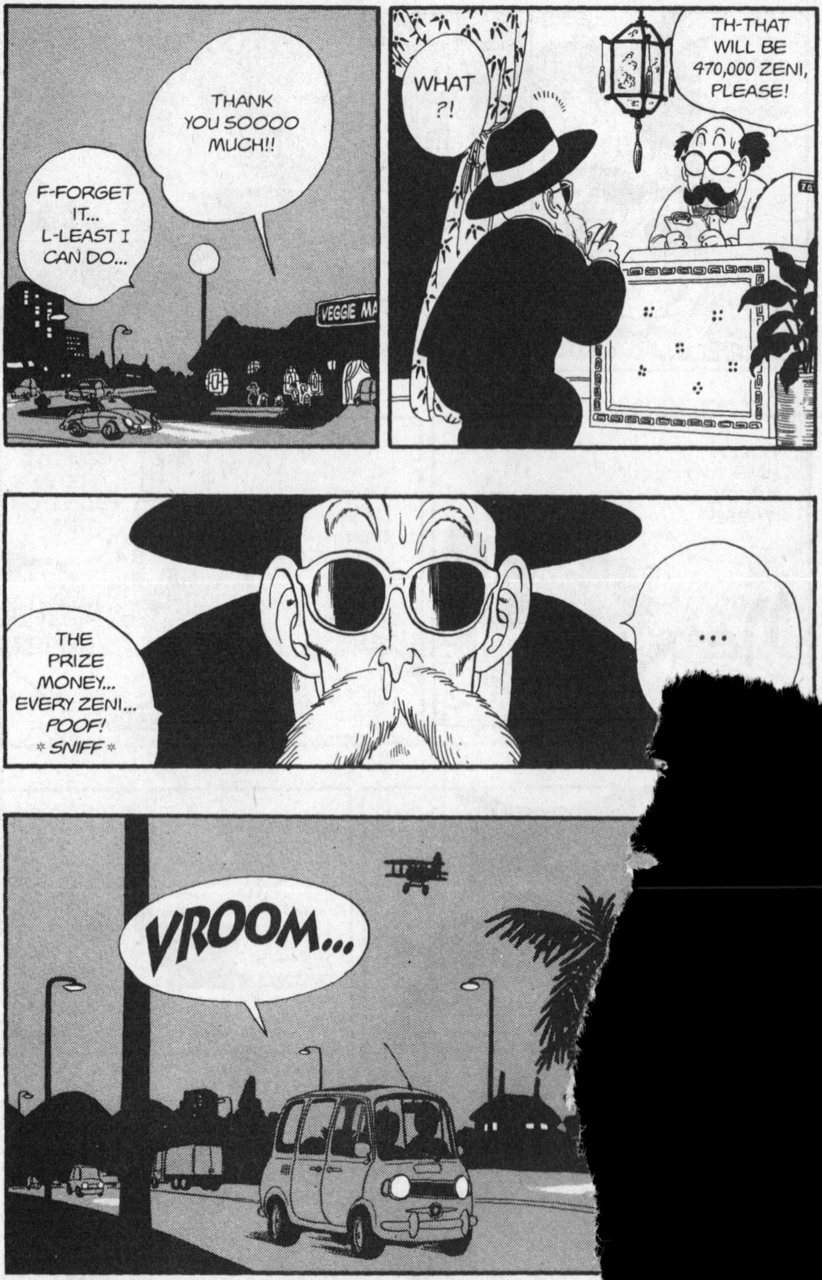
TH-THAT WILL BE 470,000 ZENI, PLEASE!
WHAT?!
THANK YOU SOOOO MUCH!!
F-FORGET IT... L-LEAST I CAN DO...
VEGGIE MA
...
THE PRIZE MONEY... EVERY ZENI... POOF! *SNIFF*
VROOM...

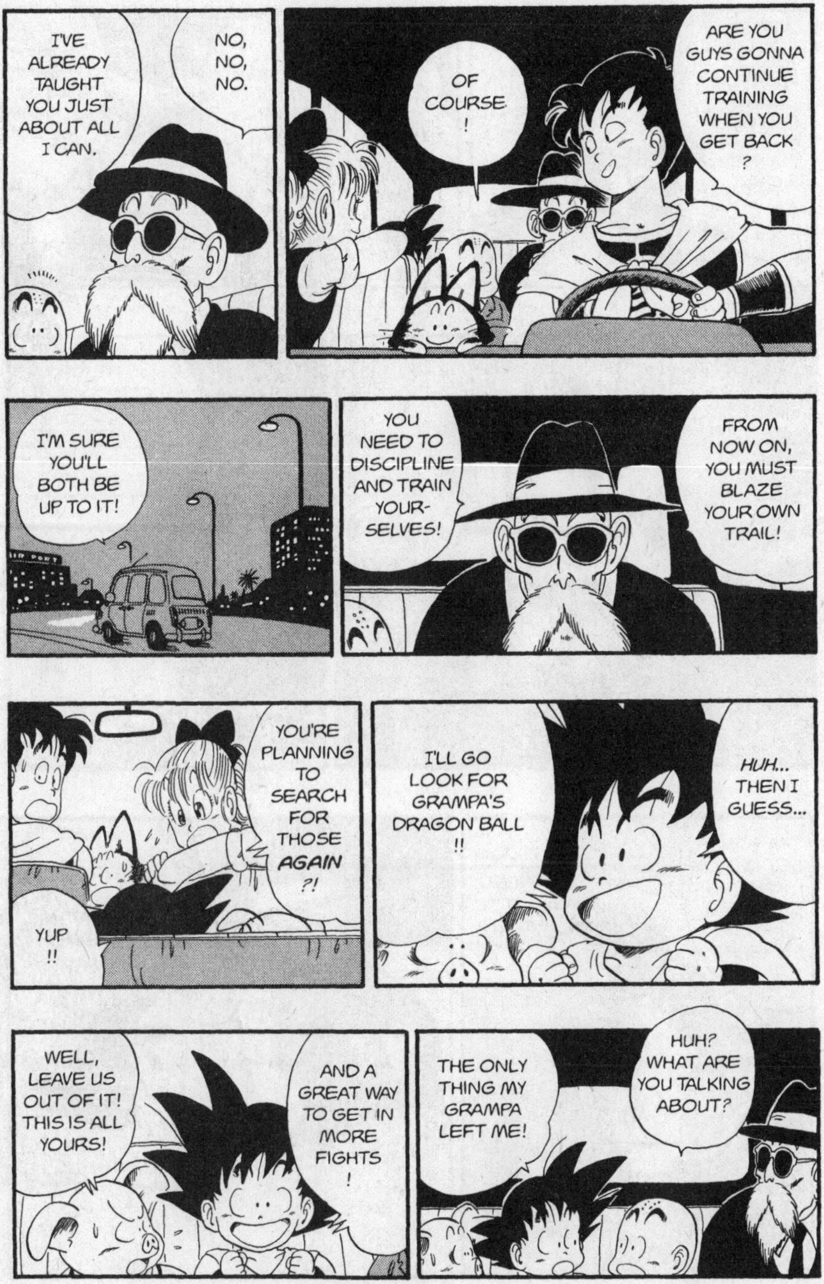
ARE YOU GUYS GONNA CONTINUE TRAINING WHEN YOU GET BACK?
OF COURSE!
NO, NO, NO.
I'VE ALREADY TAUGHT YOU JUST ABOUT ALL I CAN.
FROM NOW ON, YOU MUST BLAZE YOUR OWN TRAIL!
YOU NEED TO DISCIPLINE AND TRAIN YOUR-SELVES!
I'M SURE YOU'LL BOTH BE UP TO IT!
HUH... THEN I GUESS...
I'LL GO LOOK FOR GRAMPA'S DRAGON BALL!!
YOU'RE PLANNING TO SEARCH FOR THOSE ***AGAIN***?!
YUP!!
HUH? WHAT ARE YOU TALKING ABOUT?
THE ONLY THING MY GRAMPA LEFT ME!
AND A GREAT WAY TO GET IN MORE FIGHTS!
WELL, LEAVE US OUT OF IT! THIS IS ALL YOURS!

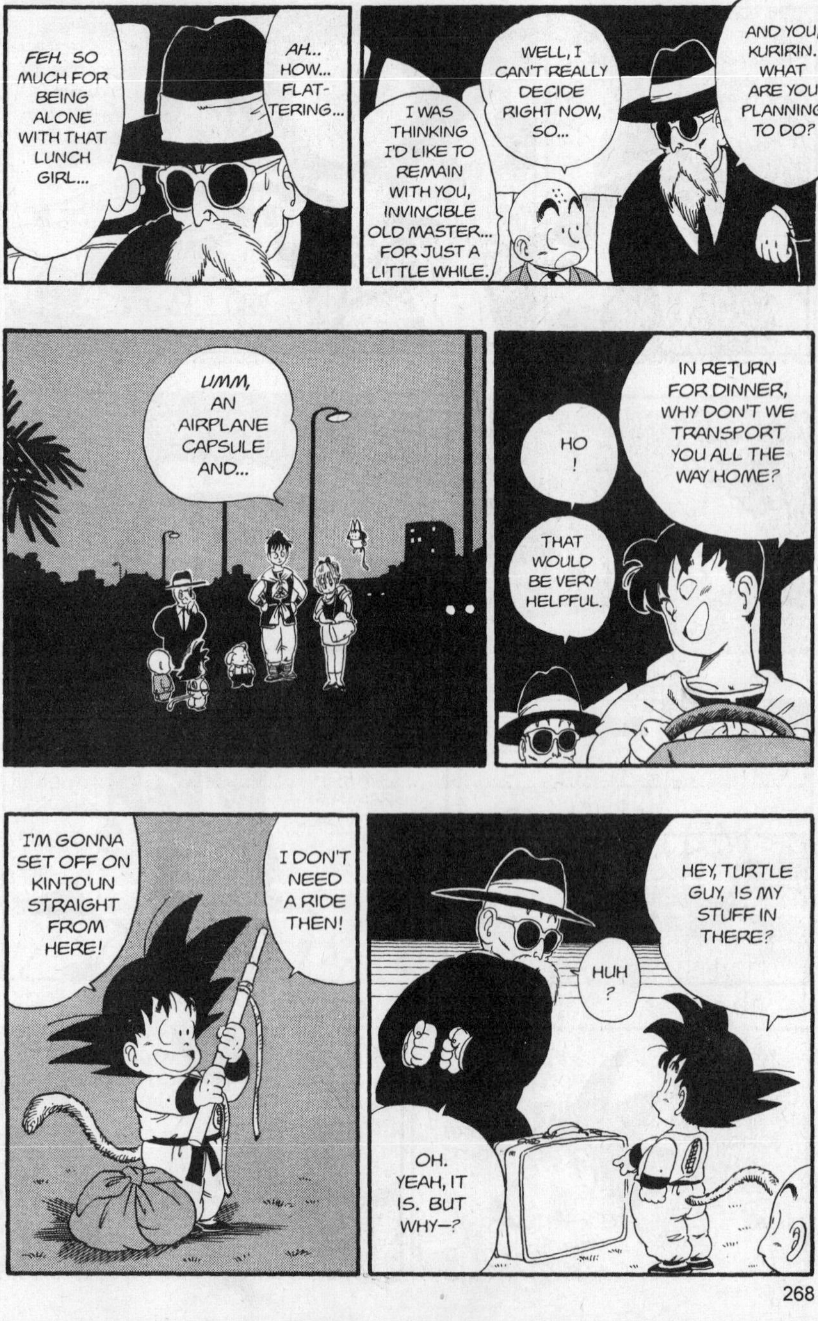
AND YOU, KURIRIN. WHAT ARE YOU PLANNING TO DO?
WELL, I CAN'T REALLY DECIDE RIGHT NOW, SO...
I WAS THINKING I'D LIKE TO REMAIN WITH YOU, INVINCIBLE OLD MASTER... FOR JUST A LITTLE WHILE.
AH... HOW... FLAT-TERING...
FEH. SO MUCH FOR BEING ALONE WITH THAT LUNCH GIRL...
IN RETURN FOR DINNER, WHY DON'T WE TRANSPORT YOU ALL THE WAY HOME?
HO!
THAT WOULD BE VERY HELPFUL.
UMM, AN AIRPLANE CAPSULE AND...
HEY, TURTLE GUY, IS MY STUFF IN THERE?
HUH?
OH. YEAH, IT IS. BUT WHY—?
I DON'T NEED A RIDE THEN!
I'M GONNA SET OFF ON KINTO'UN STRAIGHT FROM HERE!

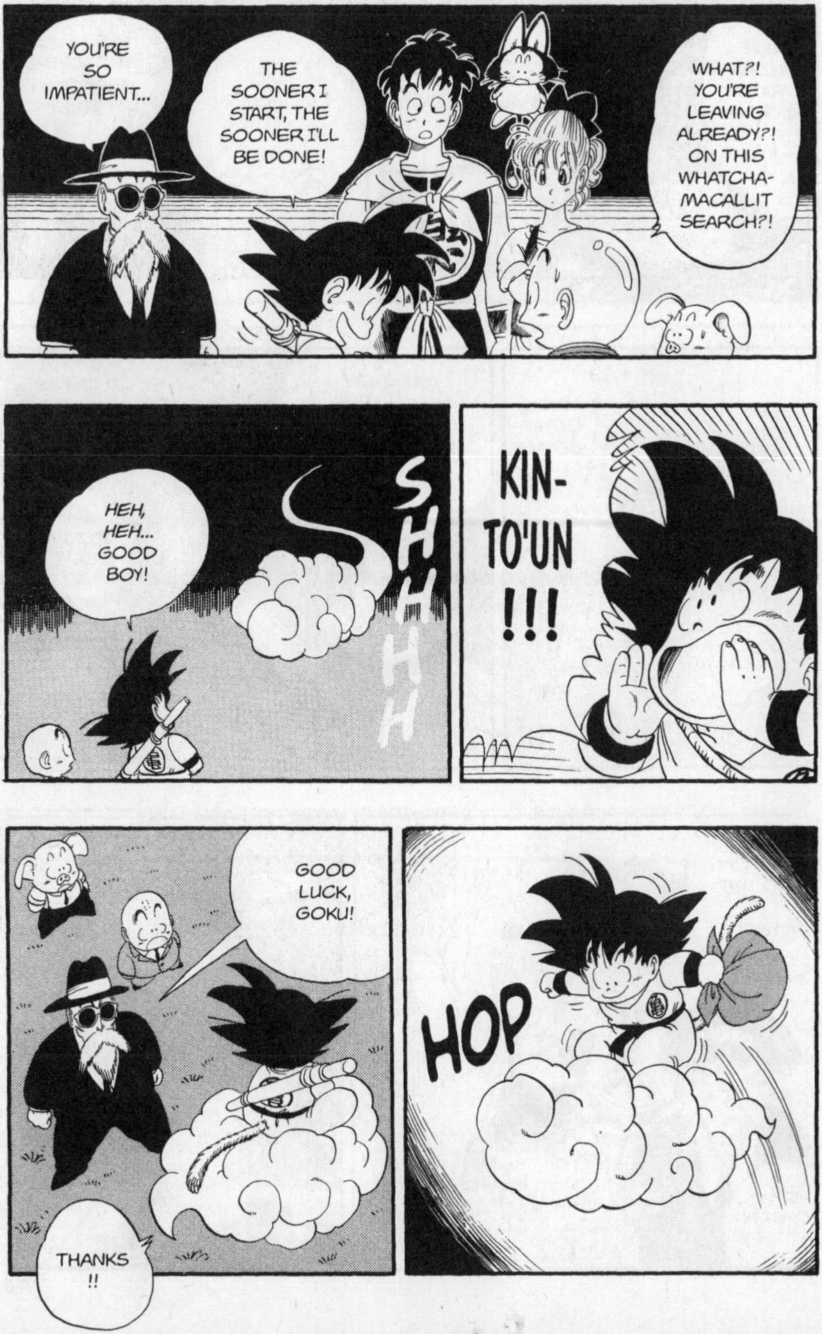
WHAT?! YOU'RE LEAVING ALREADY?! ON THIS WHATCHA-MACALLIT SEARCH?!
THE SOONER I START, THE SOONER I'LL BE DONE!
YOU'RE SO IMPATIENT...
KIN-TO'UN !!!
SHHHHH
HEH, HEH... GOOD BOY!
HOP
GOOD LUCK, GOKU!
THANKS !!

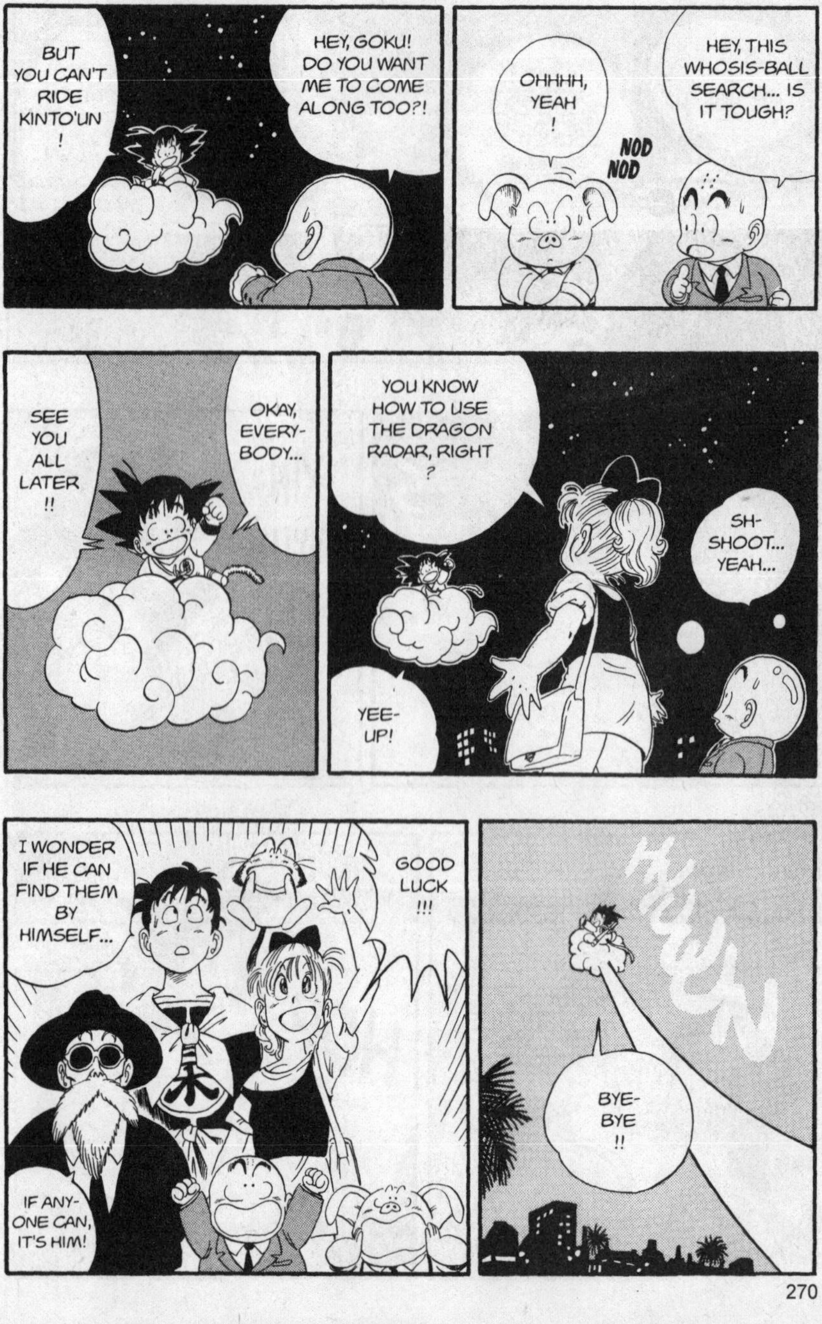
HEY, THIS WHOSIS-BALL SEARCH... IS IT TOUGH?
OHHHH, YEAH!
NOD NOD
HEY, GOKU! DO YOU WANT ME TO COME ALONG TOO?!
BUT YOU CAN'T RIDE KINTO'UN!
YOU KNOW HOW TO USE THE DRAGON RADAR, RIGHT?
SH-SHOOT... YEAH...
YEE-UP!
OKAY, EVERY-BODY...
SEE YOU ALL LATER!!
BYE-BYE!!
GOOD LUCK!!!
I WONDER IF HE CAN FIND THEM BY HIMSELF...
IF ANY-ONE CAN, IT'S HIM!

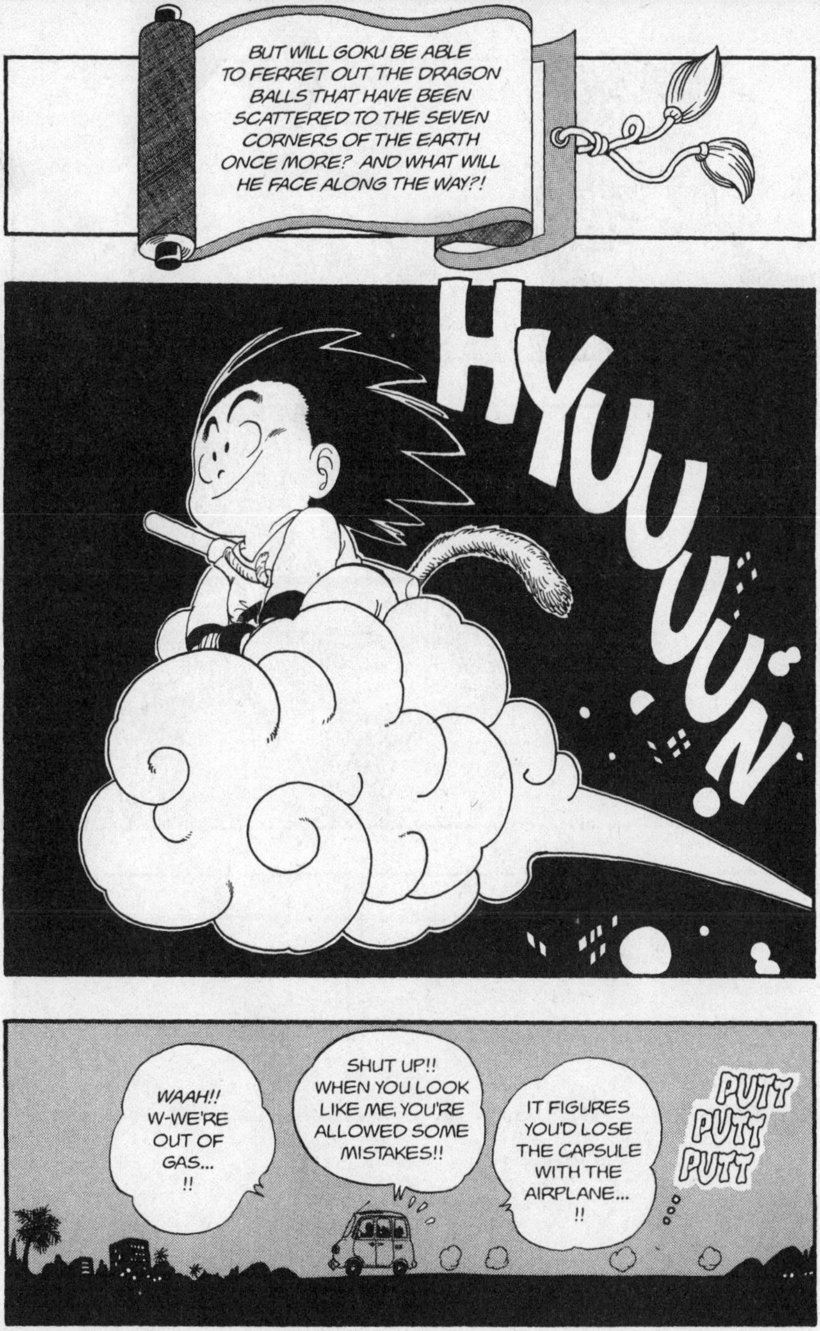
BUT WILL GOKU BE ABLE TO FERRET OUT THE DRAGON BALLS THAT HAVE BEEN SCATTERED TO THE SEVEN CORNERS OF THE EARTH ONCE MORE? AND WHAT WILL HE FACE ALONG THE WAY?!
HYUUUUN!
PUTT PUTT PUTT
IT FIGURES YOU'D LOSE THE CAPSULE WITH THE AIRPLANE... !!
SHUT UP!! WHEN YOU LOOK LIKE ME, YOU'RE ALLOWED SOME MISTAKES!!
WAAH!! W-WE'RE OUT OF GAS... !!

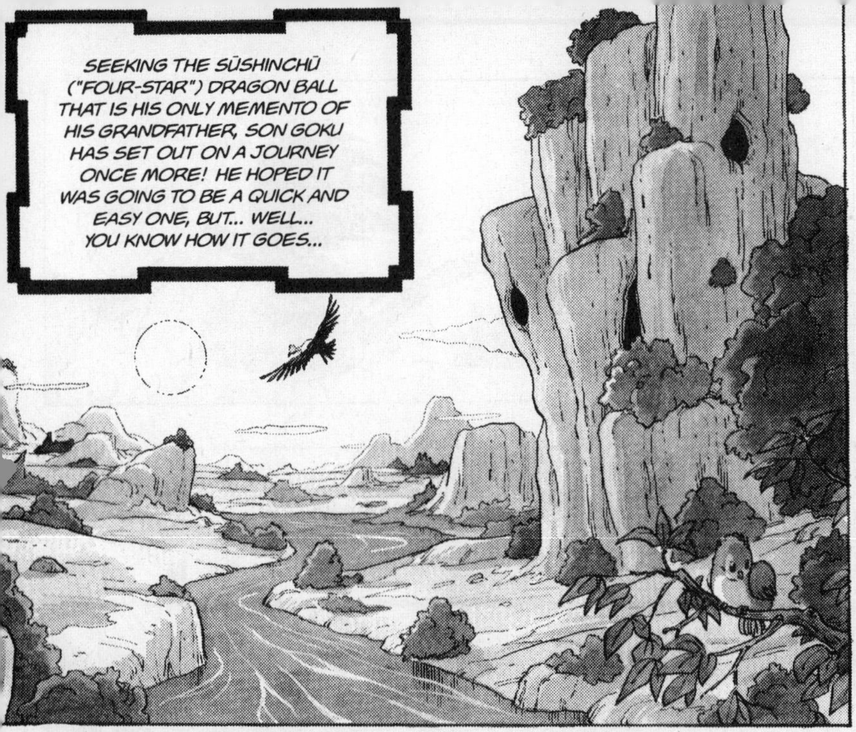
SEEKING THE SŪSHINCHŪ ("FOUR-STAR") DRAGON BALL THAT IS HIS ONLY MEMENTO OF HIS GRANDFATHER, SON GOKU HAS SET OUT ON A JOURNEY ONCE MORE! HE HOPED IT WAS GOING TO BE A QUICK AND EASY ONE, BUT... WELL... YOU KNOW HOW IT GOES...

Tale 55 · The Red Ribbon

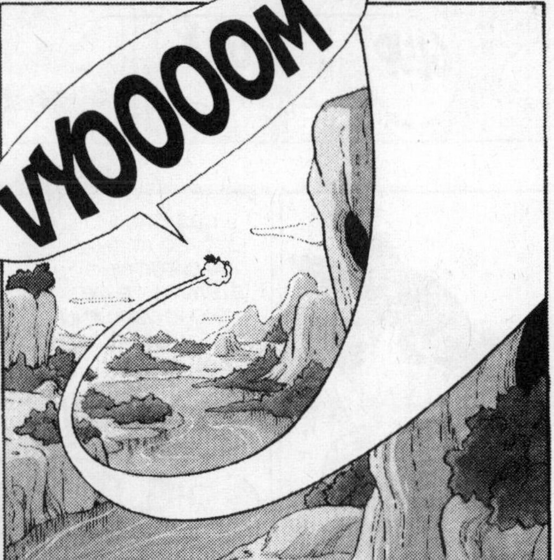
VYOOOOM

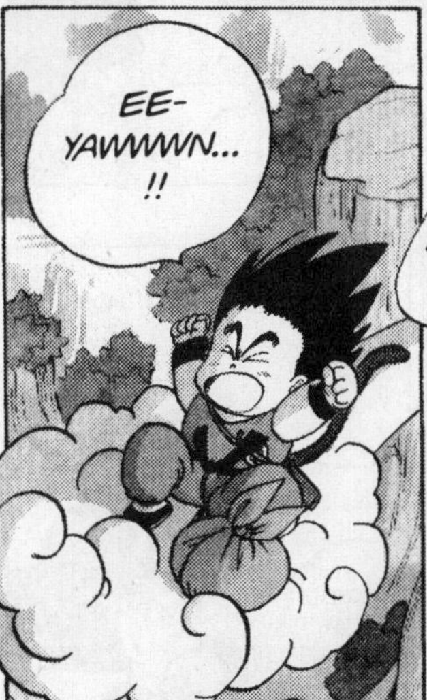
EE-YAWWWN... !!

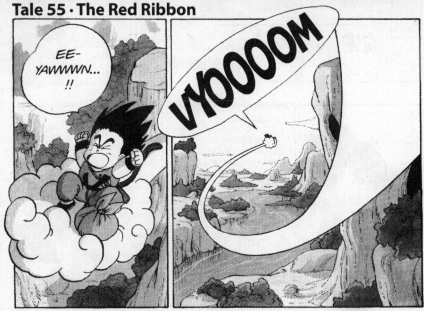

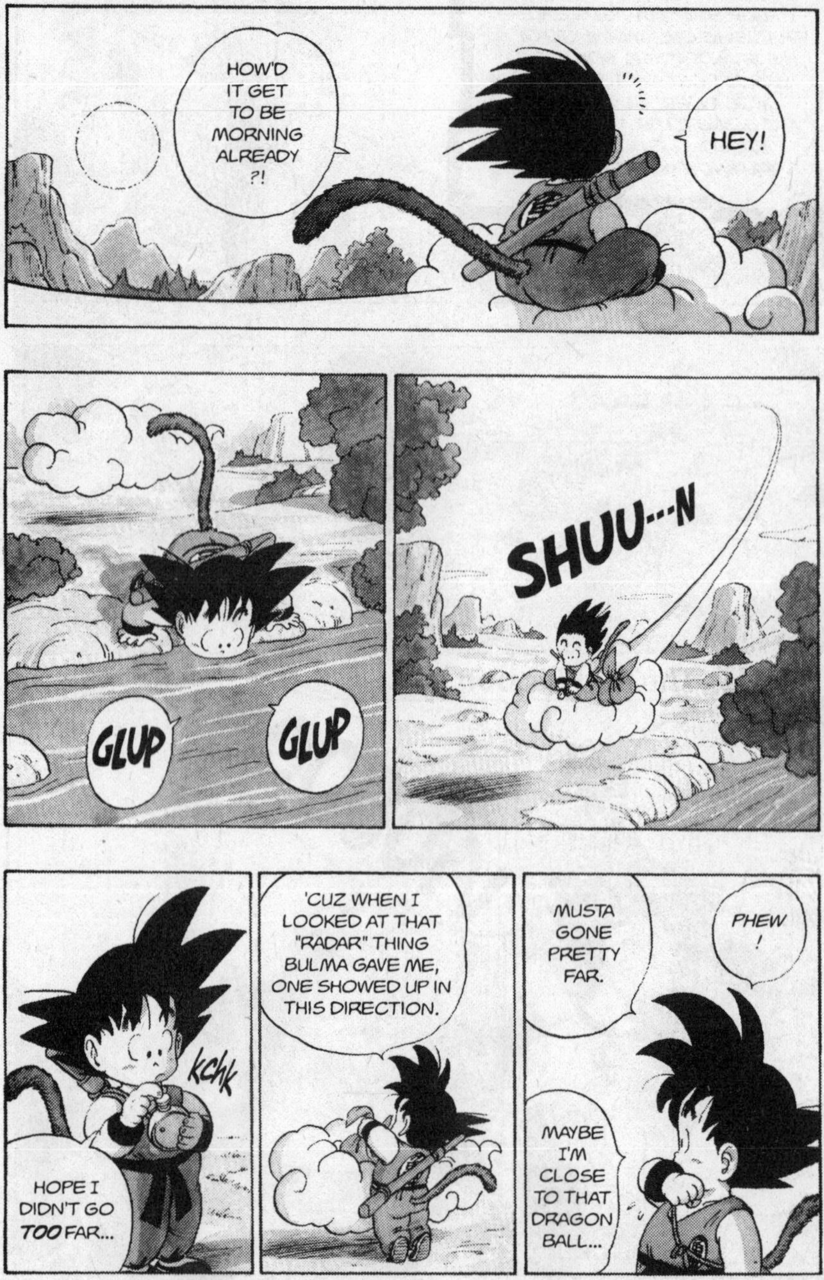
HEY!
HOW'D IT GET TO BE MORNING ALREADY ?!
SHUU---N
GLUP
GLUP
PHEW!
MUSTA GONE PRETTY FAR.
MAYBE I'M CLOSE TO THAT DRAGON BALL...
'CUZ WHEN I LOOKED AT THAT "RADAR" THING BULMA GAVE ME, ONE SHOWED UP IN THIS DIRECTION.
KCHK
HOPE I DIDN'T GO TOO FAR...

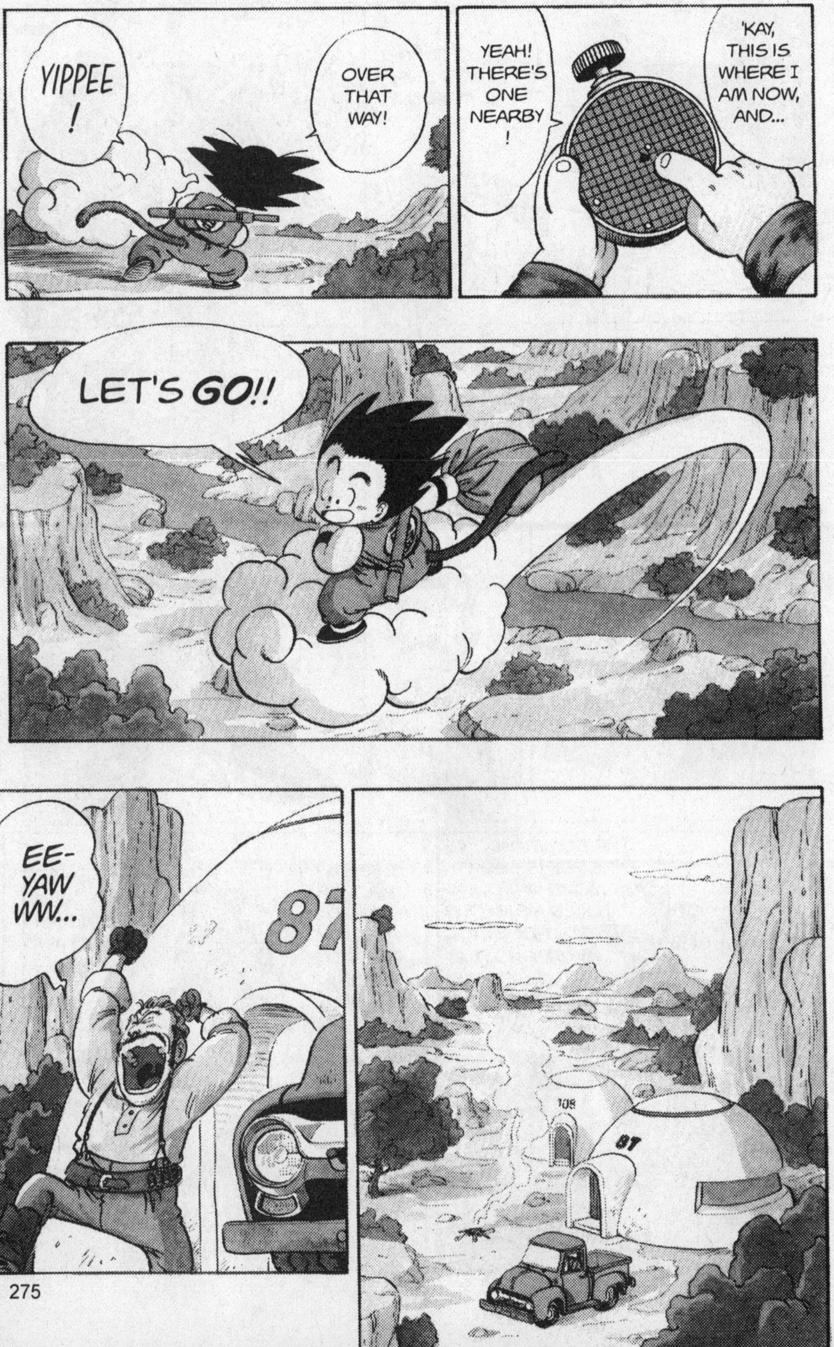
'KAY, THIS IS WHERE I AM NOW, AND...
YEAH! THERE'S ONE NEARBY!
OVER THAT WAY!
YIPPEE!
LET'S GO!!
EE-YAWWW...

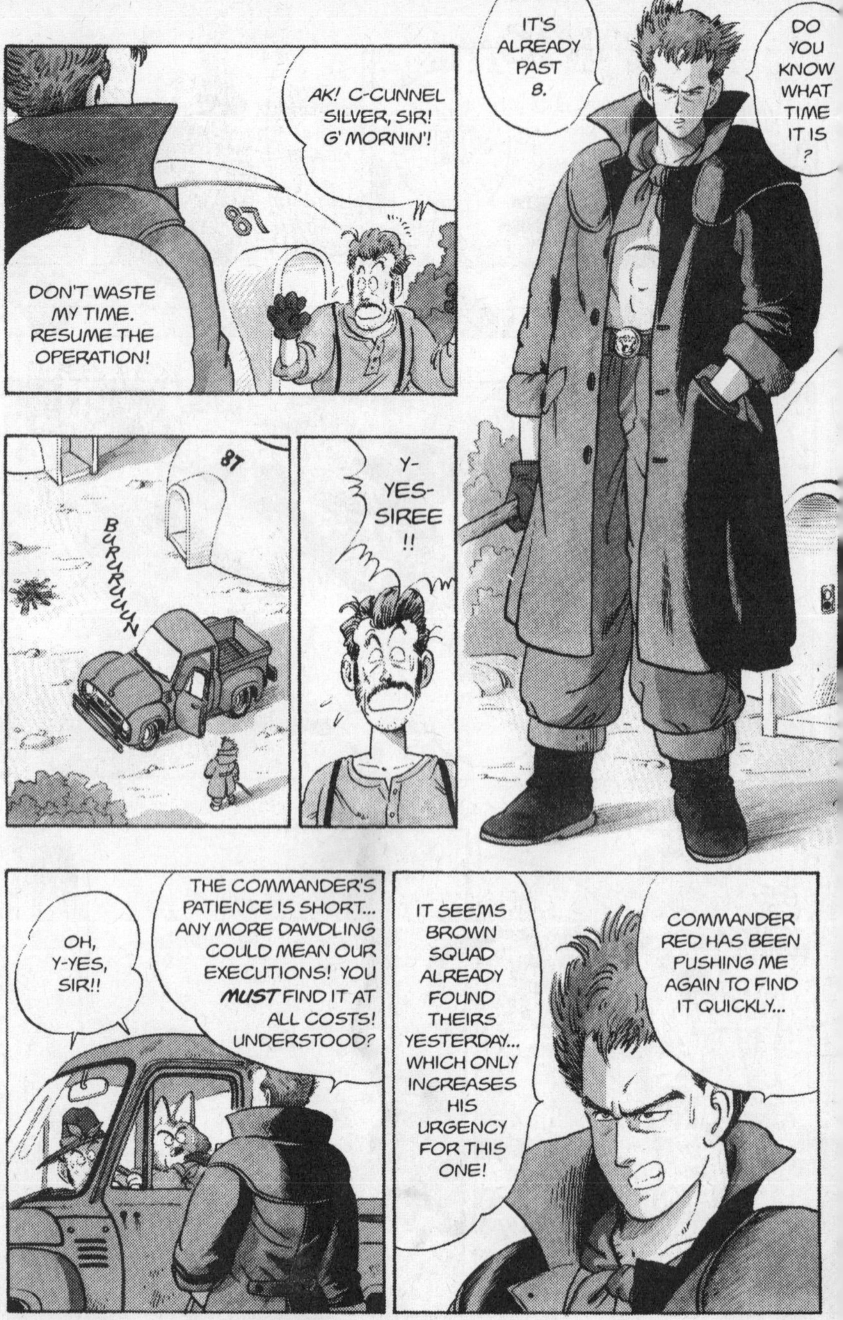
DO YOU KNOW WHAT TIME IT IS?
IT'S ALREADY PAST 8.
AK! C-CUNNEL SILVER, SIR! G' MORNIN'!
DON'T WASTE MY TIME. RESUME THE OPERATION!
Y-YES-SIREE!!
BURURUUUN
COMMANDER RED HAS BEEN PUSHING ME AGAIN TO FIND IT QUICKLY...
IT SEEMS BROWN SQUAD ALREADY FOUND THEIRS YESTERDAY... WHICH ONLY INCREASES HIS URGENCY FOR THIS ONE!
THE COMMANDER'S PATIENCE IS SHORT... ANY MORE DAWDLING COULD MEAN OUR EXECUTIONS! YOU *MUST* FIND IT AT ALL COSTS! UNDERSTOOD?
OH, Y-YES, SIR!!

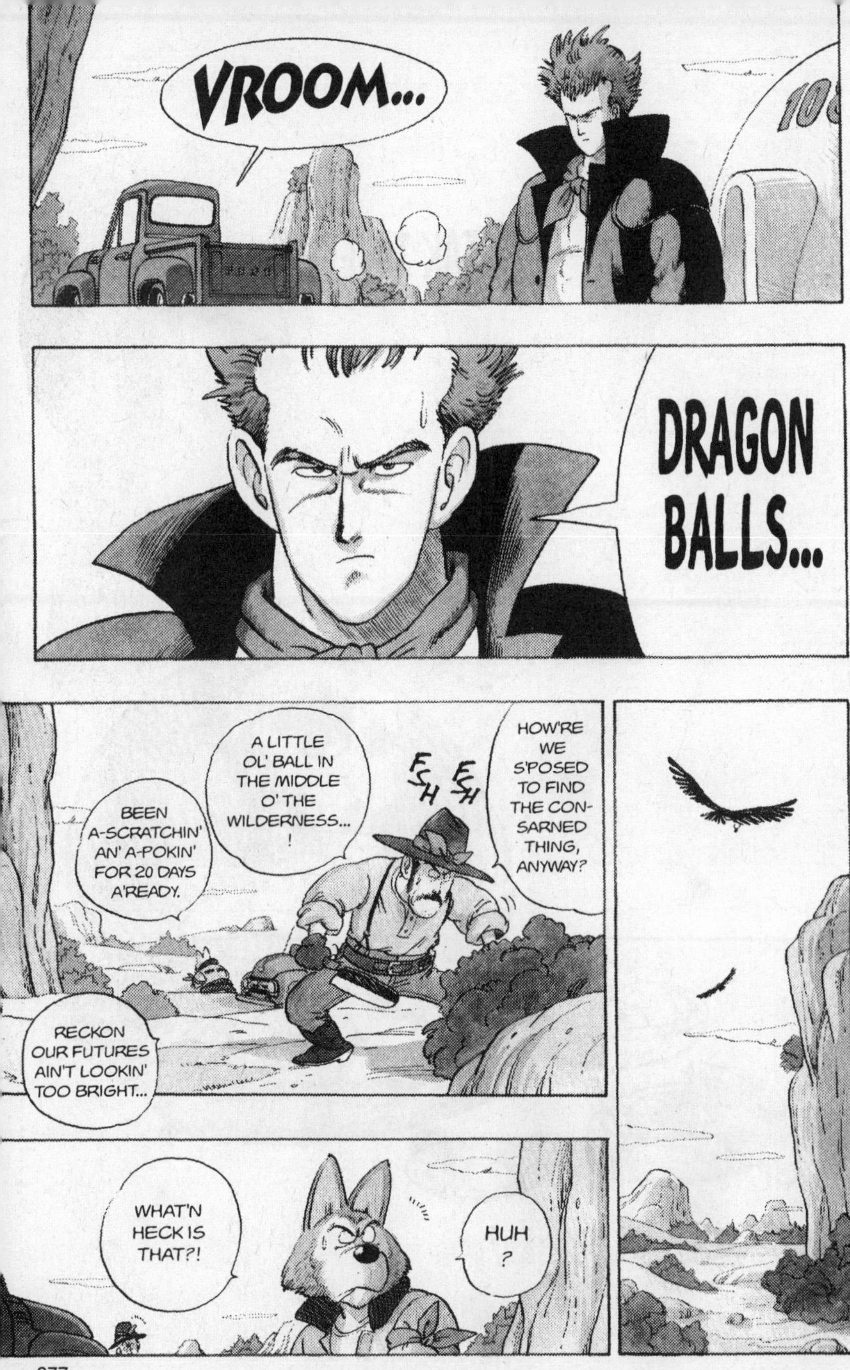
VROOM...
DRAGON BALLS...
HOW'RE WE S'POSED TO FIND THE CON-SARNED THING, ANYWAY?
FSH FSH
A LITTLE OL' BALL IN THE MIDDLE O' THE WILDERNESS...!
BEEN A-SCRATCHIN' AN' A-POKIN' FOR 20 DAYS A'READY.
RECKON OUR FUTURES AIN'T LOOKIN' TOO BRIGHT...
HUH?
WHAT'N HECK IS THAT?!

——BREAK TIME!——

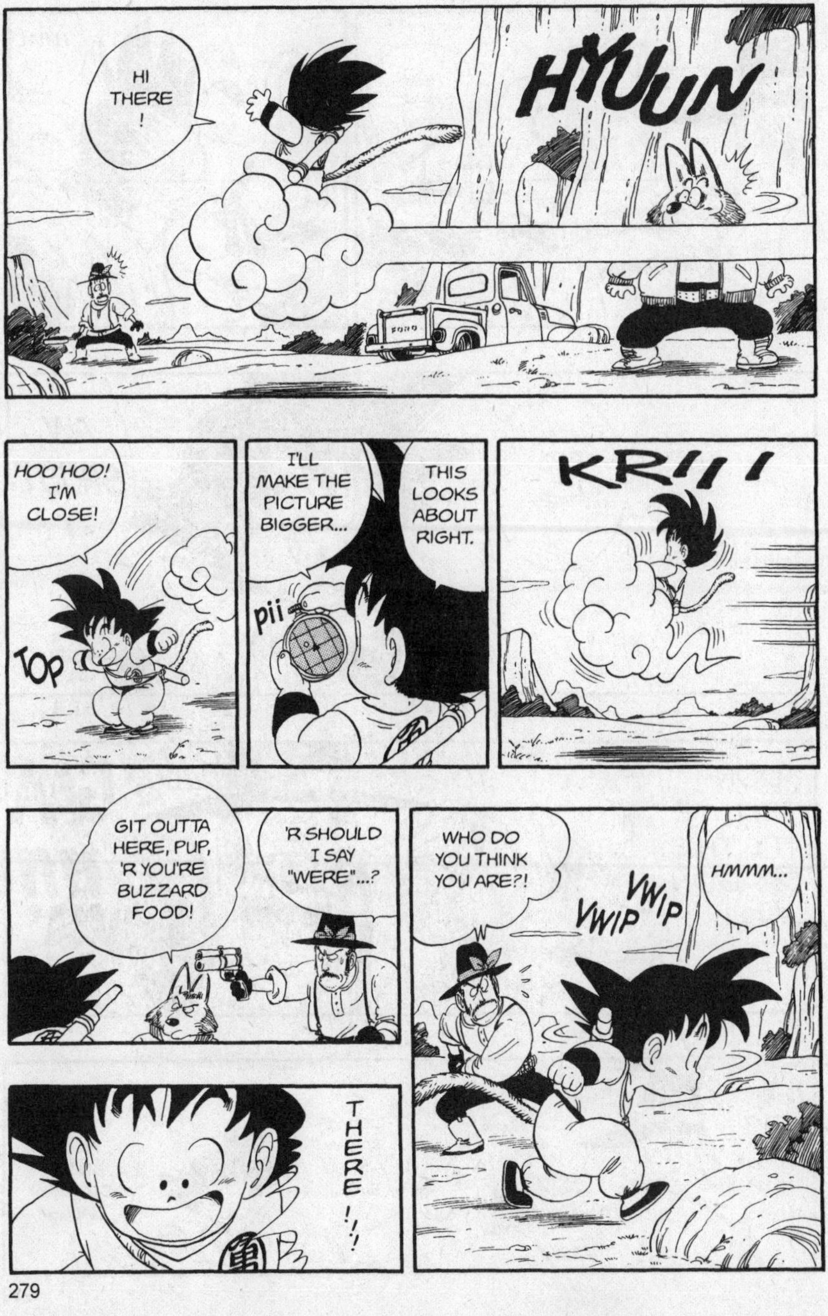
HYUUN
HI THERE !
KRIII
THIS LOOKS ABOUT RIGHT.
I'LL MAKE THE PICTURE BIGGER...
pii
HOO HOO! I'M CLOSE!
TOP
HMMM...
VWIP VWIP
WHO DO YOU THINK YOU ARE?!
'R SHOULD I SAY "WERE"...?
GIT OUTTA HERE, PUP, 'R YOU'RE BUZZARD FOOD!
THERE !!

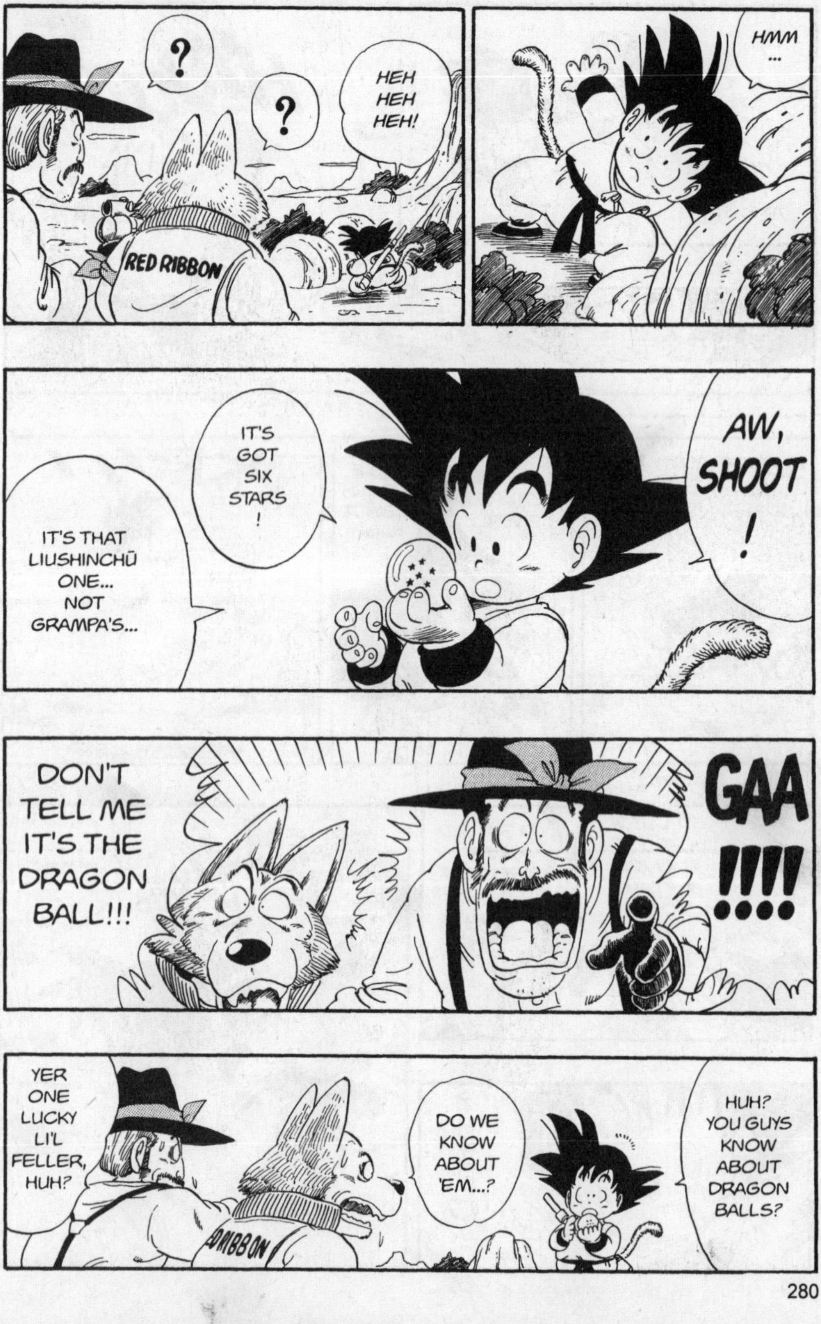
HMM ...
HEH HEH HEH!
?
?
RED RIBBON
AW, SHOOT!
IT'S GOT SIX STARS!
IT'S THAT LIUSHINCHŪ ONE... NOT GRAMPA'S...
GAA!!!!
DON'T TELL ME IT'S THE DRAGON BALL!!!
HUH? YOU GUYS KNOW ABOUT DRAGON BALLS?
DO WE KNOW ABOUT 'EM...?
YER ONE LUCKY LI'L FELLER, HUH?

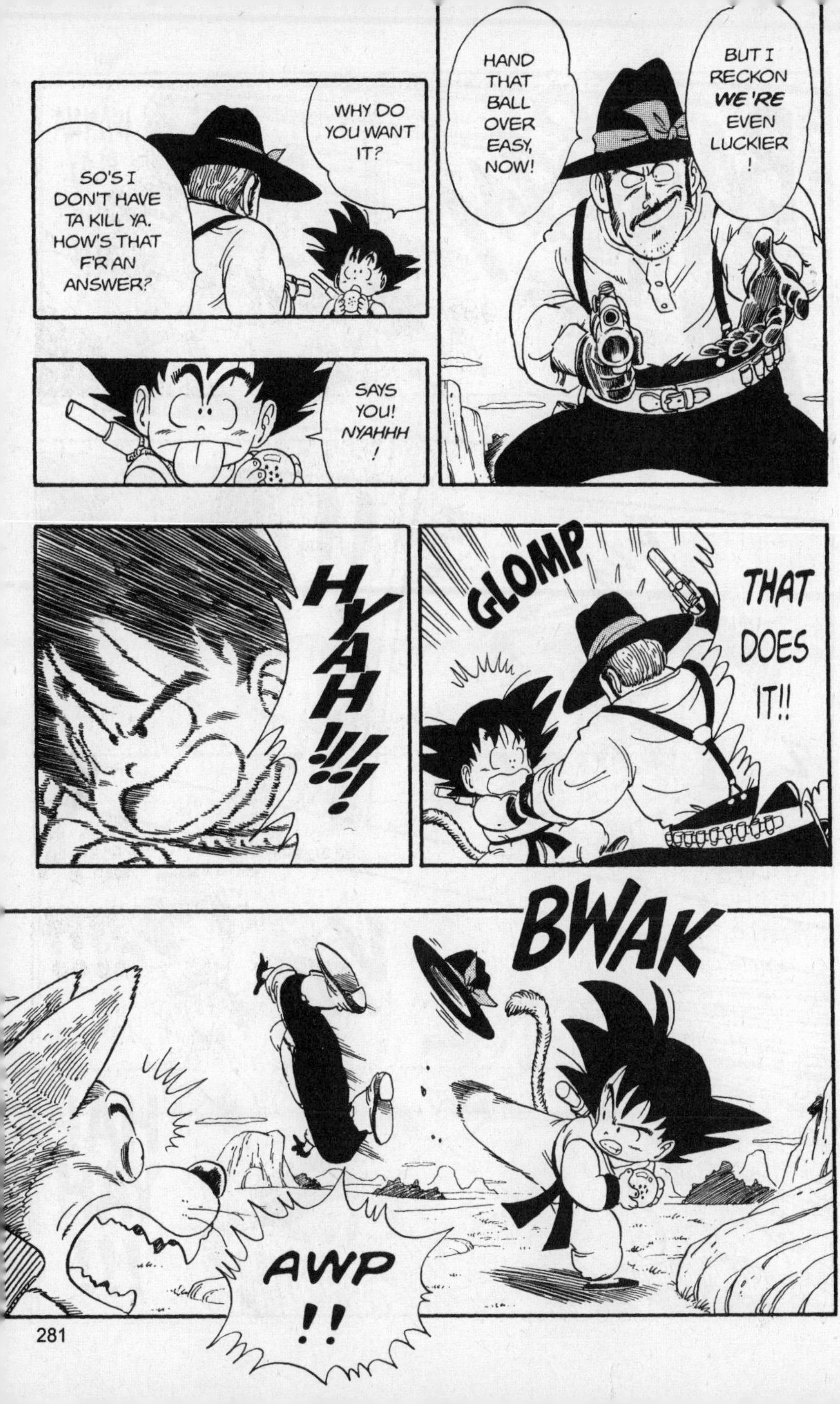
BUT I RECKON WE'RE EVEN LUCKIER!
HAND THAT BALL OVER EASY, NOW!
WHY DO YOU WANT IT?
SO'S I DON'T HAVE TA KILL YA. HOW'S THAT F'R AN ANSWER?
SAYS YOU! NYAHHH!
THAT DOES IT!!
GLOMP
HYAH!!!!
BWAK
AWP!!

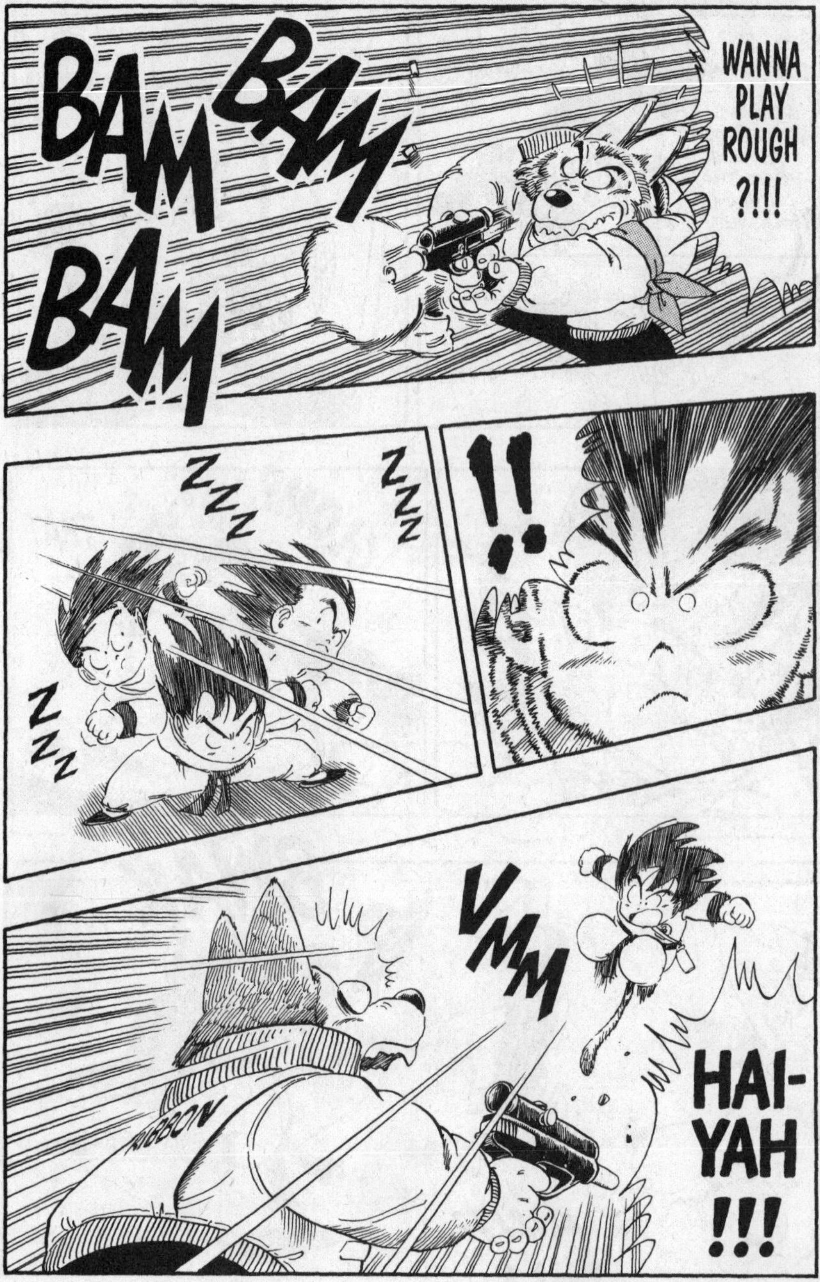

WANNA PLAY ROUGH ?!!!
BAM BAM BAM
!!
ZZZ ZZZ ZZZ
VMM
RIBBON
HAI-YAH !!!

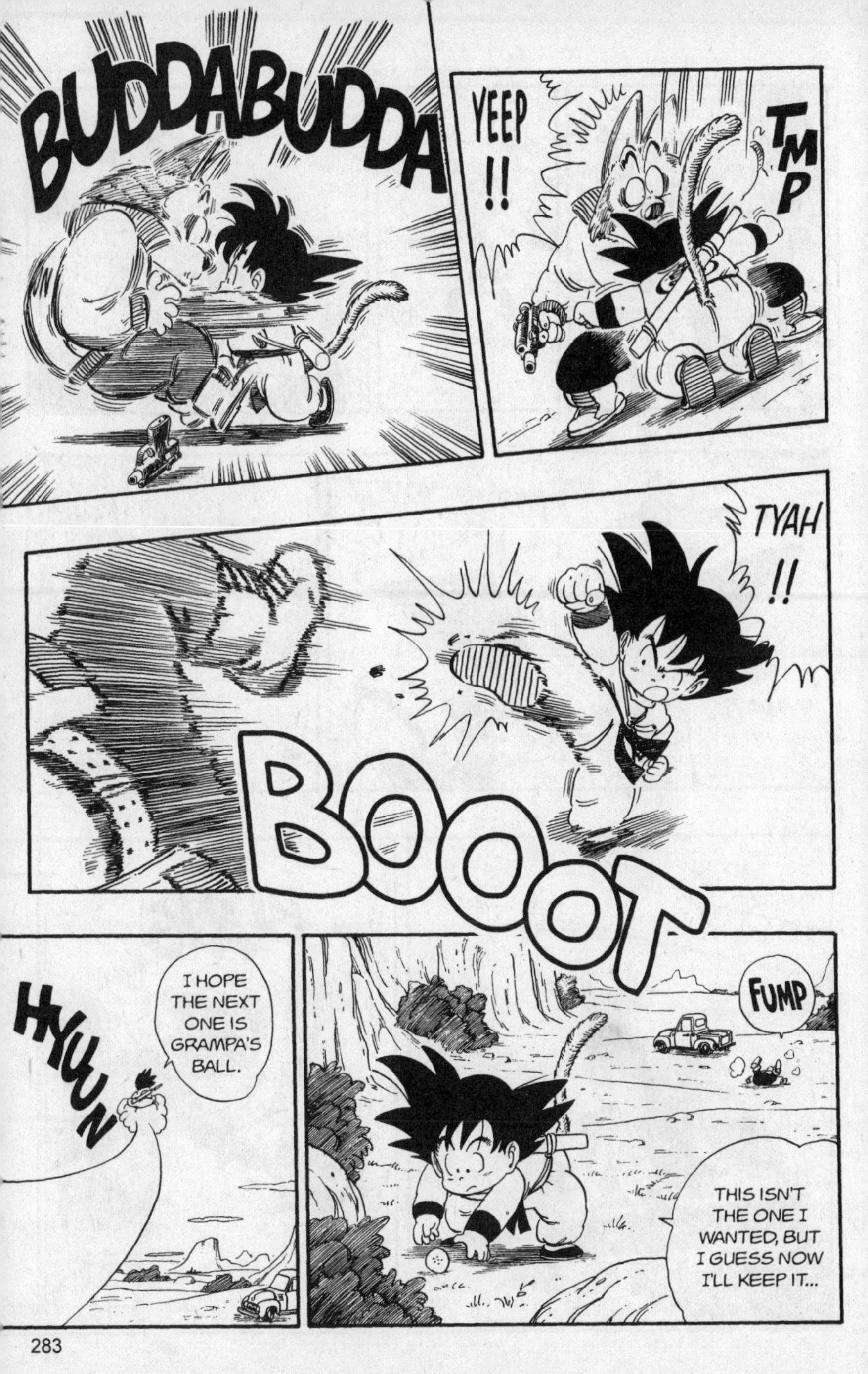
TMP
YEEP!!
BUDDABUDDA
TYAH!!
BOOOT
FUMP
THIS ISN'T THE ONE I WANTED, BUT I GUESS NOW I'LL KEEP IT...
I HOPE THE NEXT ONE IS GRAMPA'S BALL.
HYUUN

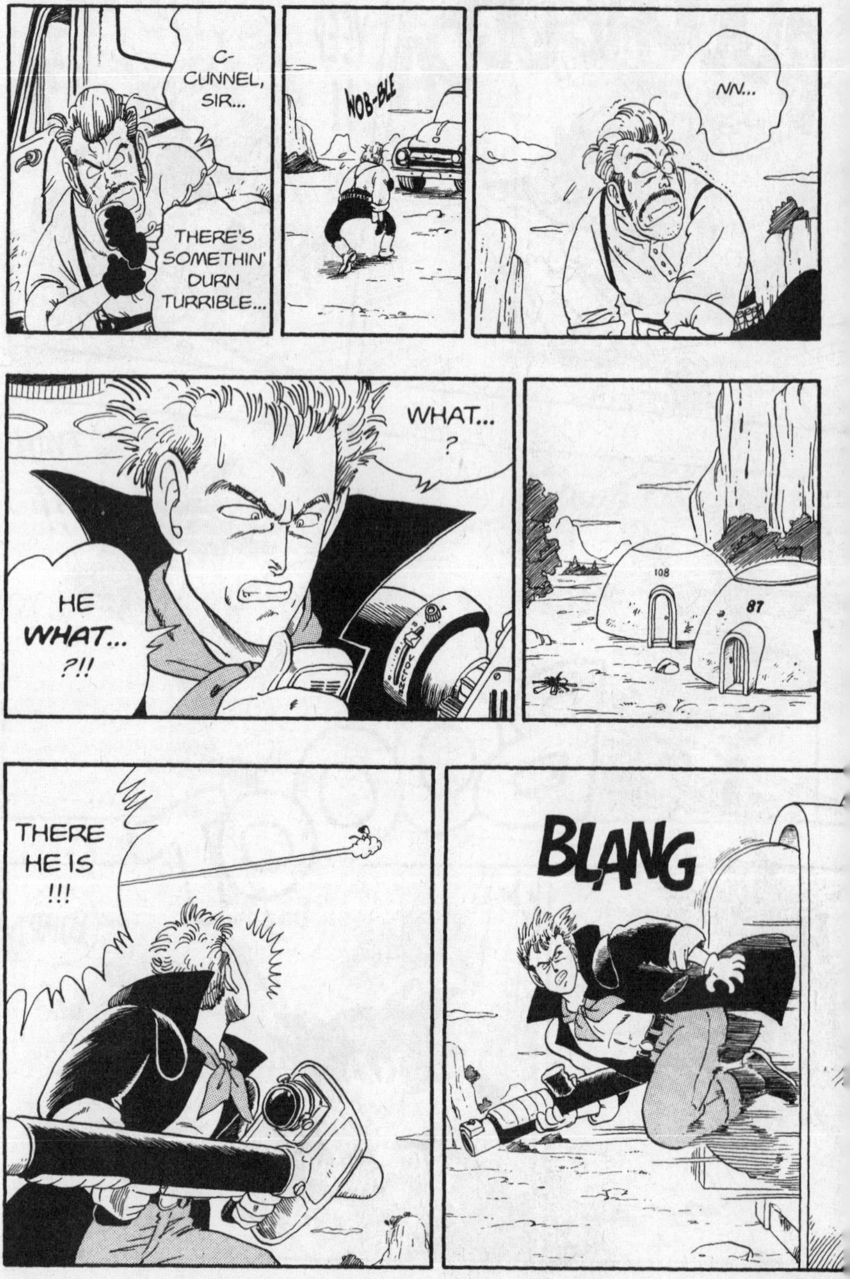
NN...
WOB-BLE
C- CUNNEL, SIR...
THERE'S SOMETHIN' DURN TURRIBLE...
108
87
WHAT... ?
HE WHAT... ?!!
BLANG
THERE HE IS !!!

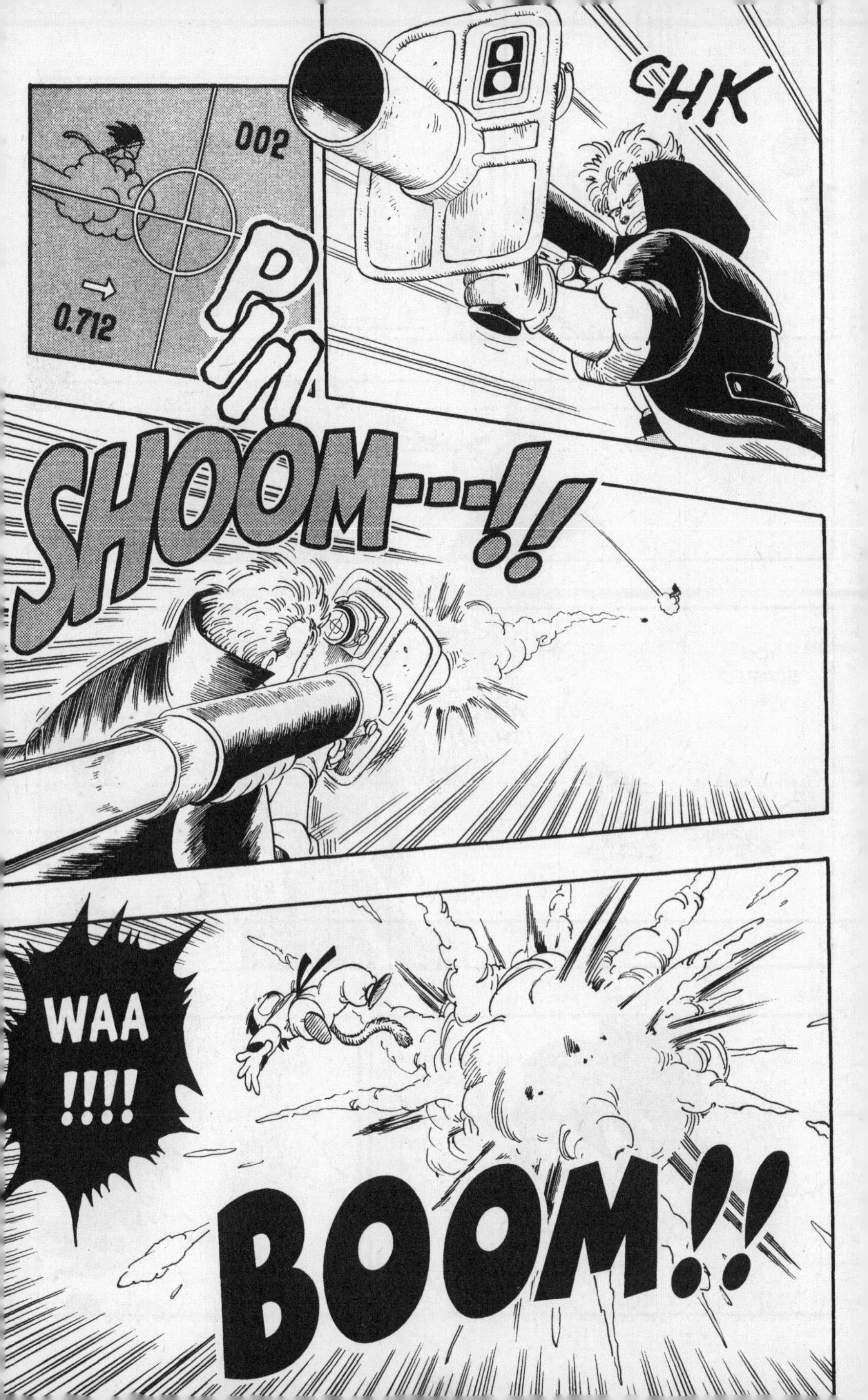
CHK
002
→
0.712
PI
SHOOM---!!
WAA !!!!
BOOM!!

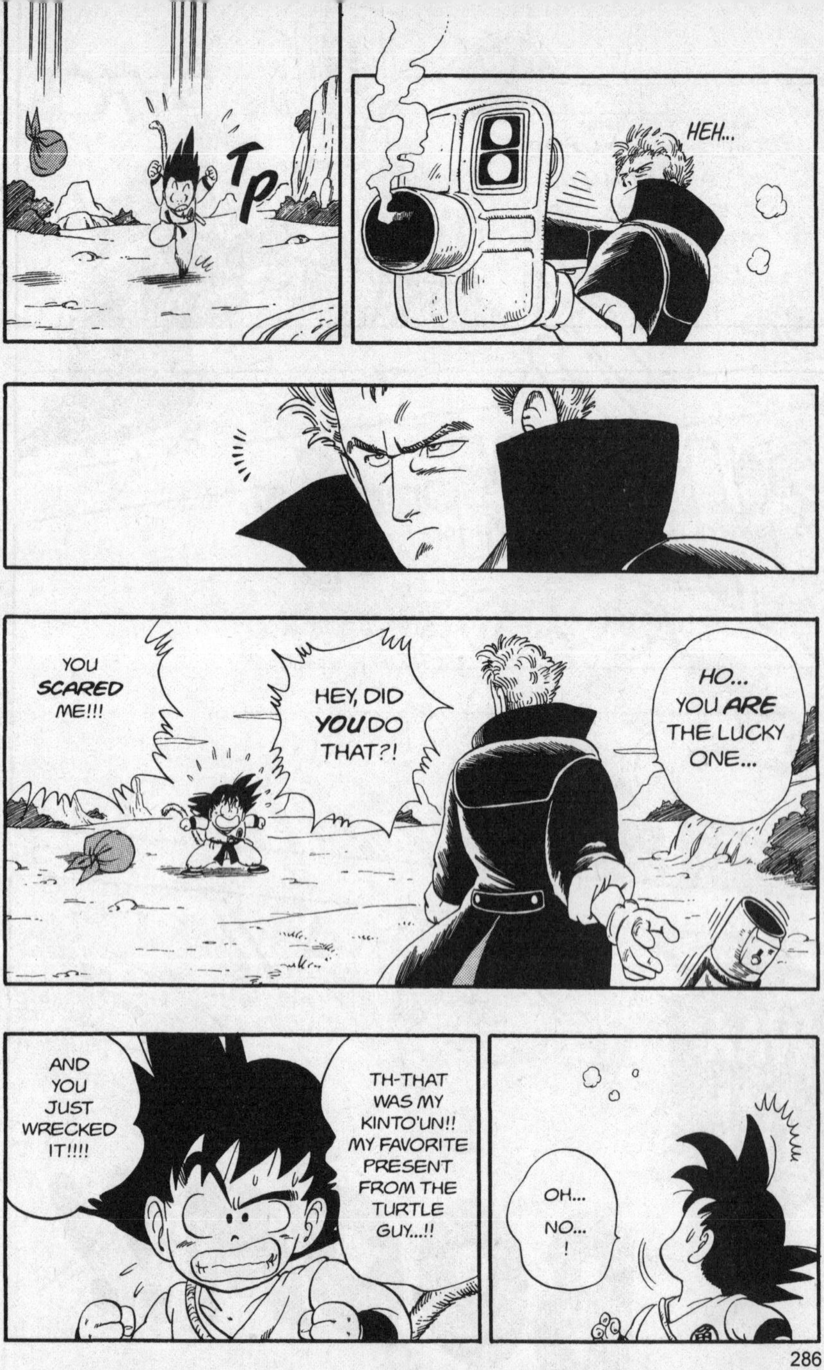
HEH...
Tp
HO... YOU **ARE** THE LUCKY ONE...
HEY, DID **YOU** DO THAT?!
YOU **SCARED** ME!!!
OH... NO... !
TH-THAT WAS MY KINTO'UN!! MY FAVORITE PRESENT FROM THE TURTLE GUY...!!
AND YOU JUST WRECKED IT!!!!

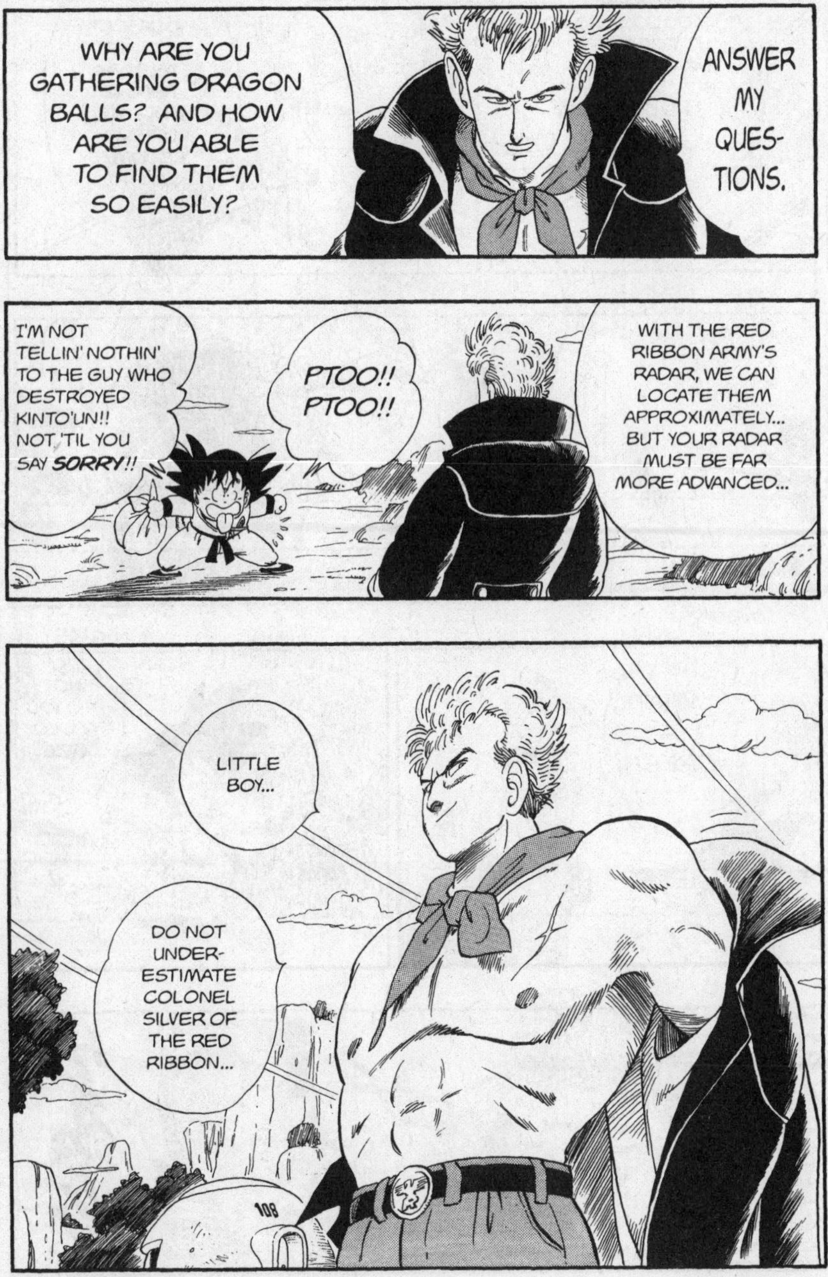
ANSWER MY QUES-TIONS.
WHY ARE YOU GATHERING DRAGON BALLS? AND HOW ARE YOU ABLE TO FIND THEM SO EASILY?
WITH THE RED RIBBON ARMY'S RADAR, WE CAN LOCATE THEM APPROXIMATELY... BUT YOUR RADAR MUST BE FAR MORE ADVANCED...
PTOO!! PTOO!!
I'M NOT TELLIN' NOTHIN' TO THE GUY WHO DESTROYED KINTO'UN!! NOT 'TIL YOU SAY **SORRY**!!
LITTLE BOY...
DO NOT UNDER-ESTIMATE COLONEL SILVER OF THE RED RIBBON...
108

Tale 56 • The Dragon Ball Scramble

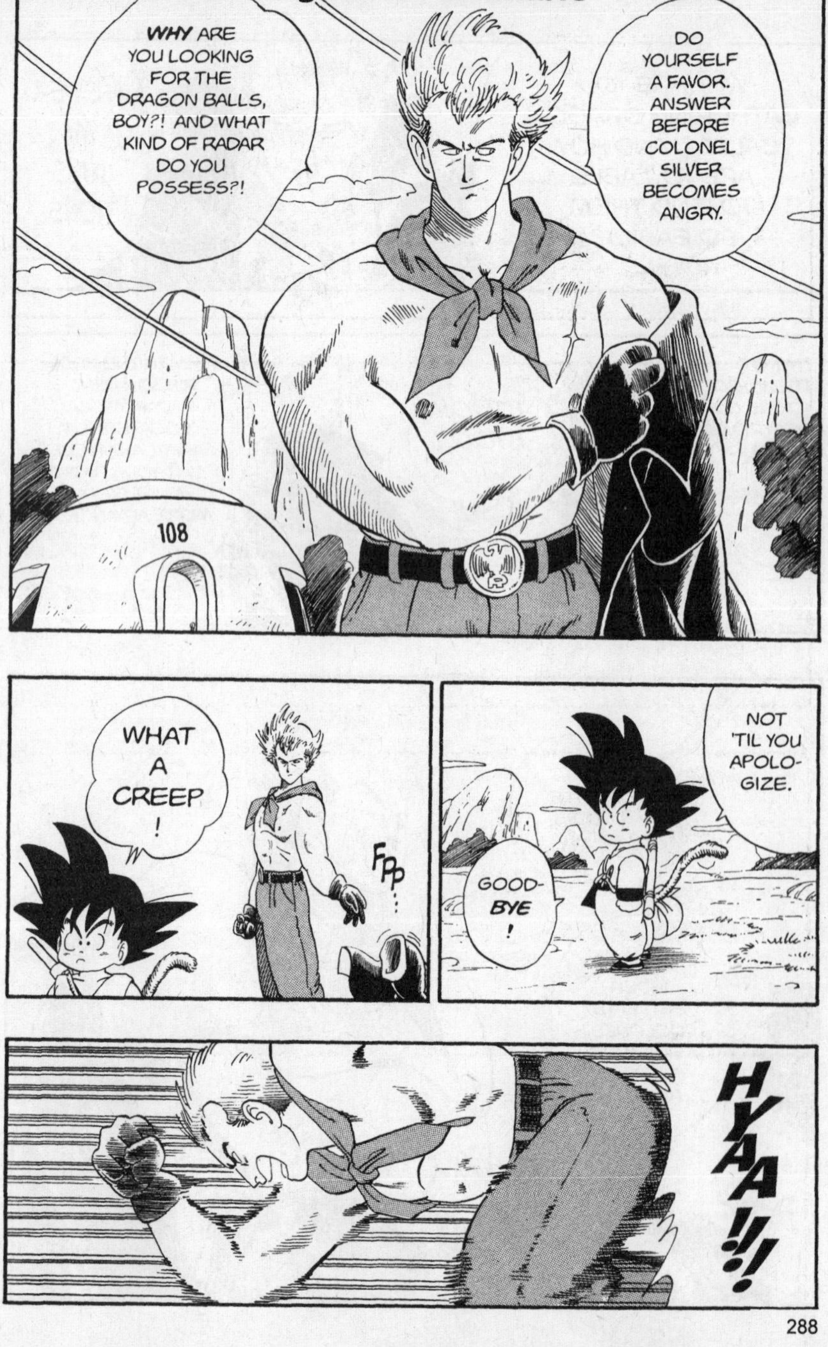

WHY ARE YOU LOOKING FOR THE DRAGON BALLS, BOY?! AND WHAT KIND OF RADAR DO YOU POSSESS?!
DO YOURSELF A FAVOR. ANSWER BEFORE COLONEL SILVER BECOMES ANGRY.
108
WHAT A CREEP!
FPP...
GOOD-BYE!
NOT 'TIL YOU APOLOGIZE.
HYAA!!!

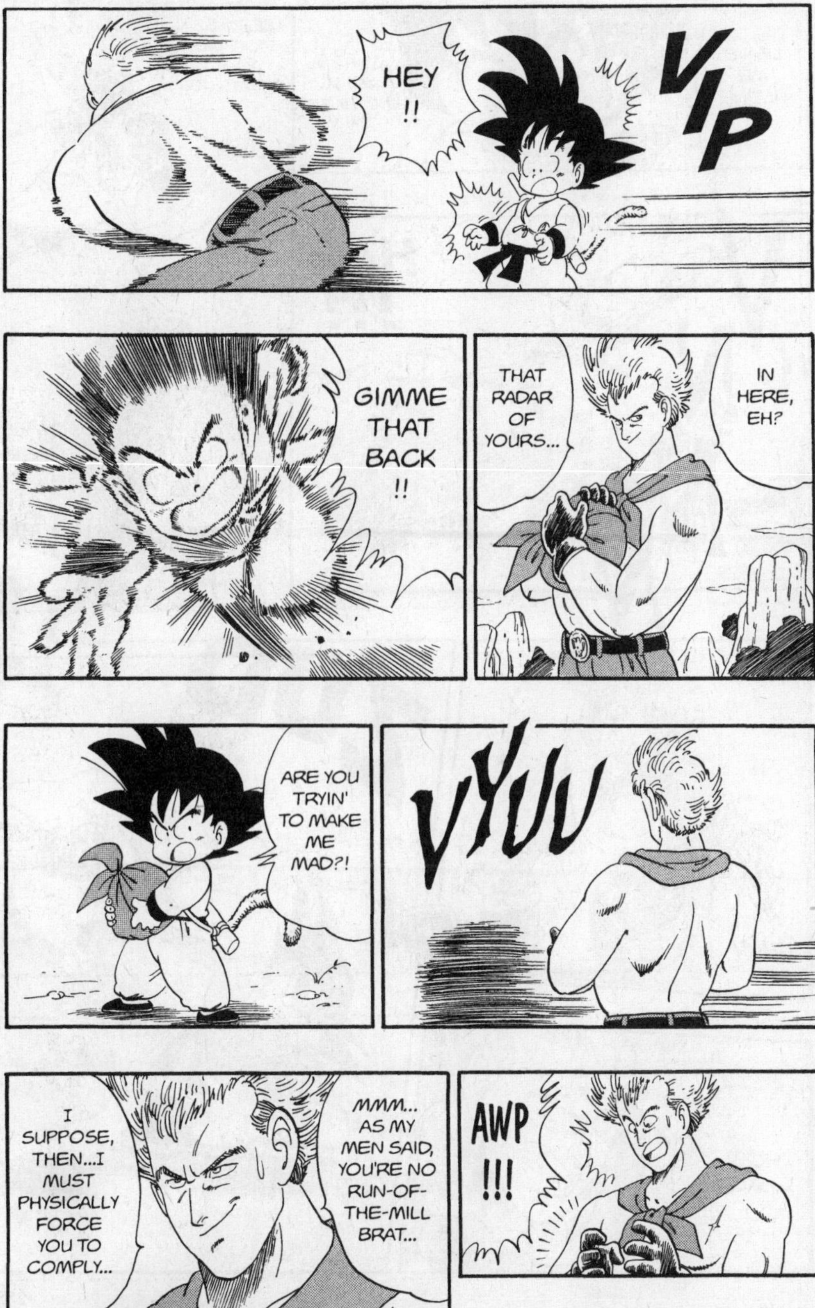
VIP
HEY !!
THAT RADAR OF YOURS...
IN HERE, EH?
GIMME THAT BACK !!
VYUU
ARE YOU TRYIN' TO MAKE ME MAD?!
AWP !!!
MMM... AS MY MEN SAID, YOU'RE NO RUN-OF-THE-MILL BRAT...
I SUPPOSE, THEN...I MUST PHYSICALLY FORCE YOU TO COMPLY...

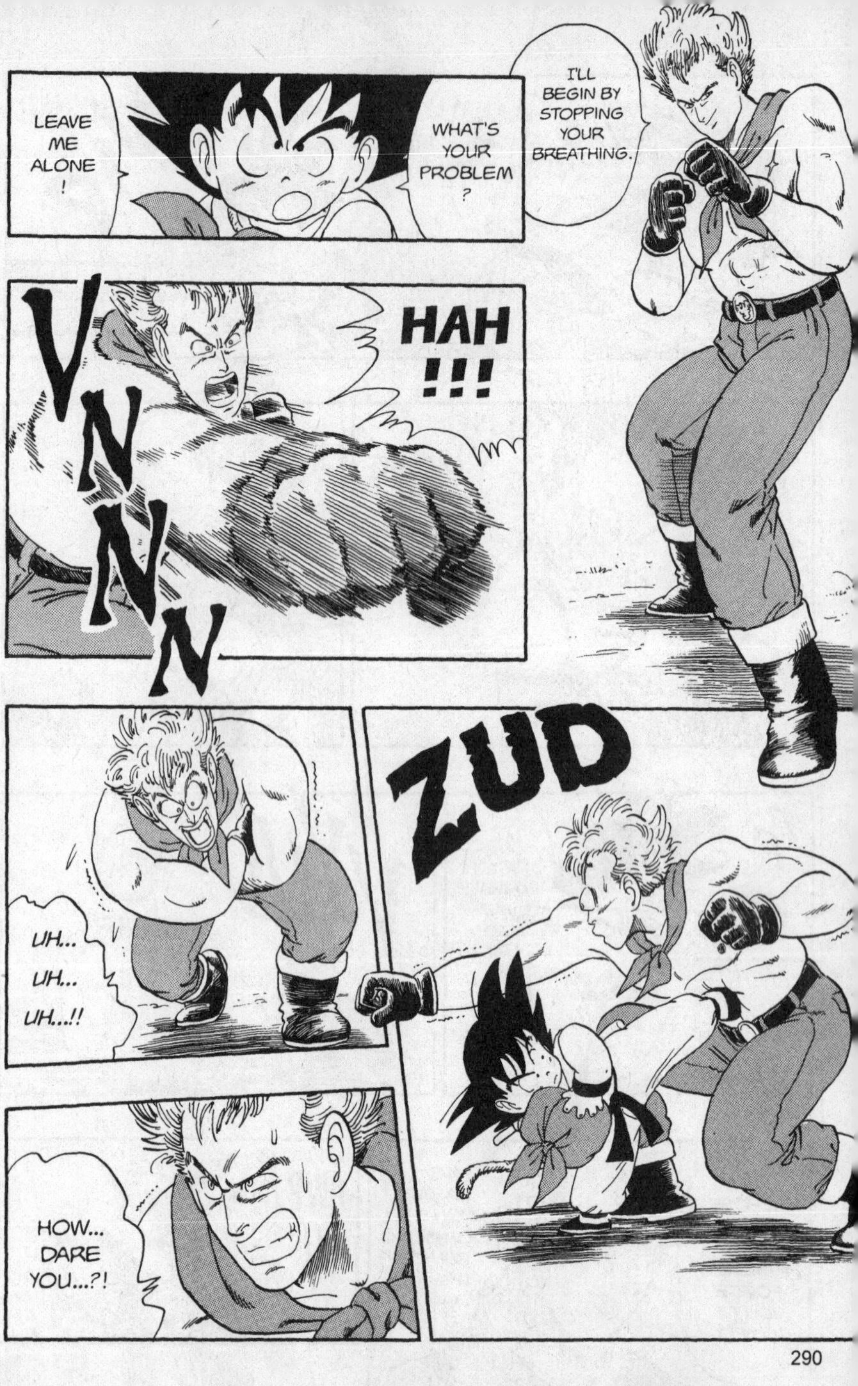
I'LL BEGIN BY STOPPING YOUR BREATHING.
WHAT'S YOUR PROBLEM ?
LEAVE ME ALONE !
HAH !!!
VNNNN
ZUD
UH... UH... UH...!!
HOW... DARE YOU...?!

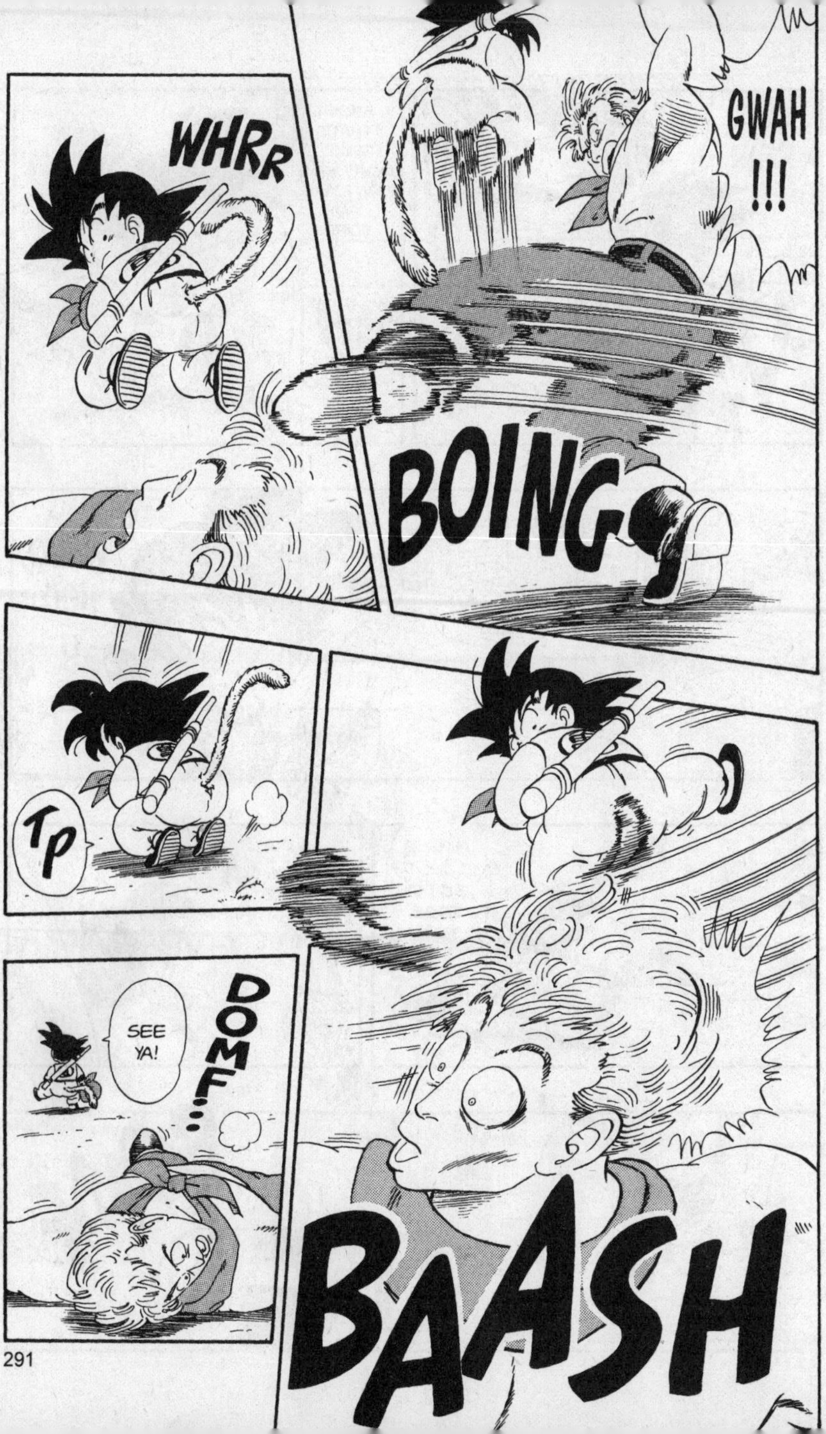
GWAH !!!
BOING
WHRR
BAASH
Tp
SEE YA!
DOMF

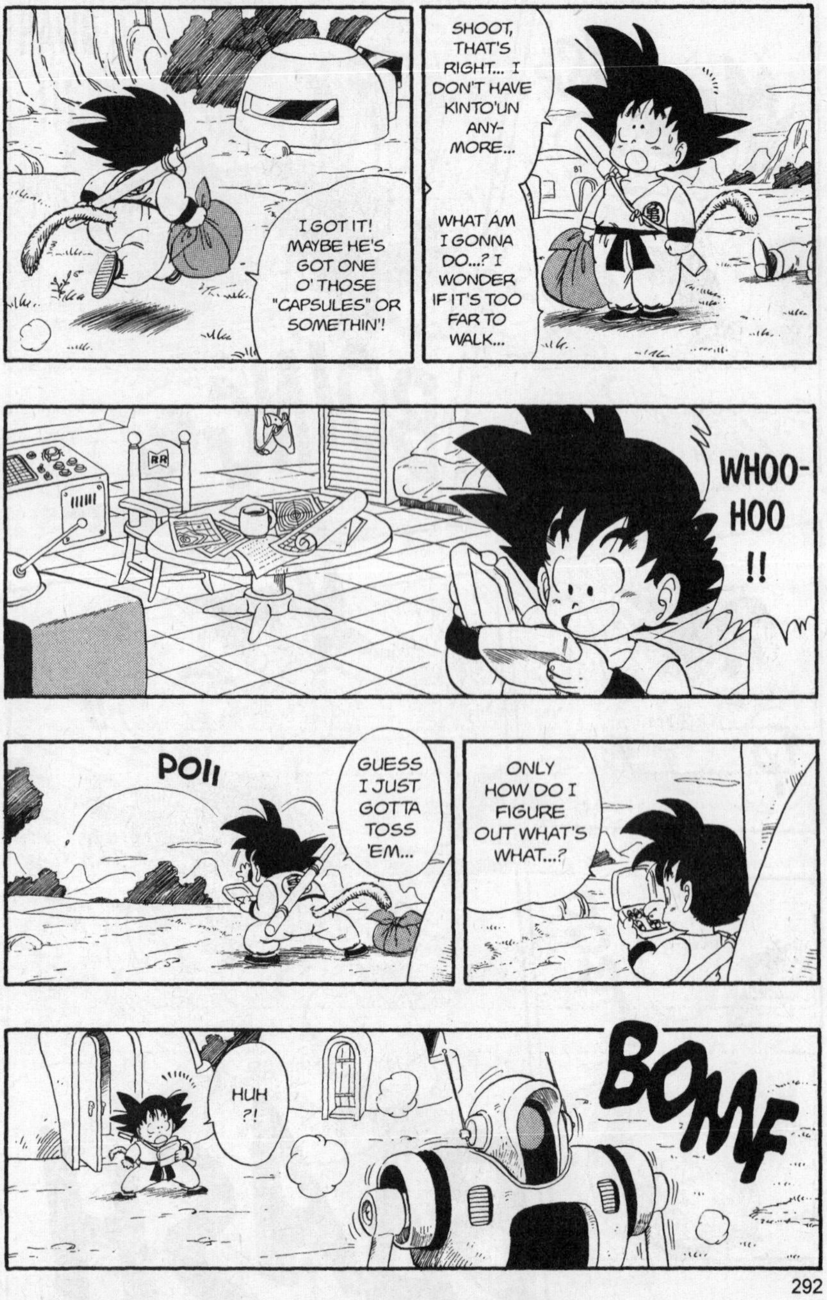
SHOOT, THAT'S RIGHT... I DON'T HAVE KINTO'UN ANYMORE...
WHAT AM I GONNA DO...? I WONDER IF IT'S TOO FAR TO WALK...
I GOT IT! MAYBE HE'S GOT ONE O' THOSE "CAPSULES" OR SOMETHIN'!
WHOO-HOO !!
ONLY HOW DO I FIGURE OUT WHAT'S WHAT...?
GUESS I JUST GOTTA TOSS 'EM...
POI
BOMF
HUH ?!

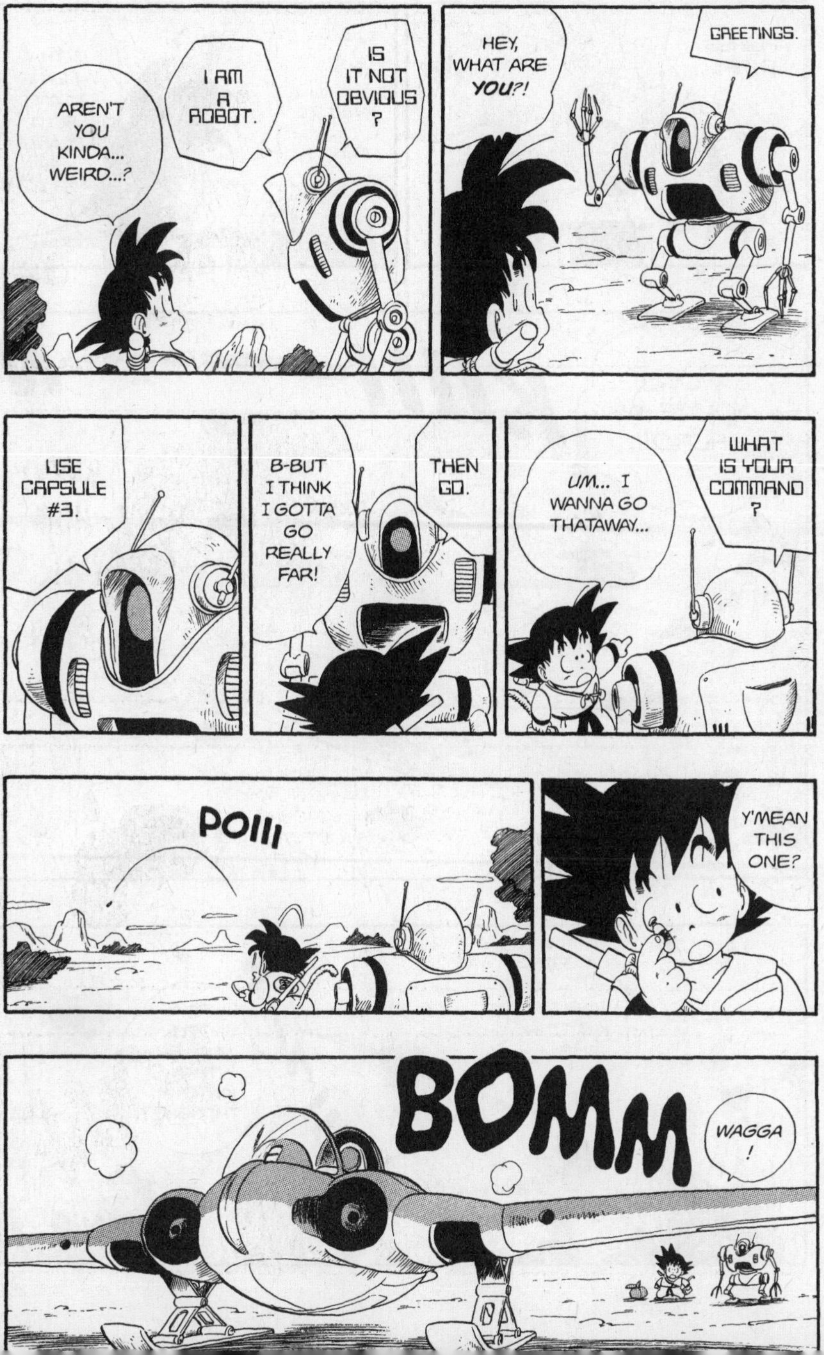
GREETINGS.
HEY, WHAT ARE *YOU*?!
IS IT NOT OBVIOUS?
I AM A ROBOT.
AREN'T YOU KINDA... WEIRD...?
WHAT IS YOUR COMMAND?
UM... I WANNA GO THATAWAY...
THEN GO.
B-BUT I THINK I GOTTA GO REALLY FAR!
USE CAPSULE #3.
Y'MEAN THIS ONE?
POIII
BOMM
WAGGA!

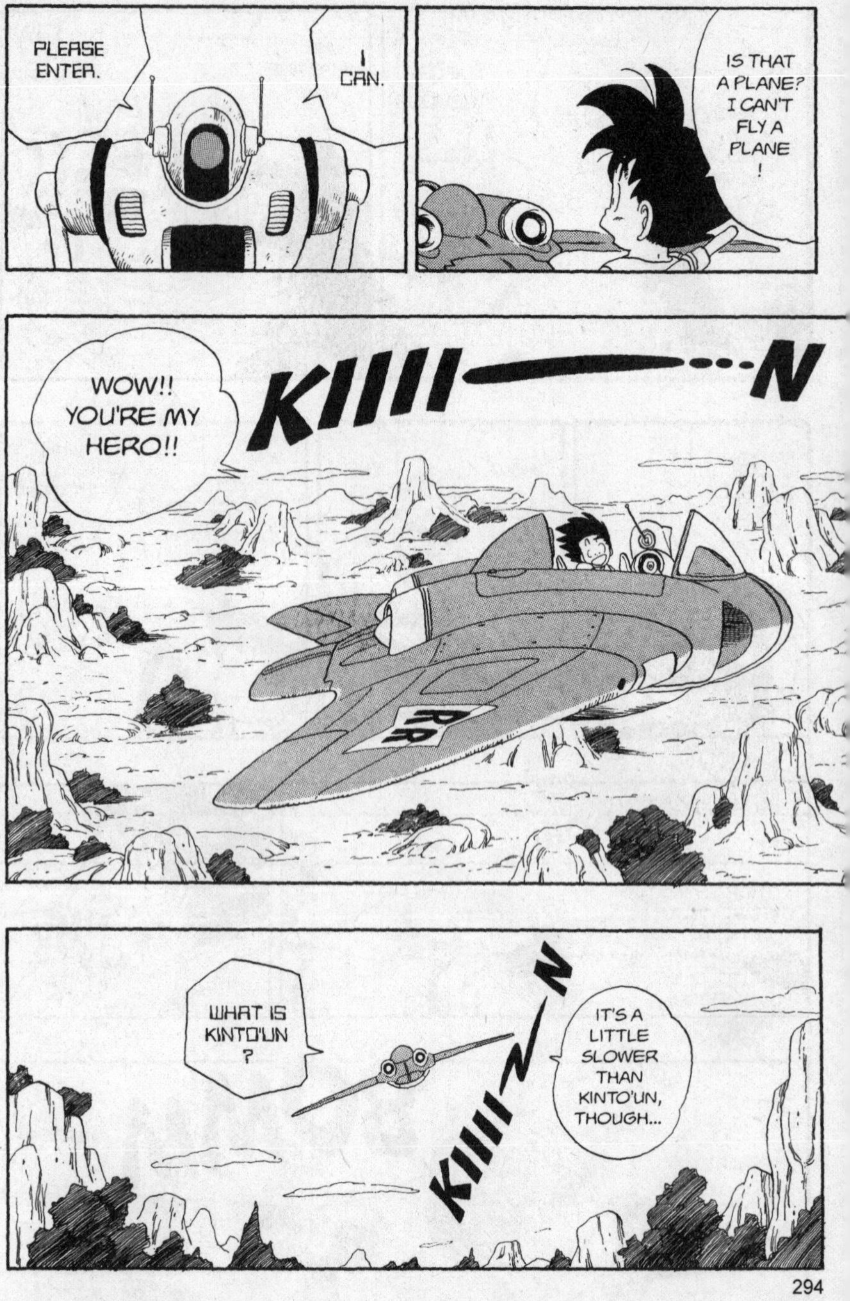
IS THAT A PLANE? I CAN'T FLY A PLANE!
I CAN.
PLEASE ENTER.
KIIII—...N
WOW!! YOU'RE MY HERO!!
IT'S A LITTLE SLOWER THAN KINTO'UN, THOUGH...
KIIII—N
WHAT IS KINTO'UN?

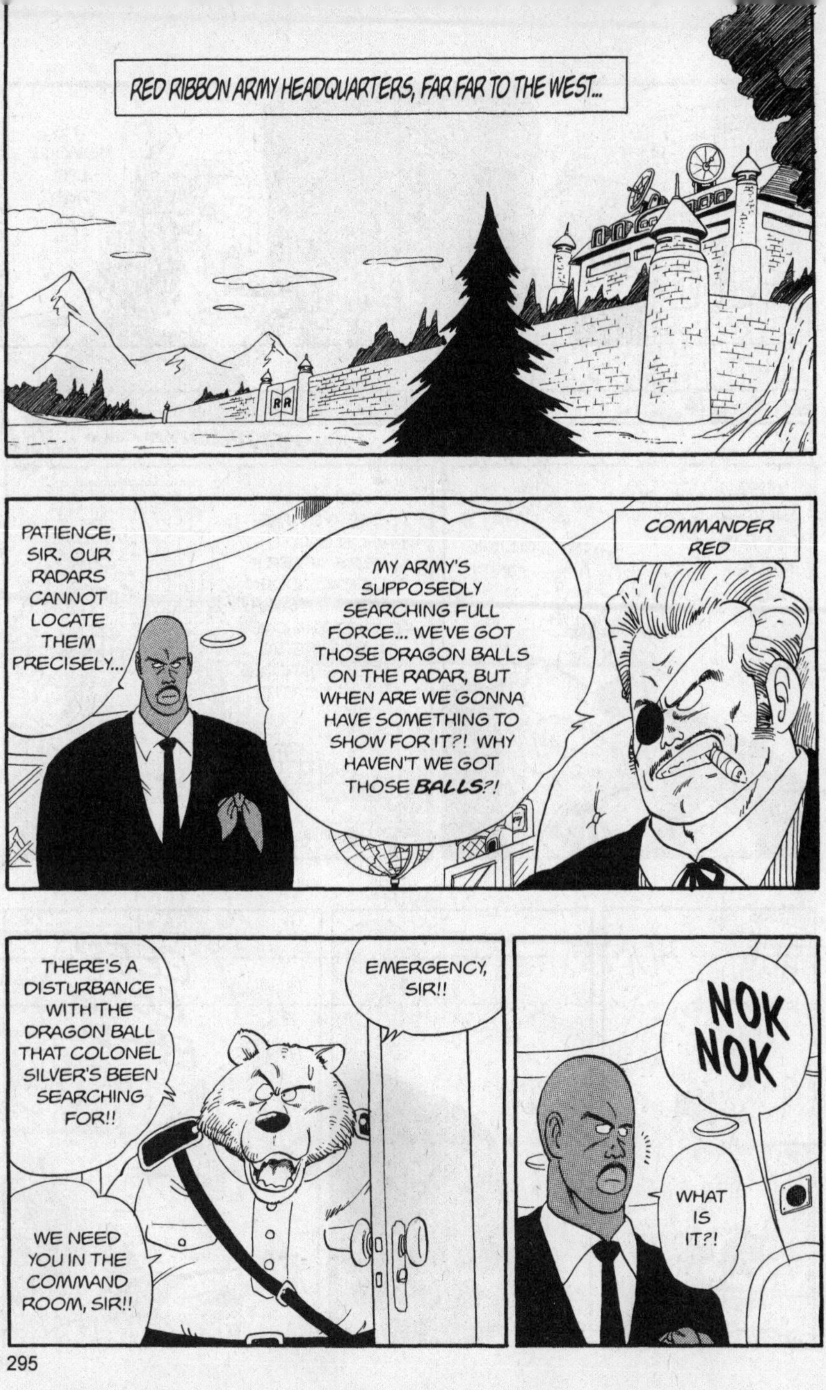
RED RIBBON ARMY HEADQUARTERS, FAR FAR TO THE WEST...
COMMANDER RED
MY ARMY'S SUPPOSEDLY SEARCHING FULL FORCE... WE'VE GOT THOSE DRAGON BALLS ON THE RADAR, BUT WHEN ARE WE GONNA HAVE SOMETHING TO SHOW FOR IT?! WHY HAVEN'T WE GOT THOSE ***BALLS***?!
PATIENCE, SIR. OUR RADARS CANNOT LOCATE THEM PRECISELY...
NOK NOK
WHAT IS IT?!
EMERGENCY, SIR!!
THERE'S A DISTURBANCE WITH THE DRAGON BALL THAT COLONEL SILVER'S BEEN SEARCHING FOR!!
WE NEED YOU IN THE COMMAND ROOM, SIR!!

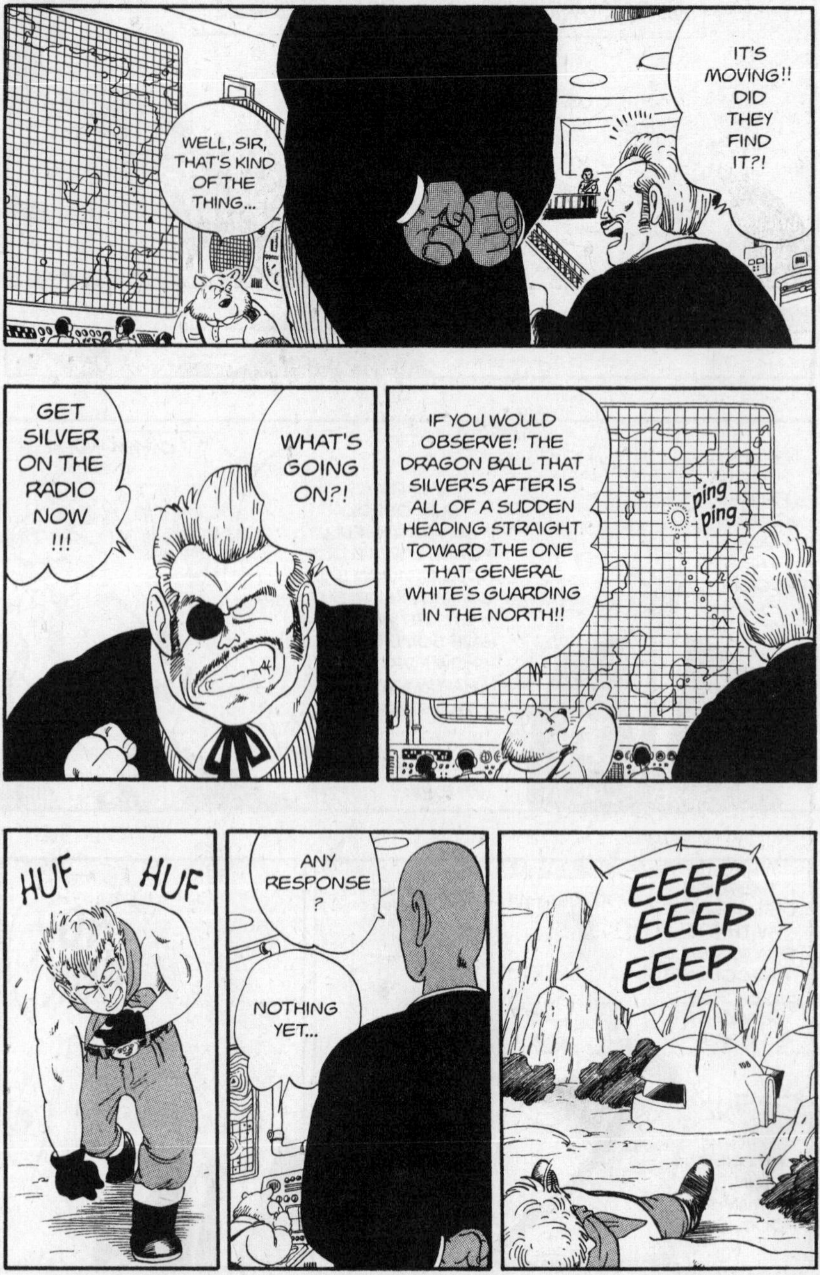
IT'S MOVING!! DID THEY FIND IT?!
WELL, SIR, THAT'S KIND OF THE THING...
IF YOU WOULD OBSERVE! THE DRAGON BALL THAT SILVER'S AFTER IS ALL OF A SUDDEN HEADING STRAIGHT TOWARD THE ONE THAT GENERAL WHITE'S GUARDING IN THE NORTH!!
ping ping
WHAT'S GOING ON?!
GET SILVER ON THE RADIO NOW !!!
EEEP EEEP EEEP
ANY RESPONSE ?
NOTHING YET...
HUF HUF

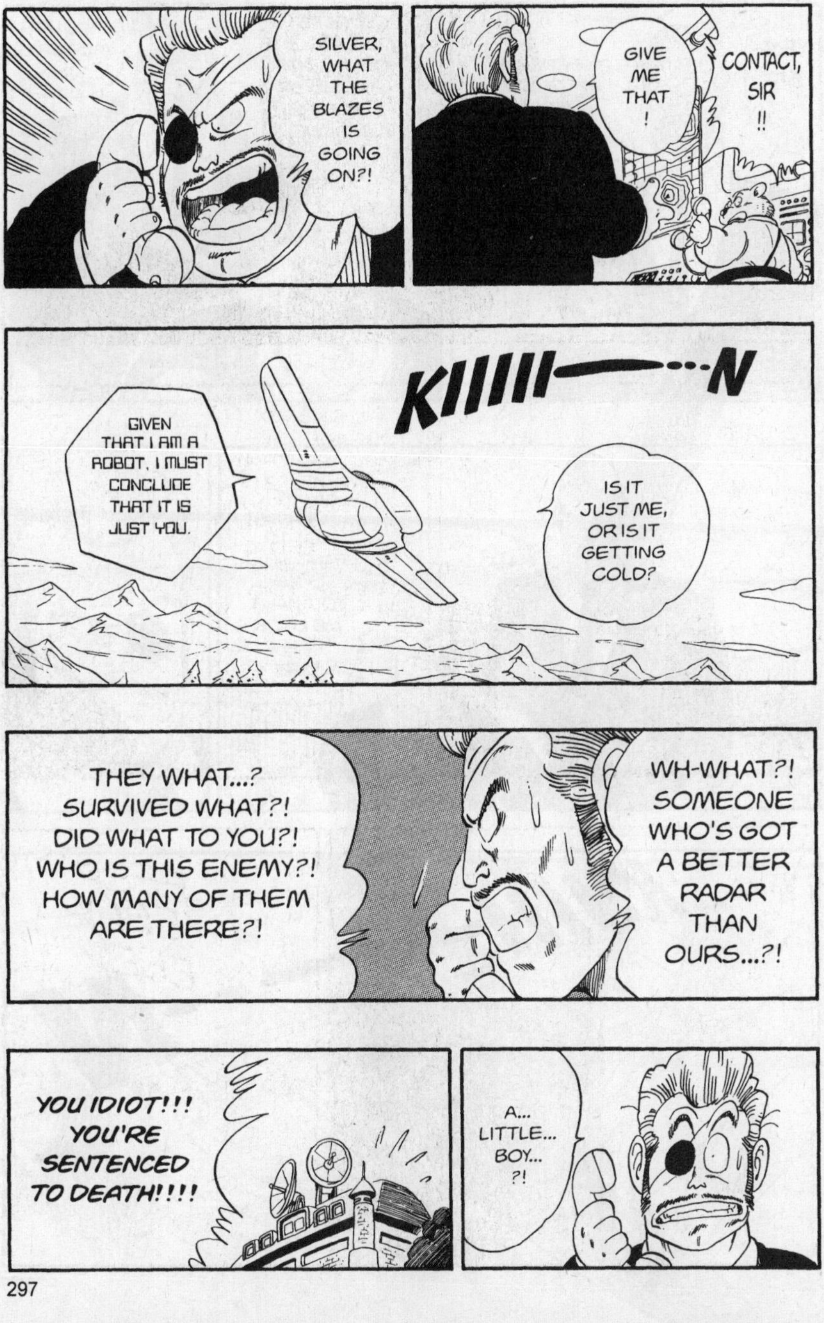
CONTACT, SIR !!
GIVE ME THAT !
SILVER, WHAT THE BLAZES IS GOING ON?!
KIIIII———N
IS IT JUST ME, OR IS IT GETTING COLD?
GIVEN THAT I AM A ROBOT, I MUST CONCLUDE THAT IT IS JUST YOU.
WH-WHAT?! SOMEONE WHO'S GOT A BETTER RADAR THAN OURS...?!
THEY WHAT...? SURVIVED WHAT?! DID WHAT TO YOU?! WHO IS THIS ENEMY?! HOW MANY OF THEM ARE THERE?!
A... LITTLE... BOY... ?!
YOU IDIOT!!! YOU'RE SENTENCED TO DEATH!!!!

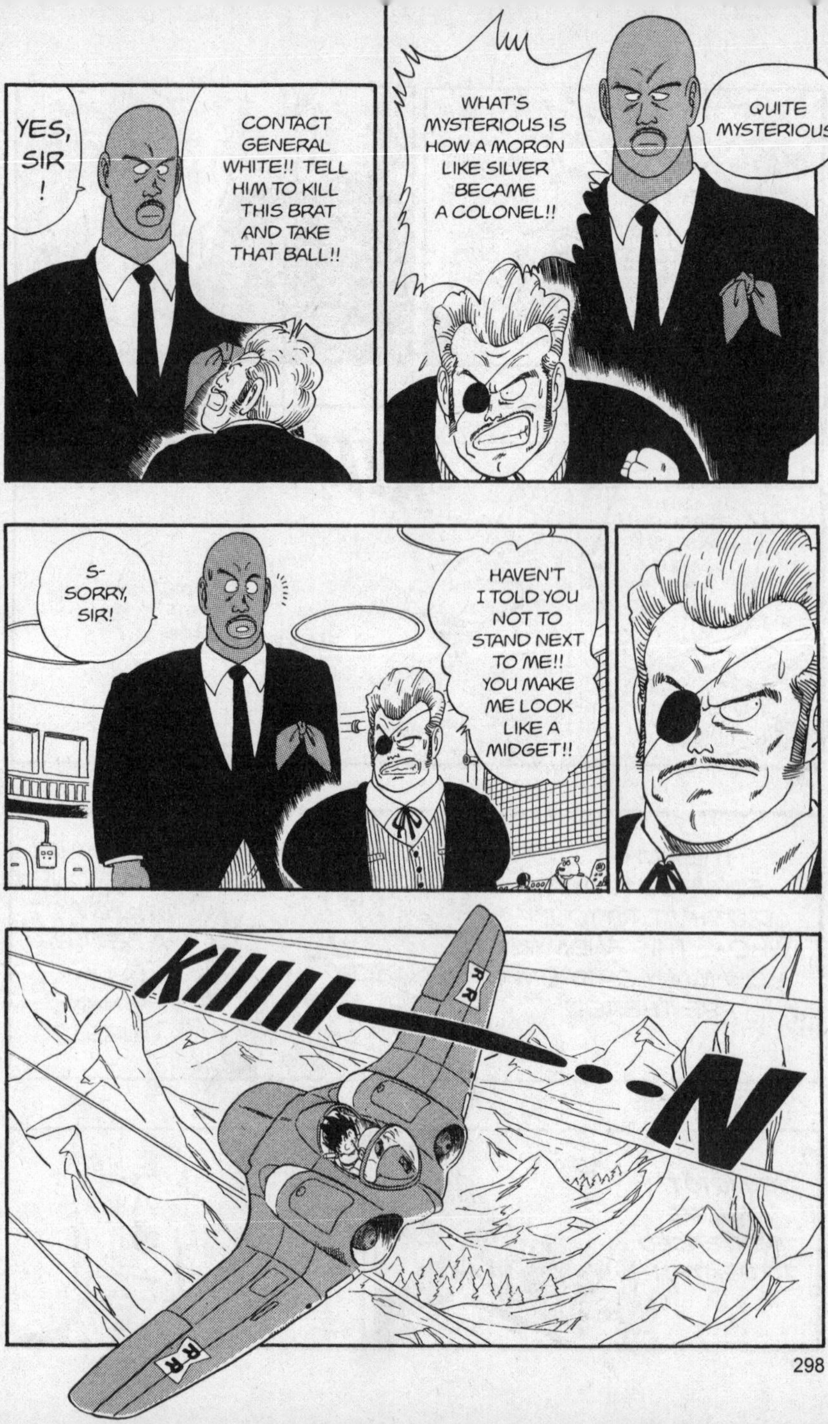
QUITE MYSTERIOUS.
WHAT'S MYSTERIOUS IS HOW A MORON LIKE SILVER BECAME A COLONEL!!
CONTACT GENERAL WHITE!! TELL HIM TO KILL THIS BRAT AND TAKE THAT BALL!!
YES, SIR !
HAVEN'T I TOLD YOU NOT TO STAND NEXT TO ME!! YOU MAKE ME LOOK LIKE A MIDGET!!
S- SORRY, SIR!
KIIIII——N

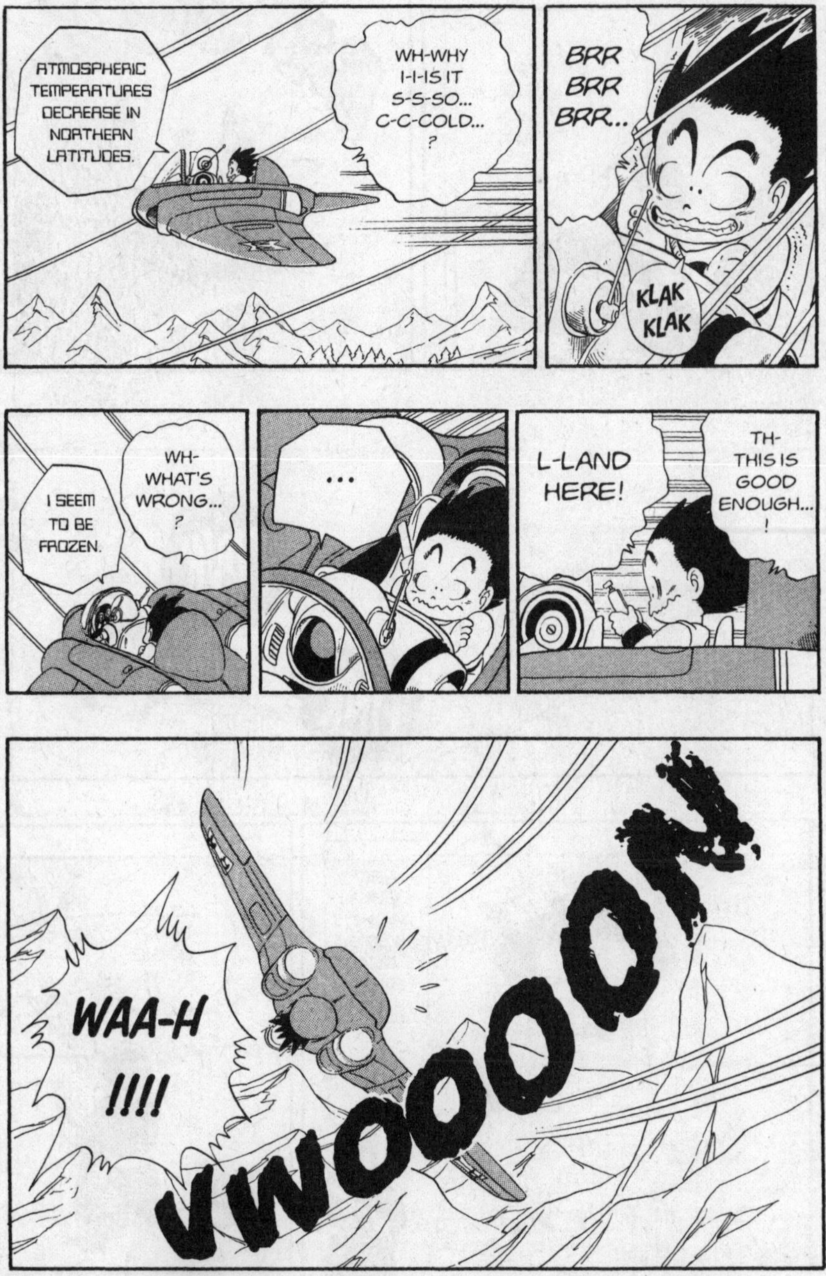
BRR
BRR
BRR...
KLAK KLAK
WH-WHY I-I-IS IT S-S-SO... C-C-COLD...?
ATMOSPHERIC TEMPERATURES DECREASE IN NORTHERN LATITUDES.
TH- THIS IS GOOD ENOUGH...!
L-LAND HERE!
...
WH- WHAT'S WRONG...?
I SEEM TO BE FROZEN.
WAA-H !!!!
VWOOOOOM

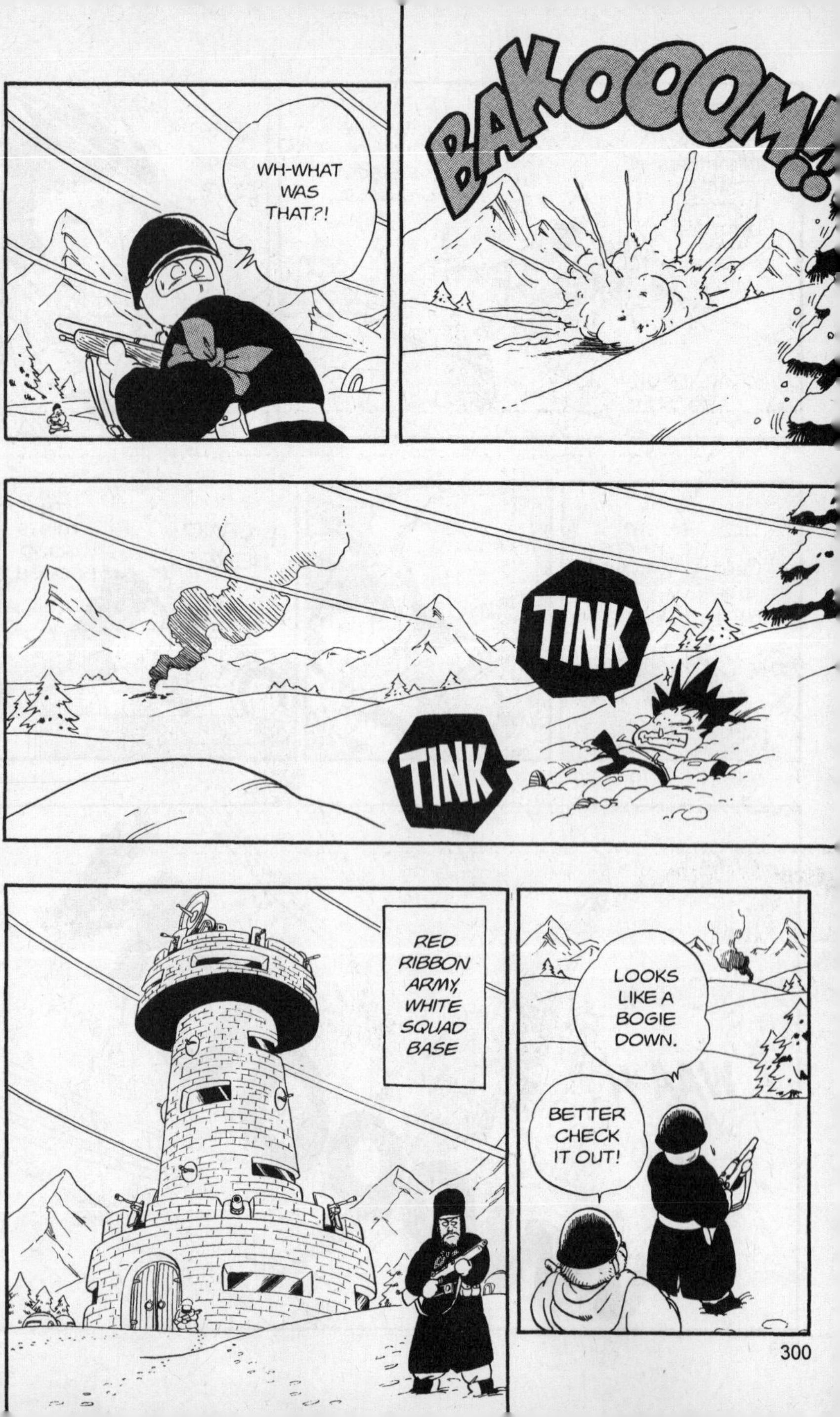
BAKOOOM!!
WH-WHAT WAS THAT?!
TINK
TINK
LOOKS LIKE A BOGIE DOWN.
BETTER CHECK IT OUT!
RED RIBBON ARMY, WHITE SQUAD BASE

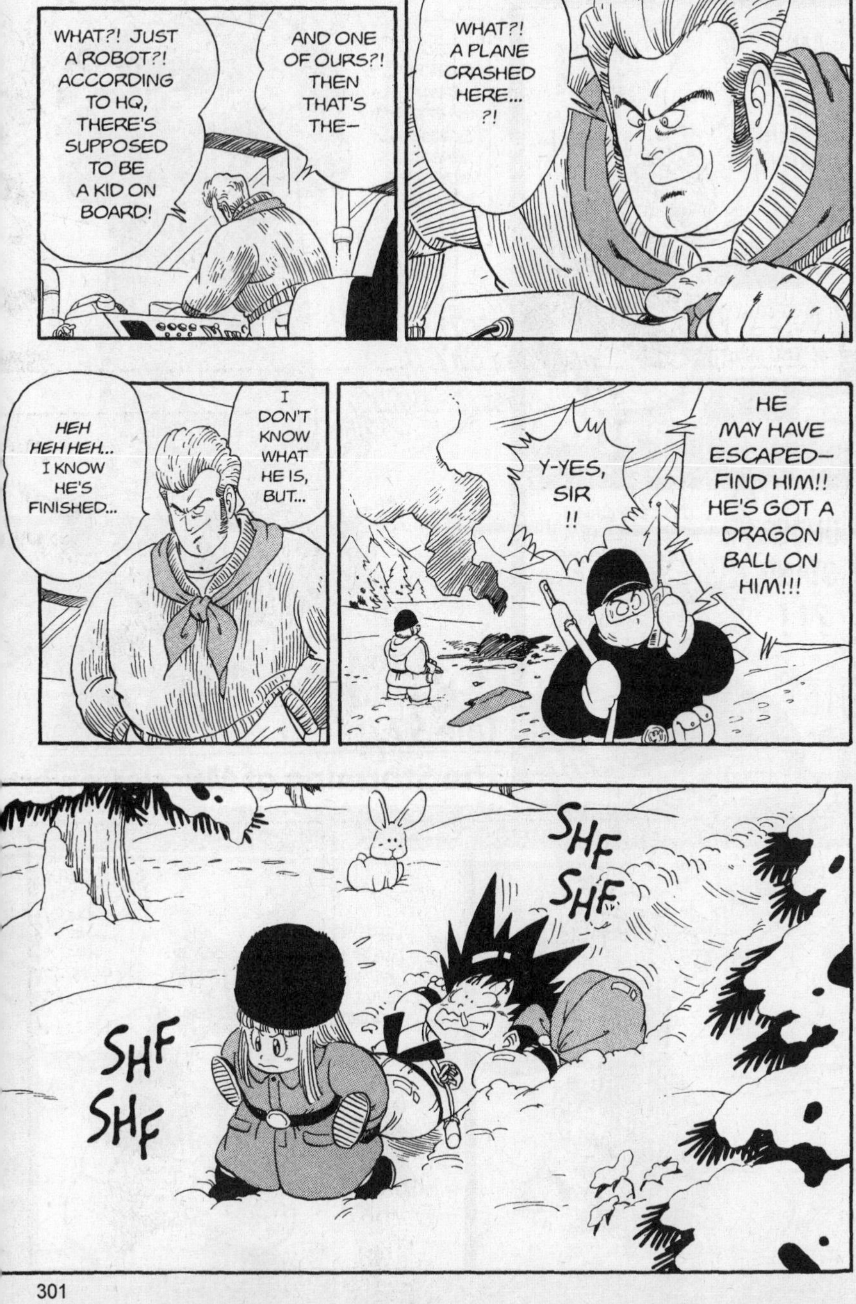

WHAT?! A PLANE CRASHED HERE... ?!
AND ONE OF OURS?! THEN THAT'S THE—
WHAT?! JUST A ROBOT?! ACCORDING TO HQ, THERE'S SUPPOSED TO BE A KID ON BOARD!
HE MAY HAVE ESCAPED— FIND HIM!! HE'S GOT A DRAGON BALL ON HIM!!!
Y-YES, SIR !!
I DON'T KNOW WHAT HE IS, BUT...
HEH HEH HEH... I KNOW HE'S FINISHED...
SHF SHF
SHF SHF

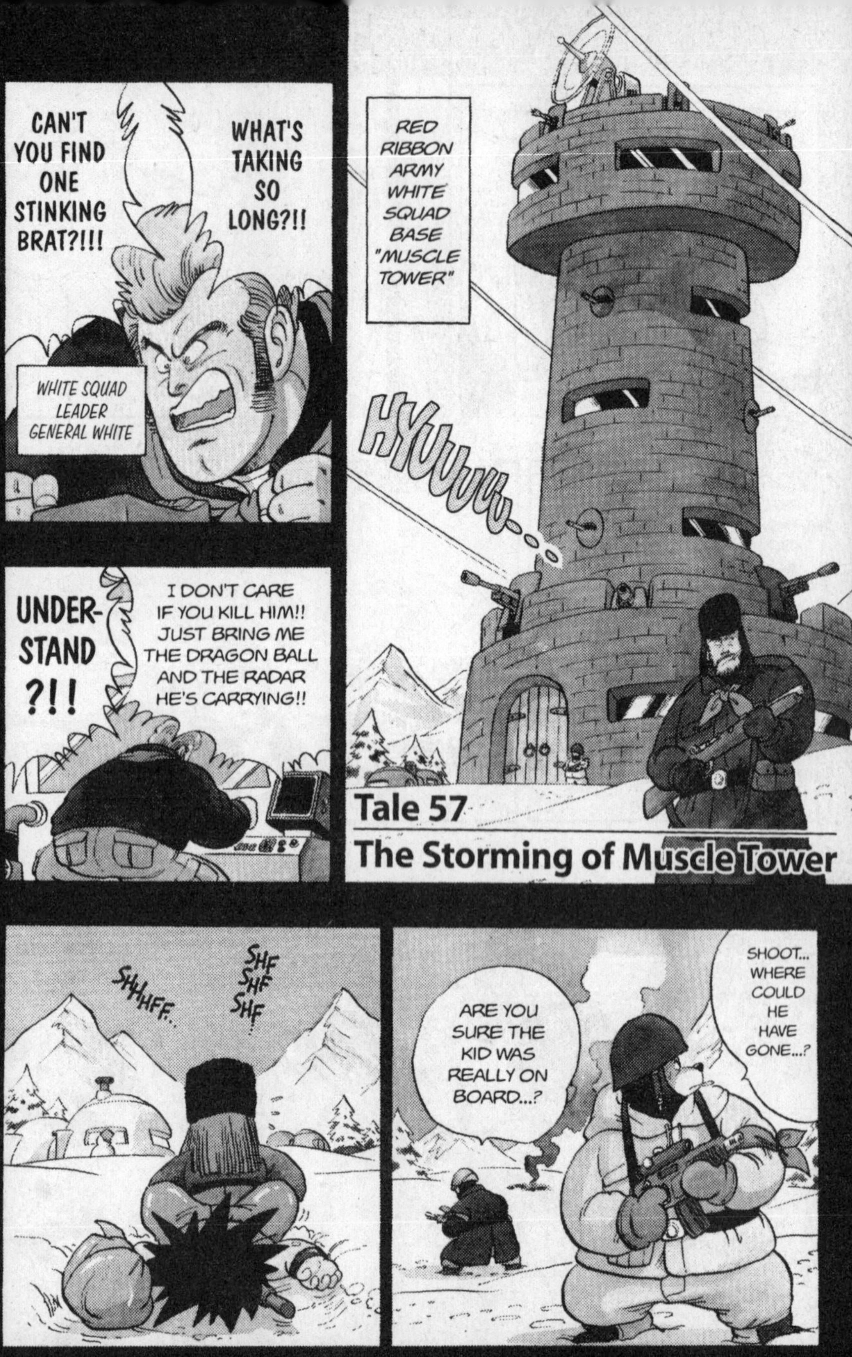
RED RIBBON ARMY WHITE SQUAD BASE "MUSCLE TOWER"
HYUUUUU...
Tale 57
The Storming of Muscle Tower
WHAT'S TAKING SO LONG?!!
CAN'T YOU FIND ONE STINKING BRAT?!!!
WHITE SQUAD LEADER GENERAL WHITE
I DON'T CARE IF YOU KILL HIM!! JUST BRING ME THE DRAGON BALL AND THE RADAR HE'S CARRYING!!
UNDER-STAND ?!!
SHOOT... WHERE COULD HE HAVE GONE...?
ARE YOU SURE THE KID WAS REALLY ON BOARD...?
SHF SHF SHF
SHHHFF...

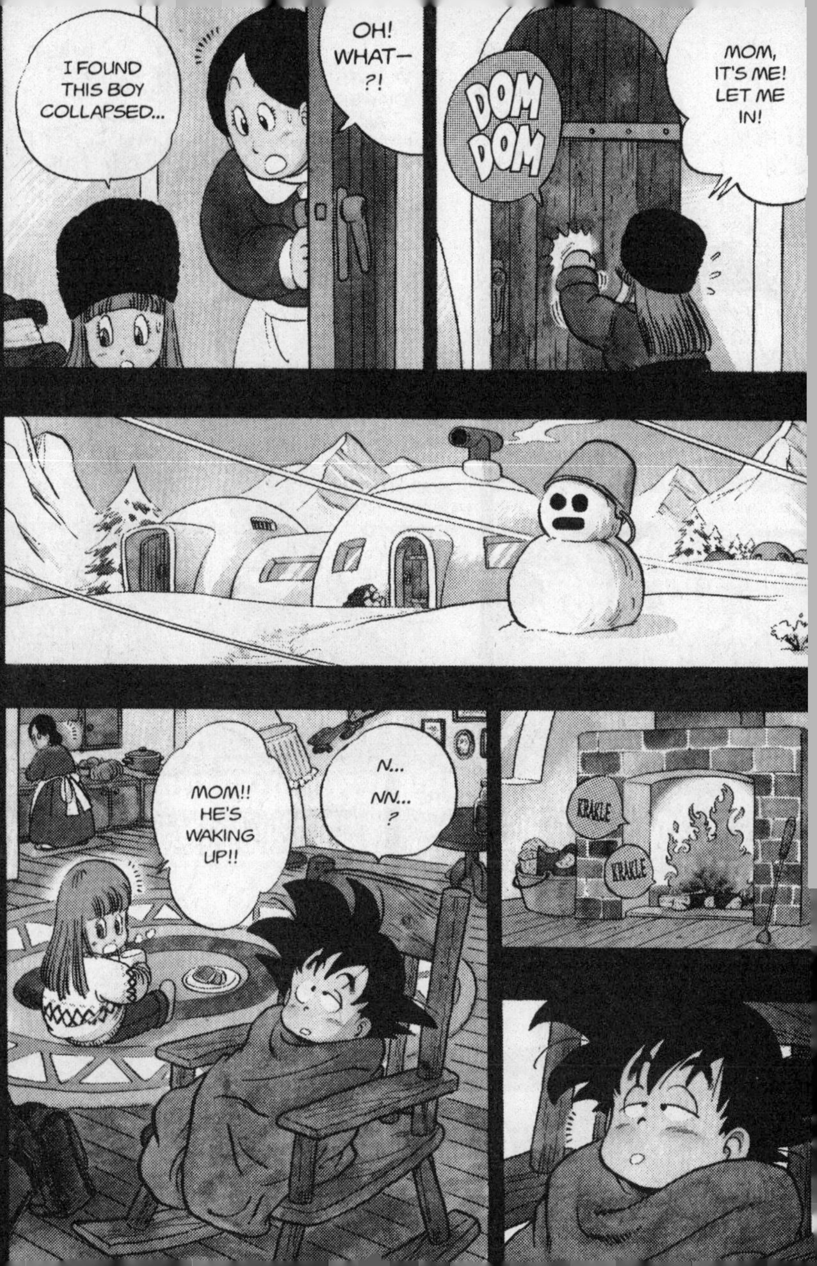
MOM, IT'S ME! LET ME IN!
DOM DOM
OH! WHAT— ?!
I FOUND THIS BOY COLLAPSED...
KRAKLE
KRAKLE
N... NN... ?
MOM!! HE'S WAKING UP!!

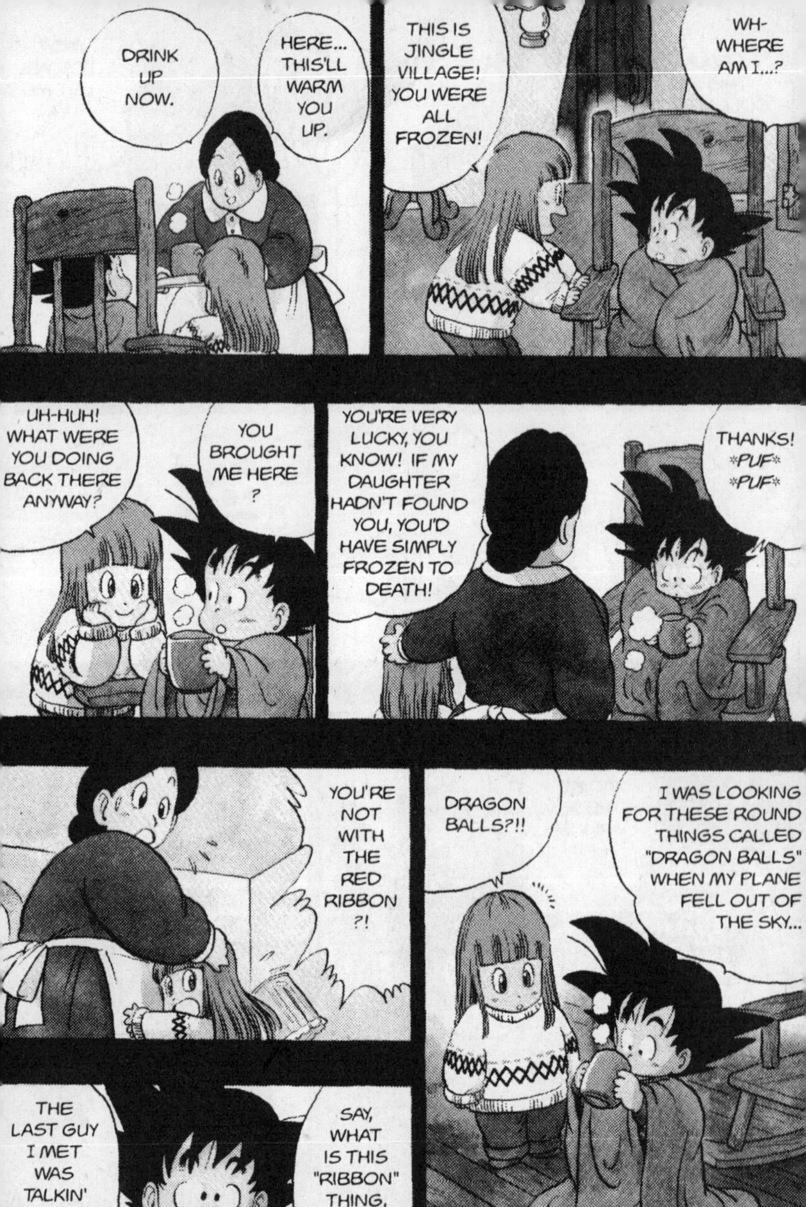
WH- WHERE AM I...?
THIS IS JINGLE VILLAGE! YOU WERE ALL FROZEN!
HERE... THIS'LL WARM YOU UP.
DRINK UP NOW.
THANKS! *PUF* *PUF*
YOU'RE VERY LUCKY, YOU KNOW! IF MY DAUGHTER HADN'T FOUND YOU, YOU'D HAVE SIMPLY FROZEN TO DEATH!
YOU BROUGHT ME HERE?
UH-HUH! WHAT WERE YOU DOING BACK THERE ANYWAY?
I WAS LOOKING FOR THESE ROUND THINGS CALLED "DRAGON BALLS" WHEN MY PLANE FELL OUT OF THE SKY...
DRAGON BALLS?!!
YOU'RE NOT WITH THE RED RIBBON?!
SAY, WHAT IS THIS "RIBBON" THING, ANYWAY?
THE LAST GUY I MET WAS TALKIN' ABOUT IT TOO...

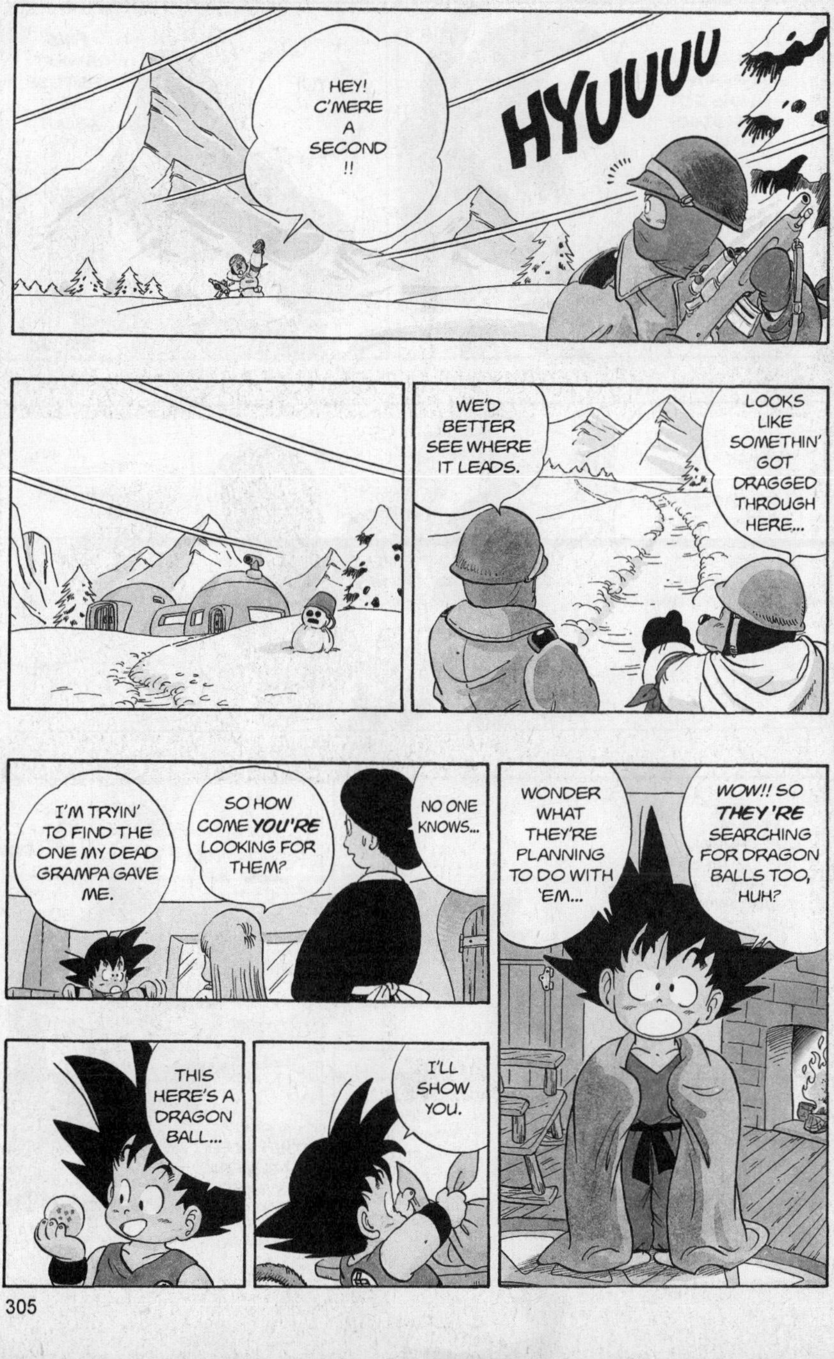
HYUUUU
HEY! C'MERE A SECOND !!
LOOKS LIKE SOMETHIN' GOT DRAGGED THROUGH HERE...
WE'D BETTER SEE WHERE IT LEADS.
WOW!! SO *THEY'RE* SEARCHING FOR DRAGON BALLS TOO, HUH?
WONDER WHAT THEY'RE PLANNING TO DO WITH 'EM...
NO ONE KNOWS...
SO HOW COME *YOU'RE* LOOKING FOR THEM?
I'M TRYIN' TO FIND THE ONE MY DEAD GRAMPA GAVE ME.
I'LL SHOW YOU.
THIS HERE'S A DRAGON BALL...

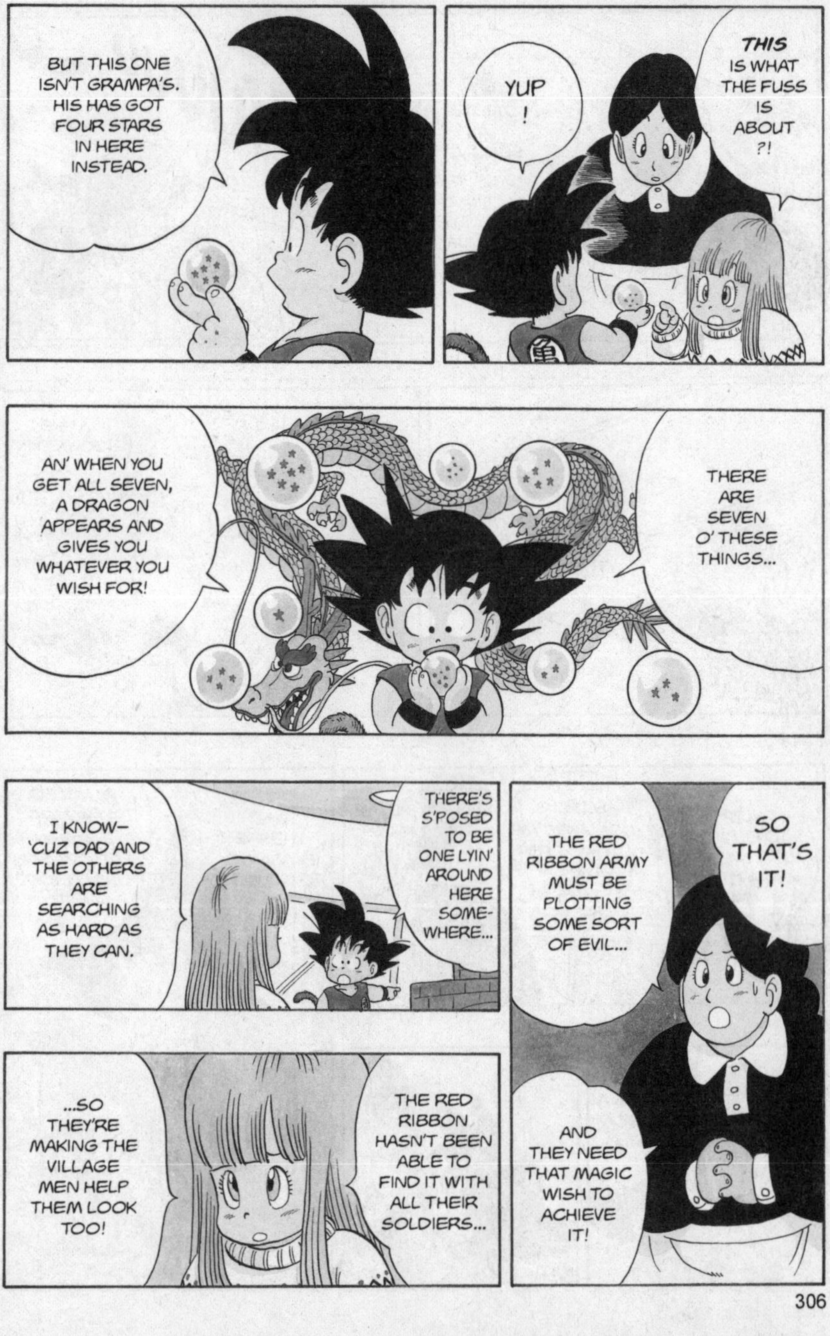
THIS IS WHAT THE FUSS IS ABOUT?!
YUP!
BUT THIS ONE ISN'T GRAMPA'S. HIS HAS GOT FOUR STARS IN HERE INSTEAD.
THERE ARE SEVEN O' THESE THINGS...
AN' WHEN YOU GET ALL SEVEN, A DRAGON APPEARS AND GIVES YOU WHATEVER YOU WISH FOR!
SO THAT'S IT!
THE RED RIBBON ARMY MUST BE PLOTTING SOME SORT OF EVIL...
AND THEY NEED THAT MAGIC WISH TO ACHIEVE IT!
THERE'S S'POSED TO BE ONE LYIN' AROUND HERE SOME-WHERE...
I KNOW— 'CUZ DAD AND THE OTHERS ARE SEARCHING AS HARD AS THEY CAN.
THE RED RIBBON HASN'T BEEN ABLE TO FIND IT WITH ALL THEIR SOLDIERS...
...SO THEY'RE MAKING THE VILLAGE MEN HELP THEM LOOK TOO!

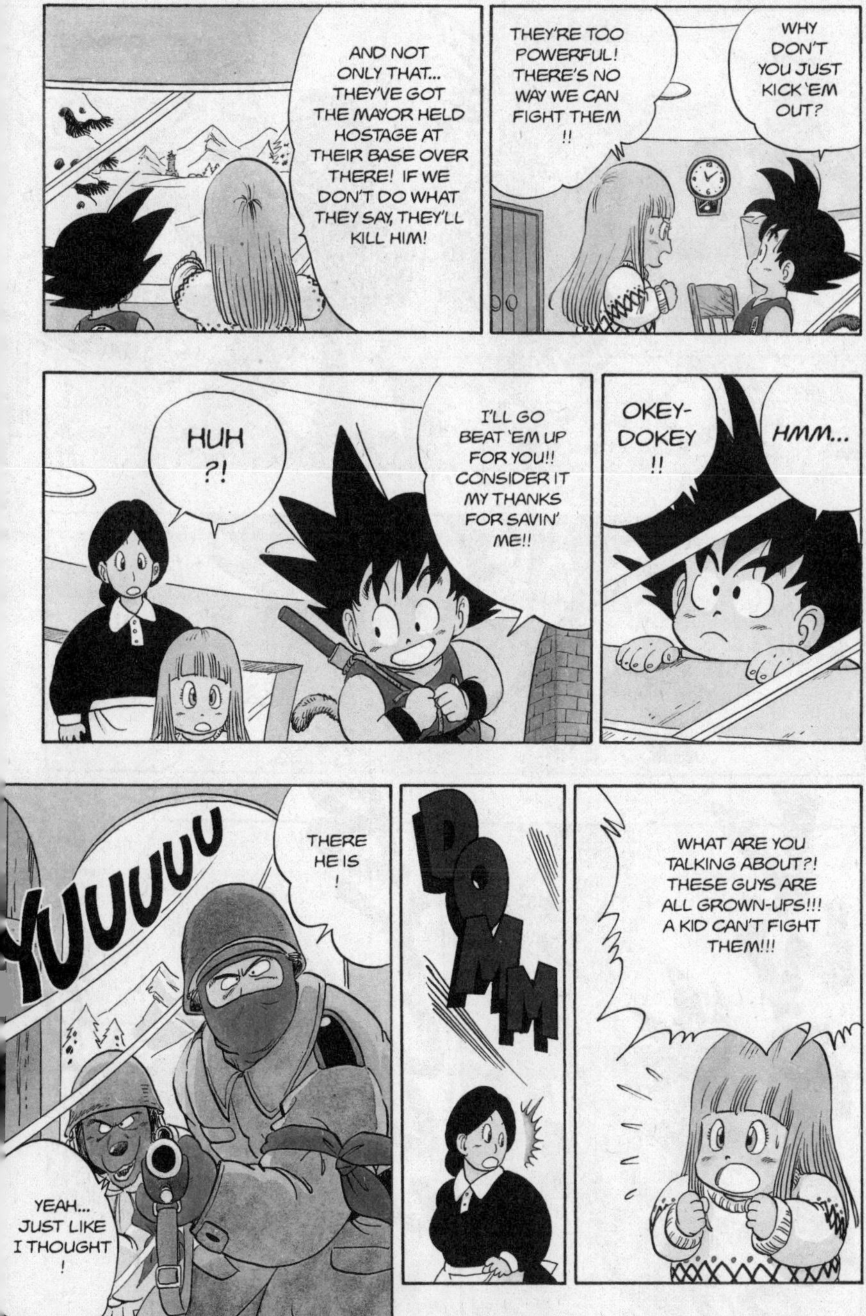
WHY DON'T YOU JUST KICK 'EM OUT?
THEY'RE TOO POWERFUL! THERE'S NO WAY WE CAN FIGHT THEM!!
AND NOT ONLY THAT... THEY'VE GOT THE MAYOR HELD HOSTAGE AT THEIR BASE OVER THERE! IF WE DON'T DO WHAT THEY SAY, THEY'LL KILL HIM!
HMM...
OKEY-DOKEY!!
I'LL GO BEAT 'EM UP FOR YOU!! CONSIDER IT MY THANKS FOR SAVIN' ME!!
HUH?!
WHAT ARE YOU TALKING ABOUT?! THESE GUYS ARE ALL GROWN-UPS!!! A KID CAN'T FIGHT THEM!!!
DOMM
THERE HE IS!
YUUUUU
YEAH... JUST LIKE I THOUGHT!

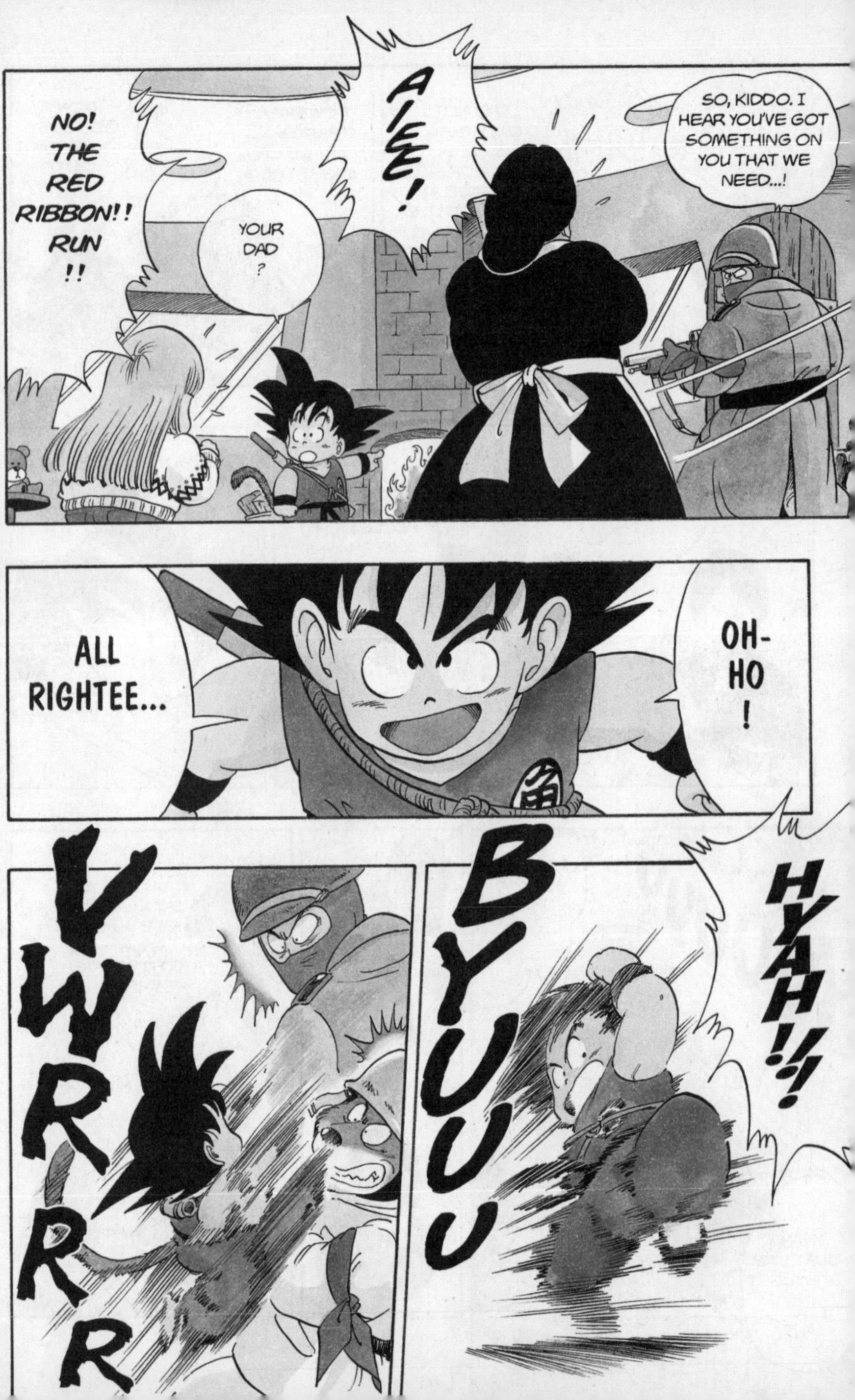
SO, KIDDO. I HEAR YOU'VE GOT SOMETHING ON YOU THAT WE NEED...!
AIEE!
YOUR DAD ?
NO! THE RED RIBBON!! RUN !!
OH-HO !
ALL RIGHTEE...
HYAH!!!
BYUUU
VWRRRR

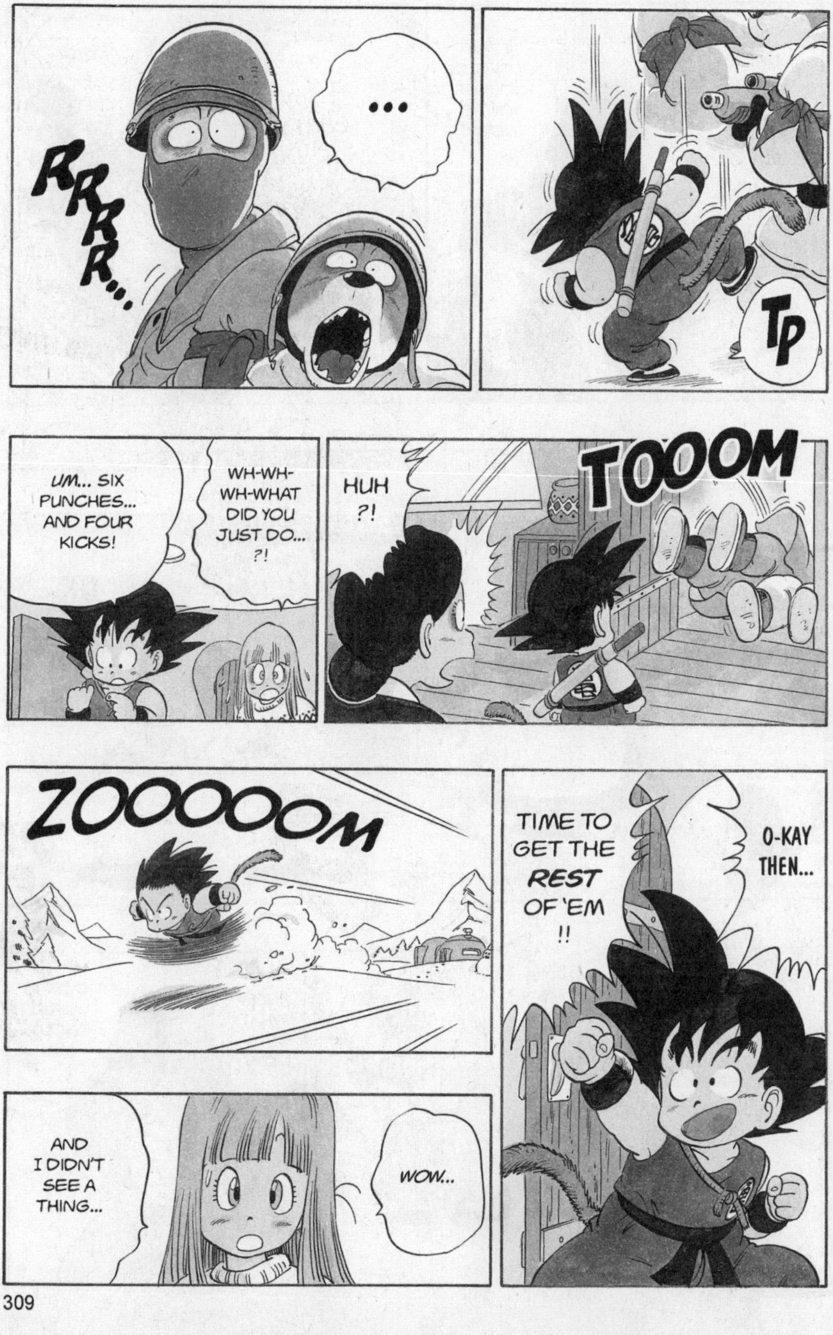
TP
RRRR...
...
TOOOM
HUH ?!
WH-WH-WH-WHAT DID YOU JUST DO... ?!
UM... SIX PUNCHES... AND FOUR KICKS!
O-KAY THEN...
TIME TO GET THE REST OF 'EM !!
ZOOOOOM
WOW...
AND I DIDN'T SEE A THING...

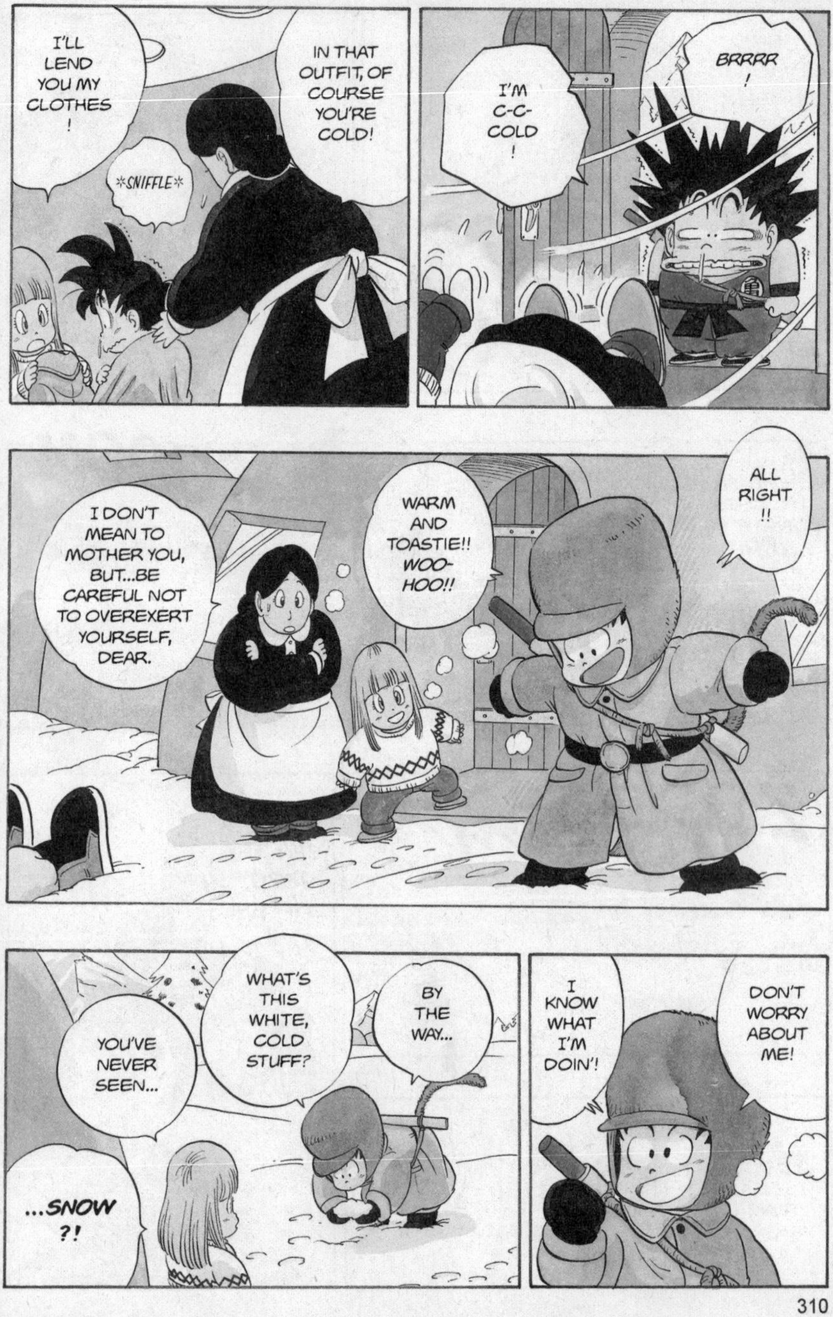
BRRRR!
I'M C-C-COLD!
IN THAT OUTFIT, OF COURSE YOU'RE COLD!
I'LL LEND YOU MY CLOTHES!
✲SNIFFLE✲
ALL RIGHT!!
WARM AND TOASTIE!! WOO-HOO!!
I DON'T MEAN TO MOTHER YOU, BUT...BE CAREFUL NOT TO OVEREXERT YOURSELF, DEAR.
DON'T WORRY ABOUT ME!
I KNOW WHAT I'M DOIN'!
BY THE WAY...
WHAT'S THIS WHITE, COLD STUFF?
YOU'VE NEVER SEEN...
...SNOW?!

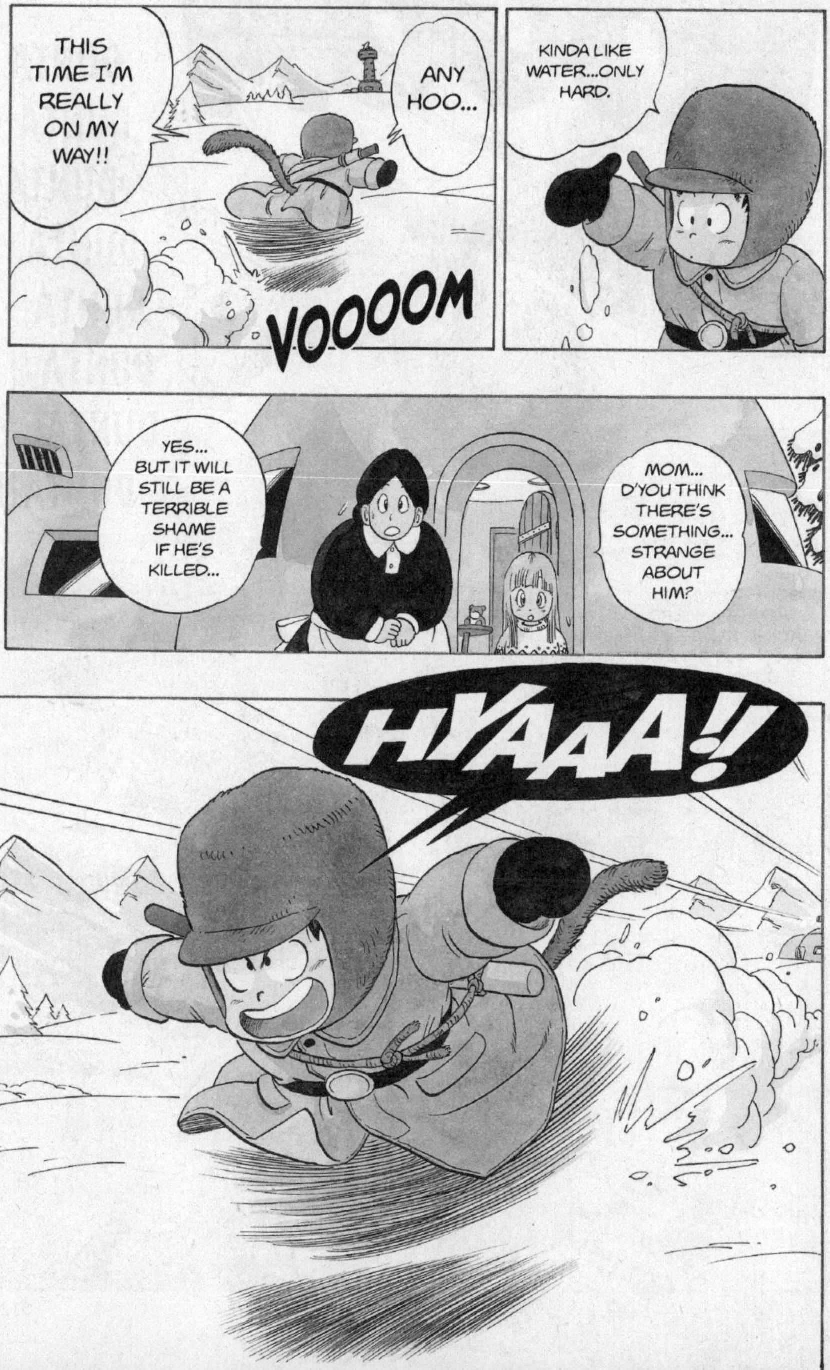
KINDA LIKE WATER...ONLY HARD.
ANY HOO...
THIS TIME I'M REALLY ON MY WAY!!
VOOOOM
MOM... D'YOU THINK THERE'S SOMETHING... STRANGE ABOUT HIM?
YES... BUT IT WILL STILL BE A TERRIBLE SHAME IF HE'S KILLED...
HYAAA!!

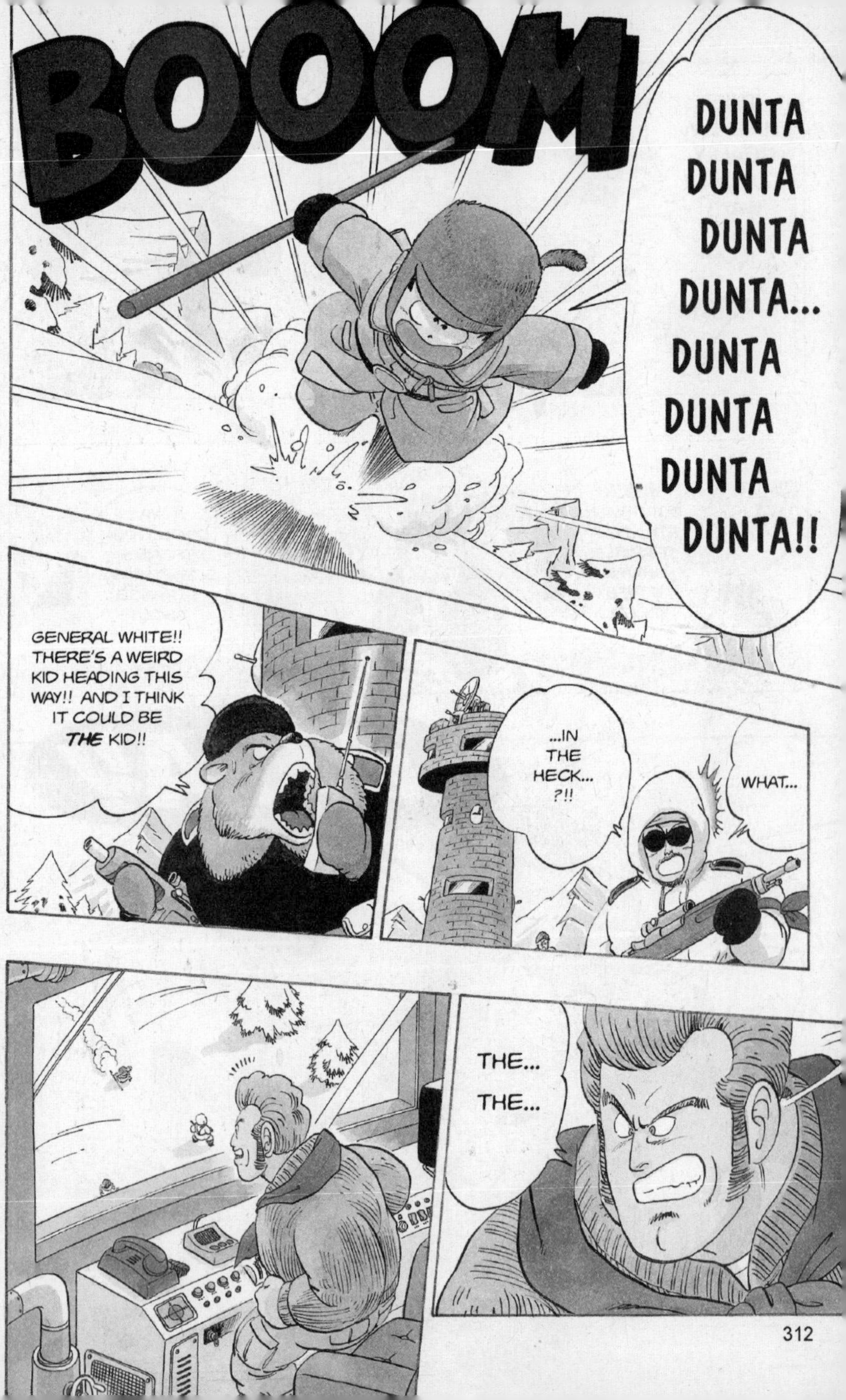
BOOOM
DUNTA DUNTA DUNTA DUNTA... DUNTA DUNTA DUNTA DUNTA!!
GENERAL WHITE!! THERE'S A WEIRD KID HEADING THIS WAY!! AND I THINK IT COULD BE *THE* KID!!
WHAT...
...IN THE HECK... ?!!
THE... THE...

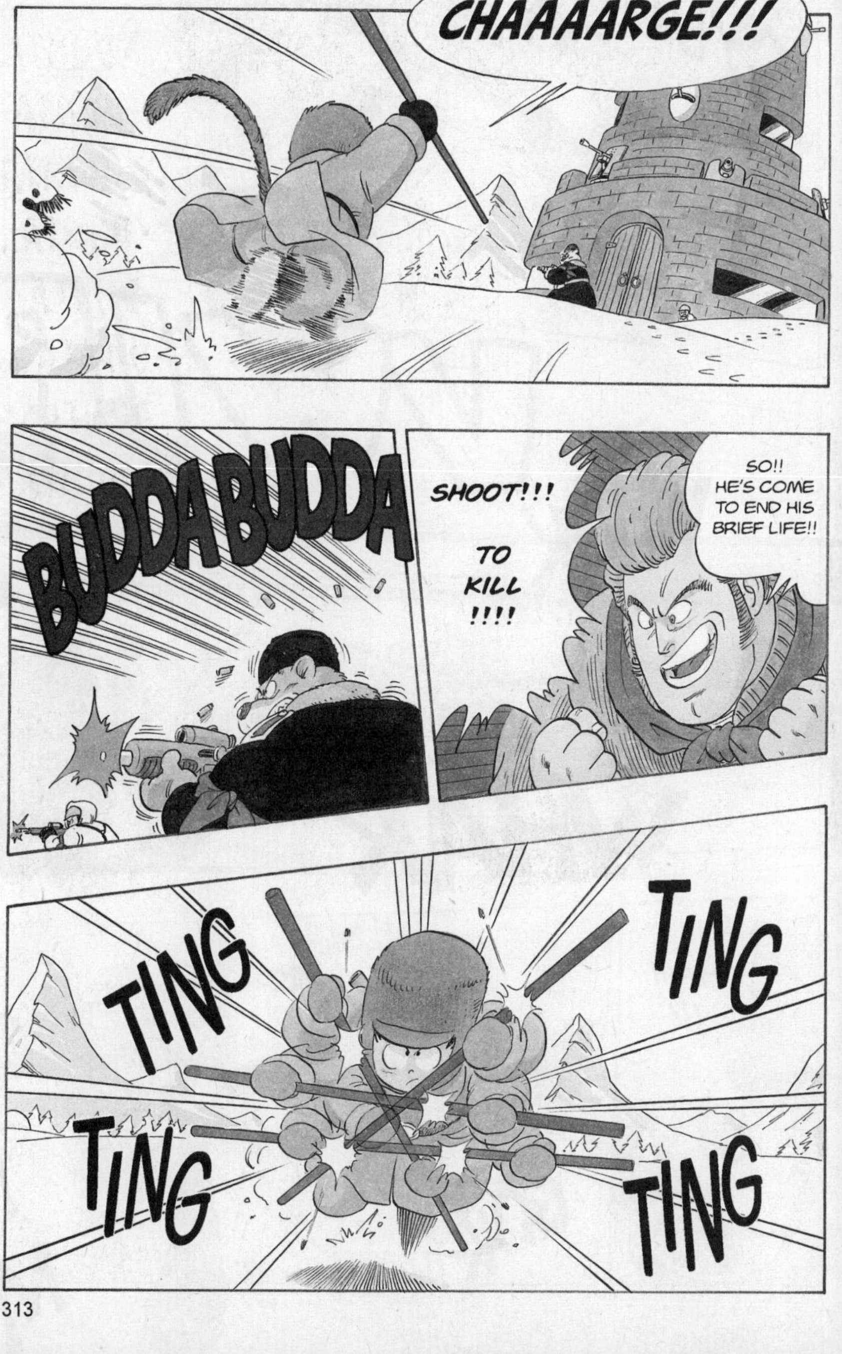
CHAAAARGE!!!
SO!! HE'S COME TO END HIS BRIEF LIFE!!
SHOOT!!!
TO KILL !!!!
BUDDA BUDDA
TING
TING
TING
TING

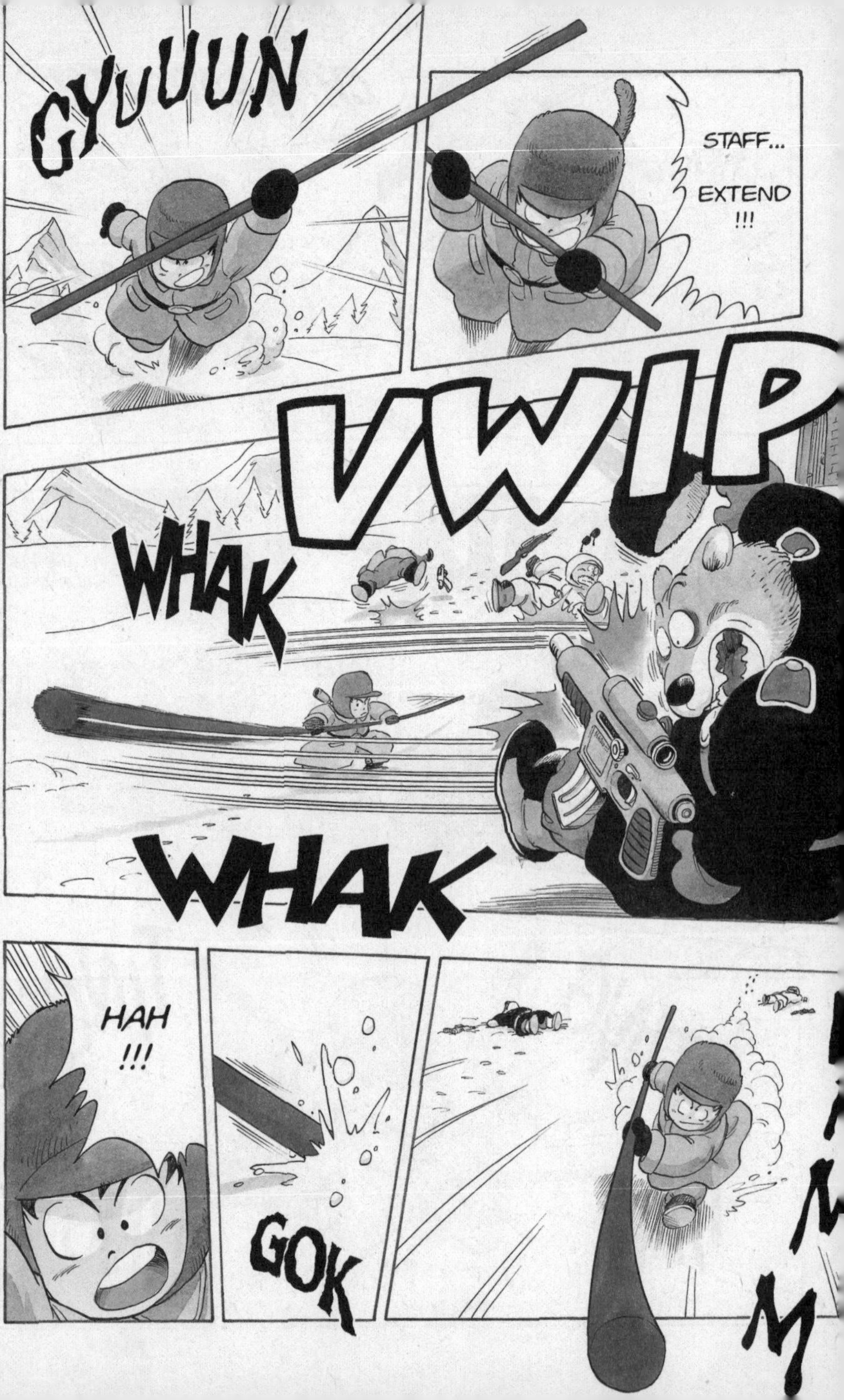
STAFF...
EXTEND !!!
GYUUUN
VWIP
WHAK
WHAK
GOK
HAH !!!

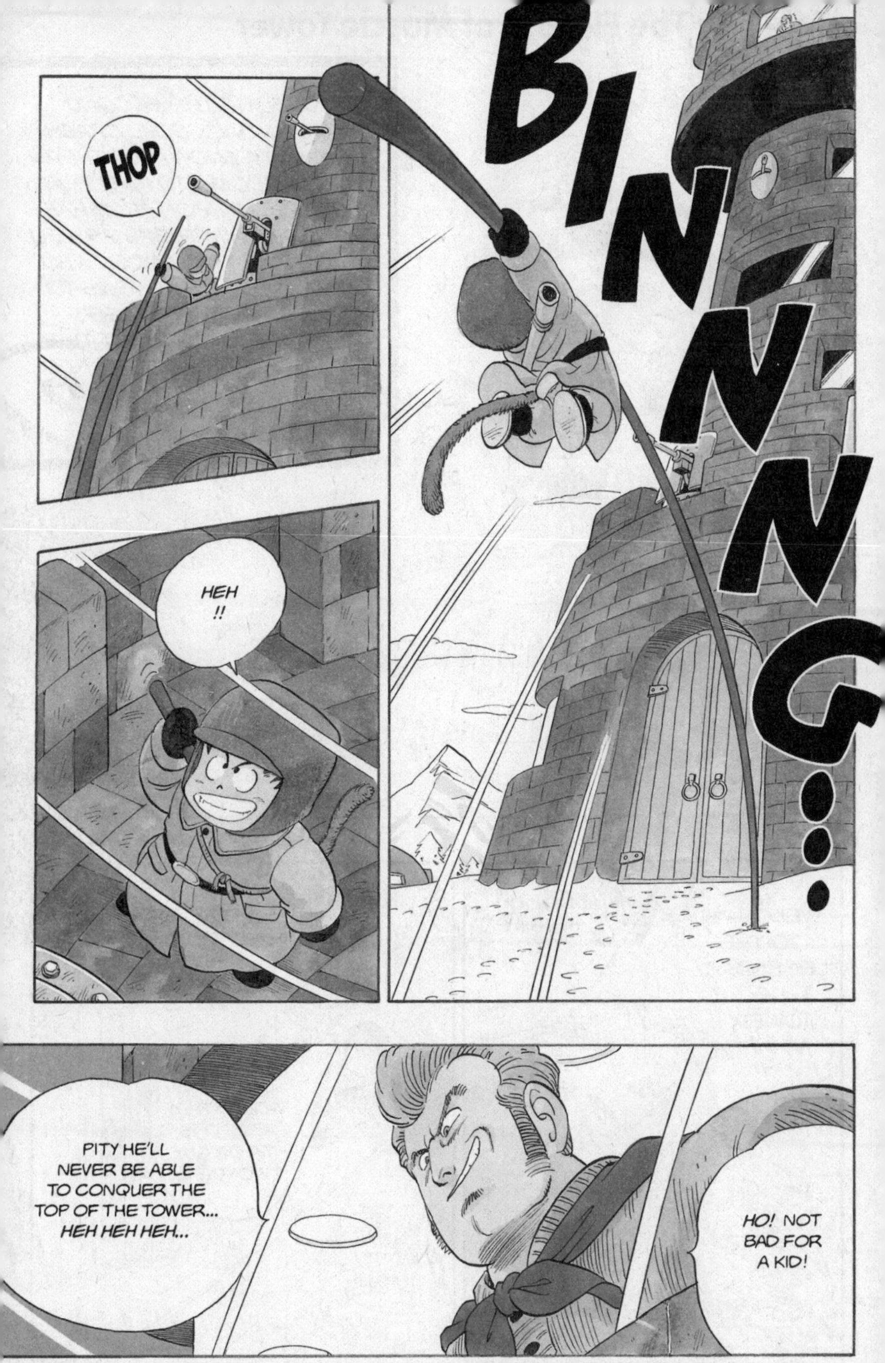
BINNNNG...!
THOP
HEH !!
HO! NOT BAD FOR A KID!
PITY HE'LL NEVER BE ABLE TO CONQUER THE TOP OF THE TOWER... HEH HEH HEH...

Tale 58 • The Flexing of Muscle Tower

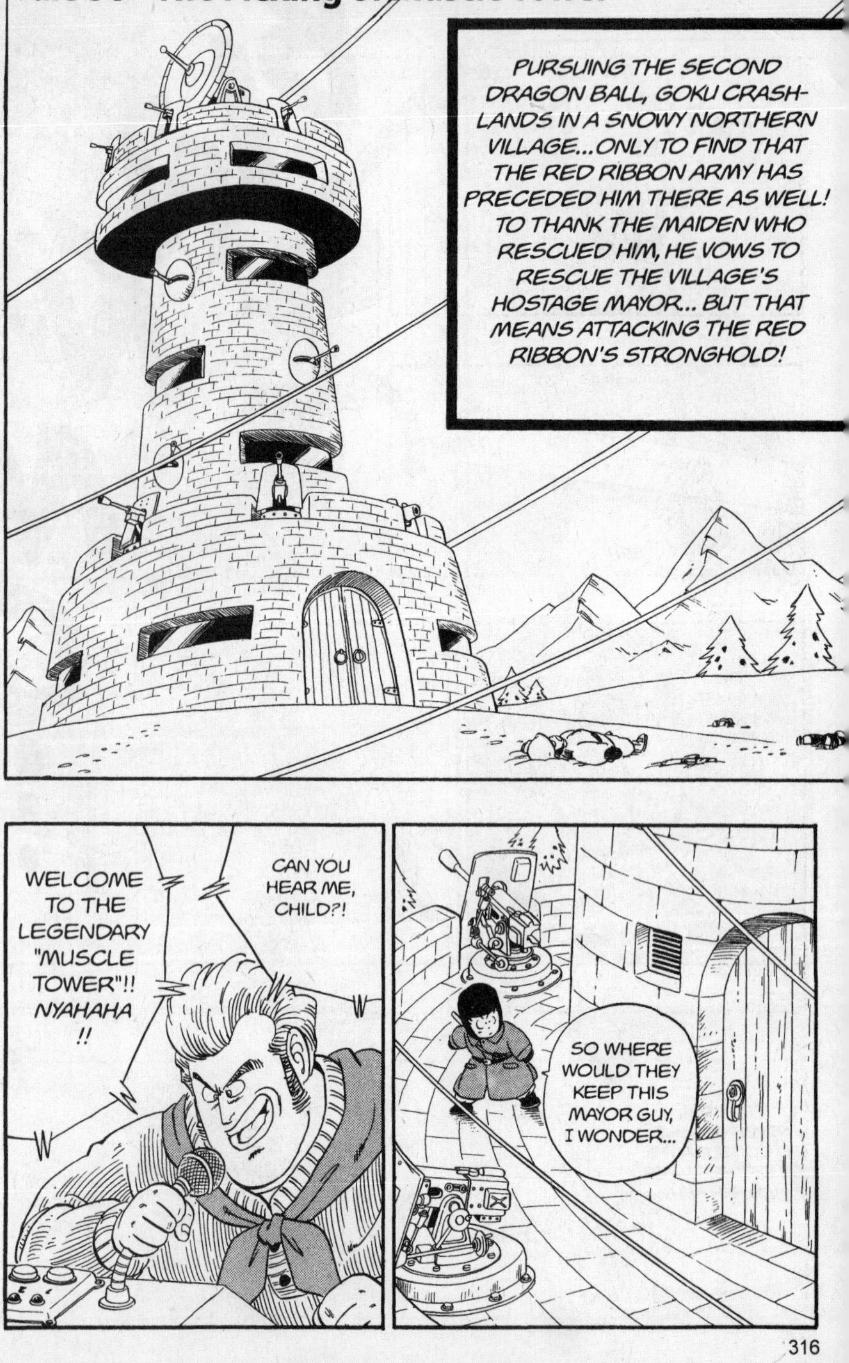

PURSUING THE SECOND DRAGON BALL, GOKU CRASH-LANDS IN A SNOWY NORTHERN VILLAGE...ONLY TO FIND THAT THE RED RIBBON ARMY HAS PRECEDED HIM THERE AS WELL! TO THANK THE MAIDEN WHO RESCUED HIM, HE VOWS TO RESCUE THE VILLAGE'S HOSTAGE MAYOR... BUT THAT MEANS ATTACKING THE RED RIBBON'S STRONGHOLD!
SO WHERE WOULD THEY KEEP THIS MAYOR GUY, I WONDER...
CAN YOU HEAR ME, CHILD?!
WELCOME TO THE LEGENDARY "MUSCLE TOWER"!! NYAHAHA !!

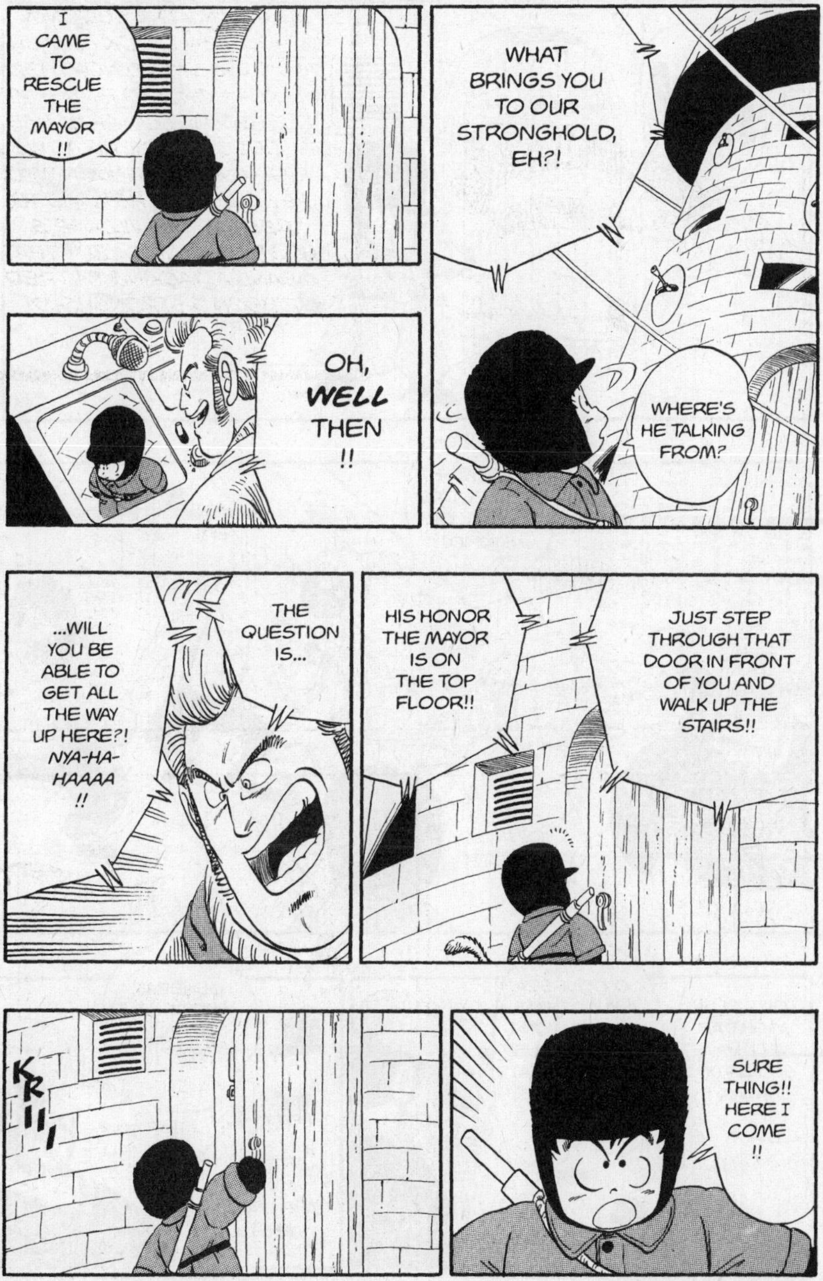
WHAT BRINGS YOU TO OUR STRONGHOLD, EH?!
WHERE'S HE TALKING FROM?
I CAME TO RESCUE THE MAYOR!!
OH, WELL THEN!!
JUST STEP THROUGH THAT DOOR IN FRONT OF YOU AND WALK UP THE STAIRS!!
HIS HONOR THE MAYOR IS ON THE TOP FLOOR!!
THE QUESTION IS...
...WILL YOU BE ABLE TO GET ALL THE WAY UP HERE?! NYA-HA-HAAAA!!
SURE THING!! HERE I COME!!
KRIII

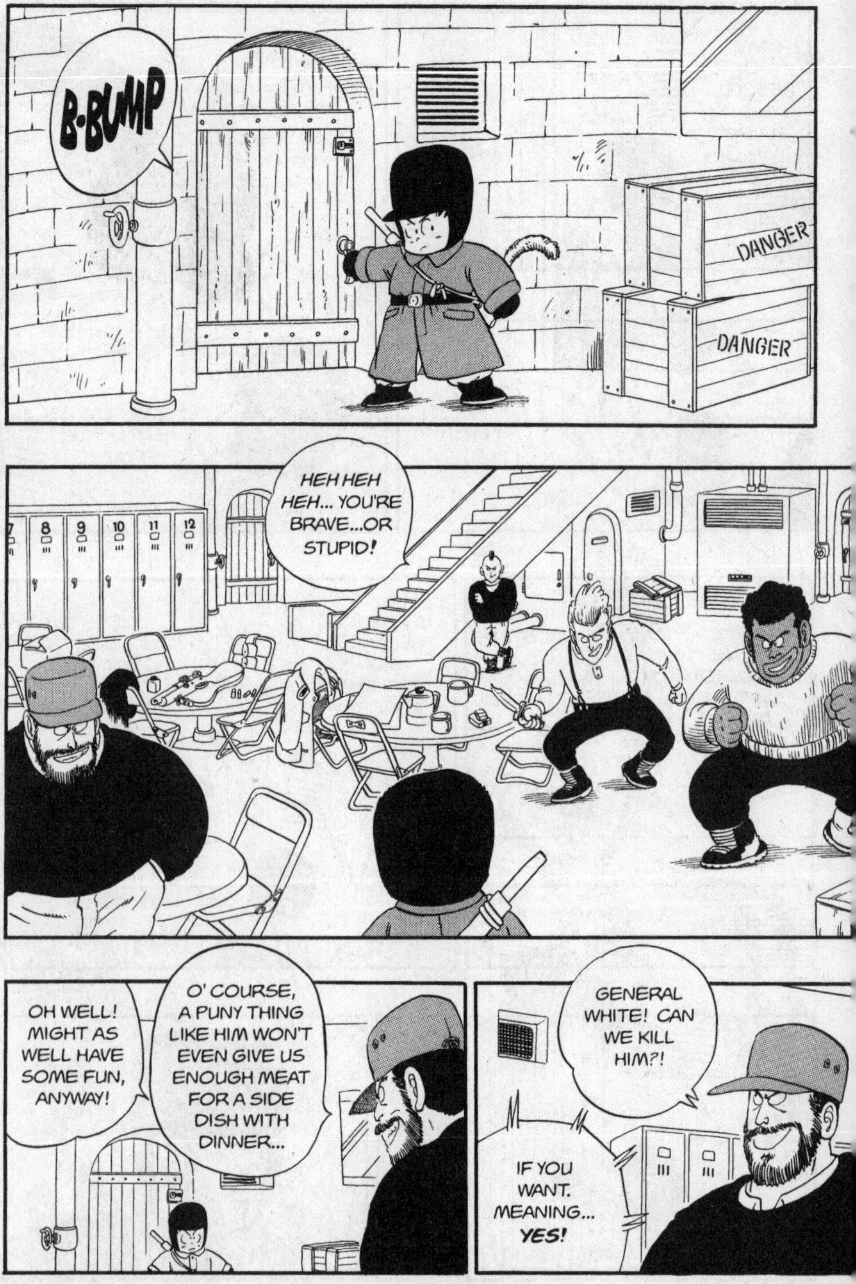
B-BUMP
DANGER
DANGER
HEH HEH HEH... YOU'RE BRAVE...OR STUPID!
GENERAL WHITE! CAN WE KILL HIM?!
IF YOU WANT. MEANING... ***YES!***
O' COURSE, A PUNY THING LIKE HIM WON'T EVEN GIVE US ENOUGH MEAT FOR A SIDE DISH WITH DINNER...
OH WELL! MIGHT AS WELL HAVE SOME FUN, ANYWAY!

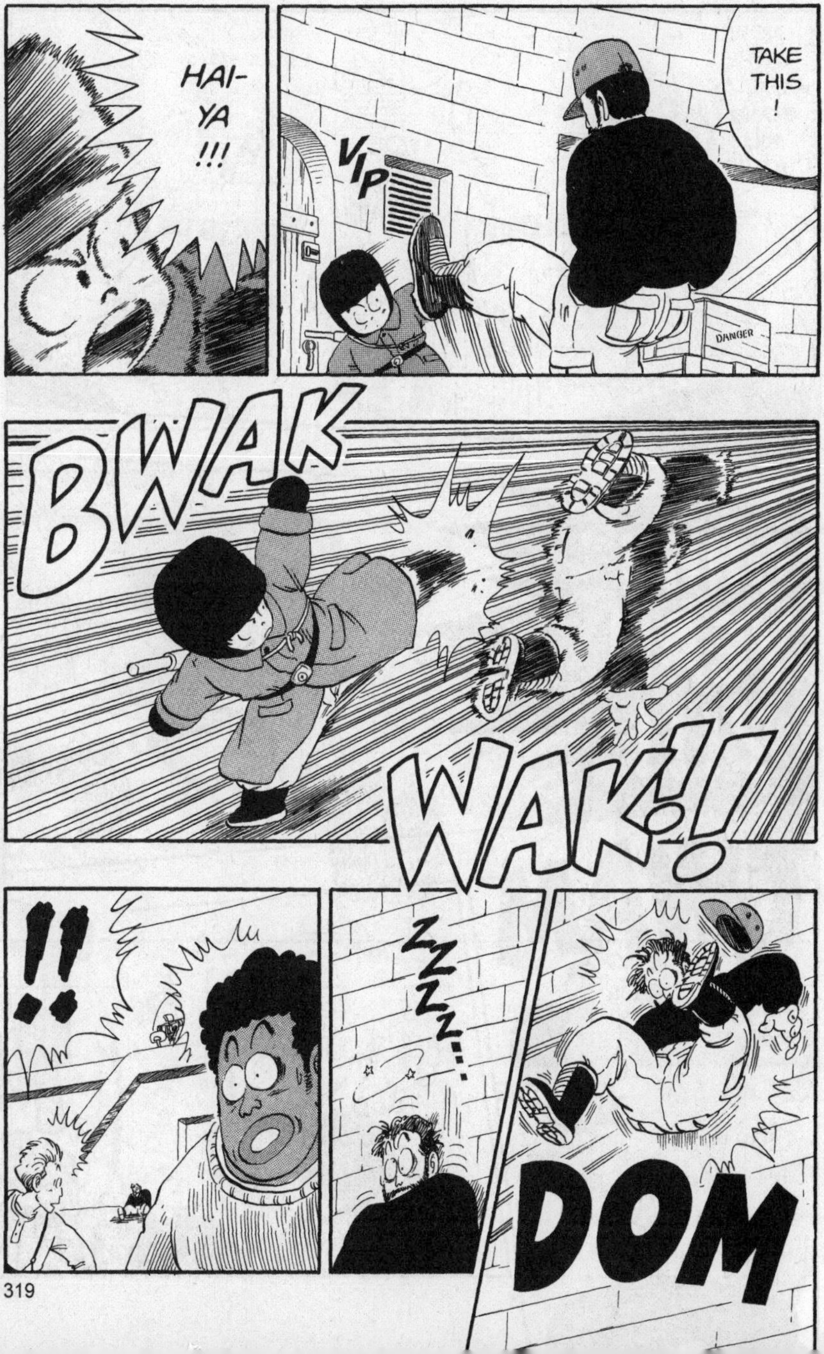
TAKE THIS !
VIP
HAI-YA !!!
DANGER
BWAK
WAK!!
ZZZZ...
DOM
!!

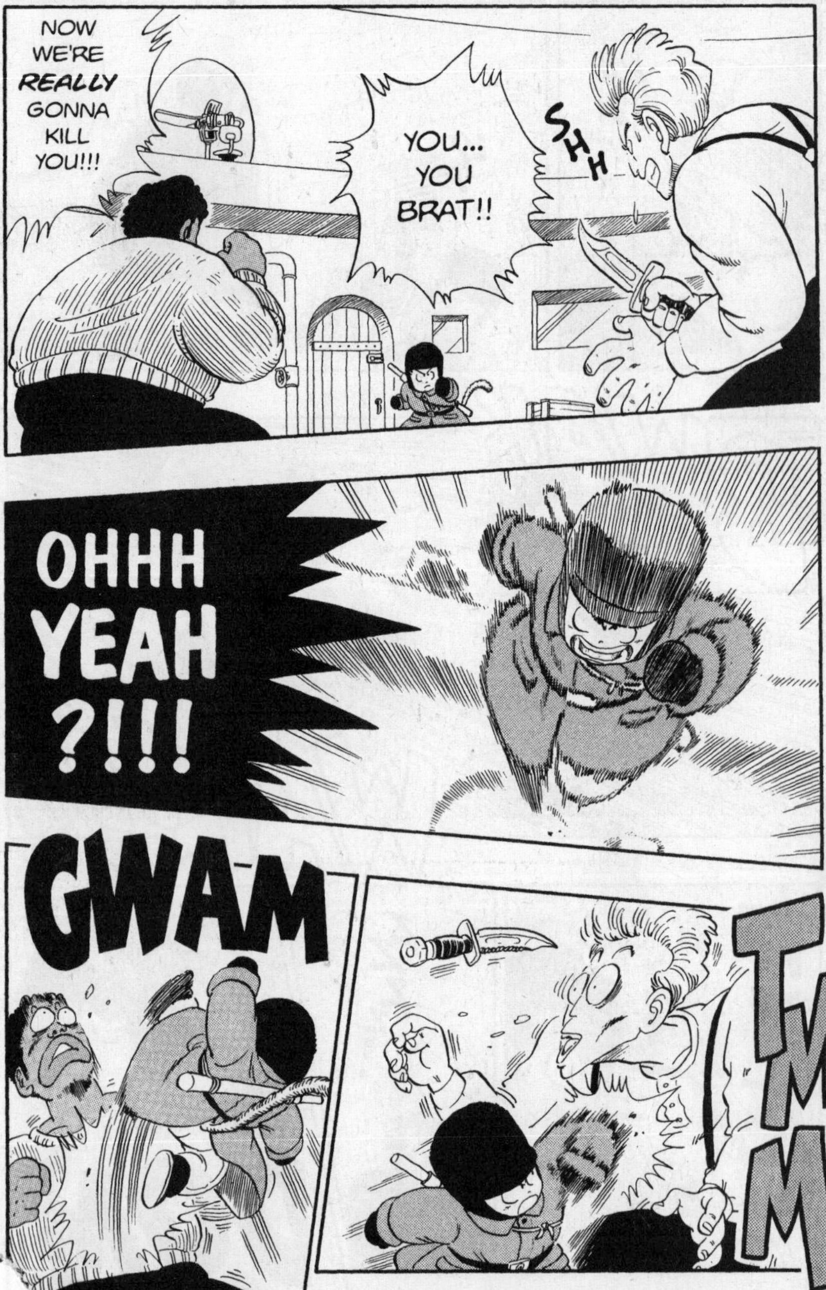
SHH
YOU... YOU BRAT!!
NOW WE'RE REALLY GONNA KILL YOU!!!
OHHH YEAH ?!!!
TMM
GWAM

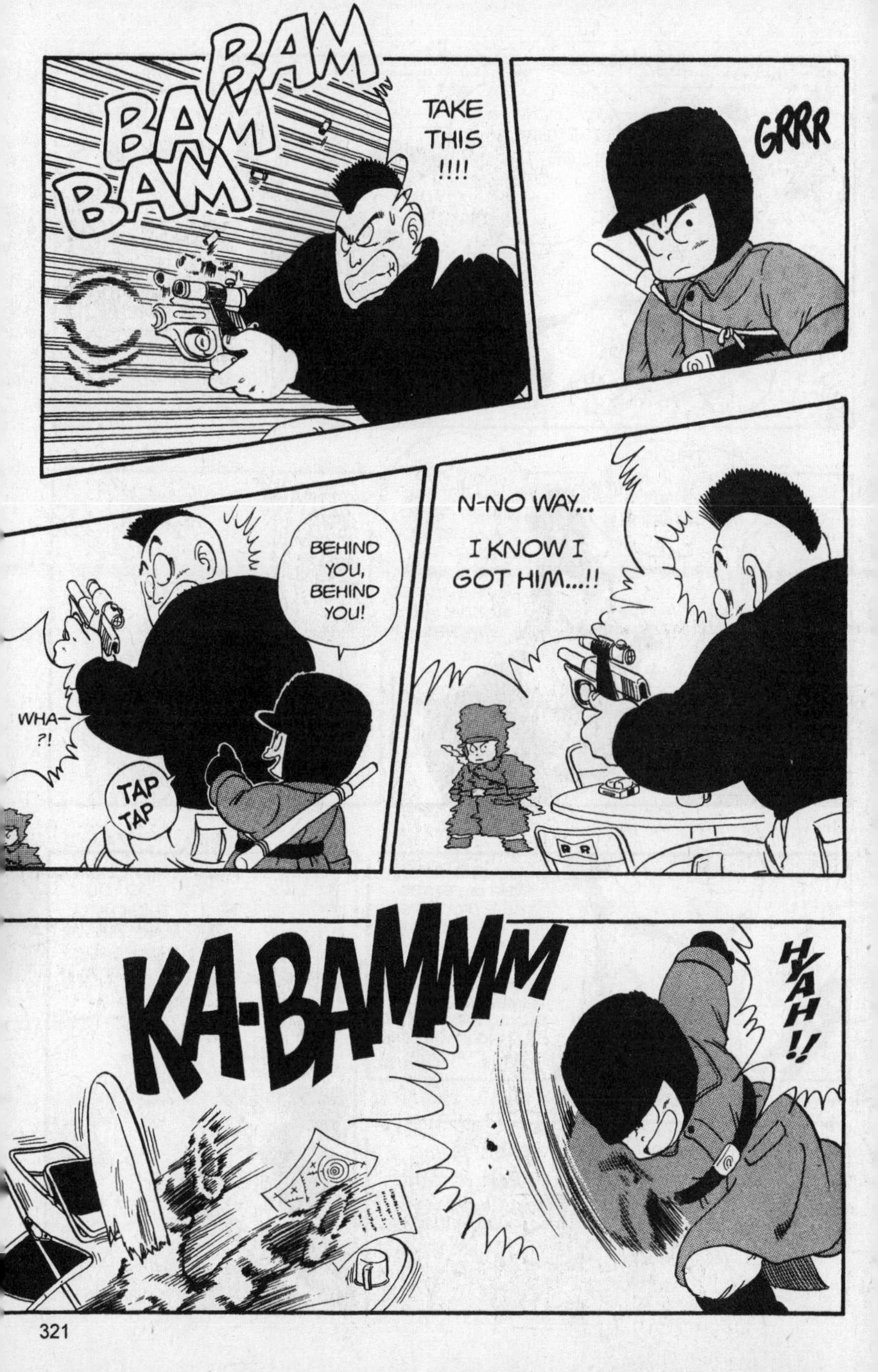
GRRR
TAKE THIS !!!!
BAM BAM BAM
N-NO WAY...
I KNOW I GOT HIM...!!
BEHIND YOU, BEHIND YOU!
WHA— ?!
TAP TAP
HYAH!!
KA-BAMMMM

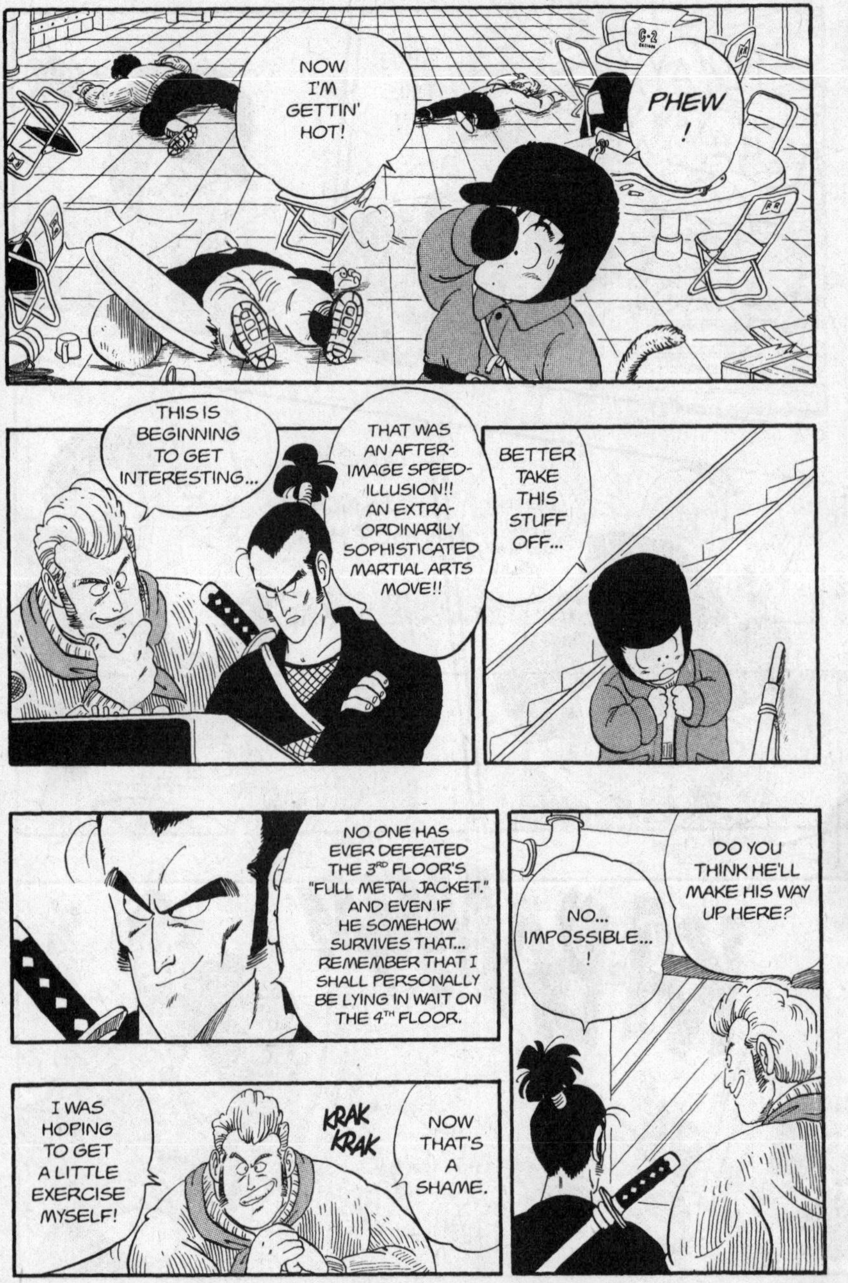
PHEW!
NOW I'M GETTIN' HOT!
BETTER TAKE THIS STUFF OFF...
THAT WAS AN AFTER-IMAGE SPEED-ILLUSION!! AN EXTRA-ORDINARILY SOPHISTICATED MARTIAL ARTS MOVE!!
THIS IS BEGINNING TO GET INTERESTING...
DO YOU THINK HE'LL MAKE HIS WAY UP HERE?
NO... IMPOSSIBLE...!
NO ONE HAS EVER DEFEATED THE 3RD FLOOR'S "FULL METAL JACKET." AND EVEN IF HE SOMEHOW SURVIVES THAT... REMEMBER THAT I SHALL PERSONALLY BE LYING IN WAIT ON THE 4TH FLOOR.
NOW THAT'S A SHAME.
KRAK KRAK
I WAS HOPING TO GET A LITTLE EXERCISE MYSELF!

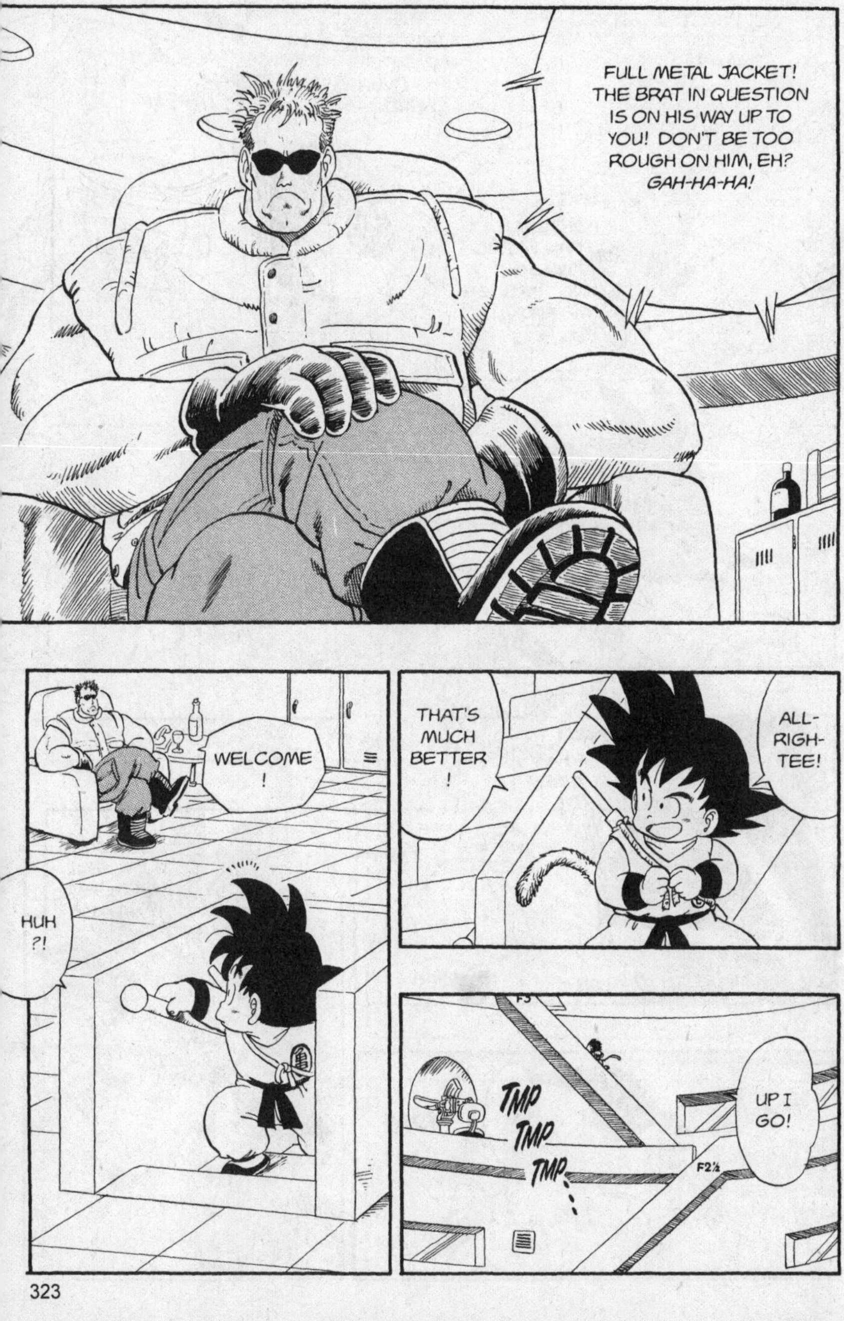
FULL METAL JACKET! THE BRAT IN QUESTION IS ON HIS WAY UP TO YOU! DON'T BE TOO ROUGH ON HIM, EH? *GAH-HA-HA!*
ALL-RIGHTEE!
THAT'S MUCH BETTER!
F3
UP I GO!
TMP
TMP
TMP
F2½
WELCOME!
HUH?!

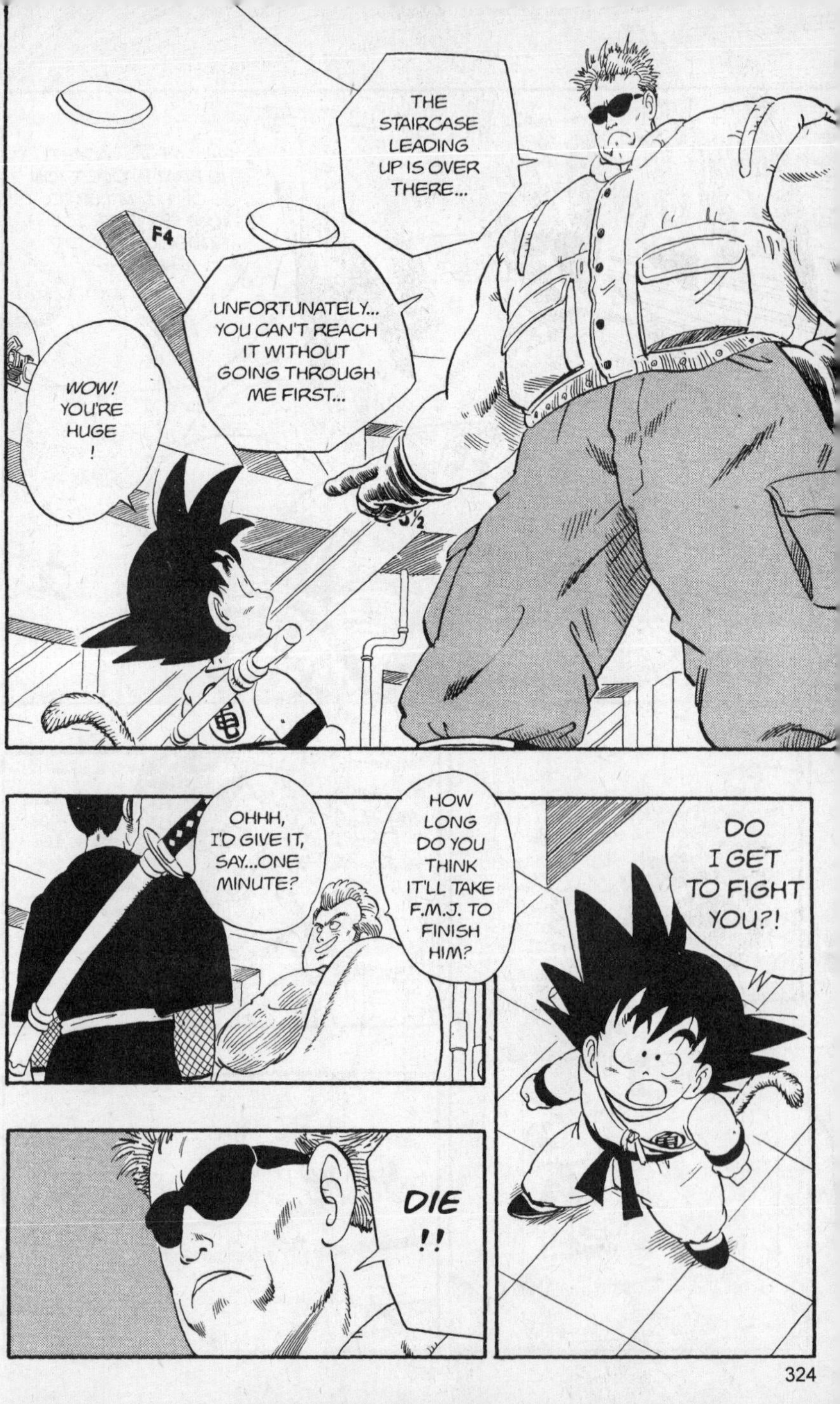
F4
THE STAIRCASE LEADING UP IS OVER THERE...
UNFORTUNATELY... YOU CAN'T REACH IT WITHOUT GOING THROUGH ME FIRST...
WOW! YOU'RE HUGE!
DO I GET TO FIGHT YOU?!
HOW LONG DO YOU THINK IT'LL TAKE F.M.J. TO FINISH HIM?
OHHH, I'D GIVE IT, SAY...ONE MINUTE?
DIE!!

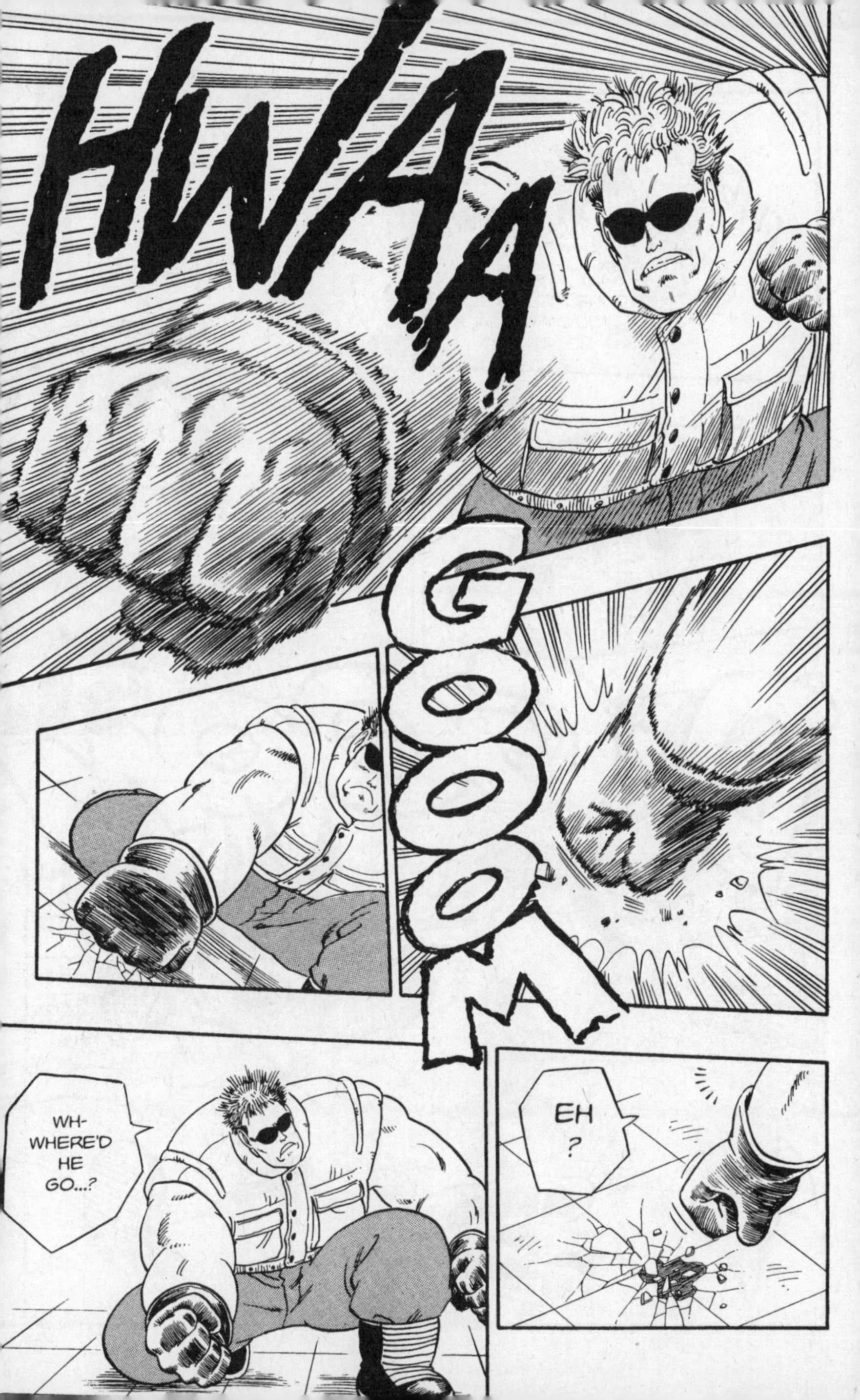
HWAA
GOOOOM
EH ?
WH- WHERE'D HE GO...?

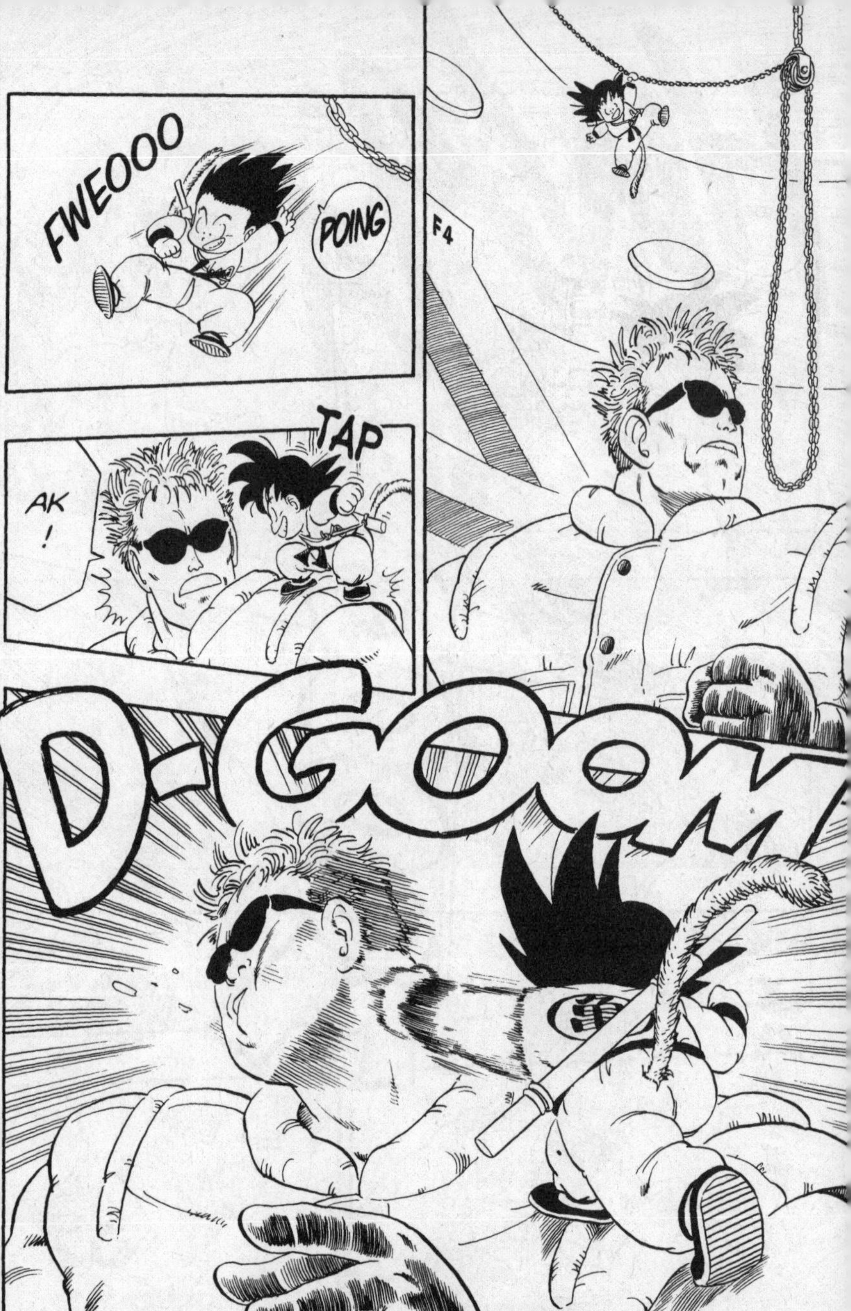
F4
FWEOOO
POING
TAP
AK!
D-GOOM

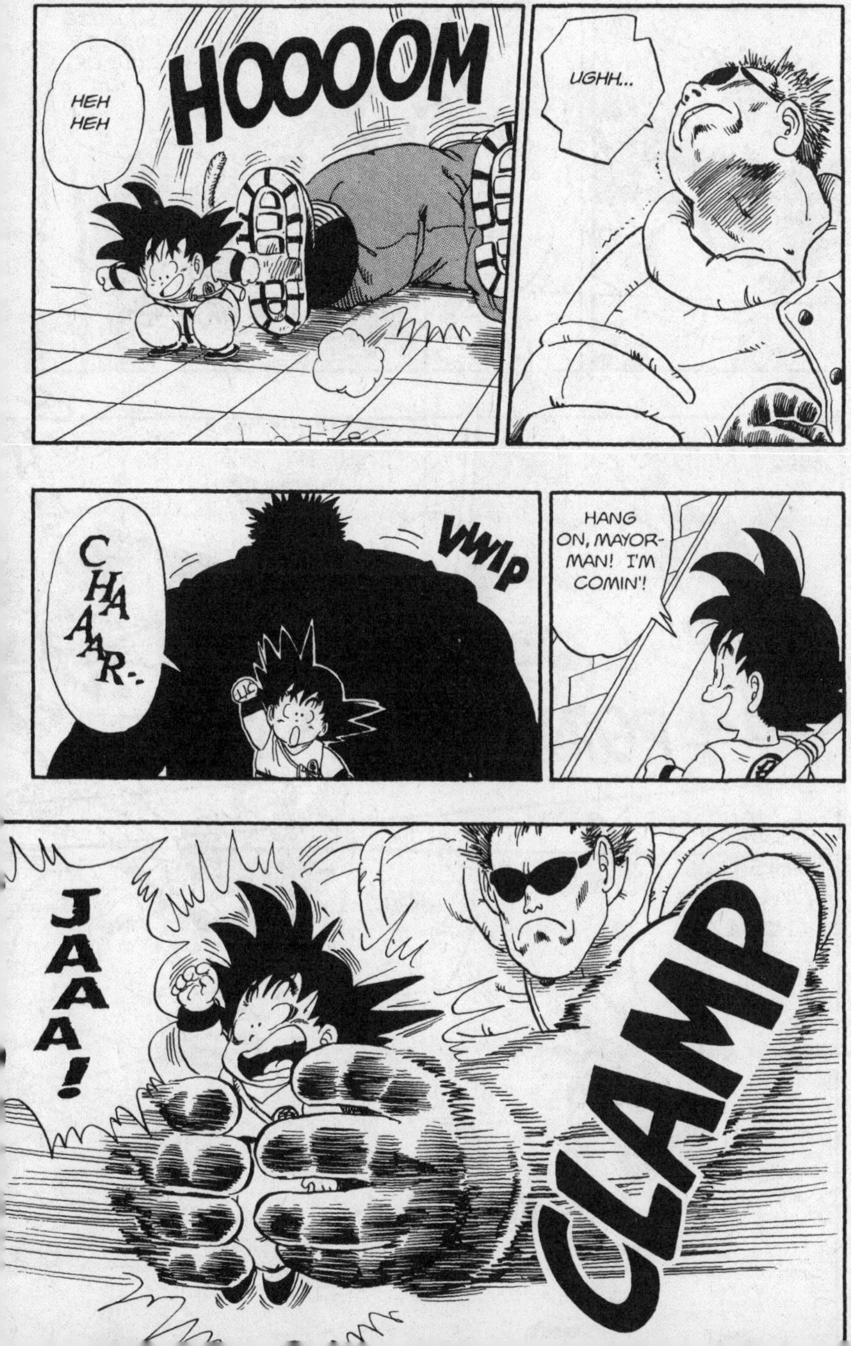
UGHH...
HOOOOM
HEH HEH
HANG ON, MAYOR-MAN! I'M COMIN'!
VWIP
CHAAAR-..
CLAMP
JAAA!

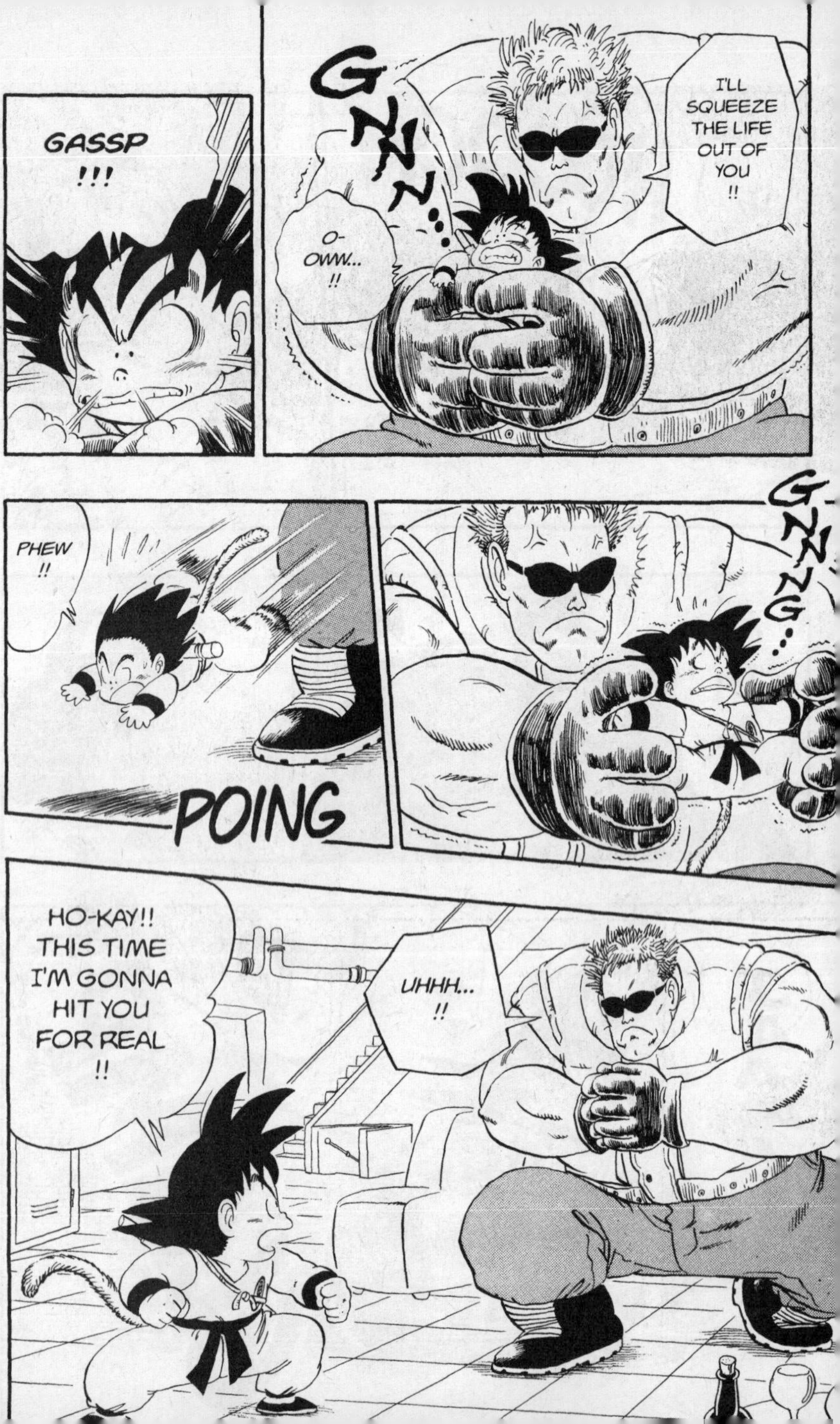
GNNN...
I'LL SQUEEZE THE LIFE OUT OF YOU !!
O-OWW... !!
GASSP !!!
GNNNG...
PHEW !!
POING
UHHH... !!
HO-KAY!! THIS TIME I'M GONNA HIT YOU FOR REAL !!

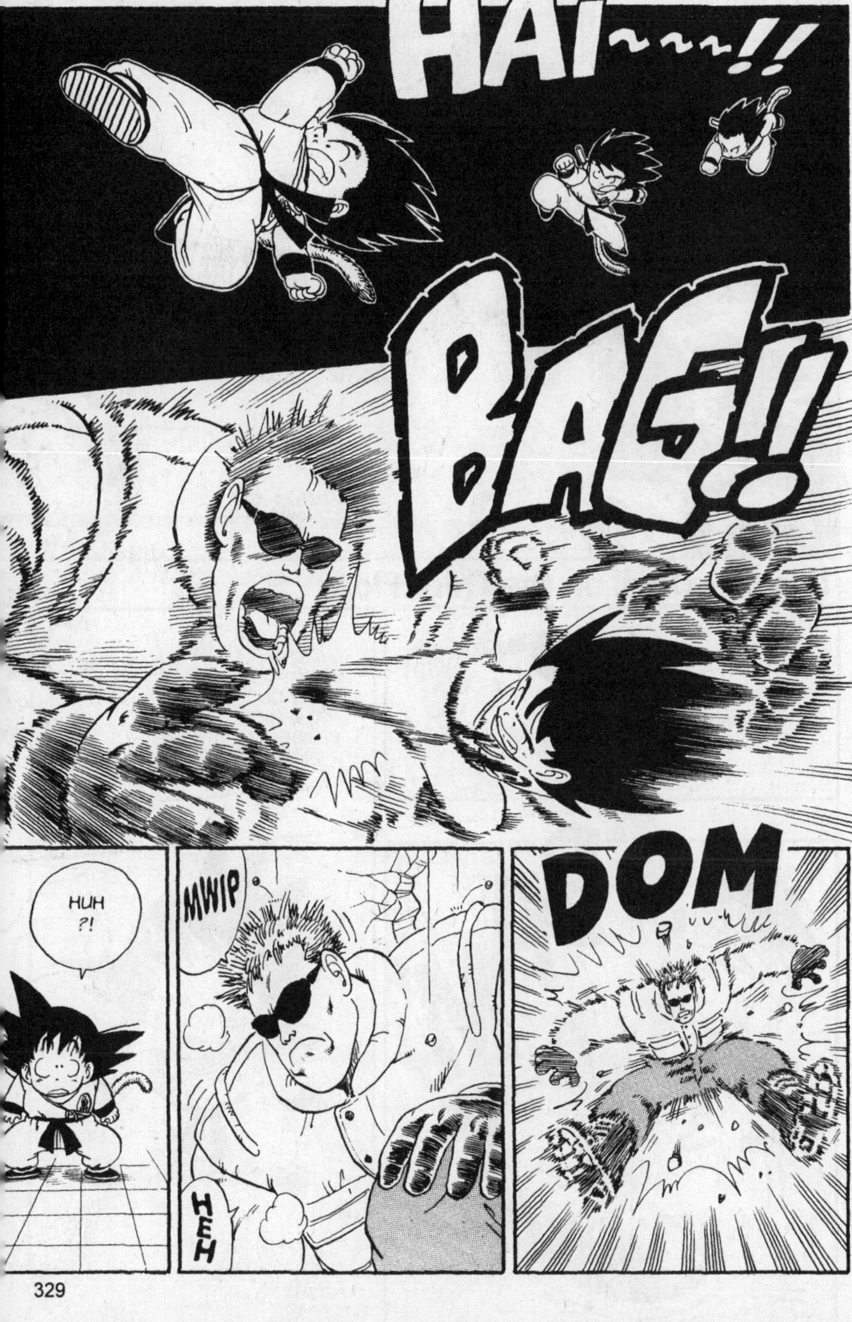
HAI~~~!!
BAG!!
DOM
MWIP
HEH
HUH ?!

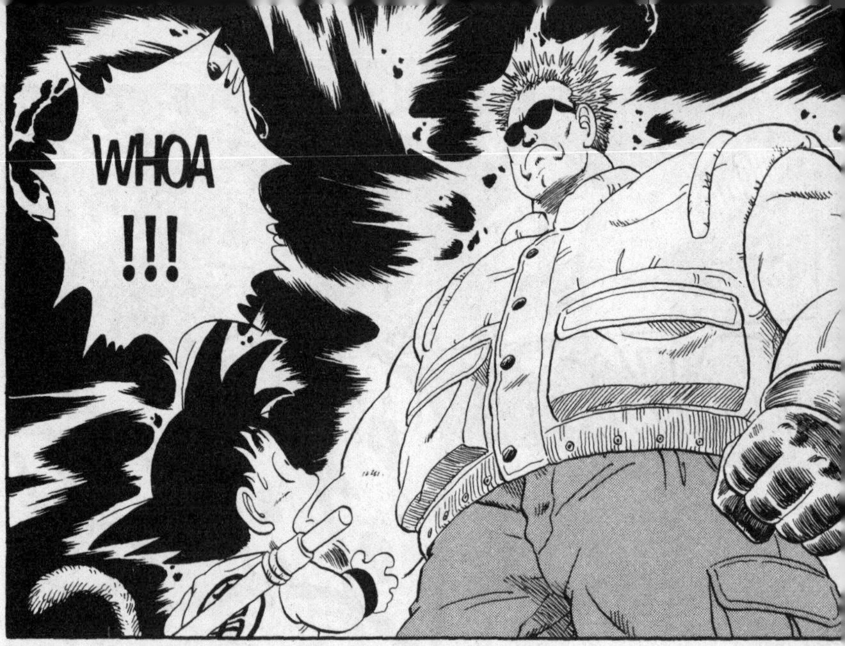
WHOA !!!

Tale 59 • Devil on the Third Floor

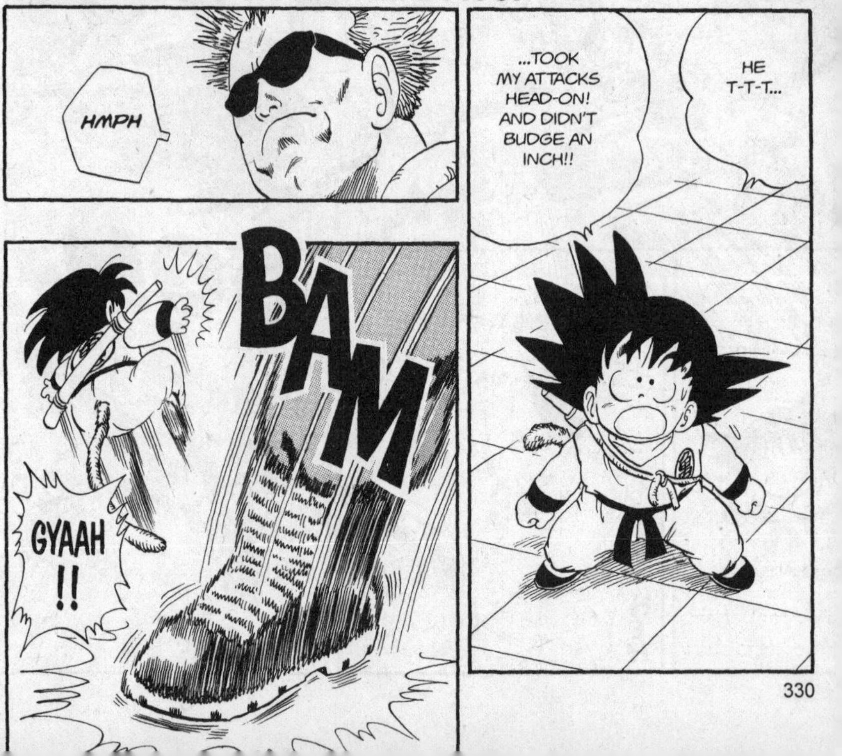
HE T-T-T...
...TOOK MY ATTACKS HEAD-ON! AND DIDN'T BUDGE AN INCH!!
HMPH
BAM
GYAAH !!

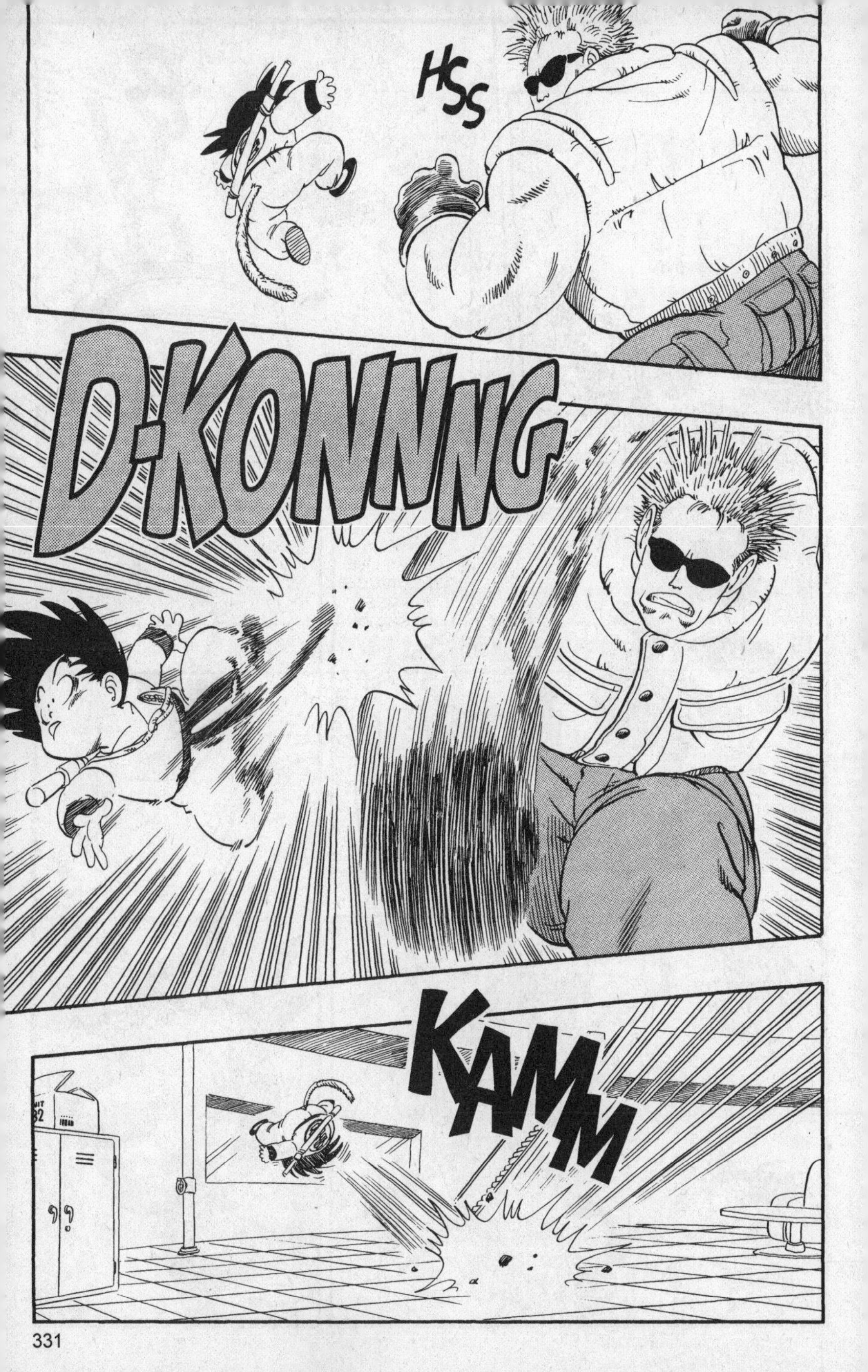
HSS
D-KONNNG
KAMM

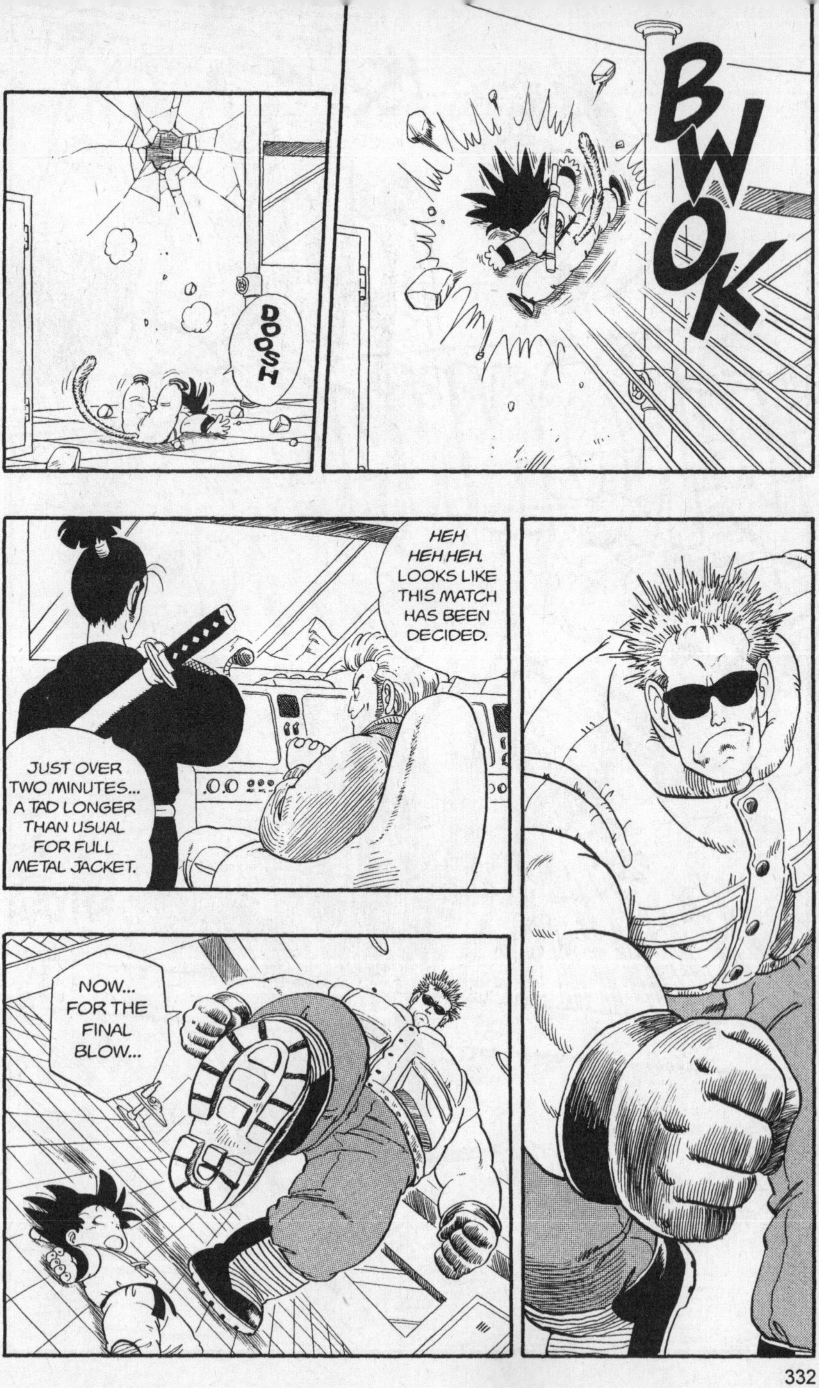
BWOK
DOOSH
HEH HEH HEH. LOOKS LIKE THIS MATCH HAS BEEN DECIDED.
JUST OVER TWO MINUTES... A TAD LONGER THAN USUAL FOR FULL METAL JACKET.
NOW... FOR THE FINAL BLOW...

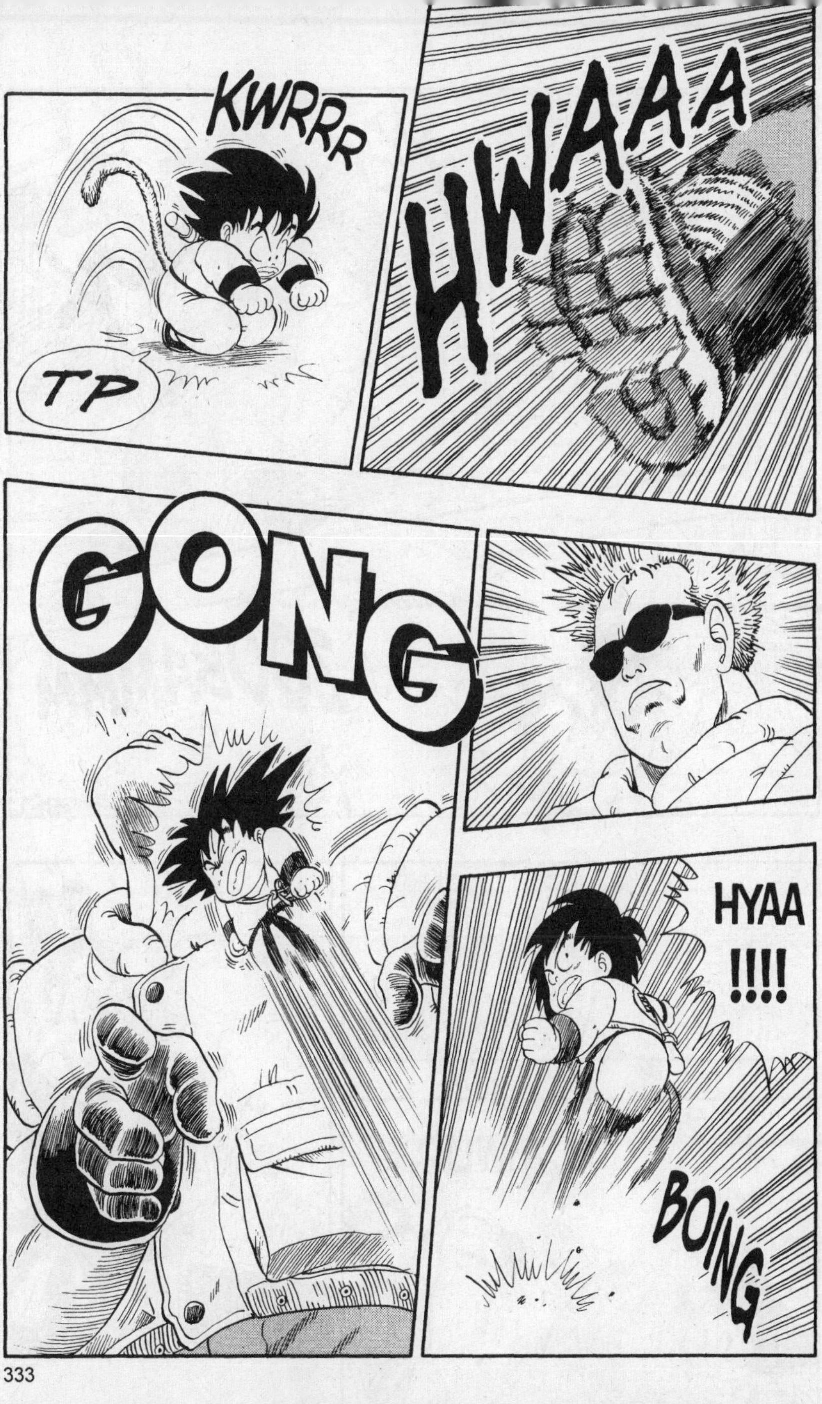
HWAAA
KWRRR
TP
HYAA !!!!
BOING
GONG

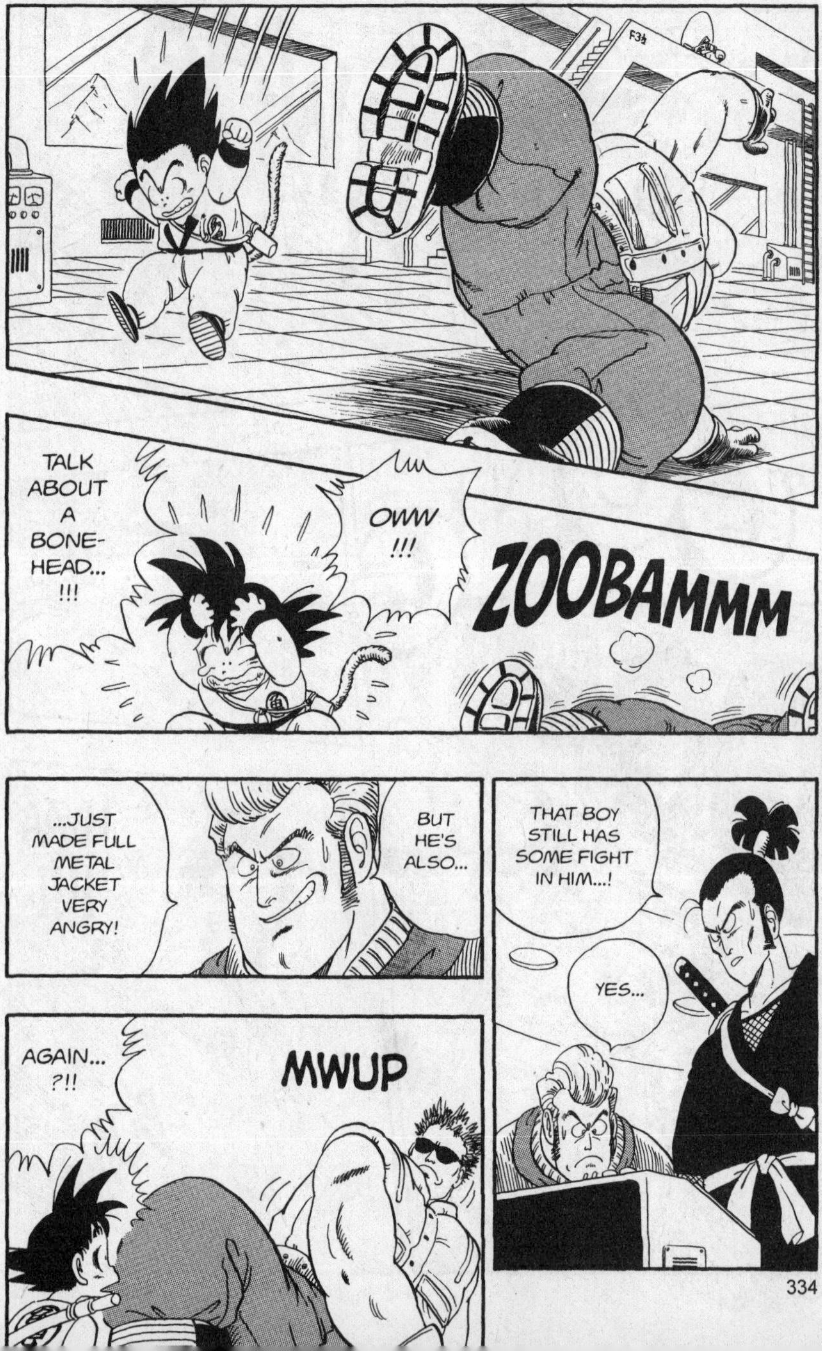
F3½
ZOOBAMMM
OWW!!!
TALK ABOUT A BONEHEAD...!!!
THAT BOY STILL HAS SOME FIGHT IN HIM...!
YES...
BUT HE'S ALSO...
...JUST MADE FULL METAL JACKET VERY ANGRY!
MWUP
AGAIN...?!!

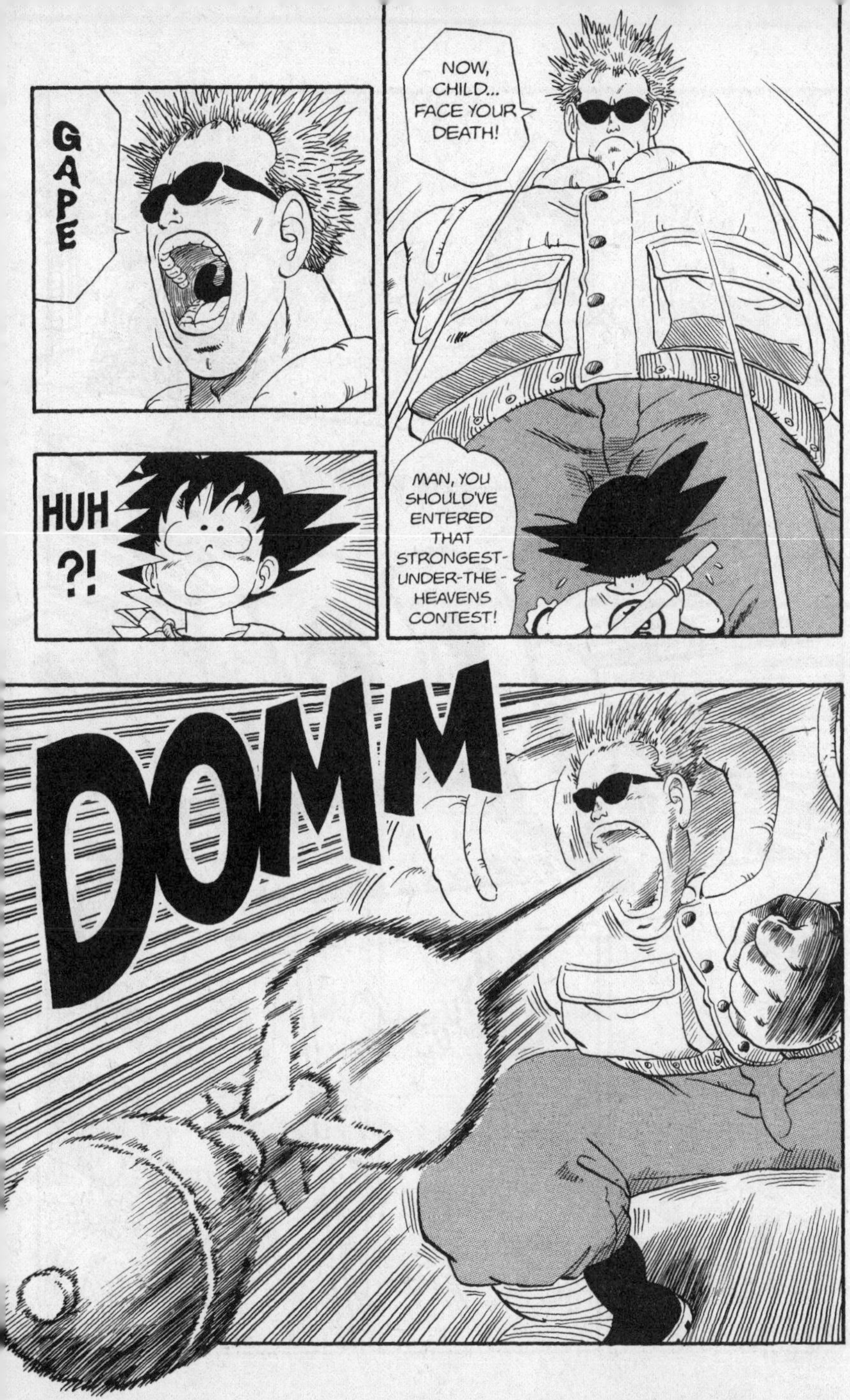
NOW, CHILD... FACE YOUR DEATH!
MAN, YOU SHOULD'VE ENTERED THAT STRONGEST-UNDER-THE-HEAVENS CONTEST!
GAPE
HUH ?!
DOMM

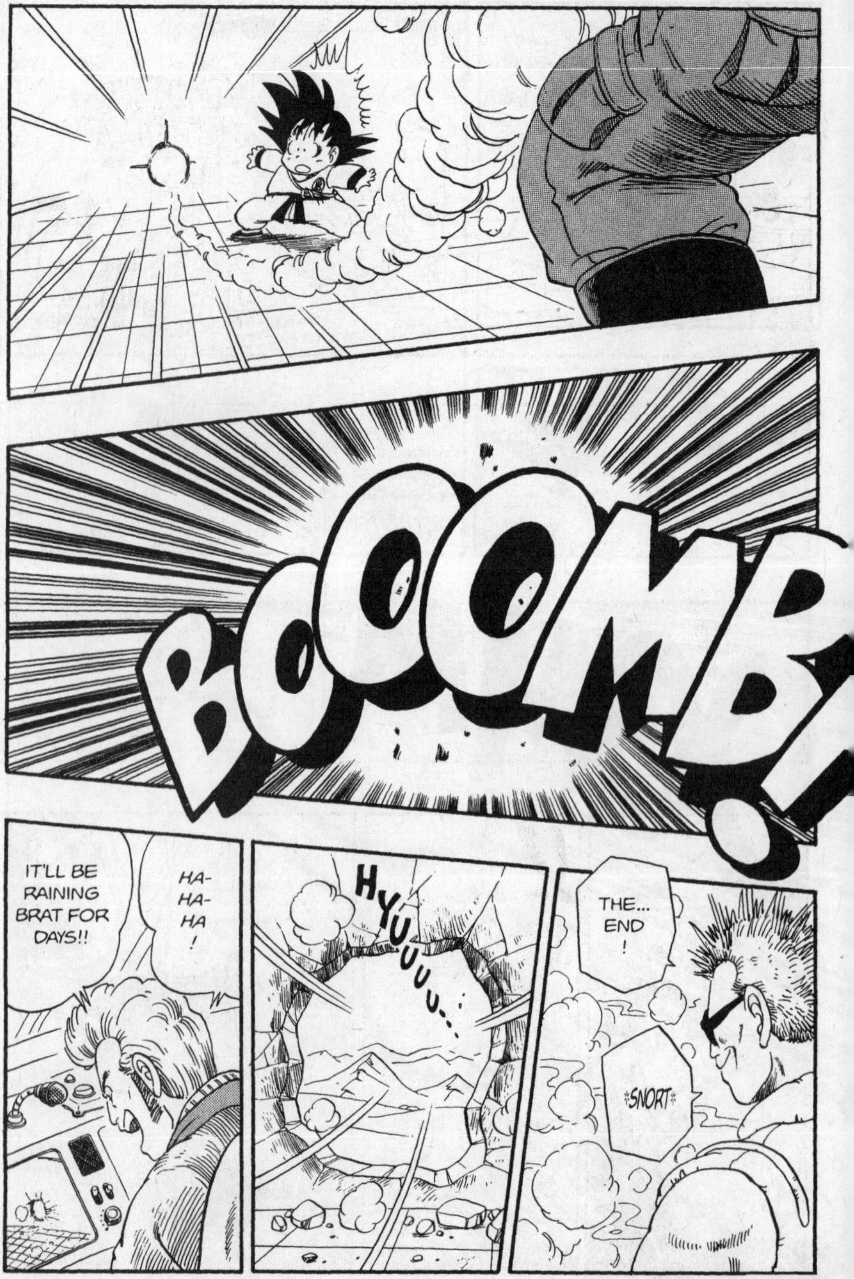
BOOOMB!!
THE... END!
SNORT
HYUUUUU...
HA-HA-HA!
IT'LL BE RAINING BRAT FOR DAYS!!

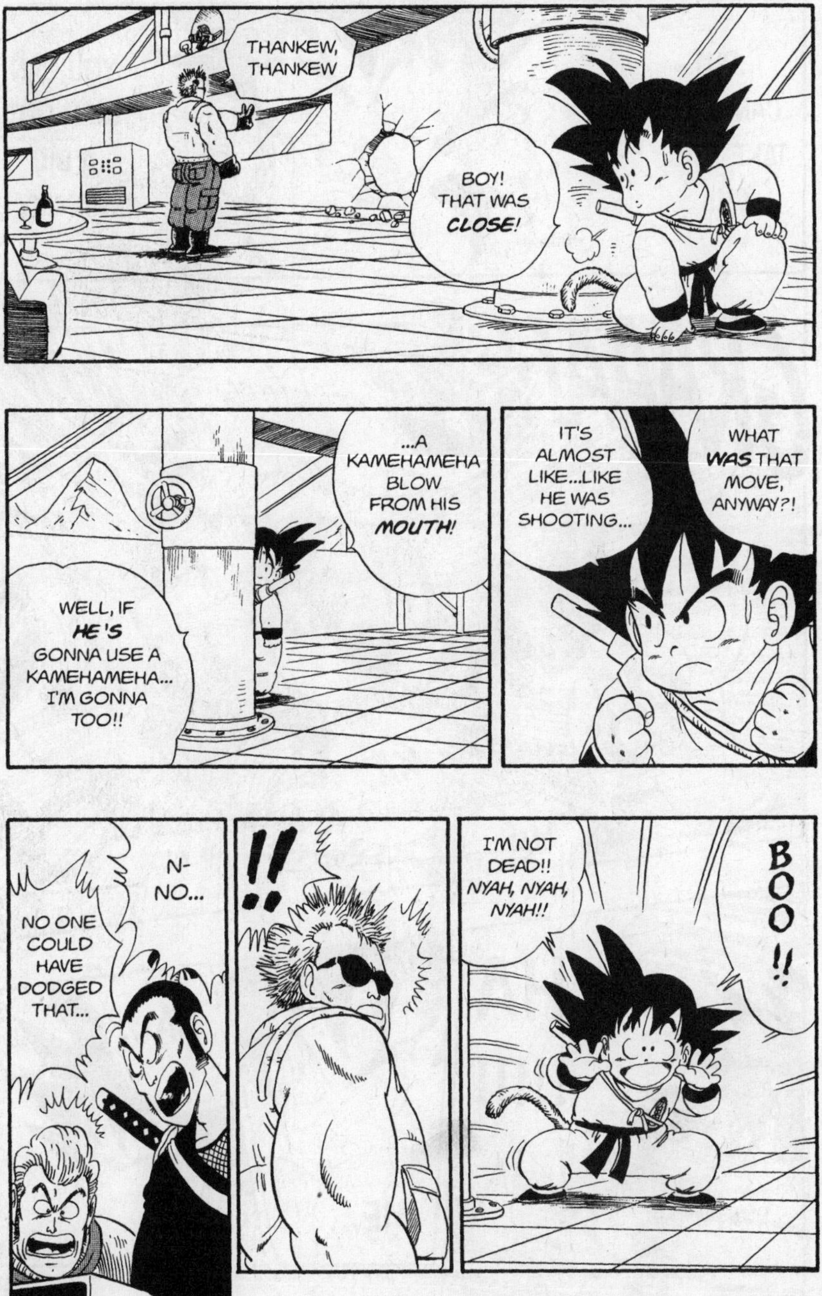
THANKEW, THANKEW
BOY! THAT WAS *CLOSE*!
WHAT **WAS** THAT MOVE, ANYWAY?!
IT'S ALMOST LIKE...LIKE HE WAS SHOOTING...
...A KAMEHAMEHA BLOW FROM HIS *MOUTH*!
WELL, IF ***HE'S*** GONNA USE A KAMEHAMEHA... I'M GONNA TOO!!
BOO!!
I'M NOT DEAD!! *NYAH, NYAH, NYAH!!*
!!
N-NO...
NO ONE COULD HAVE DODGED THAT...

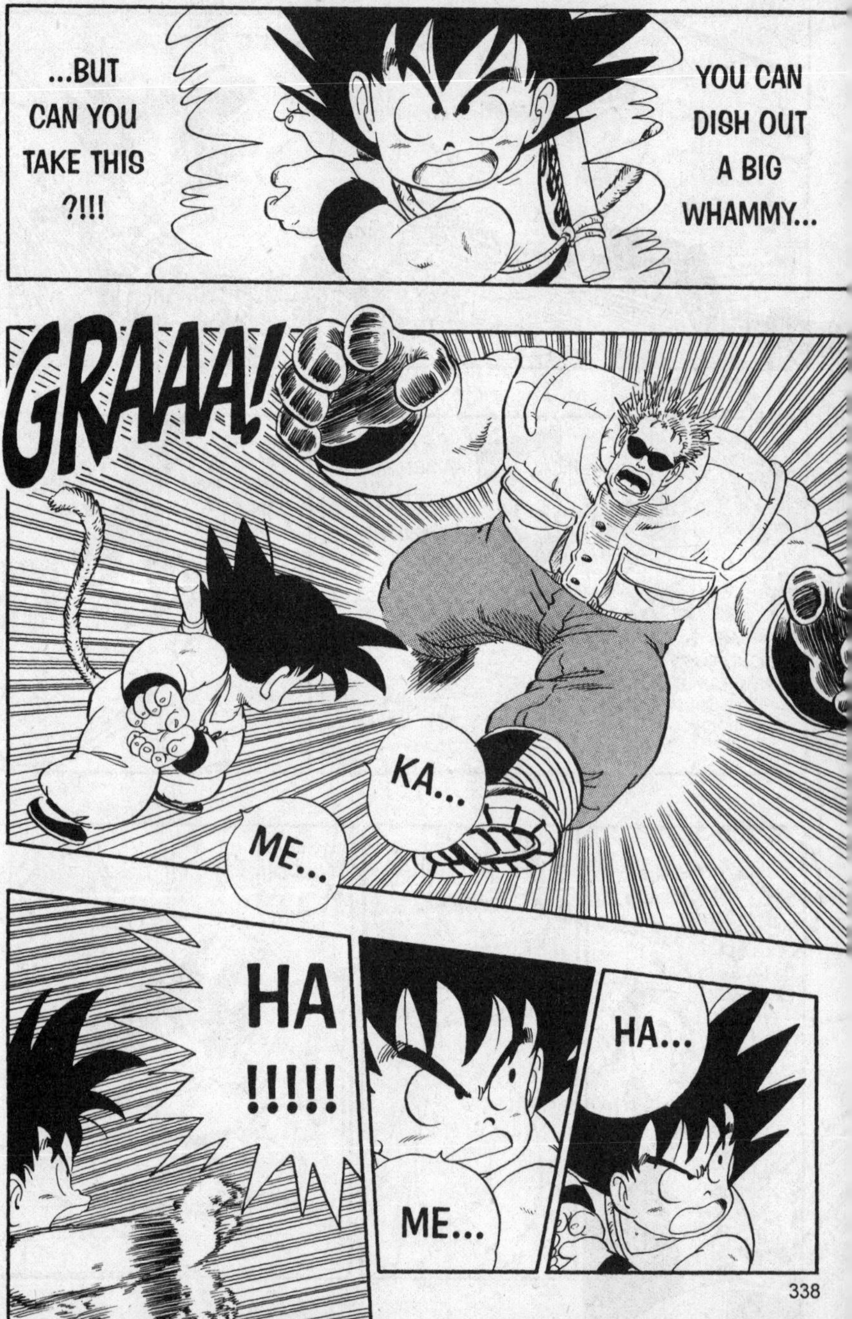
YOU CAN DISH OUT A BIG WHAMMY...
...BUT CAN YOU TAKE THIS ?!!!
GRAAA!
KA...
ME...
HA...
ME...
HA !!!!!

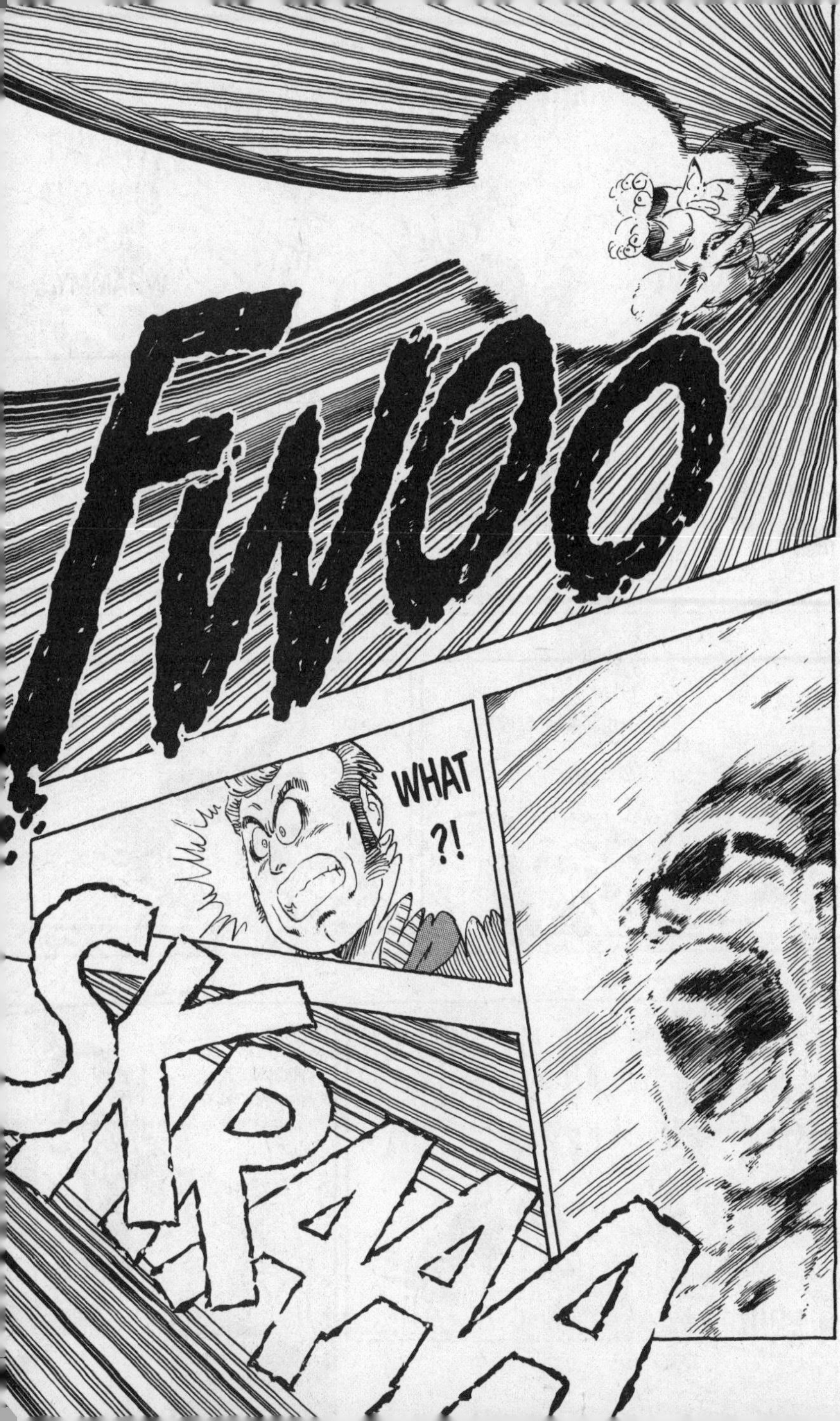
FWOO
WHAT ?!
SKRAAAA

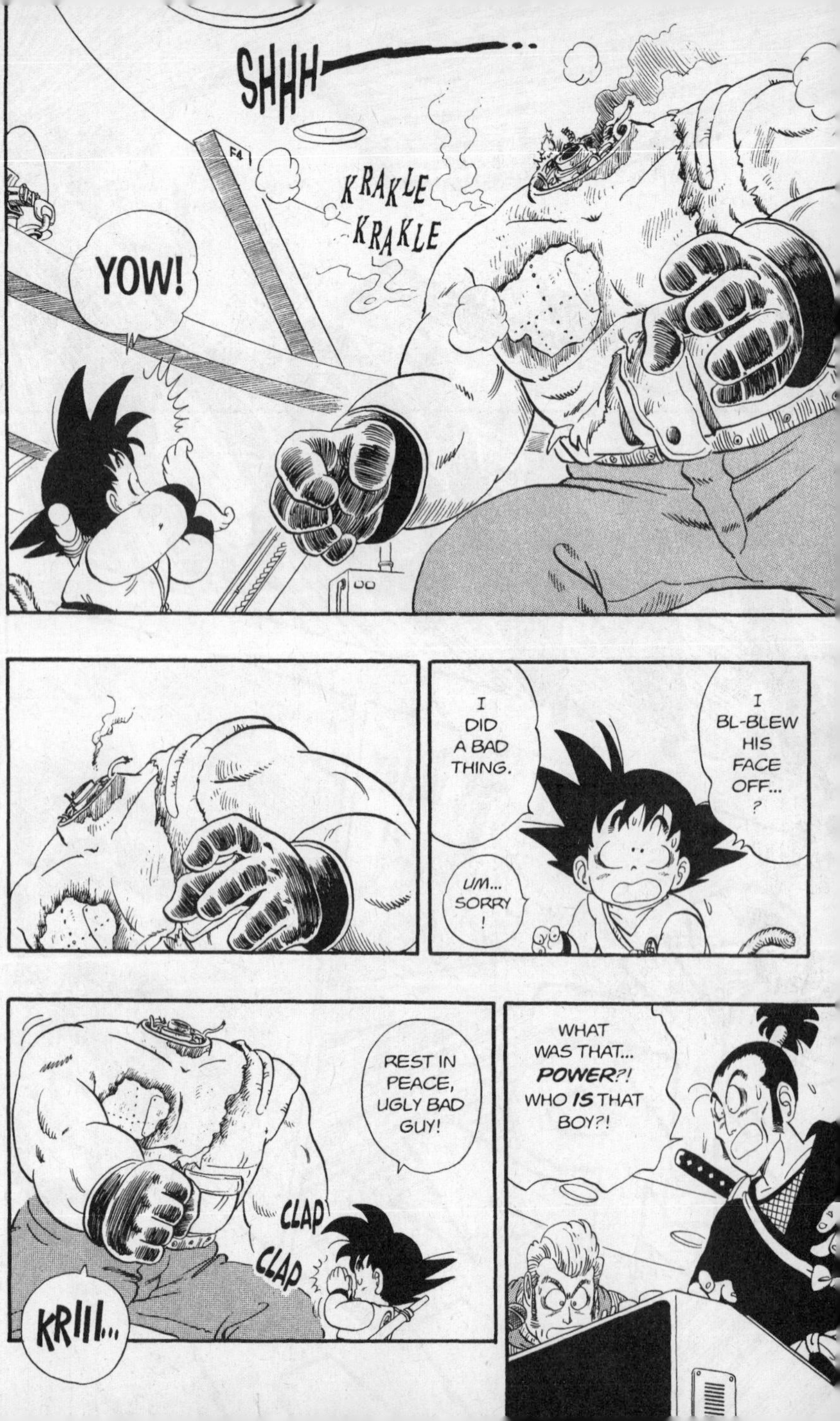
SHHH...
KRAKLE KRAKLE
YOW!
I BL-BLEW HIS FACE OFF...?
I DID A BAD THING.
UM... SORRY!
WHAT WAS THAT... **POWER**?! WHO **IS** THAT BOY?!
REST IN PEACE, UGLY BAD GUY!
CLAP
CLAP
KRIII...

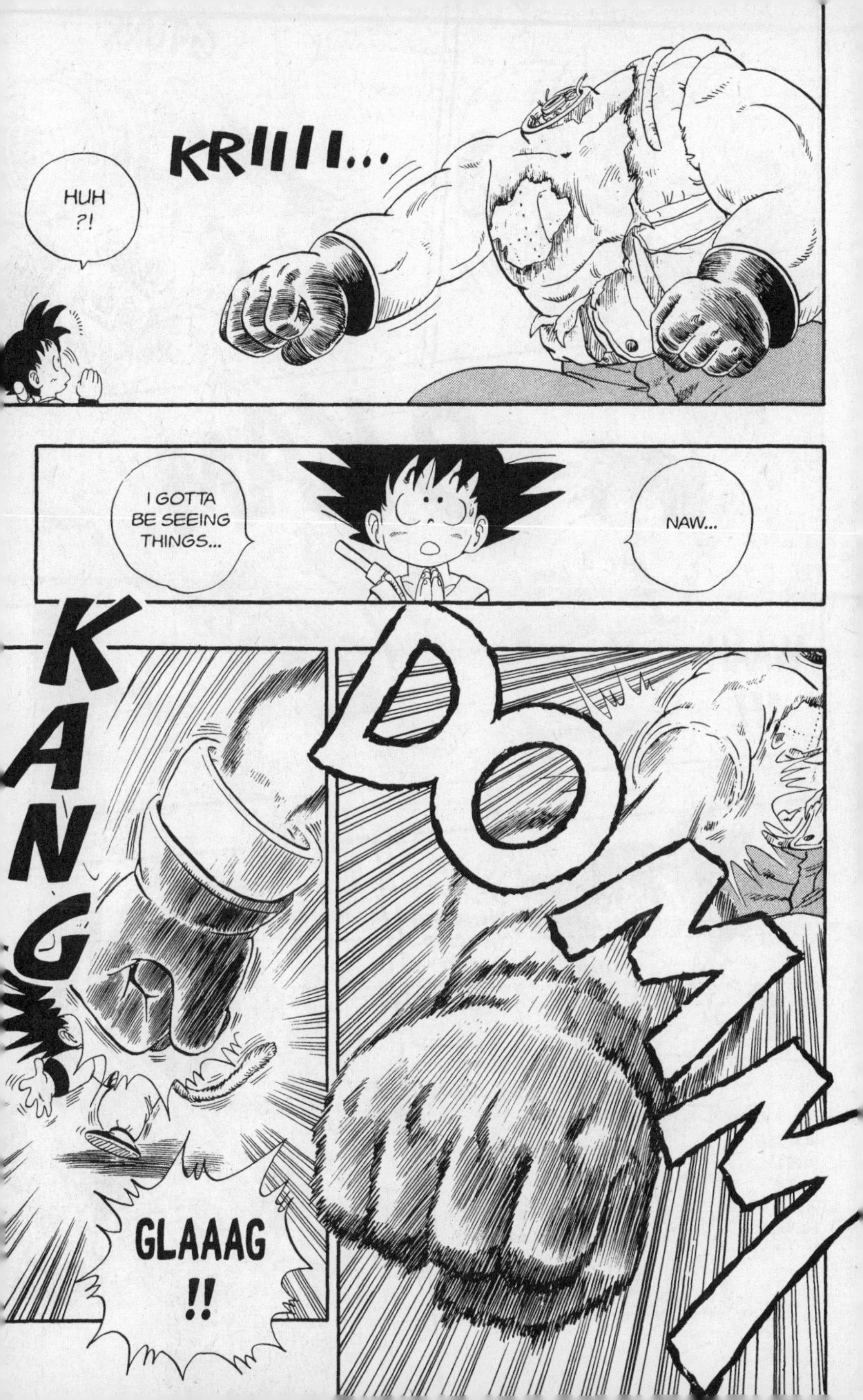
KRIIII...
HUH ?!
NAW...
I GOTTA BE SEEING THINGS...
DOMM!
KANG
GLAAG !!

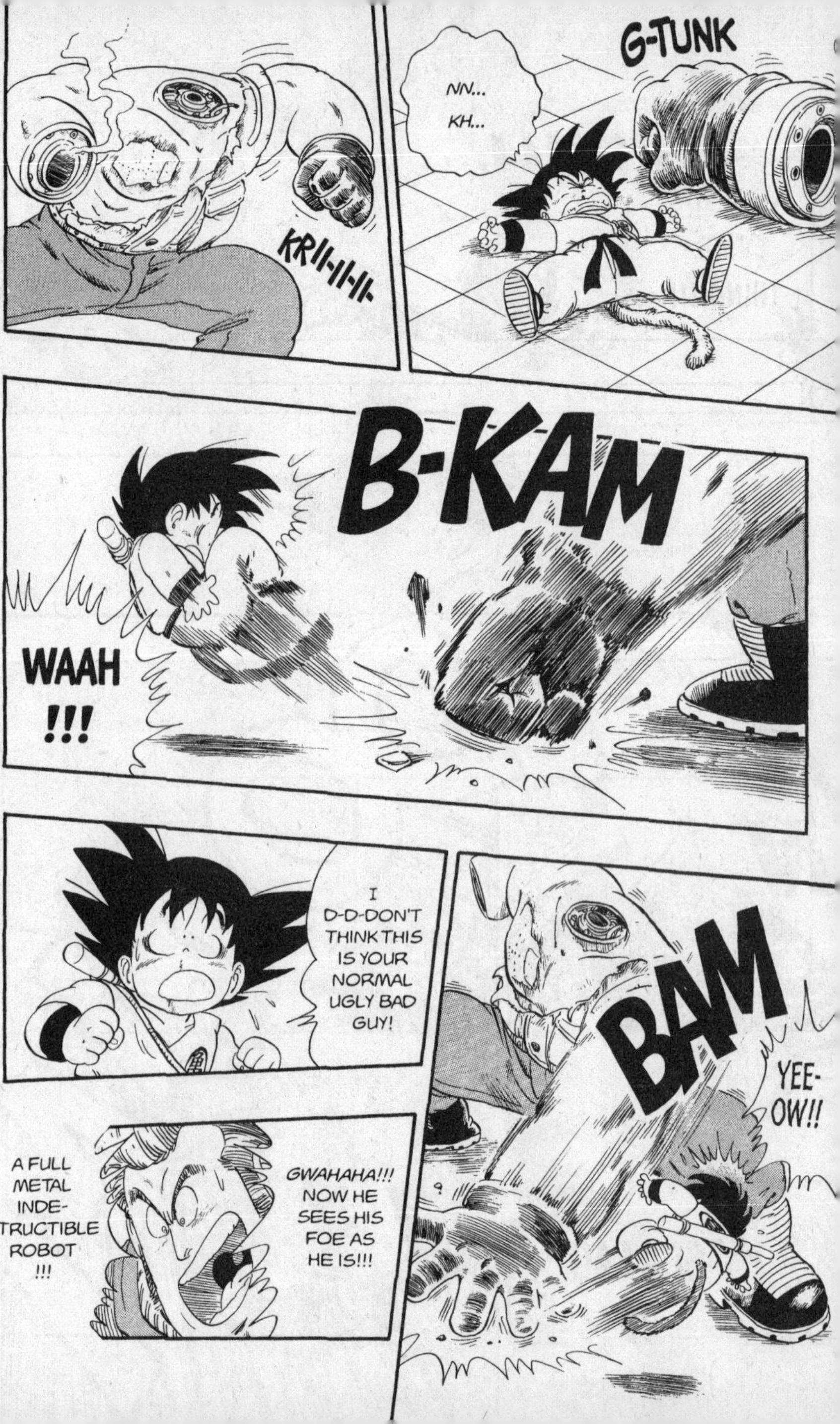
G-TUNK
NN... KH...
KRII-II-II
B-KAM
WAAH !!!
BAM
YEE-OW!!
I D-D-DON'T THINK THIS IS YOUR NORMAL UGLY BAD GUY!
GWAHAHA!!! NOW HE SEES HIS FOE AS HE IS!!!
A FULL METAL INDE-STRUCTIBLE ROBOT !!!

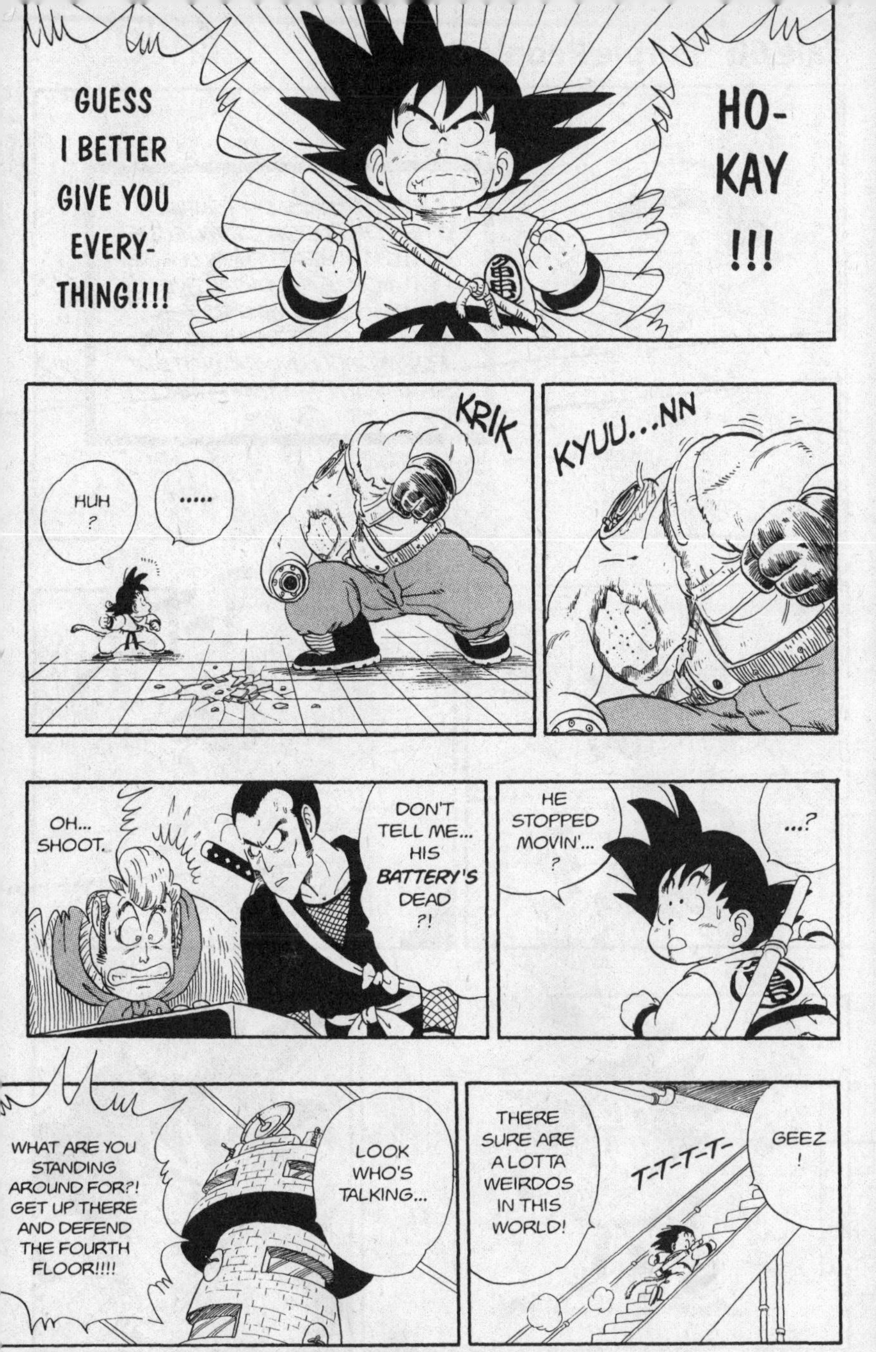
HO-KAY!!!
GUESS I BETTER GIVE YOU EVERY-THING!!!!!
KYUU...NN
KRIK
.....
HUH ?
...?
HE STOPPED MOVIN'... ?
DON'T TELL ME... HIS BATTERY'S DEAD ?!
OH... SHOOT.
GEEZ !
T-T-T-T-
THERE SURE ARE A LOTTA WEIRDOS IN THIS WORLD!
LOOK WHO'S TALKING...
WHAT ARE YOU STANDING AROUND FOR?! GET UP THERE AND DEFEND THE FOURTH FLOOR!!!!

Tale 60 • Purple People Beater

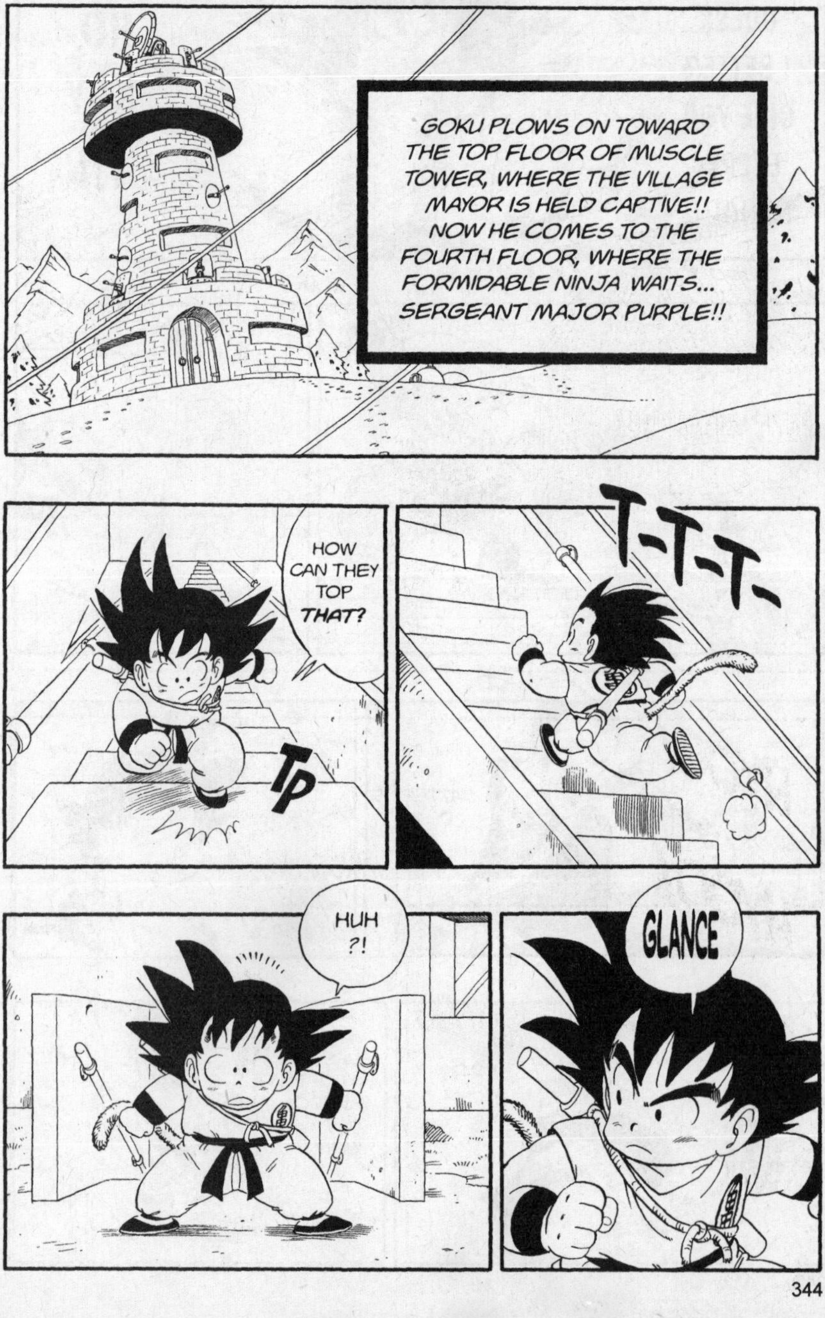
GOKU PLOWS ON TOWARD THE TOP FLOOR OF MUSCLE TOWER, WHERE THE VILLAGE MAYOR IS HELD CAPTIVE!! NOW HE COMES TO THE FOURTH FLOOR, WHERE THE FORMIDABLE NINJA WAITS... SERGEANT MAJOR PURPLE!!
T-T-T-
HOW CAN THEY TOP *THAT?*
TP
GLANCE
HUH ?!

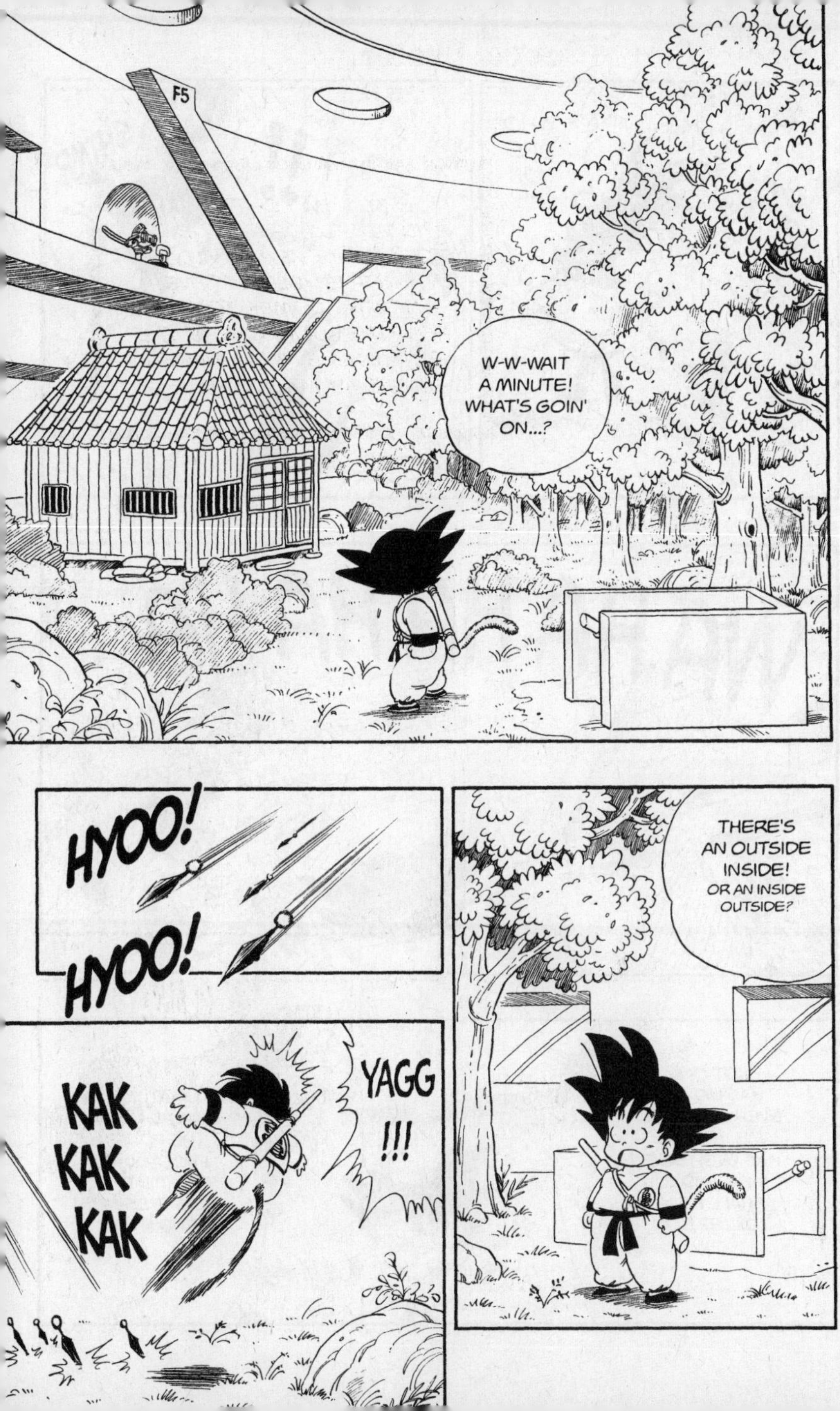

W-W-WAIT A MINUTE! WHAT'S GOIN' ON...?
THERE'S AN OUTSIDE INSIDE! OR AN INSIDE OUTSIDE?
HYOO!
HYOO!
YAGG !!!
KAK KAK KAK

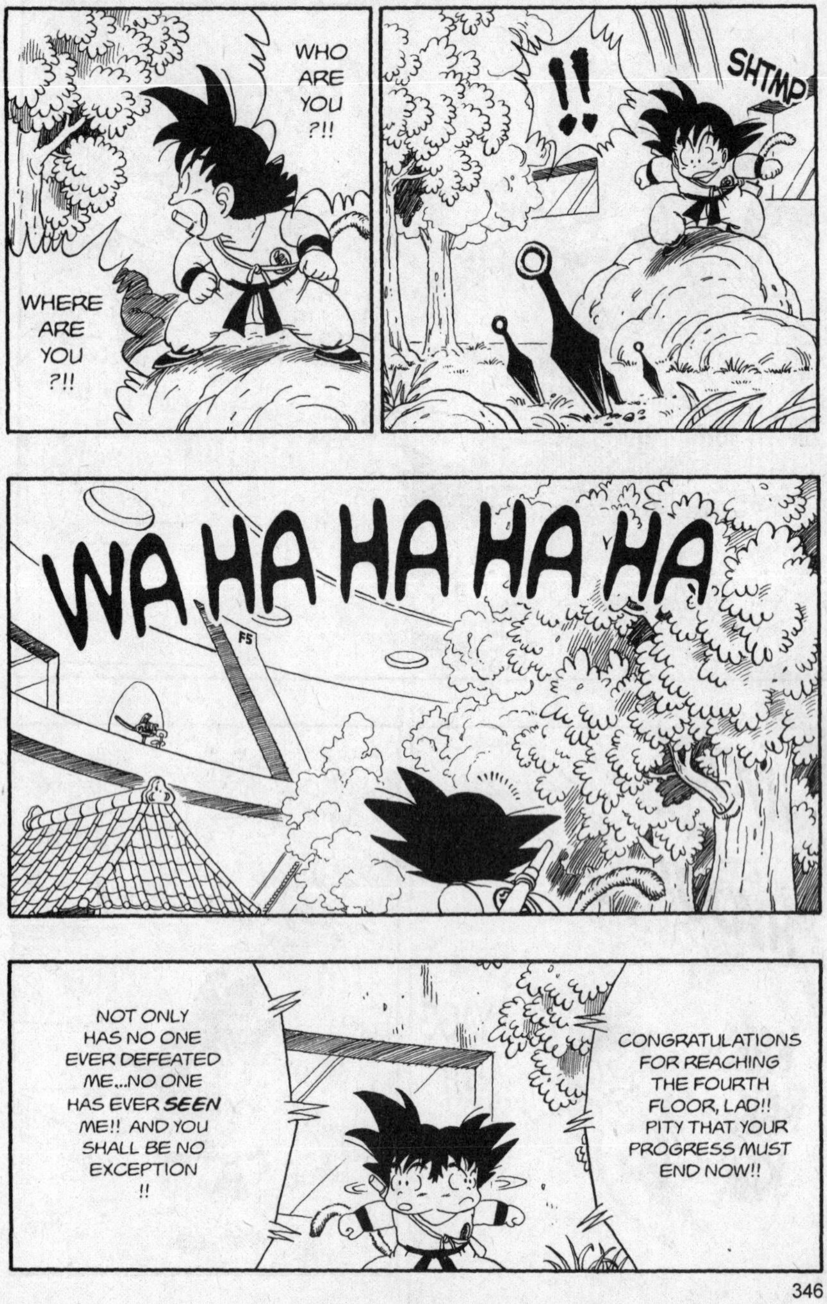
SHTMP
!!
WHO ARE YOU ?!!
WHERE ARE YOU ?!!
WA HA HA HA HA HA
F5
CONGRATULATIONS FOR REACHING THE FOURTH FLOOR, LAD!! PITY THAT YOUR PROGRESS MUST END NOW!!
NOT ONLY HAS NO ONE EVER DEFEATED ME...NO ONE HAS EVER *SEEN* ME!! AND YOU SHALL BE NO EXCEPTION !!

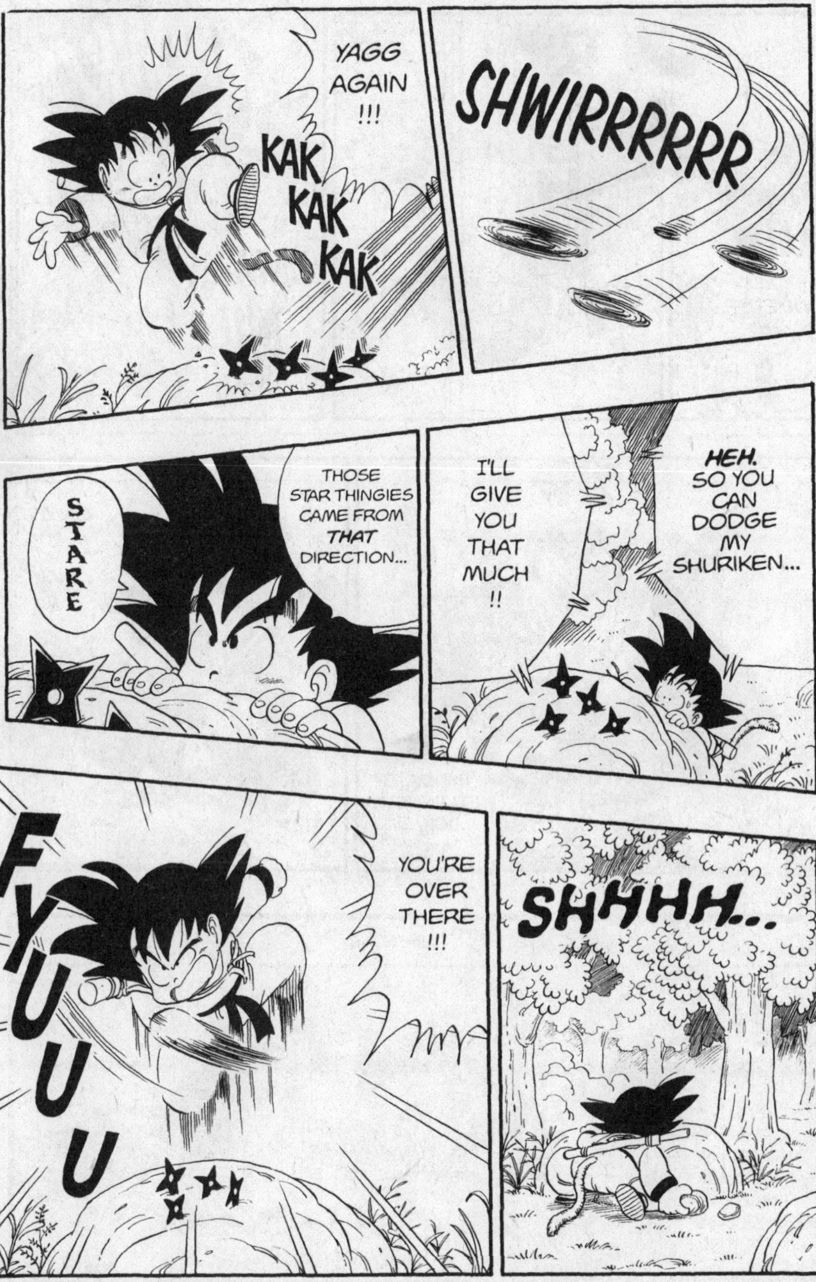
SHWIRRRRRRR
YAGG AGAIN !!!
KAK KAK KAK
HEH. SO YOU CAN DODGE MY SHURIKEN...
I'LL GIVE YOU THAT MUCH !!
THOSE STAR THINGIES CAME FROM THAT DIRECTION...
STARE
SHHHH...
YOU'RE OVER THERE !!!
FYUUUU

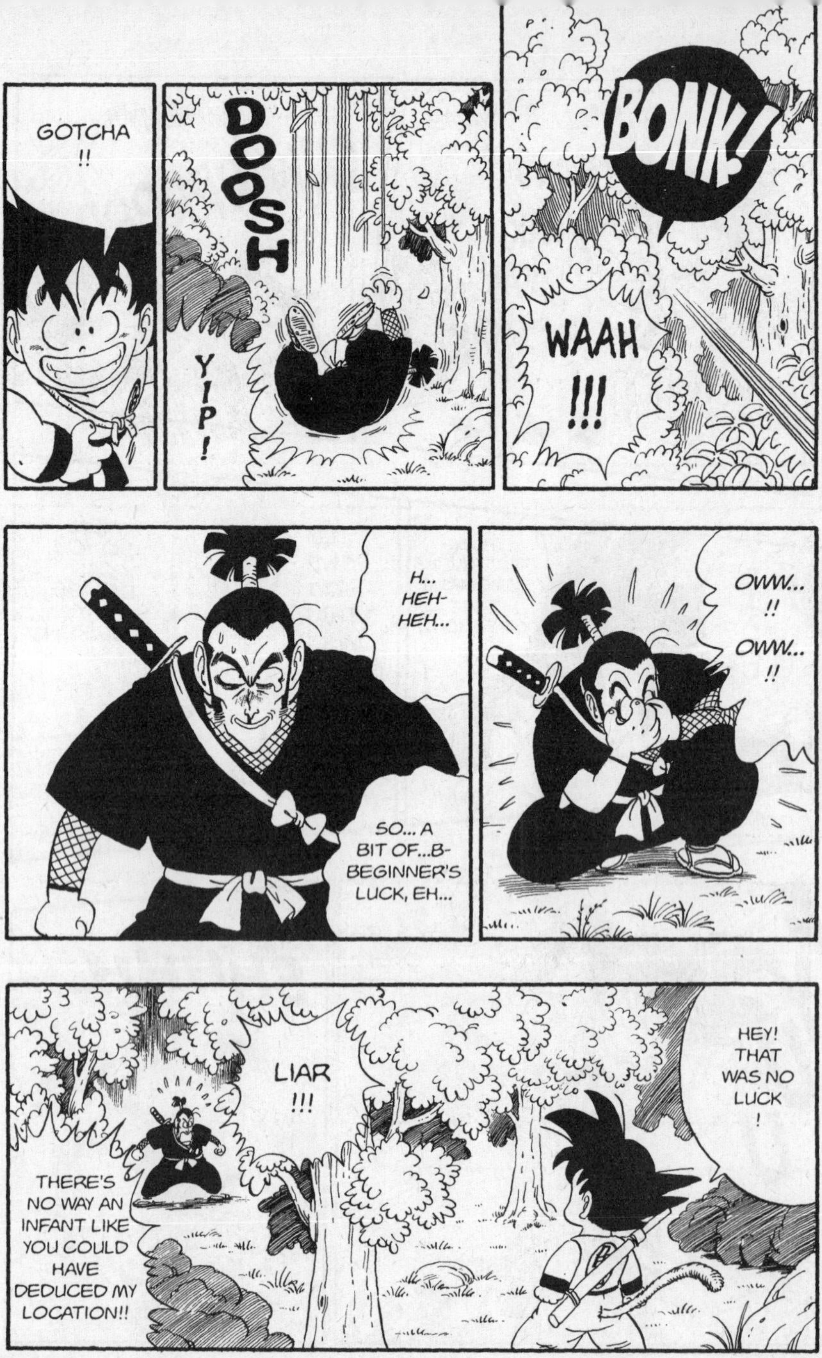
BONK!
WAAH !!!
DOOSH
YIP!
GOTCHA !!
OWW... !! OWW... !!
H... HEH-HEH...
SO... A BIT OF...B-BEGINNER'S LUCK, EH...
HEY! THAT WAS NO LUCK !
LIAR !!!
THERE'S NO WAY AN INFANT LIKE YOU COULD HAVE DEDUCED MY LOCATION!!

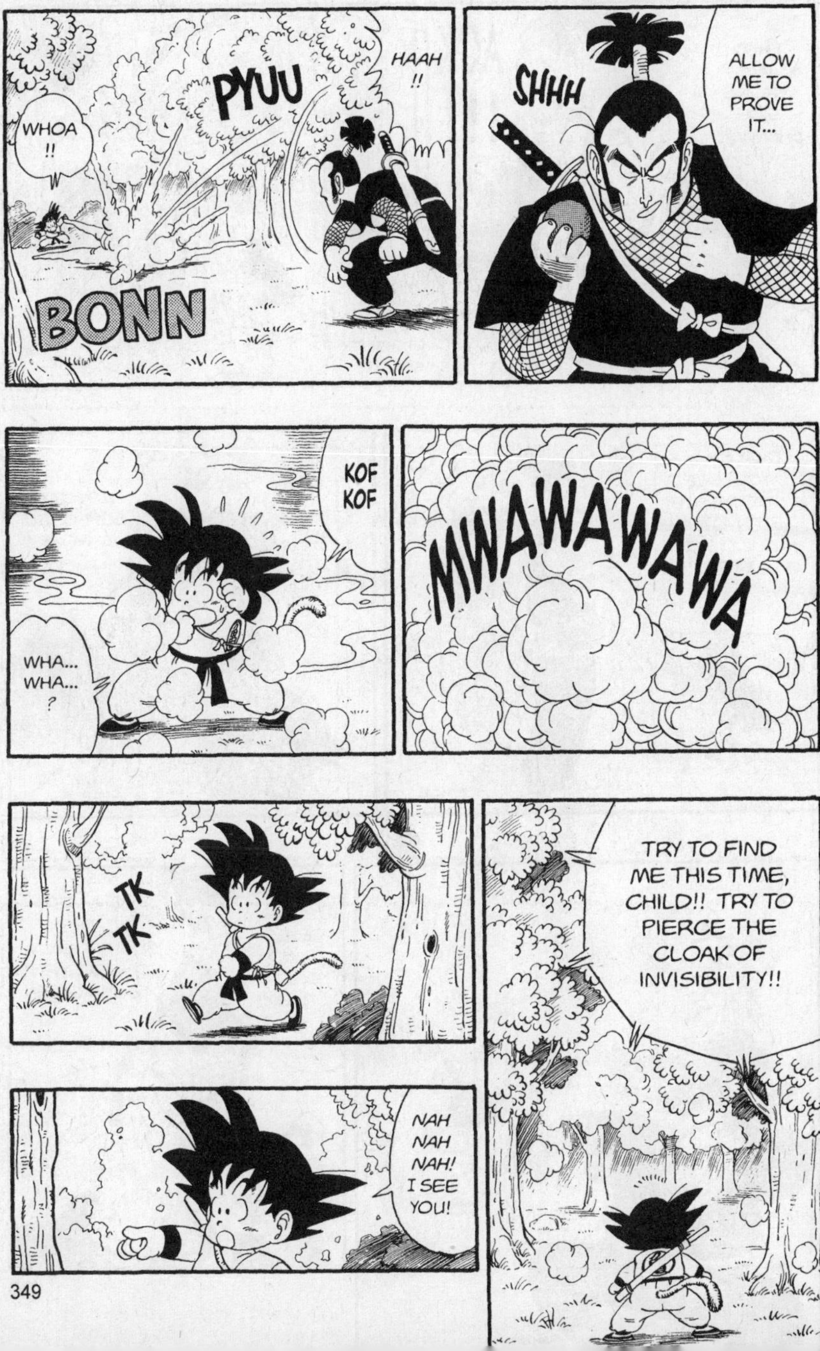
ALLOW ME TO PROVE IT...
SHHH
HAAH !!
PYUU
WHOA !!
BONN
MWAWAWAWA
KOF KOF
WHA... WHA... ?
TRY TO FIND ME THIS TIME, CHILD!! TRY TO PIERCE THE CLOAK OF INVISIBILITY!!
TK TK
NAH NAH NAH! I SEE YOU!

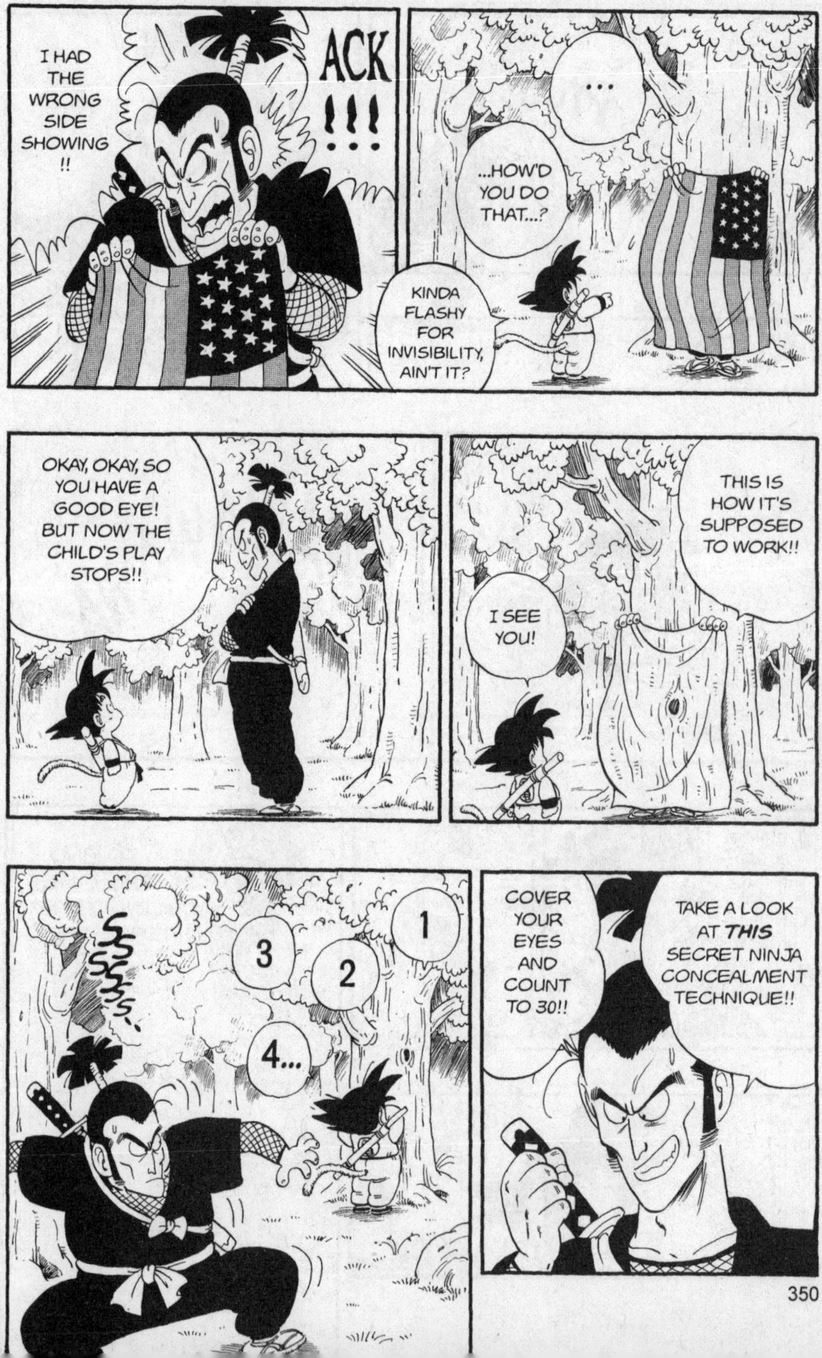
...
...HOW'D YOU DO THAT...?
KINDA FLASHY FOR INVISIBILITY, AIN'T IT?
ACK!!!...
I HAD THE WRONG SIDE SHOWING!!
THIS IS HOW IT'S SUPPOSED TO WORK!!
I SEE YOU!
OKAY, OKAY, SO YOU HAVE A GOOD EYE! BUT NOW THE CHILD'S PLAY STOPS!!
TAKE A LOOK AT **THIS** SECRET NINJA CONCEALMENT TECHNIQUE!!
COVER YOUR EYES AND COUNT TO 30!!
1
2
3
4...
SSSSSS

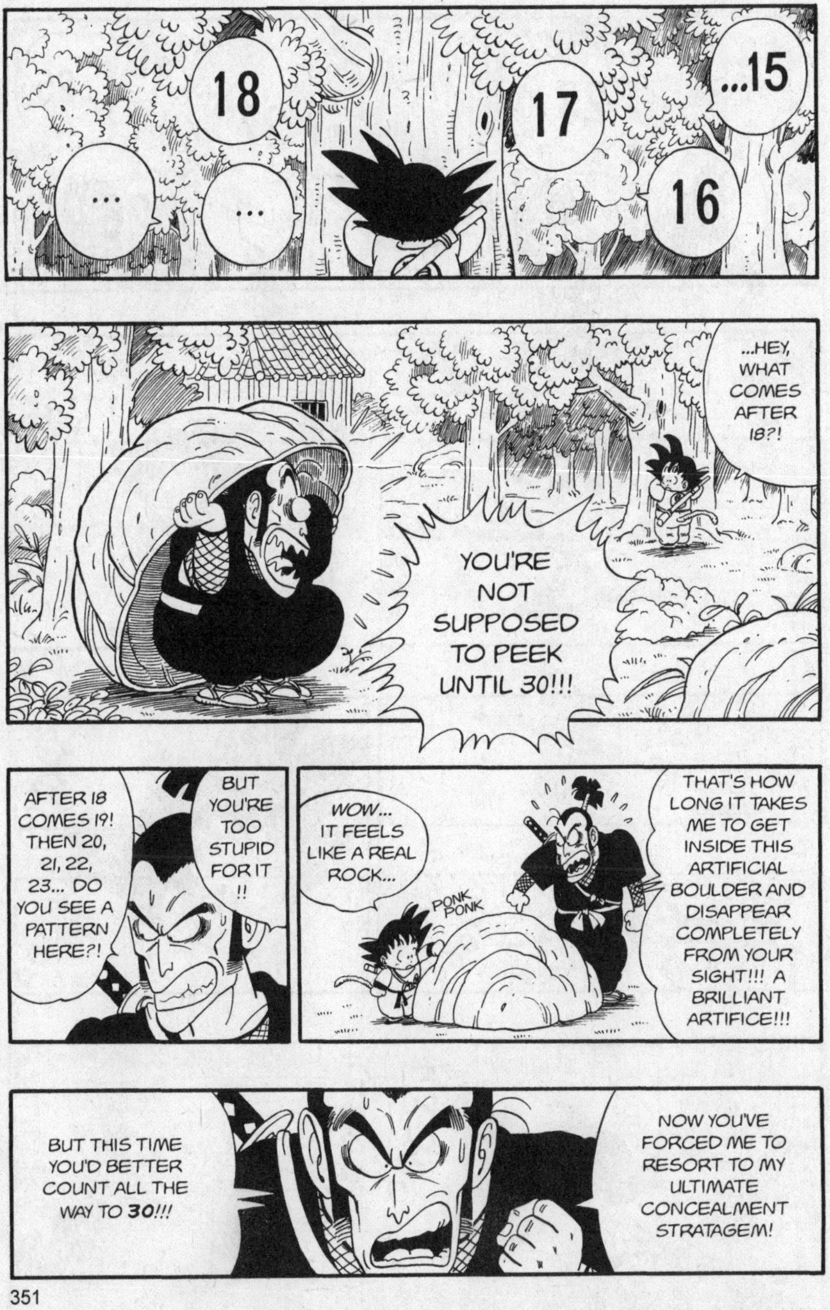

...15
16
17
18
...
...
...HEY, WHAT COMES AFTER 18?!
YOU'RE NOT SUPPOSED TO PEEK UNTIL 30!!!
THAT'S HOW LONG IT TAKES ME TO GET INSIDE THIS ARTIFICIAL BOULDER AND DISAPPEAR COMPLETELY FROM YOUR SIGHT!!! A BRILLIANT ARTIFICE!!!
WOW... IT FEELS LIKE A REAL ROCK...
PONK PONK
BUT YOU'RE TOO STUPID FOR IT!!
AFTER 18 COMES 19! THEN 20, 21, 22, 23... DO YOU SEE A PATTERN HERE?!
NOW YOU'VE FORCED ME TO RESORT TO MY ULTIMATE CONCEALMENT STRATAGEM!
BUT THIS TIME YOU'D BETTER COUNT ALL THE WAY TO 30!!!

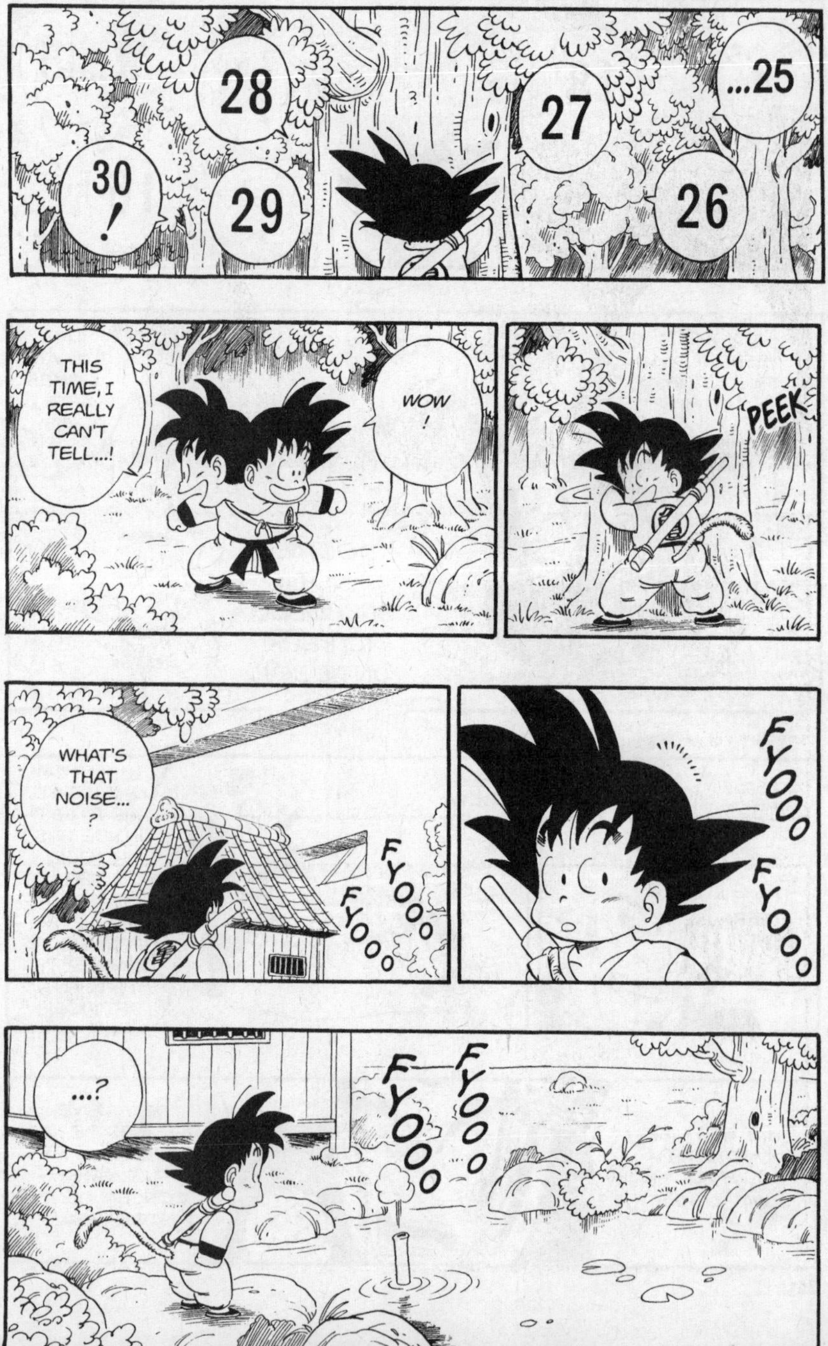
...25
26
27
28
29
30
!
PEEK
WOW
!
THIS TIME, I REALLY CAN'T TELL...!
FYOOOO
FYOOOO
WHAT'S THAT NOISE...
?
FYOOOO
FYOOOO
FYOOOO
FYOOOO
...?

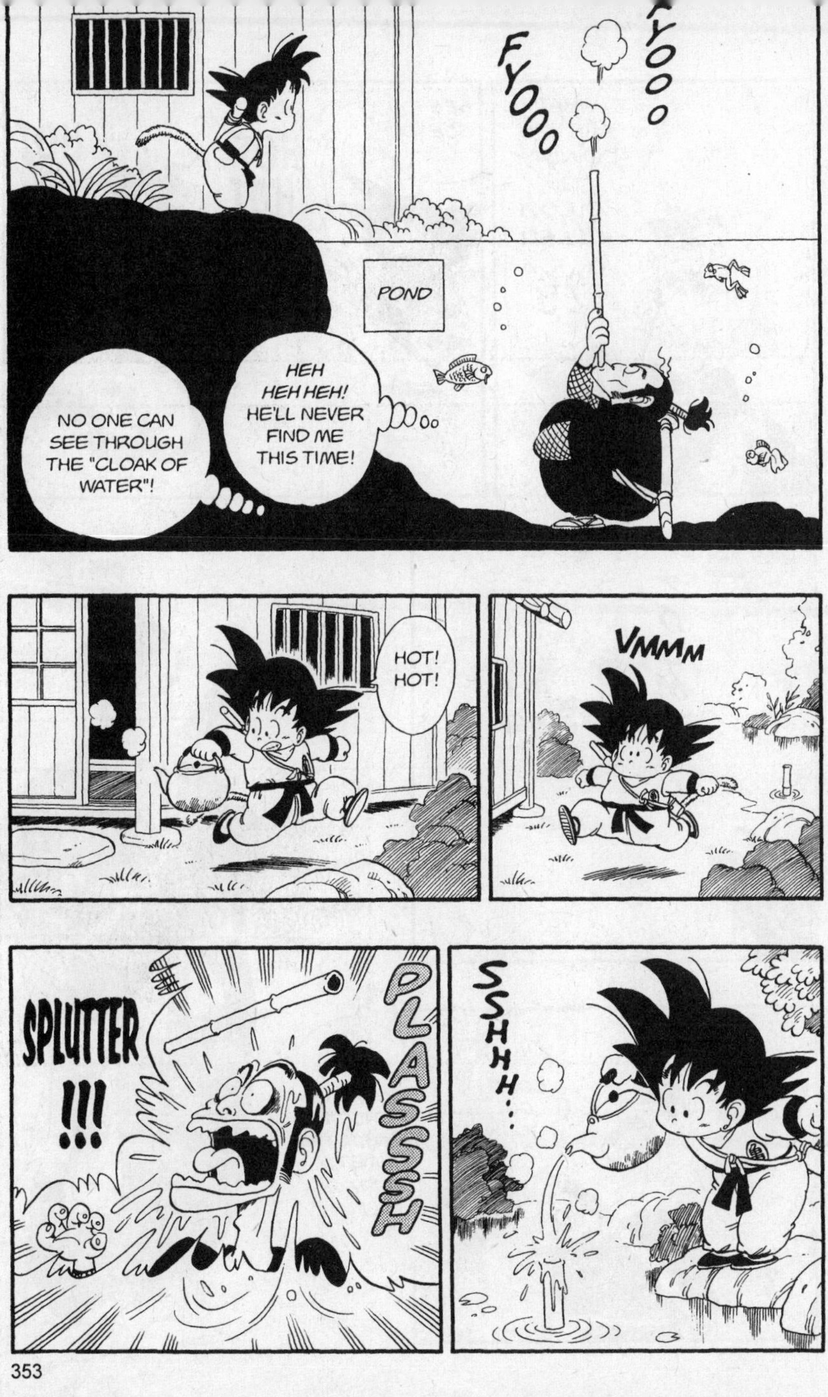
FYOOO
FYOOO
POND
HEH HEH HEH! HE'LL NEVER FIND ME THIS TIME!
NO ONE CAN SEE THROUGH THE "CLOAK OF WATER"!
VMMM
HOT! HOT!
SSHHH...
PLASSSH
SPLUTTER!!!

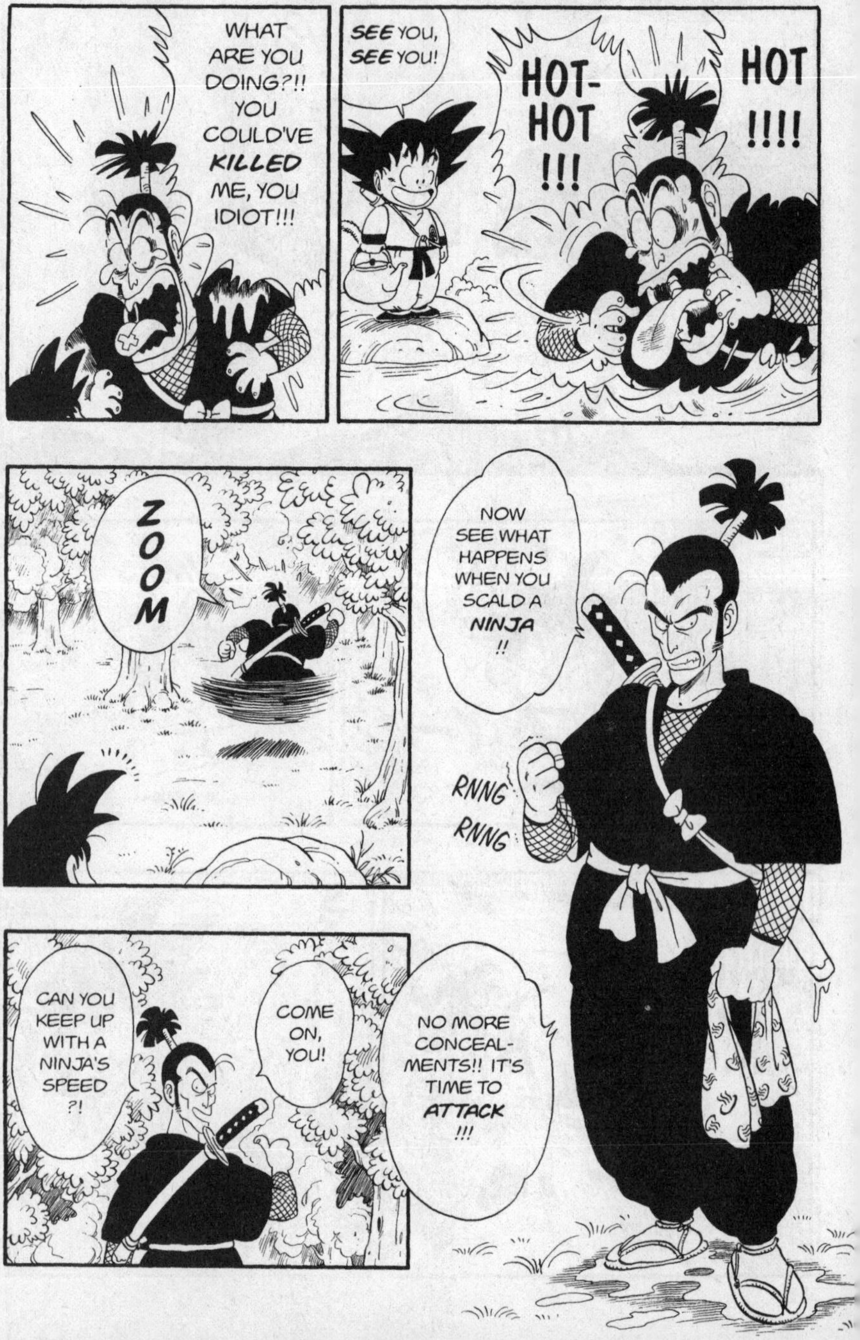
HOT !!!!
HOT-HOT !!!
SEE YOU, SEE YOU!
WHAT ARE YOU DOING?!! YOU COULD'VE KILLED ME, YOU IDIOT!!!
NOW SEE WHAT HAPPENS WHEN YOU SCALD A NINJA !!
RNNG RNNG
NO MORE CONCEAL-MENTS!! IT'S TIME TO ATTACK !!!
ZOOM
COME ON, YOU!
CAN YOU KEEP UP WITH A NINJA'S SPEED ?!

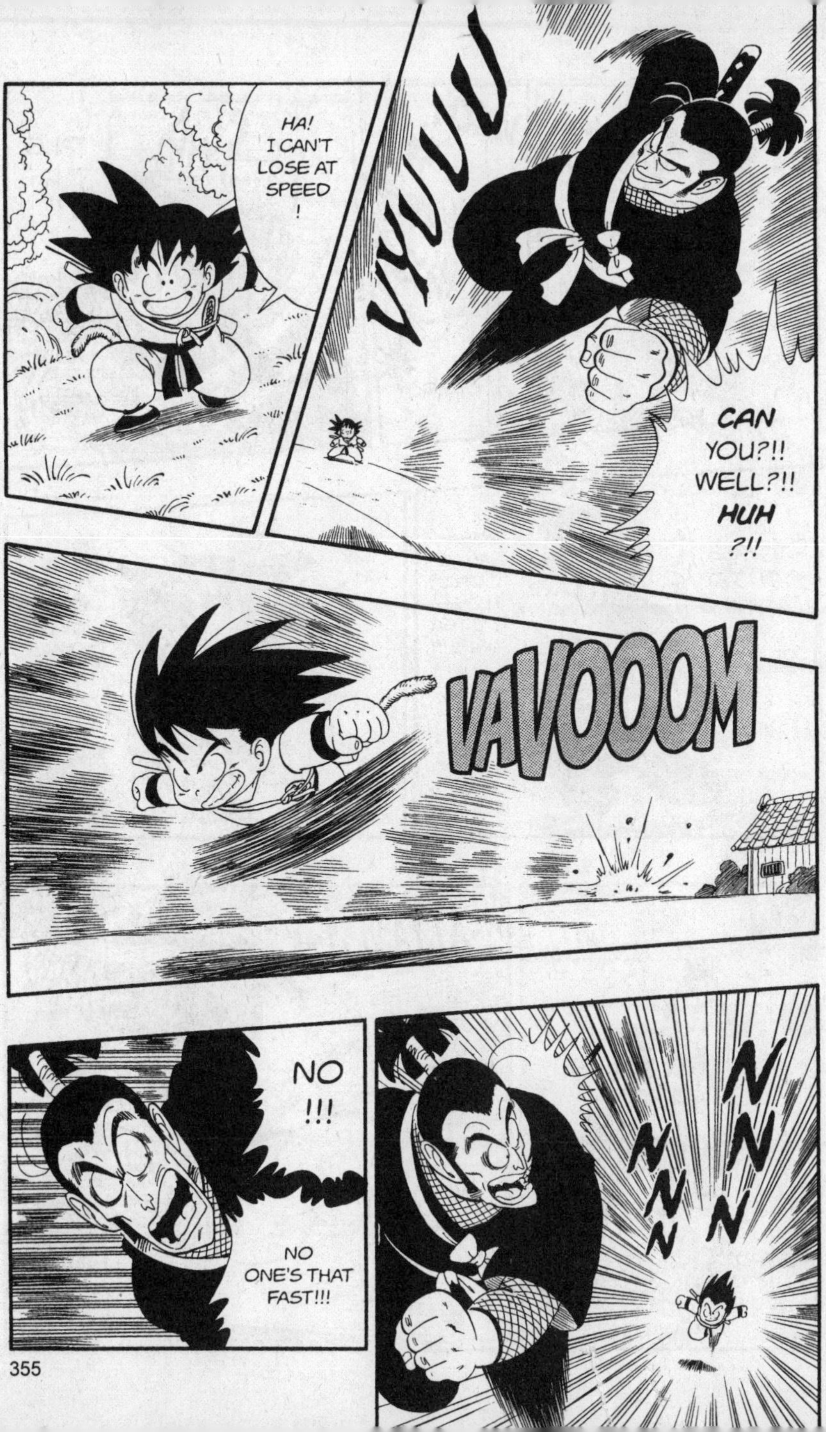
HA! I CAN'T LOSE AT SPEED !
VYUUU
CAN YOU?!! WELL?!! HUH ?!!
VAVOOOM
NO !!!
NO ONE'S THAT FAST!!!
NNNNNNNN

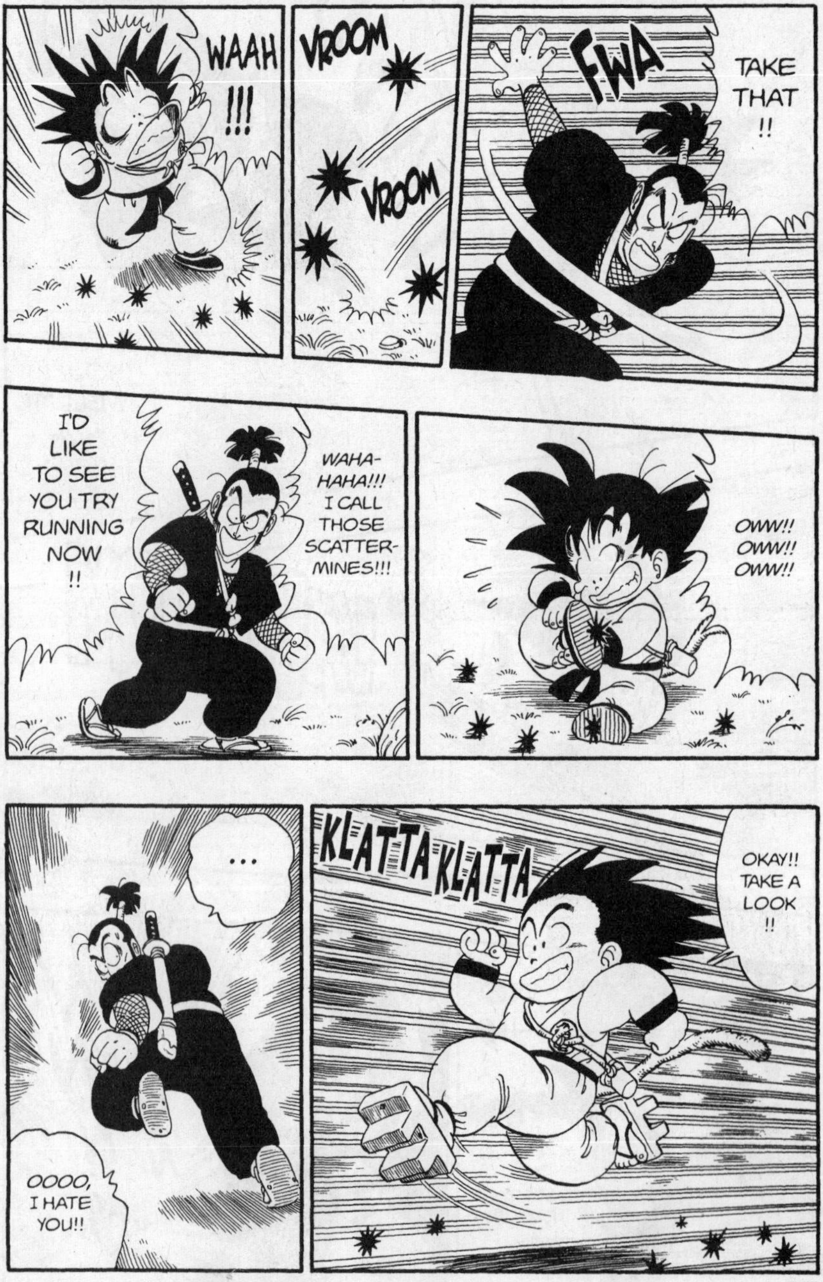
TAKE THAT!!
FWA
VROOM
VROOM
WAAH!!!
OWW!! OWW!! OWW!!
WAHA-HAHA!!! I CALL THOSE SCATTER-MINES!!!
I'D LIKE TO SEE YOU TRY RUNNING NOW!!
OKAY!! TAKE A LOOK!!
KLATTA KLATTA
...
OOOO, I HATE YOU!!

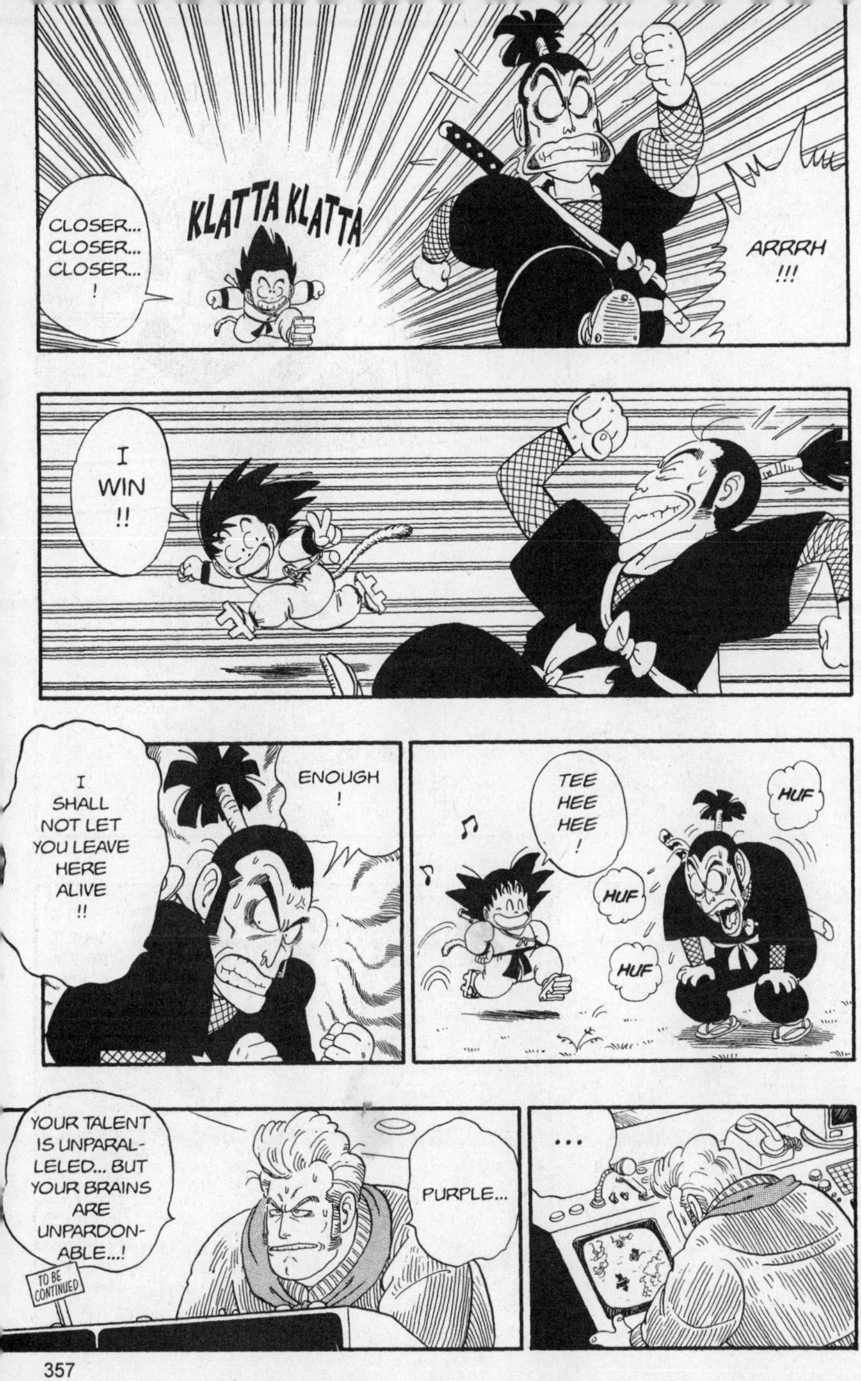
ARRRH !!!
KLATTA KLATTA
CLOSER... CLOSER... CLOSER... !
I WIN !!
HUF
TEE HEE HEE !
HUF
HUF
ENOUGH !
I SHALL NOT LET YOU LEAVE HERE ALIVE !!
...
PURPLE...
YOUR TALENT IS UNPARAL-LELED... BUT YOUR BRAINS ARE UNPARDON-ABLE...!
TO BE CONTINUED

Dragonball

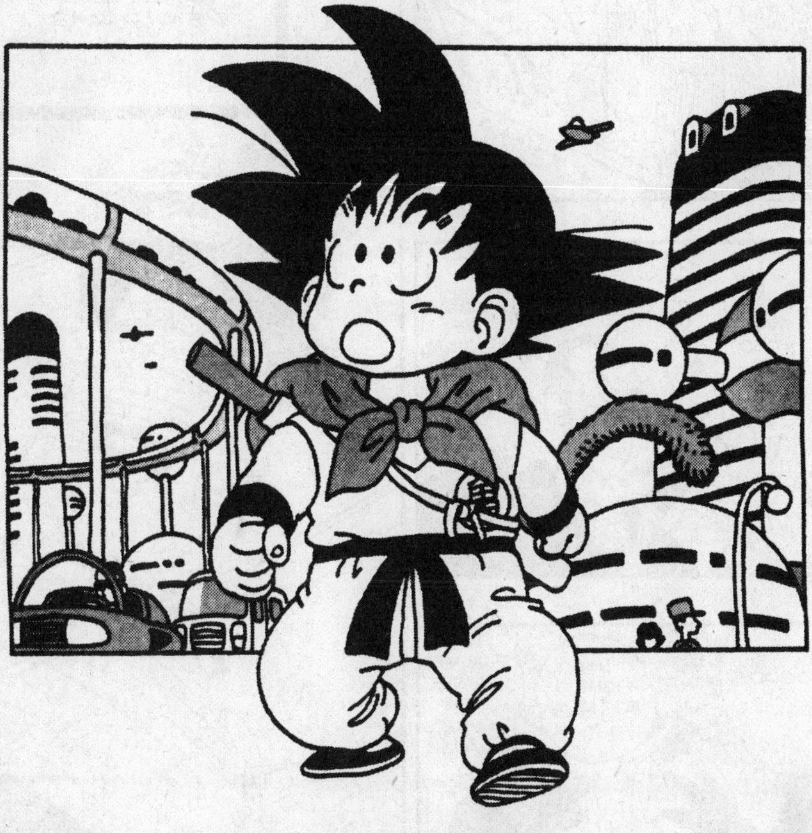

VOLUME 6

BULMA RETURNS

Tale 61 · The 4 ½ Tatami Mat Flip

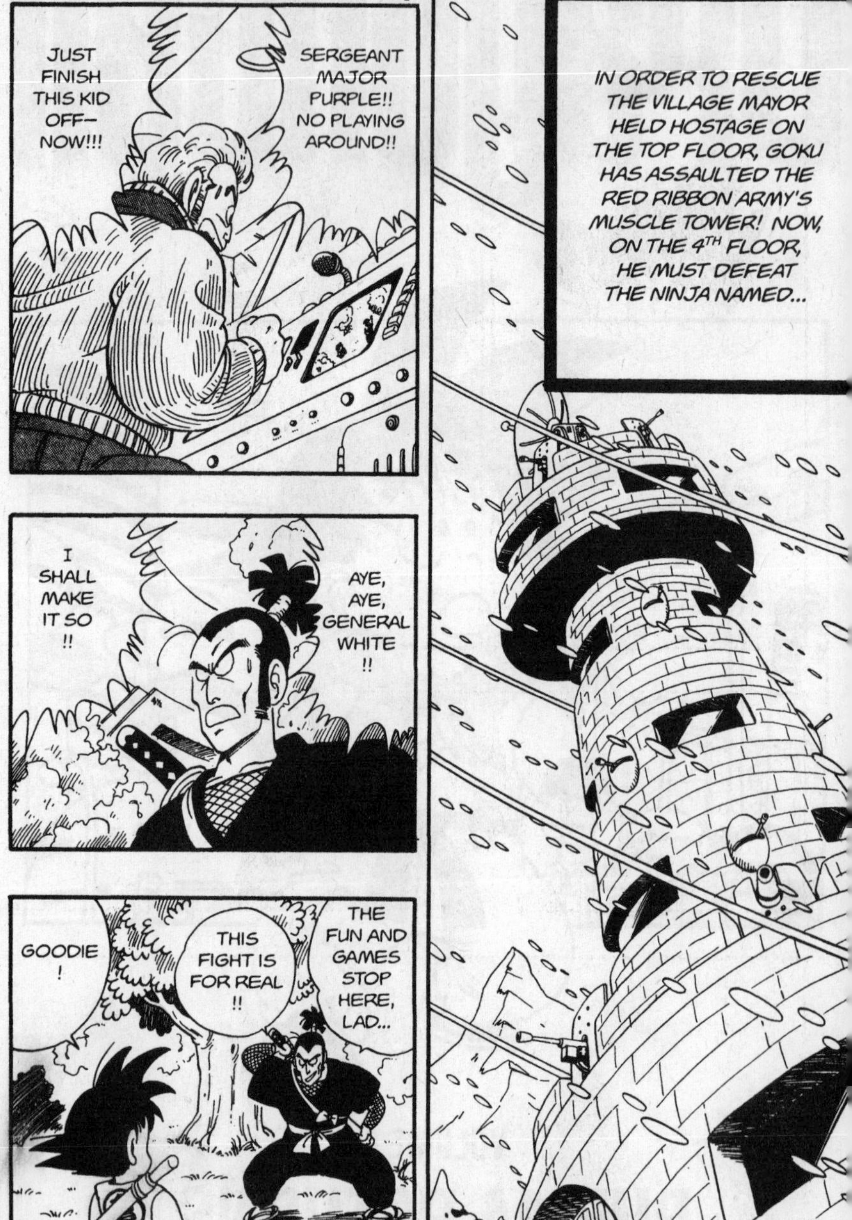
IN ORDER TO RESCUE THE VILLAGE MAYOR HELD HOSTAGE ON THE TOP FLOOR, GOKU HAS ASSAULTED THE RED RIBBON ARMY'S MUSCLE TOWER! NOW, ON THE 4TH FLOOR, HE MUST DEFEAT THE NINJA NAMED...
SERGEANT MAJOR PURPLE!! NO PLAYING AROUND!!
JUST FINISH THIS KID OFF— NOW!!!
AYE, AYE, GENERAL WHITE!!
I SHALL MAKE IT SO!!
THE FUN AND GAMES STOP HERE, LAD...
THIS FIGHT IS FOR REAL!!
GOODIE!

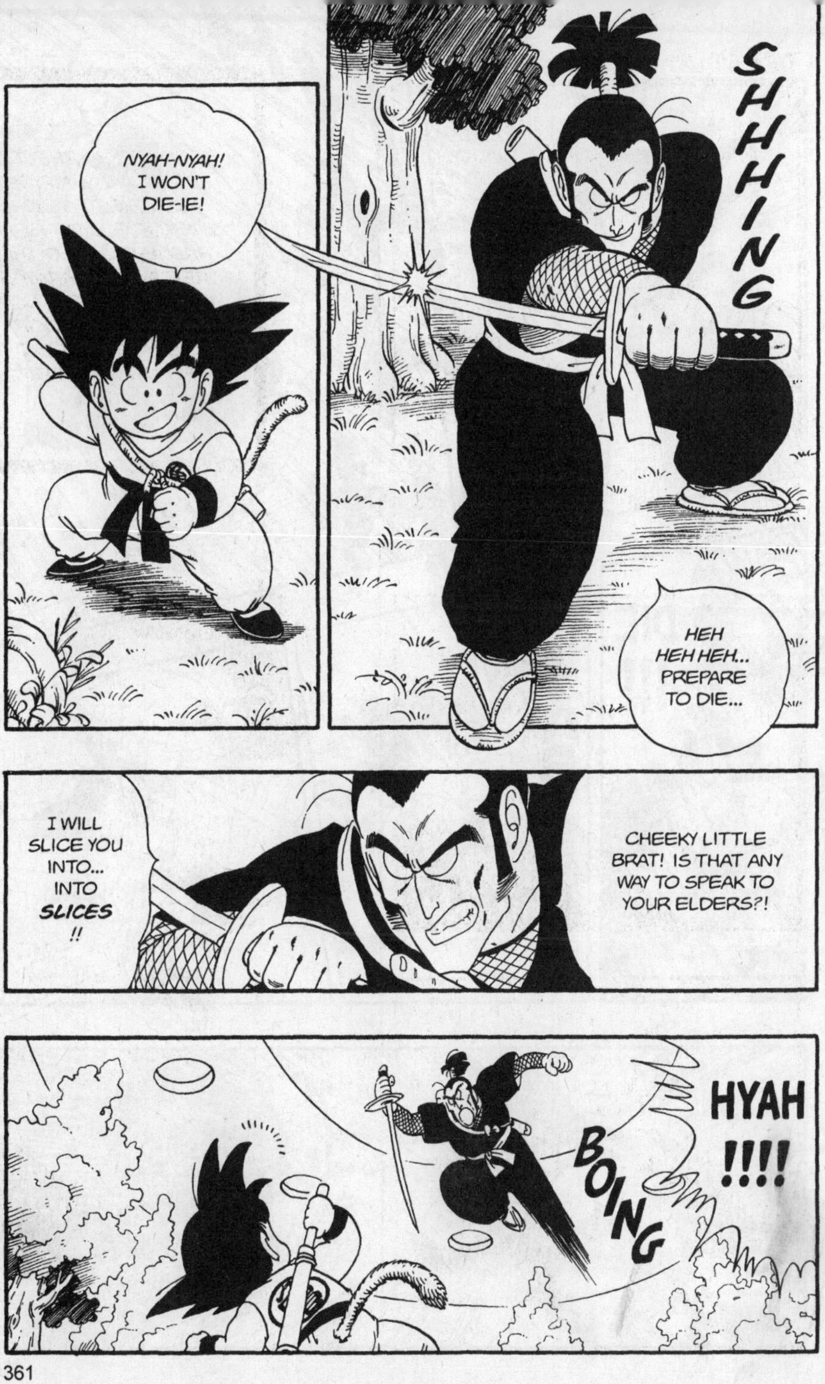
SHHHING
HEH HEH HEH... PREPARE TO DIE...
NYAH-NYAH! I WON'T DIE-IE!
CHEEKY LITTLE BRAT! IS THAT ANY WAY TO SPEAK TO YOUR ELDERS?!
I WILL SLICE YOU INTO... INTO SLICES !!
HYAH !!!!
BOING

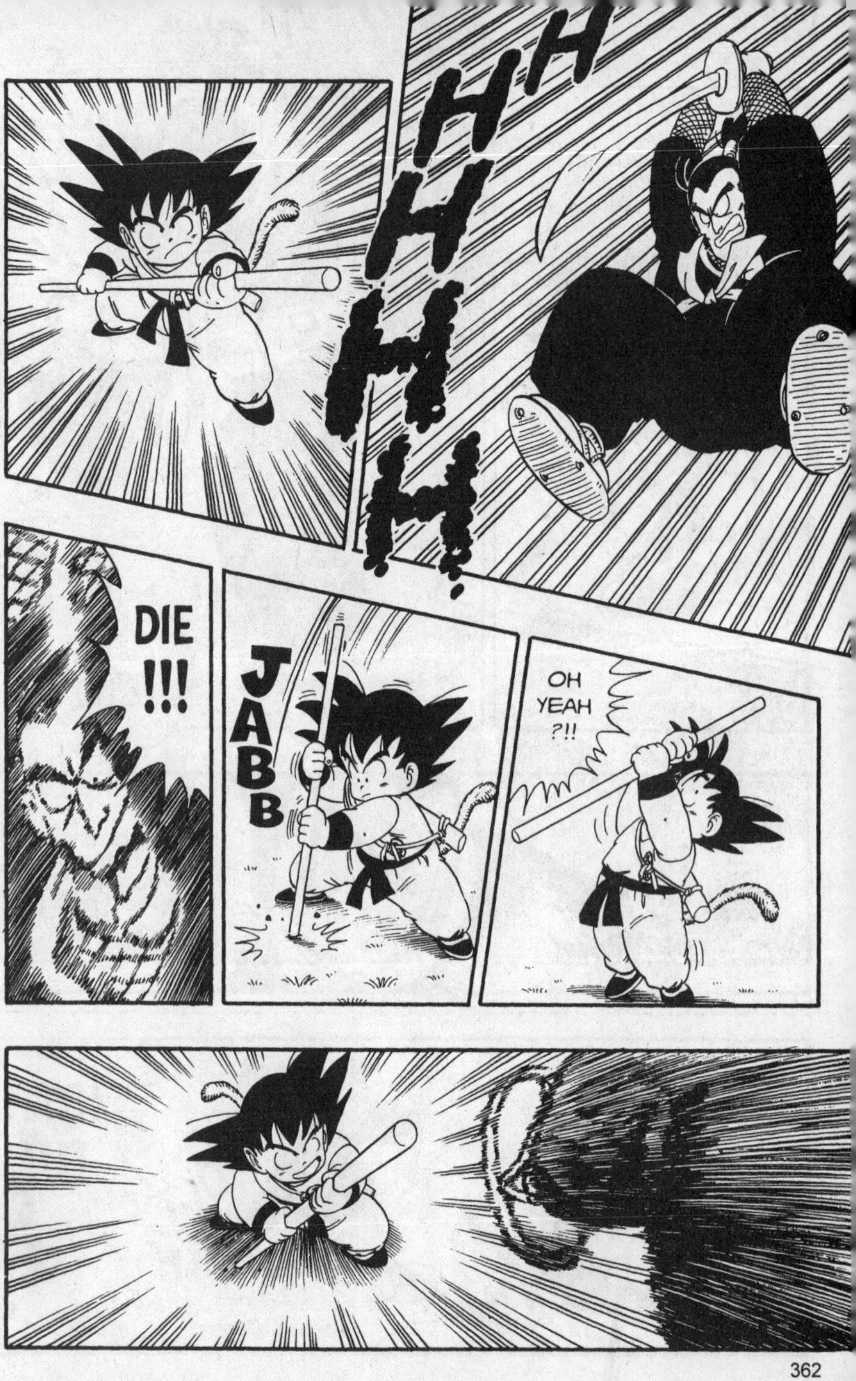
HHHHHH
OH YEAH ?!!
JABB
DIE !!!

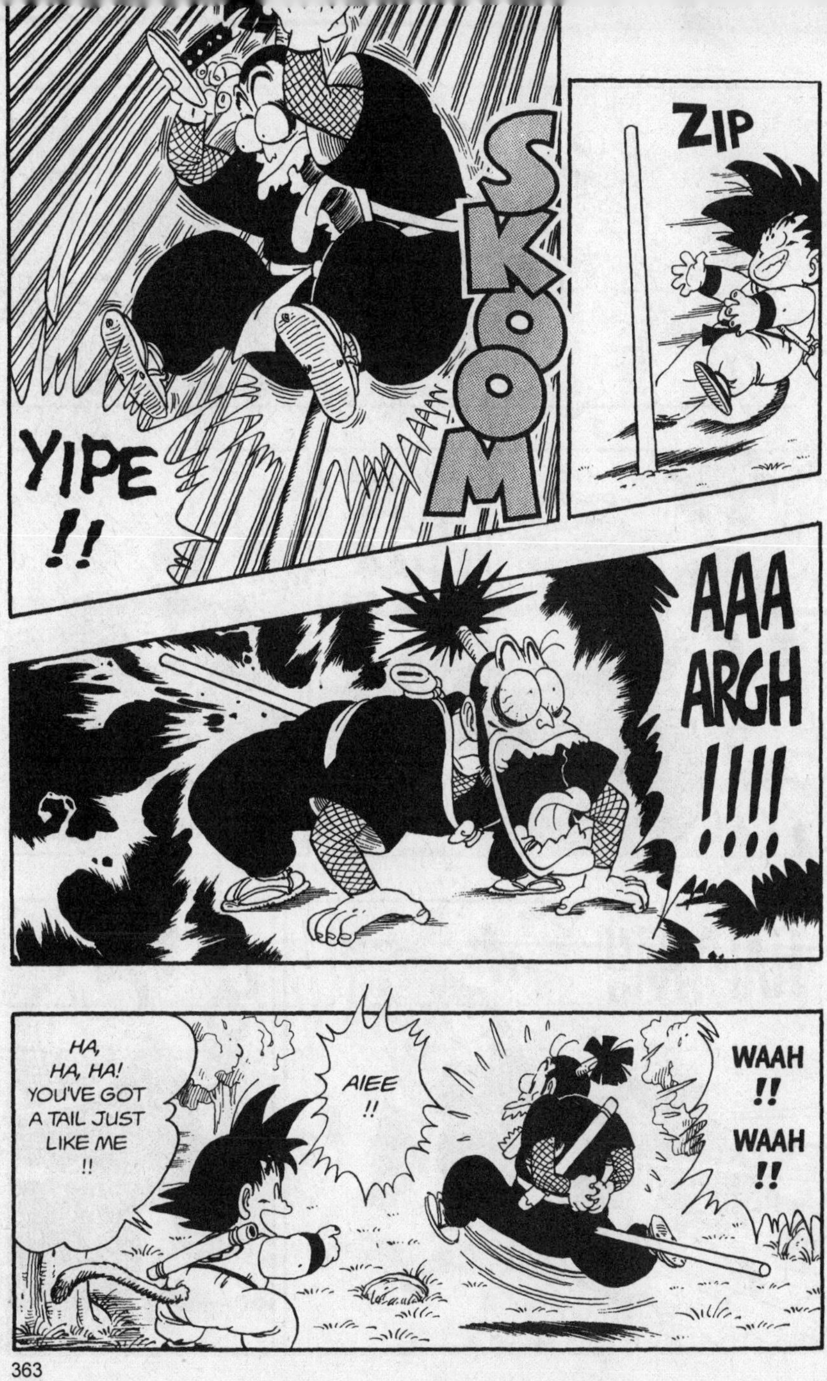
ZIP
SKOOM
YIPE !!
AAA ARGH !!!!
WAAH !! WAAH !!
AIEE !!
HA, HA, HA! YOU'VE GOT A TAIL JUST LIKE ME !!

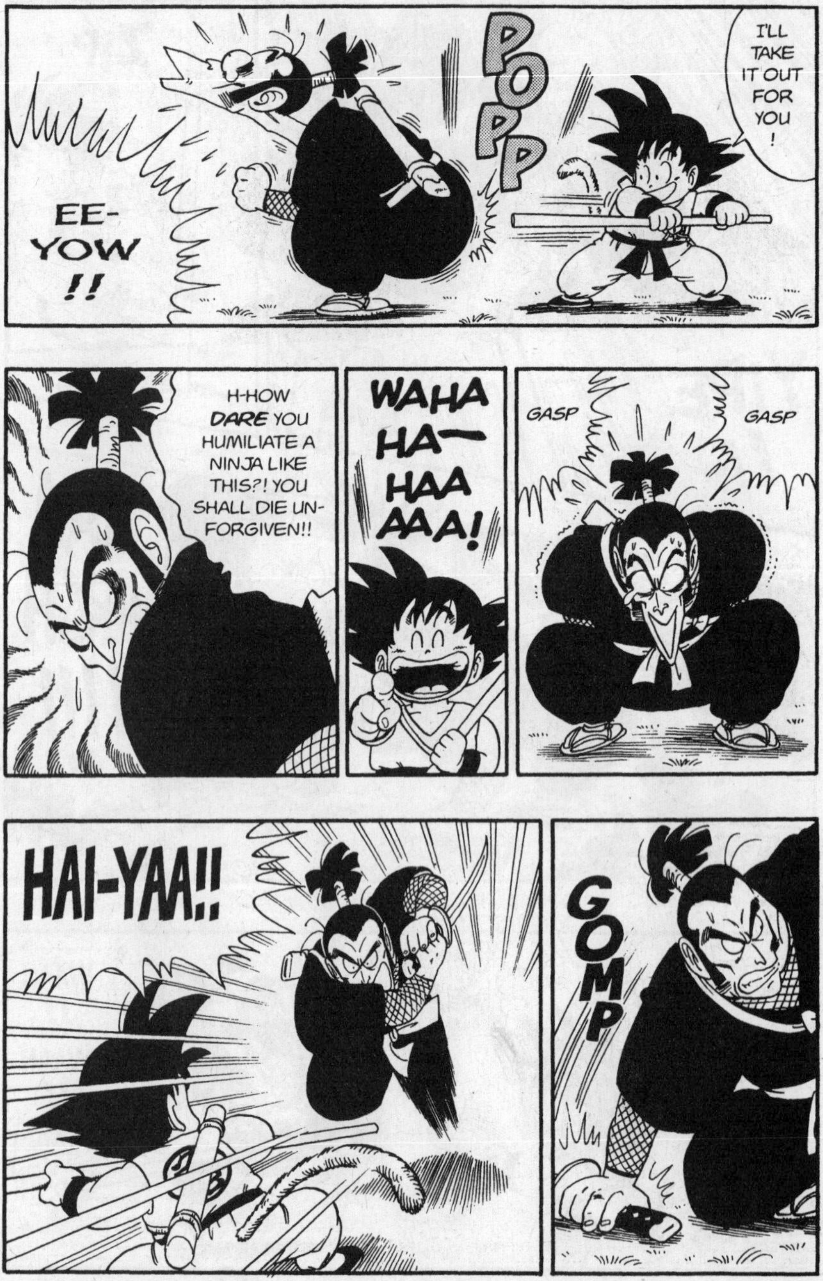

I'LL TAKE IT OUT FOR YOU!
POPP
EE-YOW!!
GASP
GASP
WAHA HA-HAA AAA!
H-HOW DARE YOU HUMILIATE A NINJA LIKE THIS?! YOU SHALL DIE UN-FORGIVEN!!
GOMP
HAI-YAA!!

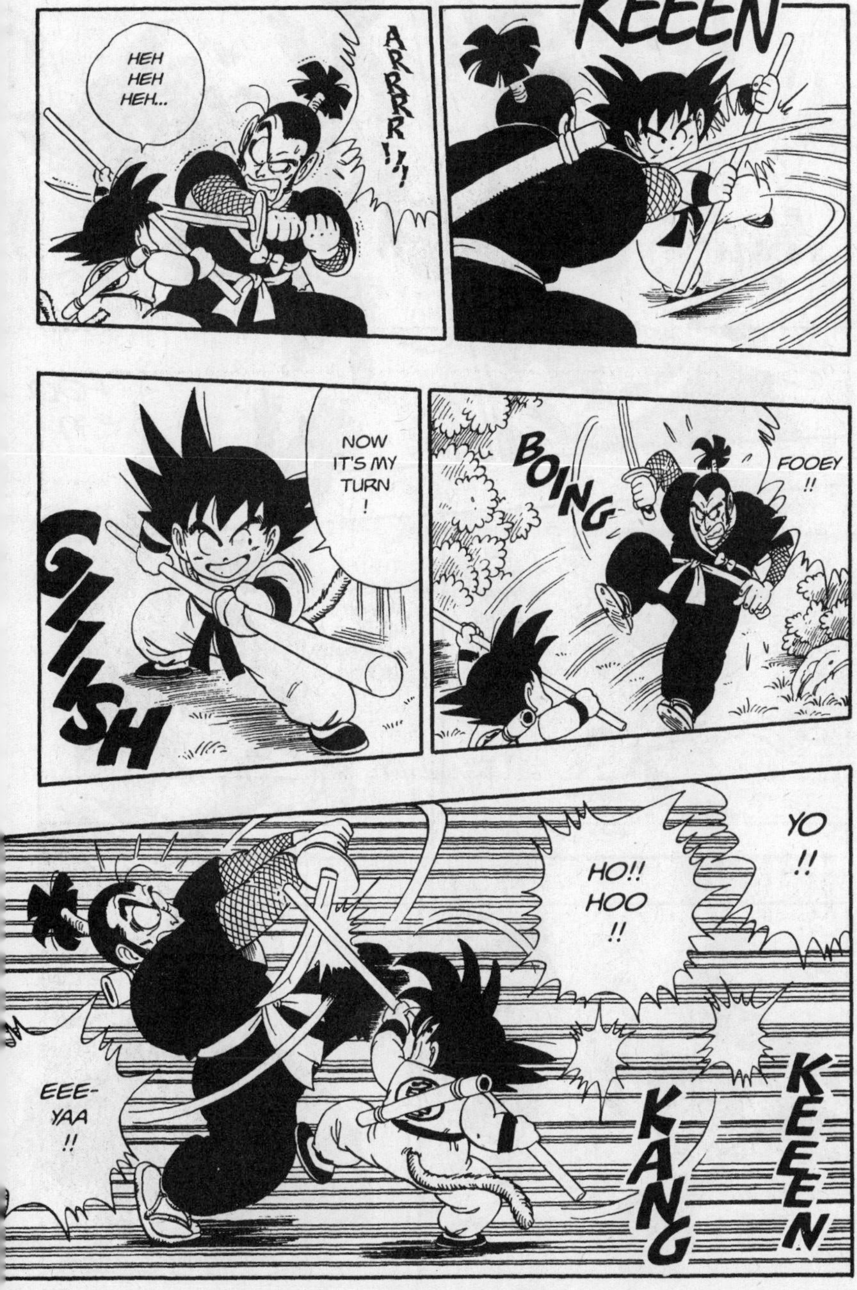
KEEEN
ARRRR!!!
HEH HEH HEH...
FOOEY!!
BOING
NOW IT'S MY TURN!
GIIISH
YO!!
HO!! HOO!!
KEEEN
KANG
EEE-YAA!!

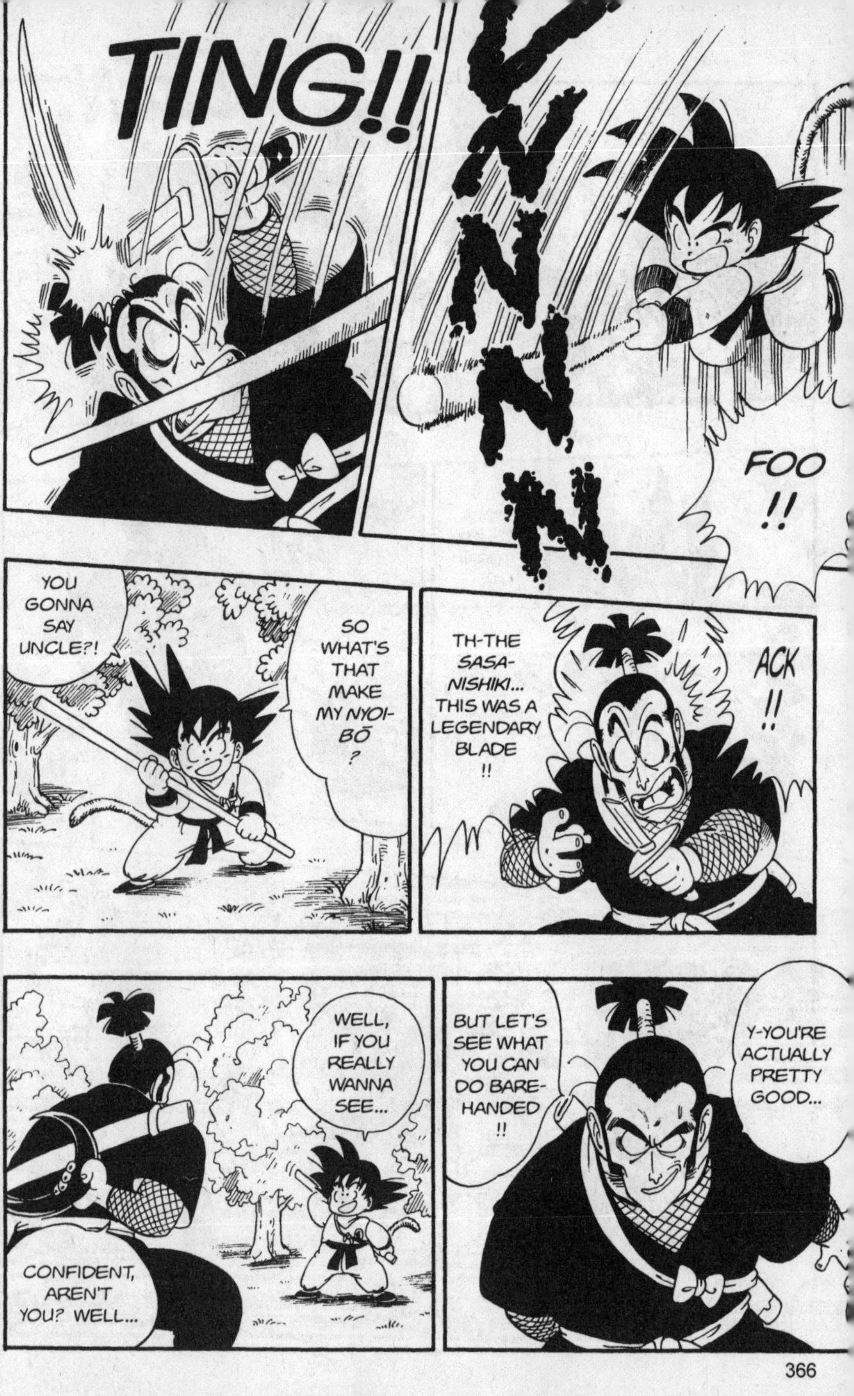
VNNNN
FOO !!
TING!!
TH-THE *SASA-NISHIKI*... THIS WAS A LEGENDARY BLADE !!
ACK !!
SO WHAT'S THAT MAKE MY *NYOI-BŌ*?
YOU GONNA SAY UNCLE?!
Y-YOU'RE ACTUALLY PRETTY GOOD...
BUT LET'S SEE WHAT YOU CAN DO BARE-HANDED !!
WELL, IF YOU REALLY WANNA SEE...
CONFIDENT, AREN'T YOU? WELL...

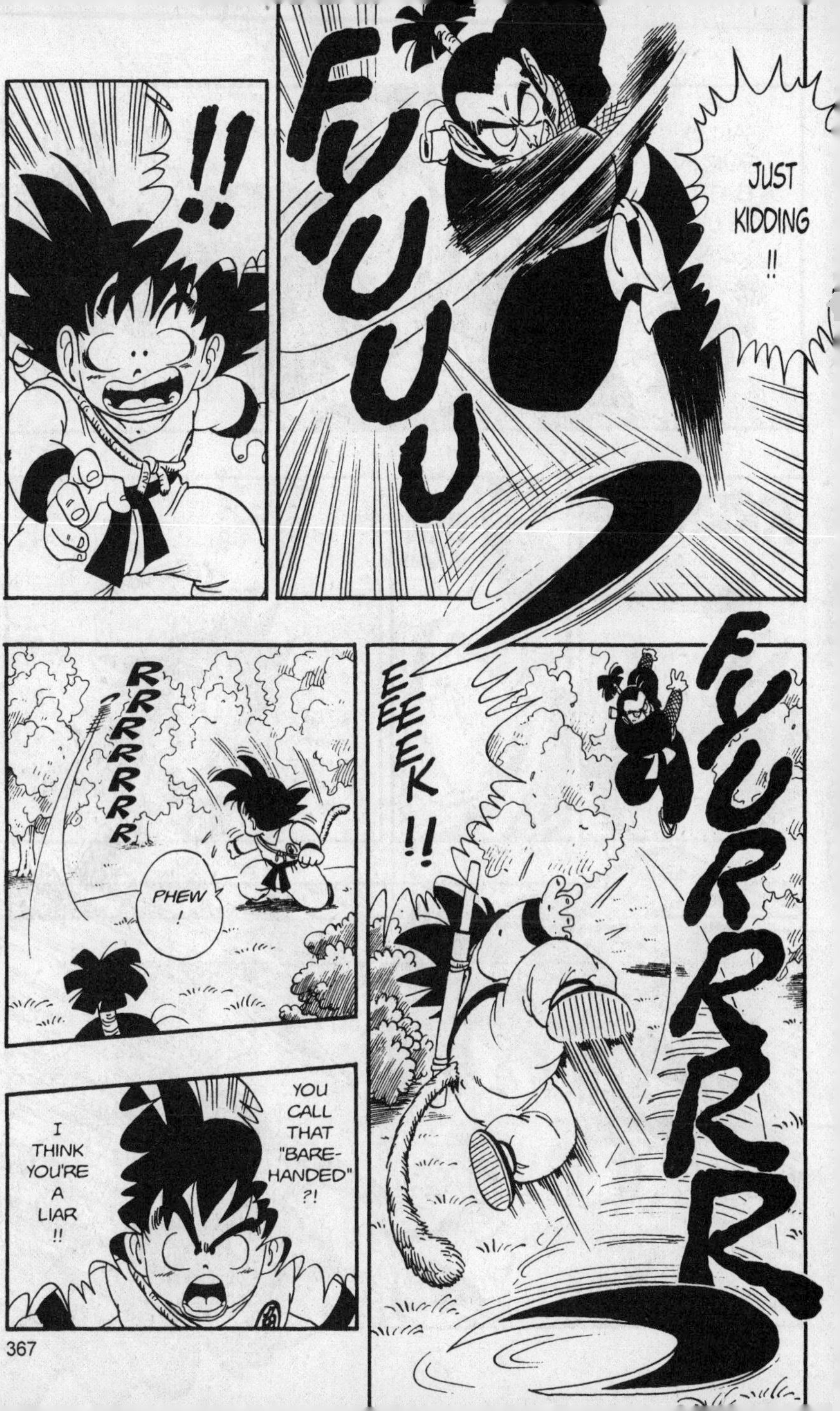
FUUUU
JUST KIDDING !!
!!
FURRRR
EEEEK !!
RRRRRRR
PHEW !
YOU CALL THAT "BARE-HANDED" ?!
I THINK YOU'RE A LIAR !!

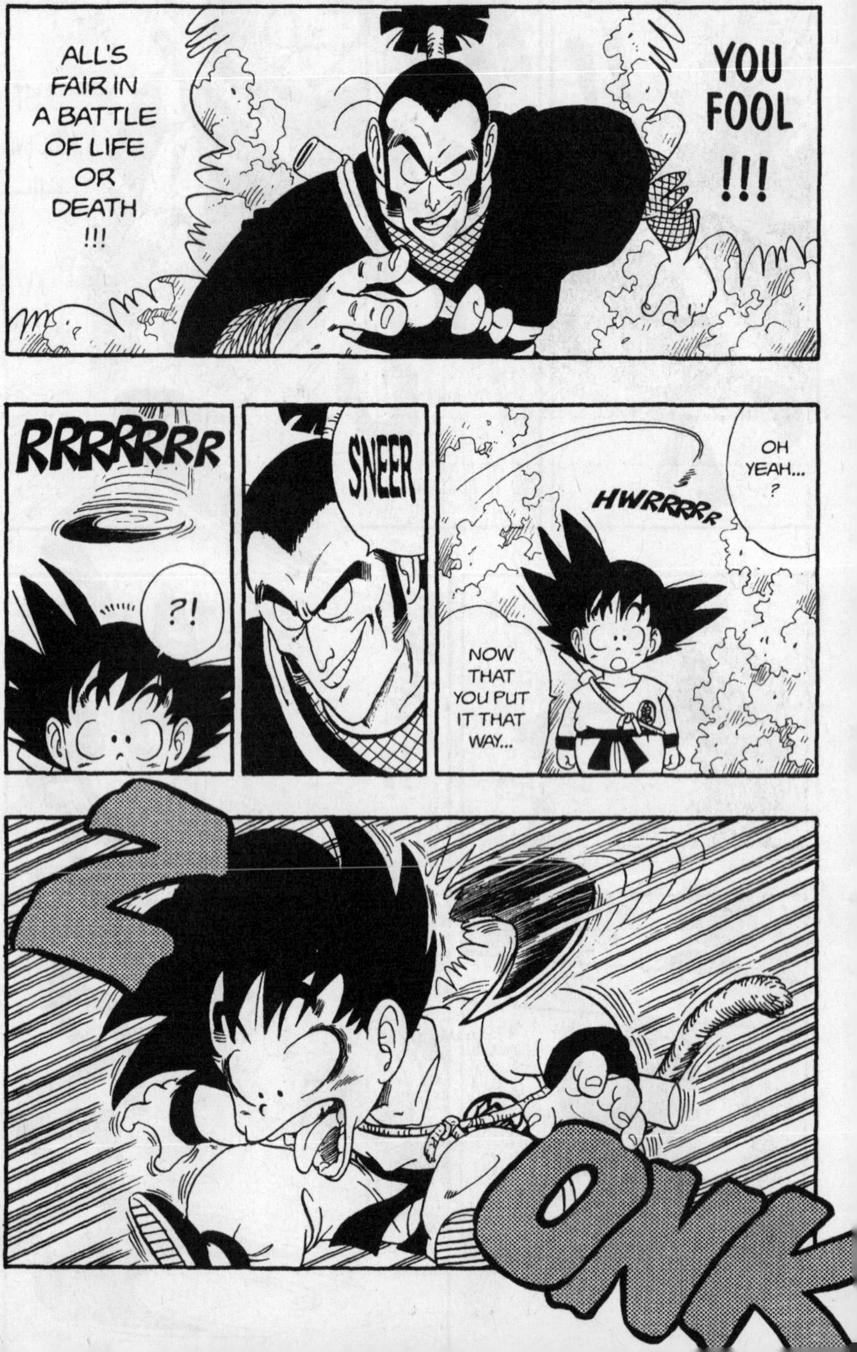
YOU FOOL !!!
ALL'S FAIR IN A BATTLE OF LIFE OR DEATH !!!
OH YEAH...?
HWRRRRRR
NOW THAT YOU PUT IT THAT WAY...
SNEER
RRRRRRR
?!
ONK

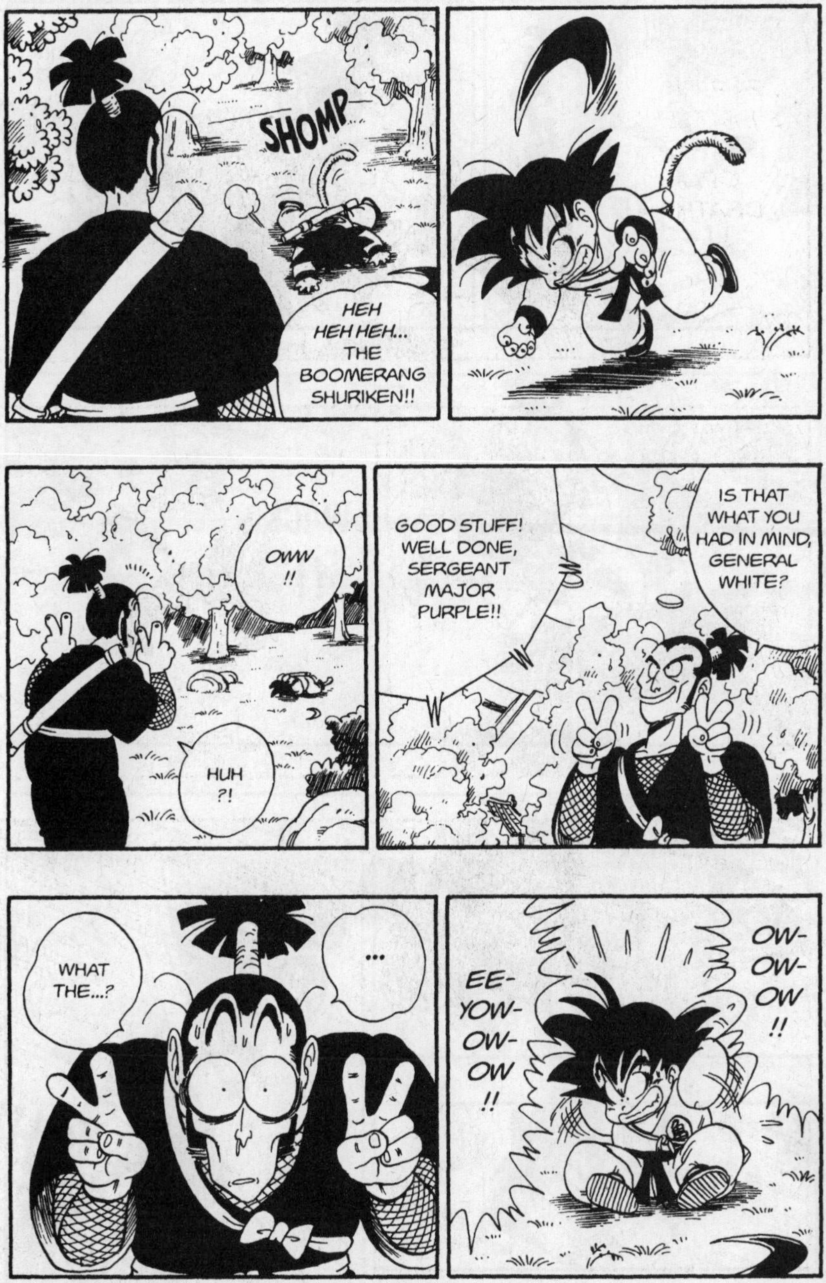
SHOMP
HEH HEH HEH... THE BOOMERANG SHURIKEN!!
IS THAT WHAT YOU HAD IN MIND, GENERAL WHITE?
GOOD STUFF! WELL DONE, SERGEANT MAJOR PURPLE!!
OWW !!
HUH ?!
OW-OW-OW !!
EE-YOW-OW-OW !!
...
WHAT THE...?

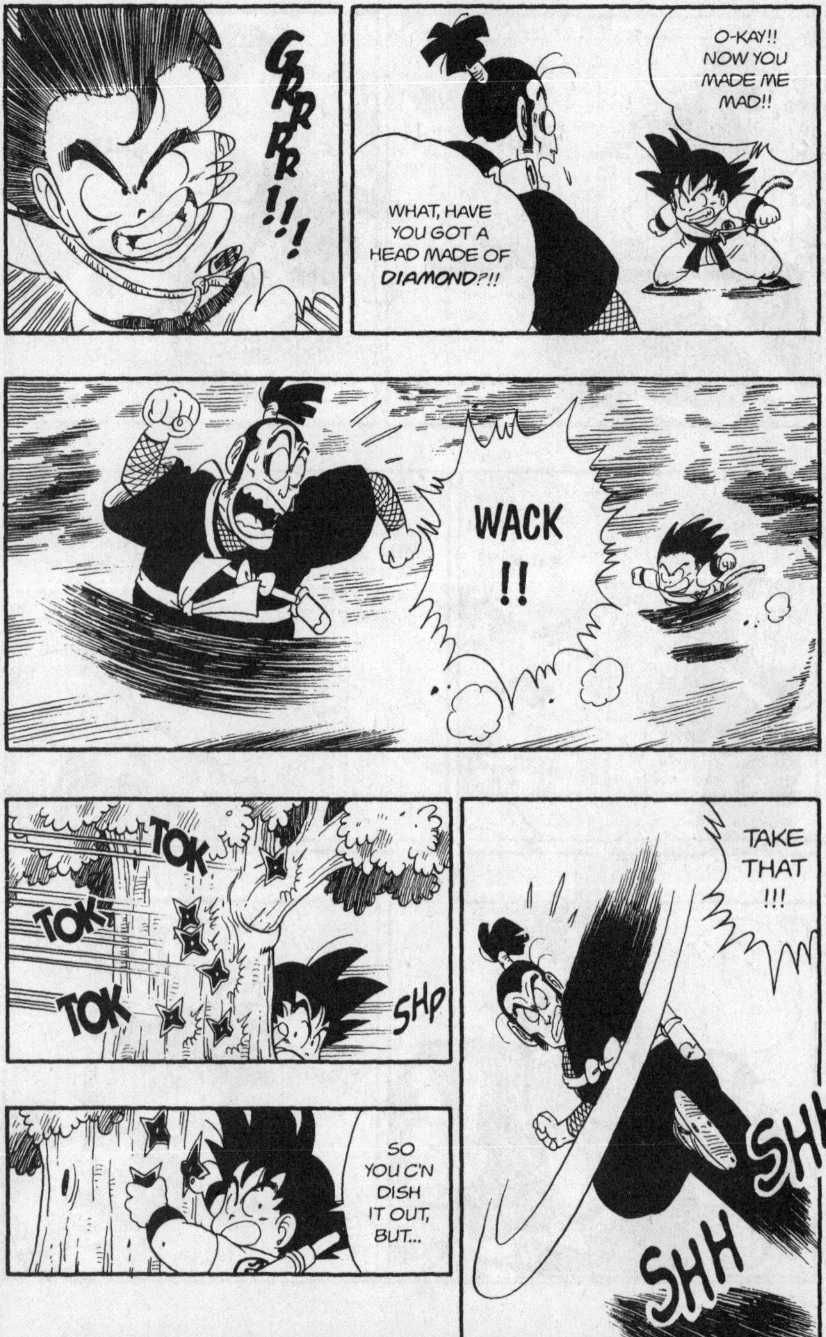
O-KAY!! NOW YOU MADE ME MAD!!
WHAT, HAVE YOU GOT A HEAD MADE OF DIAMOND?!!
GRRRR!!!
WACK !!
TAKE THAT !!!
SHH
SHH
SHH
TOK
TOK
TOK
SHP
SO YOU C'N DISH IT OUT, BUT...

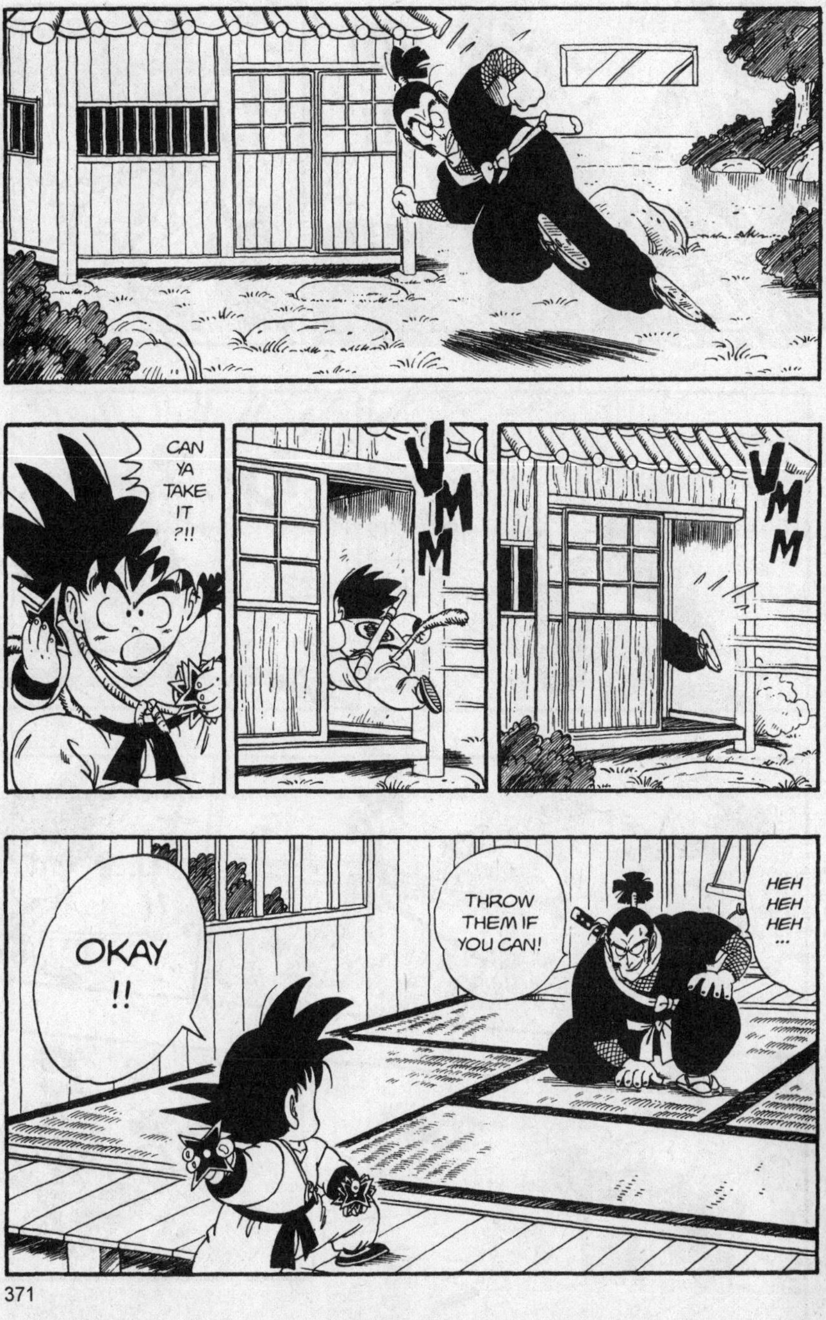
VMM
VMM
CAN YA TAKE IT ?!!
HEH HEH HEH ...
THROW THEM IF YOU CAN!
OKAY !!

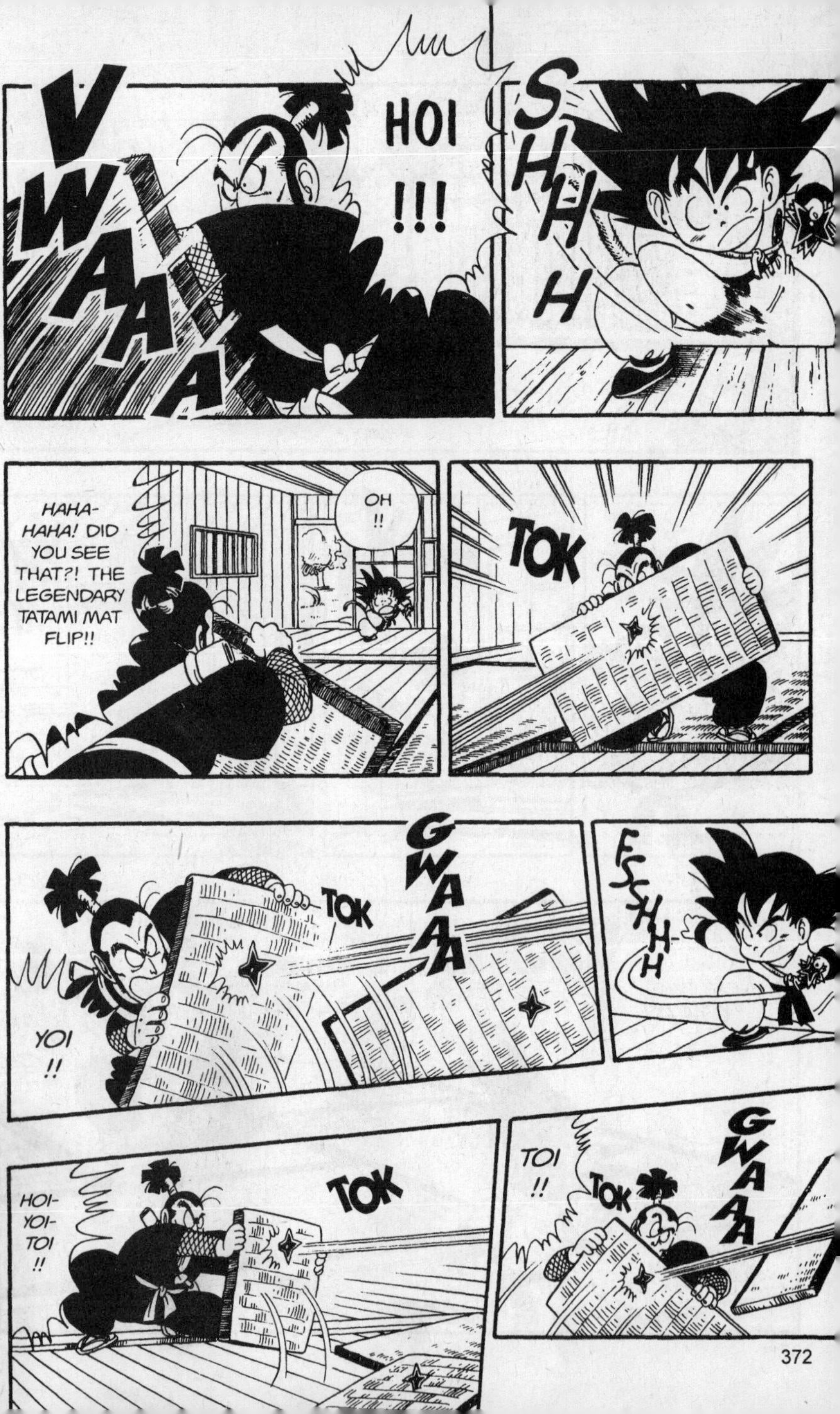
SHHHH
HOI !!!
VWAAAA
TOK
OH !!
HAHA-HAHA! DID YOU SEE THAT?! THE LEGENDARY TATAMI MAT FLIP!!
FSSHHH
GWAAA
TOK
YOI !!
GWAAA
TOK
TOI !!
TOK
HOI-YOI-TOI !!

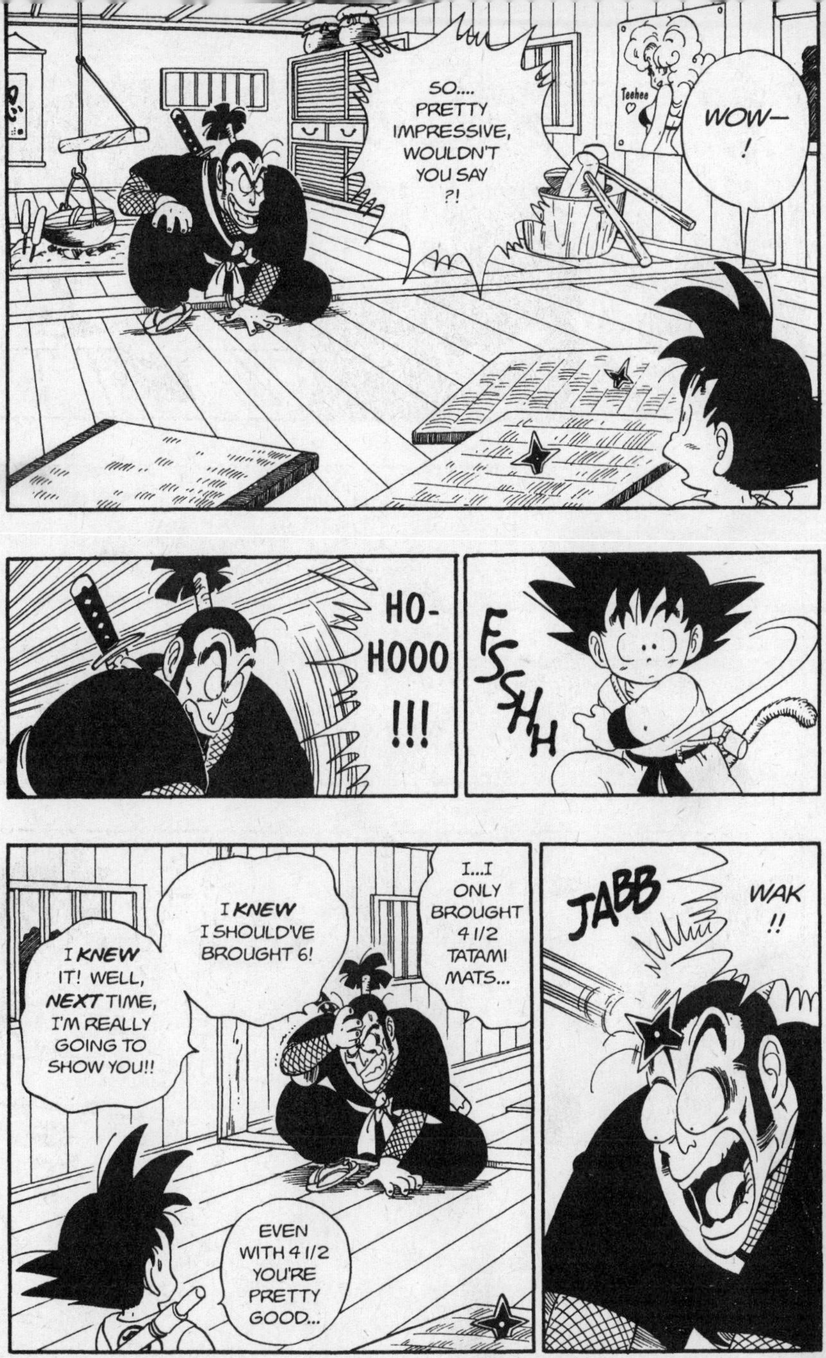
Teehee
WOW—!
SO.... PRETTY IMPRESSIVE, WOULDN'T YOU SAY ?!
FSSHH
HO-HOOO !!!
WAK !!
JABB
I...I ONLY BROUGHT 4 1/2 TATAMI MATS...
I KNEW I SHOULD'VE BROUGHT 6!
I KNEW IT! WELL, NEXT TIME, I'M REALLY GOING TO SHOW YOU!!
EVEN WITH 4 1/2 YOU'RE PRETTY GOOD...

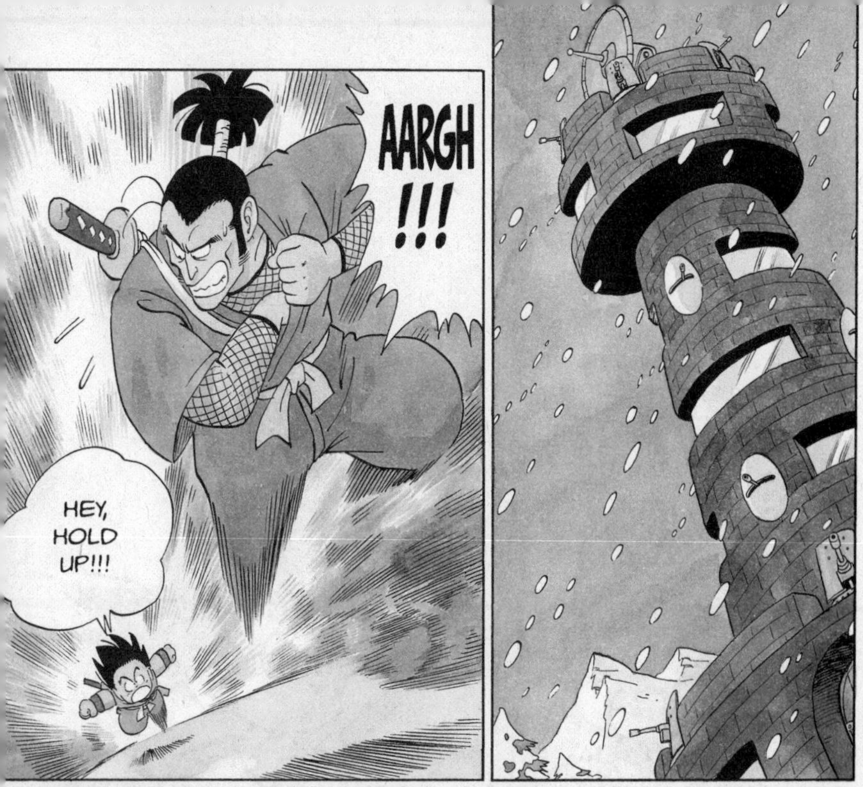
AARGH !!!
HEY, HOLD UP!!!

Tale 62 · The Ninja Split!

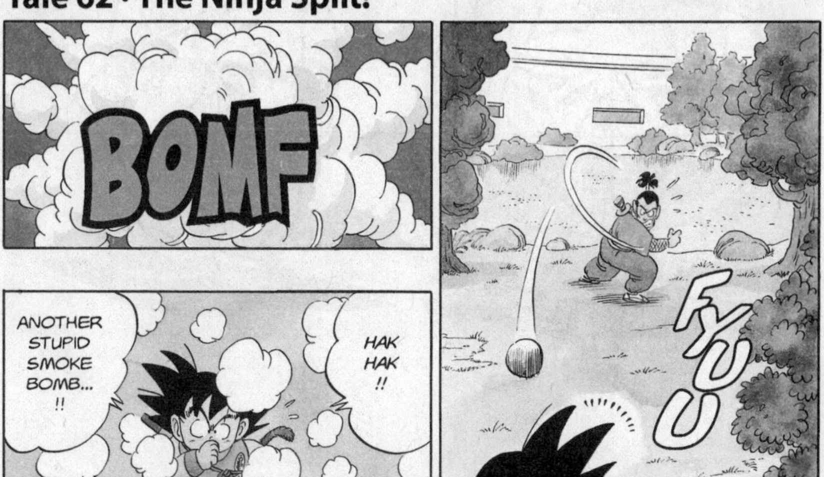
FYUU
BOMF
HAK HAK !!
ANOTHER STUPID SMOKE BOMB... !!

SON GOKU
HERO OF THE ANCIENT CHINESE FABLE **SAIYŪKI** ("JOURNEY TO THE WEST")

SON GOKU
HERO OF **DRAGON BALL**

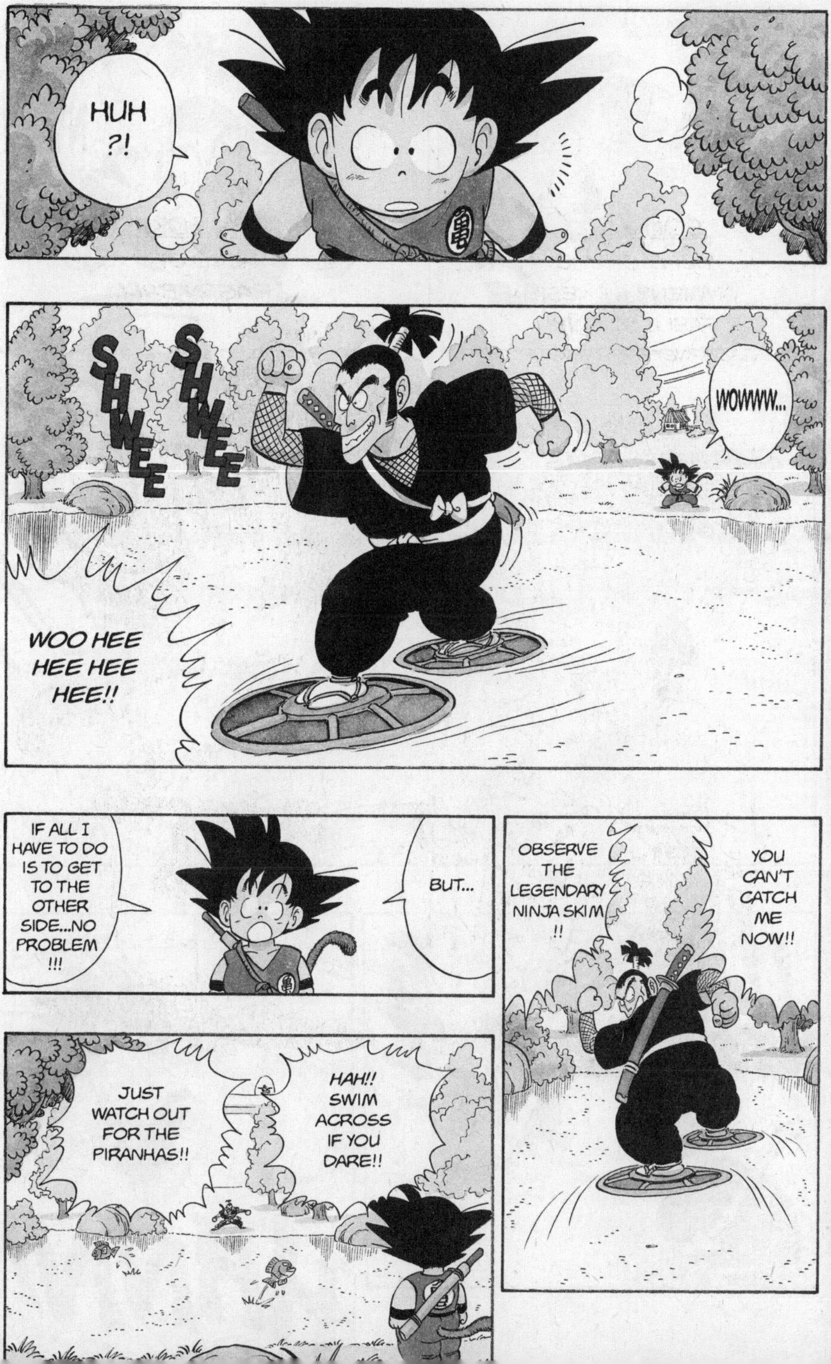
HUH ?!
WOWWW...
SHWEE SHWEE
WOO HEE HEE HEE HEE!!
YOU CAN'T CATCH ME NOW!!
OBSERVE THE LEGENDARY NINJA SKIM !!
BUT...
IF ALL I HAVE TO DO IS TO GET TO THE OTHER SIDE...NO PROBLEM !!!
HAH!! SWIM ACROSS IF YOU DARE!!
JUST WATCH OUT FOR THE PIRANHAS!!

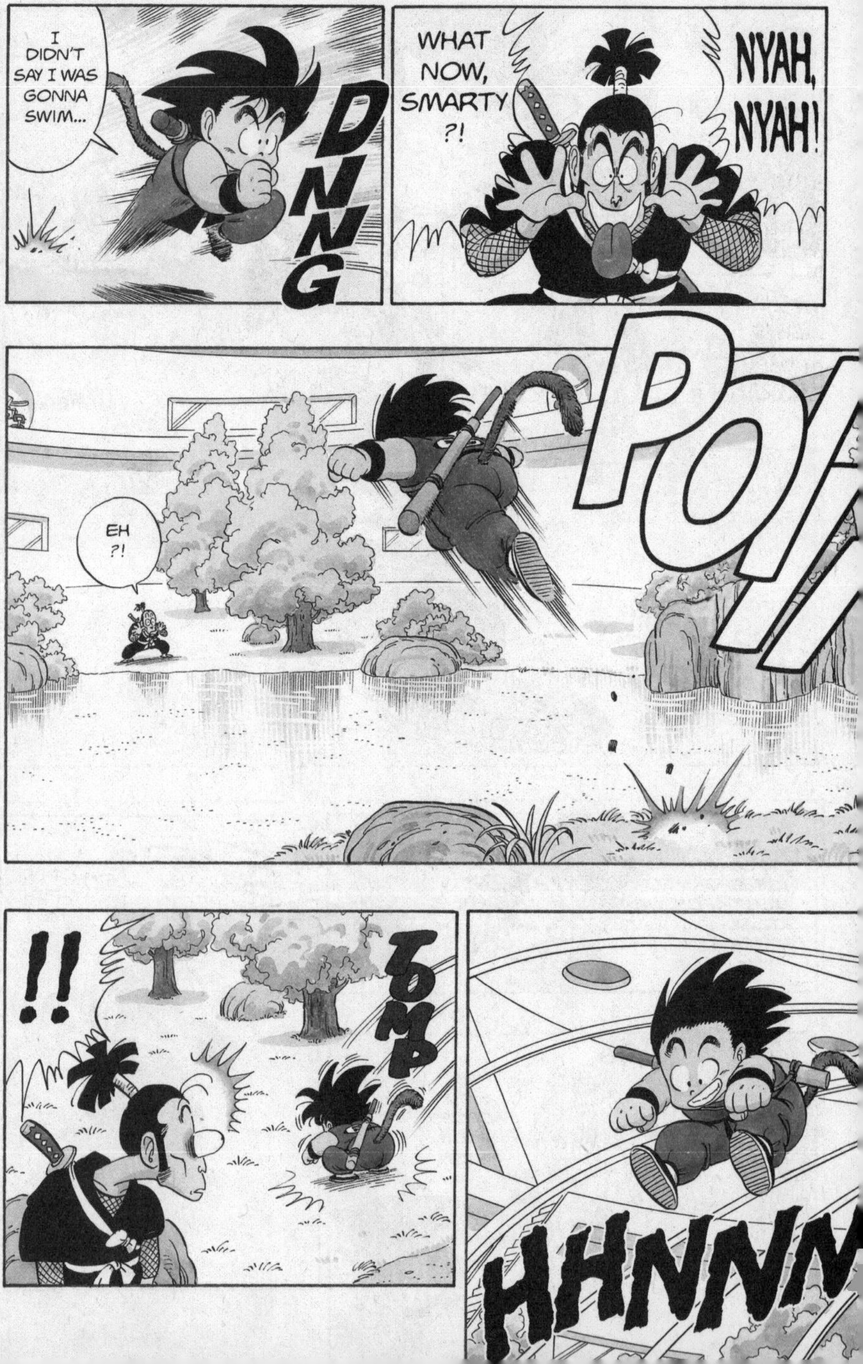

WHAT NOW, SMARTY ?!
NYAH, NYAH!
I DIDN'T SAY I WAS GONNA SWIM...
DNNG
POI
EH ?!
HHNNN
TOMP
!!

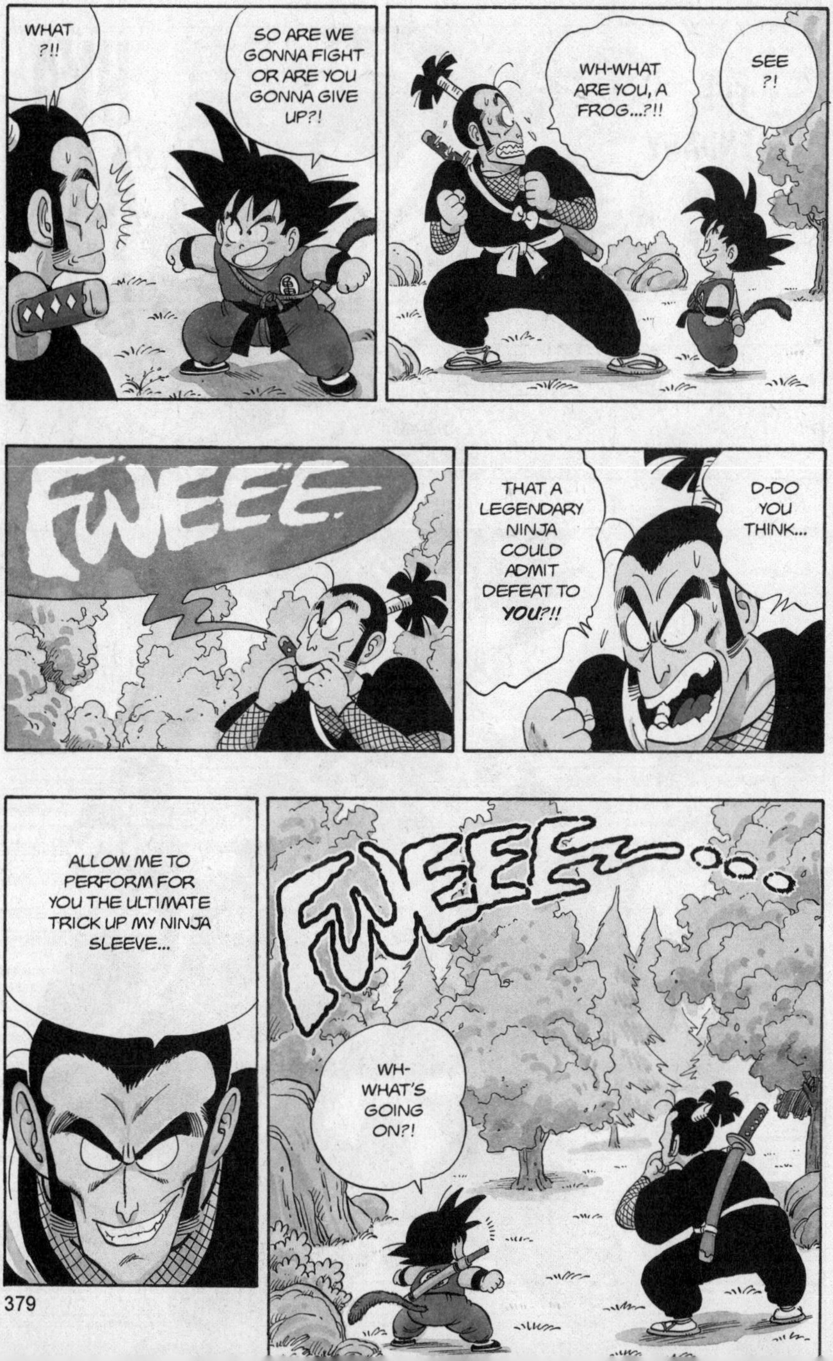
SEE ?!
WH-WHAT ARE YOU, A FROG...?!!
SO ARE WE GONNA FIGHT OR ARE YOU GONNA GIVE UP?!
WHAT ?!!
D-DO YOU THINK...
THAT A LEGENDARY NINJA COULD ADMIT DEFEAT TO YOU?!!
FWEEE
FWEEE...
WH-WHAT'S GOING ON?!
ALLOW ME TO PERFORM FOR YOU THE ULTIMATE TRICK UP MY NINJA SLEEVE...

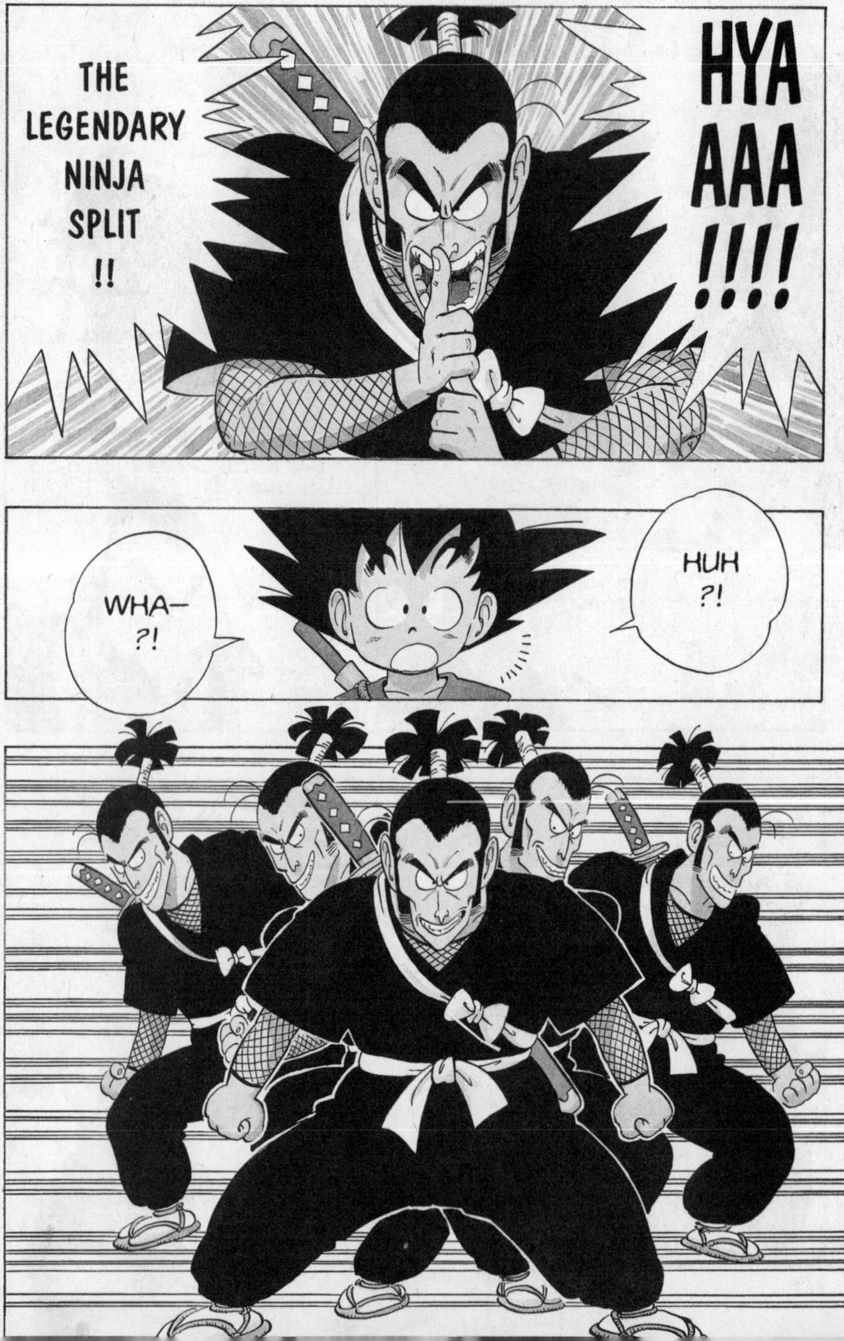

HYAAAA!!!!
THE LEGENDARY NINJA SPLIT!!
HUH?!
WHA-?!

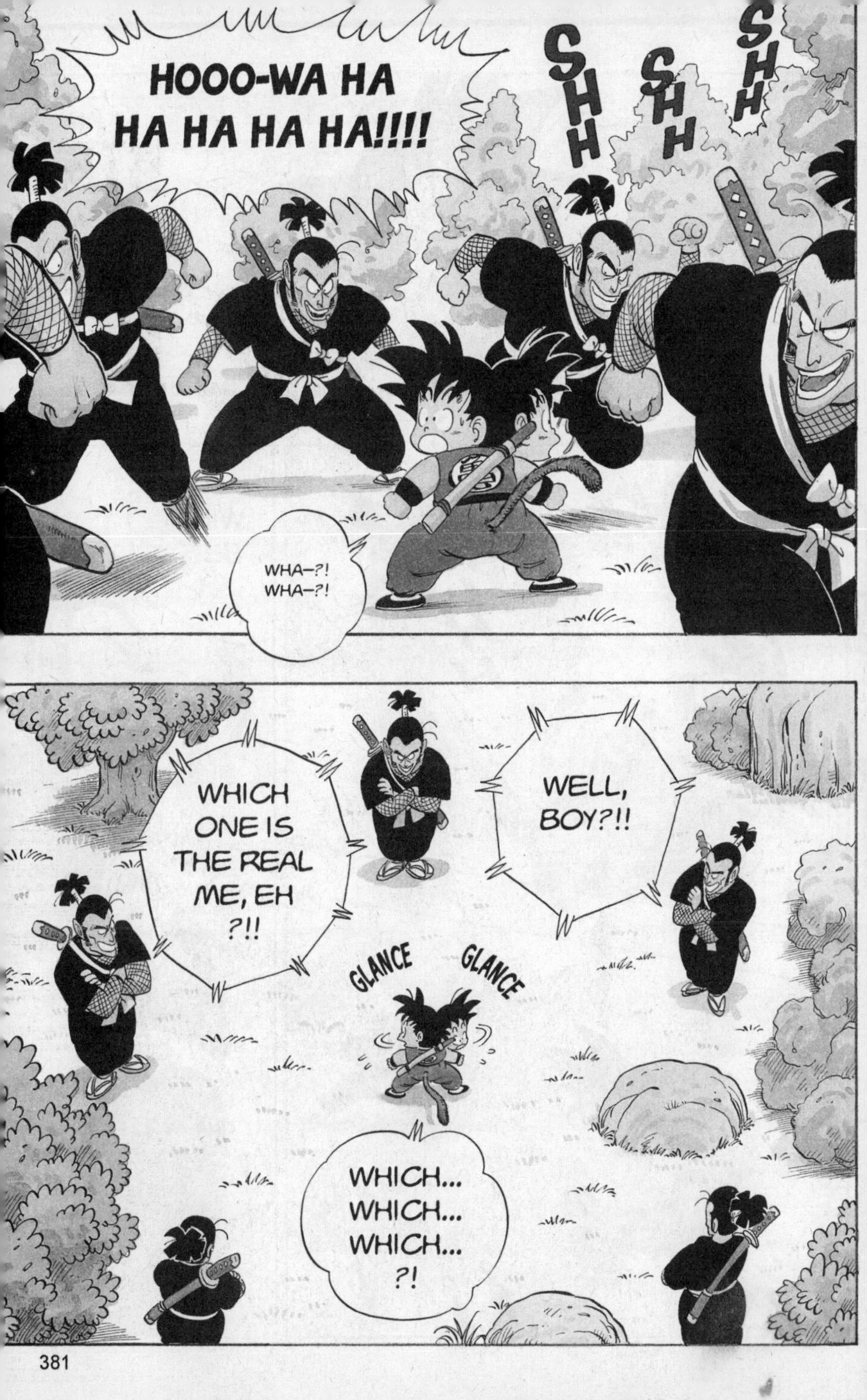
SHH
SHH
SHH
HOOO-WA HA HA HA HA HA HA!!!!
WHA-?! WHA-?!
WELL, BOY?!!
WHICH ONE IS THE REAL ME, EH ?!!
GLANCE
GLANCE
WHICH... WHICH... WHICH... ?!

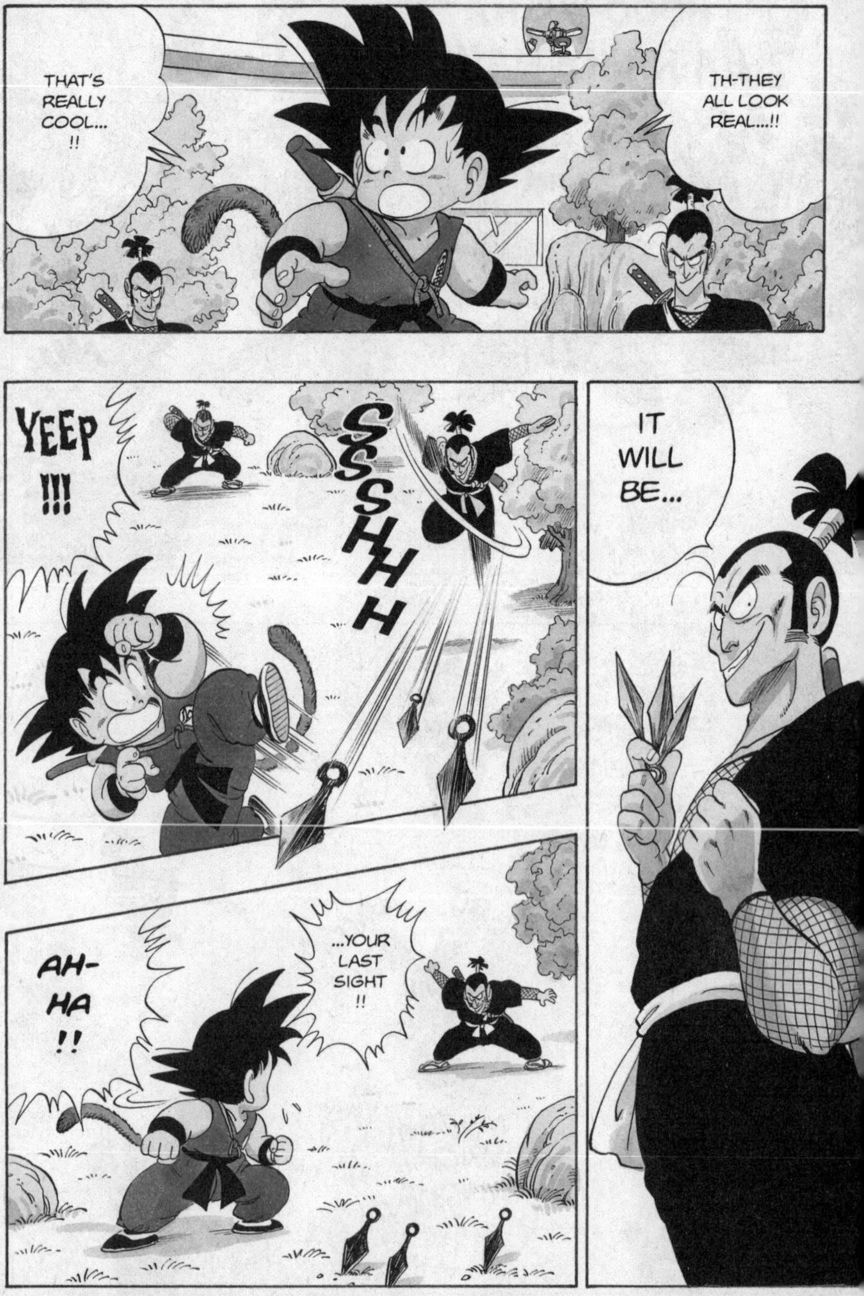
TH-THEY ALL LOOK REAL...!!
THAT'S REALLY COOL...!!
IT WILL BE...
SSHHHH
YEEP!!!
...YOUR LAST SIGHT!!
AH-HA!!

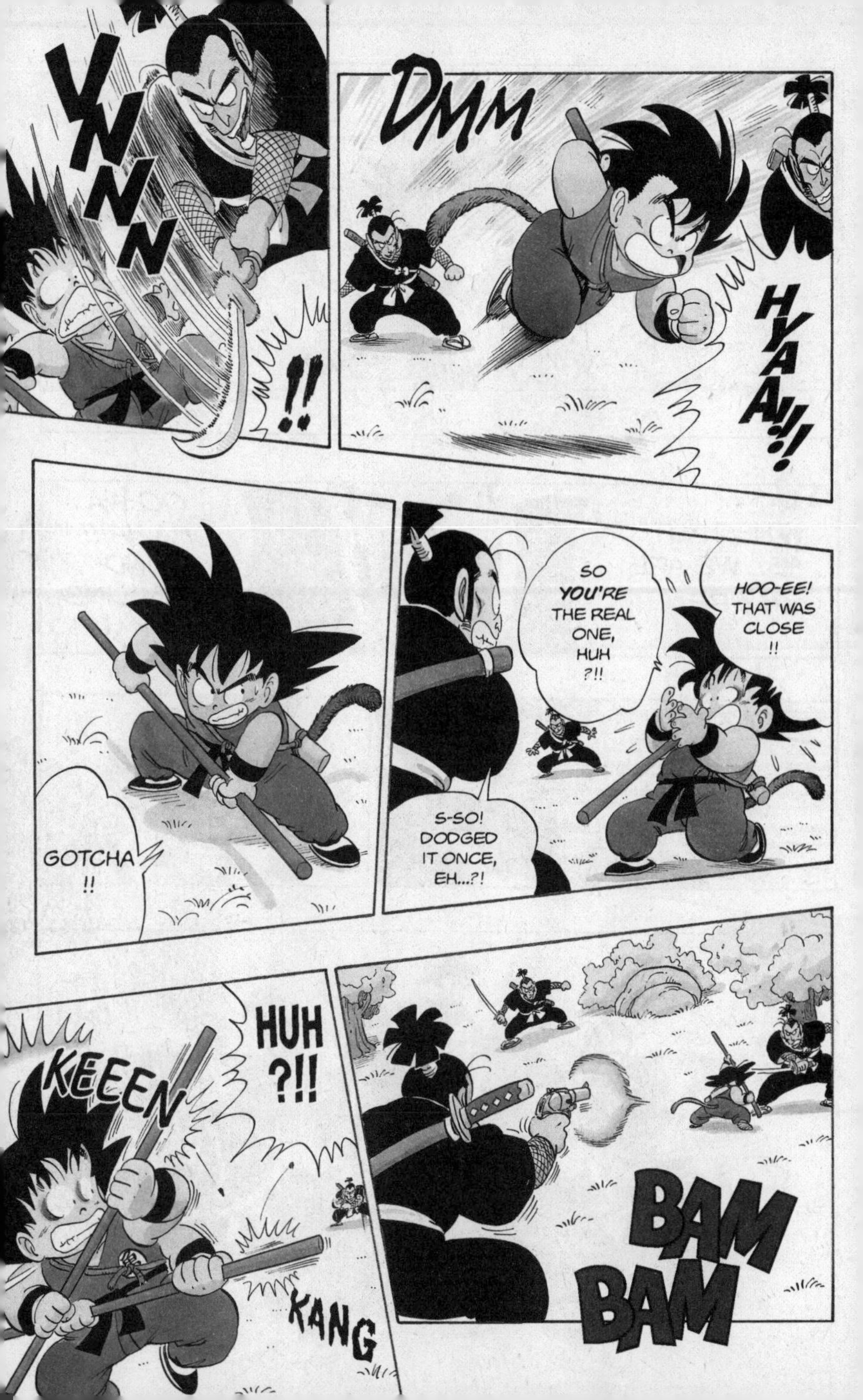
DMM
HYAA!!
VWNNN
!!
HOO-EE! THAT WAS CLOSE !!
SO YOU'RE THE REAL ONE, HUH ?!!
S-SO! DODGED IT ONCE, EH...?!
GOTCHA !!
BAM BAM
HUH ?!!
KEEEN
KANG

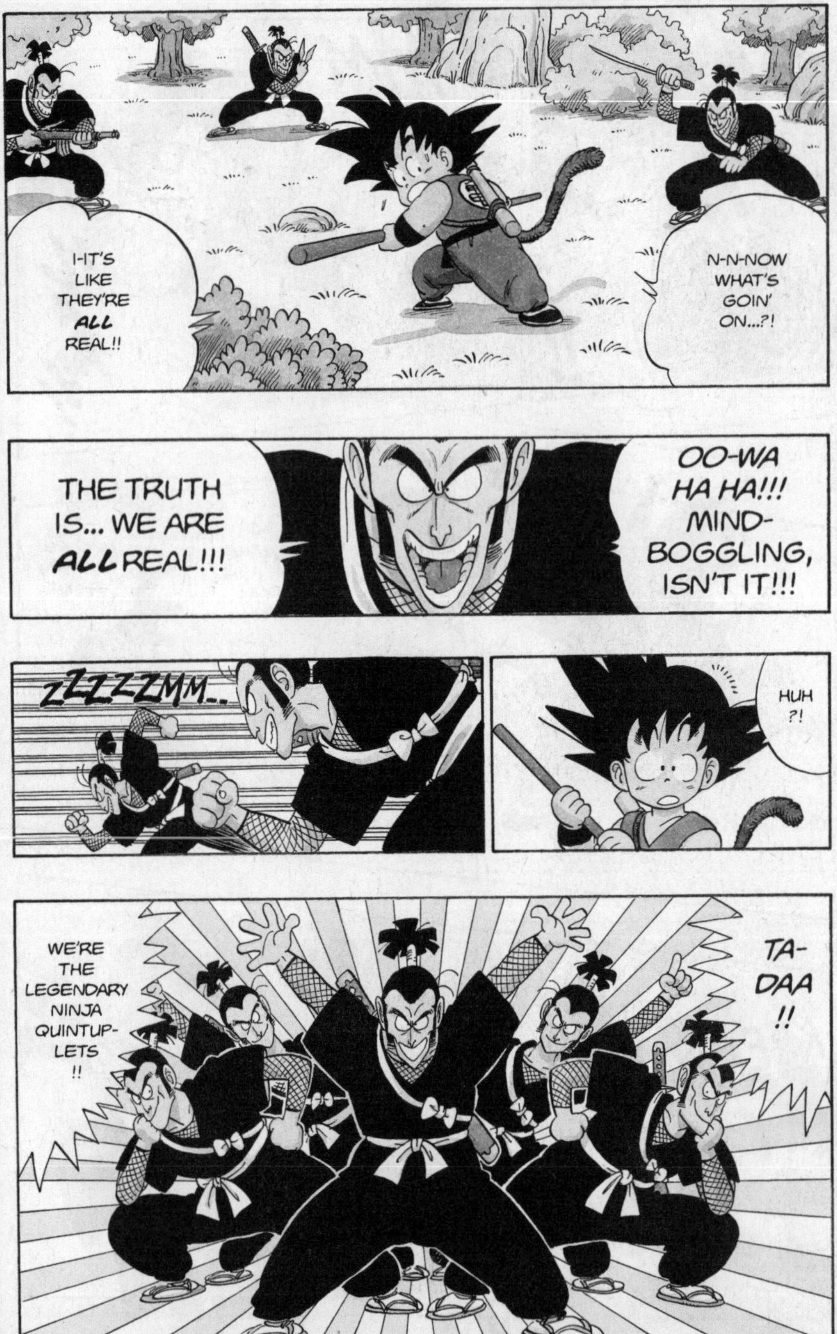
N-N-NOW WHAT'S GOIN' ON...?!
I-IT'S LIKE THEY'RE ALL REAL!!
OO-WA HA HA!!! MIND-BOGGLING, ISN'T IT!!!
THE TRUTH IS... WE ARE ALL REAL!!!
HUH ?!
ZZZZZMM..
TA-DAA !!
WE'RE THE LEGENDARY NINJA QUINTUP-LETS !!

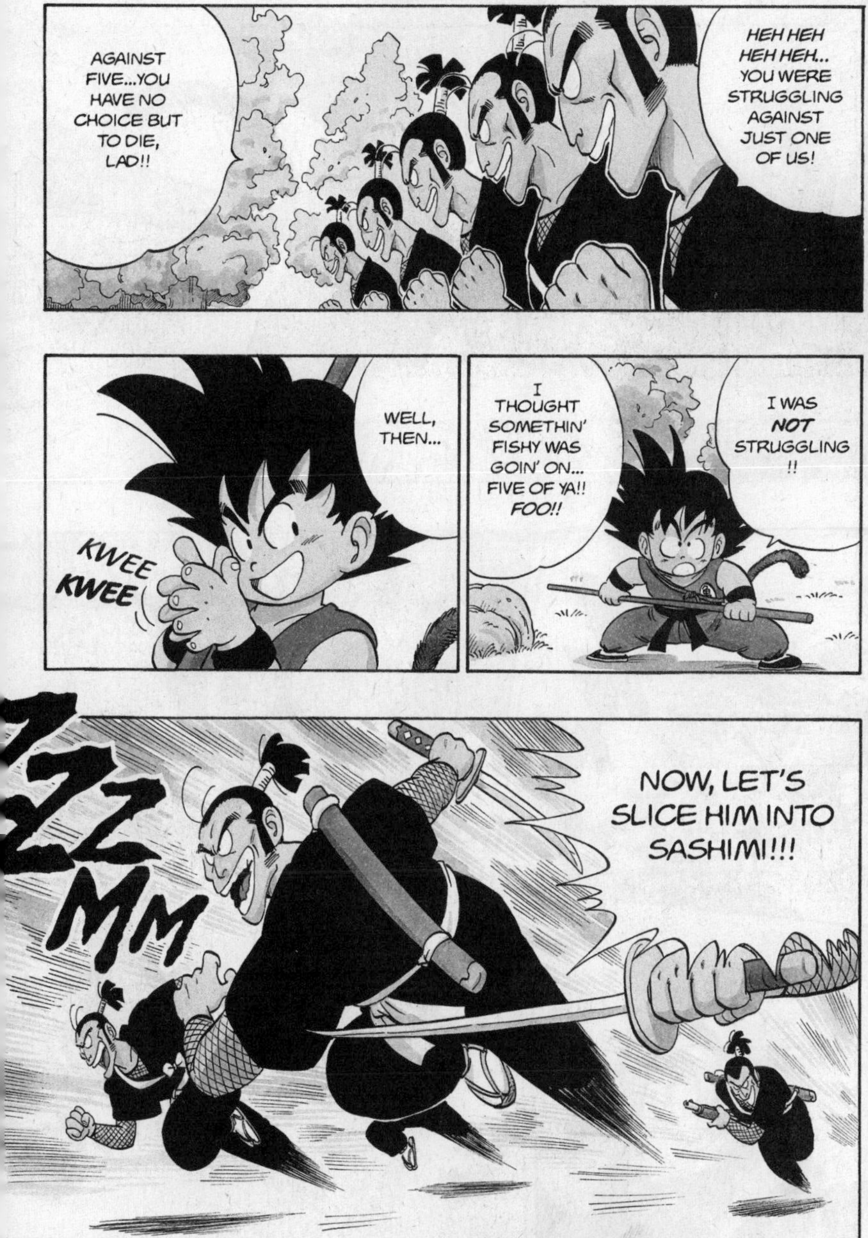
HEH HEH HEH HEH... YOU WERE STRUGGLING AGAINST JUST ONE OF US!
AGAINST FIVE...YOU HAVE NO CHOICE BUT TO DIE, LAD!!
I WAS **NOT** STRUGGLING !!
I THOUGHT SOMETHIN' FISHY WAS GOIN' ON... FIVE OF YA!! *FOO!!*
WELL, THEN...
KWEE KWEE
NOW, LET'S SLICE HIM INTO SASHIMI!!!

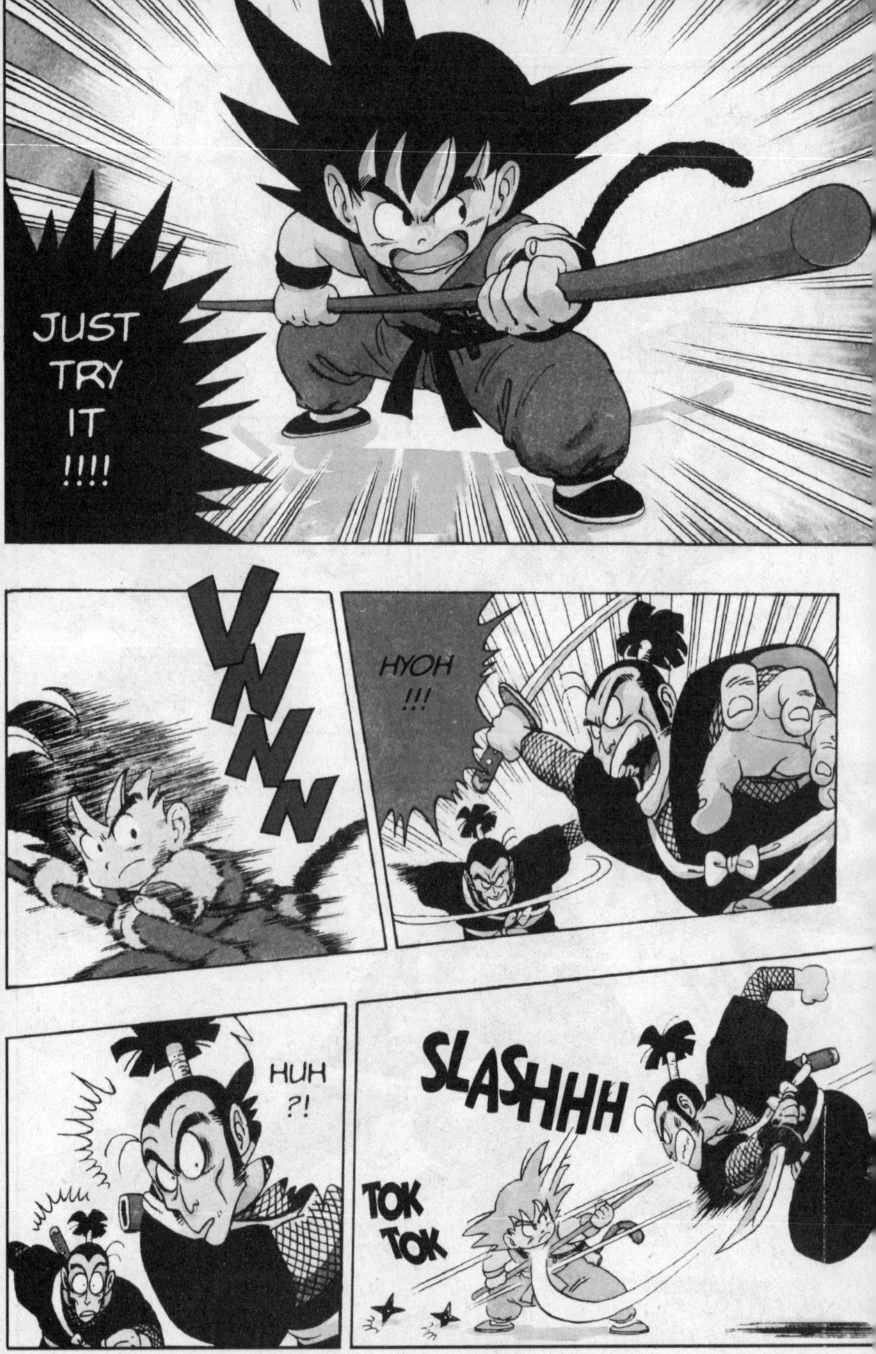
JUST TRY IT !!!!
HYOH !!!
VNNN
SLASHHH
TOK TOK
HUH ?!

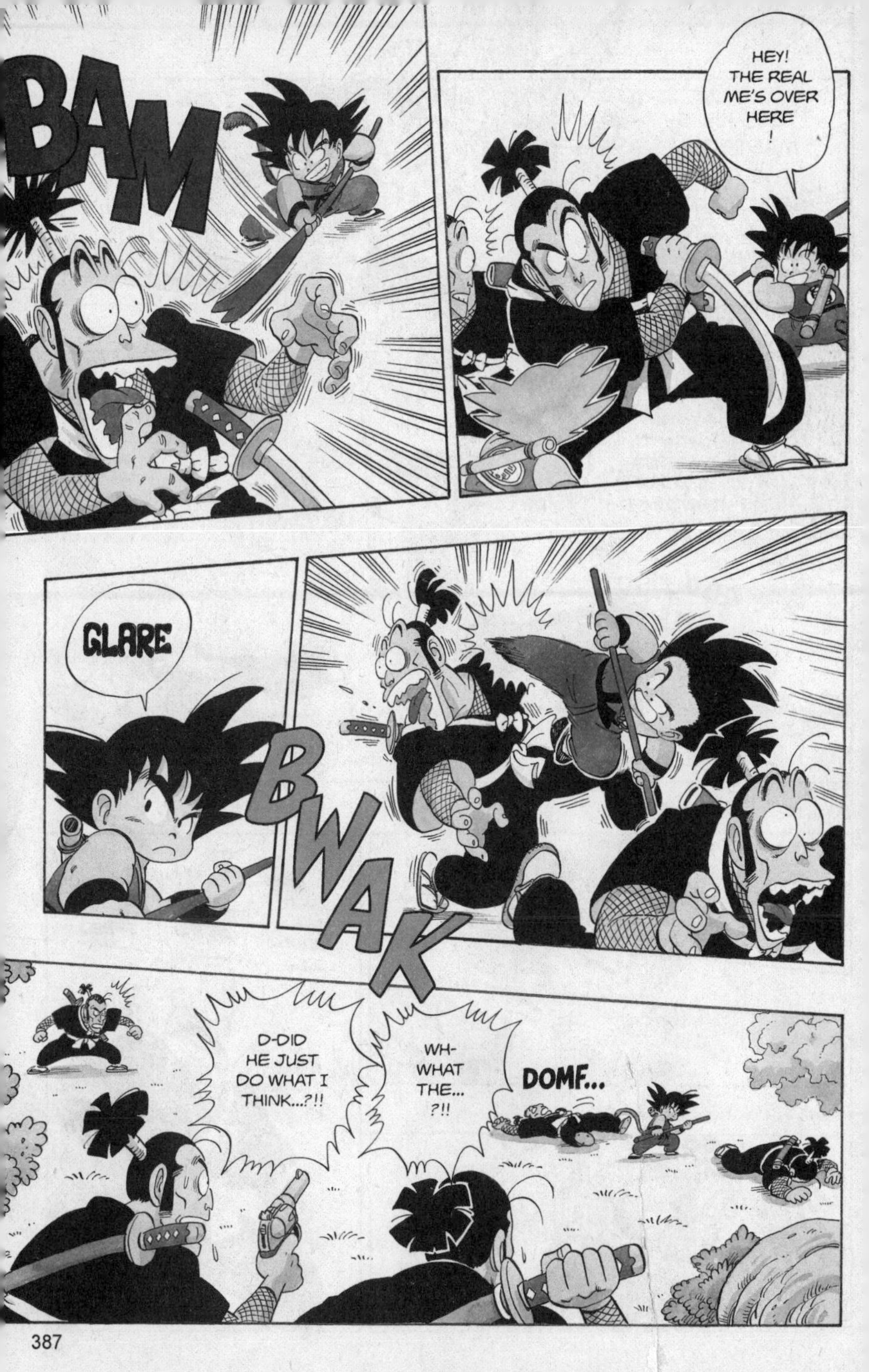
HEY! THE REAL ME'S OVER HERE !
BAM
BWAK
GLARE
DOMF...
WH- WHAT THE... ?!!
D-DID HE JUST DO WHAT I THINK...?!!

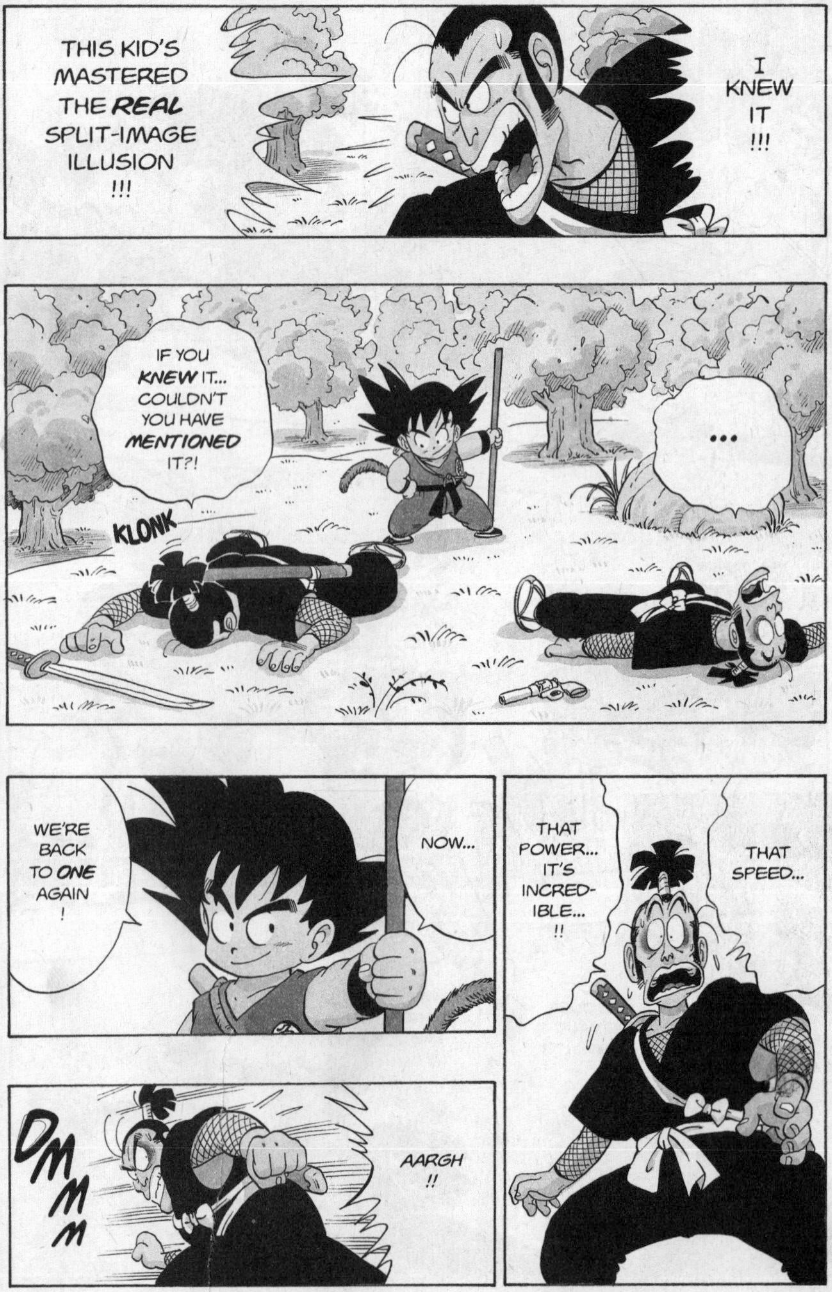
I KNEW IT !!!
THIS KID'S MASTERED THE **REAL** SPLIT-IMAGE ILLUSION !!!
IF YOU **KNEW** IT... COULDN'T YOU HAVE **MENTIONED** IT?!
KLONK
...
THAT SPEED...
THAT POWER... IT'S INCREDIBLE... !!
NOW...
WE'RE BACK TO **ONE** AGAIN !
AARGH !!
DMMMM

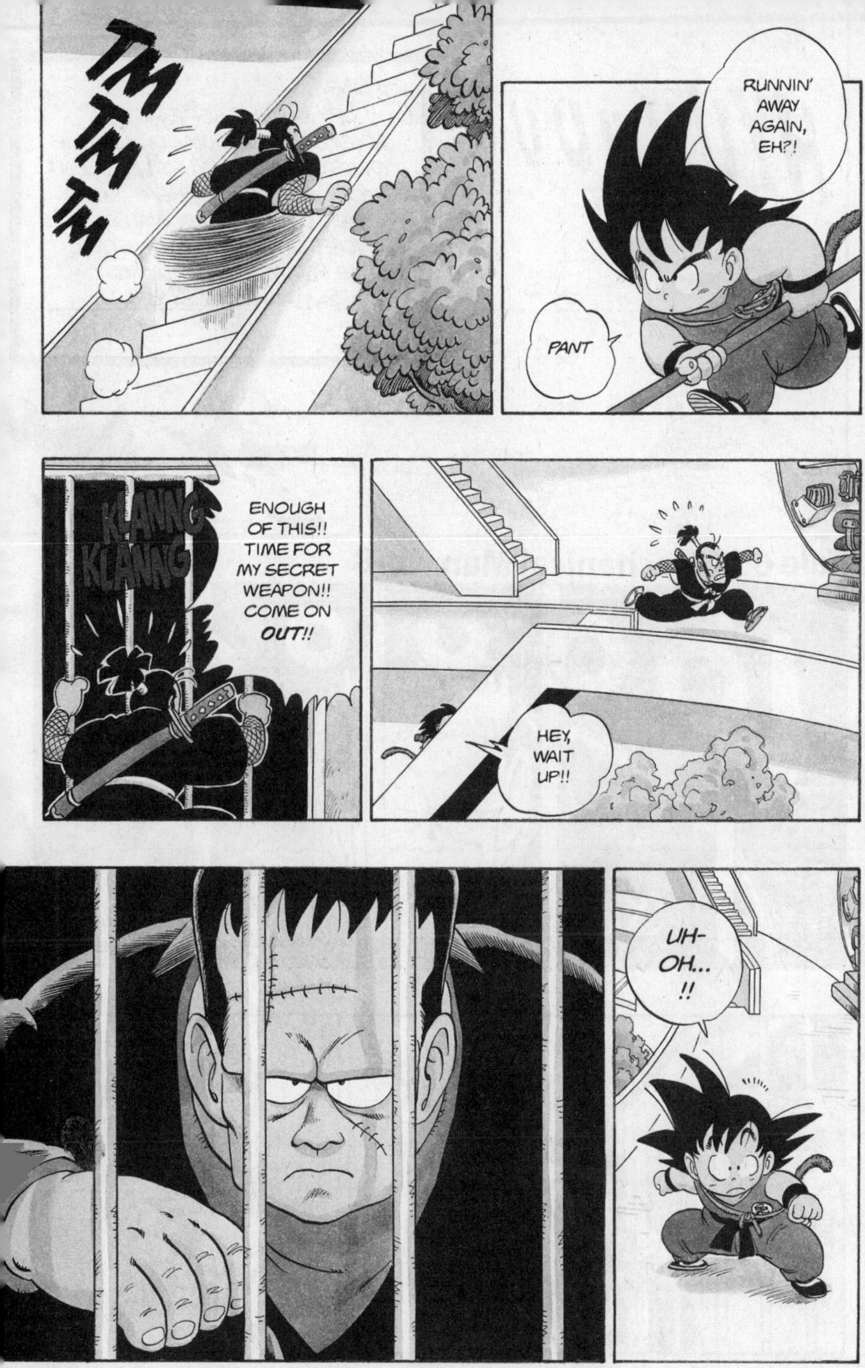
RUNNIN' AWAY AGAIN, EH?!
PANT
TM TM TM
HEY, WAIT UP!!
KLANNG KLANNG
ENOUGH OF THIS!! TIME FOR MY SECRET WEAPON!! COME ON OUT!!
UH-OH... !!

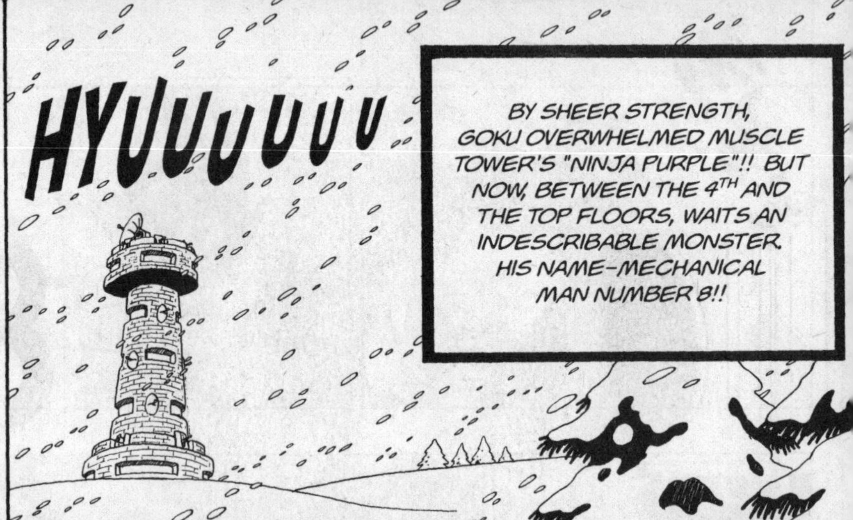
BY SHEER STRENGTH, GOKU OVERWHELMED MUSCLE TOWER'S "NINJA PURPLE"!! BUT NOW, BETWEEN THE 4TH AND THE TOP FLOORS, WAITS AN INDESCRIBABLE MONSTER. HIS NAME–MECHANICAL MAN NUMBER 8!!
HYUUUUUUU

Tale 63 • Mechanical Man No. 8

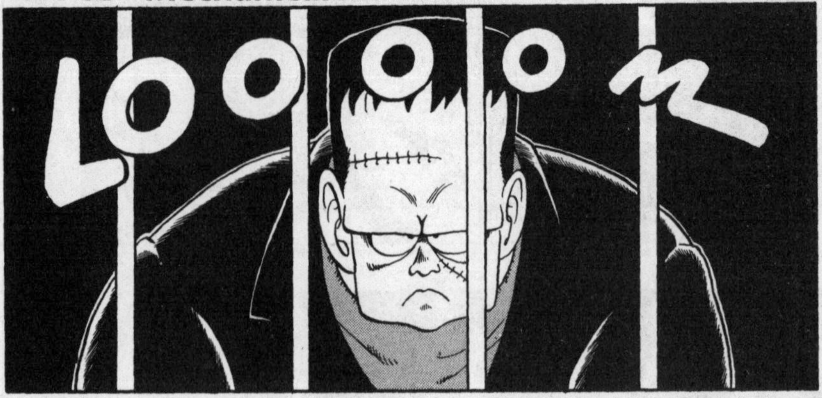
LOOOOM

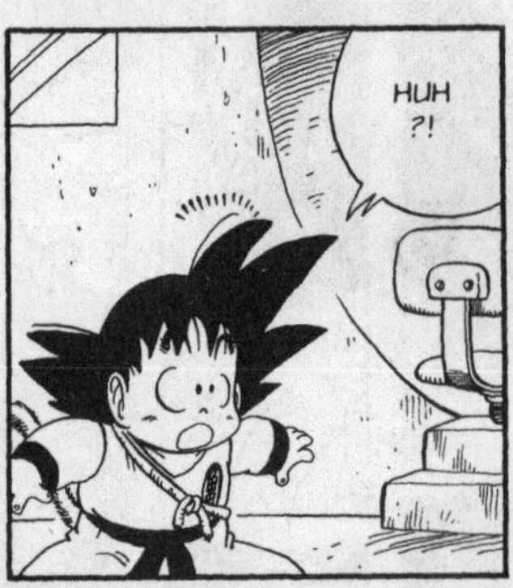
HUH ?!

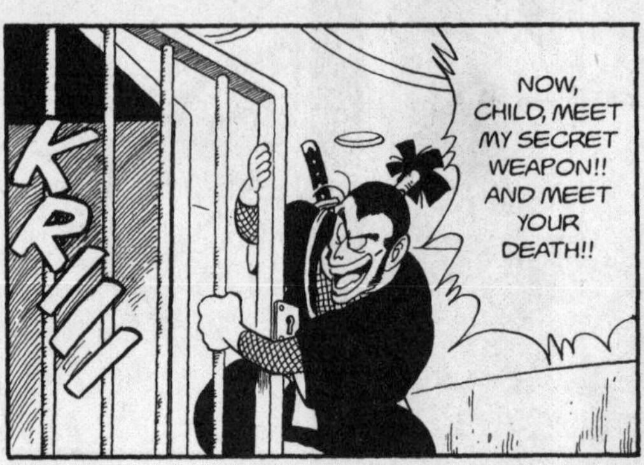
NOW, CHILD, MEET MY SECRET WEAPON!! AND MEET YOUR DEATH!!
KRIIII

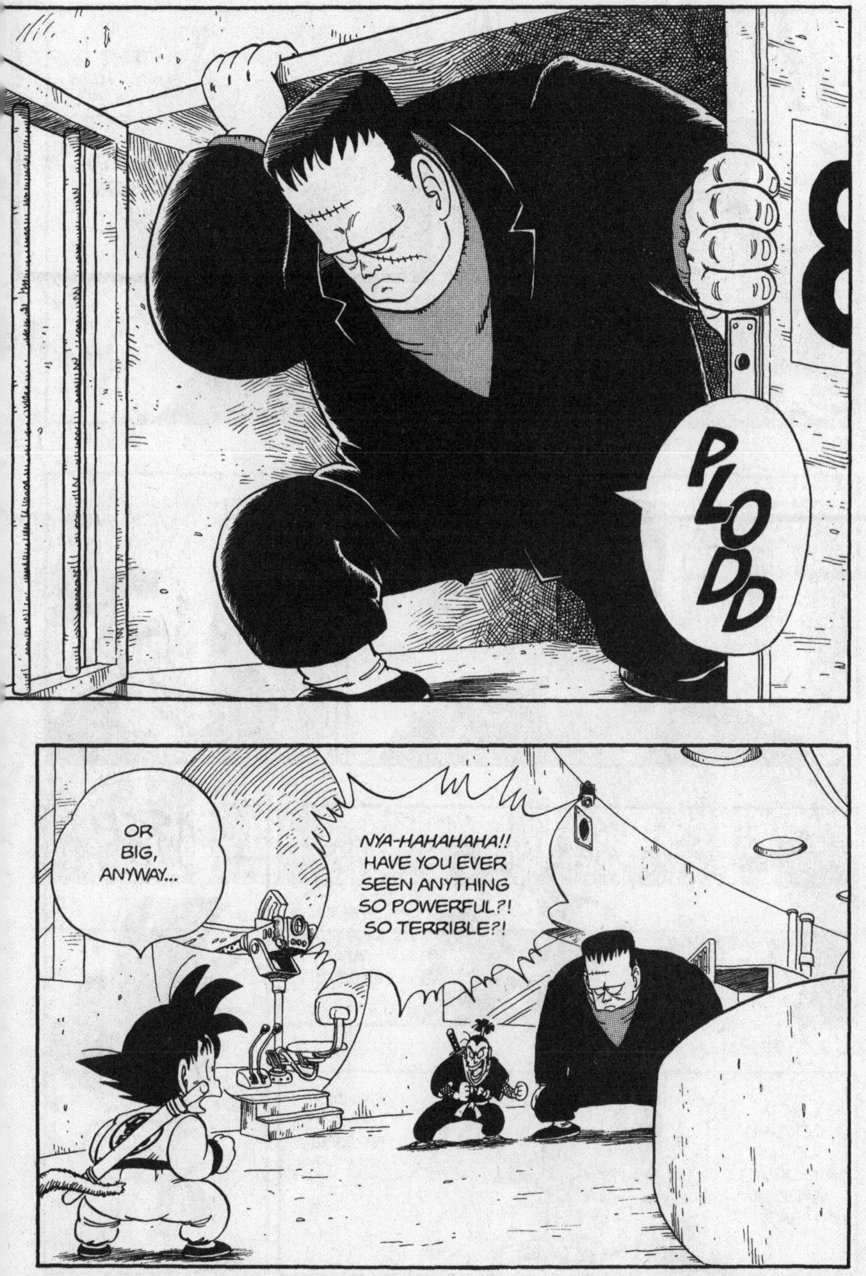
PLODD
NYA-HAHAHAHA!! HAVE YOU EVER SEEN ANYTHING SO POWERFUL?! SO TERRIBLE?!
OR BIG, ANYWAY...

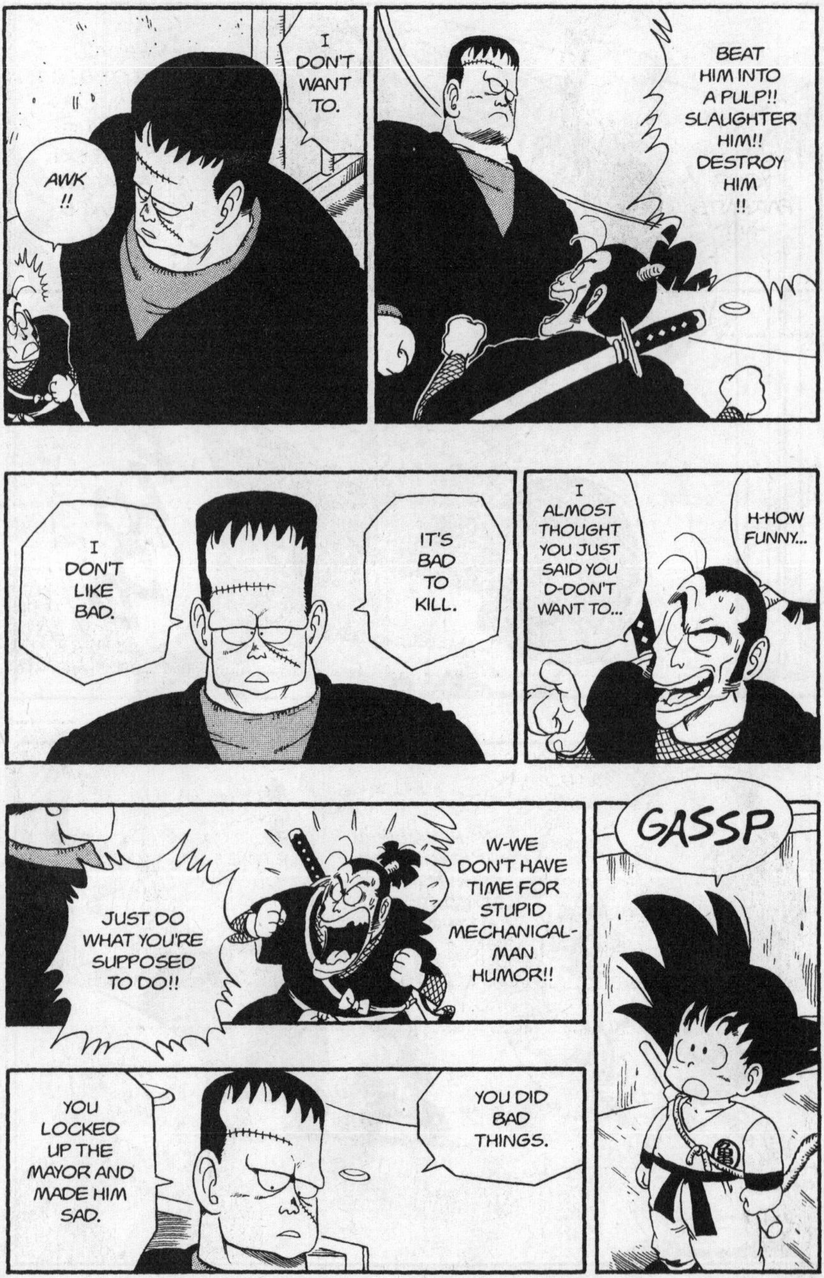
BEAT HIM INTO A PULP!! SLAUGHTER HIM!! DESTROY HIM !!
I DON'T WANT TO.
AWK !!
H-HOW FUNNY...
I ALMOST THOUGHT YOU JUST SAID YOU D-DON'T WANT TO...
IT'S BAD TO KILL.
I DON'T LIKE BAD.
GASSP
W-WE DON'T HAVE TIME FOR STUPID MECHANICAL-MAN HUMOR!!
JUST DO WHAT YOU'RE SUPPOSED TO DO!!
YOU DID BAD THINGS.
YOU LOCKED UP THE MAYOR AND MADE HIM SAD.

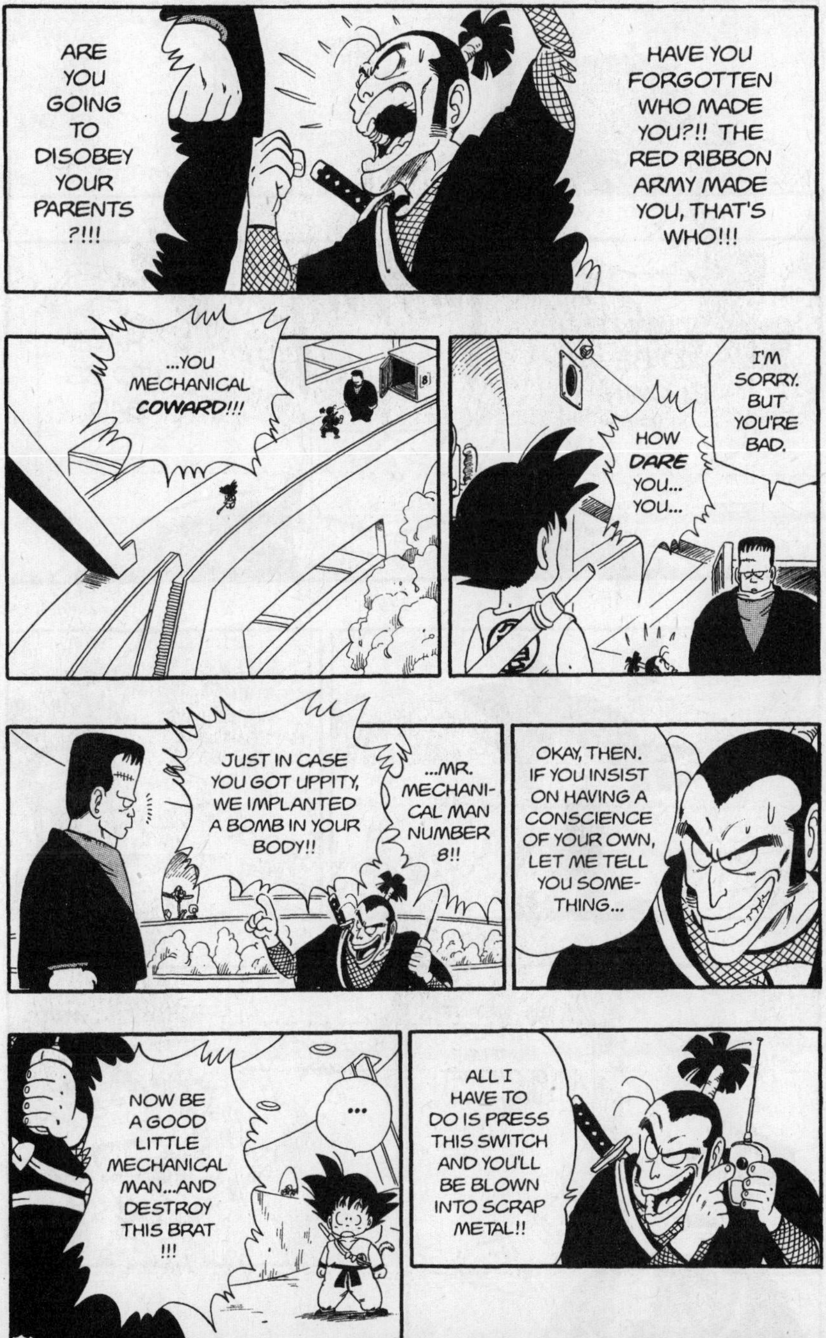
HAVE YOU FORGOTTEN WHO MADE YOU?!! THE RED RIBBON ARMY MADE YOU, THAT'S WHO!!!
ARE YOU GOING TO DISOBEY YOUR PARENTS?!!!
I'M SORRY. BUT YOU'RE BAD.
HOW DARE YOU... YOU...
...YOU MECHANICAL COWARD!!!
OKAY, THEN. IF YOU INSIST ON HAVING A CONSCIENCE OF YOUR OWN, LET ME TELL YOU SOME-THING...
...MR. MECHANI-CAL MAN NUMBER 8!!
JUST IN CASE YOU GOT UPPITY, WE IMPLANTED A BOMB IN YOUR BODY!!
ALL I HAVE TO DO IS PRESS THIS SWITCH AND YOU'LL BE BLOWN INTO SCRAP METAL!!
...
NOW BE A GOOD LITTLE MECHANICAL MAN...AND DESTROY THIS BRAT!!!
8

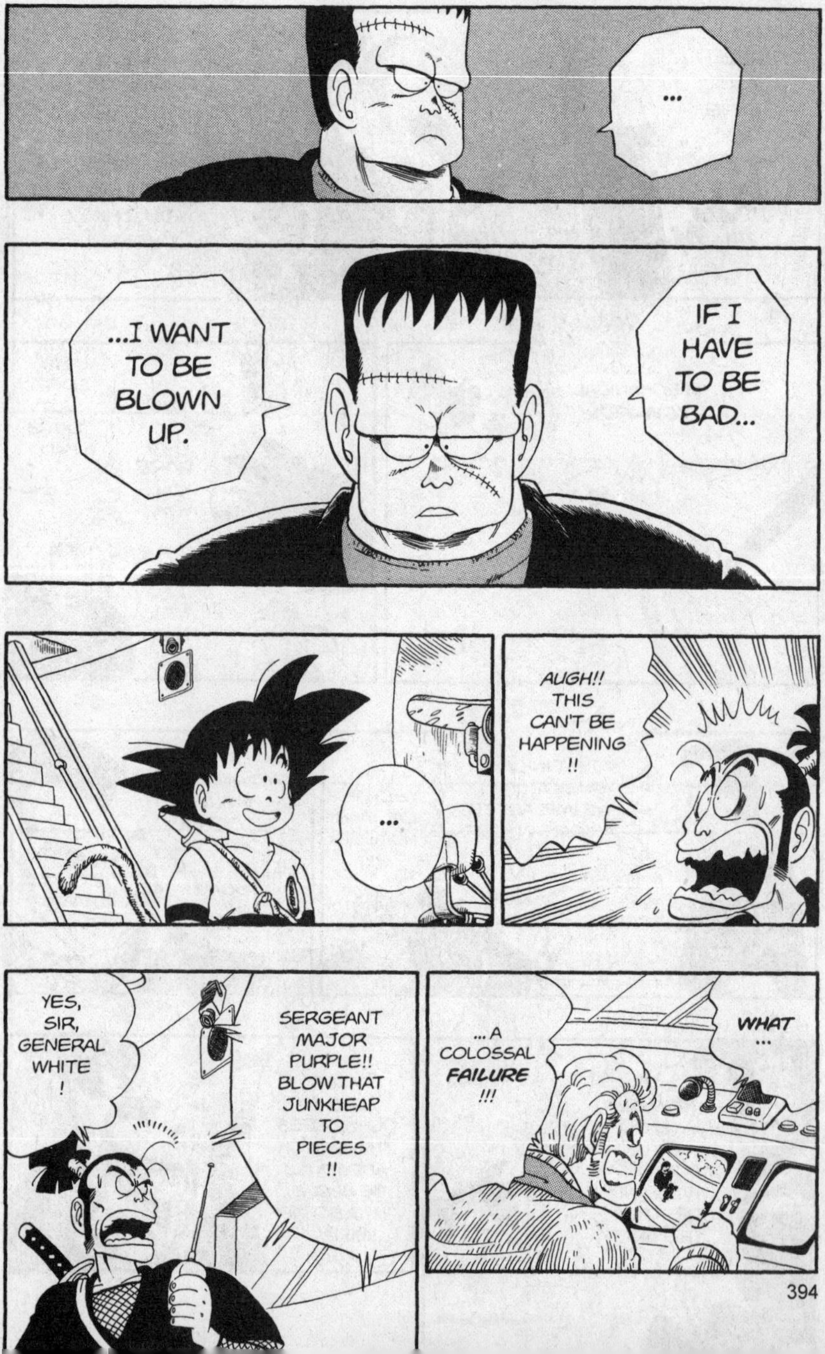
...
IF I HAVE TO BE BAD...
...I WANT TO BE BLOWN UP.
AUGH!! THIS CAN'T BE HAPPENING!!
...
WHAT...
...A COLOSSAL **FAILURE**!!!
SERGEANT MAJOR PURPLE!! BLOW THAT JUNKHEAP TO PIECES!!
YES, SIR, GENERAL WHITE!

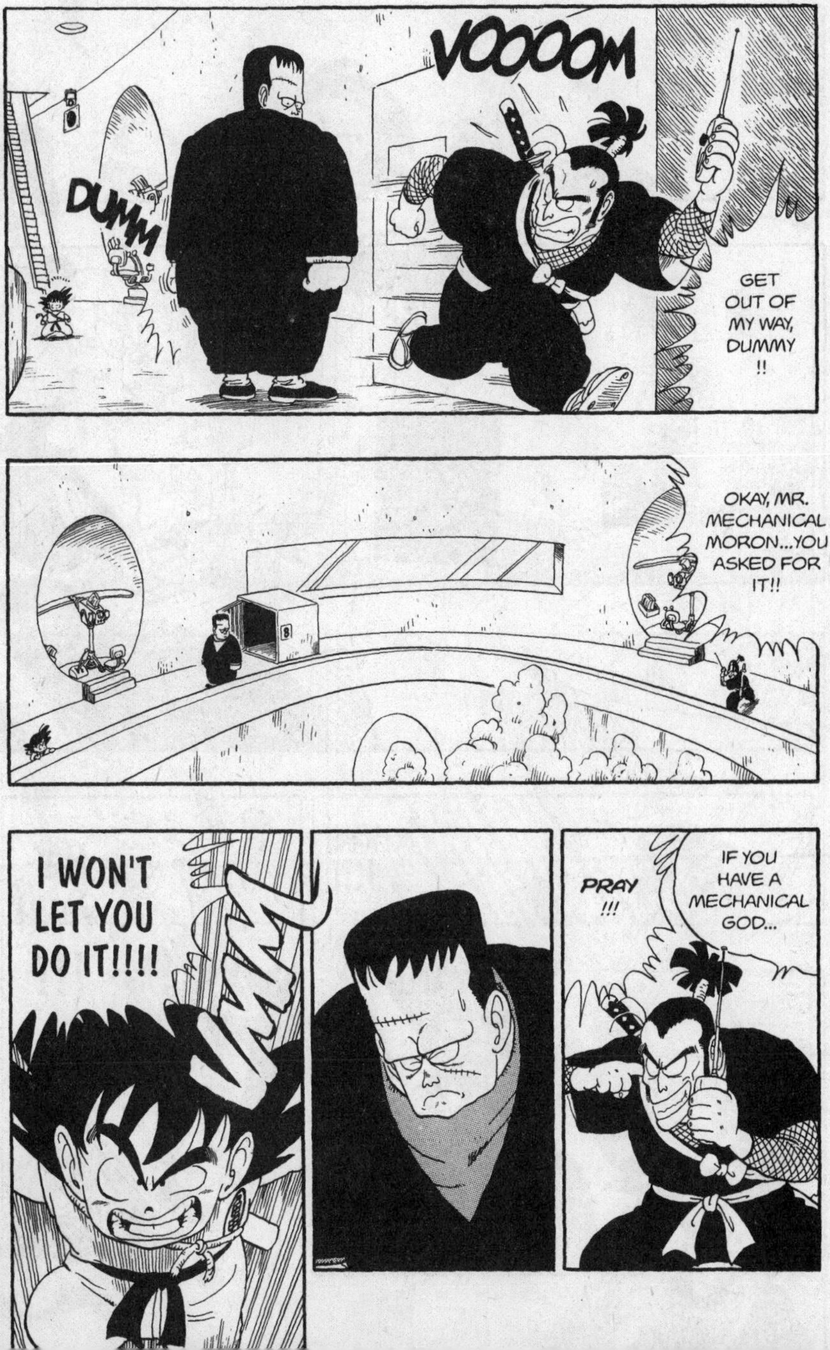
VOOOOM
GET OUT OF MY WAY, DUMMY!!
DUMM
OKAY, MR. MECHANICAL MORON...YOU ASKED FOR IT!!
IF YOU HAVE A MECHANICAL GOD...
PRAY!!!
I WON'T LET YOU DO IT!!!!

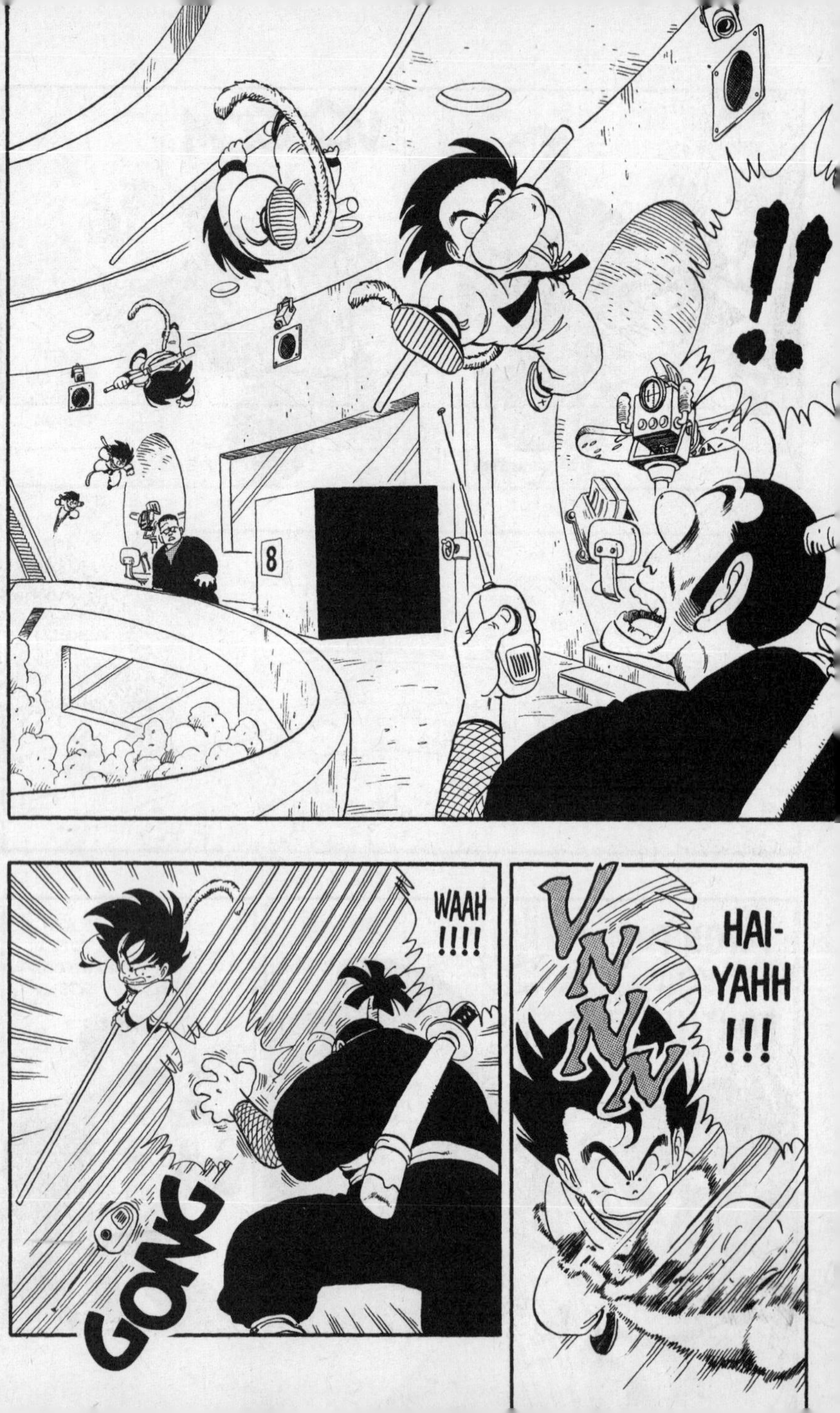
!!
8
VNNN
HAI-YAHH!!!
WAAH!!!!
GONG

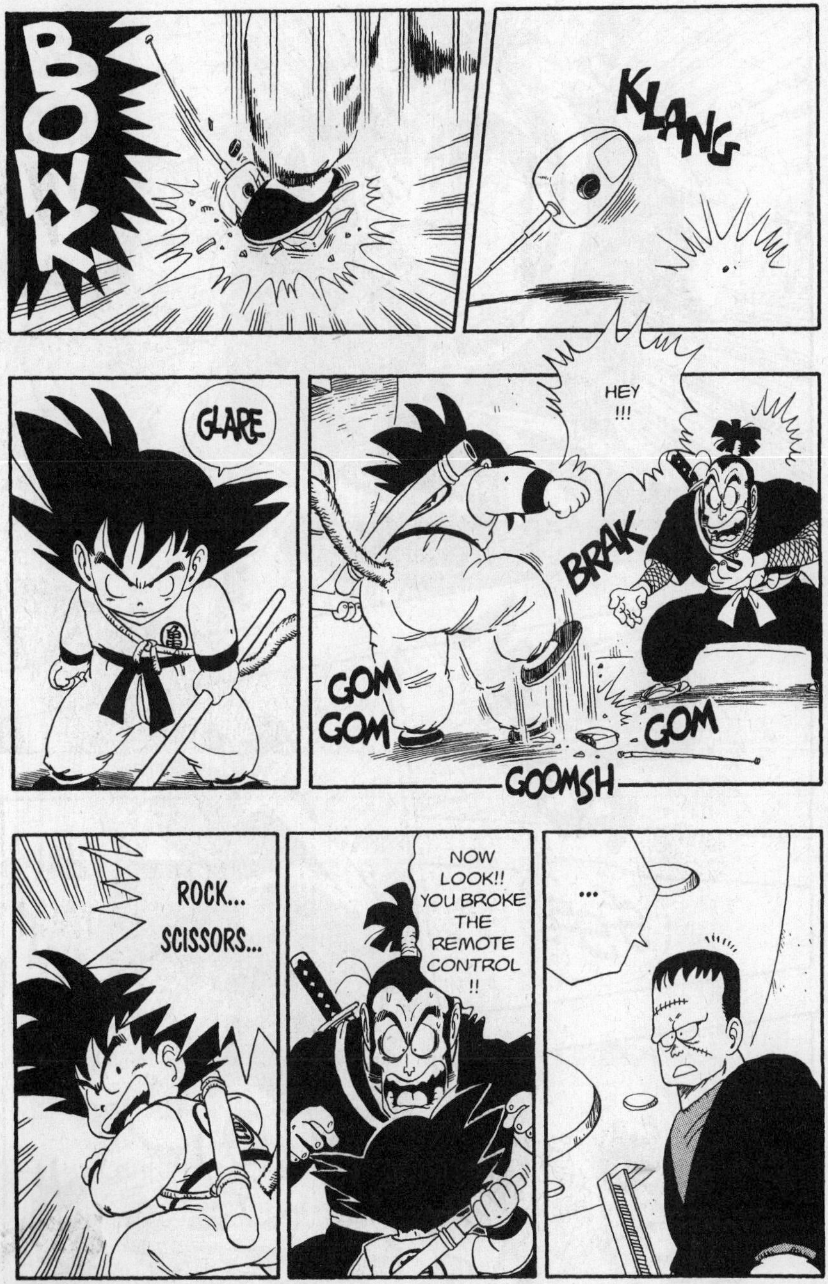
KLANG
BOWK
HEY!!!
BRAK
GOM
GOM GOM
GOOMSH
GLARE
...
NOW LOOK!! YOU BROKE THE REMOTE CONTROL!!
ROCK... SCISSORS...

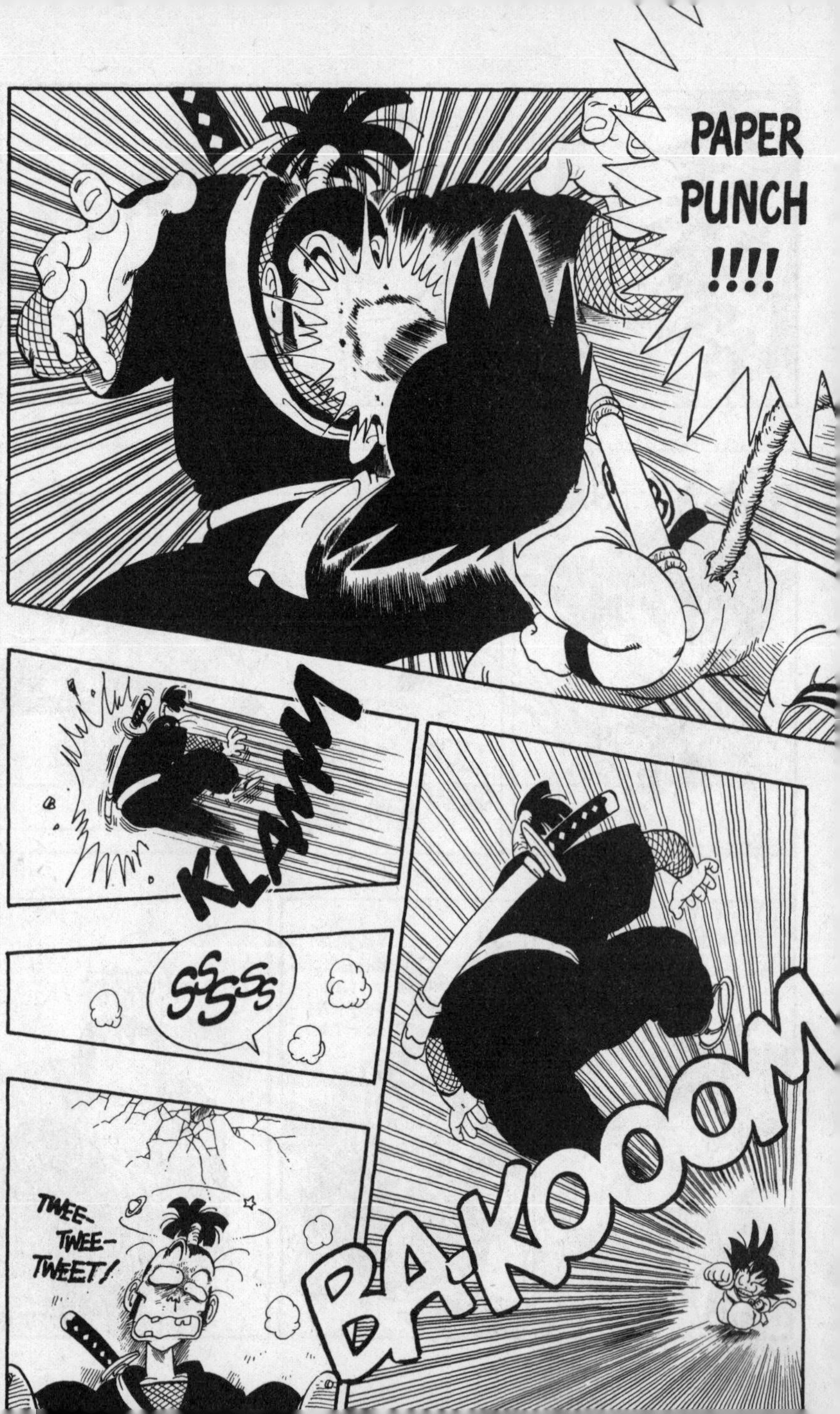
PAPER PUNCH !!!!
BA-KOOOOM
KLAMM
SSSSS
TWEE-TWEE-TWEET!

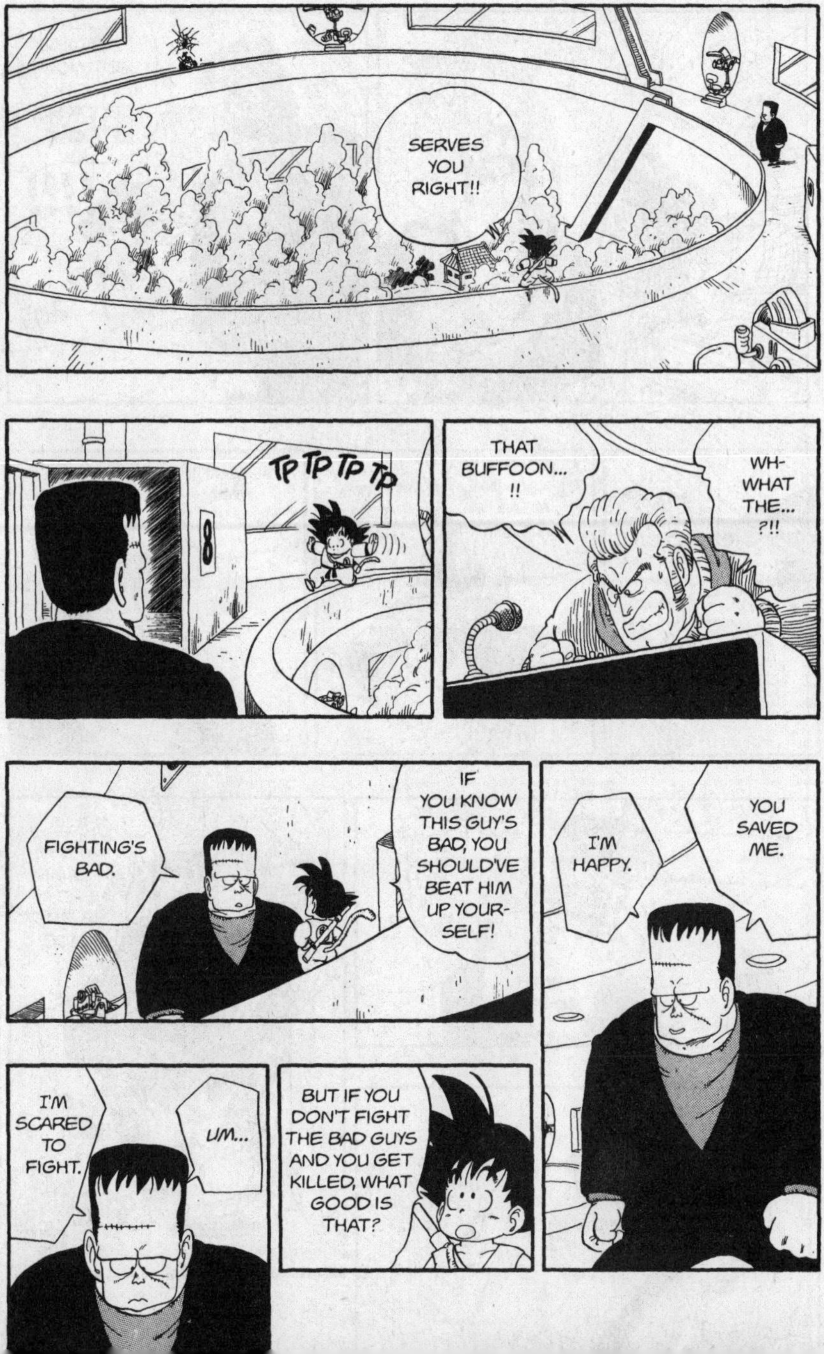
SERVES YOU RIGHT!!
WH- WHAT THE...?!!
THAT BUFFOON...!!
TP TP TP TP
YOU SAVED ME.
I'M HAPPY.
IF YOU KNOW THIS GUY'S BAD, YOU SHOULD'VE BEAT HIM UP YOUR-SELF!
FIGHTING'S BAD.
BUT IF YOU DON'T FIGHT THE BAD GUYS AND YOU GET KILLED, WHAT GOOD IS THAT?
UM...
I'M SCARED TO FIGHT.

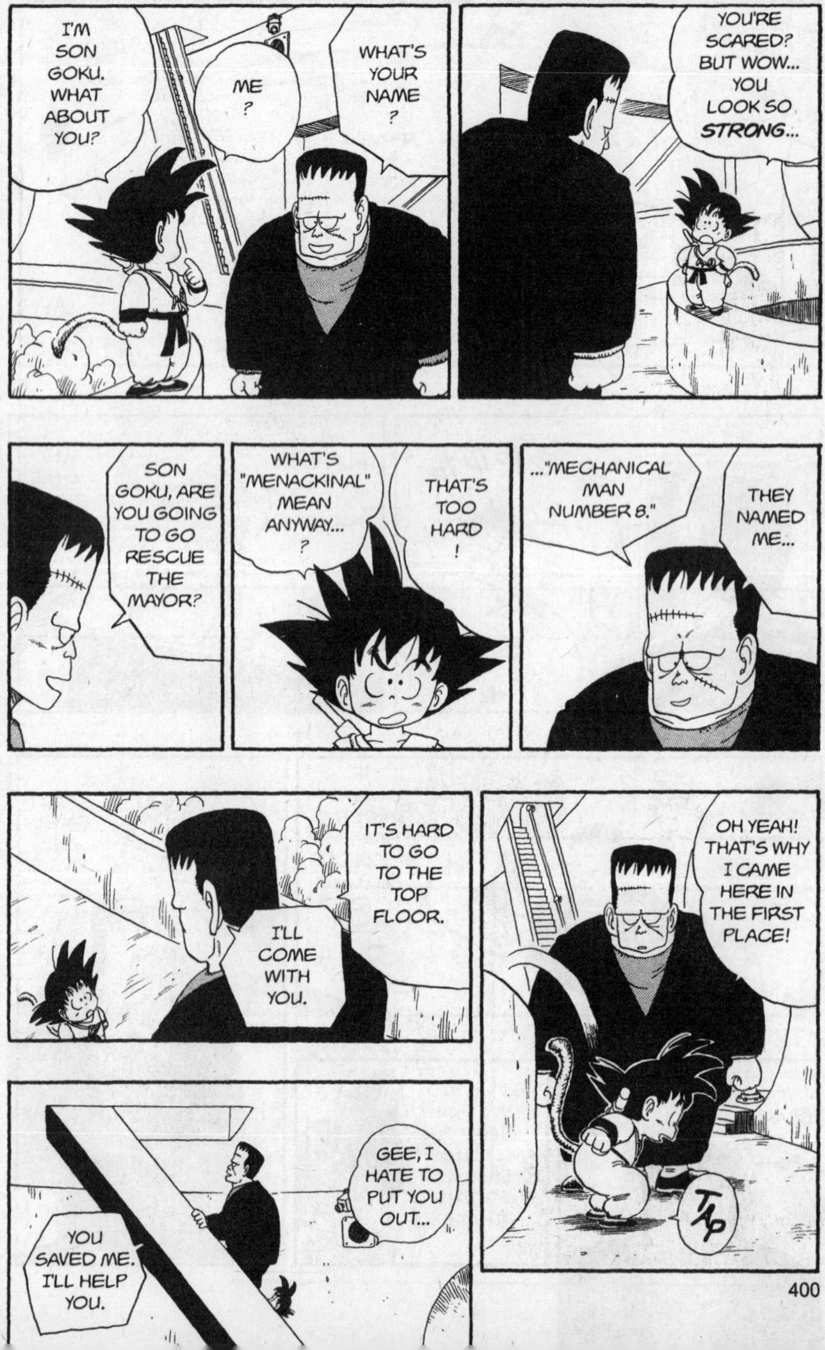
YOU'RE SCARED? BUT WOW... YOU LOOK SO STRONG...
WHAT'S YOUR NAME ?
ME ?
I'M SON GOKU. WHAT ABOUT YOU?
THEY NAMED ME...
..."MECHANICAL MAN NUMBER 8."
THAT'S TOO HARD !
WHAT'S "MENACKINAL" MEAN ANYWAY... ?
SON GOKU, ARE YOU GOING TO GO RESCUE THE MAYOR?
OH YEAH! THAT'S WHY I CAME HERE IN THE FIRST PLACE!
TAP
IT'S HARD TO GO TO THE TOP FLOOR.
I'LL COME WITH YOU.
GEE, I HATE TO PUT YOU OUT...
YOU SAVED ME. I'LL HELP YOU.

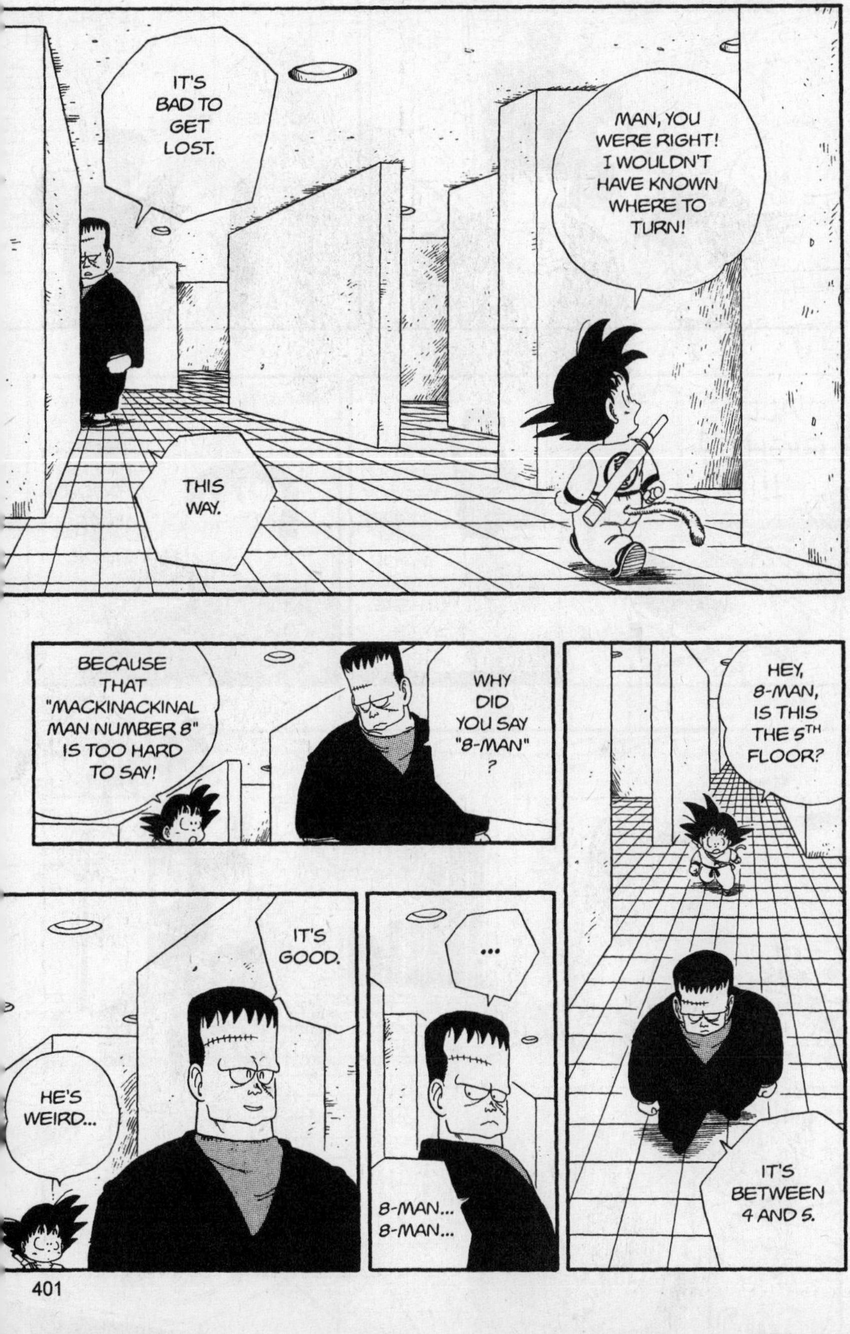
MAN, YOU WERE RIGHT! I WOULDN'T HAVE KNOWN WHERE TO TURN!
IT'S BAD TO GET LOST.
THIS WAY.
HEY, 8-MAN, IS THIS THE 5TH FLOOR?
IT'S BETWEEN 4 AND 5.
WHY DID YOU SAY "8-MAN"?
BECAUSE THAT "MACKINACKINAL MAN NUMBER 8" IS TOO HARD TO SAY!
...
8-MAN... 8-MAN...
IT'S GOOD.
HE'S WEIRD...

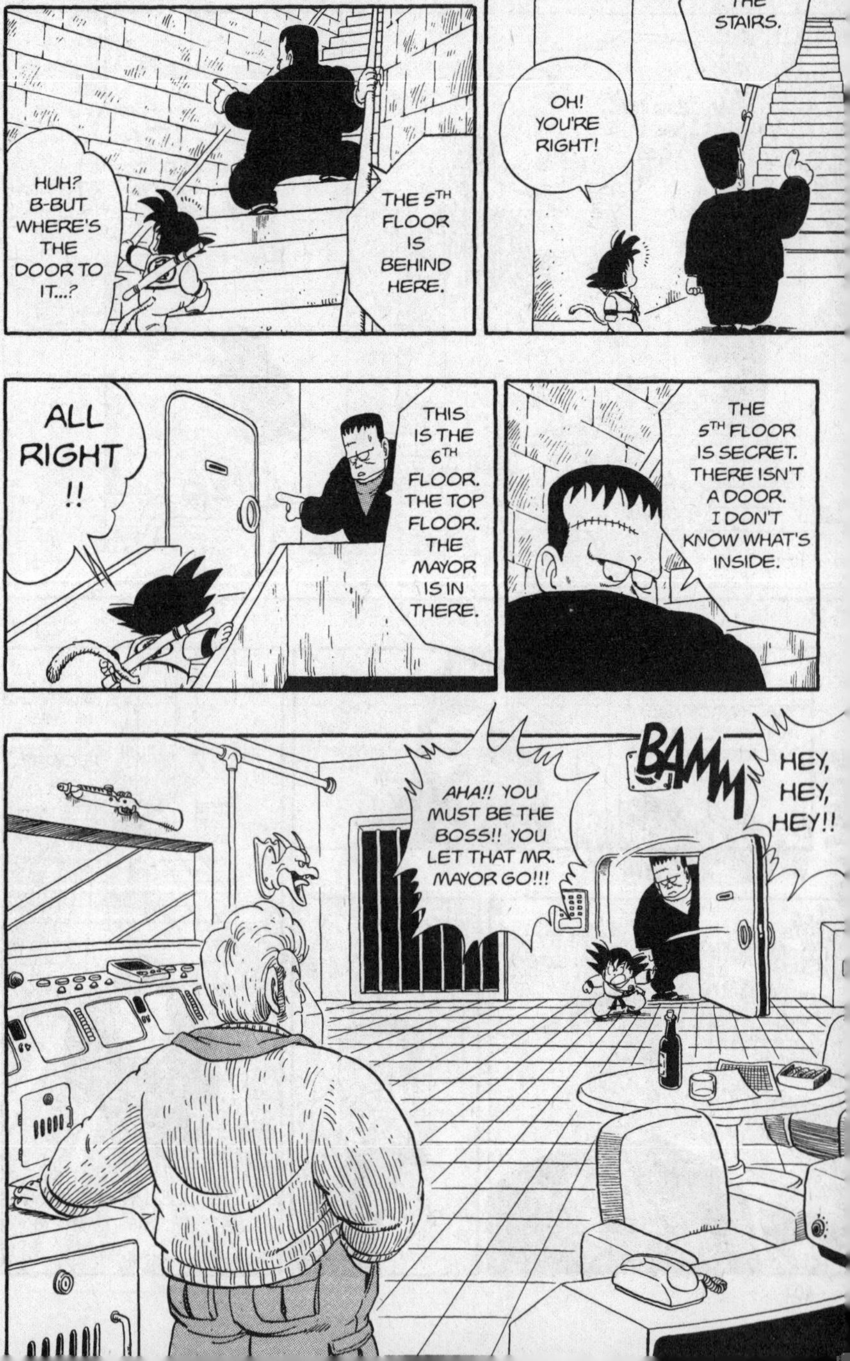
THE STAIRS.
OH! YOU'RE RIGHT!
THE 5TH FLOOR IS BEHIND HERE.
HUH? B-BUT WHERE'S THE DOOR TO IT...?
THE 5TH FLOOR IS SECRET. THERE ISN'T A DOOR. I DON'T KNOW WHAT'S INSIDE.
THIS IS THE 6TH FLOOR. THE TOP FLOOR. THE MAYOR IS IN THERE.
ALL RIGHT !!
HEY, HEY, HEY!!
BAMM
AHA!! YOU MUST BE THE BOSS!! YOU LET THAT MR. MAYOR GO!!!

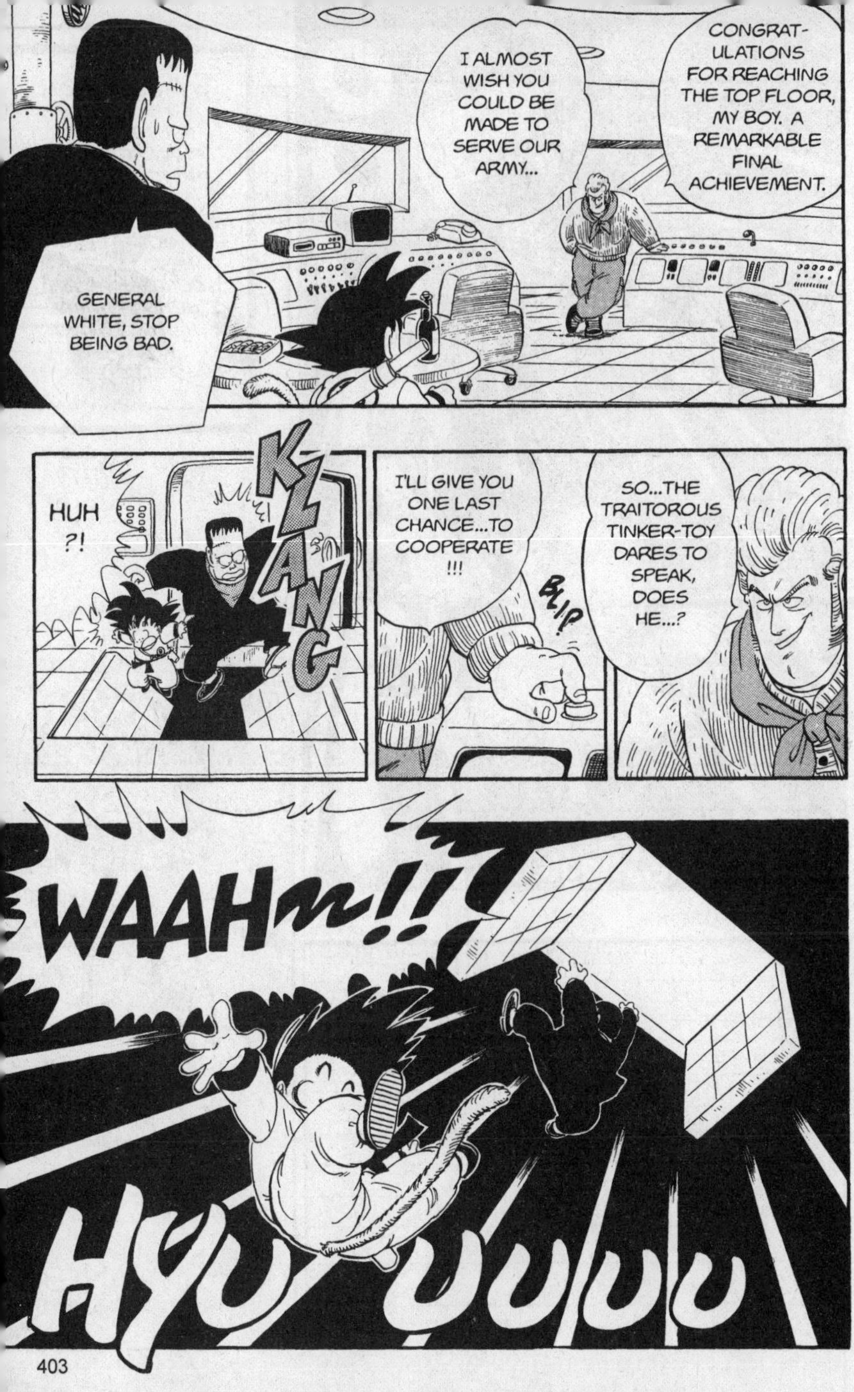
CONGRAT-ULATIONS FOR REACHING THE TOP FLOOR, MY BOY. A REMARKABLE FINAL ACHIEVEMENT.
I ALMOST WISH YOU COULD BE MADE TO SERVE OUR ARMY...
GENERAL WHITE, STOP BEING BAD.
SO...THE TRAITOROUS TINKER-TOY DARES TO SPEAK, DOES HE...?
I'LL GIVE YOU ONE LAST CHANCE...TO COOPERATE !!!
BLIP
KLANG
HUH ?!
WAAHn!!
HYUUUUUU

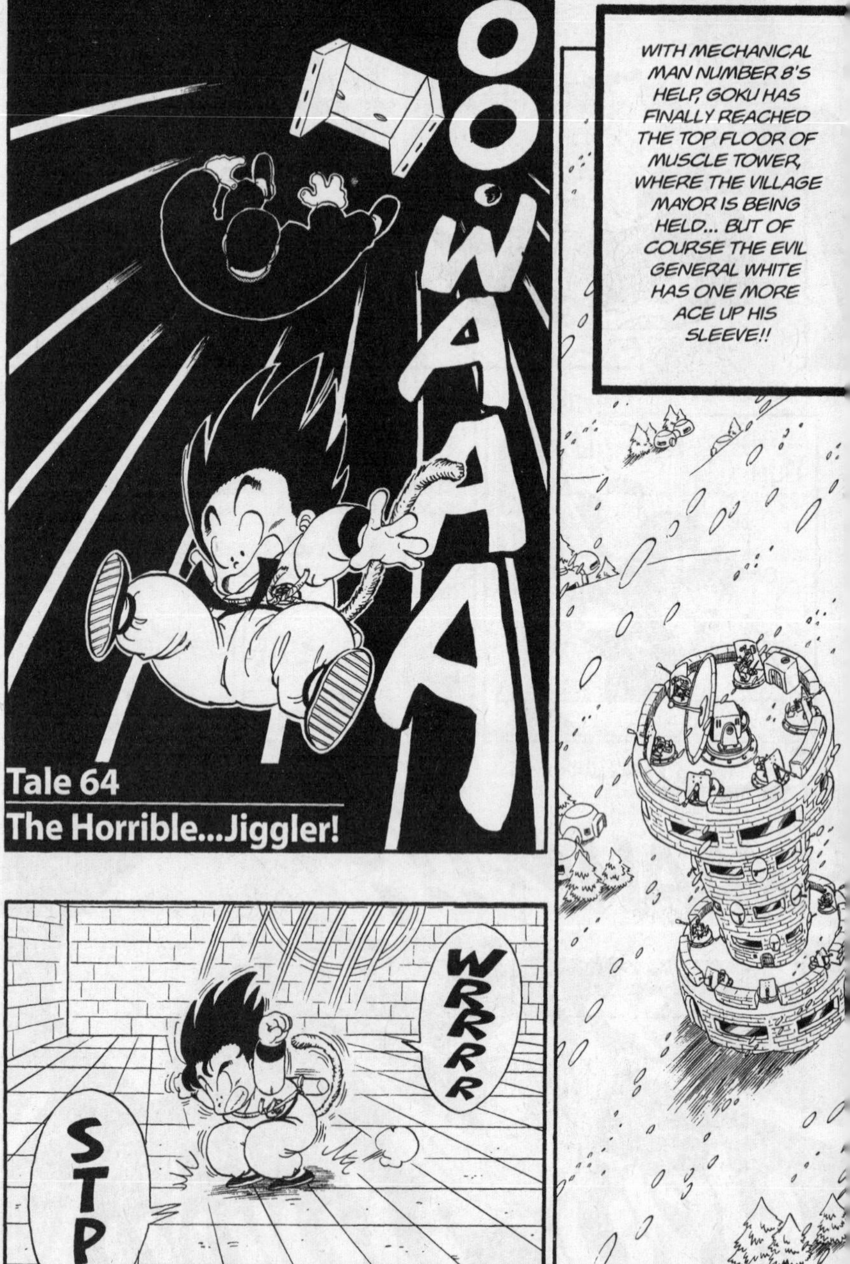
WITH MECHANICAL MAN NUMBER 8'S HELP, GOKU HAS FINALLY REACHED THE TOP FLOOR OF MUSCLE TOWER, WHERE THE VILLAGE MAYOR IS BEING HELD... BUT OF COURSE THE EVIL GENERAL WHITE HAS ONE MORE ACE UP HIS SLEEVE!!
OOWAAA
Tale 64
The Horrible...Jiggler!
WRRRR
STP

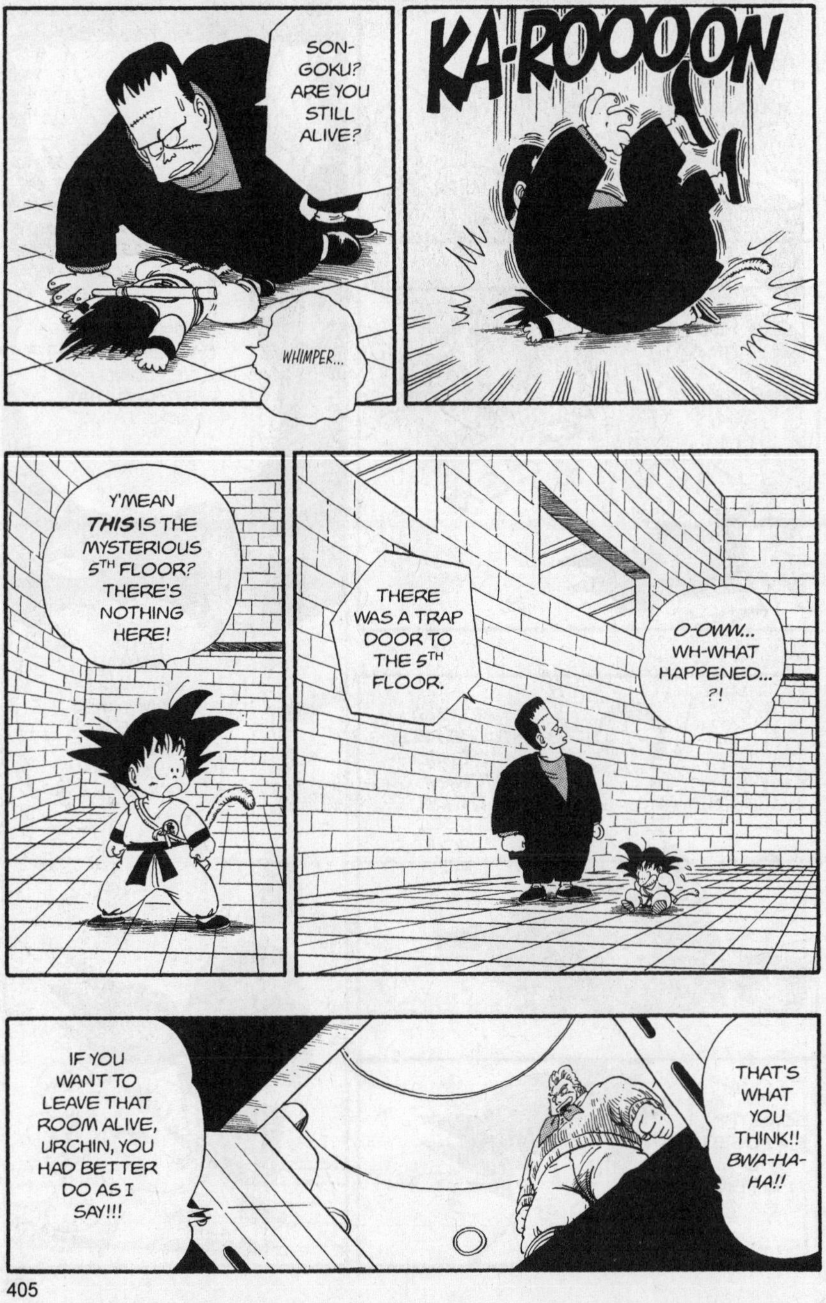
KA-ROOOOON
SON-GOKU? ARE YOU STILL ALIVE?
WHIMPER...
O-OWW... WH-WHAT HAPPENED... ?!
THERE WAS A TRAP DOOR TO THE 5TH FLOOR.
Y'MEAN THIS IS THE MYSTERIOUS 5TH FLOOR? THERE'S NOTHING HERE!
THAT'S WHAT YOU THINK!! BWA-HA-HA!!
IF YOU WANT TO LEAVE THAT ROOM ALIVE, URCHIN, YOU HAD BETTER DO AS I SAY!!!

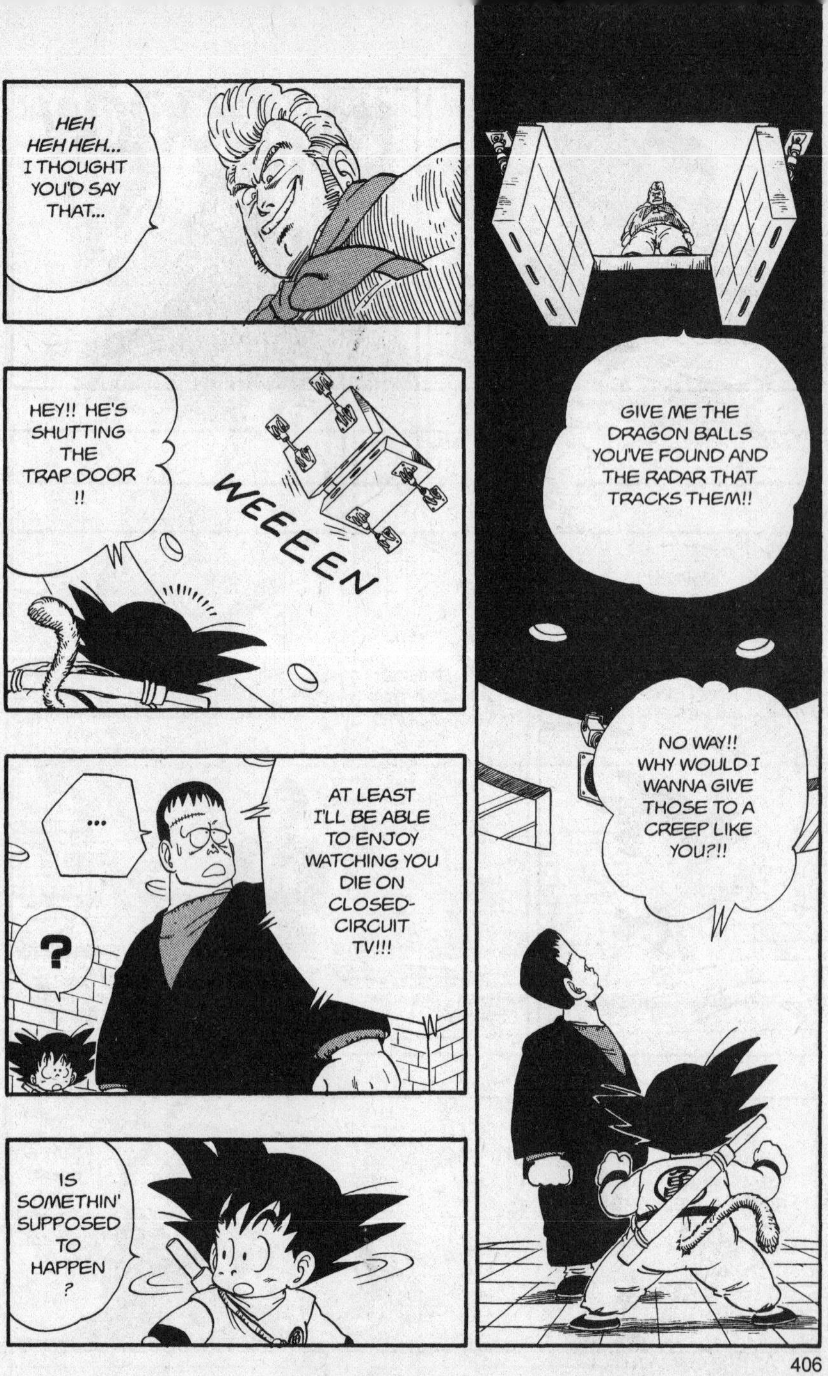
GIVE ME THE DRAGON BALLS YOU'VE FOUND AND THE RADAR THAT TRACKS THEM!!
NO WAY!! WHY WOULD I WANNA GIVE THOSE TO A CREEP LIKE YOU?!!
HEH HEH HEH... I THOUGHT YOU'D SAY THAT...
HEY!! HE'S SHUTTING THE TRAP DOOR !!
WEEEEN
AT LEAST I'LL BE ABLE TO ENJOY WATCHING YOU DIE ON CLOSED-CIRCUIT TV!!!
...
?
IS SOMETHIN' SUPPOSED TO HAPPEN ?

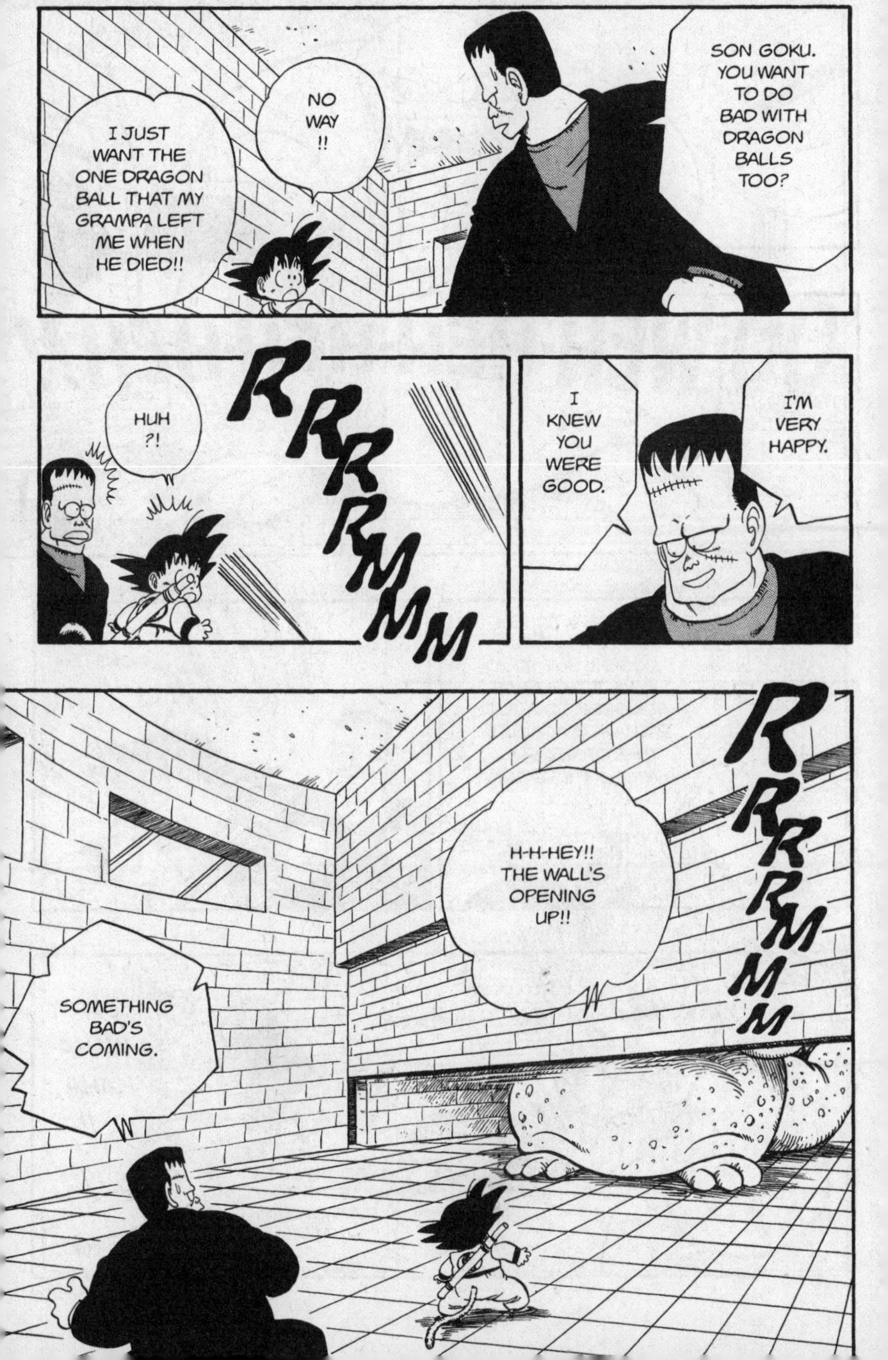

SON GOKU. YOU WANT TO DO BAD WITH DRAGON BALLS TOO?
NO WAY !!
I JUST WANT THE ONE DRAGON BALL THAT MY GRAMPA LEFT ME WHEN HE DIED!!
I'M VERY HAPPY.
I KNEW YOU WERE GOOD.
RRRRMMM
HUH ?!
RRRRMMMM
H-H-HEY!! THE WALL'S OPENING UP!!
SOMETHING BAD'S COMING.

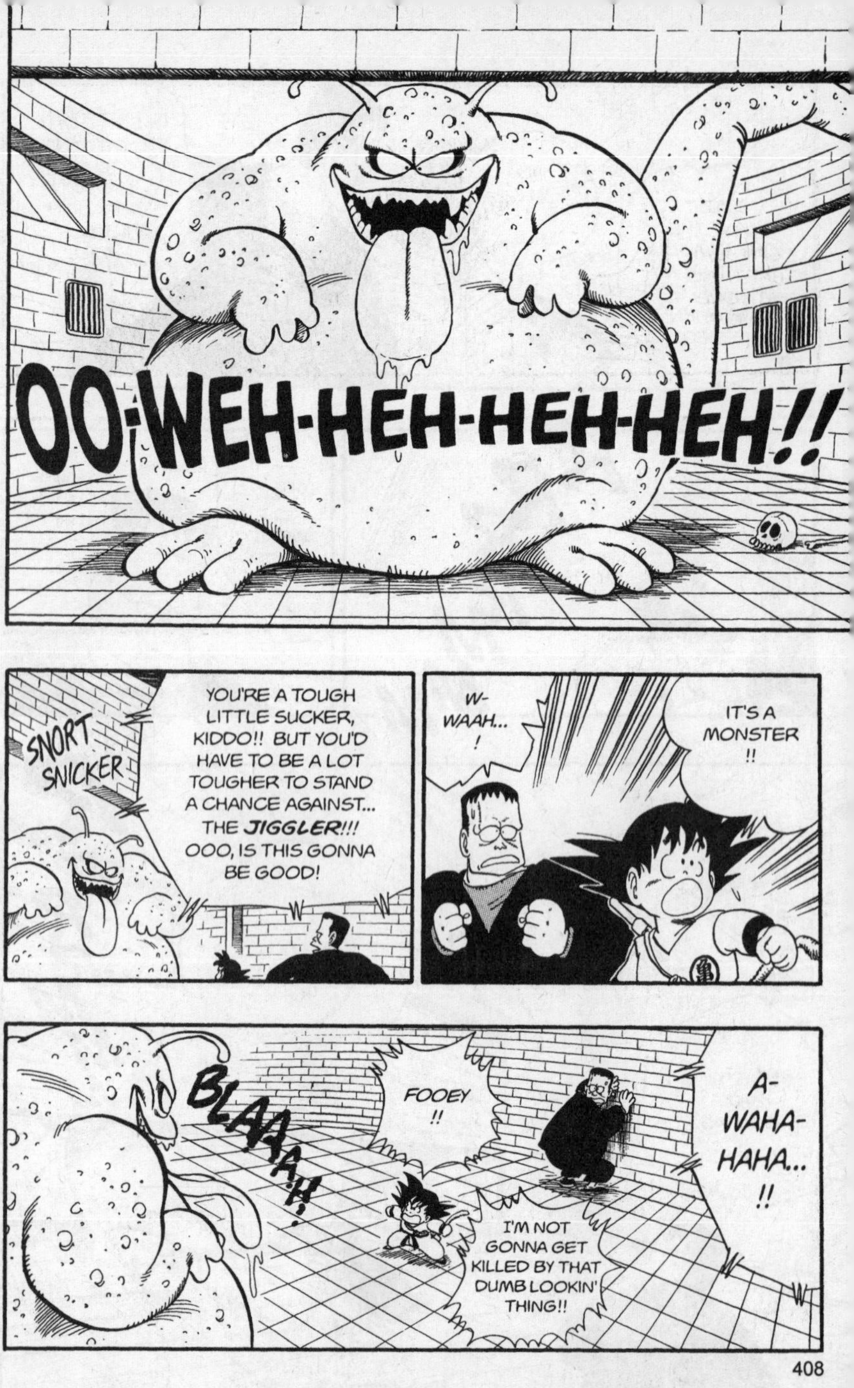
OO-WEH-HEH-HEH-HEH!!
IT'S A MONSTER !!
W-WAAH... !
YOU'RE A TOUGH LITTLE SUCKER, KIDDO!! BUT YOU'D HAVE TO BE A LOT TOUGHER TO STAND A CHANCE AGAINST... THE JIGGLER!!! OOO, IS THIS GONNA BE GOOD!
SNORT SNICKER
A-WAHA-HAHA... !!
FOOEY !!
I'M NOT GONNA GET KILLED BY THAT DUMB LOOKIN' THING!!
BLAAAAH!

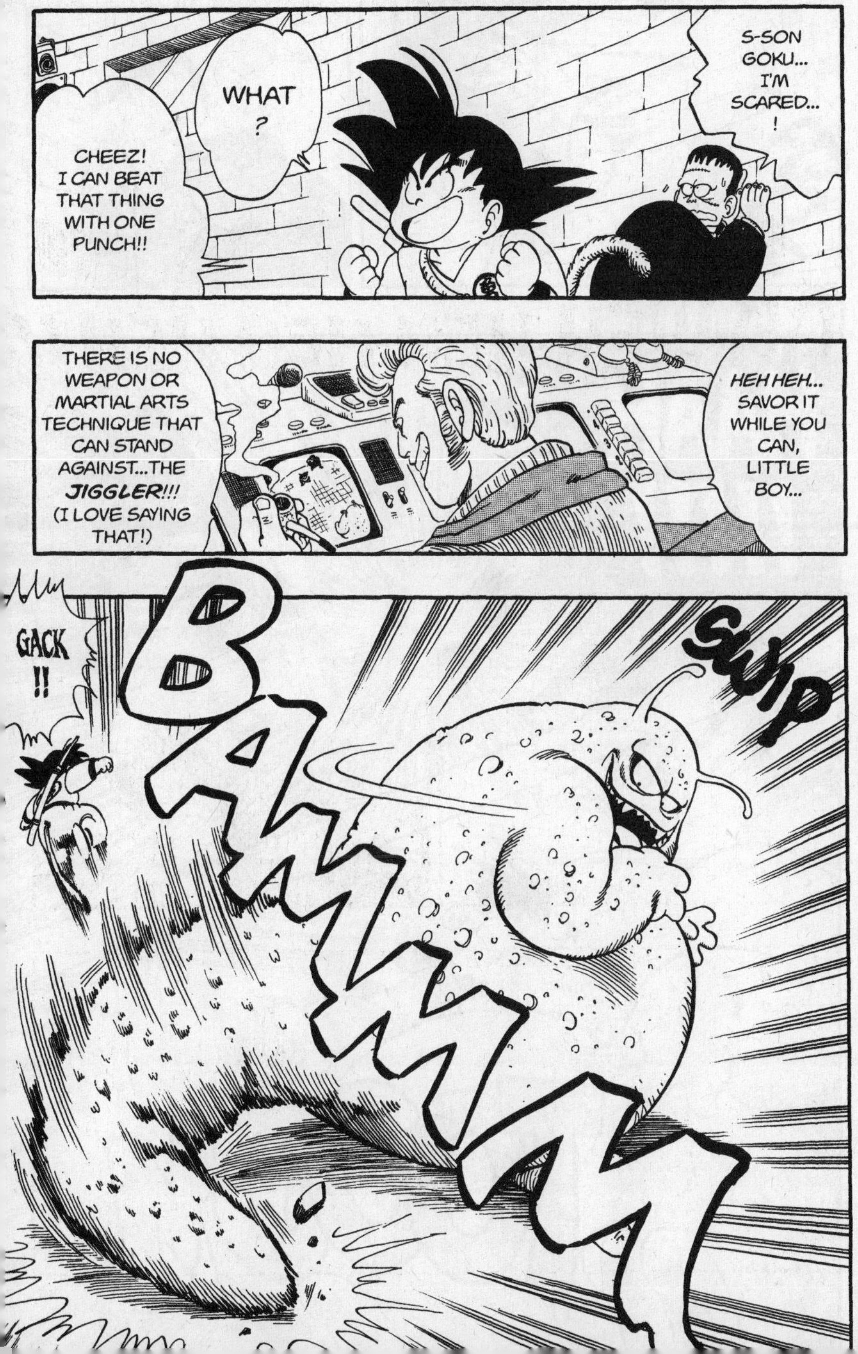
S-SON GOKU... I'M SCARED... !
WHAT ?
CHEEZ! I CAN BEAT THAT THING WITH ONE PUNCH!!
HEH HEH... SAVOR IT WHILE YOU CAN, LITTLE BOY...
THERE IS NO WEAPON OR MARTIAL ARTS TECHNIQUE THAT CAN STAND AGAINST...THE ***JIGGLER***!!! (I LOVE SAYING THAT!)
SLUP
BAMMM
GACK !!

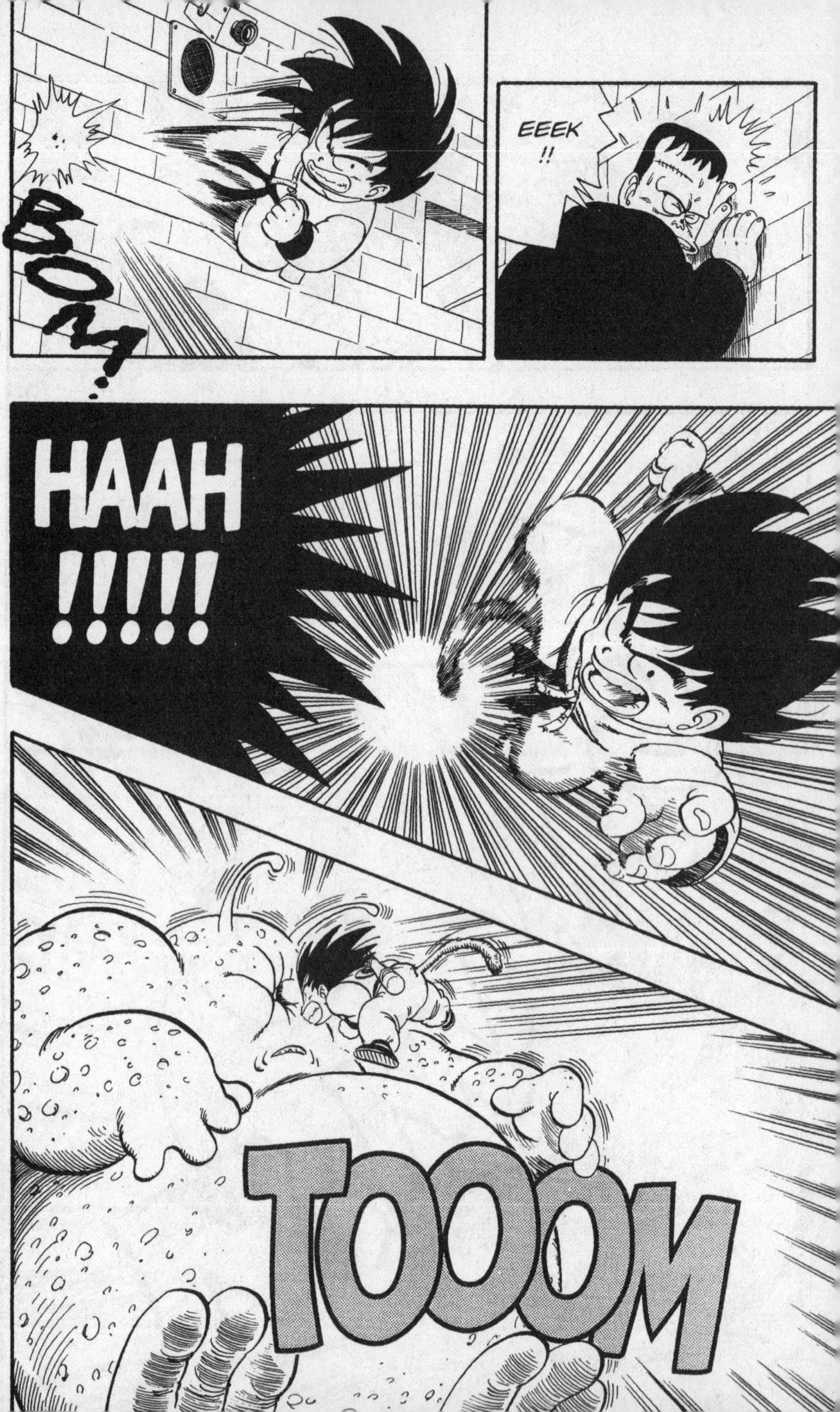
EEEK !!
BOM!
HAAH !!!!!
TOOOM

BOINNNG
HUH ?!
TP
HE HE HE HE HE
M-MY PUNCH DIDN'T BOTHER IT ONE BIT...!!
OOO-KAAY !!!
THEN TRY A KICK!!!!

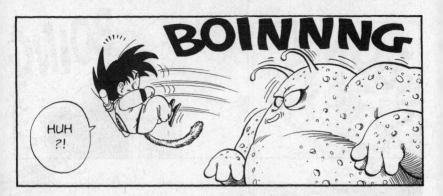

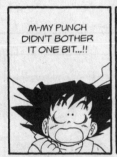

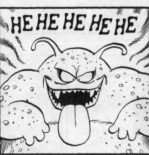

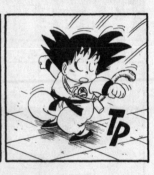

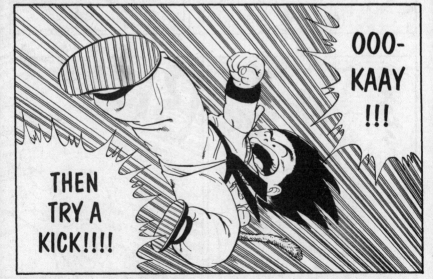

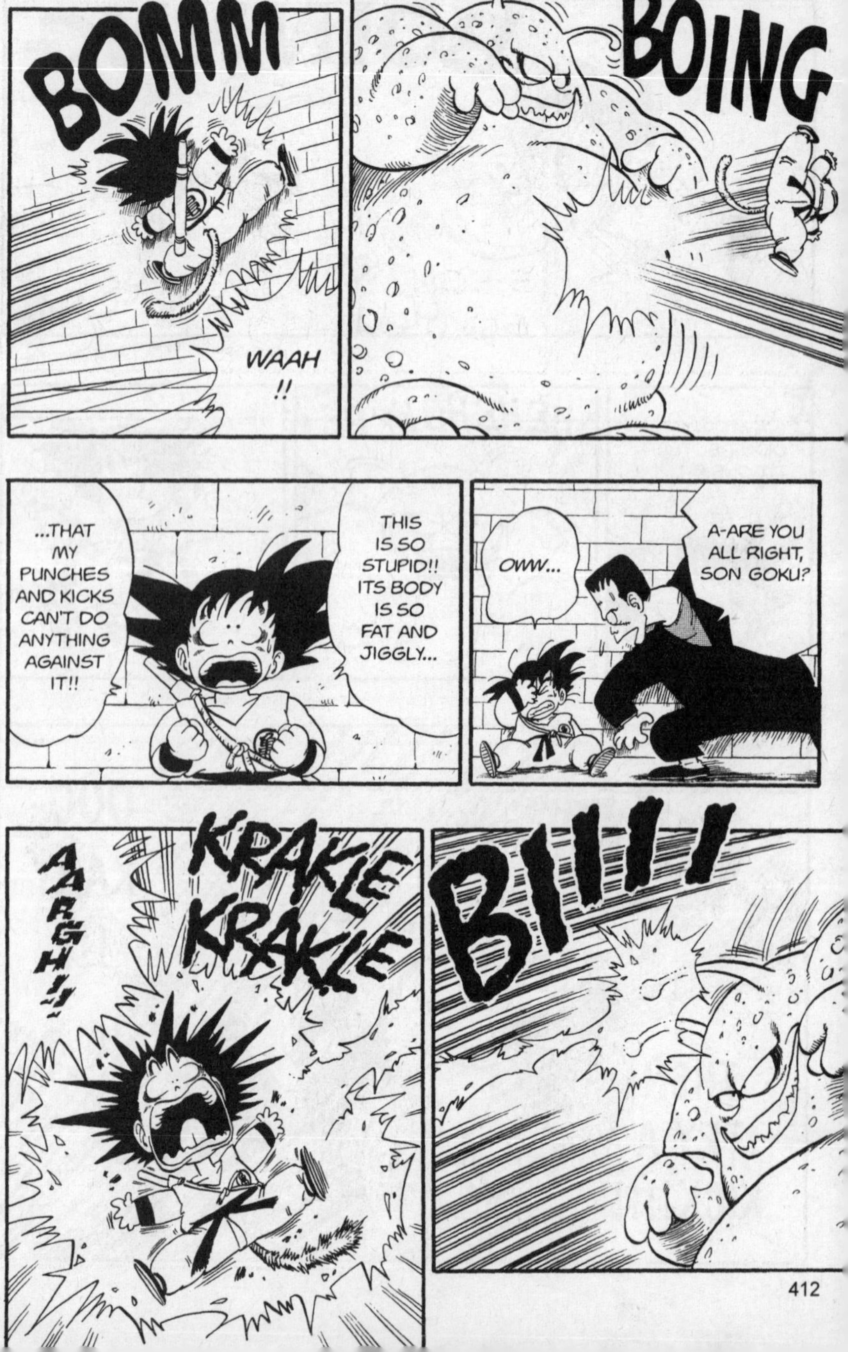
BOING
BOMM
WAAH!!
A-ARE YOU ALL RIGHT, SON GOKU?
OWW...
THIS IS SO STUPID!! ITS BODY IS SO FAT AND JIGGLY...
...THAT MY PUNCHES AND KICKS CAN'T DO ANYTHING AGAINST IT!!
BIIIII
KRAKLE KRAKLE
AARGH!!!

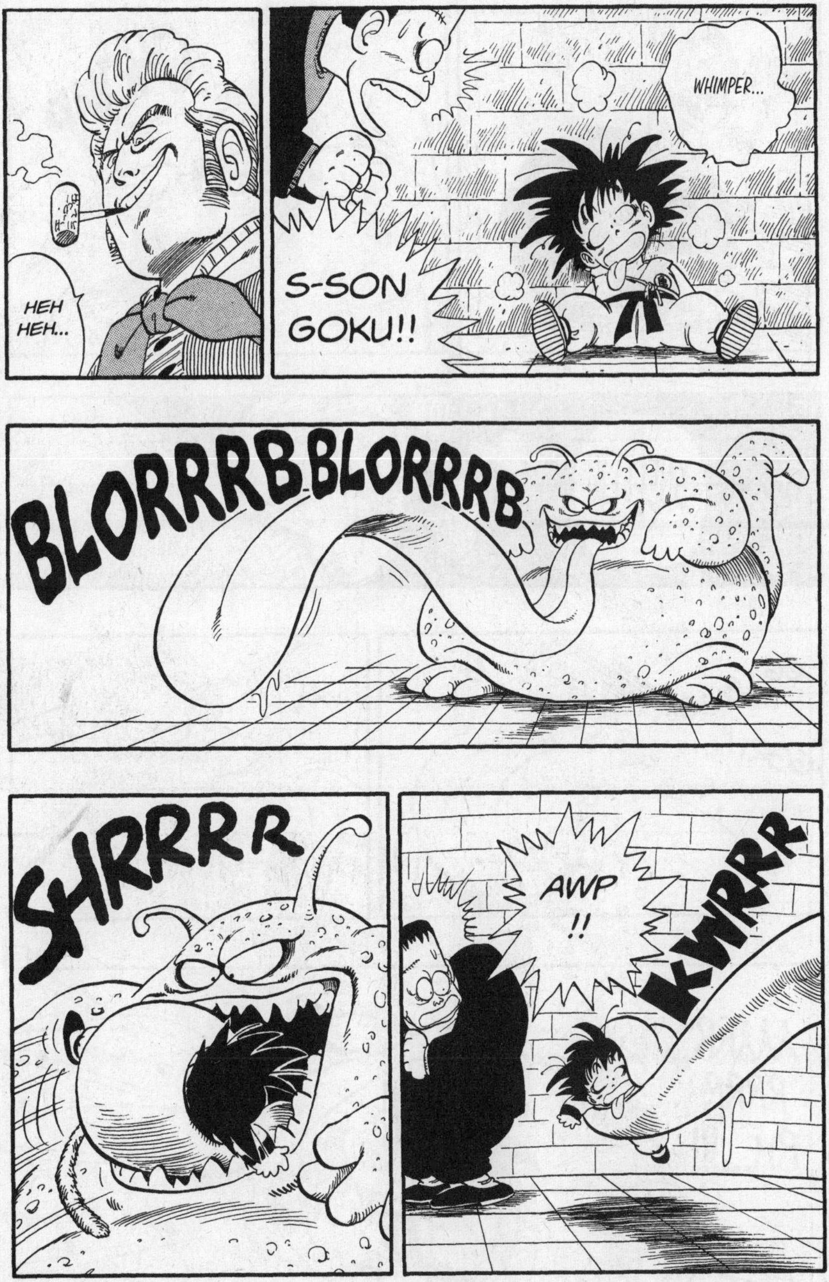
WHIMPER...
S-SON GOKU!!
HEH HEH...
BLORRRB BLORRRB
KWRRR
AWP !!
SHRRRR

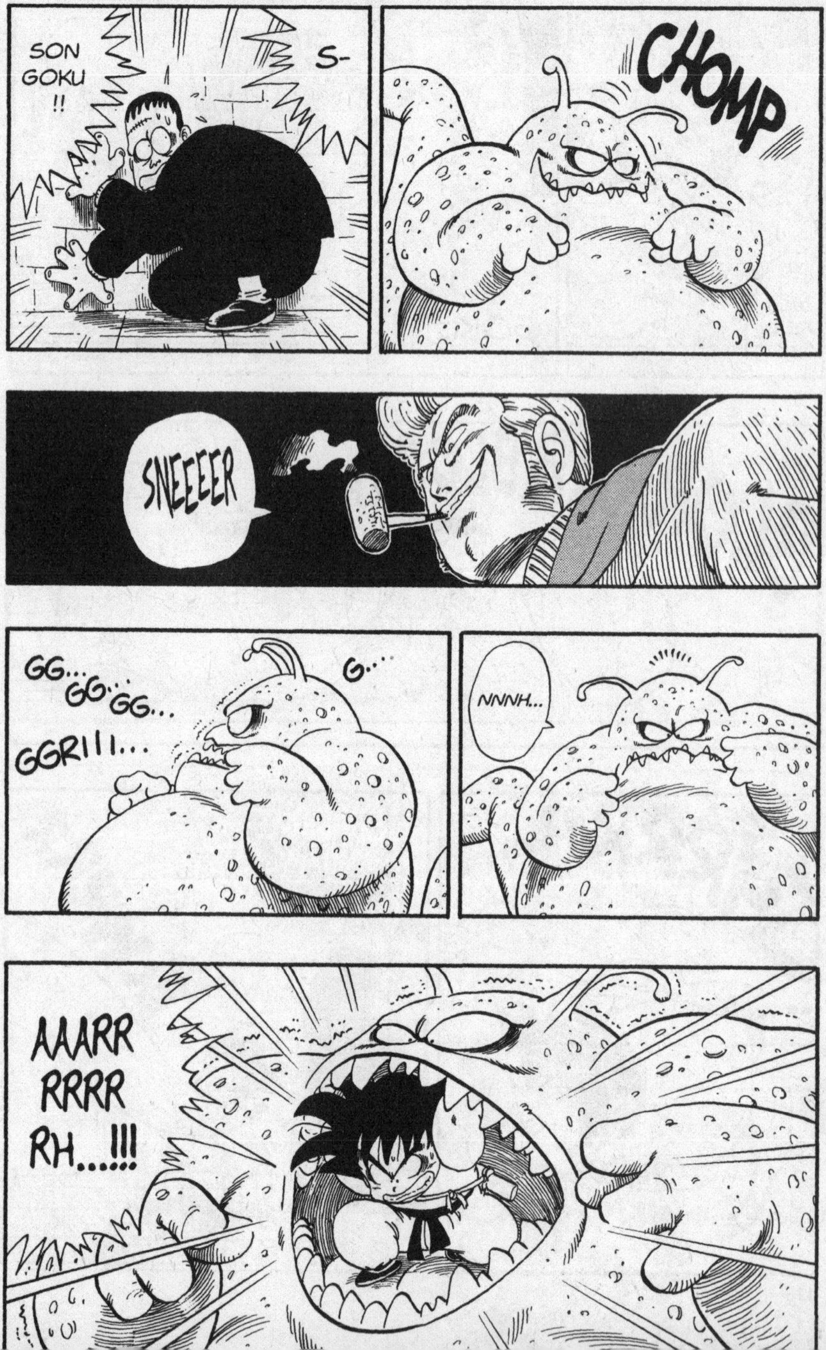
CHOMP
SON GOKU !!
S-
SNEEEER
NNNH...
G...
GG... GG... GG...
GGRIIII...
AAARR RRRR RH...!!!

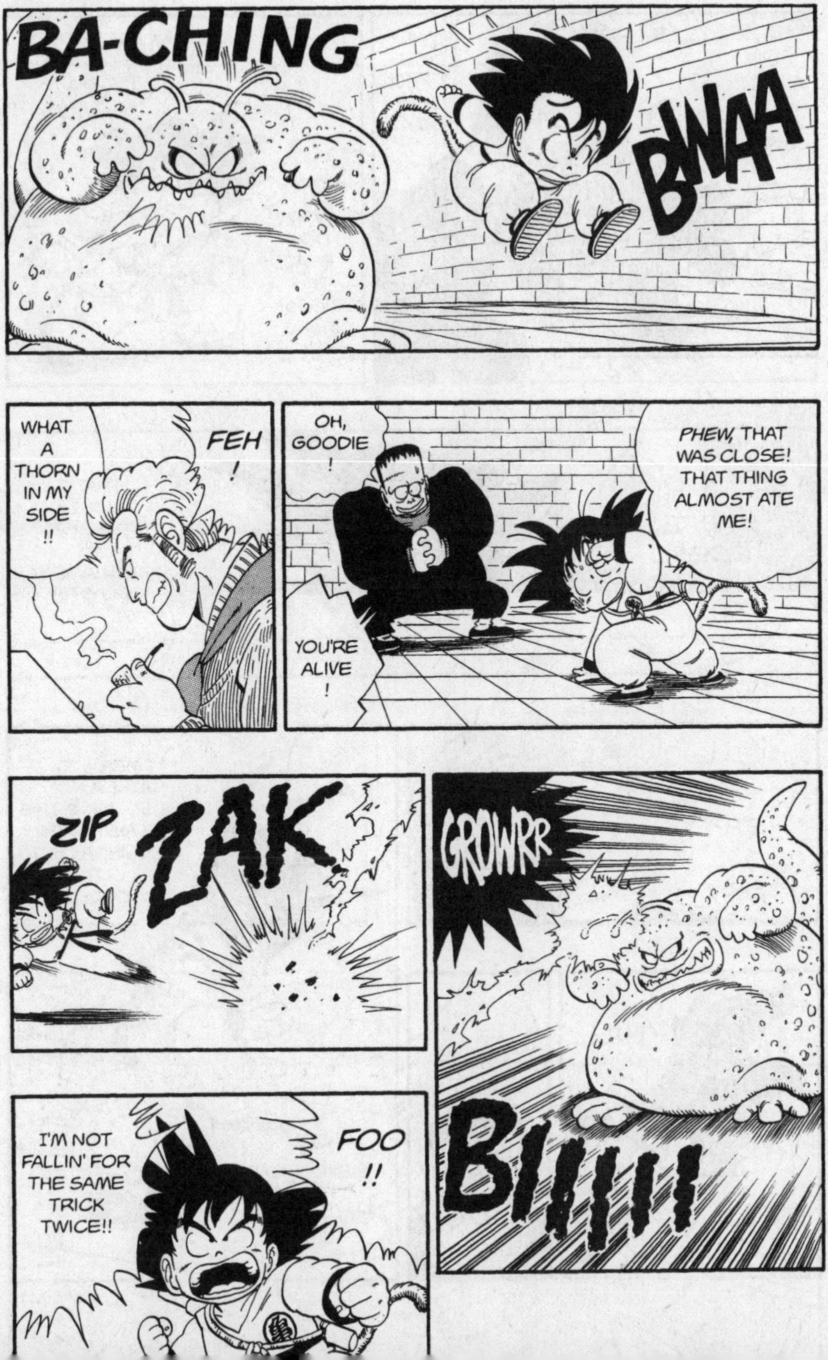
BWAA
BA-CHING
PHEW, THAT WAS CLOSE! THAT THING ALMOST ATE ME!
OH, GOODIE!
YOU'RE ALIVE!
FEH!
WHAT A THORN IN MY SIDE!!
GROWRR
BIIIII
ZIP
ZAK
FOO!!
I'M NOT FALLIN' FOR THE SAME TRICK TWICE!!

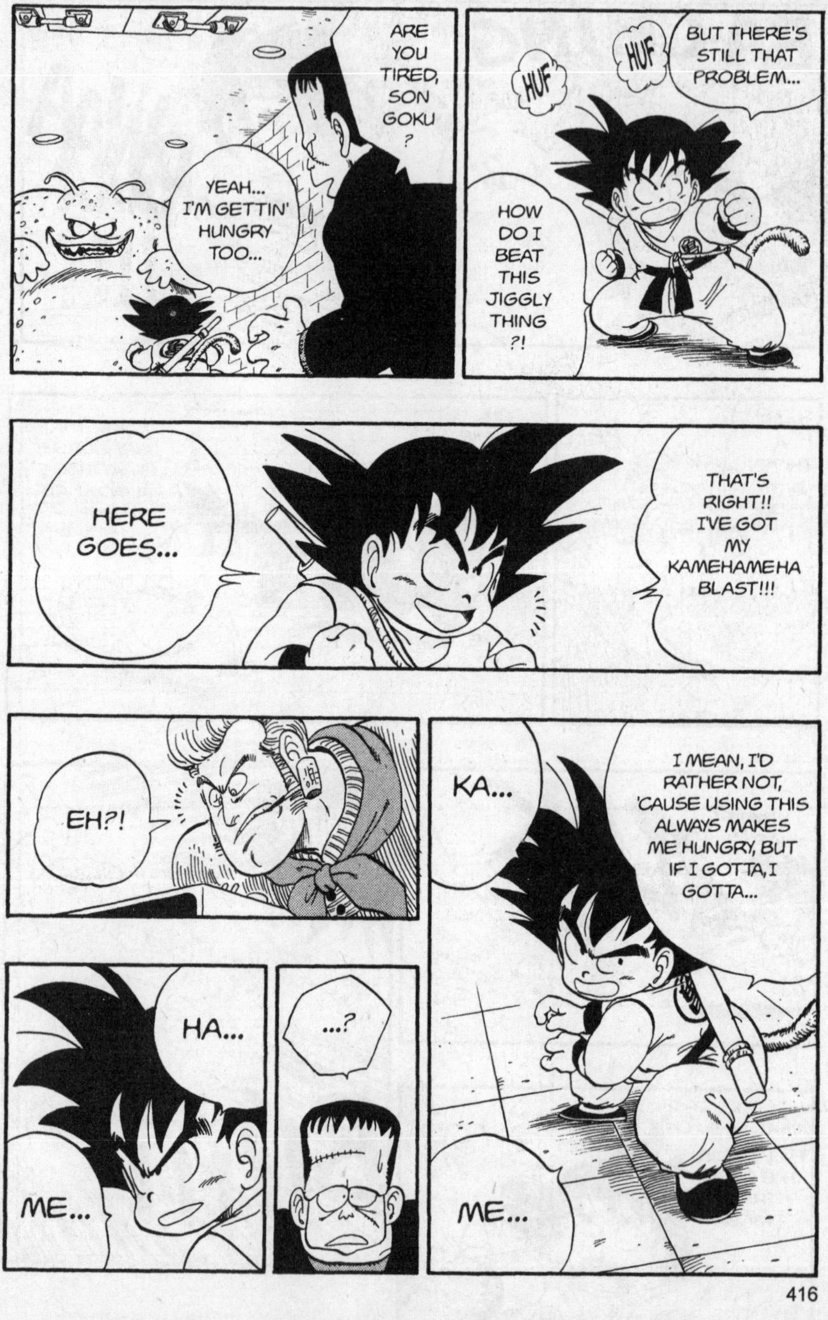
HUF
HUF
BUT THERE'S STILL THAT PROBLEM...
HOW DO I BEAT THIS JIGGLY THING ?!
ARE YOU TIRED, SON GOKU ?
YEAH... I'M GETTIN' HUNGRY TOO...
THAT'S RIGHT!! I'VE GOT MY KAMEHAMEHA BLAST!!!
HERE GOES...
I MEAN, I'D RATHER NOT, 'CAUSE USING THIS ALWAYS MAKES ME HUNGRY, BUT IF I GOTTA, I GOTTA...
KA...
ME...
EH?!
...?
HA...
ME...

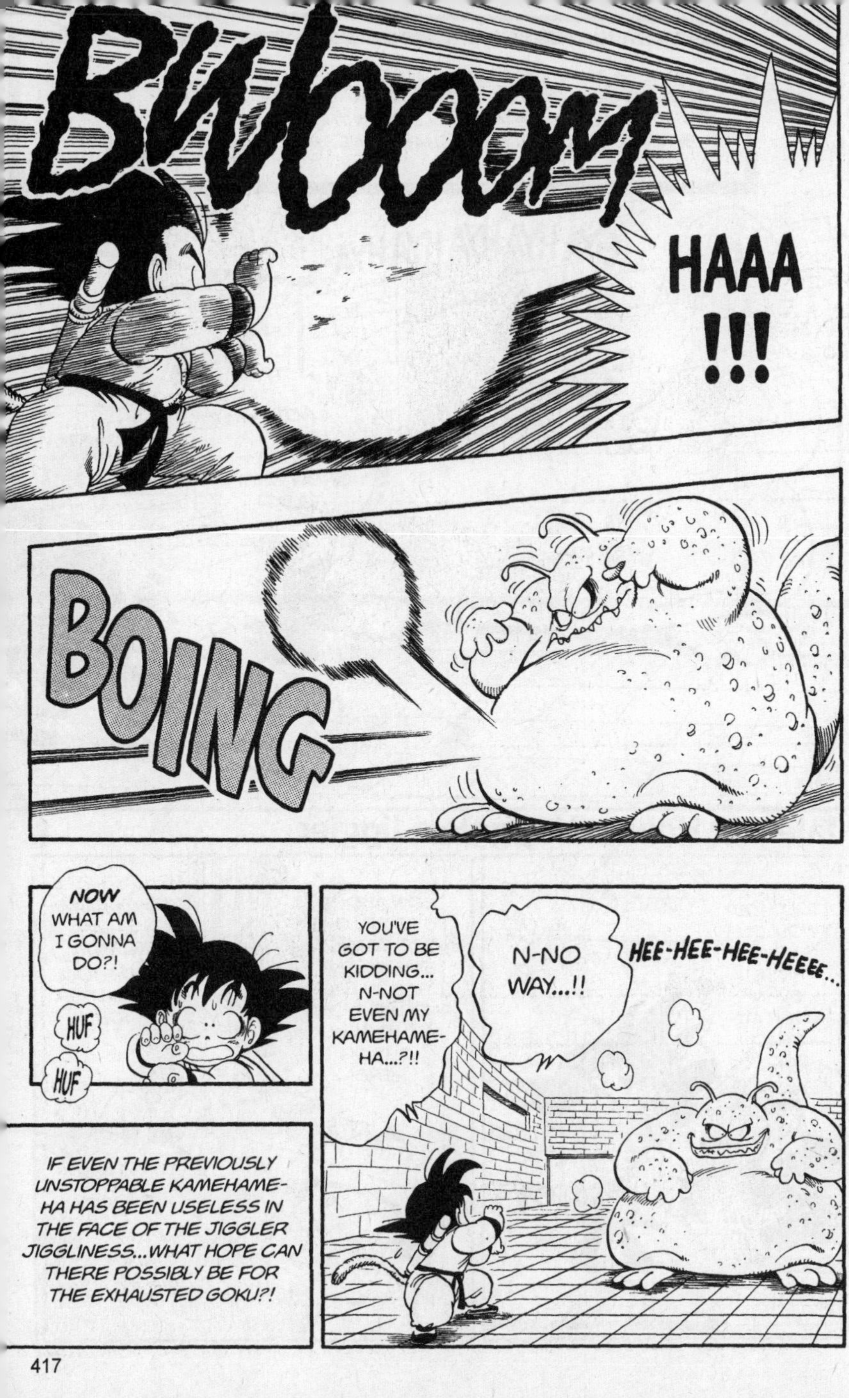
BWOOM
HAAA!!!
BOING
HEE-HEE-HEE-HEEEE...
N-NO WAY...!!
YOU'VE GOT TO BE KIDDING... N-NOT EVEN MY KAMEHAME-HA...?!!
NOW WHAT AM I GONNA DO?!
HUF
HUF
IF EVEN THE PREVIOUSLY UNSTOPPABLE KAMEHAME-HA HAS BEEN USELESS IN THE FACE OF THE JIGGLER JIGGLINESS...WHAT HOPE CAN THERE POSSIBLY BE FOR THE EXHAUSTED GOKU?!

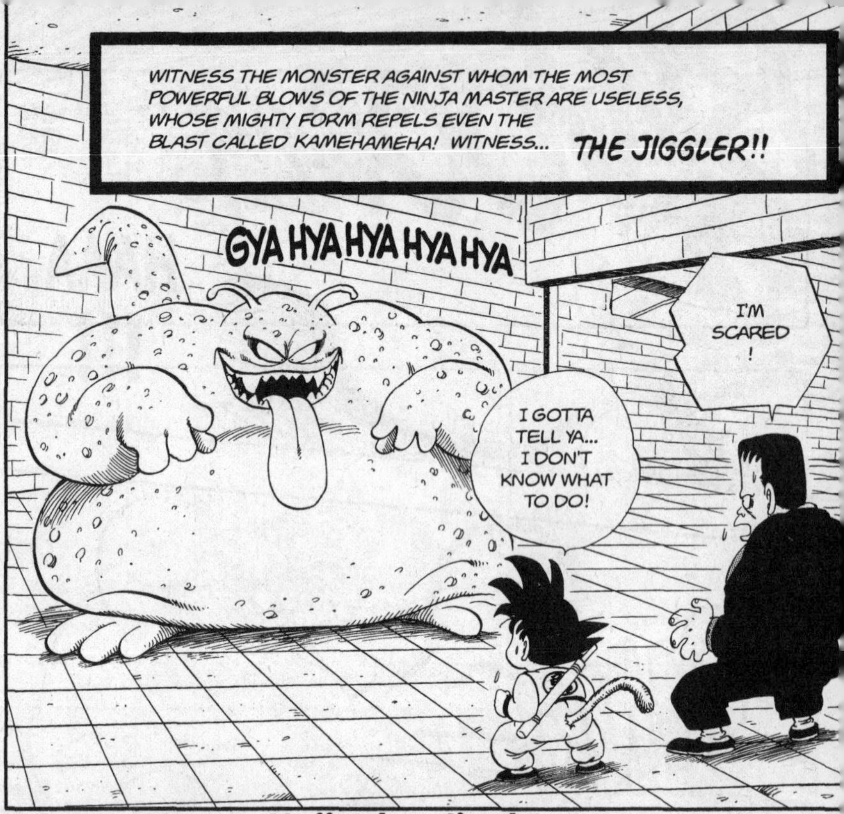
WITNESS THE MONSTER AGAINST WHOM THE MOST POWERFUL BLOWS OF THE NINJA MASTER ARE USELESS, WHOSE MIGHTY FORM REPELS EVEN THE BLAST CALLED KAMEHAMEHA! WITNESS... THE JIGGLER!!
GYA HYA HYA HYA HYA
I'M SCARED!
I GOTTA TELL YA... I DON'T KNOW WHAT TO DO!

Tale 65 • How to Unjiggle a Jiggler

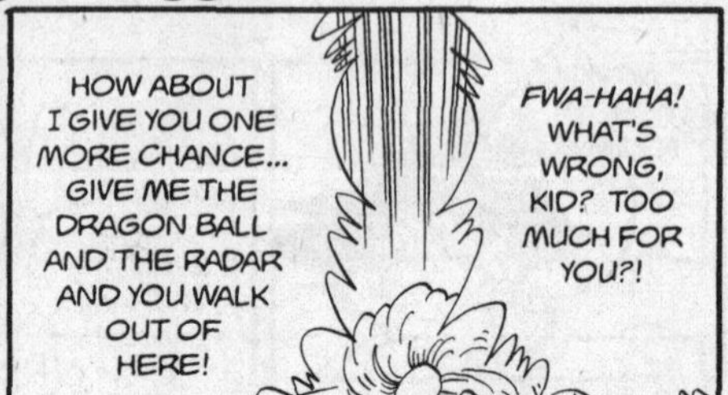
FWA-HAHA! WHAT'S WRONG, KID? TOO MUCH FOR YOU?!
HOW ABOUT I GIVE YOU ONE MORE CHANCE... GIVE ME THE DRAGON BALL AND THE RADAR AND YOU WALK OUT OF HERE!

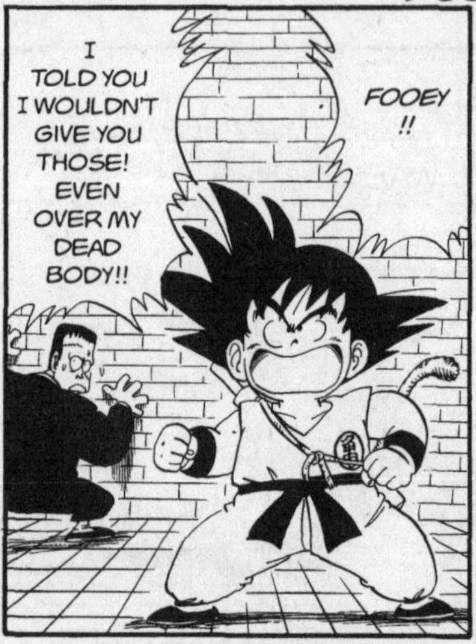
FOOEY!!
I TOLD YOU I WOULDN'T GIVE YOU THOSE! EVEN OVER MY DEAD BODY!!

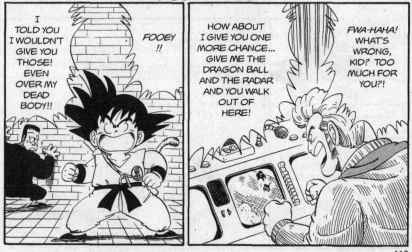

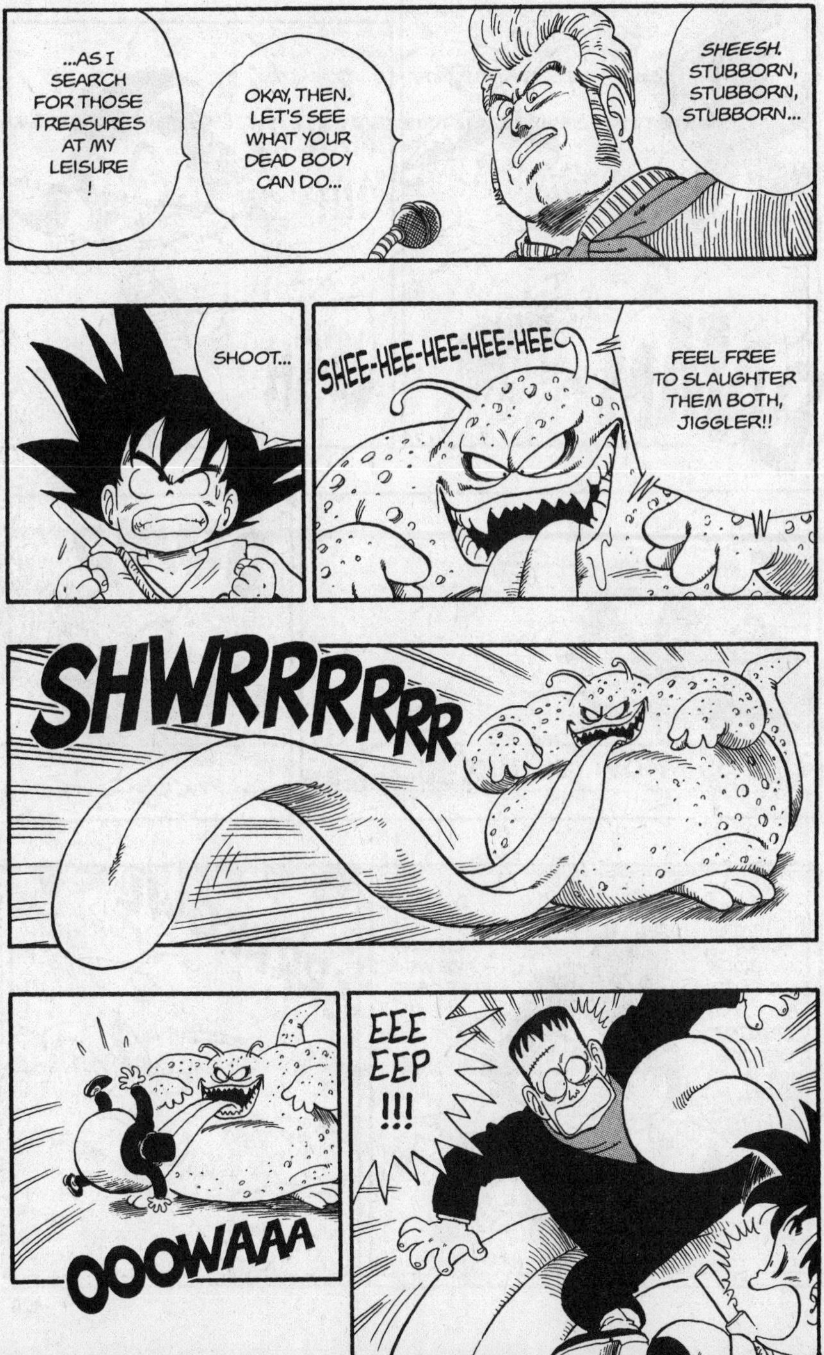
SHEESH. STUBBORN, STUBBORN, STUBBORN...
OKAY, THEN. LET'S SEE WHAT YOUR DEAD BODY CAN DO...
...AS I SEARCH FOR THOSE TREASURES AT MY LEISURE!
FEEL FREE TO SLAUGHTER THEM BOTH, JIGGLER!!
SHEE-HEE-HEE-HEE-HEE
SHOOT...
SHWRRRRRR
EEE EEP!!!
OOOWAAA

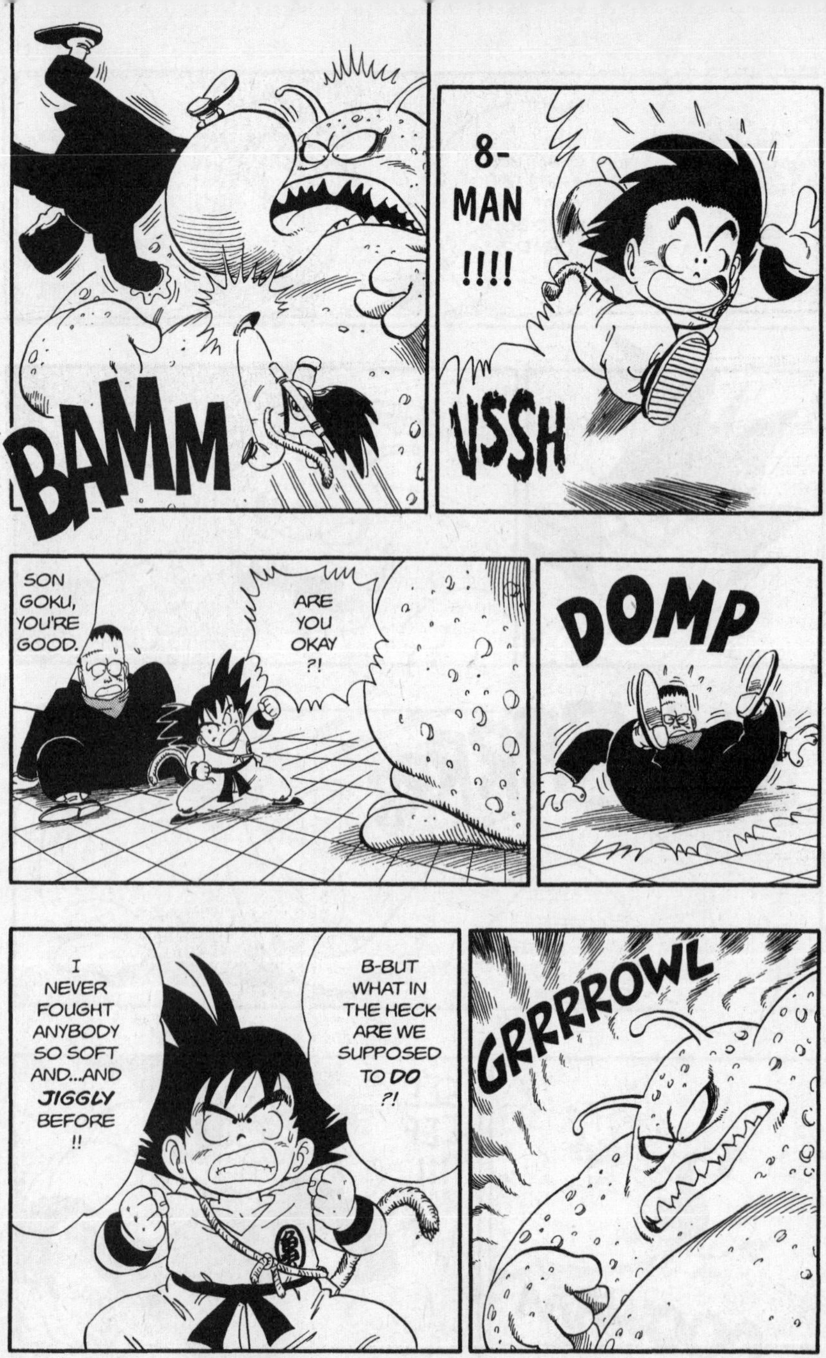
8-MAN!!!!
VSSH
BAMM
DOMP
ARE YOU OKAY?!
SON GOKU, YOU'RE GOOD.
GRRRROWL
B-BUT WHAT IN THE HECK ARE WE SUPPOSED TO *DO*?!
I NEVER FOUGHT ANYBODY SO SOFT AND...AND ***JIGGLY*** BEFORE!!

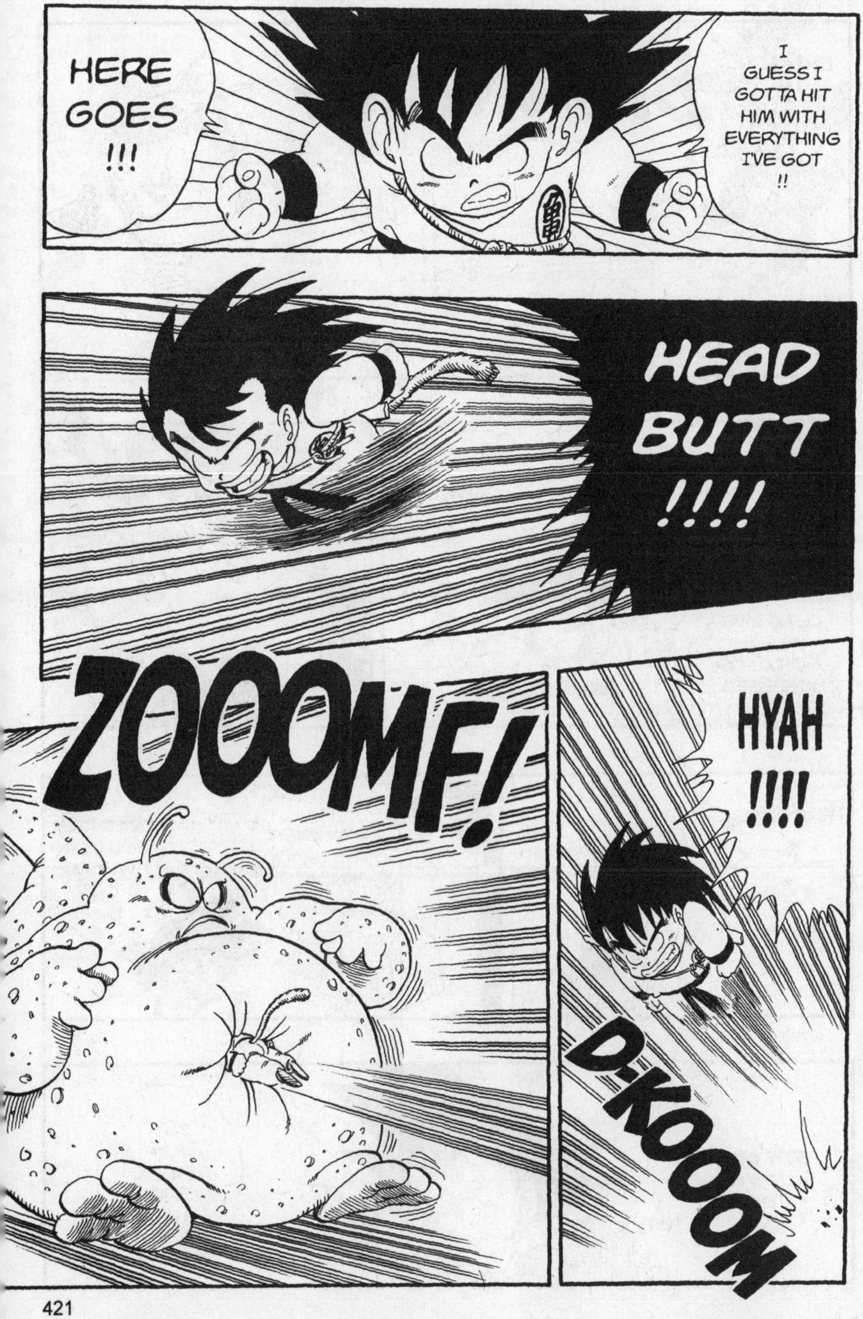
I GUESS I GOTTA HIT HIM WITH EVERYTHING I'VE GOT!!
HERE GOES!!!
HEAD BUTT!!!!
HYAH!!!!
D-KOOOM
ZOOOMF!

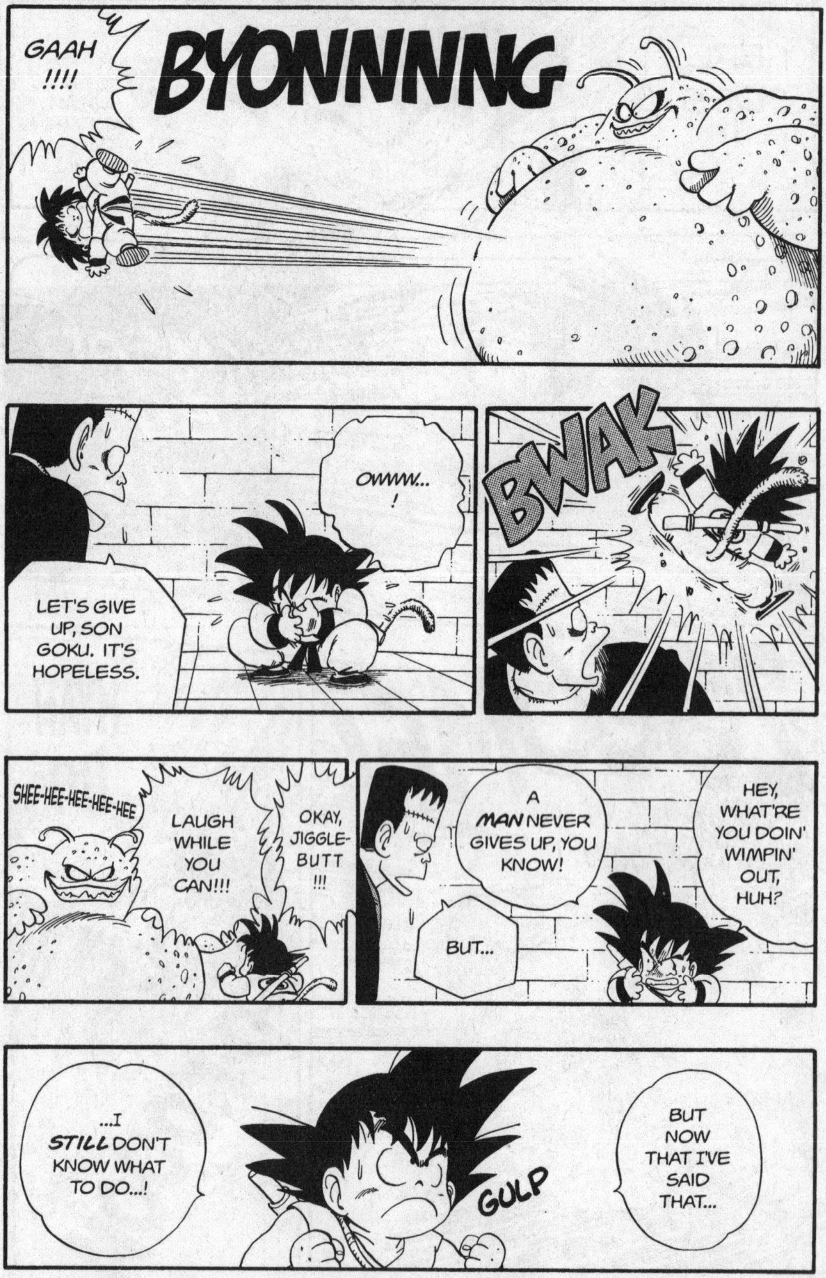
BYONNNNG
GAAH !!!!
BWAK
OWWW... !
LET'S GIVE UP, SON GOKU. IT'S HOPELESS.
HEY, WHAT'RE YOU DOIN' WIMPIN' OUT, HUH?
A MAN NEVER GIVES UP, YOU KNOW!
BUT...
OKAY, JIGGLE-BUTT !!!
LAUGH WHILE YOU CAN!!!
SHEE-HEE-HEE-HEE-HEE
BUT NOW THAT I'VE SAID THAT...
GULP
...I STILL DON'T KNOW WHAT TO DO...!

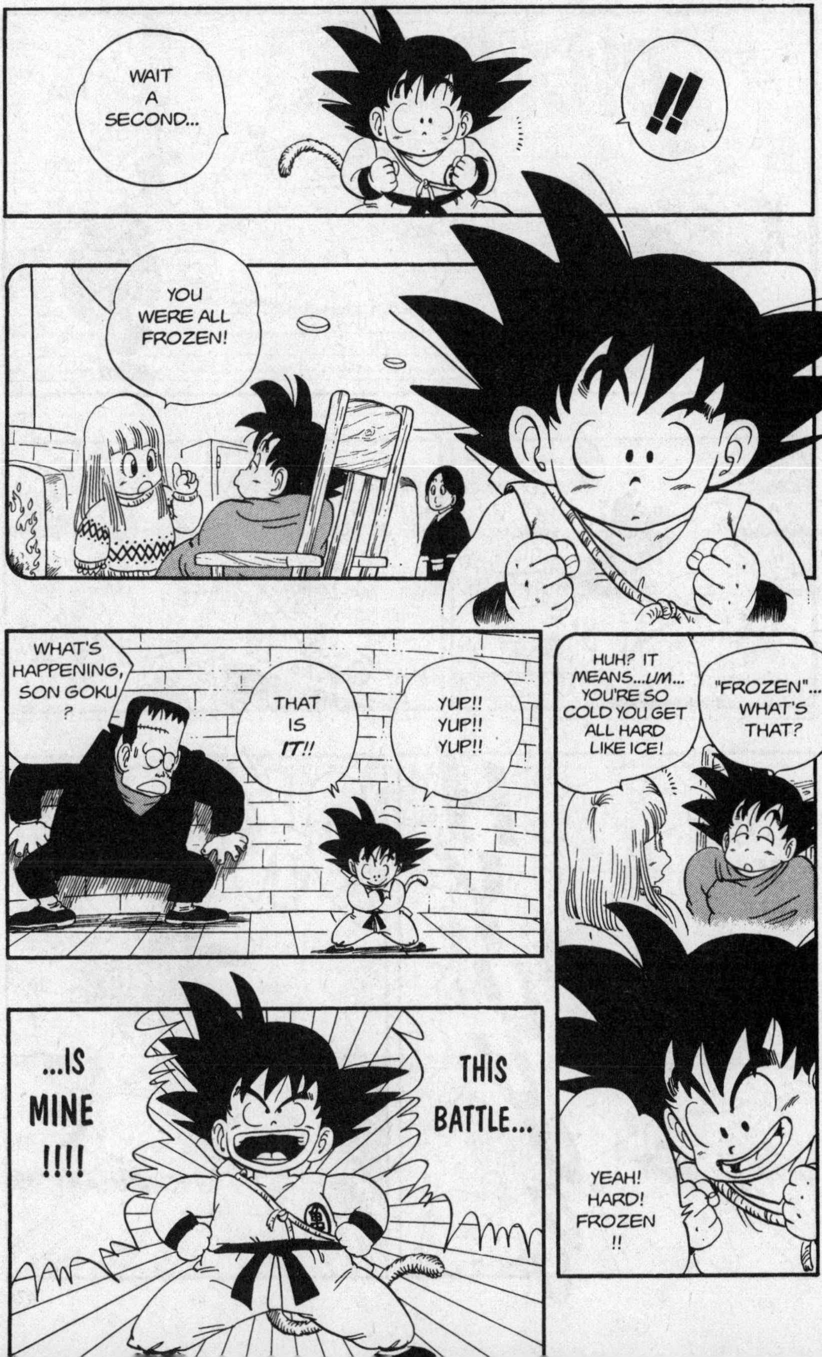
!!
WAIT A SECOND...
YOU WERE ALL FROZEN!
"FROZEN"...? WHAT'S THAT?
HUH? IT MEANS...UM... YOU'RE SO COLD YOU GET ALL HARD LIKE ICE!
YEAH! HARD! FROZEN !!
YUP!! YUP!! YUP!!
THAT IS IT!!
WHAT'S HAPPENING, SON GOKU ?
THIS BATTLE...
...IS MINE !!!!

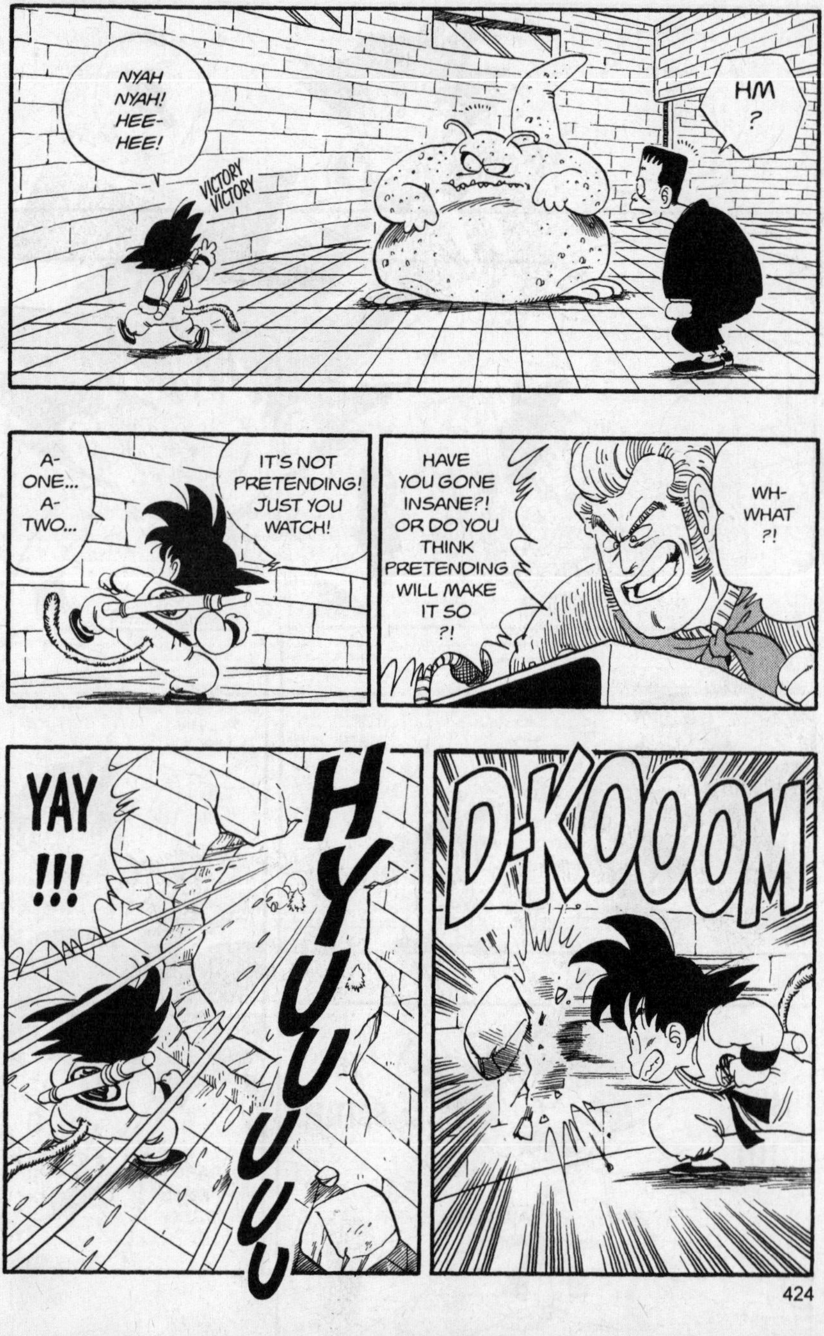
HM ?
NYAH NYAH! HEE-HEE!
VICTORY VICTORY
WH- WHAT ?!
HAVE YOU GONE INSANE?! OR DO YOU THINK PRETENDING WILL MAKE IT SO ?!
IT'S NOT PRETENDING! JUST YOU WATCH!
A-ONE... A-TWO...
D-KOOOM
HYUUUUUU
YAY !!!

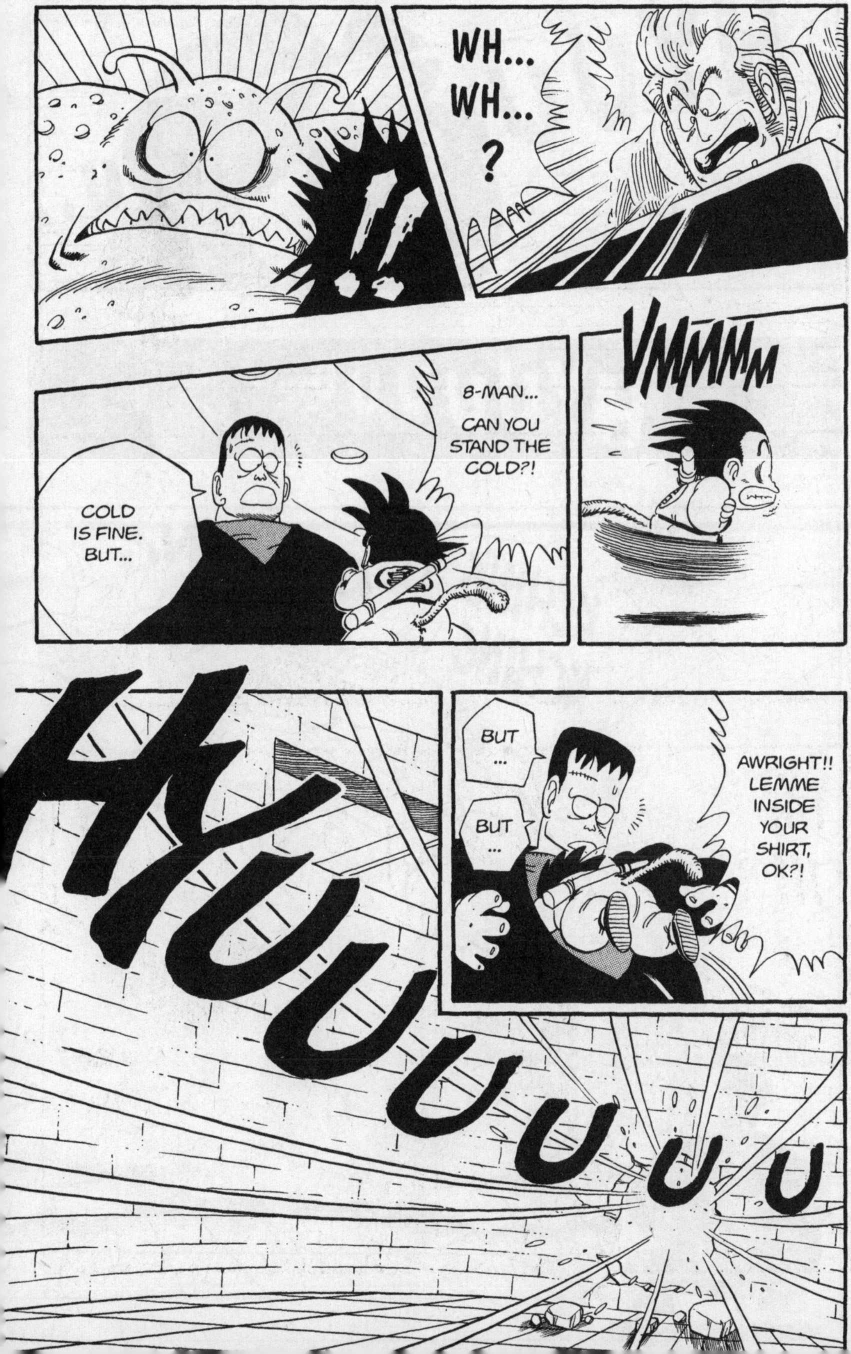
WH... WH... ?
VMMMMM
8-MAN... CAN YOU STAND THE COLD?!
COLD IS FINE. BUT...
AWRIGHT!! LEMME INSIDE YOUR SHIRT, OK?!
BUT ...
BUT ...
HYUUUUUUU

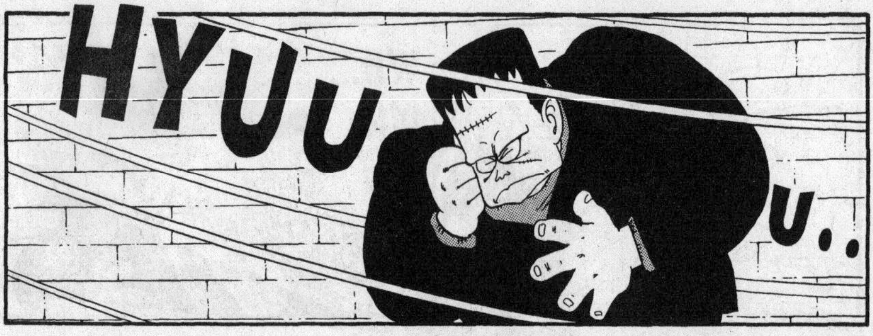
HYUUU..

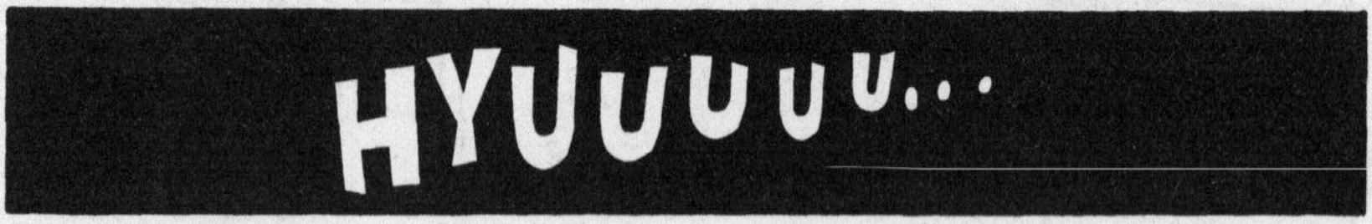
HYUUUUU...

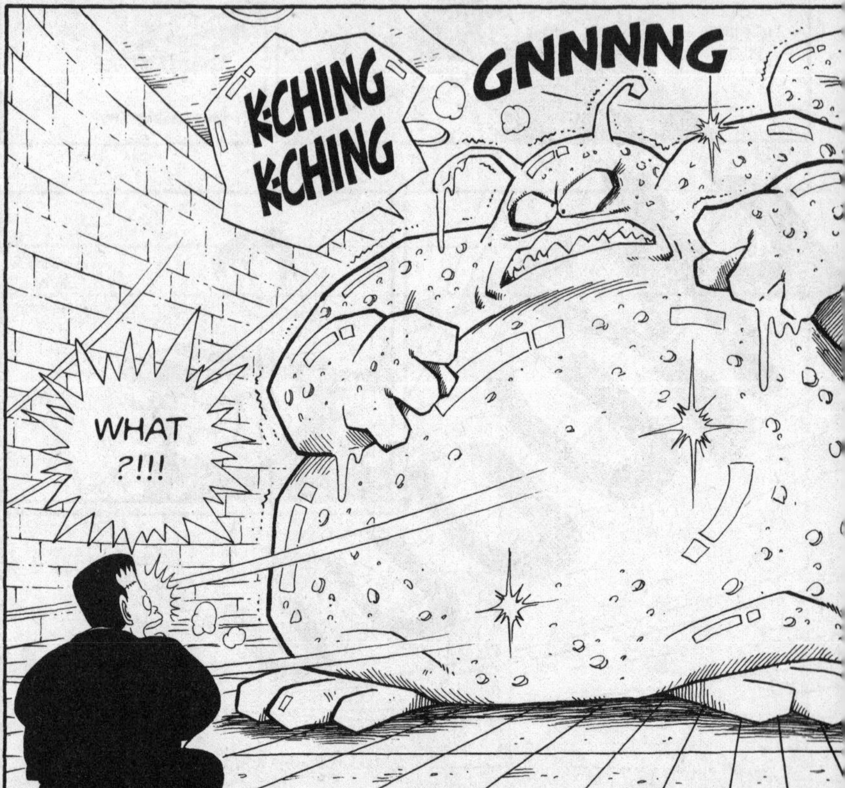
GNNNNG
K-CHING K-CHING
WHAT ?!!!

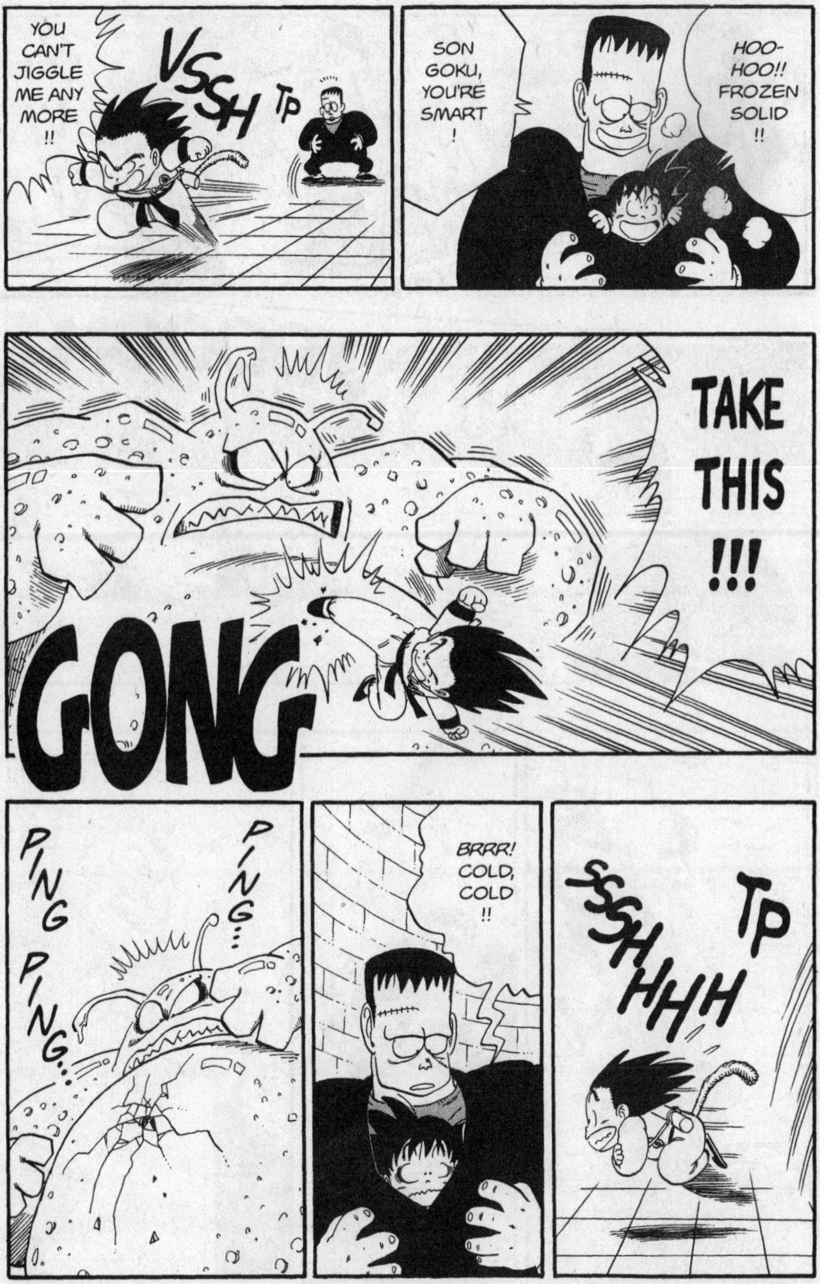
HOO-HOO!! FROZEN SOLID!!
SON GOKU, YOU'RE SMART!
VSSH
TP
YOU CAN'T JIGGLE ME ANY MORE!!
TAKE THIS!!!
GONG
TP
SSSHHHH
BRRR! COLD, COLD!!
PING
PING...
PING
PING...

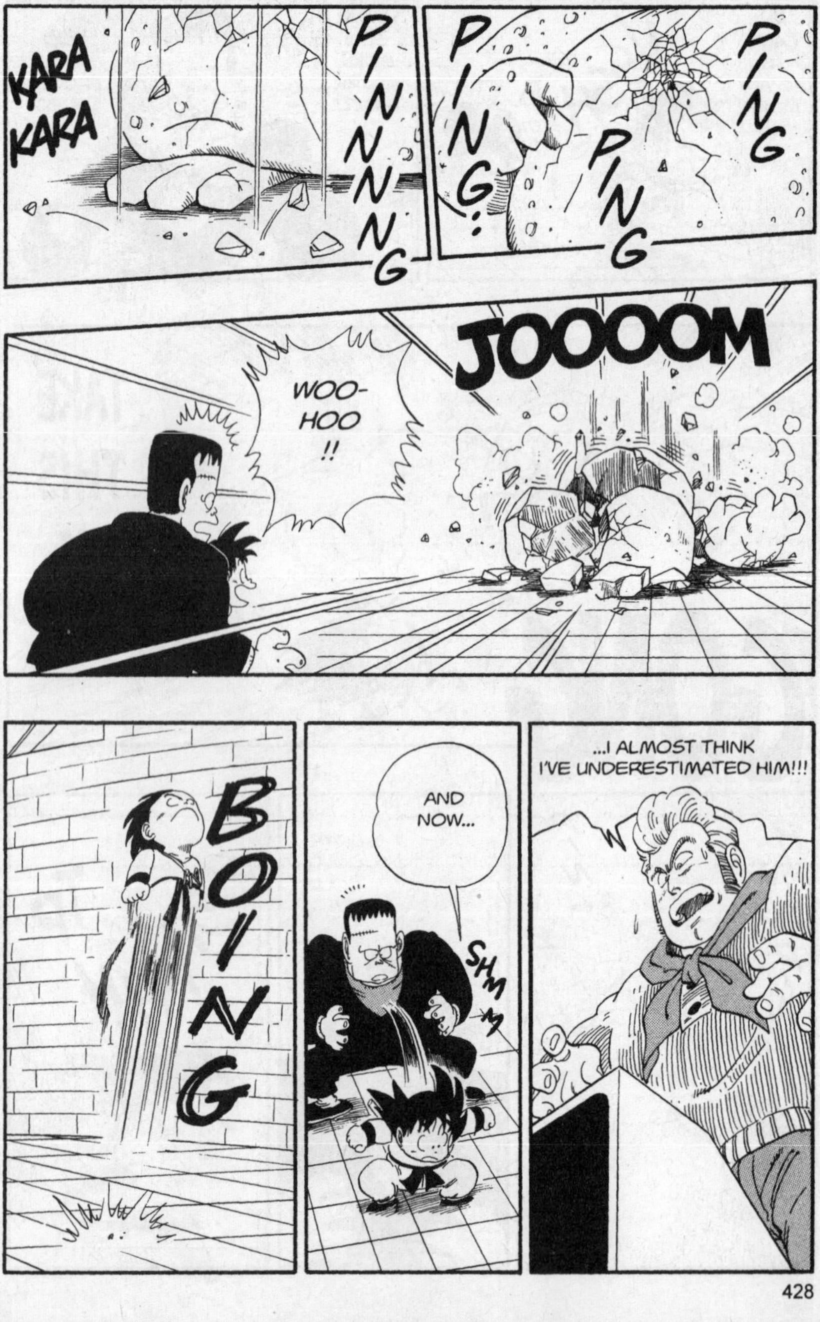
PING
PING
PING
PINNNNG
KARA
KARA
JOOOOM
WOO-HOO!!
...I ALMOST THINK I'VE UNDERESTIMATED HIM!!!
AND NOW...
SHMM
BOING

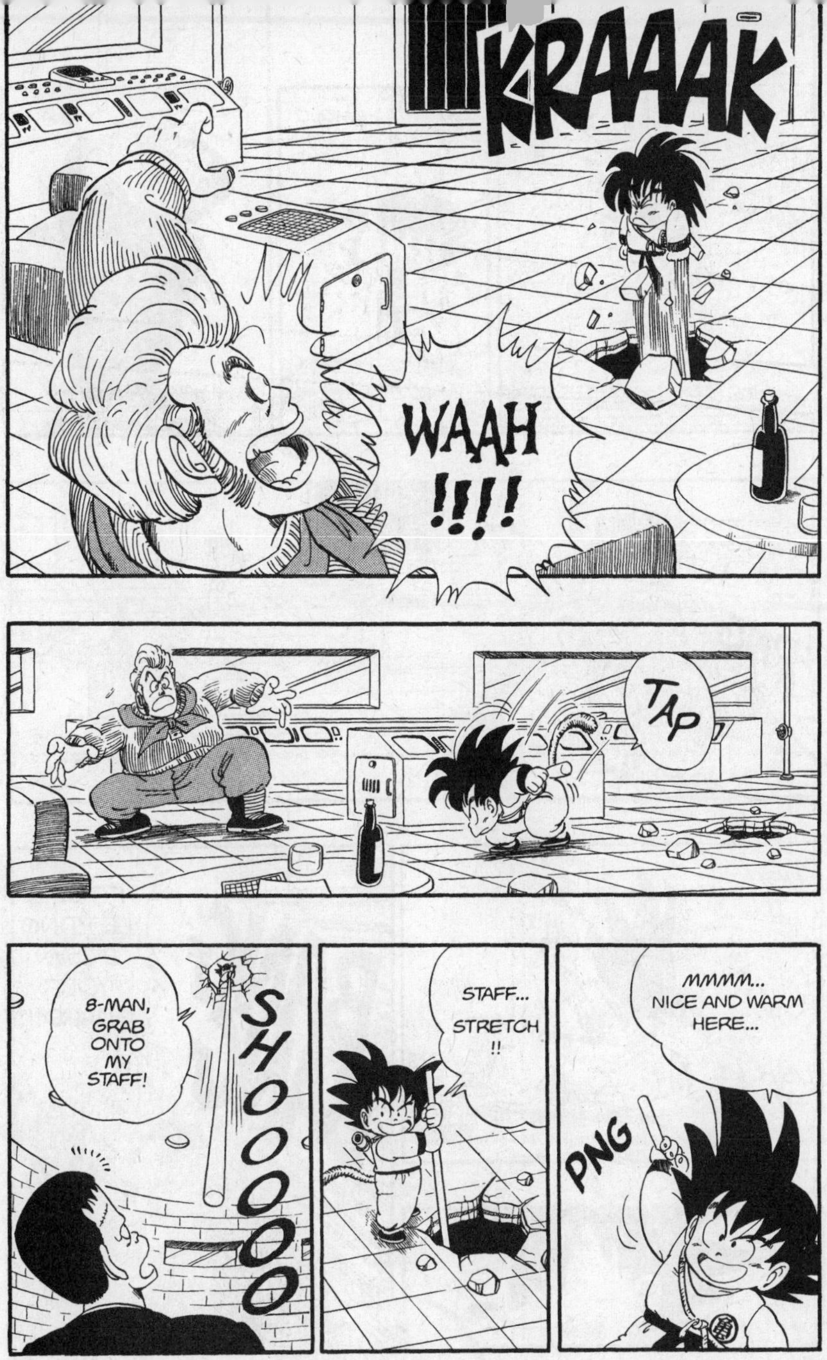
KRAAAK
WAAH !!!!
TAP
MMMM... NICE AND WARM HERE...
PNG
STAFF... STRETCH !!
8-MAN, GRAB ONTO MY STAFF!
SHOOOOO

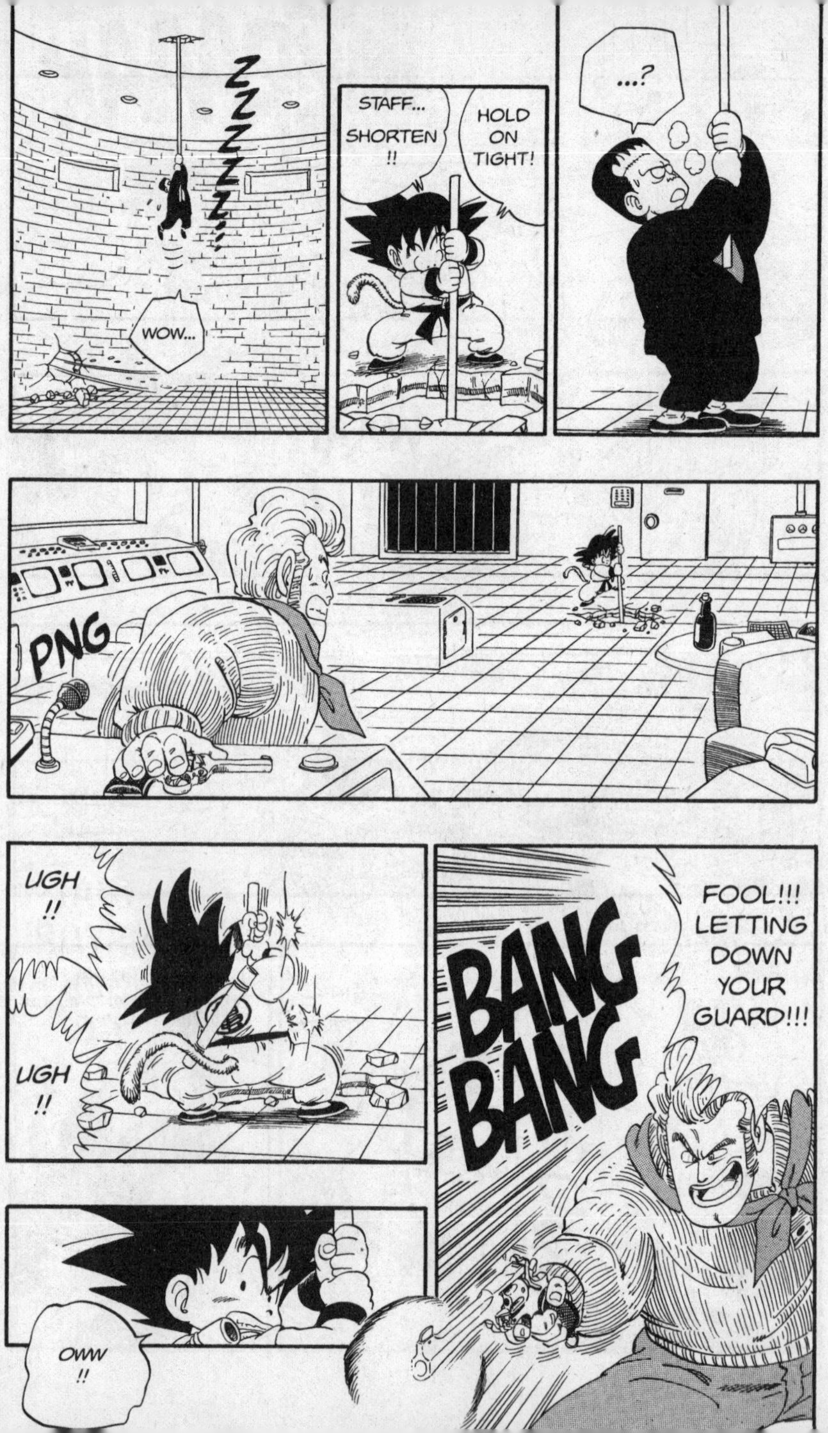
...?
HOLD ON TIGHT!
STAFF... SHORTEN !!
ZZZZZZ
WOW...
PNG
FOOL!!! LETTING DOWN YOUR GUARD!!!
BANG BANG
UGH !!
UGH !!
OWW !!

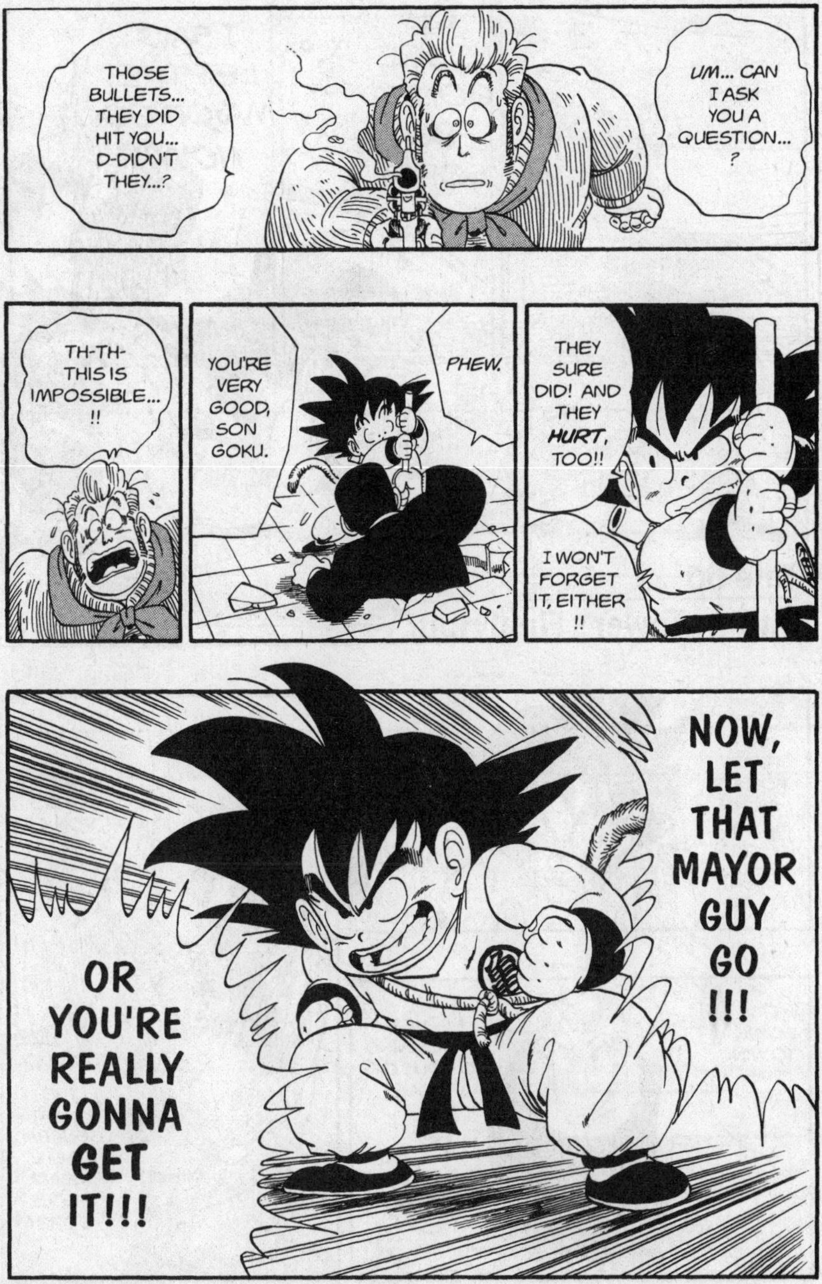
UM... CAN I ASK YOU A QUESTION... ?
THOSE BULLETS... THEY DID HIT YOU... D-DIDN'T THEY...?
THEY SURE DID! AND THEY HURT, TOO!!
I WON'T FORGET IT, EITHER !!
PHEW.
YOU'RE VERY GOOD, SON GOKU.
TH-TH-THIS IS IMPOSSIBLE... !!
NOW, LET THAT MAYOR GUY GO !!!
OR YOU'RE REALLY GONNA GET IT!!!

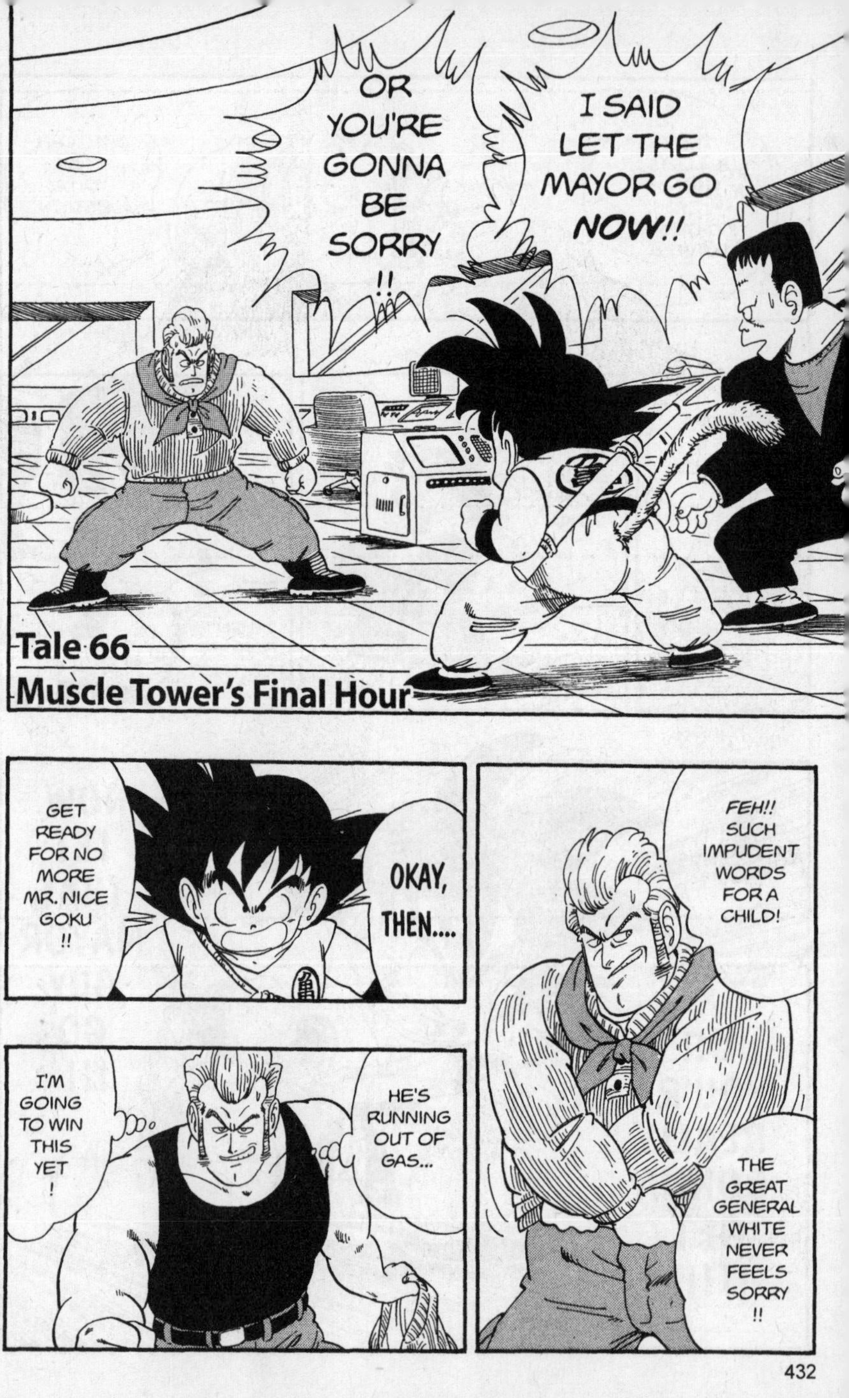
I SAID LET THE MAYOR GO NOW!!
OR YOU'RE GONNA BE SORRY!!
Tale 66
Muscle Tower's Final Hour
FEH!! SUCH IMPUDENT WORDS FOR A CHILD!
THE GREAT GENERAL WHITE NEVER FEELS SORRY!!
OKAY, THEN....
GET READY FOR NO MORE MR. NICE GOKU!!
HE'S RUNNING OUT OF GAS...
I'M GOING TO WIN THIS YET!

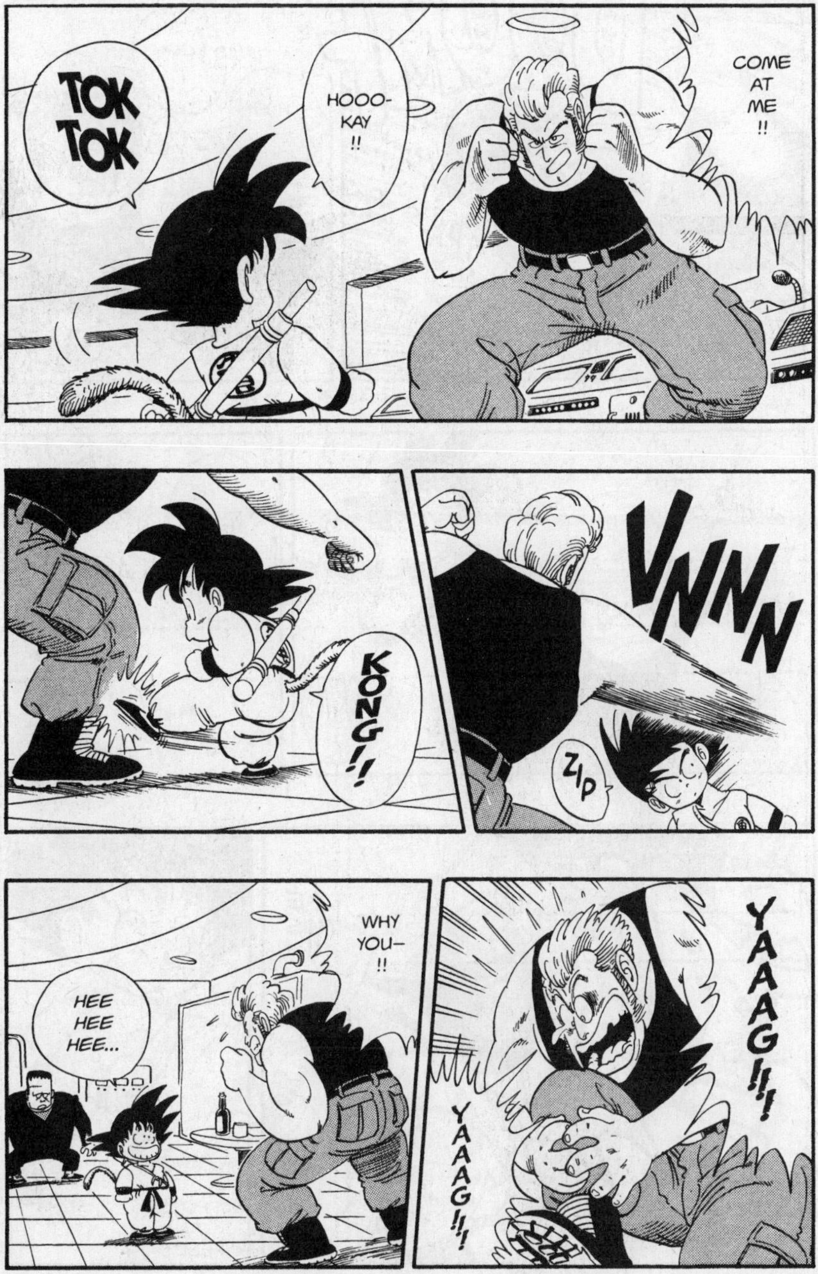
COME AT ME !!
HOOO-KAY !!
TOK TOK
VNNNN
ZIP
KONG!!
YAAAG!!!
YAAAG!!!
WHY YOU— !!
HEE HEE HEE...

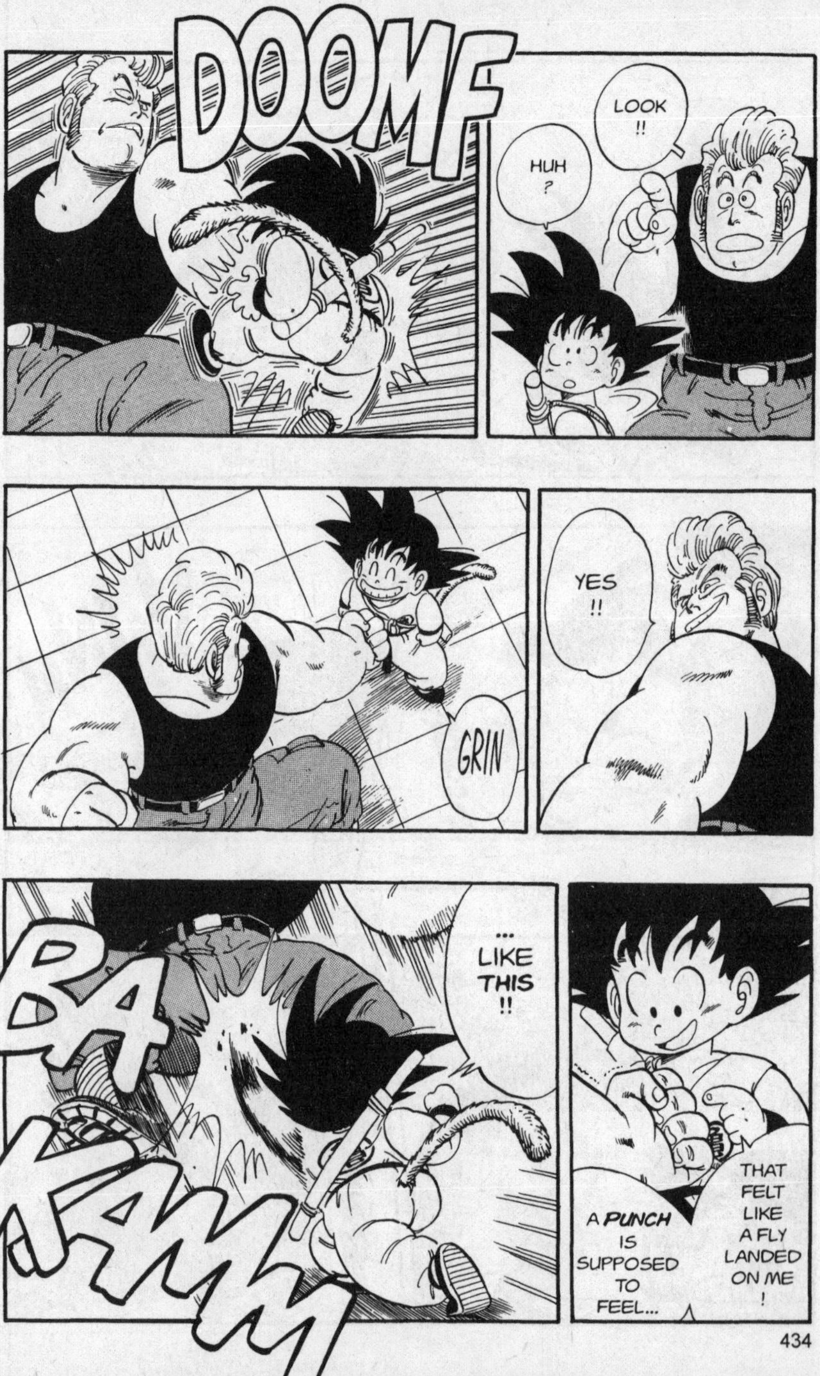
LOOK !!
HUH ?
DOOMF
YES !!
GRIN
THAT FELT LIKE A FLY LANDED ON ME !
A **PUNCH** IS SUPPOSED TO FEEL...
... LIKE THIS !!
BA KAMM

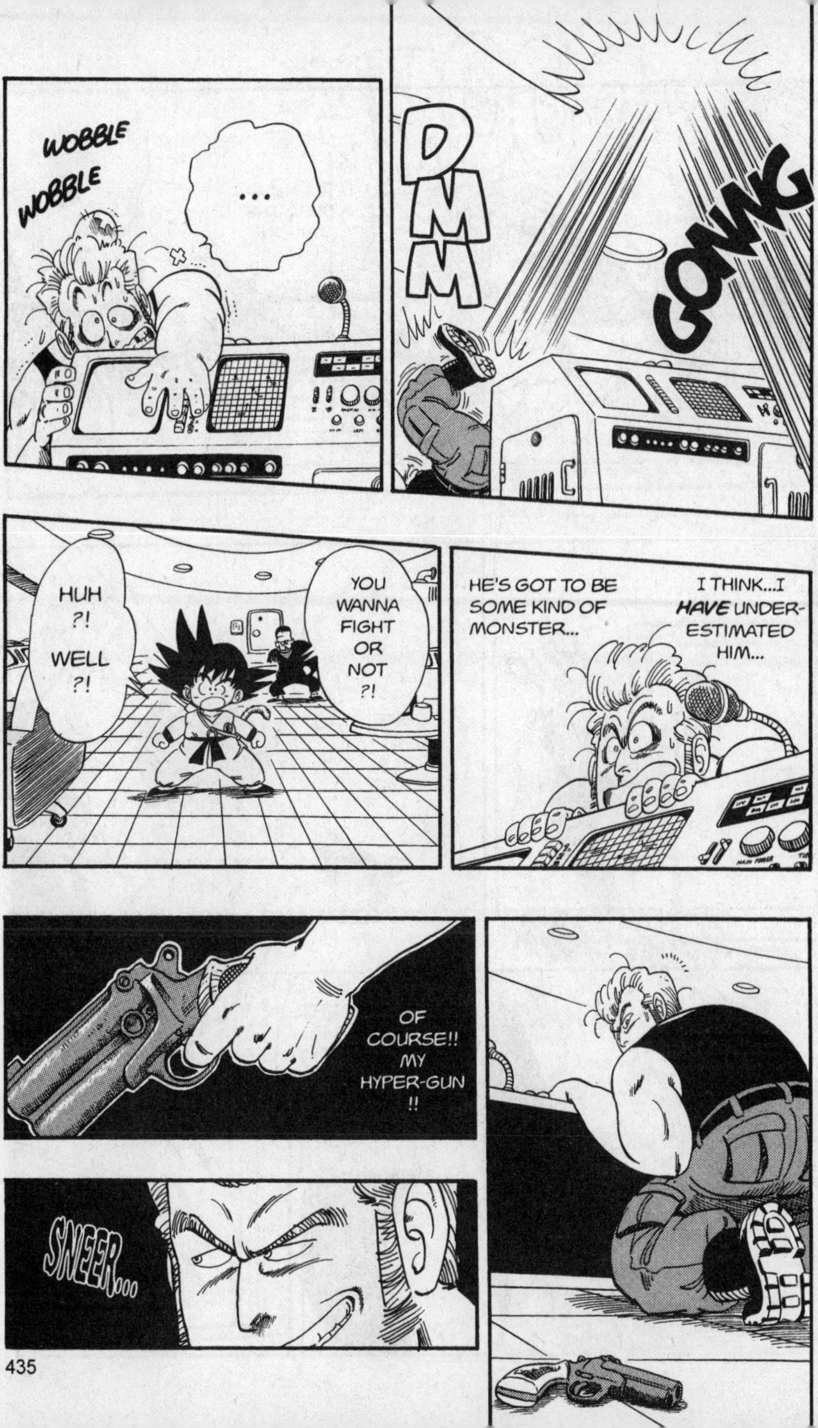

GONNG
DMMM
WOBBLE
WOBBLE
...
I THINK...I HAVE UNDERESTIMATED HIM...
HE'S GOT TO BE SOME KIND OF MONSTER...
YOU WANNA FIGHT OR NOT?!
HUH?! WELL?!
OF COURSE!! MY HYPER-GUN!!
SNEER...

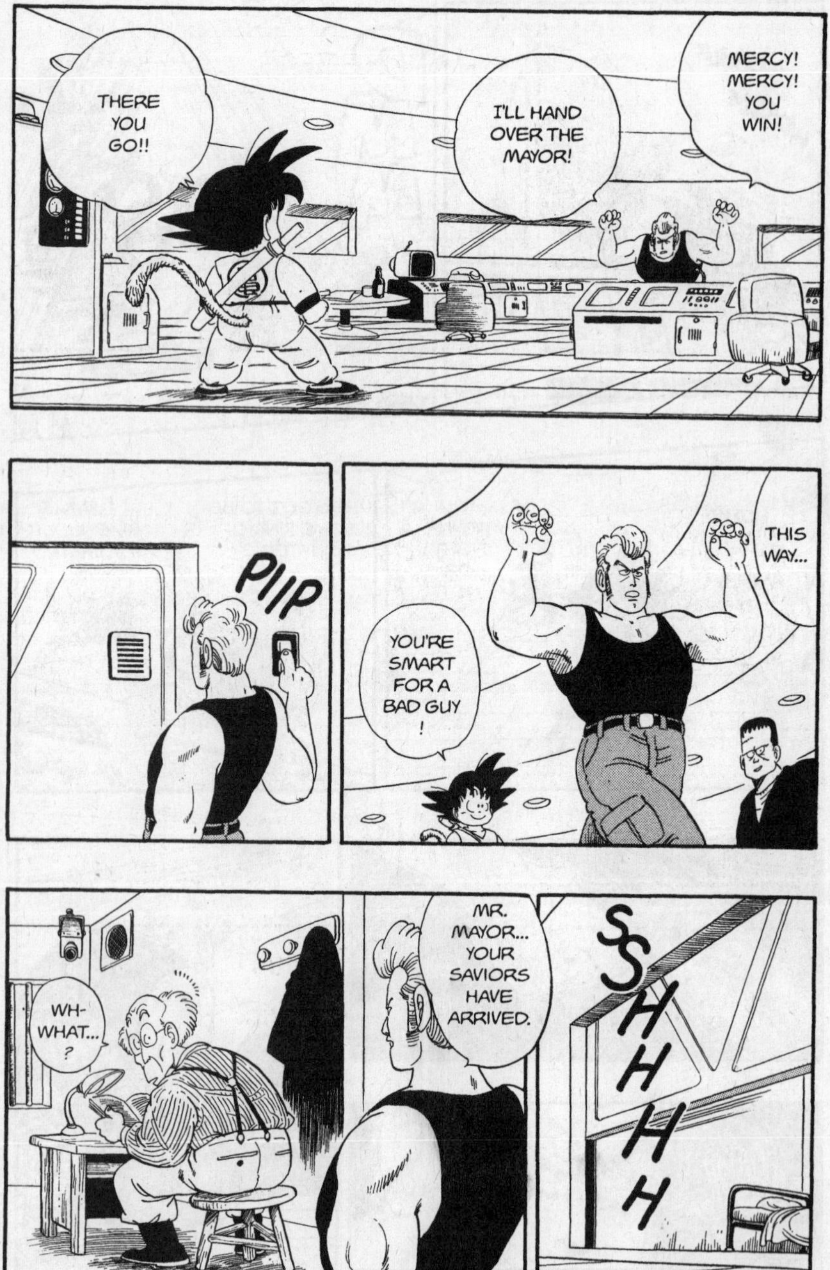
MERCY! MERCY! YOU WIN!
I'LL HAND OVER THE MAYOR!
THERE YOU GO!!
THIS WAY...
YOU'RE SMART FOR A BAD GUY!
PIIP
SSHHHH
MR. MAYOR... YOUR SAVIORS HAVE ARRIVED.
WH-WHAT...?

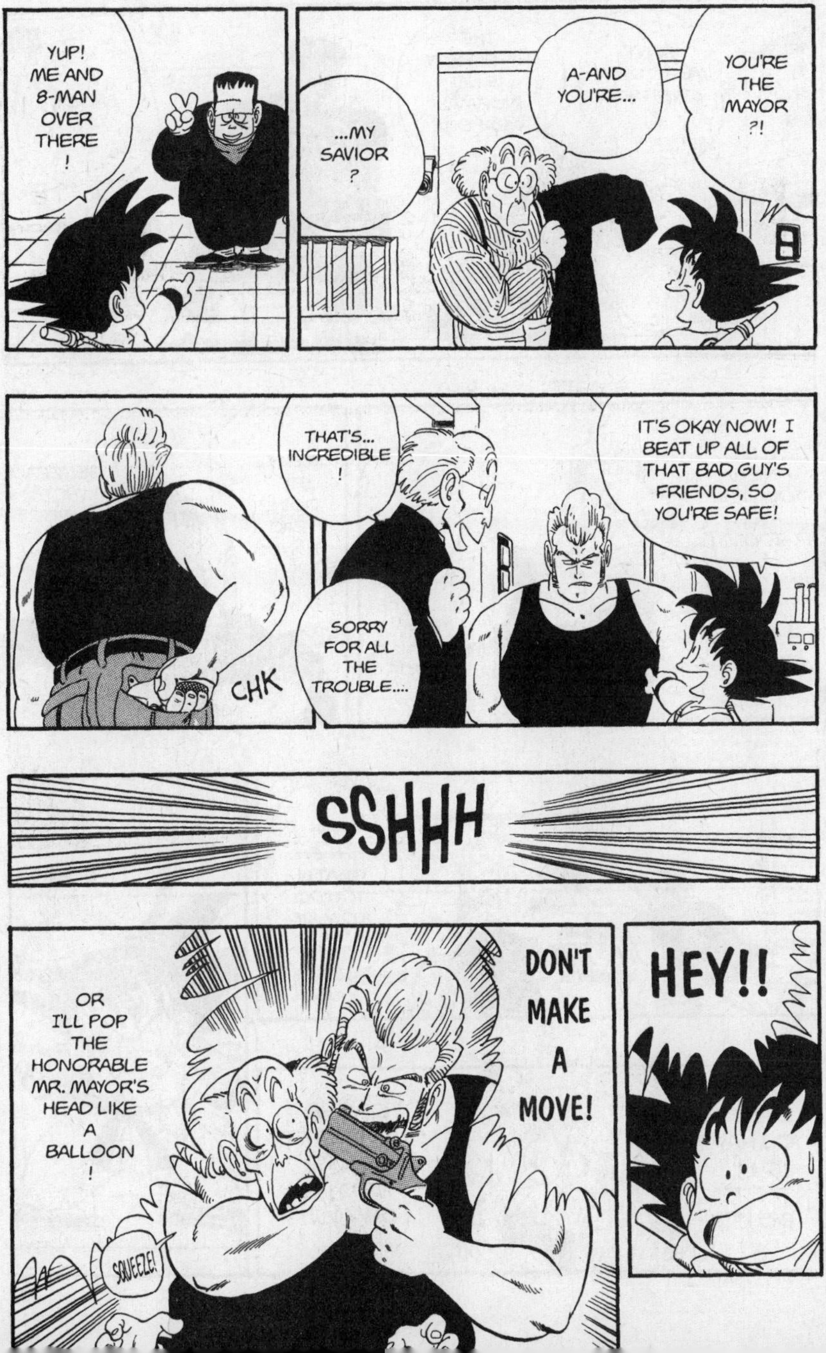
YOU'RE THE MAYOR ?!
A-AND YOU'RE...
...MY SAVIOR ?
YUP! ME AND 8-MAN OVER THERE !
IT'S OKAY NOW! I BEAT UP ALL OF THAT BAD GUY'S FRIENDS, SO YOU'RE SAFE!
THAT'S... INCREDIBLE !
SORRY FOR ALL THE TROUBLE....
CHK
SSHHH
HEY!!
DON'T MAKE A MOVE!
OR I'LL POP THE HONORABLE MR. MAYOR'S HEAD LIKE A BALLOON !
SQUEEZE!

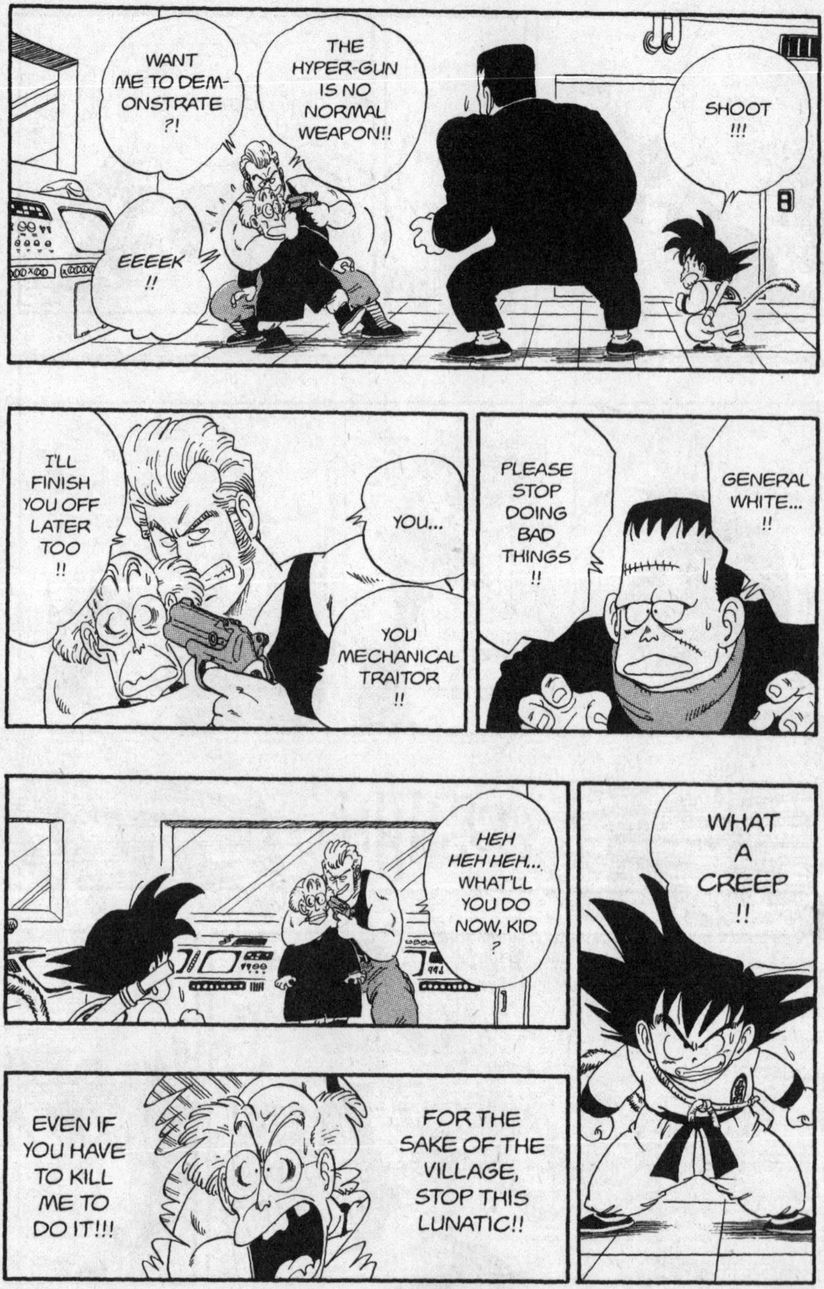
SHOOT !!!
THE HYPER-GUN IS NO NORMAL WEAPON!!
WANT ME TO DEMONSTRATE ?!
EEEEK !!
GENERAL WHITE... !!
PLEASE STOP DOING BAD THINGS !!
YOU...
YOU MECHANICAL TRAITOR !!
I'LL FINISH YOU OFF LATER TOO !!
WHAT A CREEP !!
HEH HEH HEH... WHAT'LL YOU DO NOW, KID ?
FOR THE SAKE OF THE VILLAGE, STOP THIS LUNATIC!!
EVEN IF YOU HAVE TO KILL ME TO DO IT!!!

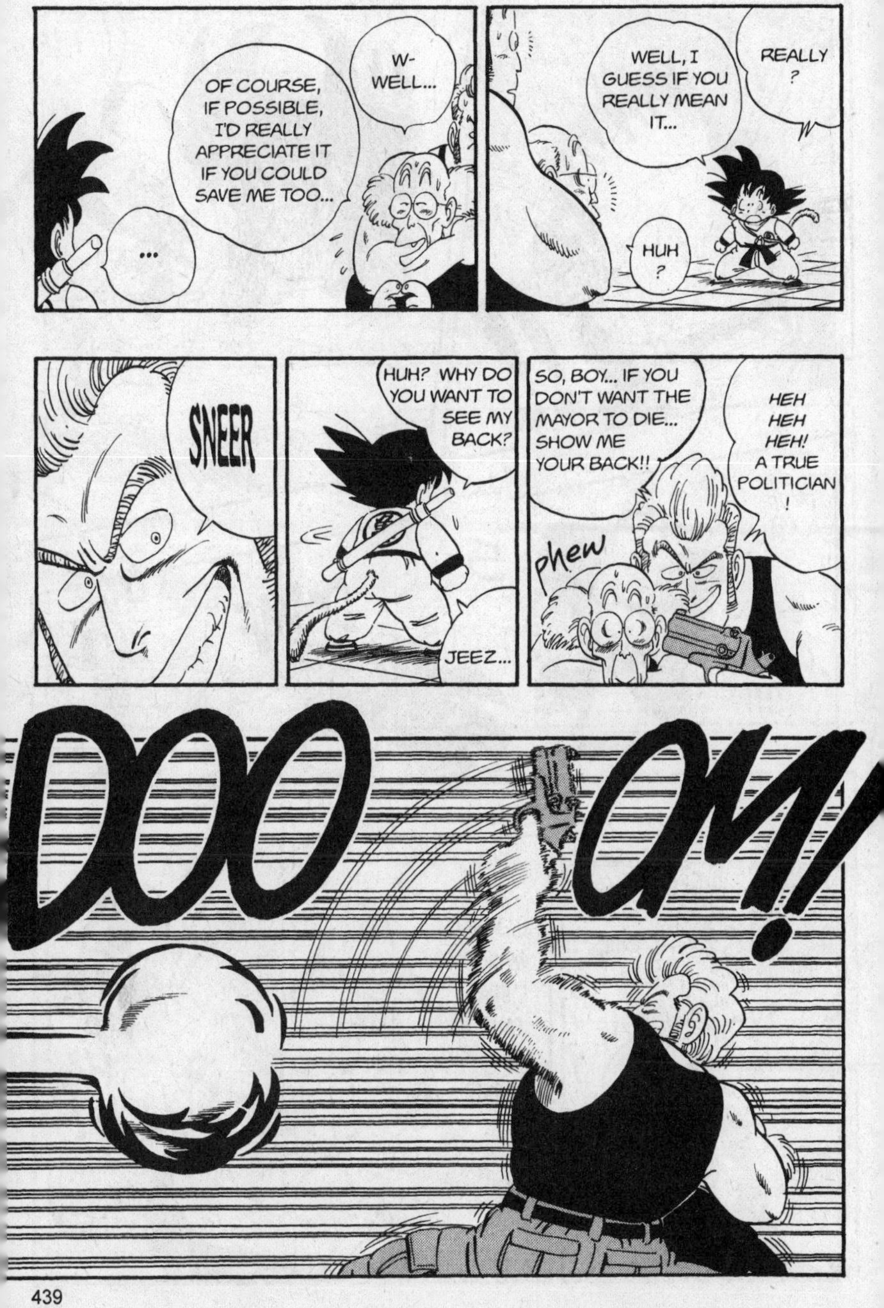
REALLY?
WELL, I GUESS IF YOU REALLY MEAN IT...
HUH?
W-WELL...
OF COURSE, IF POSSIBLE, I'D REALLY APPRECIATE IT IF YOU COULD SAVE ME TOO...
...
HEH HEH HEH! A TRUE POLITICIAN!
SO, BOY... IF YOU DON'T WANT THE MAYOR TO DIE... SHOW ME YOUR BACK!!
phew
HUH? WHY DO YOU WANT TO SEE MY BACK?
JEEZ...
SNEER
DOOOM!

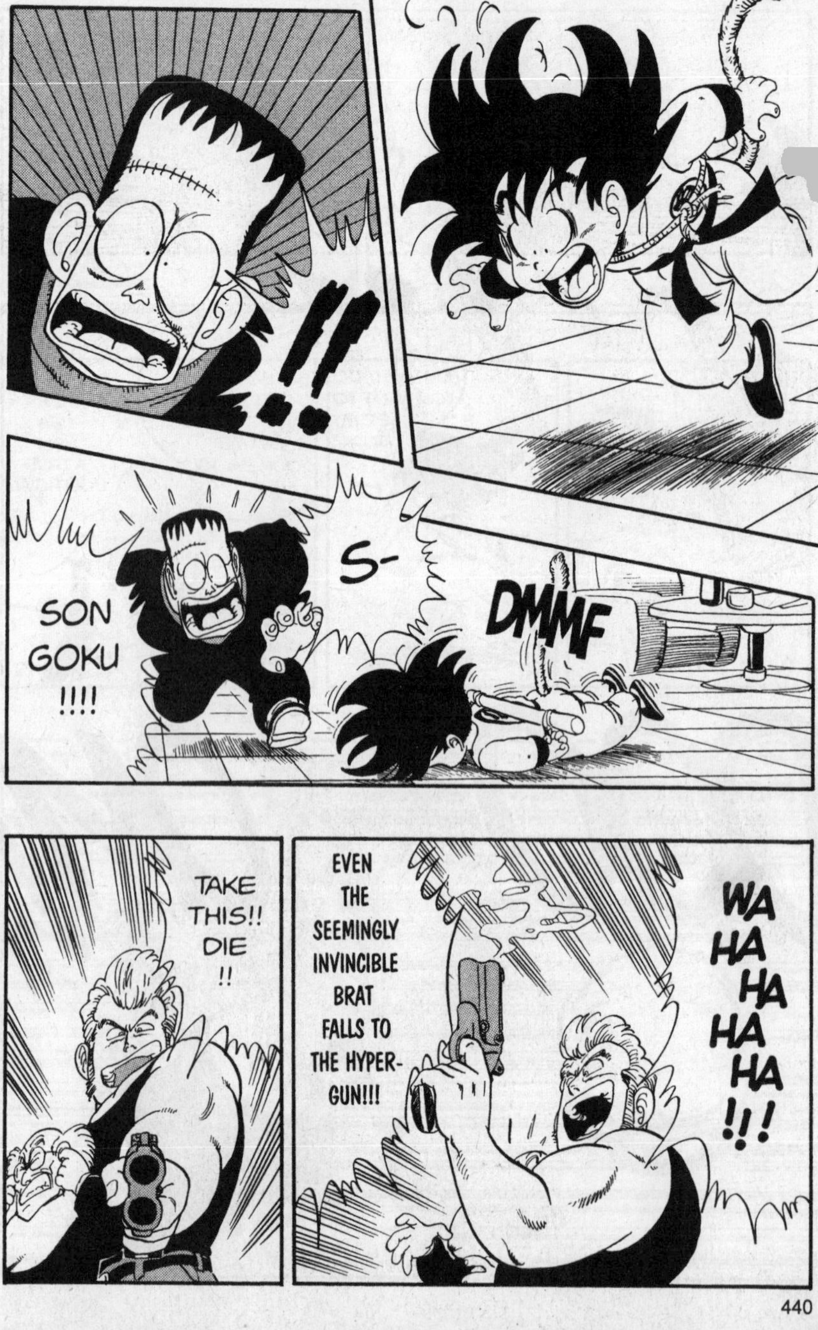
!!
DMMF
S-
SON GOKU !!!!
WA HA HA HA HA!!!
EVEN THE SEEMINGLY INVINCIBLE BRAT FALLS TO THE HYPER-GUN!!!
TAKE THIS!! DIE !!

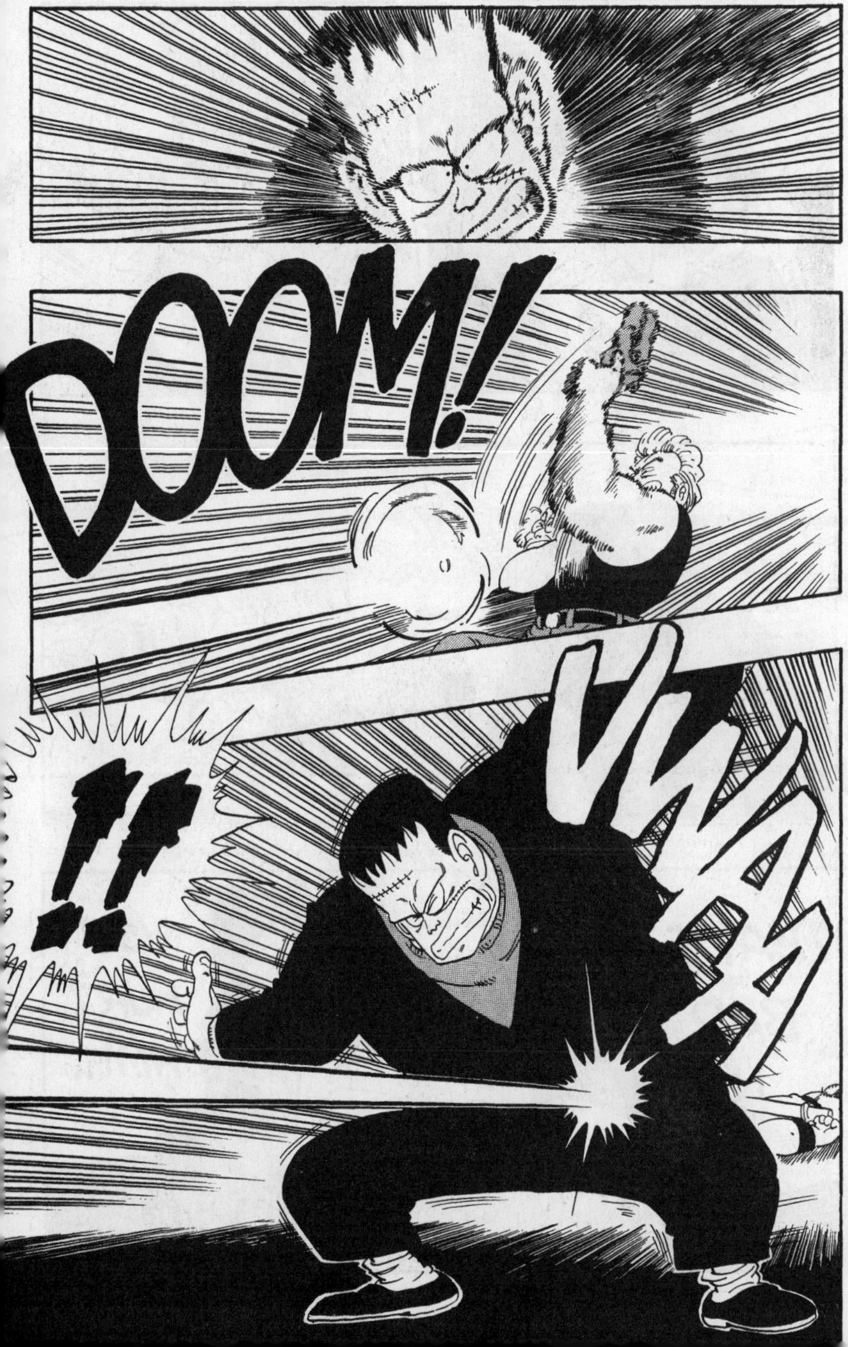
DOOM!
VWAM
!!

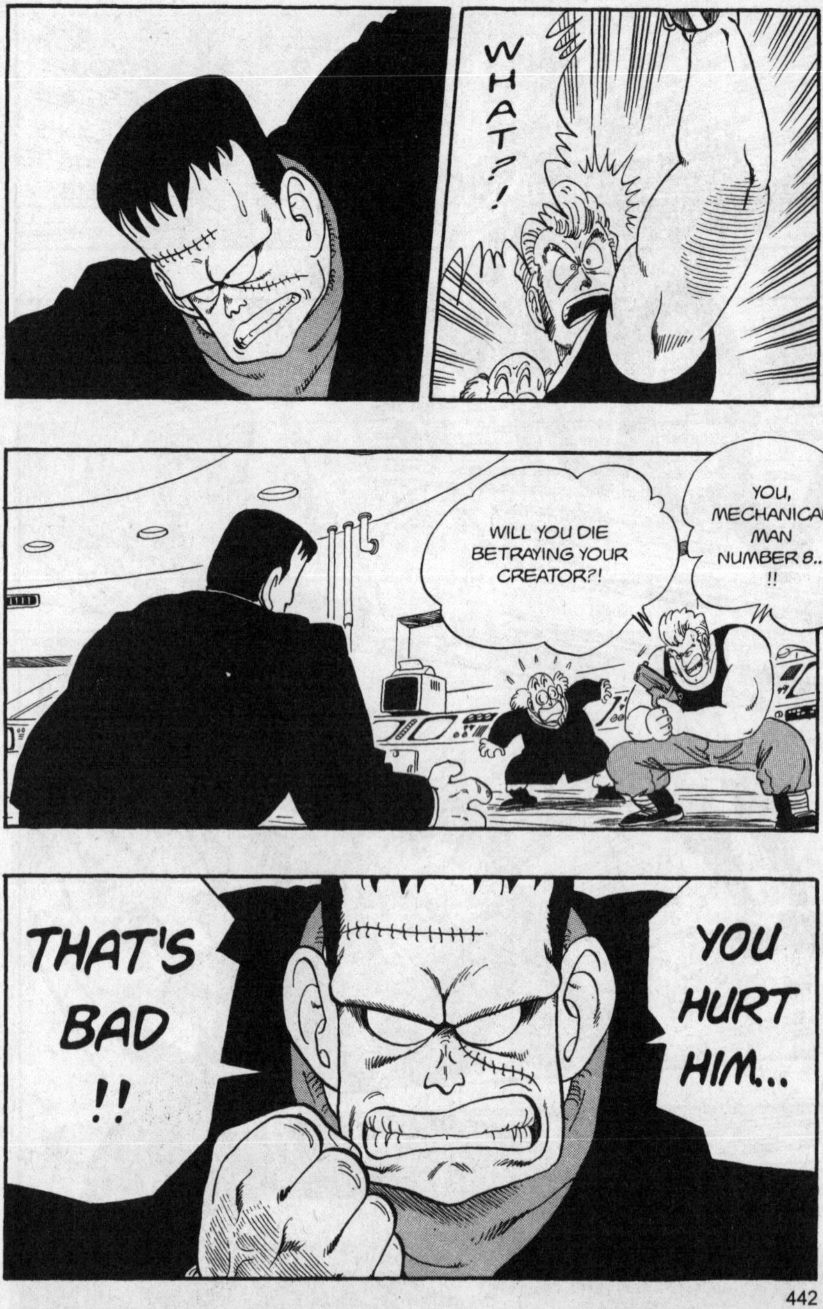
WHAT?!
YOU, MECHANICAL MAN NUMBER 8... !!
WILL YOU DIE BETRAYING YOUR CREATOR?!
YOU HURT HIM...
THAT'S BAD !!

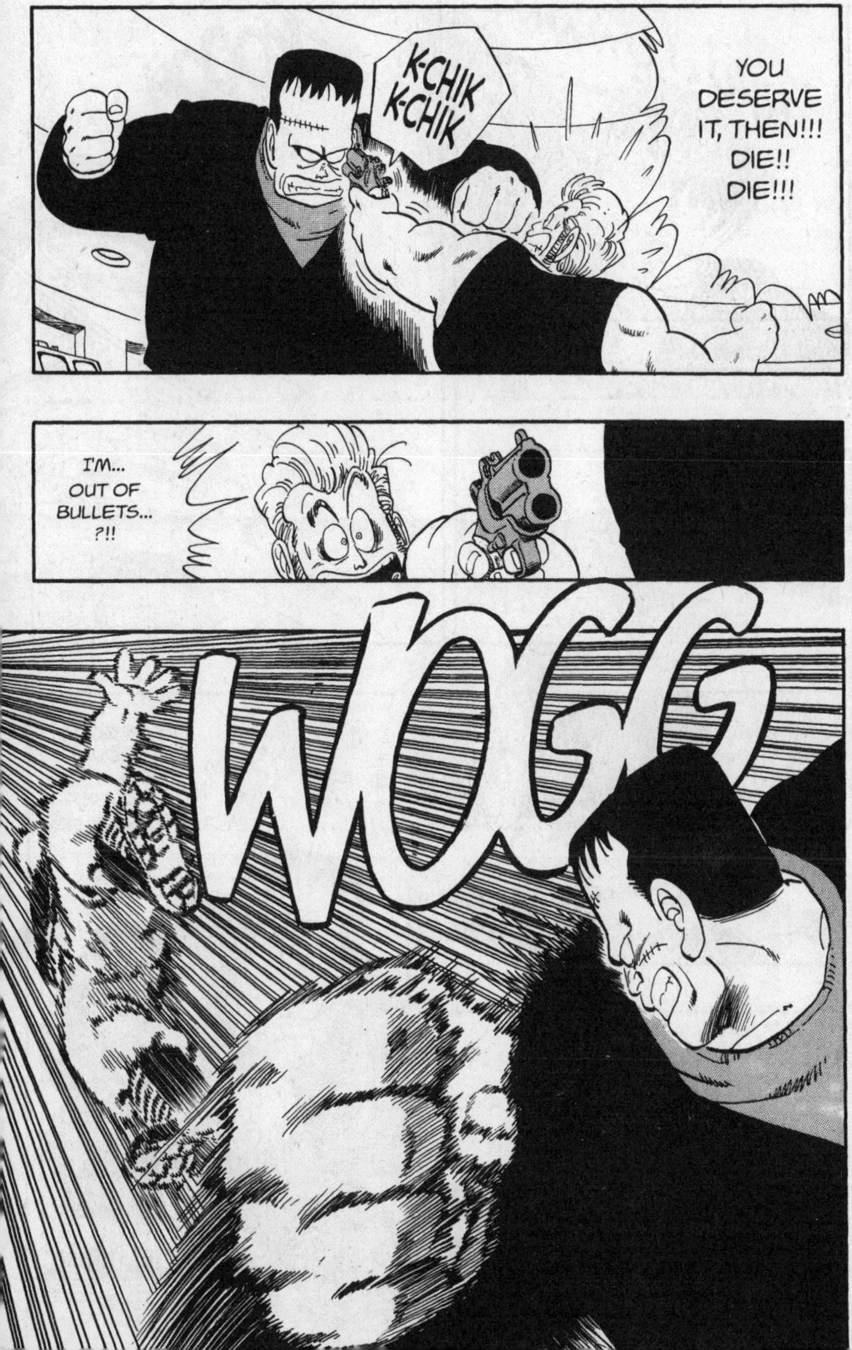
YOU DESERVE IT, THEN!!! DIE!! DIE!!!
K-CHIK K-CHIK
I'M... OUT OF BULLETS... ?!!
WOGG

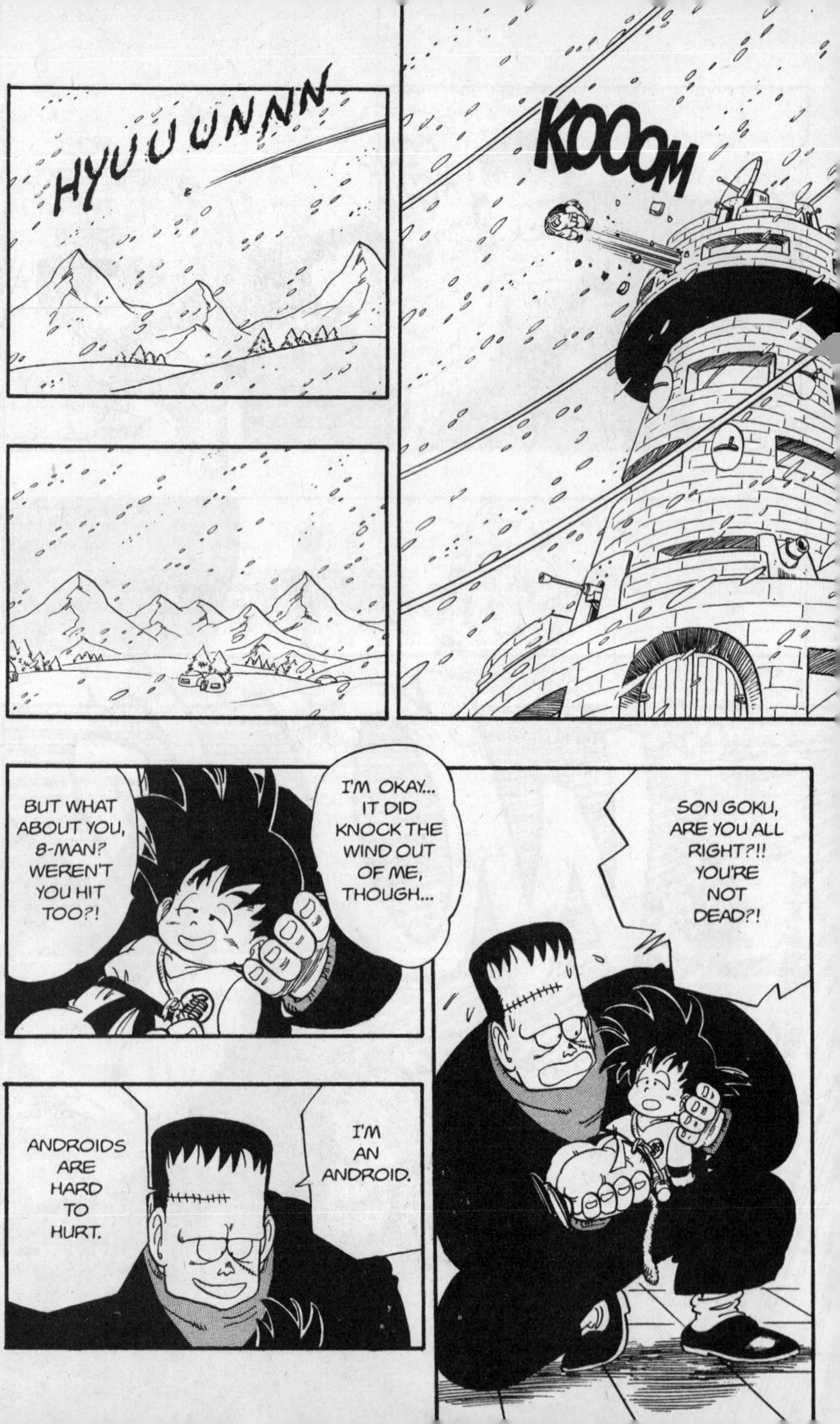
KOOOM
HYUUUNNN
SON GOKU, ARE YOU ALL RIGHT?!! YOU'RE NOT DEAD?!
I'M OKAY... IT DID KNOCK THE WIND OUT OF ME, THOUGH...
BUT WHAT ABOUT YOU, 8-MAN? WEREN'T YOU HIT TOO?!
I'M AN ANDROID.
ANDROIDS ARE HARD TO HURT.

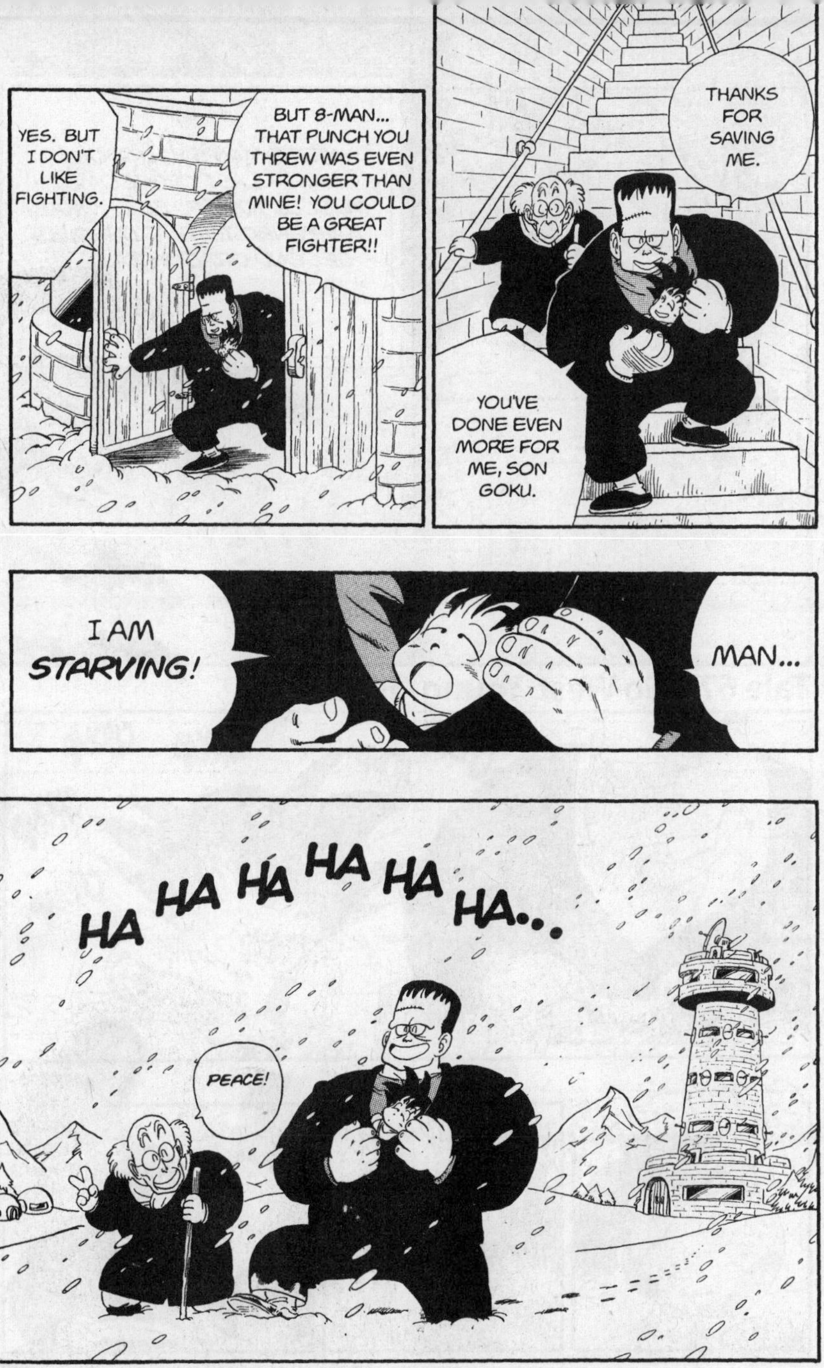
THANKS FOR SAVING ME.
YOU'VE DONE EVEN MORE FOR ME, SON GOKU.
BUT 8-MAN... THAT PUNCH YOU THREW WAS EVEN STRONGER THAN MINE! YOU COULD BE A GREAT FIGHTER!!
YES. BUT I DON'T LIKE FIGHTING.
MAN...
I AM STARVING!
HA HA HA HA HA HA...
PEACE!

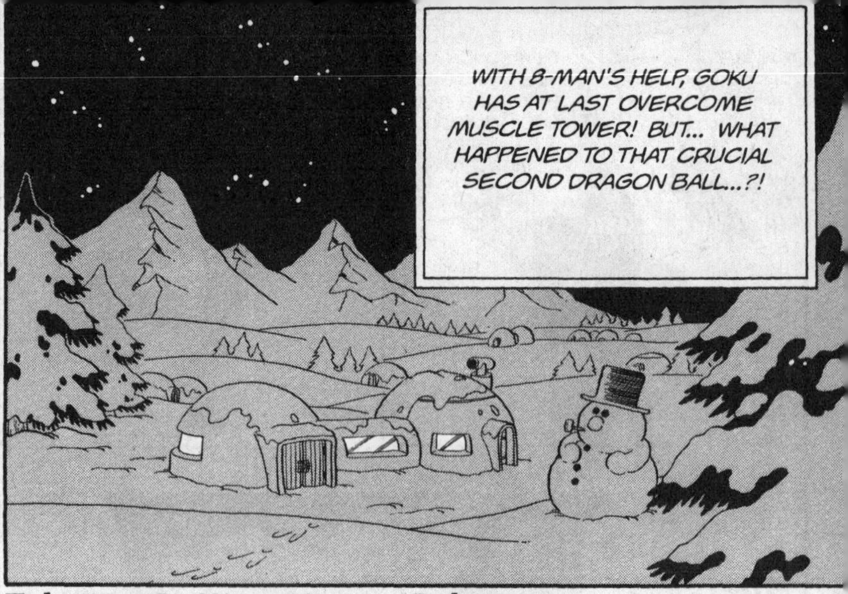
WITH 8-MAN'S HELP, GOKU HAS AT LAST OVERCOME MUSCLE TOWER! BUT... WHAT HAPPENED TO THAT CRUCIAL SECOND DRAGON BALL...?!

Tale 67 • Go West, Young Goku...

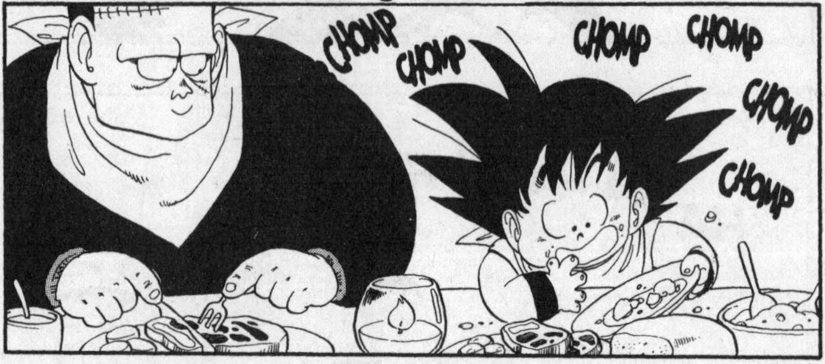
CHOMP
CHOMP
CHOMP
CHOMP
CHOMP
CHOMP

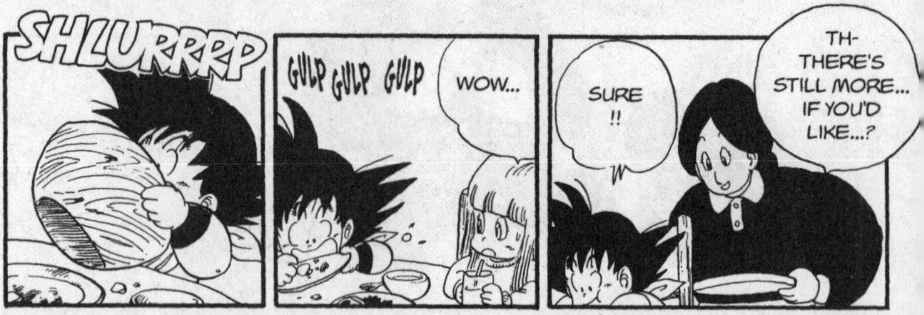
TH- THERE'S STILL MORE... IF YOU'D LIKE...?
SURE !!
WOW...
GULP GULP GULP
SHLURRRP

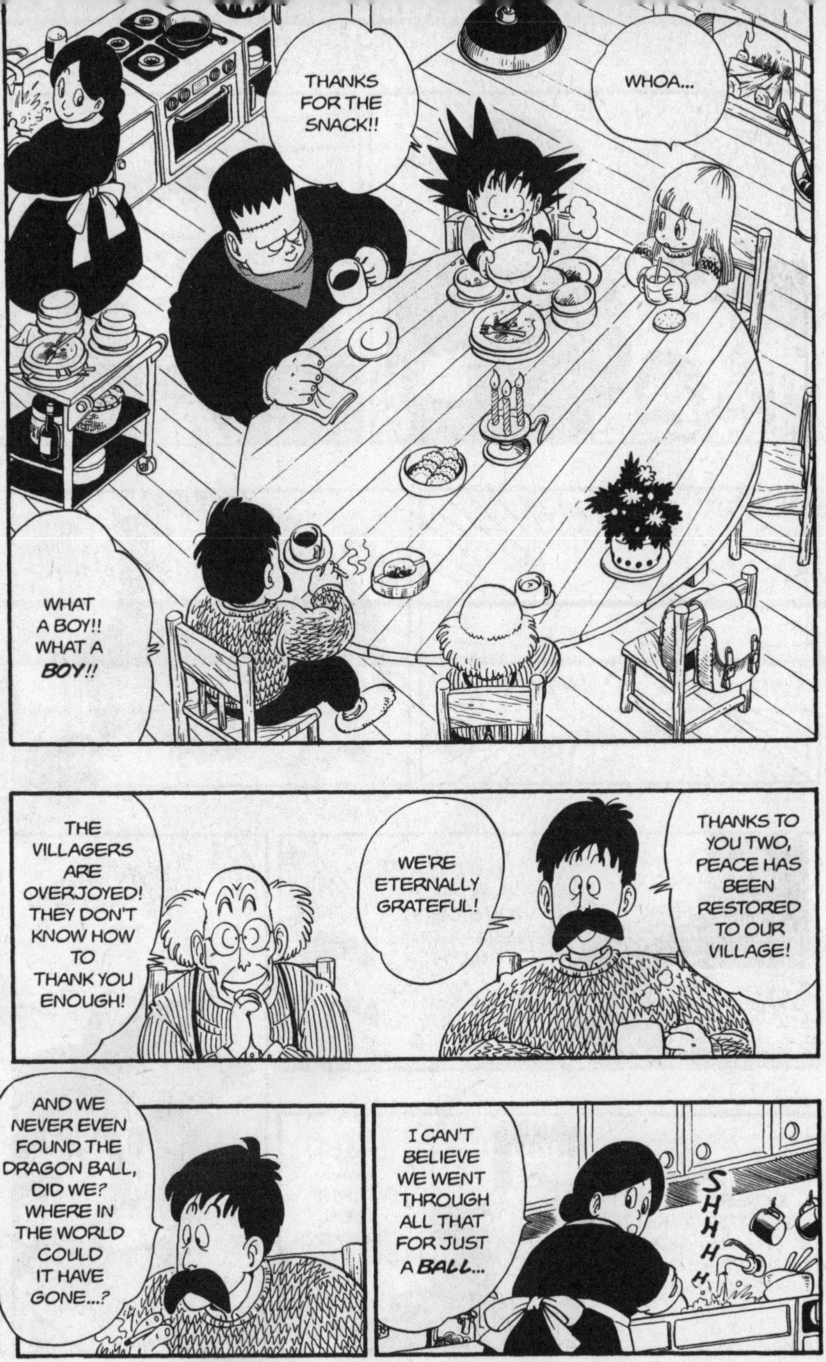
WHOA...
THANKS FOR THE SNACK!!
WHAT A BOY!! WHAT A **BOY**!!
THANKS TO YOU TWO, PEACE HAS BEEN RESTORED TO OUR VILLAGE!
WE'RE ETERNALLY GRATEFUL!
THE VILLAGERS ARE OVERJOYED! THEY DON'T KNOW HOW TO THANK YOU ENOUGH!
I CAN'T BELIEVE WE WENT THROUGH ALL THAT FOR JUST A **BALL**...
SHHHH
AND WE NEVER EVEN FOUND THE DRAGON BALL, DID WE? WHERE IN THE WORLD COULD IT HAVE GONE...?

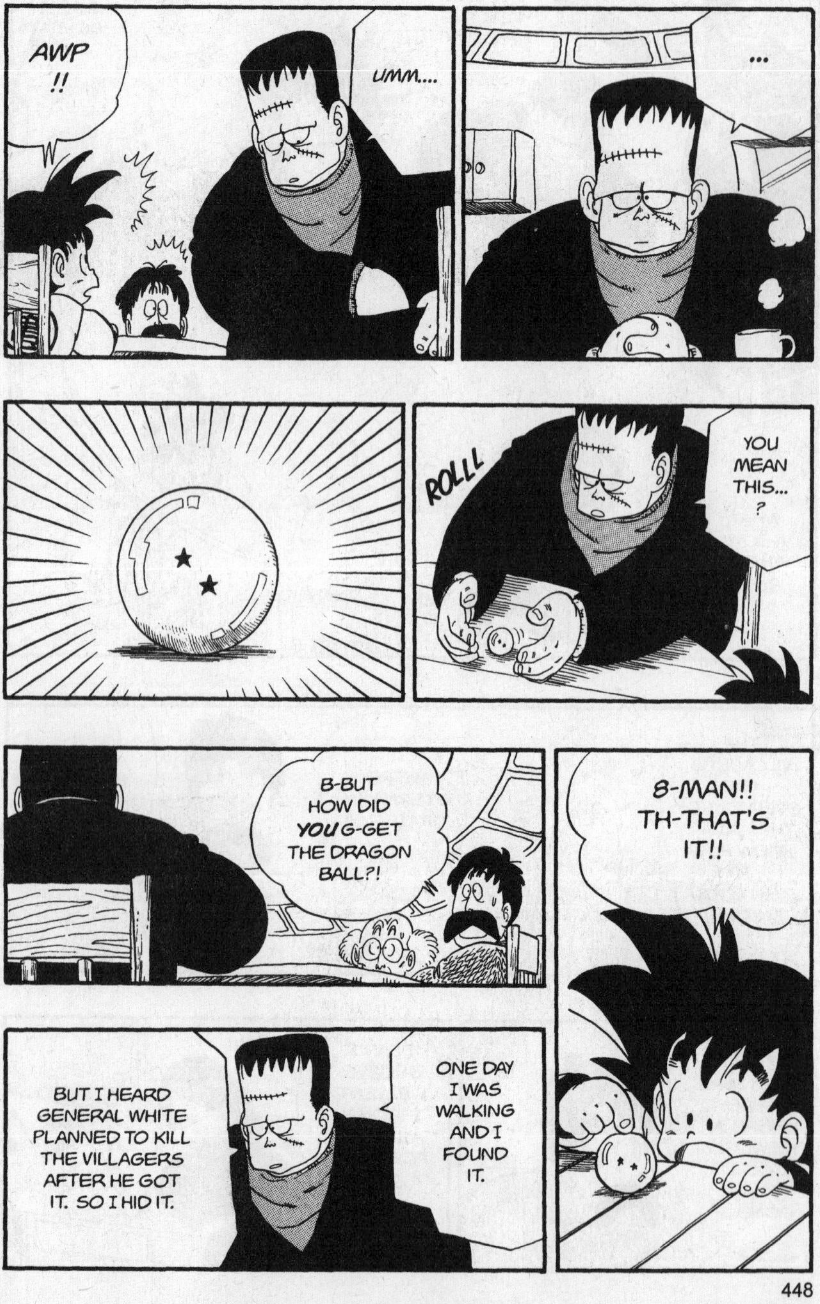
...
UMM....
AWP !!
YOU MEAN THIS... ?
ROLLL
8-MAN!! TH-THAT'S IT!!
B-BUT HOW DID YOU G-GET THE DRAGON BALL?!
ONE DAY I WAS WALKING AND I FOUND IT.
BUT I HEARD GENERAL WHITE PLANNED TO KILL THE VILLAGERS AFTER HE GOT IT. SO I HID IT.

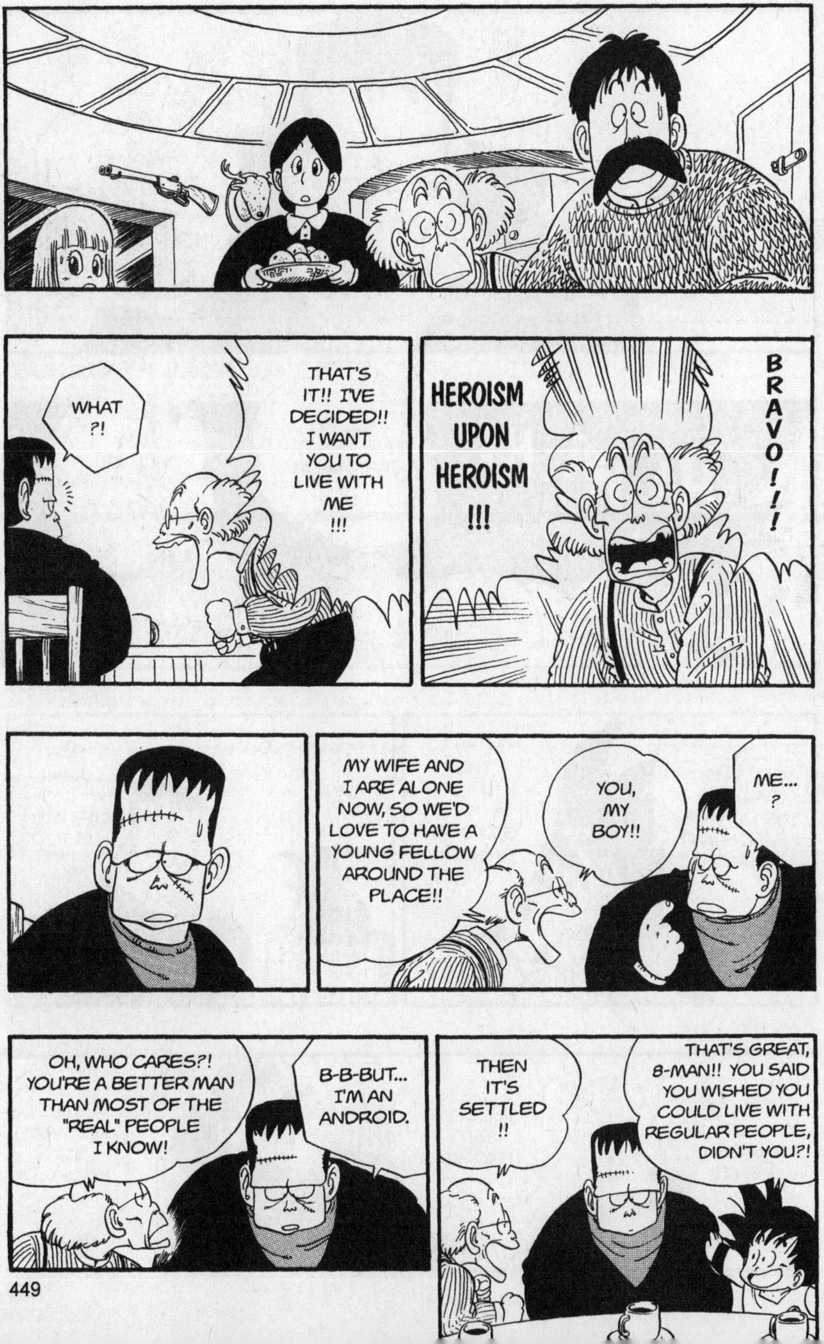
BRAVO!!!
HEROISM UPON HEROISM!!!
THAT'S IT!! I'VE DECIDED!! I WANT YOU TO LIVE WITH ME!!!
WHAT?!
ME...?
YOU, MY BOY!!
MY WIFE AND I ARE ALONE NOW, SO WE'D LOVE TO HAVE A YOUNG FELLOW AROUND THE PLACE!!
THAT'S GREAT, 8-MAN!! YOU SAID YOU WISHED YOU COULD LIVE WITH REGULAR PEOPLE, DIDN'T YOU?!
THEN IT'S SETTLED!!
B-B-BUT... I'M AN ANDROID.
OH, WHO CARES?! YOU'RE A BETTER MAN THAN MOST OF THE "REAL" PEOPLE I KNOW!

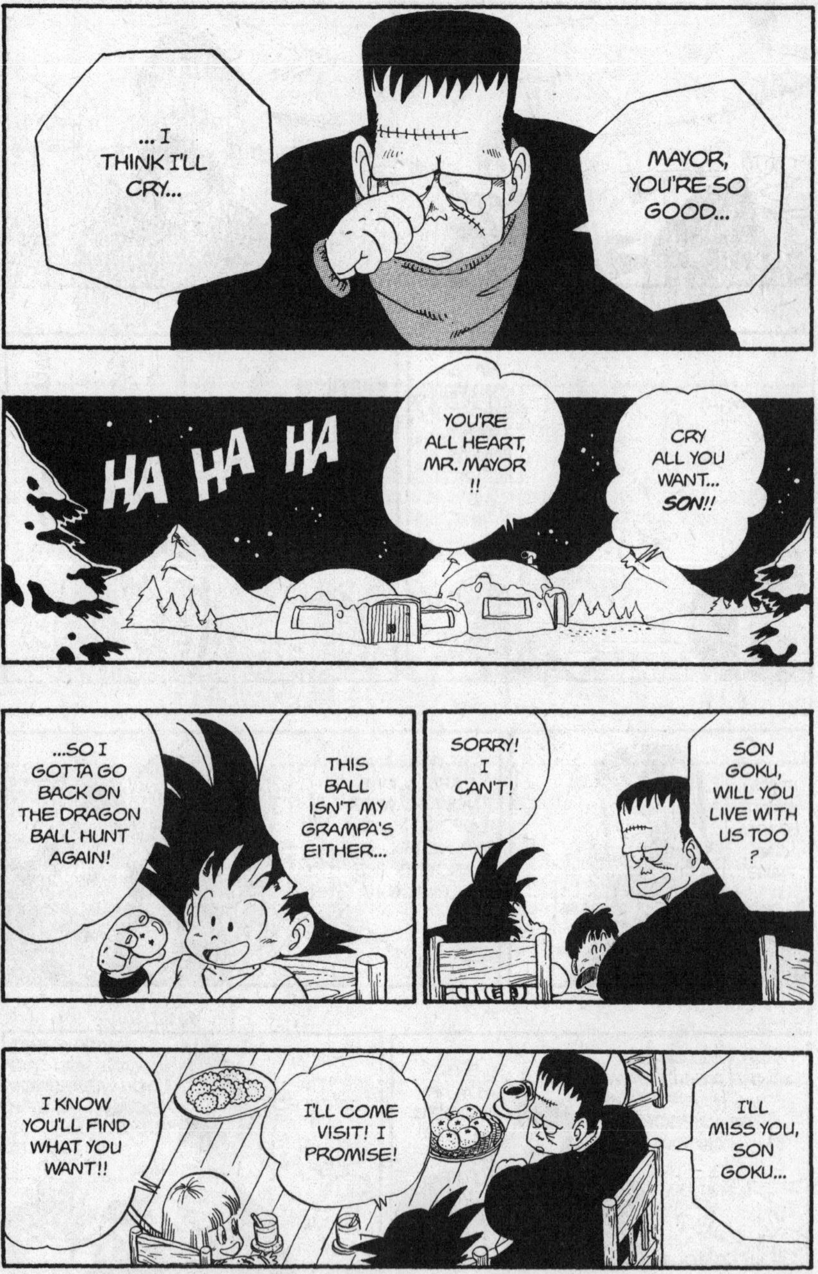
MAYOR, YOU'RE SO GOOD...
... I THINK I'LL CRY...
CRY ALL YOU WANT... SON!!
YOU'RE ALL HEART, MR. MAYOR !!
HA HA HA
SON GOKU, WILL YOU LIVE WITH US TOO ?
SORRY! I CAN'T!
THIS BALL ISN'T MY GRAMPA'S EITHER...
...SO I GOTTA GO BACK ON THE DRAGON BALL HUNT AGAIN!
I'LL MISS YOU, SON GOKU...
I'LL COME VISIT! I PROMISE!
I KNOW YOU'LL FIND WHAT YOU WANT!!

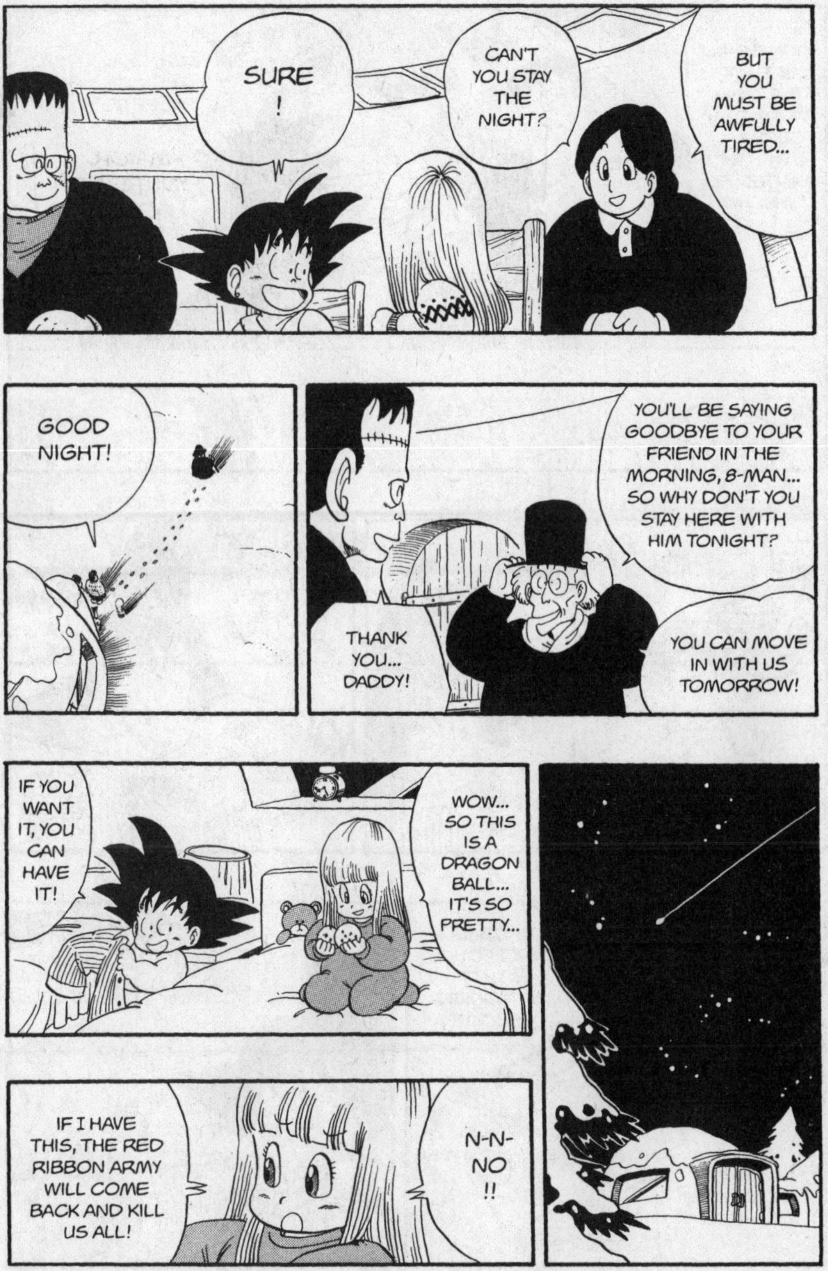
BUT YOU MUST BE AWFULLY TIRED...
CAN'T YOU STAY THE NIGHT?
SURE!
YOU'LL BE SAYING GOODBYE TO YOUR FRIEND IN THE MORNING, 8-MAN... SO WHY DON'T YOU STAY HERE WITH HIM TONIGHT?
YOU CAN MOVE IN WITH US TOMORROW!
THANK YOU... DADDY!
GOOD NIGHT!
WOW... SO THIS IS A DRAGON BALL... IT'S SO PRETTY...
IF YOU WANT IT, YOU CAN HAVE IT!
N-N-NO!!
IF I HAVE THIS, THE RED RIBBON ARMY WILL COME BACK AND KILL US ALL!

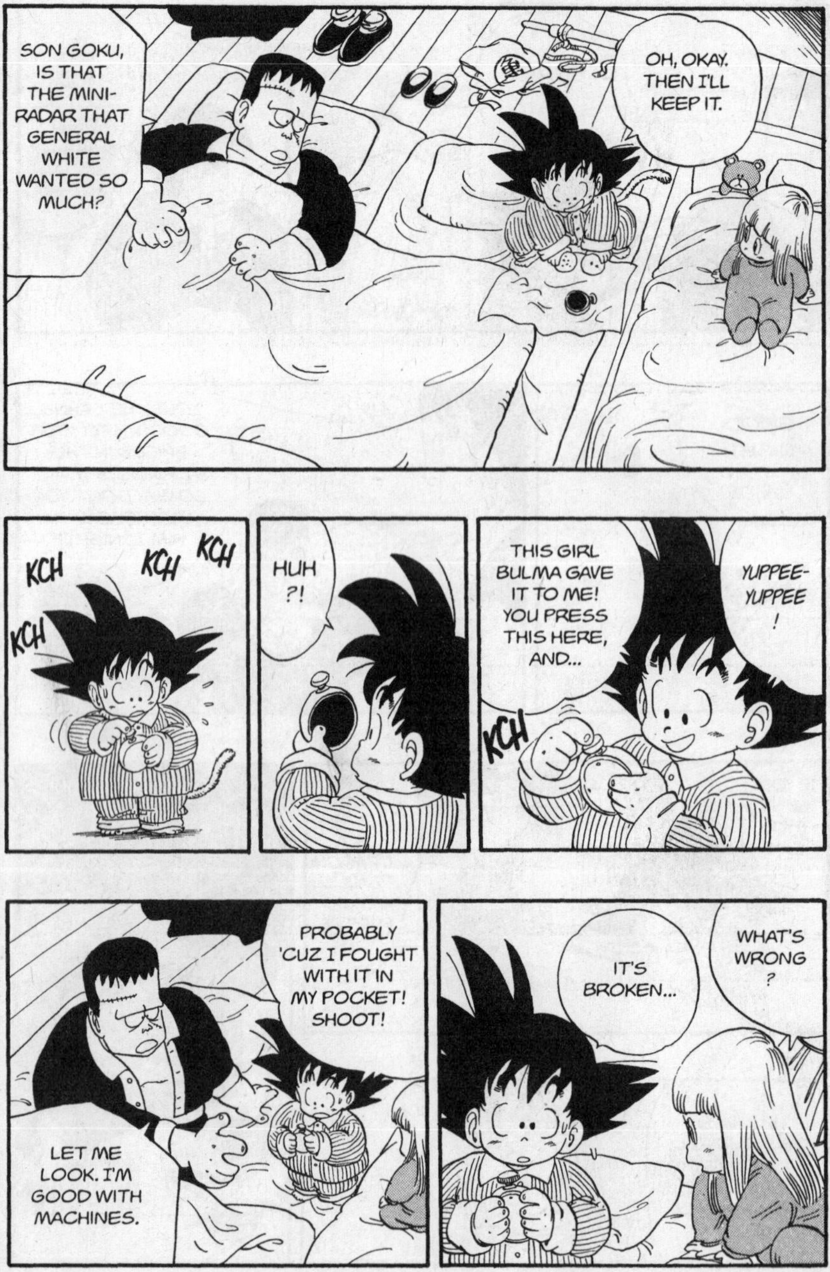
OH, OKAY. THEN I'LL KEEP IT.
SON GOKU, IS THAT THE MINI-RADAR THAT GENERAL WHITE WANTED SO MUCH?
YUPPEE-YUPPEE!
THIS GIRL BULMA GAVE IT TO ME! YOU PRESS THIS HERE, AND...
KCH
HUH ?!
KCH
KCH
KCH
KCH
WHAT'S WRONG ?
IT'S BROKEN...
PROBABLY 'CUZ I FOUGHT WITH IT IN MY POCKET! SHOOT!
LET ME LOOK. I'M GOOD WITH MACHINES.

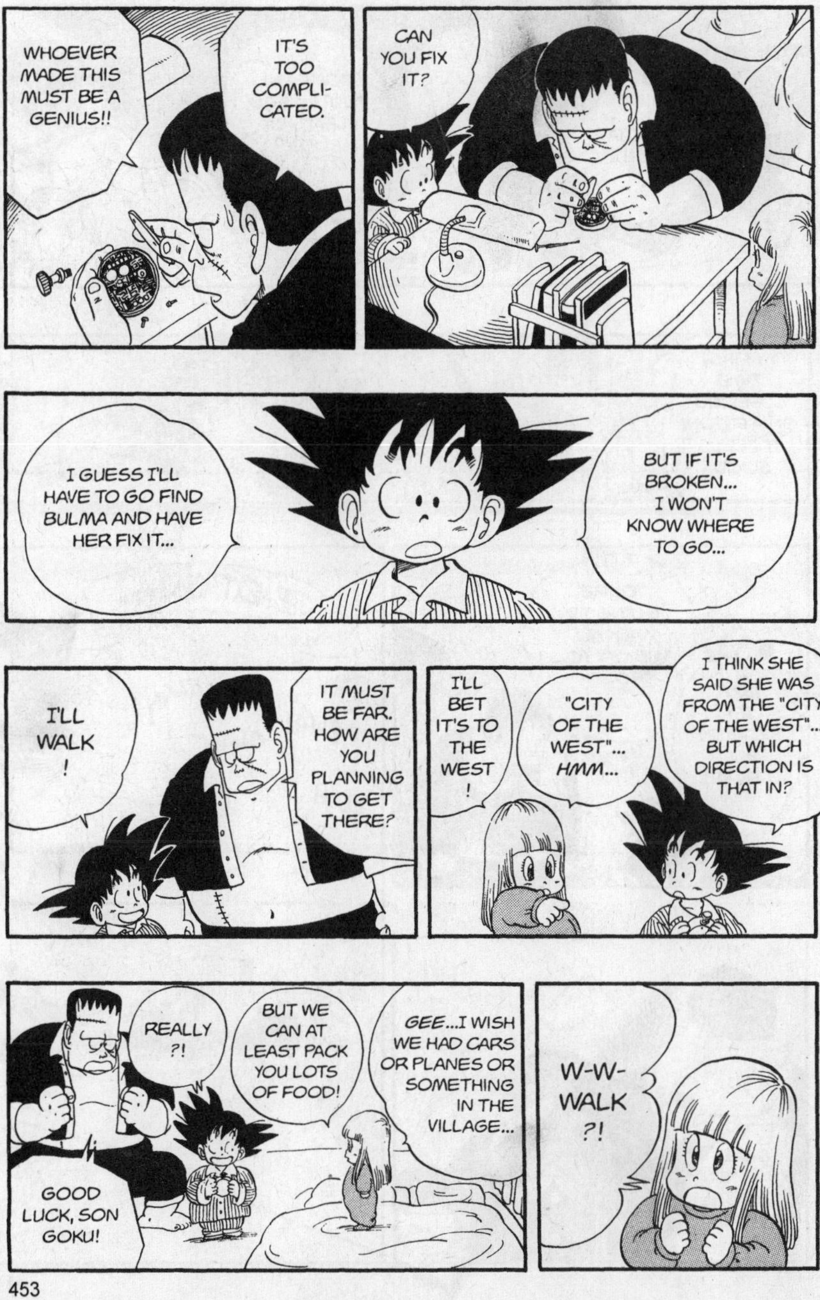
CAN YOU FIX IT?
IT'S TOO COMPLI-CATED.
WHOEVER MADE THIS MUST BE A GENIUS!!
BUT IF IT'S BROKEN... I WON'T KNOW WHERE TO GO...
I GUESS I'LL HAVE TO GO FIND BULMA AND HAVE HER FIX IT...
I THINK SHE SAID SHE WAS FROM THE "CITY OF THE WEST"... BUT WHICH DIRECTION IS THAT IN?
"CITY OF THE WEST"... *HMM*...
I'LL BET IT'S TO THE WEST!
IT MUST BE FAR. HOW ARE YOU PLANNING TO GET THERE?
I'LL WALK!
W-W-WALK?!
GEE...I WISH WE HAD CARS OR PLANES OR SOMETHING IN THE VILLAGE...
BUT WE CAN AT LEAST PACK YOU LOTS OF FOOD!
REALLY?!
GOOD LUCK, SON GOKU!

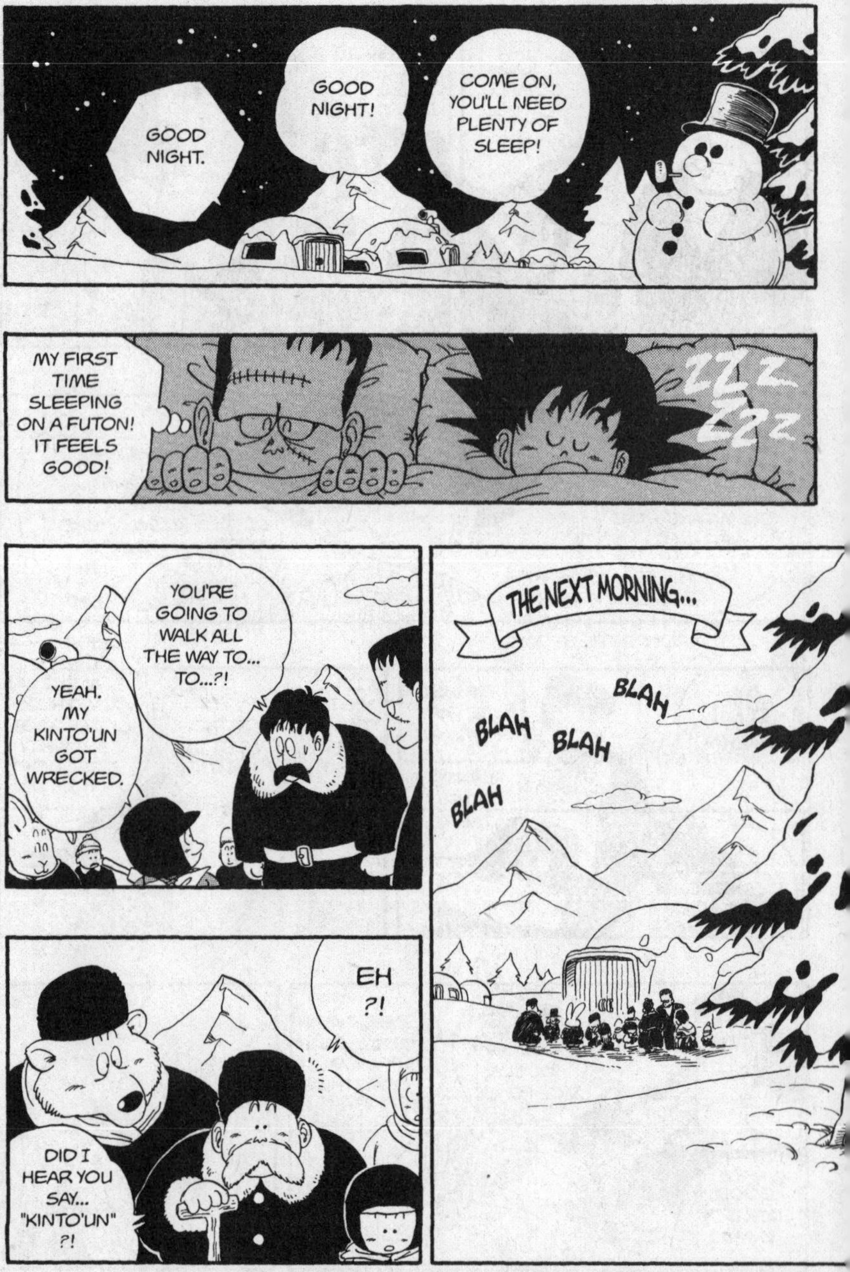
COME ON, YOU'LL NEED PLENTY OF SLEEP!
GOOD NIGHT!
GOOD NIGHT.
ZZZ ZZZ
MY FIRST TIME SLEEPING ON A FUTON! IT FEELS GOOD!
THE NEXT MORNING...
BLAH
BLAH
BLAH
BLAH
YOU'RE GOING TO WALK ALL THE WAY TO... TO...?!
YEAH. MY KINTO'UN GOT WRECKED.
EH ?!
DID I HEAR YOU SAY... "KINTO'UN" ?!

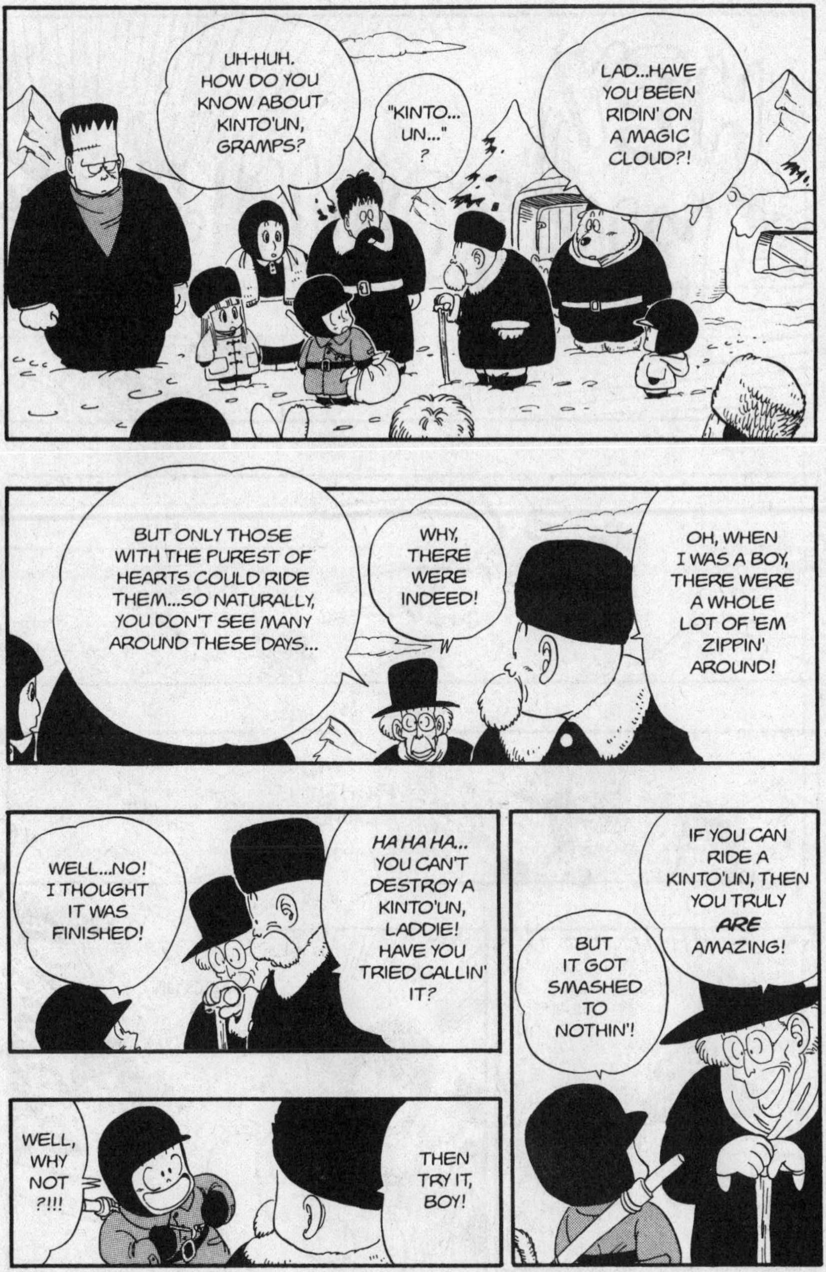
LAD...HAVE YOU BEEN RIDIN' ON A MAGIC CLOUD?!
"KINTO... UN..." ?
UH-HUH. HOW DO YOU KNOW ABOUT KINTO'UN, GRAMPS?
OH, WHEN I WAS A BOY, THERE WERE A WHOLE LOT OF 'EM ZIPPIN' AROUND!
WHY, THERE WERE INDEED!
BUT ONLY THOSE WITH THE PUREST OF HEARTS COULD RIDE THEM...SO NATURALLY, YOU DON'T SEE MANY AROUND THESE DAYS...
IF YOU CAN RIDE A KINTO'UN, THEN YOU TRULY *ARE* AMAZING!
BUT IT GOT SMASHED TO NOTHIN'!
HA HA HA... YOU CAN'T DESTROY A KINTO'UN, LADDIE! HAVE YOU TRIED CALLIN' IT?
WELL...NO! I THOUGHT IT WAS FINISHED!
THEN TRY IT, BOY!
WELL, WHY NOT ?!!!

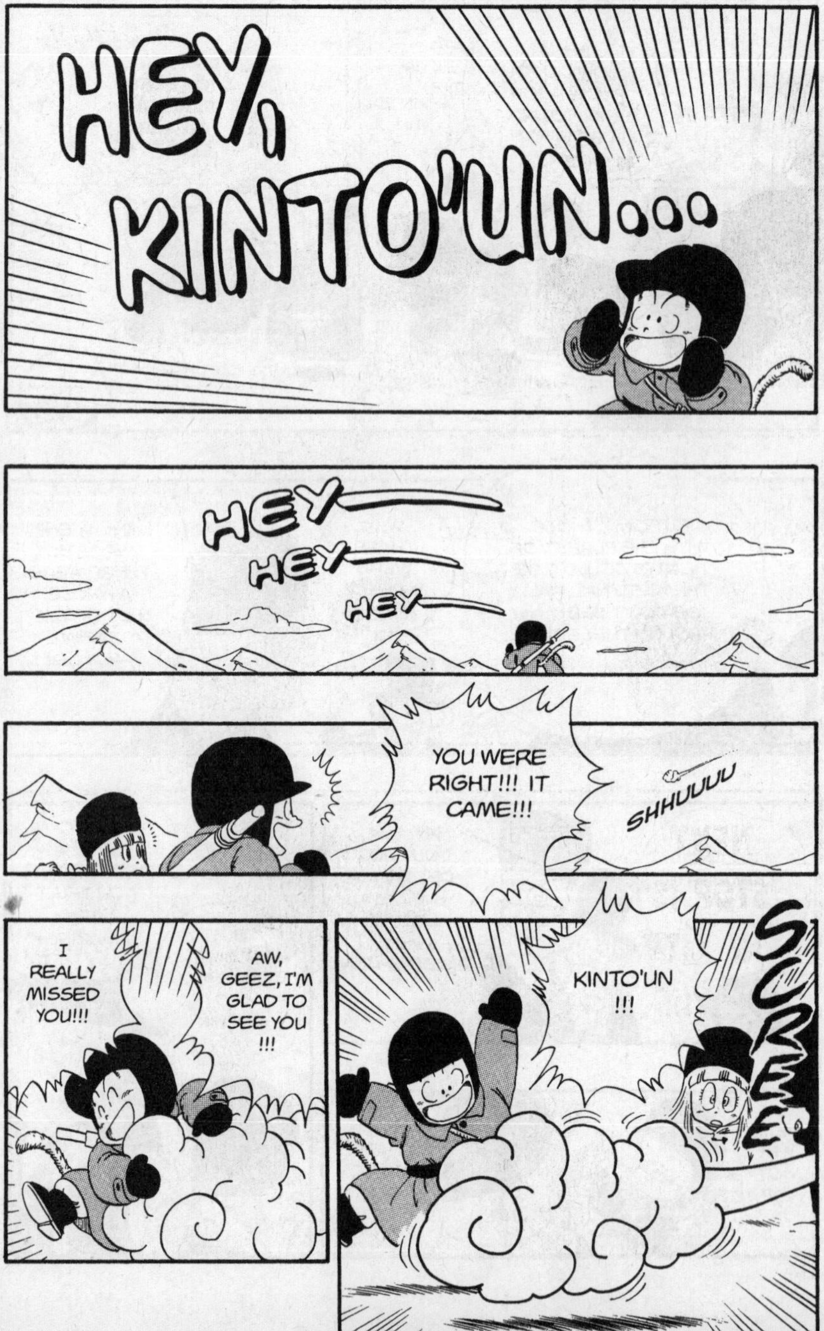
HEY, KINTO'UN...
HEY
HEY
HEY
SHHUUUU
YOU WERE RIGHT!!! IT CAME!!!
SCREEE
KINTO'UN !!!
AW, GEEZ, I'M GLAD TO SEE YOU !!!
I REALLY MISSED YOU!!!

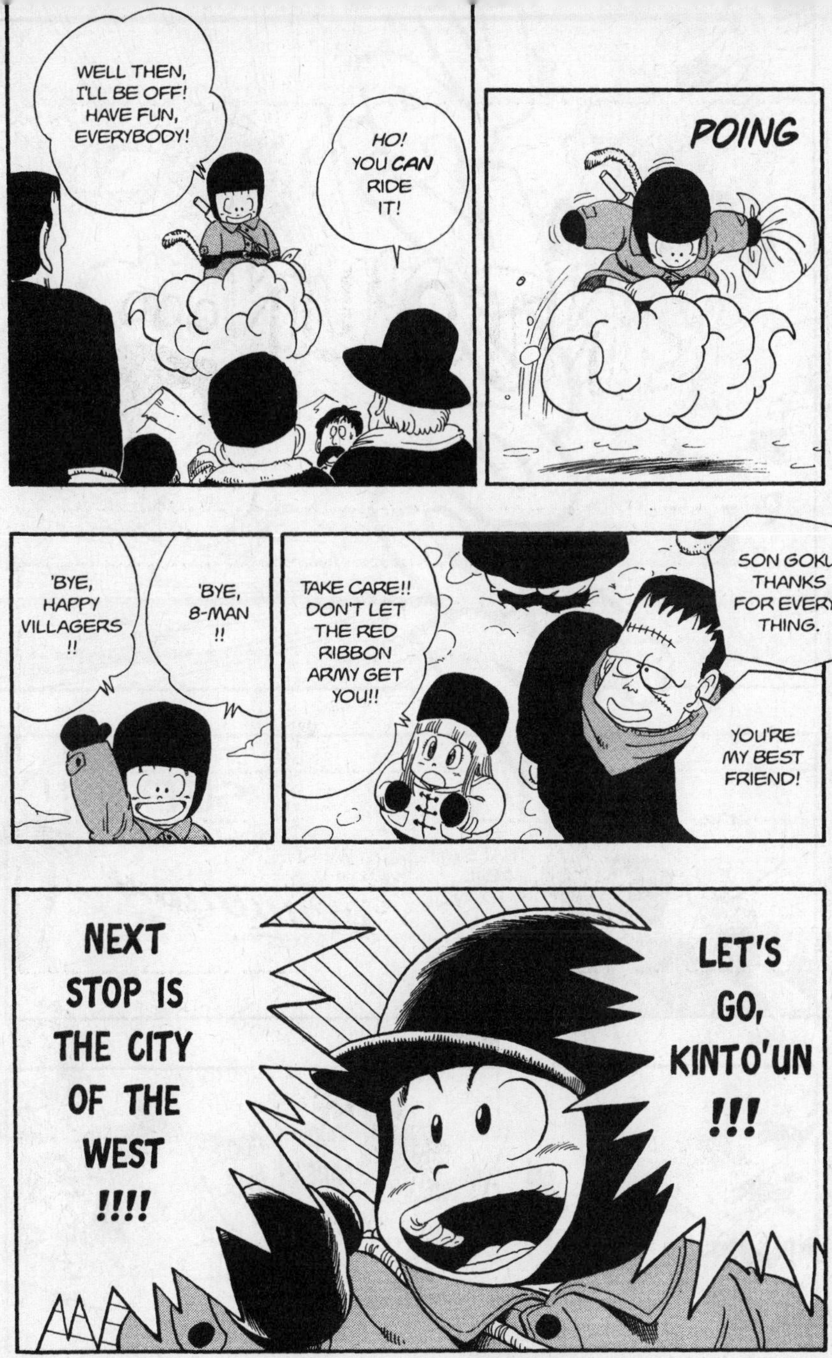
POING
HO! YOU CAN RIDE IT!
WELL THEN, I'LL BE OFF! HAVE FUN, EVERYBODY!
SON GOKU, THANKS FOR EVERYTHING.
YOU'RE MY BEST FRIEND!
TAKE CARE!! DON'T LET THE RED RIBBON ARMY GET YOU!!
'BYE, 8-MAN !!
'BYE, HAPPY VILLAGERS !!
LET'S GO, KINTO'UN !!!
NEXT STOP IS THE CITY OF THE WEST !!!!

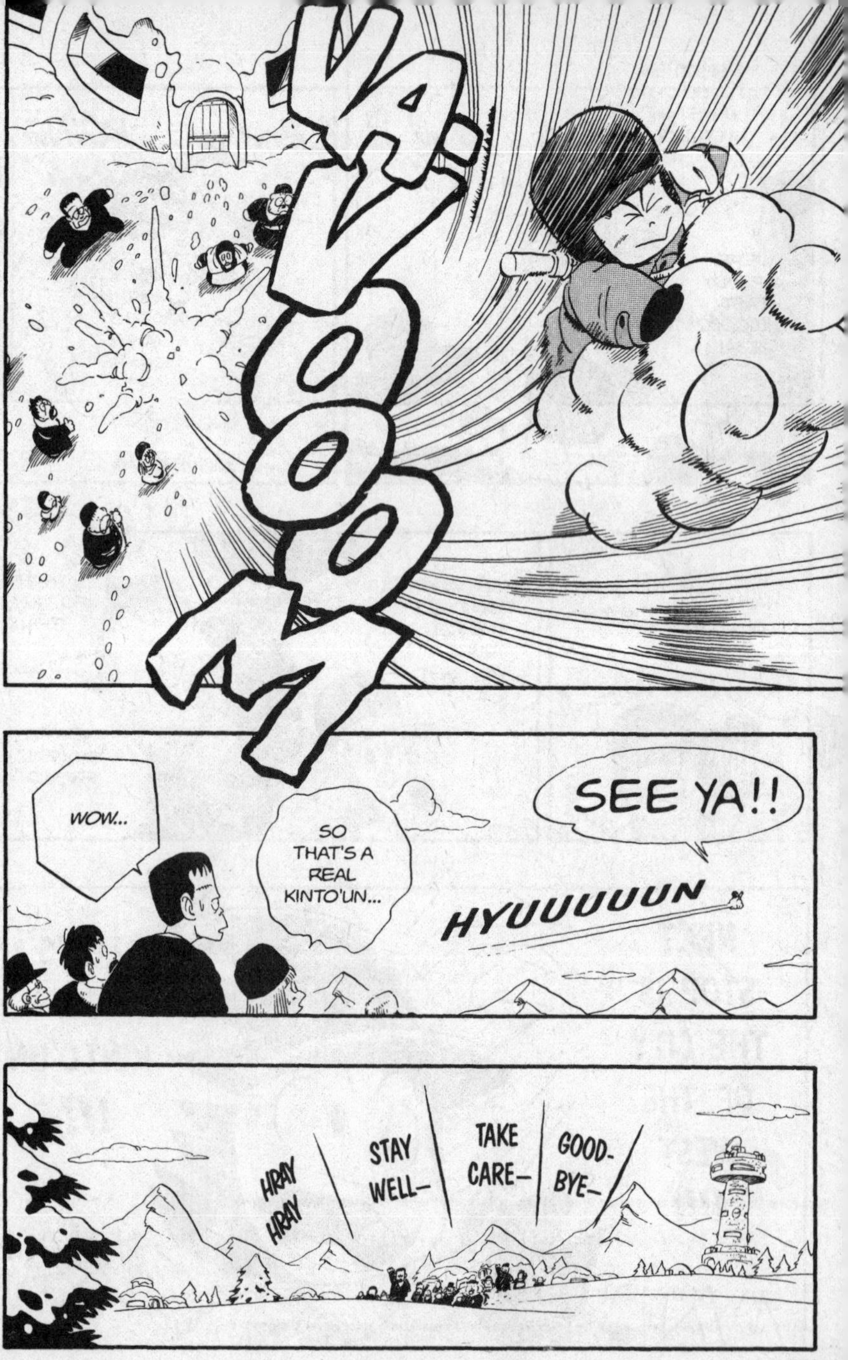
VAVOOOOM
SEE YA!!
HYUUUUUN
SO THAT'S A REAL KINTO'UN...
WOW...
GOOD-BYE-
TAKE CARE-
STAY WELL-
HRAY HRAY

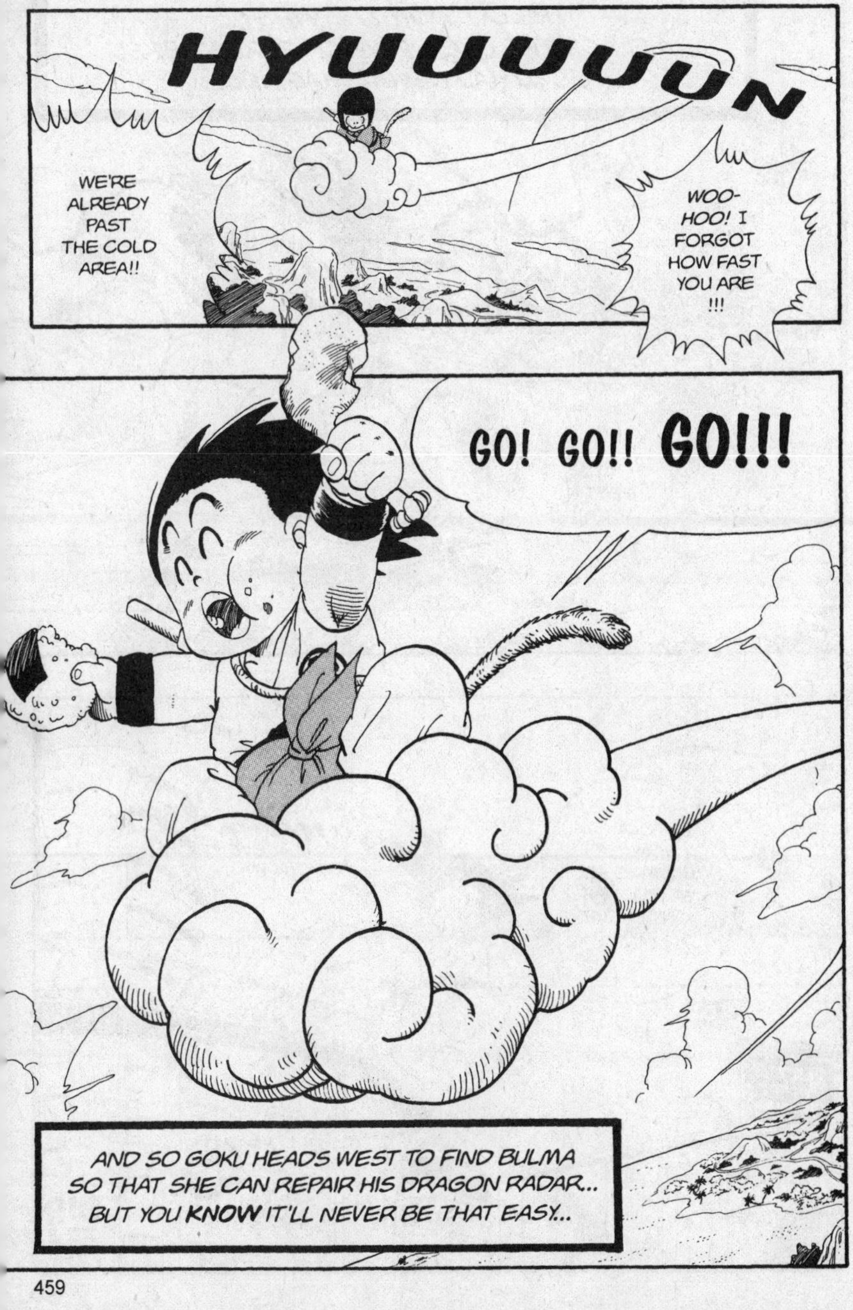
HYUUUUUUN
WOO-HOO! I FORGOT HOW FAST YOU ARE !!!
WE'RE ALREADY PAST THE COLD AREA!!
GO! GO!! GO!!!
AND SO GOKU HEADS WEST TO FIND BULMA SO THAT SHE CAN REPAIR HIS DRAGON RADAR... BUT YOU KNOW IT'LL NEVER BE THAT EASY...

Tale 68 • Monkey in the City

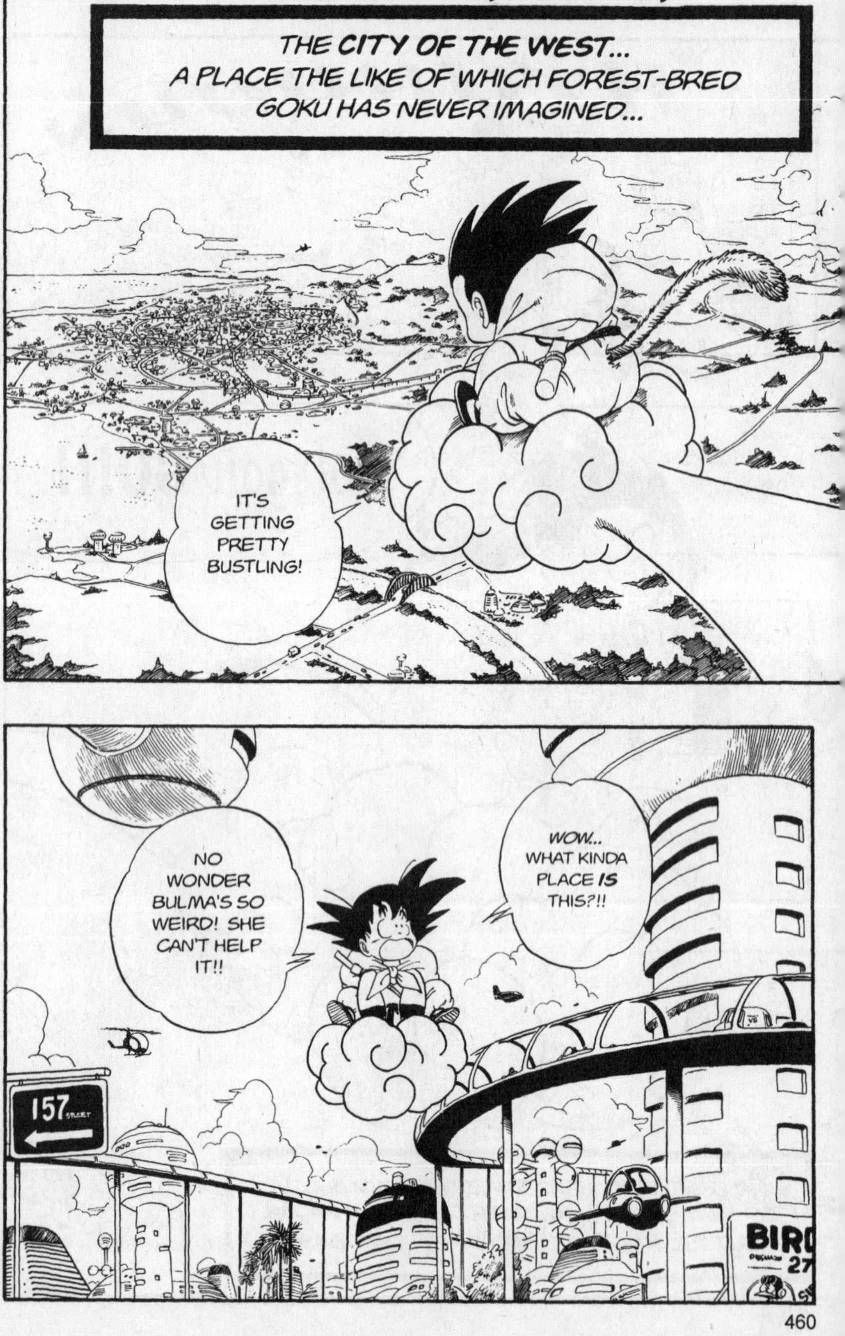
THE *CITY OF THE WEST*...
A PLACE THE LIKE OF WHICH FOREST-BRED GOKU HAS NEVER IMAGINED...
IT'S GETTING PRETTY BUSTLING!
WOW... WHAT KINDA PLACE *IS* THIS?!!
NO WONDER BULMA'S SO WEIRD! SHE CAN'T HELP IT!!
157

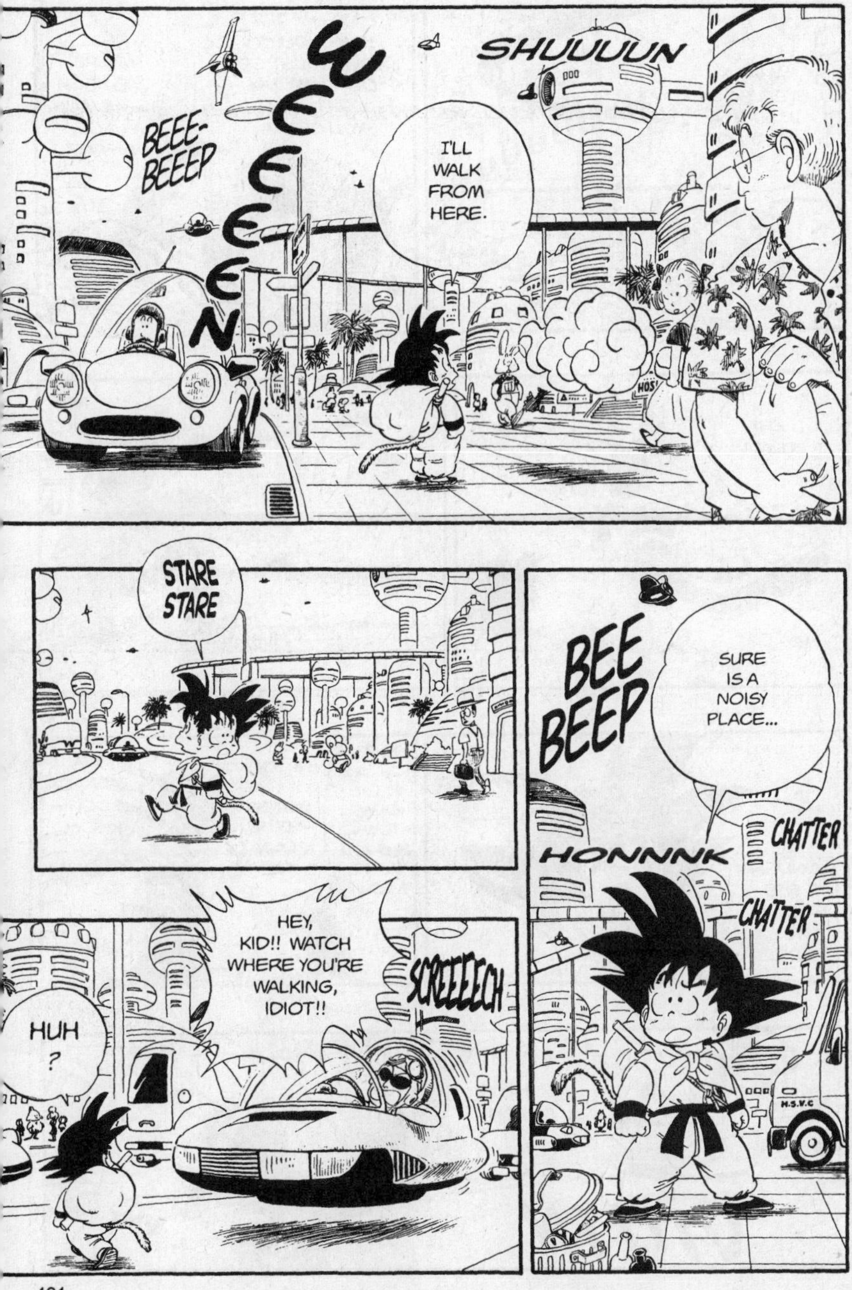
SHUUUUN
WEEEEEEN
BEEE-BEEEP
I'LL WALK FROM HERE.
BEE BEEP
SURE IS A NOISY PLACE...
CHATTER
HONNNK
CHATTER
STARE STARE
SCREEEECH
HEY, KID!! WATCH WHERE YOU'RE WALKING, IDIOT!!
HUH ?

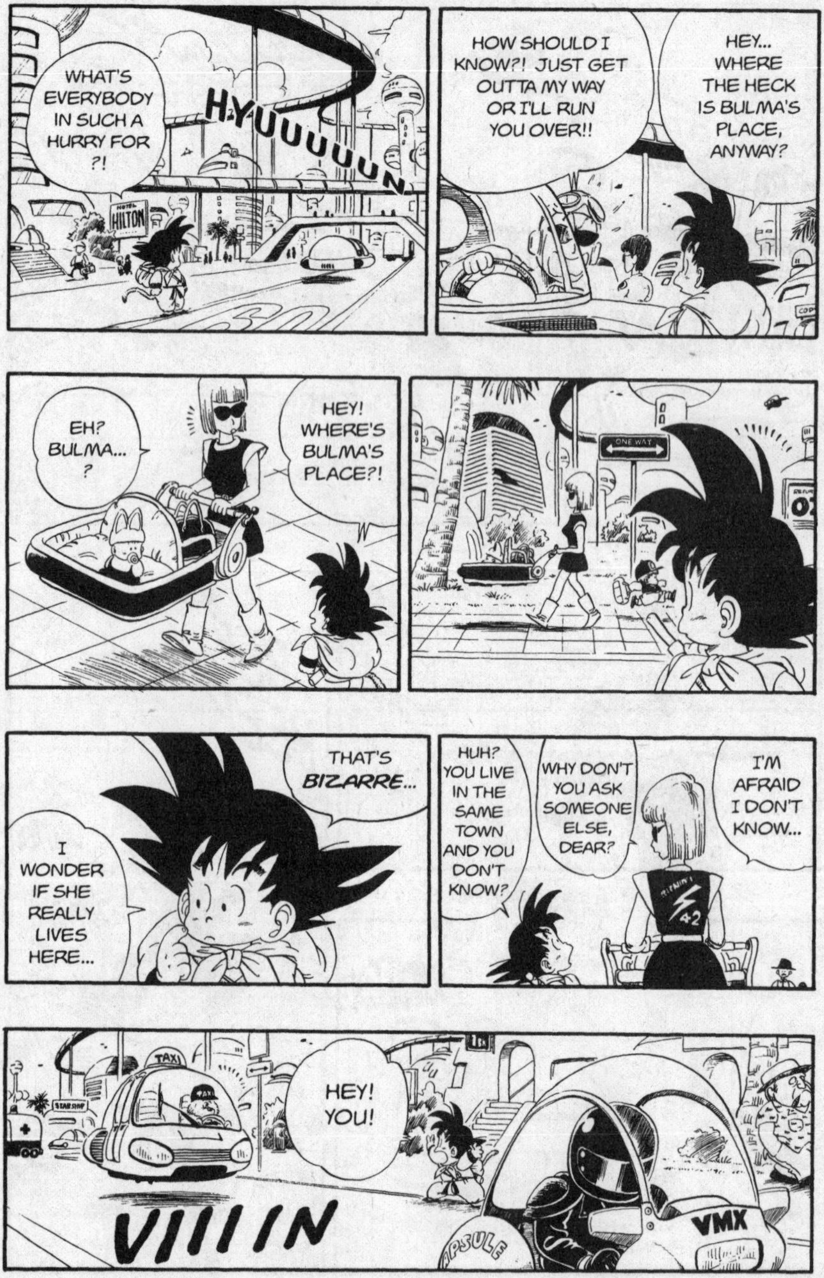
HEY... WHERE THE HECK IS BULMA'S PLACE, ANYWAY?
HOW SHOULD I KNOW?! JUST GET OUTTA MY WAY OR I'LL RUN YOU OVER!!
HYUUUUUUN
WHAT'S EVERYBODY IN SUCH A HURRY FOR ?!
HOTEL HILTON
ONE WAY
HEY! WHERE'S BULMA'S PLACE?!
EH? BULMA... ?
I'M AFRAID I DON'T KNOW...
WHY DON'T YOU ASK SOMEONE ELSE, DEAR?
HUH? YOU LIVE IN THE SAME TOWN AND YOU DON'T KNOW?
THAT'S *BIZARRE*...
I WONDER IF SHE REALLY LIVES HERE...
TAXI
HEY! YOU!
VIIIIN
VMX
CAPSULE

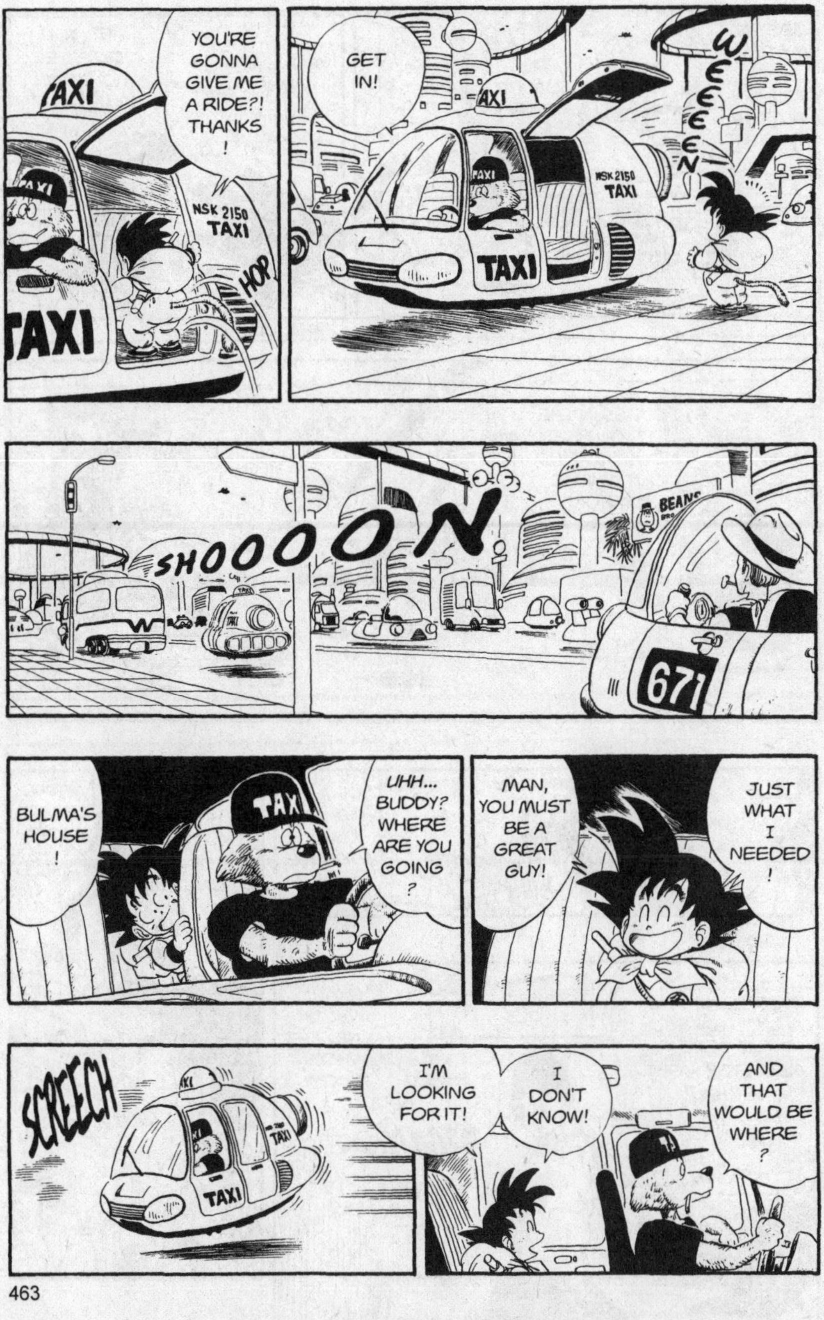
GET IN!
WEEEEEN
YOU'RE GONNA GIVE ME A RIDE?! THANKS!
NSK 2150 TAXI
HOP
SHOOOOON
BEANS
671
JUST WHAT I NEEDED!
MAN, YOU MUST BE A GREAT GUY!
UHH... BUDDY? WHERE ARE YOU GOING?
BULMA'S HOUSE!
AND THAT WOULD BE WHERE?
I DON'T KNOW!
I'M LOOKING FOR IT!
SCREECH

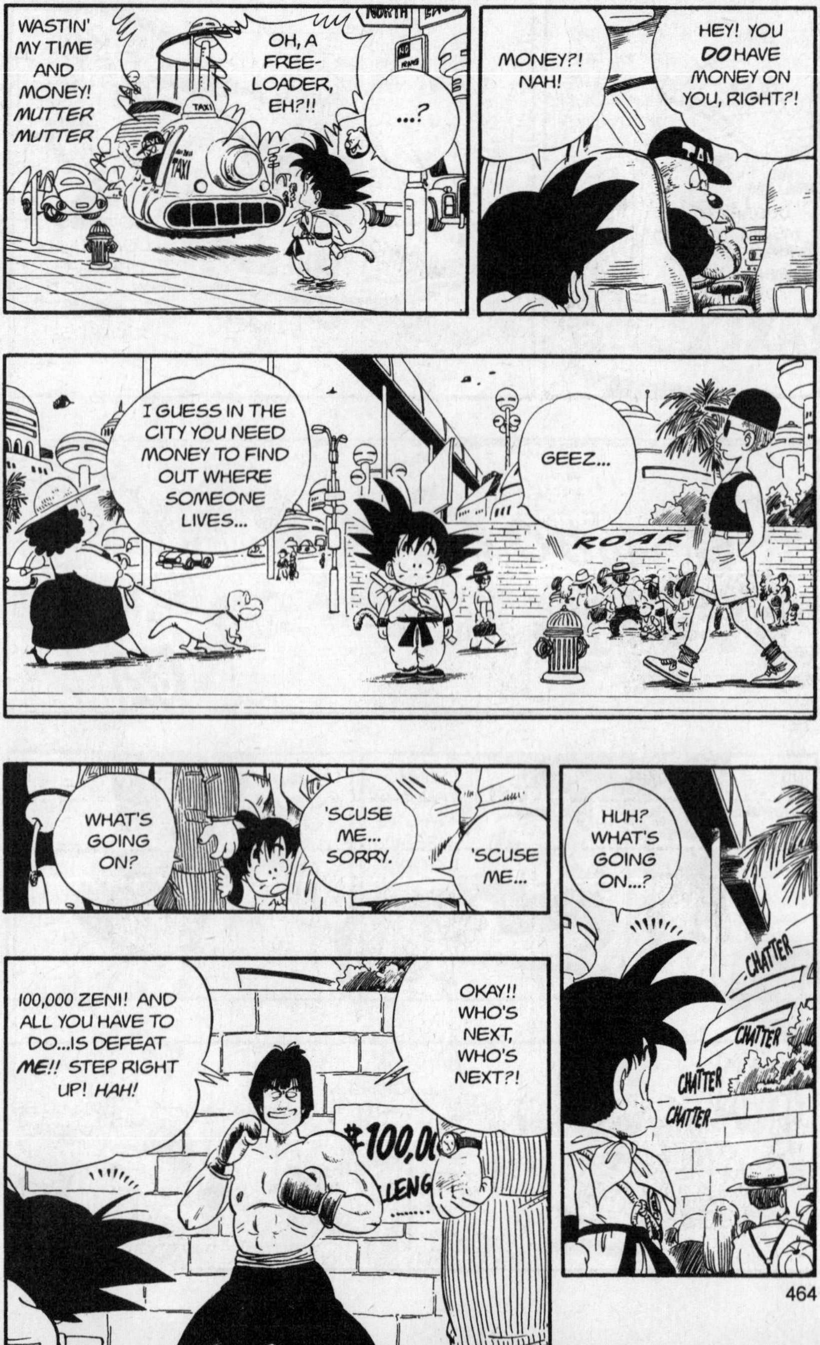
HEY! YOU DO HAVE MONEY ON YOU, RIGHT?!
MONEY?! NAH!
...?
OH, A FREE-LOADER, EH?!!
WASTIN' MY TIME AND MONEY! MUTTER MUTTER
TAXI
NORTH
GEEZ...
ROAR
I GUESS IN THE CITY YOU NEED MONEY TO FIND OUT WHERE SOMEONE LIVES...
HUH? WHAT'S GOING ON...?
CHATTER
CHATTER
CHATTER
CHATTER
'SCUSE ME...
'SCUSE ME... SORRY.
WHAT'S GOING ON?
OKAY!! WHO'S NEXT, WHO'S NEXT?!
100,000 ZENI! AND ALL YOU HAVE TO DO...IS DEFEAT ME!! STEP RIGHT UP! HAH!
$100,00
LLENG

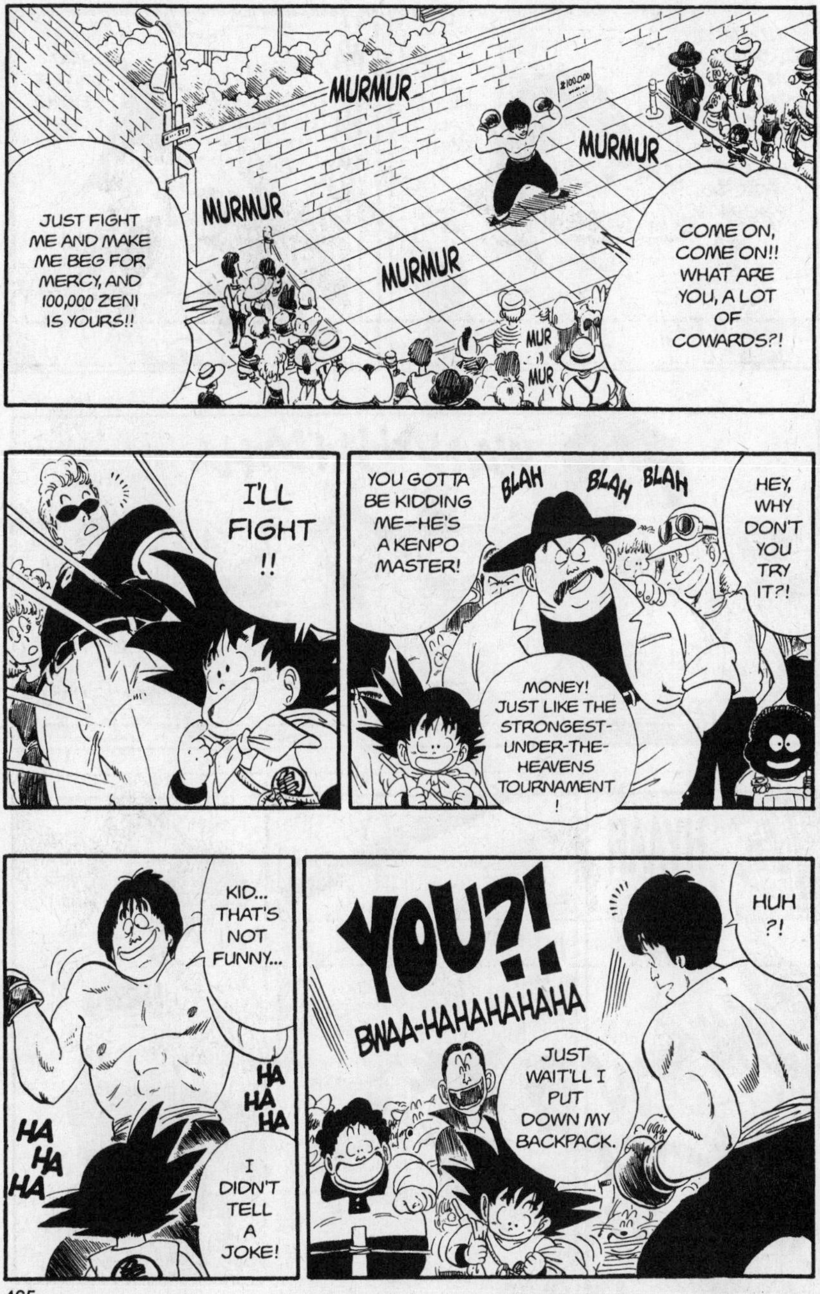
COME ON, COME ON!! WHAT ARE YOU, A LOT OF COWARDS?!
MURMUR
MURMUR
MURMUR
MURMUR
MUR MUR
JUST FIGHT ME AND MAKE ME BEG FOR MERCY, AND 100,000 ZENI IS YOURS!!
HEY, WHY DON'T YOU TRY IT?!
BLAH BLAH BLAH
YOU GOTTA BE KIDDING ME–HE'S A KENPO MASTER!
MONEY! JUST LIKE THE STRONGEST-UNDER-THE-HEAVENS TOURNAMENT!
I'LL FIGHT!!
HUH?!
YOU?!
BWAA-HAHAHAHAHA
JUST WAIT'LL I PUT DOWN MY BACKPACK.
KID... THAT'S NOT FUNNY...
HA HA HA
HA HA HA
I DIDN'T TELL A JOKE!

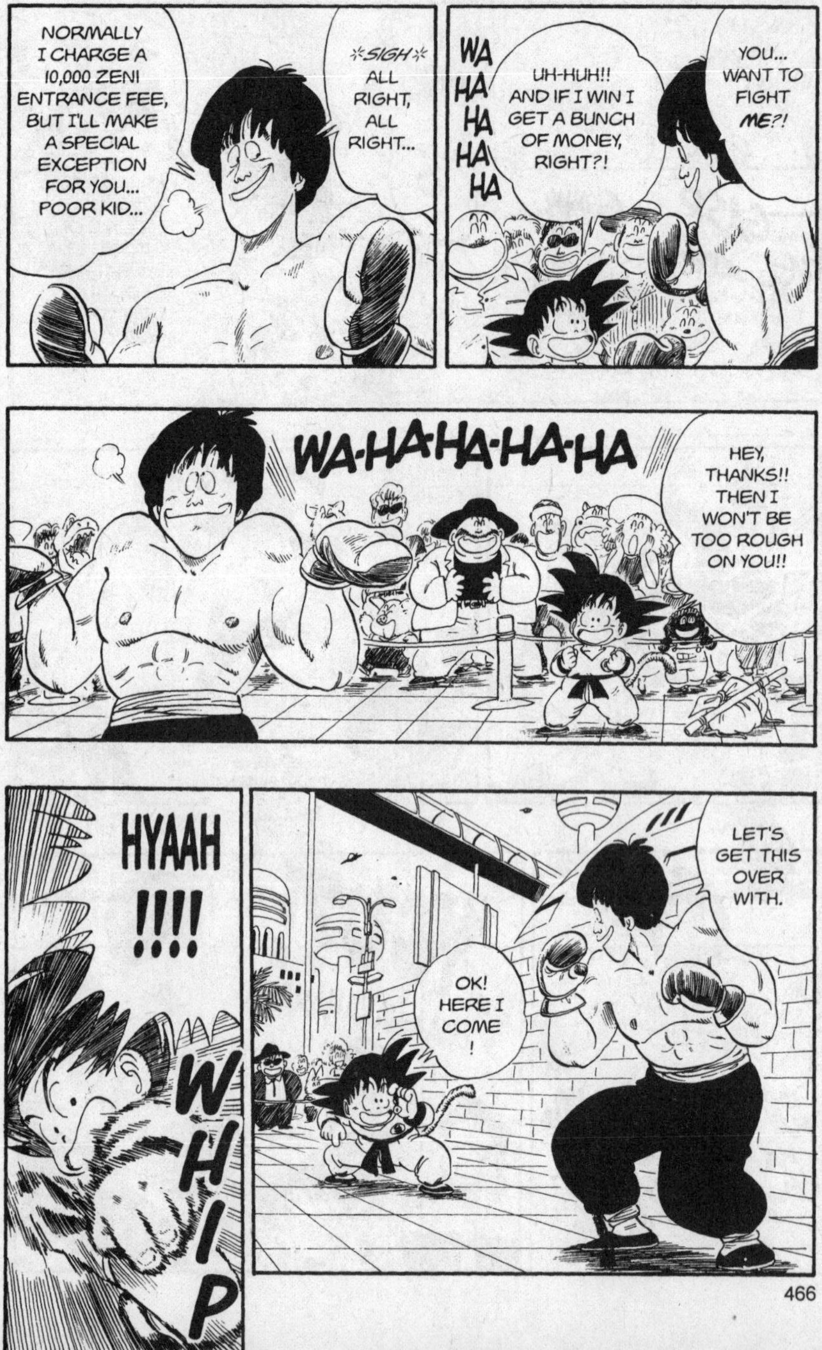
YOU... WANT TO FIGHT ME?!
UH-HUH!! AND IF I WIN I GET A BUNCH OF MONEY, RIGHT?!
WA HA HA HA HA
SIGH ALL RIGHT, ALL RIGHT...
NORMALLY I CHARGE A 10,000 ZENI ENTRANCE FEE, BUT I'LL MAKE A SPECIAL EXCEPTION FOR YOU... POOR KID...
HEY, THANKS!! THEN I WON'T BE TOO ROUGH ON YOU!!
WA-HA-HA-HA-HA
LET'S GET THIS OVER WITH.
OK! HERE I COME!
HYAAH!!!!
WHIP

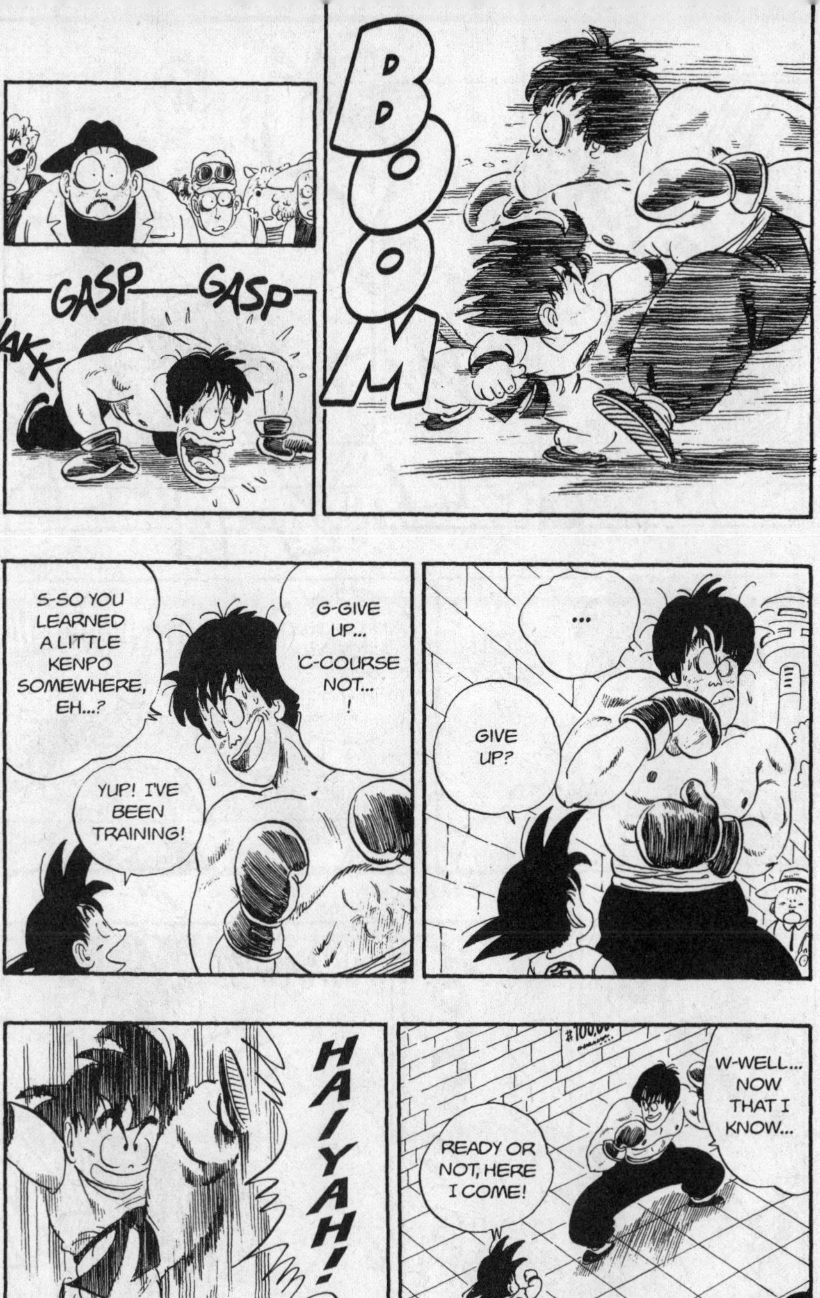
BOOOOM
GASP
GASP
HAKK
...
GIVE UP?
G-GIVE UP... 'C-COURSE NOT... !
S-SO YOU LEARNED A LITTLE KENPO SOMEWHERE, EH...?
YUP! I'VE BEEN TRAINING!
W-WELL... NOW THAT I KNOW...
READY OR NOT, HERE I COME!
HAIYAH!

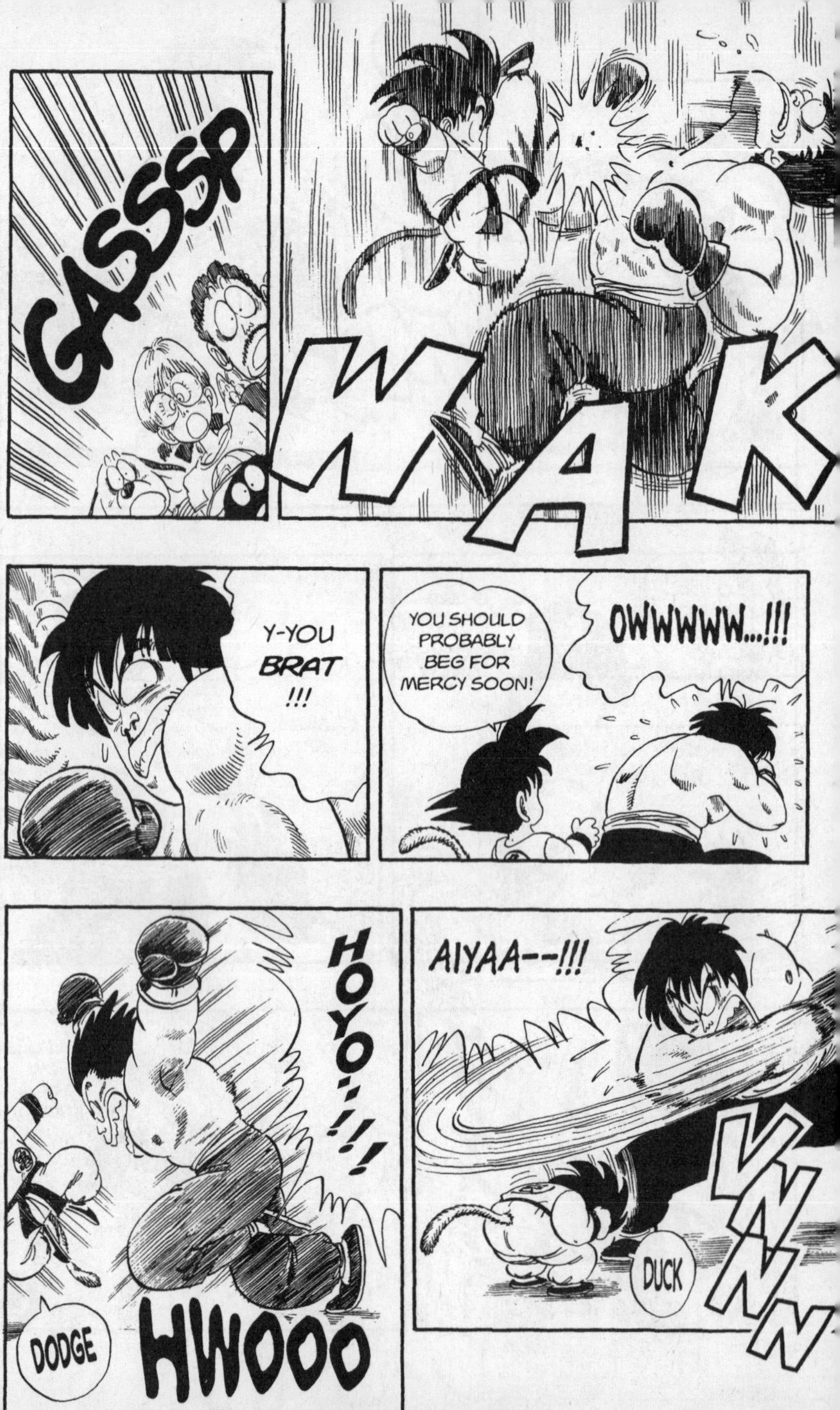
WAK
GASSSP
OWWWWW...!!!
YOU SHOULD PROBABLY BEG FOR MERCY SOON!
Y-YOU BRAT !!!
AIYAA--!!!
VNNNN
DUCK
HOYO--!!!
DODGE
HWOOO

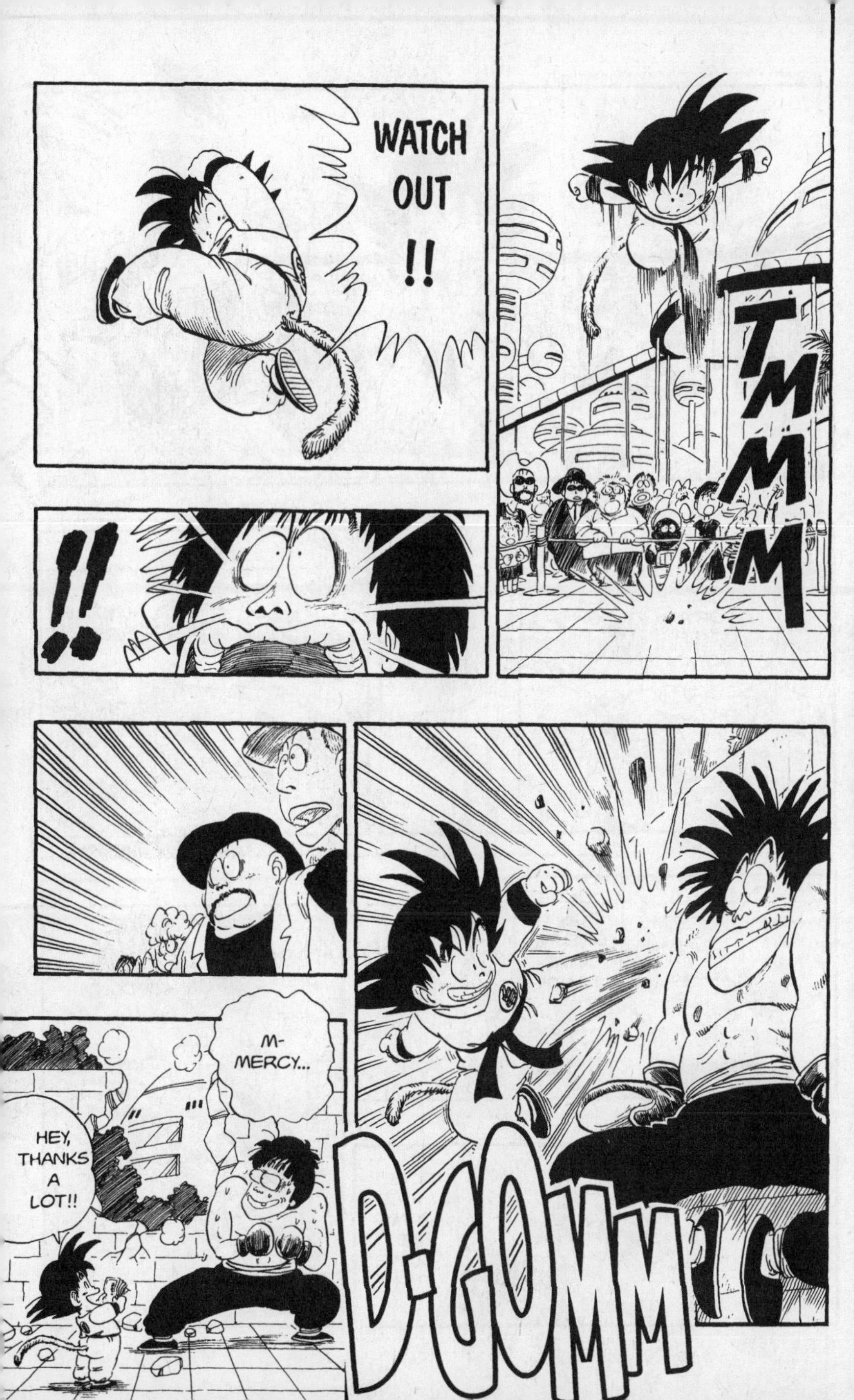
TMMM
WATCH OUT !!
!!
D-GOMM
M-MERCY...
HEY, THANKS A LOT!!

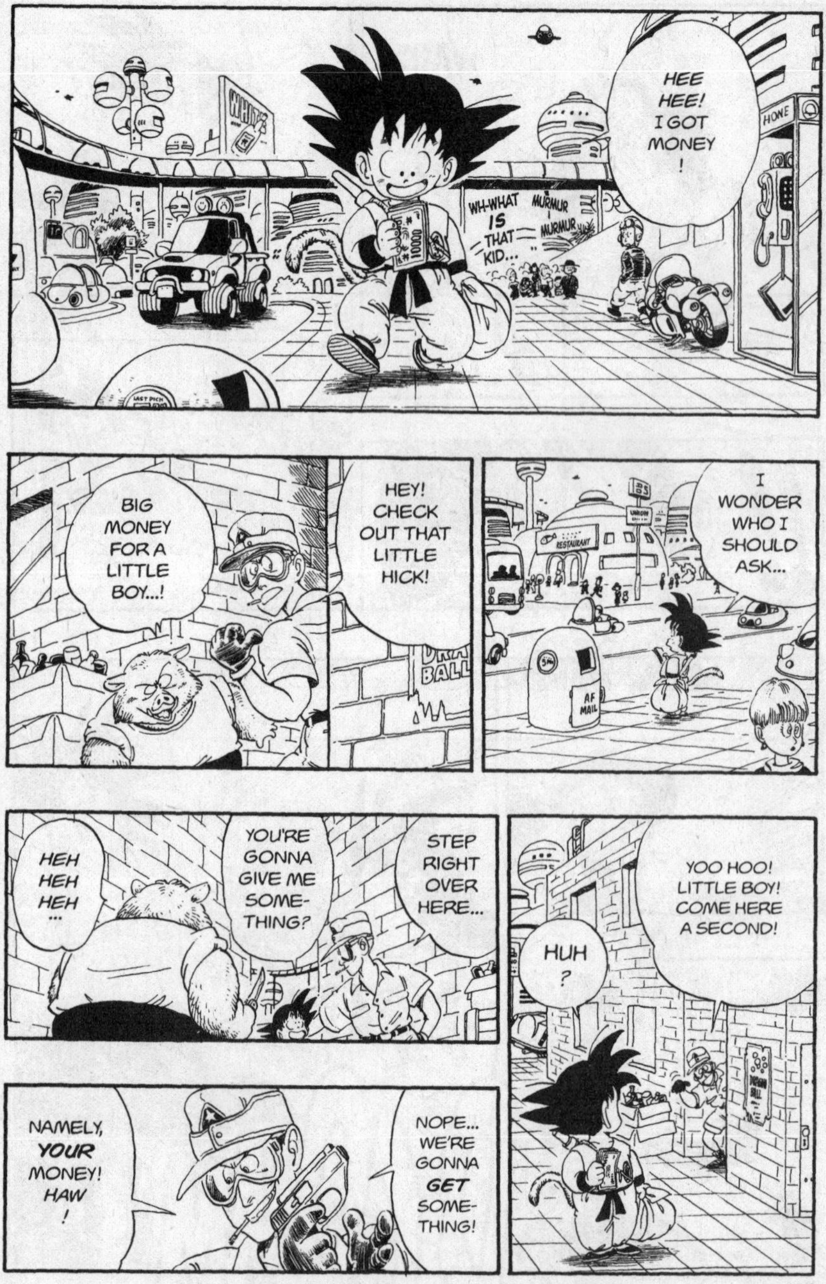
HEE HEE! I GOT MONEY!
HONE
MURMUR MURMUR
WH-WHAT IS THAT KID...
I WONDER WHO I SHOULD ASK...
RESTAURANT
AF MAIL
HEY! CHECK OUT THAT LITTLE HICK!
BIG MONEY FOR A LITTLE BOY...!
YOO HOO! LITTLE BOY! COME HERE A SECOND!
HUH?
STEP RIGHT OVER HERE...
YOU'RE GONNA GIVE ME SOMETHING?
HEH HEH HEH...
NOPE... WE'RE GONNA *GET* SOMETHING!
NAMELY, *YOUR* MONEY! HAW!

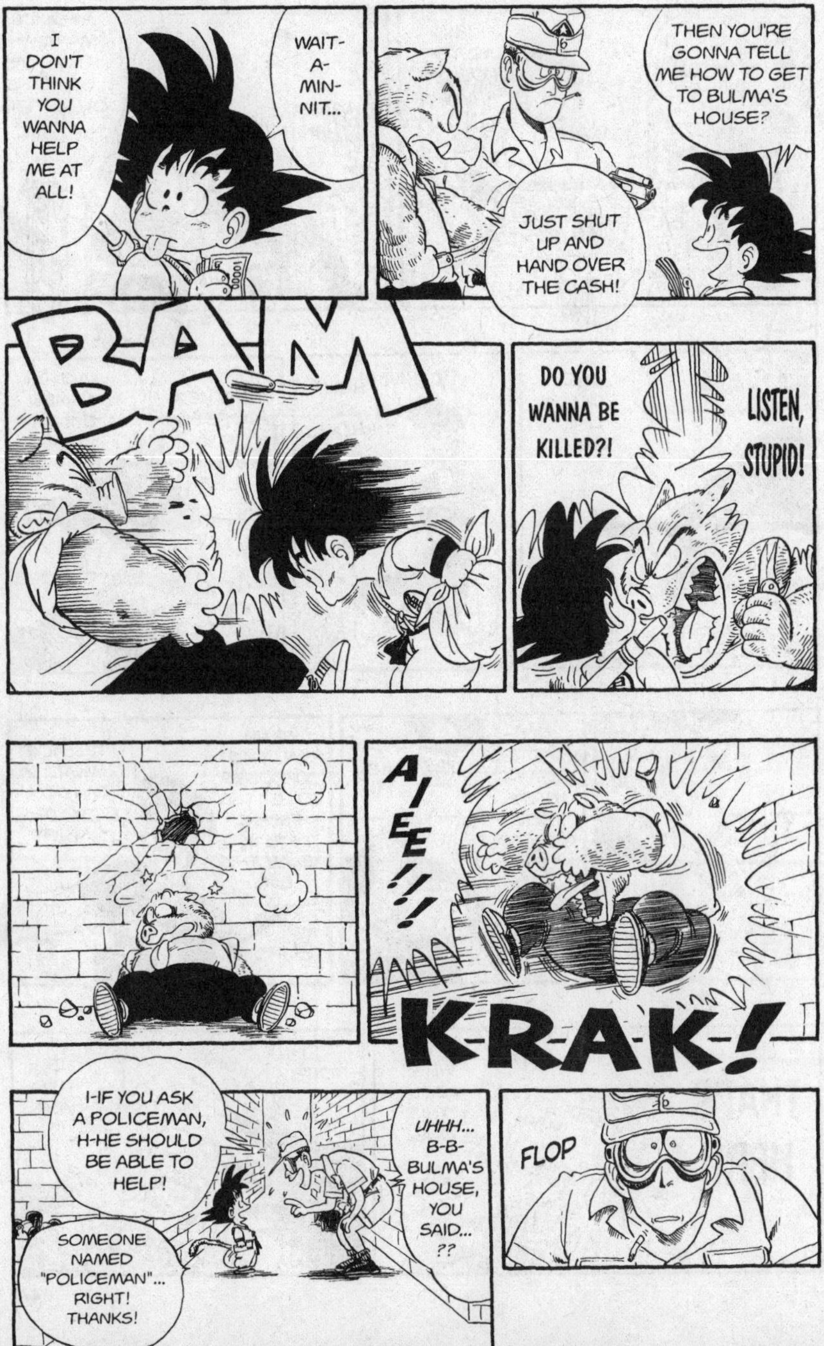
THEN YOU'RE GONNA TELL ME HOW TO GET TO BULMA'S HOUSE?
JUST SHUT UP AND HAND OVER THE CASH!
WAIT-A-MIN-NIT...
I DON'T THINK YOU WANNA HELP ME AT ALL!
LISTEN, STUPID!
DO YOU WANNA BE KILLED?!
BAM
AIEE!!!
KRAK!
FLOP
UHHH... B-B-BULMA'S HOUSE, YOU SAID...??
I-IF YOU ASK A POLICEMAN, H-HE SHOULD BE ABLE TO HELP!
SOMEONE NAMED "POLICEMAN"... RIGHT! THANKS!

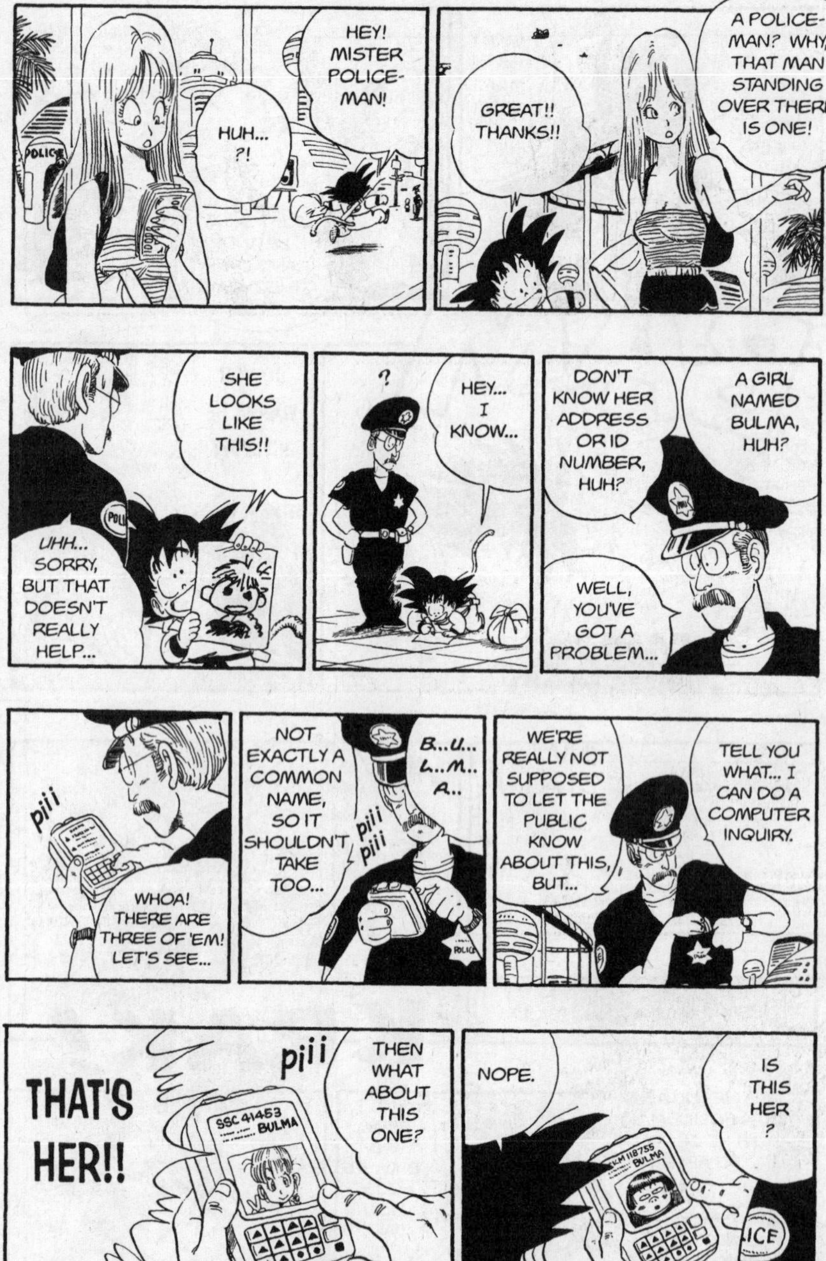
A POLICE-MAN? WHY, THAT MAN STANDING OVER THERE IS ONE!
GREAT!! THANKS!!
HEY! MISTER POLICE-MAN!
HUH...?!
A GIRL NAMED BULMA, HUH?
DON'T KNOW HER ADDRESS OR ID NUMBER, HUH?
WELL, YOU'VE GOT A PROBLEM...
?
HEY... I KNOW...
SHE LOOKS LIKE THIS!!
UHH... SORRY, BUT THAT DOESN'T REALLY HELP...
TELL YOU WHAT... I CAN DO A COMPUTER INQUIRY.
WE'RE REALLY NOT SUPPOSED TO LET THE PUBLIC KNOW ABOUT THIS, BUT...
B..U.. L..M.. A..
NOT EXACTLY A COMMON NAME, SO IT SHOULDN'T TAKE TOO...
piii piii
piii
WHOA! THERE ARE THREE OF 'EM! LET'S SEE...
IS THIS HER?
NOPE.
THEN WHAT ABOUT THIS ONE?
piii
SSC 41453 BULMA
THAT'S HER!!

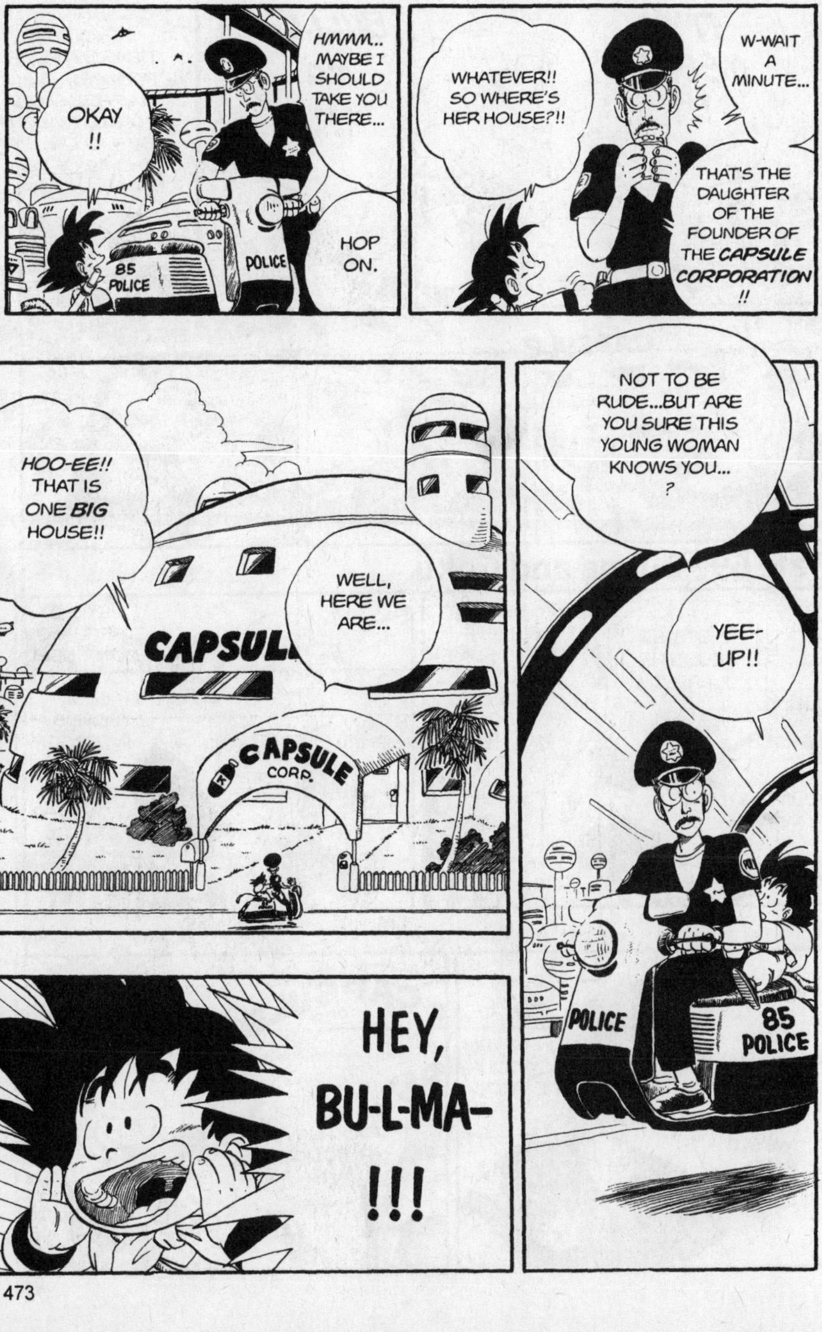
W-WAIT A MINUTE...
THAT'S THE DAUGHTER OF THE FOUNDER OF THE *CAPSULE CORPORATION* !!
WHATEVER!! SO WHERE'S HER HOUSE?!!
HMMM.. MAYBE I SHOULD TAKE YOU THERE...
POLICE
85 POLICE
HOP ON.
OKAY !!
NOT TO BE RUDE...BUT ARE YOU SURE THIS YOUNG WOMAN KNOWS YOU... ?
YEE-UP!!
POLICE
85 POLICE
WELL, HERE WE ARE...
HOO-EE!! THAT IS ONE ***BIG*** HOUSE!!
CAPSUL
CAPSULE CORP.
HEY, BU-L-MA- !!!

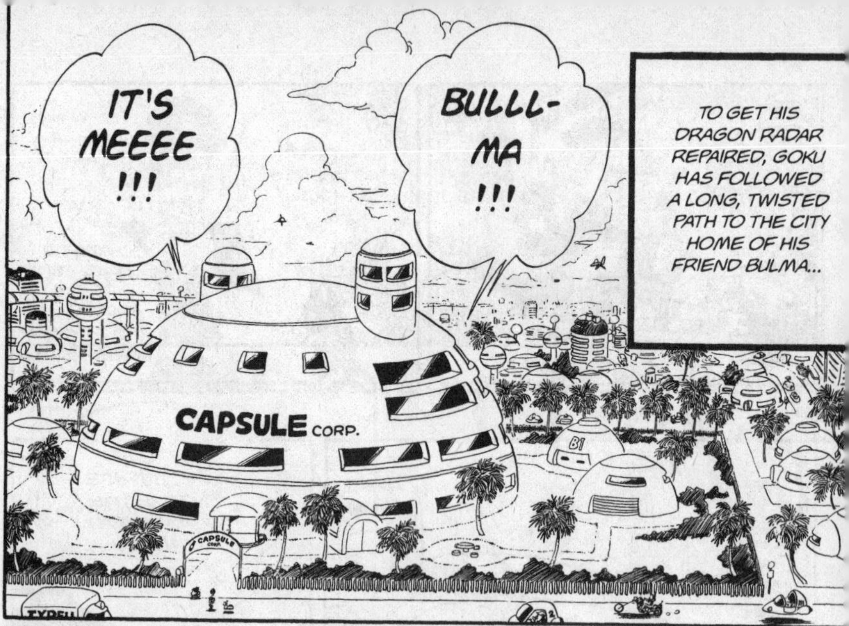
TO GET HIS DRAGON RADAR REPAIRED, GOKU HAS FOLLOWED A LONG, TWISTED PATH TO THE CITY HOME OF HIS FRIEND BULMA...
BULLL-MA !!!
IT'S MEEEE !!!
CAPSULE CORP.

Tale 69 • Bulma and Goku

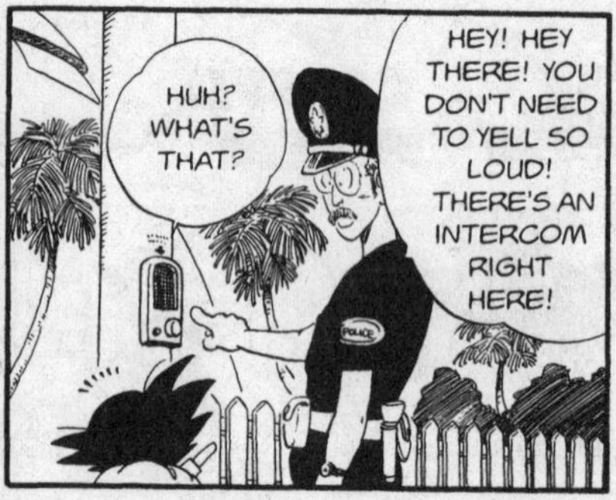
HEY! HEY THERE! YOU DON'T NEED TO YELL SO LOUD! THERE'S AN INTERCOM RIGHT HERE!
HUH? WHAT'S THAT?

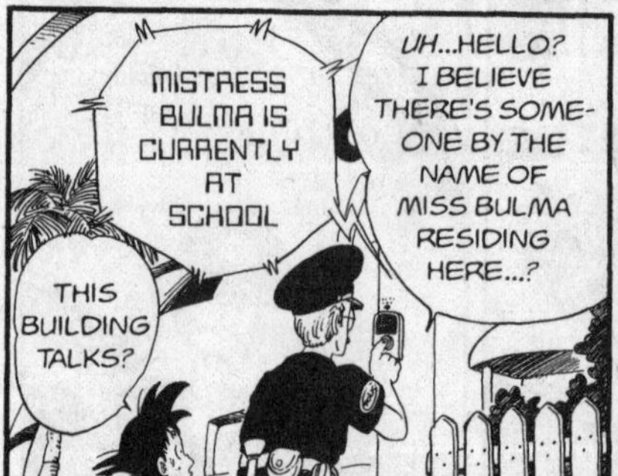
UH...HELLO? I BELIEVE THERE'S SOME-ONE BY THE NAME OF MISS BULMA RESIDING HERE...?
MISTRESS BULMA IS CURRENTLY AT SCHOOL
THIS BUILDING TALKS?

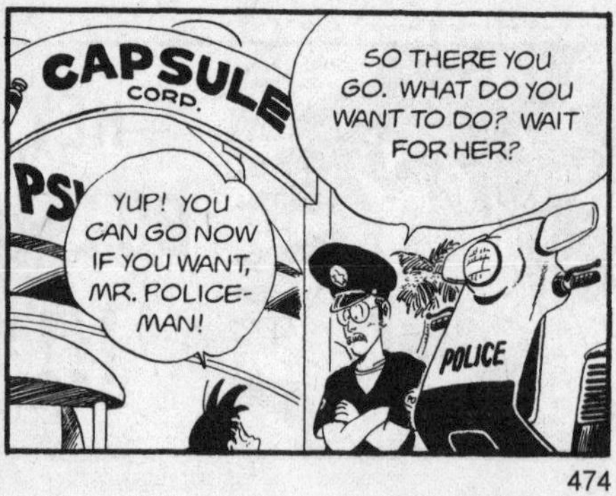
CAPSULE CORP.
SO THERE YOU GO. WHAT DO YOU WANT TO DO? WAIT FOR HER?
YUP! YOU CAN GO NOW IF YOU WANT, MR. POLICE-MAN!
POLICE

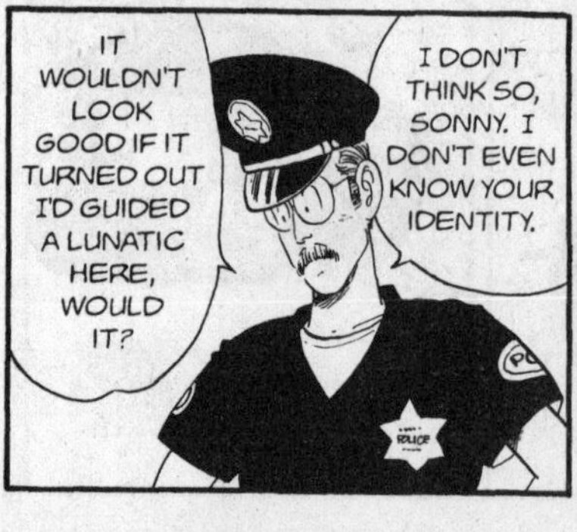
I DON'T THINK SO, SONNY. I DON'T EVEN KNOW YOUR IDENTITY.
IT WOULDN'T LOOK GOOD IF IT TURNED OUT I'D GUIDED A LUNATIC HERE, WOULD IT?

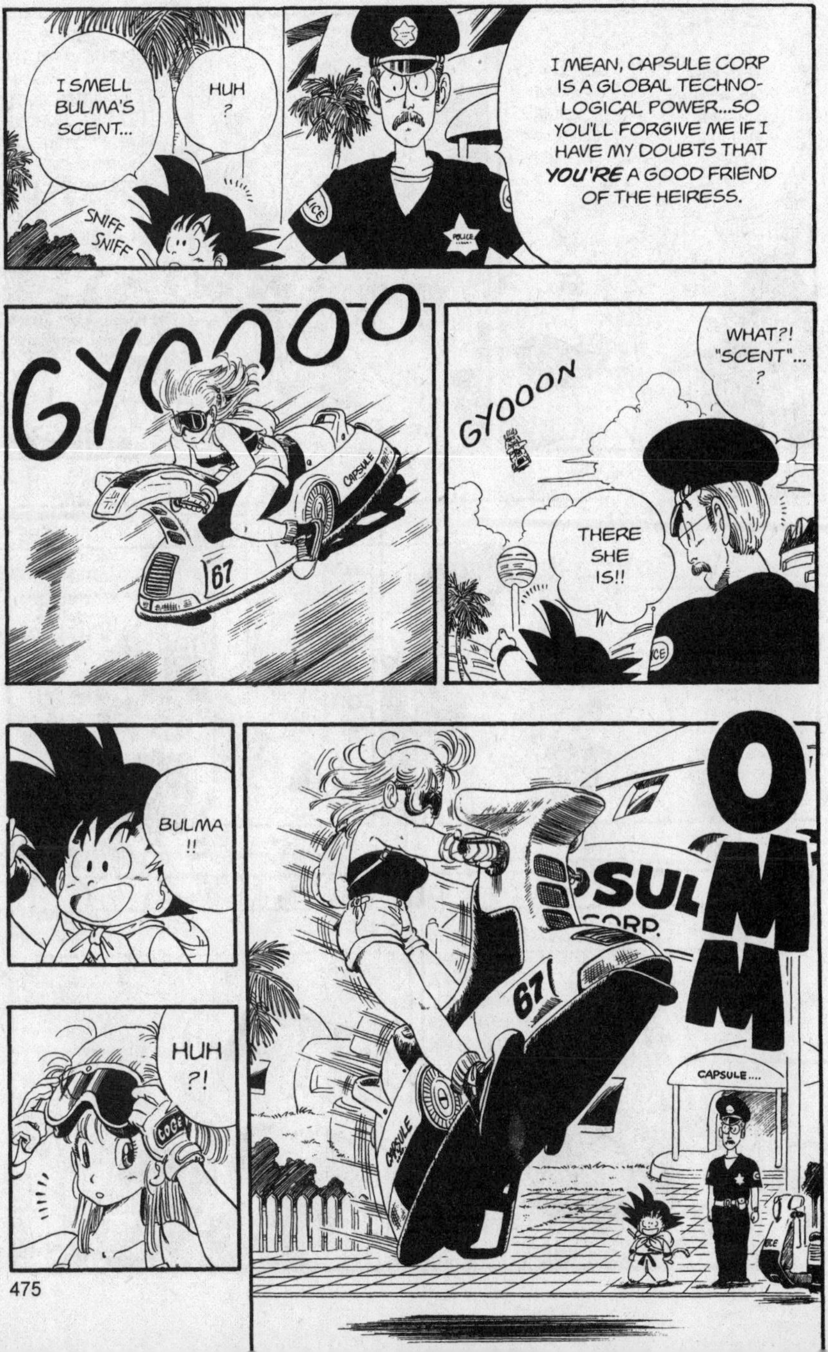
I MEAN, CAPSULE CORP IS A GLOBAL TECHNO-LOGICAL POWER...SO YOU'LL FORGIVE ME IF I HAVE MY DOUBTS THAT ***YOU'RE*** A GOOD FRIEND OF THE HEIRESS.
HUH?
I SMELL BULMA'S SCENT...
SNIFF SNIFF
WHAT?! "SCENT"...?
GYOOON
THERE SHE IS!!
GYOOOO
OMM
CAPSULE....
BULMA!!
HUH?!

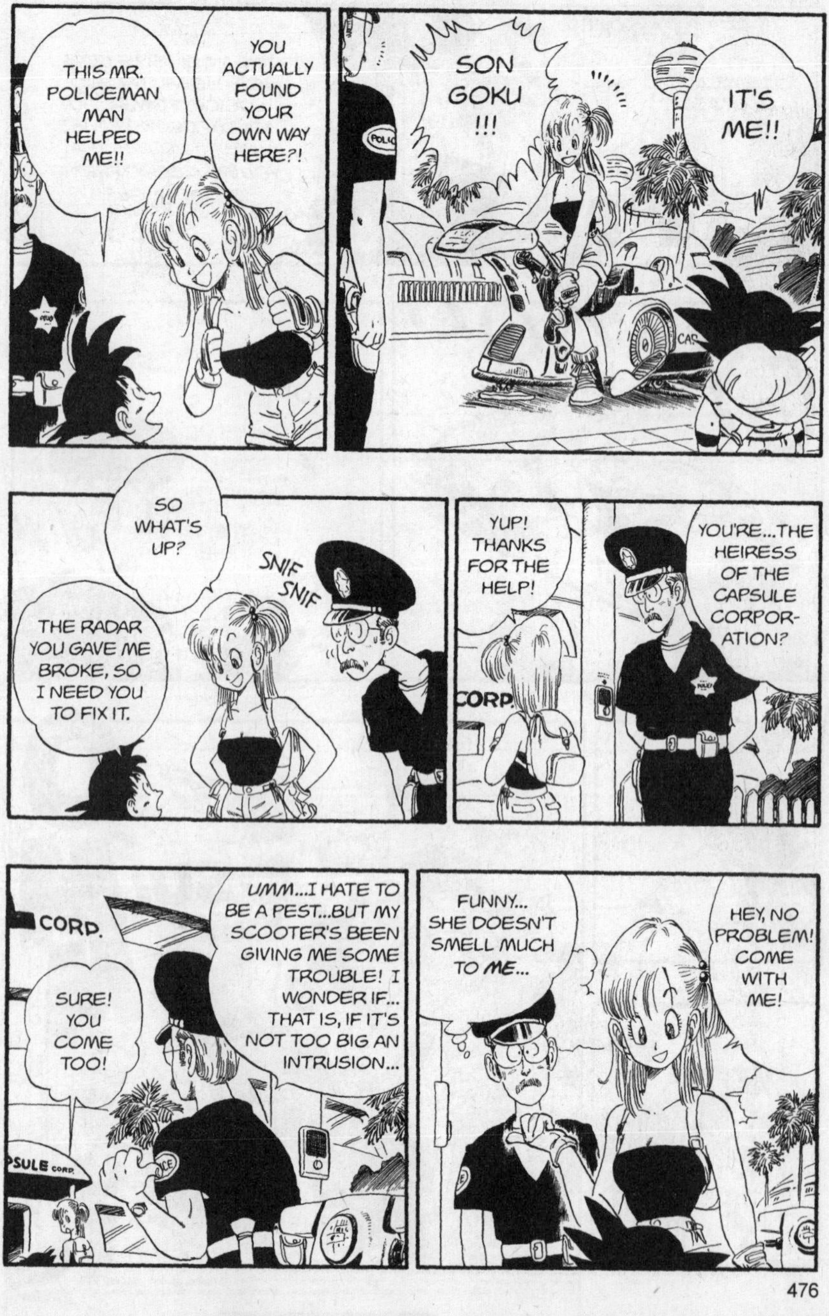
SON GOKU !!!
IT'S ME!!
YOU ACTUALLY FOUND YOUR OWN WAY HERE?!
THIS MR. POLICEMAN MAN HELPED ME!!
YOU'RE...THE HEIRESS OF THE CAPSULE CORPORATION?
YUP! THANKS FOR THE HELP!
CORP.
SO WHAT'S UP?
SNIF SNIF
THE RADAR YOU GAVE ME BROKE, SO I NEED YOU TO FIX IT.
HEY, NO PROBLEM! COME WITH ME!
FUNNY... SHE DOESN'T SMELL MUCH TO *ME*...
CORP.
UMM...I HATE TO BE A PEST...BUT MY SCOOTER'S BEEN GIVING ME SOME TROUBLE! I WONDER IF... THAT IS, IF IT'S NOT TOO BIG AN INTRUSION...
SURE! YOU COME TOO!
PSULE CORP.

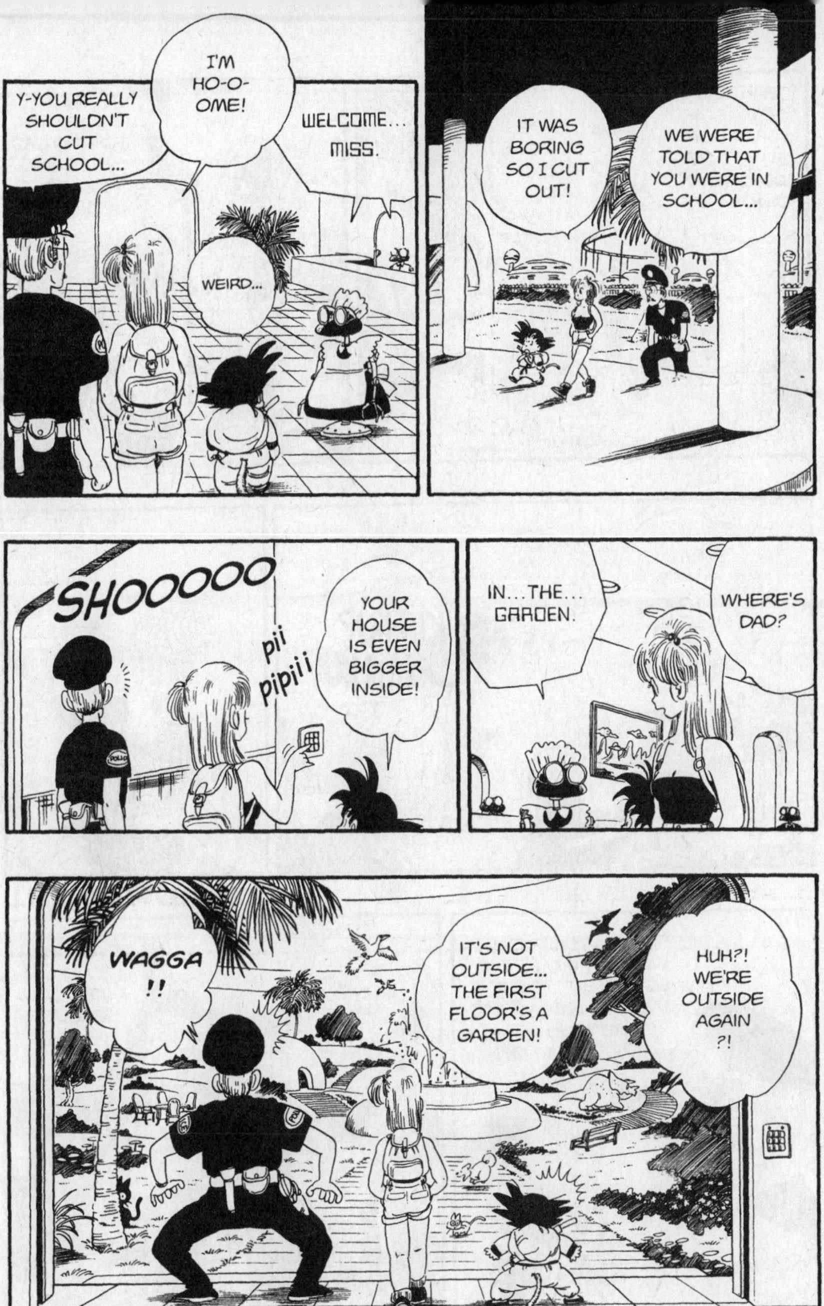
WE WERE TOLD THAT YOU WERE IN SCHOOL...
IT WAS BORING SO I CUT OUT!
WELCOME... MISS.
I'M HO-O-OME!
Y-YOU REALLY SHOULDN'T CUT SCHOOL...
WEIRD...
WHERE'S DAD?
IN... THE... GARDEN.
YOUR HOUSE IS EVEN BIGGER INSIDE!
pii pipiii
SHOOOOO
HUH?! WE'RE OUTSIDE AGAIN?!
IT'S NOT OUTSIDE... THE FIRST FLOOR'S A GARDEN!
WAGGA!!

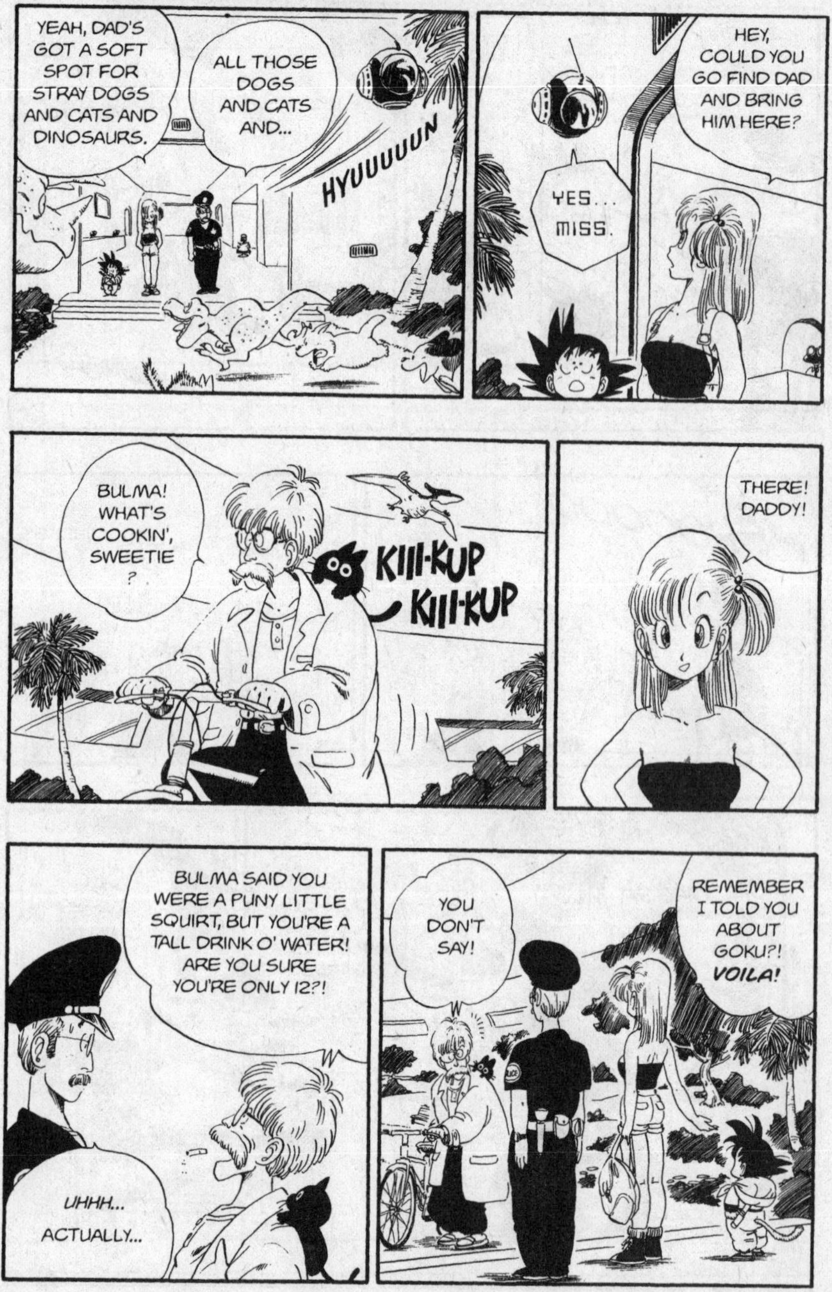
HEY, COULD YOU GO FIND DAD AND BRING HIM HERE?
YES... MISS.
ALL THOSE DOGS AND CATS AND...
YEAH, DAD'S GOT A SOFT SPOT FOR STRAY DOGS AND CATS AND DINOSAURS.
HYUUUUUN
THERE! DADDY!
BULMA! WHAT'S COOKIN', SWEETIE ?
KIII-KUP
KIII-KUP
REMEMBER I TOLD YOU ABOUT GOKU?! *VOILA!*
YOU DON'T SAY!
BULMA SAID YOU WERE A PUNY LITTLE SQUIRT, BUT YOU'RE A TALL DRINK O' WATER! ARE YOU SURE YOU'RE ONLY 12?!
UHHH... ACTUALLY...

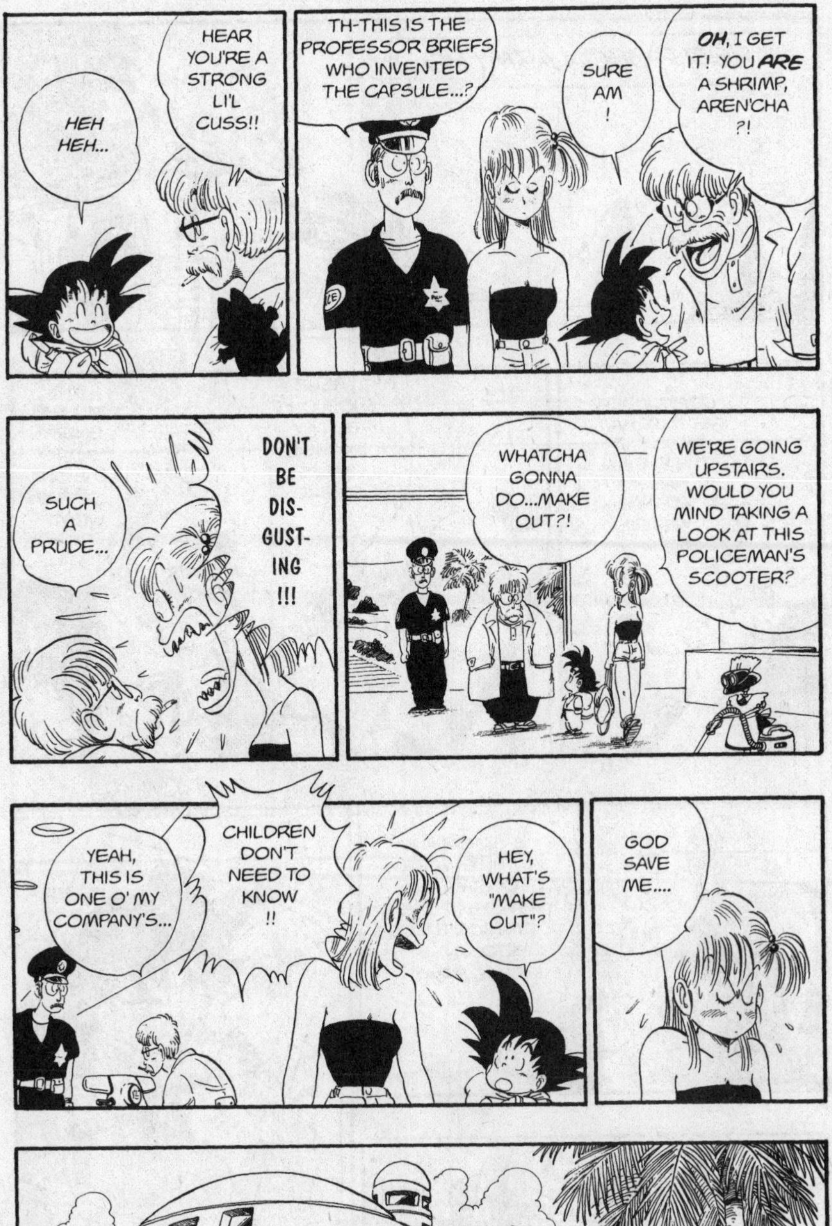
OH, I GET IT! YOU ARE A SHRIMP, AREN'CHA?!
SURE AM!
TH-THIS IS THE PROFESSOR BRIEFS WHO INVENTED THE CAPSULE...?
HEAR YOU'RE A STRONG LI'L CUSS!!
HEH HEH...
WE'RE GOING UPSTAIRS. WOULD YOU MIND TAKING A LOOK AT THIS POLICEMAN'S SCOOTER?
WHATCHA GONNA DO...MAKE OUT?!
DON'T BE DIS-GUST-ING!!!
SUCH A PRUDE...
GOD SAVE ME....
HEY, WHAT'S "MAKE OUT"?
CHILDREN DON'T NEED TO KNOW!!
YEAH, THIS IS ONE O' MY COMPANY'S...
CAPSUL

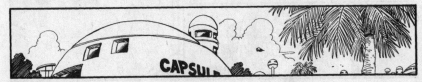

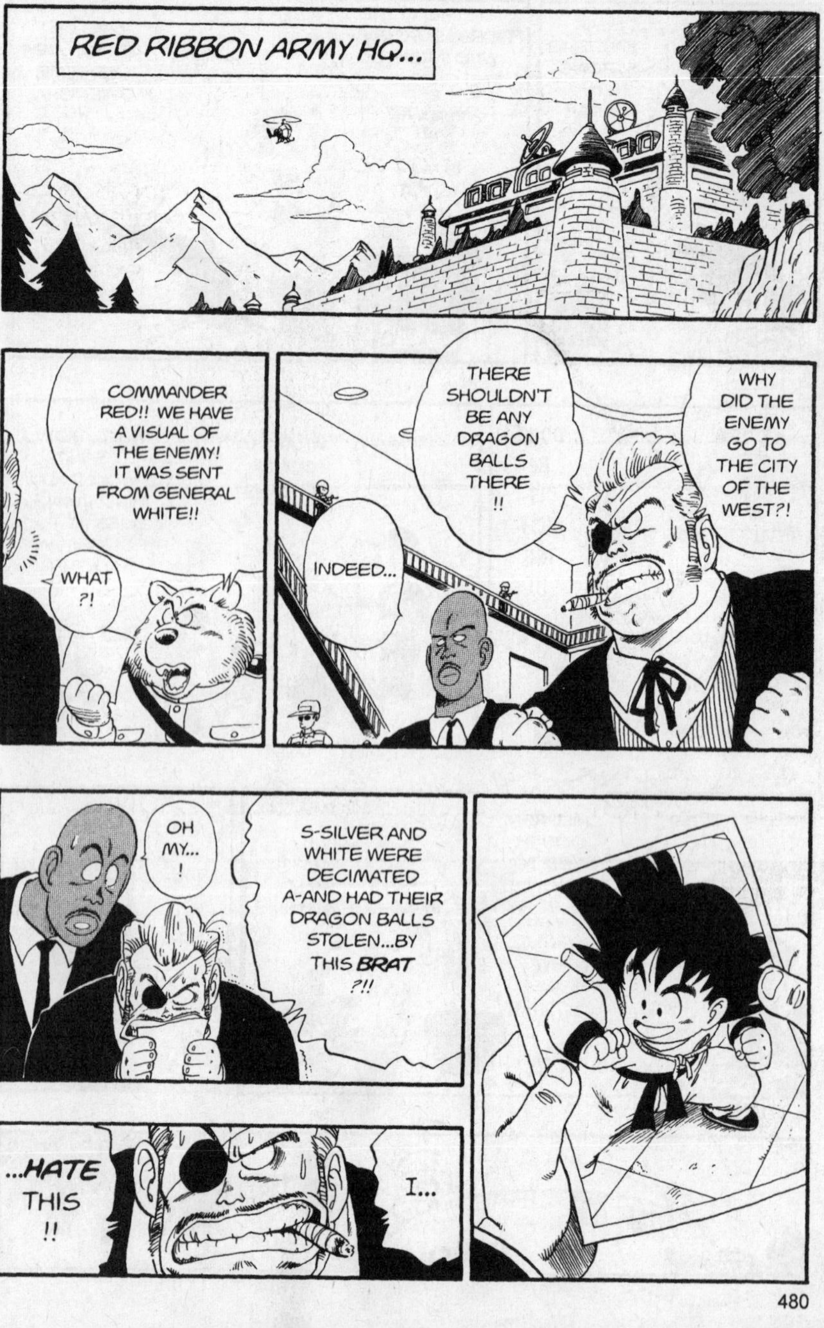

RED RIBBON ARMY HQ...
WHY DID THE ENEMY GO TO THE CITY OF THE WEST?!
THERE SHOULDN'T BE ANY DRAGON BALLS THERE !!
INDEED...
COMMANDER RED!! WE HAVE A VISUAL OF THE ENEMY! IT WAS SENT FROM GENERAL WHITE!!
WHAT ?!
S-SILVER AND WHITE WERE DECIMATED A-AND HAD THEIR DRAGON BALLS STOLEN...BY THIS BRAT ?!!
OH MY... !
I...
...HATE THIS !!

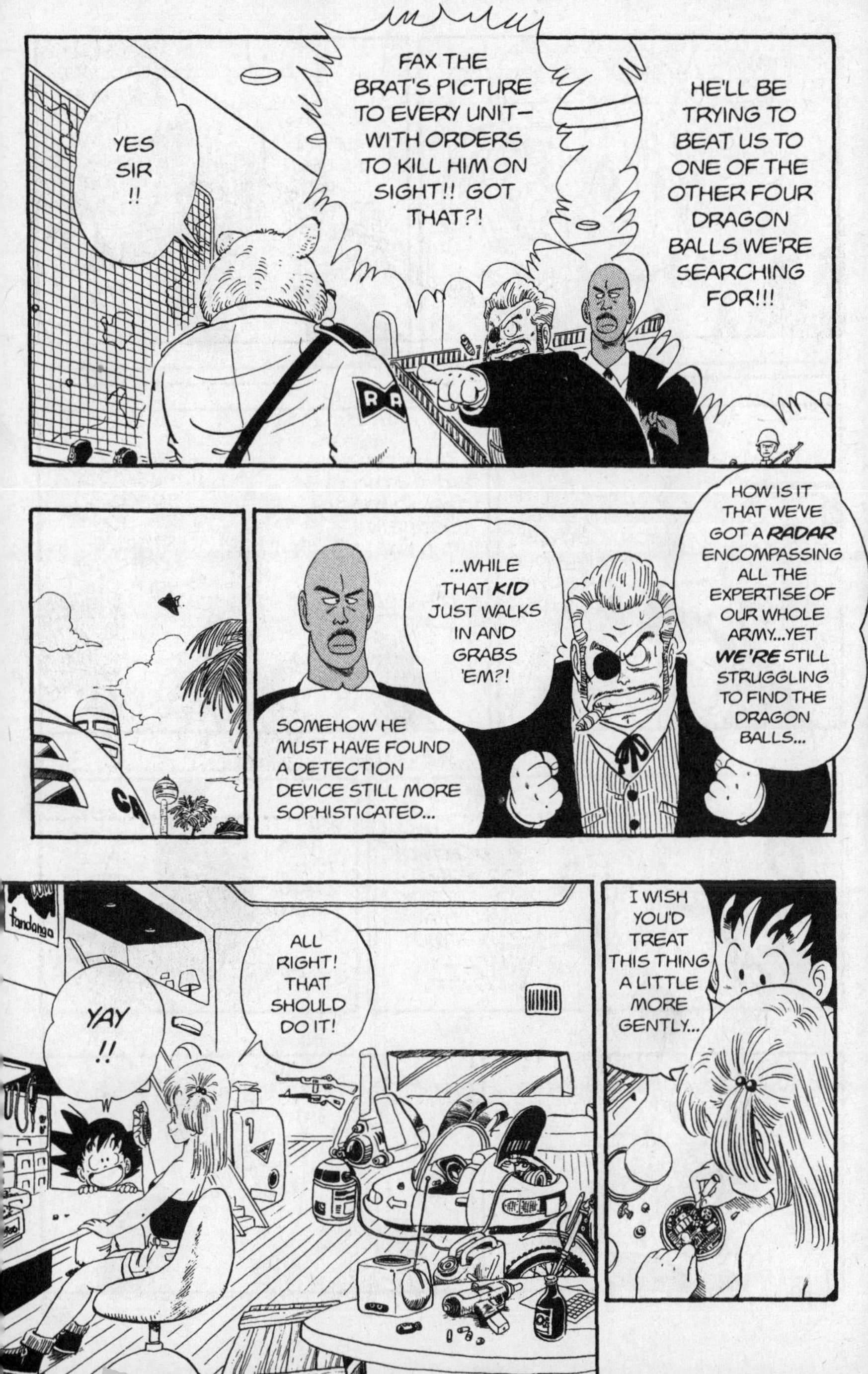
FAX THE BRAT'S PICTURE TO EVERY UNIT—WITH ORDERS TO KILL HIM ON SIGHT!! GOT THAT?!
HE'LL BE TRYING TO BEAT US TO ONE OF THE OTHER FOUR DRAGON BALLS WE'RE SEARCHING FOR!!!
YES SIR !!
HOW IS IT THAT WE'VE GOT A **RADAR** ENCOMPASSING ALL THE EXPERTISE OF OUR WHOLE ARMY...YET **WE'RE** STILL STRUGGLING TO FIND THE DRAGON BALLS...
...WHILE THAT **KID** JUST WALKS IN AND GRABS 'EM?!
SOMEHOW HE MUST HAVE FOUND A DETECTION DEVICE STILL MORE SOPHISTICATED...
I WISH YOU'D TREAT THIS THING A LITTLE MORE GENTLY...
ALL RIGHT! THAT SHOULD DO IT!
YAY !!
fandango

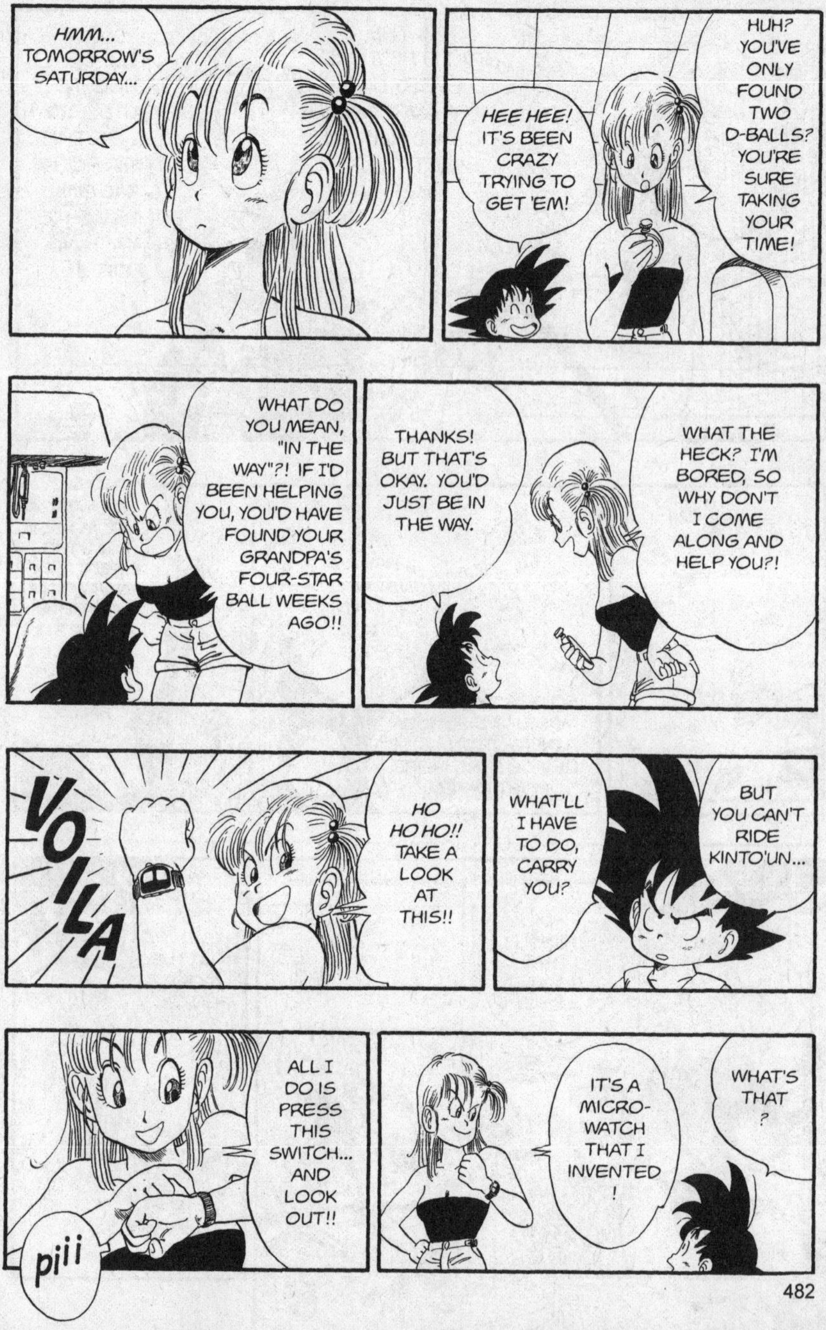
HUH? YOU'VE ONLY FOUND TWO D-BALLS? YOU'RE SURE TAKING YOUR TIME!
HEE HEE! IT'S BEEN CRAZY TRYING TO GET 'EM!
HMM... TOMORROW'S SATURDAY...
WHAT THE HECK? I'M BORED, SO WHY DON'T I COME ALONG AND HELP YOU?!
THANKS! BUT THAT'S OKAY. YOU'D JUST BE IN THE WAY.
WHAT DO YOU MEAN, "IN THE WAY"?! IF I'D BEEN HELPING YOU, YOU'D HAVE FOUND YOUR GRANDPA'S FOUR-STAR BALL WEEKS AGO!!
BUT YOU CAN'T RIDE KINTO'UN...
WHAT'LL I HAVE TO DO, CARRY YOU?
HO HO HO!! TAKE A LOOK AT THIS!!
VOILA
WHAT'S THAT ?
IT'S A MICRO-WATCH THAT I INVENTED !
ALL I DO IS PRESS THIS SWITCH... AND LOOK OUT!!
piii

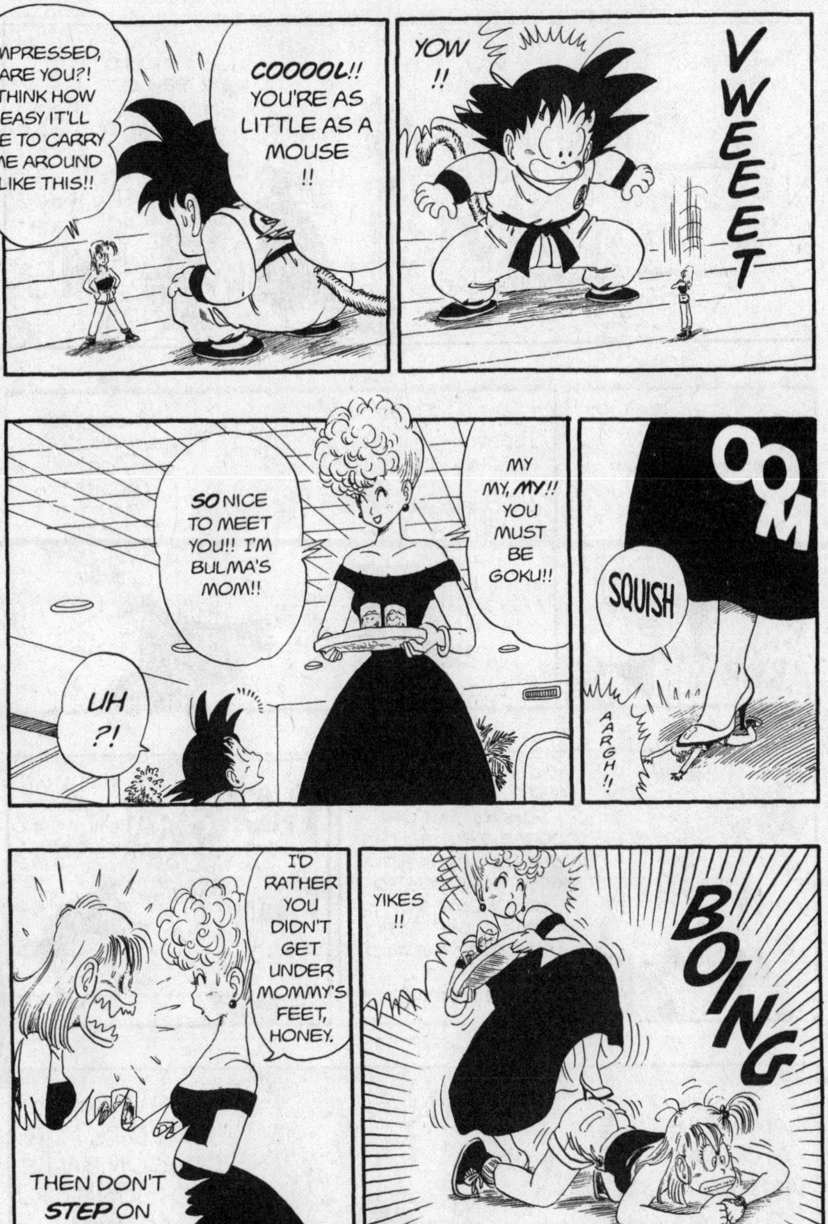
VWEEET
YOW!!
COOOOL!! YOU'RE AS LITTLE AS A MOUSE!!
IMPRESSED, ARE YOU?! THINK HOW EASY IT'LL BE TO CARRY ME AROUND LIKE THIS!!
OOM
SQUISH
AARGH!!
MY MY, MY!! YOU MUST BE GOKU!!
SO NICE TO MEET YOU!! I'M BULMA'S MOM!!
UH?!
BOING
YIKES!!
I'D RATHER YOU DIDN'T GET UNDER MOMMY'S FEET, HONEY.
THEN DON'T STEP ON ME!!!

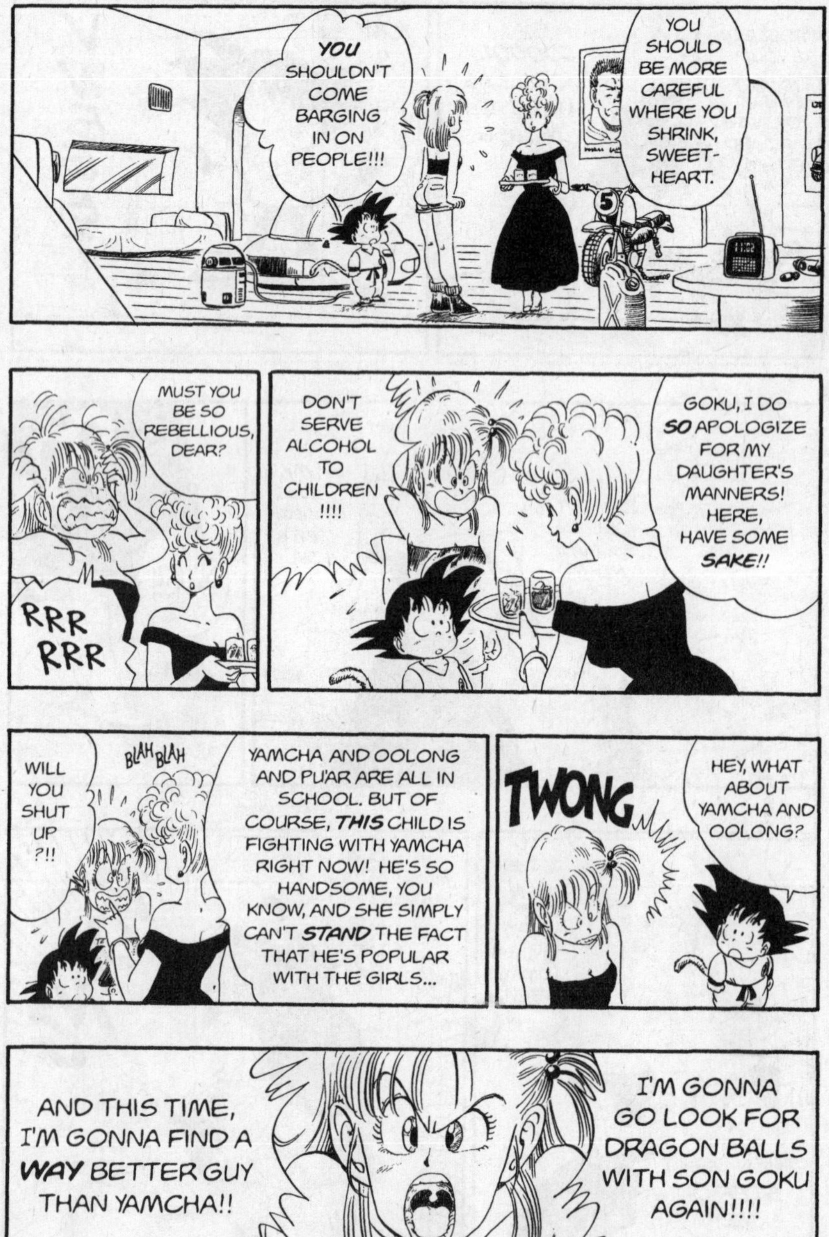
YOU SHOULD BE MORE CAREFUL WHERE YOU SHRINK, SWEET-HEART.
YOU SHOULDN'T COME BARGING IN ON PEOPLE!!!
GOKU, I DO SO APOLOGIZE FOR MY DAUGHTER'S MANNERS! HERE, HAVE SOME SAKE!!
DON'T SERVE ALCOHOL TO CHILDREN!!!!
MUST YOU BE SO REBELLIOUS, DEAR?
RRR RRR
HEY, WHAT ABOUT YAMCHA AND OOLONG?
TWONG
YAMCHA AND OOLONG AND PU'AR ARE ALL IN SCHOOL. BUT OF COURSE, THIS CHILD IS FIGHTING WITH YAMCHA RIGHT NOW! HE'S SO HANDSOME, YOU KNOW, AND SHE SIMPLY CAN'T STAND THE FACT THAT HE'S POPULAR WITH THE GIRLS...
BLAH BLAH
WILL YOU SHUT UP?!!
I'M GONNA GO LOOK FOR DRAGON BALLS WITH SON GOKU AGAIN!!!!
AND THIS TIME, I'M GONNA FIND A WAY BETTER GUY THAN YAMCHA!!

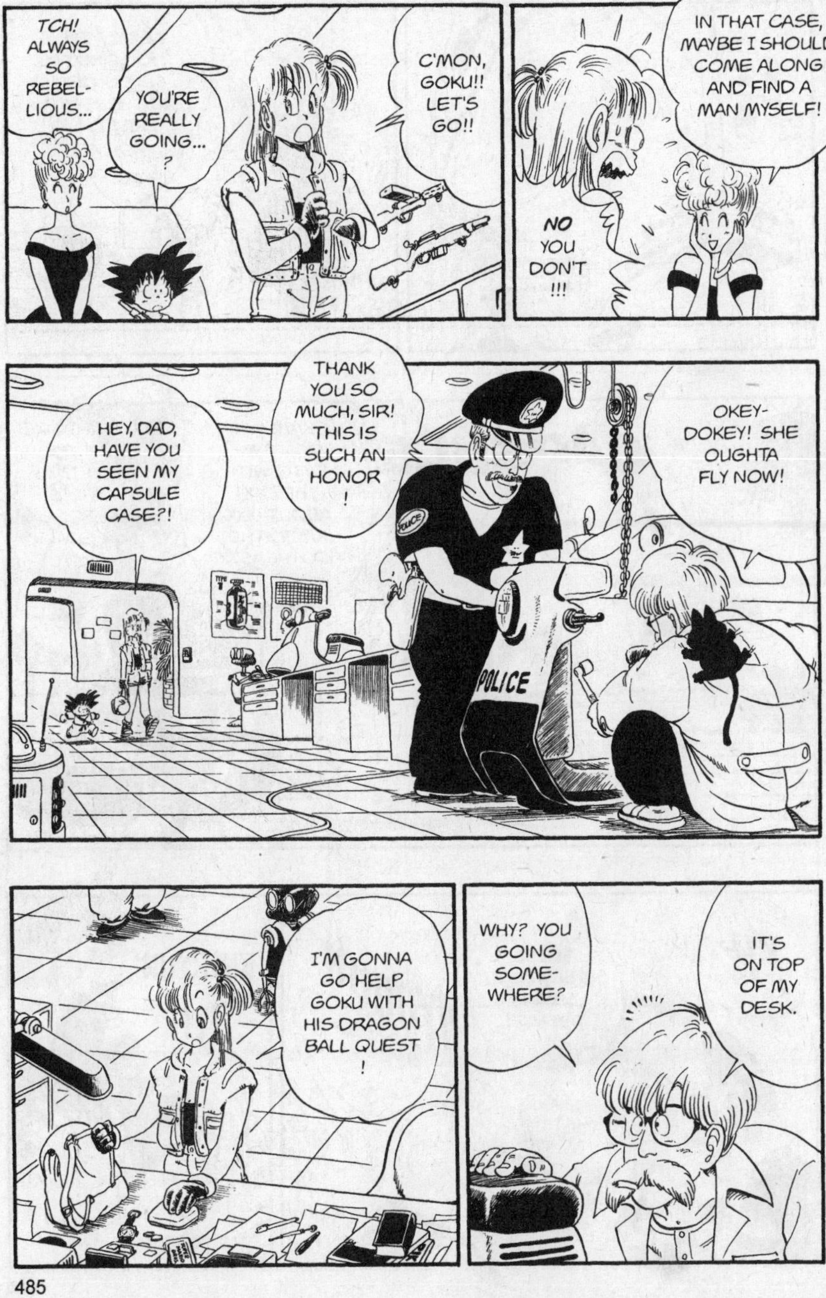
IN THAT CASE, MAYBE I SHOULD COME ALONG AND FIND A MAN MYSELF!
NO YOU DON'T!!!
C'MON, GOKU!! LET'S GO!!
TCH! ALWAYS SO REBEL-LIOUS...
YOU'RE REALLY GOING...?
OKEY-DOKEY! SHE OUGHTA FLY NOW!
THANK YOU SO MUCH, SIR! THIS IS SUCH AN HONOR!
HEY, DAD, HAVE YOU SEEN MY CAPSULE CASE?!
POLICE
IT'S ON TOP OF MY DESK.
WHY? YOU GOING SOMEWHERE?
I'M GONNA GO HELP GOKU WITH HIS DRAGON BALL QUEST!

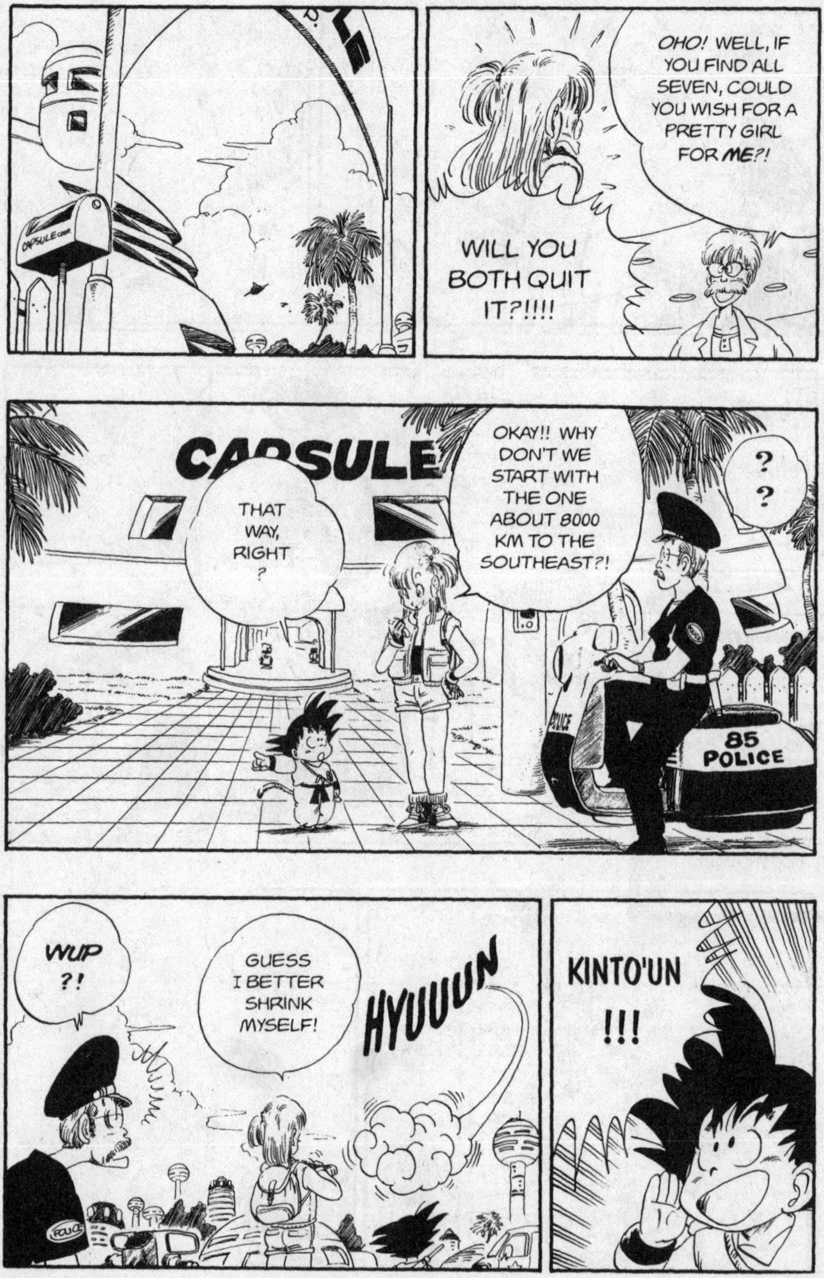
OHO! WELL, IF YOU FIND ALL SEVEN, COULD YOU WISH FOR A PRETTY GIRL FOR *ME*?!
WILL YOU BOTH QUIT IT?!!!!
CAPSULE CORP.
? ?
OKAY!! WHY DON'T WE START WITH THE ONE ABOUT 8000 KM TO THE SOUTHEAST?!
CAPSULE
THAT WAY, RIGHT?
85 POLICE
KINTO'UN !!!
HYUUUN
GUESS I BETTER SHRINK MYSELF!
WUP ?!

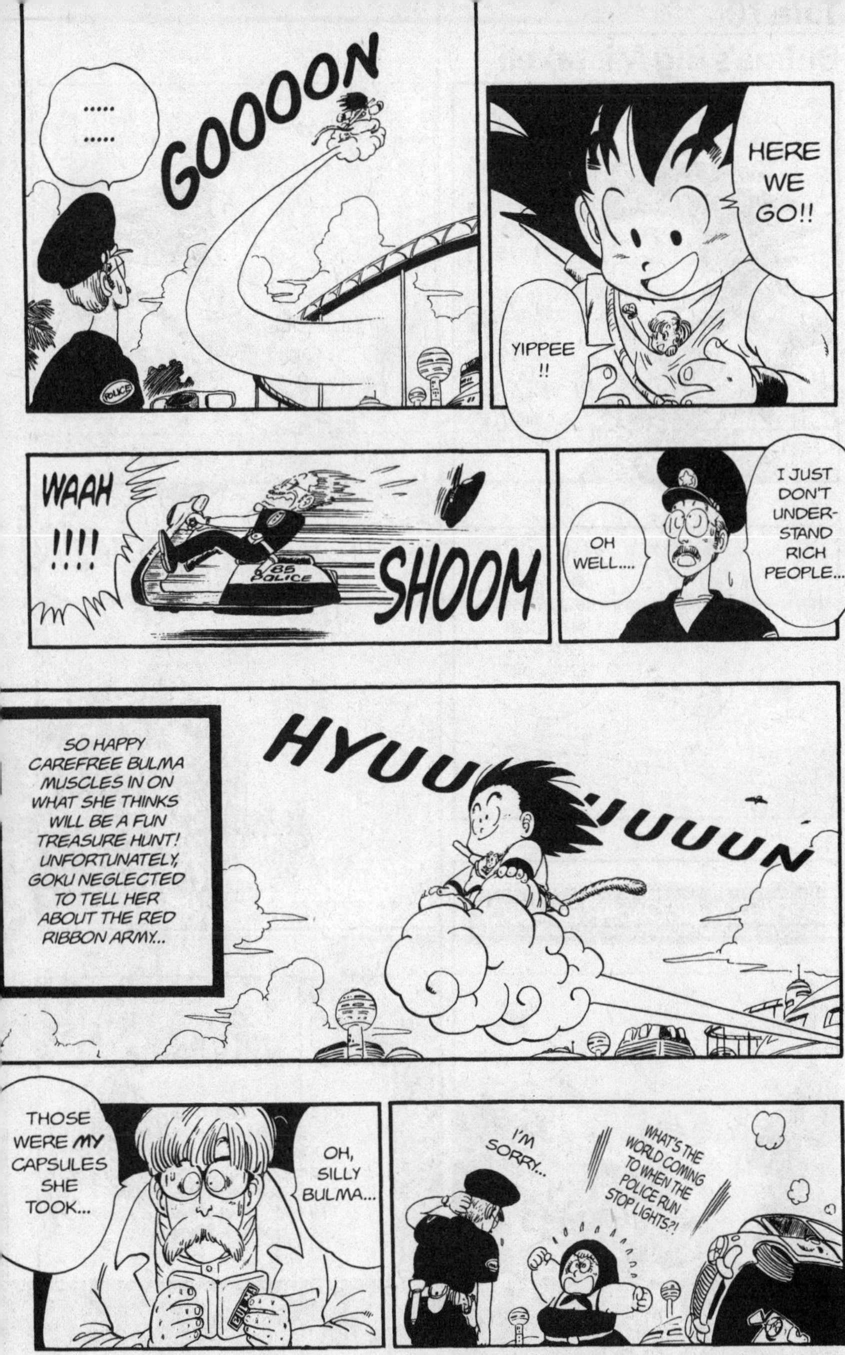
HERE WE GO!!
YIPPEE !!
.....
.....
GOOOON
I JUST DON'T UNDER-STAND RICH PEOPLE...
OH WELL....
SHOOM
WAAH !!!!
HYUUUUUUN
SO HAPPY CAREFREE BULMA MUSCLES IN ON WHAT SHE THINKS WILL BE A FUN TREASURE HUNT! UNFORTUNATELY, GOKU NEGLECTED TO TELL HER ABOUT THE RED RIBBON ARMY...
WHAT'S THE WORLD COMING TO WHEN THE POLICE RUN STOP LIGHTS?!
I'M SORRY...
THOSE WERE *MY* CAPSULES SHE TOOK...
OH, SILLY BULMA...

Tale 70
Bulma's Big Mistake!!

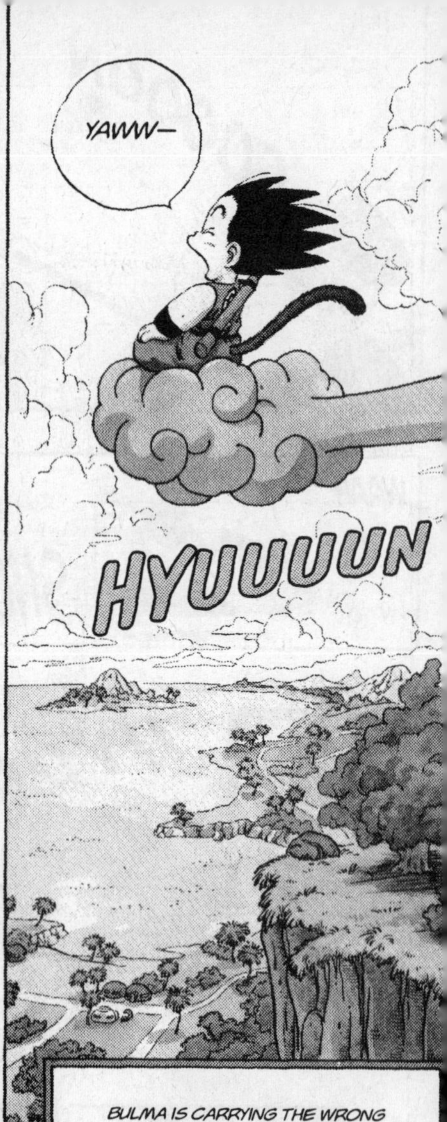
YAWW—
HYUUUUUN
BULMA IS CARRYING THE WRONG CAPSULES... AN ARMY OF CRIMINALS WANTS TO GET THE DRAGON BALLS FIRST... BUT ALL OUR HEROES KNOW IS THE LONG, GENTLE FLIGHT OF THE KINTO'UN...

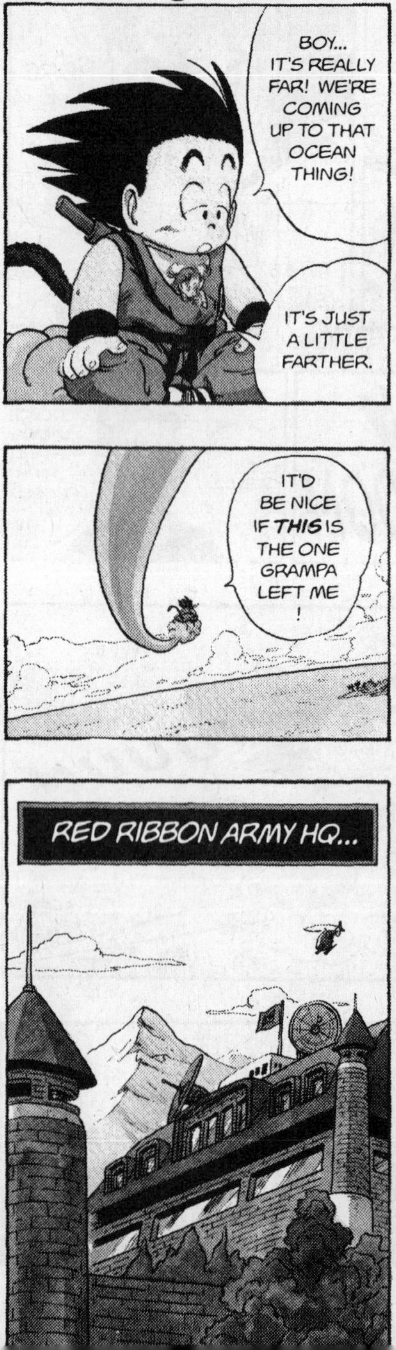
BOY... IT'S REALLY FAR! WE'RE COMING UP TO THAT OCEAN THING!
IT'S JUST A LITTLE FARTHER.
IT'D BE NICE IF THIS IS THE ONE GRAMPA LEFT ME!
RED RIBBON ARMY HQ...

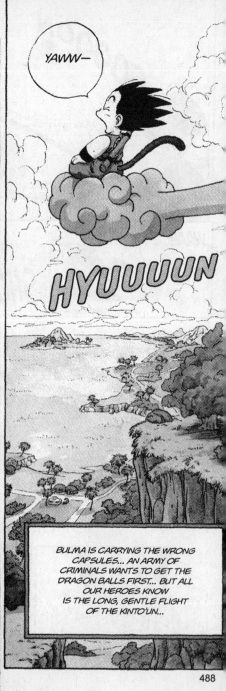

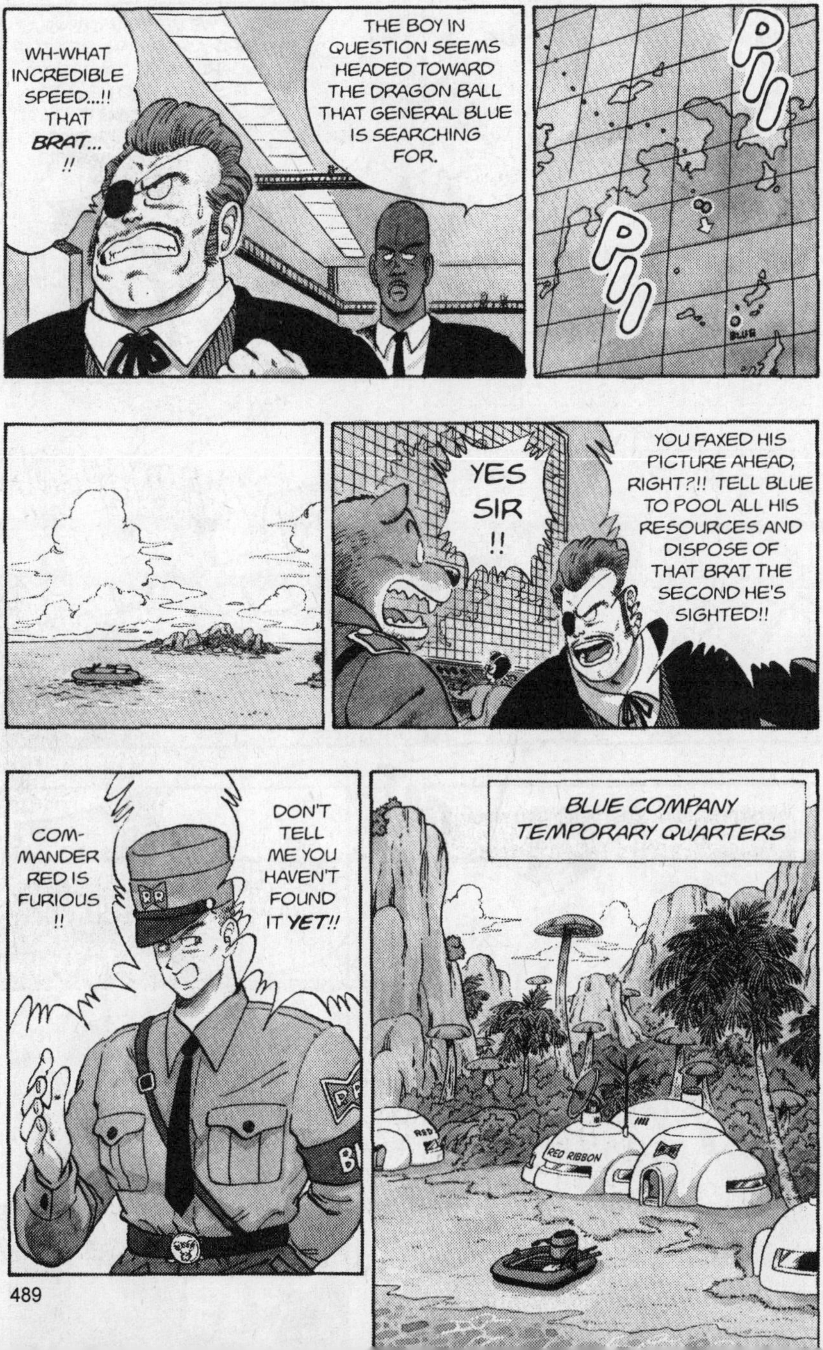
PII
PII
BLUE
THE BOY IN QUESTION SEEMS HEADED TOWARD THE DRAGON BALL THAT GENERAL BLUE IS SEARCHING FOR.
WH-WHAT INCREDIBLE SPEED...!! THAT *BRAT...* !!
YOU FAXED HIS PICTURE AHEAD, RIGHT?!! TELL BLUE TO POOL ALL HIS RESOURCES AND DISPOSE OF THAT BRAT THE SECOND HE'S SIGHTED!!
YES SIR !!
BLUE COMPANY TEMPORARY QUARTERS
RED RIBBON
DON'T TELL ME YOU HAVEN'T FOUND IT *YET*!!
COM-MANDER RED IS FURIOUS !!

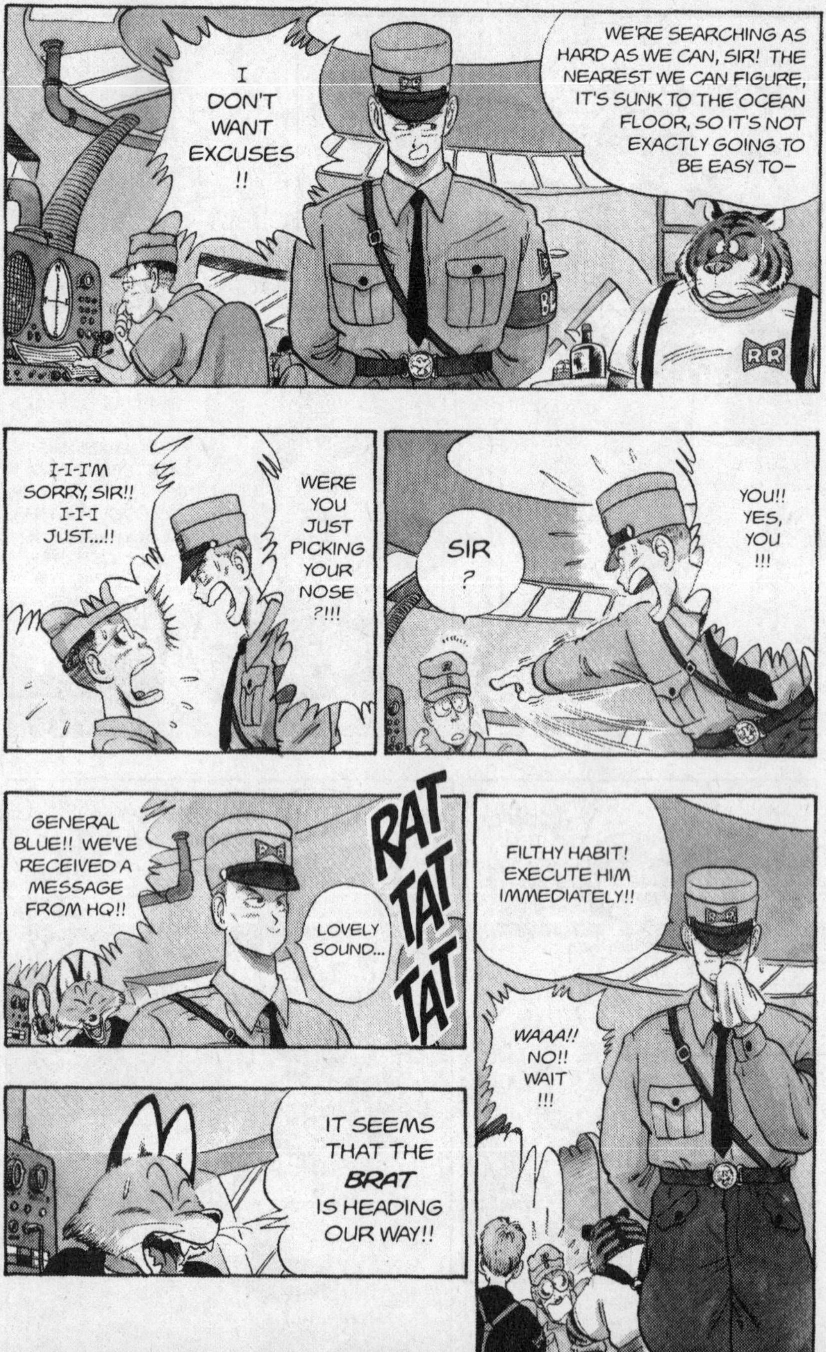
WE'RE SEARCHING AS HARD AS WE CAN, SIR! THE NEAREST WE CAN FIGURE, IT'S SUNK TO THE OCEAN FLOOR, SO IT'S NOT EXACTLY GOING TO BE EASY TO–
I DON'T WANT EXCUSES !!
YOU!! YES, YOU !!!
SIR ?
WERE YOU JUST PICKING YOUR NOSE ?!!!
I-I-I'M SORRY, SIR!! I-I-I JUST...!!
FILTHY HABIT! EXECUTE HIM IMMEDIATELY!!
WAAA!! NO!! WAIT !!!
RAT TAT TAT
LOVELY SOUND...
GENERAL BLUE!! WE'VE RECEIVED A MESSAGE FROM HQ!!
IT SEEMS THAT THE BRAT IS HEADING OUR WAY!!

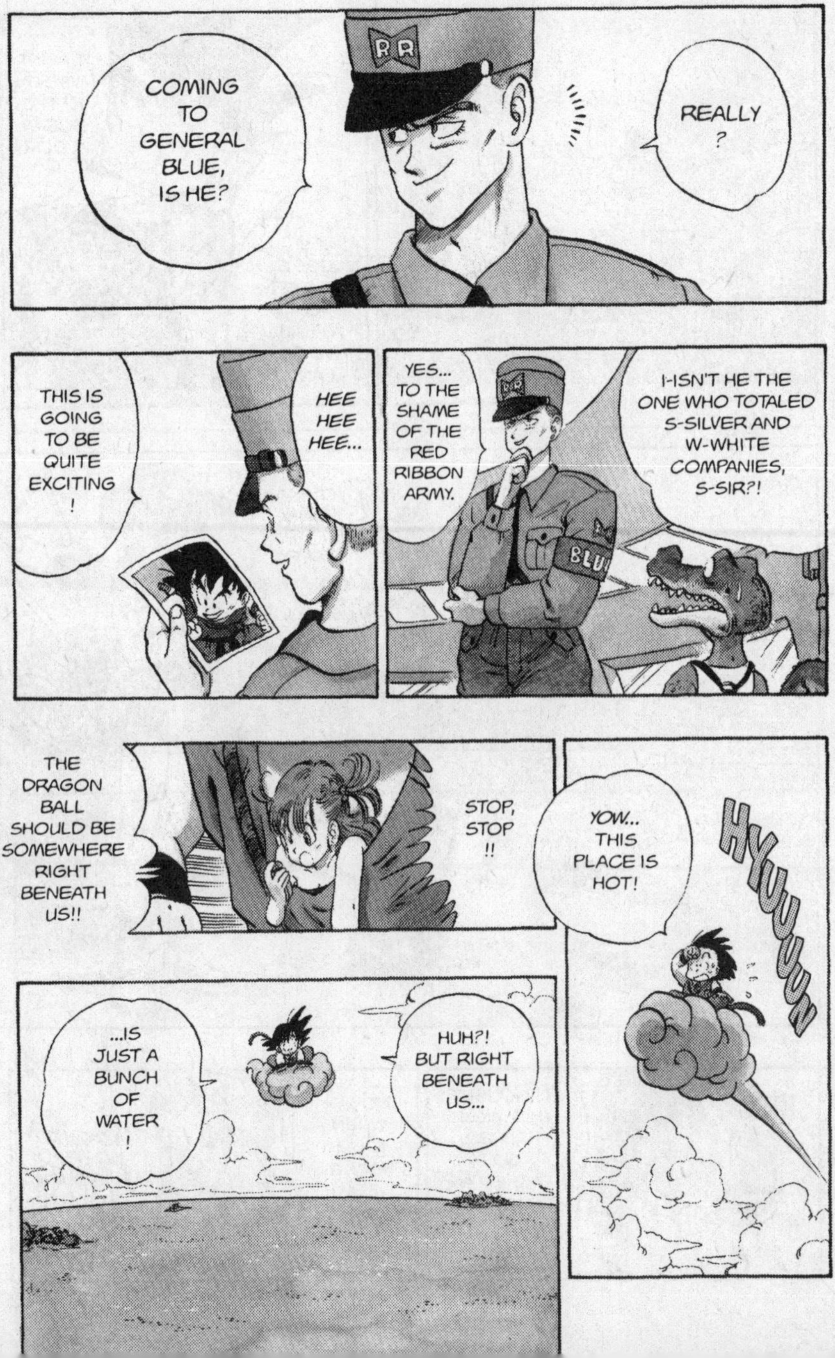
REALLY?
COMING TO GENERAL BLUE, IS HE?
I-ISN'T HE THE ONE WHO TOTALED S-SILVER AND W-WHITE COMPANIES, S-SIR?!
YES... TO THE SHAME OF THE RED RIBBON ARMY.
HEE HEE HEE...
THIS IS GOING TO BE QUITE EXCITING!
HYUUUUN
YOW... THIS PLACE IS HOT!
STOP, STOP!!
THE DRAGON BALL SHOULD BE SOMEWHERE RIGHT BENEATH US!!
HUH?! BUT RIGHT BENEATH US...
...IS JUST A BUNCH OF WATER!

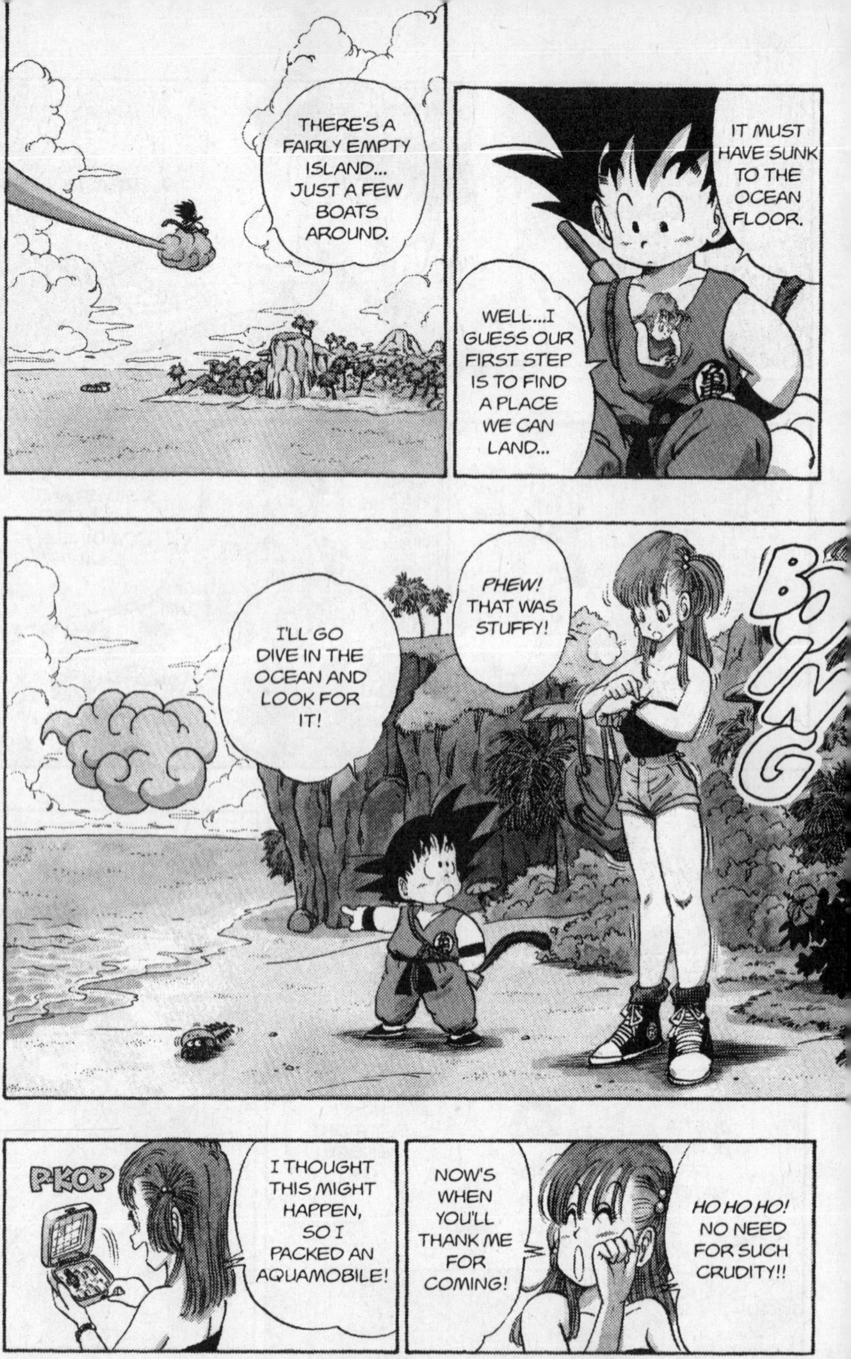
IT MUST HAVE SUNK TO THE OCEAN FLOOR.
WELL...I GUESS OUR FIRST STEP IS TO FIND A PLACE WE CAN LAND...
THERE'S A FAIRLY EMPTY ISLAND... JUST A FEW BOATS AROUND.
BOING
PHEW! THAT WAS STUFFY!
I'LL GO DIVE IN THE OCEAN AND LOOK FOR IT!
HO HO HO! NO NEED FOR SUCH CRUDITY!!
NOW'S WHEN YOU'LL THANK ME FOR COMING!
P-KOP
I THOUGHT THIS MIGHT HAPPEN, SO I PACKED AN AQUAMOBILE!

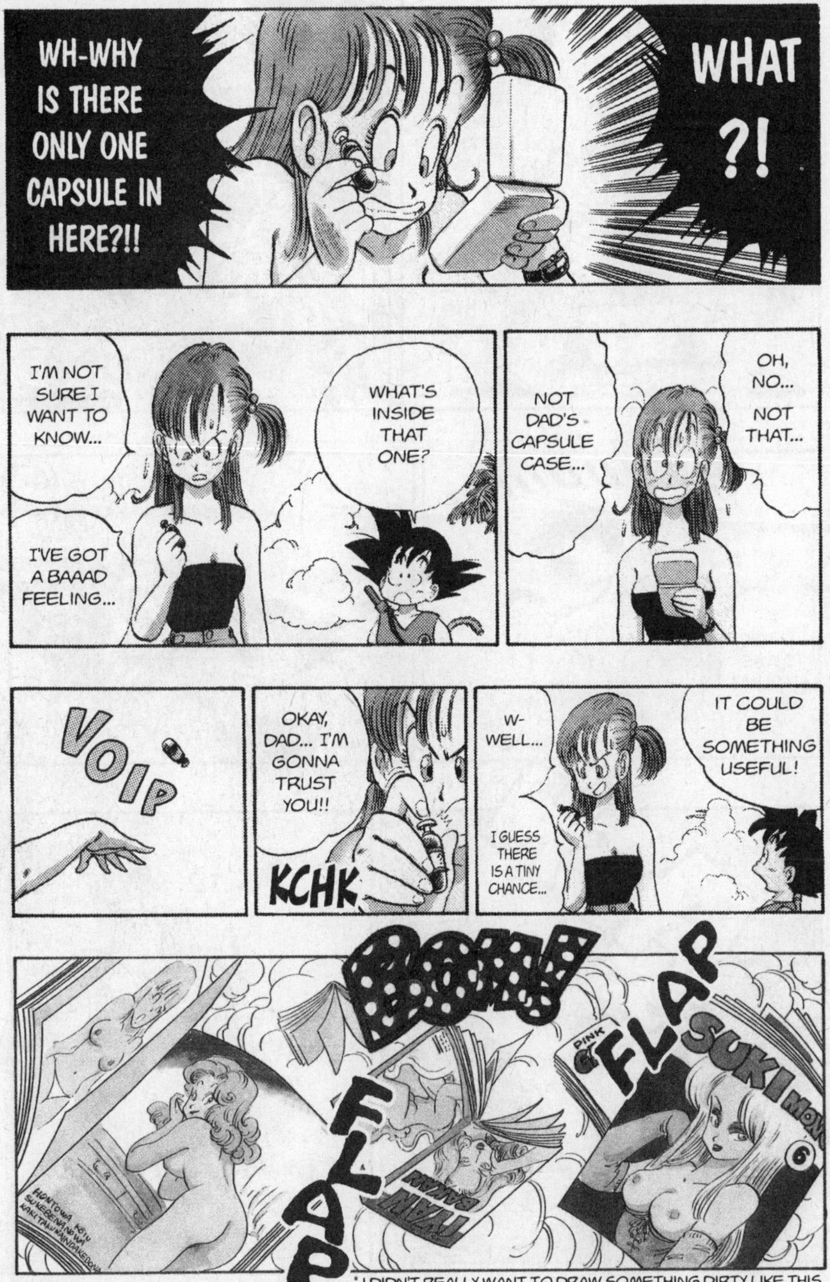
WHAT ?!
WH-WHY IS THERE ONLY ONE CAPSULE IN HERE?!!
OH, NO... NOT THAT...
NOT DAD'S CAPSULE CASE...
WHAT'S INSIDE THAT ONE?
I'M NOT SURE I WANT TO KNOW...
I'VE GOT A BAAAD FEELING...
IT COULD BE SOMETHING USEFUL!
W- WELL...
I GUESS THERE IS A TINY CHANCE...
OKAY, DAD... I'M GONNA TRUST YOU!!
KCHK
VOIP
FLAP
PINK
SUKI
FLAP
HONTOWA KOIU SUKEBENA NO WA KAKITAKUNAINDAKEDONA

* I DIDN'T REALLY WANT TO DRAW SOMETHING DIRTY LIKE THIS.

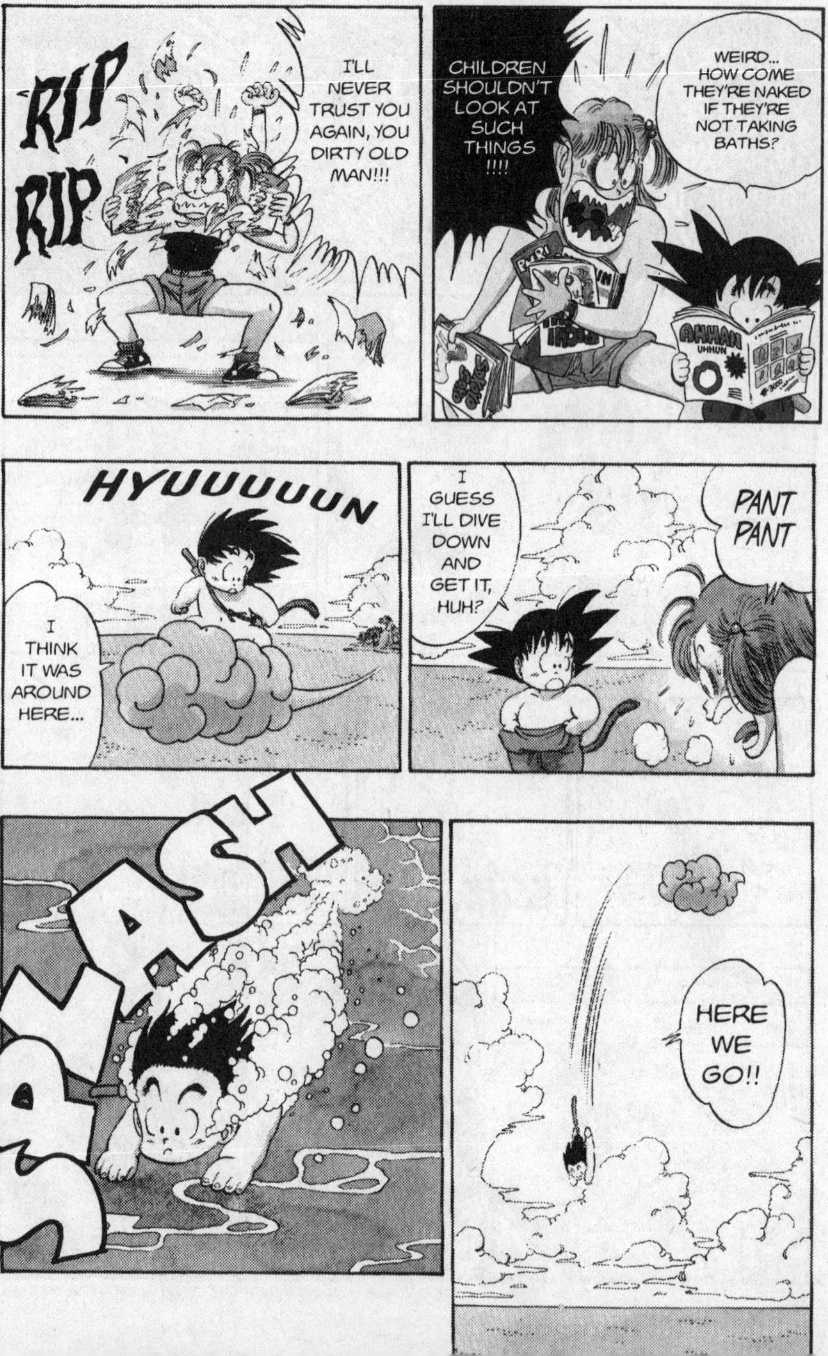
WEIRD... HOW COME THEY'RE NAKED IF THEY'RE NOT TAKING BATHS?
CHILDREN SHOULDN'T LOOK AT SUCH THINGS !!!!
I'LL NEVER TRUST YOU AGAIN, YOU DIRTY OLD MAN!!!
RIP
RIP
PANT PANT
I GUESS I'LL DIVE DOWN AND GET IT, HUH?
HYUUUUUUN
I THINK IT WAS AROUND HERE...
HERE WE GO!!
SPLASH

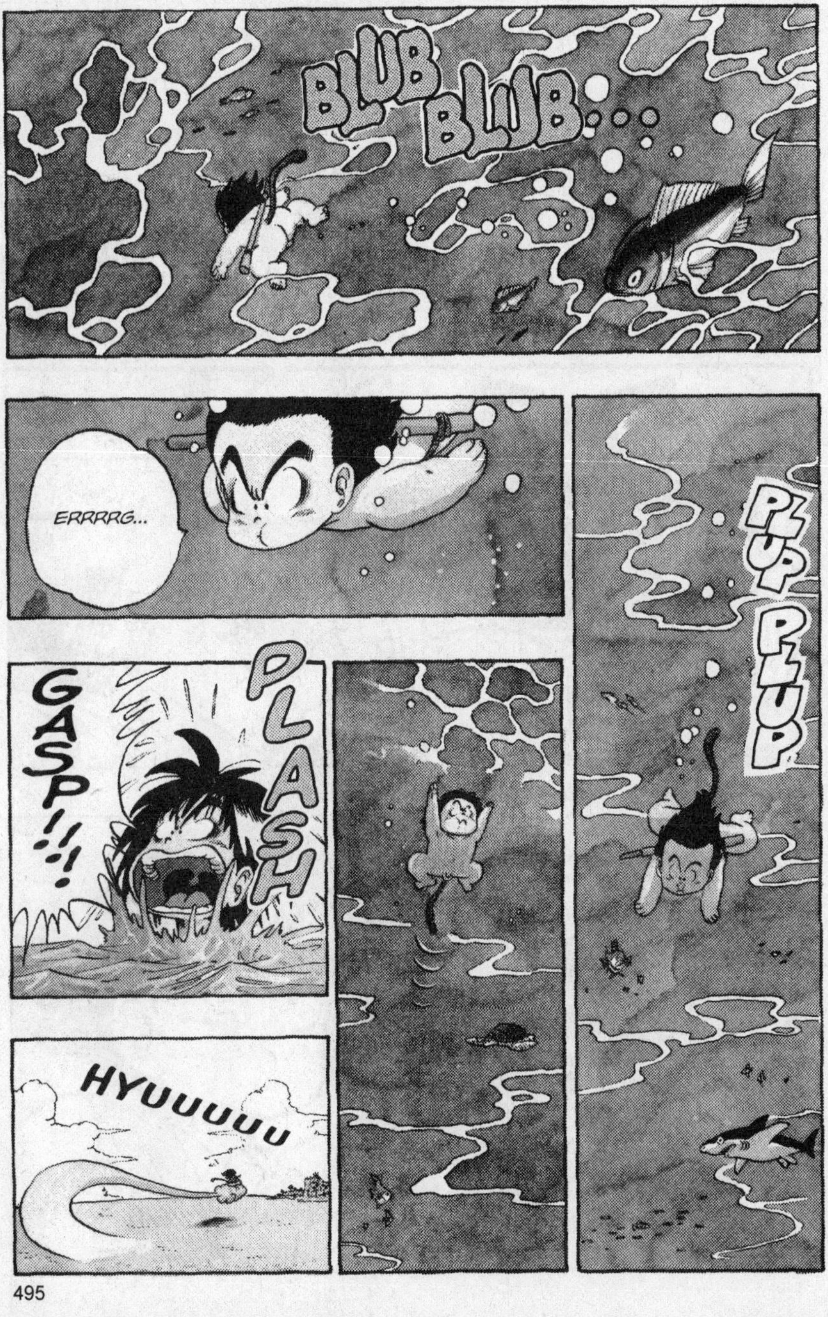
BLUB BLUB...
PLUP PLUP PLUP
ERRRRG...
PLASH
GASP!!!
HYUUUUUU

WE INTERRUPT THIS DULL STORY
FOR A THRILLING ANNOUNCEMENT!

GENERAL BLUE IS APPROACHING!!

WHAT WILL HAPPEN?! READ ON!!

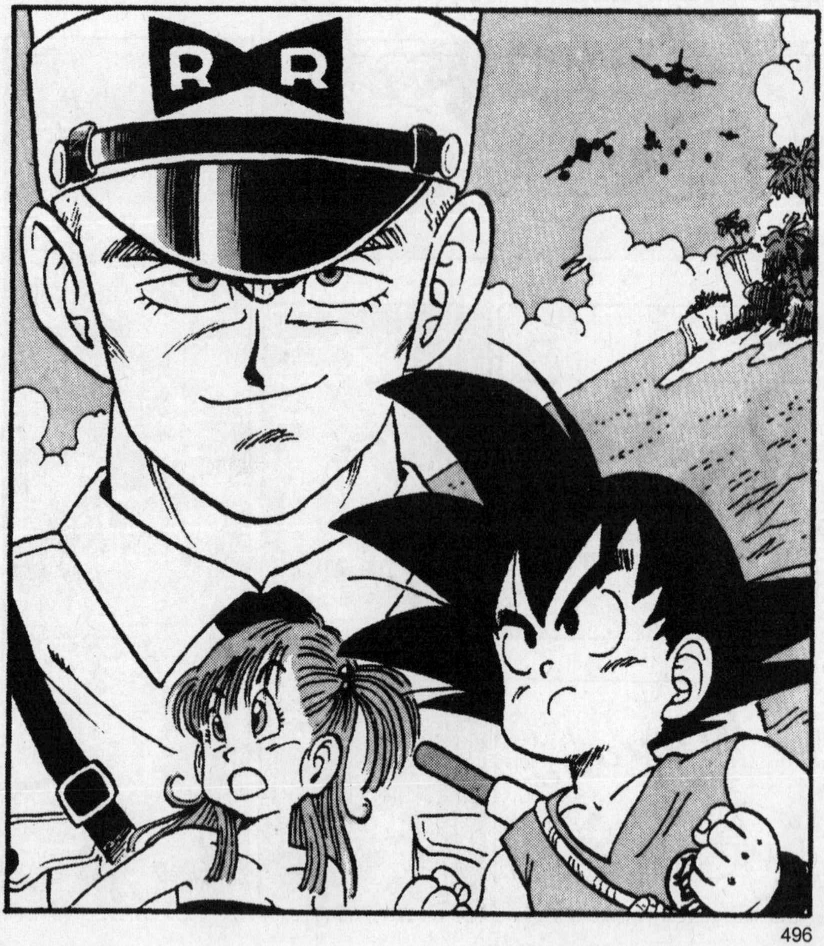
R R

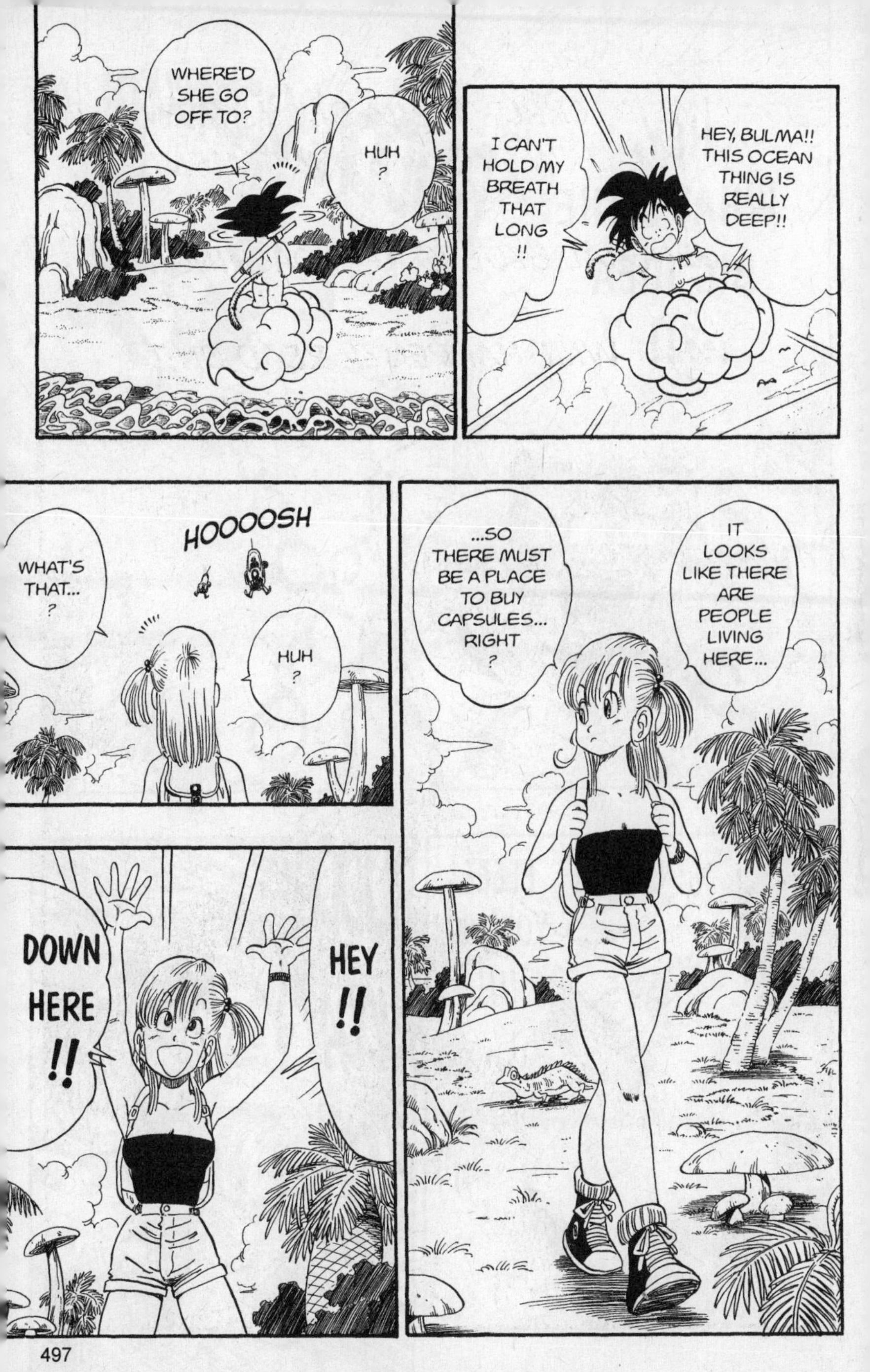
HEY, BULMA!! THIS OCEAN THING IS REALLY DEEP!!
I CAN'T HOLD MY BREATH THAT LONG !!
WHERE'D SHE GO OFF TO?
HUH ?
IT LOOKS LIKE THERE ARE PEOPLE LIVING HERE...
...SO THERE MUST BE A PLACE TO BUY CAPSULES... RIGHT ?
HOOOOSH
HUH ?
WHAT'S THAT... ?
HEY !!
DOWN HERE !!

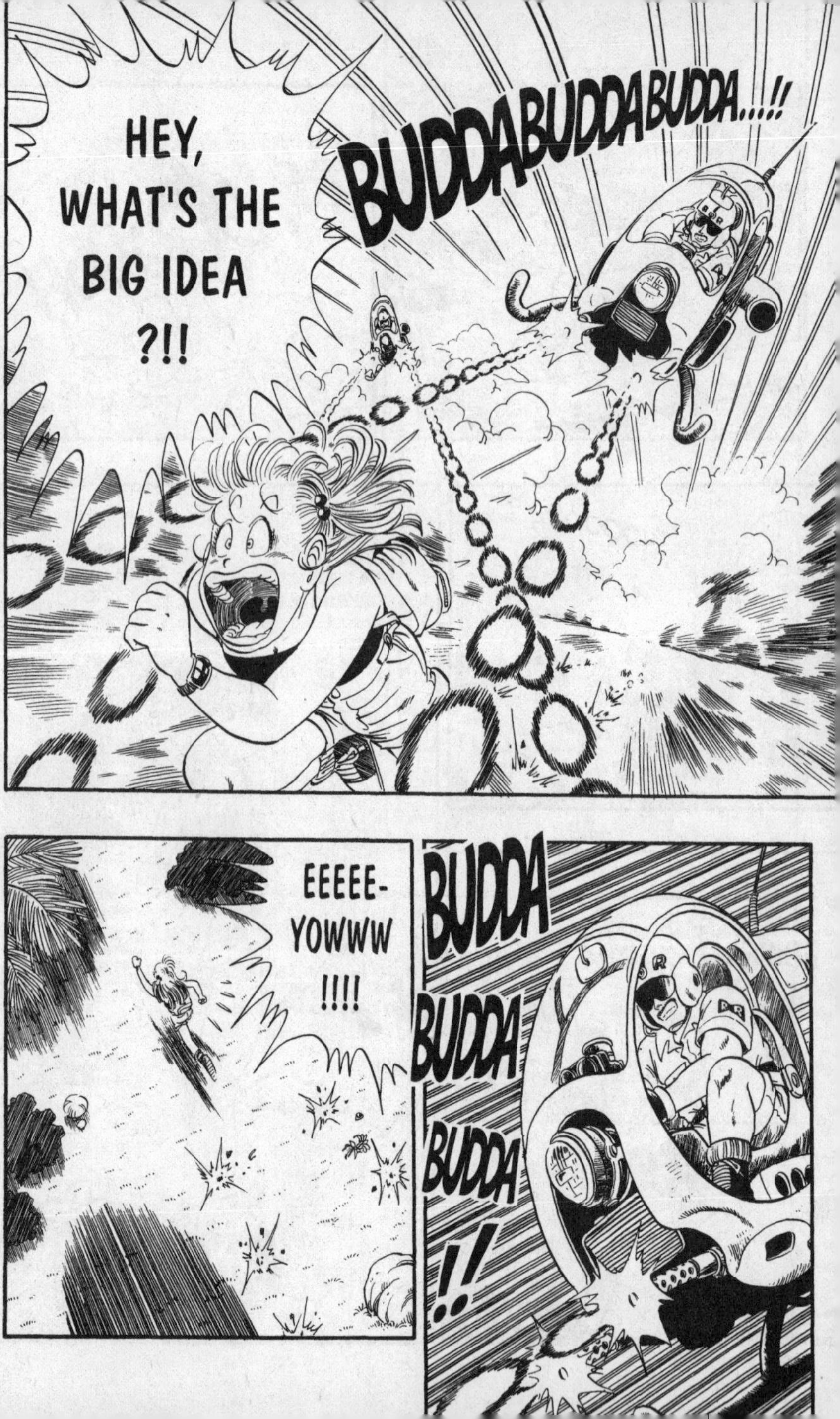
BUDDABUDDABUDDA...!!
HEY, WHAT'S THE BIG IDEA ?!!
BUDDA BUDDA BUDDA !!
EEEEE-YOWWW !!!!

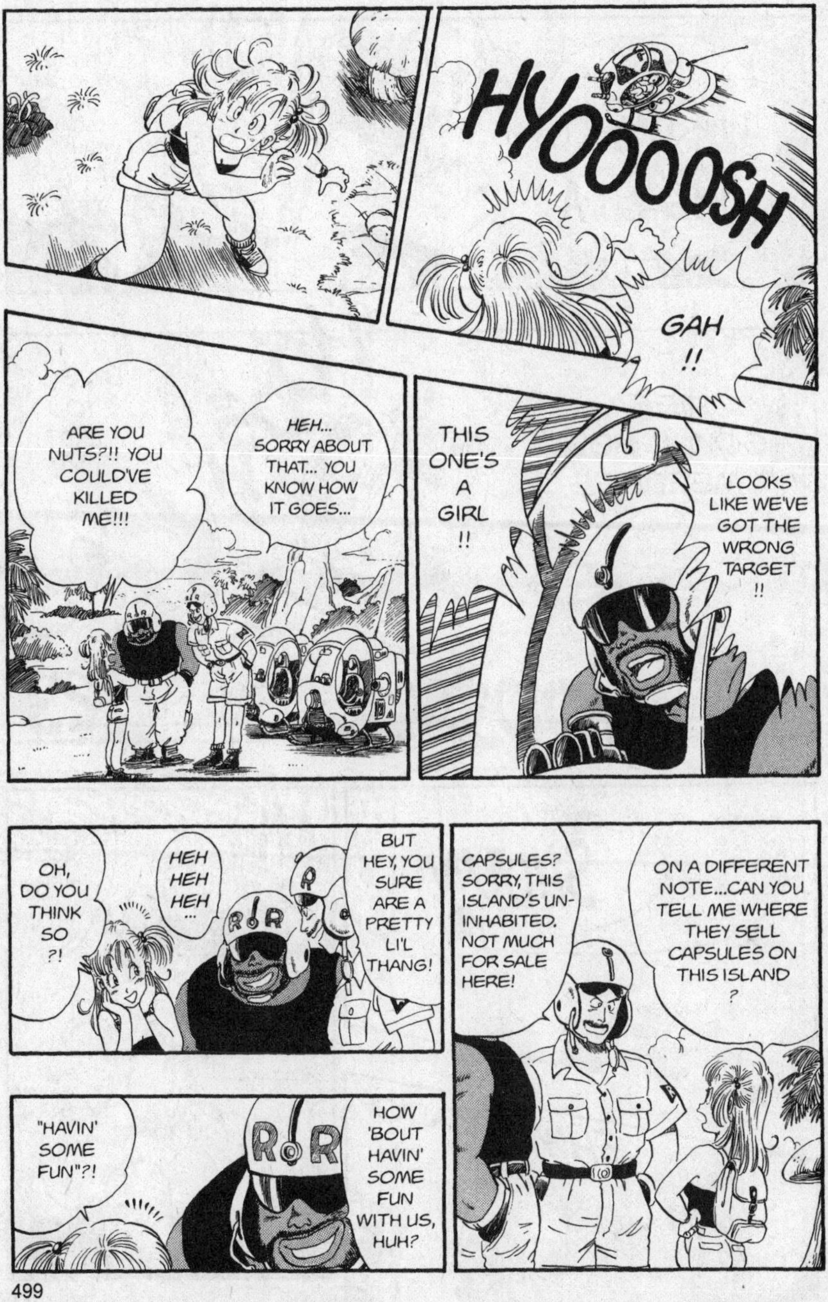
HYOOOOSH
GAH !!
LOOKS LIKE WE'VE GOT THE WRONG TARGET !!
THIS ONE'S A GIRL !!
ARE YOU NUTS?!! YOU COULD'VE KILLED ME!!!
HEH... SORRY ABOUT THAT... YOU KNOW HOW IT GOES...
ON A DIFFERENT NOTE...CAN YOU TELL ME WHERE THEY SELL CAPSULES ON THIS ISLAND ?
CAPSULES? SORRY, THIS ISLAND'S UN-INHABITED. NOT MUCH FOR SALE HERE!
BUT HEY, YOU SURE ARE A PRETTY LI'L THANG!
HEH HEH HEH ...
OH, DO YOU THINK SO ?!
HOW 'BOUT HAVIN' SOME FUN WITH US, HUH?
"HAVIN' SOME FUN"?!

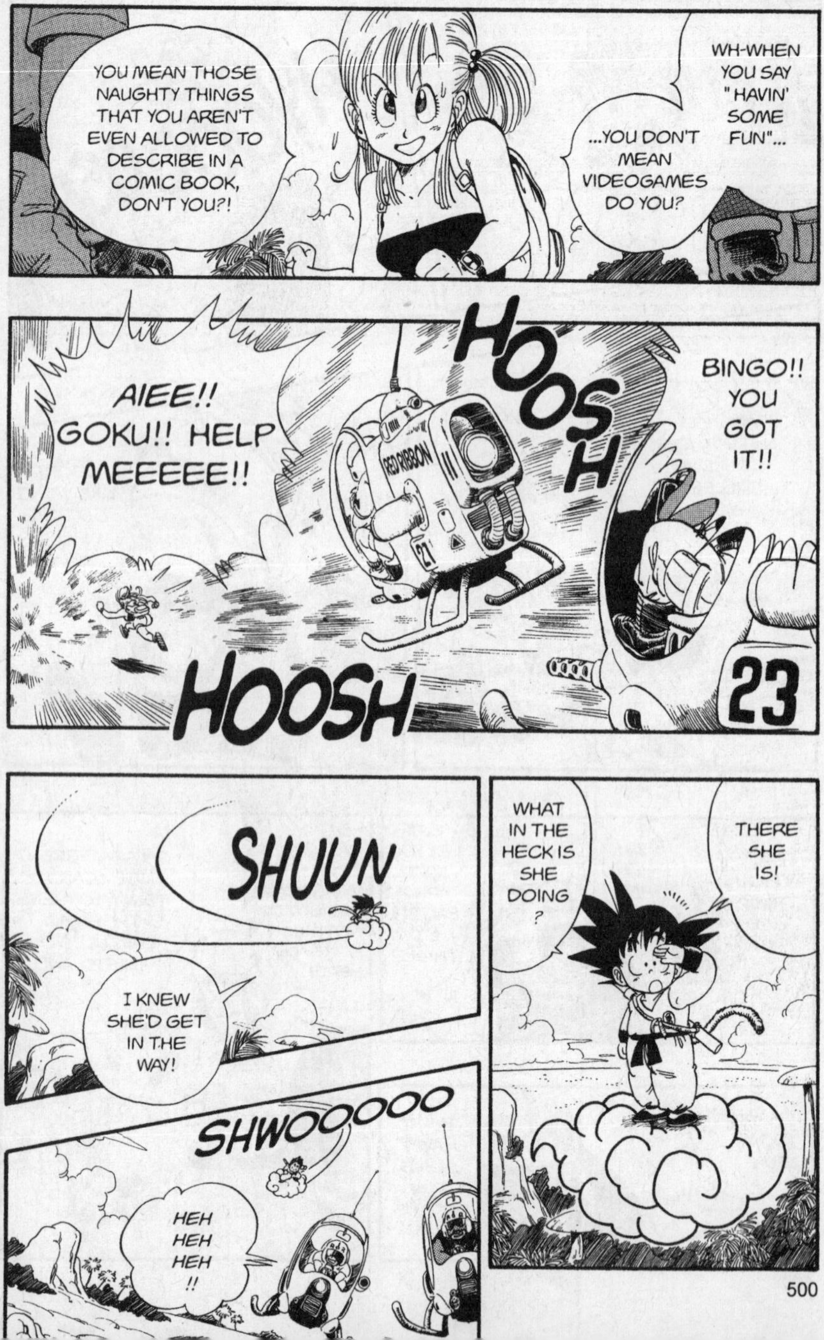
WH-WHEN YOU SAY "HAVIN' SOME FUN"...
...YOU DON'T MEAN VIDEOGAMES DO YOU?
YOU MEAN THOSE NAUGHTY THINGS THAT YOU AREN'T EVEN ALLOWED TO DESCRIBE IN A COMIC BOOK, DON'T YOU?!
HOOSH
BINGO!! YOU GOT IT!!
AIEE!! GOKU!! HELP MEEEEEE!!
RED RIBBON
23
HOOSH
THERE SHE IS!
WHAT IN THE HECK IS SHE DOING?
SHUUN
I KNEW SHE'D GET IN THE WAY!
SHWOOOOOO
HEH HEH HEH!!

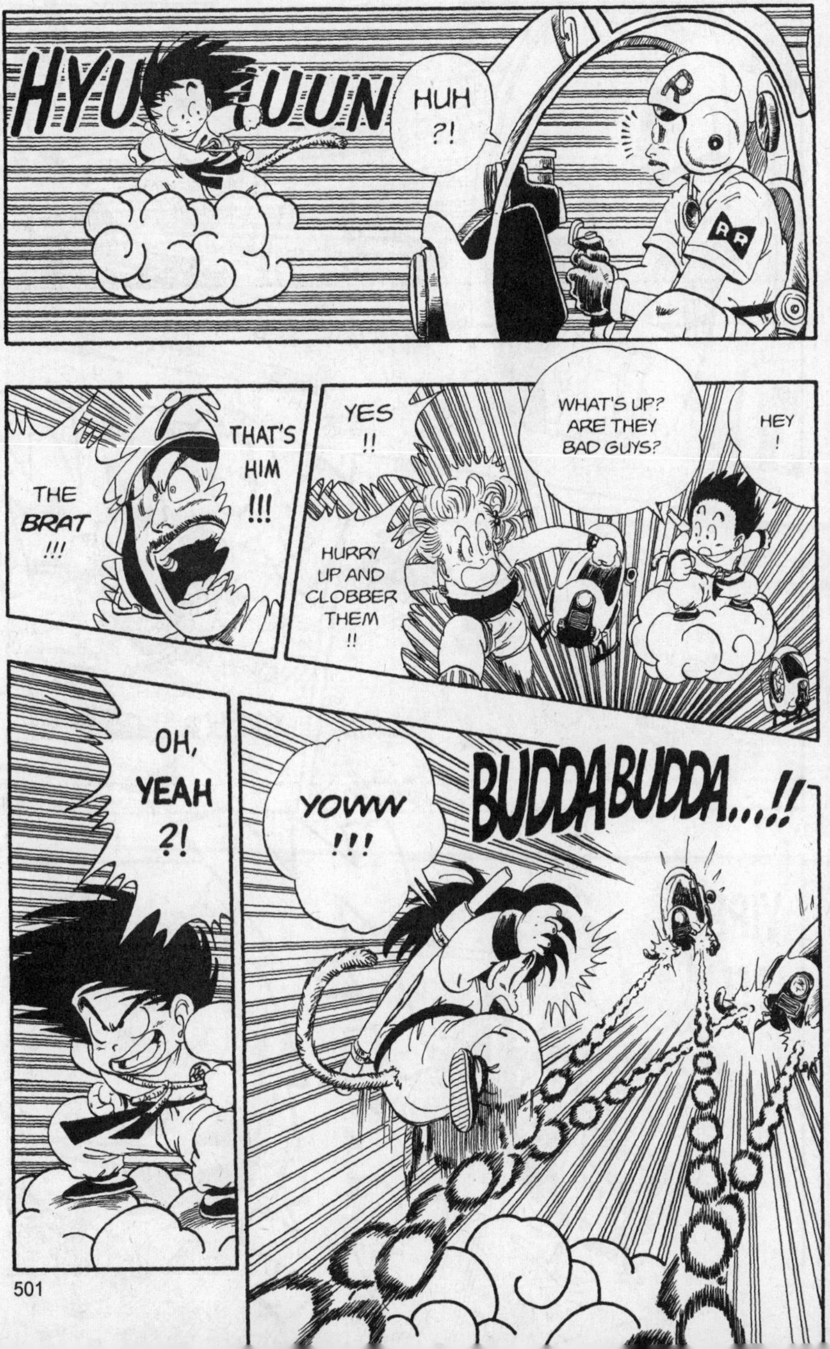
HUH ?!
HYU UUN
HEY !
WHAT'S UP? ARE THEY BAD GUYS?
YES !!
HURRY UP AND CLOBBER THEM !!
THAT'S HIM !!!
THE BRAT !!!
BUDDABUDDA...!!
YOWW !!!
OH, YEAH ?!

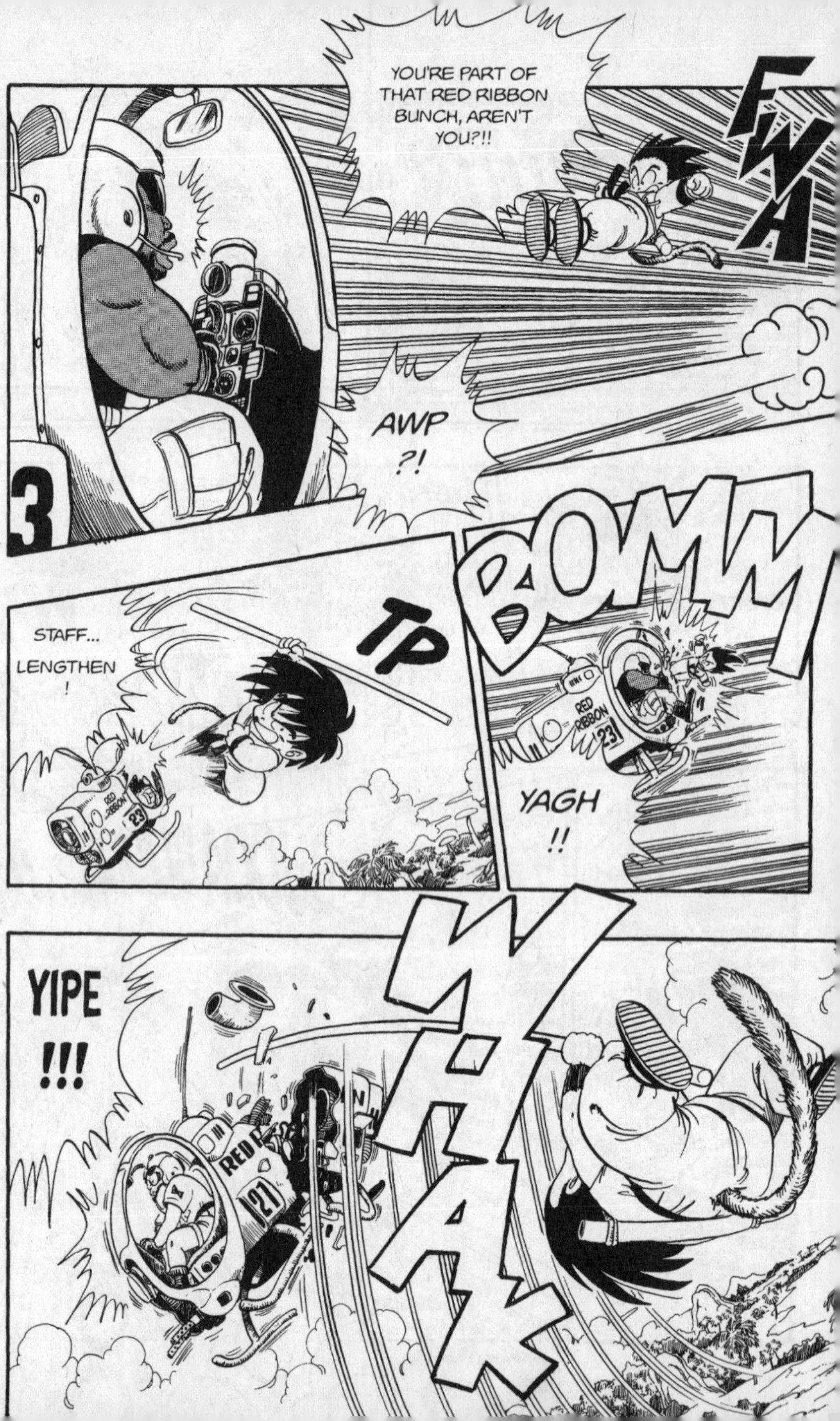
FWA
YOU'RE PART OF THAT RED RIBBON BUNCH, AREN'T YOU?!!
AWP ?!
BOMM
YAGH !!
TP
STAFF... LENGTHEN !
WHAK
YIPE !!!

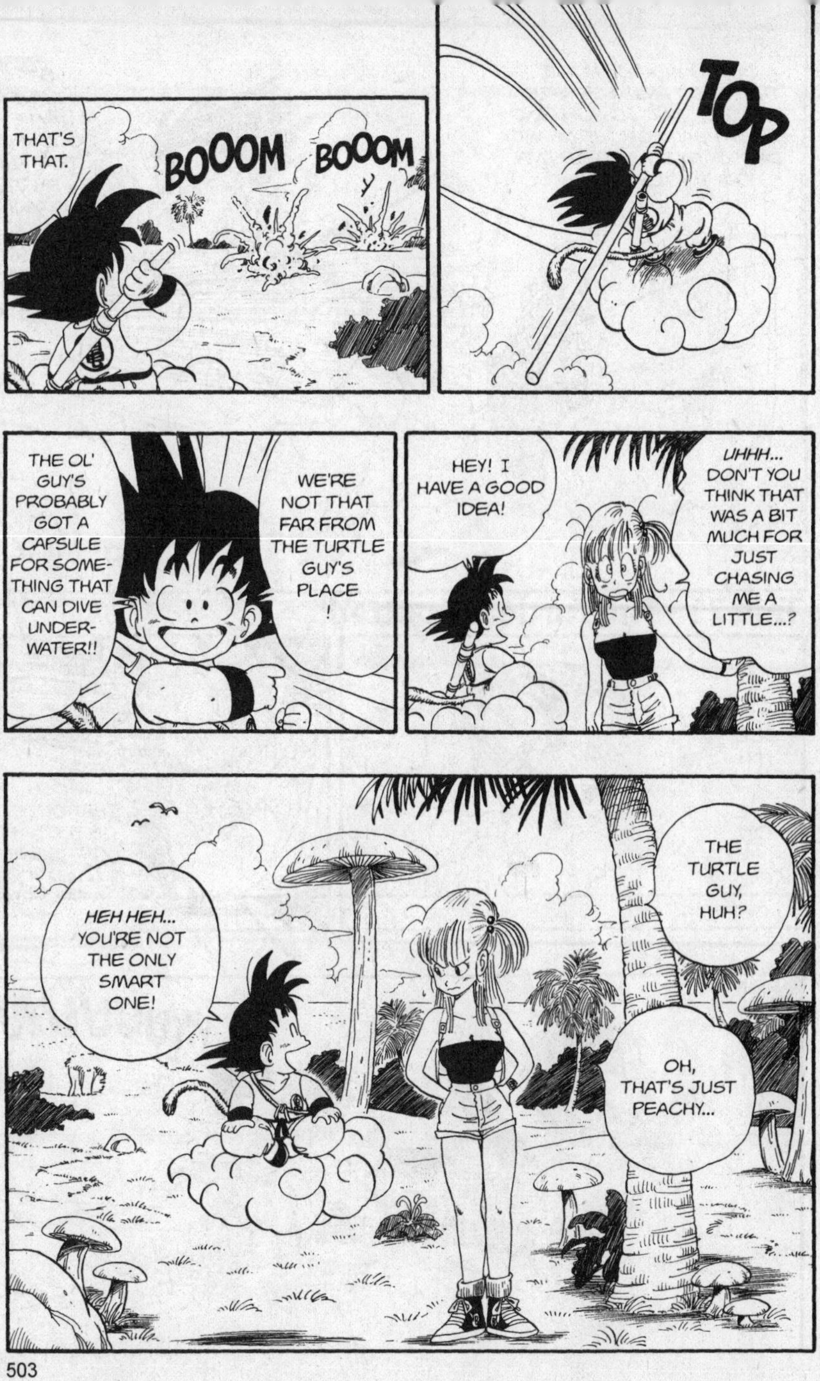
TOP
THAT'S THAT.
BOOOM
BOOOM
UHHH... DON'T YOU THINK THAT WAS A BIT MUCH FOR JUST CHASING ME A LITTLE...?
HEY! I HAVE A GOOD IDEA!
WE'RE NOT THAT FAR FROM THE TURTLE GUY'S PLACE!
THE OL' GUY'S PROBABLY GOT A CAPSULE FOR SOMETHING THAT CAN DIVE UNDERWATER!!
THE TURTLE GUY, HUH?
HEH HEH... YOU'RE NOT THE ONLY SMART ONE!
OH, THAT'S JUST PEACHY...

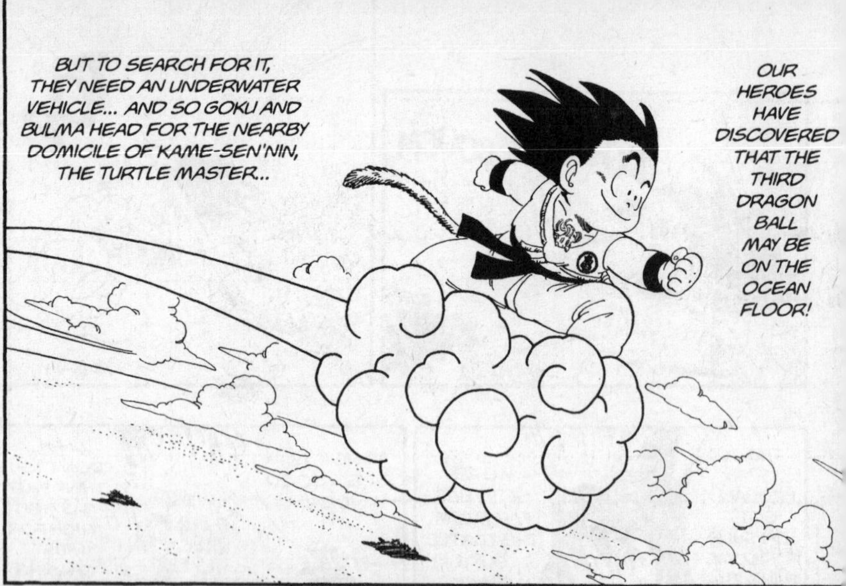
OUR HEROES HAVE DISCOVERED THAT THE THIRD DRAGON BALL MAY BE ON THE OCEAN FLOOR!
BUT TO SEARCH FOR IT, THEY NEED AN UNDERWATER VEHICLE... AND SO GOKU AND BULMA HEAD FOR THE NEARBY DOMICILE OF KAME-SEN'NIN, THE TURTLE MASTER...

Tale 71 • The Turtle Is Spotted!

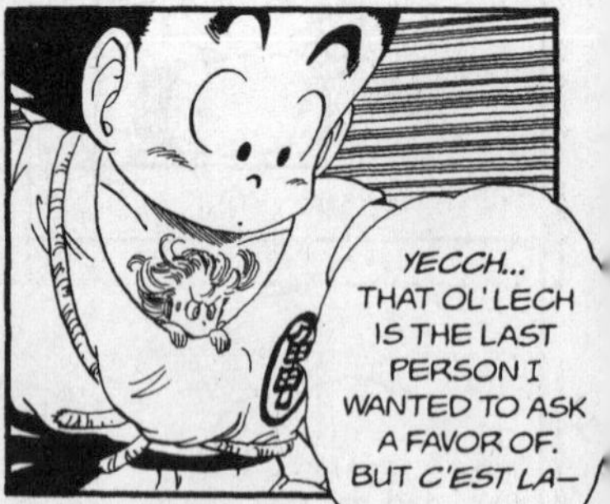
YECCH... THAT OL' LECH IS THE LAST PERSON I WANTED TO ASK A FAVOR OF. BUT C'EST LA—

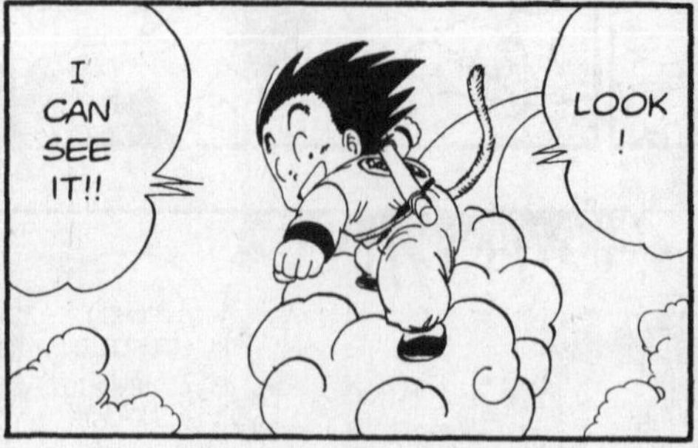
LOOK!
I CAN SEE IT!!

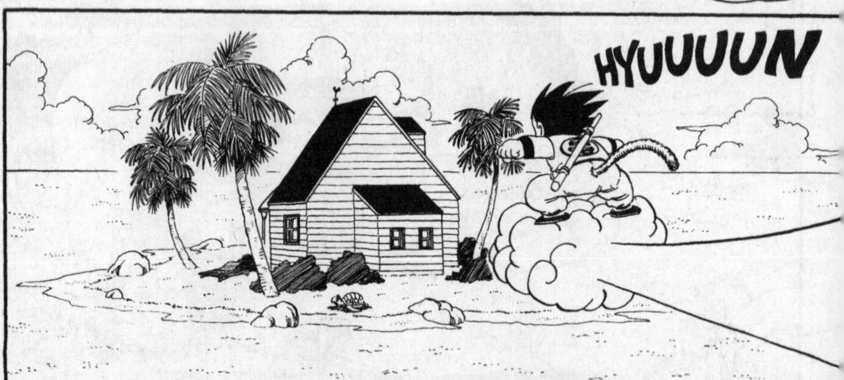
HYUUUUN

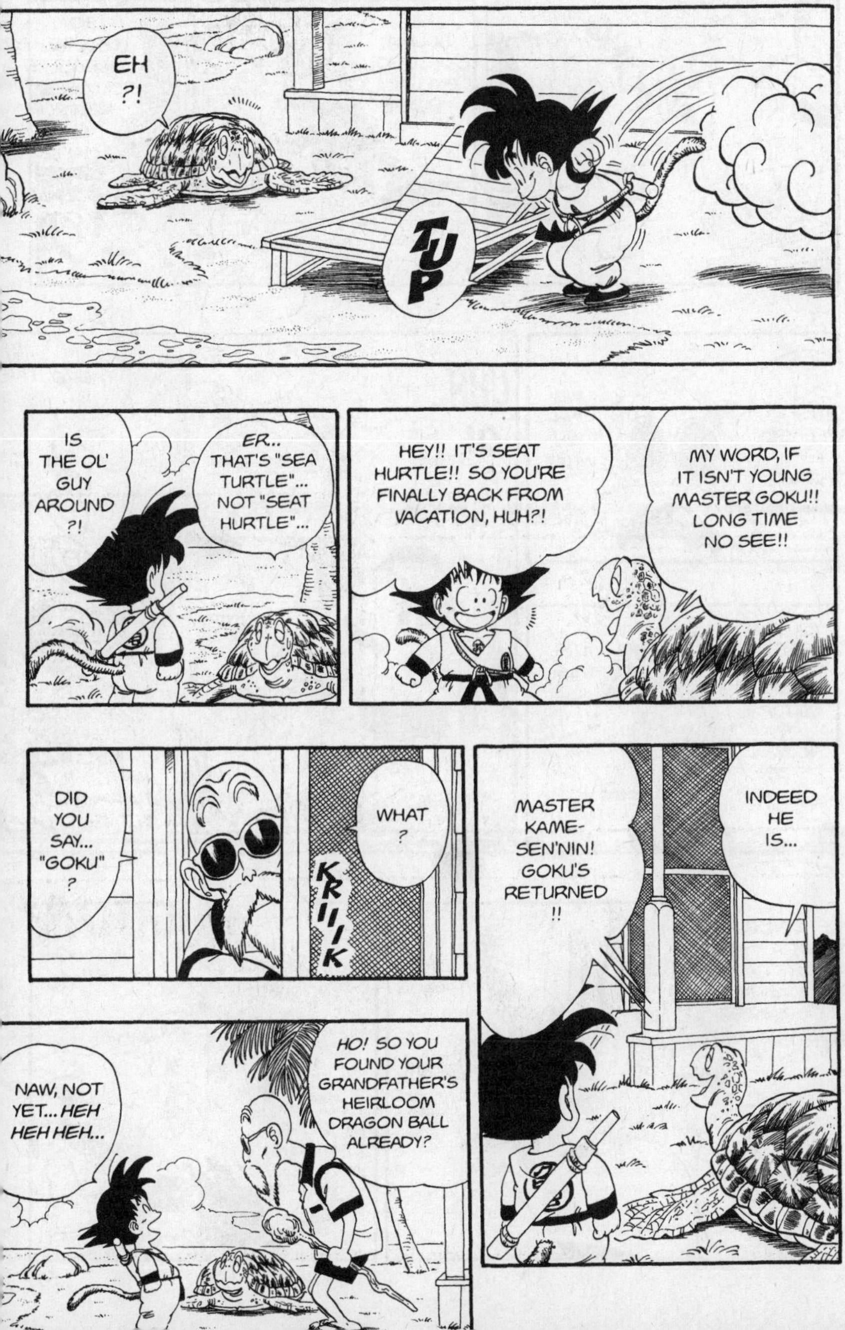
TUP
EH ?!
MY WORD, IF IT ISN'T YOUNG MASTER GOKU!! LONG TIME NO SEE!!
HEY!! IT'S SEAT HURTLE!! SO YOU'RE FINALLY BACK FROM VACATION, HUH?!
ER... THAT'S "SEA TURTLE"... NOT "SEAT HURTLE"...
IS THE OL' GUY AROUND ?!
INDEED HE IS...
MASTER KAME-SEN'NIN! GOKU'S RETURNED !!
WHAT ?
KRIIIK
DID YOU SAY... "GOKU" ?
HO! SO YOU FOUND YOUR GRANDFATHER'S HEIRLOOM DRAGON BALL ALREADY?
NAW, NOT YET... HEH HEH HEH...

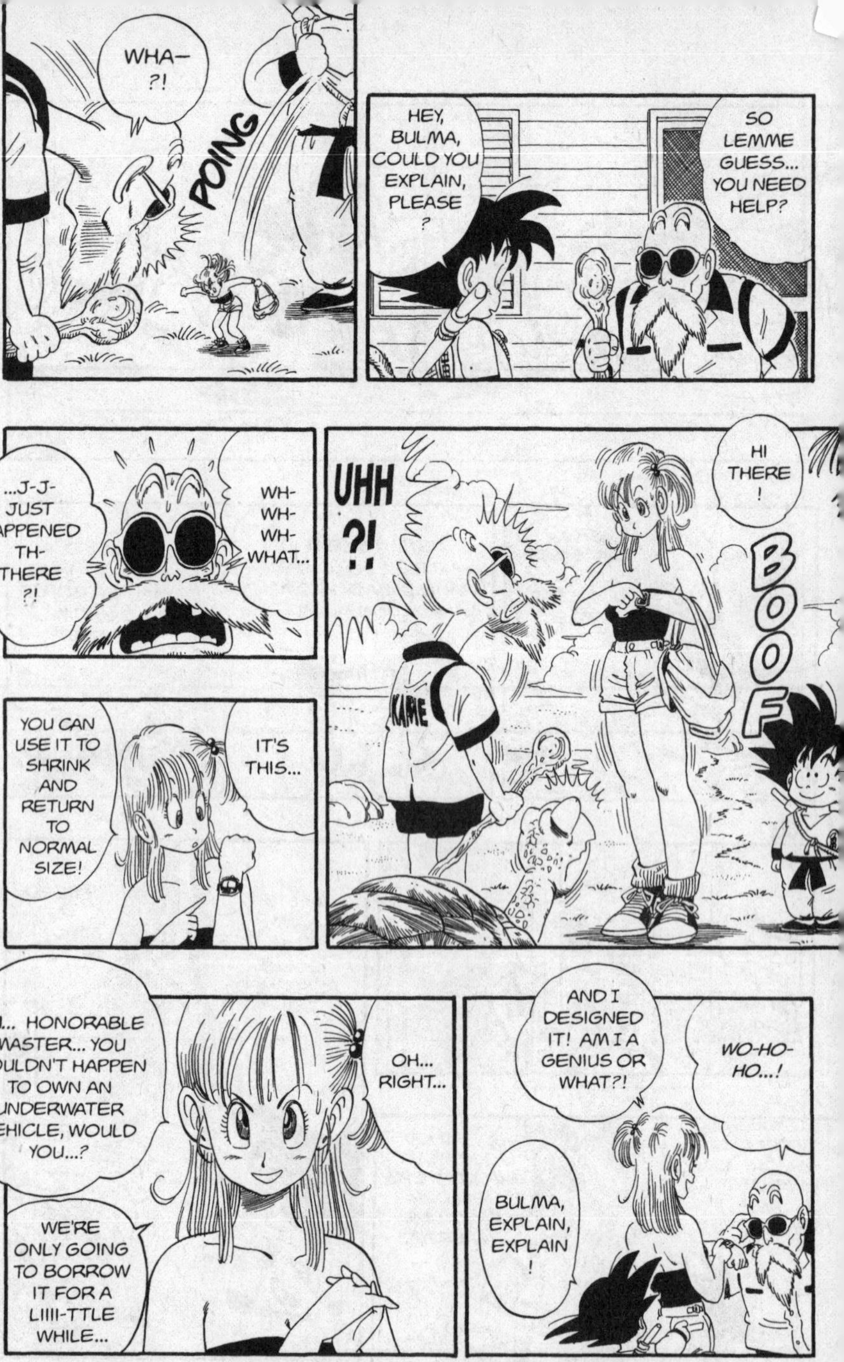
SO LEMME GUESS... YOU NEED HELP?
HEY, BULMA, COULD YOU EXPLAIN, PLEASE?
POING
WHA—?!
HI THERE!
BOOF
UHH?!
WH-WH-WH-WHAT...
...J-J-JUST HAPPENED TH-THERE?!
IT'S THIS...
YOU CAN USE IT TO SHRINK AND RETURN TO NORMAL SIZE!
WO-HO-HO...!
AND I DESIGNED IT! AM I A GENIUS OR WHAT?!
BULMA, EXPLAIN, EXPLAIN!
OH... RIGHT...
UM... HONORABLE MASTER... YOU WOULDN'T HAPPEN TO OWN AN UNDERWATER VEHICLE, WOULD YOU...?
WE'RE ONLY GOING TO BORROW IT FOR A LIIII-TTLE WHILE...

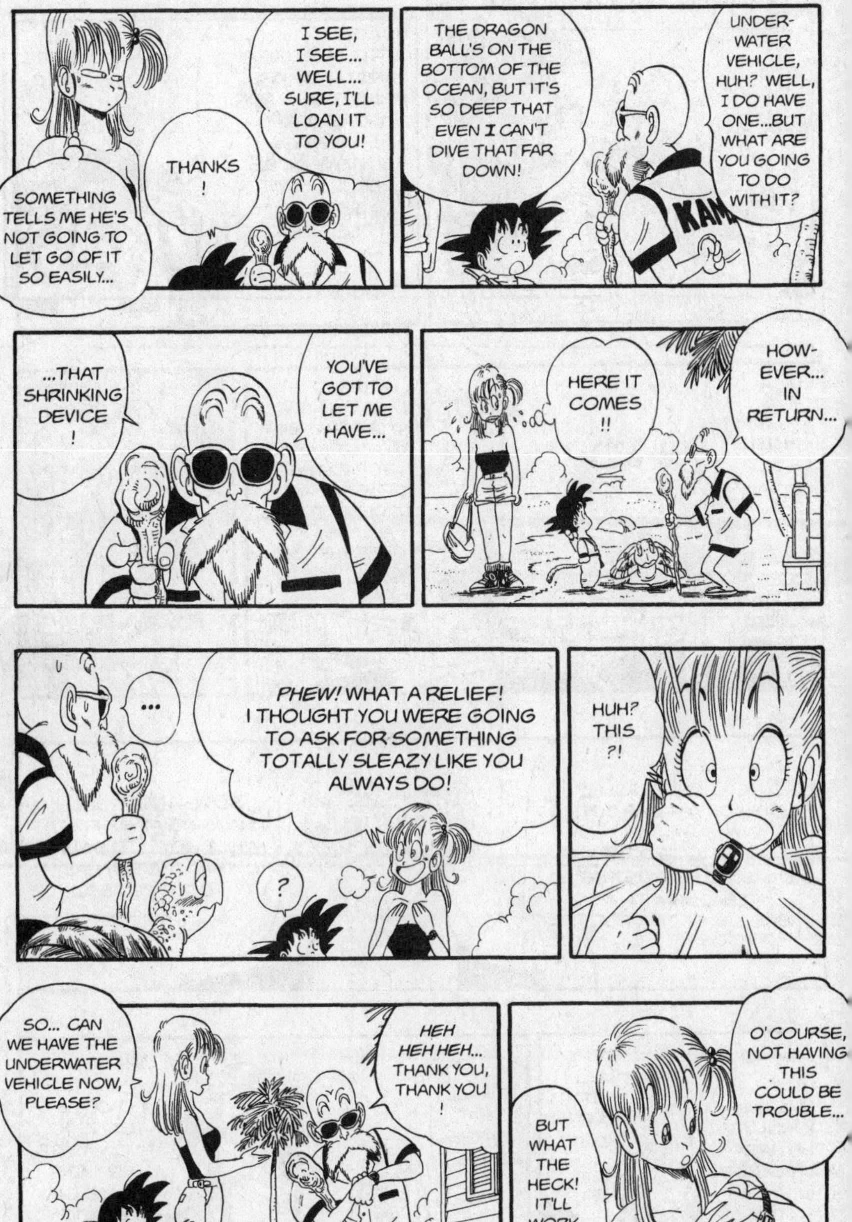
UNDER-WATER VEHICLE, HUH? WELL, I DO HAVE ONE...BUT WHAT ARE YOU GOING TO DO WITH IT?
THE DRAGON BALL'S ON THE BOTTOM OF THE OCEAN, BUT IT'S SO DEEP THAT EVEN I CAN'T DIVE THAT FAR DOWN!
I SEE, I SEE... WELL... SURE, I'LL LOAN IT TO YOU!
THANKS!
SOMETHING TELLS ME HE'S NOT GOING TO LET GO OF IT SO EASILY...
HOW-EVER... IN RETURN...
HERE IT COMES!!
YOU'VE GOT TO LET ME HAVE...
...THAT SHRINKING DEVICE!
HUH? THIS?!
PHEW! WHAT A RELIEF! I THOUGHT YOU WERE GOING TO ASK FOR SOMETHING TOTALLY SLEAZY LIKE YOU ALWAYS DO!
...
?
O'COURSE, NOT HAVING THIS COULD BE TROUBLE...
BUT WHAT THE HECK! IT'LL WORK OUT!
HEH HEH HEH... THANK YOU, THANK YOU!
SO... CAN WE HAVE THE UNDERWATER VEHICLE NOW, PLEASE?

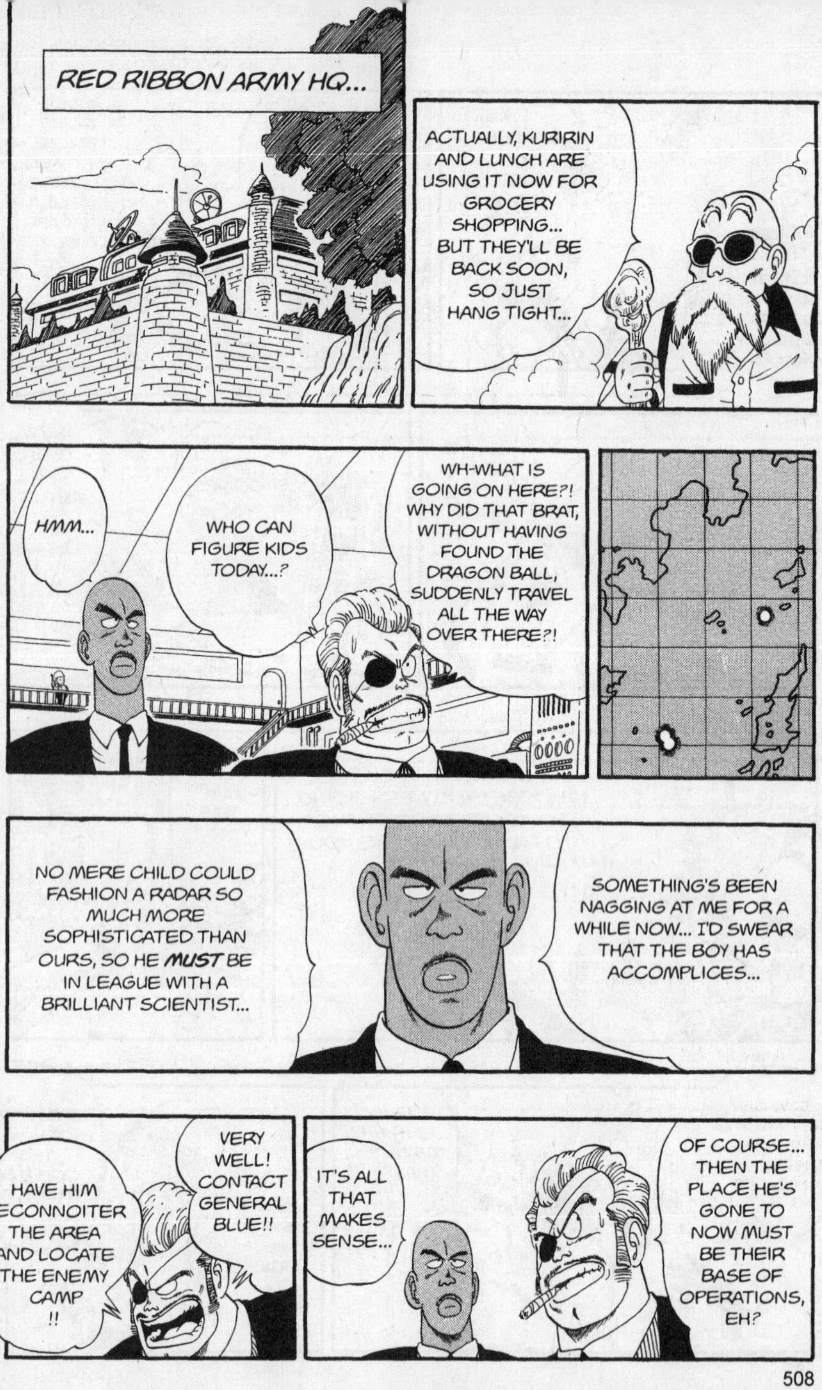
ACTUALLY, KURIRIN AND LUNCH ARE USING IT NOW FOR GROCERY SHOPPING... BUT THEY'LL BE BACK SOON, SO JUST HANG TIGHT...
RED RIBBON ARMY HQ...
WH-WHAT IS GOING ON HERE?! WHY DID THAT BRAT, WITHOUT HAVING FOUND THE DRAGON BALL, SUDDENLY TRAVEL ALL THE WAY OVER THERE?!
WHO CAN FIGURE KIDS TODAY...?
HMM...
SOMETHING'S BEEN NAGGING AT ME FOR A WHILE NOW... I'D SWEAR THAT THE BOY HAS ACCOMPLICES...
NO MERE CHILD COULD FASHION A RADAR SO MUCH MORE SOPHISTICATED THAN OURS, SO HE MUST BE IN LEAGUE WITH A BRILLIANT SCIENTIST...
OF COURSE... THEN THE PLACE HE'S GONE TO NOW MUST BE THEIR BASE OF OPERATIONS, EH?
IT'S ALL THAT MAKES SENSE...
VERY WELL! CONTACT GENERAL BLUE!!
HAVE HIM RECONNOITER THE AREA AND LOCATE THE ENEMY CAMP !!

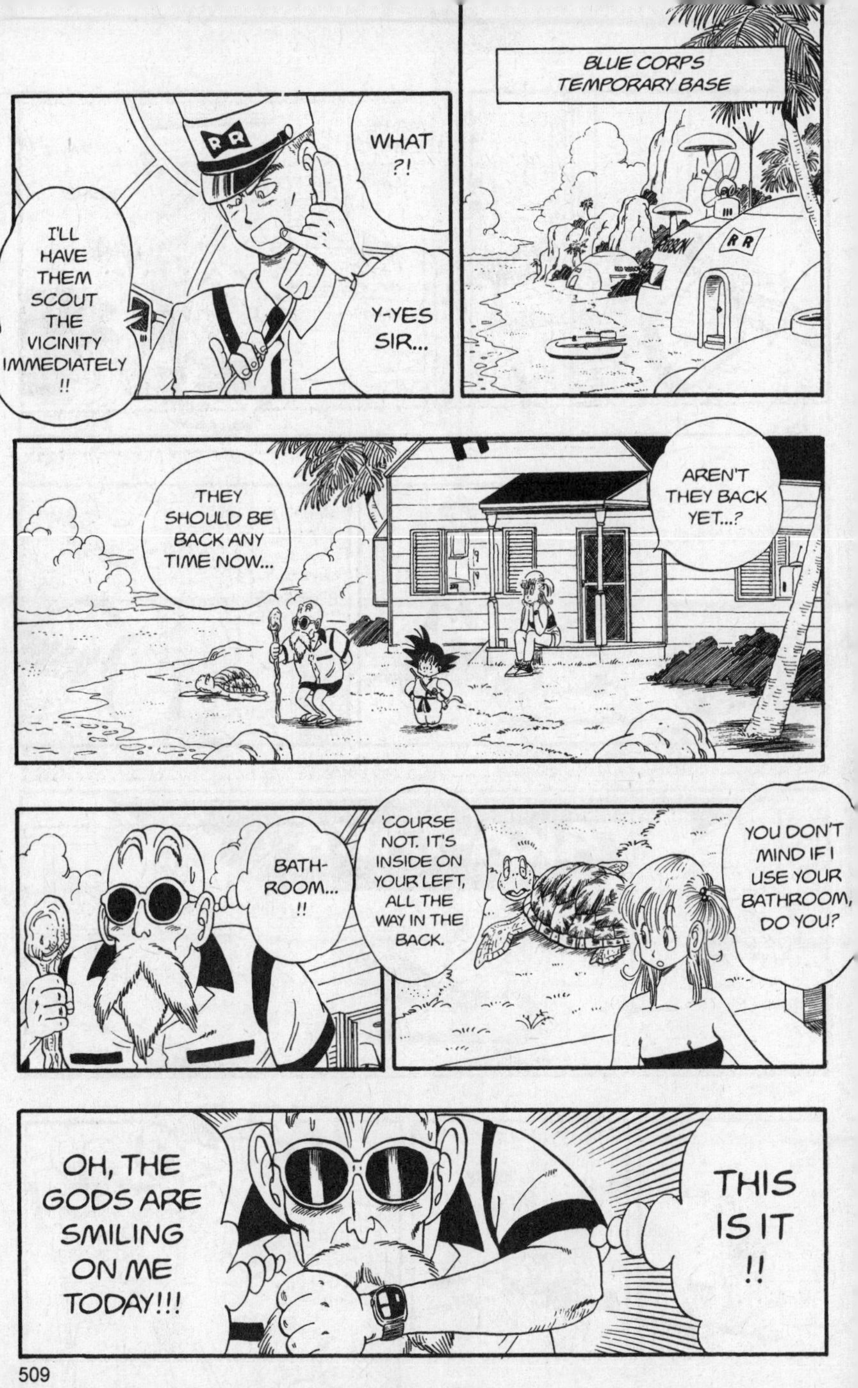

BLUE CORPS TEMPORARY BASE
WHAT ?!
Y-YES SIR...
I'LL HAVE THEM SCOUT THE VICINITY IMMEDIATELY !!
AREN'T THEY BACK YET...?
THEY SHOULD BE BACK ANY TIME NOW...
YOU DON'T MIND IF I USE YOUR BATHROOM, DO YOU?
'COURSE NOT. IT'S INSIDE ON YOUR LEFT, ALL THE WAY IN THE BACK.
BATH-ROOM... !!
THIS IS IT !!
OH, THE GODS ARE SMILING ON ME TODAY!!!

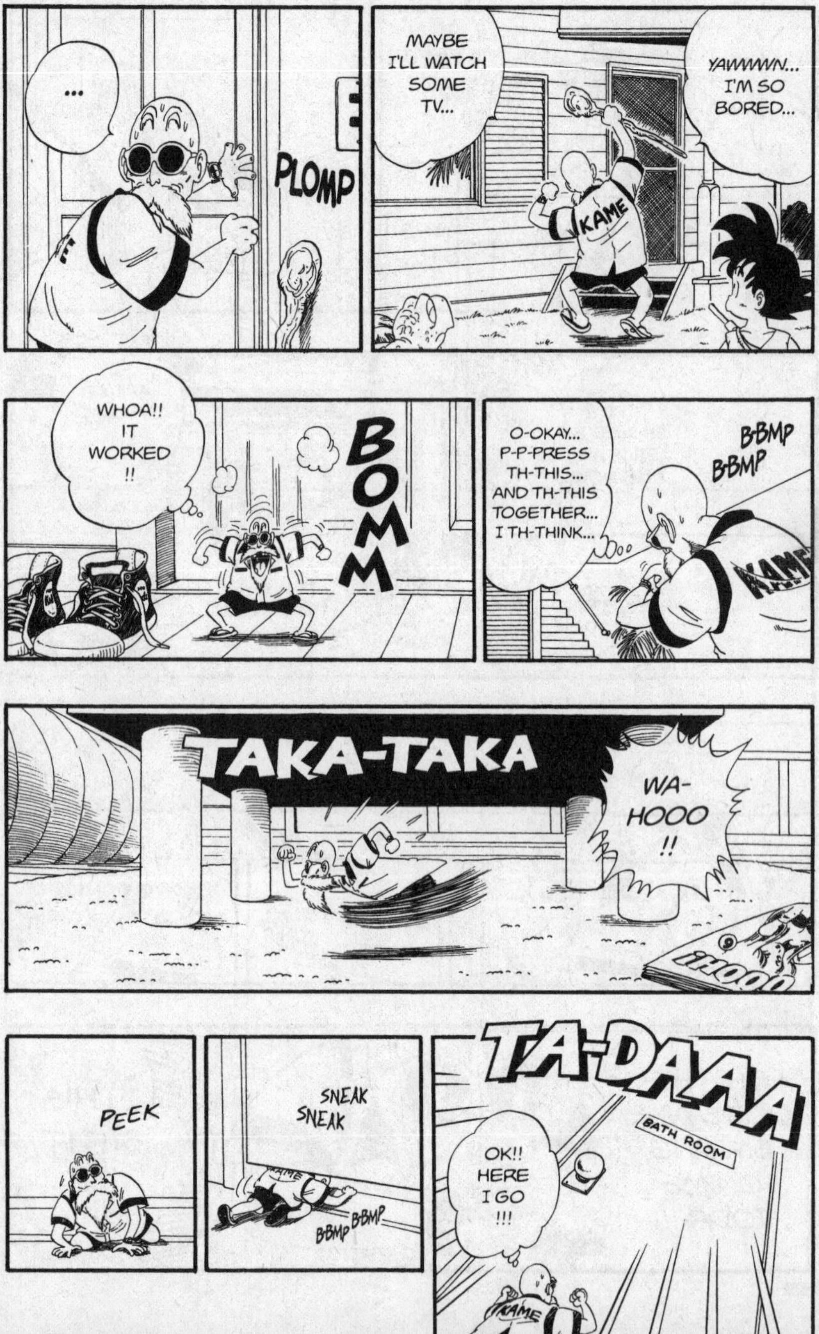
YAWWWN... I'M SO BORED...
MAYBE I'LL WATCH SOME TV...
...
PLOMP
B-BMP B-BMP
O-OKAY... P-P-PRESS TH-THIS... AND TH-THIS TOGETHER... I TH-THINK...
WHOA!! IT WORKED !!
BOMM
TAKA-TAKA
WA-HOOO !!
TA-DAAAA
BATH ROOM
OK!! HERE I GO !!!
SNEAK SNEAK
B-BMP B-BMP
PEEK

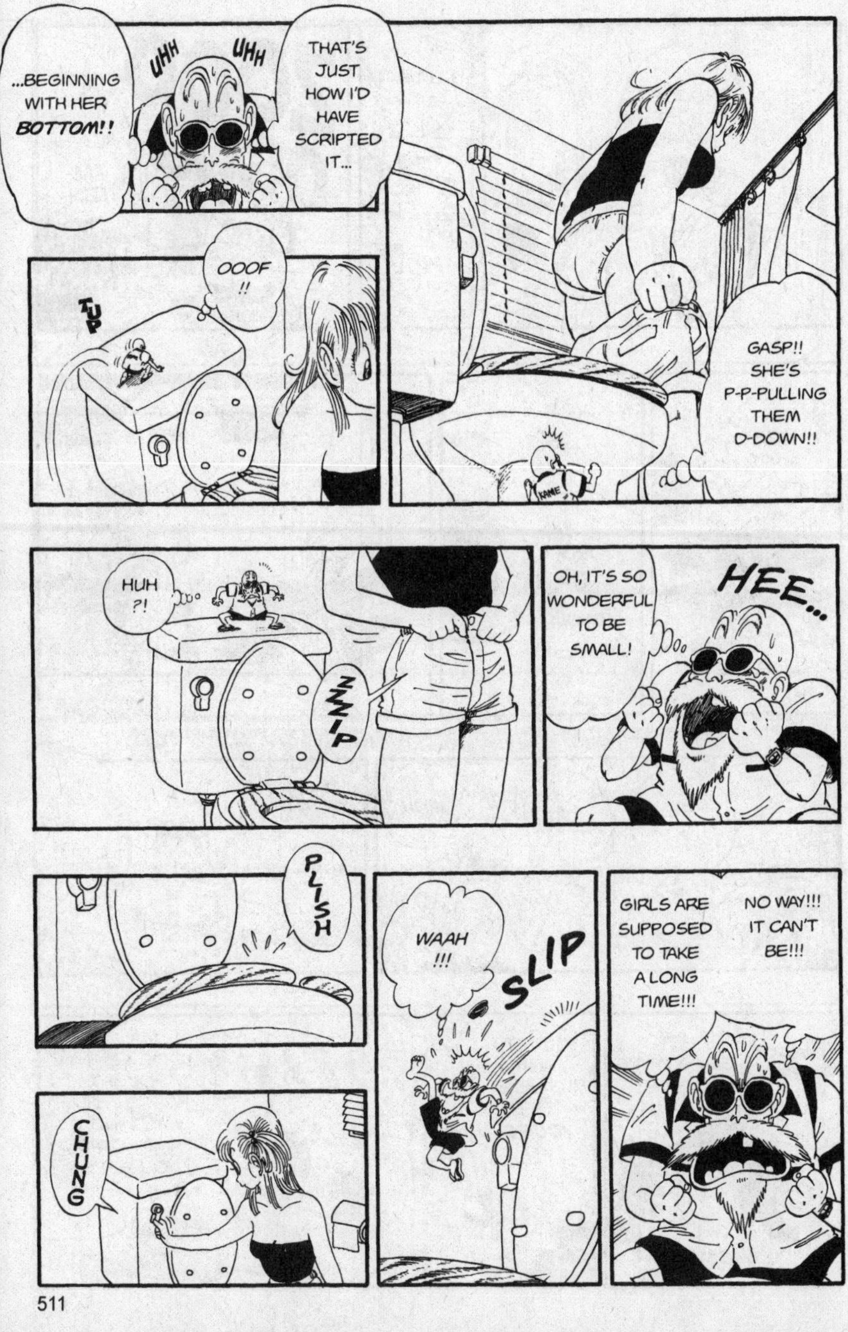
GASP!! SHE'S P-P-PULLING THEM D-DOWN!!
THAT'S JUST HOW I'D HAVE SCRIPTED IT...
UHH
UHH
...BEGINNING WITH HER BOTTOM!!
OOOF!!
TUP
HEE...
OH, IT'S SO WONDERFUL TO BE SMALL!
ZZZIP
HUH?!
NO WAY!!! IT CAN'T BE!!!
GIRLS ARE SUPPOSED TO TAKE A LONG TIME!!!
SLIP
WAAH!!!
PLISH
CHUNG

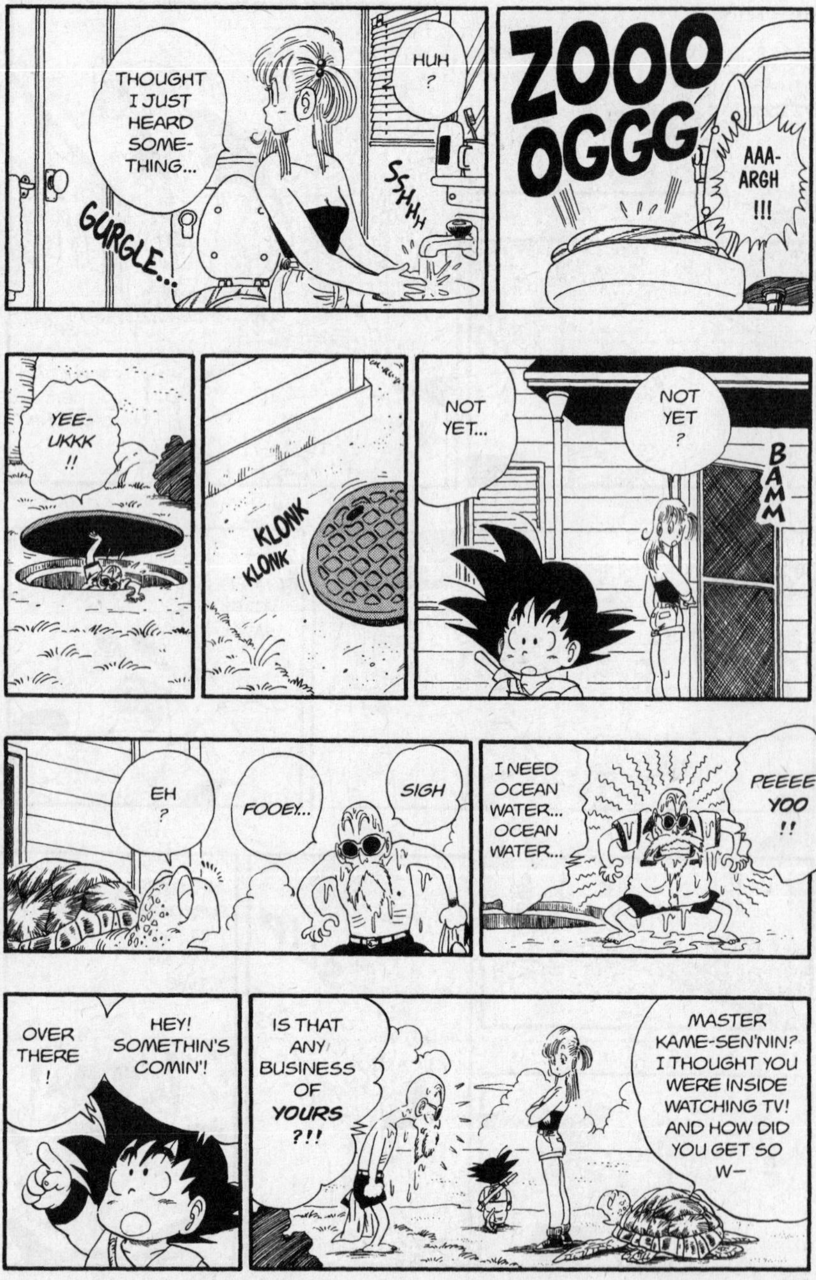
ZOOO OGGG
AAA-ARGH !!!
HUH ?
SSHHH
THOUGHT I JUST HEARD SOME-THING...
GURGLE...
NOT YET ?
BAMM
NOT YET...
KLONK KLONK
YEE-UKKK !!
PEEEE-YOO !!
I NEED OCEAN WATER... OCEAN WATER...
SIGH
FOOEY...
EH ?
MASTER KAME-SEN'NIN? I THOUGHT YOU WERE INSIDE WATCHING TV! AND HOW DID YOU GET SO W—
IS THAT ANY BUSINESS OF YOURS ?!!
HEY! SOMETHIN'S COMIN'!
OVER THERE !

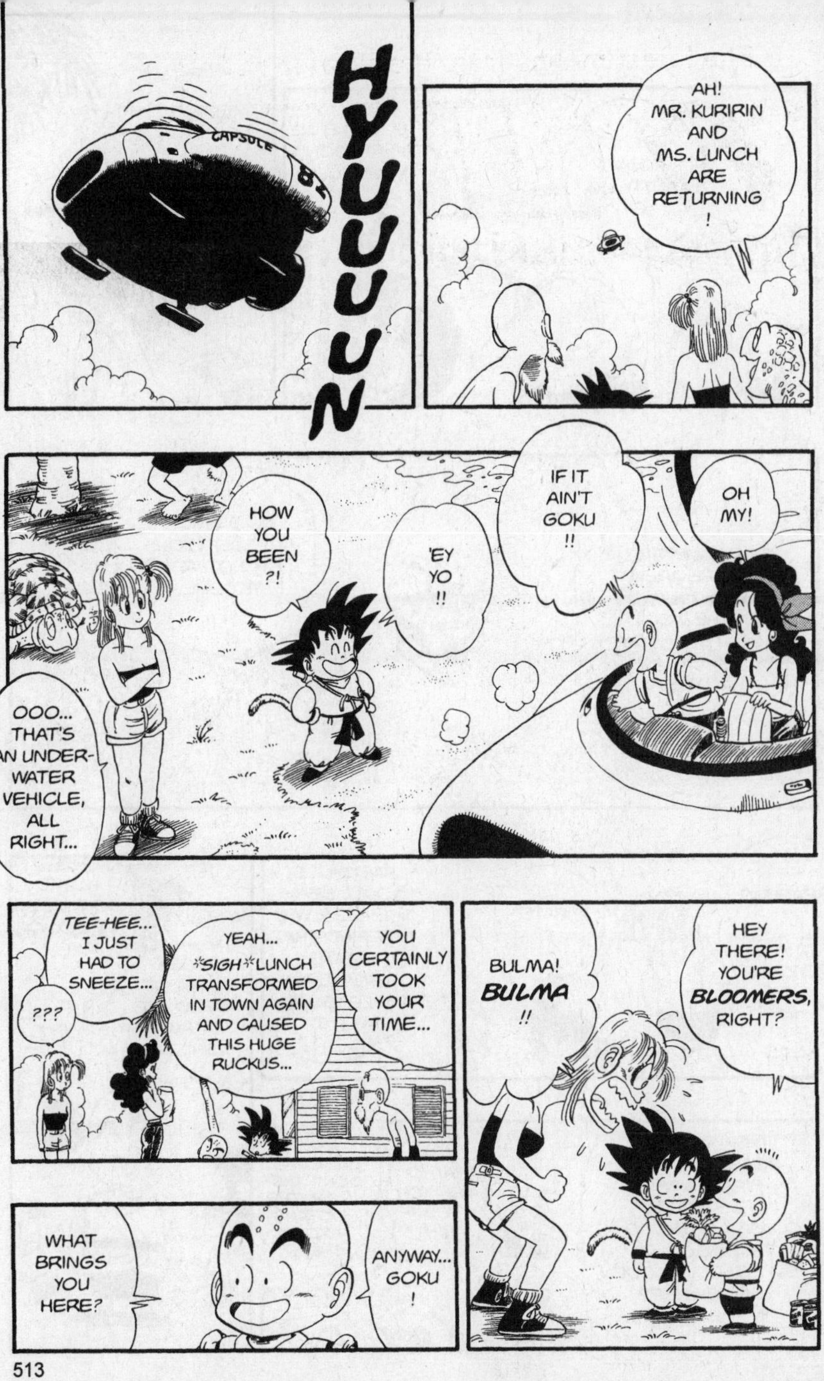
AH! MR. KURIRIN AND MS. LUNCH ARE RETURNING!
HYUUUUN
CAPSULE 82
OH MY!
IF IT AIN'T GOKU !!
'EY YO !!
HOW YOU BEEN ?!
OOO... THAT'S AN UNDER-WATER VEHICLE, ALL RIGHT...
HEY THERE! YOU'RE *BLOOMERS*, RIGHT?
BULMA! **BULMA** !!
YOU CERTAINLY TOOK YOUR TIME...
YEAH... *SIGH* LUNCH TRANSFORMED IN TOWN AGAIN AND CAUSED THIS HUGE RUCKUS...
TEE-HEE... I JUST HAD TO SNEEZE...
???
ANYWAY... GOKU !
WHAT BRINGS YOU HERE?

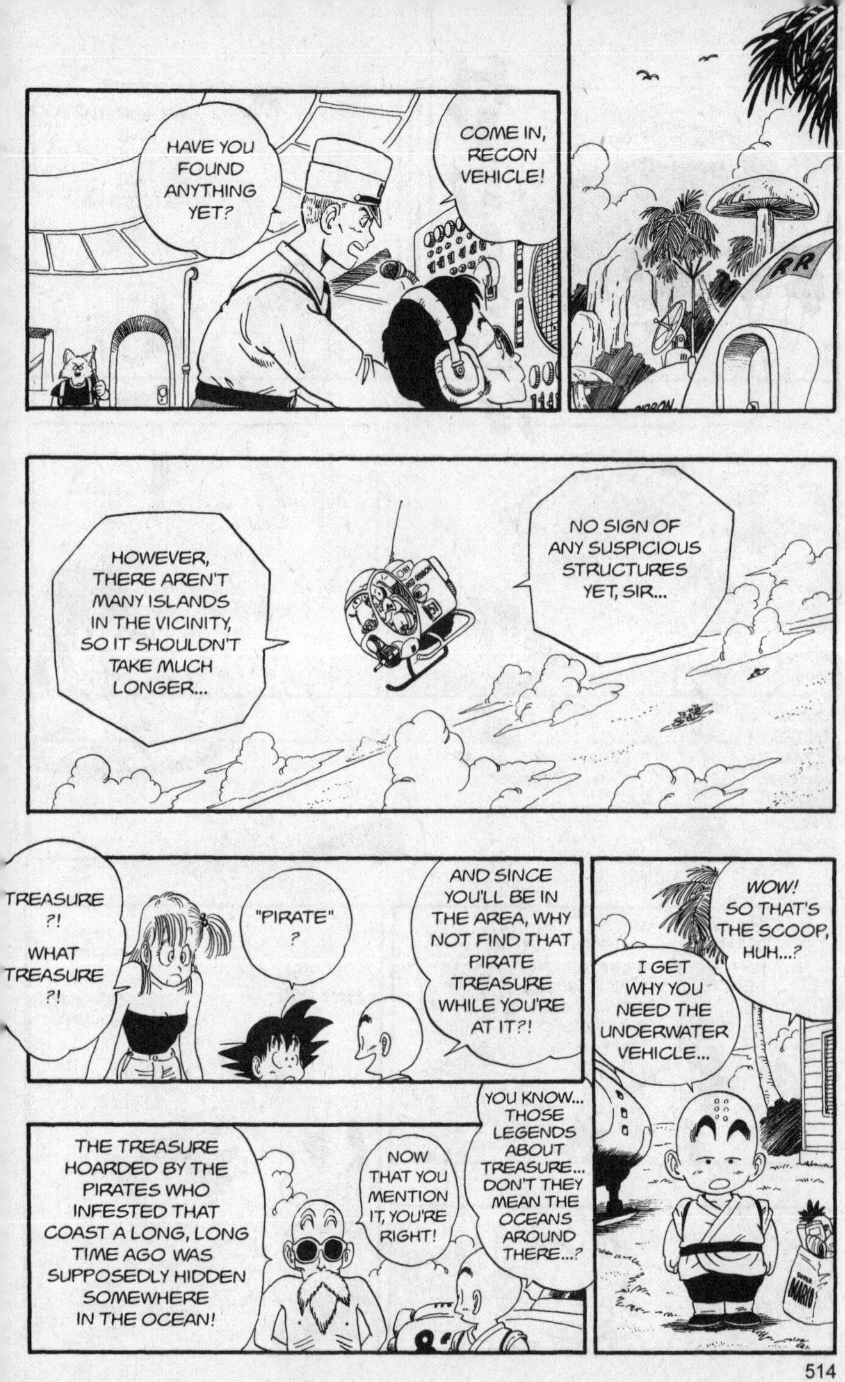
COME IN, RECON VEHICLE!
HAVE YOU FOUND ANYTHING YET?
NO SIGN OF ANY SUSPICIOUS STRUCTURES YET, SIR...
HOWEVER, THERE AREN'T MANY ISLANDS IN THE VICINITY, SO IT SHOULDN'T TAKE MUCH LONGER...
WOW! SO THAT'S THE SCOOP, HUH...?
I GET WHY YOU NEED THE UNDERWATER VEHICLE...
AND SINCE YOU'LL BE IN THE AREA, WHY NOT FIND THAT PIRATE TREASURE WHILE YOU'RE AT IT?!
"PIRATE"?
TREASURE?! WHAT TREASURE?!
YOU KNOW... THOSE LEGENDS ABOUT TREASURE... DON'T THEY MEAN THE OCEANS AROUND THERE...?
NOW THAT YOU MENTION IT, YOU'RE RIGHT!
THE TREASURE HOARDED BY THE PIRATES WHO INFESTED THAT COAST A LONG, LONG TIME AGO WAS SUPPOSEDLY HIDDEN SOMEWHERE IN THE OCEAN!

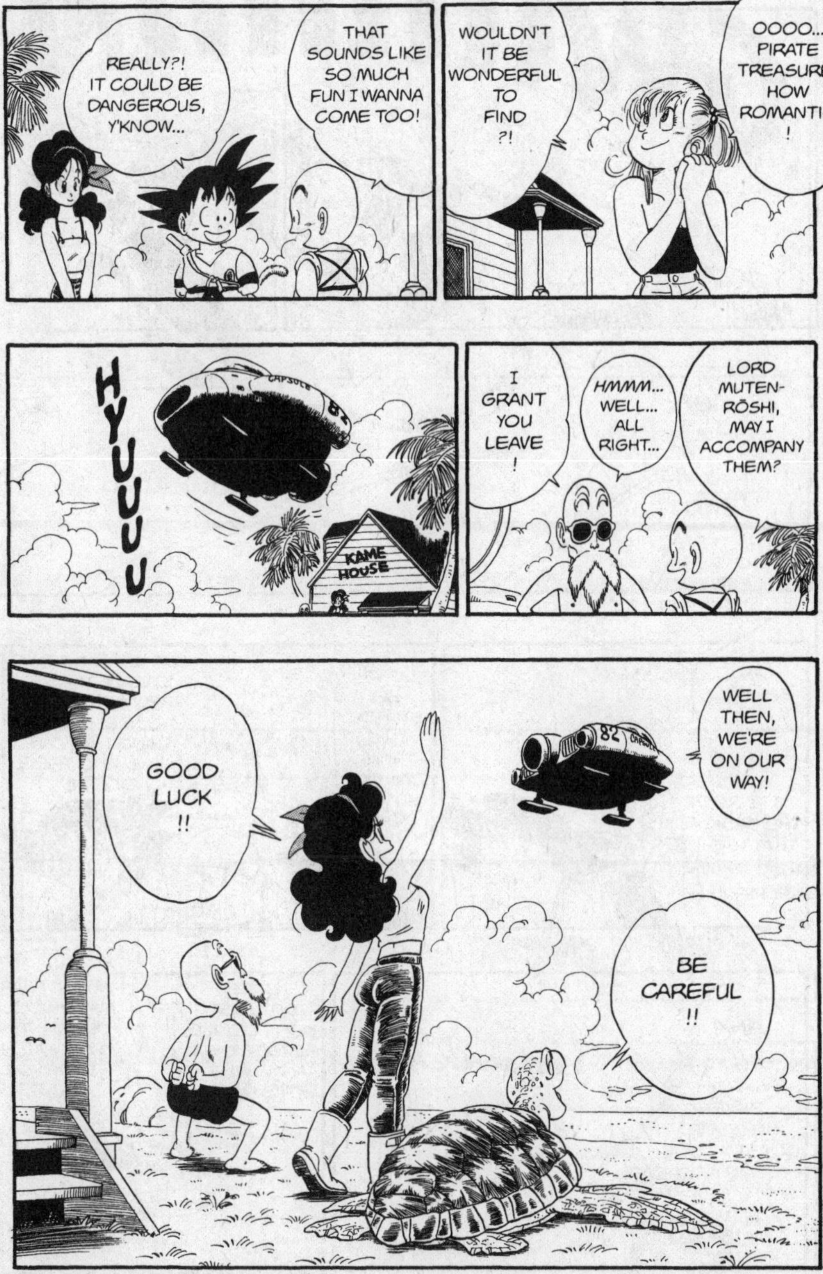
OOOO... PIRATE TREASURE! HOW ROMANTIC!
WOULDN'T IT BE WONDERFUL TO FIND ?!
THAT SOUNDS LIKE SO MUCH FUN I WANNA COME TOO!
REALLY?! IT COULD BE DANGEROUS, Y'KNOW...
LORD MUTEN-RŌSHI, MAY I ACCOMPANY THEM?
HMMM... WELL... ALL RIGHT...
I GRANT YOU LEAVE!
CAPSULE
HYUUUU
KAME HOUSE
WELL THEN, WE'RE ON OUR WAY!
82 CAPSULE
BE CAREFUL!!
GOOD LUCK!!

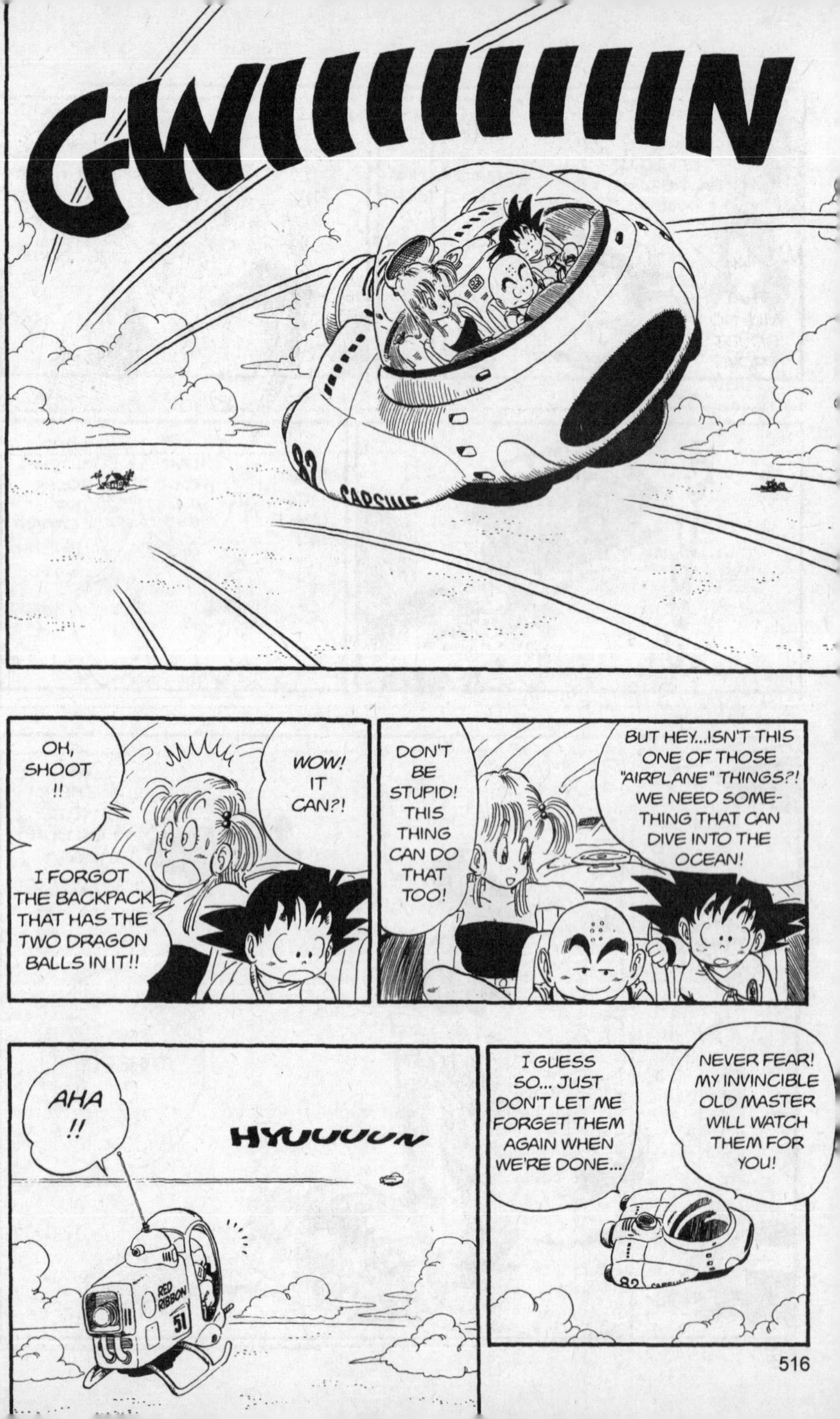
GWIIIIIIIN
82
CAPSULE
BUT HEY...ISN'T THIS ONE OF THOSE "AIRPLANE" THINGS?! WE NEED SOMETHING THAT CAN DIVE INTO THE OCEAN!
DON'T BE STUPID! THIS THING CAN DO THAT TOO!
WOW! IT CAN?!
OH, SHOOT !!
I FORGOT THE BACKPACK THAT HAS THE TWO DRAGON BALLS IN IT!!
NEVER FEAR! MY INVINCIBLE OLD MASTER WILL WATCH THEM FOR YOU!
I GUESS SO... JUST DON'T LET ME FORGET THEM AGAIN WHEN WE'RE DONE...
82
AHA !!
HYUUUUN
RED RIBBON
51

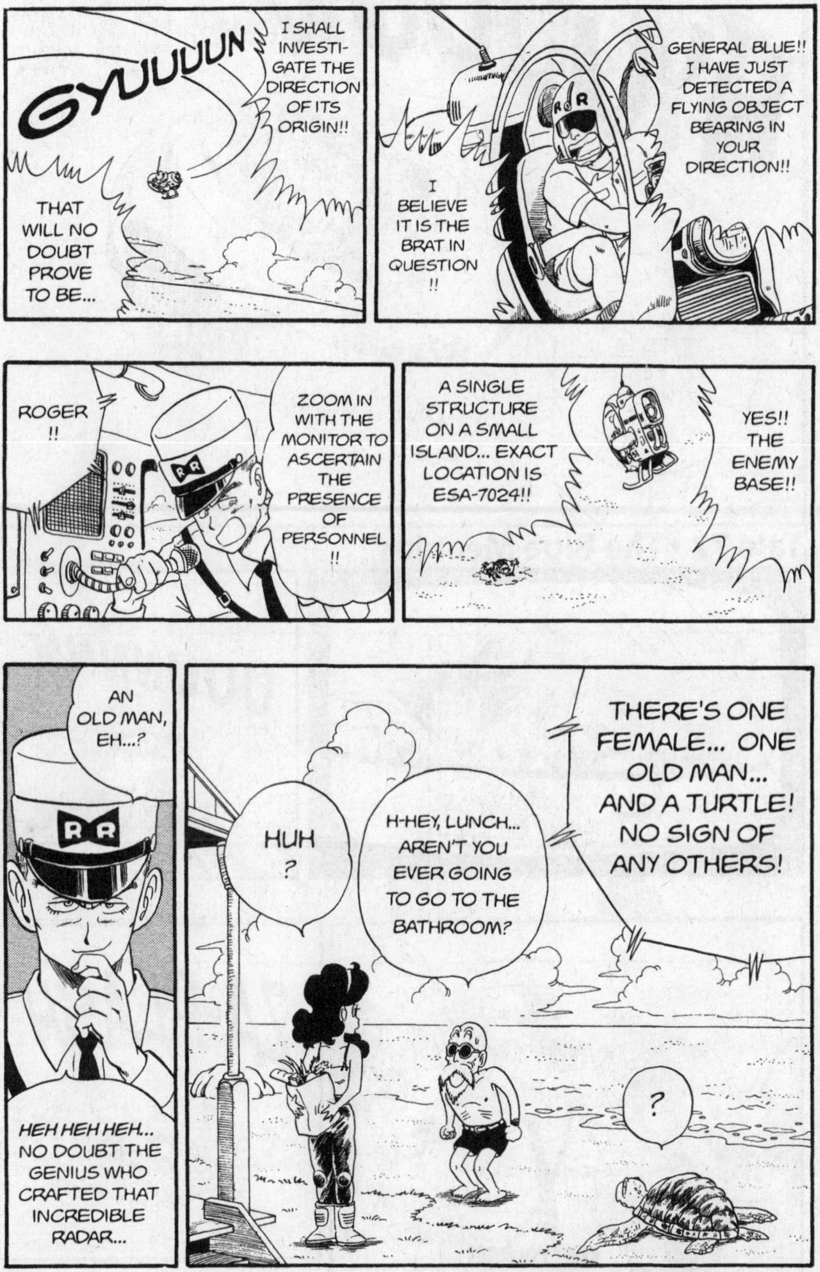
GENERAL BLUE!! I HAVE JUST DETECTED A FLYING OBJECT BEARING IN YOUR DIRECTION!!
I BELIEVE IT IS THE BRAT IN QUESTION!!
I SHALL INVESTIGATE THE DIRECTION OF ITS ORIGIN!!
GYUUUUN
THAT WILL NO DOUBT PROVE TO BE...
YES!! THE ENEMY BASE!!
A SINGLE STRUCTURE ON A SMALL ISLAND... EXACT LOCATION IS ESA-7024!!
ZOOM IN WITH THE MONITOR TO ASCERTAIN THE PRESENCE OF PERSONNEL!!
ROGER!!
THERE'S ONE FEMALE... ONE OLD MAN... AND A TURTLE! NO SIGN OF ANY OTHERS!
H-HEY, LUNCH... AREN'T YOU EVER GOING TO GO TO THE BATHROOM?
HUH?
?
AN OLD MAN, EH...?
HEH HEH HEH... NO DOUBT THE GENIUS WHO CRAFTED THAT INCREDIBLE RADAR...

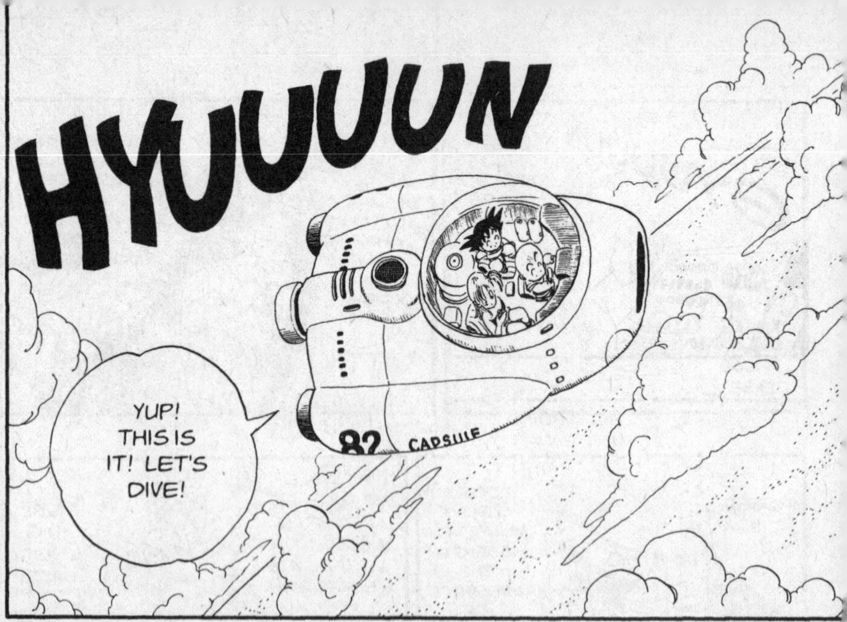
HYUUUUN
YUP! THIS IS IT! LET'S DIVE!
82 CAPSULE

Tale 72 • The Blue Meanies

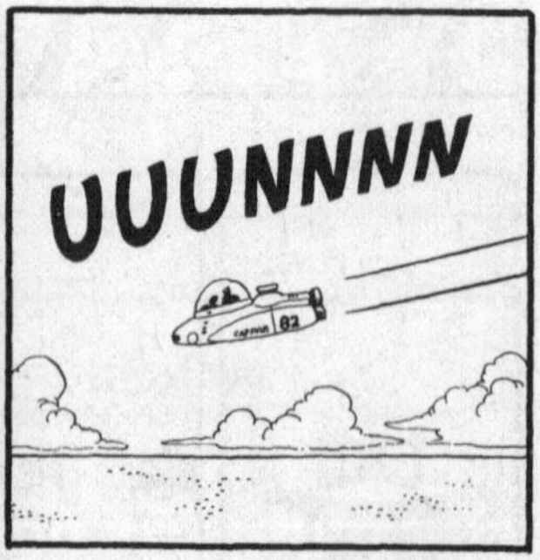
UUUNNNN

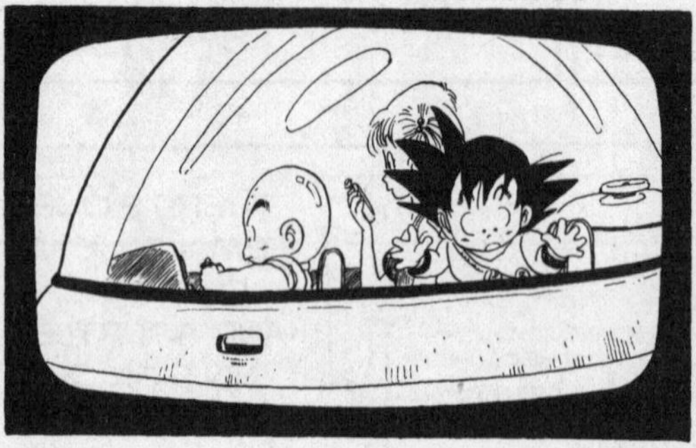

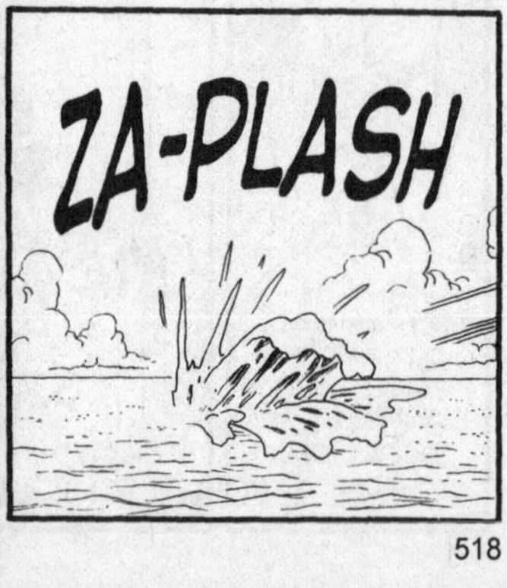
ZA-PLASH

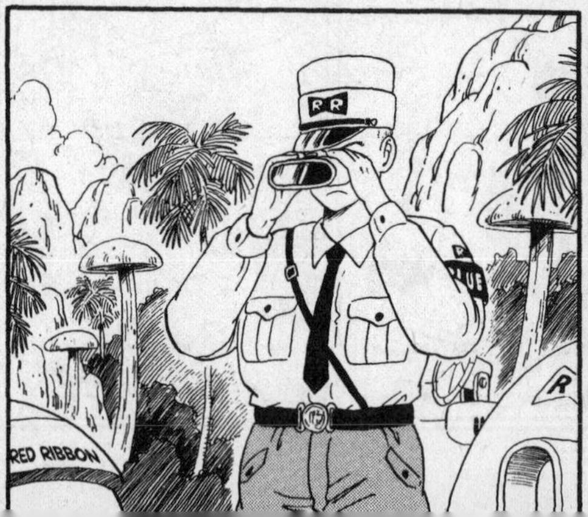
RED RIBBON

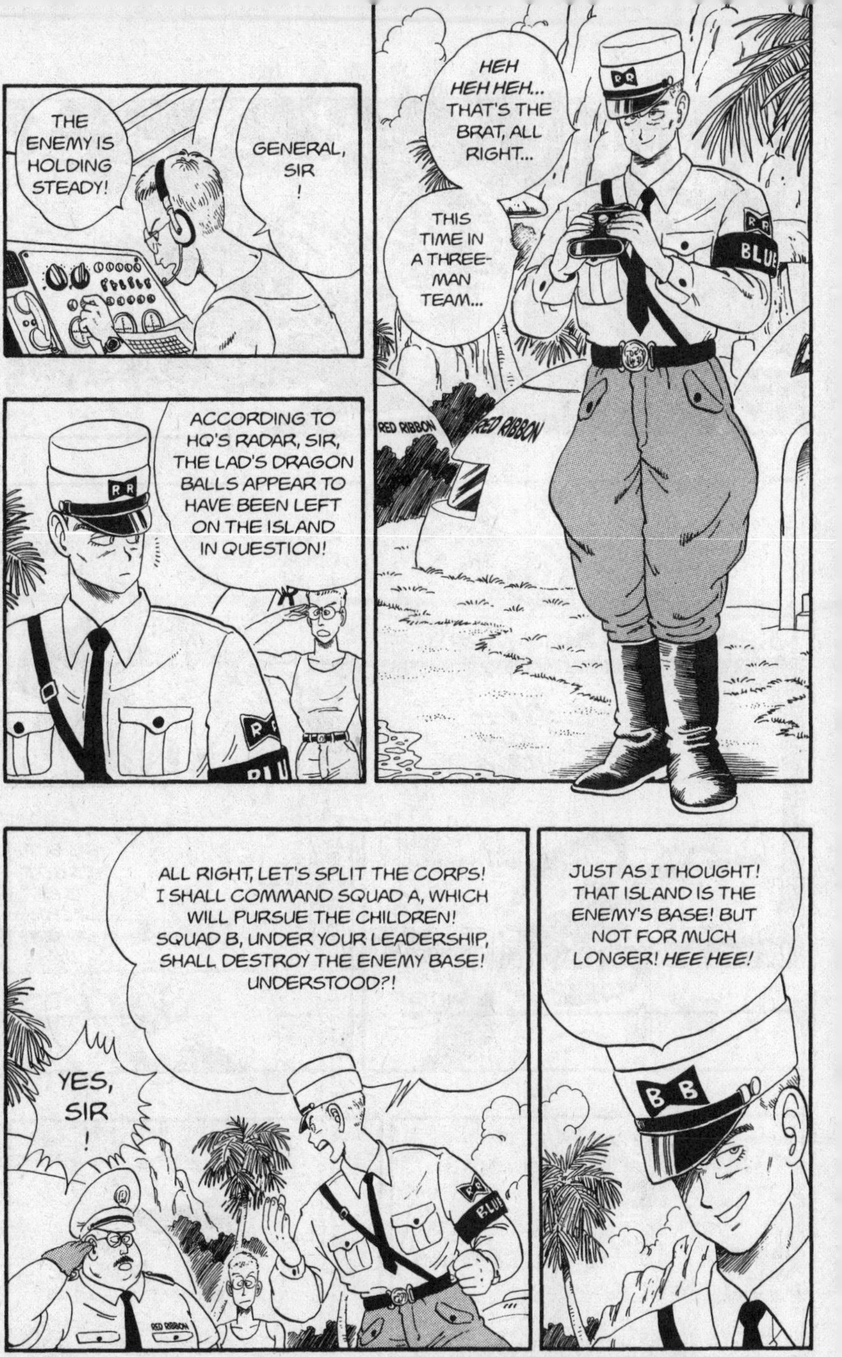
HEH HEH HEH... THAT'S THE BRAT, ALL RIGHT...
THIS TIME IN A THREE-MAN TEAM...
RED RIBBON
RED RIBBON
GENERAL, SIR !
THE ENEMY IS HOLDING STEADY!
ACCORDING TO HQ'S RADAR, SIR, THE LAD'S DRAGON BALLS APPEAR TO HAVE BEEN LEFT ON THE ISLAND IN QUESTION!
JUST AS I THOUGHT! THAT ISLAND IS THE ENEMY'S BASE! BUT NOT FOR MUCH LONGER! *HEE HEE!*
ALL RIGHT, LET'S SPLIT THE CORPS! I SHALL COMMAND SQUAD A, WHICH WILL PURSUE THE CHILDREN! SQUAD B, UNDER YOUR LEADERSHIP, SHALL DESTROY THE ENEMY BASE! UNDERSTOOD?!
YES, SIR !
RED RIBBON

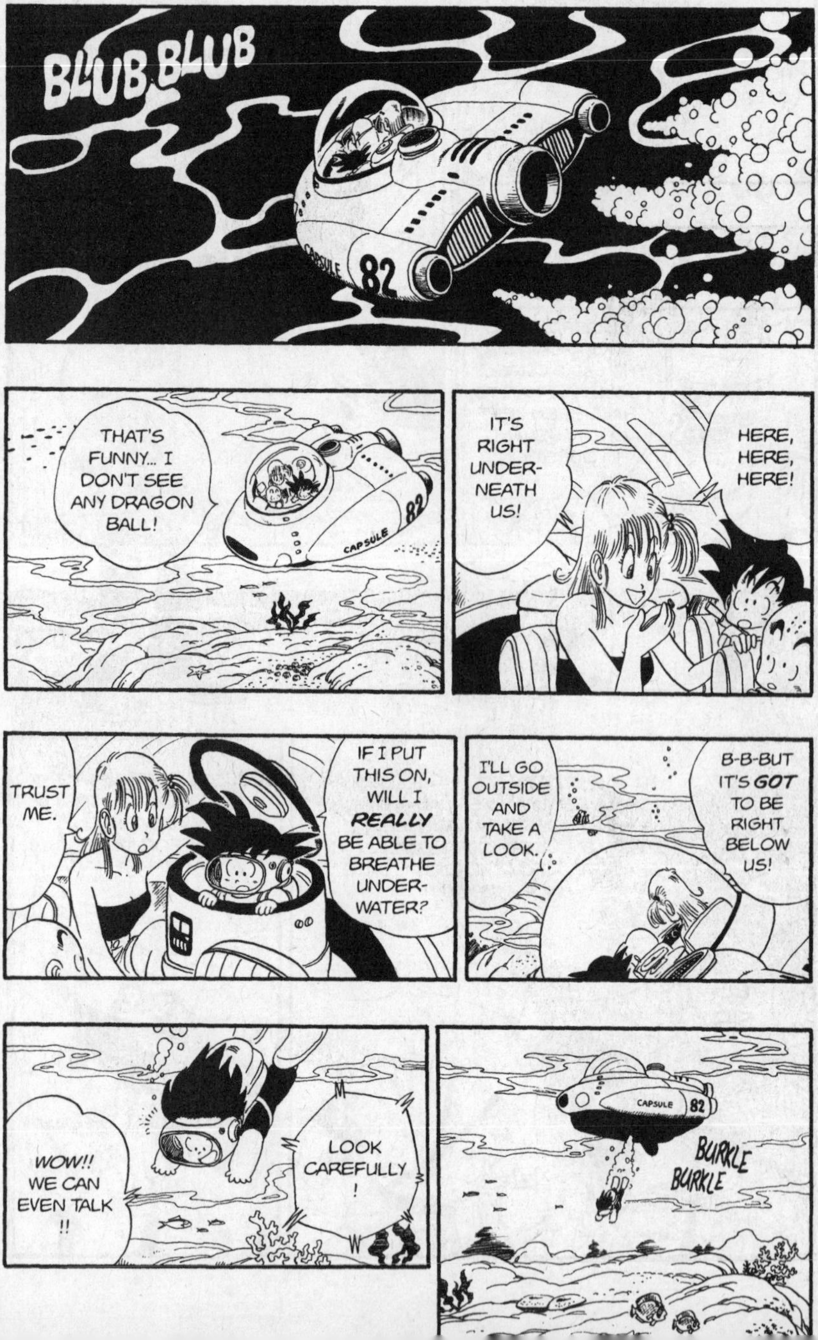
BLUB BLUB
HERE, HERE, HERE!
IT'S RIGHT UNDERNEATH US!
THAT'S FUNNY... I DON'T SEE ANY DRAGON BALL!
B-B-BUT IT'S *GOT* TO BE RIGHT BELOW US!
I'LL GO OUTSIDE AND TAKE A LOOK.
IF I PUT THIS ON, WILL I *REALLY* BE ABLE TO BREATHE UNDERWATER?
TRUST ME.
BURKLE BURKLE
LOOK CAREFULLY!
WOW!! WE CAN EVEN TALK!!

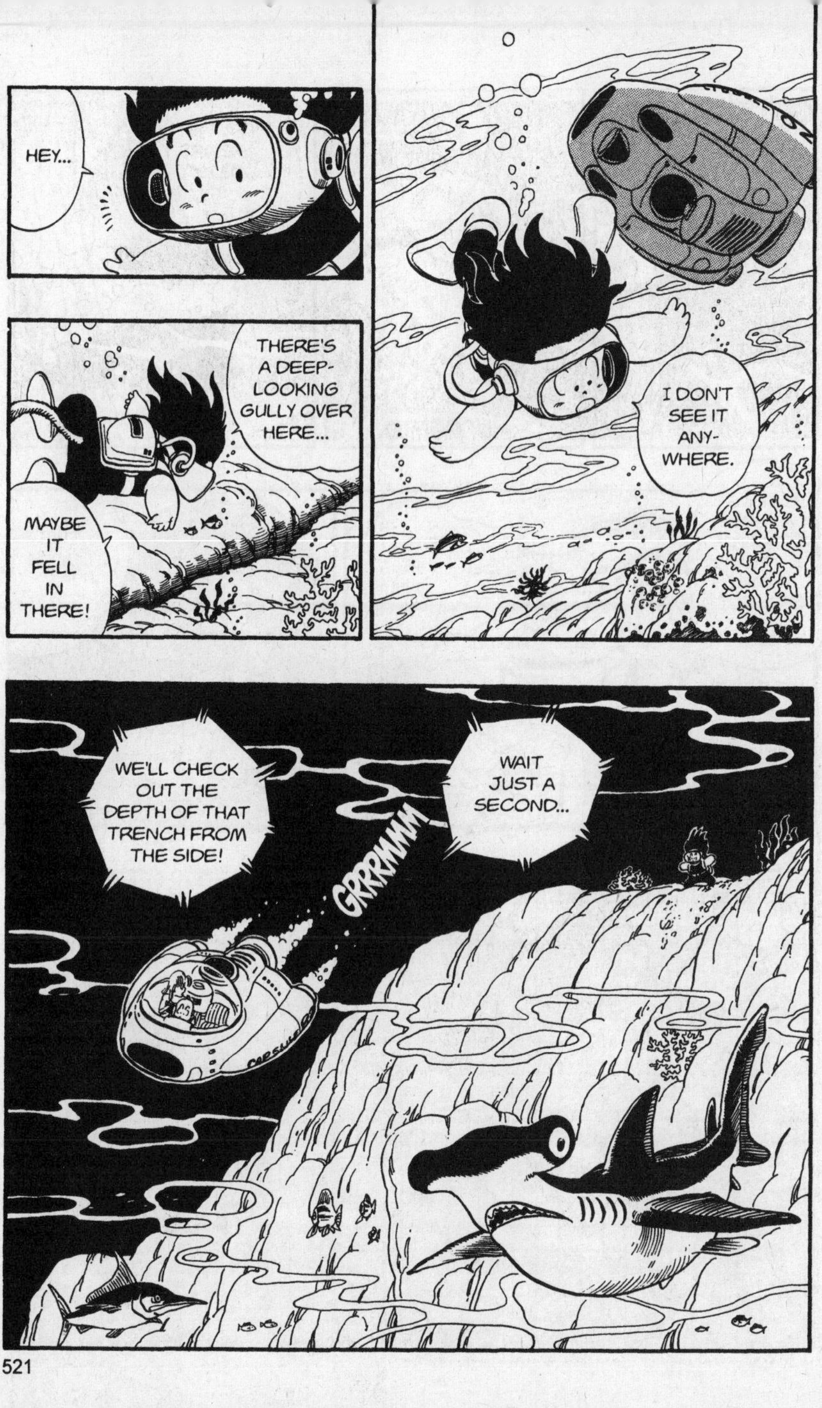
I DON'T SEE IT ANYWHERE.
HEY...
THERE'S A DEEP-LOOKING GULLY OVER HERE...
MAYBE IT FELL IN THERE!
WAIT JUST A SECOND...
WE'LL CHECK OUT THE DEPTH OF THAT TRENCH FROM THE SIDE!
GRRRMMM

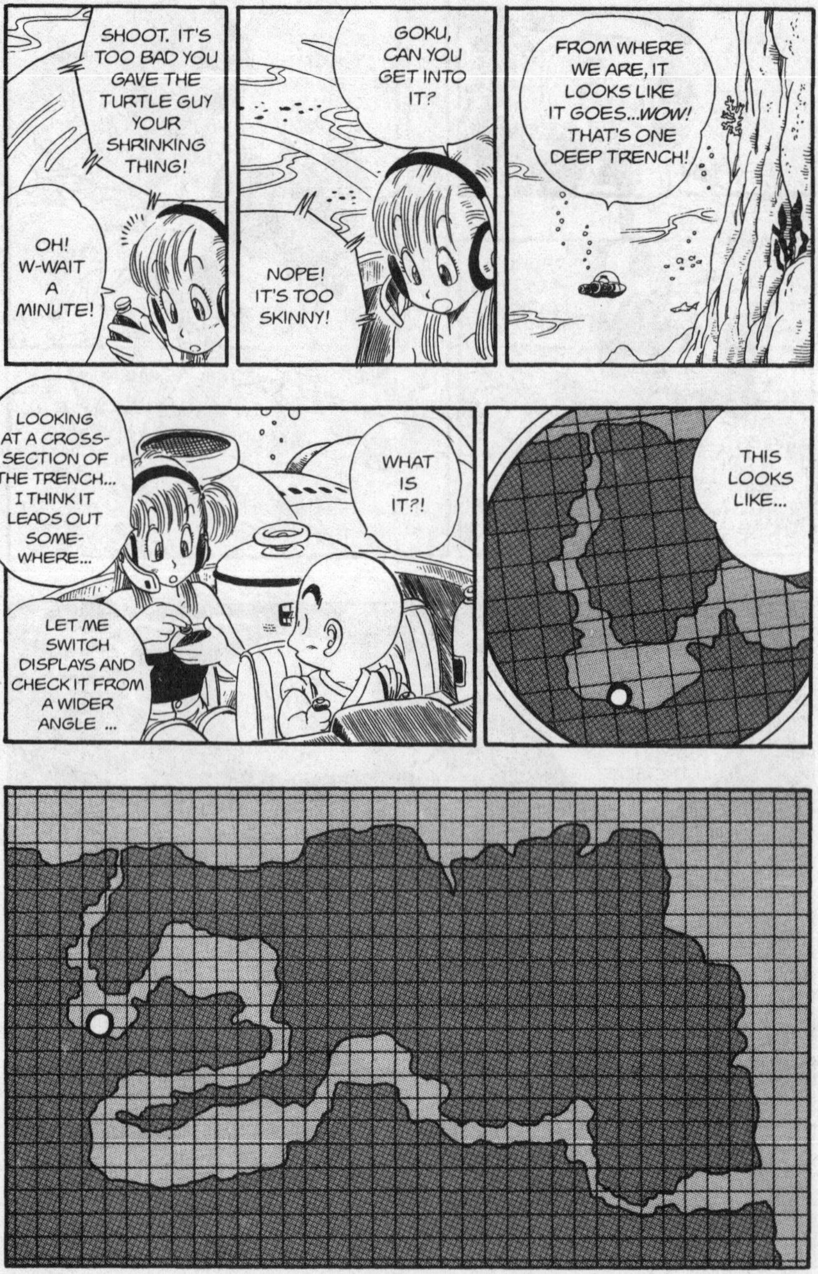
FROM WHERE WE ARE, IT LOOKS LIKE IT GOES...WOW! THAT'S ONE DEEP TRENCH!
GOKU, CAN YOU GET INTO IT?
NOPE! IT'S TOO SKINNY!
SHOOT. IT'S TOO BAD YOU GAVE THE TURTLE GUY YOUR SHRINKING THING!
OH! W-WAIT A MINUTE!
THIS LOOKS LIKE...
WHAT IS IT?!
LOOKING AT A CROSS-SECTION OF THE TRENCH... I THINK IT LEADS OUT SOMEWHERE...
LET ME SWITCH DISPLAYS AND CHECK IT FROM A WIDER ANGLE ...

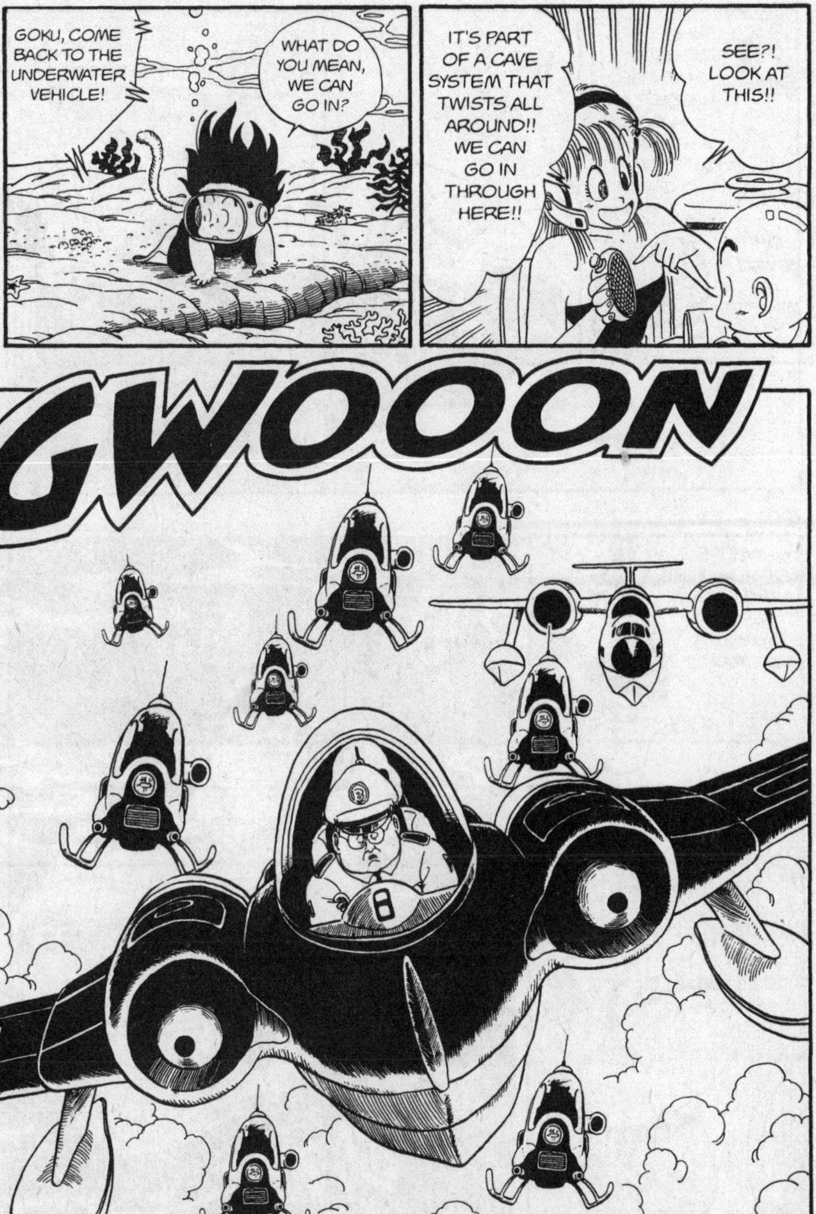
GOKU, COME BACK TO THE UNDERWATER VEHICLE!
WHAT DO YOU MEAN, WE CAN GO IN?
IT'S PART OF A CAVE SYSTEM THAT TWISTS ALL AROUND!! WE CAN GO IN THROUGH HERE!!
SEE?! LOOK AT THIS!!
GWOOON

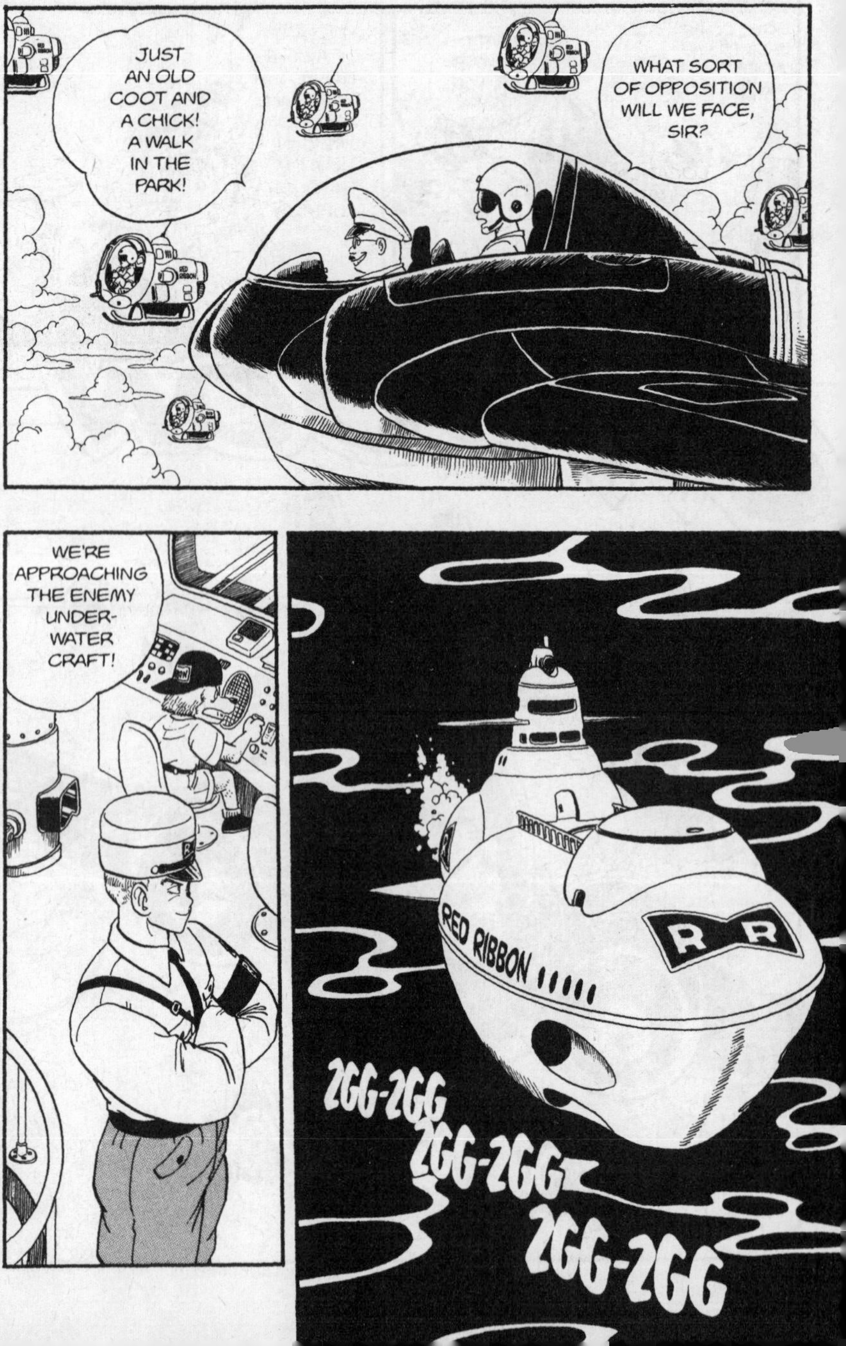
WHAT SORT OF OPPOSITION WILL WE FACE, SIR?
JUST AN OLD COOT AND A CHICK! A WALK IN THE PARK!
RED RIBBON
ZGG-ZGG
ZGG-ZGG
ZGG-ZGG
WE'RE APPROACHING THE ENEMY UNDER-WATER CRAFT!

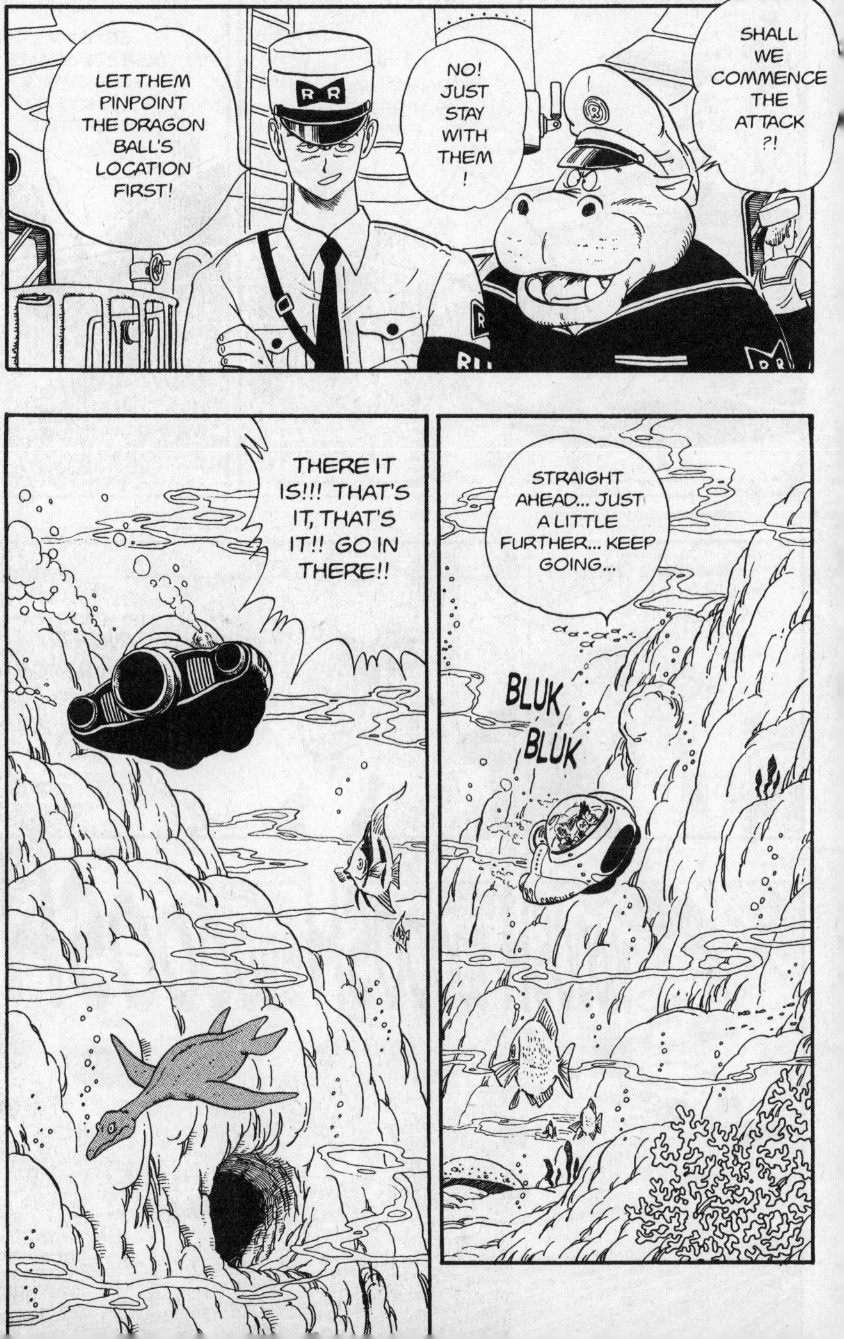
SHALL WE COMMENCE THE ATTACK ?!
NO! JUST STAY WITH THEM !
LET THEM PINPOINT THE DRAGON BALL'S LOCATION FIRST!
STRAIGHT AHEAD... JUST A LITTLE FURTHER... KEEP GOING...
BLUK BLUK
THERE IT IS!!! THAT'S IT, THAT'S IT!! GO IN THERE!!

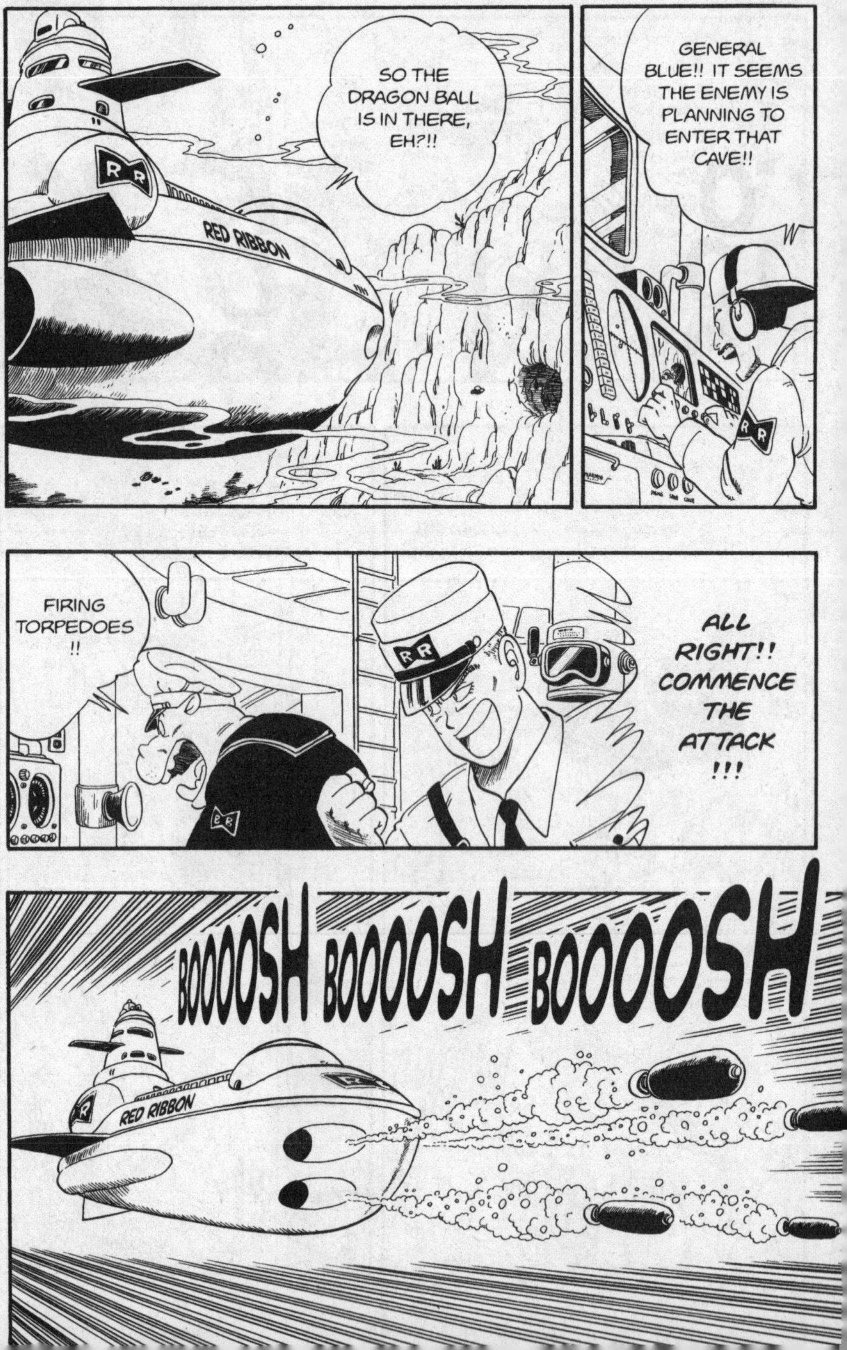
GENERAL BLUE!! IT SEEMS THE ENEMY IS PLANNING TO ENTER THAT CAVE!!
SO THE DRAGON BALL IS IN THERE, EH?!!
RED RIBBON
ALL RIGHT!! COMMENCE THE ATTACK!!!
FIRING TORPEDOES!!
BOOOSH BOOOOSH BOOOOSH
RED RIBBON

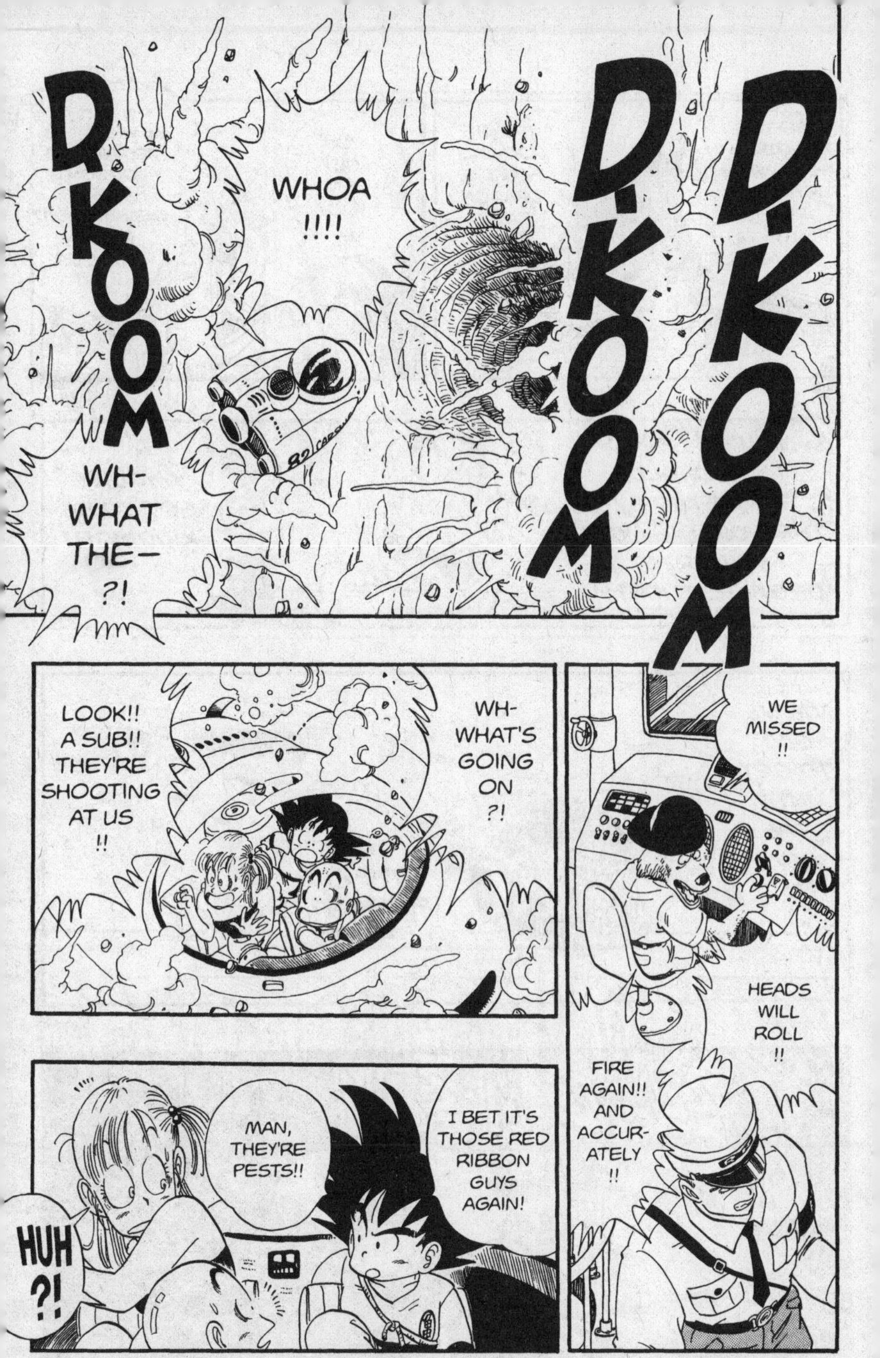
DKOOOM
DKOOM
WHOA!!!!
DKOOM
WH-WHAT THE—?!
WE MISSED!!
HEADS WILL ROLL!!
FIRE AGAIN!! AND ACCURATELY!!
WH-WHAT'S GOING ON?!
LOOK!! A SUB!! THEY'RE SHOOTING AT US!!
I BET IT'S THOSE RED RIBBON GUYS AGAIN!
MAN, THEY'RE PESTS!!
HUH?!

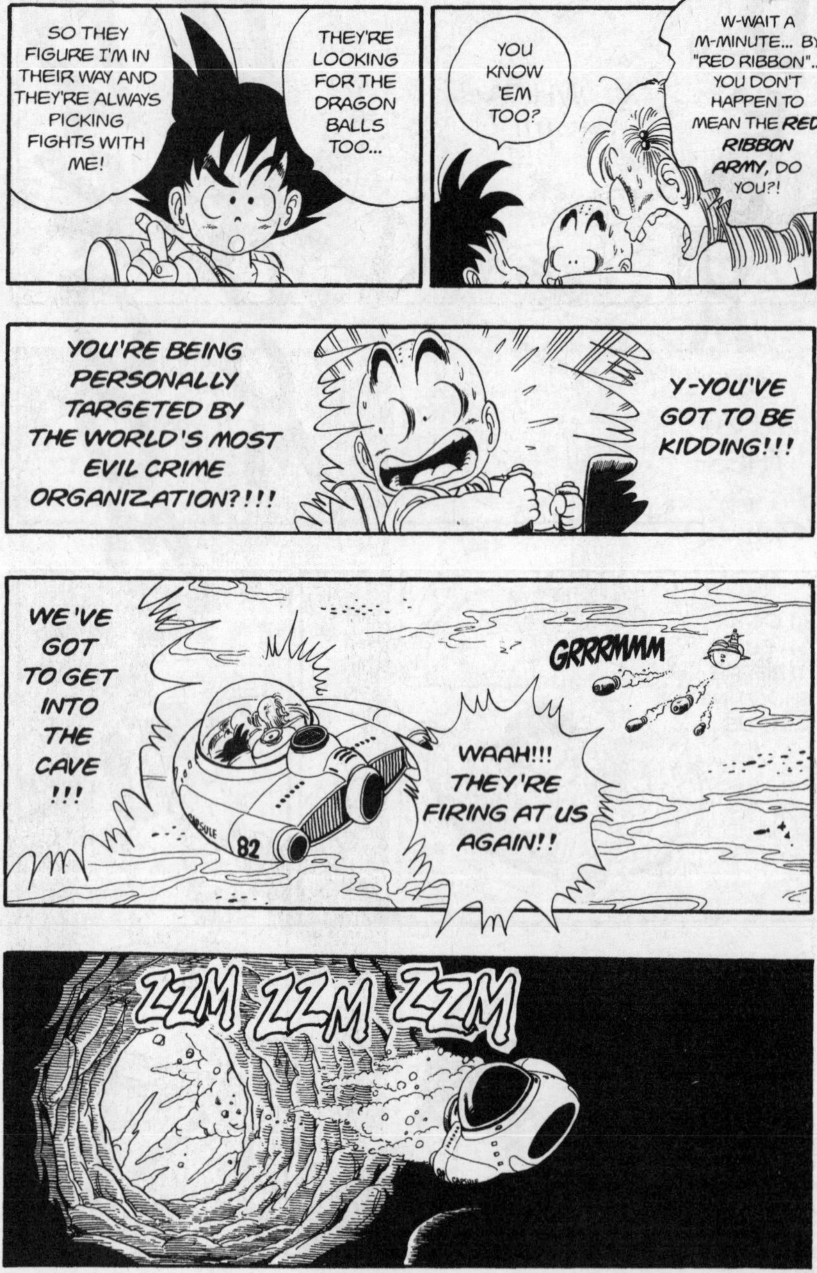
W-WAIT A M-MINUTE... BY "RED RIBBON"... YOU DON'T HAPPEN TO MEAN THE **RED RIBBON ARMY**, DO YOU?!
YOU KNOW 'EM TOO?
THEY'RE LOOKING FOR THE DRAGON BALLS TOO...
SO THEY FIGURE I'M IN THEIR WAY AND THEY'RE ALWAYS PICKING FIGHTS WITH ME!
Y-YOU'VE GOT TO BE KIDDING!!!
YOU'RE BEING PERSONALLY TARGETED BY THE WORLD'S MOST EVIL CRIME ORGANIZATION?!!!
GRRRMMM
WAAH!!! THEY'RE FIRING AT US AGAIN!!
WE'VE GOT TO GET INTO THE CAVE !!!
ZZM ZZM ZZM

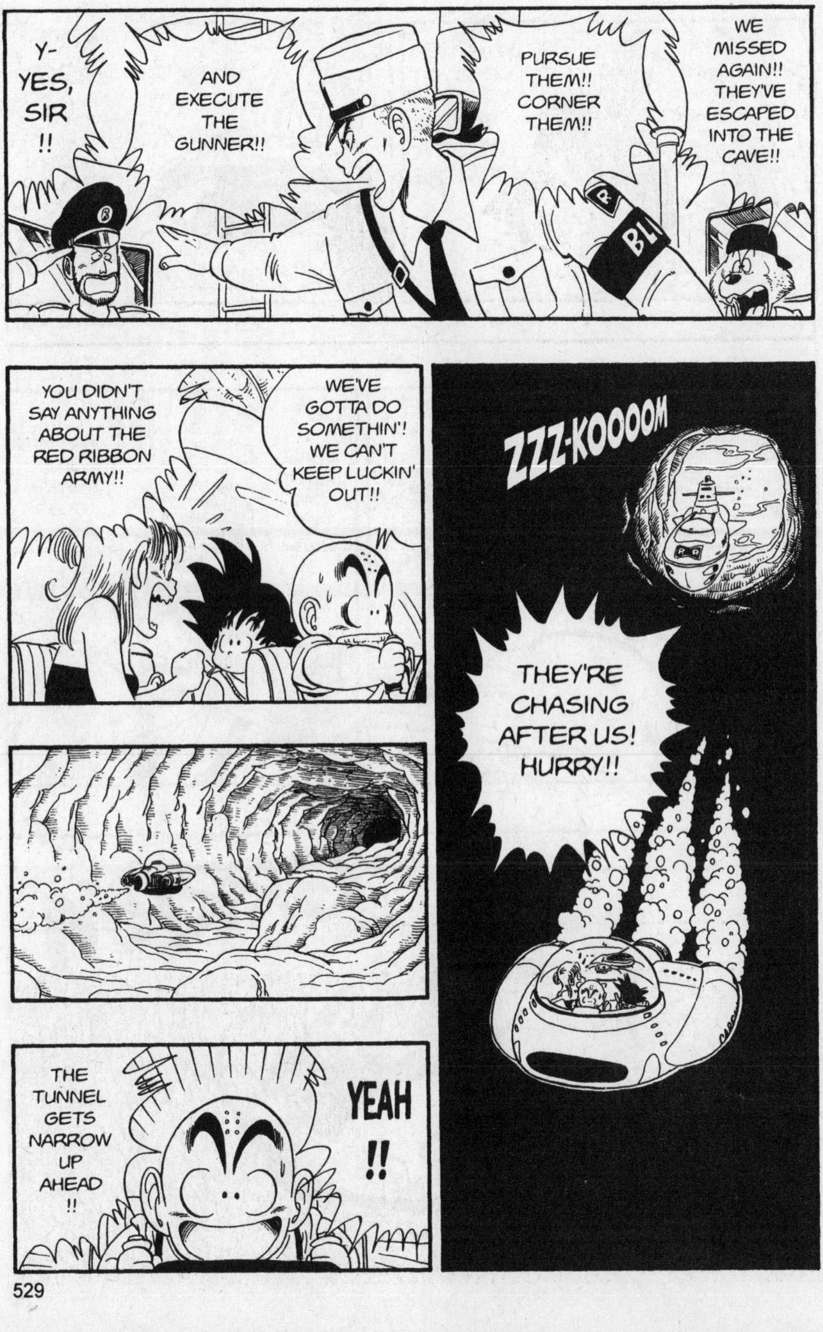
WE MISSED AGAIN!! THEY'VE ESCAPED INTO THE CAVE!!
PURSUE THEM!! CORNER THEM!!
AND EXECUTE THE GUNNER!!
Y-YES, SIR!!
ZZZ-KOOOOM
THEY'RE CHASING AFTER US! HURRY!!
WE'VE GOTTA DO SOMETHIN'! WE CAN'T KEEP LUCKIN' OUT!!
YOU DIDN'T SAY ANYTHING ABOUT THE RED RIBBON ARMY!!
YEAH!!
THE TUNNEL GETS NARROW UP AHEAD!!

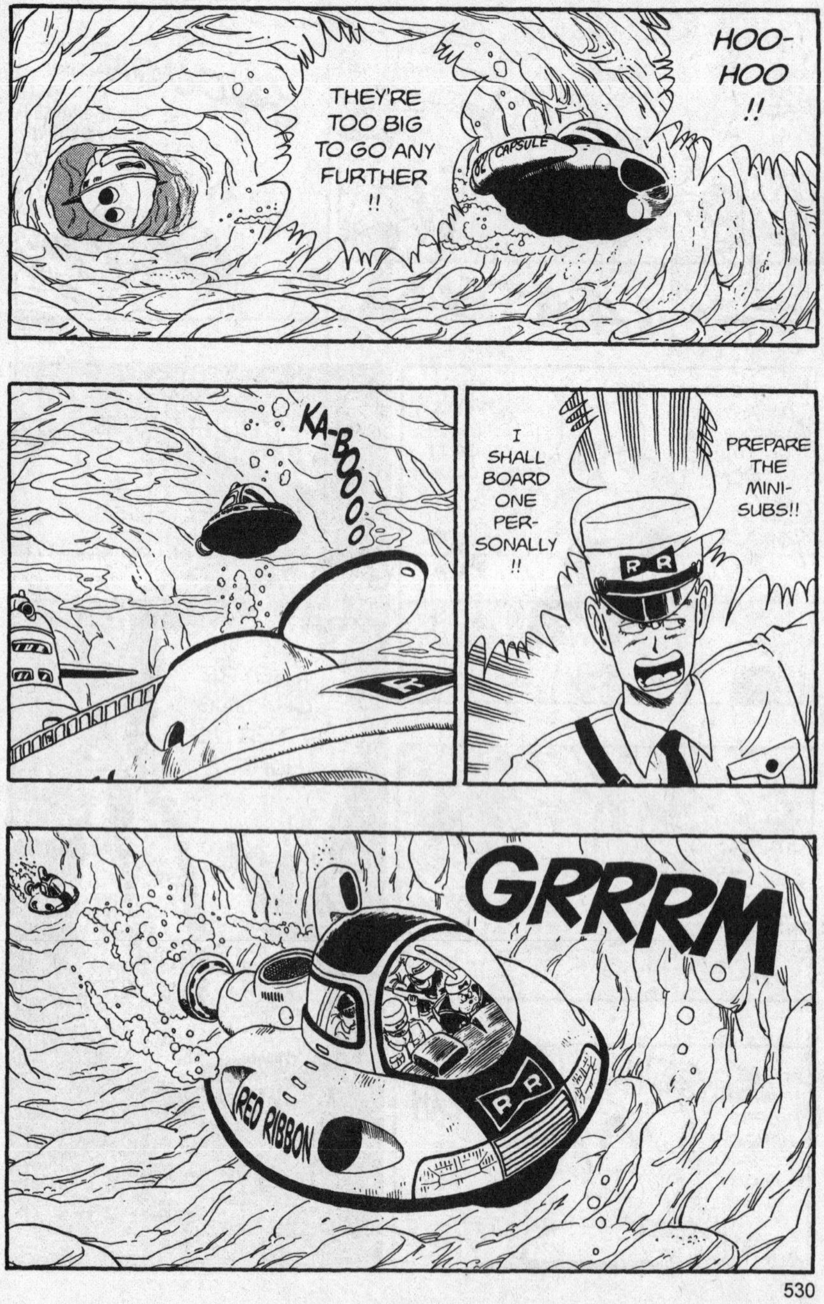
HOO-HOO !!
CAPSULE
THEY'RE TOO BIG TO GO ANY FURTHER !!
PREPARE THE MINI-SUBS!!
I SHALL BOARD ONE PERSONALLY !!
KA-BOOOOO
GRRRM
RED RIBBON

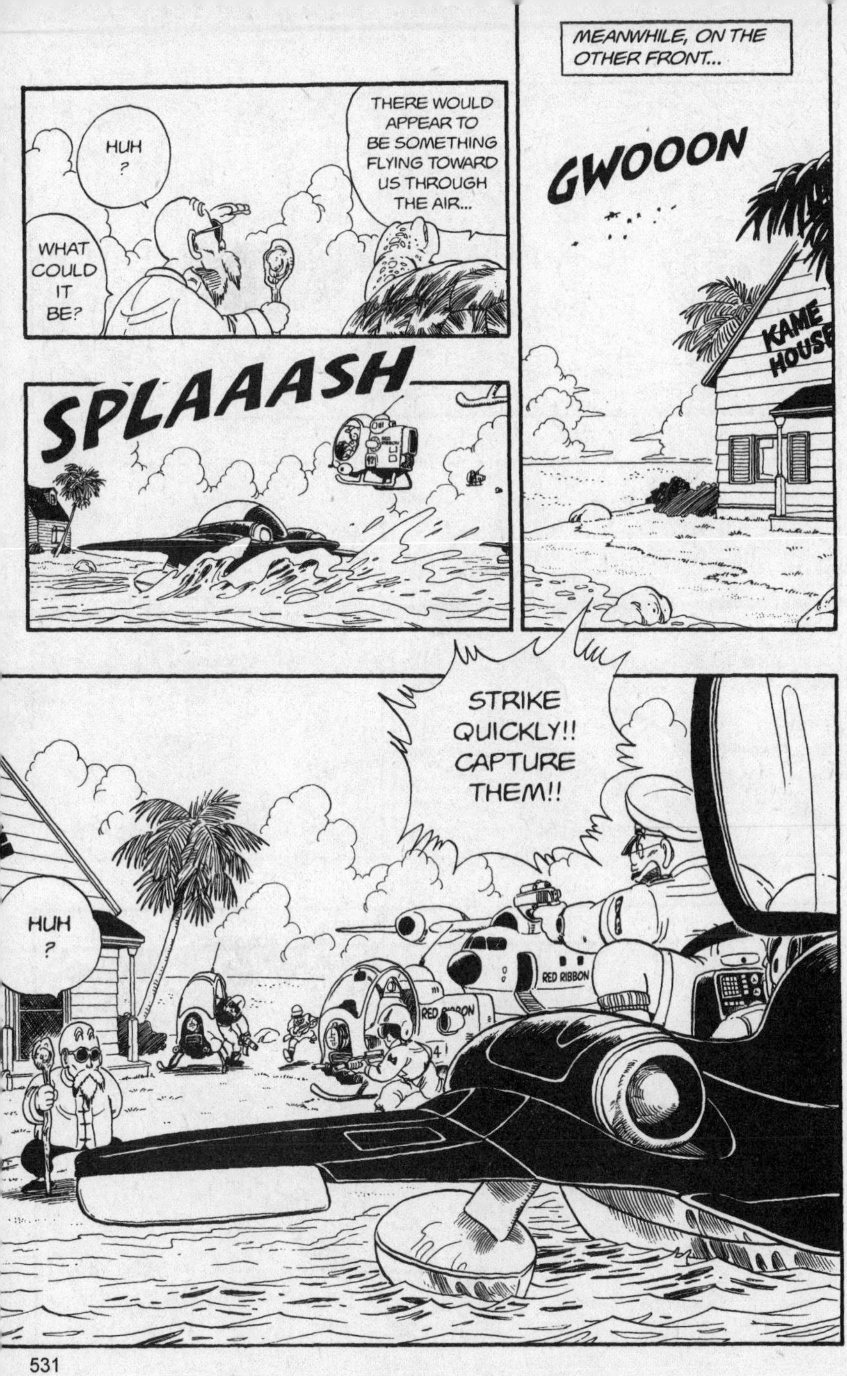
MEANWHILE, ON THE OTHER FRONT...
GWOOON
KAME HOUSE
THERE WOULD APPEAR TO BE SOMETHING FLYING TOWARD US THROUGH THE AIR...
HUH ?
WHAT COULD IT BE?
SPLAAASH
STRIKE QUICKLY!! CAPTURE THEM!!
RED RIBBON
HUH ?

TITLE PAGE
GALLERY

Following are the title pages for the individual chapters. Most of them are as they appeared during their original serialization in Japan.

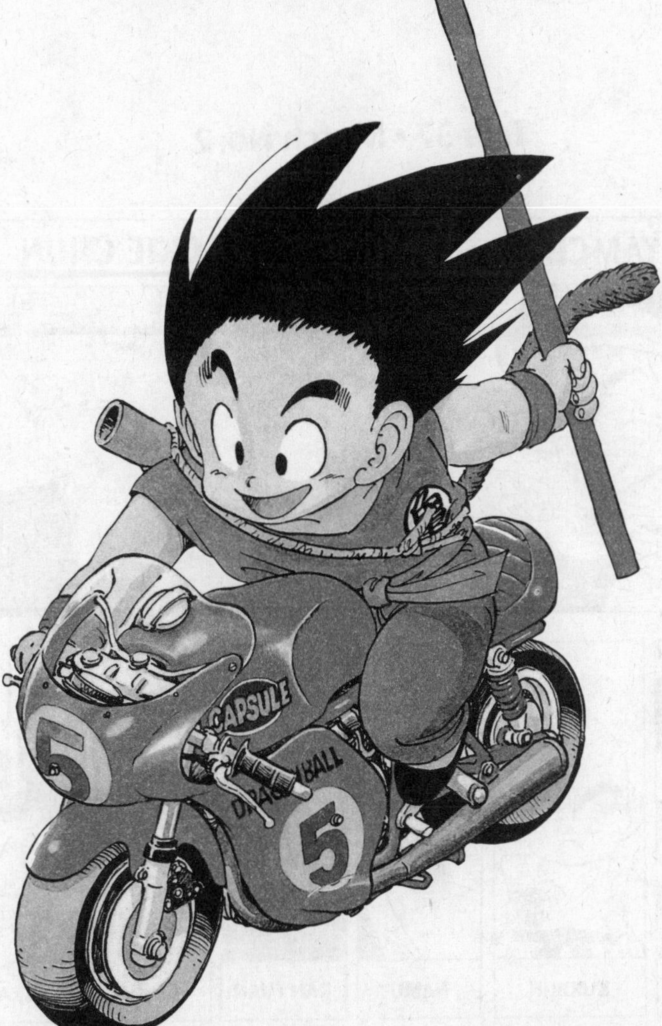
CAPSULE

ドラゴンボール

DRAGON BALL

Tale 37 • Match No. 2

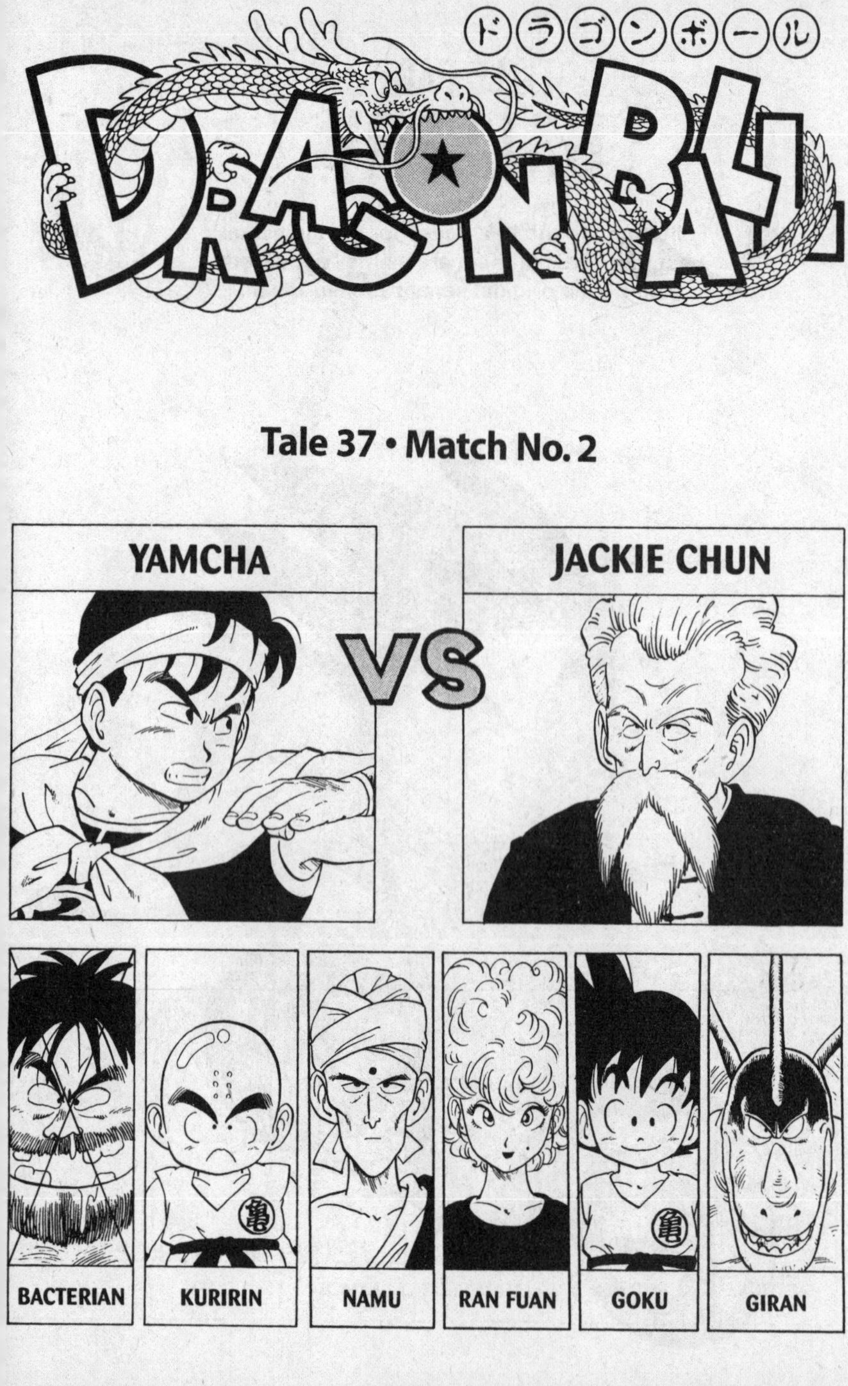
JACKIE CHUN
VS
YAMCHA
GIRAN
GOKU
RAN FUAN
NAMU
KURIRIN
BACTERIAN

ドラゴンボール

DRAGON BALL

Tale 38 · Water and Cheesecake

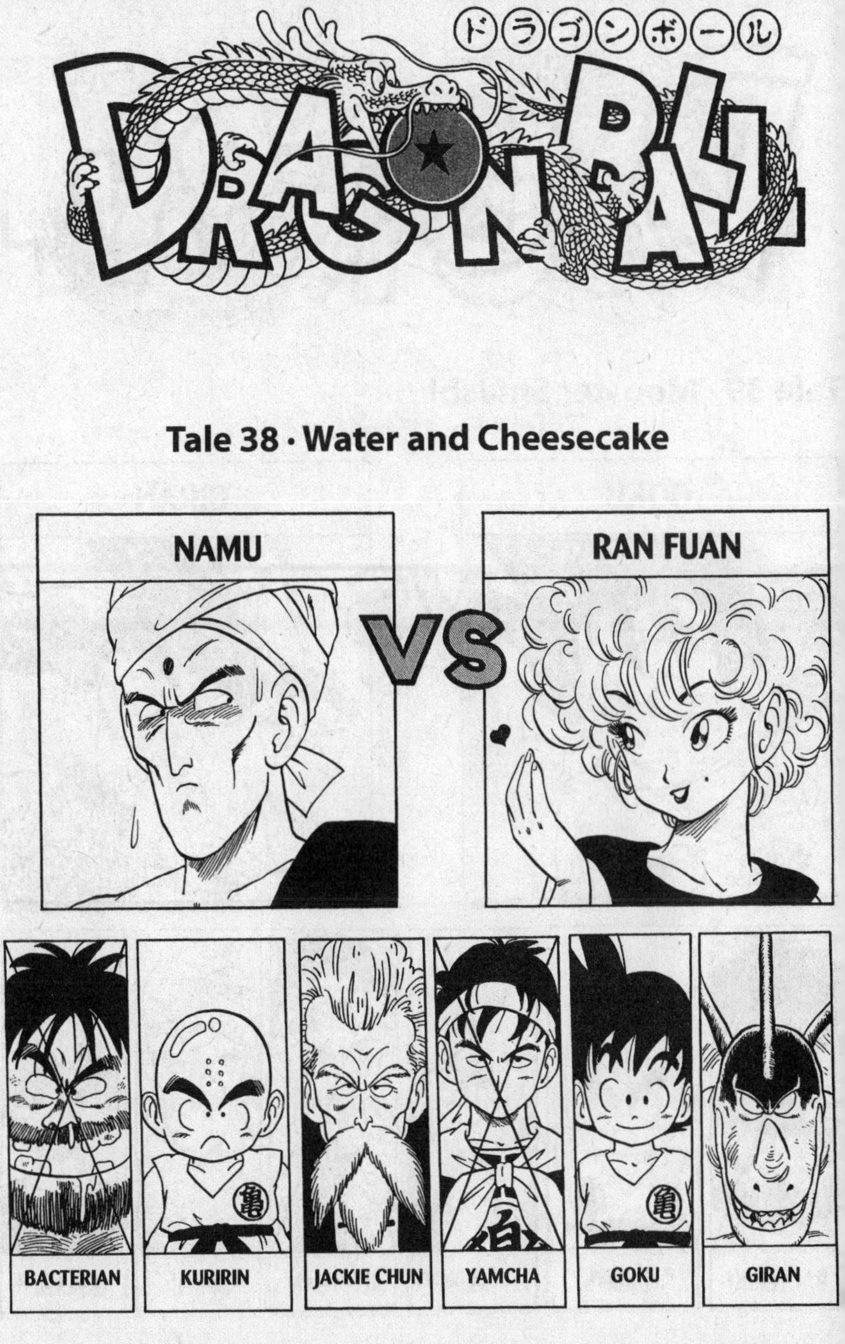

RAN FUAN
VS
NAMU
GIRAN
GOKU
YAMCHA
JACKIE CHUN
KURIRIN
BACTERIAN

ドラゴンボール

DRAGON BALL

Tale 39 · Monster Smash!

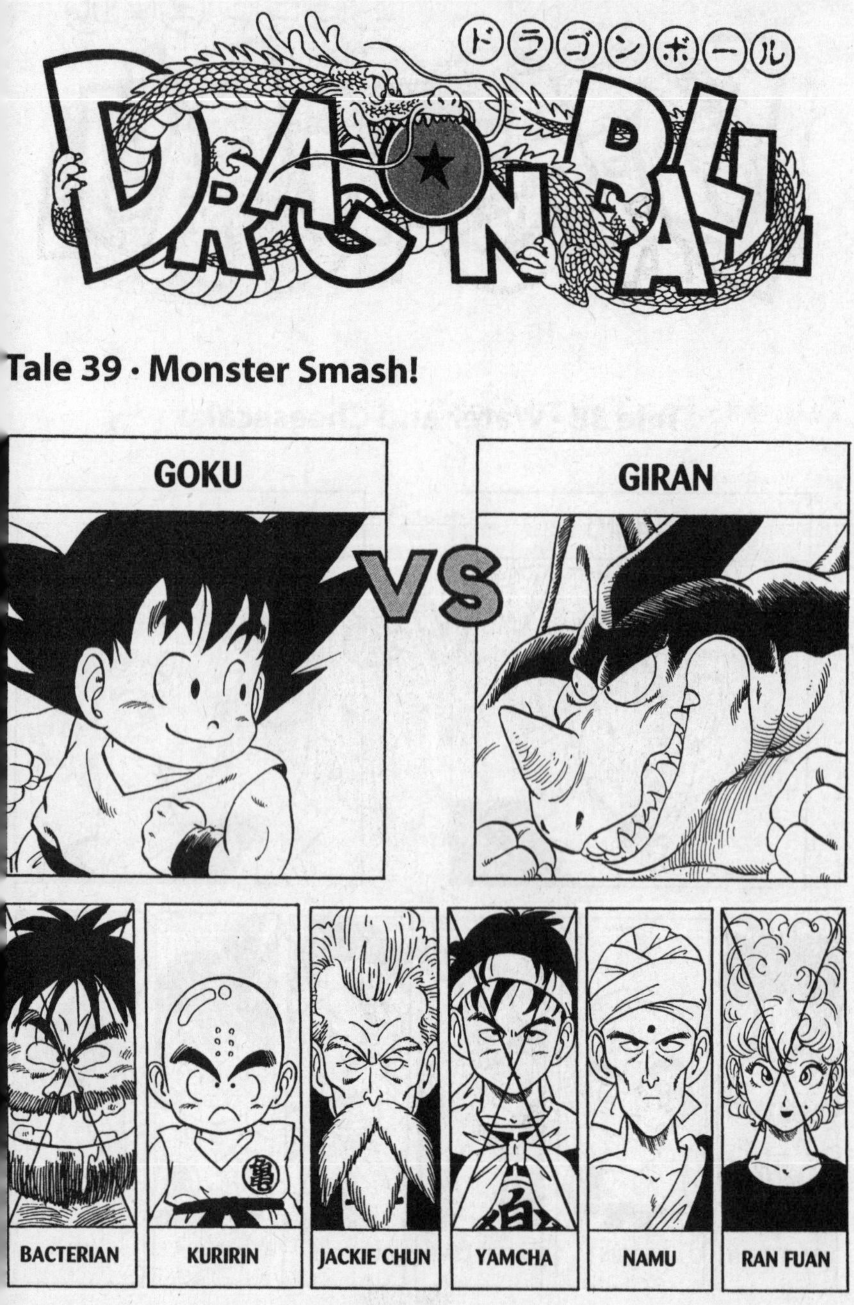
GIRAN
VS
GOKU
RAN FUAN
NAMU
YAMCHA
JACKIE CHUN
KURIRIN
BACTERIAN

ドラゴンボール

DRAGON BALL

Tale 40 · The Tail of Goku

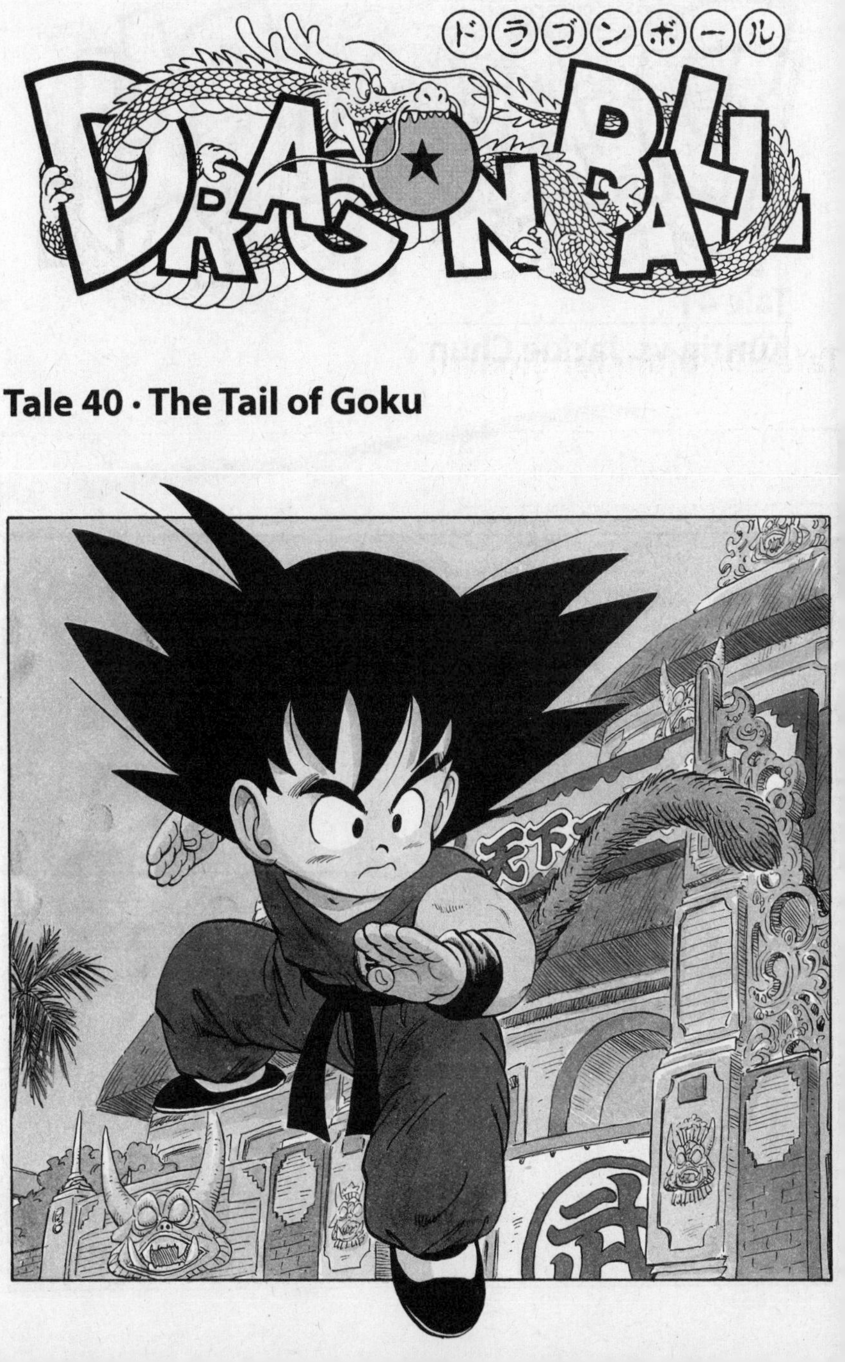
天下
武

ドラゴンボール

DRAGON BALL

Tale 41

Kuririn vs. Jackie Chun

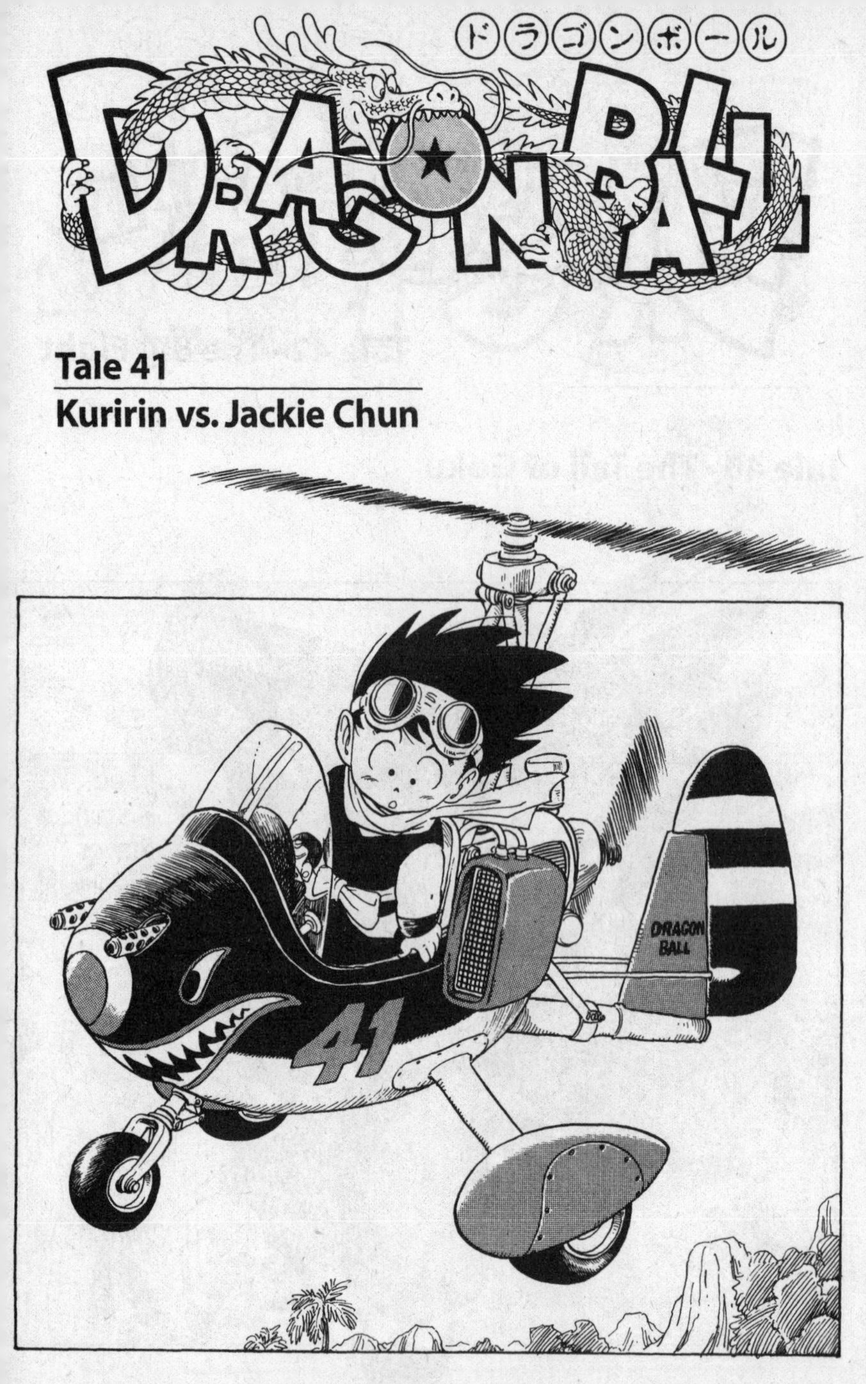
DRAGON BALL
41

ドラゴンボール

DRAGON BALL

Tale 42 · The Big Fight

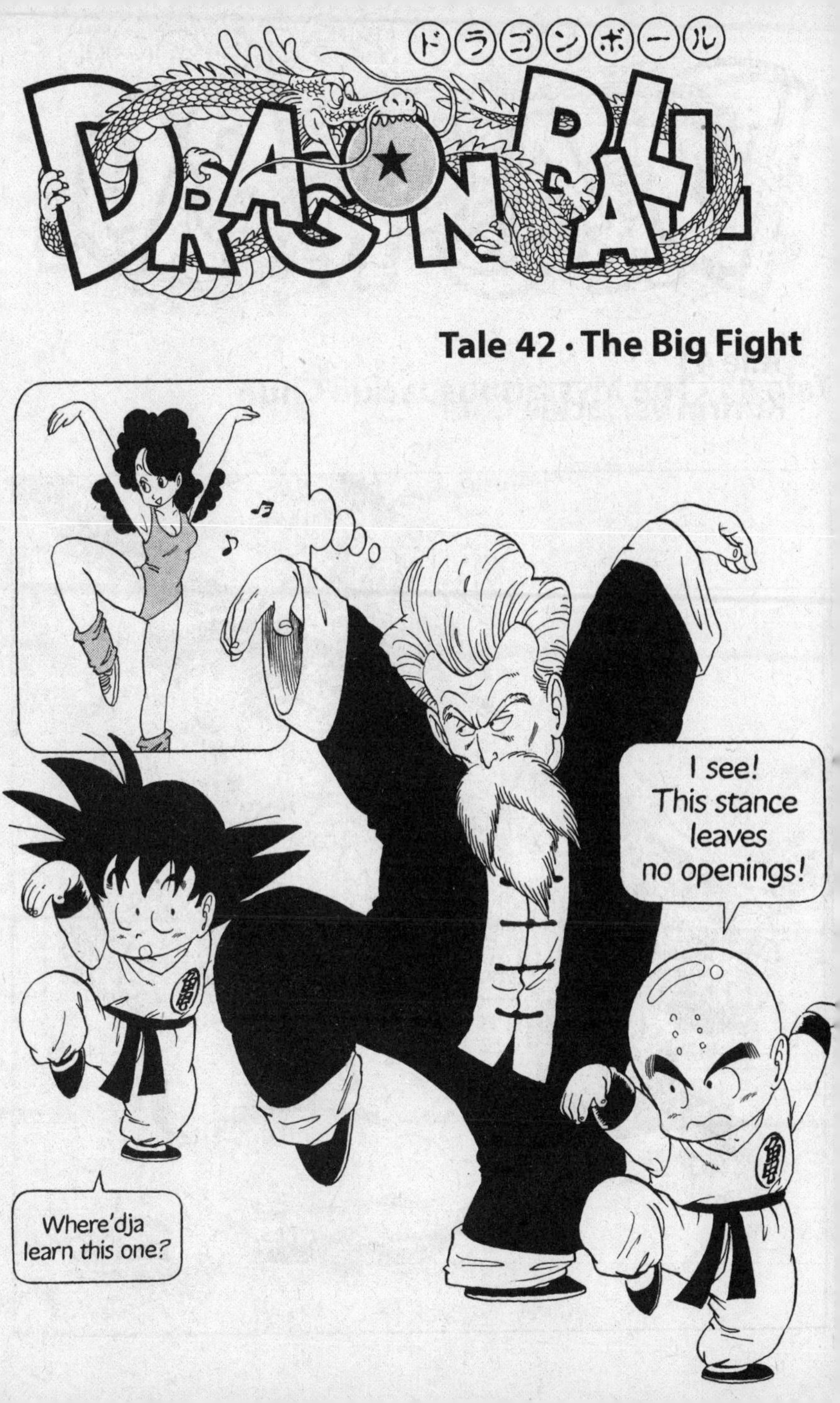
I see! This stance leaves no openings!
Where'dja learn this one?

ドラゴンボール

DRAGON BALL

Tale 43 · The Mysterious Jackie Chun

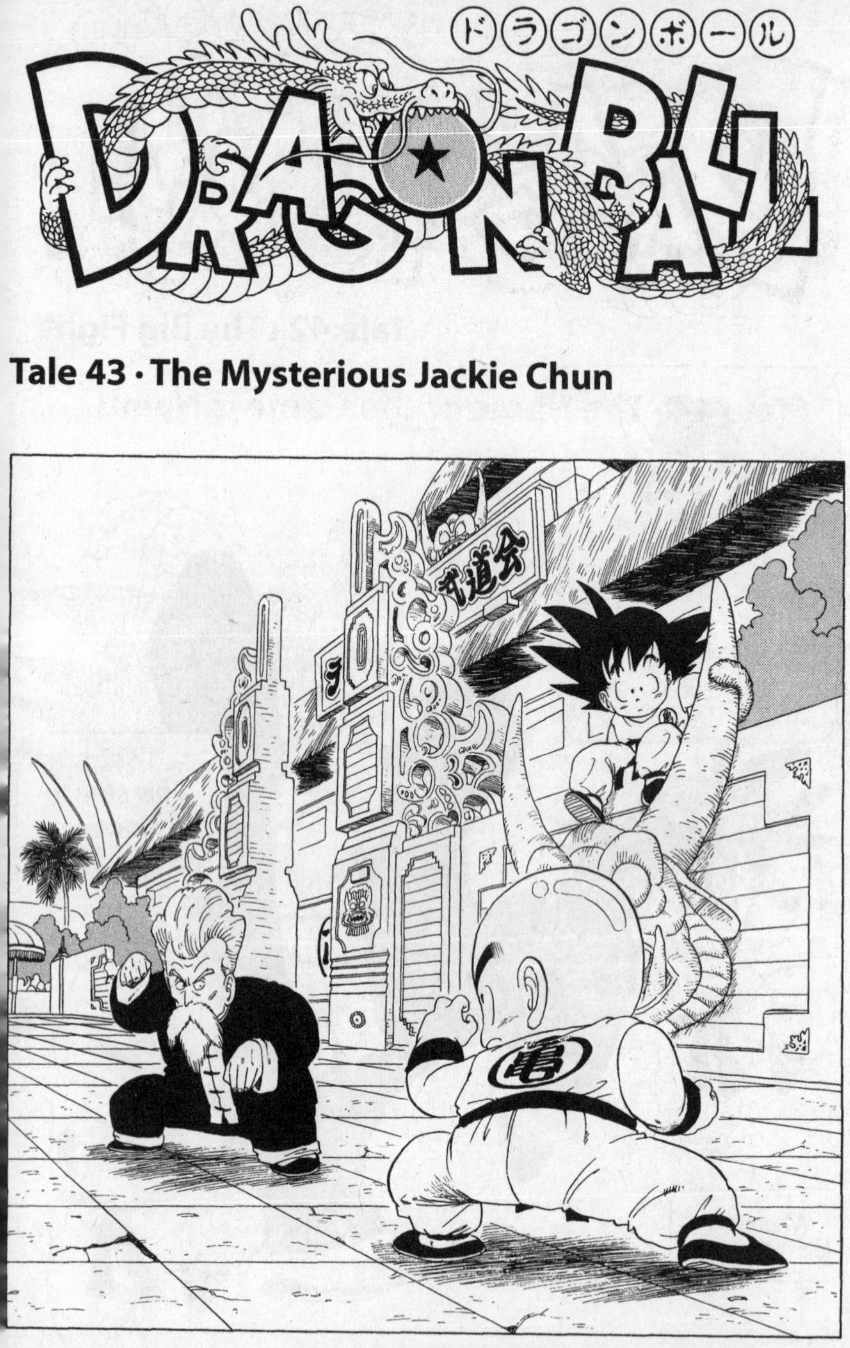
武道会
亀

ドラゴンボール

DRAGON BALL

Tale 44 · The Name of the Game Is Namu

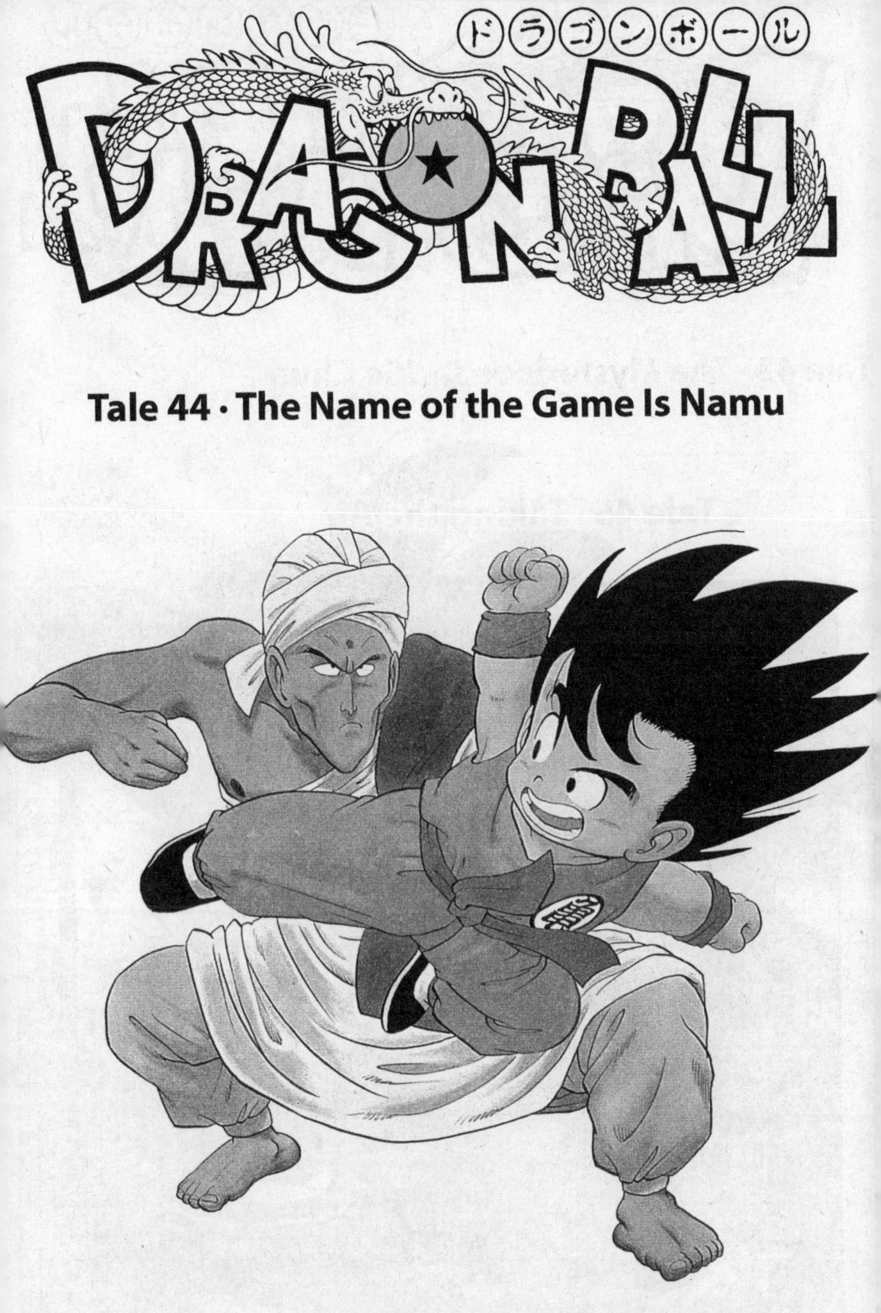

ドラゴンボール

DRAGON BALL

Tale 45 · Taking the Air

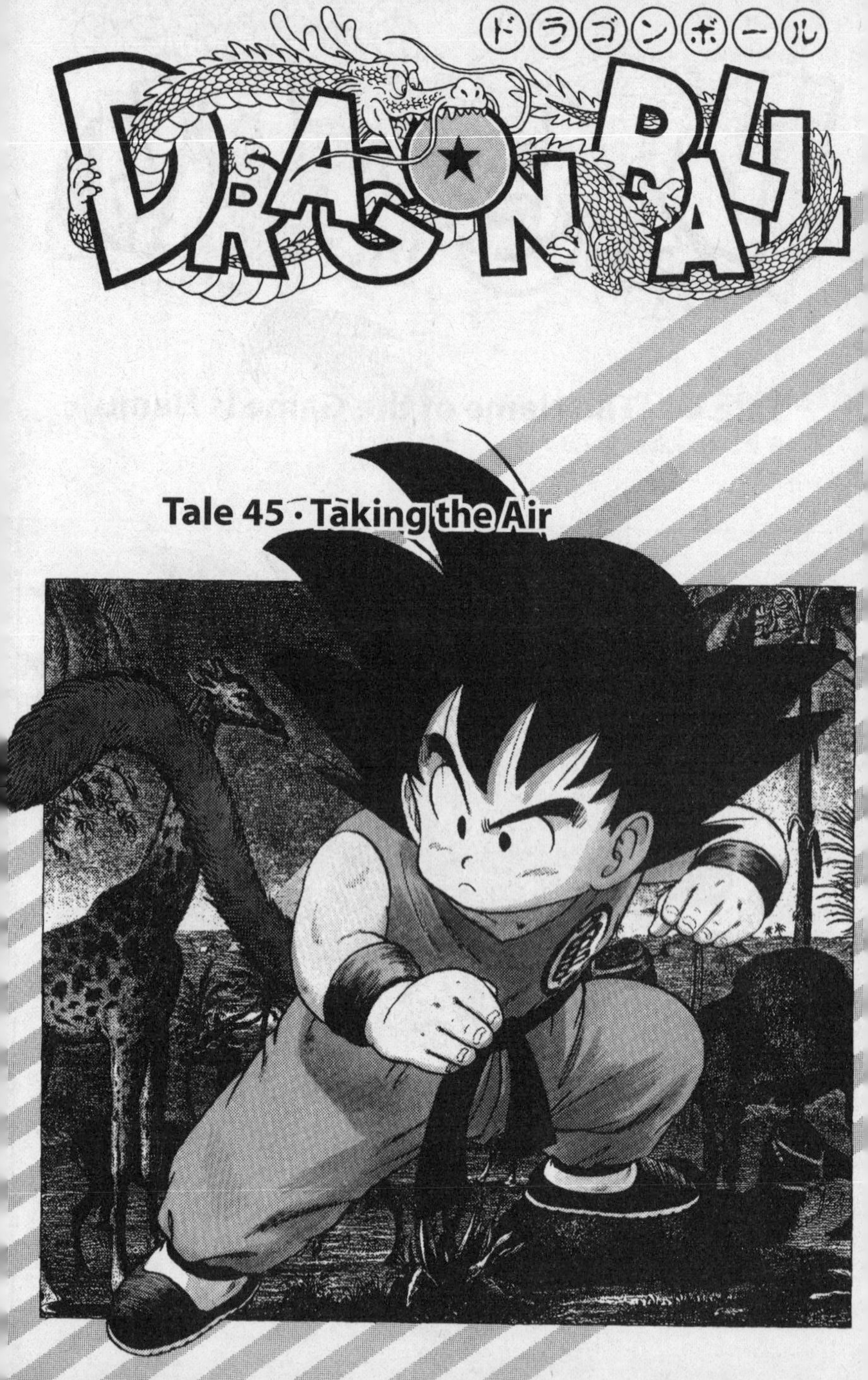

Tale 46
The Final Match

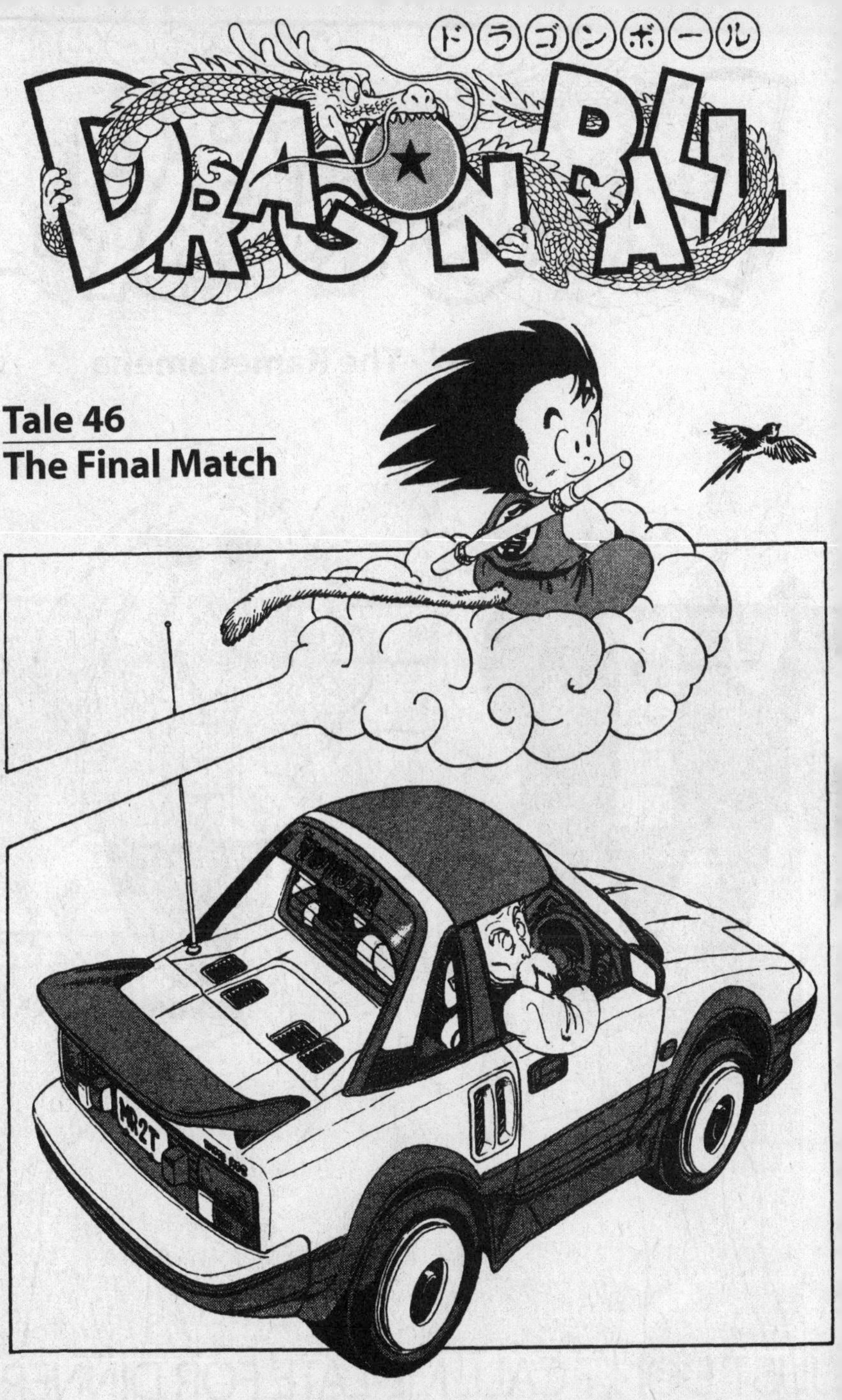
MR2T

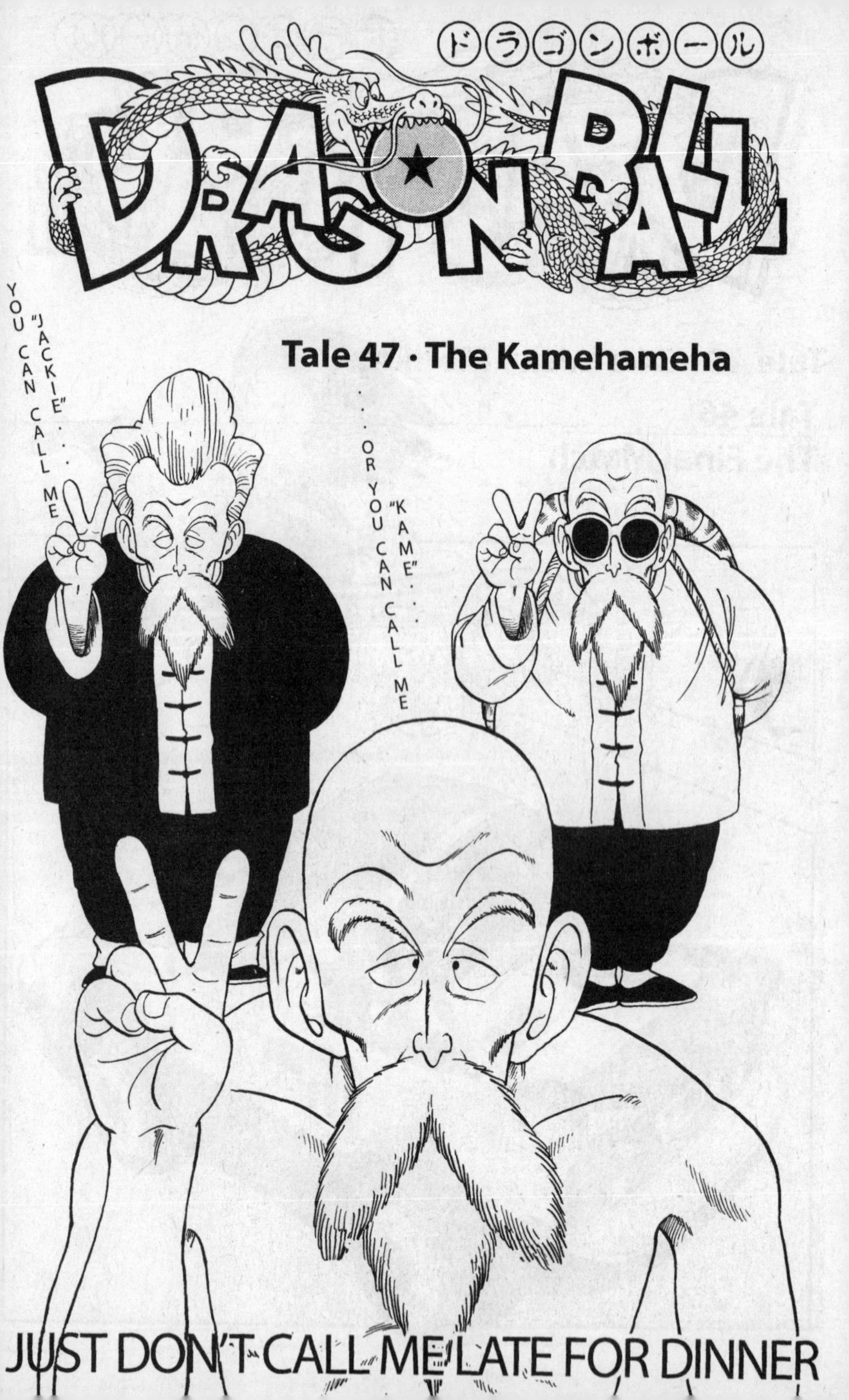
ドラゴンボール
DRAGON BALL
Tale 47 · The Kamehameha
YOU CAN CALL ME "JACKIE"...
...OR YOU CAN CALL ME "KAME"...
JUST DON'T CALL ME LATE FOR DINNER

ドラゴンボール

DRAGON BALL

Tale 48 · One Lucky Monkey

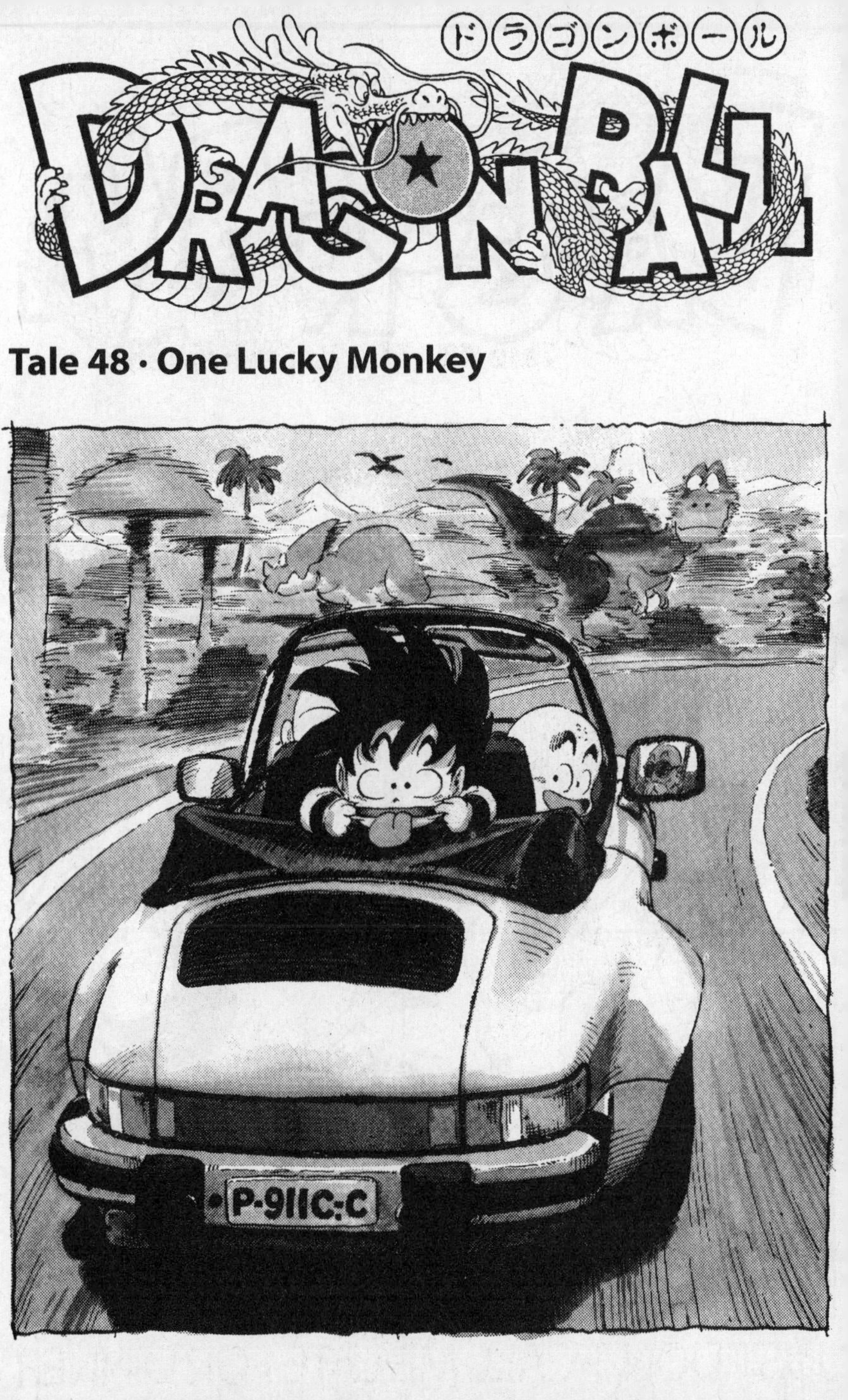
P-911C:C

Tale 49 • The Big Sleep

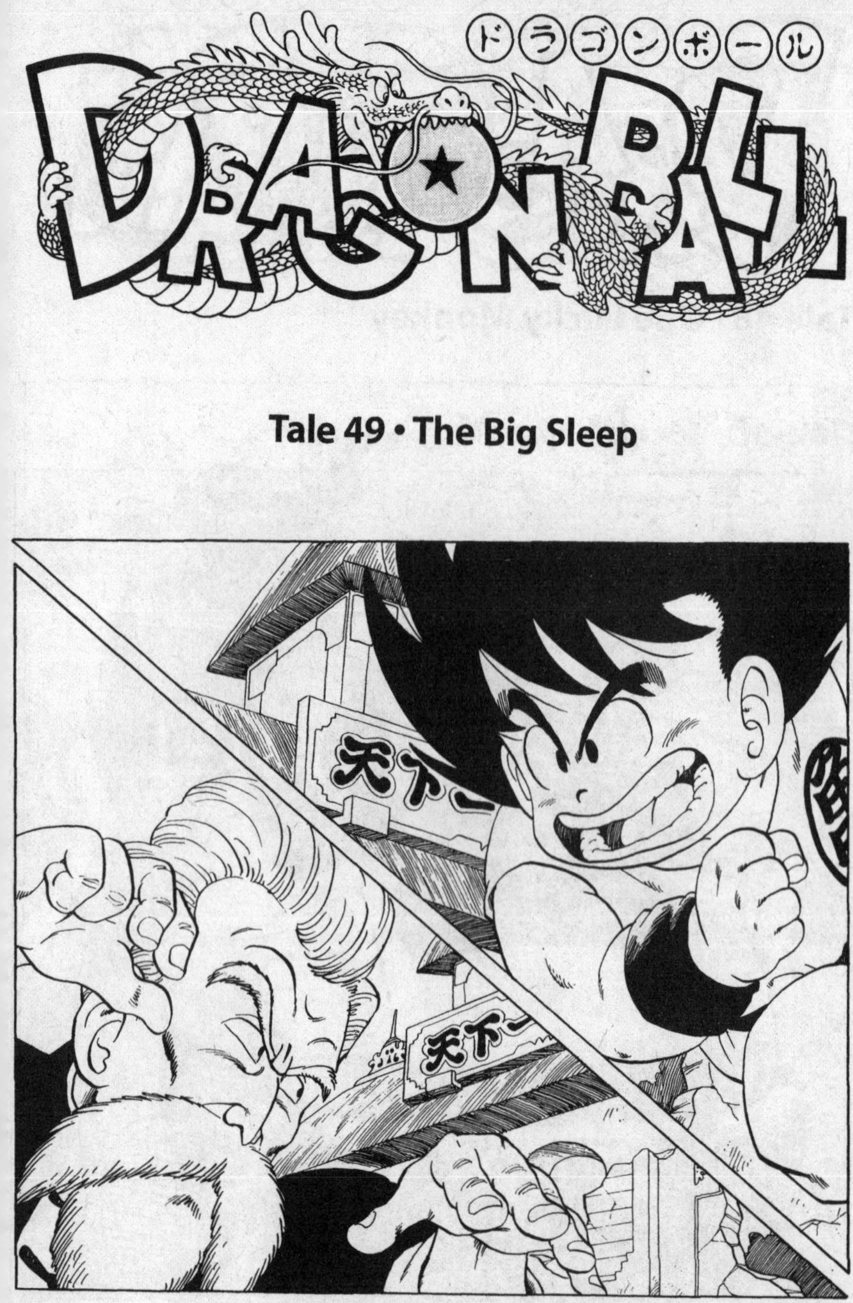
天下一
天下一

ドラゴンボール

DRAGON BALL

Tale 50 • Jackie's Shocking Secret

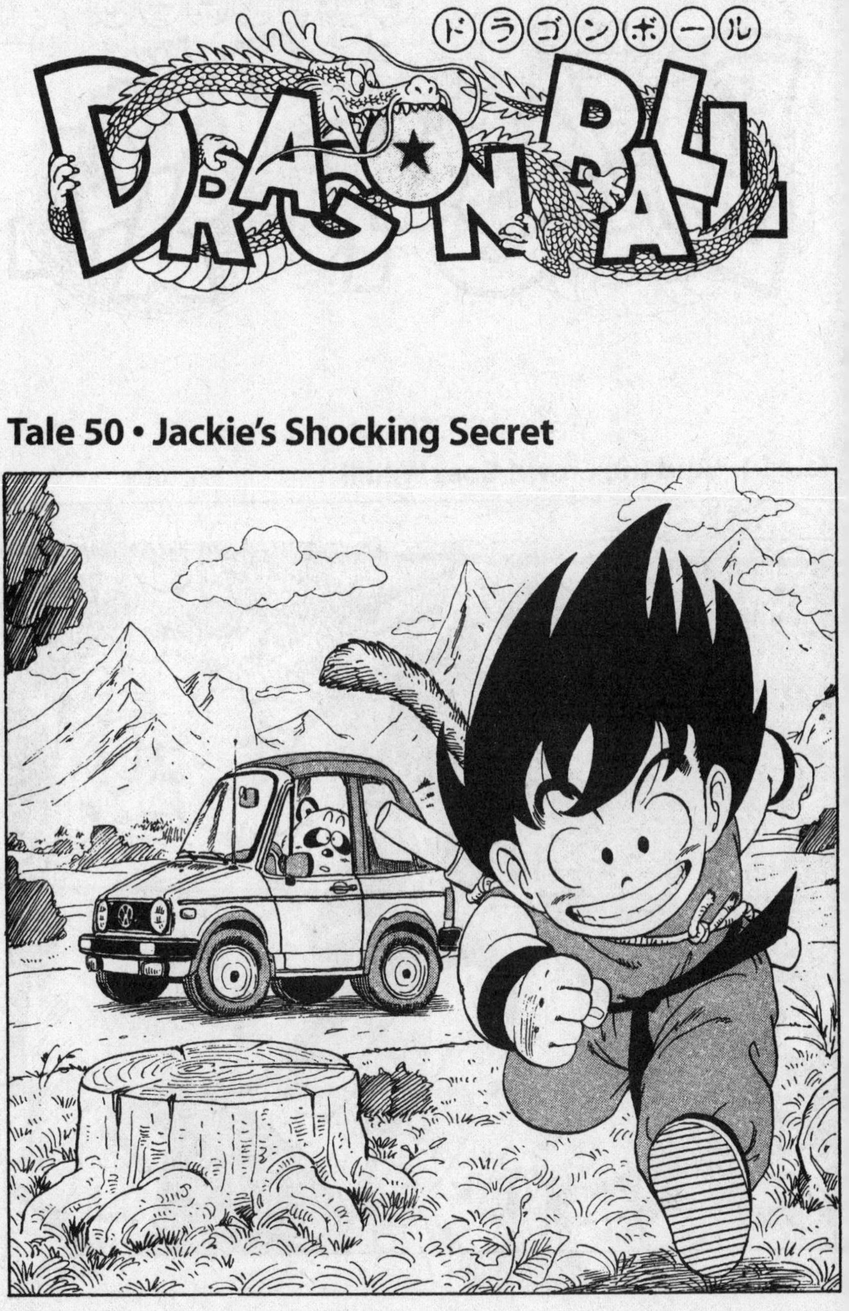

Tale 51 • And the Crowd Goes Wild!!!

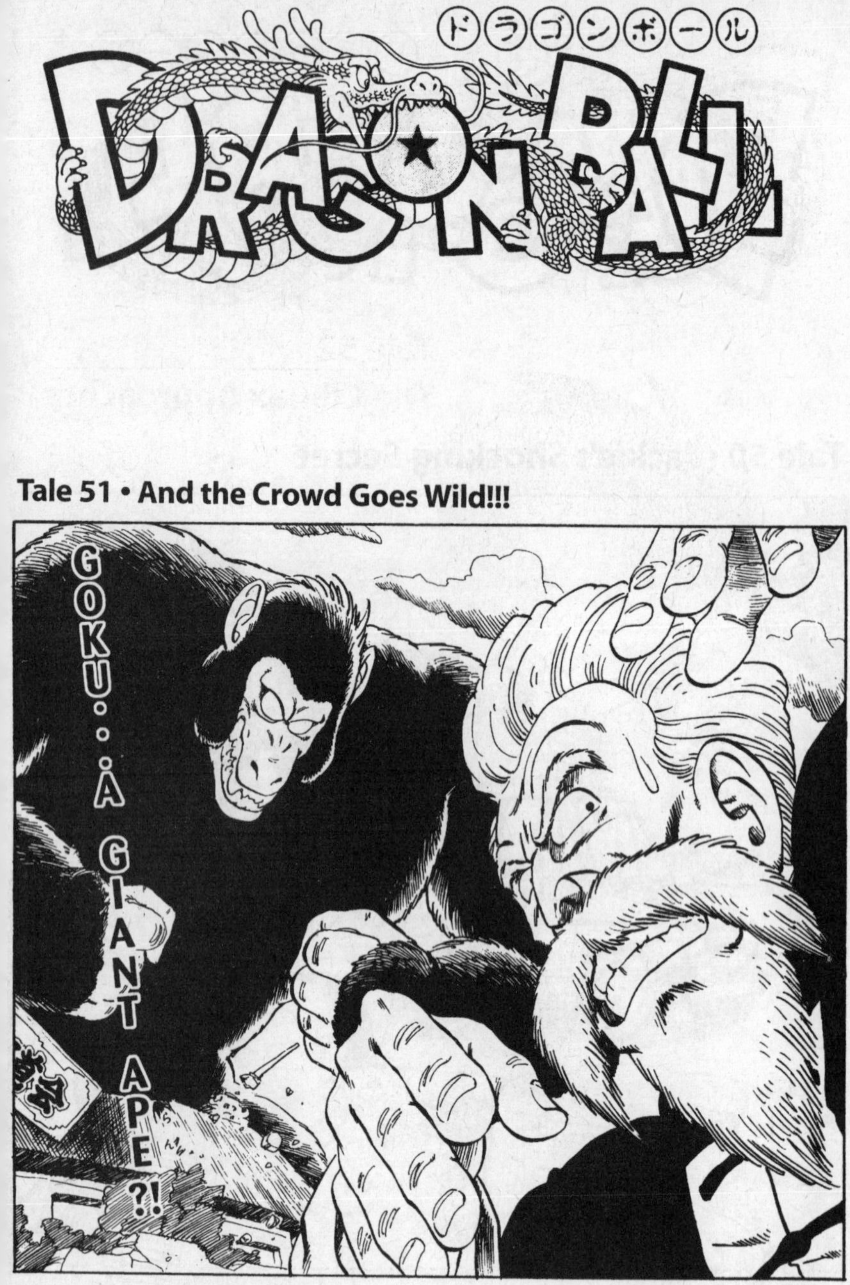
GOKU...A GIANT APE?!

ドラゴンボール

DRAGON BALL

Tale 52

The Climax Approaches

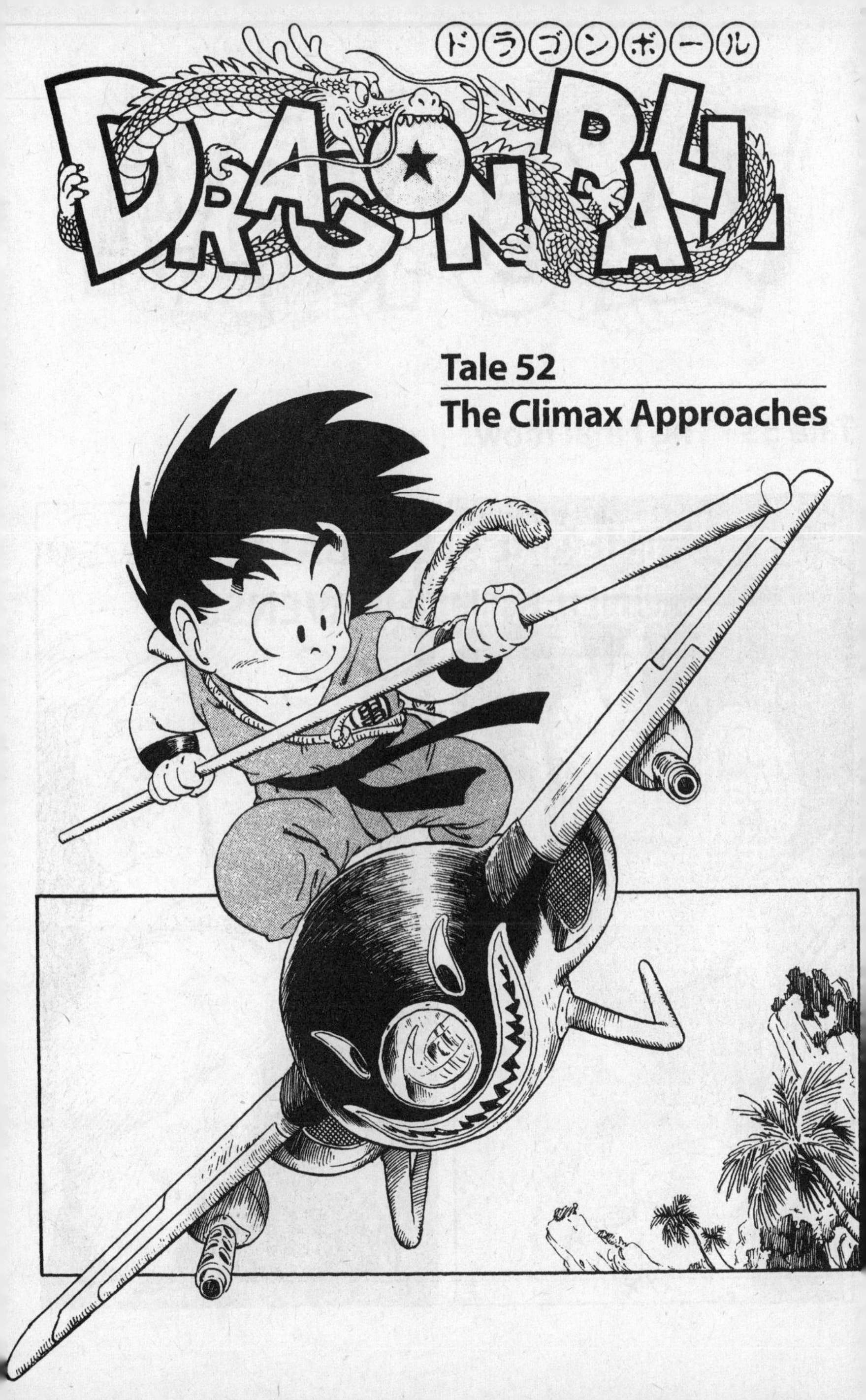

Tale 53 • The Final Blow

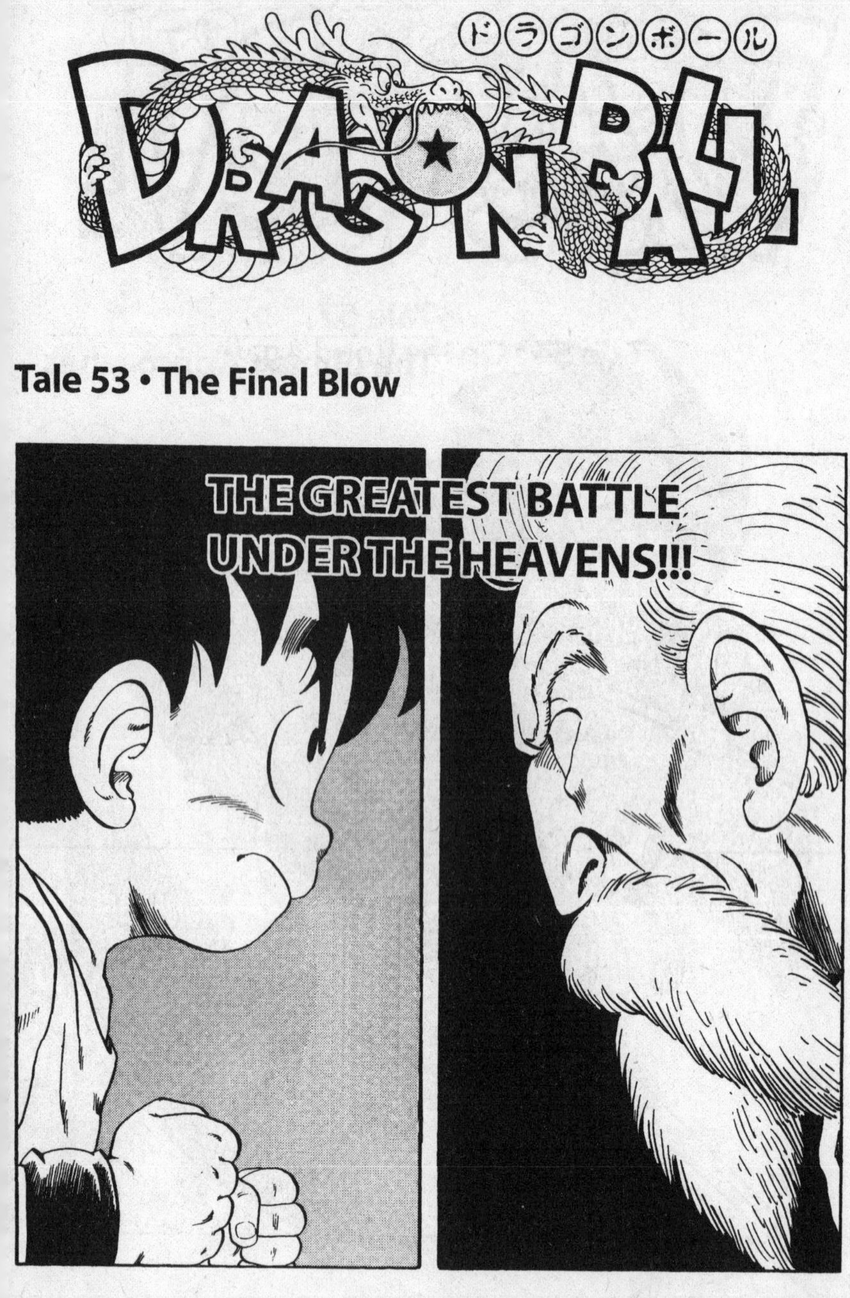
THE GREATEST BATTLE
UNDER THE HEAVENS!!!

ドラゴンボール

DRAGON BALL

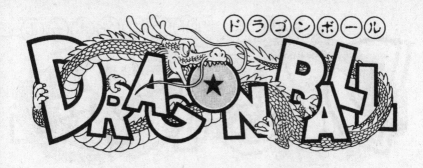

Tale 54 • On the Road Again

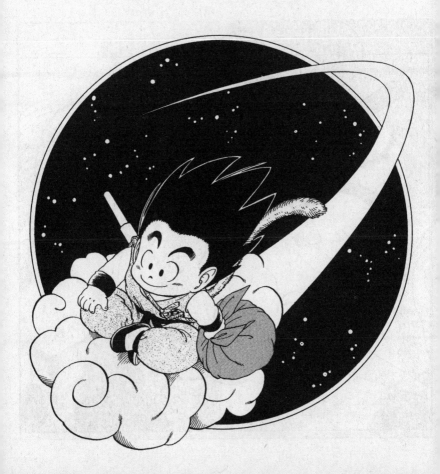

Tale 55 • The Red Ribbon

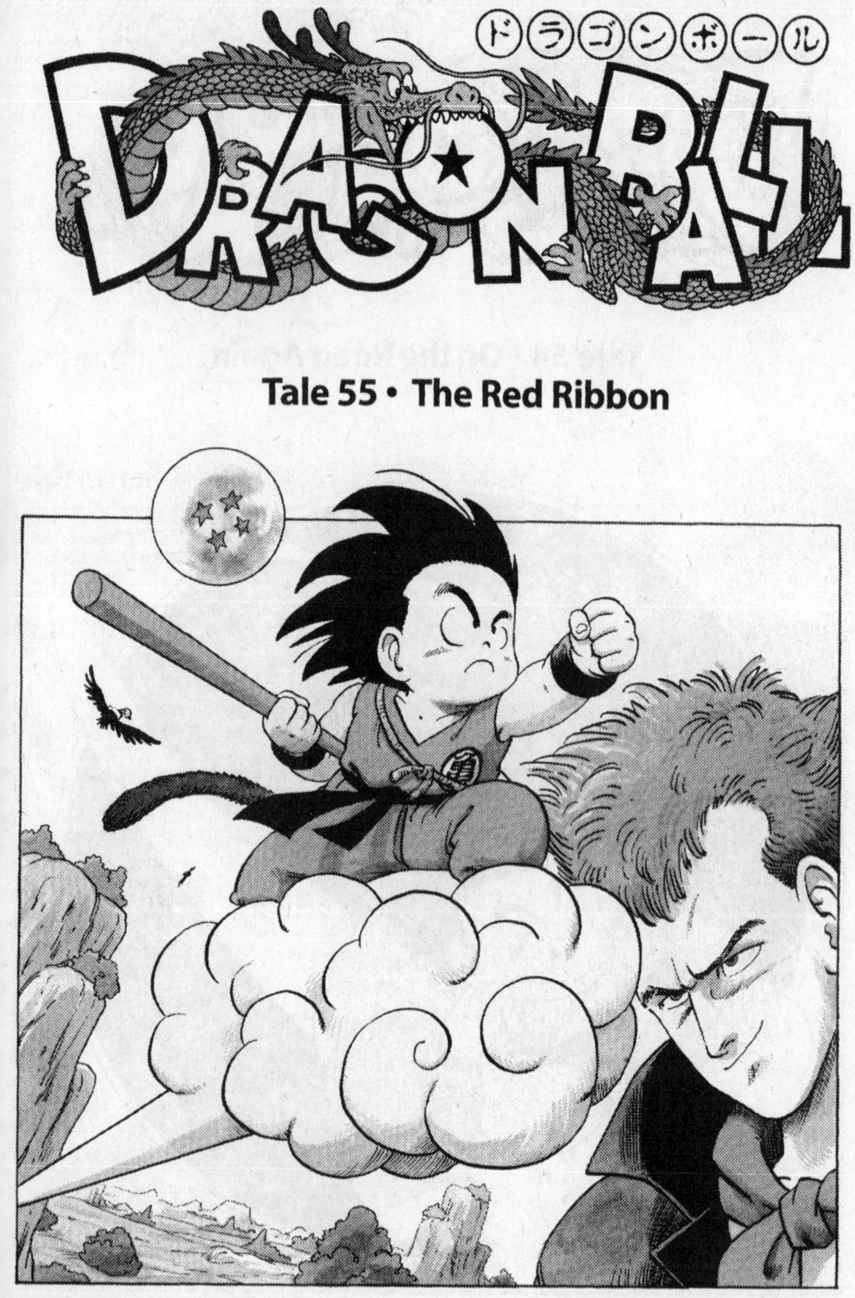

ドラゴンボール

DRAGON BALL

Tale 56 • The Dragon Ball Scramble

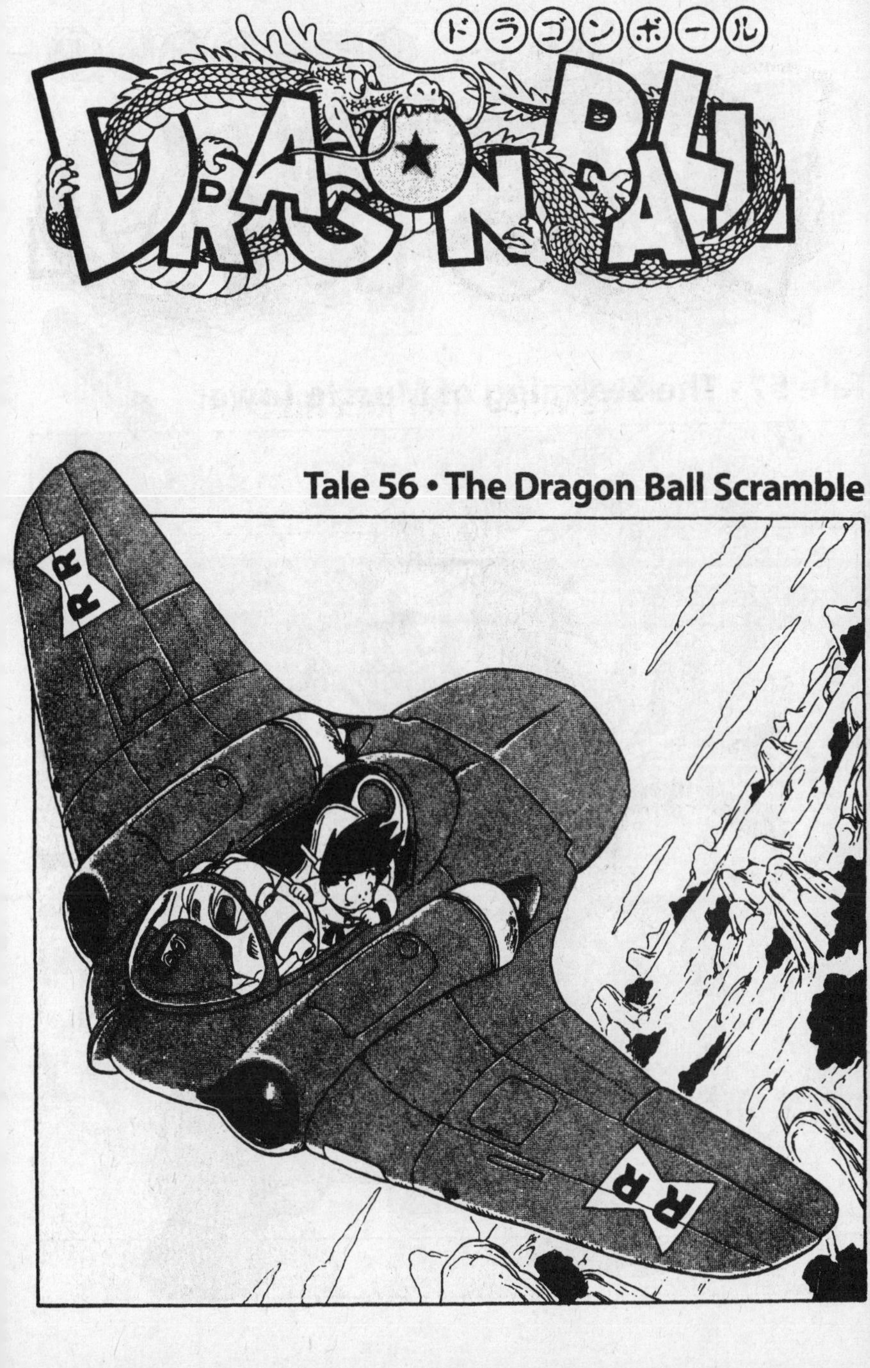
RR
RR

ドラゴンボール

DRAGON BALL

Tale 57 · The Storming of Muscle Tower

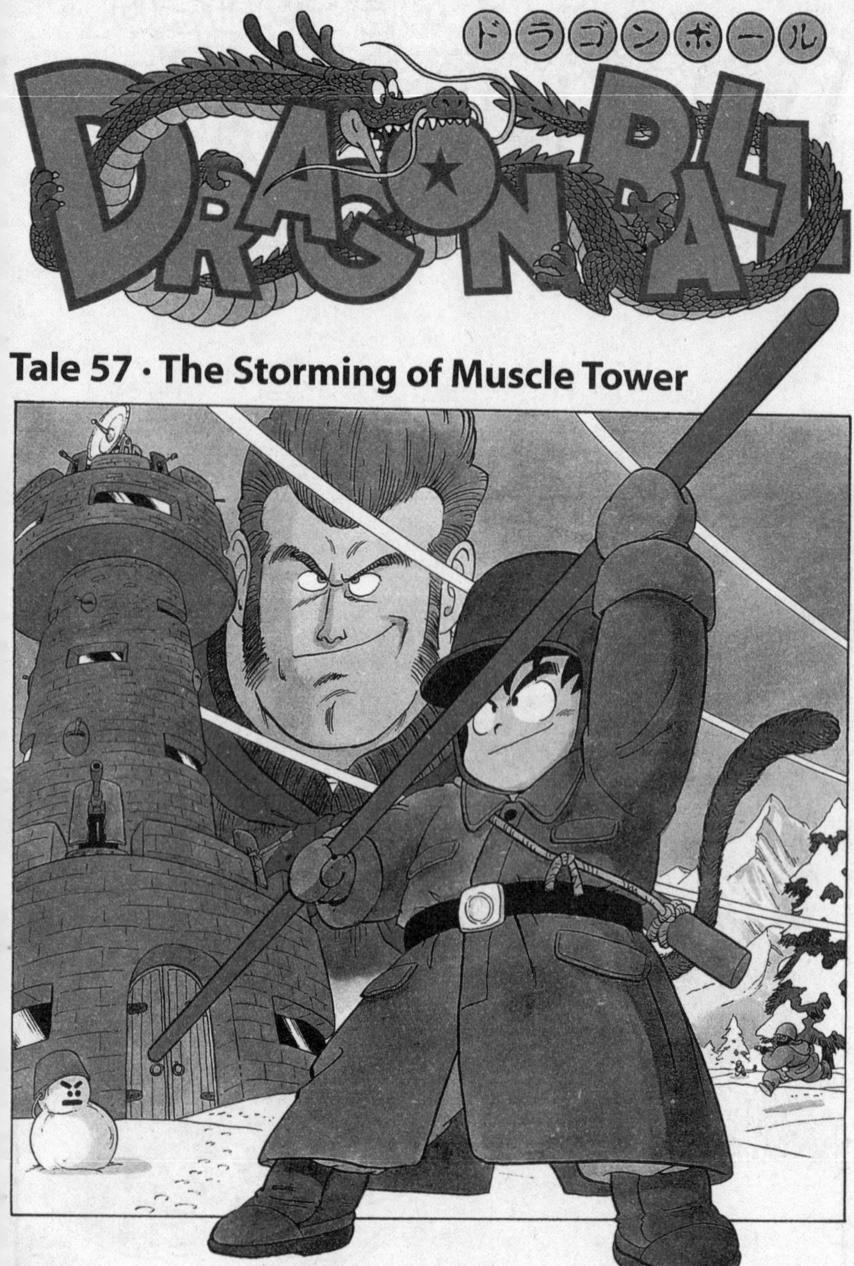

ドラゴンボール

DRAGON BALL

Tale 58 · The Flexing of Muscle Tower

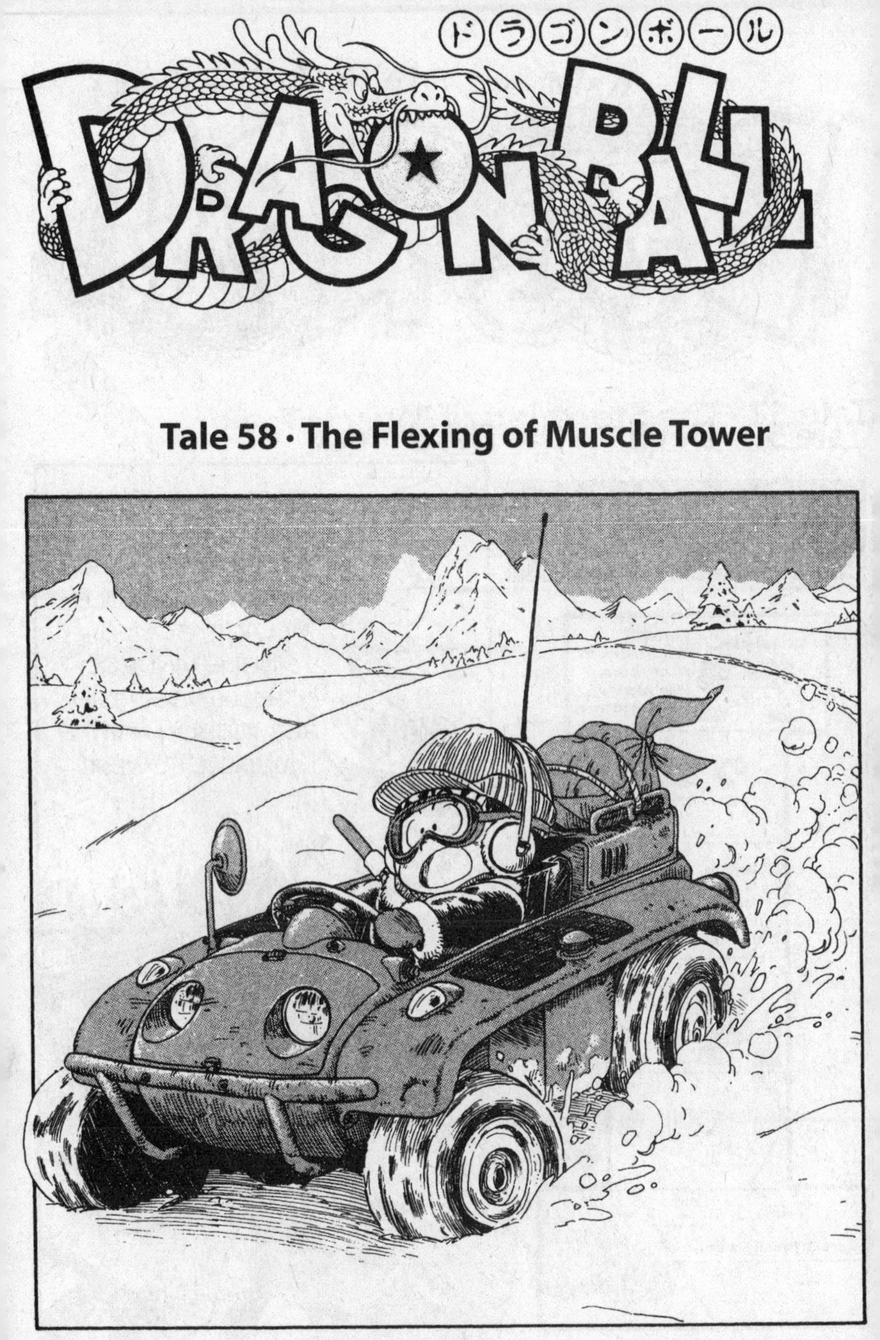

ドラゴンボール

DRAGON BALL

Tale 59 · Devil on the Third Floor

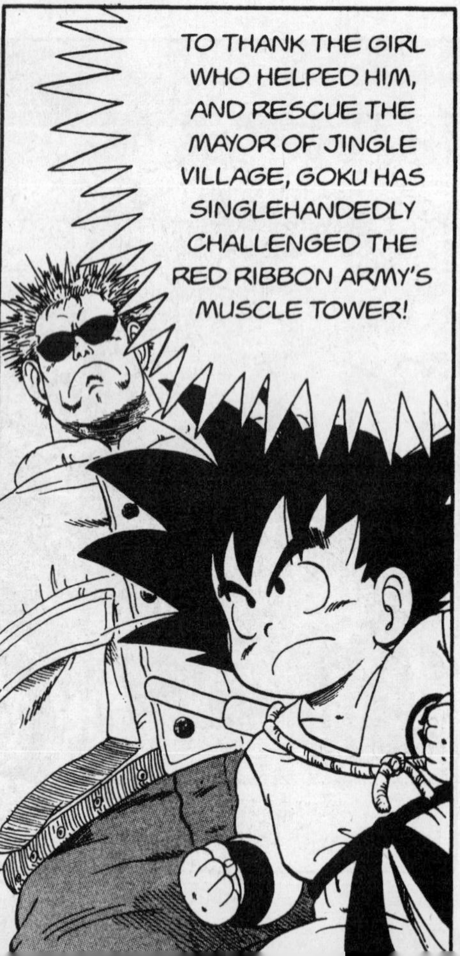
TO THANK THE GIRL WHO HELPED HIM, AND RESCUE THE MAYOR OF JINGLE VILLAGE, GOKU HAS SINGLEHANDEDLY CHALLENGED THE RED RIBBON ARMY'S MUSCLE TOWER!

This is the terrifying Muscle Tower!!!

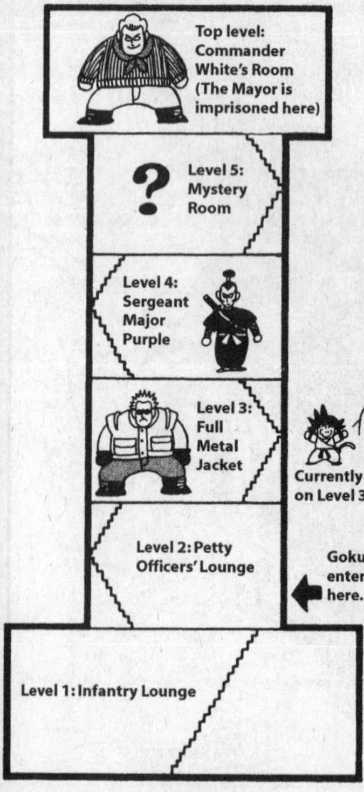
Top level: Commander White's Room (The Mayor is imprisoned here)
?
Level 5: Mystery Room
Level 4: Sergeant Major Purple
Level 3: Full Metal Jacket
Currently on Level 3
Level 2: Petty Officers' Lounge
Goku entered here.
Level 1: Infantry Lounge

Tale 60 · Purple People Beater

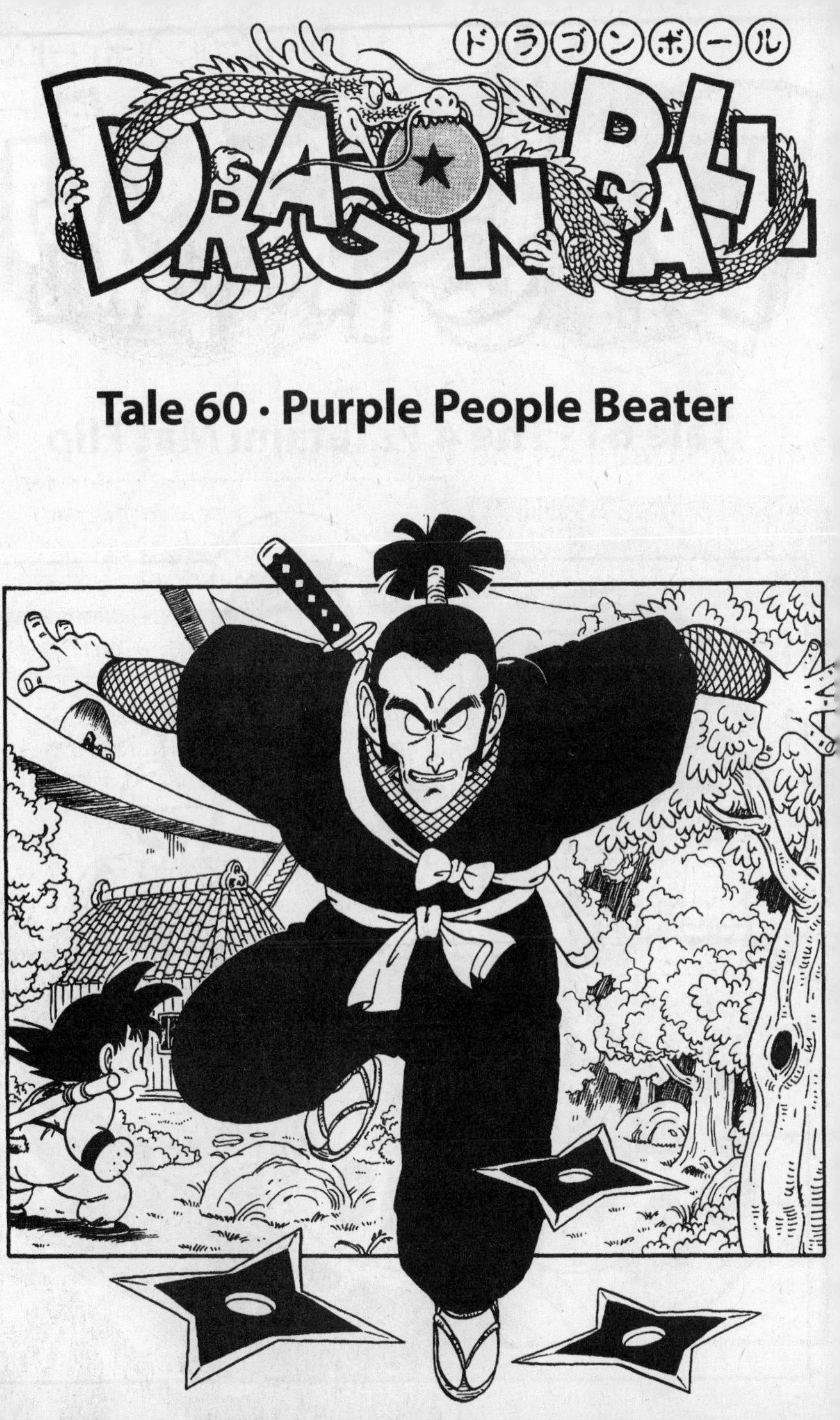

Tale 61 • The 4 ½ Tatami Mat Flip

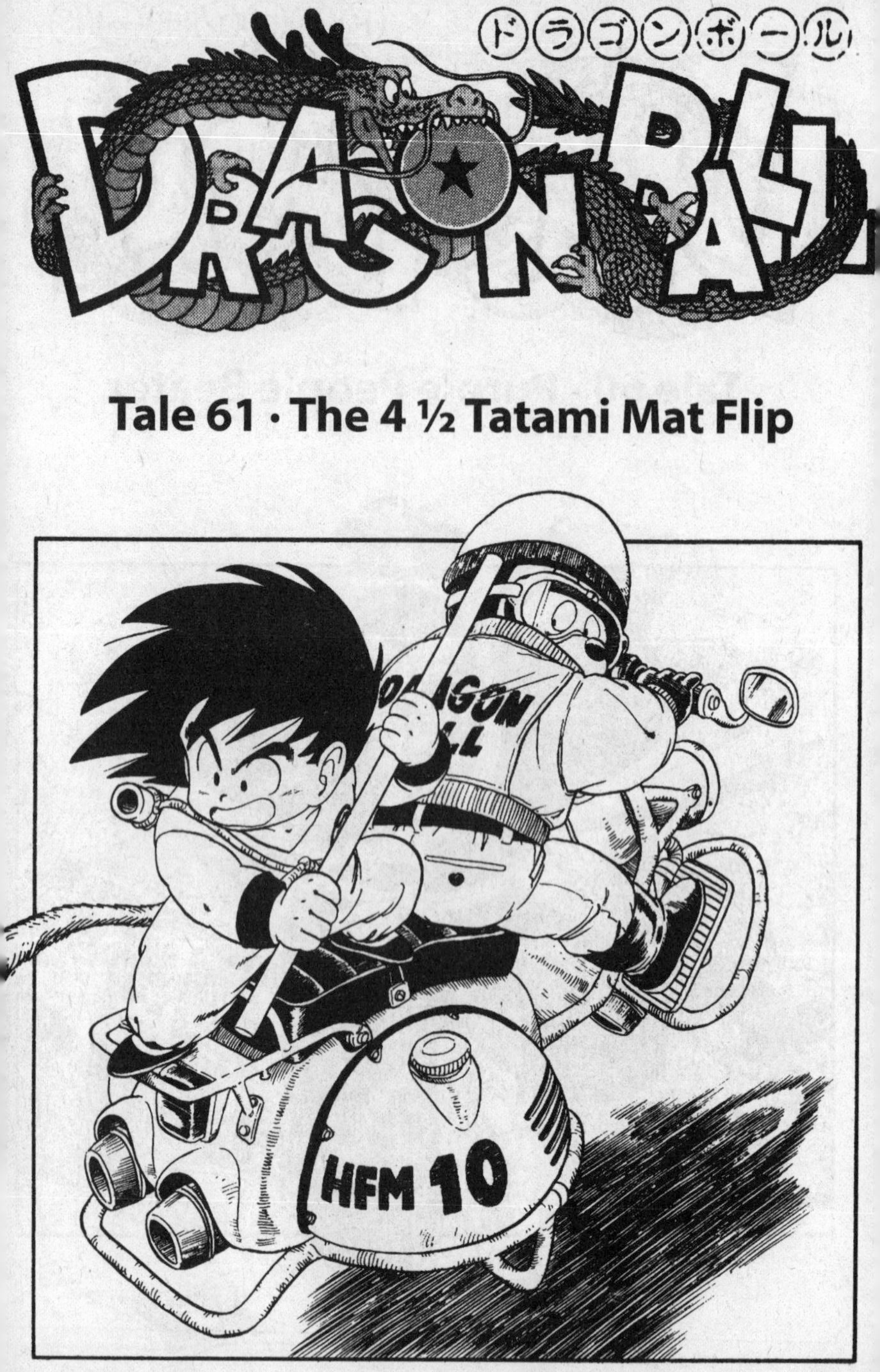
HFM 10

Tale 62 • The Ninja Split!

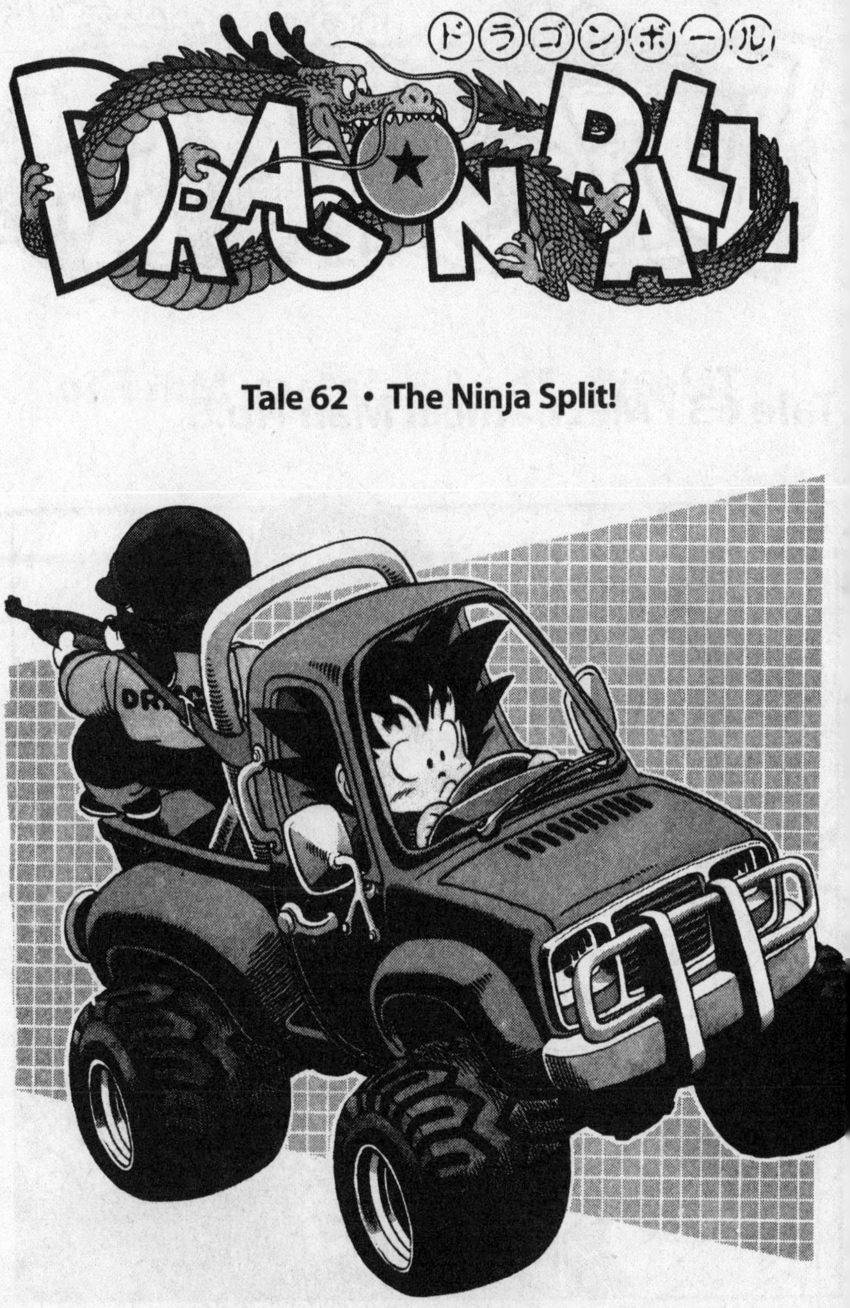

Tale 63 · Mechanical Man No.8

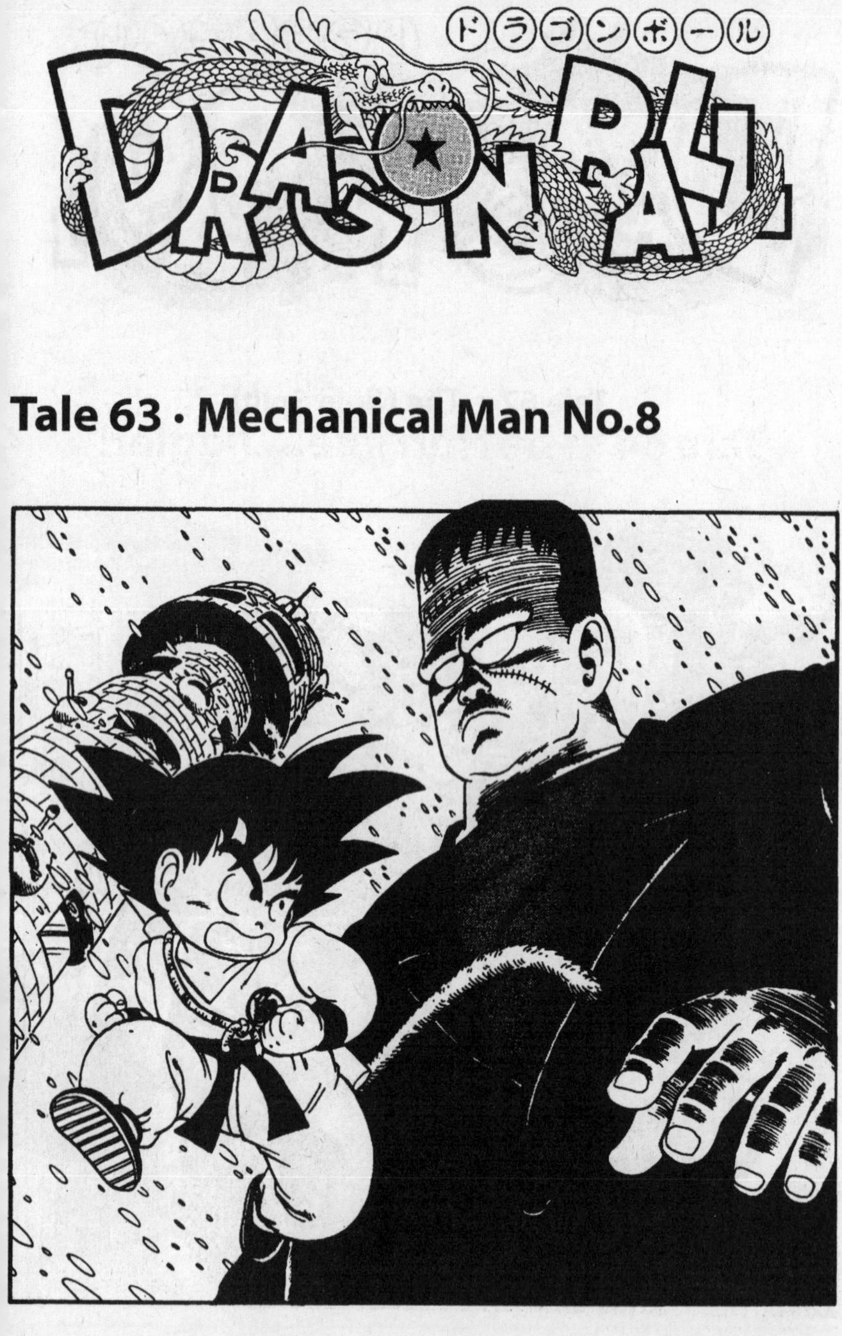

Tale 64 · The Horrible…Jiggler!

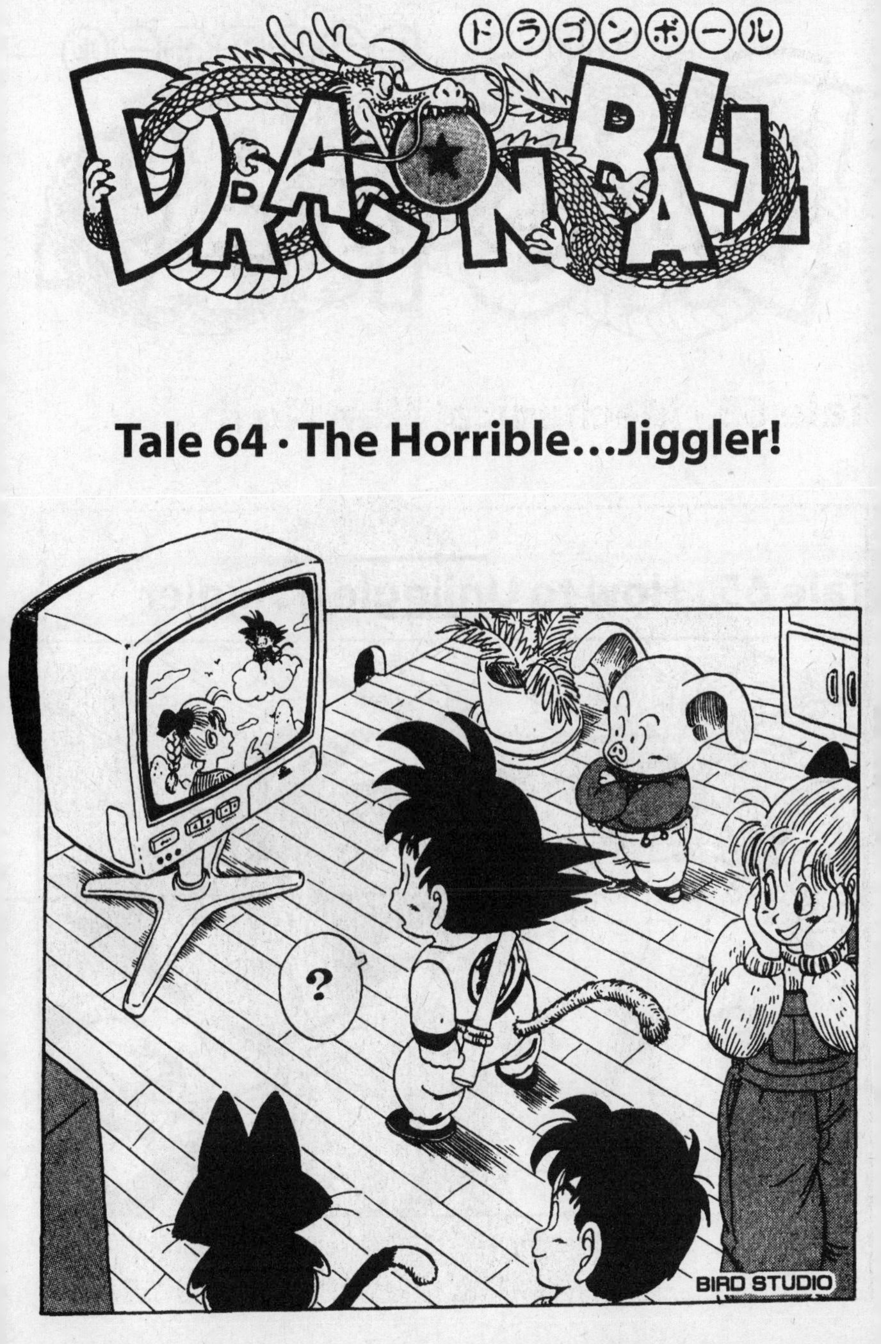
?
BIRD STUDIO

Tale 65 · How to Unjiggle a Jiggler

DRAGON BALL

ドラゴンボール

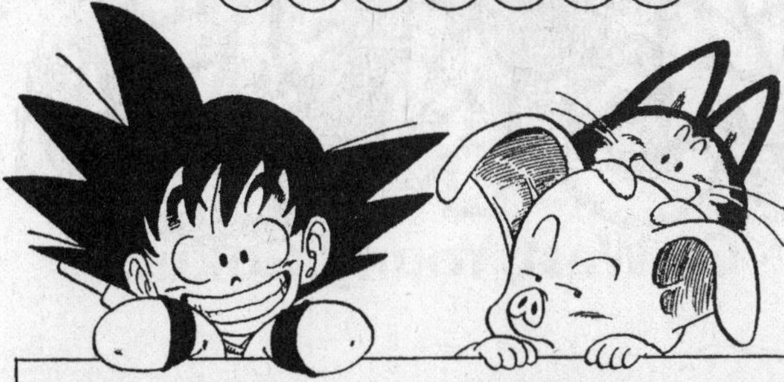

Tale 66
Muscle Tower's Final Hour

DRAGON BALL クイズスペシャルの答えだよ！

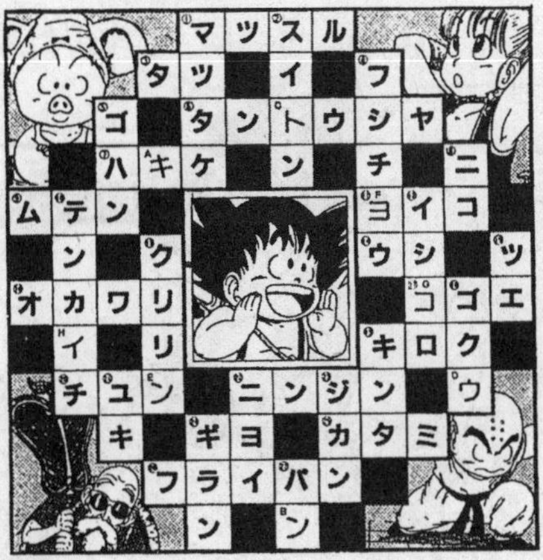

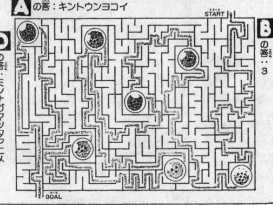

Ⓐの答：キントウンヨコイ

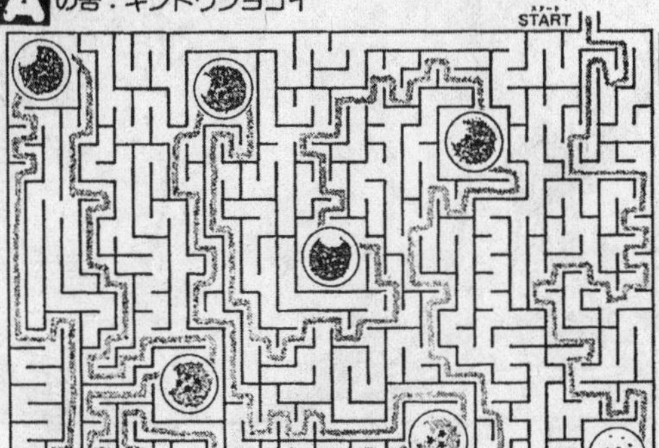

START
GOAL

Ⓑの答：3

Ⓒの答：Ⓐ7つ

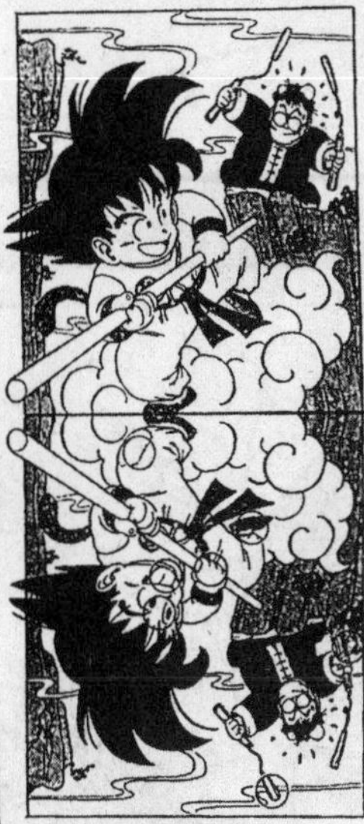

Ⓓの答：ミシナガマツタアニメ

Ⓓの悟空にバンバンされたのは何人 という設問については、「女の人で」という部分がぬけていましたので、(カ)4人(ン)3人(テ)2人、いずれも正解とします。

全部で4万2千通もの応募がありましたが正解者多数のため抽選で180名の方を当選とさせていただきました。328ページの発表をご覧ください。当選なさった方には、1カ月以内に賞品が届きますので、しばらくお待ちください。これからも応援よろしく。

※ *This page was from the time **Dragon Ball** was serialized in the magazine in Japan.*

Tale 67 · Go West, Young Goku...

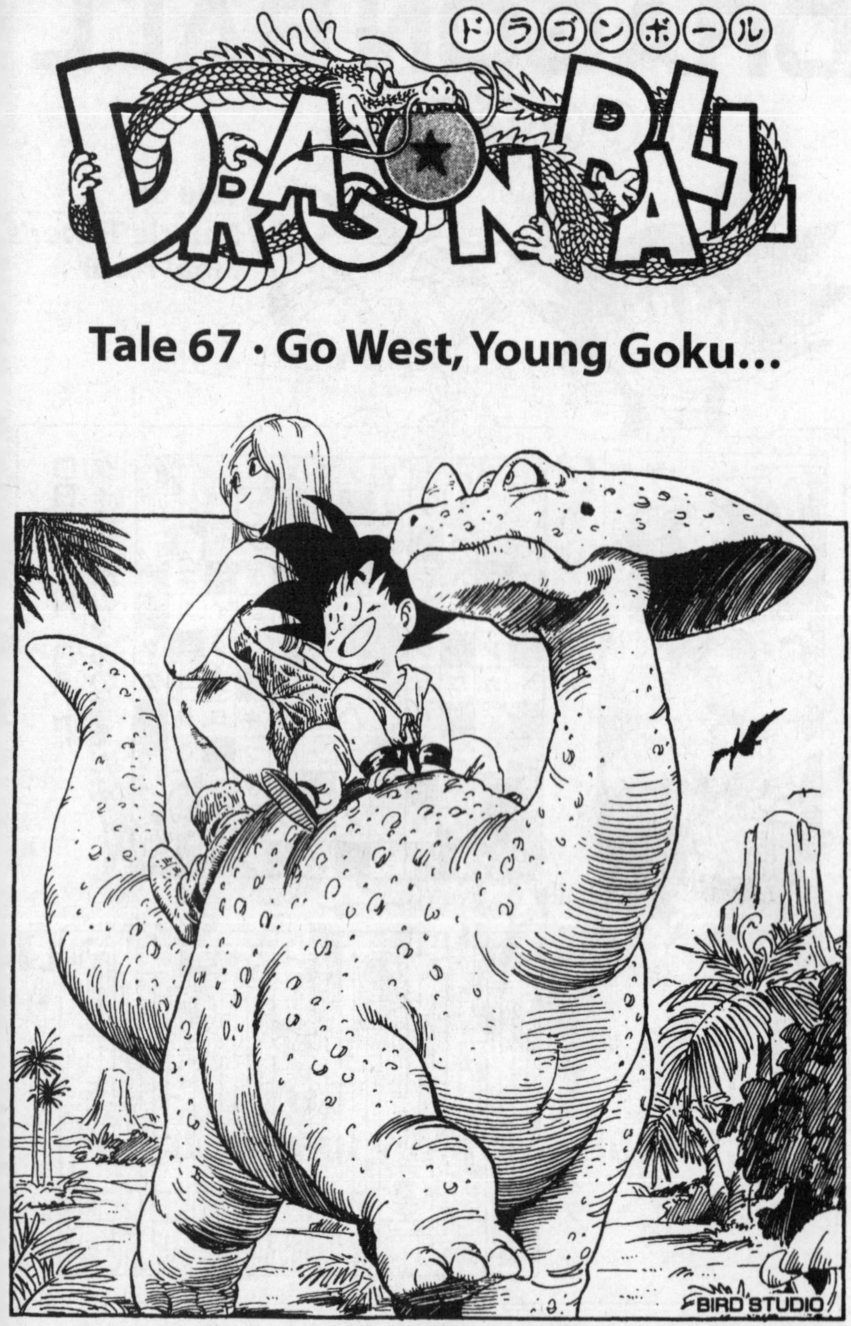
BIRD STUDIO

DRAGON BALL

Tale 68 · Monkey in the City

鳥山明
BIRD STUDIO

ドラゴンボール

DRAGON BALL

Tale 69 · Bulma and Goku

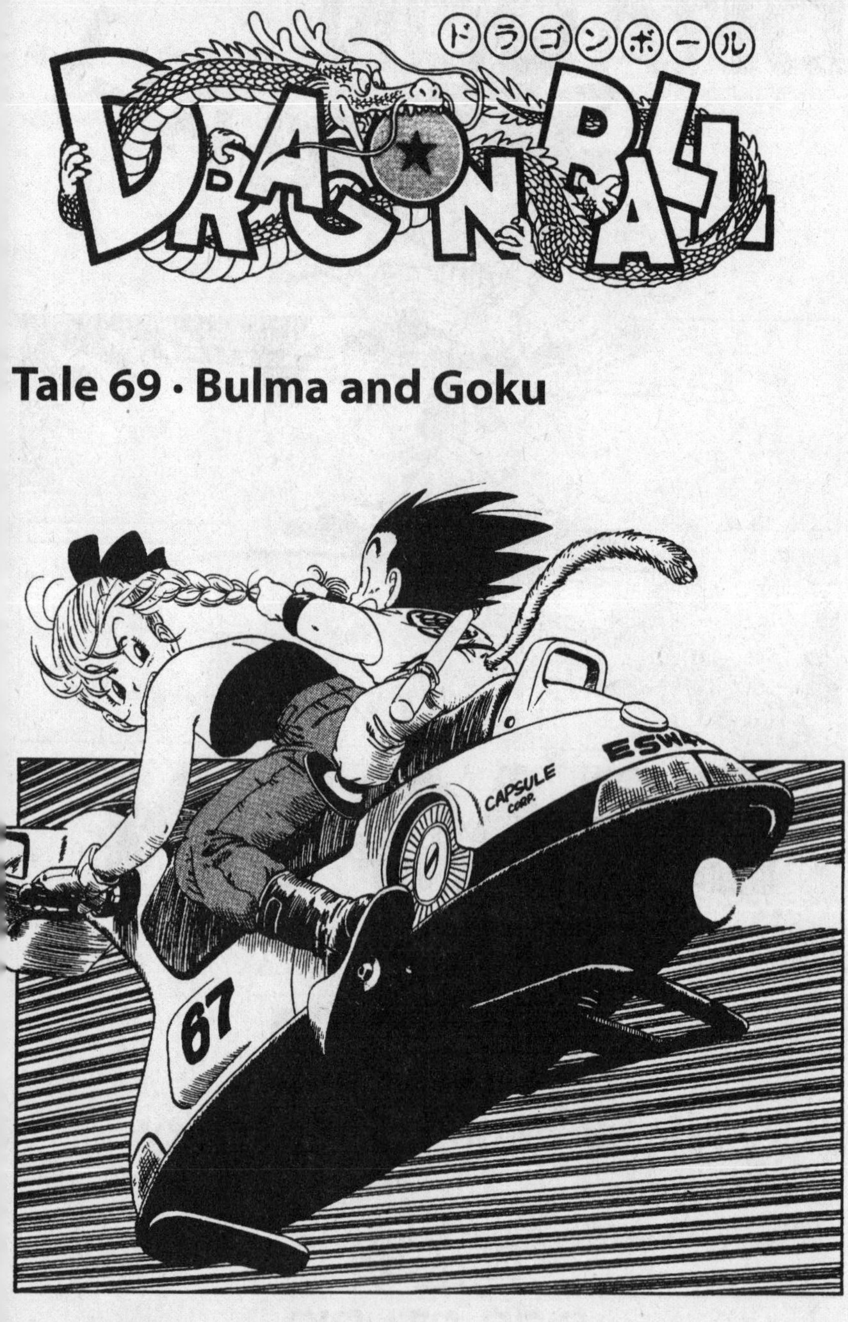
CAPSULE CORP.
67

DRAGON BALL

Tale 70 · Bulma's Big Mistake!!

Tale 71 · The Turtle Is Spotted!

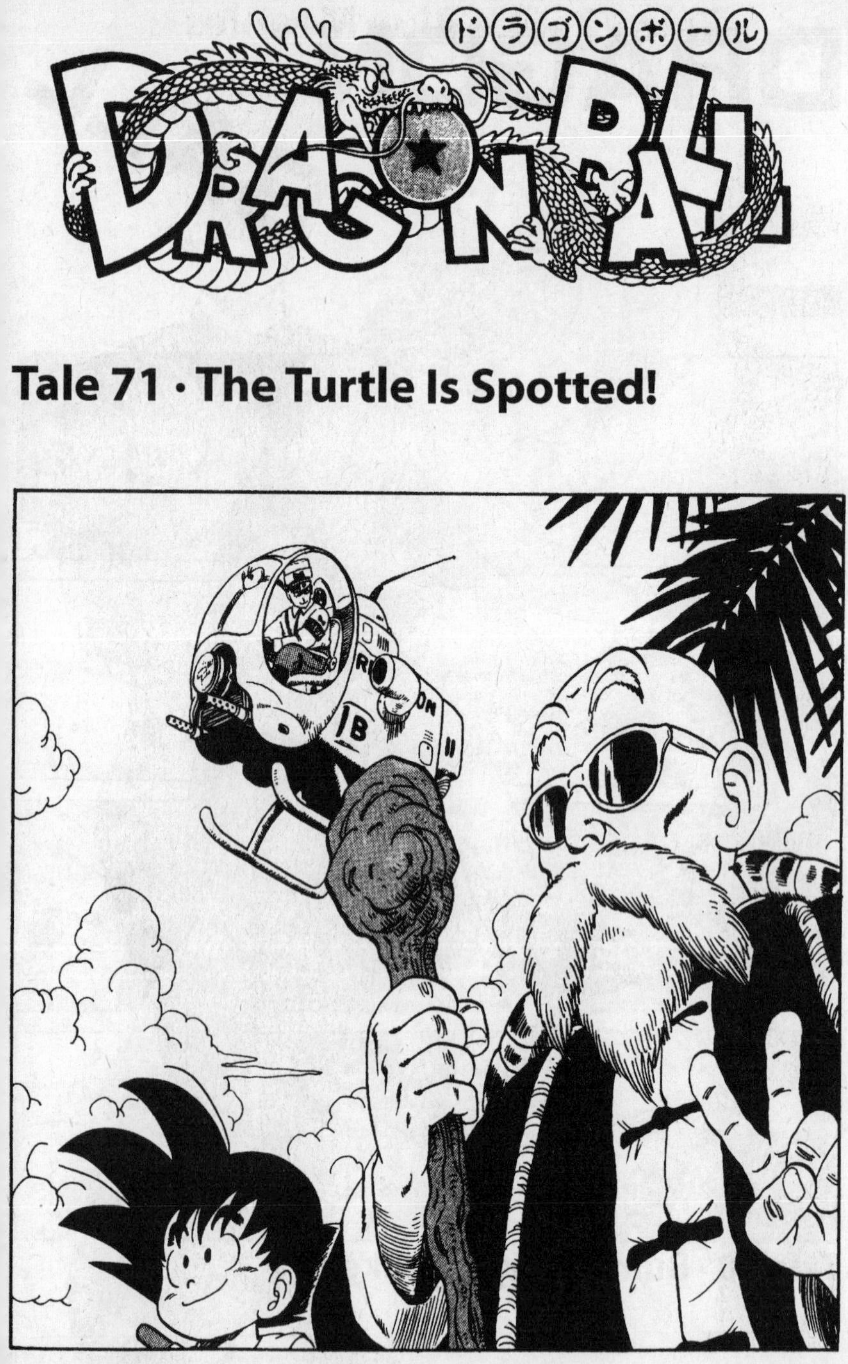

Tale 72 · The Blue Meanies

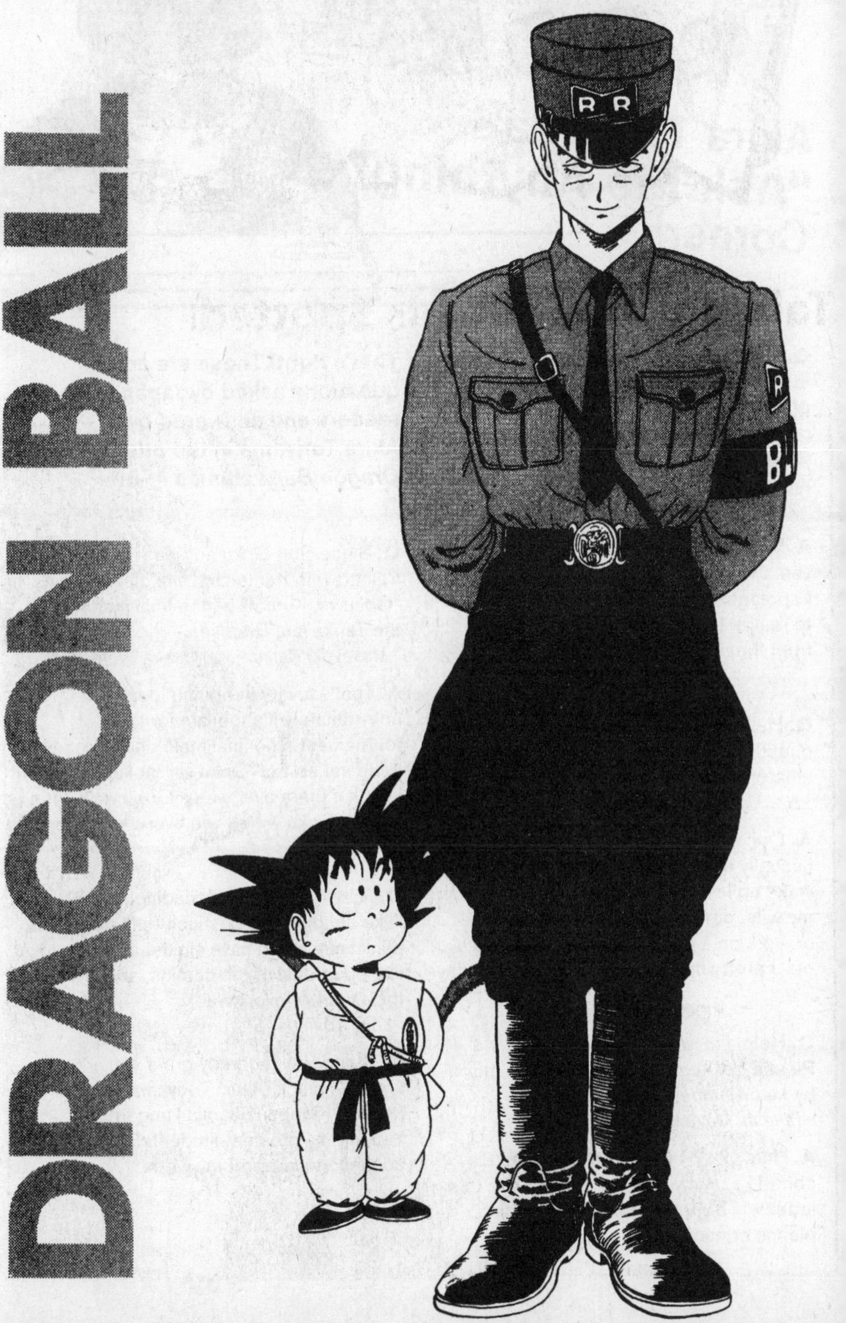
DRAGON BALL

DRAGON BALL

Akira Toriyama's "Ask Me Anything" Corner!

Q. Just so you know, I really like Oolong tea and Pu'ar tea. By the way, on page 18 of volume 1, Son Goku says to Bulma, "I never saw another human before!" Wasn't Goku's "grandpa" (the guy who raised him) a human?
–Yasuhiro Kubo, Nara Prefecture

A. W-Well…if you put it that way… yes. Oops…I made a mistake. Sorry, I apologize. You're also very smart to realize that I got the name "Pu'ar" from the name of the Chinese tea.

Q. Hello, Toriyama *Sensei*. I have a question. If you had one whole day of uninterrupted free time, what would you do?
–Naohiro Yonemoto, Tokushima Prefecture

A. Occasionally I do have a day of free time. I usually end up sleeping late and when I wake up I may go to the supermarket with my wife, or ride my bike, or see a movie, or work on a plastic model, or watch TV, or…I pretty much just putter away the day.

Q. Help! I'm running out of air! Please get some air and send it to me by *kame-hameha*. Bye.
–Takeshi Mayumi, Mie Prefecture

A. Huh…? W-What are you talking about! I assume that you didn't write this letter while you were drowning…Uh… please continue to support my work.

That's right! These are actual questions asked by Japanese readers and answered by Akira Toriyama in the original *Dragon Ball* volumes 4–6!

Q. Since Son Goku and Kuririn both trained with Kame-Sen'nin, please have "Goku vs. Kuririn" be the final match at the *Tenka'ichi Budokai*!
–Masayuki Katsumata, Osaka Prefecture

A. That's a very intriguing idea, but unfortunately it's too late for this tournament. The final match has already been set as Son Goku vs. Jackie Chun. But I think if there ever was a Goku vs. Kuririn match, Goku would win overwhelmingly.

Q. I always get a thrill reading *Dragon Ball*. I like *Dragon Ball* so much that my friends think I'm weird. I have almost all of the toys, I've bought all of the comics, and I record the TV show every week.
–Yoko Yoshida, Shizuoka Prefecture

A. Wonderful! I hereby grant you a first *dan* black belt in Toriyama School Shorinji Kempo (Shaolin kung fu). You are my greatest student! Please continue to support my work.

A. Wow! This technique is most certainly impressive. I may be able to use it in the manga. Thank you for your assistance!

Dragon of Fire Technique

Q. I always look at your manga and use them as a reference to draw my own manga. I really respect you. I have all of your manga including *Dr. Slump*, *Dragon Ball*, *Hetappi Manga Kenkyujo* (Lousy Manga Laboratory), and *Toriyama Akira Marusaku Gekijo*. I keep them to use as reference material. In particular, *Hetappi Manga Kenkyujo* greatly influenced the way I draw manga.
–Takeya Nakamura, Okinawa Prefecture

A. Thank you. You've complimented me so much I'm a bit embarrassed. Please keep up the hard work on drawing your own manga.

Q. I love *Dragon Ball*. I really like Bulma. Please continue to draw your great manga. –Mami Sato, Ibaraki Prefecture

A. Surprisingly, there are a great number of girls that say they like Bulma. Perhaps it's because her personality is a bit like a boy's. Personally, I don't really like harsh, selfish girls like Bulma.

Q. I was really happy to see Kuririn appear in the manga. (Although he hasn't made an appearance in a while.) Kuririn looks exactly like my daughter who is about to turn one year old.
–Akina Deura (my daughter),
Shizuoka Prefecture

Q. Okay, I've figured it out...*Dragon Ball* is based on the old Chinese legend *Saiyûki* (Journey to the West). Even the characters are the same: Bulma is Sanzo Hoshi, Oolong is Hakkai, Yamcha is Sagojo, and Shen Long is Sanzo Hoshi's horse. Even the order that they appear is the same. Am I wrong? I am a girl in my third year of middle school. I am afraid of the high school entrance exams! –Masae O'ouchi, Ibaraki Prefecture

A. It's true, in the beginning I set out to create a modern day version of *Saiyûki*. But soon it became difficult to remain true to the original, so I started ignoring it. So even though they have the same name, please consider my Son Goku and the monkey king Son Goku to be two different characters. However, I did get the Ox King story from *Saiyûki*. Good luck on your entrance exams!

Q. At my house we have volumes 1–24 of the *Kinnikuman* (*Ultimate Muscle*) manga and one *Kinnikuman* video.
–Naoki Koyama, Okayama Prefecture

A. Ummm...I'm sorry, Naoki. *Kinnikuman* is drawn by a person named Yudetamago...If you'd like, please take a look at *Dragon Ball*. Ha ha...ha...

Q. Hello. I really like *Dragon Ball*. I really like you too. I have a question for you. *Dr. Slump* lasted for 18 volumes. How long will *Dragon Ball* continue for?
–Eiji Harada, Okayama Prefecture

A. Hmmm...maybe for ten volumes or so. I think I'd like to make it short and sweet. But then again, there are lots of things I want to include in the story, so I don't really know.

Q. This is the first time I've written to a manga artist. Do you think that the technique I thought up is good for *Dragon Ball*? [see left].
–Tsuyoshi Maezawa, Hokkaido Prefecture

Q. What are those six marks on Kuririn's face? Is it a scar? Please tell me.
–Yasuto Tamagawa, Osaka Prefecture

A. Ah! You noticed it! The marks on Kuririn's forehead are incense burns. Sometimes you see these scars on Chinese monks in the movies. I thought I should add them because Kuririn's face is so plain.

Q. Often on the last page of *Shonen Jump*, you write about how you have pet birds. I would like to become a manga artist, and I also love animals. I would love to draw manga and have a lot of pets. *–Hiroki Yasuda, Osaka Prefecture*

A. I think it's a great thing to be an animal lover, although if you are going to have pets you should be responsible for them. In my household we have a bird, a cat, and a dog. Actually, if I could, I would also love to have a goat and a chicken.

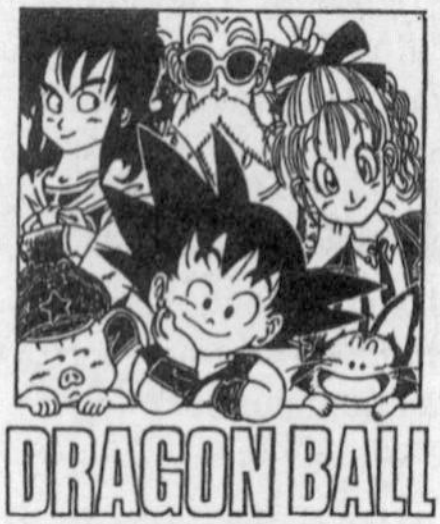
DRAGON BALL

The *Dragon Ball* New Year's Stamp

A. Thank you. So, your daughter looks exactly like Kuririn...I don't know how to respond to that. But I'm sure your daughter is very cute. By the way, does she have a nose?

Q. On the spines of the *Dragon Ball* graphic novels, so far you've drawn a Dragon Ball with one star for every volume of the series. What will you do if the series goes over seven volumes?
–Tatsuhira Koike, Saitama Prefecture

A. You're right! The spines with the drawings of the dragon and the Dragon Balls will end after the seventh volume. I am wondering myself what to do from the eighth volume on.

Q. I like Pu'ar. I told my brother that Pu'ar is a cat and he told me that Pu'ar is a mouse. Who is right?
–Nobuo Sekigawa, Kanagawa Prefecture

A. Actually, Pu'ar is neither a cat nor a mouse, but I draw him a little bit like a cat.

Q. Over New Year's break, I made a stamp using your characters [see left]. Nine months from now, I am planning on using the dragon from *Dragon Ball* to make my New Year's greeting cards.
–Kimio Nagasaki, Shizuoka Prefecture

A. This is a great stamp! I imagine it took quite a lot of work. I am really impressed. I look forward to seeing your dragon cards. Please send me one when you're finished.

Q. The caricature that you draw of yourself in the comics looks like a dirty old man, so I thought that you probably looked like a dirty old man yourself. But I saw your photograph in *Shonen Jump* and you looked very handsome.
–Yasuhiro Ando, Aichi Prefecture

A. Ha ha ha! You think so? You're right! I *do* look good! You're a great guy! Unfortunately, I just can't get too excited about a guy complimenting me like this...

AUTHOR NOTES

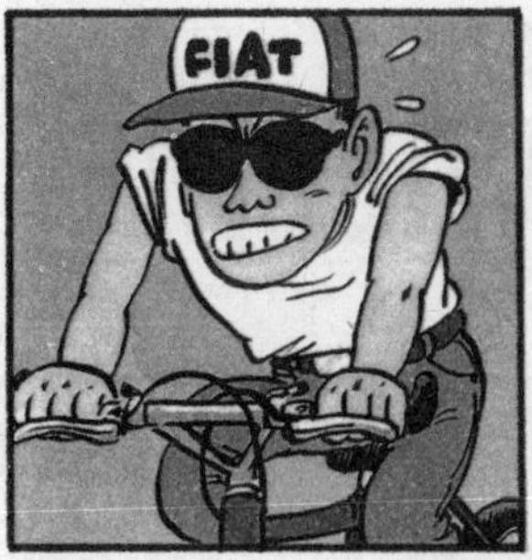
FIAT

1986

VOLUME 4

I've recently slacked off on my exercise routine, getting lazy and using the motorcycle or the car to run short errands. As a result, I now have a sizeable gut. I thought to myself, "This'll be bad if it goes on any longer!", so I made the decision that I'd at least try to get in shape by riding a bicycle. That was the theory anyway. In practice, I always end up looking at women along the way and riding slower than dirt. You couldn't really call it "exercise"...

VOLUME 5

I've mentioned this many times before, but I really hate the cold. If you turn on the heater, your head feels like it's in a daze, and if you turn it off, your hands get numb from the cold and you can't even hold your pen properly. When it gets cold I stop riding my bicycle and I only go places by car. Frankly, I'm just not that much of a cycling enthusiast. Oh, and I just want to hibernate! Spring, hurry up and get here! Every winter's day I long for you to come.

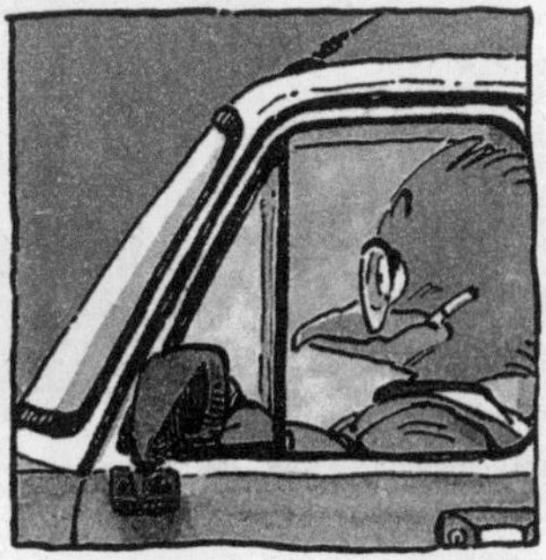

1987

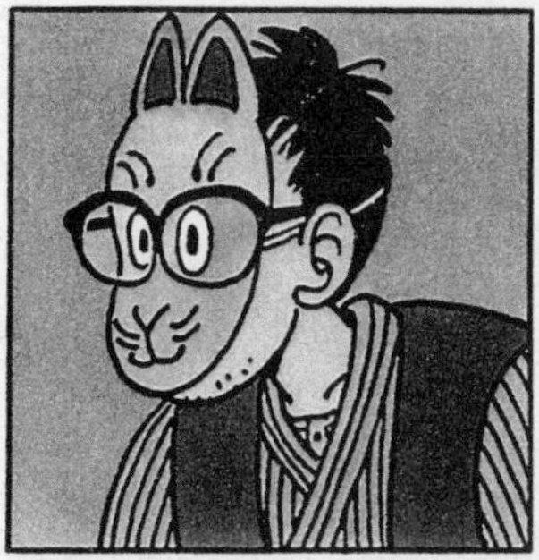

1987

VOLUME 6

Recently, the neighborhood where I live has started to get more developed, with new roads and shops being built. It's pretty convenient, but on the other hand, it's getting rarer and rarer to see weasels, pheasant or quail. The noise level has increased too. Being a country boy, I prefer a nice quiet lifestyle so I can really take it easy and reeeelax. I know it might be inconvenient in some ways, but I'd like to live way, way out in the country. This is the sort of thing that I end up thinking about.

IN THE NEXT VOLUME

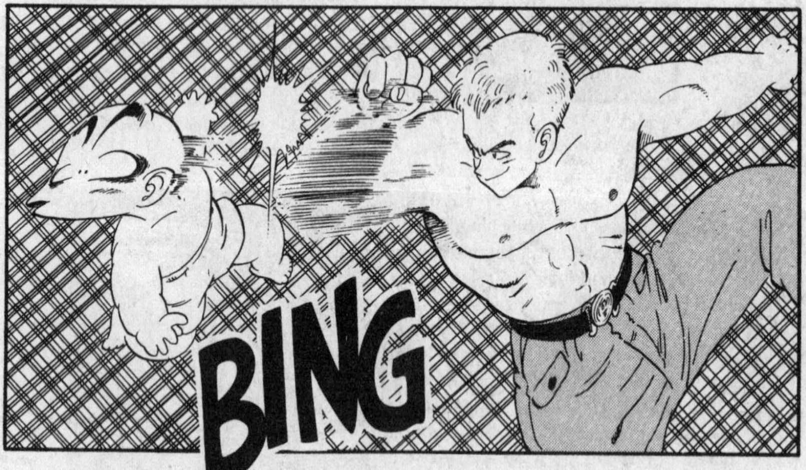
BING

The Red Ribbon Army is closing in on all sides! While Kame-Sen'nin fends off the troops that have infiltrated his island, Goku, Bulma and Kuririn try to outrun gun-toting bad guys underwater. The gang is in for a whole lot of trouble, especially when General Blue steps up with his mysterious power…